Basic Business Statistics

CONCEPTS AND APPLICATIONS

FOURTH EDITION

Basic Business Statistics

CONCEPTS AND APPLICATIONS

Mark L. Berenson
David M. Levine

Department of Statistics and Computer Information Systems
Baruch College, City University of New York

Prentice-Hall International, Inc.

ISBN 0-13-057555-0

 © 1989 by Prentice-Hall, Inc.
A Division of Simon & Schuster
Englewood Cliffs, New Jersey 07632

Printed in the United States of America

10 9 8 7 6 5 4 3 2 1

ISBN 0-13-057555-0

Prentice-Hall International (UK) Limited, *London*
Prentice-Hall of Australia Pty. Limited, *Sydney*
Prentice-Hall Canada Inc., *Toronto*
Prentice-Hall Hispanoamericana, S.A., *Mexico*
Prentice-Hall of India Private Limited, *New Delhi*
Prentice-Hall of Japan, Inc., *Tokyo*
Simon & Schuster Asia Pte. Ltd., *Singapore*
Editora Prentice-Hall do Brasil, Ltda., *Rio de Janeiro*
Prentice-Hall, Inc., *Englewood Cliffs, New Jersey*

To our wives,
Rhoda Berenson and **Marilyn Levine**
and to our children,
Kathy Berenson, Lori Berenson, and **Sharyn Levine**

Preface

When planning or revising a textbook, the authors must decide how the text will differ from those already available and what contribution it will make to the field of study. These issues are resolved in several ways in this fourth edition of *Basic Business Statistics*.

Survey Database

As in previous editions, a set of data based upon the results of a survey is included. Specifically, the data set constitutes the characteristics of 233 sampled single-family houses. This survey, used throughout the text, serves as a means of integrating the various topics, permitting a cohesive study of descriptive statistics, probability, statistical inference, and regression analysis. The use of an actual survey, examined from beginning to end, will aid the student in conducting basic research in future courses, theses, or occupational situations.

Problems

This text contains numerous problems at the end of sections as well as at the end of chapters. Many of these problems apply to realistic situations (using real data whenever possible) in various fields including accounting, economics, management, marketing, and public administration. The answers to selected problems (indicated by the symbol ●) appear at the end of the text. In addition, detailed case studies are included at the end of each of ten chapters. Moreover, at the end of most chapters, a series of database exercises pertaining to the survey is presented and indicated by the symbol □.

ACTION (⟹) and Lightning (⟋) Problems

Statistics is a living, breathing subject. It is not mere numbers crunching! Action problems enhance literacy by asking the student to write letters, memos and reports, and prepare talks. Lightning (⟋) problems are particularly thought-provoking or have no "exact" answer. Together, action and lightning problems force the reader to think and better enable the reader to understand the utility of statistical analysis as an aid to the solution of real problems in an organizational setting.

Computer Packages

A major feature of this text is the discussion of the use of such computer packages as SAS, SPSS^X, Minitab, STATGRAPHICS, and MYSTAT. Not only is output from each of these packages illustrated throughout the text, but the use of the computer as a tool for assisting in the decision-making process is interwoven in the various chapters. Extensive coverage is given to plotting data, interpreting computer output, and evaluating the assumptions of the particular statistical techniques, thereby simulating the approach used by a statistician in conducting an actual statistical analysis.

Applications to Quality and Productivity Management

It is widely recognized that the field of business has entered a new economic age, one in which competition from all over the world must be faced. This text provides detailed coverage (particularly in Chapter 19) of the management philosophy of W. Edwards Deming, the person who deserves a share of the credit for helping Japan to become known as a high-quality producer, and contains in-depth coverage of statistical process control, a topic of increasing importance in both the service and manufacturing industries.

Modern Methods

A sixth important feature of this edition is the inclusion of recently developed methods in the field of statistics. As examples, exploratory data analysis techniques, dot charts, Pareto diagrams, digidot plots, and supertables are discussed (Chapters 3 and 4); a p-value approach to hypothesis testing is used (Chapters 11–13); residual and influence analysis and model building in regression are covered (Chapters 16 and 17); and various business forecasting methods are considered (Chapter 18).

Flexibility

A final important feature is flexibility. This book is written for students taking either a one-semester or two-semester basic statistics course. There are numerous ways in which the instructor could adapt material to meet specific needs. For example, an introductory, one-semester (or two-quarter) course might consist of Chapters 1–5 (except Section 4.3), 6 (Sections 6.1 to 6.8), 7 (Sections 7.1–7.6), 8 (8.1–8.3), 9, 10 (except Section 10.7), 11 (except Section 11.11), 16 (Sections 16.1–16.7) and selections from Sections 12.1–12.2, 13.1–13.4, and 19.1–19.8. However, the material is organized so that instructors who do not wish to devote time to the questionnaire could skim or omit the data-collection phase of the survey (Chapter 2) and begin the course with Chapter 3 merely by using the results of the survey. If such a course were to emphasize inferential statistics, it could skim Chapters 1 and 2 and really begin with sections of Chapters 3, 4, 5, and 6 before covering Chapters 7 through 16. On the other hand, if the course were to primarily emphasize descriptive statistics, probability, and quality and productivity, then Chapters 1 through 6, 8 (Sections 8.1–8.3), 16 (Sections 16.1–

16.7), 18, and 19 (Sections 19.1–19.7) would be included. For a two-semester course, the entire book could be covered; descriptive statistics, probability and probability distributions, time series, and quality and productivity (Chapters 1–8, 18, 19) could be stressed in the first half and inferential statistics, correlation, regression, and multiple regression could be studied in the second half (Chapters 9 through 17). Regardless of which topics are stressed by each instructor, the primary emphasis is on the concepts of basic statistical methods and their applications to business subjects such as accounting, economics, finance, information systems, management, and marketing.

It is our hope and anticipation that the unique approaches taken in this textbook will make the study of basic statistics more meaningful, rewarding, and comprehensible for all readers.

We are extremely grateful to the many organizations and companies that generously allowed us to use their actual data for developing problems and examples throughout our text. In particular, we would like to cite Time Inc. (publisher of *Fortune*), CBS Inc. (publisher of *Road & Track*), Dun & Bradstreet Publications Corporation (publisher of *Dun's Business Month*), Crain Communications (publisher of *Crain's New York Business*), The Condé Nast Publications, Inc. (publisher of *Street and Smith's*), Consumer's Union (publisher of *Consumer Reports*), Standard & Poor's Corporation (publisher of *Standard N.Y.S.E. Stock Reports*), Brian Joiner (Joiner Associates, Inc.), M.I.T. Center for Advanced Engineering Study, CEEPress Books, The American Association of University Professors (publisher of *Academe*), OECD (publisher of *Observer*), Gale Research, Inc., Association of Research Libraries, and The College and University Personnel Association (CUPA). Moreover, we would like to thank the *Biometrika* Trustees, American Cyanamid Company, The Rand Corporation, The Chemical Rubber Company, the Institute of Mathematical Statistics, and the American Society for Testing and Materials for their kind permission to publish various tables in Appendix E. Furthermore, we would like to acknowledge the SAS Institute, SPSS Inc., Minitab Inc., STSC Inc., and SYSTAT Inc. for their permission to present computer output throughout the text.

We wish to express our thanks to Dennis Hogan, Carol Sobel, and Kate Moore of the editorial staff at Prentice-Hall and Rachel J. Witty of Letter Perfect, Inc., for their continued encouragement. We also wish to thank Professors Lou Bianco, Southeastern Massachusetts University, and John McKenzie, Babson College, and David Fluharty, Ford Motor Co., for their constructive comments during the revision of this textbook. Finally, we would like to thank our wives and children for their patience, understanding, love, and assistance in making this book a reality. It is to them that we dedicate this book.

MARK L. BERENSON
DAVID M. LEVINE

Contents

16 The Simple Linear Regression Model and Correlation 559

17 Multiple Regression Models 626

18 Index Numbers, Time Series, and Business Forecasting   **695**

Basic Business Statistics
CONCEPTS AND APPLICATIONS

1

Introduction

1.1 WHAT IS MODERN STATISTICS?

A century ago H. G. Wells commented that "statistical thinking will one day be as necessary for efficient citizenship as the ability to read and write." Each day of our lives we are exposed to a wide assortment of numerical information pertaining to such phenomena as stock market activity, unemployment rates, medical research findings, opinion poll results, weather forecasts, and sports data. Frequently, such information has a profound impact on our lives.

> The subject of **modern statistics** encompasses the collection, presentation, and characterization of information to assist in both data analysis and the decision-making process.

1.2 THE GROWTH AND DEVELOPMENT OF MODERN STATISTICS

Historically, the growth and development of modern statistics can be traced to two separate phenomena—the needs of government to collect information on its citizenry (see References 4, 5, 13, and 14) and the development of the mathematics of probability theory.

Data have been collected throughout recorded history. During the Egyptian, Greek, and Roman civilizations information was obtained primarily for the purposes of taxation and military conscription. In the Middle Ages, church institutions often kept records concerning births, deaths, and marriages. In America, various records were kept during colonial times (see Reference 14), and beginning in 1790 the Federal Constitution required the taking of a census every ten years. Today these data are used for many purposes, including congressional apportionment and the allocation of federal funds.

1.2.1 Descriptive Statistics

These and other needs for data on a nationwide basis were closely intertwined with the development of descriptive statistics.

> **Descriptive statistics** can be defined as those methods involving the collection, presentation, and characterization of a set of data in order to properly describe the various features of that set of data.

Although descriptive statistical methods are important for presenting and characterizing information (see Chapters 2 through 5), it has been the development of inferential statistical methods as an outgrowth of probability theory that has led to the wide application of statistics in all fields of research today.

1.2.2 Inferential Statistics

The initial impetus for formulation of the mathematics of probability theory came from the investigation of games of chance during the Renaissance. The foundations of the subject of probability can be traced back to the middle of the seventeenth century in the correspondence between the mathematician Pascal and the gambler Chevalier de Mere (see References 5, 8, and 9). These and other developments by such mathematicians as Bernoulli, DeMoivre, and Gauss were the forerunners of the subject of inferential statistics. However, it has only been since the turn of this century that statisticians such as Pearson, Fisher, Gosset, Neyman, Wald, and Tukey pioneered in the development of the methods of inferential statistics that are so widely applied in so many fields today.

> **Inferential statistics** can be defined as those methods that make possible the estimation of a characteristic of a population or the making of a decision concerning a population based only on sample results.

To clarify this, a few more definitions are necessary.

> A **population** (or **universe**) is the totality of items or things under consideration.
>
> A **sample** is the portion of the population that is selected for analysis.
>
> A **parameter** is a summary measure that is computed to describe a characteristic of an entire population.
>
> A **statistic** is a summary measure that is computed to describe a characteristic from only a sample of the population.

Thus, one major aspect of inferential statistics is the process of using sample statistics to draw conclusions about the true population parameters.

The need for inferential statistical methods derives from the need for sampling. As a population becomes large, it is usually too costly, too time consuming, and too cumbersome to obtain our information from the entire population. Decisions pertaining to the population's characteristics have to be based on the information contained in a sample of that population. Probability theory provides the link by ascertaining the likelihood that the results from the sample reflect the results from the population.

These ideas can be clearly seen in the example of a political poll. If the pollster wishes to estimate the percentage of the votes a candidate will receive in a particular election, he or she will not interview each of the thousands (or even millions) of voters. Instead, a sample of voters will be selected. Based on the outcome from the sample, conclusions will be drawn concerning the entire population of voters. Appended to these conclusions will be a probability statement specifying the likelihood or confidence that the results from the sample reflect the true voting behavior in the population.

1.3 ENUMERATIVE VERSUS ANALYTICAL STUDIES

The examples that we have just provided concerning inferential statistical methods allow us to make an important distinction between two types of statistical studies that are undertaken: **enumerative** studies and **analytical** studies.

> Enumerative studies involve decision-making regarding a population and/ or its characteristics.

The political poll is an example of an enumerative study since its objectives are to provide estimates of population characteristics and to take some action on that population. The listing of all the units (such as the registered voters) which belong to the population is called the **frame** (see Section 2.7) and provides the basis for the selection of the sample. Thus the focus of the enumerative study is on the counting (or measuring) of outcomes obtained from the frame.

> Analytical studies involve taking some action on a process to improve performance in the future.

The study of the outcomes of a manufacturing process taken over time is an example of an analytical study. The focus of an analytical study is on predictions of future process behavior and on understanding and improving a process. In an analytical study there is no identifiable universe, as in an enumerative study, and therefore there is also no frame. Perhaps we can highlight the distinction between enumerative and analytical studies by referring to Figure 1.1.

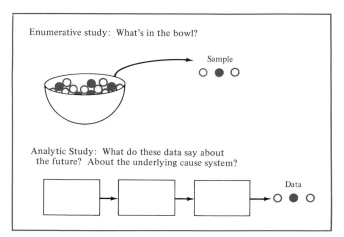

FIGURE 1.1
Enumerative vs. Analytic Study
SOURCE: Brian L. Joiner, "Transformation of the American Style of Teaching Statistics," (Madison, WI: Joiner Associates, 1986) Copyright © by Joiner Associates Inc., 1986 All Rights Reserved.

In the enumerative study the bowl represents the population. The questions of interest revolve around the issue of "What's in the bowl?". In the analytical study the questions of interest revolve around how the data collected (often over a period of time) can be used for future predictions.

The distinction between enumerative and analytical studies is an important one since the methods that have been developed primarily for enumerative studies may be misleading or incorrect for analytical studies (see References 1 and 2). In this textbook we shall develop methods that are appropriate for these two different types of studies. Some of the methods are appropriate for either type of study (see Chapters 1–8 and parts of Chapters 16 and 17). Other methods are appropriate primarily for enumerative studies (see Chapters 9–15) or primarily for analytical studies (see Chapters 18 and 19).

1.4 THE ROLE OF COMPUTER PACKAGES IN STATISTICS

In the last decade revolutionary changes have taken place in our society owing to the rapidly expanding application of computer technology. In particular, the increasing availability of the microcomputer has brought these changes into our businesses, our homes, and our classrooms. Statisticians and researchers in various disciplines can now use the computer in the application of statistical methods, particularly when large databases or highly complex computational procedures are involved.

Over this past decade groups of standardized programs have been assembled as a collection or "package" by various software developers (see References 6–7, 10–12). Multiple users of a large mainframe computer have been able to share the use of these programs with different data. Moreover, in the last four years there has been a widespread development of these statistical packages for use on a microcomputer. Certain packages that were previously available only for mainframe and minicomputers (such as SAS, SPSS[x] and Minitab) are now available in microcomputer versions, and many new packages have been specifically developed for particular brands of microcomputers.

1.5 WHY STUDY MODERN STATISTICS?

Along with the major advances in information processing, the use of statistical methods as an aid to data analysis and decision making has grown dramatically over the past decade and will continue to grow in the future. For example, the study and application of statistics are an integral part of the successful Japanese management approach to total quality control (see References 2 and 3). Some of the techniques, which are used at all organizational levels from company president to line worker, will be described in Chapter 19 of this text.

By studying modern statistics, we will obtain an appreciation for and an understanding of those techniques that are used on the numerical information we encounter in both our professional and nonprofessional lives. The concepts and methods described in this text provide a fundamental background in the subject of modern statistics and its applications in a wide variety of disciplines.

Problems

To answer the questions below you may wish to go to your library and use the following sources of reference:

Indexes
> *Business Periodical Index*
> *New York Times Index*
> *Wall Street Journal Index*

Business Magazines
> *Business Week*
> *Forbes*
> *Fortune*

General Magazines
> *Newsweek*
> *Time*
> *U.S. News & World Report*

Newspapers
> *U.S.A. Today*
> Local newspapers

General Information
> *Statistical Abstract of the United States*

For Problems 1.1 to 1.6, specify the general problem to be solved, the specific inference to be made, what the population is, and (if you are describing the results of an actual published study) what the weaknesses of the study might be. Where appropriate, tell what parameters are of primary interest and what statistics are used to arrrive at a conclusion.

1.1 Describe three applications of statistics to economics or finance.

1.2 Describe three applications of statistics to sports.

1.3 Describe three applications of statistics to political science or public administration.

1.4 Describe three applications of statistics to advertising.

1.5 Describe three applications of statistics to marketing research.

1.6 Describe three applications of statistics to medical research or health care administration.

References

1. DEMING, W. E. "On Probability as a Basis for Action" *American Statistician*, 29, 1975, pp. 146–152.
2. DEMING, W. E. *Out of the Crisis* (Cambridge, MA.: Massachusetts Institute of Technology Center for Advanced Engineering Study, 1986).
3. ISHIKAWA, K., *What is Total Quality Control? The Japanese Way* (Translated by D. J. Lu) (Englewood Cliffs, N.J.: Prentice-Hall, 1985).
4. KENDALL, M. G., AND R. L. PLACKETT, eds., *Studies in the History of Statistics and Probability*, Vol. II (London: Charles W. Griffin, 1977).

5. KIRK, R. E., ed., *Statistical Issues: A Reader for the Behavioral Sciences* (Monterey, Calif.: Brooks/Cole, 1972).
6. LEVINE, D. M., M. L. BERENSON, AND D. F. STEPHAN, *Using Minitab with Basic Business Statistics*, 2d ed. (Englewood Cliffs, N.J.; Prentice-Hall, 1986).
7. LEVINE, D. M., M. L. BERENSON, AND D. F. STEPHAN, *Using SAS with Basic Business Statistics* (Englewood Cliffs, N.J.: Prentice-Hall, 1983).
8. PEARSON, E. S., ed., *The History of Statistics in the Seventeenth and Eighteenth Centuries* (New York: Macmillan, 1978).
9. PEARSON, E. S., AND M. G. KENDALL, eds., *Studies in the History of Statistics and Probability* (Darien, Conn.: Hafner, 1970).
10. RYAN, T. A., B. L. JOINER, AND B. F. RYAN, *Minitab Student Handbook*, 2d ed. (North Scituate, Mass.: Duxbury Press, 1985).
11. *SAS User's Guide*, 1982 ed. (Raleigh, N.C.: SAS Institute, 1982).
12. *SPSS^x User's Guide* (New York: McGraw-Hill, 1983).
13. WALKER, H. M., *Studies in the History of the Statistical Method* (Baltimore: Williams & Wilkins, 1929).
14. WATTENBERG, B. E., ed., *Statistical History of the United States: From Colonial Times to the Present* (New York: Basic Books, 1976).

2

Data Collection

2.1 INTRODUCTION: THE NEED FOR RESEARCH

Throughout history human inquisitiveness has led to experimentation and research in order to aid in the **decision-making process.** This process is a common denominator to all fields of endeavor.

1. The baseball manager needs to select the correct strategy and players for a given set of conditions.
2. The personnel director wants to hire the right person for the right job.
3. The pharmaceutical manufacturer needs to determine whether a new drug is more effective than those currently in use.
4. The market researcher looks for the characteristics that distinguish a product from its competitors.
5. The potential investor wants to determine which firms within which industries are likely to have accelerated growth in a period of economic recovery.

Defining one's goals leads to considering alternative courses of action. The rational decision maker seeks to evaluate information in order to select the course of action that maximizes objectives. To the statistician or researcher, the needed information is the **data.** For a statistical analysis to be useful in the decision-making process, the input data must be appropriate. If the data are flawed by biases, ambiguities, or other types of errors, even the fanciest and most sophisticated tools would not likely be enough to compensate for such deficiencies.

2.2 SOURCES OF DATA FOR RESEARCH

There are many methods by which researchers may obtain needed data. First, they may seek data already published by governmental, industrial, or individual sources. Second, they may design an experiment to obtain the necessary data. Third, they may conduct a survey.

The federal government is a major collector of data for both public and private purposes. The Bureau of Labor Statistics is responsible for collecting data on employment as well as establishing the well-known monthly Consumer Price Index. In addition to its constitutional requirement for conducting a decennial census, the Bureau of the Census is also concerned with a variety of ongoing surveys regarding population, housing, and manufacturing and from time to time undertakes special studies on topics such as crime, travel, and health care.

A second method of obtaining needed data is through experimentation. In an experiment, strict control is exercised over the treatments given to participants. For example, in a study testing the effectiveness of toothpaste, the researcher would determine which participants in the study would use the new brand and which would not, instead of leaving the choice to the subjects. Proper experimental designs are usually the subject matter of more advanced tests, since they often involve sophisticated statistical procedures. However, in order to develop a feeling for testing and experimentation, the fundamental experimental design concepts will be considered in Chapters 11 through 14.

A third method of obtaining data is to conduct a survey. Here no control is exercised over the behavior of the people being surveyed. They are merely asked questions about their beliefs, attitudes, behaviors, and other characteristics.

If a study is to be useful, the data gathered must be *valid*; that is, the "right" responses must be assessed, and in a manner that will elicit meaningful measurements. But obtaining meaningful measurements is often "easier said than done." The process of obtaining a measurement is often governed by what is convenient, not what is needed. The measurements obtained are often only a "proxy" for the ones desired.

In order to design a survey or experiment, one must understand the different types of data and measurement levels. To demonstrate some of the issues involved in obtaining data, we will present them in the context of a survey, although most of the same issues will arise in other types of research.

2.3 OBTAINING DATA THROUGH SURVEY RESEARCH

A survey statistician will most likely want to develop an instrument that asks several questions and deals with a variety of phenomena or characteristics. These phenomena or characteristics are called **random variables.** The data, which are the observed outcomes of these random variables, may differ from response to response.

2.3.1 Types of Data

As outlined in Figure 2.1, there are basically two types of random variables yielding two types of data: **qualitative** and **quantitative.** Qualitative random variables yield **categorical** responses, while quantitative random variables yield **numerical** responses. For example, the response to the question "Do you currently own United States Government Savings Bonds?" is categorical. The choices are clearly "yes" or "no." On the other hand, responses to questions such as "To how many magazines do you currently subscribe?" or "How tall are you?" are clearly numerical. In the first case the quantitative random variable may be considered as **discrete,** while in the second case it can be thought of as **continuous.**

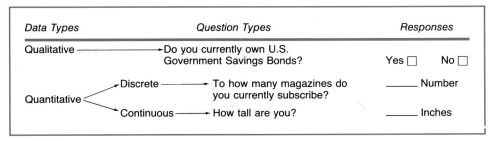

Data Types	Question Types	Responses
Qualitative ────────────→	Do you currently own U.S. Government Savings Bonds?	Yes ☐ No ☐
Quantitative ⟨ Discrete ────────→	To how many magazines do you currently subscribe?	_____ Number
Continuous ────────→	How tall are you?	_____ Inches

FIGURE 2.1
Types of data.

> **Discrete quantitative data** are numerical responses which arise from a counting process, while **continuous quantitative data** are numerical responses which arise from a measuring process.

"The number of magazines subscribed to" is an example of a discrete quantitative variable, since the response takes on one of a (finite) number of integers. The individual either currently subscribes to no magazine, one magazine, two magazines, etc. On the other hand, "the height of an individual" is an example of a continuous quantitative variable, since the response can take on any value within a continuum or interval, depending on the precision of the measuring instrument. For example, a person whose height is reported as 67 inches may be measured as $67\frac{1}{4}$ inches, $67\frac{7}{32}$ inches, or $67\frac{58}{250}$ inches if more precise instrumentation is available. Therefore, we can see that height is a continuous phenomenon which can take on any value within an interval.

It is interesting to note that theoretically no two persons could have exactly the same height, since the finer the measuring device used, the greater the likelihood of detecting differences between them. However, measuring devices used by researchers may not be sophisticated enough to detect small differences, and hence *tied observations* are often found in experimental or survey data even though the random variable is truly continuous.

2.3.2 Levels of Measurement and Types of Measurement Scales

From the above discussion, then, we see that our resulting data may also be described in accordance with the "level of measurement" attained.

In the broadest sense, all collected data are "measured" in some form. For example, even discrete quantitative data can be thought of as arising by a process of "measurement through counting." The four widely recognized levels of measurement are—from weakest to strongest level of measurement—the nominal, ordinal, interval, and ratio scales.

Nominal and Ordinal Scales

Data obtained from a qualitative variable are said to have been measured either on a nominal scale or on an ordinal scale. If the observed data are merely classified into various distinct categories in which no ordering is implied, a **nominal** level of measurement is achieved. On the other hand, if the observed data are classified into distinct categories in which ordering is implied, an **ordinal** level of measurement is attained. These distinctions are depicted in Figures 2.2 and 2.3, respectively.

Qualitative Variable	Categories
Automobile Ownership	Yes No
Type of life insurance owned	Term Endowment Straight-Life Other None
Political party affiliation	Democrat Republican Independent Other

FIGURE 2.2
Examples of nominal scaling.

Qualitative Variable	Ordered Categories
	(Lowest-Highest)
Student class designation	Freshman Sophomore Junior Senior
Product satisfaction	Very Unsatisfied Fairly Unsatisfied Neutral Fairly Satisfied Very Satisfied
Movie classification	G PG PG-13 R X
	(Highest-Lowest)
Faculty rank	Professor Associate Professor Assistant Professor Instructor
Standard & Poor's bond ratings	AAA AA A BBB BB B CCC CC C DDD DD D
Restaurant ratings	***** **** *** ** *
Student grades	A B C D F

FIGURE 2.3
Examples of ordinal scaling.

Nominal scaling is the weakest form of measurement because no attempt can be made to account for differences within a particular category or to specify any ordering or direction across the various categories. Ordinal scaling is a somewhat stronger form of measurement, because an observed value classified into one category is said to possess more of a property being scaled than does an observed value classified into another category. Nevertheless, within a particular category no attempt is made to account for differences between the classified values. Moreover, ordinal scaling is still a weak form of measurement, because no meaningful numerical statements can be made about differences between the categories. That is, the ordering implies only *which* category is "greater," "better," or "more preferred"—not *how much* "greater," "better," or "more preferred."[1]

Interval and Ratio Scales

An **interval scale** is an ordered scale in which the difference between measurements is a meaningful quantity. For example, a person who is 67 inches tall is 2 inches taller than someone who is 65 inches tall. In addition, that 2 inches is the same quantity that would be obtained if the two people were 76 and 74 inches tall, so the difference has the same meaning anywhere on the scale.

If, in addition to differences being meaningful and equal at all points on a scale, there is a true zero point so that ratios of measurements are sensible to consider, then the scale is a **ratio scale.** A person who is 76 inches tall is twice as tall as someone who is 38 inches tall; in general, then, measurements of length are ratio scales.

---

[1] College basketball and college football rankings are other examples of ordinal scaling. The differences in ability between the teams ranked first and second might not be the same as the differences in ability between the teams ranked second and third, or those ranked sixth and seventh, and so on.

Quantitative Variable	Level of Measurement
Temperature (in degrees Celsius or Fahrenheit)	Interval
Calendar time (Gregorian, Hebrew, or Islamic)	Interval
Height (in inches or centimeters)	Ratio
Weight (in pounds or kilograms)	Ratio
Age (in years or days)	Ratio
Salary (in American dollars or Japanese yen)	Ratio

FIGURE 2.4
Examples of interval and ratio scaling.

Temperature is a trickier case: Fahrenheit and centigrade (Celsius) scales are interval but not ratio; the "0" demarcation is arbitrary, not real. No one should say that 76 degrees Fahrenheit is twice as hot as 38 degrees Fahrenheit. But when measured from absolute zero, as in the Kelvin scale, temperature is on a ratio scale, since a doubling of temperature is really a doubling of the average speed of the molecules making up the substance. Figure 2.4 gives examples of interval- and ratio-scaled variables.

Data obtained from a quantitative variable are usually assumed to have been measured either on an interval scale or on a ratio scale. These scales constitute the highest levels of measurement. They are stronger forms of measurement than an ordinal scale because we are able to discern not only which observed value is the largest but also by how much.

Caution: The Need for Operational Definitions
Regardless of the level of measurement for our variables, **operational definitions** (see Reference 3) are needed to elicit the appropriate response or attain the appropriate outcome.

> An **operational definition** provides a meaning to a concept or variable that can be communicated to other individuals. It is something that has the same meaning yesterday, today, and tomorrow to all individuals.

As an example, take the word "round." Although the dictionary provides a literal meaning, what is necessary is a meaning that can actually be used in practice. Thus, the issue really is not what is round, but how far something departs from "roundness" before we say that it is not round. This needs to be defined in a way that can be consistently applied from day to day (or, for a production worker, for example, from product to product).

In the context of a survey, consider the question "What is your age?" To avoid problems of ambiguity, the researcher must develop an operational definition for the responses to the question. For example, the researcher must clarify whether age should be reported to the *nearest* birthday or as of the *last* birthday, because if your birthday is next month, you would probably choose the nearest birthday if you were turning 20; but you would be likely to report your present age if you were turning 50!

As a further example of operational definitions, consider the following recent headline in a newspaper in a suburban New York county: "Off With a Head Count: Is Suffolk more populous than Nassau? LILCO and the Census Bureau disagree."[2]

---

[2] *Newsday*, April 25, 1988.

The article included quotes from the Suffolk county executive (". . . we are confident that Suffolk is No. 1'') and the Nassau county executive ("We'll declare it a tie in the spirit of regional cooperation"). Of course, the differences in the two estimates come from the fact that the Census Bureau and the Long Island Lighting Company (LILCO) have different operational definitions used to estimate population in the two counties. The Census Bureau uses birth and death rates, migration patterns as shown on income tax returns, and a demographic formula that estimates that the average number of people per household has been shrinking in the past several years. On the other hand, for its definition, LILCO uses the number of year-round electric and gas meters, building permits, and a factor for the number of people in each house.

Problems

2.1   Explain the differences between qualitative and quantitative random variables and give three examples of each.

2.2   Explain the differences between discrete and continuous random variables and give three examples of each.

2.3   If two students both score a 90 on the same examination, what arguments could be used to show that the underlying random variable (phenomenon of interest)—test score—is continuous?

2.4   Determine whether each of the following random variables is qualitative or quantitative. If quantitative, determine whether the phenomenon of interest is discrete or continuous. Provide an operational definition for each variable.
(a) Number of telephones per household.
(b) Type of telephone.
(c) Number of long-distance calls made per month.
(d) Length (in minutes) of longest long-distance calls made per month.
(e) Color of telephone.
(f) Monthly charges (in dollars and cents) for long-distance calls made.
(g) Ownership of a cordless phone.

2.5   Suppose the following information is obtained for Peter Franklin upon his admittance to the Brandwein College infirmatory:

(1) Sex: Male
(2) Residence or Dorm: Mogelever Hall
(3) Class: Sophomore
(4) Temperature: 102.2 F° (oral)
(5) Pulse: 70 beats per minute
(6) Blood Pressure: 130/80 mgs/mm
(7) Blood Type: B Positive
(8) Known Allergies to Medicines: No
(9) Preliminary Diagnosis: Influenza
(10) Estimated Length of Stay: 3 days

Classify each of the ten responses by type of data and level of measurement. Provide an operational definition for each variable. [*Hint*: Be careful with blood presure; it's tricky.]

2.6   Give three examples of variables which are actually discrete but might be considered continuous.

2.7   For each variable in the examples of applications of statistics you mentioned in the answers to Problems 1.1–1.6 on page 5, tell whether the variable is quantitative or qualitative; whether it is discrete or continuous; what level of measurement it has; and, if it is not continuous, whether it could be treated as such.

2.8 List three examples in an area of interest to you where data are useful for decision making. What data are useful? How might they be obtained? How might the data be used in the process of making a decision?

2.9 In your own words state why temperature is an interval-scaled variable when measured in degrees Fahrenheit or centigrade, but is a ratio-scaled variable when measured from absolute zero.

2.10 One of the variables most often included in surveys is income. Sometimes the question is phrased: "What is your income (in thousands of dollars)?" In other surveys, the respondent is asked: "Is your income over $10,000? Over $20,000? Over $30,000?"
(a) For each of these cases, tell whether the variable is nominal, ordinal, interval, or ratio.
(b) In the first case, tell why income might be considered either discrete or continuous.

2.4 DESIGNING THE QUESTIONNAIRE INSTRUMENT

The general procedure for designing a questionnaire will involve

1. Choosing the broad topics which are to reflect the theme of the survey.
2. Deciding on a mode of response.
3. Formulating the questions.
4. Pilot testing and making final revisions.

To better understand this process let us consider The Real Estate Survey.

The Real Estate Survey
Suppose that the president of a large nationwide chain of real estate brokerage offices wishes to explore the possibility of opening a branch office in the central portion of Nassau County, New York, situated in an area of Long Island about twenty-five miles east of New York City. In order to obtain a profile of the communities to be served, a sample of all single-family houses is to be selected. To obtain the information on these houses, the president of the realty company hires a statistician to assist in developing a questionnaire and conducting a survey.

2.4.1 Selection of Broad Topics

Working together, the president and the statistician choose the broad topics that are to reflect the theme of the survey. The topics considered are:

1. Characteristics relating to the value and potential worth of the property.
2. Physical characteristics of the house.
3. Optional features that are present in the house.

2.4.2 Length of Questionnaire

Before very long a large number of questions will have been created. Unfortunately, however, there is an inverse relationship between the length of a questionnaire and the rate of response to the survey. That is, the longer the questionnaire, the lower will be the rate of response; the shorter the questionnaire, the higher will be the rate of response. It is, therefore, imperative that we carefully determine the merits of each question in terms of whether the question is really necessary, and if so, how to word it optimally.

Questions should be as short as possible. The response categories for qualitative questions should be nonoverlapping and complete.

2.4.3 Mode of Response

The particular questionnaire format to be selected and the specific question wording are affected by the intended mode of response. There are essentially three modes through which survey work is accomplished: personal interview, telephone interview, and mail. The personal interview and the telephone interview usually produce a higher response rate than does the mail survey—but at a higher cost. After careful consideration, the president and the statistician determine that a personal visit to each house selected in the sample is necessary in order to arrive at an accurate determination of the present worth (appraised value) of the house.

2.4.4 Formulating the Questions

Because of the inverse relationship between the length of a questionnaire and the rate of response to the survey, each question must be clearly presented in as few words as possible, and each question should be deemed essential to the survey. In addition, questions must be free of ambiguities. Operational definitions are needed to elicit the appropriate response. For example, consider the following two questions:

1. Do you smoke? Yes _____   No _____
2. How old are you? _____ years

    Question 1 has several possible ambiguities. It is not clear if the desired response pertains to cigarettes, to cigars, to pipes, or to combinations thereof. It is also not clear whether occasional smoking or habitual smoking was the primary concern of the question. If we were interested only in current cigarette consumption, perhaps it would be better to ask

    About how many cigarettes do you currently smoke each day? _____

When replying to question 2, as previously pointed out, the respondent may be confused as to whether to base the answer on the *last* birthday or the *nearest* birthday unless the appropriate operational definition is specified. This problem may be avoided, however, if the respondent is merely asked

    State your date of birth: _____   _____   _____
                            month   day   year

2.4.5 Testing the Questionnaire Instrument

Once the president and the statistician have discussed the pros and cons of each question, the instrument is properly organized and made ready for **pilot testing** so that it may be examined for clarity and length. Pilot testing on a small group of subjects is an essential phase in conducting a survey. Not only will this group of individuals be providing an estimate of the time needed for responding to the survey, but they will also be asked to comment on any perceived ambiguitites in each question and to recommend additional questions. Once the president and the statistician have evaluated these results, changes are made. If time and budget permit, a second pilot study can be undertaken on a fresh sample of respondents to further improve the document.

Figure 2.5 depicts the questionnaire devised by the president and the statistician in its final form.

Codes	REAL ESTATE SURVEY (*Please* **insert** *the value or* **circle** *the number as appropriate*)
_ _ _ _ _ 1 2 3 4 5	1. Appraised value ($000) __.__
_ _ _ _ _ 7 8 9 10 11	2. Lot Size (000 square feet) __.__
_ 13	3. Number of bedrooms __
_ _ _ 15 16 17	4. Number of bathrooms __.__
_ _ 19 20	5. Number of rooms __
_ _ 22 23	6. Age of the house (in years) __
_ _ _ _ 25 26 27 28	7. Annual taxes ($) ____
_ 30	8. Type of indoor parking facility: (0) None (1) 1-car garage (2) 2-car garage (3) 3-car garage
_ 32	9. Geographical location of the house: (1) East Meadow (2) Farmingdale (3) Levittown
_ 34	10. Architectural Style: (1) Cape (2) Expanded ranch (3) Colonial (4) Ranch (5) Split level
_ 36	11. Type of heating fuel used: (1) Gas (2) Oil
_ 38	12. Type of heating system: (1) Hot air (2) Hot water (3) Other
_ 40	13. Type of swimming pool located on the property: (1) None (2) Above ground (3) In ground
_ 42	14. Eat-in kitchen: (0) Absent (1) Present
_ 44	15. Central air conditioning: (0) Absent (1) Present
_ 46	16. Fireplace: (0) Absent (1) Present
_ 48	17. Connection to local sewer system: (0) Absent (1) Present
_ 50	18. Basement: (0) Absent (1) Present
_ 52	19. Modern kitchen: (0) Absent (1) Present
_ 54	20. Modern bathrooms: (0) Absent (1) Present
_ _ _ 56 57 58	21. Respondent Number ____

FIGURE 2.5
Questionnaire

Problems

2.11 For each of the 20 questions in the real estate survey, provide an operational definition that may be necessary to avoid ambiguity.

2.12 Why might you expect a greater response rate from a survey conducted by personal or telephone interview than from one conducted using a mailed questionnaire instrument?

2.13 Why would you expect a survey conducted by personal or telephone interview to be more costly than one conducted using a mailed questionnaire instrument?

2.14 Suppose that the director of market research at a large department store chain wanted to conduct a survey throughout a metropolitan area to determine the amount of time working women spend shopping for clothing in a typical month.

(a) Describe both the population and sample of interest and indicate the type of data the director primarily wishes to collect.

(b) Develop a first draft of the questionnaire needed in part (a) by writing a series of three qualitative questions and three quantitative questions that you feel would be appropriate for this survey. Provide operational definitions for each question.

2.15 Describe the strong and weak points of the following ways of wording a questionnaire item:

(i) In what type of residence do you live?

(ii) Do you live in a
(a) Single family house? (b) Apartment? (c) Other?

(iii) Do you live in a
(a) Single family house that you own? (b) Two–four family house that you own? (c) Coop or condominium? (d) Rented apartment? (e) Rented house?

2.16 Write a question asking how much education a person has; write three versions of the question that give different levels of detail. Describe situations in which each might be appropriate or inappropriate to use.

2.5 CHOOSING THE SAMPLE SIZE FOR THE SURVEY

Since the president and the statistician have already determined that a personal interview is the most appropriate way of obtaining their desired information, it is now necessary for them to determine the appropriate sample size for the study. Rather than taking a complete census, statistical sampling procedures have become the preferred tool in most survey situations. There are three main reasons for drawing a sample. First of all, it is usually too time consuming to perform a complete census. Second, it is too costly to do a complete census. Third, it is just too cumbersome and inefficient to obtain a complete count of the target population. (See Section 2.7.) Thus the president and the statistician decide that it is their goal to make inferences about the entire population of single family houses in these Long Island communities based on the results obtained from the sample.

After the most essential quantitative and qualitative questions in the survey have been determined, the sample size needed will be based on satisfying the question with the most stringent requirements. In our case, the president and the statistician have determined that Questions 1 and 19 are the most essential quantitative and qualitative questions, respectively. Calculation of the sample size required for a given survey is a matter that will be examined more appropriately in Chapter 10. As we shall see, the required sample size is 233 houses out of a population of 9,660 single-family houses in the geographical area of interest. However, because not everyone will be willing to respond to the survey, the president must be prepared to have a larger group of homeowners visited. If only two out of every three homeowners are expected to respond favorably (i.e., a rate of return of 67%), then 350 homeowners must be contacted in order to get 233 willing respondents.

2.6 TYPES OF SAMPLES

As depicted in Figure 2.6, there are basically two kinds of samples: the **nonprobability sample** and the **probability sample.** For most analytical studies only a non-probability

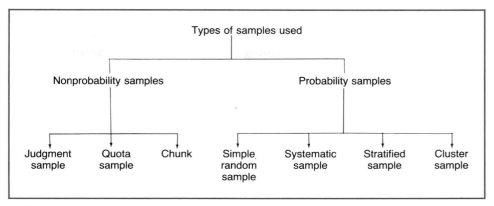

FIGURE 2.6
Types of samples.

sample such as a **judgment sample** is available. In this instance, the opinion of an expert in the subject matter of a study is crucial to being able to use the results obtained in order to make changes in a process. Some other typical procedures of nonprobability sampling are **quota sampling,** and **chunk sampling;** these are discussed in detail in specialized books on sampling methods.

In an enumerative study, the only correct way in which the researcher can make statistical inferences from a sample to a population and interpret the results probabilistically is through the use of a probability sample. A **probability sample** is one in which the subjects of the sample are chosen on the basis of known probabilities. The four types most commonly used are the **simple random sample,** the **systematic sample,** the **stratified sample,** and the **cluster sample.** The simple random sample is one in which every subject has the same chance of selection as every other subject, and in which the selection of one subject does not affect the chances that any other subject is chosen. Moreover, a simple random sample may also be construed as one in which each possible sample that is drawn had the same chance of selection as any other sample. A detailed discussion of systematic sampling, stratified sampling, and cluster sampling procedures can be found in References 1, 2, and 4.

2.7 DRAWING THE SIMPLE RANDOM SAMPLE

In this section we will be concerned with the process of selecting a simple random sample. Although it is not necessarily the most economical or efficient of the probability sampling procedures, it provides the base from which the more sophisticated procedures have evolved.

The key to proper sample selection is obtaining and maintaining an up-to-date list of all the subjects from which the sample will be drawn. Such a list is known as the **population frame.** This population listing will serve as the **target population,** so that if many different probability samples were to be drawn from such a list, hopefully each sample would be a miniature representation of the population and yield reasonable estimates of its characteristics. If the listing is inadequate because certain groups of subjects in the population were not properly included, the random probability samples will only be providing estimates of the characteristics of the *target population*—not the *actual population*—and biases in the results will occur.

To draw a simple random sample of size 350 one could conceivably record the names of each of the 9,660 homeowners in the population on separate index cards, place the index cards in a large fish bowl, thoroughly mix the cards, and then randomly select the 350 sample subjects from the fish bowl. Naturally, in order to ensure that each house (as well as each sample) has the same chance of being selected, all the index cards used must be of the same dimensions.

2.7.1 Sampling *With* or *Without Replacement* from Finite Populations

Two basic methods could be used for selecting the sample: The sample could be obtained **with replacement** or **without replacement** from the finite population. The method employed must be clearly stated by the survey statistician, since various formulas subsequently used for purposes of statistical inference are dependent upon the selection method.[3]

Let N represent the population size and n represent the sample size. When sampling with replacement, the chance that any particular subject in the population, say Judy Craven, is selected on the first draw from the fish bowl is $1/N$ (or $1/9,660$ for our example). Regardless of whoever is actually selected on the first draw, pertinent information is recorded on a master file, and then the particular index card is *replaced* in the bowl (sampling *with* replacement). The N cards in the bowl are then well shuffled and the second card is drawn. Since the first card had been replaced, the chance for selection of any particular subject, including Judy Craven, on the second draw—regardless of whether or not that individual had already been previously selected—is still $1/N$. Again the pertinent information is recorded on a master file and the index card is replaced in order to prepare for the third draw. Such a process is repeated until n, the desired sample size, is obtained. Thus, when sampling with replacement, every subject on every draw will always have the same 1 out of N chance of being selected.

But should the researcher want to have the same individual subject possibly selected more than once? When sampling from human populations, it is generally felt more appropriate to have a sample of different subjects than to permit repeated measurements of the same subject. Thus the researcher would employ the method of sampling *without* replacement, whereby once a subject is drawn, the same subject cannot be selected again. As before, when sampling without replacement, the chance that any particular subject in the population, say Judy Craven, is selected on the first draw from the fish bowl is $1/N$. Whoever is selected, the pertinent information is recorded on a master file and then the particular index card is set aside rather than replaced in the bowl (sampling *without* replacement). The remaining $N - 1$ cards in the bowl are then well shuffled, and the second card is drawn. The chance that any individual not previously selected will be selected on the second draw is now 1 out of $N - 1$. This process of selecting a card, recording the information on a master file, shuffling the remaining cards, and then drawing again continues until the desired sample of size n is obtained.

''Fish bowl'' methods of sampling, although easily understandable, are not very efficient. Less cumbersome and more scientific methods of selection are desirable.

---

[3] It is interesting to note that whether we are sampling *with replacement* from *finite* populations or sampling *without replacement* from *infinite* populations (such as some continuous, ongoing production process), the formulas used are the same.

One such method utilizes a **table of random numbers** (see Table E.1) for obtaining the sample.

2.7.2 Using a Table of Random Numbers

A table of random numbers consists of a series of digits randomly generated (by electronic impulses) and listed in the sequence in which the digits were generated (see Reference 5). Since our numeric system uses 10 digits (0, 1, 2, . . . , 9), the chance of randomly generating any particular digit is equal to the probability of generating any other digit. This probability is 1 out of 10. Hence if a sequence of 500 digits were generated, we would expect about 50 of them to be the digit 0, 50 to be the digit 1, and so on. In fact, researchers who use tables of random numbers usually test out such generated digits for randomness before employing them. Table E.1 has met all such criteria for randomness. Since every digit or sequence thereof in the table is random, we may use the table by reading either horizontally or vertically. The margins of the table designate row numbers and column numbers. The digits themselves are grouped into sequences of five for the sole purpose of facilitating the viewing of the table.

To use such a table in lieu of a fish bowl for selecting the sample, it is first necessary to assign code numbers to the individual members of the population. Suppose that a listing was obtained of the addresses and names of all $N = 9{,}660$ owners of single-family homes in the geographical area of interest. Since the population size (9,660) is a four-digit number, each assigned code number must also be four digits, so that every house has an equal chance for selection. Thus a code of 0001 is given to the first house in the population listing, a code of 0002 is given to the second house in the population listing, . . . , a code of 1752 to the one thousand seven hundred fifty-second house in the population listing, and so on until a code of 9660 is given to the Nth house in the listing.

In order to select the random sample, a random starting point for the table of random numbers (Table 2.1) must be established. One such method is to close one's eyes and strike the table of random numbers with a pencil. Suppose the statistician uses such a procedure and thereby selects row 06, column 01, as the starting point. Reading from left to right, in Table 2.1, in sequences of four digits without skipping, groups are obtained as shown.

Since $N = 9{,}660$ is the largest possible coded value, all four-digit code sequences greater than N (9661 through 9999 and 0000) are discarded. Hence the individual with code number 0033 is the first homeowner in the sample (row 06 and columns 05 through 08) because the first four-digit code sequence (9734) in row 06 was discarded. The second individual selected has code number 6488 (row 06 and columns 09 through 12). Individuals with code numbers 4720, 4334, 6391, 9363, 9411, 0959, 2470, and 7054 are selected third through tenth, respectively.

The selecting process continues in a similar manner until the desired sample size of $n = 350$ homeowners is obtained. During the selection process, if any four-digit coded sequence repeats, the subject corresponding to that coded sequence is included again as part of the sample if sampling with replacement; however, the repeating coded sequence is merely discarded if sampling without replacement. Note that the coded sequence 4205 appears in row 12, columns 33 through 36, and then again in row 21, columns 21 through 24. Since our statistician is sampling without replacement, the repeating sequences are discarded and a sample of 350 unique homeowners is obtained.

TABLE 2.1 Using a table of random numbers

Row	00000 12345	00001 67890	11111 12345	11112 67890	22222 12345	22223 67890	33333 12345	33334 67890
					Column			
01	49280	88924	35779	00283	81163	07275	89863	02348
02	61870	41657	07468	08612	98083	97349	20775	45091
03	43898	65923	25078	86129	78496	97653	91550	08078
04	62993	93912	30454	84598	56095	20664	12872	64647
05	33850	58555	51438	85507	71865	79488	76783	31708
06	[97340	03364	88472	04334	63919	36394	11095	92470
07	70543	29776	10087	10072	55980	64688	68239	20461
08	89382	93809	00796	95945	34101	81277	66090	88872
09	37818	72142	67140	50785	22380	16703	53362	44940
10	60430	22834	14130	96593	23298	56203	92671	15925
11	82975	66158	84731	19436	55790	69229	28661	13675
12	39087	71938	40355	54324	08401	26299 49420		59208
13	55700	24586	93247	32596	11865	63397 44251		43189
14	14756	23997 78643		75912	83832	32768	18928	57070
15	32166	53251	70654	92827	63491	04233	33825	69662
16	23236	73751	31888	81718	06546	83246	47651	04877
17	45794	26926	15130	82455	78305	55058	52551	47182
18	09893	20505	14225	68514	46427	56788	96297	78822
19	54382	74598 91499		14523	68479	27686	46162	83554
20	94750	89923	37089	20048	80336	94598 26940		36858
21	70297	34135	53140	33340	42050	82341	44140	82949
22	85157	47954	32979 26575		57600	40881	12250	73742
23	11100	02340	12860	74697	96644	89439	28707	25815
24	36871	50775	30592 57143		17381	68856	25853	35041
25	23913	48357	63308	16090	51690	54607	72407	55538
26	79348	36085	27973 65157		07456	22255	25626	57054
27	92074	54641	53673	54421	18130	60103	69593	49464
28	06873	21440 75593		41373	49502	17972	82578	16364
29	12478	37622	99659 31065		83613	69889	58869	29571
30	57175	55564	65411	42547	70457	03426	72937	83792
31	91616	11075	80103	07831	59309	13276	26710	73000
32	78025	73539	14621	39044	47450	03197 12787		47709
33	27587	67228	80145	10175	12822	86687	65530	49325
34	16690	20427	04251	64477	73709 73945		92396	68263
35	70183	58065	65489	31833	82093	16747	10386	59293
36	90730 35385		15679	99742	50866	78028	75573	67257
37	10934	93242	13431	24590	02770	48582	00906	58595
38	82462	30166	79613	47416	13389 80268		05085	96666
39	27463	10433	07606	16285	93699	60912	94532	95632
40	02979	52997 09079		92709	90110	47506	53693	49892
41	46888	69929	75233	52507	32097	37594	10067	67327
42	53638	83161	08289	12639	08141	12640	28437	09268
43	82433	61427	17239	89160]	19666	08814	37841	12847
44	35766	31672	50082	22795	66948	65581	84393	15890
45	10853	42581	08792	13257	61973	24450	52351	16602
46	20341	27398	72906	63955	17276	10646	74692	48438
47	54458	90542	77563	51839	52901	53355	83281	19177
48	26337	66530	16687	35179	46560	00123	44546	79896
49	34314	23729	85264	05575	96855	23820	11091	79821
50	28603	10708	68933	34189	92166	15181	66628	58599

Begin Selection
(Row 06, Column 01)

End Selection
(Row 43, Column 20)

SOURCE: Partially extracted from The Rand Corporation, *A Million Random Digits with 100,000 Normal Deviates* (New York: The Free Press, 1955).

Problems

2.17 Draw a simple random sample of one-tenth of the people living in your dormitory (or neighborhood or apartment building, etc.). Explain the procedure you used.

2.18 For a study that would involve doing personal interviews with participants (rather than mail or phone surveys) tell why a simple random sample might be less practical than some other methods.

2.19 If you wanted to determine what proportion of movies shown in the United States last year had themes based on sex or violence, how might you get a random sample to answer your question?

2.20 In a political poll to try to predict the outcome of an election, what is the population to which we usually want to generalize? How might we get a random sample from that population? From what you know about how such polls are actually conducted, what might be some problems with the sampling in these polls?

2.21 Suppose that I want to select a random sample of size 1 from a population of 3 items (which we can call A, B, and C). My rule for drawing the sample is: Flip a coin, if it is heads, pick item A; if it is tails, flip the coin again; this time, if it is heads choose B, if tails choose C. Tell why this is a random sample, but not a simple random sample.

2.22 Suppose that a population has 4 members (call them A, B, C, and D). I would like to draw a random sample of size 2, which I decide to do in the following way: Flip a coin; if it is heads, my sample will be items A and B; if it is tails, the sample will be items C and D. While this is a random sample, it is not a simple random sample. Tell why. (If you did Problem 2.21, compare the procedure described there with the procedure described in this problem.)

2.23 For a population list containing $N = 902$ individuals, what code number would you assign for
(a) The first person on the list?
(b) The fortieth person on the list?
(c) The last person on the list?

2.24 For a population of $N = 902$, verify that by starting in row 05 of the table of random numbers (Table E.1) only six rows are needed to draw a sample of size $n = 60$ *without* replacement.

2.8 OBTAINING THE RESPONSES

Now that the sample of 350 individual homeowners has been selected, the appropriate information concerning their houses must be obtained. Sufficient time must be allowed for receipt of an introductory ''cover'' letter, followed by the personal visit to perform the appraisal of the house.

The covering letter should be brief and to the point. It should state the goal or purpose of the survey, how the survey will be used, and why it is important that the respondent participates. Moreover, it should give any necessary assurance of respondent anonymity and, in our case, offer an incentive for participation.

A draft of the covering letter used by the realty company is displayed in Figure 2.7. (The final version, of course, would be typed on company stationery.) Note that the realty company has offered an incentive (either a toaster, a set of microwave cookery, or a check for $20) in order to increase the rate of response to the survey.

Problems

2.25 Write a draft of the cover letter needed for the department store survey developed in Problem 2.14 on page 16.

2.26 Write an alternative version of the cover letter shown in Figure 2.7.

December 14, 1987

Mr. and Mrs. John Q. Public
666 Lois Lane
Levittown, NY 11756

Dear Mr. and Mrs. Public:

On behalf of the B and L Realty Corporation, I am writing this letter to you to ask for your cooperation and participation in a survey that we are conducting. As a new full-service real estate company in your community, we wish to collect information that will enable us to develop a statistical profile of the communities that we will now be serving. Your home has been randomly selected from a listing of all single-family homes in your community. As part of the survey we will provide to you, free of charge, an appraisal of the present value of your house.

I would greatly appreciate it if you would allow our appraiser to visit your home for a few minutes in the near future and provide him or her with the information necessary so that an accurate appraisal can be made. As a token of appreciation, in addition to a free copy of the appraisal report, we will provide you with your choice of a toaster, a set of microwave cookery, or a cash award of $20. To set up an appointment and to arrange for delivery of your gift, please call our office at (800) 012-3456.

Sincerely,

Alan Bauman

Alan Bauman, President
B and L Realty Corporation

FIGURE 2.7
A draft of the covering letter.

2.9 DATA PREPARATION: EDITING, CODING, AND TRANSCRIBING

Once the set of data is collected it must be carefully prepared for tabular and chart presentation, analysis, and interpretation. The editing, coding, and transcribing processes are extremely important. Responses are scrutinized for completeness and for errors. If necessary, response validation is obtained by recontacting individuals whose answers appear inconsistent or unusual. In addition, responses to open-ended questions are properly classified or scored and responses to both quantitative and qualitative questions are coded for data entry.

Figure 2.8 represents the responses of John Q. Public, file code identification number 0033, who was the first homeowner selected in the sample.[4] Notice how the questionnaire responses are coded for data entry. Qualitative questions require a one-

---

[4] To facilitate data entry, each selected individual's four-digit identification number (obtained from the population listing of homes) is replaced by his or her corresponding respondent number, which specifies position in the sample selection process. For example, the first homeowner selected, John Q. Public (file code number 0033), has respondent number 001.

Question	Type of Question	Computer Code	Columns Allocated for Data Entry	John Q. Public's Responses	Coded Response
1	Appraised value	VALUE	1–5	$190,000	190.0
2	Lot Size	LOTSIZE	7–11	6,900 sq. ft.	06.90
3	Bedrooms	BED	13	4	4
4	Bathrooms	BATH	15–17	2	2.0
5	Rooms	ROOMS	19–20	8	08
6	Age in years	AGE	22–23	38	38
7	Annual taxes	TAXES	25–28	$3,750	3750
8	Type of indoor parking facility	GARAGE	30	One car garage	1
9	Geographical location	LOCATE	32	Levittown	3
10	Architectural style of house	TYPE	34	Colonial	3
11	Type of heating fuel used	FUEL	36	Oil	2
12	Type of heating system	HEAT	38	Hot water	2
13	Swimming pool	POOL	40	None	1
14	Eat-in kitchen	EIK	42	Present	1
15	Central air-conditioning	CAC	44	Absent	0
16	Fireplace	FIREPL	46	Absent	0
17	Sewer connection	SEWER	48	Present	1
18	Basement	BASE	50	Absent	0
19	Modern kitchen	MODKIT	52	Absent	0
20	Modern bathrooms	MODBATH	54	Absent	0
—	Respondent number	RESPNO	56–58	001	001

FIGURE 2.8
Coding the responses of John Q. Public, file code identification number 0033

digit code such as observed with question 10, "Architectural style of house." John Q. Public lives in a colonial and this response is given a code of 3. For quantitative questions, however, the number of spaces to allocate for a response must be based on the most extreme answers possible. For example, in question 5 two spaces are required because a house could contain more than nine rooms. However, since John Q. Public's house contains eight rooms, a coded value of 08 is recorded.

Whether we are entering data on a portable terminal or on a personal computer, it is often desirable to leave one blank space between responses to the various questions. Not only is the data format more aesthetically pleasing, but, even more important, it is easier to spot typographical errors. In our particular example, the coded responses for each homeowner takes 58 spaces (including blanks). The responses from John Q. Public are entered onto a computer terminal as depicted in Figure 2.9.[5]

Figure 2.10 on pages 24 to 29 is a printout of the data. This printout corresponds to the responses of the 233 homeowners who participated in the survey. We note that John Q. Public's responses appear first, since he was the first homeowner selected in the sample.

```
190.0 06.90 4 2.0 08 38 3750 1 3 3 2 2 1 1 0 0 1 0 0 0 001
```

FIGURE 2.9
Data entries for the responses of John Q. Public, file code identification number 0033.

---

[5] The exact format for the data will depend on the statistical package utilized (particularly when incomplete responses—i.e., **"missing values"**—are present).

```
            L                                                     M
            O                          G  L                       F           M  O  R
   V        T               R          T  A  O                    I     S     O  D  E
   A        S       B       O    A     X  A  A  Y  U  E  O  E  C  E  W  A  K  A  P
   L        I       B   A   O    A     E  G  T  P  E  A  O  I  A  P  E  S  I  T  N
   U        Z       E   T   M    G     S  E  E  E  L  T  L  K  C  L  R  E  T  H  O
   E        E       D   H   S    E     S  E  E  L  T  K  C  L  R  E  T  H     O

   190.0  06.90  4  2.0  08  38  3750  1  3  3  2  2  1  1  0  0  1  0  0  0  001
   215.0  06.00  2  2.0  07  30  2856  1  1  4  2  2  1  1  1  0  1  1  0  0  002
   160.0  06.00  3  2.0  06  35  3240  0  3  1  2  2  1  1  0  1  1  0  1  1  003
   195.0  06.00  5  2.0  08  35  4000  1  1  4  2  1  1  1  0  0  1  0  1  1  004
   163.0  07.00  3  1.0  06  39  2700  1  3  1  2  1  1  1  0  0  1  0  0  0  005
   181.0  07.00  4  1.5  07  32  3959  1  2  4  2  2  2  1  0  0  1  1  0  0  006
   220.0  09.75  4  1.5  07  60  3142  2  2  3  2  2  1  1  0  0  0  1  0  0  007
   159.9  06.00  4  1.0  07  38  2800  1  3  1  1  2  1  1  0  0  1  0  1  1  008
   160.0  06.00  2  1.0  07  35  2250  1  1  1  2  1  1  1  0  0  1  1  1  1  009
   195.0  06.00  3  2.0  07  38  2995  1  3  4  2  2  1  1  0  1  1  0  1  1  010
   165.0  09.00  4  1.0  06  32  2500  1  3  4  2  2  1  1  0  1  1  0  0  0  011
   190.0  07.00  4  2.0  06  27  2600  1  2  4  1  1  1  1  0  0  1  1  1  1  012
   180.0  11.20  4  1.0  09  32  2800  1  3  1  2  2  1  1  0  0  1  0  0  0  013
   181.0  06.00  5  2.0  10  35  2500  0  3  1  2  2  1  1  0  0  1  0  0  0  014
   160.0  05.60  3  1.0  06  37  2027  0  3  1  2  2  1  1  0  1  1  0  1  1  015
   160.0  06.50  2  1.0  05  35  2250  1  2  1  2  2  1  0  0  0  1  1  0  0  016
   185.0  06.00  3  1.5  08  37  2500  1  3  2  2  2  1  1  0  1  1  0  1  1  017
   160.0  06.00  4  1.0  06  39  2200  1  3  1  2  2  1  1  0  0  1  0  1  1  018
   176.0  06.00  4  2.0  07  37  3156  0  3  1  2  2  1  1  0  1  1  0  1  1  019
   179.9  08.70  4  1.0  06  36  2741  1  3  1  2  2  1  1  0  1  1  0  0  0  020
   147.0  06.00  4  1.0  06  39  2100  0  3  1  2  2  1  1  0  0  1  0  0  0  021
   189.0  06.50  3  2.0  07  36  2400  0  3  1  2  2  2  1  0  0  1  0  1  1  022
   176.9  06.00  4  1.5  10  30  2857  1  2  1  2  1  1  1  0  1  1  0  1  1  023
   181.0  07.00  3  1.5  07  28  3959  1  2  3  1  2  1  1  0  0  1  1  0  1  024
   151.0  06.50  3  1.0  06  35  2280  0  3  1  2  2  1  0  0  0  1  0  0  1  025
   189.0  09.41  3  1.5  06  24  2900  1  1  4  2  1  1  1  0  0  0  1  1  1  026
   170.0  06.00  3  2.0  08  38  2700  1  3  1  2  2  1  1  0  0  1  0  1  1  027
   249.0  11.25  4  2.5  08  22  4600  1  1  3  2  2  1  1  0  0  1  1  1  1  028
   267.0  09.88  6  2.5  09  33  4300  0  1  3  2  2  1  1  0  1  1  1  0  0  029
   185.0  05.82  3  1.0  06  27  3700  1  2  4  2  2  1  1  0  0  0  1  0  0  030
   269.9  10.00  4  2.0  08  28  4500  2  2  4  2  2  1  1  1  0  1  1  1  1  031
   199.9  06.00  4  2.0  06  38  2700  1  1  1  2  2  1  1  0  0  0  1  1  1  032
   180.0  06.00  3  1.5  06  35  2300  1  3  4  2  2  1  1  0  1  1  0  1  1  033
   189.9  07.20  3  2.0  07  35  2860  1  2  1  2  2  3  1  0  1  0  1  0  0  034
   299.9  07.50  4  2.5  08  14  4343  1  2  3  2  2  1  1  0  0  0  1  0  0  035
   179.9  08.00  3  1.0  07  35  2911  1  2  5  1  1  2  1  0  0  1  1  1  1  036
   210.0  10.00  3  1.5  07  30  3930  1  2  5  1  2  1  1  1  0  1  1  1  1  037
   163.0  06.00  3  1.0  06  36  1889  0  3  1  2  2  1  1  0  0  1  0  1  1  038
   159.9  06.00  3  1.0  07  39  2378  0  2  1  1  1  2  1  0  0  0  1  0  0  039
```

FIGURE 2.10
Computer listing of responses to questionnaire from a sample of homeowners.

```
        L                                              M
        O                          G  L                O        R
V       T          R         T  A  O              F    I  S  O  D  E
A       S       B  O         A  R  C  T  F  H  P   R   E  B  D  B  S
L    B  I  B  A  O  A     X  A  A  Y  U  E  O  C  E  W  A  K  A  P
U    Z  E  T  M  G  E     T  P  E  A  O  I  A  P  E  S  I  T  N
E    E  D  H  S  E  S     E  E  L  T  L  K  C  L  R  E  T  H  O

165.0  06.25  3  1.0  06  30  1800  0  2  4  2  1  1  1  0  1  1  0  1  1  040
180.0  06.00  4  1.0  08  35  2900  0  3  4  2  2  1  1  0  1  1  0  1  1  041
169.0  06.00  3  1.0  06  37  2671  1  1  4  2  1  1  1  0  0  1  0  1  1  042
179.0  06.00  3  1.0  06  35  3060  1  1  4  2  2  1  1  0  0  1  1  0  0  043
180.0  06.00  4  1.0  07  39  2400  0  3  1  2  1  1  0  0  0  1  0  1  1  044
218.0  06.00  3  2.0  07  31  3100  1  1  5  2  2  1  1  0  0  1  1  0  0  045
150.0  06.00  5  2.0  09  39  3177  1  3  1  2  2  2  1  0  0  0  0  1  1  046
247.0  08.00  4  2.0  08  30  3100  1  1  1  2  3  2  1  1  1  1  1  1  1  047
173.5  06.00  4  1.0  06  39  3000  1  3  1  2  2  1  1  0  1  1  0  1  1  048
218.0  07.40  3  2.0  07  30  3000  1  1  1  2  2  2  1  0  0  1  1  1  1  049
152.0  06.00  4  2.0  06  36  2700  1  3  1  2  2  1  1  0  0  0  0  0  1  050
299.9  05.18  4  3.5  08  15  4762  2  1  3  2  2  1  1  1  0  1  1  1  1  051
185.0  07.00  1  1.0  06  28  2700  1  2  4  2  2  1  1  0  0  1  1  1  1  052
200.0  07.50  4  2.0  08  36  3606  1  3  2  2  2  1  1  0  1  1  0  1  1  053
172.0  06.00  3  1.0  06  35  2752  1  1  4  2  2  1  1  0  0  1  0  1  1  054
230.0  07.20  3  2.5  07  31  3400  1  1  5  2  2  1  1  0  0  1  1  1  1  055
235.0  05.00  3  1.5  07  34  3148  1  1  1  2  2  1  1  0  0  0  1  1  1  056
165.9  06.00  5  2.0  07  30  3344  1  3  3  2  2  1  1  0  0  1  0  1  1  057
200.0  09.90  3  1.5  07  30  3871  1  2  5  2  2  1  1  0  0  1  1  1  1  058
190.0  06.00  4  1.5  08  44  3300  1  1  1  2  2  1  1  0  0  1  1  1  1  059
140.0  06.00  3  1.0  07  38  2450  1  3  1  2  2  1  0  0  0  0  0  1  1  060
180.0  07.20  3  1.0  05  40  1900  0  1  4  2  3  1  1  0  0  1  0  0  0  061
213.0  07.00  4  2.0  08  35  3600  0  1  4  2  2  1  1  0  0  1  1  1  1  062
115.0  18.92  3  1.0  06  16  2400  0  2  4  2  2  1  1  0  0  0  0  1  1  063
199.9  10.88  5  2.0  10  28  2540  1  2  4  2  2  1  1  0  0  1  1  0  0  064
153.0  06.18  4  1.0  06  39  2158  0  3  1  2  2  1  1  0  1  1  0  1  1  065
180.0  09.10  4  1.5  08  33  2853  1  3  2  2  2  1  1  0  1  1  0  1  1  066
162.9  06.00  4  1.0  06  38  2160  0  3  1  2  2  1  1  0  1  0  0  1  0  067
160.0  06.50  3  1.0  06  33  2500  1  3  4  2  2  1  0  0  1  1  0  0  0  068
175.0  06.00  4  1.0  06  38  2594  2  1  1  2  2  1  1  0  0  1  1  0  0  069
170.0  05.00  3  2.0  06  41  2300  1  1  1  2  3  1  1  0  0  1  1  1  1  070
155.0  06.00  4  1.0  06  35  2436  1  3  1  2  2  1  1  0  0  1  0  0  1  071
163.0  08.40  4  1.0  06  37  2400  1  3  2  2  2  1  1  0  1  1  0  0  1  072
160.0  06.00  4  2.0  06  38  2500  1  3  4  2  2  1  1  0  1  1  0  1  1  073
175.0  06.00  5  2.0  07  36  3024  1  3  1  2  2  1  1  0  0  1  1  1  1  074
176.5  06.42  4  2.0  07  39  3100  0  3  4  2  2  2  1  0  1  1  0  1  1  075
189.9  31.50  5  2.0  09  31  4200  0  2  5  2  2  1  1  0  0  1  1  1  1  076
157.9  06.00  4  1.0  06  35  1900  0  3  1  2  2  1  1  0  0  1  0  0  0  077
179.0  06.00  3  1.0  07  37  2950  1  3  2  2  2  1  1  0  1  1  0  1  1  078
215.0  07.00  4  2.0  07  35  3860  2  1  1  2  1  1  1  0  0  1  1  0  0  079
```

FIGURE 2.10 (continued)

```
        L                                                    M
        O                         G  L                  M    O    R
  V     T            R        T    A  O             F    I  S O    D    E
  A     S     B      O    A   A    R  C  T  F  H  P    R  E  B  D  B    S
  L     I     B      O    A   X    A  A  Y  U  E  O  E  C  E  W  A  K  A P
  U     Z     E      M    G   E    G  T  P  E  A  O  I  A  P  E  S  I  T N
  E     E     D      H    S   E    S  E  E  L  T  L  K  C  L  R  E  T  H O

 189.9  08.25  3  2.0  07  31  3600  1  2  4  2  2  1  1  0  0  1  1  1  080
 170.0  11.84  4  2.0  08  34  3500  0  3  3  2  2  1  1  1  0  1  0  1  1  081
 229.5  07.00  3  1.5  07  28  3500  2  1  5  1  1  1  1  0  0  1  1  1  082
 185.0  16.00  5  1.5  10  38  3200  1  3  2  2  2  2  1  0  1  1  0  1  1  083
 230.0  10.00  4  1.5  08  61  3638  2  2  3  2  2  1  1  0  1  1  1  0  0  084
 180.0  07.20  3  2.0  06  14  1582  2  1  1  2  2  1  1  0  0  1  1  1  085
 199.9  10.34  4  1.5  08  37  4079  1  3  3  2  2  1  1  0  1  1  0  1  1  086
 180.0  11.00  4  1.0  07  40  2500  1  3  1  2  2  2  1  0  0  1  0  1  1  087
 190.0  06.00  4  2.0  08  38  2890  1  3  1  2  2  1  1  0  0  1  0  1  1  088
 225.0  06.86  3  2.0  06  30  3000  0  1  4  2  2  1  1  0  1  1  1  1  1  089
 155.0  06.48  3  1.0  05  35  2483  0  1  4  2  1  1  1  0  0  0  0  0  0  090
 179.0  07.00  4  1.0  06  37  2800  1  1  2  2  2  1  1  0  1  0  0  1  1  091
 217.9  06.00  4  2.0  08  37  3460  1  3  2  2  2  3  1  0  1  1  0  1  1  092
 173.0  10.60  4  2.0  07  36  2634  0  3  1  2  2  1  1  0  0  1  0  1  1  093
 183.0  06.00  3  2.0  06  39  2708  1  2  4  2  2  2  1  0  0  1  1  1  1  094
 215.0  07.70  4  1.0  07  31  2989  1  2  5  1  1  2  1  0  0  1  1  1  1  095
 159.0  07.50  3  1.0  06  55  1814  1  2  4  2  2  1  0  0  0  1  0  1  1  096
 195.0  07.75  3  1.5  07  34  3175  1  1  5  2  2  1  1  0  0  1  1  1  1  097
 180.0  06.95  3  2.0  06  32  2800  1  2  4  2  2  2  1  0  0  1  1  1  1  098
 160.8  06.00  4  1.5  06  36  2400  1  3  4  2  2  1  1  0  1  1  0  1  1  099
 179.9  06.00  4  1.0  06  25  2750  1  1  4  2  2  1  1  0  0  0  1  0  0  100
 174.9  06.00  4  1.0  09  34  2500  1  2  1  2  2  1  1  0  0  1  1  1  1  101
 225.0  06.00  3  2.0  07  33  3701  1  1  5  2  2  1  1  0  0  1  1  1  1  102
 100.0  12.00  7  1.0  10  21  1775  0  2  4  2  2  1  1  0  0  1  1  1  1  103
 165.0  06.00  4  1.5  08  36  2640  0  3  4  2  2  2  1  0  1  0  0  1  1  104
 173.0  08.00  4  1.5  06  36  2700  0  3  4  2  1  1  1  0  1  1  0  1  1  105
 174.9  10.00  4  2.0  07  34  3000  1  2  1  2  2  1  1  0  0  1  1  1  1  106
 176.0  06.00  3  1.5  07  31  3276  1  3  1  2  2  1  1  0  0  1  0  1  1  107
 197.5  06.30  4  1.0  08  34  3454  0  1  1  2  2  1  1  0  0  1  1  1  1  108
 189.9  05.00  4  2.0  07  38  2386  1  2  1  2  2  1  1  0  0  1  1  1  1  109
 185.0  28.13  6  2.0  10  44  4000  1  3  3  2  3  1  0  0  1  0  1  0  1  110
 195.0  07.75  4  2.5  08  22  3000  1  1  4  2  2  1  1  0  0  1  1  1  1  111
 223.5  06.00  4  2.0  08  37  3200  1  3  2  2  2  3  1  0  1  1  0  1  1  112
 190.0  07.00  4  2.0  07  35  3465  2  1  1  2  1  1  1  0  0  1  1  1  1  113
 245.0  06.00  3  1.5  07  30  3900  1  1  5  2  2  1  1  1  0  1  1  0  0  114
 206.7  11.70  3  2.0  10  28  4200  1  1  5  2  1  1  1  0  0  1  1  0  0  115
 210.0  06.90  4  1.5  09  24  3500  1  2  5  2  2  2  1  0  0  1  1  0  0  116
 170.0  08.00  4  1.0  08  35  3000  1  3  4  2  2  1  1  0  1  1  0  0  0  117
 185.0  09.01  3  1.5  07  25  2400  2  2  4  2  2  1  1  0  1  0  1  1  1  118
 170.0  06.00  3  2.0  06  39  3040  1  3  4  2  2  2  1  0  1  1  0  1  1  119
```

FIGURE 2.10 (continued)

```
        L                                           M
        O                      G L              F   M O   R
V       T           R      T   A O              I S O D   E
A       S      B    O      A   R C T F H P      R E B D B S
L       I      B    A  O   A   X A A Y U E O E C E W A K A P
U       Z      E    T  M   G   E G T P E A O I A P E S I T N
E       E      D    H  S   E   S E E E L T L K C L R E T H O

199.0 10.00 3 2.0 06 38 3512 2 1 1 2 3 2 1 0 1 1 1 1 1 120
175.0 06.00 3 2.0 07 39 2800 1 3 1 2 2 1 1 0 0 1 0 1 1 121
190.0 03.55 4 2.0 06 35 2300 0 1 1 2 1 1 1 0 0 1 1 0 0 122
153.0 07.20 4 1.0 07 39 2513 1 3 1 2 2 1 0 0 0 1 0 1 1 123
190.0 05.00 3 1.5 07 85 1481 1 2 3 2 2 1 1 0 0 1 0 1 1 124
170.0 07.50 4 2.0 07 35 3616 1 3 1 2 1 1 0 0 0 1 1 1 1 125
180.0 07.00 4 2.5 07 32 2500 0 2 1 2 2 1 1 0 0 1 1 1 1 126
164.9 06.00 3 1.5 06 39 2100 0 3 1 2 2 1 1 0 0 1 0 0 0 127
192.5 06.00 4 2.0 07 35 3000 0 3 3 2 2 1 1 0 0 1 0 1 1 128
170.0 06.00 4 2.0 07 38 2500 0 3 2 2 2 1 1 0 1 1 0 1 1 129
188.0 11.12 4 2.0 07 36 4089 1 3 1 2 3 1 1 0 0 1 0 1 1 130
167.0 08.20 4 1.0 06 39 2225 0 3 4 2 2 1 1 0 1 0 0 1 1 131
297.5 12.18 5 2.5 09 24 5200 1 1 3 2 2 1 1 0 0 1 1 1 0 132
178.0 06.00 4 2.0 08 36 3250 1 3 4 2 2 3 1 0 1 1 0 1 1 133
159.9 07.80 3 1.0 06 20 3300 1 2 4 2 2 1 1 0 0 1 1 1 1 134
229.0 07.00 3 2.0 07 35 4100 1 1 3 1 2 1 1 0 0 1 0 0 0 135
215.0 07.50 4 2.0 07 35 3100 1 1 1 2 1 1 1 0 0 1 1 0 0 136
180.0 06.00 5 2.0 08 19 3500 0 3 4 2 2 1 1 0 1 1 0 1 1 137
190.0 06.78 4 2.0 06 39 2560 1 1 1 2 3 1 1 0 0 1 1 1 1 138
151.0 06.00 3 1.0 06 37 2074 0 3 1 2 2 1 1 0 0 1 0 1 1 139
239.9 06.48 4 2.5 08 16 4909 2 3 3 2 2 1 1 1 1 0 1 1 1 140
290.0 10.50 4 2.5 09 29 5000 2 1 5 2 2 1 1 0 1 1 1 0 0 141
305.0 12.10 3 2.0 09 46 3640 0 2 2 2 2 1 1 1 1 1 1 1 0 142
190.0 07.00 3 1.5 07 28 2948 1 2 5 1 1 2 1 0 0 1 1 1 1 143
310.0 07.32 4 2.5 11 32 4717 1 1 5 2 2 1 1 0 0 1 1 1 1 144
219.9 07.00 3 1.5 09 30 3200 1 2 5 1 2 1 1 0 0 1 1 0 0 145
160.0 07.85 4 2.0 07 28 2850 0 3 3 2 2 1 1 0 0 1 0 0 0 146
150.0 06.00 4 1.0 06 38 2400 1 3 1 2 2 1 1 0 0 1 0 1 1 147
189.9 07.00 5 1.5 09 28 4100 1 2 5 1 1 1 1 0 1 1 1 0 0 148
164.9 06.00 3 1.0 06 34 2836 1 3 1 2 2 1 1 0 0 1 0 0 0 149
159.9 06.00 3 1.0 06 39 2650 1 3 1 2 2 1 1 0 0 1 0 1 1 150
187.0 06.00 3 1.0 07 36 2700 1 3 1 2 2 2 1 0 0 1 0 0 0 151
160.0 12.10 5 1.0 08 37 2800 1 3 4 2 2 1 1 0 1 1 0 1 1 152
206.0 11.00 4 1.0 07 35 2886 1 1 1 2 2 1 1 0 0 1 1 0 0 153
179.9 08.40 3 2.0 06 36 2900 0 3 4 2 2 1 1 0 1 1 0 1 1 154
163.0 08.87 3 1.0 06 37 1900 1 2 4 2 3 1 1 0 1 0 1 0 0 155
170.0 06.00 4 2.0 06 32 3000 1 3 4 2 1 1 1 0 1 1 0 0 0 156
189.9 07.00 4 2.0 07 28 2935 1 2 1 2 2 1 1 0 0 1 1 1 1 157
175.0 06.00 4 2.0 07 37 3000 1 3 2 2 2 1 1 0 1 1 0 1 1 158
224.5 10.40 3 2.0 07 15 3500 2 1 4 2 2 1 1 0 0 0 1 1 1 159
```

FIGURE 2.10 (continued)

```
        L                                               M
        O                       G  L                          F        M  O  R
   V    T                 R     T  A  O                        I  S     O  D  E
   A    S     B     O        A  R  C  T  F  H  P           R  E  B  D  B  S
   L    I     B     A     O  A  X  A  A  Y  U  E  O  E  C  E  W  A  K  A  P
   U    Z     E     T     M  G  E  G  T  P  E  A  O  I  A  P  E  S  I  T  N
   E    E     D     H     S  E  S  E  E  E  L  T  L  K  C  L  R  E  T  H  O

160.0  10.00  3  1.0  06  40  2307  1  3  1  2  2  1  1  0  0  1  0  1  1  160
174.9  07.00  3  1.5  07  31  2850  1  2  5  2  2  1  1  0  0  1  1  1  1  161
177.0  06.00  5  2.0  08  39  3200  0  3  4  2  2  1  1  0  0  1  0  1  1  162
220.0  06.00  3  1.5  07  31  3000  1  1  5  2  2  1  1  0  0  1  1  1  1  163
167.8  06.00  3  1.0  07  35  3000  0  3  1  2  2  1  1  0  1  1  0  1  1  164
160.0  06.00  4  1.0  06  35  2400  0  3  1  2  2  1  1  0  0  1  0  1  1  165
270.0  10.32  3  2.5  07  26  5400  2  1  5  2  2  1  1  0  0  1  1  0  0  166
185.0  06.00  3  1.0  06  30  2500  1  2  4  2  2  1  1  0  0  1  1  1  1  167
205.0  06.00  4  1.0  08  36  2827  0  1  1  2  2  1  0  0  0  1  1  0  0  168
174.0  09.12  4  1.0  07  36  2800  0  3  2  2  2  1  1  0  1  1  0  1  1  169
169.0  06.00  4  2.0  07  37  2911  0  3  4  2  2  1  1  0  1  1  0  1  1  170
175.0  07.63  4  2.0  06  37  2800  1  3  2  2  2  1  1  0  1  1  0  1  1  171
190.0  09.00  3  2.0  07  39  2945  1  2  1  2  2  1  1  0  0  1  1  0  0  172
167.4  06.00  4  1.5  06  36  2400  1  3  4  2  2  1  1  0  1  1  0  1  1  173
192.5  06.00  3  2.5  07  27  3450  1  3  5  2  2  1  1  0  1  1  1  0  1  174
155.0  06.00  3  1.0  06  35  2200  1  3  1  2  2  1  1  0  0  1  1  1  1  175
240.0  07.00  4  2.5  08  29  4100  1  1  5  2  2  1  1  1  0  1  1  1  1  176
166.0  07.30  4  1.0  08  35  2850  0  3  1  2  2  1  1  0  0  1  0  1  1  177
210.0  12.24  5  2.0  07  30  4400  1  1  1  2  2  3  1  0  0  1  1  0  0  178
180.0  06.00  4  2.0  07  38  3048  1  3  4  2  2  1  1  0  1  1  0  1  1  179
154.0  08.40  4  2.0  06  40  2550  0  3  1  2  2  1  1  0  0  1  0  0  0  180
176.9  07.50  3  1.0  07  65  1300  1  2  3  2  3  1  1  0  0  1  1  0  0  181
214.0  05.50  4  2.0  09  23  3800  1  3  5  2  2  1  1  0  1  1  1  0  0  182
165.0  06.00  3  1.0  06  39  2500  1  3  1  2  2  1  1  0  0  1  0  1  1  183
184.0  09.10  3  1.5  07  30  4134  1  2  5  2  2  1  1  0  1  1  1  0  0  184
149.0  06.00  3  1.0  05  37  2000  0  3  1  2  2  1  1  0  0  1  0  0  0  185
215.0  07.48  3  2.0  07  35  3200  1  1  1  2  2  1  1  0  0  1  1  0  0  186
159.0  06.00  4  2.0  06  30  2400  1  3  4  2  2  1  1  0  1  1  0  0  0  187
205.0  08.00  5  2.0  10  36  2900  0  3  1  2  2  3  1  0  1  0  1  1  1  188
210.0  07.20  4  2.0  08  30  3600  1  1  1  2  2  1  1  0  0  1  1  0  0  189
171.0  10.00  3  1.5  07  30  3115  1  2  5  2  1  2  1  0  0  1  1  1  0  190
185.0  06.25  3  1.0  06  80  1000  0  2  3  1  2  1  1  0  0  1  1  1  1  191
189.0  08.00  3  1.5  09  32  3698  1  2  5  2  2  2  1  0  1  1  1  0  0  192
176.0  06.00  3  2.0  07  34  2800  1  3  1  2  2  1  1  0  1  1  0  1  1  193
229.0  10.80  4  1.0  06  36  3100  0  1  1  2  2  1  1  0  1  1  0  1  1  194
187.5  07.00  4  1.5  08  30  3815  1  2  5  2  2  1  1  0  0  1  1  1  0  195
230.0  07.30  3  1.5  07  31  3814  1  2  5  2  2  2  1  0  0  1  1  1  1  196
280.0  08.00  3  3.0  08  32  3200  1  1  5  2  2  1  1  1  0  1  1  1  1  197
198.0  06.00  5  3.0  09  33  2800  0  2  1  2  2  1  0  0  0  1  1  1  1  198
153.0  06.00  3  1.5  06  36  2650  0  3  1  2  2  1  1  0  1  1  0  1  1  199
```

FIGURE 2.10 (continued)

VALUE	LOTSIZE	BED	BATH	ROOMS	AGE	TAXES	GARAGE	LOCATE	TYPE	FUEL	HEAT	POOL	EIK	CAC	FIREPL	SEWER	BASE	MODKIT	MODBATH	RESPNO
199.9	11.00	3	2.0	10	33	2767	0	2	4	2	1	2	1	1	1	1	0	0		200
280.0	06.00	3	2.5	07	30	4058	2	1	5	2	2	1	1	0	0	1	1	1	1	201
174.5	06.00	3	1.0	06	35	2200	1	1	4	2	1	1	1	0	1	0	0	1	1	202
195.0	06.50	4	2.0	08	30	3700	0	2	1	2	2	2	1	0	1	1	1	1	1	203
185.0	04.10	3	1.0	06	38	2589	1	1	1	2	3	1	1	0	0	1	1	1	0	204
180.0	07.20	4	1.0	07	30	2900	1	1	1	2	2	1	0	0	0	1	1	0	0	205
205.0	07.50	4	2.0	07	26	3235	0	1	1	2	2	1	1	0	0	1	1	0	0	206
180.0	06.00	4	2.0	06	35	2784	1	2	1	2	1	1	1	0	0	1	1	0	0	207
190.0	06.00	4	2.0	07	39	3480	1	1	3	2	1	1	1	0	0	1	1	0	0	208
225.0	06.80	4	2.5	09	23	3600	1	2	5	2	2	1	1	0	0	1	1	1	1	209
160.0	06.00	4	1.0	07	35	2800	1	3	1	2	2	2	1	0	0	1	0	1	1	210
199.9	07.00	4	2.0	08	33	4163	2	2	5	2	1	3	1	0	1	1	1	1	1	211
180.0	08.50	3	1.0	05	35	2725	1	2	4	2	2	2	1	0	0	1	1	0	0	212
195.0	06.00	4	2.0	07	32	3000	0	1	1	2	2	1	1	0	0	1	1	0	0	213
169.5	06.00	4	2.0	07	38	2200	1	3	1	2	2	1	1	0	0	1	0	0	0	214
260.0	06.50	3	2.5	10	31	4400	0	1	5	2	2	1	1	0	1	1	1	1	1	215
175.0	06.30	3	1.0	07	39	3000	1	3	4	2	2	1	1	0	1	0	0	1	1	216
168.0	06.00	2	1.0	05	38	2400	1	1	1	2	2	1	1	0	0	1	1	1	1	217
180.0	06.00	4	1.0	06	50	2419	1	1	1	2	1	1	1	1	1	1	0	0		218
185.0	06.00	4	1.0	07	35	2200	1	1	1	1	2	1	1	0	0	1	1	1	1	219
286.5	06.00	5	2.5	11	32	4000	1	1	5	2	2	3	1	0	0	1	1	1	1	220
165.9	06.00	3	1.0	06	45	1600	0	1	1	2	2	1	1	0	0	1	1	1	1	221
265.0	06.00	3	1.0	06	31	2900	1	1	5	1	1	1	1	0	0	1	1	1	0	222
182.0	09.97	4	2.0	07	30	3739	0	2	4	2	2	1	1	0	1	0	1	0	0	223
230.0	06.00	4	2.0	06	35	3558	1	1	1	2	2	1	1	0	0	1	1	0	0	224
194.0	08.30	2	2.0	06	35	3440	1	1	4	2	2	3	1	1	1	1	1	1	1	225
295.0	12.21	5	3.0	08	28	6470	2	1	2	2	2	1	1	0	1	1	1	0	0	226
169.5	06.50	3	2.0	06	35	2303	1	1	4	2	2	1	1	0	1	1	0	0	0	227
175.0	05.40	5	1.5	08	37	3500	2	3	3	2	2	1	1	0	0	1	0	1	1	228
275.0	06.00	3	2.0	09	32	4400	2	1	5	2	2	1	1	1	1	1	1	1	1	229
150.0	06.00	3	1.0	06	37	2300	2	3	1	2	2	1	0	0	0	0	0	0	1	230
225.0	07.70	3	2.5	10	34	4100	1	1	5	2	2	1	1	0	0	1	1	0	0	231
177.5	07.00	4	2.0	07	35	3100	1	2	1	2	2	1	0	0	1	1	1	0	0	232
232.0	06.80	4	2.5	08	10	4980	1	2	3	2	2	1	1	0	0	0	1	1	1	233

FIGURE 2.10 (continued)

Problems

2.27   Code the following responses for data entry:
  (1) Height: 5 feet 2 inches   _____ inches
  (2) Weight: 97.5 pounds   _____ pounds
  (3) Date of birth: June 27, 1958   _____ years

2.28   For each case in Problem 2.27 describe the rules you used for coding. What alternatives could you have considered?

2.10   DATA COLLECTION: A REVIEW AND A PREVIEW

Once data have been collected—be it from a published source, a designed experiment, or from a survey such as we have just described—they must be organized and prepared to aid the researcher in making various analyses. In the next two chapters a variety of descriptive summary measures useful for data analysis and interpretation will be developed, various "exploratory data analysis" techniques will be described, and methods of tabular and chart presentation will be demonstrated.

Supplementary Problems

2.29   Determine whether each of the following random variables is qualitative or quantitative. If it is quantitative, determine whether the phenomenon of interest is discrete or continuous.
  (a) Automobile ownership by students
  (b) Net weight (in grams) of packaged dry cereal
  (c) Political party affiliation of civil service workers
  (d) Number of bankrupt corporations per month in the United States
  (e) Useful lifetimes (in hours) of 100-watt light bulbs
  (f) Number of on-time arrivals per hour at a large airport

2.30   Determine whether each of the following random variables is qualitative or quantitative. If it is quantitative, determine whether the phenomenon of interest is discrete or continuous. Provide an operational definition for each variable.
  (a) Brand of personal computer used
  (b) Cost of personal computer system — *quant., cont.: to the nearest $.*
  (c) Amount of time the personal computer is used per week
  (d) Primary use for the personal computer
  (e) Number of persons in the household who use the personal computer
  (f) Number of computer magazine subscriptions
  (g) Word processing package primarily used

● **2.31**   Determine whether each of the following random variables is qualitative or quantitative. If it is quantitative, determine whether the phenomenon of interest is discrete or continuous. Provide an operational definition for each variable.
  (a) Amount of money spent on clothing in the last month
  (b) Number of woman's "winter coats" owned
  (c) Favorite department store

Note: Bullet ● indicates those problems whose solutions are included in the Answers to Selected Problems. Box □ indicates those problems that refer specifically to the real estate survey.

(**d**) Amount of time spent shopping for clothing in the last month

(**e**) Most likely time period during which shopping for clothing takes place (weekday, weeknight, or weekend)

(**f**) Number of pairs of woman's gloves owned

(**g**) Primary type of transportation used for clothing shopping

2.32 Suppose the following information is obtained for Robert Keeler on his application for a home mortgage loan at the Metro Country Savings and Loan Association:

(**1**) Place of Residence: Stony Brook, New York

(**2**) Type of Residence: Single family home

(**3**) Date of Birth: April 9, 1962

(**4**) Monthly Payments: $1,427

(**5**) Occupation: Newspaper reporter/author

(**6**) Employer: Sports Daily

(**7**) Number of Years at Job: 4

(**8**) Number of Jobs in Past Ten Years: 1

(**9**) Annual Family Salary Income: $66,000

(**10**) Other Income: $16,000

(**11**) Marital Status: Married

(**12**) Number of Children: 2

(**13**) Mortgage Requested: $120,000

(**14**) Term of Mortgage: 30 years

(**15**) Other Loans: Car

(**16**) Amount of Other Loans: $8,000

Classify each of the sixteen responses by type of data and level of measurement.

2.33 Suppose that a plastic surgeon is interested primarily in studying the amount of satisfaction that former patients had with elective facial cosmetic surgery. A survey of 400 such patients is being planned.

(**a**) Describe both the population and sample of interest to the plastic surgeon.

(**b**) Describe the type of data that the plastic surgeon primarily wishes to collect.

(**c**) Develop a first draft of the questionnaire by writing a series of three qualitative questions and three quantitative questions that you feel would be appropriate for this survey. Provide an operational definition for each variable.

➠(**d**) **ACTION** Write a draft of the cover letter needed for this survey.

2.34 Suppose that the manager of the Customer Service Division of Zenith was interested primarily in determining whether customers who had purchased a video cassette recorder over the past twelve months were satisfied with their products. Using the warranty cards submitted after the purchase, the manager was planning to survey 1,425 of these customers.

(**a**) Describe both the population and sample of interest to the manager.

(**b**) Describe the type of data that the manager primarily wishes to collect.

(**c**) Develop a first draft of the questionnaire by writing a series of three qualitative questions and three quantitative questions that you feel would be appropriate for this survey. Provide an operational definition for each variable.

➠(**d**) **ACTION** Write a draft of the cover letter needed for this survey.

• **2.35** Given a population of $N = 93$, draw a sample of size $n = 15$ *without* replacement by starting in row 29 of the table of random numbers (Table E.1). Reading across the row, list the 15 coded sequences obtained.

2.36 Do Problem 2.35 by sampling *with* replacement.

2.37 For a population of $N = 1,250$, a *two-stage* usage of the table of random numbers (Table E.1) may be recommended to avoid wasting time and effort. To obtain the sample by a two-stage approach, list the four-digit coded sequences after adjusting the first digit in each sequence as follows:

If the first digit is a 0, 2, 4, 6, or 8, change the digit to 0. If the first digit is a 1, 3, 5, 7, or 9, change the digit to 1. Thus, starting in row 07 of the random numbers table (Table E.1), the sequence 7054 becomes 1054, the sequence 3297 becomes 1297, etc. Verify that only ten rows are needed to draw a sample of size $n = 60$ *without* replacement.

2.38 For a population of $N = 2,202$, a *two-stage* usage of the table of random numbers (Table E.1) may be recommended to avoid wasting time and effort. To obtain the sample by a two-stage approach, list the four-digit coded sequences after adjusting the first digit in each sequence as follows:

If the first digit is a 0, 3, or 6, change the digit to 0; if the first digit is a 1, 4, or 7, change the digit to 1; if the first digit is a 2, 5, or 8, change the digit to 2; if the first digit is a 9, discard the sequence. Thus, starting in row 07 of the random numbers table (Table E.1), the sequence 7054 becomes 1054, the sequence 3297 becomes 0297, etc. Verify that only ten rows are needed to draw a sample of size $n = 60$ *without* replacement.

2.39 For a population of $N = 4,202$, what adjustment can you suggest for a two-stage usage of the random numbers table so that each of the 4,202 individuals has the same chance of selection?

2.40 Develop a set of five quantitative and five qualitative questions that were not included in the questionnaire (Figure 2.5) and which might also have been of interest to the realty company.

2.41 Suppose that the American Kennel Club (AKC) was planning to survey 1,500 of its club members primarily to determine the percentage of its membership that currently own more than one dog. Describe both the population and sample of interest to the AKC and describe the type of data that the AKC primarily wishes to collect.

2.42 Develop a first draft of the questionnaire needed in Problem 2.41 by writing a series of three qualitative questions and three quantitative questions that you feel would be appropriate for this survey.

• 2.43 The following computerized output is extracted from a set of data similar to those collected in the real estate survey (Figure 2.10). However, each of the five lines, representing the respective responses of five particular individuals, has *at least one error* in it. Use the coded statements shown in Figures 2.5 and 2.8 on pages 15 and 23 to determine the particular recording errors in each of the five responses.

```
375.0  13.53  4  3.5  99  33  4126  2  1  5  1  1  3  1  0  1  2  1  1  1  234
212.0   7.30  4  2.0  08  39  3287  1  1  1  4  1  1  0  0  0  1  1  0  1  235
175.9   5.40  3  1.0  06  54  2716  0  4  4  2  3  1  0  0  1  1  0  0  0  236
236.5   9.75  4  0.0  07  26  3675  1  2  3  2  2  1  1  0  0  1  1  1  0  237
224.0   8.00  3  1.0  09  28  2553  1  3  5  1  2  2  2  0  0  1  1  0  0  238
```

Case Study A

Suppose that the President of the Alumni Association wishes a survey to be taken of its membership from the classes of 1985 and 1986 to determine their past achievements, current activities, and future aspirations. Toward this end, information pertaining to the following areas is desired: sex of the alumnus; major area of study; grade-point index; further educational pursuits (that is, master's degree or doctorate); current employment status; current annual salary; number of full-time positions held since graduation; annual salary anticipated in five years; political party affiliation; and marital status.

As Director of Institutional Research you are asked to write a proposal demonstrating how you plan to conduct the survey. Included in this proposal must be

1. A statement of objectives (that is, what you want to find out and why).
2. A discussion of *how* and *when* the survey will be conducted (that is, how you plan to sample 70 alumni from the list of 700 graduates in the two classes).
3. A first draft of the questionnaire instrument (containing an organized sequence of both quantitative and qualitative questions—including operational definitions for each variable, all category labelings, and column allocations for data entry).
4. A first draft of the cover letter to be used with the questionnaire.
5. A first draft of any special instructions to respondents to aid them in filling out the questionnaire.
6. A discussion of *how* you plan to "test" the questionnaire for validity and/or ambiguity.
7. A demonstration of how the responses will be coded and entered by simulating the data entry for a hypothetical respondent—John Q. Doe, graduate of the class of 1985.
8. A statement that you have taken into consideration such things as the costs involved in conducting the survey, personnel needs, and the amount of time required for implementation and completion.

References

1. COCHRAN, W. G., *Sampling Techniques*, 3d ed. (New York: Wiley, 1977).
2. DEMING, W. E., *Sample Design in Business Research* (New York: Wiley, 1960).
3. DEMING, W. E. *Out of the Crisis* (Cambridge, MA: Massachusetts Institute of Technology Center for Advanced Engineering Study, 1986).
4. HANSEN, M. H., W. N. HURWITZ, AND W. G. MADOW, *Sample Survey Methods and Theory*, Vols. I and II (New York: Wiley, 1953).
5. RAND CORPORATION, *A Million Random Digits with 100,000 Normal Deviates* (New York: Free Press, 1955).
6. *Statistical Abstract of the United States*, U.S. Department of Commerce, 1985.
7. *Survey of Current Business*, U.S. Department of Commerce, 1985.

3

Describing and Summarizing Data

3.1 INTRODUCTION: WHAT'S AHEAD

In the preceding chapter we learned how to collect data through survey research. How do we make sense out of such collected information? What are the data in Figure 2.10 telling us? How can the results ultimately be used by the president of the realty company?[1] It is obvious that collecting data is only one aspect of the subject of descriptive statistics. In this and the following chapter we shall examine the other aspects: the description, summarization, presentation, analysis, and interpretation of the data.

The goals of this chapter are

1. To develop an understanding of the properties of data and the various summary measures computed from them
2. To be able to appropriately distinguish between the use of the various summary measures

In order to introduce the relevant ideas for Chapters 3 and 4, let us suppose that a financial analyst for a major brokerage firm is interested in comparing different companies in a variety of industrial groupings in order to establish a useful portfolio for stock market investment. In particular, suppose the financial analyst starts by selecting a random sample of six companies from the (population) list of 24 in the natural resources industrial grouping.[2]

---

[1] A detailed descriptive analysis of the real estate survey—highlighted by the interpretation of computer output from several statistical software packages—will be presented in Chapter 5.

[2] See "Business Week Corporate Scoreboard," *Business Week*, March 16, 1987. Reprinted by special permission, © 1987 by McGraw-Hill, Inc. The natural resources industrial grouping comprises companies concerned with the production of coal as well as crude, integrated domestic, and international oil. Information on price to earnings was available for 24 of the companies in this industrial grouping.

Natural Resources Company	Price to Earnings Ratio
Amoco	25
Texaco	12
Chevron	23
Cyprus Minerals	28
Sun	17
Cabot	15

ie share price
dividend per share

We note that the six companies (recorded in the order in which they were selected) are presented along with their corresponding *price to earnings* (that is, PE) *ratio*. The PE ratio, defined as a company's current stock price per share divided by its annual earnings per share, permits a comparison between the market's valuation of a company and its most recent annual performance. What can be learned from such data that will assist the financial analyst with her evaluation?

PE
Ratio

3.2 EXPLORING THE DATA

Based on this sample we observe four points.

1. The data are in **raw form.** That is, the collected data seem to be in a random sequence with no apparent pattern to the manner in which the individual observations are listed.
2. Each of the PE ratios occurs only once. That is, no one of them is observed more frequently than any other.
3. The spread in the PE ratios ranges from 12 to 28.
4. There do not appear to be any unusual or extraordinary PE ratios in this sample. Arranged in numerical order, the PE ratios here are 12, 15, 17, 23, 25, 28. (If the PE ratios had been 12, 15, 17, 23, 25, 61, then 61 would have been an extreme observation, or **outlier**).

If the financial analyst were to ask us to examine the data and present a short summary of our findings, then comments similar to the four above are basically all that we could be expected to make without formal statistical training. However, we have both analyzed and interpreted what the data are trying to convey. An analysis is **objective;** we should all agree with these findings. On the other hand, an interpretation is **subjective;** we may form different conclusions when interpreting our analytical findings. From the above, points 2 through 4 are based on analysis whereas point 1 is an interpretation. With respect to the latter, no formal analytical test (see the Runs test of Chapter 15) was made—it is simply our conjecture that there is no pattern to the sequence of collected data. Moreover, our conjecture would seem to be appropriate if the sample of six companies was randomly and independently drawn from the population listing.[3] That was the case here.

Let us now see how we could add to our understanding of what the data are telling us by more formally examining three properties of quantitative data.

3.3 PROPERTIES OF QUANTITATIVE DATA

The three major properties which describe a batch of numerical data are

3 major
properties

1. Central tendency
2. Dispersion
3. Shape

---

[3] Through survey research, whether collected by mail, by telephone, or by personal interview, the observed responses are usually obtained in a random order.

In any analysis and/or interpretation, a variety of descriptive measures representing the properties of central tendency, dispersion, and shape may be used to extract and summarize the major features of the data batch. If these descriptive summary measures are computed from a sample of data, they are called **statistics;** if they are computed from an entire population of data, they are called **parameters.** Since statisticians usually take samples rather than use entire populations, our primary emphasis in this text is on statistics rather than parameters.

3.4   MEASURES OF CENTRAL TENDENCY

Most batches of data show a distinct tendency to group or cluster about a certain ''central'' point. Thus for any particular batch of data, it usually becomes possible to select some typical value or **average** to describe the entire batch. Such a descriptive typical value is a measure of central tendency or ''location.''

Four types of averages often used as measures of central tendency are the arithmetic mean, the median, the mode, and the midrange.

3.4.1   The Arithmetic Mean

The **arithmetic mean** (also called the **mean**) is the most commonly used average or measure of central tendency.[4] It is calculated by summing all the observations in a batch of data and then dividing the total by the number of items involved.

Introducing Algebraic Notation
Thus, for a sample containing a batch of n observations $X_1, X_2, \ldots, X_n$, the arithmetic mean (given by the symbol $\overline{X}$—called ''X bar'') can be written as

$$\overline{X} = \frac{X_1 + X_2 + \cdots + X_n}{n}$$

To simplify the notation, for convenience the term

$$\sum_{i=1}^{n} X_i$$

(meaning the ''summation of all the X_i values'') is conventionally used whenever we wish to add together a series of observations.[5] That is,

$$\sum_{i=1}^{n} X_i = X_1 + X_2 + \cdots + X_n$$

Using this summation notation, the arithmetic mean of the sample can be more simply expressed as

$$\overline{X} = \frac{\sum_{i=1}^{n} X_i}{n} \tag{3.1}$$

---

[4] Although the word *average* refers to any summary measure of central tendency, it is most often used synonymously for the mean.
[5] See Appendix B for a discussion of rules pertaining to summation notation.

where

$$\overline{X} = \text{sample arithmetic mean}$$

$$n = \text{sample size}$$

$$X_i = i\text{th observation of the random variable } X$$

$$\sum_{i=1}^{n} X_i = \text{``summation of'' all } X_i \text{ values in the sample (see Appendix B)}$$

For our financial analyst's sample,

$$X_1 = 25 \leftarrow \text{reported PE ratio for Amoco}$$
$$X_2 = 12 \leftarrow \text{reported PE ratio for Texaco}$$
$$X_3 = 23 \leftarrow \text{reported PE ratio for Chevron}$$
$$X_4 = 28 \leftarrow \text{reported PE ratio for Cyprus Minerals}$$
$$X_5 = 17 \leftarrow \text{reported PE ratio for Sun}$$
$$X_6 = 15 \leftarrow \text{reported PE ratio for Cabot}$$

The arithmetic mean for this sample is calculated as

$$\overline{X} = \frac{\sum_{i=1}^{n} X_i}{n} = \frac{25 + 12 + 23 + 28 + 17 + 15}{6} = 20.0$$

Note that the mean is computed as 20 even though not one particular company in the sample actually had that PE ratio. It is seen from the **dot scale** of Figure 3.1 that for this batch of data three observations are smaller than the mean and three are larger. The mean acts as a *balancing point* so that observations that are smaller balance out those that are larger.

Note that the calculation of the mean is based on all the observations (X_1, X_2, . . . , X_n) in the batch of data. No other commonly used measure of central tendency possesses this characteristic. Since its computation is based on every observation, the arithmetic mean is greatly affected by any extreme value or values. In such instances, the arithmetic mean presents a distorted representation of what the data are conveying; hence the mean would not be the best average to use for describing or summarizing such a batch of data.

To further demonstrate the characteristics of the mean, suppose the financial analyst takes a random sample of $n = 6$ companies from a list of 45 in the retailing

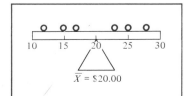

FIGURE 3.1
Dot scale representing PE ratios for six natural resource companies.

industrial grouping and another random sample of $n = 6$ companies from the list of 33 in the food processing industrial grouping.[6] The PE ratios are reported as follows:

Retailing Company	Price to Earnings Ratio
K Mart	14
Limited	42
Wickes	13
Strawbridge & Clothier	14
Dayton Hudson	16
Zayre	21

Food Processing Company	Price to Earnings Ratio
Hershey Foods	20
Flower Industries	22
Pillsbury	17
Wrigley	20
Quaker Oats	23
Hormel	18

The respective dot scales are displayed in Figures 3.2 and 3.3.

Note that the mean PE ratio for each of these samples is also 20. Nevertheless, as is observed from Figures 3.2 and 3.3, the two samples drawn here have distinctly different features—with respect to each other as well as with respect to the sample of six natural resource companies depicted in Figure 3.1. For example, four of the six companies in the sample from the retailing industrial grouping have PE ratios quite different from that of the outlier, Limited. For this sample, the arithmetic mean is presenting a distorted representation of what the data are conveying and it is not the best average to use. On the other hand, for the sample of food processing companies and the sample of natural resource companies the mean is the appropriate descriptive measure for summarizing and characterizing the respective data batches because outliers are not present. In fact, the food processing company data are quite *homogeneous*. Two of the six companies in this sample have PE ratios equivalent to the mean; furthermore, from Figures 3.1 through 3.3, it is obvious that the PE ratios of these six companies contain the least amount of scatter or variability among the three samples. In addition, it is also observed that the PE ratio data in each of the natural resource and food processing industry samples possess the property of symmetry whereas the PE ratio data for the sample of retailing companies do not. (The properties of dispersion and shape will be addressed further in Sections 3.5 and 3.6).

[6] See "Business Week Corporate Scoreboard," *Business Week*, March 16, 1987. Reprinted by special permission. © 1987 by McGraw-Hill, Inc. The retailing industrial grouping comprises department, discount, mail-order, variety, and specialty stores. The food processing industrial grouping comprises companies involved with baked goods, canned and packaged foods, dairy products, meat, and condiments. Information on price to earnings was available for 45 of the companies in the retailing industrial grouping and for 33 of the companies in the food processing industrial grouping.

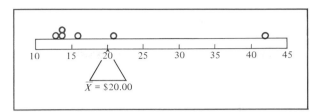

FIGURE 3.2
Dot scale representing PE ratios
for six retailing companies.

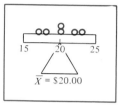

FIGURE 3.3
Dot scale representing PE ratios for six food processing companies.

3.4.2 The Median

Use when
extreme values
are observed:
outliers

The **median** is the middle value in an ordered sequence of data. If there are no ties, half of the observations will be smaller and half will be larger. The median is unaffected by any extreme observations in a batch of data. Thus whenever an extreme observation is present, it is appropriate to use the median rather than the mean to describe a batch of data.

To calculate the median from a batch of data collected in its raw form, we must first place the data in numerical order. Such an arrangement is called an **ordered array.** We then use the *positioning point formula*

$$\frac{n + 1}{2}$$

to find the place in the ordered array that corresponds to the median value.

Rule 1 If the size of the sample is an *odd* number, the median is represented by the numerical value corresponding to the positioning point—the $(n + 1)/2$ ordered observation.

Rule 2 If the size of the sample is an *even* number, then the positioning point lies between the two middle observations. The median is then the *average* of the numerical values corresponding to these two middle observations.

Even-Sized Sample
For the financial analyst's sample of six natural resources companies, the raw data were

| 25 | 12 | 23 | 28 | 17 | 15 |

The ordered array becomes

	12	15	17	23	25	28
Ordered observation	1	2	3	4	5	6

Median = 20.0

For these data, the positioning point is $(n + 1)/2 = (6 + 1)/2 = 3.5$. Therefore the median is obtained by averaging the third and fourth ordered observations:

$$\frac{17 + 23}{2} = 20.0$$

As can be seen from the ordered array, the median is unaffected by extreme observations. Regardless of whether the largest PE ratio is 28, 38, or 68 the median is still 20.0.

Odd-Sized Sample

Had the sample size been an odd number, the median would merely be represented by the numerical value given to the $(n + 1)/2$ observation in the ordered array. Thus, in the following ordered array for $n = 5$ students' GMAT scores, the median is the value of the third [that is, $(5 + 1)/2$] ordered observation—590:

	500	570	590	600	690
			↑		
			Median		
			↓		
Ordered observation	1	2	3	4	5

Ties in the Data

When computing the median, we ignore the fact that tied values may be present in the data. Suppose, for example, that the following batch of data represent the starting salaries (in thousands of dollars) for a sample of $n = 7$ accountancy majors who have recently graduated from your college:

23.1	21.6	25.0	19.8	20.5	22.7	21.6

The ordered array becomes

	19.8	20.5	21.6	21.6	22.7	23.1	25.0
				↑			
				Median			
				↓			
Ordered observation	1	2	3	4	5	6	7

For this odd-sized sample the median positioning point is the $(n + 1)/2 = $ 4th ordered observation. Thus the median is 21.6 thousand dollars, the middle value in the ordered sequence, even though the third ordered observation is also 21.6 thousand dollars.

Characteristics of the Median

To summarize, the calculation of the median value is affected by the number of observations, not by the magnitude of any extreme(s). Moreover, any observation selected at random is just as likely to exceed the median as it is to be exceeded by it.

3.4.3 The Mode   *most frequent observation*

Sometimes, when describing or summarizing a batch of data, the mode is used as a measure of central tendency. The **mode** is the value in a batch of data which appears most frequently. It is easily obtained from an ordered array. Unlike the arithmetic mean, the mode is not affected by the occurrence of any extreme values. However, the mode is not used for more than descriptive purposes because it is more variable from sample to sample than other measures of central tendency.

Using the ordered array for the PE ratio data obtained from the financial analyst's sample of six natural resources companies:

12   15   17   23   25   28

we see that there is no mode. None of the PE ratios was "most typical."

Note that there is a difference between *no mode* and a mode of 0 as illustrated in the following ordered array of noontime temperatures (°F) in Duluth during the first week of January:

Ordered array
(Duluth, Minnesota) $-4°$ $-2°$ $-1°$ $-1°$ $0°$ $0°$ $0°$ Mode = 0°

In addition, a data batch can have more than one mode, as illustrated in the following ordered array of noontime temperatures (°F) in Richmond during the first week of January:

Ordered array
(Richmond, Virginia)   21°   28°   28°   35°   41°   43°   43°

In Richmond we see there were two modes—28° and 43°. Such data are described as *bimodal*.

3.4.4 The Midrange

The **midrange** is the average of the *smallest* and *largest* observations in a batch of data. This can be written as

$$\text{Midrange} = \frac{X_{\text{smallest}} + X_{\text{largest}}}{2} \qquad (3.2)$$

Using the ordered array of PE ratios from the financial analyst's sample of six natural resource companies:

12   15   17   23   25   28

the midrange is computed from Equation (3.2) as

$$\text{Midrange} = \frac{X_{\text{smallest}} + X_{\text{largest}}}{2}$$

$$= \frac{12 + 28}{2} = 20.0$$

Despite its simplicity, the midrange must be used cautiously. Since it involves only the smallest and largest observations in a data batch, it becomes distorted as a summary measure of central tendency if an outlier is present.[7]

Nevertheless, the midrange is often used successfully as a summary measure both by financial analysts and by weather reporters, since it can give an adequate, "quick and simple" value to summarize the *entire* data batch—be it a series of daily

---

[7] For this reason we may prefer to use the *midhinge* (see Section 3.10).

closing stock prices over a whole year or a series of recorded hourly temperature readings over a whole day. In such situations, an extreme value is not likely to occur.

Problems

3.1 Which of the following statements are objective (analytic) and which are subjective (interpretive):
   (a) The average price of a home in Bergen County is $154,700.
   (b) Housing is expensive in Palo Alto.
   (c) The police in New York City are smarter, better educated, and more honest now than they were 30 years ago.
   (d) There were more burglaries per 1,000 homes reported in Chicago last year than in Des Moines.
   (e) The average score on an IQ test of students at the Wallace School of Science is 145.
   (f) Foreign product dumping is crippling our industry.
   For each subjective statement, list some objective statements which might have been used to make the interpretation given. For each objective statement, tell what interpretation might be intended by the person who made the statement.

● 3.2 Given the following two batches of data—each with samples of size $n = 7$:

Batch 1:   10   2   3   2   4   2   5
Batch 2:   20   12   13   12   14   12   15

   (a) For each batch, compute the mean, median, mode, and midrange.
   (b) Compare your results and summarize your findings.
   ✗(c) Compare the first sampled item in each batch, compare the second sampled item in each batch, and so on. Briefly describe your findings here in light of your summary in part (b).

3.3 A track coach must decide on which one of two sprinters to select for the 100-meter dash at an upcoming meet. The coach will base the decision on the results of five races between the two athletes run over a one-hour period with 15-minute rest intervals between. The following times (in seconds) were recorded for the five races:

Athlete	Race				
	1	2	3	4	5
Sharyn	12.1	12.0	12.0	16.8	12.1
Tamara	12.3	12.4	12.4	12.5	12.4

   ⟾(a) **ACTION**   Based on the data above, which of the two sprinters should the coach select? Why?
   ⟾(b) **ACTION**   Should the selection be different if the coach knew that Sharyn had fallen at the start of the fourth race? Why?
   (c) Discuss the differences in the concepts of the mean and the median as measures of central tendency and how this relates to (a) and (b).

3.4 Suppose that, owing to an error, a data batch containing the PE ratios from nine companies was recorded as 13, 15, 14, 17, 13, 16, 15, 16, and 61, where the last value should have been 16 instead of 61. Show how much the mean, median, and midrange are affected by the error (that is, compute these statistics for the "bad" and "good" data sets, and compare the results of using different estimators of central tendency).

3.5 A manufacturer of flashlight batteries took a sample of 13 from a day's production and burned them continuously until they failed. The number of hours they burned were

$$342, 426, 317, 545, 264, 451, 1049,$$
$$631, 512, 266, 492, 562, 298$$

    (a) Compute the mean, median, and midrange. Looking at the distribution of times, which descriptive measures seem best, and which worst? (And why?)

    ➡**(b) ACTION** In what ways would this information be useful to the manufacturer? Discuss.

3.6 It is stated in Section 3.5.2 that one important property of the arithmetic mean is

$$\sum_{i=1}^{n} (X_i - \overline{X}) = 0$$

    (a) Using the PE ratios from the sample of six retailing companies (see page 38), verify that this property holds.

    (b) Using the PE ratios from the sample of six food processing companies (see page 38), verify that this property holds.

3.7 Upon examining the monthly billing records of a mail-order book company, the auditor takes a sample of 20 of its unpaid accounts. The amounts owed the company were

$$\$4, \$18, \$11, \$7, \$7, \$10, \$5, \$33, \$9, \$12$$
$$\$3, \$11, \$10, \$6, \$26, \$37, \$15, \$18, \$10, \$21$$

    (a) Compute the mean, median, mode, and midrange.

    (b) If a total of 350 bills were still outstanding, use the mean to estimate the total amount owed to the company. [*Hint*: Total $= N\overline{X}$.]

    ➡**(c) ACTION** Write a draft of the memo the auditor will want to send to the chief executive officer of the mail-order book company regarding the findings.

    ✎**(d)** In what ways would this information be useful to the chief executive officer? Discuss.

3.8 You are writing a newsletter about microcomputers, and in this issue you want to describe the available printers of a certain type, called dot-matrix printers. The dollar prices of the models available are

$$575, 259, 1049, 340, 499, 675,$$
$$599, 450, 649, 475, 520, 550,$$
$$398, 490, 560, 625, 875, 749$$

    (a) What is the mean price? The median price? The midrange?

    (b) If three new models came on the market, with prices of 345, 375, and 355, what would the new mean and median prices be? Which measure changed the most, and why?

    ➡**(c) ACTION** Write the newsletter article using all the data given above.

3.9 The price of a single room on a weekday in several hotels in New York was

$$145, 210, 125, 110, 135, 90,$$
$$120, 105, 130, 124, 118, 122$$

    (a) What is the median price of a hotel room in New York? The mean price?

    ➡**(b) ACTION** How would this information be of use to a travel agent?; A convention organizer?; A tourist? Discuss.

    (c) If an additional hotel were included in the survey, and by mistake the Presidential Suite was counted (at $3,000 a day) instead of an ordinary room, what would the mean and median be?

    ✎**(d)** Discuss the reasons for the differences in your responses in **(a)** and **(c)**.

3.10   For the last ten days in June, the "Shore Special" train was late arriving at its destination by the following times (in minutes; a negative number means that the train was early by that number of minutes): -3, 6, 4, 10, -4, 124, 2, -1, 4, 1.

    ✔(a) If you were hired by the railroad as a statistician to show that the railroad is providing good service, what are some of the summary measures you would use to accomplish this?

    ✔(b) If you were hired by a TV station which was producing a documentary to show that the railroad is providing bad service, what summary measures would you use?

    ✔(c) If you were trying to be "objective" and "unbiased" in assessing the railroad's performance, which summary measures would you use? (This is the hardest part, because you cannot answer it without making additional assumptions about the relative costs of being late by various amounts of time. The field of decision theory deals with what happens when these costs are explicitly accounted for.)

3.11   In order to estimate how much water will be needed to supply the community of Falling Rock in the next decade, the town council asked the city manager to find out how much water a sample of families currently uses. The sample of 15 families used the following number of gallons (in thousands) in the past year.

11.2, 21.5, 16.4, 19.7, 14.6, 16.9, 32.2, 18.2,
13.1, 23.8, 18.3, 15.5, 18.8, 22.7, 14.0

    (a) What is the mean amount of water used per family? The median? The midrange?

    (b) Suppose that ten years from now the town council expects that there will be 45,000 families living in Falling Rock. How many gallons of water per year will be needed, if the rate of consumption per family stays the same?

    ➠**(c) ACTION**   In what ways would the information provided in **(a)** and **(b)** be useful to the town council? Discuss.

    ✔**(d)** Why might the town council have used the data from a survey rather than just measuring the total consumption in the town? (Think about what types of users are not yet included in the estimation process.)

3.5   MEASURES OF DISPERSION

A second important property which describes a batch of data is dispersion. **Dispersion** is the amount of variation or "spread" in the data. Two batches of data may differ in both central tendency and dispersion; or, as shown in Figures 3.1 and 3.3, two batches of data may have the same measures of central tendency but differ greatly in terms of dispersion. The data batch depicted in Figure 3.3 is much less variable than that depicted in Figure 3.1 (see pages 37 and 39).

    Four measures of dispersion are the range, the variance, the standard deviation, and the coefficient of variation.

3.5.1   The Range

The **range** is the difference between the largest and smallest observations in a batch of data. That is,

$$\text{Range} = X_{\text{largest}} - X_{\text{smallest}} \tag{3.3}$$

Using the ordered array for the PE ratio data from the sample of six natural resources companies:

| 12 | 15 | 17 | 23 | 25 | 28 |

the range is $28 - 12 = 16.0$.

The range measures the "total spread" in the batch of data. Although the range is a simple, easily calculated measure of dispersion, its distinct weakness is that it fails to take into account *how* the data are distributed between the smallest and largest values. This can be observed from Figure 3.4. Thus, as evidenced in scale C, it would be improper to use the range as a measure of dispersion when either one or both of its components are extreme observations.

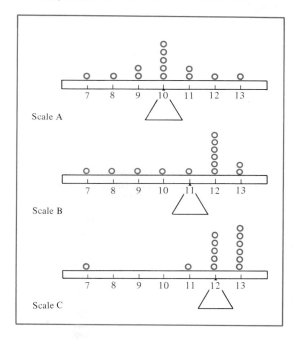

FIGURE 3.4
Comparing three data sets with the same range.

3.5.2 The Variance and the Standard Deviation

Two commonly used measures of dispersion which do take into account *how* all the values in the data are distributed are the variance and its square root, the standard deviation. These measures evaluate how the values fluctuate about the mean.

Defining the Sample Variance
The **sample variance** is "*almost*" the average of the squared differences between each of the observations in a batch of data and the mean.[8] Thus, for a sample containing

---

[8] Had the denominator been n instead of $n - 1$, the average of the squared differences "around the mean" would have been obtained. However, $n - 1$ is used here because of certain desirable mathematical properties possessed by the statistic S^2 which make it appropriate for statistical inference (see Chapter 9). Obviously, if the sample size is large, division by n or $n - 1$ doesn't make much difference.

n observations $X_1, X_2 \ldots , X_n$ the sample variance (given by the symbol S^2) can be written as:

$$S^2 = \frac{(X_1 - \overline{X})^2 + (X_2 - \overline{X})^2 + \cdots + (X_n - \overline{X})^2}{n - 1}$$

Using our summation notation, the above formulation can be more simply expressed as

$$S^2 = \frac{\sum_{i=1}^{n} (X_i - \overline{X})^2}{n - 1} \qquad (3.4)$$

where

$$\overline{X} = \text{sample arithmetic mean}$$

$$n = \text{sample size}$$

$$X_i = i\text{th value of the random variable } X$$

$$\sum_{i=1}^{n} (X_i - \overline{X})^2 = \text{summation of all the squared differences between the } X_i \text{ values and } \overline{X}$$

Defining the Sample Standard Deviation

The sample standard deviation (given by the symbol S) is simply the square root of the sample variance. That is

$$S = \sqrt{S^2} = \sqrt{\frac{\sum_{i=1}^{n} (X_i - \overline{X})^2}{n - 1}} \qquad (3.5)$$

Calculating S^2 and S

To compute the variance we

1. Obtain the difference between each observation and the mean.
2. Square each difference.
3. Add the squared results together.
4. Divide this summation by $n - 1$.

To obtain the standard deviation we merely take the square root of the variance.

For the financial analyst's sample of six natural resources companies, the raw (PE ratio) data were

25	12	23	28	17	15

and $\overline{X} = 20$.

The sample variance is computed as

$$S^2 = \frac{\sum_{i=1}^{n} (X_i - \overline{X})^2}{n - 1}$$

$$= \frac{(25 - 20)^2 + (12 - 20)^2 + \cdots + (15 - 20)^2}{6 - 1}$$

$$= \frac{196}{5}$$

$$= 39.2 \text{ (in squared units)}$$

and the sample standard deviation is computed as

$$S = \sqrt{S^2} = \sqrt{\frac{\sum_{i=1}^{n} (X_i - \overline{X})^2}{n - 1}} = \sqrt{39.2} = 6.26$$

Since in the preceding computations we are squaring the differences, *neither the variance nor the standard deviation can ever be negative.* The only time S^2 and S could be zero would be if there were no variation at all in the data—if each observation in the sample were exactly the same. In such an unusual case the range would also be zero.

But data are inherently variable—not constant. Any random phenomenon of interest that we could think of usually takes on a variety of values. For example, companies have differing PE ratios just as people have differing IQs, incomes, weights, heights, ages, pulse rates, etc. It is because data inherently vary that it becomes so important to study not only measures (of central tendency) which summarize the data but also measures (of dispersion) which reflect how the data are varying.

What the Variance and the Standard Deviation Indicate

The variance and the standard deviation are measuring the "average" scatter around the mean—that is, how larger observations fluctuate above it and how smaller observations distribute below it.

The variance possesses certain useful mathematical properties. However, its computation results in squared units—squared dollars, squared inches, etc. Thus, for practical work our primary measure of dispersion will be the standard deviation, whose value is in the original units of the data—dollars, inches, etc.

In the above PE ratio data the standard deviation is 6.26. This tells us that the *majority* of the PE ratios in this sample are clustering within 6.26 around the mean (i.e., between 13.74 and 26.26).

Why We Square the Deviations

The formulas for variance and standard deviation could not merely use

$$\sum_{i=1}^{n} (X_i - \overline{X})$$

as a numerator, because we may recall that the mean acts as a "balancing point" for observations larger and smaller than it. Therefore, the sum of the deviations about the mean is always zero;[9] that is,

$$\sum_{i=1}^{n} (X_i - \overline{X}) = 0$$

To demonstrate this, let us again refer to the PE ratio data:

25   12   23   28   17   15

Therefore,

$$\sum_{i=1}^{n} (X_i - \overline{X}) = (25 - 20) + (12 - 20) + (23 - 20) + (28 - 20)$$

$$+ (17 - 20) + (15 - 20)$$

$$= 0$$

This is depicted in the accompanying dot scale diagram displayed in Figure 3.5.

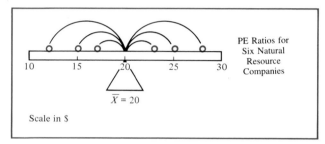

PE Ratios for Six Natural Resource Companies

Scale in $

FIGURE 3.5
The mean as a "balancing point."

As already noted, three of the observations are smaller than the mean and three are larger. Although the sum of the six deviations (5, −8, 3, 8, −3, and −5) is zero, the sum of the squared deviations allows us to study the dispersion in the data. Hence we use

$$\sum_{i=1}^{n} (X_i - \overline{X})^2$$

when computing the variance and standard deviation. In the squaring process, observations that are further from the mean get more weight than observations closer to the mean.

---

[9] Using the summation rules from Appendix B, we show the following proof:

$$\sum_{i=1}^{n} (X_i - \overline{X}) = 0$$

$$\sum_{i=1}^{n} X_i - \sum_{i=1}^{n} \overline{X} = 0$$

$$\sum_{i=1}^{n} X_i - n\overline{X} = 0$$

$$\sum_{i=1}^{n} X_i - \sum_{i=1}^{n} X_i = 0$$

The respective squared deviations for the above PE ratio data are

25   64   9   64   9   25

We note that the fourth observation ($X_4 = 28$) is 8 units higher than the mean, while the second observation ($X_2 = 12$) is 8 units lower. In the squaring process both these values contribute substantially more to the calculation of S^2 and S than do the other observations in the sample, which are closer to the mean.

Therefore we may generalize as follows:

1. The more "spread out" or dispersed the data are, the larger will be the range, the variance, and the standard deviation.
2. The more "concentrated" or homogeneous the data are, the smaller will be the range, the variance, and the standard deviation.
3. If the observations are all the same (so that there is no variation in the data), the range, variance, and standard deviation will all be zero.

Calculating S^2 and S: "Short-Cut" Formulas

The formulas for variance and standard deviation, Equations (3.4) and (3.5), are **definitional formulas,** but they are often not practical to use—even with a hand calculator. For our PE ratio data the mean is an integer—20. For more usual situations where the observations and the mean are unlikely to be integers the following "**short-cut**" formulas for the variance and the standard deviation are given for practical use:

$$S^2 = \frac{\sum_{i=1}^{n} X_i^2 - \dfrac{\left(\sum_{i=1}^{n} X_i\right)^2}{n}}{n-1} \tag{3.6}$$

$$S = \sqrt{\frac{\sum_{i=1}^{n} X_i^2 - \dfrac{\left(\sum_{i=1}^{n} X_i\right)^2}{n}}{n-1}} \tag{3.7}$$

where

$$\sum_{i=1}^{n} X_i^2 = \text{summation of the squares of each observation}$$

$$\left(\sum_{i=1}^{n} X_i\right)^2 = \text{square of the total summation}$$

The short-cut formulas, Equations (3.6) and (3.7), are identical to the definitional formulas, Equations (3.4) and (3.5). Since the denominators are the same, it is easy to show through expansion and the use of summation rules (see Appendix B) that

$$\sum_{i=1}^{n} (X_i - \overline{X})^2 = \sum_{i=1}^{n} X_i^2 - \frac{\left(\sum_{i=1}^{n} X_i\right)^2}{n}$$

Moreover, since S^2 (and S) can never be negative,

$$\sum_{i=1}^{n} X_i^2,$$

the summation of squares, must always equal or exceed

$$\left(\sum_{i=1}^{n} X_i\right)^2 \bigg/ n,$$

the square of the total summation divided by n.

Returning to the PE ratio data, the variance and standard deviation are recomputed using Equations (3.6) and (3.7) as follows:

$$S^2 = \frac{\sum_{i=1}^{n} X_i^2 - \frac{\left(\sum_{i=1}^{n} X_i\right)^2}{n}}{n - 1}$$

$$= \frac{(25^2 + 12^2 + \cdots + 15^2) - \frac{(25 + 12 + \cdots + 15)^2}{6}}{6 - 1}$$

$$= \frac{(625 + 144 + \cdots + 225) - \frac{(120)^2}{6}}{5}$$

$$= \frac{2{,}596 - 2{,}400}{5}$$

$$= \frac{196}{5} = 39.2 \quad \text{(in squared units)}$$

and

$$S = \sqrt{39.2} = 6.26.$$

3.5.3 The Coefficient of Variation

Unlike the previous measures we have studied, the **coefficient of variation** is a *relative measure* of dispersion. It is expressed as a percentage rather than in terms of the units of the particular data.

As a relative measure, the coefficient of variation is particularly useful when comparing the variability of two or more batches of data that are expressed in different units of measurement. As an example from the real estate survey of Chapter 2, suppose the president was interested in determining whether appraised value (question 1) has greater variability (on a relative basis) than does lot size (question 2). Since appraised value (in $000) is a monetary amount and lot size is in square feet, it is impossible to directly compare the two standard deviations or the two ranges for these variables. Here, however, the two coefficients of variation can be used to provide the desired answer.

The coefficient of variation, given by the symbol CV, measures the scatter in the data relative to the mean. It may be computed by

$$CV = \left(\frac{S}{\overline{X}} \right) 100\% \tag{3.8}$$

where S = standard deviation of a set of data
$\overline{X}$ = mean of a set of data

Thus, after obtaining the mean and standard deviation for the responses to both questions 1 and 2, the statistician may compute the two coefficients of variation and provide the president of the realty company with the desired answer.

The coefficient of variation is also very useful when comparing two or more sets of data which are measured in the same units but differ to such an extent that a direct comparison of the respective standard deviations is not very helpful. As an example, suppose that a potential investor was considering purchasing shares of stock in one of two companies, A or B, which are listed on the American Stock Exchange. If neither company offered dividends to its stockholders and if both companies were rated equally high (by various investment services) in terms of potential growth, the potential investor might want to consider the volatility (variability) of the two stocks to aid in the investment decision. Now suppose that each share of stock in Company A has averaged $50 over the past months with a standard deviation of $10. In addition, suppose that in this same time period the price per share for Company B stock averaged $12 with a standard deviation of $4. In terms of the actual standard deviations the price of Company A shares seems to be more volatile than that of Company B. However, since the average prices per share for the two stocks are so different, it would be more appropriate for the potential investor to consider the variability in price relative to the average price in order to examine the volatility/stability of the two stocks. For Company A the coefficient of variation is CV_A = ($10/$50)100% = 20.0%; for Company B the coefficient of variation is CV_B = ($4/$12)100% = 33.3%. Thus relative to the mean, the price of Stock B is much more variable than the price of Stock A.

Returning to the PE ratio data obtained from a sample of six natural resource companies, the coefficient of variation is

$$CV = \left(\frac{S}{\overline{X}} \right) 100\% = \left(\frac{6.26}{20.00} \right) 100\% = 31.3\%$$

That is, for this sample the relative size of the "average spread around the mean" to the mean is 31.3%.

Problems

3.12 For the PE ratio data corresponding to the sample of six retailing companies (see page 38), verify that the computation of the standard deviation is identical regardless of whether the definitional formula (3.5) or the computational formula (3.7) is used.

3.13 For the PE ratio data corresponding to the sample of six food processing companies (see page 38), verify that the computation of the standard deviation is identical regardless of whether the definitional formula (3.5) or the computational formula (3.7) is used.

● **3.14** For each data batch in Problem 3.2 on page 42:
  (a) Compute the range, variance, standard deviation, and coefficient of variation.
  (b) Compare your results and discuss your findings.
  ✐**(c)** Based on your answers to Problem 3.2 and parts (a) and (b) above, what can you generalize about the properties of central tendency and dispersion?

3.15 Using the data from Problem 3.3 on page 42, compute the range, variance, standard deviation, and coefficient of variation for each of the two athletes.

3.16 Using the data from Problem 3.4 on page 42, compute the range, variance, standard deviation, and coefficient of variation for the data batch with the error (61) and then recompute these same statistics after the PE ratio is corrected to 16.
  (a) Discuss the differences in your findings for each measure of dispersion.
  (b) Which measure seems to be affected most by the error?

3.17 For the following, refer to the data in Problem 3.5 on page 43:
  (a) Calculate the variance, standard deviation, and range.
  ✐**(b)** For many sets of data, the range is about six times the standard deviation. Is this true here? (If not, why do you think it is not?)
  ✐ ➡**(c)** **ACTION** Using the information above, what would you advise the manufacturer to do if he wanted to be able to say in advertisements that these batteries ''should last 400 hours''? (*Note*: There is no right answer to this question; the point is to consider how to make such a statement precise.)

3.18 Using the data from Problem 3.7 on page 43, compute the range, variance, standard deviation, and coefficient of variation of the amount owed to the mail-order book company.

3.19 Using all the data from parts (a) and (b) in Problem 3.8 on page 43, compute the range, variance, and standard deviation in the prices of dot-matrix printers.

3.20 Using the data from Problem 3.9 on page 43, compute the range, variance, and standard deviation of the daily prices of hotel rooms in New York. (Do not include the Presidential Suite.)

3.21 Using the data from Problem 3.10 on page 44, compute the range, variance, and standard deviation of lateness (in minutes).

3.22 Using the data from Problem 3.11 on page 44, compute the range and standard deviation in water consumption.

3.6 SHAPE

A third important property of a batch of data is its **shape**—the manner in which the data are distributed. Either the distribution of the data is **symmetrical** or it is not. If the distribution of data is not symmetrical, it is called asymmetrical or **skewed.**

To describe the shape we need only compare the mean and the median. If these two measures are equal, we may generally consider the data to be symmetrical (or *zero-skewed*). On the other hand, if the mean exceeds the median, the data may generally be described as *positive* or *right-skewed*. If the mean is exceeded by the median, those data can generally be called *negative* or *left-skewed*. That is,

Mean > median: positive or right-skewness
Mean = median: symmetry or zero-skewness
Mean < median: negative or left-skewness

Positive skewness arises when the mean is increased by some unusually high values; negative skewness occurs when the mean is reduced by some extremely low values. Data are symmetrical when there are no really extreme values in a particular direction so that low and high values balance each other out.

Figure 3.6 depicts the shapes of three data batches: the data on Scale L are negative or left-skewed (since the distortion to the left is caused by extremely small values); the data on Scale R are positive or right-skewed (since the distortion to the right is caused by extremely large values); and the data on Scale S are symmetrical (the low and high values on the scale balance, and the mean equals the median).

For our sample of six natural resources companies, the PE ratio data were displayed along the dot scale in Figure 3.1 (see page 37). The mean and the median are equal to 20, and the data appear to be symmetrically distributed around these measures of central tendency.

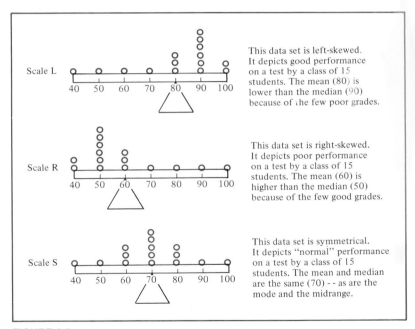

FIGURE 3.6
A comparison of three data sets differing in shape.

Problems

● **3.23**   For each data batch in Problem 3.2 on page 42:
(a) Describe the shape.
(b) Compare your results and discuss your findings.

3.24   Using the battery life data from Problem 3.5 on page 43, describe the shape.

3.25   Using the data on amount owed to the mail-order book company from Problem 3.7 on page 43, describe the shape.

3.26   Using (all) the dot-matrix printer price data from Problem 3.8 on page 43, describe the shape.

3.27   Using the hotel price data from Problem 3.9 on page 43, describe the shape. (Do not include the Presidential Suite.)

3.28   Using the train lateness data from Problem 3.10 on page 44, describe the shape.

3.29   Using the water consumption data from Problem 3.11 on page 44, describe the shape.

3.7 DEALING WITH LARGER BATCHES OF QUANTITATIVE DATA: "EXPLORATORY DATA ANALYSIS" TECHNIQUES

Figure 3.7 displays the PE ratios for *each* company in the natural resources industrial grouping. The PE ratios listed are in **raw form.** As seen from Figure 3.7, as the number of observations get large, it becomes more difficult to focus on the major features of the data. However, when the data are arranged into an **ordered array,** as in Figure 3.8, our evaluation is facilitated. It becomes easy to pick out extremes, typical values, and concentrations of values.

    In addition to the more traditional descriptive statistical techniques for analyzing quantitative data characteristics, recently developed **exploratory data analysis** meth-

Natural Resources Company	Price to Earnings Ratio
Amoco	25
Ashland Oil	12
Atlantic Richfield	20
Cabot	15
Chevron	23
Coastal	38
Cyprus Minerals	28
Exxon	11
MAPCO	17
Mitchell Energy & Development	33
Mobil	13
NACCO Industries	8
NERCO	9
Occidental Petroleum	48
Pacific Resources	10
Pennzoil	61
Phillips Petroleum	14
Pittston	50
Quaker State Oil Refining	14
Rochester & Pittsburgh Coal	10
Sun	17
Texaco	12
Unocal	20
Westmoreland Coal	13

FIGURE 3.7
Raw data pertaining to PE ratios for 24 companies in the natural resources industrial grouping.
(SOURCE: Extracted from "Business Week Corporate Scoreboard," *Business Week*, March 16, 1987, page 135. Reprinted by special permission. © 1987 by McGraw-Hill, Inc.)

8	13	23
9	14	25
10	14	28
10	15	33
11	17	38
12	17	48
12	20	50
13	20	61

FIGURE 3.8
Ordered array of PE ratios
from 24 natural resource
companies.
(SOURCE: Figure 3.7)

ods (References 4 and 5) may also be used to help us understand what information the data are conveying.

Exploratory data analysis techniques are particularly helpful when dealing with large batches of data. Although it is useful to place the raw data into an ordered array prior to computing descriptive summary measures or developing tables and charts (see Chapter 4), the greater the number of observations present in a data batch, the more cumbersome it is to form the ordered array. In such situations it becomes particularly useful to organize the data into a stem-and-leaf display in order to study their characteristics.

3.8 THE STEM-AND-LEAF DISPLAY

A **stem-and-leaf display** separates data entries into ''leading digits'' and ''trailing digits.'' For example, if the observations in the data batch all had at most two digits, then the tens column would be the leading digit and the remaining column would be the trailing digit. Thus an entry of 25 has a leading digit of 2 and a trailing digit of 5, whereas an entry of 8 has a leading digit of 0 and a trailing digit of 8.

Figure 3.9 depicts the stem-and-leaf display of PE ratios for all 24 companies in the natural resources industrial grouping. The column of numbers to the left of the vertical line is called the ''stem.'' These numbers correspond to the *leading digits* of the data. In each row the ''leaves'' branch out to the right of the vertical line, and these entries correspond to *trailing digits*.

```
0 | 89
1 | 251730440723
2 | 50380
3 | 83
4 | 8
5 | 0
6 | 1              N = 24
```

FIGURE 3.9
Stem-and-leaf display of
PE ratios from 24 natural
resource companies.
(SOURCE: Figure 3.7)

Constructing the Stem-and-Leaf Display

Using the data from Figure 3.7, the stem-and-leaf display is easily constructed. Note that the first company, Amoco, had reported a PE ratio of 25. Therefore the trailing digit of 5 is listed as the first leaf value next to the stem value of 2 (the leading digit). Moreover, the second company, Ashland Oil, had reported a PE ratio of 12. Here the trailing digit of 2 is listed as the first leaf value next to the stem value of 1. Continuing, the third company, Atlantic Richfield, had reported a PE ratio of 20 so that the trailing digit of 0 is listed as the second leaf value next to the stem value of 2.

At this point in its construction, our stem-and-leaf display appears as follows:

```
0
1 | 2
2 | 50
3
4
5
6
```

Note that two of the three companies have the same stem. As more and more companies are included, those possessing the same stems and, perhaps, even the same leaves within stems (that is, the same reported PE ratios) will be observed. Such leaf values will be recorded adjacent to the previously recorded leaves, opposite the appropriate stem—resulting in Figure 3.9.

To assist us in further examining the data, we may wish to rearrange the leaves within each of the stems by placing the digits in ascending order, row-by-row. The *revised* stem-and-leaf display is presented in Figure 3.10.

```
0 | 89
1 | 001223344577
2 | 00358
3 | 38
4 | 8
5 | 0
6 | 1              N = 24
```

FIGURE 3.10
Revised stem-and-leaf display of PE ratios from 24 natural resource companies.

Another type of rearrangement is also useful. If the researcher desires to alter the size of the stem-and-leaf display, it is flexible enough for such an adjustment. Suppose, for example, we want to increase the number of stems so that we can attain a lighter concentration of leaves on the remaining stems. This is accomplished in the stem-and-leaf display presented in Figure 3.11.

```
0H | 89
1L | 001223344
1H | 577
2L | 003
2H | 58
3L | 3
3H | 8
4L |
4H | 8
5L | 0
5H |
6L | 1              N = 24
```

FIGURE 3.11
Revised stem-and-leaf display of PE ratios from 24 natural resource companies using more stems.

Note that each stem from Figure 3.10 has been split into two new stems—one for the **low** unit digits 0, 1, 2, 3, or 4 and the other for the **high** unit digits 5, 6, 7, 8, or 9. These are represented by **L** and **H,** respectively, as indicated in the stem listings of Figure 3.11.

The (revised) stem-and-leaf display is, perhaps, the most versatile technique in descriptive statistics. It simultaneously organizes the data for further descriptive analyses and, as we will see in Chapter 4, presents the data in both tabular and chart form.

Problems

● **3.30**   Given the following stem-and-leaf display:

```
 9 | 714
10 | 82230
11 | 561776735
12 | 394282
13 | 20
```

(a) Rearrange the leaves and form the revised stem-and-leaf display.
(b) Place the data into an ordered array.
(c) Which of these two devices seems to give more information? Discuss.

3.31   Using the battery life data from Problem 3.5 on page 43
(a) Develop the ordered array.
(b) Form the stem-and-leaf display.

3.32   Using the data on amount owed to the mail-order book company from Problem 3.7 on page 43
(a) Develop the ordered array.
(b) Form the stem-and-leaf display.

3.33   Using (all) the dot-matrix printer price data from Problem 3.8 on page 43
(a) Develop the ordered array.
(b) Form the stem-and-leaf display.

3.34   Using the hotel price data (excluding the Presidential Suite) from Problem 3.9 on page 43
(a) Develop the ordered array.
(b) Form the stem-and-leaf display.

3.35   Using the water consumption data from Problem 3.11 on page 44
(a) Develop the ordered array.
(b) Form the stem-and-leaf display.

3.9   QUANTILES

Aside from the measures of central tendency, dispersion, and shape, there also exist some useful measures of "noncentral" location which are often employed when summarizing or describing the properties of large batches of quantitative data. These measures are called **quantiles.** Some of the more widely used quantiles are the **deciles** (which split the ordered data into *tenths*) and the **percentiles** (which split the ordered data into *hundredths*). For further information on these measures, see Reference 1 or 2. However, our concern here will be with the **quartiles.**

Whereas the median is a value that splits the ordered array in half (50.0% of the observations are smaller and 50.0% of the observations are larger), the quartiles are descriptive measures that split the ordered data into four quarters.

> The **first quartile, Q_1,** is the value such that 25.0% of the observations are smaller and 75.0% of the observations are larger.
>
> The **second quartile, Q_2,** is the median—50.0% of the observations are smaller and 50.0% are larger.
>
> The **third quartile, Q_3,** is the value such that 75.0% of the observations are smaller and 25.0% of the observations are larger.

To approximate the quartiles from a population containing N observations, the following *positioning point formulas* are used:[10]

$$Q_1 = \text{value corresponding to the } \frac{N + 1}{4} \text{ ordered observation.}$$

$$Q_2 = \text{median, the value corresponding to the } \frac{2(N + 1)}{4} = \frac{N + 1}{2}$$

ordered observation.

$$Q_3 = \text{value corresponding to the } \frac{3(N + 1)}{4} \text{ ordered observation.}$$

The following rules are used for obtaining the quartile values:

1. If the resulting positioning point is an integer, the particular numerical observation corresponding to that positioning point is chosen for the quartile.
2. If the resulting positioning point is halfway between two integer positioning points, the average of their corresponding values is selected.
3. If the resulting positioning point is neither an integer nor a value halfway between two other positioning points, a simple rule of thumb used to approximate the particular quartile is to round off to the nearest integer positioning point and select the numerical value of the corresponding observation.

Thus, for example, from the (revised) stem-and-leaf display (Figure 3.11) pertaining to the PE ratios of the 24 natural resource companies we have

$$Q_1 = \frac{N + 1}{4} \text{ ordered observation}$$

$$= \frac{24 + 1}{4} = 6.25 \rightarrow \text{6th ordered observation.}$$

Therefore $Q_1 = 12.0$.

$$\text{Median} = \frac{N + 1}{2} \text{ ordered observation}$$

---

[10] When dealing with a sample, we simply replace N by n in the positioning-point formulas.

$$= \frac{24 + 1}{2} = 12.5\text{th ordered observation.}$$

Therefore the median $= 16.0$.

$$Q_3 = \frac{3(N + 1)}{4} \text{ ordered observation}$$

$$= \frac{3(24 + 1)}{4} = 18.75 \rightarrow 19\text{th ordered observation.}$$

Therefore $Q_3 = 28.0$.

These quartiles, along with the smallest and largest observations, are highlighted in the accompanying stem-and-leaf display in Figure 3.12.

```
Xsmallest = 8                      0 | 89
Q1 = 12      Median = 16           1 | 001223344577
Q3 = 28                            2 | 00358
                                   3 | 38
                                   4 | 8
                                   5 | 0
Xlargest = 61                      6 | 1
```

FIGURE 3.12
Stem-and-leaf display and summary measures.

Note the following:

1. To obtain Q_1 we simply count (left to right, row by row) to the 6th ordered observation. In our data, the "leaf" is 2 so that the result is 12.
2. To obtain the median we must take the mean of the 12th and 13th ordered observations. In our data, the respective "leaves" are 5 and 7—corresponding to the PE ratios 15 and 17—so that the resulting median is 16.
3. To obtain Q_3 we simply count *down* (left to right, row by row) to the 19th ordered observation or count *up* (right to left, row by row) to the 6th ordered observation. In our data, the "leaf" is 8 so the result is 28.

Problems

- **3.36** Using the data and your results from Problem 3.30 on page 57, compute Q_1 and Q_3.
- **3.37** Using the battery life data from Problem 3.5 on page 43 and/or your results from Problem 3.31 on page 57, compute Q_1 and Q_3.
- **3.38** Using the data on amount owed to the mail-order book company from Problem 3.7 on page 43 and/or your results from Problem 3.32 on page 57, compute Q_1 and Q_3.
- **3.39** Using (all) the dot-matrix printer price data from Problem 3.8 on page 43 and/or your results from Problem 3.33 on page 57, compute Q_1 and Q_3.
- **3.40** Using the hotel price data (excluding the Presidential Suite) from Problem 3.9 on page 43 and/or your results from Problem 3.34 on page 57, compute Q_1 and Q_3.
- **3.41** Using the water consumption data from Problem 3.11 on page 44 and/or your results from Problem 3.35 on page 57, compute Q_1 and Q_3.

3.10 DESCRIPTIVE SUMMARY MEASURES USING QUARTILES

Quantiles are useful not only as measures of noncentral location; they are useful also in the development of important measures of central tendency and dispersion. In this section we describe two such measures, both of which are based on the quartiles—the midhinge and the interquartile range.

3.10.1 The Midhinge—A Measure of Central Tendency

The **midhinge** is the mean of the first and third quartiles in a batch of data. That is,

$$\text{Midhinge} = \frac{Q_1 + Q_3}{2} \qquad \textbf{(3.9)}$$

It is used to overcome potential problems introduced by extreme values in the data. For the reported PE ratio data we have

$$\text{Midhinge} = \frac{12 + 28}{2} = 20.0$$

3.10.2 The Interquartile Range—A Measure of Dispersion

The **interquartile range** (also called **midspread**) is the difference between the third and first quartiles in a batch of data. That is,

$$\text{Interquartile range} = Q_3 - Q_1 \qquad \textbf{(3.10)}$$

This simple measure considers the spread in the middle 50% of the data and thus is in no way influenced by possibly occurring extreme values.

For the PE ratio data we have

$$\text{Interquartile range} = 28 - 12 = 16.0$$

This is the range in reported PE ratios for the "middle group" of natural resource companies.

The fact that both the median (a measure of central tendency) and the interquartile range (a measure of dispersion) have the same numerical value (16) here is, of course, pure coincidence.

Problems

- **3.42** Using the data from Problem 3.30 on page 57 and your results from Problem 3.36 on page 59, compute the midhinge and the interquartile range.

3.43 Using the data from Problem 3.5 on page 43 and your results from Problem 3.37 on page 59:
   (a) Compute the midhinge and compare it with the other measures of central tendency obtained in Problem 3.5. Discuss.
   (b) Compute the interquartile range.

3.44 Using the data on amount owed to the mail-order book company from Problem 3.7 on page 43 and your results from Problem 3.38 on page 59
   (a) Compute the midhinge and compare it with the other measures of central tendency obtained in Problem 3.7. Discuss.
   (b) Compute the interquartile range.

3.45 Using (all) the dot-matrix printer price data from Problem 3.8 on page 43 and your results from Problem 3.39 on page 59
   (a) Compute the midhinge and compare it with the other measures of central tendency obtained in Problem 3.8. Discuss.
   (b) Compute the interquartile range.

3.46 Using the hotel price data (excluding the Presidential Suite) from Problem 3.9 on page 43 and your results from Problem 3.40 on page 59
   (a) Compute the midhinge and compare it with the other measures of central tendency obtained in Problem 3.9. Discuss.
   (b) Compute the interquartile range.

3.47 Using the water consumption data from Problem 3.11 on page 44 and your results from Problem 3.41 on page 59
   (a) Compute the midhinge and compare it with the other measures of central tendency obtained in Problem 3.11. Discuss.
   (b) Compute the interquartile range.

3.11 USING THE FIVE-NUMBER SUMMARY FOR THE BOX-AND-WHISKER PLOT: A GRAPHICAL TECHNIQUE

3.11.1 The Five-Number Summary

To identify and describe the major features of the data the "exploratory data analysis" approach utilizes measures of central tendency and dispersion which have the property of **resistance**—that is, statistics which are relatively insensitive to extreme values or to changes in some of the data. The median, the midhinge, and the interquartile range are three widely used resistant statistics. If we combine these resistant measures with information regarding the extremes, we have a better idea as to the shape of the distribution. A **five-number summary** then consists of

$$X_{\text{smallest}} \quad Q_1 \quad \text{median} \quad Q_3 \quad X_{\text{largest}}$$

For our PE ratio data, the five-number summary is

$$8 \quad 12 \quad 16 \quad 28 \quad 61$$

The five-number summary may now be used to study the shape of the distribution. If the data were "perfectly symmetrical," the following would be true:

symmetry

1. The distance from Q_1 to the median would equal the distance from the median to Q_3.
2. The distance from X_{smallest} to Q_1 would equal the distance from Q_3 to X_{largest}.
3. The median, the midhinge, and the midrange would all be equal. (Moreover, these measures would also equal the mean in the data.)

On the other hand, for nonsymmetrical distributions the following would be true:

1. In right-skewed distributions the distance from Q_3 to $X_{largest}$ greatly exceeds the distance from $X_{smallest}$ to Q_1.
2. In right-skewed distributions

$$\text{median} < \text{midhinge} < \text{midrange}$$

3. In left-skewed distributions the distance from $X_{smallest}$ to Q_1 greatly exceeds the distance from Q_3 to $X_{largest}$.
4. In left-skewed distributions

$$\text{midrange} < \text{midhinge} < \text{median}$$

From these rules it is obvious that our distribution of PE ratios is right-skewed. (See the stem-and-leaf display depicted in Figure 3.12 on page 59.)

3.11.2 The Box-and-Whisker Plot

In its simplest form a **box-and-whisker plot** provides a graphical representation of the data through its five-number summary. Such a plot is depicted in Figure 3.13 for the reported PE ratios of the 24 natural resources companies.

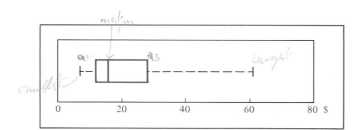

FIGURE 3.13
Box-and-whisker plot of reported PE ratios from 24 natural resource companies.

The vertical line drawn within the box represents the location of the median value in the data. Note further that the vertical line at the left side of the box represents the location of Q_1 and the vertical line at the right side of the box represents the location of Q_3. Therefore, we see that the box contains the middle 50% of the observations in the distribution. The lower 25% of the data are represented by a dashed line (that is, a **whisker**) connecting the left side of the box to the location of the smallest value, $X_{smallest}$. Similarly, the upper 25% of the data are represented by a dashed line connecting the right side of the box to $X_{largest}$.

This visual representation of the reported PE ratios depicted in Figure 3.13 indicates the right-skewness in the shape of that distribution. Not only do we observe that the vertical median line is not centered in the box, we also clearly see the disparities in the lengths of the whiskers—the dashed lines representing the lower and upper 25% of the data.

In order to illustrate how the shape of a distribution affects the box-and-whisker plot, Figure 3.14 depicts six such plots—one for each of the distributions represented in Figures 4.5 and 4.10 to 4.14, respectively. (See pages 111 to 114.)

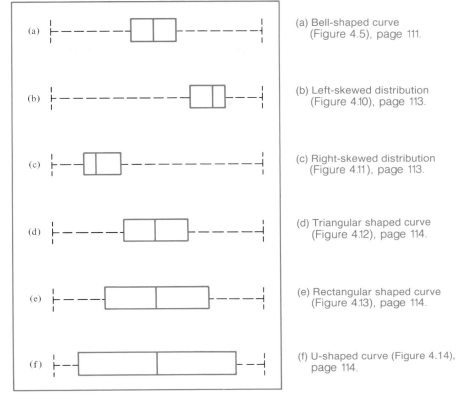

(a) Bell-shaped curve
(Figure 4.5), page 111.

(b) Left-skewed distribution
(Figure 4.10), page 113.

(c) Right-skewed distribution
(Figure 4.11), page 113.

(d) Triangular shaped curve
(Figure 4.12), page 114.

(e) Rectangular shaped curve
(Figure 4.13), page 114.

(f) U-shaped curve (Figure 4.14),
page 114.

FIGURE 3.14
Box-and-whisker plots for six hypothetical distributions.

Problems

- **3.48** Using the data from Problem 3.30 on page 57 and your results from Problem 3.36 on page 59
  (a) List the five-number summary.
  (b) Form the box-and-whisker plot and describe the shape.

  3.49 Using the battery life data from Problem 3.5 on page 43 and your results from Problem 3.37 on page 59
  (a) List the five-number summary.
  (b) Form the box-and-whisker plot and describe the shape.
  (c) Compare your answer in (b) with that from Problem 3.24 on page 54. Discuss.

  3.50 Using the data on amount owed to the mail-order book company from Problem 3.7 on page 43 and your results from Problem 3.38 on page 59
  (a) List the five-number summary.
  (b) Form the box-and-whisker plot and describe the shape.
  (c) Compare your answer in (b) with that from Problem 3.25 on page 54. Discuss.

3.51   Using (all) the dot-matrix printer price data from Problem 3.8 on page 43 and your results from Problem 3.39 on page 59

   (a) List the five-number summary.
   (b) Form the box-and-whisker plot and describe the shape.
   (c) Compare your answer in (b) with that from Problem 3.26 on page 54. Discuss.

3.52   Using the hotel price data (excluding the Presidential Suite) from Problem 3.9 on page 43 and your results from Problem 3.40 on page 59
   (a) List the five-number summary.
   (b) Form the box-and-whisker plot and describe the shape.
   (c) Compare your answer in (b) with that from Problem 3.27 on page 54. Discuss.

3.53   Using the water consumption data from Problem 3.11 on page 44 and your results from Problem 3.41 on page 59
   (a) List the five-number summary.
   (b) Form the box-and-whisker plot and describe the shape.
   (c) Compare your answer in (b) with that from Problem 3.29 on page 54. Discuss.

3.12   CALCULATING DESCRIPTIVE SUMMARY MEASURES FROM A POPULATION

In Sections 3.4 through 3.6 we examined various *statistics* that are used to describe or summarize quantitative information from a *sample*. In particular, for the PE ratios obtained from the sample of $n = 6$ natural resource companies, we used the mean, median, mode, and midrange to describe the property of central tendency; the range, variance, standard deviation, and coefficient of variation were used to describe the property of dispersion; and the relative positions of the mean and the median were used to describe the property of shape. Moreover, in the previous two sections we learned that the properties of central tendency, dispersion, and shape can also be examined through the use of exploratory data analysis techniques, particularly when the data batch is large.

Suppose, however, that our financial analyst also wishes to conduct a more *traditional* study of the PE ratios for each of the 24 companies which comprise the entire natural resources industrial grouping (that is, the *population*). The resulting measures (i.e., *parameters*) computed from the PE ratio data to summarize or describe the properties of central tendency, dispersion, and shape could then be used by the financial analyst when writing a report evaluating industrywide performance for the annual period.

3.12.1   Population Measures of Central Tendency and Dispersion

A set of descriptive measures which characterize a population of size N is given in Table 3.1.

TABLE 3.1   Descriptive measures for the population

Mean:	$\mu_x = \dfrac{\sum\limits_{i=1}^{N} X_i}{N}$	(3.11)
Midrange:	$\text{midrange} = \dfrac{X_{\text{smallest}} + X_{\text{largest}}}{2}$	(3.2A)
Range:	$\text{range} = X_{\text{largest}} - X_{\text{smallest}}$	(3.3A)
Variance:	$\sigma_x^2 = \dfrac{\sum\limits_{i=1}^{N} (X_i - \mu_x)^2}{N}$	(3.12)
Standard deviation:	$\sigma_x = \sqrt{\sigma_x^2} = \sqrt{\dfrac{\sum\limits_{i=1}^{N} (X_i - \mu_x)^2}{N}}$	(3.13)
Coefficient of variation:	$CV_{\text{pop}} = \left(\dfrac{\sigma_x}{\mu_x}\right) 100\%$	(3.14)

where N = population size

   X_i = ith value of the random variable X

$\sum\limits_{i=1}^{N} X_i$ = "summation of" all X_i values in the population

$\sum\limits_{i=1}^{N} (X_i - \mu_x)^2$ = summation of all the squared differences between the X_i values and μ_X

   The median and mode for a population of size N are respectively obtained as previously described in Sections 3.4.2 and 3.4.3 for a sample.
   From Table 3.1 we note that the population mean is given by the symbol μ_X (the Greek lower-case letter **mu subscript** X), the population variance is given by the symbol σ_X^2 (the Greek lower-case letter **sigma subscript** X "squared"), and the population standard deviation is given by the symbol σ_X. We also note that the formulas for the population variance and standard deviation differ from those for the sample in that $(n - 1)$ in the denominator of S^2 and S [see Equations (3.4) and (3.5)] is replaced by N in the denominator of σ_X^2 and σ_X.

3.12.2 Results

Using the ordered array of PE ratios for the 24 natural resources companies (Figure 3.8 on page 55) we compute the following:

Mean

$$\mu_X = \frac{\sum\limits_{i=1}^{N} X_i}{N} = \frac{521}{24} = 21.71$$

Median

$$\text{Positioning point} = \frac{N + 1}{2} \text{ ordered observation}$$

$$= \frac{24 + 1}{2} = 12.5\text{th ordered observation}$$

Thus, the median is the average of the 12th and 13th ordered observations.

$$\text{Median} = \frac{15 + 17}{2} = 16.0$$

Mode

The most frequently observed PE ratios are 10, 12, 13, 14, 17, and 20. The data are multimodal.

Midrange

$$\frac{X_{\text{smallest}} + X_{\text{largest}}}{2} = \frac{8 + 61}{2} = 34.5$$

Range

$$X_{\text{largest}} - X_{\text{smallest}} = 61 - 8 = 53.0$$

Variance

$$\sigma_X^2 = \frac{\sum_{i=1}^{N}(X_i - \mu_X)^2}{N} = \frac{(25 - 21.71)^2 + (12 - 21.71)^2 + \cdots + (13 - 21.71)^2}{24}$$

$$= 198.8733 \text{ (in squared units)}$$

Standard Deviation

$$\sigma_X = \sqrt{\sigma_X^2} = \sqrt{198.8733} = 14.10$$

Coefficient of Variation

$$\text{CV}_{\text{pop}} = \left(\frac{\sigma_X}{\mu_X}\right) 100\% = \left(\frac{14.10}{21.71}\right) 100\% = 64.9\%$$

Shape

The shape of the population is obtained either through a *relative* comparison of the mean and the median or through an evaluation of the five-number summary and box-and-whisker plot.

In the natural resources industrial grouping, the population of PE ratios can be considered as right-skewed in **shape** because the mean (21.71) exceeds the median (16.0). (Similar conclusions were drawn from the analysis of the box-and-whisker plot depicted in Figure 3.13 on page 62.)

Summarizing the Findings

Table 3.2 summarizes the results of utilizing the various descriptive measures we have investigated.

TABLE 3.2   Using descriptive measures on two data batches

	Price to Earnings Ratio	
Descriptive Measure	*Sample (n = 6)*	*Population (N = 24)*
Mean	20.0	21.71
Median	20.0	16.0
Mode	No mode	Multimodal
Midrange	20.0	34.5
Midhinge	20.0*	20.0
Q_1	15.0*	12.0
Q_3	25.0*	28.0
Range	16.0	53.0
Interquartile range	10.0*	16.0
Variance	39.20	198.8733
Standard deviation	6.26	14.10
Coefficient of variation	31.3%	64.9%
Shape	Symmetrical	Right-skewed

* See Problem 3.63 on page 72.

Aside from the midhinge, we observe that the various statistics computed from the sample of size 6 appear to differ somewhat from the corresponding characteristics obtained from the population of size 24. Why this has happened, however, is simply a function of chance. When drawing the random sample, our financial analyst properly used a table of random numbers (Table E.1) as was discussed in Section 2.7. Unfortunately—and purely by chance—the PE ratios from the selected companies are quite homogeneous and fail to account for the range of responses that exist in the entire population. This is clearly depicted on the dot-scale diagram in Figure 3.15. The sample data were not right-skewed because not one of the six companies had a PE ratio (light dots) that was among the highest 20% in the population.

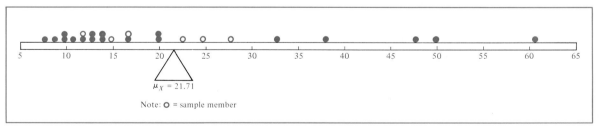

FIGURE 3.15
Dot scale showing the PE ratios for the 24 natural resources companies.
(SOURCE: Figure 3.7)

Using the Standard Deviation: The Empirical Rule

In most data batches a large portion of the observations tend to cluster somewhat near the median. In right-skewed data batches this clustering occurs to the left of (i.e., below) the median and in left-skewed data batches the observations tend to cluster to the right of (i.e., above) the median. In symmetrical data batches, of course, the observations tend to distribute equally around the median (or mean). When extreme skewness is not present and such clustering is observed in a data batch, we can use the so-called **empirical rule** to examine the property of data variability and get a better sense as to what the standard deviation is measuring.

> The **empirical rule** states that for most data batches we will find that roughly two out of every three observations (i.e., 67%) are contained within a distance of 1 standard deviation around the mean and roughly 90 to 95% of the observations are contained within a distance of 2 standard deviations around the mean.

Hence the standard deviation, as a measure of average scatter around the mean, helps us to understand how the observations distribute above and below the mean and helps us to focus on and flag unusual observations (i.e., outliers) when analyzing a batch of data.

Using the Standard Deviation: The Bienaymé-Chebyshev Rule

More than a century ago, the mathematicians Bienaymé and Chebyshev (Reference 3) independently examined the property of data variability around the mean.[11] They found that regardless of how a batch of data is distributed, the percentage of observations that are contained within distances of k standard deviations around the mean must be at least

$$\left(1 - \frac{1}{k^2}\right) 100\%$$

Therefore, for data with any shape whatsoever

1. At least $[1 - (1/2^2)]\, 100\% = 75.0\%$ of the observations must be contained within distances of ± 2 standard deviations around the mean.
2. At least $[1 - (1/3^2)]\, 100\% = 88.89\%$ of the observations must be contained within distances of ± 3 standard deviations around the mean.
3. At least $[1 - (1/4^2)]\, 100\% = 93.75\%$ of all the observations must be included within distances of ± 4 standard deviations about the mean.

Although the Bienaymé-Chebyshev rule is general in nature and applies to any kind of distribution of data, we will see in Chapter 8 that if the data form the "bell-shaped" Gaussian (i.e., normal) distribution, 68.26% of all the observations will be contained within distances of ± 1 standard deviation around the mean, while 95.44%, 99.73%, and 99.99% of the observations will be included, respectively, within distances of ± 2, ± 3, and ± 4 standard deviations around the mean. These results (among others) are summarized in Table 3.3.

Specifically, if we knew that a particular random phenomenon followed the pattern of the "bell-shaped" distribution—as many do, at least approximately—we would then know (as will be shown in Chapter 8) *exactly* how likely it is that any particular observation was close to or far from its mean. Generally, however, for any kind of distribution, the Bienaymé-Chebyshev rule tells us *at least* how likely it must be that any particular observation falls within a given distance about the mean. Such information is quite valuable in data analysis.

From Table 3.2 we recall that for the population of 24 companies in the natural

---

[11] The Bienaymé-Chebyshev rule can apply only to distances beyond ± 1 standard deviation about the mean.

TABLE 3.3   How data vary around the mean

Number of Standard Deviation Units k	Percentage of Observations Contained between the Mean and k Standard Deviations Based on		
	Bienaymé-Chebyshev Rule for Any Distribution	Gaussian Distribution	Natural Resources Company Data
1	Not calculable	Exactly 68.26%	Exactly 83.3%
2	At least 75.00%	Exactly 95.44%	Exactly 91.7%
3	At least 88.89%	Exactly 99.73%	Exactly 100.0%
4	At least 93.75%	Exactly 99.99%	Exactly 100.0%

resources industrial grouping, the mean PE ratio, μ_X, is 21.71 and the standard deviation, σ_X, is 14.10. From the ordered array (Figure 3.8) we note that 20 out of 24 companies (83.3%) had a PE ratio between $\mu_X - 1\sigma_X$ and $\mu_X + 1\sigma_X$ (that is, between 7.61 and 35.81). Moreover, we see that 22 out of 24 companies (91.7%) had a PE ratio between $\mu_X - 2\sigma_X$ and $\mu_X + 2\sigma_X$ (that is, between 0 and 49.91).[12] Finally, we note that all 24 companies (100%) had a PE ratio within $\mu_X - 3\sigma_X$ and $\mu_X + 3\sigma_X$ (that is, between 0 and 64.01). It is interesting to note that even though the PE ratio data are right-skewed in shape, the percentages of companies with PE ratios falling within two or more standard deviations about the mean are not very different from what would be expected had the data been distributed as a symmetrical, "bell-shaped" Gaussian distribution.

Problems

● **3.54**   Given the following batch of data for a population of size $N = 10$:

> 7   5   11   8   3   6   2   1   9   8

(a) Compute the mean, median, mode, midrange, and midhinge.
(b) Compute the range, interquartile range, variance, standard deviation, and coefficient of variation.
(c) Are these data skewed? If so, how?

3.55   Given the following batch of data for a population of size $N = 10$:

> 7   5   6   6   6   4   8   6   9   3

(a) Compute the mean, median, mode, midrange, and midhinge.
(b) Compute the range, interquartile range, variance, standard deviation, and coefficient of variation.
(c) Are these data skewed? If so, how?
(d) Compare the measures of central tendency to those of Problem 3.54(a). Discuss.
(e) Compare the measures of dispersion to those of Problem 3.54(b). Discuss.

---

[12] Here $\mu_X \pm 2\sigma_X$ yields the interval -6.49 to 49.91; however, a negative PE ratio is not meaningful and we record the interval as 0 to 49.91.

3.56 The following data represent the PE ratios for all 33 companies in the food processing industrial grouping listed in the ''Business Week Corporate Scoreboard.''

Company	PE Ratio
American Maize-Products	11
Borden	19
CPC International	21
Campbell Soup	18
ConAgra	17
Curtice-Burns Foods	17
Dean Foods	20
Federal	13
Flowers Industries	22
General Mills	21
Gerber Products	24
Heinz (H. J.)	21
Hershey Foods	20
Hormel (Geo. A.)	18
Hudson Foods	14
International Multifoods	17
Interstate Bakeries	17
Kellogg	25
Kraft	21
Lance	19
McCormick	18
Monfort of Colorado	8
Pilgrim's Pride	23
Pillsbury	17
Quaker Oats	23
Ralston Purina	12
Sara Lee	19
Savannah Foods & Industries	18
Seaboard	9
Smithfield Foods	15
Tyson Foods	24
Universal Foods	18
Wrigley (Wm.) Jr.	20

SOURCE: "Business Week Corporate Scoreboard," *Business Week*, March 16, 1987, pp. 125–146. Reprinted by special permission. © 1987 by McGraw-Hill, Inc.

(a) Compute
    (1) the mean   (6) the range
    (2) the median   (7) the interquartile range
    (3) the mode   (8) the variance
    (4) the midrange   (9) the standard deviation
    (5) the midhinge   (10) the coefficient of variation

(b) Form the stem-and-leaf display and box-and-whisker plot.

(c) List the five-number summary.

(d) Are these data skewed? If so, how?

(e) Compare and contrast your findings in (a) with those given in Table 3.2 (page 67) for the 24 companies comprising the natural resource industrial grouping.

(f) ACTION In what ways could this information be useful to the financial analyst? Discuss.

3.57 The following data represent the fringe benefits as a percentage of salaries paid at the 28 reporting institutions of higher learning in the state of Connecticut during the 1986–87 academic year:

Institution	Benefits as % of Salary
Albertus Magnus College	18
Asnuntuck Community College	26
Central Connecticut St. Univ.	25
Connecticut College	23
Eastern Connecticut St. Univ.	22
Fairfield University	23
Greater Hartford Comm. Coll.	26
Hartford College for Woman	19
Hartford Seminary	25
Housatonic Community College	25
Manchester Community College	26
Mattatuck Community College	21
Middlesex Community College	25
Mohegan Community College	25
Northwestern Conn. Comm. Coll.	26
Norwalk Community College	27
Quinebaug Valley Comm. Coll.	26
Sacred Heart University	26
Saint Joseph College	16
South Central Comm. College	22
Southern Conn. State Univ.	24
Trinity College	25
Tunxis Community College	25
University of Bridgeport	25
University of Connecticut	23
University of Hartford	30
Wesleyan University	28
Yale University	20

SOURCE: Data are taken from *Academe—Bulletin of the AAUP,* vol. 73, no. 2 (March–April 1987), pp. 24–25.

(a) Compute
    (1) the mean
    (2) the median
    (3) the mode
    (4) the midrange
    (5) the midhinge
    (6) the range
    (7) the interquartile range
    (8) the variance
    (9) the standard deviation
    (10) the coefficient of variation

(b) Form the stem-and-leaf display.

(c) List the five-number summary and form the box-and-whisker plot.

(d) Are these data skewed? If so, how?

(e) Analyze the data and prepare a report. Be sure to comment on whether the data are similar for community colleges and senior colleges.

⟹(f) **ACTION**   How could this information be of use to the president of one of these institutions and to its union head? Discuss.

3.58 The data at the top of page 72 represent the quarterly sales tax receipts (in $000) submitted to the comptroller of Hyersville Township for the period ending March 1988 by all 50 business establishments in that locale:

(a) Organize the data into an ordered array or stem-and-leaf display.

(b) Compute the mean, median, mode, midrange, and midhinge for this population.

(c) Compute the range, interquartile range, variance, standard deviation, and coefficient of variation for this population.

(d) Form the box-and-whisker plot and describe the shape of these quarterly sales tax receipts data.

Problem 3.58 Data

10.3	13.0	11.1	10.0	9.3
11.1	11.2	10.2	12.9	11.5
9.6	7.3	11.1	9.2	10.7
9.0	5.3	9.9	10.0	11.6
14.5	12.5	9.8	12.8	7.8
13.0	8.0	11.6	12.5	10.5
6.7	11.8	15.1	9.3	7.6
11.0	8.7	12.5	10.4	10.1
8.4	10.6	6.5	12.7	8.9
10.3	9.5	7.5	10.5	8.6

(e) What proportion of these businesses have quarterly sales tax receipts
  (1) within ± 1 standard deviation of the mean?
  (2) within ± 2 standard deviations of the mean?
  (3) within ± 3 standard deviations of the mean?

(f) Are you surprised at the results in (e)? [*Hint*: Compare and contrast your findings versus what would be expected based on the empirical rule.]

➠(g) **ACTION** Assist the comptroller of this township by writing a draft of the memo that will be sent to the Governor regarding the collected receipts.

➠(h) **ACTION** How would this information be of use to the Governor? Discuss.

Supplementary Problems

3.59 In your own words, explain the difference between raw data and an ordered array.

3.60 In your own words, explain the difference between a statistic and a parameter.

3.61 A batch of numerical data has three major properties. In your own words, define these properties and give examples of each.

3.62 Why is it advantageous to use a stem-and-leaf display instead of an ordered array?

3.63 Using the sample of $n = 6$ natural resources companies, verify the results given in Table 3.2 for the midhinge, Q_1, Q_3, and interquartile range. (See page 67.)

3.64 The following data are the monthly rental prices for a sample of 10 unfurnished studio apartments in Manhattan and a sample of 10 unfurnished studio apartments in Brooklyn Heights:

Manhattan	$955	$1000	$985	$980	$940	$975	$965	$999	$1247	$1119
Brooklyn Hts.	$750	$775	$725	$705	$694	$725	$690	$745	$575	$800

(a) For each batch of data compute the mean, median, range, standard deviation, and coefficient of variation.

Note: Problems pertaining to the real estate survey of Chapter 2 which deal with the material covered in this chapter will be presented in Chapter 5.

Note: Bullet ● indicates those problems whose solutions are included in the Answers to Selected Problems.

(b) What can be said about unfurnished studio apartments renting in Brooklyn Heights versus those renting in Manhattan?

⇒**(c)** **ACTION** How might this information be of use to an individual desiring to move into the New York City area?

● **3.65** The following data represent net income as a percent of sales during 1986 for a random sample of 15 of the "500 largest industrial corporations":

Company	Net Income to Sales (%)
Scott Paper	5.4
B F Goodrich	1.3
Harsco	4.1
Chevron	2.9
Northrop	0.7
Universal Foods	2.6
Mapco	8.5
Butler Manufacturing	0.6
Square D	7.1
Xidex	7.5
Dorsey	1.9
Washington Post	8.2
Singer	3.9
Pfizer	14.8
Snap-on Tools	9.8

SOURCE: "Fortune's Directory of the 500 Largest Industrial Corporations," *Fortune* Magazine, April 27, 1987. © 1987 Time Inc. All rights reserved.

(a) Compute

(1) the mean
(2) the median
(3) the mode
(4) the midrange
(5) the midhinge

(6) the range
(7) the interquartile range
(8) the variance
(9) the standard deviation
(10) the coefficient of variation

(b) Form the stem-and-leaf display and box-and-whisker plot.

(c) List the five-number summary.

(d) Are these data skewed? If so, how?

⇒**(e)** **ACTION** Write a memo to your economics professor summarizing your findings.

3.66 A college was conducting a *Phonothon* to raise money for the building of an Arts Center. The Provost hoped to obtain one-half million dollars for this purpose. The data below represent the amounts pledged (in $000) by all alumni who were called during the first nine nights of the campaign.

$$16, 18, 11, 17, 13, 10, 22, 15, 16$$

(a) Compute the mean, median, and standard deviation.

(b) Describe the shape of this batch of data.

(c) Estimate the total amount that will be pledged (in $000) by all alumni if the campaign is to last 30 nights. [*Hint*: Total $= N\overline{X}$.]

⇒**(d)** **ACTION** Write a memo to the Provost summarizing your findings to date and, if necessary, offering any needed recommendations.

⇒**(e)** **ACTION** How might this information assist the Provost? Discuss.

3.67 The following data represent the selling price of a sample of 25 auto alarm systems:

System	Price
Crimestopper HP2501	$399
Clifford System III	550
Alpine 8101	400
Maxiguard P-1000	370
Techne Ungo TL1600	485
Thug Bug Avenger 1001	450
Paragon K6550; KPS9200	550
VSE Digi-Guard VS8200	450
Code Alarm CA1085	325
Chapman-Lok Generation III	375
Multi Guard MGB II	300
Watchdog Trooper	260
Anes Pro 900; HL Pro 10	472
Pioneer PAS200	324
Harrison 7119; 7828	281
Automotive Security Products	455
McDermott AK012; KP-1	467
Crimestopper CS9502*	221
VSE Theftrap VS7810*	170
Auto Page MA/07S*	165
Audiovox AA9135; AA7007*	140
Sears Cat. No. 5980*	100
Anes KD5000*	99
Pioneer PAS100*	100
Wolo 612-XP*	82

* Self-installed systems.

SOURCE: Copyright 1986 by Consumers Union of United States, Inc., Mount Vernon, NY 10553. Excerpted by permission from *Consumer Reports*, October 1986, p. 661.

  (a) Set up a (revised) stem-and-leaf display for these data, and write a description of what you see.
  (b) There are two kinds of alarms, professionally installed alarms and do-it-yourself systems. Guess why the frequency distribution has two "clumps."
➡**(c) ACTION** Write an article for a local newspaper column dealing with consumer affairs in order to enlighten its readership on this matter.

3.68 The following data represent the price (in cents) per 8 ounces for a sample of 20 brands of sparkling spring and mineral water sold in New York City supermarkets:

31	40	28	30	63
35	38	33	42	22
36	68	31	32	38
34	46	34	34	28

  (a) Compute
    (1) the mean
    (2) the median
    (3) the mode
    (4) the midrange
    (5) the midhinge
    (6) the range
    (7) the interquartile range
    (8) the variance
    (9) the standard deviation
    (10) the coefficient of variation

(b) Form the stem-and-leaf display and box-and-whisker plot.

(c) List the five-number summary.

(d) Are these data skewed? If so, how?

➠(e) **ACTION** Write a memo to your economics professor summarizing your findings.

● **3.69** The following data are the book values (i.e., net worth divided by number of outstanding shares) for a random sample of 50 stocks from the New York Stock Exchange:

7	9	8	6	12	6	9	15	9	16
8	5	14	8	7	6	10	8	11	4
10	6	16	5	10	12	7	10	15	7
10	8	8	10	18	8	10	11	7	10
7	8	15	23	13	9	8	9	9	13

(a) Compute

    (1) the mean   (6) the range

    (2) the median   (7) the interquartile range

    (3) the mode   (8) the variance

    (4) the midrange   (9) the standard deviation

    (5) the midhinge   (10) the coefficient of variation

(b) Form the stem-and-leaf display and box-and-whisker plot.

(c) List the five-number summary.

(d) Are these data skewed? If so, how?

(e) Based on the Bienaymé-Chebyshev rule, between what two values would we estimate that at least 75% of the data are contained?

(f) What percentage of the data are actually contained within ± 2 standard deviations of the mean? Compare the results with those from (e).

➠(g) **ACTION** Write a memo to your economics professor summarizing your findings.

3.70 The following data represent the retail price of a sample of 26 different compact disk players:

    $329, $999, $300, $675, $350, $ 299, $199, $280, $ 900, $279, $350, $329, $299, $629, $600, $600, $600, $425, $1295, $400, $450, $1500, $600, $450, $295, $450

(a) Compute

    (1) the mean   (6) the range

    (2) the median   (7) the interquartile range

    (3) the mode   (8) the variance

    (4) the midrange   (9) the standard deviation

    (5) the midhinge   (10) the coefficient of variation

(b) Set up a box-and-whisker plot and determine whether the data are approximately right-skewed, left-skewed, or symmetric. Give reasons to justify your conclusions.

➠(c) **ACTION** If you were considering purchasing a compact disk player, how would this information assist you? What else would you want to know? Discuss.

3.71 The following data represent the retail price of a sample of 29 different brands of high fidelity video cassette recorders:

    $899, $1199, $ 850, $1000, $600, $1195, $ 750, $1595, $1050, $1200, $799, $ 700, $1500, $ 629, $899, $1150, $ 889, $ 629, $ 999, $ 650, $799, $ 900, $ 580, $ 850, $700, $ 799, $1200, $ 729, $ 899

(a) Compute

(1) the mean	(6) the range
(2) the median	(7) the interquartile range
(3) the mode	(8) the variance
(4) the midrange	(9) the standard deviation
(5) the midhinge	(10) the coefficient of variation

(b) Set up a box-and-whisker plot and determine whether the data are approximately right-skewed, left-skewed, or symmetric. Give reasons to justify your conclusions.

➠(c) **ACTION**   How might this information be of use to some friends? What would you tell them?

3.72   The following data represent the prices of a sample of 23 compact microwave ovens:

Oven	Price
General Electric JEM6	$239
J.C. Penney Cat. No. 863-1996	280
Samsung MW4530U	190
GE Omni 5 JMT20F	254
Hotpoint RE65	179
Litton Micro-Browner 1285	399
Panasonic NE5875	245
Quasar MQ5575YH	240
Amana ML40	194
Litton 1150	219
Frigidaire MC690C	139
Magic Chef M22A-6	229
Montgomery Ward 8036	199
Sears 87361	200
Toastmaster 8310	239
Toshiba ERX-5600	259
Welbilt MR5T	180
Whirlpool MW1500XP	179
White-Westinghouse KM175H	139
Emerson AT735	250
Goldstar ER503M	260
Sharp R5970	249
Emerson AMC600A	300

SOURCE: Copyright 1986 by Consumer Union of United States, Inc., Mount Vernon, NY 10553. Excerpted by permission from *Consumer Reports*, November, 1986, p. 713.

(a) Compute

(1) the mean	(6) the range
(2) the median	(7) the interquartile range
(3) the mode	(8) the variance
(4) the midrange	(9) the standard deviation
(5) the midhinge	(10) the coefficient of variation

(b) Set up a box-and-whisker plot and determine whether the data are approximately right-skewed, left-skewed, or symmetric. Give reasons to justify your conclusions.

➠(c) **ACTION**   How might this information be of use to your next-door-neighbors? What would you tell them?

3.73   The following data represent the cost per dose (in cents) of 16 different pain relievers:

Product	Cost[1] per Dose
CVS Aspirin	2.0¢
Rite-Aid Aspirin	2.4
Bayer Aspirin	6.3
Rite-Aid Acetaminophen, Regular	6.4
CVS Acetaminophen, Regular	6.8
Rite-Aid Acetaminophen, Extra-Strength	8.4
Tylenol, Regular[2]	8.7
Tylenol, Extra-Strength[2]	13.6
CVS Ibuprofen	5.0
Ibuprin[3]	5.7
Medipren[3]	6.2
Advil[3]	7.0
Nuprin[3]	7.0
Haltran[3]	9.2
Trendar Ibuprofen	9.5
Midol 200[2]	12.5

[1] *Dose: Aspirin, 2 tablets (650 milligrams); acetaminophen, 2 tablets (650 milligrams regular, 1000 milligrams extra-strength); ibuprofen, 1 tablet, (200 milligrams).*

[2] *Acetaminophen*

[3] *Ibuprofen*

SOURCE: Copyright 1987 by Consumers Union of United States, Inc., Mount Vernon, NY 10553. Excerpted by permission from *Consumer Reports*, February 1987, p. 85.

(a) Compute

(1) the mean   (6) the range
(2) the median   (7) the interquartile range
(3) the mode   (8) the variance
(4) the midrange   (9) the standard deviation
(5) the midhinge   (10) the coefficient of variation

(b) Set up a box-and-whisker plot and determine whether the data are approximately right-skewed, left-skewed, or symmetric. Give reasons to justify your conclusions.

➠**(c)** **ACTION** Write an article for a local newspaper column dealing with consumer affairs in order to enlighten its readership on this matter.

3.74 The Computer Center at your college is interested in purchasing equipment for a Statistics Laboratory. The following data represent the price for a sample of 38 IBM PC/XT compatible systems (with 640K of Random Access Memory, 10-MHz CPU, monochrome monitor, monochrome or Hercules video board, keyboard, 20 megabyte hard disk drive) that can be ordered by mail:

$ 982, $1249, $963, $1008, $920, $875, $ 999, $ 950, $1014, $1295, $ 849, $1500, $620, $1006, $1020, $857, $1095, $869, $950, $1095, $ 895, $1029, $ 878, $1295, $ 900, $949, $1199, $ 956, $929, $ 995, $899, $920, $ 949, $1249, $ 961, $ 949, $ 761, $1028

(a) Compute

(1) the mean   (6) the range
(2) the median   (7) the interquartile range
(3) the mode   (8) the variance
(4) the midrange   (9) the standard deviation
(5) the midhinge   (10) the coefficient of variation

(b) Set up a box-and-whisker plot and determine whether the data are approximately right-skewed, left-skewed, or symmetric. Give reasons to justify your conclusions.

➠**(c)** **ACTION** Write a draft of the report the Computer Center will be sending the Provost requesting purchase of ten systems.

➠**(d) ACTION** How might the Provost use this information? Discuss.

3.75 The following data represent the cost of a sample of 36 spreadsheet products available for the IBM PC, XT, AT, and compatible personal computers:

$500, $695, $195, $495, $695, $100, $350, $195, $425, $ 50, $495, $ 99,
$495, $495, $195, $259, $ 99, $199, $199, $195, $100, $180, $100, $495,
$450, $695, $ 40, $ 50, $795, $195, $ 99, $ 50, $ 50, $495, $ 99, $395

(a) Compute

(1) the mean	(6) the range
(2) the median	(7) the interquartile range
(3) the mode	(8) the variance
(4) the midrange	(9) the standard deviation
(5) the midhinge	(10) the coefficient of variation

(b) Set up a box-and-whisker plot and determine whether the data are approximately right-skewed, left-skewed, or symmetric. Give reasons to justify your conclusions.

➠**(c) ACTION** Write an article for a computer magazine in order to enlighten its readership on this matter. (Be sure to comment on ''types'' of spreadsheet products available as a reason for the disparity in the prices.)

(d) Suppose that you accidentally included a 37th spreadsheet product that cost $12,500, but was available only for IBM mainframe computers. Comment specifically on the effect of including this observation on the arithmetic mean, median, midrange, and midhinge.

3.76 The following is an ordered array representing the projections of percent changes in real GNP for the year 1988 by a sample of 42 economists:

Economist	Percent Change GNP	Economist	Percent Change GNP	Economist	Percent Change GNP
David A. Levine Sanford C. Bernstein	5.5	**Henry Kaufman** Salomon Brothers	2.7	**Jerry J. Jasinowski** Natl. Assn. of Manufacturers	1.7
Charles B. Reeder Charles Reeder Associates	4.3	**Paul W. Boltz** T. Rowe Price	2.5	**Gary Ciminero** Fleet Financial Group	1.6
Robert J. Genetski Harris Trust	3.8	**Morris Cohen** Morris Cohen and Assoc.	2.5	**Robert H. Chandross** Lloyds Bank	1.5
Rosalind Wells J. C. Penney	3.2	**William Helman** Smith Barney	2.4	**Michael H. Cosgrove** The Econoclast	1.5
Gordon B. Pye Irving Trust	3.1	**Timothy J. Sullivan** Arnhold and Bleichroeder	2.3	**David M. Blitzer** Standard and Poor's	1.4
Jerry Jordan First Interstate	3.0	**Carol A. Leisenring** CoreStates Financial	2.3	**Don P. Hilty** Chrysler	1.1
Edgar R. Fiedler Conference Board	3.0	**Robert Brusca** Nikko Securities	2.2	**Donald H. Straszheim** Merrill Lynch	1.0
David D. Hale Kemper Financial	3.0	**Alan Kellner** General Foods	2.2	**Steve Roach** Morgan Stanley	1.0
M. Cathryn Eickhoff Eickhoff Economics	3.0	**Lawrence A. Kudlow** Bear Steams	2.1	**Kenneth T. Mayland** First Pennsylvania	1.0
Peter L. Bernstein Peter L. Bernstein	2.9	**Howard Keen** Conrail	2.0	**Richard A. Stuckey** DuPont	0.9
Albert E. DePrince Marine Midland	2.8	**Viadi Catto** Texas Instruments	2.0	**Irwin L. Kellner** Manufacturer's Trust	− 1.5
Edward Yardeni Prudential-Bache	2.8	**William C. Melton** IDS Financial Services	1.8	**Robert H. Parks** Robert H. Parks and Assoc.	− 2.0
Joseph W. Duncan Dun and Bradstreet	2.7	**Maury N. Harris** Paine Webber	1.8	**A. Gary Schilling** A. Gary Schilling and Co.	− 3.0
Carl R. Palesh McCarthy, Crisante, Maffei	2.7	**Harry R. Biederman** Lockheed	1.8	**John K. Langum** Business Economics	− 3.5

SOURCE: *Business Week*, December 28, 1987, p. 111. Reprinted by special permission. © 1987 by McGraw-Hill, Inc.

(a) Compute

    (1) the mean   (6) the range

    (2) the median   (7) the interquartile range

    (3) the mode   (8) the variance

    (4) the midrange   (9) the standard deviation

    (5) the midhinge   (10) the coefficient of variation

(b) Form the stem-and-leaf display and box-and-whisker plot.

(c) List the five-number summary.

(d) Are these data skewed? If so, how?

➡**(e)** **ACTION**   Write a report based on your findings in parts (a)–(d) concerning the projected percent changes in real GNP for the year 1988. (Be sure to comment on the ''level of optimism'' these projections appear to be indicating.)

3.77 The cost (in cents) per dose of a sample of 29 regular laundry detergent products was as follows:

Product	Cost per Dose
Liquid Cheer	28¢
Tide	17
Cheer (phos.)	16
Oxydol (phos.)	18
Tide (phos.)	19
Liquid Tide	21
Dash (phos.)	26
Oxydol	15
Sears I	19
Wisk	19
Surf (phos.)	16
Era Plus	14
Dynamo 2	21
Arm & Hammer (phos.)	12
All I	26
Cheer	17
Fresh Start (phos.)	17
Sears II	28
Arm & Hammer I	13
Fresh Start	18
Dash	22
Arm & Hammer II	14
Scotch Buy (Safeway)	10
All II	16
Purex	12
Cost Cutter (Kroger) I	9
Par (Safeway)	15
Ajax	12
Cost Cutter (Kroger) II	10

SOURCE: Copyright 1987 by Consumers Union of United States, Inc., Mount Vernon, NY 10553. Excerpted by permission from *Consumer Reports*, July 1987, p. 419.

(a) Analyze the data.

➡**(b)** **ACTION**   Prepare a report summarizing your findings. In what ways might your report be of interest to the Environmental Protection Agency? To the manufacturer of *Liquid Cheer*, a high-priced product? To your own family? Discuss.

3.78 A minister speaking on a late-night radio show conjectures that ''drinking is primarily a problem in states with large urban populations, in states with legalized gambling facilities, and in states known for recreational activities.''

The following data represent the annual per capita alcohol consumption (in gallons) in all 50 states plus the District of Columbia in a recent year:

State	Per Capita Consumption	State	Per Capita Consumption
District of Columbia	5.34	Louisiana	2.63
Nevada	5.19	Michigan	2.60
New Hampshire	4.91	Maine	2.57
Alaska	3.86	North Dakota	2.55
Wisconsin	3.19	Virginia	2.55
California	3.19	South Carolina	2.50
Delaware	3.17	Georgia	2.48
Vermont	3.12	Idaho	2.43
Florida	3.12	Nebraska	2.41
Colorado	3.09	South Dakota	2.33
Arizona	3.08	Missouri	2.27
Massachusetts	3.04	Ohio	2.26
Hawaii	2.97	Pennsylvania	2.25
Montana	2.95	Indiana	2.19
Rhode Island	2.92	North Carolina	2.13
Wyoming	2.86	Iowa	2.09
Maryland	2.84	Mississippi	2.06
New Jersey	2.83	Kansas	1.95
Texas	2.82	Tennessee	1.95
Connecticut	2.80	Oklahoma	1.91
Illinois	2.77	Kentucky	1.85
New Mexico	2.75	Alabama	1.80
Washington	2.71	Arkansas	1.78
Minnesota	2.68	West Virginia	1.68
New York	2.67	Utah	1.53
Oregon	2.63		

(a) Analyze the data.

(b) Use a map of the United States to determine if any geographic patterns are present.

➡(c) **ACTION** Write a letter to the host of the radio show (based on your findings in (a) and (b)) expressing your support or disagreement with the minister's statement.

3.79 The following data represent the tuition charged (in $ thousands) at a sample of 15 private colleges in the northeast and at a sample of 15 private colleges in the midwest during the academic year 1988–89:

Northeast Colleges			Midwest Colleges		
10.5	8.9	9.6	7.9	10.6	8.4
10.1	9.3	9.1	8.2	10.1	9.2
10.0	9.7	11.2	9.1	8.5	10.7
11.0	10.4	10.5	9.3	7.5	9.5
9.8	10.0	9.9	8.8	9.3	9.8

(a) For each batch of data compute the mean, median, Q_1, Q_3, range, interquartile range, standard deviation, and coefficient of variation.

(b) For each batch of data form the stem-and-leaf display and box-and-whisker plot.

(c) List the five-number summary and interpret the shape of each data batch.

(d) Summarize your findings.

➠(e) **ACTION** Suppose you have a cousin who is a high-school senior and she seeks your advice regarding colleges in the northeast versus those in the midwest. Write her a letter based on your summary in (d).

3.80   The following data represent the amount of time (in seconds) to get from 0 to 60 mph during a road test for a sample of 17 German-made automobile models and a sample of 25 Japanese-made automobile models:

German-made Cars				Japanese-made Cars				
12.2	8.9	5.5	10.9	8.9	8.7	12.5	10.8	9.3
6.9	10.9	8.8	8.7	8.1	6.7	9.8	14.0	10.3
9.6	8.8	6.5		10.6	11.5	7.9	10.6	7.8
12.2	7.0	11.1		9.9	7.8	9.7	13.4	11.4
9.6	5.8	10.4		9.7	9.1	12.7	10.5	13.8

SOURCE: Data are extracted from *Motor Trend*, November 1987, p. 40.

 (a) Compare and contrast the acceleration times in these two samples.

➠(b) **ACTION** Write a letter to a close friend regarding your findings in (a)—assuming you knew your friend was interested in this feature when making a decision to purchase a vehicle.

3.81   The following data are the ages of a sample of 25 automobile salespeople in the United States and a sample of 25 automobile salespeople in Western Europe.

United States					Western Europe				
23	63	25	22	32	43	26	30	27	40
56	30	34	56	30	35	48	36	47	41
25	48	44	27	26	34	45	30	38	33
38	26	30	39	30	35	44	24	33	40
36	32	36	38	33	31	23	29	37	28

 (a) Compare and contrast the ages in these two samples.

 (b) Are you surprised at the results? What major socioeconomic reasons might be considered—assuming the two samples are representative of their underlying populations? Explain.

➠(c) **ACTION** Write a report to your sociology and economics professors based on your findings in (a) and (b).

3.82   The data at the top of page 82 represent the cost per pound as purchased and the cost per pound in edible meat from a sample of 19 brands of whole frozen turkey:

For each of the two variables

 (a) Compute

(1) the mean	(6) the range
(2) the median	(7) the interquartile range
(3) the mode	(8) the variance
(4) the midrange	(9) the standard deviation
(5) the midhinge	(10) the coefficient of variation

 (b) For each of the two variables, set up a box-and-whisker plot and determine whether the data are approximately right-skewed, left-skewed, or symmetric. Give reasons to justify your conclusions.

Problem 3.82 Data

Brand	Cost as Purchased	Cost of Edible Meat
Li'l Butterball	$1.16	$3.37
Jennie-O Prime Young	.76	2.00
Marval of Virginia	.72	1.97
Butterball Young	1.02	2.89
Valley Star Brand	.99	2.88
Lady Lee Young	.91	2.41
Winn Dixie Brand	1.09	2.42
Shur Fresh Brand	.89	2.45
Riverside Young	1.09	3.10
Land O Lakes Young	.88	2.66
Hebrew National Kosher	.92	2.73
Norbest Tender Timed	.97	2.53
A & P Butter Basted Young	.99	2.72
Longacre Young	.79	2.25
Lancaster Brand	.79	2.08
Empire Kosher Young	1.09	2.90
Honeysuckle White	1.07	2.89
Manor House Natural	.84	2.46
Sugarplum Prime Young	.82	2.10

SOURCE: Copyright 1987 by Consumers Union of United States, Inc., Mount Vernon, NY 10553. Excerpted by permission of *Consumer Reports*, October 1987, pp. 604–605.

➡(c) **ACTION** Write an article for a local newspaper column dealing with food in order to enlighten its readership on this matter.

(d) Suppose that you accidentally included a 20th brand of frozen turkey that consisted only of turkey breast and had a cost of $2.76 per pound as purchased and a cost of $6.54 per pound of edible meat. Comment specifically on the effect of including this observation on the arithmetic mean, median, midrange, and midhinge of each variable.

3.83 The data at the top of page 83 represent the cost (in cents) and the amount of sodium (in mgs.) of a sample of 38 brands of salted peanut butter:

For each of the two variables
(a) Compute
  (1) the mean   (6) the range
  (2) the median   (7) the interquartile range
  (3) the mode   (8) the variance
  (4) the midrange   (9) the standard deviation
  (5) the midhinge   (10) the coefficient of variation
(b) For each of the two variables, set up a box-and-whisker plot and determine whether the data are approximately right-skewed, left-skewed, or symmetric. Give reasons to justify your conclusions.
➡(c) **ACTION** Write an article for a local newspaper column dealing with food in order to enlighten its readership on this matter.
(d) Does there appear to be a difference in cost or in sodium for crunchy versus creamy salted peanut butter? Analyze.
(e) Suppose that you accidentally included a 39th brand that was "unsalted," costing 26 cents and having 3 mg of sodium per serving. Comment specifically on the effect of including this observation on the arithmetic mean, median, midrange, and midhinge of both variables in part (a).

Problem 3.83 Data

Brand	Type	Cost	Sodium
Jif	Crunchy	18	195
Skippy	Creamy	18	225
Skippy	Crunchy	18	195
Peter Pan	Crunchy	15	225
Smucker's Natural	Crunchy	21	188
Jif	Creamy	17	233
Peter Pan	Creamy	14	225
Laura Scudder's Old Fashioned	Crunchy	23	180
Real Roast	Creamy	14	240
A & P	Crunchy	13	178
Country Pure Old Fashioned	Creamy	17	225
Lady Lee (Lucky)	Crunchy	14	210
Smucker's Natural	Creamy	20	188
Kroger	Crunchy	16	255
National	Creamy	13	225
Country Pure Old Fashioned	Crunchy	17	195
Pathmark	Crunchy	12	191
Pathmark	Creamy	12	225
Food Club	Creamy	16	210
Superman	Creamy	18	225
Nu Made (Safeway)	Crunchy	17	195
Real Roast	Crunchy	14	255
Nu Made (Safeway)	Creamy	13	225
A & P	Creamy	14	225
Cost Cutter (Kroger)	Crunchy	10	205
Albertsons	Crunchy	17	180
Food Club	Crunchy	14	180
Albertsons	Creamy	14	225
Hazel Old Fashioned	Crunchy	18	203
Superman	Crunchy	16	195
Skaggs Alpha Beta	Creamy	15	210
Holsum Old Fashioned	Creamy	17	248
Kroger	Creamy	16	240
Shurfine	Creamy	12	240
Shurfine	Crunchy	13	189
P & Q (A & P)	Creamy	10	225
Cost Cutter (Kroger)	Creamy	14	194
P & Q (A & P)	Crunchy	10	195

3.84 The data at the top of page 84 refer to four features of a sample of 18 gas barbecue grills— price (in $), shelf area (in square inches), cooking grid area (in square inches), and maximum heat output (in 1000 BTU/hour):

For each variable
  (a) Compute
      (1) the mean
      (2) the median
      (3) the mode
      (4) the midrange
      (5) the midhinge
      (6) the range
      (7) the interquartile range
      (8) the variance
      (9) the standard deviation
      (10) the coefficient of variation
  (b) For each variable, set up a box-and-whisker plot and determine whether the data are

Problem 3.84 Data

Brand and Model	Price	Shelf Area	Cooking Grid	Maximum Heat Output
Weber Genesis II 439001	450	1059	405	37
Arklamatic G34534L	179	608	317	27
Nordic Ware Mark V 72450	499	196	466	42
Jacuzzi Maitre d' 40CW	404	769	334	38
Arklamatic G30432L	149	426	264	28
Char-Broil GG2068	249	856	345	40
Jacuzzi Epicurean 40AW	342	577	264	34
Sears 700 Cat. No. 10755	280	649	356	37
Charmglow Crown Classic 537X	359	586	364	35
Structo Golden Classic 77608	199	694	313	35
Ducane 2002HLPE	534	216	303	23
Char-Broil GG1466	199	743	299	31
Sunbeam 3385P	365	590	296	30
Charmglow Classic 535X	299	754	300	31
Sears 600 Cat. No. 10651	240	450	322	31
Turco Carlyle 55641	249	592	352	40
Hardwick LB3530K0T	325	294	317	29
John Deere 44G	369	139	412	39

SOURCE: Copyright 1986 by Consumers Union of United States, Inc., Mount Vernon, NY 10553. Excerpted by permission from *Consumer Reports*, June 1986, p. 360.

approximately right-skewed, left-skewed, or symmetric. Give reasons to justify your conclusions.

(c) Write an analysis of the features of the gas barbecue grills.

➠(d) **ACTION** How might this information assist a potential purchaser of a gas barbecue grill? Discuss.

3.85 The following data represent the cost (in cents), caffeine per ounce, and the cocoa mass (in percent) of a sample of 17 dark chocolate bars and 16 milk chocolate bars:

Dark Chocolate			
Bar	Cost	Caffeine	Cocoa Mass (%)
Callier Crémant	29	20	14
Sarotti Halb Bitter	37	16	13
Sarotti Extra Bitter	37	15	19
Lindt Swiss Dark	48	26	15
Tobler Tradition	50	17	19
Tobler Extra	48	22	25
Lindt Excellence	45	23	18
Bloomingdale's Dark	91	13	18
Côte d'Or Extra Superieur	34	26	19
Neiman-Marcus Dark	133	9	18
Ghirardelli Sweet Dark	37	24	17
Godiva Dark	108	10	15
Droste Bittersweet	45	13	20
Maillard Eagle Sweet	39	15	16
Whitman's Sweet Dark	26	15	15
Hershey's Special Dark	25	16	14
Perugina Luisa	54	14	17

		Milk Chocolate	
Bar	*Cost*	*Caffeine*	*Cocoa Mass* (%)
Ghirardelli	39	8	5
Cadbury's Dairy	25	2	3
Callier Gala Peter	29	16	10
Brandt	45	6	16
Sarotti	37	6	4
Tobler	48	3	4
Hershey's	22	4	4
Nestlé	32	5	4
Suchard Milka	53	5	3
Droste	45	9	2
Whitman's	23	3	5
Godiva	108	8	6
Lindt (red label)	33	4	4
Lindt (blue label)	55	1	7
Perugina Latte	54	4	5
Côte d'Or	34	10	9

SOURCE: Copyright 1986 by Consumers Union of United States, Inc., Mount Vernon, NY 10553. Excerpted by permission from *Consumer Reports*, November 1986, pp. 700–701.

For dark chocolate and milk chocolate brands separately

  (a) Compute

  (1) the mean   (6) the range

  (2) the median   (7) the interquartile range

  (3) the mode   (8) the variance

  (4) the midrange   (9) the standard deviation

  (5) the midhinge   (10) the coefficient of variation

  (b) For dark chocolate and milk chocolate brands separately, set up a box-and-whisker plot and determine whether the data are approximately right-skewed, left-skewed, or symmetric. Give reasons to justify your conclusions.

➡**(c)** **ACTION**   Write a comparitive analysis of the features of the dark chocolate and milk chocolate bars. Submit your article to your local newspaper.

3.86 The following data refer to characteristics of frankfurters (i.e., "hot dogs"). For three types of frankfurters—beef, meat (usually containing beef and pork and up to 15% poultry), and poultry—we indicate the cost (in cents) per ounce, the cost per pound of protein, the calories per frank, and sodium per frank (in mg).

	Beef Frankfurters			
Brand	*Cost per Ounce*	*Cost per Pound of Protein*	*Calories*	*Sodium*
Thorn Apple Valley Brand	11	14.23	186	495
Nathan's Famous Skinless Beef	17	21.70	181	477
Safeway Our Premium Beef	11	14.49	176	425
Eckrich Beef	15	20.49	149	322
John Morrell Jumbo Beef	10	14.47	184	482
Kroger Jumbo Dinner Beef	11	15.45	190	587
Shofar Kosher Beef	21	25.25	158	370
Mogen David Kosher Skinless Beef	20	24.02	139	322
Kahn's Jumbo Beef	14	18.86	175	479
Oscar Mayer Beef	14	18.86	148	375
Hebrew National Kosher Beef	23	30.65	152	330
Best's Kosher Beef Lower Fat	25	25.62	111	300
Smok-A-Roma Natural Smoke	7	8.12	181	386

(continued at top of page 86)

Beef Frankfurters, continued

Brand	Cost per Ounce	Cost per Pound of Protein	Calories	Sodium
Wilson Beef	9	12.74	153	401
Hygrade's Beef	10	14.21	190	645
A & P Skinless Beef	10	13.39	157	440
Best's Kosher Beef	19	22.31	131	317
Armour Beef Hot Dogs	11	19.95	149	319
Vienna Beef	19	22.90	135	298
Sinai 48 Kosher Beef	17	19.78	132	253

"Meat" Frankfurters

Brand	Cost per Ounce	Cost per Pound of Protein	Calories	Sodium
Hormel 8 Big	12	14.86	173	458
Kahn's Jumbo	12	17.32	191	506
Ball Park	12	15.20	182	473
Kroger Jumbo Dinner	10	14.01	190	545
Safeway Our Premium	11	13.92	172	496
Oscar Mayer Wieners	13	18.24	147	360
Armour Hot Dogs	10	14.12	146	387
Farmer John Wieners	9	11.83	139	386
Bryan Juicy Jumbos	11	15.41	175	507
Eckrich Lean Supreme Jumbo	15	17.40	136	393
Eckrich Jumbo	13	17.32	179	405
John Morrell	10	15.61	153	372
Eat Slim Veal	18	20.40	107	144
Hygrade's Hot Dogs	9	12.65	195	511
Scotch Buy with Chicken & Beef	7	11.17	135	405
Wilson	8	11.75	140	428
Smok-A-Roma Natural Smoke	6	9.49	138	339

Poultry Frankfurters

Brand	Cost per Ounce	Cost per Pound of Protein	Calories	Sodium
Weaver Chicken	8	10.21	129	430
Shorgood Chicken	5	6.37	132	375
Mr. Turkey	7	8.42	102	396
Louis Rich Turkey	8	9.37	106	383
Longacre Family Turkey	8	9.00	94	387
Kroger Turkey	7	8.07	102	542
Weight Watchers Turkey	9	9.39	87	359
Shenandoah Turkey Lower Fat	6	6.59	99	357
Foster Farms Jumbo Chicken	7	8.43	170	528
Manor House Turkey (Safeway)	8	8.63	113	513
Longacre Family Chicken	7	7.39	135	426
Hygrade's Grillmaster Chicken	7	7.42	142	513
Manor House Chicken (Safeway)	7	6.27	86	358
Perdue Chicken	8	9.07	143	581
Gwaltney's Great Dogs Chicken	6	7.91	152	588
Holly Farms 8 Chicken	7	8.79	146	522
Tyson Butcher's Best Chicken	6	7.18	144	545

SOURCE: Copyright 1986 by Consumers Union of United States, Inc., Mount Vernon, NY 10553. Excerpted by permission from *Consumer Reports*, June 1986, pp. 366–367.

For each type of frankfurter for each variable
  (a) Compute
  (1) the mean   (6) the range
  (2) the median   (7) the interquartile range
  (3) the mode   (8) the variance
  (4) the midrange   (9) the standard deviation
  (5) the midhinge   (10) the coefficient of variation
  (b) For each type of frankfurter for each variable, set up a box-and-whisker plot and determine whether the data are approximately right-skewed, left-skewed, or symmetric. Give reasons to justify your conclusions.
  ⟼(c) **ACTION** Write a comparative analysis of the features of the three types of frankfurters. Submit your article to your local newspaper.

3.87 The following data represent the cost per pancake (in cents), the number of calories per pancake, and the amount of sodium per pancake (in mgs.) for a sample of 30 different pancake mixes:

Mix	Cost	Calories	Sodium
Hungry Jack Buttermilk RM	4	80	190
Aunt Jemima Buttermilk RM	5	130	330
Lady Lee Old Fashioned	6	100	283
CU's recipe	4	89	156
Betty Crocker Buttermilk RM	4	93	270
Hungry Jack Extra Lights RM	3	70	163
Bisquick Buttermilk Baking Mix	6	80	233
Aunt Jemima Original	3	67	183
Betty Crocker Buttermilk CM	3	70	167
A & P RM	4	67	227
Aunt Jemima Buttermilk CM	4	87	320
Pillsbury Microwave Buttermilk	16	87	197
Aunt Jemima FB	10	67	333
Aunt Jemima Buttermilk FP	16	80	330
Aunt Jemima Buttermilk FB	10	67	287
Aunt Jemima Original FP	16	80	350
Aunt Jemima CM	3	93	320
Skaggs Alpha Beta Buttermilk	2	87	320
Hungry Jack Pan-shakes	7	67	280
Downyflake Original	18	80	250
Downyflake Buttermilk	18	80	250
A & P CM	2	93	320
Kroger	2	60	210
Hungry Jack Extra Lights CM	3	60	235
Kroger Buttermilk	3	60	210
Lady Lee Buttermilk	3	90	290
Hungry Jack Buttermilk CM	3	60	237
Dia-Mel	5	33	45
Sweet 'N Low	6	35	10
Featherweight	8	43	23

SOURCE: Copyright 1988 by Consumers Union of United States, Inc., Mount Vernon, NY 10553. Excerpted by permission from *Consumer Reports*, January 1988, pp. 22–23.

Data (displayed at the top of page 88) were also available relating to the per serving cost, calories, and sodium content of 19 different pancake syrups:
  (a) Completely analyze the data concerning pancake mixes and pancake syrups and summarize your findings.
  ⟼(b) **ACTION** If you were writing an expose that was trying to criticize pancakes, what variables and what statistical measures would you focus on, and what conclusions could you reach?

Syrup	Cost	Calories	Sodium
Camp Pure Maple (Dark Amber)	$ .90	277	37
Reese Pure Maple (Dark Amber)	1.24	269	29
Vermont Maple Orchards Pure Maple (Dark Amber)	.92	271	21
Vermont Maid (2% Maple Syrup)	.24	273	34
Golden Griddle (2% Maple Syrup)	.26	278	47
Kroger (2% Maple Syrup)	.24	276	52
Log Cabin (2% Maple Syrup)	.26	270	99
Log Cabin Country Kitchen	.19	280	63
Aunt Jemima Lite	.27	143	85
Mrs. Butterworth's Lite (Thick 'N Rich)	.25	157	160
Aunt Jemima (Extra Thick)	.26	280	134
Cost Cutter (Kroger)	.13	281	58
Mrs. Butterworth's (Thick 'N Rich)	.25	280	91
Aunt Jemima Butter Lite	.27	142	185
Kroger Buttered Syrup	.24	277	84
Kroger Lite	.24	174	244
Log Cabin Lite	.27	168	200
Karo	.19	319	123
Log Cabin Buttered Syrup	.27	284	195

SOURCE: Copyright 1988 by Consumers Union of United States, Inc., Mount Vernon, NY 10553. Excerpted by permission from *Consumer Reports*, January 1988, p. 25.

➠(c) **ACTION** If you were writing a rebuttal to (b) for the pancake industry, what response would you have?

➠(d) **ACTION** If you were trying to write an objective report for a local newspaper relating to pancakes, what conclusions would you draw?

3.88 The following ordered arrays represent the final batting averages along with the corresponding number of home runs hit by all players in the American and National Leagues having at least 350 times at bat during the 1987 season:

American League (N = 87)

Avg.	HRs	Avg.	HRs	Avg.	HRs	Avg.	HRs
.363	24	.295	9	.277	24	.259	32
.353	16	.293	20	.277	20	.259	2
.343	28	.293	3	.277	30	.259	6
.332	28	.293	28	.276	13	.257	31
.328	19	.291	17	.275	12	.257	34
.327	30	.290	22	.275	1	.257	31
.323	15	.289	19	.272	27	.256	23
.322	5	.289	49	.272	20	.256	27
.319	8	.289	32	.271	29	.256	14
.316	31	.287	5	.271	1	.253	23
.312	21	.287	4	.269	27	.252	27
.309	34	.286	5	.269	13	.252	25
.308	47	.286	23	.268	19	.251	9
.307	11	.285	34	.265	32	.250	14
.305	34	.285	34	.265	10	.250	18
.305	7	.284	16	.265	22	.249	8
.302	14	.282	26	.264	16	.248	16
.300	32	.281	11	.263	32	.247	24
.299	13	.280	9	.263	28	.246	3
.299	7	.280	18	.263	24	.245	16
.297	14	.279	2	.263	3	.244	23
.295	29	.277	4	.259	30		

National League (N = 83)

Avg.	HRs	Avg.	HRs	Avg.	HRs	Avg.	HRs
.370	7	.293	8	.280	6	.263	14
.338	27	.293	37	.279	15	.263	2
.334	26	.293	35	.278	19	.262	10
.330	18	.293	21	.277	21	.261	25
.325	9	.292	20	.277	21	.258	4
.313	20	.290	18	.276	29	.255	5
.311	10	.290	10	.275	13	.254	4
.309	12	.289	3	.273	1	.253	26
.308	35	.288	14	.273	27	.251	27
.305	13	.287	49	.273	5	.248	24
.303	0	.286	14	.272	12	.248	19
.302	7	.286	35	.272	12	.247	27
.300	15	.286	12	.272	28	.245	17
.300	18	.285	10	.271	15	.244	12
.299	9	.285	11	.270	15	.241	11
.298	26	.284	19	.267	18	.235	20
.296	11	.284	17	.266	27	.233	16
.295	44	.284	39	.265	36	.230	8
.294	16	.283	16	.265	6	.222	5
.294	16	.280	22	.264	14	.214	5
.293	17	.280	3	.264	5		

    (a) For each of these populations
        (1) Set up a stem-and-leaf display of the batting averages.
        (2) Obtain the five-number-summary of the batting averages.
        (3) Form the box-and-whisker plot of the batting averages.
    (b) For each of these populations
        (1) Set up a stem-and-leaf display of number of home runs hit.
        (2) Obtain the five-number-summary of number of home runs hit.
        (3) Form the box-and-whisker plot of number of home runs hit.
    (c) Based on your "exploratory data analyses" in (a) and (b), write a report comparing and contrasting hitting achievements in the two baseball leagues.
    ➠**(d)** ACTION How might this information be of use to the ownership of a baseball team with respect to contract offerings? Discuss.

3.89 Two sportscasters on a local radio show were debating the issue of salary and performance in professional football. Below are the ordered arrays based on number of receptions by all 32 NFC players and all 39 AFC players who caught at least 40 passes over the full 16-game (1986) season prior to the players' strike. (Receptions by running backs are indicated with an *). Also included are the corresponding figures pertaining to yardage gained, average yards per catch, and number of touchdowns scored.

Football Receptions

NFC (N = 32)				AFC (N = 39)			
Player (Team)	No.	Yards	Avg.	TD	Player (Team)	No.	Yards	Avg.	TD

Player (Team)	No.	Yards	Avg.	TD	Player (Team)	No.	Yards	Avg.	TD
Rice, Jerry, *S.F.*	86	1570	18.3	15	Christensen, Todd, *Raiders*	95	1153	12.1	8
Craig, Roger, *S.F.**	81	624	7.7	0	Toon, Al, *Jets*	85	1176	13.8	8
Smith, J. T., *St. L.*	80	1014	12.7	6	Morgan, Stanley, *N.E.*	84	1491	17.8	10
Walker, Herschel, *Dall.**	76	837	11.0	2	Anderson, Gary, *S.D.**	80	871	10.9	8
Clark, Gary, *Wash.*	74	1265	17.1	7	Collins, Tony, *N.E.**	77	684	8.9	5
Monk, Art, *Wash.*	73	1068	14.6	4	Bouza, Matt, *Ind.*	71	830	11.7	5
Bavaro, Mark, *Giants*	66	1001	15.2	4	Largent, Steve, *Sea.*	70	1070	15.3	9
Lofton, James, *G.B.*	64	840	13.1	4	Shuler, Mickey, *Jets*	69	675	9.8	4
Brown, Charlie, *Atl.*	63	918	14.6	4	Duper, Mark, *Mia.*	67	1313	19.6	11
Clark, Dwight, *S.F.*	61	794	13.0	2	Brooks, Bill, *Ind.*	65	1131	17.4	8
Quick, Mike, *Phil.*	60	939	15.7	9	Hill, Drew, *Hou.*	65	1112	17.1	5
Jordan, Steve, *Minn.*	58	859	14.8	6	Winslow, Kellen, *S.D.*	64	728	11.4	5
Ferrell, Earl, *St. L.**	56	434	7.8	3	Willhite, Gerald, *Den.**	64	529	8.3	3
Jones, James, *Det.**	54	334	6.2	1	Collinsworth, Cris, *Cinn.*	62	1024	16.5	10
Chadwick, Jeff, *Det.*	53	995	18.8	5	Givins, Earnest, *Hou.*	61	1062	17.4	3
Nelson, Darrin, *Minn.**	53	593	11.2	3	Hampton, Lorenzo, *Mia.**	61	446	7.3	3
Hill, Tony, *Dall.*	49	770	15.7	3	Clayton, Mark, *Mia.*	60	1150	19.2	10
Epps, Phillip, *G.B.*	49	612	12.5	4	Brown, Eddie, *Cinn.*	58	964	16.6	4
Jones, Mike, *N.O.*	48	625	13.0	3	Chandler, Wes, *S.D.*	56	874	15.6	4
Newsome, Tim, *Dall.**	48	421	8.8	3	Brennan, Brian, *Clev.*	55	838	15.2	6
Magee, Calvin, *T.B.*	45	564	12.5	5	Brooks, James, *Cinn.*	54	686	12.7	4
Bland, Carl, *Det.*	44	511	11.6	2	Hardy, Bruce, *Mia.*	54	430	8.0	5
Bryant, Kelvin, *Wash.**	43	449	10.4	3	Reed, Andre, *Buff.*	53	739	13.9	7
Wilder, James, *T.B.**	43	326	7.6	1	Paige, Stephone, *K.C.*	52	829	15.9	11
Gault, Willie, *Chi.*	42	818	19.5	5	Walker, Wesley, *Jets*	49	1016	20.7	12
Carter, Gerald, *T.B.*	42	640	15.2	2	Metzelaars, Pete, *Buff.*	49	485	9.9	3
Dixon, Floyd, *Atl.*	42	617	14.7	2	Riddick, Robb, *Buff.**	49	468	9.6	1
Green, Roy, *St. L.*	42	517	12.3	6	McNeil, Freeman, *Jets**	49	410	8.4	1
Sherrard, Mike, *Dall.*	41	744	18.1	5	Nathan, Tony, *Mia.**	48	457	9.5	2
Francis, Russ, *S.F.*	41	505	12.3	1	Fontenot, Herman, *Clev.**	47	559	11.9	1
Tautalatasi, Junior, *Phil.**	41	325	7.9	2	Abercrombie, Walter, *Pitt.**	47	395	8.4	2
Mitchell, Stump, *St. L.**	41	276	6.7	0	Marshall, Henry, *K.C.*	46	652	14.2	1
					Allen, Marcus, *Raiders**	46	453	9.8	2
					Watson, Steve, *Den.*	45	699	15.5	3
					Williams, Dokie, *Raiders*	43	843	19.6	8
					Fryar, Irving, *N.E.*	43	737	17.1	6
					Warner, Curt, *Sea.**	41	342	8.3	0
					Slaughter, Webster, *Clev.*	40	577	14.4	4
					Holman, Rodney, *Cinn.*	40	570	14.3	2

SOURCE: *Street & Smith's Pro Football—25th Year*, July 1987, pp. 135 and 142.

(a) Completely analyze the data and write a report comparing and contrasting performance between reception leaders in the NFC versus the AFC.

➧**(b)** ACTION   If you intended to send your report to the players' union, should you keep the two Conferences separate? Discuss when it is or is not appropriate to pool all 71 players together for one overall analysis.

➧**(c)** ACTION   One of the sportscasters has claimed that a better measure of overall performance productivity is the percentage of touchdown receptions made out of total receptions. After analyzing this variable separately for each Conference, write a letter to the radio show host agreeing with or refuting this claim.

References

1. ARKIN, H., AND R. COLTON, *Statistical Methods*, 5th ed. (New York: Barnes & Noble College Outline Series, 1970).
2. CROXTON, F., D. COWDEN, AND S. KLEIN, *Applied General Statistics*, 3d ed. (Englewood Cliffs, N.J.: Prentice-Hall, 1967).
3. KENDALL, M. G., AND A. STUART, *The Advanced Theory of Statistics*, Vol. I (London: Charles W. Griffin, 1958).
4. TUKEY, J., *Exploratory Data Analysis* (Reading, Mass.: Addison-Wesley, 1977).
5. VELLEMAN, P. F., AND D. C. HOAGLIN, *Applications, Basics, and Computing of Exploratory Data Analysis* (Boston: Duxbury Press, 1981).

Data Presentation

4.1 INTRODUCTION

As pointed out in Section 2.5, sampling saves time, money, and labor, so we usually deal with sample information rather than data from the entire population. Nevertheless, regardless of whether we are dealing with a sample or a population, as a rule of thumb, whenever a batch of data contains about 20 or more observations, the best way to examine such "mass data" is to present it in summary form by constructing appropriate tables and charts. From these we can then extract the important features of the data.

In this chapter we will demonstrate how large batches of both quantitative and qualitative data can be organized and most effectively presented in terms of tables and charts as an aid to data analysis and interpretation.

4.2 TABULATING QUANTITATIVE DATA: THE FREQUENCY DISTRIBUTION

Using either the raw data, ordered array, or stem-and-leaf display of reported PE ratios for the 24 natural resource companies presented in Figures 3.7, 3.8, and 3.9 (pages 54 and 55), the financial analyst wishes to construct the appropriate tables and charts that will enhance the report she is preparing on investment opportunities for her brokerage firm.

Regardless of whether an ordered array or a stem-and-leaf display is selected for *organizing* the data, as the number of observations gets large it becomes necessary to further condense the data into appropriate summary tables. Thus we may wish to arrange the data into *class groupings* (i.e., *categories*) according to conveniently established divisions of the range of the observations. Such an arrangement of data in tabular form is called a frequency distribution.

A **frequency distribution** is a summary table in which the data are arranged into conveniently established numerically ordered class groupings or categories.

When the data are "grouped" or condensed into frequency-distribution tables, the process of data analysis and interpretation is made much more manageable and meaningful. In such summary form the major data characteristics are very easily approximated, thus compensating for the fact that when the data are so grouped the initial information pertaining to individual observations that was previously available is lost through the grouping or condensing process.

In constructing the frequency-distribution table, attention must be given to

1. Selecting the appropriate number of class groupings for the table
2. Obtaining a suitable *class interval* or "width" of each class grouping
3. Establishing the *boundaries* of each class grouping to avoid overlapping

4.2.1 Selecting the Number of Classes

The number of class groupings to be used is primarily dependent upon the number of observations in the data. That is, larger numbers of observations require a larger number of class groups. In general, however, the frequency distribution should have at least five class groupings, but no more than 15. If there are not enough class groupings or if there are too many, little information would be obtained. As an example, a frequency distribution having but one class grouping that spans the entire range of PE ratios could be formed as follows:

PE Ratios	Number of Companies
0–70	24
Total	24

From such a summary table, however, no additional information is obtained that was not already known from scanning either the raw data or the ordered array. A table with too much data concentration is not meaningful. The same would be true at the other extreme—if a table had too many class groupings, there would be an undercon-centration of data, and very little would be learned.

4.2.2 Obtaining the Class Intervals

When developing the frequency-distribution table it is desirable to have each class grouping of equal width. To determine the width of each class, the *range* of the data is divided by the number of class groupings desired:

$$\text{width of interval} = \frac{\text{range}}{\text{number of desired class groupings}}$$

Since there are only 24 observations in our PE ratio data, we decided that seven class groupings would be sufficient. From the ordered array in Figure 3.8 (page 55), the range is computed as $61 - 8 = 53.0$, and the width of the class interval is approximated by

$$\text{width of interval} = \frac{53.0}{7} = 7.57$$

For convenience and ease of reading, the selected interval or width of each class grouping is rounded up to 10.

4.2.3 Establishing the Boundaries of the Classes

To construct the frequency-distribution table, it is necessary to establish clearly defined class boundaries for each class grouping so that the observations either in raw form or in an ordered array can be properly tallied. Overlapping of classes must be avoided.

Since the width of each class interval for the PE ratio data has been set at 10, the boundaries of the various class groupings must be established so as to include the entire range of observations. Whenever possible, these boundaries should be chosen to facilitate the reading and interpreting of data. Thus the first class interval is established from 0 to under 10, the second from 10 to under 20, etc. The data in their raw form (Figure 3.7) or from the ordered array (Figure 3.8) are then tallied into each class as shown:

PE Ratios	Frequency Tallies	
0 but less than 10	//	2
10 but less than 20	//// //// //	12
20 but less than 30	////	5
30 but less than 40	//	2
40 but less than 50	/	1
50 but less than 60	/	1
60 but less than 70	/	1
Total		24

By establishing the boundaries of each class as above, all 24 observations have been tallied into seven classes, each having an interval width of 10 without overlapping. From this ''worksheet'' the frequency distribution is presented in Table 4.1.

The main advantage of using such a summary table is that the major data characteristics become immediately clear to the reader. For example, we see from Table 4.1 that the *approximate range* of the 24 reported PE ratios is from 0 to 70, with most PE ratios tending to cluster between 10 and 20. Other descriptive measures which are obtained from grouped data will be presented in Section 4.3.

TABLE 4.1 Frequency distribution of PE ratios for 24 natural resource companies

PE Ratios	Number of Companies
0 but less than 10	2
10 but less than 20	12
20 but less than 30	5
30 but less than 40	2
40 but less than 50	1
50 but less than 60	1
60 but less than 70	1
Total	24

SOURCE: Data are taken from Figure 3.7 on page 54.

On the other hand, the major disadvantage of such a summary table is that we cannot know how the individual values are distributed within a particular class interval without access to the original data. Thus for the two companies which report PE ratios between 0 and 10, it is not clear from Table 4.1 whether the values are distributed throughout the interval, are close to 0, or are close to 10. The class midpoint, however, is the value used to represent all the data summarized into a particular interval.

> The **class midpoint** is the point halfway between the boundaries of each class and is representative of the data within that class.

The class midpoint for the interval "0 but less than 10" is 5. (The other class midpoints are, respectively, 15, 25, 35, 45, 55, and 65.)

4.2.4 Subjectivity in Selecting Class Boundaries

The selection of class boundaries for frequency-distribution tables is highly subjective. Hence for data batches which do not contain many observations, the choice of a particular set of class boundaries over another might yield an entirely different picture to the reader. For example, for the PE ratio data, using a class interval width of 15 instead of 10 (as was used in Table 4.1) may cause shifts in the way in which the batch of data distribute among the classes. This is particularly true if the number of observations in the batch is not very large.

However, such shifts in data concentration do not occur only because the width of the class interval is altered. We may keep the interval width at 10 but choose different lower and upper class boundaries. Such manipulation may also cause shifts in the way in which the data distribute—especially if the size of the batch is not very large.

Fortunately, as the number of observations in a data batch increases, alterations in the selection of class boundaries affect the concentration of data less and less.[1]

Problems

4.1   A random sample of 50 executive vice-presidents was selected from among the various public relations firms in the United States, and the annual salaries of these company officers was obtained. The salaries ranged from $52,000 to $137,000. Set up the class boundaries for a frequency distribution
(a) If 5 class intervals are desired.
(b) If 6 class intervals are desired.
(c) If 7 class intervals are desired.
(d) If 8 class intervals are desired.

● 4.2   If the annual salaries of city employees varied from $16,700 to $64,200
(a) Indicate the class boundaries of 10 classes into which these values can be grouped.
(b) What class-interval width did you choose?
(c) What are the 10 class midpoints?

---

[1] Other potential problems may also be encountered when constructing frequency-distribution tables or when preparing charts. These issues and their resolution are discussed in detail in Reference 6.

4.3 If the asking price of one-bedroom cooperative and condominium apartments in New York City varied from $103,000 to $295,000

(a) Indicate the class boundaries of 10 classes into which these values can be grouped.

(b) What class-interval width did you choose?

(c) What are the 10 class midpoints?

● **4.4** The raw data displayed below are the electric and gas utility charges during the month of July 1988 for a random sample of 50 three-bedroom apartments in Manhattan:

Raw Data on Utility Charges ($)									
96	171	202	178	147	102	153	197	127	82
157	185	90	116	172	111	148	213	130	165
141	149	206	175	123	128	144	168	109	167
95	163	150	154	130	143	187	166	139	149
108	119	183	151	114	135	191	137	129	158

(a) Form a frequency distribution
(1) having 5 class intervals.
(2) having 6 class intervals.
(3) having 7 class intervals.
[*Hint*: To help you decide how to best set up the class boundaries you should first place the raw data either in a stem-and-leaf display (by letting the leaves be the trailing digits) or in an ordered array.]

(b) Form a frequency distribution having 7 class intervals with the following class boundaries: $80 but less than $100, $100 but less than $120, and so on.

4.5 Using the ordered array in Figure 3.8 on page 55 set up the frequency distributions with the following class boundaries:

(a) 5 but less than 15, 15 but less than 25, and so on.

(b) 0 but less than 15, 15 but less than 30, and so on.

(c) 5 but less than 10, 10 but less than 15, and so on.

(d) 7.5 but less than 15, 15 but less than 22.5, and so on.

(e) Compare and contrast the different results and state whether you believe any of these distributions should be preferred to the one selected in Table 4.1 on page 94. [*Hint*: To help you decide, compare the *approximate* mode, midrange, and range for each frequency distribution to the *actual* mode, midrange, and range in the (ungrouped) data in Table 4.4 on page 101.]

4.6 Construct a frequency distribution from the mail-order book company data in Problem 3.7 on page 43.

4.7 Construct a frequency distribution from the data on prices of dot-matrix printers from the sample of 21 companies in Problem 3.8 on page 43.

4.8 Construct a frequency distribution from the PE ratios data in Problem 3.56 on page 70.

4.9 Construct a frequency distribution from the fringe benefits data in Problem 3.57 on page 71.

4.10 Construct a frequency distribution from the quarterly sales tax receipts data in Problem 3.58 on page 71.

4.11 Construct a frequency distribution from the price of auto alarm systems data in Problem 3.67 on page 74.

4.12 Construct a frequency distribution from the book value data in Problem 3.69 on page 75.

4.13 Construct a frequency distribution from the compact disk player data in Problem 3.70 on page 75.

4.14 Construct a frequency distribution from the video cassette recorder data in Problem 3.71 on page 75.

4.15 Construct a frequency distribution from the compact microwave oven data in Problem 3.72 on page 76.

4.16 Construct a frequency distribution from the IBM PC/XT compatible systems data in Problem 3.74 on page 77.

4.17 Construct a frequency distribution from the spreadsheet products data in Problem 3.75 on page 78.

4.18 Construct a frequency distribution from the GNP projections data in Problem 3.76 on page 78.

4.19 Construct a frequency distribution from the laundry detergent data in Problem 3.77 on page 79.

4.20 Construct a frequency distribution from the per capita alcoholic consumption data in Problem 3.78 on page 80.

4.21 Given the ordered arrays in the accompanying table dealing with the lengths of life (in hours) of a sample of 40 100-watt light bulbs produced by Manufacturer A and a sample of 40 100-watt light bulbs produced by Manufacturer B:

Ordered arrays of length of life of two brands of 100-watt light bulbs (in hours)

Manufacturer A				
684	697	720	773	821
831	835	848	852	852
859	860	868	870	876
893	899	905	909	911
922	924	926	926	938
939	943	946	954	971
972	977	984	1005	1014
1016	1041	1052	1080	1093

Manufacturer B				
819	836	888	897	903
907	912	918	942	943
952	959	962	986	992
994	1004	1005	1007	1015
1016	1018	1020	1022	1034
1038	1072	1077	1077	1082
1096	1100	1113	1113	1116
1153	1154	1174	1188	1230

(a) Form the frequency distribution for each brand. [*Hint*: For purposes of comparison, choose class-interval widths of $100 for each distribution.]

(b) For purposes of answering Problems 4.39, 4.57, 4.75, and 4.93, form the frequency distribution for each brand according to the following schema [if you had not already done so in part (a) of this problem]:

Manufacturer A: 650 but less than 750, 750 but less than 850, and so on
Manufacturer B: 750 but less than 850, 850 but less than 950, and so on

4.22 Construct separate frequency distributions of the ages of automobile salesmen using the data batches given in Problem 3.81 on page 81 for the United States and Western Europe.

OBTAINING DESCRIPTIVE SUMMARY MEASURES
FROM A FREQUENCY DISTRIBUTION

It is often necessary to obtain descriptive summary measures from data grouped into frequency distributions. In many cases, researchers obtain such distributions directly from reports published in magazines, newspapers, journals, etc. In these situations the original (raw) data are simply not available. In other cases where the raw data are available but a computer is not readily accessible, it becomes more and more laborious to extract the salient features of the data as the number of observations increases unless the ''mass data'' are first grouped into tables and charts. While the descriptive summary measures computed from **ungrouped** data—data in their raw form or in an ordered array—provide *actual* results, *approximations* for these descriptive measures can be obtained from **grouped** data.

Note the frequency distribution presented in Table 4.2. Since the midpoint of each class is used to represent all the observations that have been tallied into the class, the arithmetic mean may be approximated as follows:

1. Multiply each midpoint m_j by the number of observations f_j it represents.
2. Obtain the summation of these resulting products.
3. Divide this total by the number of observations.

Calculating the mean from a frequency distribution of PE ratios for all 24 natural resources companies

PE Ratios	Class Midpoints m_j	Number of Companies f_j	$m_j f_j$
0 but less than 10	5	2	10
10 but less than 20	15	12	180
20 but less than 30	25	5	125
30 but less than 40	35	2	70
40 but less than 50	45	1	45
50 but less than 60	55	1	55
60 but less than 70	65	1	65
Totals		24	$550 = \sum_{j=1}^{g} m_j f_j$

That is, for a sample of n observations

$$\overline{X} \cong \frac{\sum_{j=1}^{g} m_j f_j}{n}$$

where $\overline{X}$ = mean of the sample
$\qquad n$ = number of observations in the sample
$\qquad g$ = number of groups or classes in the frequency distribution
$\qquad m_j$ = midpoint of the jth class
$\qquad f_j$ = number of observations tallied into the jth class

while for a population of N observations

$$\mu_X \cong \frac{\sum\limits_{j=1}^{g} m_j f_j}{N} \tag{4.2}$$

Using the results from Table 4.2:

$$\mu_X \cong \frac{\sum\limits_{j=1}^{g} m_j f_j}{N} = \frac{550}{24} = 22.92$$

Thus the mean PE ratio from the population of 24 natural resources companies is approximated as 22.92.

4.3.2 Approximating Other Measures of Central Tendency

While various formulas do exist for approximating the median and mode from the frequency distribution (References 1 and 6), it is both simpler and more convenient to use other approaches. In Section 4.6 we will see that the median can be readily approximated from a chart called an **ogive.** The mode, however, can be approximated from a frequency distribution by the midpoint of the class containing the most observations. This class is the ''most typical'' or **modal class.** Thus for the 24 natural resources companies (Table 4.1), the modal class contains PE ratios from 10 to 20 and the mode is approximated as 15.

The midrange can be approximated from a frequency distribution by averaging the possible extremes—the upper boundary of the last class grouping and the lower boundary of the first class grouping. For the natural resources companies, the midrange is approximately 35 (i.e., the average of 0 and 70).

4.3.3 Approximating the Variance and Standard Deviation

To calculate the variance and standard deviation from grouped data, **definitional formulas** analogous to those given in Equations (3.4) and (3.5) for a sample and in Equations (3.12) and (3.13) for a population may be developed. Since the variance essentially measures the average of the squared differences between each observation and its mean, and since the midpoints of each class of a frequency distribution are used to represent the observations in the classes, the variance may be approximated from a frequency distribution by

1. Taking the squares of the differences between each midpoint and the mean.
2. Multiplying or ''weighting'' each of the squared differences by the respective number of observations in each class.
3. Summing these products.
4. Dividing this total by $n - 1$ in a sample or by N in a population.

Thus, for a sample we have

$$S^2 \cong \frac{\sum_{j=1}^{g} (m_j - \overline{X})^2 f_j}{n - 1} \tag{4.3}$$

where $\overline{X}$ = approximated mean
S^2 = variance of the sample
n = number of observations in the sample
g = number of groups or classes in the frequency distribution
m_j = midpoint of the jth class
f_j = number of observations tallied into the jth class

while for a population we have

$$\sigma_X^2 \cong \frac{\sum_{j=1}^{g} (m_j - \mu_X)^2 f_j}{N} \tag{4.4}$$

The standard deviation is simply the square root of the variance. For a sample we have

$$S \cong \sqrt{\frac{\sum_{j=1}^{g} (m_j - \overline{X})^2 f_j}{n - 1}} \tag{4.5}$$

while for a population we have

$$\sigma_X \cong \sqrt{\frac{\sum_{j=1}^{g} (m_j - \mu_X)^2 f_j}{N}} \tag{4.6}$$

Table 4.3 on page 101 demonstrates the computations necessary for obtaining the variance and standard deviation for the reported PE ratios from the population of 24 companies in the natural resources industry. From this table we observe that

$$\sigma_X^2 \cong \frac{\sum_{j=1}^{g} (m_j - \mu_X)^2 f_j}{N} = \frac{4{,}995.8336}{24} = 208.1597$$

and

$$\sigma_X \cong \sqrt{208.1597} = 14.43$$

The standard deviation is approximated as 14.43.

4.3.4 Approximating Other Measures of Dispersion

With grouped data the range may be approximated as the difference between the upper boundary of the last class grouping and the lower boundary of the first class grouping.

TABLE 4.3 Calculating the variance and standard deviation from a frequency distribution of PE ratios for all 24 natural resources companies

PE Ratios	Class Midpoints m_j	$(m_j - \mu_X)$	$(m_j - \mu_X)^2$	No. of Companies f_j	$(m_j - \mu_X)^2 f_j$
0 but less than 10	5	$(5 - 22.92)$	321.1264	2	642.2528
10 but less than 20	15	$(15 - 22.92)$	62.7264	12	752.7168
20 but less than 30	25	$(25 - 22.92)$	4.3264	5	21.6320
30 but less than 40	35	$(35 - 22.92)$	145.9264	2	291.8528
40 but less than 50	45	$(45 - 22.92)$	487.5264	1	487.5264
50 but less than 60	55	$(55 - 22.92)$	1,029.1264	1	1,029.1264
60 but less than 70	65	$(65 - 22.92)$	1,770.7264	1	1,770.7264
Totals				24	4,995.8336

Therefore, from Table 4.1 on page 94 the range in the reported PE ratios is approximately 70 (that is, $70 - 0$).

Whether or not the data are grouped, the coefficient of variation is still defined as a measure of relative scatter around the mean, and it may be computed from the ratio of the standard deviation to the mean. Thus, using Equation (3.14) on page 65 and the approximated (grouped data) values for σ_X and μ_X, the coefficient of variation for the PE ratios from the 24 natural resource companies may be approximated as

$$CV_{pop} \cong \left(\frac{\sigma_X}{\mu_X}\right) 100\% = \left(\frac{14.43}{22.92}\right) 100\% = 63.0\%$$

4.3.5 Comparing Descriptive Measures: Actual Values and Grouped Data Approximations

Table 4.4 presents a summary of the actual descriptive measures obtained from the raw data (see Table 3.2 on page 67) and their corresponding approximations obtained from the frequency distribution (see Table 4.1 on page 94). By scanning these results it will be clear that both the grouped-data calculations and graphical interpretations, which are much less cumbersome, yield fairly close approximations to the actual results obtained from the more laborious ungrouped-data calculations.

TABLE 4.4 A comparison of actual values and grouped data approximations

Descriptive Measure	PE Ratios of 24 Natural Resource Companies Obtained from	
	Ungrouped (Raw) Data	Grouped Data
Mean	21.71	22.92
Median	16.00	18.00*
Mode	Multimodal	15.00
Midrange	34.50	35.00
Range	53.00	70.00
Variance	198.8733	208.1597
Standard deviation	14.10	14.43
Coefficient of variation	64.9%	63.0%
Shape	Right-skewed	Right-skewed

* Obtained from the ogive in Section 4.6.

Problems

● **4.23** From the frequency distribution developed in Problem 4.4(b) on page 96 regarding utility charges

  (a) Approximate

(1) the mean	(4) the range
(2) the mode	(5) the standard deviation
(3) the midrange	(6) the coefficient of variation

  (b) Based on the Bienaymé-Chebyshev rule (Section 3.12), between what two values would we estimate that at least 75% of the data are contained?

  (c) What percentage of the data are actually contained within ± 2 standard deviations of the mean? Compare the results with those from part (b).

4.24 From the frequency distribution developed in Problem 4.6 on page 96 regarding the amount owed to a mail-order book company, approximate

  - the mean
  - the mode
  - the midrange
  - the range
  - the standard deviation
  - the coefficient of variation

4.25 From the frequency distribution developed in Problem 4.7 on page 96 regarding prices of dot-matrix printers, approximate

  - the mean
  - the mode
  - the midrange
  - the range
  - the standard deviation
  - the coefficient of variation

4.26 From the frequency distribution developed in Problem 4.8 on page 96 representing PE ratios for food processing companies, approximate

  - the mean
  - the mode
  - the midrange
  - the range
  - the standard deviation
  - the coefficient of variation

4.27 From the frequency distribution developed in Problem 4.9 on page 96 regarding fringe benefits at Connecticut colleges and universities, approximate

  - the mean
  - the mode
  - the midrange
  - the range
  - the standard deviation
  - the coefficient of variation

4.28 From the frequency distribution developed in Problem 4.10 on page 96 regarding quarterly sales tax receipts, approximate

  - the mean
  - the mode
  - the midrange
  - the range
  - the standard deviation
  - the coefficient of variation

4.29 From the frequency distribution developed in Problem 4.11 on page 96 regarding prices of auto alarm systems, approximate

  - the mean
  - the mode
  - the midrange
  - the range
  - the standard deviation
  - the coefficient of variation

4.30 From the frequency distribution developed in Problem 4.12 on page 96 regarding book values of companies listed on the NYSE, approximate

  - the mean
  - the mode
  - the midrange
  - the range
  - the standard deviation
  - the coefficient of variation

4.31 From the frequency distribution developed in Problem 4.13 on page 96 regarding prices of compact disk players, approximate

- the mean
- the mode
- the midrange

- the range
- the standard deviation
- the coefficient of variation

4.32　From the frequency distribution developed in Problem 4.14 on page 97 regarding prices of video cassette recorders, approximate
- the mean
- the mode
- the midrange

- the range
- the standard deviation
- the coefficient of variation

4.33　From the frequency distribution developed in Problem 4.15 on page 97 regarding prices of compact microwave ovens, approximate
- the mean
- the mode
- the midrange

- the range
- the standard deviation
- the coefficient of variation

4.34　From the frequency distribution developed in Problem 4.16 on page 97 regarding prices of IBM PC/XT compatible systems, approximate
- the mean
- the mode
- the midrange

- the range
- the standard deviation
- the coefficient of variation

4.35　From the frequency distribution developed in Problem 4.17 on page 97 regarding prices of spreadsheet products, approximate
- the mean
- the mode
- the midrange

- the range
- the standard deviation
- the coefficient of variation

4.36　From the frequency distribution developed in Problem 4.18 on page 97 regarding GNP projections, approximate
- the mean
- the mode
- the midrange

- the range
- the standard deviation
- the coefficient of variation

4.37　From the frequency distribution developed in Problem 4.19 on page 97 regarding laundry detergent costs per load, approximate
- the mean
- the mode
- the midrange

- the range
- the standard deviation
- the coefficient of variation

4.38　From the frequency distribution developed in Problem 4.20 on page 97 regarding per capita alcoholic consumption, approximate
- the mean
- the mode
- the midrange

- the range
- the standard deviation
- the coefficient of variation

4.39　Refer to the frequency distributions developed in Problem 4.21 on page 97 concerning life of light bulbs manufactured by two competing companies, A and B. For *each* distribution, approximate
- the mean
- the mode
- the midrange

- the range
- the standard deviation
- the coefficient of variation

4.40　Refer to the frequency distributions developed in Problem 4.22 on page 97 concerning ages of automobile salesmen in the United States and Western Europe. For *each* distribution, approximate
- the mean
- the mode
- the midrange

- the range
- the standard deviation
- the coefficient of variation

4.4 TABULATING QUANTITATIVE DATA: THE RELATIVE FREQUENCY DISTRIBUTION AND PERCENTAGE DISTRIBUTION

The frequency distribution is a summary table into which the original data are condensed or grouped to facilitate data analysis. To enhance the analysis, however, it is almost always desirable to form either the relative frequency distribution or the percentage distribution, depending on whether we prefer proportions or percentages. These two equivalent distributions are shown as Tables 4.5 and 4.6, respectively.

The **relative frequency distribution** depicted in Table 4.5 is formed by dividing the frequencies in each class of the frequency distribution (Table 4.1 on page 94) by the total number of observations. A **percentage distribution** (Table 4.6) may then be formed by multiplying each relative frequency or proportion by 100.0. Thus from Table 4.5 it is clear that the proportion of companies with reported PE ratios from 60 to under 70 is .042 while from Table 4.6 it is seen that 4.2% of the companies have such PE ratios.

TABLE 4.5 Relative frequency distribution of PE ratios for 24 natural resource companies

PE Ratios	Proportion of Companies
0 but less than 10	0.083
10 but less than 20	0.500
20 but less than 30	0.208
30 but less than 40	0.083
40 but less than 50	0.042
50 but less than 60	0.042
60 but less than 70	0.042
Total	1.000

SOURCE: Data are taken from Table 4.1.

TABLE 4.6 Percentage distribution of PE ratios for 24 natural resource companies

PE Ratios	Percentage of Companies
0 but less than 10	8.3
10 but less than 20	50.0
20 but less than 30	20.8
30 but less than 40	8.3
40 but less than 50	4.2
50 but less than 60	4.2
60 but less than 70	4.2
Total	100.0

SOURCE: Data are taken from Table 4.1.

Working with a base of 1 for proportions or 100.0 for percentages is usually more meaningful than using the frequencies themselves. Indeed, the use of the relative frequency distribution or percentage distribution becomes essential whenever one batch of data is being compared to other batches of data, especially if the numbers of observations in each batch differ.

As a case in point, let us suppose that an industrial psychologist wanted to compare daily absenteeism among the clerical workers in two department stores. If, on a given day, 9 clerical workers out of 90 in Store A were absent while 3 clerical workers out of 10 in Store B were absent, what conclusions can be drawn? It is obviously inappropriate to say that *more* absenteeism occurred in Store A. While we have observed that in Store A there were three times as many absences as there were in Store B, there were also nine times as many clerical workers employed in Store A. Hence, in these types of comparisons, we must formulate our conclusions from the *relative rates* of absenteeism, not from the actual counts. Thus it may be stated that the absenteeism rate is three times higher in Store B (30.0%) than it is in Store A (10.0%).

Suppose, when developing her report, that the financial analyst wanted to compare the PE ratios for the 24 natural resource companies with those reported from the 45 companies in the retailing industry.

Figure 4.1 on page 106 displays the PE ratios, dividend policy, and the pertinent stock exchange listing for *each* of the 45 retailing companies. We note that the PE ratio variable is *quantitative* while the dividend and stock exchange variables are *qualitative*. In this section we will be concerned only with the former; a detailed study of the categorical responses to these qualitative variables will be undertaken in Sections 4.7 through 4.9. To compare the reported PE ratios from the 24 natural resource companies with those from the 45 retailing companies we develop a percentage distribution for the latter group. This new table will then be compared with Table 4.6.

Table 4.7 depicts both the frequency distribution and the percentage distribution of the reported PE ratios from the 45 companies in the retailing industry. It is both permissible and desirable to construct one such table in lieu of two separate tables to save space.

Note that the class groupings selected in Table 4.7 match, where possible, those selected in Table 4.1 for the natural resource companies. The boundaries of the classes should match or be multiples of each other in order to facilitate comparisons.

TABLE 4.7 Frequency distribution and percentage distribution of reported PE ratios from 45 retailing companies

PE Ratios	Number of Companies	Percentage of Companies
10 but less than 20	22	48.9
20 but less than 30	12	26.7
30 but less than 40	8	17.8
40 but less than 50	2	4.4
50 but less than 60	0	0.0
60 but less than 70	0	0.0
70 but less than 80	1	2.2
Totals	45	100.0

SOURCE: Data are taken from Figure 4.1.

4.4.1 Grouped Data Comparisons: Central Tendency and Dispersion

Using the percentage distributions of Tables 4.6 and 4.7, it is now meaningful to compare the two industries in terms of their reported PE ratios. For example, from the two tables it is clear that most typically the PE ratios in each industry are clustering

Retailing Company	PE Ratio	Dividend Declaration	Stock Exchange Listing
Ames Department Stores	24	Yes	NYSE
Businessland	70	No	OTC
Carson Pirie Scott	22	Yes	NYSE
Carter Hawley Hale Stores	35	Yes	NYSE
Charming Shoppes	35	Yes	OTC
Child World	17	No	OTC
Circuit City Stores	29	Yes	NYSE
Dayton Hudson	16	Yes	NYSE
Dillard Department Stores	19	Yes	ASE
Edison Brothers Stores	12	Yes	NYSE
Family Dollar Stores	18	Yes	NYSE
Federated Department Stores	16	Yes	NYSE
Gap	29	Yes	NYSE
Hechinger	25	Yes	OTC
Highland Superstores	12	No	OTC
Home Depot	33	Yes	NYSE
Jamesway	18	Yes	NYSE
K mart	14	Yes	NYSE
Limited	42	Yes	NYSE
Longs Drug Stores	20	Yes	NYSE
Lowe's	21	Yes	NYSE
May Department Stores	19	Yes	NYSE
Melville	16	Yes	NYSE
Mercantile Stores	15	Yes	NYSE
Meyer (Fred)	13	No	OTC
Nordstrom	32	Yes	OTC
Payless Cashways	19	Yes	NYSE
Penney (J. C.)	15	Yes	NYSE
Pep Boys—Manny, Moe & Jack	34	Yes	NYSE
Perry Drug Stores	25	Yes	NYSE
Petrie Stores	19	Yes	NYSE
Price	34	No	OTC
Rite Aid	21	Yes	NYSE
Rose's Stores	16	Yes	OTC
Scotty's	19	Yes	NYSE
Sears, Roebuck	15	Yes	NYSE
Stop & Shop	22	Yes	NYSE
Strawbridge & Clothier	14	Yes	OTC
Toys "R" Us	40	No	NYSE
U.S. Shoe	30	Yes	NYSE
Wal-Mart Stores	39	Yes	NYSE
Walgreen	24	Yes	NYSE
Wickes	13	No	ASE
Woolworth (F. W.)	16	Yes	NYSE
Zayre	21	Yes	NYSE

FIGURE 4.1
Raw data pertaining to PE ratio, dividend information, and stock market listing for 45 retailing companies.

SOURCE: PE ratios are taken from "Business Week Corporate Scoreboard," *Business Week*, March 16, 1987, pp. 138–139. Reprinted by special permission. © 1987 by McGraw-Hill, Inc.

between 10 and 20. This *modal group* accounts for 50.0% of the PE ratios in the natural resource industry and 48.9% of the PE ratios in the retailing industry. From these tables we also note that for the natural resource companies the midrange is approximately 35 while the range in the reported PE ratios is approximately 70. On the other hand, for the retailing companies the midrange is approximately 45 while the range in the reported PE ratios is approximately 70.

The means, standard deviations, and coefficients of variation can also be obtained from the data in Tables 4.1 and 4.7. For the 24 natural resource companies, these measures (computed in Section 4.3) were, respectively, 22.92, 14.43, and 63.0%. For the 45 retailing companies, the respective results are 23.89, 11.78, and 49.3%.

From these summary measures we can observe the basic similarities in the distribution (structure) of PE ratios for the two particular industrial groupings. Nevertheless, there are some distinct differences. Comparing the coefficients of variation, we note that the PE ratios for the retailing companies are slightly more homogeneous (that is, heavily concentrated about the measures of central tendency) than those from the natural resource companies. While only 6.6% of the retailing companies have PE ratios of *at least* 40, 12.6% of natural resource companies report such amounts.

4.4.2 Grouped Data Comparisons: Shape

A final comparison between the PE ratio data from the two industries is based on shape. As will be indicated in Figure 4.4 (see page 110), the shapes appear to be similar—a heavy concentration of reported PE ratios under 30 with a light concentration above that amount. Hence both data batches can be described as right-skewed.

Problems

● **4.41** Form the percentage distribution from the frequency distribution developed in Problem 4.4(b) on page 96 regarding utility charges.

4.42 Form the percentage distribution from the frequency distribution developed in Problem 4.6 on page 96 regarding the amount owed to a mail-order book company.

4.43 Form the percentage distribution from the frequency distribution developed in Problem 4.7 on page 96 regarding the prices of dot-matrix printers.

4.44 Form the percentage distribution from the frequency distribution developed in Problem 4.8 on page 96 regarding PE ratios for food processing companies.

4.45 Form the percentage distribution from the frequency distribution developed in Problem 4.9 on page 96 regarding fringe benefits at Connecticut colleges and universities.

4.46 Form the percentage distribution from the frequency distribution developed in Problem 4.10 on page 96 regarding quarterly sales tax receipts.

4.47 Form the percentage distribution from the frequency distribution developed in Problem 4.11 on page 96 regarding prices of auto alarm systems.

4.48 Form the percentage distribution from the frequency distribution developed in Problem 4.12 on page 96 regarding book values of companies listed on the NYSE.

4.49 Form the percentage distribution from the frequency distribution developed in Problem 4.13 on page 96 regarding prices of compact disk players.

4.50 Form the percentage distribution from the frequency distribution developed in Problem 4.14 on page 97 regarding prices of video cassette recorders.

4.51 Form the percentage distribution from the frequency distribution developed in Problem 4.15 on page 97 regarding prices of compact microwave ovens.

4.52 Form the percentage distribution from the frequency distribution developed in Problem 4.16 on page 97 regarding prices of IBM PC/XT compatibles.

4.53 Form the percentage distribution from the frequency distribution developed in Problem 4.17 on page 97 regarding prices of spreadsheet products.

4.54 Form the percentage distribution from the frequency distribution developed in Problem 4.18 on page 97 regarding GNP projections.

4.55 Form the percentage distribution from the frequency distribution developed in Problem 4.19 on page 97 regarding laundry detergent costs per load.

4.56 Form the percentage distribution from the frequency distribution developed in Problem 4.20 on page 97 regarding per capita alcoholic consumption.

4.57 Form the percentage distributions from the frequency distributions developed in Problem 4.21 on page 97 concerning the life of light bulbs manufactured by two competing companies, A and B.

4.58 Form the percentage distributions from the frequency distributions developed in Problem 4.22 on page 97 concerning ages of automobile salesmen in the United States and in Western Europe.

4.5 GRAPHING QUANTITATIVE DATA: THE HISTOGRAM AND POLYGON

It is often said that "one picture is worth a thousand words." Indeed, statisticians have employed graphic techniques to more vividly describe batches of data. In particular, histograms and polygons are used to describe quantitative data which have been grouped into frequency, relative frequency, or percentage distributions.

4.5.1 Histograms

Histograms are vertical bar charts in which the rectangular bars are constructed at the boundaries of each class.

When plotting histograms, the random variable or phenomenon of interest is plotted along the horizontal axis; the vertical axis represents the number, proportion, or percentage of observations per class interval—depending on whether or not the particular histogram is, respectively, a frequency histogram, a relative frequency histogram, or a percentage histogram.

Vertical Axis Label	↔	Type of Chart
Number of observations	↔	**Frequency** histogram or polygon
Proportion of observations	↔	**Relative frequency** histogram or polygon
Percentage of observations	↔	**Percentage** histogram or polygon

A percentage histogram is depicted in Figure 4.2 for the reported PE ratios from all 24 companies in the natural resource industrial grouping.

When comparing two or more batches of data, however, the various histograms cannot be constructed on the same graph, because superimposing the vertical bars of one on another would cause difficulty in interpretation. For such cases it is necessary to construct relative frequency or percentage polygons.

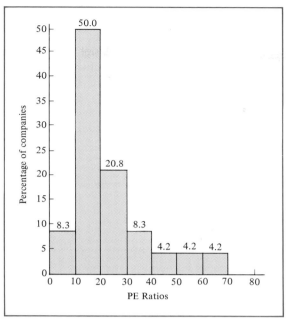

FIGURE 4.2
Percentage histogram of reported PE ratios from 24 natural resource companies.

SOURCE: Data are taken from Table 4.6.

The Stem-and-Leaf Display as a Frequency Distribution and Histogram

In Section 3.8 we commented that the (revised) stem-and-leaf display is, perhaps, the most versatile technique in descriptive statistics because it simultaneously organizes the data for further descriptive analyses and presents the data in both tabular and chart form. Thus, the (revised) stem-and-leaf display is, essentially, an ordered array, a frequency distribution, and a frequency histogram—all in one—without sacrificing the original information pertaining to the individual observations themselves.

To demonstrate these features of the stem-and-leaf display let us turn to Figure 3.10 on page 56. If we were to attach the leaves from one stem to another, consecutively, the ordered array of PE ratios for the 24 natural resource companies would be obtained. (See Figure 3.8 on page 55.) Moreover, if we were to merely tally the leaves within each stem, a frequency distribution would be constructed. (See Table 4.1 on page 94.) Finally, if we were to rotate the stem-and-leaf display 90° (that is, hold our book ''sideways''), a frequency histogram would be depicted in such a manner that the vertical bars would be represented by individual leaves on each stem. (See Figure 4.2.)

4.5.2 **Polygons**

As with histograms, when plotting polygons the phenomenon of interest is plotted along the horizontal axis while the vertical axis represents the number, proportion, or percentage of observations per class interval.[2]

---

[2] Because consecutive midpoints are connected by a series of straight lines, the polygon is sometimes ''jagged'' in appearance. If we were to make the boundaries of the classes in a frequency distribution closer together (and thereby increase the number of classes in the distribution), the jagged lines would ''smooth out.''

The **percentage polygon** is formed by letting the midpoint of each class represent the data in that class and then connecting the sequence of midpoints at their respective class percentages.

Figure 4.3 shows the percentage polygon of the reported PE ratios for the 24 natural resource companies, and Figure 4.4 compares the percentage polygons of the PE ratios for the 24 companies versus those for the 45 retailing companies. The similarities and differences in the structure of the two distributions, previously discussed when comparing Tables 4.6 and 4.7, are clearly indicated here.

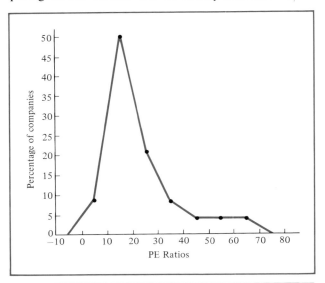

FIGURE 4.3
Percentage polygon of reported PE ratios from 24 natural resource companies. SOURCE: Data are taken from Table 4.6.

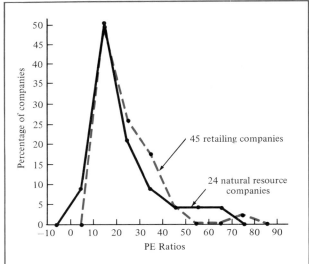

FIGURE 4.4
Percentage polygons of reported PE ratios from 24 natural resource companies and 45 retailing companies. SOURCE: Data are taken from Tables 4.6 and 4.7.

Polygon Construction

Notice that the polygon is a representation of the shape of the particular distribution. Since the area under the percentage distribution (entire curve) must be 100.0%, it is necessary to connect the first and last midpoints with the horizontal axis so as to enclose the area of the observed distribution. In Figure 4.3 this is accomplished by connecting the first observed midpoint with the midpoint of a "fictitious preceding" class (-5) having 0.0% observations and by connecting the last observed midpoint with the midpoint of a "fictitious succeeding" class (75) having 0.0% observations.

Notice, too, that when polygons (Figure 4.3) or histograms (Figure 4.2) are constructed, the vertical axis must show the true zero or "origin" so as not to distort or otherwise misrepresent the character of the data. The horizontal axis, however, does not need to specify the zero point for the phenomenon of interest. For aesthetic reasons, the range of the random variable should constitute the major portion of the chart, and when zero is not included "breaks" (‑⋀⋁‑) in the axis are appropriate.

Using Polygons for Comparing Grouped Data Batches

Polygons provide us with a useful visual aid for comparing two or more batches of data. Expanding on the dot diagram scales in Chapter 3, the properties of central tendency, dispersion, and shape can be depicted by comparing the polygons of particular distributions of data.

Figure 4.5 depicts a perfectly symmetrical bell-shaped (normal) distribution. The mean, median, mode, midrange, and midhinge are (theoretically) identical.

Figure 4.6 displays two identical normal distributions. Polygons A and B are superimposed on one another.

Figure 4.7 presents two normal distributions which differ only in central tendency. The mean, median, mode, midrange and midhinge in polygon C exceed (are to the right of) those for polygon A. (See page 112.)

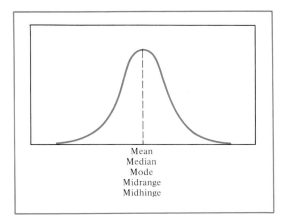

FIGURE 4.5
Bell-shaped curve.

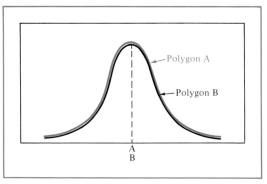

FIGURE 4.6
Two identical symmetrical bell-shaped normal distributions.

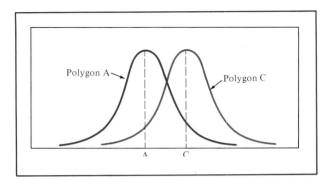

FIGURE 4.7
Two symmetrical bell-shaped normal distributions differing only in central tendency.

Figure 4.8 demonstrates two normal distributions which differ only in dispersion. The range, variance, and standard deviation in polygon D are smaller than those for polygon A.

Figure 4.9 depicts three hypothetical polygons: Polygon A is a symmetrical bell-shaped normal distribution; polygon L is negative or left-skewed (since the distortion to the left is caused by extremely small values); and polygon R is positive or right-skewed (since the distortion to the right is caused by extremely large values).

The *relative positions* of the various measures of central tendency (the mean, median, mode, midrange, and midhinge) in skewed distributions can best be examined from Figures 4.10 and 4.11.

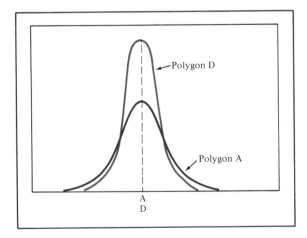

FIGURE 4.8
Two symmetric bell-shaped normal distributions differing in dispersion.

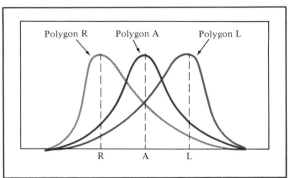

FIGURE 4.9
Three distributions differing primarily in shape.

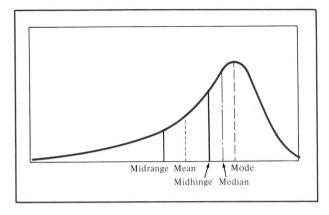

FIGURE 4.10
Left-skewed distribution.

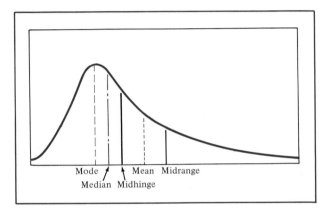

FIGURE 4.11
Right-skewed distribution.

In left-skewed distributions (Figure 4.10) the few extremely small observations distort the midrange and mean toward the left tail. Hence, we would expect the mode to be the largest value and the midrange to be the smallest. That is,

midrange < mean < midhinge < median < mode

However, in right-skewed distributions (Figure 4.11) the reverse is true. The few extremely large observations distort the midrange and the mean toward the right tail. Hence, we would expect the midrange to exceed (that is, be to the right of) all other measures. That is,

mode < median < midhinge < mean < midrange

On the other hand, in perfectly symmetric distributions the mean, median, midrange, and midhinge will all be identical. As displayed in Figures 4.12 through 4.14, the shape of the curve to the left side of these measures of central tendency is the mirror image of the shape of the curve to their right. (See page 114.)

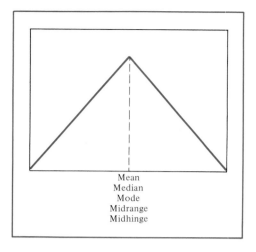

FIGURE 4.12
Triangular shaped curve.

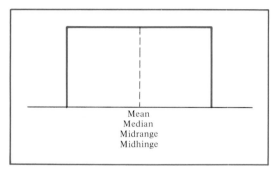

FIGURE 4.13
Rectangular shaped curve. *Note*: No mode.

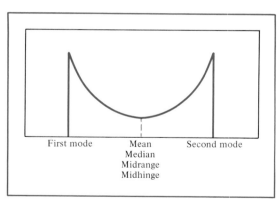

FIGURE 4.14
U-shaped curve.

Problems

● **4.59** From the percentage distribution developed in Problem 4.41 on page 107 regarding utility charges
(a) Plot the percentage histogram.
(b) Plot the percentage polygon.

4.60   From the percentage distribution developed in Problem 4.42 on page 107 regarding the amount owed to a mail-order book company
(a) Plot the percentage histogram.
(b) Plot the percentage polygon.

4.61   From the percentage distribution developed in Problem 4.43 on page 107 regarding the prices of dot-matrix printers
(a) Plot the percentage histogram.
(b) Plot the percentage polygon.

4.62   From the percentage distribution developed in Problem 4.44 on page 107 regarding PE ratios for food processing companies
(a) Plot the percentage histogram.
(b) Plot the percentage polygon.

4.63   From the percentage distribution developed in Problem 4.45 on page 107 regarding fringe benefits at Connecticut colleges and universities
(a) Plot the percentage histogram.
(b) Plot the percentage polygon.

4.64   From the percentage distribution developed in Problem 4.46 on page 107 regarding quarterly sales tax receipts
(a) Plot the percentage histogram.
(b) Plot the percentage polygon.

4.65   From the percentage distribution developed in Problem 4.47 on page 107 regarding prices of auto alarm systems
(a) Plot the percentage histogram.
(b) Plot the percentage polygon.

4.66   From the percentage distribution developed in Problem 4.48 on page 107 regarding book values of companies listed on the NYSE
(a) Plot the percentage histogram.
(b) Plot the percentage polygon.

4.67   From the percentage distribution developed in Problem 4.49 on page 107 regarding prices of compact disk players
(a) Plot the percentage histogram.
(b) Plot the percentage polygon.

4.68   From the percentage distribution developed in Problem 4.50 on page 107 regarding prices of video cassette recorders
(a) Plot the percentage histogram.
(b) Plot the percentage polygon.

4.69   From the percentage distribution developed in Problem 4.51 on page 108 regarding prices of compact microwave ovens
(a) Plot the percentage histogram.
(b) Plot the percentage polygon.

4.70   From the percentage distribution developed in Problem 4.52 on page 108 regarding prices of IBM PC/XT compatibles
(a) Plot the percentage histogram.
(b) Plot the percentage polygon.

4.71   From the percentage distribution developed in Problem 4.53 on page 108 regarding prices of spreadsheet products
(a) Plot the percentage histogram.
(b) Plot the percentage polygon.

4.72   From the percentage distribution developed in Problem 4.54 on page 108 regarding GNP projections
(a) Plot the percentage histogram.
(b) Plot the percentage polygon.

4.73 From the percentage distribution developed in Problem 4.55 on page 108 regarding laundry detergent costs per load
(a) Plot the percentage histogram.
(b) Plot the percentage polygon.

4.74 From the percentage distribution developed in Problem 4.56 on page 108 regarding per capita alcoholic consumption
(a) Plot the percentage histogram.
(b) Plot the percentage polygon.

4.75 From the percentage distributions developed in Problem 4.57 on page 108 regarding life of light bulbs
(a) Plot the percentage histograms on separate graphs.
(b) Plot the percentage polygons on one graph.

4.76 From the percentage distributions developed in Problem 4.58 on page 108 regarding ages of automobile salesmen
(a) Plot the percentage histograms on separate graphs.
(b) Plot the percentage polygons on one graph.

4.6 CUMULATIVE DISTRIBUTIONS AND CUMULATIVE POLYGONS

Two other useful methods of data presentation which facilitate analysis and interpretation are the cumulative distribution tables and the cumulative polygon charts. Both of these may be developed from either the frequency-distribution table, the relative-frequency-distribution table, or the percentage-distribution table.

4.6.1 The Cumulative Percentage Distribution

Depending on our individual preference for proportions or percentages, when comparing two or more data batches of differing size we select either the relative frequency distribution or the percentage distribution. Since we already have the percentage distributions of PE ratios for the 24 natural resource companies and the 45 retailing companies in Tables 4.6 and 4.7 (pages 104 and 107), we can use these tables to construct the respective cumulative percentage distributions for these companies as given in Tables 4.8 and 4.9.

TABLE 4.8 Cumulative percentage distribution of PE ratios from 24 natural resource companies

PE Ratios	Percentage of Companies "Less Than" Indicated Value
0	0.0
10	8.3
20	58.3
30	79.1
40	87.4
50	91.6
60	95.8
70	100.0

SOURCE: Data are taken from Table 4.6.

TABLE 4.9 Cumulative percentage distribution of PE ratios from 45 retailing companies

PE Ratios	Percentage of Companies "Less Than" Indicated Value
10	0.0
20	48.9
30	75.6
40	93.4
50	97.8
60	97.8
70	97.8
80	100.0

SOURCE: Data are taken from Table 4.7.

A **cumulative percentage distribution table** is constructed by first recording the lower boundaries of each class from the percentage distribution and then "adding in" an "extra" boundary at the end. We compute the cumulative percentages in the "*less than*" *column* by determining the percentage of observations less than each of the stated boundary values. Thus from Table 4.6, we see that 0.0% of the PE ratios in the natural resource industry are less than 0; 8.3% of the PE ratios are less than 10; 58.3% of the PE ratios are less than 20, and so on until all (100.0%) of the PE ratios are less than 70. This cumulation process is readily observed in Table 4.10.

TABLE 4.10 Forming the cumulative percentage distribution

	From Table 4.6	From Table 4.8
PE Ratios	Percentage of Companies in Class Interval	Percentage of Companies "Less Than" Lower Boundary of Class Interval
0 but less than 10	8.3	0.0
10 but less than 20	50.0	8.3
20 but less than 30	20.8	58.3 = 8.3 + 50.0
30 but less than 40	8.3	79.1 = 8.3 + 50.0 + 20.8
40 but less than 50	4.2	87.4 = 8.3 + 50.0 + 20.8 + 8.3
50 but less than 60	4.2	91.6 = 8.3 + 50.0 + 20.8 + 8.3 + 4.2
60 but less than 70	4.2	95.8 = 8.3 + 50.0 + 20.8 + 8.3 + 4.2 + 4.2
70 but less than 80	0.0	100.0 = 8.3 + 50.0 + 20.8 + 8.3 + 4.2 + 4.2 + 4.2

4.6.2 Cumulative Percentage Polygon

To construct a **cumulative percentage polygon** (also known as an **ogive**), we note that the phenomenon of interest—reported PE ratios—is again plotted on the horizontal axis, while the cumulative percentages (from the "less than" column) are plotted on the vertical axis. At each lower boundary, we plot the corresponding (cumulative) percentage value from the listing in the cumulative percentage distribution. We then connect these points with a series of straight-line segments.

Figure 4.15 on page 118 illustrates the cumulative percentage polygon of reported PE ratios for the 24 natural resource companies. The major advantage of the ogive over other charts is the ease with which we can interpolate between the plotted points.

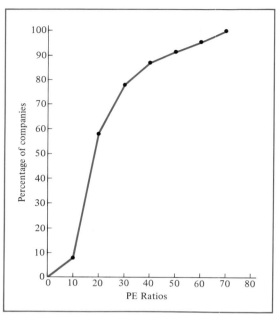

FIGURE 4.15
Cumulative percentage polygon (ogive) of PE ratios for 24 natural resource companies.

SOURCE: Data are taken from Table 4.8.

Approximating the Percentages

As one example, the financial analyst might wish to approximate the percentage of companies which report a PE ratio below a specified amount, say 15. To accomplish this, a vertical line is projected upward at 15 until it intersects the "less than" curve. The desired percentage is then approximated by reading horizontally from the point of intersection to the percentage (vertical) axis. In this case, approximately 33.0% of the natural resource companies have PE ratios under 15. (This, of course, implies that about 67.0% of the companies report PE ratios of at least 15.)

Approximating the Median

Even more important, the financial analyst may also wish to approximate various descriptive summary measures pertaining to PE ratios which correspond to particular cumulative percentages. For example, she might wish to approximate the **median** PE ratios.[3] That is, 50.0% of reported PE ratios are below what amount? To determine this, a horizontal line is drawn from the specified cumulative (50.0) percentage point until it intersects the "*less than*" curve. The desired PE ratio is then approximated by dropping a perpendicular (a vertical line) at the point of intersection to the horizontal axis. From Figure 4.15 we note that the median PE ratio is approximately 18.

Comparing Two or More Cumulative Distributions

Such approximations as the above are extremely helpful when comparing two or more

---

[3] As described in Section 3.9, other commonly considered percentage points are the 25.0% value and the 75.0% value. Moreover, a knowledge of these two values leads to approximations of the midhinge and interquartile range.

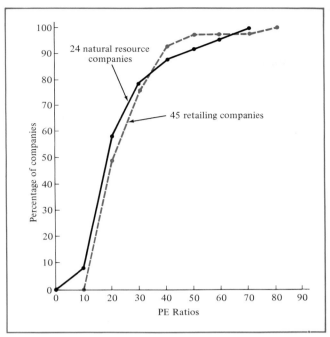

FIGURE 4.16
Ogives of PE ratios for 24 natural resource companies
and 45 retailing companies.

SOURCE: Data are taken from Tables 4.8 and 4.9.

batches of data. Figure 4.16 depicts the cumulative percentage polygons of PE ratios for both the 24 natural resource companies and the 45 retailing companies.

From Figure 4.16 we see that the median PE ratio for the retailing companies (approximately 21.0) is about three units higher than that for the natural resource companies. Other comparisons are left as an exercise for the reader (see Problem 4.95 on page 123).

Problems

● **4.77**   From the frequency distribution developed in Problem 4.4(b) on page 96 regarding utility charges
    (a) Form the cumulative frequency distribution.
    (b) Form the cumulative percentage distribution.
    (c) Plot the ogive (cumulative percentage polygon).
    (d) Approximate
        (1) the median   (3) the midhinge
        (2) Q_1 and Q_3 (4) the interquartile range
    (e) From the information in part (d) as well as your results from Problem 4.23 on page 102, determine the shape of the data.

   4.78   From the frequency distribution developed in Problem 4.6 on page 96 regarding the amount owed to a mail-order book company

      (a) Form the cumulative frequency distribution.

      (b) Form the cumulative percentage distribution.

      (c) Plot the ogive (cumulative percentage polygon).

      (d) Approximate

          (1) the median   (3) the midhinge

          (2) Q_1 and Q_3 (4) the interquartile range

      (e) From the information in part (d) as well as your results from Problem 4.24 on page 102, determine the shape of the data.

4.79   From the frequency distribution developed in Problem 4.7 on page 96 regarding prices of dot-matrix printers

      (a) Form the cumulative frequency distribution.

      (b) Form the cumulative percentage distribution.

      (c) Plot the ogive (cumulative percentage polygon).

      (d) Approximate

          (1) the median   (3) the midhinge

          (2) Q_1 and Q_3 (4) the interquartile range

      (e) From the information in part (d) as well as your results from Problem 4.25 on page 102, determine the shape of the data.

4.80   From the frequency distribution developed in Problem 4.8 on page 96 regarding PE ratios for food processing companies

      (a) Form the cumulative frequency distribution.

      (b) Form the cumulative percentage distribution.

      (c) Plot the ogive (cumulative percentage polygon).

      (d) Approximate

          (1) the median   (3) the midhinge

          (2) Q_1 and Q_3 (4) the interquartile range

      (e) From the information in part (d) as well as your results from Problem 4.26 on page 102, determine the shape of the data.

4.81   From the frequency distribution developed in Problem 4.9 on page 96 regarding fringe benefits of Connecticut colleges and universities

      (a) Form the cumulative frequency distribution.

      (b) Form the cumulative percentage distribution.

      (c) Plot the ogive (cumulative percentage polygon).

      (d) Approximate

          (1) the median   (3) the midhinge

          (2) Q_1 and Q_3 (4) the interquartile range

      (e) From the information in part (d) as well as your results from Problem 4.27 on page 102, determine the shape of the data.

4.82   From the frequency distribution developed in Problem 4.10 on page 96 regarding quarterly sales tax receipts

      (a) Form the cumulative frequency distribution.

      (b) Form the cumulative percentage distribution.

      (c) Plot the ogive (cumulative percentage polygon).

      (d) Approximate

          (1) the median   (3) the midhinge

          (2) Q_1 and Q_3 (4) the interquartile range

      (e) From the information in part (d) as well as your results from Problem 4.28 on page 102, determine the shape of the data.

4.83   From the frequency distribution developed in Problem 4.11 on page 96 regarding prices of auto alarm systems

      (a) Form the cumulative frequency distribution.

      (b) Form the cumulative percentage distribution.

      (c) Plot the ogive (cumulative percentage polygon).

   (d) Approximate
      (1) the median   (3) the midhinge
      (2) Q_1 and Q_3 (4) the interquartile range
   (e) From the information in part (d) as well as your results from Problem 4.29 on page 102, determine the shape of the data.

4.84 From the frequency distribution developed in Problem 4.12 on page 96 regarding book values of companies listed on the NYSE
   (a) Form the cumulative frequency distribution.
   (b) Form the cumulative percentage distribution.
   (c) Plot the ogive (cumulative percentage polygon).
   (d) Approximate
      (1) the median   (3) the midhinge
      (2) Q_1 and Q_3 (4) the interquartile range
   (e) From the information in part (d) as well as your results from Problem 4.30 on page 102, determine the shape of the data.

4.85 From the frequency distribution developed in Problem 4.13 on page 96 regarding prices of compact disk players
   (a) Form the cumulative frequency distribution.
   (b) Form the cumulative percentage distribution.
   (c) Plot the ogive (cumulative percentage polygon).
   (d) Approximate
      (1) the median   (3) the midhinge
      (2) Q_1 and Q_3 (4) the interquartile range
   (e) From the information in part (d) as well as your results from Problem 4.31 on page 102, determine the shape of the data.

4.86 From the frequency distribution developed in Problem 4.14 on page 97 regarding prices of video cassette recorders
   (a) Form the cumulative frequency distribution.
   (b) Form the cumulative percentage distribution.
   (c) Plot the ogive (cumulative percentage polygon).
   (d) Approximate
      (1) the median   (3) the midhinge
      (2) Q_1 and Q_3 (4) the interquartile range
   (e) From the information in part (d) as well as your results from Problem 4.32 on page 103, determine the shape of the data.

4.87 From the frequency distribution developed in Problem 4.15 on page 97 regarding prices of compact microwave ovens
   (a) Form the cumulative frequency distribution.
   (b) Form the cumulative percentage distribution.
   (c) Plot the ogive (cumulative percentage polygon).
   (d) Approximate
      (1) the median   (3) the midhinge
      (2) Q_1 and Q_3 (4) the interquartile range
   (e) From the information in part (d) as well as your results from Problem 4.33 on page 103, determine the shape of the data.

4.88 From the frequency distribution developed in Problem 4.16 on page 97 regarding prices of IBM PC/XT compatible systems
   (a) Form the cumulative frequency distribution.
   (b) Form the cumulative percentage distribution.
   (c) Plot the ogive (cumulative percentage polygon).
   (d) Approximate
      (1) the median   (3) the midhinge
      (2) Q_1 and Q_3 (4) the interquartile range

(e) From the information in part (d) as well as your results from Problem 4.34 on page 103, determine the shape of the data.

4.89 From the frequency distribution developed in Problem 4.17 on page 97 regarding prices of spreadsheet products
(a) Form the cumulative frequency distribution.
(b) Form the cumulative percentage distribution.
(c) Plot the ogive (cumulative percentage polygon).
(d) Approximate
   (1) the median
   (2) Q_1 and Q_3
   (3) the midhinge
   (4) the interquartile range
(e) From the information in part (d) as well as your results from Problem 4.35 on page 103, determine the shape of the data.

4.90 From the frequency distribution developed in Problem 4.18 on page 97 regarding GNP projections
(a) Form the cumulative frequency distribution.
(b) Form the cumulative percentage distribution.
(c) Plot the ogive (cumulative percentage polygon).
(d) Approximate
   (1) the median
   (2) Q_1 and Q_3
   (3) the midhinge
   (4) the interquartile range
(e) From the information in part (d) as well as your results from Problem 4.36 on page 103, determine the shape of the data.

4.91 From the frequency distribution developed in Problem 4.19 on page 97 regarding laundry detergent costs per load
(a) Form the cumulative frequency distribution.
(b) Form the cumulative percentage distribution.
(c) Plot the ogive (cumulative percentage polygon).
(d) Approximate
   (1) the median
   (2) Q_1 and Q_3
   (3) the midhinge
   (4) the interquartile range
(e) From the information in part (d) as well as your results from Problem 4.37 on page 103, determine the shape of the data.

4.92 From the frequency distribution developed in Problem 4.20 on page 97 regarding per capita alcoholic consumption
(a) Form the cumulative frequency distribution.
(b) Form the cumulative percentage distribution.
(c) Plot the ogive (cumulative percentage polygon).
(d) Approximate
   (1) the median
   (2) Q_1 and Q_3
   (3) the midhinge
   (4) the interquartile range
(e) From the information in part (d) as well as your results from Problem 4.38 on page 103, determine the shape of the data.

4.93 From the frequency distributions developed in Problem 4.21 on page 97 regarding life of light bulbs
(a) Form the cumulative frequency distributions.
(b) Form the cumulative percentage distributions.
(c) Plot the ogives (cumulative percentage polygons) on one graph.
(d) For the two groups, approximate
   (1) the median
   (2) Q_1 and Q_3
   (3) the midhinge
   (4) the interquartile range
(e) From the information in part (d) as well as your results from Problem 4.39 on page 103, determine the shapes of the two data batches.

4.94   From the frequency distributions developed in Problem 4.22 on page 97 regarding ages of automobile salesmen
(a) Form the cumulative frequency distributions.
(b) Form the cumulative percentage distributions.
(c) Plot the ogives (cumulative percentage polygons) on one graph.
(d) For the two groups, approximate
   (1) the median   (3) the midhinge
   (2) Q_1 and Q_3 (4) the interquartile range
(e) From the information in part (d) as well as your results from Problem 4.40 on page 103, determine the shapes of the two data batches.

4.95   Examine Figure 4.16 on page 119.
(a) 10.0% of the PE ratios in each industry are below what amounts?
(b) 25.0% of the PE ratios in each industry are below what amounts?
(c) 75.0% of the PE ratios in each industry are below what amounts?
(d) 90.0% of the PE ratios in each industry are below what amounts?
(e) What percentage of the PE ratios in each industry are below 25?
(f) What percentage of the PE ratios in each industry are below 45?
(g) Discuss your findings.
➡(h) **ACTION**   How might your information be of assistance to the financial analyst? Discuss.

4.7 GRAPHING QUANTITATIVE DATA IN SEQUENCE: THE DIGIDOT PLOT

Thus far in this chapter in our discussions on graphical methods we have not in any way taken into account the sequential order in which the data have been collected. In many situations, particularly in accountancy, economics, and finance, the analyst is interested in studying a set of data collected on a regular daily, weekly, monthly, quarterly, or yearly basis so that it would be natural to plot the outcomes (be they stock price indices, industrywide sales revenues, corporate earnings, etc.) on a graph in which the (horizontal) X axis represents a given period of time. This subject of **time series analysis** is presented in Chapter 18. In other circumstances, particularly in the management of process and product quality, the analyst is also interested in studying the outcomes in a set of data collected in sequential order (be they the number of hourly arrivals of cars at a toll booth, the percentage of defective batteries in consecutive samples of fifty, the amount of fill in consecutive one-liter apple juice bottles, etc.). The subject of **statistical control of process and product quality** is discussed in Chapter 19 and a variety of **control charts** are introduced therein. In this section, as an introduction to these important subjects, we use the PE ratios for the 24 companies in the natural resources industrial grouping (see Figure 3.7 on page 54) in order to illustrate that plotting the data in sequential order can enhance an analysis.

The PE ratio data listed in Figure 3.7 appear to be in raw form. Although the companies are listed in alphabetical order, we should not expect that the PE ratios pertaining to these companies would follow any observable ordered pattern. (In fact, a major assumption in the inferential procedures we shall be discussing in Chapters 10 through 15 will be that our collected sample observations are randomly and independently drawn.) Here, then, it would be of interest to graphically evaluate whether the PE ratio data are actually in raw form or whether some unsuspected relationship exists between a company name and its PE ratio.

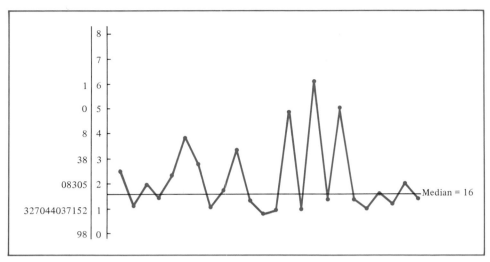

FIGURE 4.17
Hunter's digidot plot of PE ratios for 24 natural resource companies listed alphabetically.

Displaying Hunter's Digidot Plot

The data from Figure 3.7 have been organized into a stem-and-leaf display (Figure 3.9 on page 55), tabulated into a frequency distribution (Table 4.1 on page 94), and displayed graphically as a histogram (Figure 4.2 on page 109). Although it is obvious that the PE ratios in this industrial grouping are right-skewed and tend to cluster in the teens, no information regarding potential patterns in the sequential ordering of the obtained PE ratios is possible from these summary displays. To remedy this, Figure 4.17 depicts a digidot plot, a useful graphic device recently developed by Hunter (Reference 8).

The **digidot plot** simultaneously presents a stem-and-leaf display and a graph of the observations in the sequential order in which they are obtained. A horizontal line over the sequence at the expected median value permits an easy reference for observing any patterns. For example, had there been a positive trend in the observations over the ordered sequence in which they were collected, the graph would indicate a rise from left to right. For a negative trend, the graph would be reversed.

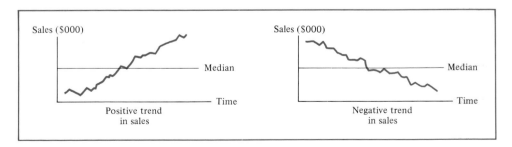

In these situations then we would visually observe long sequences of values on one side of the median followed by long sequences of values on the other side of the median.

Inspecting Figure 4.17 we find, as would be assumed, that there is no evidence of any pattern in the graph. There is no relationship (nor should there be) between alphabetical order and PE ratio. The longest consecutive sequence of PE ratios above the median is 3 (observations 5, 6, and 7) and the longest consecutive sequence below the median is also 3 (observations 11, 12, and 13). On the other hand, the higher swings of the graph above the median line as compared to the distances below it demonstate the right skewness in this batch of data.

Constructing Hunter's Digidot Plot

Comparing the stem-and-leaf display in Figure 3.9 (page 55) with that shown in the above digidot plot, we note that they would be identical if we were to turn one of them upside down! Thus, in constructing the stem-and-leaf portion of the digidot plot we note that the leaves are branching off to the left of the stems instead of to the right. Moreover, note that the stems are listed high to low from top to bottom instead of low to high as in Figure 3.9. This is done for graphical convenience since the (vertical) Y axis of a graph goes from high to low, top to bottom.

To construct the digidot plot we use graph paper. To the left of the vertical axis we indicate the stems along with "tick marks" for the PE ratios on the vertical scale. To the left of the stems we draw another vertical line to permit placement of the leaves. We then simultaneously construct the stem-and-leaf portion and graph the PE ratios in the order in which they are listed from Figure 3.7. These ratios are plotted from left to right, with equal distances between. The consecutive dots are then connected and the median line is drawn through the ordered sequence. In Figure 4.17, the median PE ratio line is plotted from the vertical axis at the value 16.0. Here the actual median is plotted because the intent was to check an assumption in a batch of data already obtained. On the other hand, for production processes that are being monitored in progress (that is, the plots are being made interactively), the expected median would be plotted initially so that it would provide for a visual interpretation of patterns over time.

Problems

4.96 A manufacturer of men's jeans uses a machine that can be adjusted to vary the length of the material being produced. Suppose the production plan is to produce jeans that have a length of 34 inches. The machine is then adjusted to produce jeans with an average length of 34 inches. A sample of 30 consecutive pairs of jeans is selected from the production process and their lengths are recorded below in row sequence (from left to right):

34.02	34.06	34.05	34.01	33.91	33.76	33.89	33.98	33.88	33.96
33.85	33.94	33.91	34.03	34.05	34.00	33.97	33.84	33.74	33.85
33.94	33.99	34.03	34.10	34.02	33.95	33.96	34.01	33.93	33.82

(a) Form a digidot plot for these data.

(b) What conclusions can you reach about whether the manufacturing process is in control?

4.97 Victor Sternberg was training for a 5K race. As part of his training regimen he ran a quarter-mile interval for speed on the track for 27 consecutive days prior to the race and kept a record of his time trials. The data on page 126 are his quarter-mile times (in seconds):

	Sunday	Monday	Tuesday	Wednesday	Thursday	Friday	Saturday
1st Week	90	91	89	88	88	86	84
2nd Week	85	84	83	84	83	82	80
3rd Week	80	81	81	79	79	78	76
4th Week	79	78	75	74	73	72	RACE

(a) Form a digidot plot for these time trials. (Use the median for this 27-day period.)

(b) What can be concluded from this plot? Discuss.

4.8 TABULATING QUALITATIVE DATA: THE SUMMARY TABLE

When dealing with qualitative phenomena the categorical responses may be tallied into **summary tables** and then graphically displayed as either **bar charts, pie charts,** or **dot charts.**

To illustrate the development of a summary table, let us consider the data obtained by the financial analyst regarding the stock market listings for the various companies in the retailing industry. From Figure 4.1 on page 106 we see that of the 45 retailing companies, 33 are traded on the New York Stock Exchange (NYSE), 2 are traded on the American Stock Exchange (ASE), and 10 are traded on the over-the-counter list (OTC). This information is presented in the accompanying frequency and percentage summary table, Table 4.11.

TABLE 4.11 Frequency and percentage summary table pertaining to stock exchange listing for 45 companies

Stock Exchange Listing	Number of Companies	Percentage of Companies
NYSE	33	73.3
ASE	2	4.4
OTC	10	22.2
Totals	45	99.9*

* Error in rounding.
SOURCE: Data are taken from Figure 4.1.

From Table 4.11 we may conclude that the overwhelming majority of companies (73.3%) in the retailing industry are traded on the New York Stock Exchange.

4.9 GRAPHING QUALITATIVE DATA: BAR, PIE, AND DOT CHARTS

To express this information graphically, either the more traditional percentage bar chart (Figure 4.18) or percentage pie chart (Figure 4.19) can be displayed, or the more modern percentage dot chart (Figure 4.20) can be developed.

The purpose of graphical presentation is to display data accurately and clearly. Figures 4.18, 4.19, and 4.20 all attempt to convey the same information with respect to stock market listing. Whether these charts succeed, however, has been a matter of

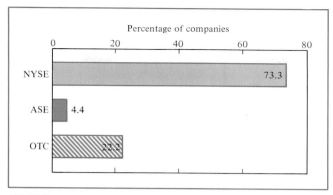

FIGURE 4.18
Percentage bar chart depicting stock exchange listing
for 45 retailing companies. SOURCE: Data are taken from Table 4.11.

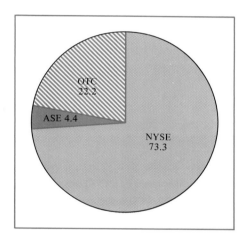

FIGURE 4.19
Percentage pie chart depicting stock exchange
listing for 45 retailing companies.
SOURCE: Data are taken from Table 4.11.

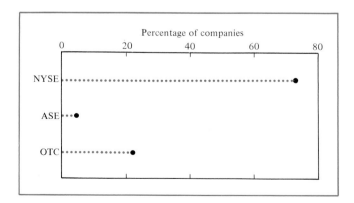

FIGURE 4.20
Percentage dot chart depict-
ing stock exchange listing for
45 retailing companies.
SOURCE: Data are taken from
Table 4.11.

much concern in the past few years (see References 2–5, 7, 9). In particular, recent research in the human perception of graphs (Reference 5) suggests that the dot chart portrays the information best while the pie chart presents the weakest display. Nevertheless, the selection of a particular chart is still highly subjective and often dependent upon the aesthetic preferences of the researcher.

4.9.1 The Bar Chart

To construct bar charts the following suggestions are made:

1. For categorical responses that are qualitative, the bars should be constructed horizontally as in Figure 4.18; for categorical responses that are numerical the bars should be constructed vertically.
2. All bars should have the same width (as in Figure 4.18) so as not to mislead the reader. Only the lengths may differ.
3. Spaces between bars should range from one-half the width of a bar to the width of a bar.
4. Scales and guidelines are useful aids in reading a chart and should be included.
5. The axes of the chart should be clearly labeled.
6. Any ''keys'' to interpreting the chart may be included within the body of the chart or below the body of the chart.
7. The title of the chart appears below the body.
8. Footnotes or source notes, when appropriate, are given following the title of the chart.

4.9.2 The Pie Chart

To construct pie charts we may use both the compass and the protractor—the former to draw the circle, the latter to measure off the appropriate pie sectors. Since the circle has 360°, the protractor may be used to divide up the pie based on the percentage ''slices'' desired. As an example, in Figure 4.19, 22.2% of the retailing companies are traded on the over-the-counter list (OTC). Thus, we would multiply 360 by 0.222, mark off the resulting 80° with the protractor, and then connect the appropriate points to the center of the pie, forming a slice comprising 22.2% of the area. In such a manner the entire pie chart can be constructed.

4.9.3 The Dot Chart

When constructing dot charts, simplicity and sparsity of adornment result in greater clarity. The following suggestions are made:

1. The light dotted lines should be constructed horizontally, as in Figure 4.20, adjacent to the various categories of the variable being studied.
2. Spacing between the light dotted lines (i.e., between the categories) should be equal.
3. Horizontal scales showing the frequency count at the bottom of the frame or the percentages at the top of the frame should be included as in Figure 4.20. The axes should be clearly labeled.
4. The title of the chart appears below the body.
5. Footnotes or source notes, as appropriate, appear after the title of the chart along with any ''keys'' to interpreting the chart.

Problems

• **4.98**   A well-known newspaper conducted a telephone poll of New Yorkers' attitudes toward New York City. A total of 419 persons were selected in a simple random sample. The following data reflected the responses to a question regarding the adequacy of police and fire protection:

Is the police and fire protection in your neighborhood adequate?	
Yes	293
No	80
Don't know or refused to answer	46
Total	419

(a) Convert the data to percentages and construct
   (1) a bar chart
   (2) a pie chart
   (3) a dot chart
(b) Which of these charts do you prefer to use here? Why?
➠(c) **ACTION**   What are these data telling you? Write an article for this newspaper.

4.99   The board of directors of a large housing cooperative wish to investigate the possibility of hiring a supervisor for an outdoor playground. All 616 households in the cooperative were polled, with each household having one vote, regardless of its size. The following data were collected:

Should the co-op hire a supervisor?	
Yes	146
No	91
Not sure	58
No response	321
Total	616

(a) Convert the data to percentages and construct
   (1) a bar chart
   (2) a pie chart
   (3) a dot chart
(b) Which of these charts do you prefer to use here? Why?
(c) Eliminating the "no response" group, convert the 295 responses to percentages and construct
   (1) a bar chart
   (2) a pie chart
   (3) a dot chart
➠(d) **ACTION**   Based on your findings in (a) and (c), what would you recommend that the board of directors do? Write a letter to the president of the board.

4.100   The following table on page 130 represents the market shares (in percent) held by cigarette manufacturers during a recent year:

Manufacturer	Market Share (in %)
Philip Morris	37.89
Reynolds	32.61
Brown & Williamson	10.83
Lorillard	8.22
American	6.87
Liggett	3.58
Total	100.00

(a) Construct a bar chart.
(b) Construct a pie chart.
(c) Construct a dot chart.
(d) Which of these charts do you prefer to use here? Why?
➡(e) **ACTION** Describe these sales results in a brief report and suggest some ways American could consider for improving its market share position.

4.101 Dataquest has provided market share estimates for producers of IBM and IBM compatible spreadsheet software based on sales during 1986. Suppose, in validating these figures, your company, an independent consulting firm, develops the following table:

Spreadsheet	Market Share (in %)
Lotus 1-2-3	62.5
Symphony (integrated program)	10.0
Multiplan	9.6
VP Planner	6.7
SuperCalc4	6.4
All others	4.8
Total	100.0

(a) Construct a bar chart.
(b) Construct a pie chart.
(c) Construct a dot chart.
(d) Which of these charts do you prefer to use here? Why?
➡(e) **ACTION** Describe these sales results in a brief report and suggest some ways SuperCalc4 could consider for improving its market share position.

4.102 According to Beverage Digest, sales in the soft drink industry reached $38 billion dollars for the year 1987. Suppose, in validating these findings, your company, an independent consulting firm, develops the table displayed at the top of page 131 representing the market share (in percent) held by the leading brands of soft drinks sold in the United States for that year.
(a) Construct a bar chart.
(b) Construct a pie chart.
(c) Construct a dot chart.
(d) Which of these charts do you prefer to use here? Why?
➡(e) **ACTION** Write a report summarizing the above data and offer suggestions as to how the Royal Crown Cola Company might enhance its market share position.
(f) **(Class Project)** Let each student in the class respond to the question: "Which soft drink do you most prefer?" so that the teacher may tally the results into a summary table on the blackboard.

Soft Drink Brands	Market Share (in %)
Classic Coke	19.8
Pepsi	18.9
Diet Coke	7.8
Diet Pepsi	4.7
Dr. Pepper	4.3
Sprite	3.5
7-Up	3.4
Mountain Dew	2.9
Caffeine-Free Diet Coke	1.8
RC Cola	1.6
Coke	1.5
All others	29.8
Total	100.00

(Note that all these figures are within 0.1% of those reported by *Beverage Digest*).

(1) Convert the data to percentages and construct a bar chart, a pie chart, and a dot chart.

➡(2) **ACTION** Compare and constrast the findings from the class with those obtained nationally based on market shares. What do you conclude? Discuss.

4.103 A report by Wharton Econometric Forecasting Associates, Inc. indicated the total value of all goods and services produced in Long Island (i.e., Nassau and Suffolk Counties in New York) by each sector of the economy in the year 1987. The total was 17.3 billions of dollars. Suppose, in validating these findings, your company, an independent consulting firm, develops the following table:

Economic Sector	Percent of Long Island GNP in 1987
Agriculture	0.8
Construction	4.6
Finance, Insurance, R.E.	19.8
Government	5.7
Manufacturing	20.2
Services	21.7
Transportation & Utilities	8.3
Wholesale & Retail Trade	18.8
Total	99.9*

* Due to rounding.

(a) Construct a bar chart.
(b) Construct a pie chart.
(c) Construct a dot chart.
(d) Which of these charts do you prefer to use here? Why?
➡(e) **ACTION** Describe these results in a brief report to your supervisor.

4.104 The U.S. Department of Energy has reported the following information concerning the market share (in percent) of crude oil production held by countries in the years 1976 and 1986. (See page 132.)

	Percent Market Share	
Country	1976	1986
OPEC:		
Saudi Arabia	15.0	8.8
Iran	8.7	2.7
Iraq	4.0	3.0
Other OPEC	26.3	17.5
Britain	0.5	4.7
Canada	2.3	2.8
China	2.9	4.7
Mexico	1.4	4.7
Norway	0.5	1.7
U.S.	14.0	16.0
U.S.S.R.	17.0	21.0
Others	7.4	12.4
Totals	100.0	100.0

    (a) Construct bar charts for each year.
    (b) Construct pie charts for each year.
    (c) Construct dot charts for each year.
    (d) Which of these charts do you prefer to use here? Why?
➠**(e)** **ACTION**   Write a report describing the changing patterns in crude oil production over the ten-year period. Can you list any worldwide events since 1970 that may have contributed to these changes?

4.105   The U.S. Commerce Department reported the following information for the year 1986 regarding imports and exports:

	Exports from U.S.		Imports into U.S.	
Country	Billions $	%	Billions $	%
Britain	11.4	5.3	16.0	4.1
Canada	45.3	20.9	68.7	17.7
France	7.2	3.3	10.5	2.7
Italy	4.8	2.2	11.3	2.9
Japan	26.9	12.4	85.5	22.1
Mexico	12.4	5.7	17.6	4.5
Netherlands	7.8	3.6	4.3	1.1
South Korea	6.4	2.9	13.5	3.5
Taiwan	5.5	2.5	21.3	5.5
West Germany	10.6	4.9	26.1	6.7
Others	79.0	36.3	112.3	29.0
Totals	217.3	100.0	387.1	99.8*

* Due to rounding.

Using the percentages
    (a) Construct separate bar charts for imports and exports.
    (b) Construct separate pie charts for imports and exports.
    (c) Construct separate dot charts for imports and exports.
    (d) Which of these charts do you prefer to use here? Why?
➠**(e)** **ACTION**   Analyze the data and write a memo to your economics professor based on your findings.

4.10 GRAPHING QUALITATIVE DATA: THE PARETO DIAGRAM

The **Pareto diagram** is a special type of histogram or vertical bar chart in which the categorical responses are plotted in the descending rank order of their frequencies and combined with a cumulative polygon on the same scale. The main principle behind this graphical device is its ability to flag the "vital few" from the "trivial many" and thereby permit the researcher to focus on the important responses. Hence the chart achieves its greatest utility when the qualitative variable of interest contains many categories. The Pareto diagram is widely used in the statistical control of process and product quality (see Chapter 19).

To illustrate the Pareto diagram, we may observe that in Figure 4.18 the bar chart pertaining to stock exchange listing presents the categories as NYSE, ASE, and OTC. Since the OTC contains a much higher percentage of these companies than the ASE, a Pareto diagram may be formed by changing the ordering. Such a plot is depicted in Figure 4.21. From the lengths of the vertical bars we observe that approximately three out of every four of these companies in the retailing industry are listed on the NYSE. Moreover, from the cumulative polygon we note that more than 95 percent of these companies are listed on either the NYSE or OTC.

In constructing the Pareto diagram, the vertical axis contains the percentages (from 100 on top to 0 on bottom) and the horizontal axis contains the categories of interest. The bars must be of equal width and, for visual impact (Reference 9), we suggest that the bars be of the same tint. The point on the cumulative percentage polygon for each category is centered at the midpoint of each respective bar. Hence, when studying a Pareto diagram, we should be focusing on two things—the magnitudes of the differences in adjacent descending categories and the cumulative percentages of these adjacent categories.

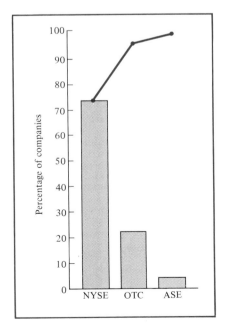

FIGURE 4.21
Pareto diagram depicting stock exchange listing for 45 retailing companies.
SOURCE: Data are taken from Table 4.11 on page 126.

Problems

4.106 Refer to the data in Problem 4.102 on page 130 regarding percent market share attained by soft drink brands.

(a) Form a Pareto diagram.

(b) Which of the graphs seems to give the most visual impact—the Pareto diagram here or one of the charts drawn in parts (a)–(c) of Problem 4.102? Discuss.

4.107 Refer to the data in Problem 4.105 on page 132 regarding imports and exports.

(a) Set up a table based on "balance of trade." That is, for each country, calculate the value of import dollars minus export dollars—yielding either a trade deficit or a trade surplus.

(b) For those countries with which the United States has a trade deficit (i.e., import dollars are more than export dollars), form a Pareto diagram.

(c) Summarize your findings.

➠**(d)** **ACTION** Write a report for your social sciences professor based on your findings in (c). List potential social, political, cultural, and/or economic reasons that may have led to this trade deficit.

4.108 The consulting firm of Holzmacher, McLendon and Murrel reported on daily water consumption per household in the South Farmingdale (New York) Water District during the summer of 1986. The results of their study indicate the following:

Reason for Water Usage	No. Gallons per Day
Bathing and Showering	99
Dishwashing	13
Drinking and Cooking	11
Laundering	33
Lawn Watering	150
Toilet	88
Misc.	20
Total	414

(a) Form a Pareto diagram.

(b) Summarize your findings.

➠**(c)** **ACTION** If the town council were concerned about future water shortages, write a letter based on your findings in (b) pinpointing problem areas and proposing legislation which might conserve water through changes in personal habits.

4.109 In a recent year the U.S. Fire Administration reported on the leading causes of residential fire deaths:

Cause of Death	Percentage
Appliances/Equipment	4.9
Children playing with fire	6.4
Cooking	6.3
Electrical fires	5.0
Heating	12.9
Incendiary	6.7
Open flame/Candles	3.0
Smoking	22.0
Spread from original site	1.1
Unknown origin	31.7
Total	100.0

(a) Form a Pareto diagram.

(b) Summarize your findings.

(c) Reconstruct the above table after removing the "unknown origins" category and form a new Pareto diagram.

(d) Summarize your findings.

➡(e) **ACTION** Write an article for the "daily living" section of your local newspaper based on your findings in (b) and (d) in order to enlighten the readership on this matter.

● **4.110** In a survey conducted by the Computer Intelligence Corp., companies categorized in eleven industrial groupings indicated an interest in purchasing mainframe computers in the coming year. Suppose, in validating their findings, your company, an independent consulting firm, develops the following table indicating the percentage of sampled companies in each industrial grouping interested in such purchases:

Industrial Grouping	*Percent of Companies Interested*
Agriculture/Mining/Construction	2
Banking/Savings & Loan	8
Business services	4
Discrete manufacturing	17
Electrical data processing services	7
Finance/Insurance	9
Government	11
Medical/Education	14
Process manufacturing	11
Transportation/Utilities	7
Wholesale/Retail	10
Total	100

(a) Form a Pareto diagram.

(b) Summarize your findings.

(c) What must be assumed about the sizes of these industrial groupings in order for your findings in (b) to be useful?

➡(d) **ACTION** Suppose you were a stockholder at IBM, which controls 92 percent of the mainframe computer market. Write a letter to the public relations officer of IBM suggesting areas in which the company should concentrate its advertising and promotional activities based on your findings in (b) and response in (c).

4.111 J. D. Power & Associates surveyed more than 25,000 owners of '87 model cars registered in November and December 1986 to determine the numbers and types of problems buyers encountered during the first few months. An analysis of their New Car Initial Quality Study was given in *Motor Trend* in its September 1987 issue (see page 38). Suppose, in validating these findings, your company, an independent consulting firm, conducts a similar study and provides the table displayed at the top of page 136 for the automobile industry as a whole as well as a breakdown of domestic versus Japanese automobiles.

(a) Form a Pareto diagram for each. [*Hint*: Recompute the percentages for each by dividing the given percentage values by the total of the percentages taken over all the types of problems for a particular group.]

(b) Analyze the data for the industry as a whole.

(c) Compare and contrast initial car performance of domestic versus Japanese automobiles.

➡(d) **ACTION** Write an article for the consumers page of your local newspaper based on your findings in (b) and (c) in order to enlighten future car purchasers on this matter.

Type of Problem	Percentage of Cars with Problems		
	Industry	Domestic	Japanese
Body	13	14	11
Brakes	7	5	8
Electrical/accessories	21	23	16
Engine	17	19	11
Exterior paint/moldings	14	16	12
Interior	14	16	11
Squeaks/rattles	15	15	14
Steering/handling	5	5	4
Temperature control	6	5	5
Transmission	7	7	7
Water leaks	5	7	3
Wind noise	10	11	9

4.11 TABULARIZING QUALITATIVE DATA: CROSS-CLASSIFICATION TABLES AND SUPERTABLES

4.11.1 The Cross-Classification Table

It is often desirable to examine the categorical responses to two qualitative variables simultaneously. For example, the financial analyst might be interested in examining whether or not there is any "pattern" or relationship between the dividend record of a retailing company and the stock exchange on which it is traded. Table 4.12 depicts this information for all 45 companies in the industry. Such two-way tables of cross classification are also known as **contingency tables** and will be studied once again in Chapters 6 and 13.

TABLE 4.12 Cross-classification table of dividend policy and stock exchange listing for 45 retailing companies

Dividend Declaration	Stock Exchange Listing			Totals
	NYSE	ASE	OTC	
Yes	32	1	5	38
No	1	1	5	7
Totals	33	2	10	45

To construct Table 4.12, for example, the joint responses for each of the 45 companies with respect to dividend declaration and stock exchange are tallied into one of the six possible "cells" of the table. Thus from Figure 4.1 (on page 106), the first company (Ames Department Stores) declares a dividend and is traded on the New York Stock Exchange. These responses were tallied into the cell composed of the first row and first column. The second company (Businessland) does not declare a dividend and is traded on the over-the-counter list. These responses were tallied into the cell composed of the second row and third column. The remaining 43 joint responses were recorded in a similar manner.

In order to explore any possible pattern or relationship between dividend policy and stock exchange listing, it is useful to first convert these results into percentages based on

1. The overall total (i.e., 45 companies in the retailing industry).
2. The row totals (i.e., yes or no).
3. The column totals (i.e., NYSE, ASE, or OTC).

This is accomplished in Tables 4.13, 4.14, and 4.15, respectively.

We will highlight some of the many findings present in these tables for the companies comprising the retailing industry. From Table 4.13 we note that

1. 84.4% of the companies declare a dividend.
2. 73.3% of the companies trade on the New York Stock Exchange.
3. 71.1% of the companies declare a dividend and trade on the New York Stock Exchange.

From Table 4.14 we note that

1. 84.2% of those companies which declare a dividend trade on the New York Stock Exchange.
2. 71.4% of those companies which do not declare a dividend trade on the over-the-counter list.

TABLE 4.13 Cross-classification table of dividend policy and stock exchange listing (percentages based on overall total—45 companies)

| | Stock Exchange Listing | | | |
Dividend Declaration	NYSE	ASE	OTC	Totals
Yes	71.1	2.2	11.1	84.4
No	2.2	2.2	11.1	15.5
Totals	73.3	4.4	22.2	99.9*

* Error due to rounding.

TABLE 4.14 Cross-classification table of dividend policy and stock exchange listing for 45 retailing companies (percentages based on row totals)

| | Stock Exchange Listing | | | |
Dividend Declaration	NYSE	ASE	OTC	Totals
Yes	84.2	2.6	13.2	100.0
No	14.3	14.3	71.4	100.0
Totals	73.3	4.4	22.2	99.9*

* Errors due to rounding.

From Table 4.15 on page 138 we note that

1. 97.0% of the companies that trade on the New York Stock Exchange declare dividends.
2. 50.0% of the companies that trade on either the American Stock Exchange or the over-the-counter list declare dividends.

The tables, therefore, indicate a pattern; companies in the retailing industry are likely to trade on the New York Stock Exchange and declare dividends.

TABLE 4.15 Cross-classification table of dividend policy and stock exchange listing for 45 retailing companies (percentages based on column totals)

| | Stock Exchange Listing | | | |
Dividend Declaration	NYSE	ASE	OTC	Totals
Yes	97.0	50.0	50.0	84.4
No	3.0	50.0	50.0	15.6
Totals	100.0	100.0	100.0	100.0

4.11.2 The Supertable

A recently developed technique for presenting qualitative data is the supertable (see Reference 9). A **supertable** is essentially a collection of cross-classification tables for the same column variable and categories. However, as many row variables as desired are included for comparison against the column variable. The data in each cell of the table are always given as a percentage of its corresponding row total. This permits line-by-line comparisons for the categories *within* a particular row variable as well as for the categories *among* the various row variables.

Table 4.16 presents a supertable which investigates possible relationships between a variety of financial performance variables and the stock exchange listing for the 45 companies in the retailing industry.

Note the similarity between the top part of Table 4.16 and the cross-classification table presented as Table 4.14.

TABLE 4.16 A supertable for studying possible relationships between market performance and stock exchange listing for 45 retailing companies

| Variables and Category Percentages | Stock Exchange Listing | | |
	NYSE	ASE	OTC
Dividend Declaration:			
Yes (84%)	84.2%	2.6%	13.2%
No (16%)	14.3%	14.3%	71.4%
Annual earnings per share:			
Above $2 (29%)	84.6%	7.7%	7.7%
At or Below $2 (71%)	68.8%	3.1%	28.1%
Change in profits over past year:			
Up (67%)	73.3%	6.7%	20.0%
Unchanged (7%)	33.3%	0.0%	66.7%
Down (27%)	83.3%	0.0%	16.7%
Current price to earnings ratio:			
Above 20 (49%)	77.3%	0.0%	22.7%
At or Below 20 (51%)	69.6%	8.7%	21.7%

Problems

4.112 Researchers were looking at the relationship between the type of college which was attended and the level of job which people who graduated in 1960 held at the time of the study. The researchers examined only graduates who went into industry. The cross-tabulation of the data is presented below:

Management Level	Type of College		
	Ivy League	Other Private	Public
High (Sr. V-P or above)	45	62	75
Middle	231	563	962
Low	254	341	732

(a) Construct a table with either row or column percentages, depending on which you think is more informative.

(b) Interpret the results of the study.

(c) What other variable or variables might you want to know before advising someone to attend an Ivy League or other private school if he or she wants to get to the top in business?

4.113 People returning from vacations in different countries were asked how they enjoyed their vacation. Their responses are as follows

Country	Response to Country			
	Yuck	So-So	Good	Great
England	5	32	65	45
Italy	3	12	32	43
France	8	23	28	25
Guatemala	9	12	6	2

(a) Construct a table of row proportions.

(b) What would you conclude from this study?

4.114 One of the earliest supertables developed by Tufte (Reference 9) appeared in the *New York Times* following the 1980 presidential election. A similar table based on that election appears on page 140. There are numerous deficiencies throughout this table.

(a) Examine each row variable and point out any deficiencies with respect to
   (1) headings or labels
   (2) possibly missing categories
   (3) incorrect percentages
   (4) possible recording errors

(b) Discuss the importance of proper data presentation.

4.115 Develop (in outline form) a supertable corresponding to cigarette smoking based on gender, age group, occupation level, and education level.

Supertable portraying the electorate (based on 12,752 interviews with voters at their polling places)

	Carter	Reagan	Anderson
Party affiliation			
Democrats (43%)	66	26	6
Independents (23%)	30	54	12
Republicans (28%)	11	84	4
Race			
Blacks (10%)	82	14	3
Hispanics (2%)	54	36	7
Whites (88%)	36	55	8
Religion			
Catholic (25%)	40	51	7
Jewish (5%)	45	39	14
Protestant (46%)	37	56	6
Born-again white Protestant (17%)	34	61	4
Female (49%)	45	46	7
Male (51%)	37	54	7
Region of residence			
East (32%)	43	47	8
South (27%)	44	51	3
Midwest (20%)	41	51	6
West (11%)	35	52	10
Family income			
Less than $10,000 (13%)	50	41	6
$10,000–$14,999 (14%)	47	42	8
$15,000–$24,999 (30%)	38	53	7
$25,000–$50,000 (24%)	32	58	8
Over $50,000 (5%)	25	65	8
Occupation			
Professional or manager (40%)	33	56	9
Clerical, sales or other white-collar (11%)	42	48	8
Blue-collar worker (17%)	46	47	5
Agriculture (3%)	29	66	3
Looking for work (3%)	55	35	7
Labor union involvement			
Labor union household (26%)	47	44	7
No member of household in union (62%)	35	55	8
More important problem			
Unemployment (39%)	51	40	7
Inflation (44%)	30	60	9

4.12 DATA PRESENTATION: AN OVERVIEW

Data presentation is an essential element of any large-scale statistical investigation. In this chapter we have become familiar with a variety of techniques for tabularizing and charting both quantitative and qualitative data. As we shall see in Chapter 5, the rapid developments in computer technology over the past decade have resulted in major advances in computer graphics capabilities, and tables and charts of high quality are now obtainable from a variety of computer software.

Supplementary Problems

4.116 Explain the differences between frequency distributions, relative frequency distributions, and percentage distributions.

4.117 When comparing two or more sets of data with different sample sizes, why is it necessary to compare their respective relative frequency or percentage distributions?

4.118 The raw data displayed below are the starting salaries for a random sample of 100 computer science or computer systems majors who earned their baccalaureate degrees during the year 1988:

Starting Salaries ($000)

24.2	29.9	23.4	23.0	25.5	22.0	33.9	20.4	26.6	24.0
28.9	22.5	18.7	32.6	26.1	26.2	26.7	20.4	22.2	24.7
18.6	18.5	19.6	24.4	24.8	27.8	27.6	27.2	20.8	22.1
19.7	25.3	28.2	34.2	32.5	30.8	26.8	20.6	21.2	20.7
25.2	25.7	32.2	28.8	24.7	18.7	20.5	25.5	19.1	25.5
22.1	27.5	25.8	25.2	25.6	25.2	25.2	27.9	18.9	37.3
29.9	23.2	19.8	20.8	29.5	27.6	21.2	38.7	21.3	24.8
32.3	20.1	26.8	25.4	26.3	21.2	19.5	22.8	21.7	25.3
32.3	28.1	27.5	25.3	19.3	27.4	26.4	20.9	34.5	25.9
31.4	27.4	27.3	20.6	31.8	25.8	25.2	21.9	26.8	26.5

   (a) Place the raw data in a stem-and-leaf display. [*Hint*: Let the leaves be the tenths digits.]
   (b) Place the raw data in an ordered array.
   (c) Form the frequency distribution and percentage distribution.
   (d) Plot the frequency histogram.
   (e) Plot the percentage polygon.
   (f) Form the cumulative percentage distribution.
   (g) Plot the ogive (cumulative percentage polygon).
➠(h) **ACTION**   Write a brief report to your computer professor.

4.119 Refer to Problem 4.118 and use the frequency distribution and ogive constructed in parts (c) and (g).
   (a) Approximate
      (1) the mean   (5) the range
      (2) the median   (6) the interquartile range
      (3) the mode   (7) the standard deviation
      (4) Q_1 and Q_3 (8) the coefficient of variation
   (b) Approximate the midrange and midhinge. Determine the shape of the data. Discuss.
   (c) Based on the Bienaymé-Chebyshev rule, between what two values would we estimate that at least 75% of the data are contained?
   (d) What percentage of the data are actually contained within ± 2 standard deviations of the mean? Compare the results with those from (c).
➠(e) **ACTION**   Summarize your findings here and in Problem 4.118(h) in a letter to a friend at another college who is majoring in computer systems.

Note: Problems pertaining to the real estate survey of Chapter 2 which deal with the material covered in this chapter will be presented in Chapter 5.

4.120   Refer to Problem 3.83 on page 82 regarding cost and sodium concentration of salted peanut butter brands.

    (a) Using the cost data for the 38 sampled brands
        (1) Form the frequency and percentage distributions in the same table.
        (2) Plot the percentage polygon.
        (3) Form the cumulative percentage distribution.
        (4) Plot the percentage ogive.
        (5) Approximate

• the mean	• the range
• the median	• the interquartile range
• the mode	• the variance
• the midrange	• the standard deviation
• the midhinge	• the coefficient of variation

        (6) Compare and contrast your approximations with the actual results computed from the ungrouped data in Problem 3.83(a).

    (b) Using the sodium data for the 38 sampled brands, repeat (a)(1) to (a)(6).

    ➠**(c) ACTION**   Based on (a) and (b) above, what enhancements to your newspaper article [Problem 3.83(c)] would you include? Discuss.

• 4.121   Given the batches of data below based on closing stock price for random samples of 25 issues traded on the American Exchange and 50 issues traded on the New York Exchange

American Exchange (25 issues)	New York Exchange (50 issues)	
$ 6.88	$36.50	$26.00
.75	23.50	19.00
3.88	8.25	46.00
4.12	57.50	23.50
11.88	27.12	22.62
15.88	3.75	12.88
16.50	25.00	5.50
8.75	15.50	37.50
9.25	36.12	9.88
7.50	6.00	59.12
5.38	9.12	35.25
14.38	33.38	20.62
2.50	22.50	24.00
4.88	8.75	80.50
6.38	8.62	29.38
33.62	5.75	3.75
4.88	21.88	64.75
9.00	6.12	14.25
2.00	25.00	46.38
20.00	15.88	4.75
14.25	24.00	25.00
4.00	10.88	35.00
15.25	18.75	9.00
2.38	53.88	12.38
49.50	20.38	31.00

    (a) Using interval widths of $10, form the frequency distribution and percentage distribution for each batch.

    (b) Plot the frequency histogram for each batch.

    (c) On one graph, plot the percentage polygon for each batch.

      (d) Form the cumulative percentage distribution for each batch.

      (e) On one graph, plot the ogive (cumulative percentage polygon) for each batch.

      ➠**(f)** **ACTION** Write a brief report comparing and contrasting the two batches.

• 4.122 Refer to Problem 4.121 and use the frequency distributions and ogives constructed in parts (a) and (e).

      (a) Approximate for each

(1) the mean	(6) the range
(2) the median	(7) the interquartile range
(3) the mode	(8) the variance
(4) the midrange	(9) the standard deviation
(5) the midhinge	(10) the coefficient of variation

      ➠**(b)** **ACTION** Compare and contrast the two sets of results and summarize your findings here and in Problem 4.121(f). Write a report for your economics professor.

4.123 Refer to Problem 3.88 on page 88 regarding baseball batting averages and home runs hit by all players in the American and National Leagues with at least 350 batting appearances.

      (a) Using the batting average data separately for the two groups

          (1) Form the frequency and percentage distributions in the same table for the American League players.

          (2) Repeat (1) for the National League players.

          (3) Plot the percentage polygons on the same graph.

          (4) Form the cumulative percentage distribution for the American League players.

          (5) Repeat (4) for the National League players.

          (6) Plot the percentage ogives on the same graph.

          (7) Approximate for each data batch

• the mean	• the range
• the median	• the interquartile range
• the mode	• the variance
• the midrange	• the standard deviation
• the midhinge	• the coefficient of variation

          (8) Compare and contrast your approximations with the actual results computed from the ungrouped data in Problem 3.88(a).

      (b) Using the home run data separately for the two groups, repeat (a)(1) to (a)(7) and then compare and contrast your approximations with the actual results computed from the ungrouped data in Problem 3.88(b).

      ➠**(c)** **ACTION** Suppose you were a sportscaster for a local television station. Based on (a) and (b) above as well as your report in Problem 3.88(c), how would you communicate a summary of your findings to the television audience?

4.124 Refer to Problem 3.89 on page 89 regarding receptions, yardage, average yardage, touchdowns, and percentage of receptions for touchdowns by all 32 NFC players and all 39 AFC players who caught at least 40 passes during the season.

      (a) Enhance your *exploratory data analysis* in Problem 3.89(a) by constructing appropriate tables and charts and by computing appropriate summary approximations.

      ➠**(b)** **ACTION** A caller to the local radio show asked the sportscasters if running backs are comparable to other receivers (i.e., split ends, wide receivers, tight ends) with respect to overall performance-productivity (i.e., percentage of touchdown receptions made out of total receptions). How would you respond?

4.125 A wholesale appliance distributing firm wished to study its accounts receivable for two successive months. Two independent samples of 50 accounts were selected for each of the two months. The results have been summarized in the table displayed at the top of page 144:

Frequency distributions for accounts receivable

Amount	March Frequency	April Frequency
$ 0– under $2,000	6	10
$ 2,000– under $4,000	13	14
$ 4,000– under $6,000	17	13
$ 6,000– under $8,000	10	10
$ 8,000– under $10,000	4	0
$10,000– under $12,000	0	3
Totals	50	50

(a) Plot the frequency histogram for each month.
(b) On one graph, plot the percentage polygon for each month.
(c) Form the cumulative percentage distribution for each month.
(d) On one graph, plot the ogive (cumulative percentage polygon) for each month.
➠(e) **ACTION**   Write a brief report comparing and contrasting the accounts receivable of the two months.

4.126   Refer to Problem 4.125 and use the frequency distributions of ''accounts receivable in two consecutive months.''
(a) Approximate for each

    (1) the mean   (6) the range
    (2) the median   (7) the interquartile range
    (3) the mode   (8) the variance
    (4) the midrange   (9) the standard deviation
    (5) the midhinge   (10) the coefficient of variation

➠(b) **ACTION**   Compare and contrast the two sets of results and summarize your findings here and in Problem 4.125(e). Write a memo to the firm's vice-president of finance on this matter.

4.127   A home-heating-oil delivery firm wished to compare how fast the oil bills were paid in two adjacent Westchester County (New York) communities. A random sample of 50 vouchers from Bronxville and 100 vouchers from Mt. Vernon were selected, and the number of days between delivery and payment were recorded as shown in the following table:

Frequency distributions of payment records for home-heating-oil bills in two communities

Number of Days	Bronxville Frequency	Mt. Vernon Frequency
0–4	4	6
5–9	14	21
10–14	16	24
15–19	10	30
20–24	5	7
25–29	1	6
30–34	0	6
Totals	50	100

(a) Plot the percentage histogram for each community.
(b) On one graph, plot the percentage polygon for each community.
(c) Form the cumulative percentage distribution for each community.
(d) On one graph, plot the ogive (cumulative percentage polygon) for each community.
➠(e) **ACTION**   Write a brief report comparing and contrasting the number of days between delivery and payment in the two communities.

4.128 Refer to Problem 4.127 and use the frequency distributions of "payment records of home-heating-oil bills in two communities."

    (a) Approximate for each

(1) the mean	(6) the range
(2) the median	(7) the interquartile range
(3) the mode	(8) the variance
(4) the midrange	(9) the standard deviation
(5) the midhinge	(10) the coefficient of variation

    ➡**(b)** **ACTION** Compare and contrast the two sets of results and summarize your findings here and in Problem 4.127(e). Write a memo to the firm's vice-president of finance on this matter.

    ➡**(c)** **ACTION** If it is the firm's policy to flag all bills more than one month due and to initiate promotional strategies in any region where at least 10% of the bills are more than one month due, what additional statement(s) should be appended to the memo in (b)?

4.129 Wisconsin Power & Light was interested in improving the efficiency of gas home-heating systems and you are hired to participate in the investigation of this problem. To obtain a better understanding of the problem, you decide to survey current energy consumption in single-family homes.

    The following frequency distribution represents the average energy consumption (in BTUs) per single-family home over a two-week period for a random sample of 90 homes throughout the state of Wisconsin:

Energy Consumption (BTUs)	No. Homes
2.4 but less than 4.8	2
4.8 but less than 7.2	6
7.2 but less than 9.6	25
9.6 but less than 12.0	29
12.0 but less than 14.4	16
14.4 but less than 16.8	8
16.8 but less than 19.2	3
19.2 but less than 21.6	1
Total	90

    (a) Completely analyze the data.

    ➡**(b)** **ACTION** Write a preliminary report for the chief executive officer.

4.130 You are employed as a quality-control engineer at Chrysler Corporation and, in an effort to improve the quality of your company's products, you wish to compare various design features of U.S. and foreign-made automobile models.

    The table on page 146 contains the cumulative distributions and cumulative percentage distributions of steering turn revolutions (lock-to-lock) for a sample of 45 U.S. manufactured compact/small car automobile models and for a sample of 92 foreign-made compact/small car automobile models. Based on these data, answer the following questions:

    (a) How many models of U.S.-made automobiles have 4.5 or more revolutions?

    (b) What is the percentage of U.S.-made automobiles with less than 3.5 revolutions?

    (c) Which group of car models—U.S. made or foreign made—have the wider range in steering turn revolutions?

    (d) How many foreign-made automobile models have steering turn revolutions between 3.50 and 3.99 (inclusive)?

    (e) Use the cumulative distributions to construct the frequency distributions and percentage distributions for each group of car models.

    (f) On one graph, plot the two percentage ogives.

⟳(g) **ACTION** Write a brief report comparing and contrasting the steering turn revolutions information for the two groups of car models.

Cumulative frequency and percentage distributions for the number of steering turn revolutions for U.S.-manufactured and foreign-made compact/small car automobile models

Steering Turn Revolutions	U.S.-Made Automobile Models "Less Than" Indicated Values		Foreign-Made Automobile Models "Less Than" Indicated Values	
	Number	Percentage	Number	Percentage
2.0	0	0.0	0	0.0
2.5	1	2.2	3	3.3
3.0	5	11.1	15	16.3
3.5	16	35.6	44	47.8
4.0	33	73.3	85	92.4
4.5	43	95.6	91	98.9
5.0	44	97.8	92	100.0
5.5	44	97.8	92	100.0
6.0	44	97.8	92	100.0
6.5	45	100.0	92	100.0

SOURCE: Data are extracted from *Road & Track*, vol. 34, no. 7 (March 1983), pp. 70–73.

4.131 Refer to Problem 4.130 and use the frequency distributions and ogives of "steering turn revolutions" that were constructed in parts (e) and (f).
    (a) Approximate for each distribution
        (1) the mean   (6) the range
        (2) the median   (7) the interquartile range
        (3) the mode   (8) the variance
        (4) the midrange   (9) the standard deviation
        (5) the midhinge   (10) the coefficient of variation
  ⟳**(b)** **ACTION** Compare and contrast the two sets of results and summarize your findings here and in Problem 4.130(g). Write a memo to your supervisor regarding this matter.

4.132 The table on page 147 contains the cumulative frequency distributions and cumulative percentage distributions of average annual salaries (excluding fringe benefits) earned by full professors at the institutions of higher learning in California and Massachusetts in a recent year. Based on these data, answer the following questions:
    (a) How many institutions in California have average annual salaries for full professors of $40,000 or more?
    (b) What is the percentage of institutions in California with average annual salaries for full professors less than $30,000?
    (c) Which state has a larger range in average salaries?
    (d) How many institutions in Massachusetts have average annual salaries for full professors of at least $35,000 but less than $40,000?
    (e) Does California or Massachusetts have more institutions with average annual salaries less than $30,000?

(f) Does California or Massachusetts have a greater percentage of institutions with average annual salaries less than $30,000?

(g) Use the cumulative distributions to construct the frequency distributions and percentage distributions for each state.

(h) On one graph, plot the two percentage ogives.

➡(i) **ACTION** Write a brief report comparing and contrasting the salary information for the two states.

Cumulative distributions and cumulative percentage distributions comparing average annual salaries earned by full professors at the institutions of higher learning in California and Massachusetts

Average Salary (in $000)	California Institutions "Less Than" Indicated Value		Massachusetts Institutions "Less Than" Indicated Value	
	Number	Percentage	Number	Percentage
15	0	0.0	0	0.0
20	0	0.0	1	2.2
25	2	3.1	1	2.2
30	7	10.9	8	17.8
35	15	23.4	21	46.7
40	21	32.8	24	53.3
45	47	73.4	33	73.3
50	50	78.1	42	93.3
55	58	90.6	43	95.5
60	61	95.3	45	100.0
65	64	100.0	45	100.0

SOURCE: Data are taken from "The Annual Report on the Economic Status of the Profession: 1986–1987," *Academe—Bulletin of the AAUP*, vol. 73, no. 2 (March–April 1987).

4.133 Refer to Problem 4.132 and use the frequency distributions and ogives that were constructed in parts (g) and (h).

(a) Approximate for each distribution

(1) the mean   (6) the range

(2) the median   (7) the interquartile range

(3) the mode   (8) the variance

(4) the midrange   (9) the standard deviation

(5) the midhinge   (10) the coefficient of variation

➡(b) **ACTION** Compare and contrast the two sets of results and summarize your findings here and in Problem 4.132(i). Write a letter to your sister, a doctoral student in economics who has expressed interest in a teaching career either in the northeast or in California, discussing this matter. Be sure to include in your letter a discussion of other variables that need to be considered for this eventual decision.

4.134 You are employed as an analyst for a major building developer who is interested in constructing a shopping mall in either Centerport or Northport—two adjacent communities on the north shore of Long Island in Suffolk County, New York.

The figure on page 148 contains the cumulative relative frequency polygons (ogives) of family incomes for two random samples of 200 families each drawn from the two communities. Based on these data, answer each of the following questions:

Cumulative relative frequency polygons of family incomes for two communities.

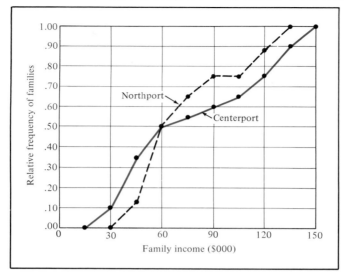

(a) How many of the families in Centerport have incomes of $120,000 or more?
(b) What is the percentage of families in Centerport with incomes of less than $90,000?
(c) Which sample has a larger range of incomes?
(d) How many of the families in Northport have an income of at least $90,000 but less than $105,000?
(e) Does Centerport or Northport have more family incomes of $60,000 or above?
(f) What percentage of Centerport families earn less than $60,000?
(g) What percentage of Centerport families earn $60,000 or more?
(h) Which community has more incomes below $120,000?
(i) Use the ogives to construct the relative frequency distribution and frequency distribution for each community.
(j) On one graph plot the two relative frequency polygons.
⇒(k) **ACTION** Write a brief report comparing and contrasting your two income distributions.

4.135 Refer to Problem 4.134 and use the frequency distributions of family income in Centerport and Northport that were constructed in (i).
(a) Approximate for each

(1) the mean	(6) the range
(2) the median	(7) the interquartile range
(3) the mode	(8) the variance
(4) the midrange	(9) the standard deviation
(5) the midhinge	(10) the coefficient of variation

⇒(b) **ACTION** Compare and contrast the two sets of results and summarize your findings here and in Problem 4.134(k). Write a memo to the firm's vice-president of finance regarding this matter.

4.136 You are working for an independent consulting agency hired by a well-known realty company specializing in sales of homes in the Pocono Mountains in northeast Pennsylvania. Your task is to evaluate mortgage rates held by homeowners in two popular communities.
The figure on page 149 contains the percentage ogives of mortgages held by 100 homeowners sampled in Penn Estates and 200 homeowners sampled in Hemlock Farms—two Pocono communities. Based on these data, answer each of the following questions:

Percentage ogives of mortgage rates for 100 homeowners in Penn Estates and 200 homeowners in Hemlock Farms.

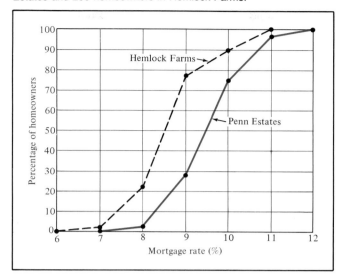

(a) What is the range in mortgage rates held by the Penn Estates homeowners?

(b) What is the range in mortgage rates held by the Hemlock Farms homeowners?

(c) Fifty percent of the Penn Estates homeowners held mortgages with rates of less than what amount?

(d) Fifty percent of the Hemlock Farms homeowners held mortgages with rates of less than what amount?

(e) What percentage of the Penn Estates homeowners held mortgages with rates of at least 9 but less than 10%?

(f) What percentage of the Hemlock Farms homeowners held mortgages with rates of less than 10%?

(g) How many of the Penn Estates homeowners held mortgages with rates of 11% or more?

(h) Which community contains the largest percentage of homeowners who held mortgages with rates below 8.5%?

(i) Use the ogives to construct the percentage distribution and the frequency distribution for each of the samples.

(j) Plot the two percentage polygons on one graph.

➠**(k)** **ACTION**   Write a brief report comparing and contrasting your two distributions. What seems to be apparent about the mortgage rates in these two communities? What reason(s) may be attributed to this? *Hint:* One of these communities has been steadily growing for 20 years; the other has been rapidly growing for 10 years.

4.137 Refer to Problem 4.136, and use the frequency distributions of ''mortgages held by homeowners in two communities'' that were constructed in (i).

(a) Approximate for each

(1) the mean	(6) the range
(2) the median	(7) the interquartile range
(3) the mode	(8) the variance
(4) the midrange	(9) the standard deviation
(5) the midhinge	(10) the coefficient of variation

➠**(b)** **ACTION**   Compare and contrast the two sets of results and summarize your findings here and in Problem 4.136(k). Write a memo to your supervisor regarding this matter.

• **4.138** Gross sales receipts (in thousands of dollars) are recorded daily for Ethel's, a dress boutique in New York City, over the 29-day period February 1–February 29, 1988:

	Monday	Tuesday	Wednesday	Thursday	Friday	Saturday	Sunday
Wk 1:	3.3	3.7	3.0	3.5	3.4	5.7	5.0
Wk 2:	3.9	3.8	3.6	3.9	5.6	6.8	3.9
Wk 3:	7.2	4.3	3.8	4.5	3.2	6.6	5.1
Wk 4:	3.1	3.3	3.2	4.2	3.7	6.2	5.4
Wk 5:	4.0						

(Note that federal and state holidays are boxed)

(a) Analyze the data. Describe anything unusual.

(b) Does there appear to be any pattern in gross sales receipts over time?

4.139 **(Student Project)** Choose a stock listed on the NYSE and, starting on a Monday, record its daily closing price for a full four-week (i.e., 20-day) period in which the stock market is open. Also record the changes in closing price from the previous trading session over this four-week period.

(a) Analyze each batch of data.

(b) Does there seem to be a pattern in the closing prices of the stock over this time period?

(c) Does there seem to be a pattern in the changes in closing prices over time?

➡(d) **ACTION** Write a memo to your economics professor based on your findings in (b) and (c).

4.140 Explain the differences between histograms, polygons, and ogives (cumulative polygons).

4.141 Explain the differences between histograms and bar charts.

4.142 Explain the differences between bar charts, pie charts, dot charts, and Pareto diagrams.

4.143 Explain the differences between ogives and Pareto diagrams.

4.144 Explain the differences between stem-and-leaf displays and digidot plots.

4.145 Based on sales during a recent year, the following data represent the market shares (in percent) held by the leading types of nonprescription pain relievers sold in the United States:

Pain Reliever	Market Share (in %)
Tylenol	30
Anacin	15
Aspirin	10
Bufferin	8
Excedrin	8
All others	29
Totals	100

(a) Construct a bar chart.

(b) Construct a pie chart.

(c) Construct a dot chart.

(d) Form a Pareto diagram.

(e) Which of these graphs do you prefer to use here? Why?

(f) **(Class Project)** Let each student in the class respond to the question: "Which pain reliever do you most prefer?" so that the teacher may tally the results into a summary table on the blackboard.

   (1) Convert the data to percentages and construct an appropriate graph.

  ➡(2) **ACTION** Compare and contrast the findings from the class with those obtained nationally based on market shares. What do you conclude? How may a particular company take advantage of your findings (assuming, of course, that the results from your class prove to be representative of those from college audiences in general)?

4.146 According to Legg-Mason-Wood-Walker Inc., annual revenues in the overnight mail delivery business exceed $6 billion dollars. Suppose, in validating their findings, your company, an independent consulting firm, develops the following table representing the market shares (in percent) held by overnight mail deliverers (of packages weighing 70 pounds or less) during the year 1986:

Deliverer	Market Share (in %)
Federal Express	52.8
United Parcel Service	13.2
U.S. Postal Service	8.0
Purolator Courier	7.4
Airborne Freight	6.6
Emery Air Freight	2.9
DHL Worldwide Express	2.5
All others	6.6
Total	100.0

(a) Construct a bar chart.
(b) Construct a pie chart.
(c) Construct a dot chart.
(d) Form a Pareto diagram.
(e) Which of these graphs do you prefer to use here? Why?
(f) Analyze the data.
➠(g) **ACTION** Based on your findings in (f) write an article for the "daily living" column of your local newspaper in order to enlighten the readership on this matter.

4.147 In college-textbook production it becomes very costly to make changes beyond intermediate stages in the process and authors are asked to judiciously scrutinize their manuscripts in the earlier stages in order to avoid major alterations. Suppose you are hired to assist the production editor at Prentice Hall in monitoring problems in the production process so that company policy on this matter can be enhanced. A sample of ten "quantitative type" texts reveals the following information regarding the type and number of manuscript corrections on a per-chapter basis at the galley proof stage (which comes between the initial submission and editing of the manuscript and the setting of the actual book pages).

Type of Corrections	Number of Corrections	Percentage of Corrections
Author's alterations	15	20.8
Grammar, punctuation, and spelling changes	25	34.7
Spacing corrections	3	4.2
Wrong position of words, tables, and figures	6	8.3
Wrong style of type	17	23.6
Other corrections	6	8.3
Totals	72	99.9*

* Error in rounding.

It should be noted that except for author's alterations, all other corrections are the result of errors made by the editor and compositor in the typesetting process.

(a) Form the appropriate graph to pinpoint the ''vital few'' from the ''trivial many.''

➡(b) **ACTION** Analyze the data and write a memo to the production editor pinpointing editorial problems.

4.148 Environmental conservation is a national issue of major importance. It has been said that Americans threw out 227.1 million tons of garbage last year, enough to fill one of the World Trade Center's Twin Towers from bottom to top every day. Typically, disposal of garbage is achieved through landfills (87 percent), incineration (7 percent), and recycling (5 percent).

Suppose that the consulting firm at which you are employed provides the following table showing the percentage breakdown of the sources of waste:

Source	Percentage
Paper and paperboard	37.1
Yard waste	17.9
Glass	9.7
Metals	9.6
Food waste	8.1
Plastics	7.2
Wood	3.8
Rubber and leather	2.5
Textiles	2.1
All other	2.0
Total	100.0

(a) Form the appropriate graph to pinpoint the ''vital few'' from the ''trivial many.''

(b) Analyze the data and summarize your findings.

➡(c) **ACTION** Write a letter to the Environmental Protection Agency based on your findings and request government information on the potential for recycling for each of the items.

4.149 In March 1987, Harley Davidson Inc., the sole surviving motorcycle manufacturer in the United States, requested the U.S. International Tariff Commission to withdraw tariff protections that were granted in 1983 to save it from bankruptcy because of Japanese competition. The special tariffs had been imposed for a five-year period by President Reagan in April 1983 in order to give the company time to execute planned changes in manufacturing practices and in product improvements. Since Harley's motorcycles are up to 50 percent more expensive than competing Japanese models, the tariffs followed a sliding scale that added 45 percent to the cost of the Japanese imports with large engines during the year 1983, with a decline to 10 percent in the year ending April 1988.

Based on sales during two different years (1986 and 1983), the following data represent market shares (in percent) held by competing manufacturers of large-engine motorcycles (i.e., in excess of 700 cubic centimeters) sold in the United States.

Manufacturer	Percent Market Share	
	1986	1983
Honda	36.9	50.4
Harley	19.4	12.5
Yamaha	16.1	15.2
Suzuki	12.0	8.5
Kawasaki	11.9	11.3
BMW	3.4	1.6
All others	0.3	0.5
Totals	100.0	100.0

(a) For each year construct an appropriate graph and analyze the data.

➡(b) **ACTION**   Based on the above information, if you had been a Harley Davidson stock-holder, would you have supported the company's early request to remove the tariffs? Draft a letter to the chief executive officer expressing your opinions.

4.150   A political poll of 1,500 registered voters in the State of New York yielded the following breakdown for party affiliation and union membership.

Party Affiliation	Union Membership		
	Yes	No	No, Not Employed
Democrat	371	19	208
Independent	263	88	93
Republican	89	222	147

(a) Construct a table of column proportions.

(b) What would you conclude from these results? (Be sure to comment on differences between nonunion individuals based on whether or not they are employed).

(c) What other variables would you want to know regarding employment in order to enhance your findings?

4.151   **(Class Project)**   Let each student in the class be cross-classified based on gender (male, female) and current employment status (yes, no) so that the results are tallied on the blackboard.

(a) Construct a table with either row or column percentages, depending on which you think is more informative.

(b) What would you conclude from this study?

(c) What other variables would you want to know regarding employment in order to enhance your findings?

4.152   Develop (in outline form) a supertable corresponding to job promotion based on gender, race, age group, education level, and occupation level.

4.153   Develop (in outline form) a supertable corresponding to graduate-school intent based on gender, race, age group, employment status, college major, and college grade-point average.

References

1. ARKIN, H., AND R. COLTON, *Statistical Methods*, 5th ed. (New York: Barnes & Noble College Outline Series, 1970).

2. CHAMBERS, J. M., W. S. CLEVELAND, B. KLEINER, AND P. A. TUKEY, *Graphical Methods for Data Analysis* (Boston: Duxbury Press, 1983).

3. CLEVELAND, W. S., "Graphs in Scientific Publications," *The American Statistician*, vol. 38 (November 1984), pp. 261–269.

4. CLEVELAND, W. S., "Graphical Methods for Data Presentation: Full Scale Breaks, Dot Charts, and Multibased Logging," *The American Statistician*, vol. 38 (November 1984), pp. 270–280.

5. CLEVELAND, W. S., AND R. McGILL, "Graphical Perception: Theory, Experimentation, and Application to the Development of Graphical Methods," *Journal of the American Statistical Association*, vol. 79 (September 1984), pp. 531–554.

6. CROXTON, F., D. COWDEN, AND S. KLEIN, *Applied General Statistics*, 3d ed. (Englewood Cliffs, N.J.: Prentice-Hall, 1967).

7. EHRENBERG, A. S. C., "Rudiments of Numeracy," *Journal of the Royal Statistical Society*, Series A, vol. 140 (1977), pp. 277–297.

8. HUNTER, J. S., "The Digidot Plot," *The American Statistician*, vol. 42 (February 1988), p. 54.

9. TUFTE, E. R., *The Visual Display of Quantitative Information* (Cheshire, Conn.: Graphics Press, 1983).

10. WAINER, H., "How to Display Data Badly," *The American Statistician*, vol. 38 (May 1984), pp. 137–147.

5

Using the Computer for Descriptive Statistical Analysis

5.1 INTRODUCTION AND OVERVIEW

When dealing with large batches of data, we may use the computer to assist us in our descriptive statistical analysis. In this chapter we will demonstrate how various statistical software can be used for organizing, summarizing, and characterizing quantitative data as well as presenting both quantitative and qualitative data in tabular and chart form.

By learning how to access a statistical package, such as Minitab, MYSTAT, SAS, SPSS[x], or STATGRAPHICS, we will be able to take advantage of recent technological progress and gain an appreciation for the assistance the computer may give us in solving statistical problems—particularly those involving large numbers of variables or large data batches. (See References 1–8.) To accomplish this, let us return to the real estate survey that was developed in Chapter 2.

In an initial analysis of the survey data (Figure 2.10), let us suppose that answers to the following are of particular concern to the president of the realty company:

    A. *General Question*: What is the average appraised value of all single-family homes in this geographical area (see real estate survey, question 1)?

    B. *Specific Question*: Are there differences in the average appraised value among single-family homes situated in East Meadow, Farmingdale, and Levittown (see real estate survey, questions 1 and 9)?

    C. *General Question*: What types of single-family homes are primarily found in this geographical area (see real estate survey, question 10)?

    D. *Specific Question*: What percentage of single-family homes in this geographical area are designed in a split-level style (see real estate survey, question 10)?

    E. *General Question*: Is there a relationship between community location and architectural style (see real estate survey, questions 9 and 10)?

    F. *Specific Question*: Is there a relationship between having a modern kitchen facility and modern bathrooms (see real estate survey, questions 19 and 20)?

These questions raised by the president require a detailed descriptive statistical analysis of the 233 responses to the real estate survey. This analysis will be the subject of the remaining sections of this chapter.[1]

5.2   USING STATISTICAL PACKAGES FOR QUANTITATIVE DATA

In response to question A—which deals with quantitative data—the following would be desired: a set of descriptive summary measures, a stem-and-leaf display, frequency and percentage distributions, a box-and-whisker plot, and a histogram or polygon. Figure 5.1 presents computer output displaying the needed descriptive summary measures. This output was obtained by accessing Minitab. In addition, Figure 5.2 depicts the stem-and-leaf display from MYSTAT, Figure 5.3 (page 158) shows the frequency and percentage distributions from SPSS[x], and Figures 5.4, 5.5, and 5.6, respectively, present the box-and-whisker plot, histogram, and ogive using STATGRAPHICS (pages 159–161).

```
MTB > describe 'value'

                    N       MEAN    MEDIAN    TRMEAN     STDEV    SEMEAN
value             233     190.85    181.00    187.90     34.54      2.26

                  MIN        MAX        Q1        Q3
value          100.00     310.00    169.50    202.50
```

FIGURE 5.1
Summary measures from Minitab output.
NOTE: FIGURE 5.1
We should be familiar with all the summary measures obtained from the Minitab output except TRMEAN (which is beyond the scope of this text) and SEMEAN (which will be studied in Chapter 9).

From the various computer output, a response to the president's first general question can be made. The various tables and charts indicate that the distribution of appraised values is slightly right-skewed. The mean appraisal is almost 191 thousand dollars; the median is 181 thousand dollars. A substantial majority of appraisals (79.4%) fall between 156.31 thousand dollars and 225.39 thousand dollars (that is, the interval formed from $\overline{X} \pm S$). In addition (from the five-number summary), although the appraisals range in value from 100 to 310 thousand dollars, the "midspread" or interquartile range is from 169.5 to 202.5 thousand dollars. Furthermore, only 6.9% of the appraisals exceed 250 thousand dollars.

To respond to question B—a comparison of appraised values among single-family homes in East Meadow, Farmingdale, and Levittown—a sorting of the quantitative responses into the three geographic locations is required. This process can be performed by accessing any of these statistical packages. Once that is achieved, types of output similar to that presented in Figures 5.1 through 5.6 would be needed for each group separately. To highlight this, Figure 5.7 (pages 162–163) presents the set of descriptive summary measures and Figures 5.8 and 5.9 (pages 163 and 164) respectively depict the stem-and-leaf displays and the box-and-whisker plots for each of the geographic

[1] In practice, the statistician would likely use one or two statistical packages when performing the descriptive statistical analysis. However, computer output from several packages is presented here so that we may demonstrate some of the useful features of these packages.

```
            STEM AND LEAF PLOT OF VARIABLE:      VALUE    , N =   233

MINIMUM IS:          100.000
LOWER HINGE IS:         169.500
MEDIAN IS:           181.000
UPPER HINGE IS:         200.000
MAXIMUM IS:          310.000


                    10    0
                    11    5
              ***OUTSIDE VALUES***
                    14    0
                    14    79
                    15    0001123334
                    15    5557999999
                    16    0000000000002333344
                    16  H 55555677789999
                    17    00000001233344444
                    17    5555555666667789999999
                    18  M 00000000000000000111234
                    18    5555555555778999999999
                    19    00000000000224
                    19    55555578999999
                    20  H 00
                    20    55566
                    21    000034
                    21    555557889
                    22    0034
                    22    5555999
                    23    00002
                    23    59
                    24    0
                    24    5
              ***OUTSIDE VALUES***
                    24    79
                    26    0579
                    27    05
                    28    006
                    29    05799
                    30    5
                    31    0
```

FIGURE 5.2
Stem-and-leaf display from MYSTAT output.

NOTE: FIGURE 5.2
When splitting a stem into two stems based on low (L) and high (H) digits as on pages 56 and 57, MYSTAT does not label the low and high groups. MYSTAT separates outliers with the reference ***OUTSIDE VALUES*** and also indicates the group containing the median (M), and the groups containing the hinges (H)—which approximate the quartiles, Q_1 and Q_3. It should also be pointed out that in some situations a stem can be split into five stems based on lowest two digits (*), twos and threes (T), fours and fives (F), sixes and sevens (S), and highest two digits (.).

locations. The output displayed in these respective figures was obtained by accessing SAS, Minitab, and STATGRAPHICS.

From Figures 5.7 through 5.9, it appears that the appraised values are typically highest in East Meadow and lowest in Levittown. With respect to dispersion, the appraisals in East Meadow and Farmingdale are less homogeneous than those in Levittown—a reflection of the uniformity in the planning of that latter community. The three distributions of appraised values, however, are each approximately symmetrical in shape.

```
VALUE

VALUE LABEL              VALUE      FREQUENCY      PERCENT

100  -  119.9              1            2           0.9
120  -  139.9              2            0           0.0
140  -  159.9              3           23           9.9
160  -  179.9              4           75          32.2
180  -  199.9              5           73          31.3
200  -  219.9              6           22           9.4
220  -  239.9              7           18           7.7
240  -  259.9              8            4           1.7
260  -  279.9              9            6           2.6
280  -  299.9             10            8           3.4
300  -  319.9             11            2           0.9
                                    -----------   -------
                         TOTAL          233         100.0

VALID CASES      233    MISSING CASES            0
```

FIGURE 5.3
Frequency and percentage distributions from SPSS^x output.

5.3 USING STATISTICAL PACKAGES FOR QUALITATIVE DATA

In response to question C—which deals with qualitative data—a summary table and pie chart are desired.[2] Figure 5.10 (page 165) presents computer output displaying the needed summary table obtained from accessing SPSS^x; Figure 5.11 (page 165) displays a bar chart from STATGRAPHICS regarding type of architectural style for single-family houses.

From the summary table and bar chart the specific question (D) raised by the president can also be addressed. Typically, the style of house in this geographical area is Cape (41.6%) or ranch (25.8%). In addition, the split-level style accounts for 16.3% of the houses here.

5.4 USING STATISTICAL PACKAGES FOR CROSS-TABULATIONS

In response to questions E and F—both of which deal with pairs of qualitative variables—tables of cross-classifications are desired. Figures 5.12 (page 166) and 5.13 (page 167) respectively display the needed computer output obtained from accessing SAS.

From these cross-classification tables the two questions raised by the president can be addressed. We observe from the "large" (3-by-5) cross-classification table in Figure 5.12 that, in general, there appears to be a relationship between community location and architectural style. The percentage corresponding to the architectural style categories differ substantially from row to row (i.e., the community location categories). In particular, we note from the cells of the table that certain combinations of the two variables stand out. Compared with others, the combinations "Levittown"

---

[2] As of this writing, none of the popular statistical packages include either the recently developed digidot plot presented in Section 4.7, the dot chart presented in Section 4.9.3, or the supertable described in Section 4.11.2.

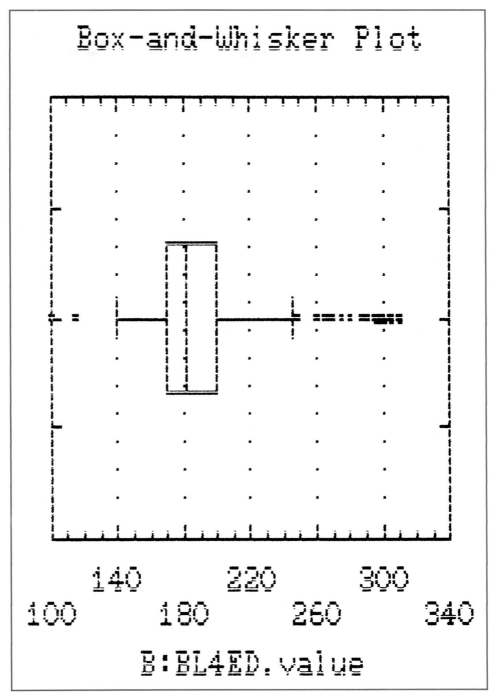

FIGURE 5.4
Box-and-whisker plot from STATGRAPHICS output.

NOTE: FIGURE 5.4
Outliers are flagged separately outside the whiskers of the box-and-whisker plot.

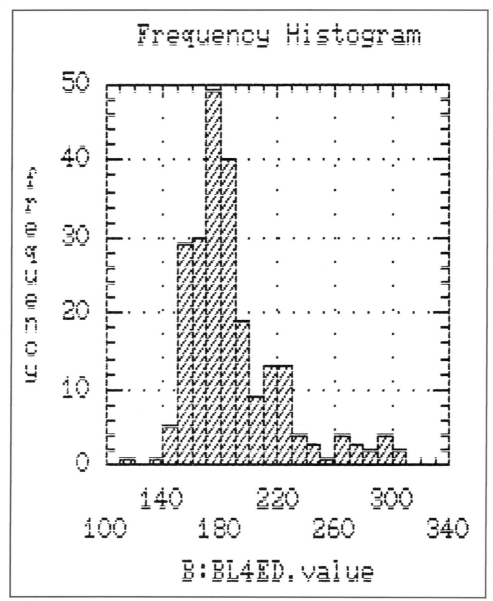

FIGURE 5.5
Frequency histogram from STATGRAPHICS output.

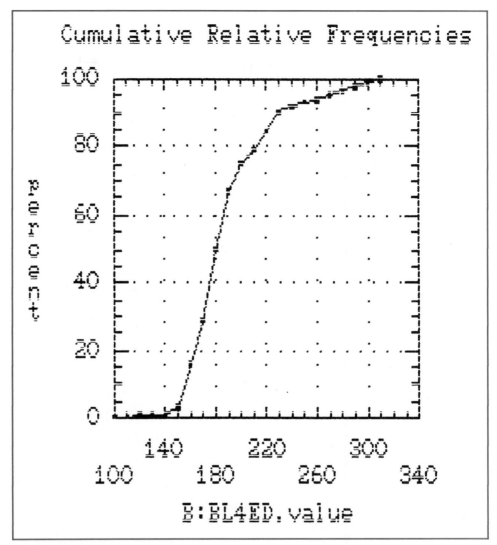

FIGURE 5.6
Percentage ogive from STATGRAPHICS output.

NOTE: FIGURES 5.3, 5.5, and 5.6
As we have discussed in Section 4.2.4 on page 95, there is much subjectivity in selecting class boundaries in frequency distributions. Hence we note that the frequency and percentage distributions obtained by SPSS[x] in Figure 5.3 do not match the histogram and ogive obtained by STATGRAPHICS in Figures 5.5 and 5.6. Each statistical package is programmed differently for establishing the boundaries of the classes in a frequency distribution. However, we could control for this by exercising certain options. We then could set up the lower and upper boundaries of the classes as we desire and our output would be consistent.

GEOGRAPHICAL LOCATION=EAST MEADOW

UNIVARIATE

VARIABLE=VALUE   APRRAISED VALUE

MOMENTS

N	74	SUM WGTS	74
MEAN	215.227	SUM	15926.8
STD DEV	38.4944	VARIANCE	1481.82
SKEWNESS	0.758809	KURTOSIS	-0.245744
USS	3536050	CSS	108173
CV	17.8855	STD MEAN	4.47488
T:MEAN=0	48.0967	PROB>¦T¦	0.0001
SGN RANK	1387.5	PROB>¦S¦	0.0001
NUM \= 0	74		

QUANTILES(DEF=4)				EXTREMES	
100% MAX	310	99%	310	LOWEST	HIGHEST
75% Q3	231.25	95%	295.625	155	290
50% MED	208.35	90%	280	160	295
25% Q1	185	10%	171	165.9	297.5
0% MIN	155	5%	167.475	168	299.9
		1%	155	169	310

RANGE	155
Q3-Q1	46.25
MODE	190

GEOGRAPHICAL LOCATION=FARMINGDALE

UNIVARIATE

VARIABLE=VALUE   APRRAISED VALUE

MOMENTS

N	60	SUM WGTS	60
MEAN	191.333	SUM	11480
STD DEV	32.6027	VARIANCE	1062.94
SKEWNESS	1.069	KURTOSIS	4.54196
USS	2259220	CSS	62713.2
CV	17.0397	STD MEAN	4.20899
T:MEAN=0	45.4582	PROB>¦T¦	0.0001
SGN RANK	915	PROB>¦S¦	0.0001
NUM \= 0	60		

QUANTILES(DEF=4)				EXTREMES	
100% MAX	305	99%	305	LOWEST	HIGHEST
75% Q3	199.9	95%	268.005	100	230
50% MED	186.25	90%	229.5	115	232
25% Q1	178.1	10%	160.3	159	269.9
0% MIN	100	5%	159.045	159.9	299.9
		1%	100	159.9	305

RANGE	205
Q3-Q1	21.8
MODE	189.9

FIGURE 5.7
Summary measures from SAS output.

```
GEOGRAPHICAL LOCATION=LEVITTOWN

UNIVARIATE

VARIABLE=VALUE              APRRAISED VALUE

                       MOMENTS

N                    99   SUM WGTS        99
MEAN            172.341   SUM          17061.8
STD DEV         16.9209   VARIANCE     286.318
SKEWNESS        1.18914   KURTOSIS     2.55663
USS             2968514   CSS          28059.1
CV              9.81826   STD MEAN     1.70062
T:MEAN=0        101.341   PROB>|T|      0.0001
SGN RANK           2475   PROB>|S|      0.0001
NUM \= 0             99


            QUANTILES(DEF=4)                    EXTREMES

100% MAX    239.9    99%    239.9   LOWEST    HIGHEST
 75% Q3       180    95%      205     140        205
 50% MED      170    90%    192.5     147        214
 25% Q1       160    10%      153     149      217.9
  0% MIN      140     5%      150     150      223.5
                      1%      140     150      239.9
RANGE        99.9
Q3-Q1          20
MODE          160
```

FIGURE 5.7 (continued)

NOTE: FIGURE 5.7

As we see from the output under the headings of MOMENTS, QUANTILES, and EX-TREMES, SAS provides an extensive set of summary measures, many of which we have not learned so far. The summary measures of interest to us are highlighted in color.

```
Stem-and-leaf of value      locate = 1     N = 74
Leaf Unit = 10

     1      1 5
    13      1 666667777777
    33      1 88888889999999999999
   (13)     2 0000111111111
    28      2 22222222333
    17      2 4444
    13      2 66677
     8      2 8889999
     1      3 1


Stem-and-leaf of value      locate = 2     N = 60
Leaf Unit = 10

     2      1 01
     2      1
     5      1 555
    16      1 66677777777
   (31)     1 88888888888888888888888999999999
    13      2 01111
     8      2 22333
     3      2
     3      2 6
     2      2 9
     1      3 0
```

FIGURE 5.8
Stem-and-leaf displays from Minitab output.

```
Stem-and-leaf of value       locate = 3        N = 99
Leaf Unit = 10

   19       1  444555555555555555
  (52)      1  6666666666666666666666666677777777777777777777777777
   28       1  888888888888888999999
    6       2  0011
```

FIGURE 5.8 (continued)

NOTE: FIGURE 5.8
In a Minitab stem-and-leaf display the numbers in the first column are cumulated counts of
the values up to the median class. In the first panel, the (13) means that there are thirteen
values in the median class. The numbers written below the (13) are the cumulated
counts—starting from the largest value back to the median class.

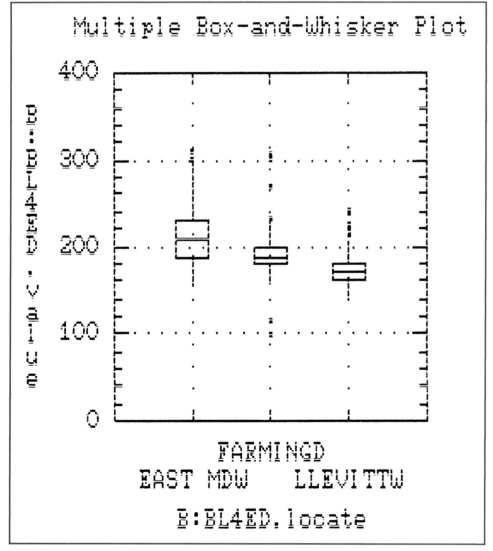

FIGURE 5.9
Box-and-whisker plots from STATGRAPHICS output.

```
TYPE          ARCHITECTURAL STYLE OF HOUSE

VALUE LABEL                    VALUE        FREQUENCY        PERCENT

CAPE                             1              97             41.6
EXPANDED RANCH                   2              15              6.4
COLONIAL                         3              23              9.9
RANCH                            4              60             25.8
SPLIT LEVEL                      5              38             16.3
                                          ---------        -------
                            TOTAL             233            100.0
```

FIGURE 5.10
Summary table from SPSS[x] output.

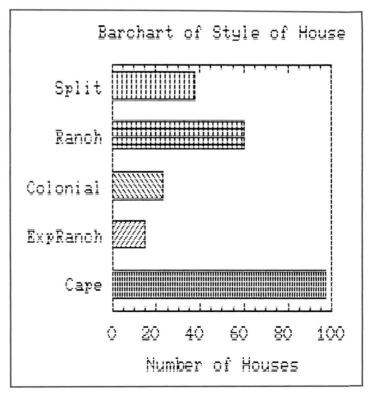

FIGURE 5.11
Bar chart from STATGRAPHICS output.

```
TABLE OF LOCATE BY TYPE

LOCATE(GEOGRAPHICAL LOCATION)          TYPE(TYPE OF HOUSE)

FREQUENCY    ^
  PERCENT    ^
  ROW PCT    ^
  COL PCT    ^CAPE     ^EXPANDED^COLONIAL^RANCH    ^SPLIT
             ^         ^ RANCH  ^        ^         ^              ^TOTAL
  -----------+--------+--------+--------+--------+--------^--------------
EAST MEADOW  ^    31  ^     2  ^     6  ^    16^ ^    19  ^    74
             ^  13.30 ^  0.86  ^  2.58  ^  6.87^   8.15   ^31.76
             ^  41.89 ^  2.70  ^  8.11  ^ 21.62^  25.68   ^
             ^  31.96 ^ 13.33  ^ 26.09  ^ 26.67^  50.00   ^
  -----------+--------+--------+--------+--------+--------^--------------
FARMINGDALE  ^    14  ^     1  ^     8  ^    20^ ^    17  ^    60
             ^   6.01 ^  0.43  ^  3.43  ^  8.58^   7.30   ^25.75
             ^  23.33 ^  1.67  ^ 13.33  ^ 33.33^  28.33   ^
             ^  14.43 ^  6.67  ^ 34.78  ^ 33.33^  44.74   ^
  -----------+--------+--------+--------+--------+--------^--------------
LEVITTOWN    ^    52  ^    12  ^     9  ^    24^ ^     2  ^    99
             ^  22.32 ^  5.15  ^  3.86  ^ 10.30^   0.86   ^42.49
             ^  52.53 ^ 12.12  ^  9.09  ^ 24.24^   2.02   ^
             ^  53.61 ^ 80.00  ^ 39.13  ^ 40.00^   5.26   ^
  -----------+--------+--------+--------+--------+--------^--------------
TOTAL            97        15       23       60       38   ^   233
               41.63      6.44     9.87    25.75    16.31    100.00
```

FIGURE 5.12
Cross-classification tables from SAS output.

and "Cape," "Levittown" and "expanded ranch," "Farmingdale" and "ranch," "Farmingdale" and "split-level," and "East Meadow" and "split-level" each appear with far greater frequency than should be expected if the two variables were not related. In a similar vein, the combinations "Farmingdale" and "Cape" and "Levittown" and "Split-level" are conspicuously absent.[3] Interestingly, from the "small" 2-by-2 cross-classification table displayed in Figure 5.13, the relationship betwen the row and column variables is even easier to observe. Here it is obvious that houses (redecorated) with modern kitchen facilities are also likely to have modern bathrooms and vice versa.

5.5 THE COMPUTER AND THE RESEARCHER: INTERACTING ROLES

To this point we have studied how collected data are prepared, summarized, characterized, and presented. In particular, in this chapter we have demonstrated how appropriate computer software can assist us in the descriptive statistical analysis of our data. Thus the major role of the statistician or researcher is to analyze and interpret results. The role of the computer is to assist in this process. The computer is an extremely helpful tool which can easily and rapidly store, organize, and process information and provide us with summary results, tables, and charts. Nevertheless, we must bear in mind that the computer is only a tool.

To properly interact with the computer, the researcher must not only be familiar with the particular software package in use, but must also correctly select statistical procedures which are appropriate for the tasks at hand. For example, pie charts and

---

[3] The topic of *statistical independence* will be covered in depth in Chapters 6 and 13.

```
TABLE OF MODKIT BY MODBATH

MODKIT(MODERN KITCHEN)
              MODBATH(MODERN BATHROOMS)

FREQUENCY^
EXPECTED ^
DEVIATION^
  PERCENT ^
  ROW PCT ^
  COL PCT ^ABSENCE ^PRESENCE^    TOTAL
---------+--------+--------+
ABSENCE  ^     72 ^      8 ^       80
         ^   27.1 ^   52.9 ^
         ^   44.9 ^  -44.9 ^
         ^   30.90 ^   3.43 ^    34.33
         ^   90.00 ^  10.00 ^
         ^   91.14 ^   5.19 ^
---------+--------+--------+
PRESENCE ^      7 ^    146 ^      153
         ^   51.9 ^  101.1 ^
         ^  -44.9 ^   44.9 ^
         ^   3.00 ^  62.66 ^    65.67
         ^   4.58 ^  95.42 ^
         ^   8.86 ^  94.81 ^
---------+--------+--------+
TOTAL          79      154       233
             33.91    66.09   100.00
```

FIGURE 5.13
Cross-classification tables from SAS output.

NOTE: FIGURES 5.12 & 5.13
SAS provides the user with numerous options when developing a cross-classification table. Invoking such options, as we see from the output in Figure 5.13, each cell contains six pieces of information—the frequency or cell count (highlighted in color), the "expected" frequency (to be discussed in Chapter 13), the deviation (i.e., the difference between the frequency and the expected frequency), the percent (i.e., the cell frequency as a percentage of the grand total), the row percent (i.e., the cell frequency as a percentage of the row total), and the column percent (i.e., the cell frequency as a percentage of the column total). The cross-classification table in Figure 5.12 is presented without invoking the expected frequency and deviation options. Note that this one table takes the place of four tables. (See Tables 4.12–4.15 on pages 136–138.)

cross-classification tables are for use *only* on qualitative data. It is improper to request pie charts or cross-classifications for continuous quantitative variables unless they have been first categorized into classes as in a frequency-distribution or supertable. On the other hand, means, medians, ranges, and standard deviations should be used *only* for quantitative variables. It is completely inappropriate to instruct the computer to give such summary results for qualitative variables like geographic location or architectural style. The output would be meaningless.

We shall see throughout this text, as we both demonstrate and interpret a variety of computer output corresponding to the topics to be studied in the chapters ahead, that it is crucial that the researcher use the computer in a manner consistent with correct statistical methodology.

Database Exercises

The following problems refer to the sample data obtained from the questionnaire of Figure 2.5 and presented in Figure 2.10. They should be solved (to the greatest extent possible) with the aid of an available computer package.

Suppose you are hired as a research assistant to the president of the realty company. From the responses to the questions dealing with quantitative variables in the real estate survey (see pages 24–29), in Problems 5.1 through 5.53 which follow,

(a) Obtain for each group

(1) the mean
(2) the median
(3) the midrange
(4) the midhinge

(5) the range
(6) the interquartile range
(7) the standard deviation
(8) the coefficient of variation

(b) In each group

(1) List the raw data.
(2) Form the ordered array.
(3) Form the stem-and-leaf display.
(4) Form the frequency and percentage distributions.
(5) Form the cumulative percentage distribution.
(6) Form the digidot plot (using the sample median).

(c) On one graph

(1) Plot the percentage polygons.
(2) Plot the ogives.

➡(d) ACTION Write a memo to the president of the realty company comparing and contrasting the groups and discussing your findings.

☐ **5.1** Examine appraised value based on type of indoor parking facility (questions 1 and 8).

☐ **5.2** Examine appraised value based on geographical location (questions 1 and 9).

☐ **5.3** Examine appraised value based on architectural style (questions 1 and 10).

☐ **5.4** Examine appraised value based on type of heating fuel used (questions 1 and 11).

☐ **5.5** Examine appraised value based on type of heating system (questions 1 and 12).

☐ **5.6** Examine appraised value based on type of swimming pool (questions 1 and 13).

☐ **5.7** Examine appraised value based on absence or presence of an eat-in kitchen (questions 1 and 14).

☐ **5.8** Examine appraised value based on absence or presence of central air-conditioning (questions 1 and 15).

☐ **5.9** Examine appraised value based on absence or presence of a fireplace (questions 1 and 16).

☐ **5.10** Examine appraised value based on absence or presence of a connection to the local sewer system (questions 1 and 17).

☐ **5.11** Examine appraised value based on absence or presence of a basement (questions 1 and 18).

☐ **5.12** Examine appraised value based on absence or presence of a modern kitchen (questions 1 and 19).

☐ **5.13** Examine appraised value based on absence or presence of modern bathroom facilities (questions 1 and 20).

☐ **5.14** Examine lot size based on geographic location (questions 2 and 9).

☐ **5.15** Examine number of bedrooms based on geographic location (questions 3 and 9).

☐ **5.16** Examine number of bedrooms based on architectural style (questions 3 and 10).

☐ **5.17** Examine number of bathrooms based on geographic location (questions 4 and 9).

☐ **5.18** Examine number of bathrooms based on architectural style (questions 4 and 10).

☐ **5.19** Examine number of rooms based on geographic location (questions 5 and 9).

☐ **5.20** Examine number of rooms based on architectural style (questions 5 and 10).

☐ **5.21** Examine number of rooms based on type of heating fuel used (questions 5 and 11).

☐ **5.22** Examine number of rooms based on type of heating system (questions 5 and 12).

☐ **5.23** Examine number of rooms based on type of swimming pool (questions 5 and 13).

☐ **5.24** Examine number of rooms based on absence or presence of an eat-in kitchen (questions 5 and 14).

☐ **5.25** Examine number of rooms based on absence or presence of central air-conditioning (questions 5 and 15).

☐ **5.26** Examine number of rooms based on absence or presence of a fireplace (questions 5 and 16).

☐ **5.27** Examine number of rooms based on absence or presence of a basement (questions 5 and 18).

☐ **5.28** Examine age of house based on type of indoor parking facility (questions 6 and 8).

☐ **5.29** Examine age of house based on geographic location (questions 6 and 9).

☐ **5.30** Examine age of house based on architectural style (questions 6 and 10).

☐ **5.31** Examine age of house based on type of heating fuel used (questions 6 and 11).

☐ **5.32** Examine age of house based on type of heating system (questions 6 and 12).

☐ **5.33** Examine age of house based on type of swimming pool (questions 6 and 13).

☐ **5.34** Examine age of house based on absence or presence of an eat-in kitchen (questions 6 and 14).

☐ **5.35** Examine age of house based on absence or presence of central air-conditioning (questions 6 and 15).

☐ **5.36** Examine age of house based on absence or presence of a fireplace (questions 6 and 16).

☐ **5.37** Examine age of house based on absence or presence of a connection to a local sewer system (questions 6 and 17).

☐ **5.38** Examine age of house based on absence or presence of a basement (questions 6 and 18).

☐ **5.39** Examine age of house based on absence or presence of a modern kitchen (questions 6 and 19).

☐ **5.40** Examine age of house based on absence or presence of modern bathroom facilities (questions 6 and 20).

☐ **5.41** Examine annual taxes based on type of indoor parking facility (questions 7 and 8).

☐ **5.42** Examine annual taxes based on geographic location (questions 7 and 9).

☐ **5.43** Examine annual taxes based on architectural style (questions 7 and 10).

☐ **5.44** Examine annual taxes based on type of heating fuel used (questions 7 and 11).

☐ **5.45** Examine annual taxes based on type of heating system (questions 7 and 12).

☐ **5.46** Examine annual taxes based on type of swimming pool (questions 7 and 13).

☐ **5.47** Examine annual taxes based on absence or presence of an eat-in kitchen (questions 7 and 14).

☐ **5.48** Examine annual taxes based on absence or presence of central air-conditioning (questions 7 and 15).

☐ **5.49** Examine annual taxes based on absence or presence of a fireplace (questions 7 and 16).

☐ **5.50** Examine annual taxes based on absence or presence of a connection to a local sewer system (questions 7 and 17).

☐ **5.51** Examine annual taxes based on absence or presence of a basement (questions 7 and 18).

☐ **5.52** Examine annual taxes based on absence or presence of a modern kitchen (questions 7 and 19).

☐ **5.53** Examine annual taxes based on absence or presence of modern bathroom facilities (questions 7 and 20).

Suppose you are hired as a research assistant to the president of the realty company. From the responses to the questions dealing with qualitative variables in the real estate survey (see pages 24–29), in Problems 5.54 through 5.64 which follow

  (a) Form
    (1) a summary table and bar chart.
    (2) a pie chart.
➡ (b) **ACTION**   Write a memo to the president of the realty company discussing your findings.

☐ **5.54** Examine type of indoor parking facility (question 8).

☐ **5.55** Examine type of heating fuel used (question 11).

☐ **5.56** Examine type of heating system (question 12).

☐ **5.57** Examine type of swimming pool (question 13).

☐ **5.58** Examine absence or presence of an eat-in kitchen (question 14).

☐ **5.59** Examine absence or presence of central air-conditioning (question 15).

☐ **5.60** Examine absence or presence of a fireplace (question 16).

☐ **5.61** Examine absence or presence of a connection to a local sewer system (question 17).

☐ **5.62** Examine absence or presence of a basement (question 18).

☐ **5.63** Examine absence or presence of a modern kitchen (question 19).

☐ **5.64** Examine absence or presence of modern bathroom facilities (question 20).

Suppose you are hired as a research assistant to the president of the realty company. From the responses to the questions dealing with qualitative variables in the real estate survey (see pages 24–29), in Problems 5.65 through 5.90 which follow

  (a) Form a contingency table and analyze the data.
➡ (b) **ACTION**   Write a memo to the president of the realty company discussing your findings.

☐ **5.65** Cross-classify type of indoor parking facility (question 8) with architectural style (question 10).

☐ **5.66** Cross-classify geographic location (question 9) with type of heating fuel used (question 11).

☐ **5.67** Cross-classify geographic location (question 9) with type of heating system (question 12).

☐ **5.68** Cross-classify geographic location (question 9) with type of swimming pool (question 13).

☐ **5.69** Cross-classify geographic location (question 9) with eat-in kitchen (question 14).

☐ **5.70** Cross-classify geographic location (question 9) with central air-conditioning (question 15).

☐ **5.71** Cross-classify geographic location (question 9) with fireplace (question 16).

☐ **5.72** Cross-classify geographic location (question 9) with connection to a local sewer system (question 17).

☐ **5.73** Cross-classify geographic location (question 9) with basement (question 18).

☐ **5.74** Cross-classify geographic location (question 9) with modern kitchen (question 19).

☐ **5.75** Cross-classify geographic location (question 9) with modern bathroom facilities (question 20).

☐ **5.76** Cross-classify architectural style (question 10) with type of heating fuel used (question 11).

☐ **5.77** Cross-classify architectural style (question 10) with type of heating system (question 12).

☐ **5.78** Cross-classify architectural style (question 10) with type of swimming pool (question 13).

☐ **5.79** Cross-classify architectural style (question 10) with eat-in kitchen (question 14).

☐ **5.80** Cross-classify architectural style (question 10) with central air-conditioning (question 15).

☐ **5.81** Cross-classify architectural style (question 10) with fireplace (question 16).

☐ **5.82** Cross-classify architectural style (question 10) with connection to a local sewer system (question 17).

☐ **5.83** Cross-classify architectural style (question 10) with basement (question 18).

☐ **5.84** Cross-classify architectural style (question 10) with modern kitchen (question 19).

☐ **5.85** Cross-classify architectural style (question 10) with modern bathroom facilities (question 20).

☐ **5.86** Cross-classify type of heating fuel used (question 11) with type of heating system (question 12).

☐ **5.87** Cross-classify type of swimming pool (question 13) with connection to a local sewer system (question 17).

☐ **5.88** Cross-classify type of swimming pool (question 13) with modern kitchen (question 19).

☐ **5.89** Cross-classify type of swimming pool (question 13) with modern bathroom facilities (question 20).

☐ **5.90** Cross-classify central air-conditioning (question 15) with fireplace (question 16).

Case Study B

The board of directors of a well-known diversified company is contemplating the development of a fund. It will cater to the needs of clients interested in stocks which, over the years, have continuously demonstrated growth in dividend payments.

As senior research analyst for the company you are given the responsibility of investigating the market performance of stocks having outstanding dividend records. Being wary of the stock market's fallibility as a result of "Black Monday" October 1987, you have decided to first "historically explore" financial data from a recent year in order to monitor whether the portfolio of stocks you would have chosen then would be successful now. Using the data compiled for *Dun's Business Month* by Moody's Investors Service in 1984, you "explore" the list of the 120 top corporate performers (based on ten-year dividend growth rate). The data are presented in Table 5.1 (see pages 172–175).

Certain key questions have now come to mind and you have written down the following:

1. Are there differences in earnings per share between top corporate performers traded on the New York Stock Exchange versus those traded elsewhere (that is, on the American Stock Exchange or on the NASDAQ over-the-counter list)?

2. For the same two groups, are there differences in
   a. Yield?
   b. Stock price?
   c. Net income?
   d. Return on equity?

3. For the group of 120 stocks possessing outstanding dividend records, do the 60 companies having the "best" ten-year dividend growth rate differ in earnings per share from those 60 companies having the "second-best" ten-year dividend growth rate?

4. For the same groups, are there differences in
   a. Yield?
   b. Stock price?
   c. Net income?
   d. Return on equity?

5. Using such criteria as earnings per share, yield, stock price, net income, and return on equity, how would this group of 120 stocks compare against a random sample of 120 other stocks not enjoying such outstanding dividend records?

You are scheduled to make an oral presentation and submit a written preliminary report to the board of directors in ten days. Knowing that your findings and recommendations will significantly affect the board's decision to establish such a fund and to choose the appropriate stocks to constitute its portfolio, you set out to answer the aforementioned questions.

If your company's computer is available, you will be able to use all appropriate descriptive statistical methods with which you are familiar. If the computer is not available, you will have to limit yourself to presentations of summary tables and charts and to descriptive summary measures which are obtained from these tables and charts.

TABLE 5.1 Top corporate performers

Rank	Company	Where Traded	1984 Dividend	1974 Dividend	Ten-Year Dividend Growth Rate	Stock Price	Yield
1	Texas Oil & Gas Corp.	NYSE	$ .18	$ .0011	65.5%	$ $21\frac{1}{4}$	0.8%
2	Church's Fried Chicken, Inc.	NYSE	.80	.021	43.5	28	2.9
3	Amer. Indemnity Financial Corp.	OTC	1.12	.0397	39.7	$18\frac{1}{2}$	6.1
4	RPM, Inc.	OTC	.56	.022	38.2	$15\frac{1}{4}$	3.7
5	Servicemaster Industries, Inc.	OTC	1.04	.055	33.6	$32\frac{1}{4}$	3.2
6	United Energy Resources, Inc.	NYSE	2.48	.15	32.4	$25\frac{1}{8}$	9.9
7	Levi Strauss & Co.	NYSE	1.85	.12	31.5	$27\frac{1}{2}$	6.7
8	Harland (John H.) Co.	NYSE	.92	.06	31.4	$45\frac{3}{4}$	2.0
9	Moore McCormack Res., Inc.	NYSE	1.04	.07	31.0	$22\frac{1}{8}$	4.7
10	Parsons Corp.	NYSE	1.00	.067	31.0	$31\frac{5}{8}$	3.2
11	Keystone International, Inc.	NYSE	.48	.003	30.4	16	3.0
12	Rite Aid Corp.	NYSE	.41	.03	29.9	$25\frac{1}{4}$	1.6
13	Guardian Industries Corp.	NYSE	.32	.024	28.7	$21\frac{5}{8}$	1.5
14	Hospital Corp. of America	NYSE	.50	.038	28.7	$40\frac{7}{8}$	1.2
15	Dorsey Corp.	NYSE	1.20	.10	28.2	$30\frac{3}{4}$	3.9
16	Schlumberger Limited	NYSE	1.20	.091	28.1	$45\frac{3}{8}$	2.6
17	United Industrial Corp.	NYSE	.48	.0509	27.8	$19\frac{1}{2}$	2.5
18	Acme Electric Corp.	NYSE	.32	.0269	27.7	$10\frac{3}{8}$	3.1
19	Anixter Bros., Inc.	NYSE	.28	.025	26.9	$17\frac{3}{4}$	1.6
20	Revco D. S., Inc.	NYSE	.80	.071	26.9	$29\frac{5}{8}$	2.7
21	Equitable Bancorporation	OTC	.72	.064	26.5	19	3.8
22	Dart & Kraft, Inc.	NYSE	4.24	.409	26.0	$80\frac{5}{8}$	5.3
23	Betz Laboratories, Inc.	OTC	1.20	.11	25.9	31	3.9
24	Baker International Corp.	NYSE	.92	.094	25.7	$17\frac{1}{4}$	5.3
25	Ohio Mattress Co.	NYSE	.40	.041	25.6	16	2.5
26	Great Lakes Chemical Corp.	ASE	.40	.038	25.4	$34\frac{1}{4}$	1.2
27	Lee Enterprises, Inc.	NYSE	.80	.077	25.4	$24\frac{1}{2}$	3.3
28	Flowers Industries, Inc.	NYSE	.36	.038	24.8	$15\frac{3}{8}$	2.4
29	Halliburton Co.	NYSE	1.80	.20	24.6	$31\frac{5}{8}$	5.7
30	General Cinema Corp.	NYSE	.40	.0387	24.3	$25\frac{5}{8}$	1.6
31	Nucor Corp.	NYSE	.36	.04	24.2	$29\frac{1}{4}$	1.2
32	Philip Morris, Inc.	NYSE	3.40	.375	24.2	$77\frac{7}{8}$	4.4
33	Trion, Inc.	OTC	.09	.0097	24.2	$7\frac{1}{2}$	1.2
34	Hunt Manufacturing Co.	NYSE	.44	.0512	24.0	$22\frac{7}{8}$	1.9
35	Sunwest Financial Services, Inc.	OTC	1.40	.155	24.0	$32\frac{1}{4}$	4.4
36	Pay 'N Pak Stores, Inc.	NYSE	.60	.069	23.9	$15\frac{5}{8}$	3.8
37	Roadway Services, Inc.	OTC	1.00	.114	23.9	$28\frac{1}{2}$	3.5
38	Big Three Industries, Inc.	NYSE	.80	.10	23.1	$21\frac{5}{8}$	3.7
39	Knight Ridder Newspapers, Inc.	NYSE	.64	.08	23.1	$27\frac{1}{2}$	2.3
40	Smith International, Inc.	NYSE	.96	.12	23.1	$14\frac{5}{8}$	6.6
41	Tyler Corp.	NYSE	.70	.0875	23.1	$29\frac{1}{2}$	2.4
42	Baxter Travenol Laboratories, Inc.	NYSE	.33	.04	23.0	$13\frac{1}{2}$	2.4
43	Fort Howard Paper Co.	NYSE	1.48	.181	23.0	$59\frac{3}{4}$	2.5
44	American Recreation Centers, Inc.	OTC	.16	.018	22.8	$9\frac{1}{2}$	1.7
45	Telephone & Data Systems, Inc.	ASE	.39	.05	22.8	$9\frac{3}{8}$	4.2
46	Commerce Clearing House, Inc.	OTC	1.92	.23	22.6	$67\frac{1}{2}$	2.9
47	Duplex Products, Inc.	ASE	.84	.107	22.6	$26\frac{1}{2}$	3.2
48	Hewlett-Packard Co.	NYSE	.22	.025	22.5	$37\frac{1}{8}$	0.6
49	Gannett Co., Inc.	NYSE	1.28	.169	22.4	$44\frac{3}{8}$	2.9
50	Hutton (E. F.) Group, Inc.	NYSE	.80	.107	22.3	$30\frac{1}{2}$	2.6
51	Allied Bancshares, Inc.	OTC	.80	.1067	22.2	$24\frac{1}{8}$	3.3
52	First Maryland Bancorp.	OTC	1.60	.213	22.0	28	5.7
53	Jostens, Inc.	NYSE	.80	.1508	21.9	$18\frac{7}{8}$	4.2
54	West Co., Inc. (The)	NYSE	.44	.058	21.9	$18\frac{3}{4}$	2.4
55	Kelly Services, Inc.	OTC	.64	.079	21.8	25	2.6
56	Abbott Laboratories	NYSE	1.20	.162	21.7	$40\frac{1}{8}$	3.0
57	Cincinnati Financial Corp.	OTC	2.20	.294	21.7	$70\frac{1}{4}$	3.1
58	Entex, Inc.	NYSE	1.30	.177	21.6	$19\frac{3}{4}$	6.6
59	Heck's Inc.	NYSE	.28	.04	21.5	$11\frac{7}{8}$	2.4
60	Shoney's Inc.	OTC	.16	.023	21.4	$33\frac{5}{8}$	0.5

Earnings Per Share	1983 Payout	Annual Sales (Millions)	Net Income (Millions)	Return on Sales	Shareholders' Equity (Millions)	Return on Equity
$ 1.41	9.9%	$ 1,871.2	$ 295.7	15.8%	$ 1,192.8	24.8%
1.66	42.8	464.1	31.6	6.8	241.5	13.1
1.55	72.3	78.9	2.2	2.8	37.8	5.8
1.09	41.1	154.2	8.4	5.4	54.5	15.4
1.17	70.7	700.6	25.6	3.7	58.5	43.8
1.04	234.6	4,034.7	28.9	0.7	897.8	3.2
4.61	36.9	2,731.2	194.5	7.1	1,053.7	18.5
2.46	30.9	188.9	20.7	11.0	92.7	22.3
1.04	100.0	423.4	9.1	2.2	373.5	2.4
1.85	47.3	839.8	45.7	5.4	204.5	22.3
.79	56.5	110.4	12.5	11.3	85.5	14.6
1.76	18.2	1,223.2	74.2	6.1	323.7	22.9
1.68	15.5	464.8	38.1	8.2	212.2	18.0
2.80	13.7	3,917.0	243.2	6.2	1,570.9	15.5
3.02	38.1	446.5	10.1	2.3	81.9	12.3
3.73	26.3	5,797.4	1,084.2	18.7	5,818.8	18.6
1.64	23.6	288.2	16.7	5.8	77.7	21.5
0.63	50.2	66.0	2.3	3.5	20.1	11.5
0.72	31.9	525.9	10.3	2.0	183.5	5.6
2.54	25.9	2,227.5	93.4	4.2	447.2	20.9
1.28	41.8	265.1	14.4	5.4	160.1	9.0
7.92	48.5	9,714.0	435.1	4.5	2,922.7	14.9
2.08	45.2	266.9	33.1	12.4	161.7	20.5
0.91	—	1,837.6	63.5	—	1,044.1	—
0.70	41.9	98.8	7.7	7.8	37.8	20.4
1.63	18.4	225.9	23.8	10.5	141.4	16.8
1.64	38.1	172.5	22.7	13.2	119.3	19.0
.83	0.4	522.3	19.2	3.7	116.1	16.5
2.66	62.0	5,522.1	314.8	5.7	3,571.5	8.8
2.62	10.5	928.6	98.5	10.6	259.1	38.0
1.98	14.6	542.5	27.9	5.1	258.1	10.8
7.17	38.7	12,975.9	903.5	7.0	4,033.7	22.4
0.63	11.9	20.8	2.0	9.6	8.8	22.7
1.35	28.1	85.0	6.1	7.2	37.1	16.4
4.04	29.5	193.6	18.0	9.3	124.5	14.5
1.11	49.3	250.0	10.0	4.0	93.6	10.7
2.47	33.4	1,252.9	99.2	7.9	528.8	18.8
1.07	67.3	668.8	45.3	6.8	615.7	7.4
1.80	29.7	1,473.3	119.4	8.1	807.9	14.8
4.17	—	697.0	94.6	—	545.3	—
1.88	33.2	960.9	18.4	1.9	175.2	10.5
1.54	17.6	1,842.5	218.0	11.9	1,151.1	18.9
3.78	33.3	785.9	106.9	13.6	754.7	14.2
0.69	14.9	21.4	1.7	7.9	16.9	10.1
0.92	38.1	87.6	6.9	7.9	65.6	10.5
2.77	60.6	388.9	24.9	6.4	86.7	28.7
2.33	31.8	219.0	8.7	4.0	68.0	12.8
1.69	9.5	4,710.0	423.0	9.2	2,887.0	15.0
2.40	50.0	1,703.6	191.6	11.2	1,022.2	18.7
4.42	17.2	2,172.0	110.6	5.1	602.6	18.4
2.55	27.5	719.0	98.8	13.7	457.0	21.6
3.65	41.1	339.2	19.2	5.7	221.3	8.7
1.67	39.1	440.4	33.8	7.7	170.6	19.8
2.08	18.3	190.4	16.3	8.6	96.3	16.9
1.34	35.5	524.4	17.4	3.3	89.4	19.5
2.86	33.6	2,927.9	347.6	11.9	1,417.9	24.5
6.32	29.2	438.2	46.7	10.7	305.3	15.3
2.76	45.3	1,221.7	60.5	5.0	274.8	22.0
1.03	26.2	435.0	9.5	2.2	113.3	8.4
1.16	12.9	397.8	23.2	5.8	138.0	16.8

TABLE 5.1 (Continued)

Rank	Company	Where Traded	1984 Dividend	1974 Dividend	Ten-Year Dividend Growth Rate	Stock Price	Yield
61	Cross (A. T.) Co.	ASE	$ 1.32	$ .184	21.2%	$ 27$\frac{3}{8}$	4.8%
62	Masco Corp.	NYSE	.56	.073	21.2	24$\frac{3}{4}$	2.3
63	Multimedia, Inc.	OTC	.60	.089	21.0	34$\frac{1}{4}$	1.8
64	Communications Industries, Inc.	OTC	.36	.053	20.8	22$\frac{1}{4}$	1.6
65	Deluxe Check Printers, Inc.	NYSE	1.76	.235	20.8	51$\frac{1}{2}$	3.4
66	Payless Drug Store Northwest, Inc.	NYSE	.34	.046	20.8	21$\frac{3}{8}$	1.6
67	Dean Foods Co.	NYSE	.48	.07	20.7	26$\frac{3}{8}$	1.8
68	Houston Natural Gas Corp.	NYSE	2.00	.30	20.6	46	4.4
69	Lewis (Palmer G.) Co., Inc.	OTC	.28	.042	20.5	7$\frac{5}{8}$	3.7
70	Rollins, Inc.	NYSE	.46	.071	20.5	8$\frac{7}{8}$	5.2
71	WD-40 Co.	OTC	.88	.1333	20.5	19$\frac{1}{4}$	4.6
72	Pioneer Corp.	NYSE	1.24	.194	20.4	27$\frac{1}{4}$	4.6
73	Bowl America, Inc.	ASE	.38	.06	20.1	10$\frac{1}{2}$	3.6
74	Lear Siegler, Inc.	NYSE	1.80	.28	20.1	44$\frac{1}{8}$	4.1
75	Daniel Industries, Inc.	NYSE	.18	.029	20.0	18$\frac{3}{8}$	1.0
76	Super Value Stores, Inc.	NYSE	.68	.103	20.0	29	2.4
77	Kaman Corp.	OTC	.56	.0817	19.9	22	2.6
78	Heileman (G.) Brewing Co.	NYSE	.48	.076	19.7	16$\frac{1}{4}$	3.0
79	Block (H. R.), Inc.	NYSE	2.40	.36	19.6	43$\frac{5}{8}$	5.5
80	Lomas & Nettleton Financial Corp.	NYSE	1.16	.18	19.6	29	4.0
81	Heinz (H. J.) & Co.	NYSE	1.60	.247	19.4	40$\frac{1}{2}$	4.0
82	Jack Eckerd Corp.	NYSE	1.00	.17	19.4	27$\frac{1}{2}$	3.6
83	AMP, Inc.	NYSE	.64	.11	19.3	31$\frac{5}{8}$	2.0
84	O'Sullivan Corp.	ASE	.60	.094	19.3	30$\frac{5}{8}$	2.0
85	Pioneer Hi-bred International	OTC	.80	.1334	19.3	29$\frac{1}{4}$	2.7
86	Century Telephone Enterprises, Inc.	NYSE	.78	.135	19.2	8$\frac{3}{4}$	8.9
87	Dexter Corp.	NYSE	.80	.128	19.2	21$\frac{1}{8}$	3.8
88	Core Industries, Inc.	NYSE	.52	.089	19.1	12$\frac{3}{8}$	4.2
89	Barry Wright Corp.	NYSE	.60	.095	19.0	28$\frac{5}{8}$	2.1
90	Chemed Corp.	NYSE	1.48	.26	19.0	27$\frac{1}{8}$	5.5
91	Melville Corp.	NYSE	1.32	.231	19.0	37$\frac{3}{4}$	3.5
92	Affiliated Publications, Inc.	ASE	.80	.1422	18.9	46	1.7
93	K Mart Corp.	NYSE	1.24	.215	18.8	35	3.6
94	Millipore Corp.	OTC	.44	.075	18.8	32$\frac{3}{4}$	1.4
95	Dover Corp.	NYSE	.82	.14	18.7	37	2.2
96	Alco Standard Corp.	NYSE	1.16	.21	18.6	28$\frac{7}{8}$	4.0
97	Mine Safety Appliances Corp.	OTC	.88	.145	18.6	56$\frac{1}{2}$	1.6
98	American Hospital Supply Corp.	NYSE	1.12	.20	18.5	28$\frac{3}{4}$	3.9
99	United States Tobacco Co.	NYSE	1.44	.2633	18.5	34$\frac{5}{8}$	4.2
100	Provident Life & Accident Ins. Co.	OTC	2.88	.52	18.4	73	3.9
101	P. H. H. Group, Inc.	NYSE	.88	.16	18.3	24$\frac{3}{8}$	3.6
102	Progressive Corp.	OTC	.16	.03	18.2	36$\frac{3}{8}$	0.4
103	Albertsons, Inc.	NYSE	.68	.125	18.1	28$\frac{1}{8}$	2.4
104	Citizens Fidelity Corp.	OTC	.92	.17	18.1	23$\frac{7}{8}$	3.9
105	Colt Industries, Inc.	NYSE	2.20	.417	18.1	51$\frac{3}{8}$	4.3
106	Russell Corp.	ASE	.30	.057	18.1	12$\frac{1}{8}$	2.5
107	American Business Products, Inc.	NYSE	.56	.107	18.0	22$\frac{3}{4}$	2.5
108	Lance, Inc.	OTC	1.16	.2178	18.0	30$\frac{3}{4}$	3.8
109	Morrison Knudson Co., Inc.	NYSE	1.40	.264	18.0	30	4.7
110	Omark Industries, Inc.	NYSE	1.04	.198	18.0	23$\frac{3}{4}$	4.4
111	Owens & Minor, Inc.	OTC	.36	.0705	17.7	14	2.6
112	Protective Corp.	OTC	1.24	.24	17.7	33$\frac{1}{2}$	3.7
113	Seaway Food Town, Inc.	OTC	.68	.133	17.7	12$\frac{1}{4}$	5.6
114	Farmers Group, Inc.	OTC	1.52	.30	17.6	46	3.3
115	Dennison Manufacturing Co.	NYSE	1.20	.225	17.5	22$\frac{1}{2}$	5.3
116	Burdy Corp.	NYSE	.84	.169	17.4	14$\frac{1}{8}$	6.0
117	Consolidated Edison Co. of N.Y.	NYSE	2.12	.425	17.4	29$\frac{1}{8}$	7.3
118	McGraw-Hill, Inc.	NYSE	1.24	.25	17.4	41$\frac{3}{4}$	3.0
119	Capital Holding Corp.	NYSE	1.48	.30	17.3	39	3.8
120	General Signal Corp.	NYSE	1.80	.35	17.2	46$\frac{1}{4}$	3.9

Earnings Per Share	1983 Payout	Annual Sales (Millions)	Net Income (Millions)	Return on Sales	Shareholders' Equity (Millions)	Return on Equity
$ 1.90	60.5%	$ 118.4	$ 15.6	13.2%	$ 80.1	19.5%
1.93	22.8	1,059.4	106.5	10.1	728.8	14.6
2.15	24.2	269.7	35.1	13.0	224.5	15.6
1.18	26.3	64.2	10.8	16.8	64.8	16.7
3.37	36.8	619.7	76.6	12.4	284.9	26.9
1.35	18.2	852.9	24.7	2.9	129.7	19.0
1.61	22.9	834.2	22.1	2.6	108.7	20.3
4.66	38.4	2,962.3	190.2	6.4	1,381.0	13.8
0.67	38.8	121.0	1.8	1.5	27.0	6.7
0.63	72.8	262.3	15.6	5.9	34.1	45.7
1.07	71.7	50.2	8.0	15.9	22.2	36.0
1.95	60.5	1,025.4	72.9	7.1	403.8	18.1
1.07	32.1	16.7	1.7	10.2	9.9	17.2
4.96	31.8	1,941.7	85.1	4.4	569.3	14.9
0.36	46.7	154.3	3.5	2.3	99.1	3.5
2.08	27.9	5,922.6	76.7	1.3	384.7	19.9
1.82	21.4	475.8	12.8	2.7	89.1	14.4
2.15	20.9	1,325.6	56.9	4.3	239.3	23.8
3.88	50.6	415.6	48.0	11.6	237.4	20.2
2.35	38.7	240.0	34.3	14.3	162.8	21.1
3.40	35.8	3,953.7	237.5	6.0	1,139.6	20.9
1.91	50.3	2,325.0	71.7	3.1	568.2	12.6
1.52	34.9	1,515.4	163.1	10.8	800.8	20.4
1.98	22.1	108.7	8.6	7.9	34.5	24.9
1.37	52.6	505.4	43.7	8.6	352.3	12.4
1.07	71.0	99.5	9.3	9.3	85.1	10.9
1.77	41.5	561.4	27.3	4.9	186.1	14.7
0.74	63.5	130.0	7.3	5.6	85.1	8.6
1.57	28.1	162.1	13.6	8.4	89.0	15.3
2.17	62.7	271.3	17.3	6.4	80.9	21.4
3.36	32.4	3,923.2	176.2	4.5	831.2	21.2
2.80	22.9	293.8	22.2	7.6	123.0	18.0
3.80	27.9	18,597.9	492.3	2.6	2,940.1	16.7
1.52	25.0	292.4	20.6	7.0	192.8	10.7
2.18	33.0	1,009.6	77.5	7.6	502.7	15.4
2.72	41.5	2,785.9	57.3	2.1	427.1	13.4
3.65	18.9	312.7	13.5	4.3	141.9	9.5
2.86	33.6	3,310.5	211.9	6.4	1,396.8	15.2
2.42	47.9	382.7	70.6	18.4	260.0	27.2
9.54	26.8	1,148.8	88.1	7.7	687.6	12.8
2.30	34.3	538.4	36.4	6.8	211.7	17.2
2.81	5.4	268.5	22.6	8.4	79.7	28.4
2.15	26.7	4,279.3	70.3	1.6	391.8	17.9
2.38	33.6	235.3	28.8	12.2	175.6	16.4
4.01	49.9	1,576.1	99.3	6.3	466.8	21.3
1.35	21.0	318.6	26.6	8.3	173.3	15.3
1.59	28.5	236.1	9.0	3.8	64.1	14.0
2.30	45.7	308.3	28.7	9.3	142.4	20.2
3.97	33.3	2,165.9	41.5	1.9	325.5	12.8
2.01	50.7	297.3	14.6	4.9	144.5	10.1
1.41	22.0	255.2	3.0	1.2	29.3	10.2
3.80	31.4	178.6	20.6	11.5	118.8	17.3
1.58	41.1	472.3	3.4	0.7	38.0	8.9
4.06	33.5	382.2	137.6	36.0	917.4	15.0
2.07	47.7	628.7	31.4	5.0	211.0	14.9
1.01	79.2	211.5	12.0	5.7	131.6	9.1
4.16	45.2	5,515.6	536.8	9.7	3,703.7	14.5
2.52	42.9	1,295.1	126.4	9.8	616.6	20.5
4.38	32.0	1,272.7	122.3	9.6	953.3	12.8
3.16	53.2	1,574.9	89.6	5.7	846.0	10.6

References

1. LEVINE, D. M., M. L. BERENSON, AND D. F. STEPHAN, *Using Minitab with Basic Business Statistics*, 2d ed. (Englewood Cliffs, N.J.: Prentice-Hall, 1986).
2. LEVINE, D. M., M. L. BERENSON, AND D. F. STEPHAN, *Using the SPSS Batch System with Basic Business Statistics* (Englewood Cliffs, N.J.: Prentice-Hall, 1983).
3. LEVINE, D. M., M. L. BERENSON, AND D. F. STEPHAN, *Using SAS with Basic Business Statistics* (Englewood Cliffs, N.J.: Prentice-Hall, 1983).
4. *MYSTAT User's Guide* (Evanston, Ill., SYSTAT, Inc., 1988).
5. RYAN, T. A., B. L. JOINER, AND B. F. RYAN, *Minitab Student Handbook*, 2d ed. (North Scituate, Mass.: Duxbury Press, 1985).
6. *SAS User's Guide*, 1982 ed. (Raleigh, N.C.: SAS Institute, 1982).
7. *SPSS^X User's Guide* (New York: McGraw-Hill, 1983).
8. *STATGRAPHICS User's Guide* (Rockville, Md., STSC, Inc., 1986).

Basic Probability

6.1 INTRODUCTION

In this chapter we begin to study various rules of basic probability that can be used to evaluate the chance of occurrence of different phenomena. These rules will be expanded so that we can use probability theory in making inferences about population parameters based only on sample statistics.

6.2 OBJECTIVE AND SUBJECTIVE PROBABILITY

What do we mean by the word probability? **Probability** is the likelihood or chance that a particular event will occur. It could refer to

1. The chance of picking a black card from a deck of cards.
2. The chance that a house selected at random from the real estate survey has a modern kitchen.
3. The chance that a new consumer product on the market will be successful.

Each of these examples refers to one of three approaches to the subject of probability. The first is often called the **a priori classical probability** approach. Here the probability of success is based upon a prior knowledge of the process involved. In the simplest case, when each outcome is equally likely, this chance of occurrence of the event may be defined as follows:

$$\text{probability of occurrence} = \frac{X}{T} \qquad (6.1)$$

where
  X = the number of outcomes for which the event we are looking for occurs
  T = the total number of possible outcomes

For example, in finding the probability of picking a black card from a deck of cards (and defining black as a "success") the correct answer would be 26/52 or 1/2, since there are 26 black cards in a standard deck of cards.

What does this probability tell us? If we replace each card after it is drawn, does it mean that one out of the next two cards will be black? No, on the contrary, we cannot say for sure what will happen on the next several selections. However, we can say that in the long run, if this selection process is followed on a "large" number of trials, the proportion of black cards selected will approach .50.

In this first example, the number of successes and the number of outcomes is known from the composition of the deck of cards. On the other hand, in the second approach to probability, called the **empirical classical probability** approach, although the probability is still defined as the ratio of the number of favorable outcomes to the total number of outcomes, these outcomes are based upon observed data, not upon prior knowledge of a process.

In our second example, from the real estate survey, the probability that a house has a modern kitchen can be found by selecting a random sample of houses from the entire population. In Chapter 2 such a sample of 233 houses was selected (see Figure 2.10). Of these 233 houses, 80 had a modern kitchen. Therefore, the probability that a house selected at random has a modern kitchen (that is, the probability of occurrence) is 80/233 or .343.

The third approach to probability is called the **subjective probability** approach. Whereas in the previous two approaches the probability of a favorable event was computed *objectively*—either from prior knowledge or from actual data—*subjective* probability refers to the chance of occurrence assigned to an event by a particular individual. This chance may be quite different from the subjective probability assigned by another individual. For example, the inventor of a new toy may assign quite a different probability to the chance of success for the toy than the president of the company that is considering marketing the toy. The assignment of subjective probabilities to various events is usually based upon a combination of an individual's past experience, personal opinion, and analysis of a particular situation. Subjective probability is especially useful in making decisions in situations in which the probability of various events cannot be determined empirically.

Problems

6.1 Distinguish between classical probability and subjective probability.
6.2 Give three examples of a priori classical probability.
6.3 Give three examples of empirical classical probability.
6.4 Give three examples of subjective probability.

6.3 BASIC PROBABILITY CONCEPTS

6.3.1 Sample Spaces and Events

The basic elements of probability theory are the outcomes of the process or phenomenon under study. Each possible type of occurrence is referred to as an event.

A **simple event** can be described by a single characteristic. The collection of all the possible events is called the **sample space.**

We can achieve a better understanding of these terms by referring to several examples. First, let us examine the standard deck of 52 playing cards (Figure 6.1) in which there are four suits (diamonds, spades, hearts, and clubs) each of which has 13 different cards (ace, king, queen, jack, ten, nine, eight, seven, six, five, four, three, two).

If we are to randomly select a card from the deck

1. What is the probability the card is black?
2. What is the probability the card is an ace?
3. What is the probability the card is a black ace?
4. What is the probability the card is black *or* an ace?
5. If we knew that the card selected was black, what is the probability that it is also an ace?

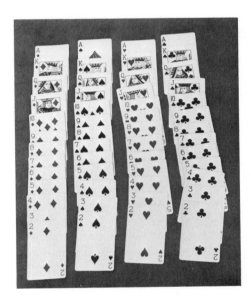

FIGURE 6.1
Standard deck of 52 playing cards.

As a second example, let us refer to the data collected in the real estate survey discussed in Chapter 2. Suppose that from the total sample of 233 houses we pick a single house at random.

1. What is the probability that the house has a modern kitchen?
2. What is the probability that the house has modern bathrooms?
3. What is the probability that the house has a modern kitchen *and* has modern bathrooms?
4. What is the probability that the house has a modern kitchen *or* has modern bathrooms?
5. Suppose that we knew that the house had a modern kitchen. What then would be the probability that it also had modern bathrooms?

In the case of the deck of cards, the sample space consists of the entire deck of 52 cards, made up of various events, depending on how they are classified. For example, if the events are classified by suit, then there are four events: diamond, spade, heart, and club. If the events are classified by card value, there are 13 events: ace, king, . . . , and two. On the other hand, from the real estate survey, the sample space is based on the responses obtained concerning the 233 houses in the survey. Since each question of interest here is divided into two categories, the simple events are as follows:

1. For question 19 pertaining to a modern kitchen, the two simple events are presence of a modern kitchen and absence of a modern kitchen.
2. For question 20 pertaining to modern bathrooms, the two simple events are presence of modern bathrooms and absence of modern bathrooms.

The manner in which the sample space is subdivided depends on the types of probabilities that are to be determined. With this in mind, it is of interest to define both the complement of an event and a joint event as follows:

The **complement of event** *A* includes all events that are not part of event *A*. It is given by the symbol *A'*.

The complement of the event "black" would consist of all those cards that were not black (that is, all the red cards). The complement of spade would contain all cards that were not spades (that is, diamonds, hearts, and clubs). The complement of presence of a modern kitchen is, of course, absence of a modern kitchen.

A **joint event** is an event that has two or more characteristics.

The event "black ace" is a joint event, since the card must be both black *and* ace in order to qualify as a black ace. In a similar manner, the event "presence of a modern kitchen and presence of modern bathrooms" is a joint event, since the house must have a modern kitchen *and* also have modern bathrooms.

6.3.2 Contingency Tables and Venn Diagrams

There are several ways in which a particular sample space can be viewed. The first method involves assigning the appropriate events to a table of cross-classifications. Such a table is also called a **contingency table** (see Section 4.11).

If the two variables of interest for the card example were "presence of ace" and "color of card," the contingency table would look as shown in Table 6.1.

TABLE 6.1   Contingency table for face-color variables

	Red	Black	Totals
Ace	2	2	4
Non-ace	24	24	48
Totals	26	26	52

The values in each cell of the table were obtained by subdividing the sample space of 52 cards according to the number of aces and the color of the card. It can be noted that if the row and column (margin) totals are known, only one cell entry in this 2 × 2 table is needed in order to obtain the entries in the remaining three cells.

The contingency table for the 233 houses in the real estate survey is developed by referring back to Figure 5.13 or by using a computer package to cross-classify the two variables. This is displayed as Table 6.2.

As we have seen in Section 4.11, a contingency table provides a clear presentation of the number of possible outcomes of the relevant variables.

The second way of presenting the sample space is by using a **Venn diagram.**

TABLE 6.2   Contingency table for modern kitchen–modern bathrooms

Modern Kitchen	Modern Bathrooms		
	Present	Absent	Totals
Present	72	8	80
Absent	7	146	153
	79	154	233

This diagram graphically represents the various events as "unions" and "intersections" of circles.

Figure 6.2 represents a typical Venn diagram for a two-variable situation, with each variable having only two events (A and A', B and B'). The circle on the left (the lighter one) represents all events that are part of A. The circle on the right (the darker one) represents all events that are part of B. The area contained within circle A *and* circle B (center area) is the **intersection** of A and B (written as $A \cap B$), since this area is part of A *and* is also part of B. The total area of the two circles is the **union** of A and B (written as $A \cup B$) and contains all outcomes that are part of event A, part of event B, or part of both A and B. The area in the diagram outside $A \cup B$ contains those outcomes that are neither part of A nor part of B.

In order to develop a Venn diagram, A and B must be defined. It does not matter which event is defined as A or B, as long as we are consistent in evaluating the various events.

For the card-playing example, the events can be defined as follows:

$$A = \text{ace} \qquad B = \text{black}$$
$$A' = \text{non-ace} \qquad B' = \text{red}$$

In drawing the Venn diagram (see Figure 6.3), the value of the intersection of A *and* B must be determined so that the sample space can be divided into its parts. $A \cap B$ consists of all black aces in the deck (that is, the two outcomes ace of clubs and ace of spades).

Since there are two black aces, the remainder of event A (ace) consists of the red aces (there are two). The remainder of event B (black cards) consists of all black cards that are not aces (there are 24). The remaining cards are those that are neither black nor ace (there are also 24).

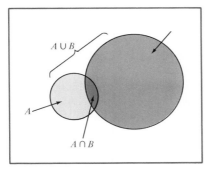

FIGURE 6.2
Venn diagram for events A and B.

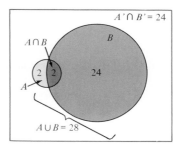

FIGURE 6.3
Venn diagram for card-deck example.

Problems

6.5 Explain the difference between a simple event and a joint event and provide an example of each.

6.6 Explain the difference between union and intersection and provide an example of each.

● **6.7** A manager of a women's store wishes to determine the relationship between the type of customer and the type of payment. She has collected the following data:

	Payment	
Customer	Credit	Cash
Regular	70	50
Nonregular	40	40

(a) Give an example of a simple event.
(b) Give an example of a joint event.
(c) What is the complement of cash payment?
(d) Why is "regular customer who makes a cash payment" a joint event?
(e) Set up the Venn diagram.

6.8 The purchase of many consumer goods may involve various degrees of preplanning. Items such as a pair of slacks or a suit may be the result of a few days' or weeks' planning. Other more expensive purchases, such as a car or a house, may require planning ahead for a year or more before actual buying takes place.

Numerous intensive studies have been conducted of consumer planning for the purchase of durable goods such as television sets, refrigerators, washing machines, stoves, and automobiles. In one such study, 1,000 individuals in a randomly selected sample were asked whether they were planning to buy a new television in the next 12 months. A year later the same persons were interviewed again to find out whether they actually bought a new television. The response to both interviews is cross-tabulated in the table below:

	Buyers	Nonbuyers	Totals
Planned to buy	200	50	250
Did not plan to buy	100	650	750
Totals	300	700	1,000

(a) Give an example of a simple event.
(b) Give an example of a joint event.
(c) What is the complement of "planned to buy"?
(d) Set up a Venn diagram.

● **6.9** A sample of 500 respondents was selected in a large metropolitan area in order to determine various information concerning consumer behavior. Among the questions asked was, "Do you enjoy shopping for clothing?" Of 240 males, 136 answered yes. Of 260 females, 224 answered yes.

(a) Set up a 2 × 2 table or a Venn diagram to evaluate the probabilities.
(b) Give an example of a simple event.
(c) Give an example of a joint event.
(d) What is the complement of "enjoy shopping for clothing"?

6.10 Of 250 employees of a tobacco company, a total of 130 smoke cigarettes. There are 150 males working for this company; 85 of the males smoke cigarettes.
 (a) Set up a 2 × 2 table or a Venn diagram to evaluate the probabilities.
 (b) Give an example of a simple event.
 (c) Give an example of a joint event.
 (d) What is the complement of ''smokes cigarettes''?

6.11 The Statistics Association at a large state university would like to determine whether there is a relationship between a student's interest in statistics and his or her ability in mathematics. A random sample of 200 students is selected and they are asked whether their ability in mathematics and interest in statistics is low, average, or high. The results were as follows:

Interest in Statistics	Ability in Mathematics			
	Low	Average	High	Totals
Low	60	15	15	90
Average	15	45	10	70
High	5	10	25	40
Totals	80	70	50	200

 (a) Give an example of a simple event.
 (b) Give an example of a joint event.
 (c) Why is ''high interest in statistics'' and ''high interest in mathematics'' a joint event?

6.4 SIMPLE (MARGINAL) PROBABILITY

Thus far we have focused upon the meaning of probability and on defining and illustrating several sample spaces. We shall now begin to answer some of the questions posed in the previous sections by developing rules for obtaining different types of probability.

The most obvious rule for probabilities is that they range in value from 0 to 1. An impossible event has probability 0 of occurring, while a certain event has probability 1 of occurring. **Simple probability** refers to the probability of occurrence of a simple event, $P(A)$, such as

- The probability of selecting a black card.
- The probability of selecting an ace.
- The probability of having a modern kitchen.
- The probability of having modern bathrooms.

We have already noted that the probability of selecting a black card is 26/52 or 1/2, since there are 26 black cards in the 52-card deck.

How would we find the probability of picking an ace from the deck? We would find the number of aces in the deck by totaling the black aces and the red aces in the deck:

$$P(\text{ace}) = \frac{\text{number of aces in deck}}{\text{number of cards in deck}}$$

$$= \frac{\text{number of red aces } + \text{ number of black aces}}{\text{total number of cards}}$$

$$= \frac{2 + 2}{52} = \frac{4}{52}$$

Simple probability is also called **marginal probability** since the total number of successes (aces in this case) can be obtained from the appropriate margin of the contingency table (see Table 6.1).

The probability of an ace, $P(A)$, also could be obtained from the Venn diagram (Figure 6.3 on page 181) by looking at the number of outcomes contained in circle A. There are four: two contained in $A \cap B$ and two outside of $A \cap B$. This, of course, gives us the same result as analyzing the contingency table.

Let us refer to the second example. We want to find the probability that a randomly selected house has a modern kitchen.

This probability can be determined by referring to the contingency table (Table 6.2 on page 181):

$$P(\text{having a modern kitchen}) = \frac{\text{number of houses having a}}{\text{total number of houses in}}$$
$$\phantom{P(\text{having a modern kitchen})} = \frac{\text{modern kitchen}}{\text{the sample}}$$

$$= \frac{80}{233} = .343$$

Problems

- **6.12** Referring to Problem 6.7 on page 182, if a customer is selected at random, what is the probability that
  (a) The customer is a regular?
  (b) The customer pays with credit?
  (c) The customer pays with cash?
  (d) The customer is a nonregular?

  6.13 Referring to Problem 6.8 on page 182, if an individual is selected at random, what is the probability that in the last year he or she
  (a) Has bought a new television?
  (b) Planned to buy a new television?
  (c) Did not plan to buy a new television?
  (d) Has not bought a new television?

- **6.14** Referring to Problem 6.9 on page 182, what is the probability that a respondent chosen at random
  (a) Is a male?
  (b) Enjoys shopping for clothing?
  (c) Is a female?
  (d) Does not enjoy shopping for clothing?

  6.15 Referring to Problem 6.10 on page 183, what is the probability that an employee chosen at random
  (a) Is a male?
  (b) Smokes cigarettes?
  (c) Is a female?
  (d) Does not smoke cigarettes?

  6.16 Referring to Problem 6.11 on page 183, if a student is selected at random, what is the probability that he or she

(a) Has a high ability in mathematics?
(b) Has an average interest in statistics?
(c) Has a low ability in mathematics?
(d) Has a high interest in statistics?

6.5 JOINT PROBABILITY

Whereas marginal probability refers to the occurrence of simple events, **joint probability** refers to phenomena containing two or more events, such as the probability of a black ace, a red queen, or of houses that have a modern kitchen and modern bathrooms.

Recall that a joint event *A and B* means that both event *A and* event *B* must occur simultaneously. Referring to Table 6.1, those cards that are black *and* ace consist only of the outcomes in the single cell, ''black ace.'' Since there are two black aces, the probability of picking a card that is a black ace is

$$P(\text{black } and \text{ ace}) = \frac{\text{number of black aces}}{\text{number of cards in deck}}$$

$$= \frac{2}{52}$$

This result can also be obtained by examining the Venn diagram of Figure 6.3 on page 181. The joint event *''A and B''* (black ace) consists of the intersection $(A \cap B)$ of events *A* (ace) and *B* (black), which contains two outcomes. Therefore the probability of a black ace is equal to 2/52.

The probability of choosing a house that has a modern kitchen and has modern bathrooms would be obtained from Table 6.2 in the following manner:

$$P(\text{modern kitchen } and \text{ modern bathrooms}) = \frac{72}{233}$$

since there are 72 houses that have a modern kitchen and modern bathrooms.

Now that we have discussed the concept of joint probability, the marginal probability of a particular event can be viewed in an alternative manner. We have already shown that the marginal probability of an event consists of a set of joint probabilities. For example, if *B* consists of two events, B_1 and B_2, then we can observe that $P(A)$, the probability of event *A*, consists of the joint probability of event *A* occurring with event B_1 and the joint probability of event *A* occurring with event B_2. Thus, in general,

$$P(A) = P(A \text{ and } B_1) + P(A \text{ and } B_2) + \cdots + P(A \text{ and } B_k) \qquad (6.2)$$

where $B_1, B_2 \ldots, B_k$ are mutually exclusive and collectively exhaustive events.

That is, none of the B_i can occur at the same time (**mutually exclusive**) and at least one of the B_i must occur (**collectively exhaustive**). For example, being male *and* being female are mutually exclusive and collectively exhaustive events. No one is both, and everyone is one or the other.

Therefore, the probability of an ace can be expressed as follows:

$$P(\text{ace}) = P(\text{ace } and \text{ red}) + P(\text{ace } and \text{ black})$$

$$= \frac{2}{52} + \frac{2}{52}$$

$$= \frac{4}{52}$$

This is, of course, the same result that we would obtain if we added up the frequency for outcomes that made up the simple event "ace."

Problems

- **6.17** Referring to Problem 6.7 on page 182, what is the probability that if a customer is selected at random
  - **(a)** The customer is regular *and* buys on credit?
  - **(b)** The customer is nonregular *and* pays cash?
  - **(c)** The customer is regular *and* pays cash?

- **6.18** Referring to Problem 6.8 on page 182, what is the probability that in the last year he or she
  - **(a)** Planned to buy *and* actually bought a new television?
  - **(b)** Planned to buy *and* actually did not buy a new television?
  - **(c)** Did not plan to buy *and* actually did not buy a new television?

- **6.19** Referring to Problem 6.9 on page 182, what is the probability that a respondent chosen at random
  - **(a)** Is a female *and* enjoys shopping for clothing?
  - **(b)** Is a male *and* does not enjoy shopping for clothing?
  - **(c)** Is a male *and* enjoys shopping for clothing?

- **6.20** Referring to Problem 6.10 on page 183, what is the probability that an employee chosen at random
  - **(a)** Is a female *and* smokes cigarettes?
  - **(b)** Is a male *and* does not smoke cigarettes?
  - **(c)** Is a female *and* does not smoke cigarettes?

- **6.21** Referring to Problem 6.11 on page 183, what is the probability that a student chosen at random
  - **(a)** Has a low ability in mathematics *and* a low interest in statistics?
  - **(b)** Has a high ability in mathematics *and* an average interest in statistics?
  - **(c)** Has a high ability in mathematics *and* a high interest in statistics?

6.6 ADDITION RULE

Having developed a means of finding the probability of event *A* and the probability of event "*A and B*," we should like to examine a rule (the **addition rule**) that is used for finding the probability of event "*A or B*." This rule for obtaining the probability of the union of *A* and *B* considers the occurrence of either event *A* or event *B* or both *A* and *B*.

The event "black or ace" would include all cards that were black, were aces, or were black aces. Moreover, the event "presence of modern kitchen or presence of modern bathrooms" would include all houses that had a modern kitchen, had modern bathrooms, or had both these characteristics.

Suppose we refer to this latter example. Each cell of the contingency table (Table

6.2 on page 181) can be examined to determine whether it is part of the event in question. If we want to study the event "presence of modern kitchen *or* presence of modern bathrooms," from Table 6.2, the cell "presence of a modern kitchen *and* absence of modern bathrooms" is part of the event, since it includes those houses that have a modern kitchen. The cell "absence of a modern kitchen *and* presence of modern bathrooms" is included because it contains houses that have modern bathrooms. Finally, the cell "presence of a modern kitchen *and* presence of modern bathrooms" has both the characteristics of interest.

Therefore, the probability can be obtained as follows:

$$
\begin{aligned}
P(\text{modern kitchen } or \text{ modern bathrooms}) = \; & P(\text{presence of modern kitchen } and \text{ absence of modern bathrooms}) \\
& + P(\text{absence of modern kitchen } and \text{ presence of modern bathrooms}) \\
& + P(\text{presence of modern kitchen } and \text{ presence of modern bathrooms}) \\
= \; & \frac{8}{233} + \frac{7}{233} + \frac{72}{233} = \frac{87}{233}
\end{aligned}
$$

The computation of $P(A \cup B)$, the probability of the event *A or B*, can be expressed in the following **general addition rule:**

$$
P(A \cup B) = P(A \; or \; B) = P(A) + P(B) - P(A \; and \; B) \qquad \textbf{(6.3)}
$$

Applying this addition rule to the previous example, we obtain the following result:

$$
\begin{aligned}
P(\text{modern kitchen } or \text{ modern bathrooms}) = \; & P(\text{modern kitchen}) \\
& + P(\text{modern bathrooms}) \\
& - P(\text{modern kitchen } and \text{ modern bathrooms}) \\
= \; & \frac{80}{233} + \frac{79}{233} - \frac{72}{233} = \frac{87}{233}
\end{aligned}
$$

The addition rule is to take the probability of *A* and add it to the probability of *B*; the intersection of *A and B* must then be subtracted from this total because it has already been included twice in computing the probability of *A* and of *B*. This can be clearly demonstrated by referring to the contingency table. If the outcomes of the event "presence of a modern kitchen" are added to those of the event "presence of modern bathrooms," then the joint event "presence of modern kitchen *and* presence of modern bathrooms" (the intersection) has been included in each of these events. Therefore, since this has been "double counted," it must be subtracted to provide the correct result.

6.6.1 Mutually Exclusive Events

In certain circumstances, however, the joint probability need not be subtracted because it is equal to zero. Such situations occur when no outcomes exist for a particular event. For example, suppose that we wanted to know the probability of picking from a standard deck of 52 playing cards a single card that was either a heart *or* a spade. Using the addition rule, we have the following:

$$P(\text{heart } or \text{ spade}) = P(\text{heart}) + P(\text{spade}) - P(\text{heart } and \text{ spade})$$

$$= \frac{13}{52} + \frac{13}{52} - \frac{0}{52}$$

$$= \frac{26}{52}$$

Certainly we realize that the probability that a card will be both a heart *and* a spade simultaneously is zero, since in a standard deck each card may take on only one particular suit. The intersection in this case is nonexistent (called the **null set**) because it contains no outcomes, since heart and spade cannot occur simultaneously in the same card.

As mentioned previously, whenever the joint probability does not contain any outcomes, the events involved are considered to be *mutually exclusive*. This refers to the fact that the occurrence of one event (a heart) means that the other event (a spade) cannot occur. Thus, the addition rule for mutually exclusive events reduces to

$$P(A \text{ or } B) = P(A) + P(B) \tag{6.4}$$

6.6.2 Collectively Exhaustive Events

Now consider what the probability would be of selecting a card that was red *or* black. Since red and black are mutually exclusive events, using Equation (6.4) we would have

$$P(\text{red } or \text{ black}) = P(\text{red}) + P(\text{black})$$

$$= \frac{26}{52} + \frac{26}{52} = \frac{52}{52} = 1.0$$

The probability of red *or* black adds up to 1.0. This means that the card selected must be red or black, since they are the only colors in a standard deck. Since one of these events must occur, they are considered to be *collectively exhaustive* events.

Problems

6.22 Explain the difference between mutually exclusive events and collectively exhaustive events and give an example of each.

6.23 For each of the following, tell whether the events which are created are (i) mutually exclusive (ii) collectively exhaustive. If they are not, either reword the categories to make them mutually exclusive and collectively exhaustive or tell why this would not be useful.
(a) Registered voters were asked whether they registered as Republican or Democrat.
(b) Respondents were classified on car ownership into the categories American, European, Japanese, none.
(c) People were asked, "Do you currently live in (i) an apartment (ii) a house?"

   (d) A product was classified as defective or not defective.
   (e) People were asked, ''Do you intend to purchase a color television in the next six months?
   (i) Yes (ii) No

✎ **6.24** The probability of each of the following events is zero. For each, tell why. Tell what common characteristic of these events makes their probability zero.
   (a) A person who is registered as a Republican and a Democrat.
   (b) A product that is defective and not defective.
   (c) A house that is heated by oil and by natural gas.

● **6.25** Referring to Problem 6.7 on page 182, if a customer is selected at random, what is the probability that
   (a) The customer is regular *or* pays cash?
   (b) The customer is nonregular *or* pays on credit?
   (c) The customer pays cash *or* pays on credit?

   6.26 Referring to Problem 6.8 on page 182, if an individual is selected at random, what is the probability that in the last year he or she
   (a) Planned to buy a new television *or* actually bought a new television?
   (b) Did not plan to buy a new television *or* did not actually buy a new television?
   (c) Planned to buy a new television *or* did not plan to buy a new television?

● **6.27** Referring to Problem 6.9 on page 182, what is the probability that a respondent chosen at random
   (a) Is a female *or* enjoys shopping for clothing?
   (b) Is a male *or* does not enjoy shopping for clothing?
   (c) Is a male *or* a female?

   6.28 Referring to Problem 6.10 on page 183, what is the probability that an employee chosen at random
   (a) Is male *or* smokes cigarettes?
   (b) Is female *or* does not smoke cigarettes?
   (c) Smokes cigarettes *or* does not smoke cigarettes?

   6.29 Referring to Problem 6.11 on page 183, what is the probability that a student selected at random
   (a) Has a high interest in statistics *or* a high ability in mathematics?
   (b) Has an average interest in statistics *or* a low ability in mathematics?
   (c) Has a low interest in statistics *or* an average interest in statistics? Are these two events mutually exclusive? Why?
   (d) Has a low ability in mathematics *or* an average ability in mathematics *or* a high ability in mathematics? Are these events mutually exclusive? Why? Are they also collectively exhaustive? Why?

6.7 CONDITIONAL PROBABILITY

Each example that we have studied thus far in this chapter has involved the probability of a particular event when sampling from the entire sample space. However, how would we find various probabilities if certain information about the events involved were already known? For example, if we were told that the card was black, what would be the probability that the card was an ace? Or if we were told that the house had modern bathrooms, what then would be the probability that it also had a modern kitchen?

   When we are computing the probability of a particular event A, given information about the occurrence of another event B, this probability is referred to as **conditional probability,** $P(A|B)$. The conditional probability $P(A|B)$ can be defined as follows:

$$P(A|B) = \frac{P(A \text{ and } B)}{P(B)} \tag{6.5}$$

where $P(A \text{ and } B)$ = joint probability of A and B
$P(B)$ = marginal probability of B

Rather than using Equation (6.4) for finding conditional probability, we can use the contingency table or Venn diagram. In the first example, we wish to find $P(\text{ace}|\text{black})$. Here the information is given that the card is black. Therefore, the sample space does not consist of all 52 cards in the deck; it consists only of the black cards. Of the 26 black cards, two are aces. Therefore, the probability of an ace, given that we know the card is black, is

$$P(\text{ace}|\text{black}) = \frac{\text{number of black aces}}{\text{number of black cards}}$$

$$= \frac{2}{26}$$

This result (2/26) can also be obtained by using Equation (6.5) as follows: If

$$P(A|B) = \frac{P(A \text{ and } B)}{P(B)}$$

$$\text{event } A = \text{ace}$$

$$\text{event } B = \text{black}$$

then

$$P(\text{ace}|\text{black}) = \frac{P(\text{ace and black})}{P(\text{black})}$$

$$= \frac{2/52}{26/52}$$

$$= \frac{2}{26}$$

Let us now examine the second example mentioned, that of determining $P(\text{modern kitchen}|\text{modern bathrooms})$. Since the information given is that the house contains modern bathrooms, the sample space is reduced to those 79 houses. Of these 79 houses, from Table 6.2 we may observe that 72 have a modern kitchen. Therefore, the probability that the house has a modern kitchen given that it has modern bathrooms may be computed as follows:

$$P(\text{modern kitchen}|\text{modern bathrooms}) = \frac{\begin{array}{c}\text{number of houses that have}\\ \text{a modern kitchen } and\\ \text{modern bathrooms}\end{array}}{\begin{array}{c}\text{number of houses that have}\\ \text{modern bathrooms}\end{array}}$$

$$= \frac{72}{79}$$

Again, Equation (6.5) would provide the same answer, as follows:

$$P(A|B) = \frac{P(A \text{ and } B)}{P(B)}$$

where event A = presence of a modern kitchen
event B = presence of modern bathrooms

$$P(\text{modern kitchen}|\text{modern bathrooms}) = \frac{P(\text{modern kitchen and modern bathrooms})}{P(\text{modern bathrooms})}$$

$$= \frac{72/233}{79/233}$$

$$= \frac{72}{79}$$

Decision Trees

In Table 6.2 on page 181, the houses were classified according to presence or absence of a modern kitchen and also modern bathrooms. An alternative way to view the breakdown of the possibilities into four cells is through the use of a **decision tree**. Figure 6.4 consists of a decision tree for the data of Table 6.2.

In Figure 6.4 beginning at the left with the entire set of houses, there are two "branches" according to whether a modern kitchen is present or absent. Each of these branches has two subbranches, corresponding to whether modern bathrooms are present or absent. The probabilities placed at the end of the initial branches represent the marginal probabilities of A [that is, $P(A)$] and A' [that is, $P(A')$], while the probabilities at the end of each of the four subbranches represent the joint probability for each combination of events A and B. The conditional probability can be obtained by dividing

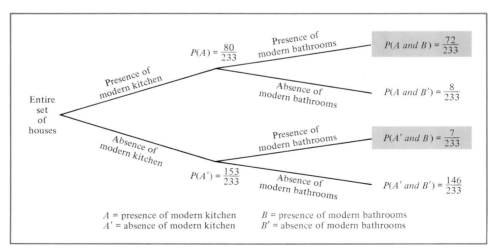

FIGURE 6.4
Decision tree for the data of Table 6.2.

the joint probability of interest by the appropriate marginal probability. For example, to obtain the $P(\text{modern kitchen}|\text{modern bathrooms})$ we would take $P(\text{modern kitchen } and \text{ modern bathrooms})$ and divide it by $P(\text{modern bathrooms})$. From Figure 6.4, we would have

$$P(A|B) = \frac{P(A \text{ and } B)}{P(B)}$$

$$P(\text{modern kitchen}|\text{modern bathrooms}) = \frac{72/233}{72/233 + 7/233}$$

$$= \frac{72/233}{79/233}$$

$$= \frac{72}{79}$$

Note that the denominator, $P(B)$, is the sum of the probabilities of the two appropriate joint events, $P(A \text{ and } B) + P(A' \text{ and } B)$—the probability of presence of modern kitchen *and* presence of modern bathrooms plus the probability of absence of modern kitchen *and* presence of modern bathrooms.

Statistical Independence

It has been observed that in the first example the probability that the card picked is an ace, given that we know it is black, is 2/26. We may remember that the probability of picking an ace out of the deck, $P(\text{ace})$, was 4/52, which reduces to 2/26. This result reveals some important information. The prior knowledge that the card was black did not affect the probability that the card was an ace. This characteristic is called **statistical independence** and can be defined as follows:

$$P(A|B) = P(A) \tag{6.6}$$

where $P(A|B)$ = conditional probability of A given B
$P(A)$ = marginal probability of A

Thus we may note that two events A and B are statistically independent if and only if $P(A|B) = P(A)$.

Here, "color of the card" and "being an ace" are statistically independent events. Knowledge of one event in no way affects the probability of the second event.

We should also like to determine whether having a modern kitchen is independent of having modern bathrooms. The proportion of those houses that have modern bathrooms that also have a modern kitchen is $72/79 = .911$, while the proportion of all houses that have a modern kitchen is $80/233 = .343$. This result reveals some important information: the prior knowledge of the presence of modern bathrooms has affected our prediction of the presence of a modern kitchen. Thus, from a statistical perspective we can state that these two events can be considered to be associated, i.e., not independent. The proportion of houses having a modern kitchen is not the same as the proportion of houses having a modern kitchen given that they also have modern bathrooms.

Problems

- **6.30** Referring to Problem 6.7 on page 182
    - **(a)** Assume that we know the customer is a regular. What is the probability then that he or she will buy on credit?
    - **(b)** Assume we know the customer has paid cash. What is the probability then that he or she is a regular customer?
    - **(c)** Are the two events, being a regular customer and paying on credit, statistically independent? Explain.
- **6.31** Referring to Problem 6.8 on page 182
    - **(a)** If the respondent planned to buy a new television, what is the probability that he or she actually bought one?
    - **(b)** If the respondent did not plan to buy a new television, what is the probability that he or she did not buy a new television?
    - **(c)** Are planning to buy a new television and actually buying one statistically independent? Explain.
- **6.32** Referring to Problem 6.9 on page 182
    - **(a)** Suppose the respondent chosen is a female. What then is the probability that she does not enjoy shopping for clothing?
    - **(b)** Suppose the respondent chosen enjoys shopping for clothing. What then is the probability that the individual is a male?
    - **(c)** Are enjoying shopping for clothing and the gender of the individual statistically independent? Explain.
- **6.33** Referring to Problem 6.10 on page 183
    - **(a)** Suppose we meet a female employee of the company. What then is the probability that she does not smoke cigarettes?
    - **(b)** Suppose we meet a male employee of the company. What then is the probability that he smokes cigarettes?
    - **(c)** Are cigarette smoking and the gender of the individual statistically independent? Explain.
- **6.34** Referring to Problem 6.11 on page 183
    - **(a)** Assume we know that the person selected has a high ability in mathematics. What is the probability that this individual has a high interest in statistics?
    - **(b)** Assume we know that the person selected has an average ability in mathematics. What is the probability that this individual has a low interest in statistics?
    - **(c)** Are interest in statistics and ability in mathematics statistically independent? Explain.

6.8 MULTIPLICATION RULE

The formula for conditional probability can be manipulated algebraically so that the joint probability (*A and B*) can be determined from the conditional probability of an event. From Equation (6.5) we have

$$P(A|B) = \frac{P(A \text{ and } B)}{P(B)}$$

Solving for the joint probability (*A and B*), we have the **general multiplication rule:**

$$P(A \text{ and } B) = P(A|B)P(B) \tag{6.7}$$

To demonstrate the use of this multiplication rule we turn to an example. Suppose that 20 marking pens are displayed in a stationery store. Six are red and 14 are blue. We are to randomly select two markers from the set of 20. What is the probability that both markers selected are red? Here the multiplication rule can be used in the following way:

$$P(A \text{ and } B) = P(A|B)P(B)$$

Therefore if

$$A_R = \text{second marker selected is red}$$

$$B_R = \text{first marker selected is red}$$

we have

$$P(A_R \text{ and } B_R) = P(A_R|B_R)P(B_R)$$

The probability that the first marker is red is 6/20, since six of the 20 markers are red. However, the probability that the second marker is also red depends on the result of the first selection. If the first marker is not returned to the display after its color is determined (sampling *without* replacement), then the number of markers remaining will be 19. If the first marker is red, the probability that the second also is red is 5/19, since five red markers remain in the display. Therefore, using Equation (6.7), we have the following:

$$P(A_R \text{ and } B_R) = \left(\frac{6}{20}\right)\left(\frac{5}{19}\right)$$

$$= \frac{30}{380} = .079$$

However, what if the first marker selected is returned to the display after its color is determined? Then the probability of picking a red marker on the second selection is the same as on the first selection (sampling *with* replacement), since there are six red markers out of 20 in the display. Therefore, we have the following:

$$P(A_R \text{ and } B_R) = P(A_R|B_R)P(B_R)$$

$$= \left(\frac{6}{20}\right)\left(\frac{6}{20}\right)$$

$$= \frac{36}{400} = .09$$

This example of sampling *with* replacement illustrates that the second selection is independent of the first, since the second probability was not influenced by the first selection. Therefore, the **multiplication rule for independent events** can be expressed as follows [by substituting $P(A)$ for $P(A|B)$]:

$$P(A \text{ and } B) = P(A)P(B) \tag{6.8}$$

If this rule holds for two events, A and B, then A and B are statistically independent. Therefore, there are two ways to determine statistical independence.

1. Events *A* and *B* are statistically independent if and only if $P(A|B) = P(A)$.
2. Events *A* and *B* are statistically independent if and only if $P(A \text{ and } B) = P(A)P(B)$.

It should be noted that for a 2×2 contingency table, if this is true for one joint event, it will be true for all joint events. For example, if the probability of a card being an ace is independent of it being black, then the probability of it being an ace is independent of it being red, the probability of not being an ace is independent of it being black, and the probability of not being an ace is independent of it being red.

Now that we have discussed the multiplication rule, we can write the formula for marginal probability (6.1) as follows. If

$$P(A) = P(A \text{ and } B_1) + P(A \text{ and } B_2) + \cdots + P(A \text{ and } B_k)$$

then, using the multiplication rule, we have

$$P(A) = P(A|B_1)P(B_1) + P(A|B_2)P(B_2) + \cdots + P(A|B_k)P(B_k) \quad \textbf{(6.9)}$$

where $B_1, B_2 \ldots, B_k$ are *k* mutually exclusive and collectively exhaustive events.

We may illustrate this formula by referring to Table 6.1 on page 180. Using Equation (6.9), we may compute the probability of an ace as follows:

$$P(A) = P(A|B_1)P(B_1) + P(A|B_2)P(B_2)$$
$$= \left(\frac{2}{26}\right)\left(\frac{26}{52}\right) + \left(\frac{2}{26}\right)\left(\frac{26}{52}\right)$$
$$= \frac{2}{52} + \frac{2}{52}$$
$$= \frac{4}{52}$$

Problems

- **6.35** Referring to Problem 6.7 on page 182, use Equation (6.8) to determine whether being a regular customer and buying on credit are statistically independent.

  6.36 Referring to Problem 6.8 on page 182, use Equation (6.8) to determine whether planning to buy a new television and actually buying one are statistically independent.

- **6.37** Referring to Problem 6.9 on page 182, use Equation (6.8) to determine whether enjoying shopping for clothing is statistically independent of the gender of the individual.

  6.38 Referring to Problem 6.10 on page 183, use Equation (6.8) to determine whether cigarette smoking is statistically independent of the gender of the individual.

  6.39 Referring to Problem 6.11 on page 183, use Equation (6.8) to determine whether ability in mathematics is statistically independent of interest in statistics.

  6.40 Suppose you believe that the probability that you will get an A in Statistics is .6, and the probability that you will get an A in Organizational Behavior is .8. If these events are independent, what is the probability that you will get an A in both Statistics and Organizational Behavior? Give some plausible reasons why these events may not be independent, even though the teachers of these two subjects may not communicate about your work.

6.41 A standard deck of cards is being used to play a game. There are four suits (hearts, diamonds, clubs, and spades), each having 13 cards (ace, 2, 3, 4, 5, 6, 7, 8, 9, 10, jack, queen, and king), making a total of 52 cards. This complete deck is thoroughly mixed, and you will receive the first two cards from the deck *without* replacement.
(a) What is the probability that both cards are queens?
(b) What is the probability that the first card is a 10 *and* the second card is a 5 *or* 6?
(c) If we were sampling *with* replacement, what would be the answer in (a)?
(d) In the game of blackjack the picture cards (jack, queen, king) count as 10 points while the ace counts as either 1 or 11 points. All other cards are counted at their face value. Blackjack is achieved if your two cards sum to 21 points. What is the probability of getting blackjack in this problem?

6.42 A bin contains two defective tubes and five good tubes. Two tubes are randomly selected from the bin *without* replacement.
(a) What is the probability that both tubes are defective?
(b) What is the probability that the first tube selected is defective *and* the second tube is good?

6.43 A box of nine baseball gloves contains two left-handed gloves and seven right-handed gloves.
(a) If two gloves are randomly selected from the box *without* replacement, what is the probability that
(1) both gloves selected will be right-handed?
(2) there will be one right-handed glove *and* one left-handed glove selected?
(b) If three gloves are selected, what is the probability that all three will be left-handed?
(c) If we were sampling *with* replacement, what would be the answers to (a)(1) and (b)?

6.44 A shipment of 10 dolls contains three boy dolls and seven girl dolls.
(a) If two dolls are selected from the shipment *without* replacement, what is the probability that
(1) both dolls selected will be girls?
(2) there will be one girl doll *and* one boy doll?
(3) the first doll selected will be a girl and the second doll selected will be a boy?
(b) Compare your answers for parts (a)(2) and (a)(3) and explain why they are different.

6.9 BAYES' THEOREM

Conditional probability takes into account information about the occurrence of one event to predict the probability of another event. This concept can be extended to "revise" probabilities based on new information and to determine the probability that a particular effect was due to a specific cause. The procedure for revising these probabilities is known as **Bayes' theorem** [since it was originally developed by Rev. Thomas Bayes (1702–1761); see Reference 2].

Bayes' theorem can be applied to the following problem: The marketing manager of a toy manufacturing firm is planning to introduce a new toy into the market. In the past, 40% of the toys introduced by the company have been successful, and 60% have not been successful. Before the toy is actually marketed, market research is conducted and a report, either favorable or unfavorable, is compiled. In the past, 80% of the successful toys received favorable reports and 30% of the unsuccessful toys also received favorable reports. The marketing manager would like to know the probability that the new toy will be successful if it receives a favorable report.

Bayes' theorem can be developed from the definitions of conditional and marginal probability in the following manner:

$$P(A \text{ and } B) = P(A|B)P(B) \tag{6.10a}$$

but also

$$P(A \text{ and } B) = P(B|A)P(A) \qquad \textbf{(6.10b)}$$

From Equations (6.10a and 6.10b) we have

$$P(B|A)P(A) = P(A|B)P(B)$$

so that, by dividing by $P(A)$, we get

$$P(B|A) = \frac{P(A|B)P(B)}{P(A)} \qquad \textbf{(6.10c)}$$

From Equation (6.9), however,

$$P(A) = P(A|B_1)P(B_1) + P(A|B_2)P(B_2) + \cdots + P(A|B_k)P(B_k)$$

so that **Bayes' theorem** is

$$P(B_i|A) = \frac{P(A|B_i)P(B_i)}{P(A|B_1)P(B_1) + P(A|B_2)P(B_2) + \cdots + P(A|B_k)P(B_k)} \qquad \textbf{(6.10d)}$$

where B_i is the ith event out of k mutually exclusive events.

Now we can use Bayes' theorem to solve the toy manufacturer's problem. Let

event S = successful toy   event F = favorable report

event S' = unsuccessful toy   event F' = unfavorable report

and

$$P(S) = .40 \qquad P(F|S) = .80$$
$$P(S') = .60 \qquad P(F|S') = .30$$

Then

$$\begin{aligned}
P(S|F) &= \frac{P(F|S)P(S)}{P(F|S)P(S) + P(F|S')P(S')} \\
&= \frac{(.80)(.40)}{(.80)(.40) + (.30)(.60)} \\
&= \frac{.32}{.32 + .18} = \frac{.32}{.50} \\
&= .64
\end{aligned}$$

The probability of a successful toy, given that a favorable report was received, is .64. Thus the probability of an unsuccessful toy, given that a favorable report was received, is .36, since there are only two possible events.

$$\begin{aligned}
P(S'|F) &= 1 - P(S|F) \\
&= 1 - .64 = .36
\end{aligned}$$

The denominator of Bayes' theorem represents the marginal probability of event F, in this case a favorable market research report. Therefore, the proportion of toys that receive favorable market research reports is .50.

The computation of the probabilities is summarized in Table 6.3 and displayed in the form of a decision tree in Figure 6.5.

TABLE 6.3 Bayes' theorem calculations for toy manufacturer's problem

Events S_i	Prior Probability $P(S_i)$	Conditional Probability $P(F\|S_i)$	Joint Probability $P(F\|S_i)P(S_i)$	Revised Probability $P(S_i\|F)$
S = successful toy	.40	.80	.32	.32/.50 = .64 = $P(S\|F)$
S' = unsuccessful toy	.60	.30	.18	.18/.50 = .36 = $P(S'\|F)$
			.50	

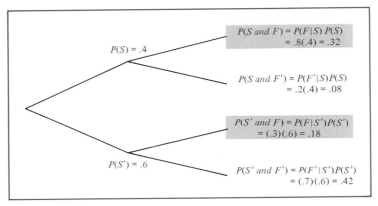

FIGURE 6.5
Decision tree for the toy manufacturer's problem.

Referring to the data collected in the real estate survey, Bayes' theorem can also be utilized to determine the conditional probability that a house that has a modern kitchen will also have modern bathrooms, P(modern bathrooms|modern kitchen) based on information about the proportion of houses that have modern bathrooms that also have a modern kitchen, P(modern kitchen|modern bathrooms).

event A = presence of modern kitchen   event B = presence of modern bathrooms

event A' = absence of a modern kitchen   event B' = absence of modern bathrooms

From Table 6.2 we have

$$P(B) = 79/233 \qquad P(A|B) = 72/79$$

$$P(B') = 154/233 \qquad P(A|B') = 8/154$$

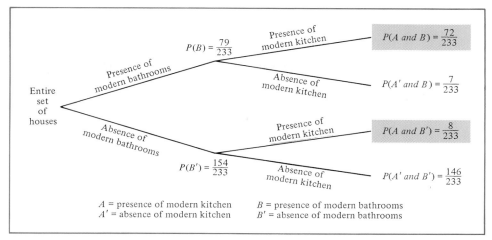

FIGURE 6.6
Decision tree for determining P(modern bathrooms|modern kitchen).

Therefore

$$P(B|A) = \frac{P(A|B)P(B)}{P(A|B)P(B) + P(A|B')P(B')}$$

$$= \frac{(72/79)(79/233)}{(72/79)(79/233) + (8/154)(154/233)}$$

Thus

$$P(B|A) = \frac{72/233}{80/233} = \frac{72}{80} = .90$$

These computations are summarized in the decision tree depicted in Figure 6.6. We may note that the only difference between Figures 6.6 and 6.4 (page 191) is the order of the branches. In Figure 6.4 the first branch refers to $P(A)$ whereas in Figure 6.6 the first branch refers to $P(B)$.

Problems

6.45 A television station would like to measure the ability of its weather forecaster. Past data have been collected that indicate the following:

1. The probability the forecaster predicted sunshine on sunny days is .80.
2. The probability the forecaster predicted sunshine on rainy days is .40.
3. The probability of a sunny day is .60.

Find the probability that
(a) It will be sunny given that the forecaster has predicted sunshine.
(b) The forecaster will predict sunshine.

● **6.46** An advertising executive is studying television viewing habits of married men and women during prime-time hours. Based on past viewing records he has determined that during prime time husbands are watching television 60% of the time. It has also been determined that when the husband is watching television, 40% of the time the wife is also watching. When the husband is not watching television, 30% of the time the wife is watching television. Find the probability that

(a) If the wife is watching television, the husband is also watching television.

(b) The wife is watching television during prime time.

6.47 The Olive Construction Co. is determining whether it should submit a bid for the construction of a new shopping center. In the past, Olive's main competitor, Base Construction Co., has submitted bids 70% of the time. If Base Construction Co. does not bid on a job, the probability that the Olive Construction Co. will get the job is .50; if Base Construction Co. does bid on a job, the probability that the Olive Construction Co. will get the job is .25.

(a) If the Olive Construction Co. gets the job, what is the probability that the Base Construction Co. did not bid?

(b) What is the probability that Olive Construction Co. will get the job?

• **6.48** The editor of a major textbook publishing company is trying to decide whether to publish a proposed new business statistics textbook. Previous textbooks published indicate that 10% are huge successes, 20% are modest successes, 40% break even, and 30% are losers. However, before a publishing decision is made, the book will be reviewed. In the past, 99% of the huge successes received favorable reviews. 70% of the moderate successes received favorable reviews, 40% of the break-even books received favorable reviews, and 20% of the losers received favorable reviews.

(a) If the proposed text receives a favorable review, how should the editor revise the probabilities of the various outcomes to take this information into account?

(b) What proportion of textbooks receive favorable reviews?

6.49 A municipal bond rating service has three rating categories (A, B, and C). In the past year, of the municipal bonds issued throughout the country, 70% have been rated A, 20% have been rated B, and 10% have been rated C. Of the municipal bonds rated A, 50% were issued by cities, 40% by suburbs, and 10% by rural areas. Of the municipal bonds rated B, 60% were issued by cities, 20% by suburbs, and 20% by rural areas. Of the municipal bonds rated C, 90% were issued by cities, 5% by suburbs, and 5% by rural areas.

(a) If a new municipal bond is to be issued by a city, what is the probability that it will receive an A rating?

(b) What proportion of the municipal bonds are issued by cities?

(c) What proportion of the municipal bonds are issued by suburbs?

6.10 COUNTING RULES

Each rule of probability that we have discussed has involved the counting of the number of favorable outcomes and the total number of outcomes. In many instances, however, because of the large number of possibilities, it is not feasible to list each of the outcomes. In these circumstances, rules for counting have been developed. Five different counting rules will be discussed here.

First of all, suppose that a coin was being flipped 10 times. How would we determine the number of different possible outcomes (the sequences of heads and tails)?

Counting Rule 1: If any one of k different mutually exclusive and collectively exhaustive events can occur on each of n trials, the number of possible outcomes is equal to

$$k^n \qquad\qquad (6.11)$$

If a coin (having two sides) is tossed 10 times, the number of outcomes is 2^{10} = 1,024. If a die (having six sides) is rolled twice, the number of different outcomes is $6^2 = 36$.

The second counting rule is a more general version of the first. To illustrate this rule, suppose that the number of possible events is different on some of the trials. For example, a state motor vehicle department would like to know how many license plate numbers would be available if the license plate consisted of three digits followed by two letters. The fact that three values are digits (each having 10 possible outcomes) while two positions are letters (each having 26 outcomes) leads to the second rule of counting.

Counting Rule 2: If there are k_1 events on the first trial, k_2 event on the second trial, . . . , and k_n events on the nth trial, then the number of possible outcomes is

$$(k_1)(k_2) \cdots (k_n) \tag{6.12}$$

Thus if a license plate consisted of three digits followed by two letters, the total number of possible outcomes would be $(10)(10)(10)(26)(26) = 676,000$. Taking another example, if a restaurant menu had a choice of four appetizers, ten entrees, three beverages, and six desserts, the total number of possible dinners would be $(4)(10)(3)(6)$ = 720.

The third counting rule involves the computation of the number of ways that a set of objects can be arranged in order. If a set of six textbooks is to be placed on a shelf, how can we determine the number of ways in which the six books may be arranged? We may begin by realizing that any of the six books could occupy the first position on the shelf. Once the first position is filled, there are five books to choose from in filling the second. This assignment procedure is continued until all the positions are occupied. The total number of arrangements would be equal to $(6)(5)(4)(3)(2)(1)$ = 720. This situation can be generalized as counting rule 3.

Counting Rule 3: The number of ways that all n objects can be arranged in order is

$$n! = n(n - 1) \cdots (1) \tag{6.13}$$

where $n!$ is called n *factorial* and $0!$ is defined as 1.

The number of ways that six books could be arranged is

$$n! = (6)(5)(4)(3)(2)(1)$$
$$= 720$$

In many instances we need to know the number of ways in which a subset of the entire group of objects can be arranged in order. Each possible arrangement is called a **permutation.**

For example, modifying the previous problem, if six textbooks are involved, but there is room for only four books on the shelf, how many ways can these books be arranged on the shelf?

Counting Rule 4: Permutations: The number of ways of arranging X objects selected from n objects in order is

$$\frac{n!}{(n-X)!} \tag{6.14}$$

Therefore, the number of ordered arrangements of four books selected from six books is equal to

$$\frac{n!}{(n-X)!} = \frac{6!}{(6-4)!} = \frac{6!}{2!} = \frac{6(5)(4)(3)(2)(1)}{2(1)} = 360$$

Finally, in many situations we are not interested in the *order* of the outcomes but only in the number of ways that X objects can be selected out of n objects, *irrespective of order*. This rule is called the rule of **combinations.**

Counting Rule 5: Combinations: The number of ways of selecting X objects out of n objects, irrespective of order, is equal to

$$\frac{n!}{X!(n-X)!} \tag{6.15}$$

This expression may be denoted by the symbol $\binom{n}{X}$.

Comparing this rule to the previous one, we see that it differs only in the inclusion of a term $X!$ in the denominator. This is because when we counted permutations, all of the arrangements of the X objects were distinguishable; with combinations, the $X!$ possible arrangements of objects are irrelevant. Therefore, the number of combinations of four books selected from six books is expressed by

$$\frac{n!}{X!(n-X)!} = \frac{6!}{4!(6-4)!} = \frac{6!}{4!2!} = \frac{6(5)(4)(3)(2)(1)}{4(3)(2)(1)(2)(1)} = 15$$

6.11 SUMMARY

In this chapter we have examined various rules of probability as well as applications of these rules to a variety of problems. Probability theory is the foundation of statistical inference. These concepts will be extended to more complicated situations in subsequent chapters so that methodology can be developed to use descriptive summary measures in order to make inferences about populations.

Problems

- **6.50** A lock on a bank vault consists of three dials, each with 30 positions. In order for the vault to open when closed, each of the three dials must be in the correct position.
  (a) How many different possible "dial combinations" are there for this lock?
  (b) What is the probability that if you randomly select a position on each dial, you will be able to open the bank vault?
  (c) Explain why "dial combinations" are not mathematical combinations expressed by Equation (6.14)?

- **6.51** **(a)** If a coin is tossed seven times, how many different outcomes are possible?
  (b) If a die is tossed seven times, how many different outcomes are possible?
  (c) Discuss the differences in your answers to (a) and (b).

- **6.52** A famous fast-food restaurant has a menu that consists of ten entrees, two vegetables, four beverages, and three desserts. How many different meals (consisting of one entree, vegetable, beverage, and dessert) can be ordered at this restaurant?

- **6.53** A particular brand of women's jeans can be ordered in seven different sizes, three different colors, and three different styles. How many different jeans would have to be ordered if a store wanted to have one pair of each type?

- **6.54** The Daily Double at the local racetrack consists of picking the winners of the first two races. If there are 10 horses in the first race and 13 horses in the second race, how many Daily Double possibilities are there?

- **6.55** There are six teams in the Eastern Division of the National League: Chicago, Montreal, New York, Philadelphia, Pittsburgh, and St. Louis. How many different orders of finish are there in which the teams can place? Do you *really* believe that all these orders are equally likely? Discuss.

- **6.56** A gardener has seven rows available in his vegetable garden to place tomatoes, eggplant, peppers, cucumbers, beans, lettuce, and squash. Each vegetable will be allotted one and only one row. How many ways are there to position these vegetables in his garden?

- **6.57** A basketball team must schedule a game with each of three different teams. There are five different dates available for games. How many different schedules can be made?

- **6.58** The Big Triple at the local racetrack consists of picking the correct order of finish of the first three horses in the ninth race. If there are 12 horses entered in today's ninth race, how many Big Triple outcomes are there?

- **6.59** The Quinella at the local racetrack consists of picking the horses that will place first and second in a race irrespective of order. If eight horses are entered in a race, how many Quinella combinations are there?

- **6.60** A student has seven books that she would like to place in an attaché case. However, only four books can fit into the attaché case. Regardless of the arrangement, how many ways are there of placing four books into the attaché case?

- **6.61** A daily lottery is to be conducted in which two winning numbers are to be selected out of 100 numbers? How many different combinations of winning numbers are possible?

Supplementary Problems

- **6.62** In evaluating conditional probabilities and using Bayes' Theorem, which do you prefer— summary tables such as Table 6.3 or decision trees such as Figure 6.5? Why?

6.63 When rolling a die once, what is the probability that
   (a) The face of the die is odd?
   (b) The face is even *or* odd?
   (c) The face is even *or* a one?
   (d) The face is odd *or* a one?
   (e) The face is both even *and* a one?
   (f) Given the face is odd, it is a one?

• **6.64** The director of a large employment agency wishes to study various characteristics of its job applicants. A sample of 200 applicants has been selected for analysis. Seventy applicants have had their current jobs for at least five years; 80 of the applicants are college graduates; 25 of the college graduates have had their current jobs at least five years.
   (a) What is the probability that an applicant chosen at random
      (1) Is a college graduate?
      (2) Is a college graduate *and* has held the current job less than five years?
      (3) Is a college graduate *or* has held the current job at least five years?
   (b) Given that a particular employee is a college graduate, what is the probability that he or she has held the current job less than five years?
   (c) Determine whether being a college graduate *and* holding the current job for at least five years are statistically independent.
      [*Hint*: Set up a 2 × 2 table or a Venn diagram or a decision tree to evaluate the probabilities.]

6.65 Suppose that a survey has been undertaken to determine if there is a relationship between place of residence and ownership of a foreign-made automobile. A random sample of 200 car owners from large cities, 150 from suburbs, and 150 from rural areas was selected with the following results:

	Type of Area			
Car Ownership	*Large City*	*Suburb*	*Rural*	*Totals*
Own foreign car	90	60	25	175
Do not own foreign car	110	90	125	325
Totals	200	150	150	500

   (a) If a car owner is selected at random, what is the probability that he or she
      (1) Owns a foreign car?
      (2) Lives in a suburb?
      (3) Owns a foreign car *or* lives in a large city?
      (4) Lives in a large city *or* a suburb?
      (5) Lives in a large city *and* owns a foreign car?
      (6) Lives in a rural area *or* does not own a foreign car?
   (b) Assume we know that the person selected lives in a suburb. What is the probability that he or she owns a foreign car?
   (c) Is area of residence statistically independent of whether the person owns a foreign car? Explain.

6.66 A nationwide market research study was undertaken to determine the preferences of various age groups of males for different sports. A random sample of 1,000 men was selected and each individual was asked to indicate his favorite sport. The results were as follows (see page 205):

Age Group	Sport				
	Baseball	Football	Basketball	Hockey	Totals
Under 20	26	47	41	36	150
20–29	38	84	80	48	250
30–39	72	68	38	22	200
40–49	96	48	30	26	200
50 and over	134	44	18	4	200
Totals	366	291	207	136	1,000

    (a) If a respondent is selected at random, what is the probability that he
        (1) Prefers baseball?
        (2) Is between 20 and 29 years old?
        (3) Is between 20 and 29 years old *and* prefers basketball?
        (4) Is at least 50 years of age *or* prefers baseball?
    (b) Assume that the person selected is under 20 years old. What is the probability that he prefers hockey?

6.67 An art director for a magazine has 12 pictures to choose from for 5 positions in her magazine.
    (a) How many different sets of 5 pictures could she choose from the 12 available pictures?
    (b) Once she has picked her 5 pictures, in how many ways can she arrange them in the magazine?
    (c) How many permutations are there of 12 objects taken 5 at a time? [Show how this answer is related to your answers to (a) and (b).]

Database Exercises

The following problems refer to the sample data obtained from the questionnaire of Figure 2.5 on page 15 and presented in Figure 2.10 on pages 24–29. They should be solved with the aid of an available computer package.

☐ **6.68** Set up a cross-classification table of whether the house has an eat-in kitchen (question 14) and whether it has a modern kitchen (question 19).
    (a) What is the probability that a randomly selected house
        (1) Has an eat-in kitchen?
        (2) Does not have a modern kitchen?
        (3) Has an eat-in kitchen *and* a modern kitchen?
        (4) Has an eat-in kitchen *or* a modern kitchen?
    (b) Assume that we know that the house has an eat-in kitchen. What then is the probability that it has a modern kitchen?
    (c) Is the presence of an eat-in kitchen statistically independent of the presence of a modern kitchen? Explain.

☐ **6.69** Set up a cross-classification table of whether the house has an eat-in kitchen (question 14) and whether it has a basement (question 18).
    (a) What is the probability that a randomly selected house
        (1) Has an eat-in kitchen?
        (2) Has a basement?
        (3) Does not have an eat-in kitchen *and* does not have a basement?
        (4) Has an eat-in kitchen *or* has a basement?

(b) Suppose we know that the house has a basement. What then is the probability that it has an eat-in kitchen?

(c) Is the presence of an eat-in kitchen statistically independent of the presence of a basement? Explain.

□ **6.70** Set up a cross-classification table of whether the house has central air-conditioning (question 15) and whether it has a fireplace (question 16).

(a) What is the probability that a randomly selected house
   (1) Does not have central air-conditioning?
   (2) Has a fireplace?
   (3) Has central air-conditioning *and* does not have a fireplace?
   (4) Has central air-conditioning *or* has a fireplace?

(b) Suppose we know that the house has a fireplace. What then is the probability that it has central air-conditioning?

(c) Is the presence of central air-conditioning statistically independent of the presence of a fireplace? Explain.

□ **6.71** Set up a cross-classification table of whether the house has central air-conditioning (question 15) and whether it has a modern kitchen (question 19).

(a) What is the probability that a randomly selected house
   (1) Has central air-conditioning?
   (2) Has a modern kitchen?
   (3) Has central air-conditioning *and* does not have a modern kitchen?
   (4) Has central air-conditioning *or* has a modern kitchen?

(b) Suppose we know that a house has a modern kitchen. What then is the probability that it has central air-conditioning?

(c) Is the presence of central air-conditioning statistically independent of the presence of a modern kitchen? Explain.

□ **6.72** Set up a cross-classification table of whether the house has a fireplace (question 16) and whether it has a basement (question 18).

(a) What is the probability that a randomly selected house
   (1) Has a fireplace?
   (2) Does not have a basement?
   (3) Does not have a fireplace *and* does not have a basement?
   (4) Has a fireplace *or* does not have a basement?

(b) Assume we know that the house has a basement. What then is the probability that it has a fireplace?

(c) Is the presence of a fireplace statistically independent of the presence of a basement?

□ **6.73** Set up a cross-classification table of the geographic location of the house (question 9) and whether the house has a fireplace (question 16).

(a) What is the probability that a randomly selected house
   (1) Has a fireplace?
   (2) Is located in East Meadow?
   (3) Is located in East Meadow *and* has a fireplace?
   (4) Is located in Farmingdale *or* in Levittown?
   (5) Is located in Levittown *or* does not have a fireplace?

(b) Assume we know that a house is located in East Meadow. What then is the probability that it has a fireplace?

(c) Is geographic location statistically independent from presence of a fireplace? Explain.

□ **6.74** Set up a cross-classification table of the geographic location of the house (question 9) and whether the house has a connection to a local sewer system (question 17).

(a) What is the probability that a randomly selected house
   (1) Has a local sewer connection?
   (2) Is located in East Meadow?

(3) Is located in East Meadow *and* does not have a local sewer connection?
(4) Is located in Farmingdale *or* in Levittown?
(5) Is located in Levittown *or* does not have a local sewer connection?

(b) Assume we know that a house is located in East Meadow. What then is the probability that it has a local sewer connection?

(c) Is geographic location statistically independent from presence of a local sewer connection? Explain.

□ **6.75** Set up a cross-classification table of the architectural style of house (question 10) and the presence of a fireplace (question 16).

(a) What is the probability that a randomly selected house
(1) Has a fireplace?
(2) Is a Cape?
(3) Is a split level *and* has a fireplace?
(4) Is a Cape *or* a colonial *or* a split level?
(5) Is a Cape *or* does not have a fireplace?

(b) Assume we know that a house is a split level. What then is the probability that it has a fireplace?

(c) Is type of house statistically independent from presence of a fireplace? Explain.

□ **6.76** Set up a cross-classification table of the architectural style of house (question 10) and the presence of a modern kitchen (question 19).

(a) What is the probability that a randomly selected house
(1) Has a modern kitchen?
(2) Is a Cape?
(3) Is a split level *and* has a modern kitchen?
(4) Is a Cape *or* a colonial *or* a split level?
(5) Is a Cape *or* does not have a modern kitchen?

(b) Assume we know that a house is a split level. What then is the probability that it has a modern kitchen?

(c) Is type of house statistically independent from presence of a modern kitchen? Explain.

□ **6.77** Set up a cross-classification table of the type of heating fuel used (question 11) and whether the house has a basement (question 18).

(a) What is the probability that a randomly selected house
(1) Has gas heat?
(2) Does not have a basement?
(3) Uses oil heat *and* does not have a basement?
(4) Uses oil heat *or* does not have a basement?

(b) Assume we know that the house has a basement. What then is the probability that it uses oil heat?

(c) Is the type of heating fuel used statistically independent of the presence of a basement?

□ **6.78** Set up a cross-classification table of the type of swimming pool (question 13) and the presence of a fireplace (question 16).

(a) What is the probability that a randomly selected house
(1) Has an above-ground swimming pool?
(2) Has a fireplace?
(3) Has an in-ground swimming pool *and* has a fireplace?
(4) Has an above-ground *or* an in-ground swimming pool?
(5) Does not have a swimming pool *or* does not have a fireplace?

(b) Assume we know that a house has an in-ground swimming pool. What then is the probability that it has a fireplace?

(c) Is type of swimming pool statistically independent from presence of a fireplace? Explain.

□ **6.79** Set up a cross-classification table of the type of indoor parking facility (question 8) and the geographic location of the house (question 9).

    (a) What is the probability that a randomly selected house
        (1) Has a one-car garage?
        (2) Is located in East Meadow?
        (3) Is located in East Meadow *and* has a one-car garage?
        (4) Is located in Farmingdale *or* in Levittown?
        (5) Is located in Levittown *or* does not have a garage?
    (b) Assume we know that a house is located in East Meadow. What then is the probability that it has a two-car garage?
    (c) Is type of garage statistically independent of the geographic location? Explain.

□ **6.80** Set up a cross-classification table of the geographic location of the house (question 9) and the architectural style of house (question 10).
    (a) What is the probability that a randomly selected house
        (1) Is a Cape?
        (2) Is located in East Meadow?
        (3) Is located in East Meadow *and* is a Cape?
        (4) Is located in Farmingdale *or* in Levittown?
        (5) Is located in Levittown *or* is a ranch?
    (b) Assume we know that a house is located in East Meadow. What then is the probability that it is a Cape?
    (c) Is geographic location statistically independent from the type of house? Explain.

□ **6.81** Set up a cross-classification table of the architectural style of house (question 10) and the type of swimming pool (question 13).
    (a) What is the probability that a randomly selected house
        (1) Does not have a swimming pool?
        (2) Is a Cape?
        (3) Is a split level *and* has an above-ground swimming pool?
        (4) Is a Cape *or* a colonial *or* a split level?
        (5) Has an above-ground pool *or* an in-ground pool?
        (6) Is a Cape *or* does not have a swimming pool?
    (b) Assume we know that a house is a split level. What then is the probability that it has an in-ground pool?
    (c) Is type of house statistically independent from the type of swimming pool? Explain.

□ **6.82** Set up a cross-classification table of the type of heating fuel used (question 11) and the type of heating system (question 12).
    (a) What is the probability that a randomly selected house
        (1) Has gas heat?
        (2) Has a hot-water heating system?
        (3) Uses oil heat *and* a hot-air heating system?
        (4) Uses oil heat *or* a hot-water heating system?
    (b) Assume we know that the house has a hot-water heating system. What then is the probability that it uses oil heat?
    (c) Is the type of heating fuel used statistically independent of the type of heating system used? Explain.

□ **6.83** Set up a cross-classification table of the geographic location of the house (question 9) and the type of swiming pool (question 13).
    (a) What is the probability that a randomly selected house
        (1) Does not have a swimming pool?
        (2) Is located in East Meadow?
        (3) Is located in East Meadow *and* does not have a swimming pool?
        (4) Is located in Farmingdale *or* in Levittown?
        (5) Is located in Levittown *or* has an above-ground pool?

(b) Assume we know that a house is located in East Meadow. What then is the probability that it has an in-ground pool?

(c) Is geographic location statistically independent from the type of swimming pool? Explain.

References

1. HAYS, W. L., *Statistics for the Social Sciences* 3d ed. (New York: Holt, Rinehart and Winston, 1981).
2. KIRK, R. E., ed., *Statistical Issues*: *A Reader for the Behavioral Sciences* (Belmont, Calif.: Wadsworth, 1972).
3. MOSTELLER, F., R. Rourke, and G. Thomas, *Probability with Statistical Applications*, 2d ed. (Reading, Mass.: Addison-Wesley, 1970).

7

Some Important Discrete Probability Distributions

7.1 INTRODUCTION: WHAT'S AHEAD

In the preceding chapter we established various rules of probability and examined some counting techniques. In this chapter we will utilize this information to develop the concept of mathematical expectation and to explore various probability models which represent discrete phenomena of interest.

The goals of this chapter are

1. To develop an understanding of the concept of mathematical expectation and its applications in decision making.
2. To gain an appreciation of the need for various discrete probability distributions.
3. To acquire the ability to use the binomial, hypergeometric, and Poisson probability distributions in decision making.

7.2 THE PROBABILITY DISTRIBUTION FOR A DISCRETE RANDOM VARIABLE

As discussed in Section 2.3, a quantitative random variable is some phenomenon of interest whose responses or outcomes may be expressed numerically. Such a random variable may also be classified as discrete or continuous—the former arising from a counting process and the latter from a measuring process. This chapter deals with various probability distributions which represent discrete random variables. As an example from the real estate survey developed in Chapter 2, responses to the question about (total) number of rooms pertain to a probability distribution for a discrete random variable.

We may define the probability distribution for a discrete random variable as follows:

A **probability distribution for a discrete random variable** is a mutually exclusive listing of all possible numerical outcomes for that random variable such that a particular probability of occurrence is associated with each outcome.

Assuming that a fair six-sided die will not stand on edge or roll out of sight (*null events*), Table 7.1 represents the probability distribution for the outcomes of a single roll of the fair die. Since all possible outcomes are included, this listing is complete (or *collectively exhaustive*) and thus the probabilities must sum up to 1. We can then use this table to obtain various probabilities for the rolling of a fair die.

TABLE 7.1   Theoretical probability distribution of the results of rolling one fair die

Face of Outcome		Probability
1	⚀	1/6
2	⚁	1/6
3	⚂	1/6
4	⚃	1/6
5	⚄	1/6
6	⚅	1/6
	Total	1

The probability of a face ⚁ is

$$P\left(⚁\right) = 1/6$$

Using the addition rule for mutually exclusive events, the probability of an odd face is

$$P(\text{odd}) = P\left(⚀\right) + P\left(⚂\right) + P\left(⚄\right)$$

$$= 1/6 + 1/6 + 1/6 = 3/6$$

Moreover, the probability of a face of ⚁ or less is

$$P\left(⚁ \text{ or less}\right) = P\left(⚀\right) + P\left(⚁\right) = 1/6 + 1/6 = 2/6$$

And the probability of a face larger than $\left(⚅\right)$ is

$$P\left(> ⚅\right) = 0$$

7.3 MATHEMATICAL EXPECTATION

In order to summarize a discrete probability distribution we shall compute its major characteristics—the mean and the standard deviation.

7.3.1 Expected Value of a Discrete Random Variable

The mean (μ_X) of a probability distribution is the **expected value** of its random variable.

> The **expected value of a discrete random variable** may be considered as its weighted average over all possible outcomes—the "weights" being the probability associated with each of the outcomes.

This summary measure can be obtained by multiplying each possible outcome X_i by its corresponding probability $P(X_i)$ and then summing up the resulting products. Thus, the expected value of the discrete random variable X, symbolized as $E(X)$, may be expressed as follows:

$$\mu_X = E(X) = \sum_{i=1}^{N} X_i P(X_i) \tag{7.1}$$

where X = discrete random variable of interest
X_i = ith outcome of X
$P(X_i)$ = probability of occurrence of the ith outcome of X
$i = 1, 2, \ldots, N$

For the theoretical probability distribution of the results of rolling one fair die (Table 7.1), the expected value of the roll may be computed as

$$
\begin{aligned}
\mu_X = E(X) = \sum_{i=1}^{N} X_i P(X_i) &= (1)(1/6) + (2)(1/6) + (3)(1/6) \\
&\quad + (4)(1/6) + (5)(1/6) + (6)(1/6) \\
&= 1/6 + 2/6 + 3/6 + 4/6 + 5/6 + 6/6 \\
&= 21/6 = 3.5
\end{aligned}
$$

Notice that the expected value of the results of rolling a fair die is not "literally meaningful," since we can never obtain a face of 3.5. However, we can expect to observe the six different faces with equal likelihood so that, in the long run, over many rolls, the average value would be 3.5.

To make this particular situation meaningful, however, we introduce the following carnival game: How much money should we be willing to put up in order to have the opportunity of rolling a fair die if we were to be paid, in dollars, the amount on the face of the die? Since the expected value of a roll of a fair die is 3.5, the expected long-run payoff is $3.50 per roll. That is, on any particular roll our payoff will be $1.00, $2.00, . . . , or $6.00, but over many, many rolls the payoff can be expected to average out to $3.50 per roll. Now if we want the game to be fair, neither we nor our opponent (the "house") should have an advantage. Thus we should be willing to pay $3.50 per roll to play. If the house wants to charge us $4.00 per roll we can expect to lose from such gambling, on the average, $.50 per roll over time, and unless we derive some intrinsic satisfaction (costing on the average $.50 per roll), we should refrain from participating in such a game.

Usually, though, in any casino or carnival-type game the expected long-run payoff to the participant is negative, otherwise the house would not be in business (References 6 and 7). Such games as Craps, Under-or-over-seven, Chuck-a-luck, or Roulette (see Reference 6) attract large numbers of participants and, in each case, the expected return over time favors the house.[1]

7.3.2 Variance and Standard Deviation of a Discrete Random Variable

The **variance (σ_X^2) of a discrete random variable** may be defined as the weighted average of the squared discrepancies between each possible outcome and its mean—the "weights" being the probabilities of each of the respective outcomes.

This summary measure can be obtained by multiplying each possible squared discrepancy $(X_i - \mu_X)^2$ by its corresponding probability $P(X_i)$ and then summing up the resulting products. Hence, the variance of the discrete random variable X may be expressed as follows:

$$\sigma_X^2 = \sum_{i=1}^{N} (X_i - \mu_X)^2 P(X_i) \tag{7.2}$$

where X = discrete random variable of interest
$\quad X_i$ = ith outcome of X
$\quad P(X_i)$ = probability of occurrence of the ith outcome of X
$\quad i = 1, 2, \ldots, N$

Moreover, the **standard deviation (σ_X) in the probability distribution of a discrete random variable** is given by

$$\sigma_X = \sqrt{\sum_{i=1}^{N} (X_i - \mu_X)^2 P(X_i)} \tag{7.3}$$

For the theoretical probability distribution of the results of rolling one fair die (Table 7.1) the variance and the standard deviation may be computed by

$$
\begin{aligned}
\sigma_X^2 &= \sum_{i=1}^{N} (X_i - \mu_X)^2 P(X_i) \\
&= (1 - 3.5)^2(1/6) + (2 - 3.5)^2(1/6) \\
&\quad + (3 - 3.5)^2(1/6) + (4 - 3.5)^2(1/6) \\
&\quad + (5 - 3.5)^2(1/6) + (6 - 3.5)^2(1/6) \\
&= 2.9166
\end{aligned}
$$

---

[1] Since a decision maker who acts rationally would want to maximize gains or minimize losses, rational persons would freely partake in such transactions only if something other than expected monetary value were the ultimate criterion. The concept of the **expected utility of money** is discussed in References 3 and 10. It is the criterion which rational participants are considering, implicitly or explicitly, when they partake in such games. On the other hand, however, the house uses the expected-monetary-value criterion when it participates in such games.

and

$$\sigma_X = 1.71$$

In terms of our carnival game, the mean payoff per roll is \$3.50 with a standard deviation of \$1.71. According to the Bienaymé-Chebyshev rule (Section 3.12), the majority of our payoffs would be expected to be within $\sqrt{2} = 1.414$ standard deviations of the mean (that is, $\mu_X \pm 1.414\ \sigma_X$). Most likely, then, on a per roll basis we would expect a payoff between \$1.00 and \$5.00 [that is, these are the integer outcomes between the values $3.50 \pm 1.414\ (1.71)$] and not win very frequently if it is costing us \$4.00 per roll to play.

7.3.3 Expected Value of a Function of a Random Variable: Expected Monetary Value

As prospective participants in the carnival game, the most important question that we had to address was whether or not it was *profitable* for us to play the game. To answer this question, we had to realize that the random variable of interest from the "gambling viewpoint" was not really X, the *outcome on the face of the die* (as in Table 7.1), but rather V, the *dollar value* associated with the resulting outcome from rolling the die. Thus, for participating in the game, the values for V ranged from $-\$3$ to $+\$2$ since it cost \$4 for every roll of the die (see Table 7.2).

TABLE 7.2   Theoretical probability distribution representing the dollar value for participating in carnival game

Result (X)	Dollar Value (V)	Probability
· 1	−3	1/6
2	−2	1/6
3	−1	1/6
4	0	1/6
5	1	1/6
6	2	1/6
		$\overline{1}$

For purposes of decision making, the objective is to compare the **expected monetary values** (denoted by $E(V)$ or EMV) among alternative strategies (such as "play the carnival game" versus "don't play"). The expected monetary value indicates the average profit that would be gained if a particular strategy were selected in many decision-making situations (such as "play the game many times"). Hence to play the game

$$E(V) = \sum_{i=1}^{N} V_i P(V_i) = (-3)(1/6) + (-2)(1/6) + \cdots + (2)(1/6)$$
$$= -.50$$

while not playing the game

$$E(V) = 0$$

Thus our long-run expected payoff for participating is negative. On the average, we'd be losing 50 cents each time we decide to roll the die.[2]

Assigning Probabilities

To compute the expected monetary value for the various strategies, a set of probabilities must be assigned to the mutually exclusive and collectively exhaustive listing of outcomes or events. In many cases, no information is available about the probability of occurrence of the various events and, thus, equal probabilities are assigned. In other instances, the probabilities of the events can be estimated in several ways. First, information may be available from past experience that can be used for estimating the probabilities. Second, a subjective assessment of the likelihood of the various events may be given by managers or other supervisory personnel. Third, the probabilities of the events could follow a particular discrete probability distribution such as the uniform, binomial, hypergeometric, or Poisson distribution. These latter models will be the subject matter of the remainder of this chapter.

Problems

● **7.1** Given the following probability distributions:

Distribution A		Distribution B	
X	P(X)	X	P(X)
0	.50	0	.05
1	.20	1	.10
2	.15	2	.15
3	.10	3	.20
4	.05	4	.50

    (a) Compute the mean for each distribution.
    (b) Compute the standard deviation for each distribution.
    ➠**(c)** **ACTION**   Compare and contrast the results in parts (a) and (b). Discuss what you have learned.

7.2 Given the following probability distributions:

Distribution C		Distribution D	
X	P(X)	X	P(X)
0	.20	0	.10
1	.20	1	.20
2	.20	2	.40
3	.20	3	.20
4	.20	4	.10

---

[2] Over an evening in which the die is rolled 100 times, we'd be expected to "take in" $350 but "pay out" $400. Thus, at the end of play we'd be expected to lose $50 on the 100 rolls—an average of 50 cents per roll (or $12\frac{3}{4}$ cents per dollar "wagered").

(a) Compute the mean for each distribution.

(b) Compute the standard deviation for each distribution.

➠(c) **ACTION** Compare and contrast the results in parts (a) and (b). Discuss what you have learned.

7.3 Using the company records for the past 500 working days, the manager of Silverman Motors, a suburban automobile dealership, has summarized the number of cars sold per day into the following table:

Number of Cars Sold per Day	Frequency of Occurrence
0	40
1	100
2	142
3	66
4	36
5	30
6	26
7	20
8	16
9	14
10	8
11	2
Total	500

(a) Form the empirical probability distribution (that is, relative frequency distribution) for the discrete random variable X, the number of cars sold per day.

(b) Compute the mean or expected number of cars sold per day.

(c) Compute the standard deviation.

(d) What is the probability that on any given day
   (1) fewer than 4 cars will be sold?
   (2) at most 4 cars will be sold?
   (3) at least 4 cars will be sold?
   (4) exactly 4 cars will be sold?
   (5) more than 4 cars will be sold?

➠(e) **ACTION** Write a letter to the manager discussing the dealership's performance over the past 500 working days.

7.4 An employee for a vending concession at a ball park must choose between working behind the "hot dog counter" and receiving a fixed sum of $50 for the evening versus walking around the stands selling beer on a commission basis. If the latter is chosen the employee can make $90 on a warm night, $70 on a moderate night, $45 on a cool night, and $15 on a cold night. At this time of year the probabilities of a warm, moderate, cool, or cold night are, respectively, 0.1, 0.3, 0.4, and 0.2.

(a) Determine the mean or expected value to be earned by selling beer that evening.

(b) Compute the standard deviation.

➠(c) **ACTION** Which product should the employee sell? Why?

7.5 A state lottery is to be conducted in which 10,000 tickets are to be sold for $1 each. Six winning tickets are to be randomly selected: one grand-prize winner of $5,000, one second-prize winner of $2,000, one third-prize winner of $1,000, and three other winners of $500 each.

(a) Compute the expected value of playing this game.

➠(b) **ACTION** Would you play this game? Why?

● 7.6 Let us consider rolling a pair of six-sided dice. The random variable of interest represents the sum of the two numbers (that is, faces) that occur when the pair of fair dice are rolled. The probability distribution is given on page 217:

X	P(X)
2	1/36
3	2/36
4	3/36
5	4/36
6	5/36
7	6/36
8	5/36
9	4/36
10	3/36
11	2/36
12	1/36
	1

(a) Determine the mean or expected sum from rolling a pair of fair dice.

(b) Compute the variance and the standard deviation.

The game of Craps deals with the rolling of a pair of fair dice. A *field bet* in the game of Craps is a one-roll bet and is based on the outcome of the pair of dice. For every $1.00 bet you make: you can lose the $1.00 if the sum is 5, 6, 7, or 8; you can win $1.00 if the sum is 3, 4, 9, 10, or 11; or you can win $2.00 if the sum is either 2 or 12.

(c) Form the probability distribution function representing the different outcomes that are possible in a field bet.

(d) Determine the mean of this probability distribution.

(e) What is the player's expected long-run profit (or loss) from a $1.00 field bet? Interpret.

(f) What is the expected long-run profit (or loss) to the house from a $1.00 field bet? Interpret.

➡(g) **ACTION** Would you play this game and make a field bet?

7.7 In the carnival game Under-or-over-seven a pair of fair dice are rolled once and the resulting sum determines whether or not the player wins or loses his or her bet. For example, the player can bet $1.00 that the sum is under 7—that is, 2, 3, 4, 5, or 6. For such a bet the player will lose $1.00 if the outcome equals or exceeds 7 or will win $1.00 if the result is under 7. Similarly, the player can bet $1.00 that the sum is over 7—8, 9, 10, 11, or 12. Here the player wins $1.00 if the result is over 7 but loses $1.00 if the result is 7 or under. A third method of play is to bet $1.00 on the outcome 7. For this bet the player will win $4.00 if the result of the roll is 7 and lose $1.00 otherwise.

(a) Form the probability distribution function representing the different outcomes that are possible for a $1.00 bet on being under 7.

(b) Form the probability distribution function representing the different outcomes that are possible for a $1.00 bet on being over 7.

(c) Form the probability distribution function representing the different outcomes that are possible for a $1.00 bet on 7.

(d) Prove that the expected long-run profit (or loss) to the player is the same—no matter which method of play is used.

➡(e) **ACTION** Would you prefer to play Under-or-over-seven or make a field bet in Craps (Problem 7.6)? Why?

7.8 Why does the term *expected value* have that name, even though in many cases (such as our carnival game on page 212) you will never see the expected value as the result of any single experiment? (That is, in what sense is a value which never occurs expected?)

7.9 Suppose an author is trying to choose between two publishing companies that are competing for the marketing rights to her new novel. Prentice-Hall has offered the author $10,000 plus $2 for each book sold. Random House has offered the author $2,000 plus $4 for each book sold. The author estimates the distribution of demand for this book as displayed at the top of page 218:

Number of Books Sold	Probability
1,000	.45
2,000	.20
5,000	.15
10,000	.10
50,000	.10

⟶**ACTION**   Using the expected-monetary-value criterion, determine whether the author should sell the marketing rights to Prentice-Hall or to Random House. Discuss.

● **7.10**   The Islander Fishing Co. purchases clams for $1.00 per pound from Peconic Bay fishermen for sale to various New York restaurants for $1.50 per pound. Any clams not sold to the restaurants by the end of the week can be sold to a local soup company for $.25 per pound. The probabilities of various levels of demand are as follows:

Demand (pounds)	Probability
500	.2
1,000	.4
2,000	.4

[*Hint*: The company can purchase 500 pounds, 1,000 pounds, or 2,000 pounds.]

⟶**ACTION**   Using the expected-monetary-value criterion, determine the optimal number of pounds of clams that the company should purchase from the fishermen. Discuss.

7.11   The LeFleur Garden Center chain purchases Christmas trees from a supplier for sale during the holiday season. The trees are purchased for $6.00 each and are sold for $12.00 each. Any trees not sold can be disposed of for $3.00 each. The probability of various levels of demand is as follows:

Demand (number of trees)	Probability
100	.2
200	.6
500	.2

[*Hint*: The chain can purchase trees in lots of 100, 200, or 500.]

⟶**ACTION**   Using the expected-monetary-value criterion, determine the number of trees that the chain should purchase from the supplier. Discuss.

● **7.12**   A city street vendor with a stand outside a large office building must determine whether to sell ice cream or soda today. The vendor believes that the profit made will depend upon the weather. The payoff table is as follows:

Event	Strategy	
	Sell Soda	Sell Ice Cream
Cool weather	+$40	+$20
Warm weather	+$55	+$80

Based upon her past experience at this time of the year, the vendor estimates the probability of warm weather as .60.

➠**ACTION** Determine whether the vendor should sell soda or sell ice cream based upon the expected-monetary-value criterion. Discuss.

7.13 An investor has a certain amount of money available to invest now. Three alternative portfolio selections are available. The estimated profits of each portfolio under each economic condition are indicated in the following payoff table:

Event	Porfolio Selection		
	A	B	C
Economy declines	+ $500	− $2,000	− $7,000
No change	+ $1,000	+ $2,000	− $1,000
Economy expands	+ $2,000	+ $5,000	+ $20,000

Based upon his own past experience, the investor assigns the following probabilities to each economic condition:

$$P(\text{economy declines}) = .30$$
$$P(\text{no change}) = .50$$
$$P(\text{economy expands}) = .20$$

➠**ACTION** Determine the best portfolio selection for the investor according to the expected-monetary-value criterion. Discuss.

7.14 Shop-Quik Supermarkets purchases large quantities of white bread for sale during a week. The bread is purchased for 65 cents per loaf and is sold for 90 cents per loaf. Any loaves of bread not sold by the end of the week can be sold to a local thrift shop for 50 cents per loaf. Based on past demand, the probability of various levels of demand is as follows:

Demand (Loaves)	Probability
6,000	.1
8,000	.5
10,000	.3
12,000	.1

[*Hint*: Bread can be purchased in quantities of 6,000 loaves, 8,000 loaves, 10,000 loaves, or 12,000 loaves.]

➠**ACTION** Using the expected-monetary-value criterion, determine the optimal number of loaves of bread that should be purchased. Discuss.

7.4 DISCRETE PROBABILITY DISTRIBUTION FUNCTIONS

The probability distribution for a discrete random variable may be

1. A *theoretical* listing of outcomes and probabilities (as in Table 7.1), which can be obtained from a mathematical model representing some phenomenon of interest.
2. An *empirical* listing of outcomes and their observed relative frequencies.
3. A *subjective* listing of outcomes associated with their subjective or ''contrived'' probabilities representing the degree of conviction of the decision maker as to the likelihood of the possible outcomes (as discussed in Section 6.2).

In this chapter we will be concerned mainly with the first kind of probability distribution—the listing obtained from a mathematical model representing some phenomenon of interest.

> A **model** is considered to be a miniature representation of some underlying phenomenon. In particular, a mathematical model is a mathematical expression representing some underlying phenomenon. For discrete random variables, this mathematical expression is known as a **probability distribution function.**

When such mathematical expressions are available, the exact probability of occurrence of any particular outcome of the random variable can be computed. In such cases, then, the entire probability distribution can be obtained and listed. For example, the probability distribution function represented in Table 7.1 is one in which the discrete random variable of interest is said to follow the **uniform probability distribution.** This type of mathematical model will be discussed in Section 7.5. In addition, other types of mathematical models have been developed to represent various discrete phenomena which occur in the social and natural sciences, in medical research, and in business. The more useful of these represent data characterized by the **binomial probability distribution,** the **hypergeometric probability distribution,** and the **Poisson probability distribution.** Each of these discrete distributions will also be discussed in this chapter.

7.5 UNIFORM DISTRIBUTION

A uniform probability distribution reflecting the possible outcomes of a roll of a single fair die was presented in Table 7.1. *The essential characteristic of the uniform distribution is that all outcomes of the random variable are equally likely to occur.* Thus the probability that the face $\boxed{\because}$ of the fair die turns up is the same as that for any other result—1/6—since there are six possible outcomes.

The mathematical expression representing the probability that a discrete random variable X, which follows the uniform distribution, takes on a particular value x from among a series of consecutive integer values is given by

$$P(X = x) = \frac{1}{(b - a) + 1} \qquad (7.4)$$

where b = largest possible outcome of X
$\quad\ a$ = smallest possible outcome of X
$\quad\ X = a, a + 1, a + 2, \ldots, b$

In the die example, $b = 6$ and $a = 1$, so that the probability that X takes on a particular value in this interval is

$$P(X = x) = \frac{1}{(6 - 1) + 1} = \frac{1}{6}$$

Although the mean and the standard deviation for any discrete random variable could be computed from Equations (7.1) and (7.3), simpler methods exist for making these summary computations when the random variable is considered to be uniformly distributed. In such cases the mean or expected value of the random variable X can be shown to be

$$\mu_X = E(X) = \frac{a + b}{2} \tag{7.5}$$

and the standard deviation is obtained from

$$\sigma_X = \sqrt{\frac{[(b - a) + 1]^2 - 1}{12}} \tag{7.6}$$

Applications of uniformly distributed random variables are found in the development of lotteries and other forms of gaming; in the generation of random numbers for engineering and/or simulation experiments; and, as was discussed in Section 7.3.3, in the assessment of one's ''prior probabilities'' or ''prior beliefs'' regarding the outcome of some future event for decision-making purposes.

Problems

7.15 For the uniform distribution displayed in Table 7.1 on page 211 ($b = 6$ and $a = 1$), verify that Equation (7.5) yields the same result for μ_X as was obtained in Section 7.3.1 using Equation (7.1).

7.16 For the uniform distribution displayed in Table 7.1 on page 211 ($b = 6$ and $a = 1$), verify that Equation (7.6) yields the same result for σ_X as was obtained in Section 7.3.2 using Equation (7.3).

7.17 List the uniform distribution that represents the single-digit numbers (0 through 9) generated in a table of random numbers (Section 2.7.2).
⟾**ACTION** Compare this theoretical distribution against the empirical relative frequency distribution formed by tallying all 200 digits which appear in the first five rows of Table E.1. Discuss.

7.6 BINOMIAL DISTRIBUTION

One discrete probability distribution function which is extremely useful for describing many phenomena is the binomial distribution. The binomial model also plays a particularly important role as an approximation to the hypergeometric distribution (which we shall consider in Section 7.7.2).

The binomial distribution possesses four essential properties:

1. The possible observations may be obtained by two different sampling methods. Either each observation may be considered as having been selected from an **infinite population without replacement** or from a **finite population with replacement**.

2. Each observation may be classified into one of two mutually exclusive and collectively exhaustive categories, usually called *success* and *failure*.

3. The probability of an observation's being classified as success, p, is constant from observation to observation. Thus, the probability of an observation's being classified as failure, $1 - p$, is constant over all observations.

4. The outcome (that is, success or failure) of any observation is independent of the outcome of any other observation.

The discrete random variable or phenomenon of interest which follows the binomial distribution is the number of successes obtained in a sample of n observations. Thus the binomial distribution has enjoyed numerous applications:

- *In games of chance*:
  What is the probability that red will come up 15 or more times in 19 spins of the roulette wheel?

- *In product quality control*:
  What is the probability that in a sample of 20 tires of the same type none will be defective if 8% of all such tires produced at a particular plant are defective?

- *In education*:
  What is the probability that a student can pass a ten-question multiple-choice exam (each containing four choices) if the student guesses on each question? (Passing is defined as getting 60% of the items correct—that is, getting at least six out of ten items correct.)

- *In finance*:
  What is the probability that a particular stock will show an increase in its closing price on a daily basis over the next ten (consecutive) trading sessions if stock market price changes really are random?

In each of these examples the four properties of the binomial distribution are clearly satisfied. For the roulette example, a particular set of spins may be construed as the sample taken from an infinite population of spins without replacement. When spinning the roulette wheel, each observation is categorized as red (success) or not red (failure). The probability of spinning red, p, on an American roulette wheel is 18/38 and is assumed to remain stable over all observations. Thus the probability of failure (spinning black or green), $1 - p$, is 20/38 each and every time the roulette wheel spins. Moreover, the roulette wheel has no memory—the outcome of any one spin is independent of preceding or following spins, so that, for example, the probability of obtaining red on the 32nd spin, given that the previous 31 spins were all red, remains equal to p, 18/38, if the roulette wheel is a fair one (see Figure 7.1 on page 223).[3]

In the product quality-control example, the sample of tires is also selected without replacement from an ongoing production process, an infinite population of manufactured tires.[4] As each tire in the sample is inspected, it is categorized as defective or non-defective.[5] Over the entire sample of tires the probability of any particular tire's being

---

[3] It has been reported (Reference 9) that one time at Monte Carlo red came up on 32 consecutive spins. The probability of such an occurrence is indeed a very small number—$(18/37)^{32}$ = .0000000000969. The Monte Carlo roulette wheel, like other European wheels, has 37 equal-sized sectors—18 red, 18 black, and one green.

[4] As an example of a binomial random variable arising from sampling with replacement from a finite population, consider the probability of obtaining two clubs in five draws from a randomly shuffled deck of cards, where the selected card is replaced and the deck well shuffled after each draw.

[5] Note that when we are looking for defective tires, the discovery of such an event is deemed a success. This is one of the instances referred to above where, for statistical purposes, the term "success" may refer to business failures, deaths due to a particular illness, and other phenomena that, in nonstatistical terminology, would be deemed unsuccessful.

FIGURE 7.1
American roulette wheel.

classified as defective, p, is .08, so that the probability of any tire being categorized as nondefective, $1 - p$, is .92. The production process is assumed to be stable. This is the case if

1. The machinery producing the tires does not wear down.
2. The raw materials used are uniform.
3. The labor is consistent.

Moreover, for such a production process, the probability of one tire's being classified as defective or nondefective is independent of the classification for any other tire.

Similar statements pertaining to the binomial distribution's properties (characteristics) in the education example and in the finance example can be made as well. This is left to the reader. (See Problems 7.18 and 7.19 on page 230).

The four examples of binomial probability models described above are distinguished by the parameters n and p. Each time a set of parameters—the number of observations in the sample, n, and the probability of success, p—is specified, a particular binomial probability distribution can be generated.

- For the roulette example, $n = 19$ and $p = 18/38$.
- For the quality-control example, $n = 20$ and $p = .08$.
- For the education example, $n = 10$ and $p = 1/4$.
- For the finance example, $n = 10$ and $p = 1/2$.

7.6.1 Development of the Mathematical Model

As another example of a phenomenon which satisfies the conditions of the binomial distribution, and one which is convenient for intuitively deriving an expression for the probabilities which arise in binomial problems, we shall return to the rolling of a fair die which was discussed in Section 7.2. Here, however, we consider success to be the outcome face ⚁ and failure to be any other outcome. Suppose we are now interested in three rolls of this same die in order to determine how frequently the face ⚁ is obtained.[6] What might occur? None of the rolls might land on ⚁; one of the rolls may be a ⚁; two of the rolls may land on ⚁; or all three rolls may land on ⚁. Can the binomial random variable, the number of ⚁ faces occurring on three rolls of a fair die, take on any other value? Obviously not! If we roll the same die three times and are interested in how often a particular value (face ⚁) occurs, that value cannot exceed the number of rolls n, nor can it be lower than zero. Hence the range of a binomial random variable is from 0 to n.

Suppose then, for example, that we roll a fair die three times and observe the following result:

First Roll	Second Roll	Third Roll
⚁	Not 5	⚁

We now wish to determine the probability of this occurrence; that is, what is the probability of obtaining two successes (face ⚁) in three rolls in the *particular sequence* above? Since it may be assumed that rolling dice is a stable process, the probability that each roll occurs as above is

First Roll	Second Roll	Third Roll
$p = 1/6$	$1 - p = 5/6$	$p = 1/6$

Since each outcome is independent of the others, the probability of obtaining the given sequence is

$$p(1 - p)p = p^2(1 - p)^1 = p^2(1 - p) = (1/6)^2(5/6) = 5/216$$

Thus out of 216 possible and equally likely outcomes from rolling a fair die three times, five will have the face ⚁ as the first and last roll, with a face other than ⚁ (that is, ⚀, ⚂, ⚃, ⚄, or ⚅) as the middle roll, and the particular sequence above will be obtained.

Now, however, we may ask how many different sequences are there for

[6] Three rolls of the same die is equivalent to one roll of each of three dice. See Problem 7.21 on the game of Chuck-a-luck (page 230).

obtaining two faces of ⊡ out of $n = 3$ rolls of the die? Using Equation (6.15) from Section 6.10, we have

$$\binom{n}{X} = \frac{n!}{X!(n-X)!} = \frac{3!}{2!(3-2)!} = 3$$

such sequences. These three possible sequences are

sequence 1 = ⊡ [Not 5] ⊡ with probability $p(1-p)p = p^2(1-p)^1 = 5/216$
sequence 2 = ⊡ ⊡ [Not 5] with probability $pp(1-p) = p^2(1-p)^1 = 5/216$
sequence 3 = [Not 5] ⊡ ⊡ with probability $(1-p)pp = p^2(1-p)^1 = 5/216$

Therefore, the probability of obtaining exactly two faces of ⊡ from three rolls of a die is equal to

(number of possible sequences) × (probability of a particular sequence)
(3) × (5/216) = 15/216 = .0694

A similar, intuitive derivation can be obtained for the other three possible outcomes of the random variable—no face ⊡ , one face ⊡ , or all three faces ⊡ . However, as n, the number of observations, gets large, this type of intuitive approach becomes quite laborious, and a mathematical model is more appropriate. In general, the following mathematical model represents the binomial probability distribution for obtaining the number of successes (X), given a knowledge of the parameters n and p:

$$P(X = x \mid n, p) = \frac{n!}{x!(n-x)!} p^x (1-p)^{n-x} \tag{7.7}$$

where $P(X = x \mid n, p)$ = the probability that $X = x$, given a knowledge of n and p
n = sample size
p = probability of success
$1 - p$ = probability of failure
x = number of successes in the sample ($X = 0, 1, 2, \ldots, n$)

We note, however, that the generalized form shown in Equation (7.7) is merely a restatement of what we had intuitively derived above.

The binomial random variable X can have any integer value from 0 through n. In Equation (7.7) the product

$$p^x(1-p)^{n-x}$$

tells us the probability of obtaining exactly x successes out of n observations *in a particular sequence*, while the term

$$\frac{n!}{x!(n-x)!}$$

tells us *how many sequences* or arrangements (i.e., *combinations*—see Section 6.10) of the *x* successes out of *n* observations are possible. Hence, given the number of observations *n* and the probability of success *p*, we may determine the probability of *x* successes:

$$P(X = x|n, p) = \text{(number of possible sequences)}$$
$$\times \text{(probability of a particular sequence)}$$
$$= \frac{n!}{x!(n - x)!} p^x(1 - p)^{n-x}$$

by substituting the desired values for *n*, *p*, and *x* and computing the result.

Thus, as above, the probability of obtaining exactly two faces of ⚁ from three rolls of a die is

$$P\left(X = 2|n = 3, p = \frac{1}{6}\right) = \frac{3!}{2!(3 - 2)!}\left(\frac{1}{6}\right)^2\left(1 - \frac{1}{6}\right)^{3-2}$$
$$= \frac{3!}{2!1!}\left(\frac{1}{6}\right)^2\left(\frac{5}{6}\right)^1$$
$$= (3)\left(\frac{1}{6}\right)\left(\frac{1}{6}\right)\left(\frac{5}{6}\right) = \frac{15}{216} = .0694$$

Such computations may become quite tedious, especially as *n* gets large. However, we may obtain the probabilities directly from Table E.7 and thereby avoid any computational drudgery. Table E.7 provides, for various selected combinations of the parameters *n* and *p*, the probabilities that the binomial random variable takes on values of *X* = 0, 1, 2, . . . , *n*. However, the reader should be cautioned that the *p* values in Table E.7 are taken to only two decimal places; thus, in some circumstances, due to rounding errors, the probabilities will only be approximations to the true result. As a case in point, for our dice-rolling experiment, we first find in Table E.7 the combination *n* = 3 with *p* rounded to .17. To obtain the approximate probability of exactly two successes, we read the probability corresponding to the row *X* = 2, and the result is .0720 (as demonstrated in Table 7.3 on page 227).[7] Thus Table E.7 has given us an approximate answer to the true probability, .0694, obtained from Equation (7.7) using the fraction 1/6 = *p* rather than the rounded decimal value .17.

7.6.2 Characteristics of the Binomial Distribution

Each time a set of parameters—*n* and *p*—is specified, a particular binomial probability distribution can be generated. This can be readily seen by examining Table E.7 for various combinations of *n* and *p*.

Shape
We note that a binomial distribution may be symmetric or skewed. Whenever *p* = .5, the binomial distribution will be symmetric regardless of how large or small the value of *n*. However, when *p* ≠ .5, the distribution will be skewed. The closer *p* is to .5 and the larger the number of observations, *n*, the less skewed the distribution will be.

---

[7] Note that for *p* > .5, we read across the bottom and up the right-hand side of the table.

TABLE 7.3 Obtaining a binomial probability

n	X	0.01	0.02	0.03	0.04	0.05	0.06	0.07	0.08	0.09	0.10	0.11	0.12	0.13	0.14	0.15	0.16	0.17	0.18
2	0	0.9801	0.9604	0.9409	0.9216	0.9025	0.8836	0.8649	0.8464	0.8281	0.8100	0.7921	0.7744	0.7569	0.7396	0.7225	0.7056	0.6889	0.6724
	1	0.0198	0.0392	0.0582	0.0768	0.0950	0.1128	0.1302	0.1472	0.1638	0.1800	0.1958	0.2112	0.2262	0.2408	0.2550	0.2680	0.2822	0.2952
	2	0.0001	0.0004	0.0009	0.0016	0.0025	0.0036	0.0049	0.0064	0.0081	0.0100	0.0121	0.0144	0.0169	0.0196	0.0225	0.0256	0.0289	0.0324
3	0	0.9703	0.9412	0.9127	0.8847	0.8574	0.8306	0.8044	0.7787	0.7536	0.7290	0.7050	0.6815	0.6585	0.6361	0.6141	0.5927	0.5718	0.5514
	1	0.0294	0.0576	0.0847	0.1106	0.1354	0.1590	0.1816	0.2031	0.2236	0.2430	0.2614	0.2788	0.2952	0.3106	0.3251	0.3387	0.3513	0.3631
	2	0.0003	0.0012	0.0026	0.0046	0.0071	0.0102	0.0137	0.0177	0.0221	0.0270	0.0323	0.0380	0.0441	0.0506	0.0574	0.0645	0.0720	0.0797
	3	0.0000	0.0000	0.0000	0.0001	0.0001	0.0002	0.0003	0.0005	0.0007	0.0010	0.0013	0.0017	0.0022	0.0027	0.0034	0.0041	0.0049	0.0058
4	0	0.9606	0.9224	0.8853	0.8493	0.8145	0.7807	0.7481	0.7164	0.6857	0.6561	0.6274	0.5997	0.5729	0.5470	0.5220	0.4979	0.4746	0.4521
	1	0.0388	0.0753	0.1095	0.1416	0.1715	0.1993	0.2252	0.2492	0.2713	0.2916	0.3102	0.3271	0.3424	0.3562	0.3685	0.3793	0.3888	0.3970
	2	0.0006	0.0023	0.0051	0.0088	0.0135	0.0191	0.0254	0.0325	0.0402	0.0486	0.0575	0.0669	0.0767	0.0870	0.0975	0.1004	0.1195	0.1307
	3	0.0000	0.0000	0.0001	0.0002	0.0005	0.0008	0.0013	0.0019	0.0027	0.0036	0.0047	0.0061	0.0076	0.0094	0.0115	0.0138	0.0163	0.0191
	4	0.0000	0.0000	0.0000	0.0000	0.0000	0.0000	0.0000	0.0000	0.0001	0.0001	0.0001	0.0002	0.0003	0.0004	0.0005	0.0007	0.0008	0.0010

P

SOURCE: Extracted from Table E.7.

Thus the distribution of the number of occurrences of red in 19 spins of the roulette wheel is only slightly skewed to the right, since $p = 18/38$. On the other hand, with small p the distribution will be highly right-skewed—as is observed for the distribution of the number of defective tires in a sample of 20 where $p = .08$. For very large p, the distribution would be highly left-skewed.

We leave it to the reader to verify the effect of n and p on the shape of the distribution by plotting the histogram in Problem 7.24(c). However, to summarize the above characteristics, three binomial distributions are depicted in Figure 7.2 on page 229. Panel A represents the probability of obtaining the face ⚁ on three rolls of a fair die; Panel B represents the probability of obtaining "heads" on three tosses of a fair coin; and panel C represents the probability of obtaining "heads" on four tosses of a fair coin. Thus a comparison of panel A with panel B demonstrates the effect on shape when the sample sizes are the same but the probabilities for success differ. Moreover, a comparison of panel B with C shows the effect on shape when the probabilities for successes are the same but the sample sizes differ.

The Mean

The mean of the binomial distribution can be readily obtained as the product of its two parameters, n and p. That is, instead of using Equation (7.1), which holds for all discrete probability distributions, for data that are binomially distributed we simply compute

$$\mu_X = E(X) = np \qquad (7.8)$$

Intuitively, this makes sense. For example, if we spin the roulette wheel 19 times, how frequently should we "expect" the color red to come up? On the average, over the long run, we would theoretically expect

$$\mu_X = E(X) = np = (19)\left(\frac{18}{38}\right) = 9$$

occurrences of red in 19 spins—the same result that would be obtained from the more general expression shown in Equation (7.1).

The Standard Deviation

The standard deviation of the binomial distribution is easily calculated using the formula

$$\sigma_X = \sqrt{np(1 - p)} \qquad (7.9)$$

Referring to our roulette wheel example, we simply compute

$$\sigma_X = \sqrt{(19)\left(\frac{18}{38}\right)\left(\frac{20}{38}\right)} = \sqrt{4.7368} = 2.18$$

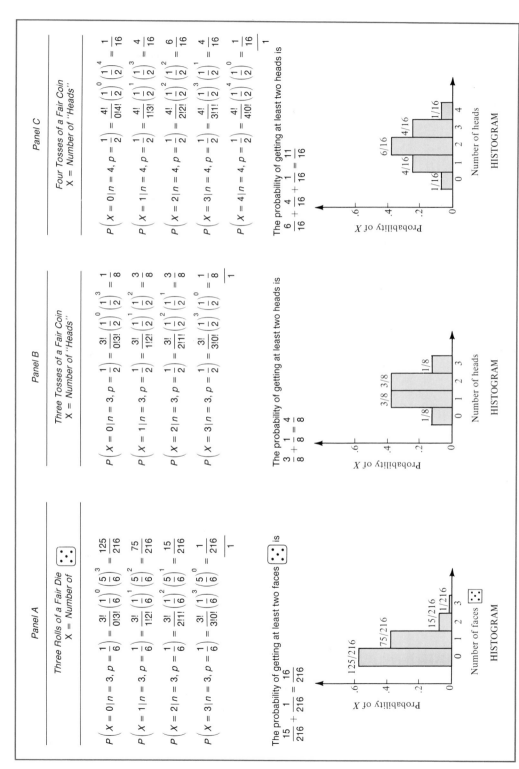

FIGURE 7.2
Comparison of three binomial distributions.

—the same result that would be obtained from the more general expression shown in Equation (7.3).

Summary

In this section we have developed the binomial model as a useful discrete probability distribution in its own right. The binomial distribution, however, plays an even more important role when it is used to approximate the hypergeometric probability distribution, as will be described in the next section. It is in this latter capacity that the binomial is used in statistical inference problems regarding estimating or testing proportions (as will be discussed in Chapters 9 through 11).

Problems

7.18 Describe how the four properties of the binomial distribution could be satisfied in the education example on page 222.

7.19 Describe how the four properties of the binomial distribution could be satisfied in the finance example on page 222.

7.20 Using Table E.7 determine the following:
(a) If $n = 4$ and $p = .12$, then $P(X = 0 | n = 4, p = .12) = ?$
(b) If $n = 10$ and $p = .40$, then $P(X = 9 | n = 10, p = .40) = ?$
(c) If $n = 15$ and $p = .50$, then $P(X = 8 | n = 15, p = .50) = ?$
(d) If $n = 7$ and $p = .83$, then $P(X = 6 | n = 7, p = .83) = ?$
(e) If $n = 9$ and $p = .90$, then $P(X = 9 | n = 9, p = .90) = ?$

7.21 In the carnival game of Chuck-a-luck three fair dice are rolled after the player has placed a bet on the occurrence of a particular face of the dice, say ⚃. For every $1.00 bet that you place you can lose the $1.00 if none of the three dice shows the face ⚃; you can win $1.00 if one die shows the face ⚃; you can win $2.00 if two of the dice show the face ⚃; or you can win $3.00 if all three dice show the face ⚃.
  (a) Form the probability distribution function representing the different monetary values (winnings or losses) that are possible (from one roll of the three dice). [*Hint*: Review Section 7.6.1 and see Figure 7.2 (panel A).]
  (b) Determine the mean of this probability distribution.
  (c) What is the player's expected long-run profit (or loss) from a $1.00 bet? Interpret.
  (d) What is the expected long-run profit (or loss) to the house? Interpret.
  ⟹(e) **ACTION** Would you play Chuck-a-luck and make a bet? Discuss.

7.22 It is known that 30% of the defective parts produced in a certain manufacturing process can be made satisfactory by rework.
  (a) What is the probability that in a batch of six such defective parts at least three can be satisfactorily reworked?
  (b) What is the probability that none of them can be reworked?
  (c) What is the probability that all of them can be reworked?

7.23 Based on past experience, the main printer in a university computer center is operating properly 90% of the time. If a random sample of ten inspections are made
  (a) What is the probability that the main printer is operating properly
    (1) exactly nine times?
    (2) at least nine times?
    (3) at most nine times?

(4) more than nine times?

(5) fewer than nine times?

(b) How many times can the main printer be expected to operate properly?

● **7.24** The probability that a patient fails to recover from a particular operation is .1.

(a) What is the probability that exactly two of the next eight patients having this operation will not recover?

(b) What is the probability that at most one patient of the eight will not recover?

(c) Using the probabilities extracted from Table E.7, plot the histogram for this binomial distribution.

7.25 Based upon past experience, 7% of all luncheon expense vouchers are in error.

(a) If a random sample of five vouchers are selected, what is the probability that

(1) exactly one is in error?

(2) at least two are in error?

(3) no more than two are in error?

(b) What assumptions about the probability distribution are necessary to solve (a)?

7.7 HYPERGEOMETRIC DISTRIBUTION

Both the binomial distribution and the hypergeometric distribution are concerned with the same thing—the number of successes in a sample containing n observations. What differentiates these two discrete probability distributions is the manner in which the data are obtained. For the binomial model, the sample data are drawn *with* replacement from a finite population or *without* replacement from an infinite population (as discussed in Section 2.7.1). On the other hand, for the hypergeometric model, the sample data are drawn *without* replacement from a finite population. Hence, while the probability of success, p, is constant over all observations of a binomial experiment, and the outcome of any particular observation is independent of any other, the same cannot be said for a hypergeometric experiment; here the outcome of one observation is affected by the outcomes of the previous observations.

To illustrate this point, let us consider the problem referred to in footnote 4 on page 222. Suppose that we wish to determine the probability of obtaining two clubs in five draws from a thoroughly shuffled standard deck of 52 cards (see Figure 6.1 on page 179). Here the population, $N = 52$, is finite. To determine the probability, however, we must know whether the sample of $n = 5$ cards is drawn with or without replacement.

In the former, a single card would be selected, observed, and replaced, and then the 52-card deck would be reshuffled prior to the subsequent draw. In such cases p, the probability of success—selecting a club—is $13/52 = 1/4$ throughout the experiment. (In fact, theoretically, the same card could even be selected each time.) Moreover, the outcome of one draw is independent of the outcome of any other draw. This type of problem is binomial, and the following probability is obtained:

$$P(X = 2 | n = 5, p = 13/52) = \frac{n!}{x!(n - x)!} p^x (1 - p)^{n-x}$$
$$= [5!/2!3!](13/52)^2(39/52)^3 = .2637$$

For the *particular* arrangement shown in Figure 7.3 (see page 232), the following probability of its occurrence is computed:

$$pp(1 - p)(1 - p)(1 - p) = p^2(1 - p)^3$$
$$= (13/52)^2(39/52)^3 = .02637$$

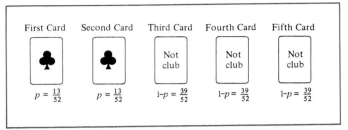

FIGURE 7.3
Sample with replacement (binomial).

However, $\binom{5}{2} = 10$ such arrangements are possible. Therefore, regardless of arrangement, the probability of obtaining two clubs is $(10)(.02637) = .2637$.

On the other hand, if five selections are made without replacement, the probability of success, p, changes from draw to draw—depending on which previous cards have already been selected. Since we are sampling without replacement, a particular card drawn once cannot be selected again. From this, the hypergeometric probability may be intuitively described. Depending on what type of cards have already been selected, Figure 7.4 shows the set of changing probabilities observed for this particular arrangement. From Figure 7.4 we note

p_1 = probability of success on the first card drawn

p_2 = probability of success on the second card drawn, given success on the first card drawn

$1 - p_3$ = probability of failure on the third card drawn, given success on the first two cards drawn

$1 - p_4$ = probability of failure on the fourth card drawn, given two successes and one failure previously

$1 - p_5$ = probability of failure on the fifth card drawn, given two successes and two failures previously

Extending our multiplication and counting rules (Sections 6.8 and 6.10), the probability of such an occurrence is

$$p_1 p_2 (1 - p_3)(1 - p_4)(1 - p_5) = (13/52)(12/51)(39/50)(38/49)(37/48)$$
$$= .02743$$

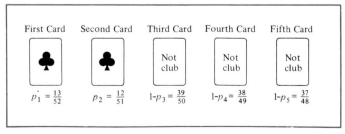

FIGURE 7.4
Sample without replacement (hypergeometric).

and thus, with ten such arrangements possible, the probability of observing two clubs out of five cards when sampling without replacement is .2743.

7.7.1 Development of the Mathematical Model

As the sample size n gets larger, however, such an intuitive formulation becomes tedious so we need another approach to describe and develop the hypergeometric probability distribution.

Using Equation (6.15) for combinations, we may determine that there are

$$\binom{N}{n} = \frac{N!}{n!(N-n)!} = \frac{52!}{5!47!} = 2{,}598{,}960$$

different but equally likely ways to draw a sample of five cards from a standard 52-card deck. Of these 2,598,960 possible arrangements, how many different ways can we select two clubs and three nonclubs (that is, either diamonds, hearts, or spades) as our sample of $n = 5$ cards from a population of $N = 52$ cards of which there are 13 clubs and 39 nonclubs? There are $\binom{13}{2} = 13!/2!11! = 78$ different ways of obtaining two clubs out of 13 that exist in the population. Also, there are $\binom{39}{3} = $ 39!/3!36! = 9,139 different ways of obtaining three nonclubs out of 39 nonclubs in the population. Now, using counting rule 2 in Section 6.10, the total number of ways to select the desired sample containing two clubs and three nonclubs is $78 \times 9{,}139 = 712{,}842$. Hence the probability of obtaining the desired sample is 712,842/2,598,960 = .2743.

In general, a mathematical expression of the hypergeometric distribution for obtaining X successes, given a knowledge of the parameters n, N, and A, is

$$P(X = x | n, N, A) = \frac{\binom{A}{x}\binom{N-A}{n-x}}{\binom{N}{n}}$$

$$= \frac{\dfrac{A!}{x!(A-x)!} \times \dfrac{(N-A)!}{(n-x)!(\{N-A\}-\{n-x\})!}}{\dfrac{N!}{n!(N-n)!}}$$

(7.10)

where $P(X = x | n, N, A) = $ the probability that $X = x$, given a knowledge of n, N, and A

$n = $ sample size

$N = $ population size

$A = $ number of successes in the population

$N - A = $ number of failures in the population

$x = $ number of successes in the sample

The number of successes in the sample, x, cannot exceed the number of successes in the population, A, or the sample size, n. Thus the range of the hypergeometric random variable is limited to the sample size (as was the range for the binomial random variable) or to the number of successes in the population—whichever is smaller.

Using Equation (7.10) in the example above, we would have

$$P(X = 2 | n = 5, N = 52, A = 13) = \frac{\binom{13}{2}\binom{39}{3}}{\binom{52}{5}}$$

$$= \frac{\frac{13!}{2!11!} \times \frac{39!}{3!36!}}{\frac{52!}{5!47!}}$$

$$= .2743$$

7.7.2 Characteristics of the Hypergeometric Distribution

Since p can be considered the probability or true proportion of successes in the population, it can also be written as

$$p = \frac{A}{N} = \frac{\text{number of successes in population}}{\text{population size}} \qquad (7.11)$$

Moreover, the true proportion of failures in the population is then

$$1 - p = \frac{N - A}{N} \qquad (7.12)$$

Shape

Like the binomial distribution, the hypergeometric distribution may also be symmetric or skewed. Whenever $p = .5$, the hypergeometric distribution will be symmetric regardless of how large or small the value of n; however, when $p \neq .5$, the distribution will be skewed. The degree of skewness will vary—depending on the proximity of p to .5 and the size of n.

The Mean

Like the binomial distribution, the mean for the hypergeometric distribution can be computed from

$$\mu_X = E(X) = np \qquad (7.13)$$

The Standard Deviation

On the other hand, the standard deviation for the hypergeometric distribution is obtained from

$$\sigma_X = \sqrt{np(1 - p)} \cdot \sqrt{\frac{N - n}{N - 1}} \tag{7.14}$$

where the expression $\sqrt{\dfrac{N - n}{N - 1}}$ is a **finite population correction factor** which arises

because of the process of sampling without replacement from finite populations. (This correction factor will be discussed in greater detail in Section 9.4.)

7.7.3 Using the Binomial Distribution to Approximate the Hypergeometric Distribution

Figure 7.5 on page 236 permits us to compare the theoretical results of an experiment obtained from the binomial model against those from the hypergeometric distribution. Panel A represents the binomial probability distribution generated by considering the number of clubs obtained in a sample of five cards selected with replacement, while panel B depicts the hypergeometric distribution generated when sampling without replacement. The comparative results are fairly similar because the sample size $n = 5$ represents but a small portion (9.6%) of the population size $N = 52$.

As a rule of thumb, when sampling without replacement from a finite population, if the sample size is less than 5% of the population size (that is, $n < .05N$), we may use the binomial probability distribution to approximate the hypergeometric distribution. The results will be quite similar, and the binomial model is much less cumbersome. The importance of this application of the binomial distribution should not be overlooked, since much sample survey work (such as that undertaken by the statistician in developing the real estate questionnaire presented in Chapter 2) deals with hypergeometric type data. Estimation and hypothesis testing for the proportion of successes will be studied in Chapters 10 and 11.

Problems

7.26 Determine the following:
  (a) If $n = 4$, $N = 10$, and $A = 5$, then $P(X = 3|n, N, A) = ?$
  (b) If $n = 4$, $N = 6$, and $A = 3$, then $P(X = 1|n, N, A) = ?$
  (c) If $n = 5$, $N = 12$, and $p = .25$, then $P(X = 0|n, N, A) = ?$
  (d) If $n = 3$, $A = 3$, and $p = .3$, then $P(X = 3|n, N, A) = ?$

7.27 Refer to Problem 7.26:
  (a) Compute the mean, variance, and standard deviation for the hypergeometric distribution described in (a).

Sampling with Replacement (Binomial)　　　　　*Sampling without Replacement (Hypergeometric)*

$$P(X = 0 \mid n = 5,\ p = 13/52) = \binom{5}{0}\left(\frac{13}{52}\right)^0\left(\frac{39}{52}\right)^5 = .23730$$

$$P(X = 0 \mid n = 5,\ N = 52,\ A = 13) = \frac{\binom{13}{0}\binom{39}{5}}{\binom{52}{5}} = .22153$$

$$P(X = 1 \mid n = 5,\ p = 13/52) = \binom{5}{1}\left(\frac{13}{52}\right)^1\left(\frac{39}{52}\right)^4 = .39551$$

$$P(X = 1 \mid n = 5,\ N = 52,\ A = 13) = \frac{\binom{13}{1}\binom{39}{4}}{\binom{52}{5}} = .41142$$

$$P(X = 2 \mid n = 5,\ p = 13/52) = \binom{5}{2}\left(\frac{13}{52}\right)^2\left(\frac{39}{52}\right)^3 = .26367$$

$$P(X = 2 \mid n = 5,\ N = 52,\ A = 13) = \frac{\binom{13}{2}\binom{39}{3}}{\binom{52}{5}} = .27428$$

$$P(X = 3 \mid n = 5,\ p = 13/52) = \binom{5}{3}\left(\frac{13}{52}\right)^3\left(\frac{39}{52}\right)^2 = .08789$$

$$P(X = 3 \mid n = 5,\ N = 52,\ A = 13) = \frac{\binom{13}{3}\binom{39}{2}}{\binom{52}{5}} = .08154$$

$$P(X = 4 \mid n = 5,\ p = 13/52) = \binom{5}{4}\left(\frac{13}{52}\right)^4\left(\frac{39}{52}\right)^1 = .01465$$

$$P(X = 4 \mid n = 5,\ N = 52,\ A = 13) = \frac{\binom{13}{4}\binom{39}{1}}{\binom{52}{5}} = .01073$$

$$P(X = 5 \mid n = 5,\ p = 13/52) = \binom{5}{5}\left(\frac{13}{52}\right)^5\left(\frac{39}{52}\right)^0 = \frac{.00098}{1}$$

$$P(X = 5 \mid n = 5,\ N = 52,\ A = 13) = \frac{\binom{13}{5}\binom{39}{0}}{\binom{52}{5}} = \frac{.00050}{1}$$

The probability of getting two or fewer clubs out of five cards is $.23730 + .39551 + .26367 = .89648$

The probability of getting two or fewer clubs out of five cards is $.22153 + .41142 + .27428 = .90723$.

Mean: $\mu_X = np = (5)\left(\frac{13}{52}\right) = 1.25$

Mean: $\mu_X = np = (5)\left(\frac{13}{52}\right) = 1.25$

Standard deviation: $\sigma_X = \sqrt{np(1 - p)}$

$$= \sqrt{(5)\left(\frac{13}{52}\right)\left(\frac{39}{52}\right)} = .97$$

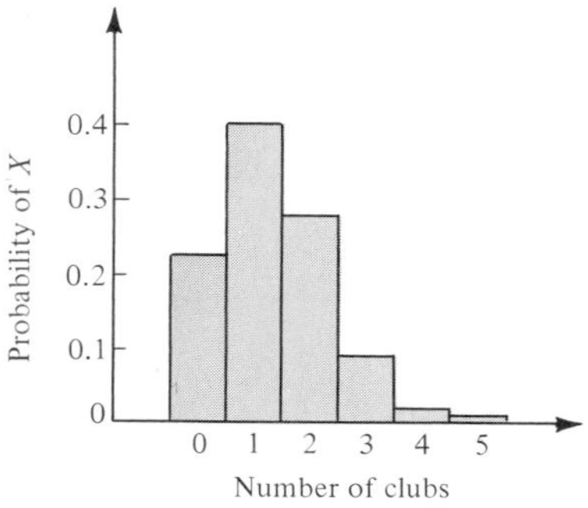

Standard deviation: $\sigma_X = \sqrt{np(1 - p)} \cdot \sqrt{\dfrac{N - n}{N - 1}}$

$$= \sqrt{(5)\left(\frac{13}{52}\right)\left(\frac{39}{52}\right)} \cdot \sqrt{\frac{52 - 5}{52 - 1}}$$

$$= .93$$

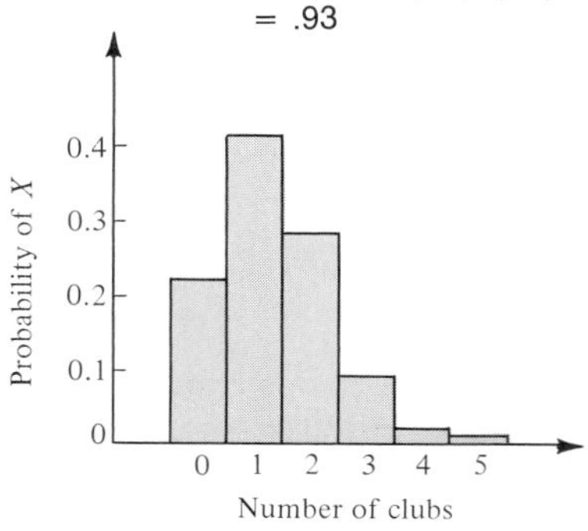

Number of clubs

HISTOGRAM

Number of clubs

HISTOGRAM

FIGURE 7.5
Comparing the binomial and hypergeometric distributions.

(b) Compute the mean, variance, and standard deviation for the hypergeometric distribution described in (b).

(c) Compute the mean, variance, and standard deviation for the hypergeometric distribution described in (c).

(d) Compute the mean, variance, and standard deviation for the hypergeometric distribution described in (d).

• **7.28** An auditor for the Internal Revenue Service is selecting a sample of six tax returns from persons in a particular profession for possible audit. If two or more of these indicate "improper" deductions, the entire group (population) of 100 tax returns will be audited.

(a) What is the probability that the entire group will be audited if the true percentage of improper returns is

(1) 25?

(2) 30?

(b) Discuss the differences in your results depending on the true percentage of improper returns.

7.29 The dean of a business school wishes to form an executive committee of five from among the 40 tenured faculty members at the school. The selection is to be random, and at the school there are eight tenured faculty members in accounting.

(a) What is the probability that the committee will contain

(1) none of them?

(2) at least one of them?

(3) not more than one of them?

(b) How many tenured faculty members in accounting would be expected?

7.30 From an inventory of 48 cars being shipped to local automobile dealers 12 have had defective radios installed.

(a) What is the probability that one particular dealership receiving eight cars

(1) obtains all with defective radios?

(2) obtains none with defective radios?

(3) obtains at least one with a defective radio?

(b) How many cars containing defective radios would be expected?

7.8 POISSON DISTRIBUTION

The Poisson distribution is another discrete probability distribution function which has many important practical applications. Not only are numerous discrete phenomena represented by a **Poisson process,** but the Poisson model is also used for providing approximations to the binomial distribution (as will be described in Section 7.8.4).

The following are some examples of Poisson-distributed phenomena:

• *Number of calls per hour* coming into the switchboard of a police station.

• *Number of car arrivals per day* at a toll bridge.

• *Number of business failures per week* in the state of California.

• *Number of major industrial strikes per year* in the United Kingdom.

• *Number of chips per cookie* in a pack of Marilyn's chocolate-chip cookies.

• *Number of defects per batch* in a production process.

• *Number of runs per inning* of a baseball game.

• *Number of turnovers per quarter* of a professional basketball game.

And, of course, the "classic" example,

• *Number of deaths per year per corps* due to being kicked in the head by a horse in the Prussian cavalry.[8]

---

[8] Ehrenberg (Reference 2) demonstrates quite clearly how the data obtained by the military historian von Bortkewitsch (1898) are approximated (fitted) by the Poisson distribution (see Problem 13.58).

In each of the above cases, the discrete random variable—*number of "successes" per unit* (that is, per interval of time, length, area, etc.)—is representative of a Poisson process.

> A **Poisson process** is said to exist if we can observe discrete events in a continuous interval (of time, length, area, etc.) in such a manner that if we shorten the interval sufficiently
>
> 1. The probability of observing exactly one success in the interval is stable.
> 2. The probability of observing two or more successes in the interval is 0.
> 3. The occurrence of a success in any one interval is statistically independent of that in any other interval.

To better understand the Poisson process, suppose we examine the number of calls per hour coming into the switchboard of a police station in a large metropolis. Any incoming call is a discrete event at a particular point over the continuous one-hour interval. Over such an interval of time we might receive on average 180 incoming calls. Now if we were to "break up" the one-hour interval into 3,600 consecutive one-second intervals

1. The expected (or average) number of incoming calls in any one-second interval would be .05.
2. The probability of receiving more than one call in any one-second interval is 0.
3. Receiving a particular call in any one-second interval has no effect on (i.e., is statistically independent of) receiving a call in any other one-second interval.

7.8.1 The Mathematical Model

It is interesting to note that the Poisson distribution has but one parameter, which we will call λ (the Greek lower-case letter **lambda**). While the Poisson random variable *X* refers to the *number of successes per unit*, the parameter of λ refers to the *average or expected number of successes per unit*. Moreover, we note that in theory the Poisson random variable ranges from 0 to ∞.

The mathematical expression[9] for the Poisson distribution for obtaining *X* successes, given that λ successes are expected, is

$$P(X = x|\lambda) = \frac{e^{-\lambda}\lambda^x}{x!} \qquad (7.15)$$

where $P(X = x|\lambda)$ = the probability that $X = x$ given a knowledge of λ
  λ = expected number of successes
  e = mathematical constant approximated by 2.71828
  x = number of successes per unit

---

[9] See References 1 and 4 for a more mathematically rigorous development of the Poisson distribution.

7.8.2 Characteristics

Shape
Each time the parameter λ is specified, a particular Poisson probability distribution can be generated. A Poisson distribution will be right-skewed when λ is small and will approach symmetry (with a peak in the center) as λ gets large.

The Mean and the Standard Deviation
An interesting property of the Poisson distribution is that mean μ_X and variance σ_X^2 are each equal to the parameter λ. Thus,

$$\mu_X = E(X) = \lambda \tag{7.16}$$

and

$$\sigma_X = \sqrt{\lambda} \tag{7.17}$$

7.8.3 Applications of the Poisson Model

To demonstrate some applications of the Poisson model let us return to our switchboard problem: If, on the average, the switchboard receives .05 incoming calls per *second*, what is the probability that in any given *minute* exactly two phone calls will be received? Moreover, what is the chance that more than two phone calls will be received?

To solve these we must convert from seconds into minutes.

		Conversions				
Avg. per Second		Avg. per Minute		Avg. per Hour		Avg. per Day
.05	$\leftrightarrow$	3.0	$\leftrightarrow$	180.0	$\leftrightarrow$	4320.0

λ, the expected number of calls per minute, is 3.0. Now, using Equation (7.15), we have, for the first question

$$P(X = 2|\lambda = 3.0) = \frac{e^{-3.0}(3.0)^2}{2!} = \frac{9}{(2.71828^3)(2)} = .2240.$$

However, hand calculations are not necessary here. Referring to Table E.6, the tables of the Poisson distribution, the result is easily obtained. As displayed in Table 7.4 (page 240), which is a replica of Table E.6, only the values of λ and X are needed. Hence, the probability of receiving exactly two incoming calls, given that 3.0 are expected, is .2240. To answer the second question—the probability that in any given minute more than two phone calls will be received—we have

$$P(X > 2|\lambda = 3.0) = P(X = 3|\lambda = 3.0) + P(X = 4|\lambda = 3.0) + \cdots$$
$$+ P(X = \infty|\lambda = 3.0)$$

TABLE 7.4   Obtaining a Poisson probability

X					λ					
	2.1	2.2	2.3	2.4	2.5	2.6	2.7	2.8	2.9	3.0
0	.1225	.1108	.1003	.0907	.0821	.0743	.0672	.0608	.0550	.0498
1	.2572	.2438	.2306	.2177	.2052	.1931	.1815	.1703	.1596	.1494
2	.2700	.2681	.2652	.2613	.2565	.2510	.2450	.2384	.2314	.2240
3	.1890	.1966	.2033	.2090	.2138	.2176	.2205	.2225	.2237	.2240
4	.0992	.1082	.1169	.1254	.1336	.1414	.1488	.1557	.1662	.1680
5	.0417	.0476	.0538	.0602	.0668	.0735	.0804	.0872	.0940	.1008
6	.0146	.0174	.0206	.0241	.0278	.0319	.0362	.0407	.0455	.0504
7	.0044	.0055	.0068	.0083	.0099	.0118	.0139	.0163	.0188	.0216
8	.0011	.0015	.0019	.0025	.0031	.0038	.0047	.0057	.0068	.0081
9	.0003	.0004	.0005	.0007	.0009	.0011	.0014	.0018	.0022	.0027
10	.0001	.0001	.0001	.0002	.0002	.0003	.0004	.0005	.0006	.0008
11	.0000	.0000	.0000	.0000	.0000	.0001	.0001	.0001	.0002	.0002
12	.0000	.0000	.0000	.0000	.0000	.0000	.0000	.0000	.0000	.0001

SOURCE: Extracted from Table E.6.

Since all the probabilities in a probability distribution must sum to 1, the terms on the right side of the equation can be expressed as

$$1 - P(X \leq 2 | \lambda = 3.0)$$

Thus

$$P(X > 2 | \lambda = 3.0) = 1 - \{P(X = 0 | \lambda = 3.0) + P(X = 1 | \lambda = 3.0) + P(X = 2 | \lambda = 3.0)\}$$

Now, using Equation (7.20), we have

$$P(X > 2 | \lambda = 3.0) = 1 - \left\{ \frac{e^{-3.0}(3.0)^0}{0!} + \frac{e^{-3.0}(3.0)^1}{1!} + \frac{e^{-3.0}(3.0)^2}{2!} \right\}$$

From Table E.6 (or its replica, Table 7.4) we can readily obtain the probabilities of 0, 1, or 2 successes, given a mean of 3.0 successes. Therefore,

$$P(X > 2 | \lambda = 3.0) = 1 - \{.0498 + .1494 + .2240\}$$
$$= 1 - .4232 = .5768$$

Thus we see that there is roughly a 42.3% chance that two or fewer calls will be received by the switchboard per minute. Therefore, a 57.7% chance exists that three or more calls will be received.

7.8.4   Using the Poisson Distribution to Approximate the Binomial Distribution

For those situations in which n is very large and p is very small,[10] the Poisson distribution may be used to approximate the binomial distribution. From Equation (7.7) on page

---

[10] But what constitutes large n and small p? A rule of thumb used by some statisticians (see, for example, Reference 5) is that the Poisson approximation to the binomial distribution is appropriate for combinations of $n \geq 20$ with $p \leq .05$. However, we will see from Figure 7.6 that rather good approximations are obtained for $n = 20$ and $p = .08$. In addition, we should note here that when n is large but p is not very small, appropriate approximations to the binomial distribution can be obtained from the normal distribution. This will be discussed in Section 8.4.

225 it is clearly seen that as *n* gets large, the computations for the binomial distribution become tedious. However, for those situations in which *p* is also very small, the following mathematical expression for the Poisson model may be used to facilitate the computations and give a good approximation to the true (binomial) result:

$$P(X = x|n, p) \cong \frac{e^{-np}(np)^x}{x!}$$

(7.18)

where $P(X = x|n, p)$ = the probability that $X = x$, given a knowledge of *n* and *p*
$\quad\quad\quad\quad\quad n$ = sample size
$\quad\quad\quad\quad\quad p$ = true probability of success
$\quad\quad\quad\quad\quad e$ = base of the Naperian (natural) logarithmic system—
$\quad\quad\quad\quad\quad\quad$ a mathematical constant approximated by 2.71828
$\quad\quad\quad\quad\quad x$ = number of successes in the sample

It was noted that the Poisson random variable may theoretically range from 0 to ∞. However, when used as an approximation to the binomial distribution, the Poisson random variable—the number of successes out of *n* observations—clearly cannot exceed the sample size *n*. Moreover, with large *n* and small *p*, Equation (7.18) implies that the probability of observing a large number of successes becomes small and approaches zero quite rapidly. Hence because of the severe degree of right-skewness in such a probability distribution, no difficulty arises when employing the Poisson approximation to the binomial.

Characteristics

As mentioned previously, an interesting characteristic about the Poisson distribution is that the mean μ_X and the variance σ_X^2 are each equal to λ. Therefore, when using the Poisson distribution to approximate the binomial model, we may compute the mean

$$\mu_X = E(X) = \lambda = np$$

(7.19)

and we may approximate the standard deviation

$$\sigma_X = \sqrt{\lambda} \cong \sqrt{np}$$

(7.20)

We note that the standard deviation given by Equation (7.20) agrees with that given for the binomial model [Equation (7.9)] when *p* is close to zero so that $(1 - p)$ is close to one.

Application

To illustrate the use of the Poisson approximation for the binomial, we compute the probability of obtaining exactly one defective tire from a sample of 20 if 8% of the tires manufactured at a particular plant are defective. Thus from Equation (7.18) we have

$$P(X = 1|n = 20, p = .08) \cong \frac{e^{-(20)(.08)}[(20)(.08)]^1}{1!} = \frac{e^{-1.6}(1.6)^1}{1}$$

However, rather than having to use the natural logarithmic system to determine this probability, tables of the Poisson distribution (Table E.6) can be employed. Referring to these tables, the only values necessary are the parameter λ and the desired number of successes X. Since in the above example $\lambda = 1.6$ and $X = 1$, we have from Table E.6,

$$P(X = 1|\lambda = 1.6) = .3230$$

This is shown in Table 7.5 (which is a replica of Table E.6).

TABLE 7.5   Obtaining a Poisson probability

X	1.1	1.2	1.3	1.4	1.5	1.6	1.7	1.8	1.9	2.0
0	.3329	.3012	.2725	.2466	.2231	.2019	.1827	.1653	.1496	.1353
1	.3662	.3614	.3543	.3452	.3347	.3230	.3106	.2975	.2842	.2707
2	.2014	.2169	.2303	.2417	.2510	.2584	.2640	.2678	.2700	.2707
3	.0738	.0867	.0998	.1128	.1255	.1378	.1496	.1607	.1710	.1804
4	.0203	.0260	.0324	.0395	.0471	.0551	.0636	.0723	.0812	.0902

SOURCE: Extracted from Table E.6.

Had the true distribution, the binomial, been employed instead of the approximation, we would compute

$$P(X = 1|n = 20, p = .08) = \binom{20}{1}(.08)^1(.92)^{19} = .3282$$

This computation, though, is tedious. Clearly, with Table E.7 available, one could argue that we should look up the binomial probability directly for $n = 20$, $p = .08$, and $X = 1$ and not bother calculating it or using the Poisson approximation. On the other hand, Table E.7 shows binomial probabilities only for particular n from 2 through 20, so that for $n > 20$ the Poisson approximation should certainly be used if p is very small.

To summarize our findings, Figure 7.6 compares the binomial distribution (panel A) and its Poisson approximation (panel B) for the number of defective tires in a sample of 20. The similarities of the two results are clearly evident, thus demonstrating the usefulness of the Poisson approximation.

Problems

7.31   Using Table E.6, determine the following:
(a) If $\lambda = 2.5$, then $P(X = 2|\lambda = 2.5) = ?$
(b) If $\lambda = 8.0$, then $P(X = 8|\lambda = 8.0) = ?$
(c) If $\lambda = 0.5$, then $P(X = 1|\lambda = 0.5) = ?$
(d) If $\lambda = 3.7$, then $P(X = 0|\lambda = 3.7) = ?$
(e) If $\lambda = 4.4$, then $P(X = 7|\lambda = 4.4) = ?$

Panel A	Panel B
Binomial Distribution*	*Poisson Distribution†*

$P(X = 0 \mid n = 20, p = .08) = .1887$

$P(X = 0 \mid n = 20, p = .08) = \dfrac{e^{-1.6}(1.6)^0}{0!} = .2019$

$P(X = 1 \mid n = 20, p = .08) = .3282$

$P(X = 1 \mid n = 20, p = .08) = \dfrac{e^{-1.6}(1.6)^1}{1!} = .3230$

$P(X = 2 \mid n = 20, p = .08) = .2711$

$P(X = 2 \mid n = 20, p = .08) = \dfrac{e^{-1.6}(1.6)^2}{2!} = .2584$

$P(X = 3 \mid n = 20, p = .08) = .1414$

$P(X = 3 \mid n = 20, p = .08) = \dfrac{e^{-1.6}(1.6)^3}{3!} = .1378$

$P(X = 4 \mid n = 20, p = .08) = .0523$

$P(X = 4 \mid n = 20, p = .08) = \dfrac{e^{-1.6}(1.6)^4}{4!} = .0551$

$P(X = 5 \mid n = 20, p = .08) = .0145$

$P(X = 5 \mid n = 20, p = .08) = \dfrac{e^{-1.6}(1.6)^5}{5!} = .0176$

$P(X = 6 \mid n = 20, p = .08) = .0032$

$P(X = 6 \mid n = 20, p = .08) = \dfrac{e^{-1.6}(1.6)^6}{6!} = .0047$

$P(X = 7 \mid n = 20, p = .08) = .0005$

$P(X = 7 \mid n = 20, p = .08) = \dfrac{e^{-1.6}(1.6)^7}{7!} = .0011$

$P(X = 8 \mid n = 20, p = .08) = .0001$

$P(X = 8 \mid n = 20, p = .08) = \dfrac{e^{-1.6}(1.6)^8}{8!} = .0002$

$P(X = 9 \mid n = 20, p = .08) = .0000$

$P(X = 9 \mid n = 20, p = .08) = \dfrac{e^{-1.6}(1.6)^9}{9!} = .0000$

$P(X = 10 \mid n = 20, p = .08) = \dfrac{e^{-1.6}(1.6)^{10}}{10!} = .0000$

$\vdots$

$\vdots$

$P(X = 20 \mid n = 20, p = .08) = \underline{.0000}$
1

$P(X = 20 \mid n = 20, p = .08) = \dfrac{e^{-1.6}(1.6)^{20}}{20!} = \underline{.0000}$
$\phantom{P(X = 20 \mid n = 20, p = .08) = \dfrac{e^{-1.6}(1.6)^{20}}{20!} = }1$

The probability of discovering two or more defective tires is
$1 - [P(X = 0) + P(X = 1)].$
$1 - [.1887 + .3282] = .4831$

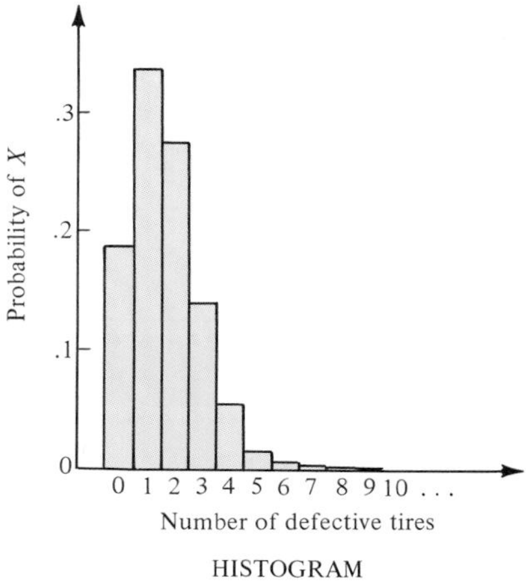

The probability of discovering two or more defective tires is approximately
$1 - [P(X = 0) + P(X = 1)].$
$1 - [.2019 + .3230] = .4751$

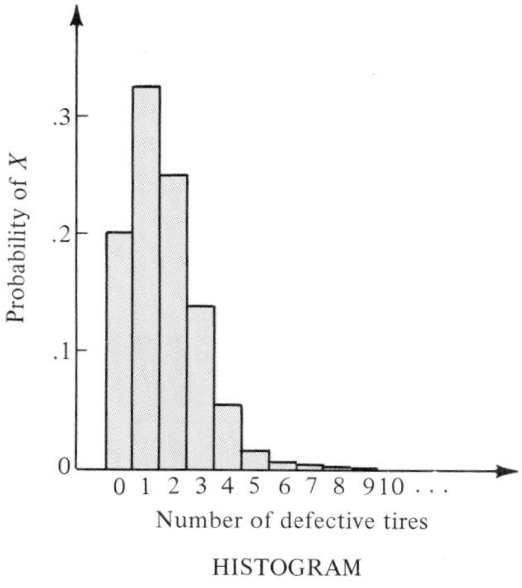

FIGURE 7.6
Binomial distribution and its Poisson approximation.

* The binomial probabilities are taken from Table E.7.
† The Poisson probabilities are taken from Table E.6.

7.32 The average number of claims per hour made to the Gnecco & Trust Insurance Company for damages or losses incurred in moving is 3.1. What is the probability that in any given hour

(a) Fewer than three claims will be made?

(b) Exactly three claims will be made?

(c) Three or more claims will be made?

(d) More than three claims will be made?

7.33 The average number of cars per minute stopping for gas at a particular service station along the New Jersey Turnpike is 1.2. What is the probability that in any given minute

(a) Fewer than two cars will stop for gas?

(b) More than three cars will stop for gas?

(c) Fewer than two cars or more than three cars will stop for gas?

(d) Either two or three cars will stop for gas?

7.34 Based upon past records, the average number of two-car accidents within a New York City police precinct is 3.4 per day. What is the probability that there will be

(a) At least six such accidents in this precinct on any given day?

(b) Not more than two such accidents in this precinct on any given day?

(c) Fewer than two such accidents in this precinct on any given day?

(d) At least two but no more than six such accidents in this precinct on any given day?

● **7.35** The quality control manager of Marilyn's Cookies is inspecting a batch of chocolate-chip cookies that have just been baked. If the production process is in control, the average number of chip parts per cookie is 6.0. What is the probability that in any particular cookie being inspected

(a) Fewer than five chip parts will be found?

(b) Exactly five chip parts will be found?

(c) Five or more chip parts will be found?

(d) Four or five chip parts will be found?

7.36 Refer to Problem 7.35. How many cookies in a batch of 100 being sampled should the manager expect to discard if company policy requires that all chocolate-chip cookies sold must have at least four chocolate-chip parts?

7.37 A natural gas exploration company averages 4 strikes (that is, natural gas is found) per 100 holes drilled. If 20 holes are to be drilled, what is the probability that

(a) Exactly 1 strike will be made?

(b) At least 2 strikes will be made?

Solve this problem using two different probability distributions (the binomial and the Poisson) and briefly compare and explain your results.

7.38 Based upon past experience, 2% of the telephone bills mailed to suburban households are incorrect. If a sample of 20 bills is selected, find the probability that at least one bill will be incorrect. Do this using two probability distributions (the binomial and the Poisson) and briefly compare and explain your results.

Supplementary Problems

7.39 Using the summation rules (see Appendix B) show that the expression for σ_X^2 given in Equation (7.2) can also be written as

$$\sigma_X^2 = \sum_{i=1}^{N} X_i^2 P(X_i) - \mu_X^2$$

Verify your results using the data presented in Table 7.1 on page 211.

7.40   The owner of a large home-heating-oil delivery company would like to determine whether to offer a solar heating installation service to its customers. The owner of the company has determined that a startup cost of $150,000 would be necessary, but a profit of $2,000 can be made on each solar heating system installed. The owner estimates the probability of various demand levels as follows:

Number of Units Installed	Probability
50	.4
100	.3
200	.3

➠**ACTION**   Using the expected-monetary-value criterion, determine whether the company should offer this solar heating installation service.

7.41   A bakery wishes to make orange Halloween cakes. Each cake costs $2.00 to make and is sold for $3.50. Any cakes not sold during the day *cannot* be sold at a later time. Based on past experience, the baker estimates the demand for these cakes will be either 5, 10, or 15 with probabilities of .6, .3, and .1, respectively.

[*Hint*: The baker can make 5, 10, or 15 cakes.]

➠**ACTION**   Using the expected-monetary-value criterion, determine the number of cakes that the baker should make.

7.42   The producer of a nationally distributed brand of potato chips would like to determine the feasibility of changing the product package from a cellophane bag to an unbreakable container. The product manager believes that there would be three possible national market responses to a change in product package: weak, moderate, and strong. The payoffs, in increased or decreased profit as compared to the current product package, are the following:

Event	Strategy	
	Use New Package	Keep Old Package
Weak national response	− $4,000,000	0
Moderate national response	+ $1,000,000	0
Strong national response	+ $5,000,000	0

Based upon past experience, the product manager assigns the following probabilities to the different levels of national response:

$$P(\text{weak national response}) = .30$$

$$P(\text{moderate national response}) = .60$$

$$P(\text{strong national response}) = .10$$

➠**ACTION**   Using the expected-monetary-value criterion, determine whether the new product package should be adopted.

7.43   A businessman would like to determine whether it would be profitable to establish a gardening service in a local suburb. The businessman believes that there are four possible levels of demand for this gardening service:

   1. Very low demand—1% of the households would use the service.
   2. Low demand—5% of the households would use the service.

3. Moderate demand—10% of the households would use the service.
4. High demand—25% of the households would use the service.

Based upon past experience in other suburbs, the businessman assigns the following probabilities to the various demand levels:

$$P(\text{very low demand}) = .20$$
$$P(\text{low demand}) = .50$$
$$P(\text{moderate demand}) = .20$$
$$P(\text{high demand}) = .10$$

The businessman has calculated the following profits or losses of this garden service for each demand level (over a period of 1 year):

	Strategy	
Demand	Provide Garden Service	No Garden Service
Very low ($p = .01$)	−$10,000	0
Low ($p = .05$)	−$1,000	0
Moderate ($p = .10$)	+$8,000	0
High ($p = .25$)	+$20,000	0

➠**(a) ACTION** Using the expected-monetary-value criterion, determine whether the gardening service should be instituted in this suburb.

    Suppose the businessman decides that, prior to a final decision, a survey of households in this suburb should be taken to determine demand for this gardening service. If a random sample of 20 households is selected and three would use this gardening service

(b) Revise the prior probabilities of the businessman in light of this sample information. [*Hint:* Use the binomial distribution and Bayes' Theorem (Section 6.9) to determine the conditional probability of this outcome given a particular level of demand.]

    Note: This process is called **Bayesian decision-making** (see References 8 and 10).

➠**(c) ACTION** Use these revised probabilities along with the expected-monetary-value criterion to determine whether the businessman should institute this gardening service.

✗ **7.44** The manufacturer of a brand of inexpensive felt tip pens maintains a production process that produces 10,000 pens per day. In order to maintain the highest quality of this product, the manufacturer guarantees free replacement of any defective pen sold. It has been calculated that each defective pen produced costs 20¢ for the manufacturer to replace. Based upon past experience, four rates of producing defective pens are possible:

1. Very low—1% of the pens produced are defective.
2. Low—5% of the pens produced are defective.
3. Moderate—10% of the pens produced are defective.
4. High—20% of the pens produced are defective.

    The manufacturer can reduce the rate of defective pens produced by having a mechanic fix the machines at the end of the day. This mechanic can reduce the defective rate to 1%, but his services will cost $80.

    A payoff table based upon the daily production of 10,000 pens, indicating the replacement costs for each of two alternatives (calling in the mechanic and not calling in the mechanic), is presented on page 247:

Defective Rate	Action	
	Do Not Call Mechanic	Call Mechanic
Very low (1%)	$ 20	$100
Low (5%)	$100	$100
Moderate (10%)	$200	$100
High (20%)	$400	$100

Based upon past experience, each defective rate is assumed to be equally likely to occur.

➠(a) **ACTION** Using the expected monetary-value criterion, determine whether to call the mechanic.

The manufacturer decides that prior to a final decision a random sample of pens should be studied. Thus, at the end of a particular day's production, a random sample of 15 pens is selected, of which 2 are defective.

➠(b) **ACTION** The manufacturer wishes to use the **Bayesian decision-making approach** (References 8 and 10) by revising prior probabilities to take into account the sample information. Use the expected-monetary-value criterion to determine whether to call the mechanic. [*Hint*: Use the binomial distribution and Bayes' Theorem (Section 6.9) to determine the conditional probability of this sample outcome, given a particular defective rate.]

7.45 Based upon past experience, 15% of the bills of a large mail-order book company are incorrect. A random sample of three current bills is selected.
  (a) What is the probability that
    (1) exactly two bills are incorrect?
    (2) no more than two bills are incorrect?
    (3) at least two bills are incorrect?
  (b) What assumptions about the probability distribution are necessary to solve this problem?

7.46 The quality control manager of Ruby's Gambling Equipment Company which manufactures dice for sale to gambling casinos must ensure the "fairness" of the dice prior to shipment. Suppose that a particular die is rolled 20 times.

  (a) What is the probability that the die lands on an odd face (that is, ⚀ , ⚂ , or ⚄)
    (1) exactly 17 times?
    (2) at least 17 times?
    (3) at most 17 times?
    (4) more than 17 times?
    (5) fewer than 17 times?
  (b) How many times can the die be expected to land on an odd face if the die is truly a fair one?

7.47 Abe Lincoln said that "you can't please all the people all the time." Suppose that you can please each individual nine times out of ten and that there are eight people you want to please.
  (a) Calculate
    (1) The probability that you'll please all of them.
    (2) The probability that you'll please at least six of them.
    (3) The probability that you'll please four or fewer.
  (b) Use an appropriate table to check your calculations of the probability distribution.
  (c) What is the expected number of people you will please? How likely is it that you will please exactly that number?
  ✗(d) What is the standard deviation of the number of people you will please? From this and the expected value, find out approximately how many people you will please at least three-fourths of the time.

- **7.48** Suppose that on a very long arithmetic test, Donna would get 70% of the items right.
    - **(a)** For a ten-item quiz, calculate
        - (1) The probability that Donna will get at least seven items right.
        - (2) The probability that Donna will get less than six items right (and therefore fail the quiz).
        - (3) The probability that Donna will get nine or ten items right (and get an A on the quiz).
    - **(b)** Use an appropriate table to check your calculations of the probability distribution.
    - **(c)** What is the expected number of items that Donna will get right? What proportion of the time will she get that number right?
    - **(d)** What is the standard deviation of the number of items that Donna will get right? Compare the proportion of time that Donna will be within two standard deviations according to the distribution you just calculated with the same probability calculated from the Bienaymé-Cheybshev inequality.

  7.49 If Teri were to take a ten-question true-false quiz and has to guess on each question
    - **(a)** Calculate
        - (1) The probability that Teri will get at least seven items right.
        - (2) The probability that Teri will get less than six items right (and therefore fail the quiz).
        - (3) The probability that Teri will get nine or ten items right (and get an A on the quiz).
    - **(b)** What is the expected number of items that Teri will get right? What proportion of the time will she get that number right if she always has to guess on each question?
    - **(c)** Compare and contrast your answers with those in parts (a) and (c) of Problem 7.48. Discuss.
    - ✏**(d)** Is it reasonable to assume that Teri will *always* have to guess on each question? Describe situations where this might occur.

  7.50 Hapless Hal has decided to try to find a suitable mate through a video dating service. The service promises to arrange four dates for Hal with women who are matched with him on various personality characteristics and interests. Although the service claims a ''95% success rate,'' meaning that 95% of their customers enjoy at least two of their four dates, Hal has been fooled by slick con artists in the past, so he decides to use his newly learned information on the binomial distribution to help him decide whether to sign up for the service. To do this, Hal knows he must assume some value for the probability of a date being ''successful.'' He decides to try several different values, but to start with, he chooses $p = 1/3$.
    - **(a)** Find the probability for Hal's chances of having 0, 1, 2, 3, and 4 successful dates.
    - **(b)** Using the information from (a), find the probability that at least two of the dates will be successful; that at least three of the dates will be successful.
    - **(c)** Recalculate the above probabilities using the more pessimistic estimate of $p = 1/10$, and the more optimistic estimate of $p = 1/2$.
    - **(d)** How *sensitive* is the expected probability of success to Hal's estimate of p? That is, how much does the probability of at least two successful dates vary when p changes from 1/10 to 1/3, and from 1/3 to 1/2?

  7.51 The typing pool at Drucker, Gershfeld & Gold (a large law firm) contains 25 secretaries, 10 of whom have been with the firm for more than five years. The executive officer of the firm wishes to randomly select three secretaries for assignment to a new case.
    - **(a)** What is the probability that
        - (1) none of the secretaries will have over five years of experience?
        - (2) one of the secretaries will have over five years of experience?
        - (3) two of the secretaries will have over five years of experience?
        - (4) all three of the secretaries will have over five years of experience?
    - **(b)** Why is this a probability distribution?
    - **(c)** What discrete model does this represent?
    - **(d)** Compute the mean and the standard deviation from Equations (7.1) and (7.3) and then verify your computations by applying the direct formulas peculiar to this discrete model.

7.52 In the game of Keno the player is given a card containing 80 numbers as indicated below:

1	2	3	4	5	6	7	8	9	10
11	12	13	14	15	16	17	18	19	20
21	22	23	24	25	26	27	28	29	30
31	32	33	34	35	36	37	38	39	40
41	42	43	44	45	46	47	48	49	50
51	52	53	54	55	56	57	58	59	60
61	62	63	64	65	66	67	68	69	70
71	72	73	74	75	76	77	78	79	80

In each game the player may choose up to (and including) 15 different numbers and indicates this selection by "marking the spots" (that is, placing an X through the chosen numbers) on the card. Play occurs when 20 balls are drawn (without replacement) from a bowl containing 80 numbered balls corresponding to the numbered spots on a card. There are many ways to play Keno. The amount that is won depends on the method of play, the casino played in, the amount wagered, and how many of the drawn balls have numbers matching those that the player had selected. The following rules govern play at a particular Las Vegas casino:

If 1 spot is marked, the player receives $3.00 for a $1.00 wager if 1 of the 20 balls drawn out of 80 matches the particular spot selected. The $1.00 is lost otherwise.

If 2 spots are marked, the player receives $12.00 for a $1.00 wager if 2 of the 20 balls drawn out of 80 match the particular spots selected. The $1.00 is lost otherwise.

If 3 spots are marked, the player receives $1.00 for the $1.00 wager (that is, "breaks even") if 2 of the 20 balls drawn match the particular spots selected; however, the player receives $43.00 if 3 of the 20 balls drawn match the 3 particular spots selected. The $1.00 is lost otherwise.

Some other schemes are given below for $1.00 wagers. The values in the table represent the amount received by the player for the corresponding number of matches.

Number of Spots Marked	Number of Matches				
	2	3	4	5	· · ·
4	$1.00	$4.00	$114.00		
5		$1.50	$ 21.50	$485.50	
⋮					

If 15 spots are marked, the player receives the following for a $1.00 wager; $1.50 for 6 matches; $7.00 for 7 matches; $21.50 for 8 matches; $107.00 for 9 matches; $285.50 for 10 matches; $2,143.00 for 11 matches; $7,143.00 for 12 matches; $21,428.50 for 13 matches; $25,000.00 for 14 matches; or $25,000.00 for all 15 matches. The $1.00 is lost otherwise.

(a) Form the probability distribution function representing the different outcomes that are possible for a $1.00 wager wherein 1 spot is marked.

(b) Form the probability distribution function representing the different outcomes that are possible for a $1.00 wager wherein 2 spots are marked.

(c) Form the probability distribution function representing the different outcomes that are possible for a $1.00 wager wherein 3 spots are marked.

(d) Form the probability distribution function representing the different outcomes that are possible for a $1.00 wager wherein 4 spots are marked.

(e) Form the probability distribution function representing the different outcomes that are possible for a $1.00 wager wherein 5 spots are marked.

(f) Form the probability distribution function representing the different outcomes that are possible for a $1.00 wager wherein 15 spots are marked.

(g) Determine the expected long-run profit (or loss) to the player who continually marks
  (1) 1 spot as in (a)
  (2) 2 spots as in (b)
  (3) 3 spots as in (c)
  (4) 4 spots as in (d)
  (5) 5 spots as in (e)
  (6) 15 spots as in (f).

➡(h) **ACTION** Based on your findings, is it ''better'' (that is, more profitable or less costly) in the long run to continually mark 1 spot?, 2 spots?, 3 spots? . . . , 15 spots? In other words, does the method of play matter in the game of Keno ? Discuss this in a letter to a friend.

➡(i) **ACTION** Would you prefer to play Keno or Chuck-a-luck (Problem 7.21 on page 230) or Under-or-over seven (Problem 7.7 on page 217) or make a field bet in Craps (Problem 7.6 on page 216)? Why?

• **7.53** The manufacturer of the disk drives used in one of the well-known brands of microcomputers expects only 2% of the disk drives to malfunction during the microcomputer's warranty period.

(a) In a sample of ten disk drives, what is the probability that
  (1) none will malfunction during the warranty period?
  (2) exactly one will malfunction during the warranty period?
  (3) at least two will malfunction during the warranty period?

(b) Solve (a)(1), (a)(2), and (a)(3) using the Poisson distribution as an approximation of the binomial distribution and briefly compare your results.

(c) In a sample of 50 disk drives, what is the *approximate* probability that
  (1) none will malfunction during the warranty period?
  (2) exactly one will malfunction during the warranty period?
  (3) at least two will malfunction during the warranty period?

(d) What assumptions are needed in order to use the two probability distributions in this problem?

7.54 One out of every 100 light bulbs produced by the Lori Lighting Co. fails before the end of a one-week period when left burning continuously. One bulb is installed on each of the 50 floors of a large apartment building in New York City. What is the *approximate* probability that

(a) One bulb will be burned out at the end of the week?

(b) More than three of the bulbs will be burned out at the end of the week?

(c) Fewer than three of the bulbs will be burned out at the end of the week?

(d) Three of the bulbs will be burned out at the end of the week?

7.55 S. J. Prais reported that the average number of industrial strikes per year in large firms in the United Kingdom is 0.4 [''The strike-proneness of large plants in Britain,'' *Journal of the Royal Statistical Society*, A, 141 (1978), pp. 368–384]. What is the probability that in any one year there will be

(a) no major strike?

(b) at least one major strike?

(c) exactly one major strike?

(d) at most two major strikes?

7.56 Over the 1988 season the Entes Valley High School soccer team averaged 3.7 goals per game for 20 games.

(a) What is the probability that in any one game the team would score
  (1) at most two goals?
  (2) no goals?
  (3) five or more goals?
  (4) two or three goals?

✗(b) If Entes Valley's opponents averaged 2.1 goals per game in their meetings is it possible for you to determine how many of these games Entes Valley won? Discuss.

7.57 The Educational Computer Center of a well-known university has 300 computer terminals set up for student usage on a daily basis. The probability that any terminal will require servicing on a particular day is .015.

    (a) What is the probability that on a particular day

        (1) at most two terminals will require servicing?

        (2) at least five terminals will require servicing?

        (3) three or four terminals will require servicing?

    (b) If the Educational Computer Center's policy is to perform maintenance operations on all 300 terminals whenever ten or more require servicing on a given day, how many times a year would you expect this to occur if the facility is available for student usage throughout the year?

References

1. DERMAN, C., L. J. GLESER, AND I. OLKIN, *A Guide to Probability Theory and Application* (New York: Holt, Rinehart and Winston, 1973).

2. EHRENBERG, A. S. C., *Data Reduction: Analyzing and Interpreting Statistical Data* (London: Wiley, 1975).

3. GORDON, G., AND I. PRESSMAN, *Quantitative Decision Making for Business*, 2d ed. (Englewood Cliffs, N.J.: Prentice-Hall, 1983).

4. LARSEN, R. J., AND M. L. MARX, *An Introduction to Mathematical Statistics and Its Applications*, 2d ed. (Englewood Cliffs, N.J.: Prentice-Hall, 1986).

5. MILLER, I., AND J. E. FREUND, *Probability and Statistics for Engineers*, 2d ed. (Englewood Cliffs, N.J.: Prentice-Hall, 1977).

6. SCARNE, J., *Scarne's New Complete Guide to Gambling* (New York: Simon and Schuster, 1974).

7. THORP, E. O., *Beat the Dealer* (New York: Random House, 1962).

8. VALINSKY, D., "Statistics," in C. HEYEL, ed., *The Encyclopedia of Management* (New York: Van Nostrand Reinhold, 1963).

9. WEAVER, W., "Probability," in A. SHUCHMAN, ed., *Scientific Decision Making in Business* (New York: Holt, Rinehart and Winston, 1963).

10. WINKLER, R. L., *Introduction to Bayesian Inference and Decision* (New York: Holt, Rinehart and Winston, 1972).

The Normal Distribution

8.1 MATHEMATICAL MODELS OF CONTINUOUS RANDOM VARIABLES: THE PROBABILITY DENSITY FUNCTION

Now that we have studied several discrete probability distribution functions, we may turn our attention to the **continuous probability density functions**—those that arise due to some measuring process on various phenomena of interest. Continuous models have important applications in engineering and the physical sciences as well as in business and the social sciences. Some examples of continuous random phenomena are: height, weight, time between arrivals (of telephone calls into a switchboard), and customer servicing times. Moreover, from the real estate survey developed in Chapter 2, responses to questions regarding appraised value, lot size, age of house, and annual taxes also pertain to probability density functions for continuous random variables.

When a mathematical expression is available to represent some underlying continuous phenomenon, the probability that various values of the random variable occur within certain ranges or intervals may be calculated. However, the *exact* probability of a *particular value* is zero.

As an example, the probability distribution represented in Table 8.1 is obtained by categorizing a distribution in which the continuous random phenomenon of interest is said to follow the **Gaussian** or "bell-shaped" **normal probability density function.** If the nonoverlapping (mutually exclusive) listing contains all possible class intervals (is collectively exhaustive), the probabilities will again sum to 1. This is demonstrated in Table 8.1. Such a probability distribution may be considered as a relative frequency distribution as described in Section 4.4, where, except for the two open-ended classes, the midpoint of every other class interval represents the data in that interval.

Unfortunately, obtaining probabilities or computing expected values and the standard deviations for continuous phenomena involves mathematical expressions which require a knowledge of integral calculus and are beyond the scope of this book. Nevertheless, one continuous probability density function which we shall focus upon has been deemed so important for applications that special probability tables (such as Table E.2) have been devised in order to eliminate the need for what otherwise would require laborious mathematical computations. This particular continuous probability density function is known as the **Gaussian** or **normal distribution.**

TABLE 8.1   Thickness of 10,000 brass washers manufactured by a large company

Thickness (inches)	Relative Frequency or Probability
Under .0180	48/10,000 = .0048
.0180 < .0182	122/10,000 = .0122
.0182 < .0184	325/10,000 = .0325
.0184 < .0186	695/10,000 = .0695
.0186 < .0188	1198/10,000 = .1198
.0188 < .0190	1664/10,000 = .1664
.0190 < .0192	1896/10,000 = .1896
.0192 < .0194	1664/10,000 = .1664
.0194 < .0196	1198/10,000 = .1198
.0196 < .0198	695/10,000 = .0695
.0198 < .0200	325/10,000 = .0325
.0200 < .0202	122/10,000 = .0122
.0202 or above	48/10,000 = .0048
Total	1.0000

8.2   THE NORMAL DISTRIBUTION

8.2.1   Importance of the Normal Distribution

The normal distribution is vitally important in statistics for three main reasons:

1. Numerous continuous phenomena seem to follow it or can be approximated by it.
2. We can use it to approximate various discrete probability distributions and thereby avoid much computational drudgery (Section 8.4).
3. It provides the basis for *classical statistical inference* because of its relationship to the *central limit theorem* (Chapter 9).[1]

8.2.2   Properties of the Normal Distribution

The normal distribution has several interesting theoretical properties. Among these are

1. It is "bell-shaped" and symmetrical in its appearance.
2. Its measures of central tendency (mean, median, mode, midrange, and midhinge) are all identical.
3. Its "middle spread" is equal to 1.33 standard deviations.[2] That is, the interquartile range is contained within an interval of two-thirds of a standard deviation below the mean to two-thirds of a standard deviation above the mean.
4. Its associated random variable has an infinite range ($-\infty < X < +\infty$).

In actual practice some of the variables we observe may only approximate these theoretical properties. This occurs for two reasons: (1) the underlying population distribution may be only approximately normal; and (2) any actual sample may deviate from the theoretically expected characteristics. For some phenomenon which may be approximated by the normal distribution model:

---

[1] This third (and most important) point will be developed in Chapter 9 and emphasized in Chapters 10 through 15.

[2] Thus, for normally distributed data, if the interquartile range equals 1.33 standard deviations, then the standard deviation equals three-fourths of the interquartile range.

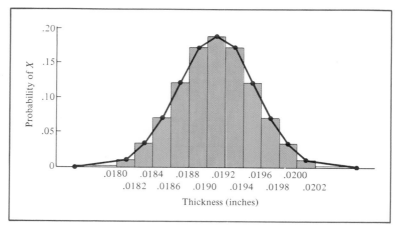

FIGURE 8.1
Relative frequency histogram and polygon of the thickness of 10,000 brass washers. SOURCE: Data are taken from Table 8.1

1. Its polygon may be only approximately "bell-shaped" and symmetrical in appearance.
2. Its measures of central tendency may differ slightly from each other.
3. The value of its interquartile range may differ slightly from 1.33 standard deviations.
4. Its *practical range* will not be infinite but will generally lie within 3 standard deviations above and below the mean. (That is, range $\approx$ 6 standard deviations.)[3]

As a case in point, let us refer to Figure 8.1, which depicts the relative frequency histogram and polygon for the distribution of the thickness of 10,000 brass washers presented in Table 8.1. For these data, the first three theoretical properties of the normal distribution seem to have been satisified; however, the fourth does not hold. The random variable of interest, thickness, cannot possibly take on values of zero or below, nor can a washer be so thick that it becomes unusable. From Table 8.1 we note that only 48 out of every 10,000 brass washers manufactured can be expected to have a thickness of .0202 inch or more, while an equal number can be expected to have a thickness under .0180 inch. Thus the chance of randomly obtaining a washer so thin or so thick is .0048 + .0048 = .0096—or almost 1 in 100.

We shall leave it to the reader to verify (see Problem 8.4 on page 269) that 99.04% of these manufactured washers can be expected to have a thickness between .0180 and .0202 inch—that is, 2.59 standard deviations (distances) above and below the mean.

Caution: What about other data sets? Not all continuous random variables are normally distributed. That is, the reader must be cautioned that often the continuous random phenomenon we may be interested in studying neither will follow the normal distribution nor can be adequately approximated by it. In such a case the four "practical" properties described above will not hold. While some methods for studying such continuous phenomena are outside the scope of this text (see References 1 and 2), other (distribution-free) techniques which do not depend on the particular form of the underlying random variable will be discussed in Chapter 15. Nevertheless, Problem

---

[3] Thus, for normally distributed data, if the range approximately equals 6 standard deviations, then the standard deviation approximately equals one-sixth the range.

8.5 (on page 270) will give the reader the opportunity to decide whether a given data set seems to approximate the normal distribution sufficiently to permit it to be examined using the methodology of this chapter.

8.2.3 The Mathematical Model

The mathematical model or expression representing a probability density function is denoted by the symbol $f(X)$. For the normal distribution, the model used to obtain the desired probabilities is

$$f(X) = \frac{1}{\sqrt{2\pi}\,\sigma_X}\, e^{-(1/2)[(X - \mu_X)/\sigma_X]^2} \tag{8.1}$$

where e is the mathematical constant approximated by 2.71828

π is the mathematical constant approximated by 3.14159

μ_X is the population mean

σ_X is the population standard deviation

X is any value of the continuous random variable, where $-\infty < X < +\infty$

Let us examine the components of the normal probability density function in Equation (8.1). Since e and π are mathematical constants, the probabilities of the random variable X are only dependent upon the two parameters of the normal distribution—the population mean μ_X and the population standard deviation σ_X. Every time we specify a *particular combination* of μ_X and σ_X, a *different* normal probability distribution will be generated—each having its own set of probabilities. We illustrate this in Figure 8.2, where three different normal distributions are depicted. Distributions A and B have the same mean (μ_X) but have different standard deviations. On the other hand, distributions A and C have the same standard deviation (σ_X) but have different means. Furthermore, distributions B and C depict two normal probability density functions which differ with respect to both μ_X and σ_X.

Unfortunately, the mathematical expression in Equation (8.1) is computationally tedious. To avoid such computations, it would be useful to have a set of tables that would provide the desired probabilities. However, since an infinite number of combinations of the parameters μ_X and σ_X exist, an infinite number of tables would be required.

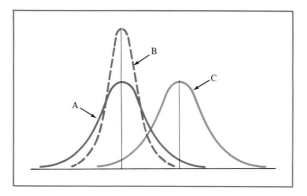

FIGURE 8.2
Three normal distributions having differing parameters μ_X and σ_X.

8.2.4 **Standardizing the Normal Distribution**

Fortunately, by *standardizing* the data, we will only need one table. (See Table E.2.) By using the **transformation formula:**

$$Z = \frac{X - \mu_X}{\sigma_X} \qquad\qquad (8.2)$$

any normal random variable X is converted to a standardized normal random variable Z. While the original data for the random variable X had mean μ_X and standard deviation σ_X, the standardized random variable Z will always have mean $\mu_Z = 0$ and standard deviation $\sigma_Z = 1$.

> A **standardized normal distribution** is one whose random variable Z always has a mean $\mu_Z = 0$ and a standard deviation $\sigma_Z = 1$.

Substituting in Equation (8.1), we see that the probability density function of a standard normal variable Z is

$$f(Z) = \frac{1}{\sqrt{2\pi}}\, e^{-(1/2)Z^2} \qquad\qquad (8.1a)$$

Thus, we can always convert any set of normally distributed data to its standardized form and then determine its desired probabilities from the table of the standardized normal distribution.

To see how the transformation formula (8.2) may be applied and how we may then use the results to read probabilities from the table of the standardized normal distribution (Table E.2), let us consider the following problem.

Suppose a consultant was investigating the time it took factory workers to assemble a particular part in a Volvo automobile plant and determined the data (time in seconds) to be normally distributed with a mean μ_X of 75 seconds and a standard deviation σ_X of 6 seconds.

Transforming the Data

We see from Figure 8.3 that every measurement X has a corresponding standardized measurement Z obtained from the transformation formula (8.2). Hence from Figure 8.3 it is clear that a time of 81 seconds required for a factory worker to complete the task is equivalent to 1 standardized unit (that is, 1 *standard deviation*) above the mean, since

$$Z = \frac{81 - 75}{6} = +1$$

while a time of 57 seconds required for a worker to assemble the part is equivalent to 3 standardized units (that is, 3 *standard deviations*) below the mean because

$$Z = \frac{57 - 75}{6} = -3$$

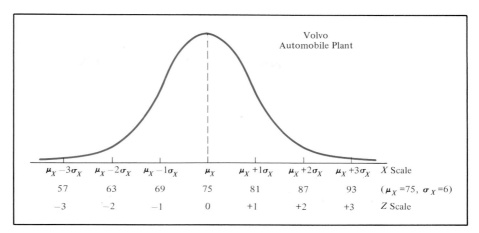

FIGURE 8.3
Transformation of scales.

Thus, the standard deviation has become the unit of measurement. In other words, a time of 81 seconds is 6 seconds (i.e., 1 standard deviation) higher or "slower" than the average time of 75 seconds while a time of 57 seconds is 18 seconds (i.e., 3 standard deviations) lower or "faster" than the average time.

Suppose now that the consultant conducted the same time-and-motion study at a BMW automobile plant, where the workers were trained to assemble the part by a different method using different equipment. Suppose that at this plant she determined that the time to perform the task was normally distributed with mean μ_X of 60 seconds and standard deviation σ_X of 3 seconds. The data are depicted in Figure 8.4 on page 258. In comparison with the aforementioned results at the Volvo automobile plant, we note, for example, that at this automobile plant a time of 57 seconds to complete the task is only 1 standard deviation below the mean for the group, since

$$Z = \frac{57 - 60}{3} = -1$$

Moreover, a time of 63 seconds is 1 standard deviation above the mean time for assemblage, since

$$Z = \frac{63 - 60}{3} = +1$$

while a time of 51 seconds is 3 standard deviations below the group mean because

$$Z = \frac{51 - 60}{3} = -3$$

8.2.5 Using the Normal Probability Tables

The two bell-shaped curves in Figures 8.3 and 8.4 depict the relative frequency polygons for the normal distributions representing the time (in seconds) for all factory workers to assemble a part at two particular automobile plants. Since at each plant the times to assemble the part are known for every factory worker, the data represent the entire

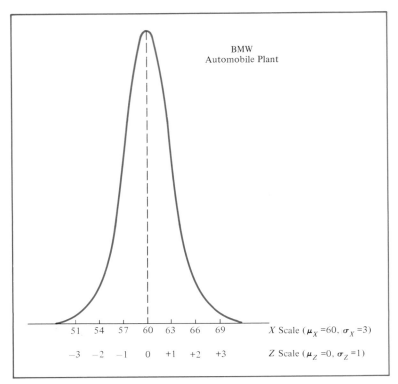

FIGURE 8.4
A different transformation of scales.

population at a particular plant, and therefore the *probabilities* or proportion of area under the curve must add up to 1. Clearly, then, the area under the curve between any two reported time values represents but a portion of the total area possible.

Suppose the consultant wishes to determine the probability that a factory worker selected at random from the Volvo automobile plant should require between 75 and 81 seconds to complete the task. That is, what is the likelihood that the worker's time is between the plant mean and one standard deviation above this mean? This answer is found by using Table E.2.

Table E.2 represents the probabilities or areas under the normal curve calculated from the mean μ_X to the particular values of interest X. Using Equation (8.2), this corresponds to the probabilities or areas under the standardized normal curve from the mean ($\mu_Z = 0$) to the transformed values of interest Z. Only positive entries for Z are listed in the table, since for such a symmetrical distribution with zero mean, the area from the mean to $+Z$ (that is, Z standard deviations above the mean) must be identical to the area from the mean to $-Z$ (that is, Z standard deviations below the mean).

To use Table E.2 we note that all Z values must first be recorded to two decimal places. Thus our particular Z value of interest is recorded as $+1.00$. To read the probability or area under the curve from the mean to $Z = +1.00$, we scan down the Z column from Table E.2 until we locate the Z value of interest (in tenths). Hence we stop in the row $Z = 1.0$. Next we read across this row until we intersect the column that contains the hundredths place of the Z value. Therefore, in the body of the table the tabulated probability for $Z = 1.00$ corresponds to the intersection of the row $Z =$

TABLE 8.2 Obtaining an area under the normal curve

Z	.00	.01	.02	.03	.04	.05	.06	.07	.08	.09
0.0	.0000	.0040	.0080	.0120	.0160	.0199	.0239	.0279	.0319	.0359
0.1	.0398	.0438	.0478	.0517	.0557	.0596	.0636	.0675	.0714	.0753
0.2	.0793	.0832	.0871	.0910	.0948	.0987	.1026	.1064	.1103	.1141
0.3	.1179	.1217	.1255	.1293	.1331	.1368	.1406	.1443	.1480	.1517
0.4	.1554	.1591	.1628	.1664	.1700	.1736	.1772	.1808	.1844	.1879
0.5	.1915	.1950	.1985	.2019	.2054	.2088	.2123	.2157	.2190	.2224
0.6	.2257	.2291	.2324	.2357	.2389	.2422	.2454	.2486	.2518	.2549
0.7	.2580	.2612	.2642	.2673	.2704	.2734	.2764	.2794	.2823	.2852
0.8	.2881	.2910	.2939	.2967	.2995	.3023	.3051	.3078	.3106	.3133
0.9	.3159	.3186	.3212	.3238	.3264	.3289	.3315	.3340	.3365	.3389
1.0	.3413	.3438	.3461	.3485	.3508	.3531	.3554	.3577	.3599	.3621
1.1	.3643	.3665	.3686	.3708	.3729	.3749	.3770	.3790	.3810	.3830

SOURCE: Extracted from Table E.2.

1.0 with the column $Z = .00$ as shown in Table 8.2 (which is a replica of Table E.2). This probability is .3413. As depicted in Figure 8.5, there is a 34.13% chance that a factory worker selected at random from the Volvo automobile plant will require between 75 and 81 seconds to assemble the part.

On the other hand, we know from Figure 8.4 that at the BMW automobile plant a time of 63 seconds is 1 standardized unit above the mean time of 60 seconds. Thus the likelihood of a randomly selected factory worker at the BMW automobile plant completing the assemblage in between 60 and 63 seconds is also .3413.[4] These results are clearly illustrated in Figure 8.6 (page 260), which demonstrates that regardless of the mean μ_X and standard deviation σ_X of a particular set of normally distributed data, a transformation to a standardized scale can always be made from Equation (8.2), and, by using Table E.2, any probability or portion of area under the curve can be obtained. From Figure 8.6 we see that the probability or area under the curve from 60 to 63 seconds at the BMW automobile plant is identical to the probability or area under the curve from 75 to 81 seconds at the Volvo automobile plant.

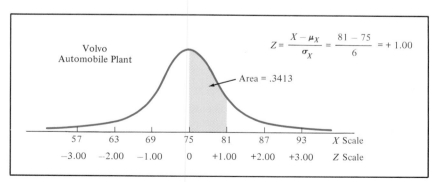

FIGURE 8.5
Determining the area between the mean and Z from a standardized normal distribution.

---

[4] Mathematically this may be expressed as $P(60 \le X \le 63) = P(0 \le Z \le 1) = .3413$.

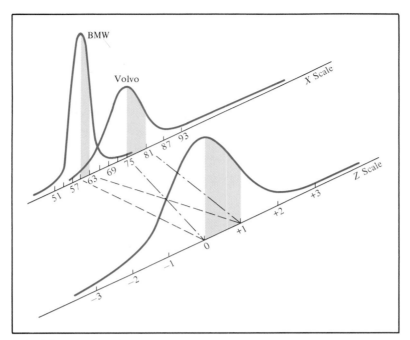

FIGURE 8.6
Demonstrating a transformation of scales for corresponding portions under two curves.

8.3 APPLICATIONS

Now that we have learned to use Table E.2 in conjunction with Equation (8.2), many different types of probability questions pertaining to the normal distribution can be resolved. To illustrate this, let us suppose that the consultant raises the following questions with regard to assembling a particular part at the Volvo automobile plant:

1. What is the probability that a randomly selected factory worker can assemble the part in under 75 seconds or in over 81 seconds?
2. What is the probability that a randomly selected factory worker can assemble the part in 69 to 81 seconds?
3. What is the probability that a randomly selected factory worker can assemble the part in under 62 seconds?
4. What is the probability that a randomly selected factory worker can assemble the part in 62 to 69 seconds?
5. How many seconds must elapse before 50% of the factory workers assemble the part?
6. How many seconds must elapse before 10% of the factory workers assemble the part?
7. What is the interquartile range (in seconds) expected for factory workers to assemble the part?

8.3.1 Finding the Probabilities Corresponding to Known Values

We recall from Section 8.2.4 that the assembly time data at the Volvo automobile plant are normally distributed with a mean μ_X of 75 seconds and a standard deviation

σ_X of 6 seconds. In responding to questions 1 through 4, we shall use this information as we seek to determine the probabilities associated with various measured values.

Question 1: Finding $P(X < 75$ or $X > 81)$

How can we determine the probability that a randomly selected factory worker will perform the task in under 75 seconds or over 81 seconds? Since we have already determined the probability that a randomly selected factory worker will need between 75 and 81 seconds to assemble the part, it is obvious from Figure 8.5 on page 259 that our desired probability must be its *complement*; that is, $1 - .3413 = .6587$.

Another way of viewing this problem, however, is to separately obtain both the probability of assembling the part in under 75 seconds and the probability of assembling the part in over 81 seconds and then use the *addition rule for mutually exclusive events* [Equation (6.4)] to obtain the desired result. This is depicted in Figure 8.7.

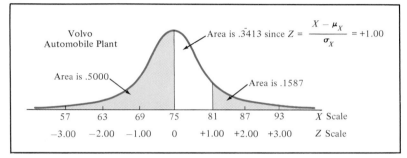

FIGURE 8.7
Finding $P(X < 75$ or $X > 81)$.

Since the mean and median are theoretically the same for normally distributed data, it is clear that 50% of the workers can assemble the part in under 75 seconds.[5] To show this, from Equation (8.2) we have

$$Z = \frac{X - \mu_X}{\sigma_X} = \frac{75 - 75}{6} = 0.00$$

Using Table E.2, we see that the area under the normal curve from the mean to $Z = 0.00$ is .0000. Hence the area under the curve less than $Z = 0.00$ must be $.5000 - .0000 = .5000$ (which happens to be the area for the entire left side of the distribution from the mean to $Z = -\infty$, as shown in Figure 8.7).

Now we wish to obtain the probability of assembling the part in over 81 seconds. But Equation (8.2) only gives the areas under the curve from the mean to Z, not from Z to $+\infty$. Thus we find the probability from the mean to Z and subtract this result from .5000 to obtain the desired answer. Since we know that the area or portion of the curve from the mean to $Z = +1.00$ is .3413, the area from $Z = +1.00$ to $Z = +\infty$ must be $.5000 - .3413 = .1587$. Hence the probability that a randomly selected

---

[5] Unlike the case of discrete random variables where the wording of the problem is so essential, we note that for continuous random variables there is much more flexibility in the wording. Hence there are two ways to state our result: We can say that 50% of the workers can assemble the part in *under 75 seconds* or we can say that 50% of the workers can assemble the part in *75 seconds or less*. Semantics are unimportant, because with continuous random variables the probability of assembling the part in exactly 75 seconds (or any other exactly specified time) is 0.

factory worker will perform the task in under 75 or over 81 seconds, $P(X < 75$ or $X > 81)$, is $.5000 + .1587 = .6587$.

Question 2: Finding $P(69 \leq X \leq 81)$

Suppose that we are now interested in determining the probability that a randomly selected factory worker can complete the part in 69 to 81 seconds, that is, $P(69 \leq X \leq 81)$. We note from Figure 8.8 that one of the values of interest is above the mean assemblage time of 75 seconds while the other value is below it. Since our transformation formula (8.2) permits us only to find probabilities from a *particular value of interest to the mean*, we can obtain our desired probability in three steps:

1. Determine the probability from the mean to 81 seconds.
2. Determine the probability from the mean to 69 seconds.
3. Sum up the two mutually exclusive results.

For this example, we already completed step 1; the area under the normal curve from the mean to 81 seconds is .3413. To find the area from the mean to 69 seconds (step 2), we have

$$Z = \frac{X - \mu_X}{\sigma_X} = \frac{69 - 75}{6} = -1.00$$

Table E.2 shows only positive entries for Z. Because of symmetry, it is clear that the area from the mean to $Z = -1.00$ must be identical to the area from the mean to $Z = +1.00$. Discarding the negative sign, then, we look up (in Table E.2) the value $Z = 1.00$ and find the probability to be .3413. Hence, from step 3, the probability that the part can be assembled in between 69 and 81 seconds is $.3413 + .3413 = .6826$. This is displayed in Figure 8.8.

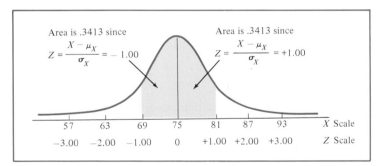

FIGURE 8.8
Finding $P(69 \leq X \leq 81)$.

Generalizing from the Standard Normal Distribution

The above result is rather important. If we may generalize for a moment, we can see that for any normal distribution there is a .6826 chance that a randomly selected item will fall within ±1 standard deviation above or below the mean. Moreover, we will leave it to the reader to verify from Table E.2 (see Problem 8.3 on page 269) that there is a .9544 chance that any randomly selected normally distributed observation will fall within ±2 standard deviations above or below the mean and a .9973 chance that the observation will fall between ±3 standard deviations above or below the mean.

For our particular automobile plant, this tells us that slightly more than two out

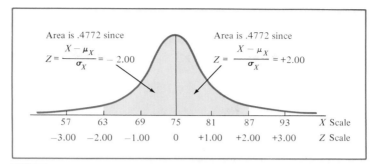

FIGURE 8.9
$P(63 \le X \le 87)$.

of every three factory workers (68.26%) can be expected to complete the task within ± 1 standard deviation from the mean. Moreover, from Figure 8.9, slightly more than 19 out of every 20 factory workers (95.44%) can be expected to complete the assemblage within ± 2 standard deviations from the mean (that is, between 63 and 87 seconds), and, from Figure 8.10, practically all factory workers (99.73%) can be expected to assemble the part within ± 3 standard deviations from the mean (that is, between 57 and 93 seconds).

From Figure 8.10 it is indeed quite unlikely (.0027 or only 27 factory workers in 10,000) that a randomly selected factory worker will be so fast or so slow that he or she could be expected to complete the assemblage of the part in under 57 seconds or over 93 seconds. Thus it is clear why $6\sigma_X$ (that is, 3 standard deviations above the mean to 3 standard deviations below the mean) is often used as a *practical approximation* of the range for normally distributed data.

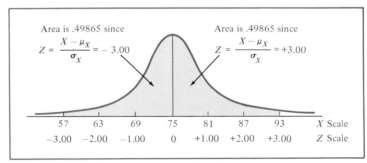

FIGURE 8.10
$P(57 \le X \le 93)$.

Question 3: Finding $P(X < 62)$

To obtain the probability that a randomly selected factory worker can assemble the part in under 62 seconds we should examine the shaded region of Figure 8.11 on page 264. The transformation formula (8.2) only permits us to find areas under the standardized normal distribution from the mean to Z, not from Z to $-\infty$. Thus, we must find the probability from the mean to Z and subtract this result from .5000 to obtain the desired answer.

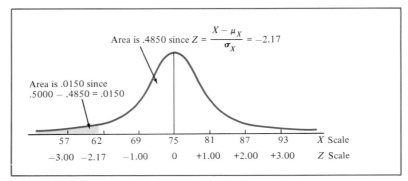

FIGURE 8.11
Finding $P(X < 62)$.

To determine the area under the curve from the mean to 62 seconds, we have

$$Z = \frac{X - \mu_X}{\sigma_X} = \frac{62 - 75}{6} = \frac{-13}{6} - 2.17$$

Neglecting the negative sign, we look up the Z value of 2.17 in Table E.2 by matching the appropriate Z row (2.1) with the appropriate Z column (.07) as shown in Table 8.3 (a replica of Table E.2).

Therefore, the resulting probability or area under the curve from the mean to 2.17 standard deviations below it is .4850. Hence the area from $Z = -2.17$ to $Z = -\infty$ must be $.5000 - .4850 = .0150$. This is indicated in Figure 8.11.

TABLE 8.3 Obtaining an area under the normal curve

Z	.00	.01	.02	.03	.04	.05	.06	.07	.08	.09
0.0	.0000	.0040	.0080	.0120	.0160	.0199	.0239	.0279	.0319	.0359
0.1	.0398	.0438	.0478	.0517	.0557	.0596	.0636	.0675	.0714	.0753
0.2	.0793	.0832	.0871	.0910	.0948	.0987	.1026	.1064	.1103	.1141
0.3	.1179	.1217	.1255	.1293	.1331	.1368	.1406	.1443	.1480	.1517
0.4	.1554	.1591	.1628	.1664	.1700	.1736	.1772	.1808	.1844	.1879
⋮	⋮	⋮	⋮	⋮	⋮	⋮	⋮	⋮	⋮	⋮
2.0	.4772	.4778	.4783	.4788	.4793	.4798	.4803	.4808	.4812	.4817
2.1	.4821	.4826	.4830	.4834	.4838	.4842	.4846	.4850	.4854	.4857
2.2	.4861	.4864	.4868	.4871	.4875	.4878	.4881	.4884	.4887	.4890
2.3	.4893	.4896	.4898	.4901	.4904	.4906	.4909	.4911	.4913	.4916
2.4	.4918	.4920	.4922	.4925	.4927	.4929	.4931	.4932	.4934	.4936

SOURCE: Extracted from Table E.2.

Question 4: Finding $P(62 \leq X \leq 69)$
As a final illustration of determining probabilities from the standardized normal distribution, suppose we wish to find how likely it is that a randomly selected factory worker can complete the task in 62 to 69 seconds? Since both values of interest are below the mean, we see from Figure 8.12 that the desired probability (or area under the curve between the two values) is less than .5000. Since our transformation formula (8.2) only permits us to find probabilities from a *particular value of interest to the mean*, we can obtain our desired probability in three steps:

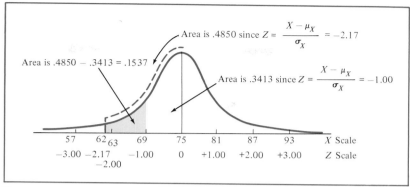

FIGURE 8.12
Finding $P(62 \le X \le 69)$

1. Determine the probability or area under the curve from the mean to 62 seconds.
2. Determine the probability or area under the curve from the mean to 69 seconds.
3. Subtract the smaller area from the larger (to avoid double counting).

For this example, we have already completed steps 1 and 2 in answering questions 3 and 2, respectively. The area from the mean to 62 seconds is .4850, while the area from the mean to 69 seconds is .3413. Hence, from step 3, by subtracting the smaller area from the larger one we determine that there is only a .1437 probability of randomly selecting a factory worker who could be expected to complete the task in between 62 and 69 seconds. That is,

$$P(62 \le X \le 69) = P(62 \le X \le 75) - P(69 \le X \le 75)$$
$$= .4850 - .3413$$
$$= .1437$$

8.3.2 Finding the Values Corresponding to Known Probabilities

In our previous applications regarding normally distributed data we have sought to determine the probabilities associated with various measured values. Now, however, suppose we wish to determine particular values of the variables of interest which correspond to known probabilities. As examples, let us respond to questions 5 through 7.

Question 5
To determine how many seconds elapse before 50% of the factory workers assemble the part, we should examine Figure 8.13 on page 266. Since this time value corresponds to the median, and the mean and median are equal in all symmetric distributions, the median must be 75 seconds.

Question 6
To determine how many seconds elapse before 10% of the factory workers assemble the part, we should focus on Figure 8.14 on page 266.

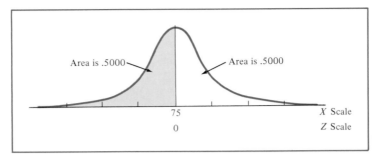

FIGURE 8.13
Finding *X*.

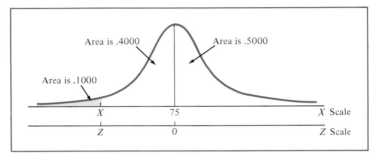

FIGURE 8.14
Finding *Z* to determine *X*.

Since 10% of the factory workers are expected to complete the task in under *X* seconds, then 90% of the workers would be expected to require *X* seconds or more to do the job. From Figure 8.14 it is clear that this 90% can be broken down into two parts—times (in seconds) above the mean (that is, 50%) and times between the mean and the desired value *X* (that is, 40%). While we do not know *X*, we can easily determine the corresponding standardized value *Z*, since the area under the normal curve from the standardized mean 0 to this *Z* must be .4000. Using the body of Table

TABLE 8.4   Obtaining a *Z* value corresponding to a particular area under the normal curve

Z	*.00*	*.01*	*.02*	*.03*	*.04*	*.05*	*.06*	*.07*	*.08*	*.09*
0.0	.0000	.0040	.0080	.0120	.0160	.0199	.0239	.0279	.0319	.0359
0.1	.0398	.0438	.0478	.0517	.0557	.0596	.0636	.0675	.0714	.0753
0.2	.0793	.0832	.0871	.0910	.0948	.0987	.1026	.1064	.1103	.1141
0.3	.1179	.1217	.1255	.1293	.1331	.1368	.1406	.1443	.1480	.1517
0.4	.1554	.1591	.1628	.1664	.1700	.1736	.1772	.1808	.1844	.1879
⋮	⋮	⋮	⋮	⋮	⋮	⋮	⋮	⋮	⋮	⋮
1.0	.3413	.3438	.3461	.3485	.3508	.3531	.3554	.3577	.3599	.3621
1.1	.3643	.3665	.3686	.3708	.3729	.3749	.3770	.3790	.3810	.3830
1.2	.3849	.3869	.3888	.3907	.3925	.3944	.3962	.3980	.3997	.4015
1.3	.4032	.4049	.4066	.4082	.4099	.4115	.4131	.4147	.4162	.4177
1.4	.4192	.4207	.4222	.4236	.4251	.4265	.4279	.4292	.4306	.4319

SOURCE: Extracted from Table E.2.

E.2, we search for the area or probability .4000. The closest result is .3997 as shown in Table 8.4 (a replica of Table E.2).

Working from this area to the margins of the table, we see that the Z value corresponding to the particular Z row (1.2) and Z column (.08) is 1.28. However, from Figure 8.14, the Z value must be recorded as a negative (that is, $Z = -1.28$), since it is below the standardized mean of 0.

Once Z is obtained, we can now use the transformation formula (8.2) to determine the value of interest, X. Since

$$Z = \frac{X - \mu_X}{\sigma_X} \qquad (8.2)$$

then

$$X = \mu_X + Z\sigma_X \qquad (8.3)$$

Substituting, we compute

$$X = 75 + (-1.28)(6) = 67.32 \text{ seconds}$$

Thus we could expect that 10% of the workers will be able to complete the task in less than 67.32 seconds.

As a review, to find a *particular* value associated with a known probability we must take the following steps:

1. Sketch the normal curve and then place the values for the means (μ_X and μ_Z) on the respective X and Z scales.
2. Split the appropriate half of the normal curve into two parts—the portion from the desired X to the mean and the portion from the desired X to the tail.
3. Shade the area of interest.
4. Using Table E.2, determine the appropriate Z value corresponding to the area under the normal curve from the desired X to the mean μ_X.
5. Using Equation (8.3), solve for X; that is,

$$X = \mu_X + Z\sigma_X$$

Question 7

To obtain the interquartile range we must first find the value for Q_1 and the value for Q_3; then we must subtract the former from the latter.

To find the first quartile value, we must determine the time (in seconds) for which only 25% of the factory workers can be expected to assemble the part faster. This is depicted in Figure 8.15 on page 268.

Although we do not know Q_1, we can easily obtain the corresponding standardized value Z, since the area under the normal curve from the standardized mean 0 to this Z must be .2500. Using the body of Table E.2, we search for the area or probability .2500. The closest result is .2486, as shown in Table 8.5 on page 268 (which is a replica of Table E.2).

Working from this area to the margins of the table, we see that the Z value corresponding to the particular Z row (0.6) and Z column (.07) is 0.67. However, from

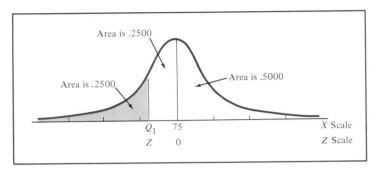

FIGURE 8.15
Finding Q_1.

Figure 8.15, the Z value must be recorded as a negative (that is, $Z = -0.67$), since it lies to the left of the standardized mean of 0.

Once Z is obtained, the final step is to use Equation (8.3). Hence,

$$Q_1 = X = \mu_X + Z\sigma_X$$
$$= 75 + (-0.67)(6)$$
$$= 75 - 4$$
$$= 71 \text{ seconds}$$

To find the third quartile, we must determine the time (in seconds) for which 75% of the factory workers can be expected to assemble the part faster (and 25% could complete the task slower). This is displayed in Figure 8.16 on page 269.

From the symmetry of the normal distribution, our desired Z value must be $+0.67$ (since Z lies to the right of the standardized mean of 0). Therefore, using Equation (8.3), we compute

$$Q_3 = X = \mu_X + Z\sigma_X$$
$$= 75 + (+0.67)(6)$$
$$= 75 + 4$$
$$= 79 \text{ seconds}$$

TABLE 8.5 Obtaining a Z value corresponding to a particular area under the normal curve

Z	.00	.01	.02	.03	.04	.05	.06	.07	.08	.09
0.0	.0000	.0040	.0080	.0120	.0160	.0199	.0239	.0279	.0319	.0359
0.1	.0398	.0438	.0478	.0517	.0557	.0596	.0636	.0675	.0714	.0753
0.2	.0793	.0832	.0871	.0910	.0948	.0987	.1026	.1064	.1103	.1141
0.3	.1179	.1217	.1255	.1293	.1331	.1368	.1406	.1443	.1480	.1517
0.4	.1554	.1591	.1628	.1664	.1700	.1736	.1772	.1808	.1844	.1879
0.5	.1915	.1950	.1985	.2019	.2054	.2088	.2123	.2157	.2190	.2224
0.6	.2257	.2291	.2324	.2357	.2389	.2422	.2454	.2486	.2518	.2549
0.7	.2580	.2612	.2642	.2673	.2704	.2734	.2764	.2794	.2823	.2852
0.8	.2881	.2910	.2939	.2967	.2995	.3023	.3051	.3078	.3106	.3133
0.9	.3159	.3186	.3212	.3238	.3264	.3289	.3315	.3340	.3365	.3389
1.0	.3413	.3438	.3461	.3485	.3508	.3531	.3554	.3577	.3599	.3621
1.1	.3643	.3665	.3686	.3708	.3729	.3749	.3770	.3790	.3810	.3830

SOURCE: Extracted from Table E.2.

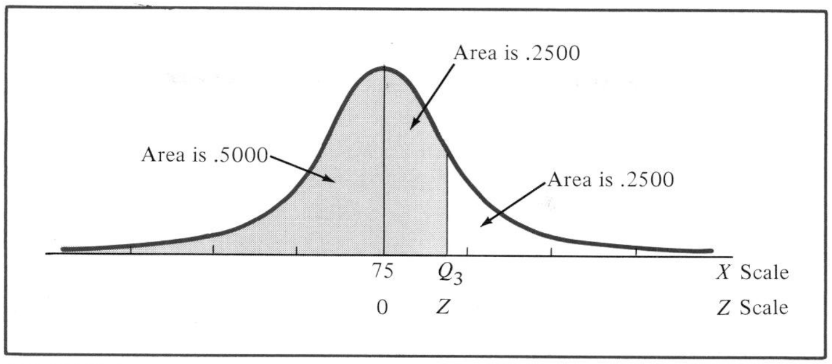

FIGURE 8.16
Finding Q_3.

The interquartile range or "middle spread" of the distribution is

$$\text{interquartile range} = Q_3 - Q_1$$
$$= 79 - 71$$
$$= 8 \text{ seconds}$$

Problems

8.1 Given a standardized normal distribution having mean of 0 and standard deviation of 1 (Table E.2).
(a) What is the probability that
 (1) Z is less than 1.57?
 (2) Z exceeds 1.84?
 (3) Z is between 1.57 and 1.84?
 (4) Z is less than 1.57 or greater than 1.84?
 (5) Z is between -1.57 and 1.84?
 (6) Z is less than -1.57 or greater than 1.84?
(b) What is the value of Z if 50.0% of all possible Z values are larger?
(c) What is the value of Z if only 2.5% of all possible Z values are larger?
(d) Between what two values of Z (symmetrically distributed around the mean) will 68.26% of all possible Z values be contained?

● **8.2** Given a standardized normal distribution (with mean of 0 and standard deviation of 1), determine the following probabilities:
(a) $P(Z > +1.34) = ?$ (d) $P(Z < -1.17) = ?$
(b) $P(Z \leq +1.17) = ?$ (e) $P(-1.17 \leq Z \leq +1.34) = ?$
(c) $P(0 \leq Z \leq +1.17) = ?$ (f) $P(-1.17 \leq Z \leq -0.50) = ?$

8.3 Verify the following:
(a) The area under the normal curve between the mean and 2 standard deviations above and below it is .9544.
(b) The area under the normal curve between the mean and 3 standard deviations above and below it is .9973.

8.4 The thickness of a batch of 10,000 brass washers of a certain type manufactured by a large company is normally distributed with a mean of .0191 inch and with a standard deviation of .000425 inch. Verify that 99.04% of these washers can be expected to have a thickness between .0180 and .0202 inch.

8.5 Using the following data sets decide whether or not the random variable of interest appears to be approximately normally distributed:
- **(a)** PE ratios of food processing companies (Problem 3.56 on page 70).
- **(b)** Fringe benefits as a percent of salaries (Problem 3.57 on page 71).
- **(c)** Quarterly sales tax receipts (Problem 3.58 on page 71).
- **(d)** Selling price of auto alarm systems (Problem 3.67 on page 74).
- **(e)** Projected changes in GNP (Problem 3.76 on page 78).
- **(f)** Cost per dose of laundry detergent (Problem 3.77 on page 79).
- **(g)** Alcoholic consumption (Problem 3.78 on page 80).
- **(h)** Sodium content of salted peanut butter brands (Problem 3.83 on page 82).
- **(i)** Calories in pancake mixes (Problem 3.87 on page 87).
- **(j)** Batting averages in the American League (Problem 3.88 on page 88).
- **(k)** Starting salaries (Problem 4.118 on page 141).

8.6 Monthly food expenditures for families of four in a large city average $420 with a standard deviation of $80. Assuming that the monthly food expenditures are normally distributed
- **(a)** What percentages of these expenditures are less than $350?
- **(b)** What percentages of these expenditures are between $250 and $350?
- **(c)** What percentages of these expenditures are between $250 and $450?
- **(d)** What percentages of these expenditures are less than $250 or greater than $450?
- **(e)** Determine Q_1 and Q_3 from the normal curve.
- ➠**(f) ACTION** Write a letter to your economics professor regarding your findings.

8.7 The length of time needed to service a car at Miller's Automotive Service Station is normally distributed with mean $\mu_X = 4.5$ minutes and standard deviation $\sigma_X = 1.1$ minutes.
- **(a)** What is the probability that a randomly selected car will require
  - (1) more than 6 minutes of service or under 5 minutes of service?
  - (2) between 3.5 and 5.6 minutes of service?
  - (3) at most 3.5 minutes of service?
- **(b)** What is the servicing time such that only 5% of all cars require more than this amount of time?
- ➠**(c) ACTION** If you were hired as a consultant, what would you tell the owner of Miller's?

8.8 The reaction time to a certain psychological experiment is normally distributed with mean $\mu_X = 20$ seconds and standard deviation $\sigma_X = 4$ seconds.
- **(a)** What is the probability that a subject has a reaction time between 14 and 30 seconds?
- **(b)** What is the probability that a subject has a reaction time between 25 and 30 seconds?
- **(c)** What percentage of subjects have reaction times over 14 seconds?
- **(d)** What is the reaction time such that only 1% of all subjects are faster?
- **(e)** What is the reaction time representing Q_3?

8.9 A set of final examination grades in an introductory statistics course was found to be normally distributed with a mean of 73 and a standard deviation of 8.
- **(a)** What is the probability of getting at most a grade of 91 on this exam?
- **(b)** What percentage of students scored between 65 and 89?
- **(c)** What percentage of students scored between 81 and 89?
- **(d)** What is the final exam grade if only 5% of the students taking the test scored higher?
- **(e)** If the professor "curves" (gives A's to the top 10% of the class regardless of the score), are you better off with a grade of 81 on this exam or a grade of 68 on a different exam where the mean is 62 and the standard deviation is 3? Show statistically and explain.

8.10 At a well-known business school the grade-point indexes of its 1,000 undergraduates are approximately normally distributed with mean $\mu_X = 2.83$ and standard deviation $\sigma_X = .38$.
- **(a)** What is the probability that a randomly selected student has a grade-point index between 2.00 and 3.00?

(b) What percentage of the student body are on probation—that is, have grade-point indexes below 2.00?

(c) How many students at this school are expected to be on the dean's list—that is, have grade-point indexes equal to or exceeding 3.20?

(d) What grade-point index will be exceeded by only 15% of the student body?

8.11 The number of days between billing and payment of charge accounts at Groshen's, a large department store, is approximately normally distributed with a mean of 18 days and standard deviation of 4 days.

(a) What proportion of the bills will be paid

   (1) between 12 and 18 days?

   (2) between 20 and 23 days?

   (3) in less than 8 days?

   (4) in 12 or more days?

(b) Within how many days will 99.5% of the bills be paid?

➠(c) **ACTION** If you were hired as a consultant, what would you tell the vice president of finance at Groshen's?

8.12 Show that for normally distributed data the interquartile range is approximately equal to 1.33 standard deviations.

8.13 Show that for normally distributed data the standard deviation can be approximated as .75 times the interquartile range.

8.14 Suppose that an intelligence test is constructed to have a normal distribution with a mean of 100 and a standard deviation of 15.

(a) Draw a picture of a normal curve with a mean of 100, and mark the absicssa (horizontal axis) where scores of 70, 85, 100, 115, and 130 should be.

(b) What proportion of people have IQ scores

   (1) Less than 100?

   (2) Less than 115?

   (3) Greater than 130?

   (4) Greater than 145?

(c) What proportion of people have IQ scores

   (1) Between 85 and 115?

   (2) Between 70 and 130?

(d) If IQ scores were reported instead on a scale with a mean of 500 and a standard deviation of 100 (like SAT scores), what would scores of 400, 500, and 600 have been on the original IQ scale?

8.15 Suppose that the length of time it takes one variety of seeds of a plant to germinate is normally distributed with a mean of 15 days and a standard deviation of 4 days.

(a) What proportion of the seeds should germinate

   (1) Within 19 days?

   (2) Within 23 days?

(b) By what day should three-fourths of the seeds have germinated?

(c) Suppose that by the 15th day only 60% of the seeds have germinated; would you worry about having a bad bunch of seeds? Discuss.

8.16 Suppose that the amount of time it takes the Internal Revenue Service (IRS) to send refunds to taxpayers is normally distributed with a mean of 12 weeks and a variance of 9.

(a) What proportion of taxpayers should get a refund

   (1) Within 6 weeks?

   (2) Within 9 weeks?

(b) What proportion of refunds will be sent more than 15 weeks after the IRS receives the tax return?

(c) How long will it take before 90% of taxpayers get their refunds?

8.4 THE NORMAL DISTRIBUTION AS AN APPROXIMATION TO VARIOUS DISCRETE PROBABILITY DISTRIBUTIONS

In the previous section we demonstrated the importance of the normal probability density function because of the numerous phenomena which seem to follow it or whose distributions can be approximated by it. In this section we shall demonstrate another important aspect of the normal distribution—how it may be used to approximate various important discrete probability distribution functions such as the binomial, the hypergeometric, and the Poisson.

8.4.1 Need for a Correction for Continuity Adjustment

There are two major reasons to employ a **correction for continuity adjustment** here.

First, recall that a discrete random variable can take on only specified values whereas a continuous random variable used to approximate it can take on any values whatsoever within a continuum or interval around those specified values. Hence, when using the normal distribution to approximate such discrete distribution functions as the binomial, the hypergeometric, or the Poisson, more accurate approximations of the probabilities are likely to be obtained if a correction for continuity adjustment is employed.

Second, recall that with a continuous distribution (such as the normal), the probability of obtaining a *particular* value of a random variable is zero. On the other hand, when the normal distribution is used to approximate a discrete distribution, a correction for continuity adjustment can be employed so that we may approximate the probability of a specific value of the discrete distribution.

As a case in point, consider an experiment in which we toss a fair coin 12 times and observe the number of heads. Suppose we want to compute the probability of obtaining *exactly* 4 heads. Whereas a discrete random variable can have only a specified value (such as 4), a continuous random variable used to approximate it could take on any values whatsoever within an interval around that specified value, as demonstrated on the accompanying scale:

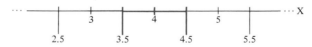

The correction for continuity adjustment requires the adding or subtracting of 0.5 from the value or values of the discrete random variable X as needed. Hence to use the normal distribution to approximate the probability of obtaining *exactly* 4 heads (i.e., $X = 4$), we would find the area under the normal curve from $X = 3.5$ to $X = 4.5$, the lower and upper boundaries of 4. Moreover, to determine the approximate probability of observing *at least* 4 heads, we would find the area under the normal curve from $X = 3.5$ and above since, on a continuum, 3.5 is the lower boundary of X. Similarly, to determine the approximate probability of observing *at most* 4 heads, we would find the area under the normal curve from $X = 4.5$ and below since, on a continuum, 4.5 is the upper boundary of X.

When using the normal distribution to approximate discrete probability distribution functions, we see that semantics becomes important again. To determine the approximate probability of observing *fewer* than 4 heads, we would find the area under the normal curve from $X = 3.5$ and below; to determine the approximate probability of observing *more than* 4 heads, we would find the area under the normal curve from $X = 4.5$ and above; and to determine the approximate probability of observing 4 *through* 7 heads, we would find the area under the normal curve from $X = 3.5$ to $X = 7.5$. The reader will have an opportunity to obtain these results in Problem 8.17 on page 279.

8.4.2 Approximating the Binomial Distribution

In Section 7.6.2 we stated that the binomial distribution will be symmetric (like the normal distribution) whenever $p = .5$. When $p \neq .5$ the binomial distribution will not be symmetric. However, the closer p is to .5 and the larger the number of sample observations n, the more symmetric the distribution becomes.

On the other hand, the larger the number of observations in the sample, the more tedious it is to compute the exact probabilities of success by use of Equation (7.7). Fortunately, though, whenever the sample size is large, the normal distribution can be used to approximate the exact probabilities of success that otherwise would have to be obtained through laborious computations.

As one rule of thumb this normal approximation can be used whenever both of the following two conditions are met:

1. The product of the two parameters n and p equals or exceeds 5.
2. The product $n(1 - p)$ equals or exceeds 5.

We recall from Section 7.6.2 that the mean of the binomial distribution is given by

$$\mu_X = np$$

while the standard deviation of the binomial distribution is obtained from

$$\sigma_X = \sqrt{np(1 - p)}$$

Substituting into the transformation formula (8.2).

$$Z = \frac{X - \mu_X}{\sigma_X}$$

we have

$$Z = \frac{X - np}{\sqrt{np(1 - p)}}$$

so that, for large enough n, the random variable Z is approximately normally distributed.

Hence, to find approximate probabilities corresponding to the values of the discrete random variable X we have

$$Z = \frac{x_a - np}{\sqrt{np(1 - p)}} \tag{8.4}$$

where $\mu_X = np$, mean of the binomial distribution

$\sigma_X = \sqrt{np(1 - p)}$, standard deviation of the binomial distribution

x_a = adjusted number of successes, x, for the discrete random variable X, such that $x_a = x - .5$ or $x_a = x + .5$ as needed

and the approximate probabilities of success are obtained from Table E.2, the table of the standardized normal distribution.

Example

To illustrate this, suppose, in the product quality-control example (described on page 222), that a sample of $n = 1,600$ tires of the same type are obtained at random from an ongoing production process in which 8% of all such tires produced are defective. What is the probability that in such a sample *not more than* 150 tires will be defective?

Since both $np = (1,600)(.08) = 128$ and $n(1 - p) = (1,600)(.92) = 1,472$ exceed 5, we may use the normal distribution to approximate the binomial:

$$Z = \frac{x_a - np}{\sqrt{np(1 - p)}} = \frac{150.5 - 128}{\sqrt{(1,600)(.08)(.92)}} = \frac{22.5}{10.85} = +2.07$$

Here, x_a, the adjusted number of successes, is 150.5. Hence the approximate probability that X does not exceed this value corresponds, on the standardized Z scale, to a value of not more than $+2.07$. This is depicted in Figure 8.17.

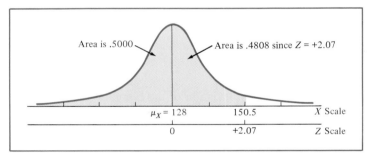

FIGURE 8.17
Approximating the binomial distribution.

Using Table E.2, the area under the curve between the mean and $Z = +2.07$ is .4808, so that the approximate probability is given by $.5000 + .4808 = .9808$.

Under the binomial distribution the probability of obtaining not more than 150 defective tires consists of all events up to and including 150 defectives—that is, $P(X \le 150) = P(X = 0) + P(X = 1) + \cdots + P(X = 150)$, and the true probability may be laboriously computed from

$$\sum_{X=0}^{150} \binom{1,600}{X} (.08)^X (.92)^{1,600 - X}$$

To appreciate the amount of work saved by using the normal approximation to the binomial model in lieu of the exact probability computations, just imagine making the following 151 computations from Equation (7.7) before summing up the results:

$$\binom{1,600}{0}(.08)^0(.92)^{1,600} + \binom{1,600}{1}(.08)^1(.92)^{1,599}$$

$$+ \cdots + \binom{1,600}{150}(.08)^{150}(.92)^{1,450}$$

Obtaining a Probability Approximation for an Individual Value

Suppose that we now want to compute the probability of obtaining *exactly* 150 defectives. In such a problem, the correction for continuity defines the integer value of interest to range from one-half unit below it to one-half unit above it. In our problem, the probability of obtaining 150 defective tires would be defined as the area (under the normal curve) between 149.5 and 150.5. Thus by using Equation (8.4), the probability can be approximated as follows:

$$Z = \frac{150.5 - 128}{\sqrt{(1,600)(.08)(.92)}} = +2.07$$

and

$$Z = \frac{149.5 - 128}{\sqrt{(1,600)(.08)(.92)}} = +1.98$$

From Table E.2, we note that the area under the normal curve from the mean to $X = 150.5$ is .4808 while the area under the curve from the mean to $X = 149.5$ is .4761. Thus as depicted in Figure 8.18, the approximate probability of obtaining 150 defective tires is the difference in the two areas, .0047.

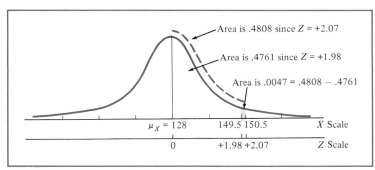

FIGURE 8.18
Approximating an exact binomial probability.

8.4.3 Approximating the Hypergeometric Distribution

The normal approximation to the hypergeometric distribution is also used whenever both $np \geq 5$ and $n(1 - p) \geq 5$. In fact we may recall from Sections 7.6 and 7.7 that the only distinction in the application of the hypergeometric distribution and the binomial distribution is that the latter deals with problems in which sampling is accomplished with replacement from a finite population or without replacement from an infinite population, while the hypergeometric distribution deals with problems in which sampling is achieved without replacement from a finite population.

We recall from Section 7.7.2 that the mean of the hypergeometric distribution is given by

$$\mu_X = np$$

while the standard deviation of the hypergeometric distribution is obtained from

$$\sigma_X = \sqrt{np(1-p)} \cdot \sqrt{\frac{N-n}{N-1}}$$

Substituting into the transformation formula (8.2),

$$Z = \frac{X - \mu_X}{\sigma_X}$$

we have

$$Z = \frac{X - np}{\sqrt{np(1-p)} \cdot \sqrt{\frac{N-n}{N-1}}}$$

so that, for large enough n, the random variable Z is approximately normally distributed.

Hence, to find approximate probabilities corresponding to the values of the discrete random variable X we have

$$Z = \frac{x_a - np}{\sqrt{np(1-p)} \cdot \sqrt{\frac{N-n}{N-1}}} \tag{8.5}$$

where $\mu_X = np$, the mean of the hypergeometric distribution

$\sigma_X = \sqrt{np(1-p)} \cdot \sqrt{\frac{N-n}{N-1}}$, the standard deviation of the hypergeometric distribution

x_a = adjusted number of successes, x, for the discrete random variable X, such that $x_a = x - .5$ or $x_a = x + .5$ as needed.

and the approximate probabilities of success are obtained from Table E.2.

We note here though that such a computation for the standard deviation in Equation (8.5) is necessary only when the sample size, selected without replacement from a finite population, is large in comparison to the population size. In Section 7.7.3 we stated as a rule of thumb that this is considered to occur if the sample size equals or exceeds 5% of the population size. For much sample survey work, however, when sampling without replacement from a finite population, the sample size is usually small when compared with the population (that is, $n < .05N$). In these cases we may neglect the expression $\sqrt{\dfrac{N-n}{N-1}}$, the **finite population correction factor,** and thereby consider the problem identical to that of the normal approximation to the binomial distribution given by Equation (8.4).

To illustrate this with the real estate survey of Chapter 2, suppose we consider the following: What is the probability of obtaining 79 *or more* houses having at least one fireplace in a sample of 233 houses if, in the population of 9,660 houses listed by the realty company, 35.0% of them (3,381) have at least one fireplace? Here,

$n = 233$ and $N = 9{,}660$. Since $n < .05N$, the expression $\sqrt{\dfrac{N-n}{N-1}}$ may be neglected. Using Equation (8.4) in lieu of Equation (8.5), we compute:

$$Z = \frac{x_a - np}{\sqrt{np(1-np)}} = \frac{78.5 - (233)(.35)}{\sqrt{(233)(.35)(.65)}} = \frac{78.5 - 81.55}{7.28} = -0.42$$

Here, x_a, the adjusted number of successes, is 78.5. Hence the approximate probability that X will exceed this value corresponds, on the standardized Z scale, to a value of at least -0.42. This is depicted in Figure 8.19.

From Figure 8.19 and Table E.2, the probability of obtaining 79 or more houses having at least one fireplace in a sample of 233 houses is approximated by .1628 + .5000 = .6628.

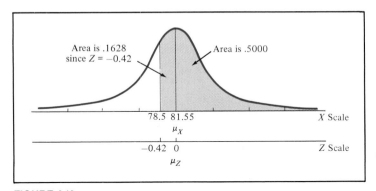

FIGURE 8.19
Approximating the hypergeometric distribution.

8.4.4   Approximating the Poisson Distribution

The normal distribution may also be used to approximate the Poisson model whenever the parameter λ, the expected number of successes, equals or exceeds 5. Since the value of the mean and the variance of a Poisson distribution are the same, we have

$$\mu_X = \lambda$$

and

$$\sigma_X = \sqrt{\lambda}$$

and by substituting into the transformation formula (8.2),

$$Z = \frac{X - \mu_X}{\sigma_X}$$

we have

$$Z = \frac{X - \lambda}{\sqrt{\lambda}}$$

so that, for large enough n, the random variable Z is approximately normally distributed.

Hence, to find approximate probabilities corresponding to the values of the discrete random variable X we have

$$Z = \frac{(x_a - \lambda)}{\sqrt{\lambda}} \qquad (8.6)$$

where λ = expected number of successes or mean of the Poisson distribution

$\sigma_X = \sqrt{\lambda}$, the standard deviation of the Poisson distribution

x_a = adjusted number of successes, x, for the discrete random variable X, such that $x_a = x - .5$ or $x_a = x + .5$ as needed.

and the approximate probabilities of success are obtained from Table E.2.

To illustrate this let us suppose that at an automobile plant the average number of work stoppages per day due to equipment problems during the production process is 12.0. What then is the approximate probability of having 15 *or fewer* work stoppages due to equipment problems on any given day? From Equation (8.6) we have

$$Z = \frac{x_a - \lambda}{\sqrt{\lambda}} = \frac{15.5 - 12.0}{\sqrt{12.0}} = +1.01$$

Here, x_a, the adjusted number of successes, is 15.5. Hence the approximate probability that X does not exceed this value corresponds, on the standardized Z scale, to a value of not more than $+1.01$. This is depicted in Figure 8.20. From Figure 8.20 and Table E.2, we note that the area under the normal curve from the mean to 15.5 is .3438. Hence the area up to 15.5 is $.5000 + .3438 = .8438$. Therefore, the approximate

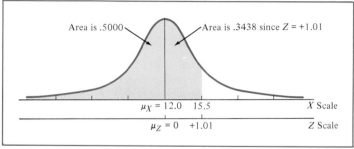

FIGURE 8.20
Approximating the Poisson distribution.

probability of having 15 or fewer work stoppages due to equipment problems on any given day is .8438. This approximation compares quite favorably to the exact Poisson probability, .8445, obtained from Equation (7.15) on page 238 or from Table E.6.

8.4.5 Large Sample Sizes: Neglecting the Correction for Continuity Adjustment

We have seen from the second example in Section 8.4.2 that if we are interested in obtaining probability approximations for individual values of the random variable, then it is, of course, necessary to use the correction for continuity adjustment. On the other hand, for other types of probability approximations, no hard and fast rule exists for using the correction for continuity adjustment. Since it is known that the advantages of increased accuracy become minimal with larger sample sizes and since the employment of the correction for continuity adjustment increases the computational complexity of our work, the correction for continuity will not be used in the remainder of this text. In most instances, our sample sizes will be large enough so that differences in the approximations obtained when using or not using the correction for continuity adjustment will be negligible.

Problems

● **8.17**   Consider an experiment in which we toss a fair coin 12 times and observe the number of heads.
  (a) Use Equation (7.7) on page 225 or Table E.7 to determine the probability of observing
    (1) 4 heads
    (2) at least 4 heads
    (3) at most 4 heads
    (4) fewer than 4 heads
    (5) more than 4 heads
    (6) 4 through 7 heads
  (b) Use the normal approximation to the binomial distribution [Equation (8.4)] to approximate the probabilities in (a)(1)–(a)(6).
  ⇒**(c)** **ACTION**   Compare and contrast your findings in (a) and (b). Discuss why it is permissible to use the normal approximation to the binomial distributions in part (b).

8.18   For overseas flights, an airline has three different choices on its dessert menu—ice cream, apple pie, and chocolate cake. Based on past experience the airline feels that each dessert is equally likely to be chosen.
  (a) If a random sample of four passengers is selected, what is the probability that at least two will choose ice cream for dessert?
  (b) If a random sample of 21 passengers is selected, what is the *approximate* probability that at least two will choose ice cream for dessert?

8.19   Based upon past experience, 40% of all customers at Miller's Automotive Service Station pay for their purchases with a credit card.
  (a) If a random sample of three customers is selected, what is the probability that
    (1) none pay with a credit card?
    (2) two pay with a credit card?
    (3) at least two pay with a credit card?
    (4) not more than two pay with a credit card?

(b) If a random sample of 200 customers is selected, what is the *approximate* probability that
   (1) at least 75 pay with a credit card?
   (2) not more than 70 pay with a credit card?
   (3) between 70 and 75 customers, inclusive, pay with a credit card?

➡**(c) ACTION** Based on part (b), if you were hired as a consultant, what would you tell the owner of Miller's?

8.20 The dean of a business school wishes to form a faculty senate of 20 members from among the faculty of 100. The selection is to be random and at the school 25 of the faculty members are in accounting. You are asked to assist in the drawing.
   (a) What is the *approximate* probability that the faculty senate body will contain
      (1) at least two accounting faculty?
      (2) between two and six accounting faculty?
   (b) How many accounting faculty would be expected in the faculty senate?
   ➡**(c) ACTION** Suppose no accounting faculty were selected and inquiries by that department are made. Prepare a draft of a letter for the dean justifying the drawings that were made.

8.21 On average, 10.0 persons per minute are waiting for an elevator in the lobby of a large office building between the hours of 8 A.M. and 9 A.M.
   (a) What is the probability that in any one-minute period at most four persons are waiting?
   (b) What is the *approximate* probability that in any one-minute period at most four persons are waiting?
   (c) Compare your results in (a) and (b).

● **8.22** The number of cars arriving per minute at a toll booth on a particular bridge is Poisson distributed with $\mu_X = 2.5$.
   (a) What is the probability that in any given minute
      (1) no cars arrive?
      (2) not more than two cars arrive?
   (b) If μ_X, the expected number of cars arriving at the toll booth per ten-minute interval, is 25.0, what is the *approximate* probability that in any given ten-minute period
      (1) not more than 20 cars arrive?
      (2) between 20 and 30 cars arrive?

8.23 Cars arrive at Kenny's Car Wash at a rate of nine per half-hour.
   (a) What is the probability that in any given half-hour period at least three cars arrive?
   (b) What is the *approximate* probability that in any given half-hour period at least three cars arrive?
   (c) Compare your results in (a) and (b).

8.5 SUMMARY AND OVERVIEW

In this chapter we have thoroughly examined one particularly important continuous distribution, the normal probability density function. In particular, the normal distribution was shown to be useful in its own right and also useful as an approximation of various discrete models. In the next chapter we shall investigate how the normal distribution provides the basis for classical statistical inference.

Supplementary Problems

✗ **8.24** Suppose the Governor projects that, on a weekly basis, a State Football Lottery Program he has proposed is expected to average 10.0 million dollars in profits (to be turned over to the state for educational programs) with a standard deviation of 2.5 million dollars. Suppose further that the weekly profits data are assumed to be (approximately) normally distributed. The following questions may be raised (or anticipated at the Governor's next press conference):

1. What is the probability that on any given week profits will be between 10.0 and 12.5 million dollars?
2. What is the probability that on any given week profits will be between 7.5 and 10.0 million dollars?
3. What is the probability that on any given week profits will be between 7.5 and 12.5 million dollars?
4. What is the probability that on any given week profits will be at least 7.5 million dollars?
5. What is the probability that on any given week profits will be under 7.5 million dollars?
6. What is the probability that on any given week profits will be between 12.5 and 14.3 million dollars?
7. Fifty percent of the time weekly profits (in millions of dollars) are expected to be above what value?
8. Ninety percent of the time weekly profits (in millions of dollars) are expected to be above what value?
9. What is the interquartile range in weekly profits expected from the State Football Lottery Program?

➠**ACTION** You have been hired as a consultant. Prepare responses for the Governor on these nine anticipated questions and write a report discussing your overall findings.

8.25 Toby's Trucking Company determined that on an annual basis the distance traveled per truck is normally distributed with a mean of 50.0 thousand miles and a standard deviation of 12.0 thousand miles.

(a) What proportion of trucks can be expected to travel between 34.0 and 50.0 thousands of miles in the year?
(b) What is the probability that a randomly selected truck travels between 34.0 and 38.0 thousands of miles in the year?
(c) What percentage of trucks can be expected to travel either below 30.0 or above 60.0 thousands of miles in the year?
(d) How many of the 1,000 trucks in the fleet are expected to travel between 30.0 and 60.0 thousands of miles in the year?
(e) How many miles will be traveled by at least 80% of the trucks?

8.26 Plastic bags used for packaging produce are manufactured so that the breaking strength of the bag is normally distributed with a mean of 5 pounds per square inch and a standard deviation of 1.5 pounds per square inch.

(a) What proportion of the bags produced have a breaking strength
 (1) between 5 and 5.5 pounds per square inch?
 (2) between 3.2 and 4.2 pounds per square inch?
 (3) at least 3.6 pounds per square inch?
 (4) less than 3.17 pounds per square inch?
(b) Between what two values symmetrically distributed around the mean will 95% of the breaking strengths fall?

8.27 Helen H. is 67 inches tall and weighs 135 pounds. If the heights of women are normally distributed with $\mu_H = 65$ inches and $\sigma_H = 2.5$ inches and if the weights of women are normally distributed with $\mu_W = 125$ pounds and $\sigma_W = 10$ pounds, determine whether Helen's more unusual characteristic is her height or her weight. Discuss.

8.28 The net weight of boxes of packaged cereal follows the normal distribution with mean $\mu_X = 368$ grams. Find the standard deviation σ_X if 98% of the boxes have a net weight below 400 grams.

8.29 The toll charge for telephone calls to Central America follows the normal distribution with mean $\mu_X = \$21.00$. Find the standard deviation σ_X if 80% of the calls have a toll charge above $17.50.

● **8.30** A statistical analysis of 1,000 long-distance telephone calls made from the headquarters of Johnson & Shurgot Corp. indicates that the length of these calls is normally distributed with $\mu_X = 240$ seconds and $\sigma_X = 40$ seconds.

  (a) What percentage of these calls lasted less than 180 seconds?
  (b) What is the probability that a particular call lasted between 180 and 300 seconds?
  (c) How many calls lasted less than 180 seconds or more than 300 seconds?
  (d) What percentage of the calls lasted between 110 and 180 seconds?
  (e) What is the length of a particular call if only 1% of all calls are shorter?
  (f) If the researcher could not assume that the data were normally distributed, what then would be the probability that a particular call lasted between 180 and 300 seconds? [*Hint:* Recall the Bienaymé–Chebyshev rule in Section 3.12.2.]
  (g) Discuss the differences in your answers to (b) and (f).
  ⇒**(h)** ACTION   If you were hired as a consultant, write a memo to the vice president of finance regarding your findings in parts (a)–(e).

● **8.31** It is known that one out of every three people entering Groshen's (a large department store) will make at least one purchase.

  (a) If a random sample of $n = 5$ persons is selected, what is the probability that
    (1) two or more of them will make at least one purchase?
    (2) at most four of them will make at least one purchase?
  (b) If a random sample of $n = 81$ persons is selected, what is the *approximate* probability that
    (1) 30 or more of them will make at least one purchase?
    (2) at most 40 of them will make at least one purchase?

8.32 The famous parapsychologist Professor Sy Klops decides to investigate whether people can read minds. He makes up five cards, each of which has a different symbol on it. When a subject comes to be tested, Klops picks up a card at random and asks the subject to guess which symbol is on the card. Klops then records whether the subject is correct or not, shuffles the cards again, and repeats the procedure. (Each such cycle on which one of two outcomes can occur is sometimes called a *trial*.)

  (a) Suppose each subject is given 5 trials. Calculate what proportion of people tested will be expected to get none right, one right, and so on.
  ⇒**(b)** ACTION   In the situation described in (a), if the Professor tests 1,000 people and says that 5 "show promise for having telepathic powers" because they got all 5 trials correct, would you agree or disagree, and why?
  ⇒**(c)** ACTION   Now suppose that the Professor uses more trials for each subject, so that everyone is tested on 50 trials. Discuss whether or not you think he can use the normal approximation to the binomial distribution.
  (d) Regardless of your answer to (c), use the normal approximation to the binomial to estimate the probability that someone will get at least 15 right by chance.

8.33 Servicing records indicate that 50% of all new automobiles purchased of a particular brand will require some type of repair within the 90-day warranty period. For a random sample of $n = 12$ such new automobiles, use the binomial distribution to determine

  (a) The probability that eight or nine of them will require repair within the 90-day warranty period.
  (b) The probability that not more than two of them will require repair within the 90-day warranty period.

Use the normal approximation to the binomal distribution to determine

  (c) the *approximate* probability that eight or nine of them will require repair within the 90-day warranty period.

(d) the *approximate* probability that not more than two of them will require repair within the 90-day warranty period.

➠**(e)** **ACTION** Discuss the differences in your answers in (a) versus (c) and in (b) versus (d).

● **8.34** Based on past experience the dispatcher of Toby's Trucking Company estimates that on any given day 20% of the trucks will arrive at their destinations more than one hour late. There are 1,000 trucks in the fleet.

(a) If a sample of ten trucks is selected, what is the probability that at most one arrives more than one hour late?

(b) If a sample of 100 trucks is selected, what is the *approximate* probability that at most ten arrive more than one hour late?

● **8.35** What is the (*approximate*) probability that a student could pass a 100-question true-false examination if the student were to guess on each question? (*Note*: To pass, the student must get at least 60 questions right.)

8.36 What is the (*approximate*) probability that a student would get exactly 60 questions right on a 100-question true-false examination if the student were to guess on each question?

● **8.37** Senator Phil E. Bluster believes that for a particular bill, each senator has a .75 probability of voting in favor of it. If 51 (out of 100) votes are needed for the bill to pass, and each senator decides independently how to vote, calculate

(a) The probability that the bill will pass (i.e., that at least 51 senators will vote for it).

(b) The probability that at least 67 senators will vote for it.

(c) The probability that at least 76 senators will vote for it.

8.38 Suppose that the average number of goals per game scored by the Baruch College Statesmen's soccer team last season was 2.5.

(a) What is the probability that in any one game
  (1) no goal will be scored?
  (2) at least five goals will be scored?
  (3) three or four goals will be scored?

(b) What is the *approximate* probability that over a 20-game season
  (1) a total of 40 through 60 goals will be scored?
  (1) a total of 40 or fewer goals will be scored?
  (3) a total of 60 or more goals will be scored?

8.39 The average number of accidents per day in a well-known tire factory is 3.2.

(a) What is the probability that in any one day
  (1) exactly four accidents will occur?
  (2) more than four accidents will occur?
  (3) at least four accidents will occur?
  (4) either three or four accidents will occur?

(b) What is the probability that in any five-day period
  (1) exactly 20 accidents will occur?
  (2) more than 20 accidents will occur?
  (3) at least 20 accidents will occur?
  (4) 15 through 20 accidents will occur?

(c) What is the *approximate* probability that in any five-day period
  (1) exactly 20 accidents will occur?
  (2) more that 20 accidents will occur?
  (3) at least 20 accidents will occur?
  (4) 15 through 20 accidents will occur?

➠**(d)** **ACTION** Compare and contrast your findings in (a), (b), and (c). Discuss.

The average number of stray dogs caught per day by the local ASPCA patrol is 2.2.
  (a) What is the probability that in any one day
    (1) exactly two stray dogs will be caught?
    (2) more than two stray dogs will be caught?
    (3) at least two stray dogs will be caught?
    (4) either two or three stray dogs will be caught?
  (b) What is the probability that in any five-day period
    (1) exactly ten stray dogs will be caught?
    (2) more than ten stray dogs will be caught?
    (3) at least ten stray dogs will be caught?
    (4) 10 through 15 stray dogs will be caught?
  (c) What is the *approximate* probability that in any five-day period
    (1) exactly ten stray dogs will be caught?
    (2) more than ten stray dogs will be caught?
    (3) at least ten stray dogs will be caught?
    (4) 10 through 15 stray dogs will be caught?
➠(d) **ACTION** Compare and contrast your findings in (a), (b), and (c). Discuss.

8.41 The average number of work stoppages per hour in a production process is 0.8.
  (a) What is the probability that in any one hour
    (1) exactly two stoppages will occur?
    (2) at most two stoppages will occur?
    (3) fewer than two stoppages will occur?
    (4) one or two stoppages will occur?
  (b) What is the probability that in any one eight-hour shift
    (1) exactly 16 stoppages will occur?
    (2) at most 16 stoppages will occur?
    (3) fewer than 16 stoppages will occur?
    (4) 8 through 16 stoppages will occur?
  (c) What is the *approximate* probability that in any one eight-hour shift
    (1) exactly 16 stoppages will occur?
    (2) at most 16 stoppages will occur?
    (3) fewer than 16 stoppages will occur?
    (4) 8 through 16 stoppages will occur?
➠(d) **ACTION** Compare and contrast your findings in (a), (b), and (c). Discuss.

8.42 Based upon past experience, 7% of all luncheon expense vouchers are in error. If a random sample of 400 vouchers is selected, what is the *approximate* probability that:
  (a) exactly 25 are in error?
  (b) fewer than 25 are in error?
  (c) between 20 and 25 (inclusive) are in error?

8.43 On a Saturday morning, an average of 8.5 customers arrive at a particular suburban bank every 10 minutes.
  (a) What is the probability that in any given 10-minute period:
    (1) exactly 5 customers arrive?
    (2) no more than 5 customers arrive?
  (b) What is the *approximate* probability that in any given 10-minute period:
    (1) exactly 5 customers arrive?
    (2) no more than 5 customers arrive?
  (c) Compare your results in (a)(1) versus (b)(1) and (a)(2) versus (b)(2).

Case Study C

There are nine basic betting strategies in roulette. These are presented below along with the corresponding odds.

As examples, in strategy 1 a $1 bet on any particular number results in a loss of the dollar or a profit of $35 (that is, a payoff of $36 including the $1 bet) while in strategy 9 a $1 bet on "even–odd" or "red–black" or "1 to 18"–"19 to 36" results in a loss of the dollar or a profit of a dollar (that is, a payoff of $2 including the $1 bet).

Suppose that you were planning a trip to a casino offering the game of roulette with the aforementioned betting strategies and odds. A friend who is a mathematical statistics major has hinted to you that the various betting strategies may not all be equal and that perhaps there is at least one which may give the player a greater advantage

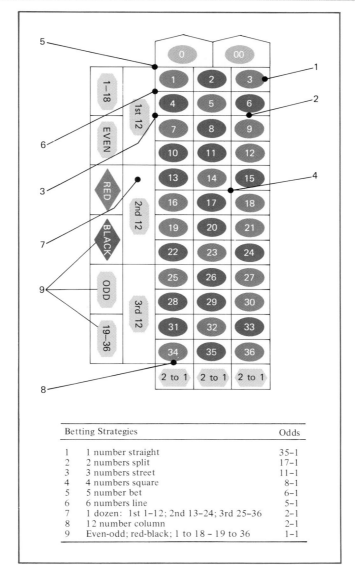

Betting Strategies		Odds
1	1 number straight	35–1
2	2 numbers split	17–1
3	3 numbers street	11–1
4	4 numbers square	8–1
5	5 number bet	6–1
6	6 numbers line	5–1
7	1 dozen: 1st 1–12; 2nd 13–24; 3rd 25–36	2–1
8	12 number column	2–1
9	Even-odd; red-black; 1 to 18 – 19 to 36	1–1

or disadvantage. Using the results of mathematical expectation, you decide to check out the various betting strategies based on your intent to make only $1 bets and then write a letter to your friend explaining your findings.

As you are preparing your letter while relaxing at the hotel pool, you overhear a heated conversation on the best method of attempting to maximize profits in 200 plays of the roulette game if one were to continually make $1 bets on each game and not worry about the consequences (that is, the possibility of losing much or all of the $200). The two people were arguing over whether it is a better strategy to bet "one number" (strategy 1) on each play or to continually bet a "three-number street" (strategy 3) on each play or a particular color such as "red" (strategy 9) on each play. Since you just happen to have your table of the normal distribution with you, you decide to analyze these possibilities and impress your friend with your mathematical and statistical abilities by describing your findings in your letter.

References

1. DERMAN, C., L. J. GLESER, AND I. OLKIN, *A Guide to Probability Theory and Application* (New York: Holt, Rinehart and Winston, 1973).
2. LARSEN, R. J., AND M. L. MARX, *An Introduction to Mathematical Statistics and Its Applications*, 2d ed. (Englewood Cliffs, N.J.: Prentice-Hall, 1986).

Sampling Distributions

9.1 THE NEED FOR SAMPLING DISTRIBUTIONS

A major goal of data analysis is to use statistics such as the sample mean and the sample proportion in order to estimate the corresponding *true* values in the population. The process of generalizing these sample results to the population is referred to as **statistical inference.** In the preceding three chapters we have examined basic rules of probability and investigated various probability distributions such as the uniform, binomial, hypergeometric, Poisson, and normal distributions. In this chapter we shall use these rules of probability along with our knowledge of probability distributions to begin focusing on how certain statistics (such as the mean or proportion) can be utilized in making inferences about the true population parameters.

We should realize that in enumerative studies a researcher is concerned with drawing conclusions about a population, not about a sample. As examples, a political pollster would be interested in the sample results only as a way of estimating the actual proportion of the votes that each candidate will receive from the population of voters. Likewise, an auditor, in selecting a sample of vouchers, is interested only in using the sample mean for estimating the population average amount. Moreover, in our real estate survey, the statistician would utilize sample information as a way of drawing inferences about the population of single-family houses. Thus in each of these situations, the sample is used for drawing conclusions about the population.

In practice, a single sample of a predetermined size is selected at random from the population. The items that are to be included in the sample are determined through the use of a random number generator, such as a table of random numbers (see Section 2.7). Hypothetically, in order to be able to use the sample statistic to estimate the population parameter, we should examine every possible sample that could have occurred. If this selection of all possible samples actually were to be done, the distribution of the results would be referred to as a **sampling distribution.** Although in practice only one such sample is actually selected, the concept of a sampling distribution must be examined so that probability theory can be used in making inferences about the population values.

9.2 SAMPLING DISTRIBUTION OF THE MEAN

9.2.1 Why the Arithmetic Mean?

In Chapter 3 we discussed several measures of central tendency. Undoubtedly, the most widely used (if not always the best) measure of central tendency is the arithmetic mean. This is particularly the case if the population can be assumed to be normally distributed.

Among several important mathematical properties (see Reference 2) of the arithmetic mean for a normal distribution are

1. Unbiasedness
2. Efficiency
3. Consistency

The first property, **unbiasedness,** involves the fact that the average of all the possible sample means (of a given sample size n) will be equal to the population mean μ_X.

This property can be demonstrated empirically by looking at the following example: A population of four typists were asked to type the same page of a manuscript. The number of errors made by each typist were:

Typist	Number of Errors
A	3
B	2
C	1
D	4

This population distribution is shown in Figure 9.1.

We may recall from Section 3.12 that when the data from a population are available, the mean can be computed from

$$\mu_X = \frac{\sum_{i=1}^{N} X_i}{N} \qquad (9.1)$$

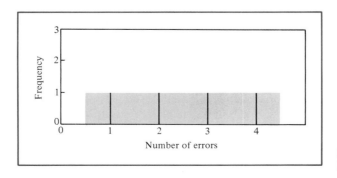

FIGURE 9.1
Number of errors made by a population of four typists.

and the standard deviation can be computed from

$$\sigma_X = \sqrt{\frac{\sum_{i=1}^{N}(X_i - \mu_X)^2}{N}}$$
(9.2)

Thus,

$$\mu_X = \frac{3 + 2 + 1 + 4}{4} = 2.5 \text{ errors}$$

and

$$\sigma_X = \sqrt{\frac{(3 - 2.5)^2 + \cdots + (4 - 2.5)^2}{4}} = 1.12 \text{ errors}$$

If samples of two typists are selected *with* replacement from this population, there are 16 possible samples that could be selected ($N^n = 4^2 = 16$). These possible sample outcomes are shown in Table 9.1.

TABLE 9.1 All 16 samples of $n = 2$ typists from a population of $N = 4$ typists when sampling with replacement

Sample	Typists	Sample Outcomes	Sample Mean $\bar{X}_i$
1	A, A	3, 3	$\bar{X}_1 = 3$
2	A, B	3, 2	$\bar{X}_2 = 2.5$
3	A, C	3, 1	$\bar{X}_3 = 2$
4	A, D	3, 4	$\bar{X}_4 = 3.5$
5	B, A	2, 3	$\bar{X}_5 = 2.5$
6	B, B	2, 2	$\bar{X}_6 = 2$
7	B, C	2, 1	$\bar{X}_7 = 1.5$
8	B, D	2, 4	$\bar{X}_8 = 3$
9	C, A	1, 3	$\bar{X}_9 = 2$
10	C, B	1, 2	$\bar{X}_{10} = 1.5$
11	C, C	1, 1	$\bar{X}_{11} = 1$
12	C, D	1, 4	$\bar{X}_{12} = 2.5$
13	D, A	4, 3	$\bar{X}_{13} = 3.5$
14	D, B	4, 2	$\bar{X}_{14} = 3$
15	D, C	4, 1	$\bar{X}_{15} = 2.5$
16	D, D	4, 4	$\bar{X}_{16} = 4$
			$\mu_{\bar{X}} = 2.5 = \mu_X$

If all these 16 sample means are averaged, the mean of these values ($\mu_{\bar{X}}$) is equal to 2.5, which is the mean of the population, μ_X.

On the other hand, if sampling was being done *without* replacement, there would be six possible samples of two typists:

$$\frac{N!}{n!(N-n)!} = \frac{4!}{2!2!} = 6$$

These six possible samples are listed in Table 9.2.

TABLE 9.2 All six possible samples of $n = 2$ typists from a population of $N = 4$ typists when sampling without replacement

Sample	Typists	Sample Outcomes	Sample Mean $\bar{X}_i$
1	A, B	3, 2	$\bar{X}_1 = 2.5$
2	A, C	3, 1	$\bar{X}_2 = 2$
3	A, D	3, 4	$\bar{X}_3 = 3.5$
4	B, C	2, 1	$\bar{X}_4 = 1.5$
5	B, D	2, 4	$\bar{X}_5 = 3$
6	C, D	1, 4	$\bar{X}_6 = 2.5$
			$\mu_{\bar{X}} = 2.5 = \mu_X$

In this case, also, the average of all sample means ($\mu_{\bar{X}}$) is equal to the population mean, 2.5. Therefore we have shown that the sample arithmetic mean is an unbiased estimator of the population mean.

The second property possessed by the mean, **efficiency,** refers to the precision of the sample statistic as an estimator of the population parameter. For distributions such as the normal, the arithmetic mean is considered to be more stable from sample to sample than are other measures of central tendency. For any size sample the mean will, on the average, come closer to the population mean than any other unbiased estimator, so that the sample mean is a ''better'' estimate of the population mean.

The third property, **consistency,** refers to the effect of the sample size on the usefulness of an estimator. As the sample size increases, the variation of the sample mean from the population mean becomes smaller and smaller so that the sample arithmetic mean becomes a better estimate of the population mean.

9.2.2 Standard Error of the Mean

The fluctuation in the average number of typing errors which was obtained when sampling with replacement from all 16 possible samples is illustrated in Figure 9.2.

In this small example, although we can observe a good deal of fluctuation in the sample mean—depending on which typists were selected—there is not nearly as much fluctuation as in the actual population itself. The fact that the sample means are less variable than the population data follows directly from the **law of large numbers.** A particular sample mean averages together all the values in the sample. A population may consist of individual outcomes that can take on a wide range of values from extremely small to extremely large. However, if an extreme value falls into the sample, although it will have an effect on the mean, the effect will be reduced since it is being averaged in with all the other values in the sample. Moreover, as the sample size increases, the effect of a single extreme value gets even smaller, since it is being averaged with more observations.

This phenomenon is expressed statistically in the value of the standard deviation of the sample mean. This is the measure of variability of the mean from sample to sample

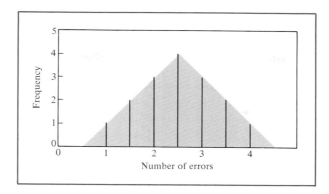

FIGURE 9.2
Sampling distribution of the average number of errors for samples of two typists.

and is referred to as the **standard error of the mean,** $\sigma_{\bar{X}}$. When sampling with replacement, the standard error of the mean is equal to

$$\sigma_X = \frac{\sigma_X}{\sqrt{n}} \qquad (9.3)$$

the standard deviation of the population divided by the square root of the sample size. Therefore, as the sample size increases, the standard error of the mean will decrease by a factor equal to the square root of the sample size. This relationship between the standard error of the mean and the sample size will be further examined in Chapter 10 when we address the issue of sample size determination.

9.2.3 Sampling from Normal Populations

Now that we have introduced the idea of a sampling distribution and mentioned the standard error of the mean, we need to explore the question of what distribution the sample mean $\bar{X}$ will follow. It can be shown that if we sample *with* replacement from a population that is normally distributed with mean μ_X and standard deviation σ_X, the sampling distribution of the mean will also be normally distributed for *any size n* with mean $\mu_{\bar{X}} = \mu_X$ and have a standard error of the mean $\sigma_{\bar{X}} = \sigma_X/\sqrt{n}$.

In the most elementary case, if we draw samples of size $n = 1$, each possible sample mean is a single observation from the population, since

$$\bar{X} = \frac{\sum_{i=1}^{n} X_i}{n} = \frac{X_i}{1} = X_i$$

If we know that the population is normally distributed with mean μ_X and standard deviation σ_X, then of course the sampling distribution of $\bar{X}$ for samples of $n = 1$ must also follow the normal distribution with mean $\mu_{\bar{X}} = \mu_X$ and standard error of the mean $\sigma_X = \sigma_X/\sqrt{n} = \sigma_X/\sqrt{1} = \sigma_X$. In addition, we note that as the sample size increases, the sampling distribution of the mean still follows a normal distribution with mean $\mu_{\bar{X}} = \mu_X$. However, as the sample size increases, the standard error of the mean decreases, so that a larger proportion of sample means are closer to the population

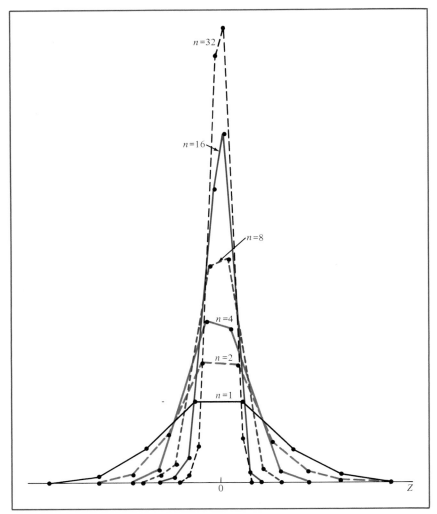

FIGURE 9.3
Sampling distributions of the mean from 500 samples of size n = 1, 2, 4, 8, 16,
and 32 selected from a normal population.

mean. This can be observed by referring to Figure 9.3. In this figure, 500 samples of size 1, 2, 4, 8, 16, and 32 were randomly selected from a normally distributed population. We can see clearly from the polygons in Figure 9.3 that while the sampling distribution of the mean is approximately[1] normal for each sample size, the sample means are distributed more tightly around the population mean as the sample size is increased.

We may obtain a deeper insight into the concept of the sampling distribution of the mean if we examine the following: Suppose that the packaging equipment in a manufacturing process that is filling 368-gram (thirteen-ounce) packages of cereal is set so that the amount of cereal in the box is normally distributed with a mean of 368

[1] We must remember that "only" 500 samples out of an infinite number of samples have been selected, so that the sampling distributions shown are only approximations of the true distributions.

grams. From past experience, the standard deviation of the population is known to be 15 grams.

If a sample of 25 boxes is randomly selected from the many thousands that are filled in a day, and the average weight is computed for this sample, what type of result could be expected?

For example, do you think that the sample mean would be 368 grams? 200 grams? 365 grams? The sample acts as a "miniature representation" of the population, so that if the values in the population were normally distributed, the values in the sample should be approximately normally distributed. Moreover, if the population mean is 368 grams, the sample mean has a good chance of being "close to" 368 grams.

To explore this problem even further, how can we determine the probability that the sample of 25 boxes will have a mean between 365 and 368 grams? We know from our study of the normal distribution (Section 8.2) that the area between any value X and the population mean μ_X can be found by converting to standardized Z units:

$$Z = \frac{X - \mu_X}{\sigma_X} \qquad (9.4)$$

and finding the appropriate value in the table of the normal distribution (Table E.2). In the examples in Section 8.2, we were studying how any single value X deviates from the mean. Now in the cereal-fill example, the value involved is a sample mean $\overline{X}$, and we wish to determine the likelihood of obtaining a sample mean between 365 and the population mean of 368. Thus, by substituting $\overline{X}$ for X, $\mu_{\overline{X}}$ for μ_X and $\sigma_{\overline{X}}$ for σ_X, we have

$$Z = \frac{\overline{X} - \mu_{\overline{X}}}{\sigma_{\overline{X}}} = \frac{\overline{X} - \mu_X}{\dfrac{\sigma_X}{\sqrt{n}}} \qquad (9.5)$$

Note that, based on the property of unbiasedness, it is always true that $\mu_{\overline{X}} = \mu_X$.

To find the area between 365 and 368 grams (Figure 9.4) we have

$$Z = \frac{\overline{X} - \mu_X}{\dfrac{\sigma_X}{\sqrt{n}}} = \frac{365 - 368}{\dfrac{15}{\sqrt{25}}} = \frac{-3}{3} = -1.00$$

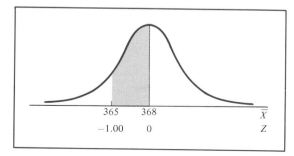

FIGURE 9.4
Diagram of normal curve needed to find area between 365 and 368 grams.

Looking up 1.00 in Table E.2, we find an area of .3413. Therefore, 34.13% of all the possible samples of size 25 would have a sample mean between 365 and 368 grams.

We must realize that this is not the same as saying that a certain percentage of *individual* boxes will have between 365 and 368 grams. In fact, that percentage can be computed from Equation (9.4) as follows:

$$Z = \frac{X - \mu_X}{\sigma_X} = \frac{365 - 368}{15} = \frac{-3}{15} = -0.20$$

The area corresponding to $Z = -.20$ in Table E.2 is .0793. Therefore, 7.93% of the *individual* boxes are expected to contain between 365 and 368 grams. Comparing these results, we may observe that many more *sample means* than *individual boxes* will be between 365 and 368 grams. This result can be explained by the fact that each sample consists of 25 different values, some small and some large. The averaging process dilutes the importance of any individual value, particularly when the sample size is large. Thus, the chance that the mean of a sample of 25 will be "close to" the population mean is greater than the chance that a *single individual* value will be.

How would these results be affected by using a different sample size, such as 100 boxes instead of 25? Here we would have the following:

$$Z = \frac{\overline{X} - \mu_X}{\dfrac{\sigma_X}{\sqrt{n}}} = \frac{365 - 368}{\sqrt{100}} = \frac{-3}{1.5} = -2.00$$

From Table E.2, the area under the normal curve from the mean to $Z = -2.00$ is .4772. Therefore 47.72% of the samples of size 100 would be expected to have means between 365 and 368 grams, as compared with only 34.13% for samples of size 25.

Instead of determining the proportion of sample means that are expected to fall within a certain interval, we might be more interested in finding out the interval within which a fixed proportion of the samples (means) would fall. For example, suppose we wanted to find an interval around the population mean that will include 95% of the sample means based on samples of 25 boxes. The 95% could be divided into two equal parts, half below the mean and half above the mean (see Figure 9.5). Analogous to Section 8.3 we are determining a distance below and above the population mean containing a specific area of the normal curve. From Equation (9.5) we have

$$Z_L = \frac{\overline{X}_L - \mu_X}{\dfrac{\sigma_X}{\sqrt{n}}}$$

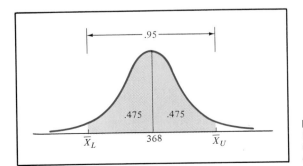

FIGURE 9.5
Diagram of normal curve needed to find upper and lower limits to include 95% of sample means.

where $Z_L = -Z$ and

$$Z_U = \frac{\overline{X}_U - \mu_X}{\frac{\sigma_X}{\sqrt{n}}}$$

where $Z_U = +Z$. Therefore, the lower value of $\overline{X}$ is

$$\overline{X}_L = \mu_X - Z\frac{\sigma_X}{\sqrt{n}} \tag{9.6a}$$

while the upper value of $\overline{X}$ is

$$\overline{X}_U = \mu_X + Z\frac{\sigma_X}{\sqrt{n}} \tag{9.6b}$$

Since $\sigma_X = 15$ and $n = 25$ and the value of Z corresponding to an area of .475 from the center of the normal curve is 1.96, the lower and upper values of $\overline{X}$ can be found as follows:

$$\overline{X}_L = 368 - (1.96)\frac{15}{\sqrt{25}} = 368 - 5.88 = 362.12$$

$$\overline{X}_U = 368 + (1.96)\frac{15}{\sqrt{25}} = 368 + 5.88 = 373.88$$

Our conclusion would be that 95% of all sample means based on samples of 25 boxes should fall between 362.12 and 373.88 grams.

9.2.4 Sampling from Nonnormal Populations

In the preceding section we explored the sampling distribution of the mean for the case in which the population itself was normally distributed. However, we should realize that in many instances either we will know that the population is not normally distributed or we may believe that it is unrealistic to assume a normal distribution. Thus, we need to examine the sampling distribution of the mean for populations that are not normally distributed. This issue brings us to an important theorem in statistics, the **central limit theorem.**

> **Central Limit Theorem:** As the sample size (number of observations in each sample) gets "large enough," the sampling distribution of the mean can be approximated by the normal distribution. This is true regardless of the shape of the distribution of the individual values in the population.

What sample size is "large enough"? A great deal of statistical research has gone into this issue. As a general rule, statisticians have found that for most population distributions, once the sample size is at least 30, the sampling distribution of the mean will be approximately normal. However, we may be able to apply the central limit theorem for even smaller sample sizes if some knowledge of the population is available (for example, if the distribution is symmetric).

The application of the central limit theorem to different populations can be illustrated by referring to Figures 9.6 to 9.8. Each of the depicted sampling distributions has been obtained by using the computer to select 500 different samples from their respective population distributions. These samples were selected for varying sizes $n = 2, 4, 8, 16, 32$) from three different continuous distributions (normal, uniform, and exponential). See pages 297, 298, 299.

The first figure, Figure 9.6, illustrates the sampling distribution of the mean selected from a normal population. In the previous section we stated that if the population is normally distributed, the sampling distribution of the mean will be normally distributed regardless of the sample size. An examination of the sampling distributions shown in Figure 9.6 gives empirical evidence to this statement. For each sample size studied, the sampling distribution of the mean is approximately normally distributed (see footnote 1 on page 292).

The second figure, Figure 9.7, presents the sampling distribution of the mean based upon a population that follows a continuous uniform (rectangular) distribution. As depicted in part (a), for samples of size $n = 1$, each value in the population is equally likely. However, when samples of only two are selected, there is a "peaking" or "central limiting" effect already working. Thus in this case we can observe somewhat more values "close to" the mean of the population than far out at the extremes. Moreover, as the sample size increases, the sampling distribution of the mean rapidly approaches a normal distribution. Once there are samples of at least eight observations, the sample mean approximately follows a normal distribution.

Finally, the third figure, Figure 9.8, exemplifies the sampling distribution of the mean obtained from a highly right-skewed population, called the exponential distribution (Reference 2). From Figure 9.8 we note that as the sample size increases, the sampling distribution becomes less skewed. When samples of size 16 are taken, the distribution of the mean is slightly skewed, while for samples of size 32 the sampling distribution of the mean appears to be normally distributed.

We may now use the results obtained from our well-known statistical distributions (normal, uniform, exponential) to summarize our conclusions as follows:

1. For most population distributions, regardless of shape, the sampling distribution of the mean will be approximately normally distributed if samples of at least 30 observations are selected.
2. If the population distribution is fairly symmetric, the sampling distribution of the mean will be approximately normal if samples of at least 15 observations are selected.
3. If the population is normally distributed, the sampling distribution of the mean will be normally distributed regardless of the sample size.

The central limit theorem, then, is of crucial importance in using statistical inference to draw conclusions about a population. It allows the researcher to make inferences about the population mean without having to know the specific shape of the population distribution.

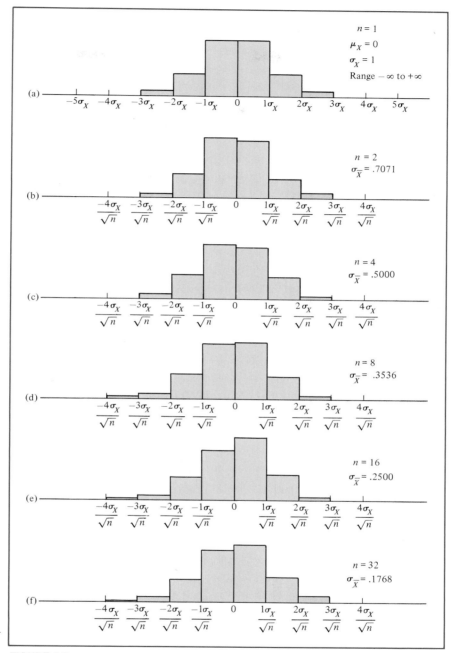

FIGURE 9.6
Normal distribution and the sampling distribution of the mean from 500 samples of size $n = 2, 4, 8, 16, 32$.

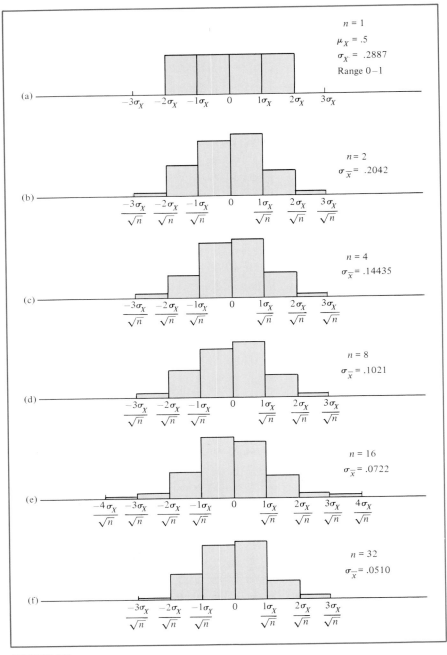

FIGURE 9.7
Continuous uniform (rectangular) distribution and the sampling distribution of the
mean from 500 samples of size $n = 2, 4, 8, 16, 32$.

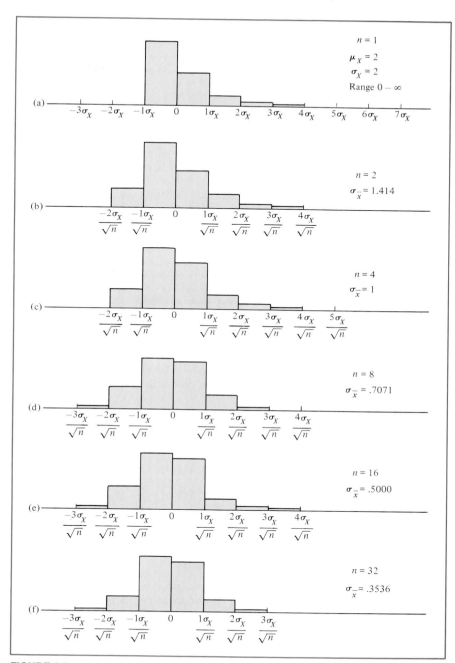

FIGURE 9.8
Exponential distribution and the sampling distribution of the mean from 500
samples of size n = 2, 4, 8, 16, 32.

Problems

9.1 Explain why a statistician would be interested in drawing conclusions about a population rather than merely describing the results of a sample.

9.2 Distinguish between a probability distribution and a sampling distribution.

9.3 For each of the following three populations indicate what the sampling distribution for samples of 25 would consist of
  (a) Travel expense vouchers for a university for an academic year.
  (b) Absentee records (days absent/year) in 1988 for employees of a large manufacturing company.
  (c) Yearly sales (in gallons) of unleaded gasoline at Exxon service stations.

9.4 The following data represent the number of days absent per year in a population of six employees of a small company:

$$1, 3, 6, 7, 7, 12$$

  (a) Assuming that you sample *without* replacement
    (1) select all possible samples of size 2 and set up the sampling distribution of the mean.
    (2) compute the mean of all the sample means and also compute the population mean. Are they equal? What property is this called?
    (3) do parts (1) and (2) for all possible samples of size 3.
    (4) compare the shape of the sampling distribution of the mean obtained in parts (1) and (3). Which sampling distribution seems to have the least variability? Why?
  (b) Assuming that you sample *with* replacement, do parts (1)–(4) of part (a) and compare the results. Which sampling distributions seem to have the least variability, those in part (a) or part (b)? Why?

9.5 Referring to the data of Problem 3.56 on page 70 (the PE ratios for all 33 companies in the food processing industry), and assuming that you sample without replacement
  (a) Select all possible samples of size 2 and set up the sampling distribution of the mean.
  (b) Compute the mean of all the sample means and also compute the population mean. Are they equal? What is this property called?

• **9.6** Paper bags used for packaging groceries are manufactured so that the breaking strength of the bag is normally distributed with a mean of 5 pounds per square inch and a standard deviation of 1 pound per square inch.
  (a) What proportion of the bags produced have a breaking strength between 5 and 5.5 pounds per square inch?
  (b) What proportion of the bags produced have a breaking strength between 4 and 4.1 pounds per square inch?
  (c) If many random samples of 16 bags are selected
    (1) what would the mean and the standard error of the mean be expected to equal?
    (2) what distribution would the sample means follow?
    (3) what proportion of the sample means would be between 5 and 5.5 pounds per square inch?
    (4) what proportion of the sample means would be between 4 and 4.1 pounds per square inch?
  (d) Compare the answers of (a) to (c)(3), and (b) to (c)(4). Discuss.
  (e) Which is more likely to occur—an individual value above 5.5 pounds per square inch, a sample mean above 5.25 pounds per square inch in a sample of size 4, or a sample mean above 5.1 pounds per square inch in a sample of size 25? Explain.

9.7 Long-distance telephone calls are normally distributed with $\mu_X = 8$ minutes and $\sigma_X = 2$ minutes. If random samples of 25 calls were selected

(a) Compute $\sigma_{\bar{X}}$

(b) What proportion of the sample means would be between 7.8 and 8.2 minutes?

(c) What proportion of the sample means would be between 7.5 and 8 minutes?

(d) If random samples of 100 calls were selected

    (1) what proportion of the sample means would be between 7.8 and 8.2 minutes?

    (2) explain the difference in the results of (b) and (d)(1).

✎ (e) Which is more likely to occur—an individual value above 11 minutes, a sample mean above 9 minutes in a sample of 25 calls, or a sample mean above 8.6 minutes in a sample of 100 calls? Explain.

● **9.8** The amount of time a bank teller spends with each customer has a population mean $\mu_X = 3.10$ minutes and standard deviation $\sigma_X = .40$ minutes. If a random sample of 16 customers is selected

(a) What is the probability that the average time spent per customer will be at least 3 minutes?

(b) There is an 85% chance that the sample mean will be below how many minutes?

(c) What assumption must be made in order to solve (a) and (b)?

(d) If a random sample of 64 customers is selected

    (1) there is an 85% chance that the sample mean will be below how many minutes?

    (2) what assumption must be made in order to solve (d)(1)?

✎ (e) Which is more likely to occur—an individual time below 2 minutes, a sample mean above 3.4 minutes in a sample of 16 customers, or a sample mean below 2.9 minutes in a sample of 64 customers? Explain.

✎ **9.9** A large chain of home improvement centers stocks a nationally known brand of portable electric drills. In order to achieve maximum volume discount, the drill will be reordered for all stores at the same time. The inventory reorder decision is to reorder when the average inventory at a sample of stores is below 25 drills. Based on past data, the standard deviation is assumed to be 10 drills. If a random sample of 25 stores is selected, what is the probability that the drill will be reordered

(a) When the true average inventory of all stores is 20 drills?

(b) When the true average inventory of all stores is 30 drills?

(c) What assumption must be made in (a) and (b)?

(d) What would be your answer to (a) and (b) if the sample size was increased to 36?

9.3 SAMPLING DISTRIBUTION OF THE PROPORTION

In our discussion of sampling distributions thus far we have focused on the distribution of the mean of quantitative variables. On the other hand, when examining qualitative variables, the characteristic that is usually considered is the proportion of successes. As examples, in our survey the statistician might be interested in estimating the proportion of houses that have a modern kitchen. A political pollster might be interested in estimating the true proportion of votes that will be obtained by a particular candidate. Finally, the quality control manager might like to determine the true rate of occurrence of a particular type of defect.

In several previous chapters we have briefly discussed qualitative variables. In Equation (6.1) on page 177 we defined the (population) proportion of successes p as

$$p = \frac{\text{number of successful outcomes}}{\text{total number of outcomes}}$$

while in Chapter 7 we saw that the number of successes in a sample of size n followed a binomial distribution expressed as follows:

$$P(X = x \text{ successes}) = \frac{n!}{x!(n-x)!} p^x (1-p)^{n-x}$$

where the average number of successes μ_X was equal to np and the standard deviation of the number of successes σ_X was equal to $\sqrt{np(1-p)}$.

Now, instead of expressing the variable in terms of number of successes X, we can readily convert the variable to proportion of successes by dividing by n, the sample size. Thus we have

$$p_S = \frac{X}{n} = \frac{\text{number of successes}}{\text{sample size}} \qquad \text{(9.7)}$$

The average (or expected proportion of successes μ_{p_S}) is equal to p, while the standard deviation of the proportion of successes σ_{p_S} is equal to $\sqrt{p(1-p)/n}$. In Section 8.4 we said that when the sample size was large, the binomial distribution could be approximated by the normal distribution. The general rule of thumb was that if np and $n(1-p)$ each were at least 5, the normal distribution provided a good approximation to the binomial distribution. In most cases in which inferences are being made about the proportion, the sample size is substantial enough to meet the conditions for using the normal approximation (see Reference 1). Thus, in many instances, we may use the normal distribution to evaluate the sampling distribution of the proportion. Let us refer to the following example.

The manager of the local branch of a savings bank has determined that 40% of all depositors have multiple accounts at the bank. If a random sample of 200 depositors is selected, what is the probability that the sample proportion of depositors with multiple accounts will be between .40 and .43?

Since the sampling distribution of the proportion can be assumed to be normally distributed,[2] we have

$$Z = \frac{\overline{X} - \mu_{\overline{X}}}{\sigma_{\overline{X}}}$$

and because we are dealing with sample proportions (not sample means)

$$p_S = \text{sample proportion}$$

$$p = \text{population proportion}$$

$$\sigma_{p_S} = \sqrt{\frac{p(1-p)}{n}}$$

and, substituting p_S for $\overline{X}$, $\mu_{p_S} = p$ for $\mu_{\overline{X}}$, and $\sigma_{p_S} = \sqrt{p(1-p)/n}$ for $\sigma_{\overline{X}}$, we have

$$Z \cong \frac{p_S - p}{\sqrt{\dfrac{p(1-p)}{n}}} \qquad \text{(9.8)}$$

---

[2] When working with the sampling distribution of the proportion for very large samples, the continuity correction factor (see Section 8.4) is usually omitted, since it will have minimal effect on the results.

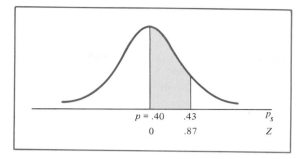

FIGURE 9.9
Diagram of normal curve needed to find the area between the proportions .40 and .43.

Substituting,

$$Z \cong \frac{p_s - p}{\sqrt{\dfrac{p(1-p)}{n}}}$$

$$= \frac{.43 - .40}{\sqrt{\dfrac{.40(.60)}{200}}} = \frac{.03}{\sqrt{\dfrac{.24}{200}}}$$

$$= \frac{.03}{.0346} = 0.87$$

Using Table E.2, the area under the normal curve from $Z = 0$ to $Z = .87$ is .3078. Therefore the probability of obtaining a sample proportion between .40 and .43 is .3078. This means that if the true proportion of successes in the population were .40, then 30.78% of the samples of size 200 would be expected to have sample proportions between .40 and .43. (See Figure 9.9.)

As with quantitative data, knowledge of the sampling distribution will allow inferences to be made about a population proportion based only upon the proportion of successes in a single sample. These concepts of inference will be developed further in the next two chapters.

Problems

- **9.10** Historically, 10% of a large shipment of machine parts are defective. If random samples of 400 parts are selected, what proportion of the samples will have
  - **(a)** Between 9% and 10% defective parts?
  - **(b)** Less than 8% defective parts?
  - **(c)** If a sample size of only 100 was selected, what would your answers have been in (a) and (b)?
  - ✓**(d)** Which is more likely to occur—a percent defective above 13% in a sample of 100 or a percent defective above 10.5% in a sample of 400? Explain.

  9.11 A political pollster is conducting an analysis of sample results in order to make predictions on election night. Assuming a two-candidate election, if a specific candidate receives at least 55% of the vote in the sample, then that candidate will be forecast as the winner of the election. If

a random sample of 100 voters is selected, what is the probability that a candidate will be forecasted as the winner when
   (a) The true percentage of his vote is 50.1%?
   (b) The true percentage of his vote is 60%?
   (c) The true percentage of his vote is 49%?
   (d) If the sample size was increased to 400, what would be your answer to (a), (b), and (c)? Discuss.

9.12 Based on past data, 30% of the credit card purchases at a large department store are for amounts above $100. If random samples of 100 credit card purchases are selected
   (a) What proportion of samples are likely to have between 20% and 30% of the purchases over $100?
   (b) Within what symmetrical limits of the population percentage will 95% of the sample percentages fall?

9.13 Suppose that a marketing experiment is to be conducted in which students are to taste two different brands of soft drink. Their task is to correctly identify the brand tasted. If random samples of 200 students are selected and it is assumed that the students have no ability to distinguish between the two brands
   (a) What proportion of the samples will have between 50% and 60% of the identifications correct?
   (b) Within what symmetrical limits of the population percentage will 90% of the sample percentages fall?
   (c) What is the probability of obtaining a sample percentage of correct identifications in excess of 65%?
   ✔(d) Which is more likely to occur—more than 60% correct identifications in a sample of 200 or more than 55% correct identifications in a sample of 1,000? Explain.
   [*Hint*: If an individual has no ability to distinguish between the two soft drinks, then each one is equally likely to be selected.]

9.14 Historically, 93% of the deliveries of an overnight mail service arrive before 10:30 on the following morning. If random samples of 500 deliveries are selected, what proportion of the samples will have
   (a) Between 93% and 95% of the deliveries arriving before 10:30 on the following morning?
   (b) More than 95% of the deliveries arriving before 10:30 on the following morning?
   (c) If a sample size of 1,000 were selected, what would your answers be in (a) and (b)?
   ✔(d) Which is more likely to occur—more than 95% of the deliveries in a sample of 500 arriving before 10:30 on the following morning or less than 90% in a sample of 1,000 arriving before 10:30 on the following morning? Explain.

9.4   SAMPLING FROM FINITE POPULATIONS

The central limit theorem and the standard errors of the mean and the proportion were based upon the premise that the samples selected were chosen *with* replacement. However, in virtually all survey research, sampling is conducted *without* replacement from populations that are of a finite size N. In these cases, particularly when the sample size n is not small as compared with the population size N ($n/N > .05$; i.e., more than 5% of the population is sampled), a **finite population correction factor** **(fpc)** should be used in defining the standard error of the mean and the standard error of the proportion. The finite population correction factor may be expressed as[3]

---

[3] The finite population correction factor essentially expresses the proportion of observations that have not been included in the sample $\left(1 - \dfrac{n}{N} = \dfrac{N-n}{N}\right)$. This result is approximately equal to $\dfrac{N-n}{N-1}$ when N is large.

$$\text{fpc} = \sqrt{\frac{N - n}{N - 1}} \qquad\qquad \textbf{(9.9)}$$

where n = sample size
 N = population size

Therefore, when dealing with means, we have

$$\sigma_{\bar{X}} = \frac{\sigma_X}{\sqrt{n}} \sqrt{\frac{N - n}{N - 1}} \qquad\qquad \textbf{(9.10)}$$

and when we are referring to proportions, we have

$$\sigma_{p_S} = \sqrt{\frac{p(1 - p)}{n}} \cdot \sqrt{\frac{N - n}{N - 1}} \qquad\qquad \textbf{(9.11)}$$

Examining the formula for the finite population correction factor, we see that the numerator will always be smaller than the denominator, so the correction factor will be less than 1. Since this is multiplied by the standard error, the standard error becomes smaller when corrected. That is, we get more accurate estimates because we are sampling a large segment of the population.

We may illustrate the application of the finite population correction factor by referring back to the two problems discussed in this chapter. In Section 9.2.3, a sample of 25 cereal boxes was selected from a filling process. Suppose that a population of 2,000 boxes were filled on this particular day. Using the finite population correction factor we would have

$$\sigma_X = 15, n = 25, N = 2,000$$

$$\sigma_{\bar{X}} = \frac{\sigma_X}{\sqrt{n}} \sqrt{\frac{N - n}{N - 1}}$$

$$= \frac{15}{\sqrt{25}} \sqrt{\frac{2,000 - 25}{2,000 - 1}}$$

$$= (3)\sqrt{(.988)} = 2.982$$

The probability of obtaining a sample whose mean is between 365 and 368 grams is computed as follows:

$$Z = \frac{\bar{X} - \mu_{\bar{X}}}{\sigma_{\bar{X}}} = \frac{-3}{2.982} = -1.01$$

From Table E.2 the approximate area under the normal curve is .3438.

It is evident in this example that the use of the finite population correction factor had a very small effect on the standard error of the mean and the subsequent area under the normal curve, since the sample was only 1.25% of the population size.

In the example concerning the local savings bank (Section 9.3), suppose that there were a total of 1,000 different depositors at the bank. The previous sample of size 200 out of this finite population results in the following:

$$\sigma_{p_S} = \sqrt{\frac{p(1-p)}{n}} \cdot \sqrt{\frac{N-n}{N-1}}$$

$$= \sqrt{\frac{.4(.6)}{200}} \cdot \sqrt{\frac{1,000-200}{1,000-1}}$$

$$= \sqrt{\frac{.24}{200}} \cdot \sqrt{\frac{800}{999}} = \sqrt{\frac{.24}{200}} \cdot \sqrt{.801}$$

$$= .0346(.895) = .031$$

Thus $Z = .03/.031 = 0.97$, and, from Table E.2, the appropriate area under the normal curve is .3340. In this example, the use of the finite population correction factor had a moderate effect on the standard error of the proportion and on the area under the normal curve, since the sample size is 20% (that is, $n/N = .20$) of the population.

Problems

- **9.15** Referring to Problem 9.6 on page 300, if the population consisted of 200 paper bags, what would be your answer to part (c) of that problem?
- **9.16** Referring to Problem 9.8 on page 301, if there were a population of 500 customers, what would be your answers to (a) and (b) of that problem?
- **9.17** Referring to Problem 9.9 on page 301, if the chain had a total of 250 stores, what would be your answers to (a) and (b) of that problem?
- **9.18** Referring to Problem 9.10 on page 303, if the shipment included 5,000 machine parts, what would be your answers to (a) and (b) of that problem?
- **9.19** Referring to Problem 9.14 on page 304, if the population consisted of 10,000 deliveries, what would be your answers to (a) and (b) of that problem?

9.5 SUMMARY AND OVERVIEW

In this chapter we have examined the distribution of the sample mean and the sample proportion. The importance of the normal distribution in statistics has been further emphasized by examining the central limit theorem. We have seen that knowledge of a population distribution is not always necessary in drawing conclusions from a sampling distribution of the mean or proportion. These concepts are central to the development of statistical inference. The main objective of statistical inference is to take information based only upon a sample and use this information to draw conclusions and make decisions about various population values. The statistical techniques developed to achieve these objectives are discussed in the next four chapters (confidence intervals and tests of hypotheses).

Supplementary Problems

• **9.20** A soft-drink machine is regulated so that the amount dispensed is normally distributed with $\mu_X = 7$ ounces and $\sigma_X = .5$ ounce. If samples of nine cups are taken, what value will be exceeded by 95% of the sample means?

9.21 The number of hours of life of a type of transistor battery is normally distributed with $\mu_X = 100$ hours and $\sigma_X = 20$ hours.
(a) What proportion of the batteries will last between 100 and 115 hours?
(b) If random samples of 16 batteries are selected, what proportion of the sample means will be
    (1) between 100 and 115 hours?
    (2) more than 90 hours?
    (3) Within what limits around the population mean will 90% of sample means fall?
(c) Is the central limit theorem necessary to answer (1), (2), and (3)? Explain.

9.22 The number of customers per week at each store of a supermarket chain has a population mean of $\mu_X = 5,000$ and standard deviation $\sigma_X = 500$. If a random sample of 25 stores is selected
(a) What is the probability that the sample mean will be below 5,075 customers per week?
(b) Within what limits around the population mean can we be 95% certain that the sample mean will fall?

9.23 **(Class Project)** The table of random numbers is an example of a uniform distribution since each digit is equally likely to occur. Starting in the row corresponding to the day of the month in which you were born, use the table of random numbers (Table E.1) to take *one digit* at a time. Select samples of size $n = 2$, $n = 5$, $n = 10$. Compute the sample mean $\overline{X}$ of each sample. For each sample size, each student should select five different samples so that a frequency distribution of the sample means can be developed for the results of the entire class. What can be said about the shape of the sampling distribution for each of these sample sizes?

9.24 **(Class Project)** A coin having one side "heads" and the other side "tails" is to be flipped ten times and the number of heads obtained is to be recorded. If each student performs this experiment five times, a frequency distribution of the number of "heads" can be developed from the results of the entire class. Does this distribution seem to approximate the normal distribution?

9.25 **(Class Project)** The number of cars waiting in line at a car wash is distributed as follows:

Length of Waiting Line (number of cars)	Probability
0	.25
1	.40
2	.20
3	.10
4	.04
5	.01

The table of random numbers can be used to select samples from this distribution by assigning numbers as described at the top of page 308:

1. Start in the row corresponding to the day of the month in which you were born.

2. *Two-digit* random numbers are to be selected.

3. If a random number between 00 and 24 is selected, record a length of 0; if between 25 and 64, record a length of 1; if between 65 and 84, record a length of 2; if between 85 and 94, record a length of 3; if between 95 and 98, record a length of 4; if it is 99, record a length of 5.

Select samples of size $n = 2$, $n = 10$, $n = 25$. Compute the sample mean for each sample. For example, if a sample size 2 results in random numbers 18 and 46, these would correspond to lengths of 0 and 1, respectively, producing a sample mean of 0.5. If each student selects five different samples for each sample size, a frequency distribution of the sample means (for each sample size) can be developed from the results of the entire class. What conclusions can you draw about the sampling distribution of the mean as the sample size is increased?

9.26 **(Class Project)** The table of random numbers can be used to simulate the operation of an urn of different colored balls as follows:

1. Start in the row corresponding to the day of the month in which you were born.

2. *One-digit* numbers are to be selected.

3. If a random digit between 0 and 6 is selected, consider the ball to be white; if a random digit is a 7, 8, or 9, consider the ball to be red.

Select samples of 10, 25, and 50 digits. In each sample, count the number of white balls and compute the proportion of white balls in the sample. If each student in the class selects five different samples for each sample size, a frequency distribution of the proportion of white balls (for each sample size) can be developed from the results of the entire class. What conclusions can be drawn about the sampling distribution of the proportion as the sample size is increased?

References

1. COCHRAN, W. G., *Sampling Techniques*, 3d ed. (New York: Wiley, 1977).
2. LARSEN, R. L., AND M. L. MARX, *An Introduction to Mathematical Statistics and Its Applications*, 2d ed. (Englewood Cliffs, N.J.: Prentice-Hall, 1986).

10

Estimation

10.1 POINT AND CONFIDENCE INTERVAL ESTIMATES

Statistical inference is the process of using sample results to draw conclusions about the characteristics of a population. In this chapter we shall examine statistical procedures that will enable us to *estimate* the true population mean and the true population proportion.

There are two major types of estimates: **point estimates** and **interval estimates.** A point estimate consists of a single sample statistic that is used to estimate the true population parameter. For example, the sample mean $\overline{X}$ is a point estimate of the population mean μ_X, while the sample variance S^2 is a point estimate of the population variance σ_X^2. Recall from Section 9.2.1 that the sample mean $\overline{X}$ possessed the highly desirable properties of unbiasedness and efficiency. Although in practice only one sample is selected, we know that the average value of all possible sample means is the true population parameter[1] (μ_X). Since we realize that the sample statistic ($\overline{X}$) varies from sample to sample (i.e., it depends on the elements selected in the sample), we need to provide for a more informative estimate of the true population characteristic. To accomplish this we shall develop an interval estimate of the true population mean by taking into account the sampling distribution of the mean. The interval that we construct will have a specified *confidence* or probability of correctly estimating the true value of the population parameter. Similar interval estimates will also be developed for the true population proportion p.

---

[1] It is for this reason that the denominator of the sample variance is $n - 1$ instead of n, so that S^2 will be an unbiased estimator of σ_X^2; that is, if

$$S^2 = \frac{\sum_{i=1}^{n} (X_i - \overline{X})^2}{n - 1} \text{ and } \sigma_X^2 = \frac{\sum_{i=1}^{N} (X_i - \mu_X)^2}{N}$$

then $E(S^2) = \sigma_X^2$, and therefore S^2 is an unbiased estimator of σ_X^2.

10.2   CONFIDENCE INTERVAL ESTIMATION OF THE MEAN (σ_X KNOWN)

In Section 9.2 we observed that from either the central limit theorem or knowledge of the population distribution we could determine the percentage of sample means that fell within certain distances of the population mean. For instance, in Section 9.2.3, in the example involving the filling of cereal boxes (in which $\mu_X = 368$, $\sigma_X = 15$, and $n = 25$) we observed that 95% of all sample means would fall between 362.12 and 373.88 grams.

The type of reasoning in this statement (*deductive reasoning*) is exactly opposite to the type of reasoning that is needed here (*inductive reasoning*). In statistical inference we must take the results of a single sample and draw conclusions about the population, not vice versa. In practice, the population mean is the unknown quantity that is to be estimated. Suppose, for example, in the cereal-filling process, that the true population mean μ_X was unknown but the true population standard deviation σ_X was known to be 15 grams. Thus, rather than taking $\mu_X \pm (1.96) \sigma_X/\sqrt{n}$ to find the upper and lower limits around μ_X as in Section 9.2, let us determine the consequences of substituting the sample mean $\overline{X}$ for the unknown μ_X and using $\overline{X} \pm (1.96) \sigma_X/\sqrt{n}$ as an interval within which we estimate the unknown μ_X. Although in practice a single sample mean $\overline{X}$ is observed, we need to develop a *hypothetical* set of examples in order to understand the full meaning of the interval estimate that shall be obtained.

In the first case, suppose that the sample mean was 362.3 grams. The interval developed to estimate μ_X would be $362.3 \pm (1.96)(15)/\sqrt{25}$ or 362.3 ± 5.88. That is, the estimate of μ_X would be

$$356.42 \leq \mu_X \leq 368.18$$

Since the population mean μ_X (equal to 368) is included *within* the interval, we observe that this sample has led to a correct statement about μ_X (see Figure 10.1).

To continue our hypothetical example, suppose that for a different sample the mean was 369.5. The interval developed from this sample would be $369.5 \pm (1.96)(15)/\sqrt{25}$ or 369.5 ± 5.88. That is, the estimate of μ_X would be

$$363.62 \leq \mu_X \leq 375.38$$

Since the true population mean μ_X (equal to 368) is also included within this interval, we conclude that this statement about μ_X is correct.

Now, before we begin to think that we will *always* make correct statements about μ_X from the sample $\overline{X}$, let us estimate a third hypothetical sample, in which the sample mean is equal to 360 grams. The interval developed here would be $360 \pm (1.96)(15)/\sqrt{25}$ or 360 ± 5.88. In this case, the estimate of μ_X is

$$354.12 \leq \mu_X \leq 365.88$$

Observe that this estimate is *not* a correct statement, since the population mean μ_X is not included in the interval developed from this sample. Thus we are faced with a dilemma. For some samples the interval estimate of μ_X will be correct, while for others it will be incorrect. In addition, we must also realize that in practice we select only *one* sample, and since we do not know the true population mean, we cannot determine whether our particular statement is correct. What we can do in order to resolve this dilemma is to determine the proportion of samples producing intervals that result in correct statements about the population mean μ_X. In order to do this we need to examine

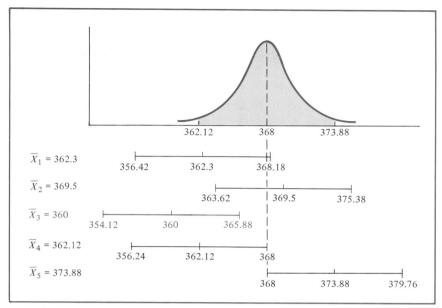

FIGURE 10.1
Confidence interval estimates for five different samples of size $n = 25$ taken
from a population where $\mu_X = 368$ and $\sigma_X = 15$.

two other hypothetical samples: the case in which $\overline{X} = 362.12$, and the case in which
$\overline{X} = 373.88$. If $\overline{X} = 362.12$, the interval will be $362.12 \pm (1.96)(15)/\sqrt{25}$ or 362.12
± 5.88. That is

$$356.24 \leq \mu_X \leq 368.00$$

Since the population mean of 368 is at the upper limit of the interval, the statement
is a correct one.

Finally, if $\overline{X} = 373.88$, the interval will be $373.88 \pm (1.96)(15)/\sqrt{25}$ or 373.88
± 5.88. That is,

$$368.00 \leq \mu_X \leq 379.76$$

In this case, since the population mean of 368 is included at the lower limit of the
interval, the statement is a correct one.

Thus, from these examples (see Figure 10.1) we can determine that if the sample
mean falls anywhere between 362.12 and 373.88 grams, the population mean will be
included *somewhere* within the interval. However, we know from our discussion of
the sampling distribution in Section 9.2.3 that 95% of the sample means fall between
362.12 and 373.88 grams. Therefore, 95% of all sample means will include the
population mean within the interval developed. The interval from 362.12 to 373.88 is
referred to as a 95% **confidence interval.**

> In general a 95% **confidence interval estimate** can be interpreted to mean
> that if all possible samples of the same size n were taken, 95% of them
> would include the true population mean somewhere within the interval
> around their sample means, while only 5% of them would not.

Since only one sample is selected in practice and μ_X is unknown, we never know for sure whether the specific interval obtained includes the population mean. However, we can state that we have 95% confidence that we have selected a sample whose interval does include the population mean.

In our examples we had 95% confidence of including the population mean within the interval. In some situations we might desire a higher degree of assurance (such as 99%) of including the population mean within the interval. In other cases we might be willing to accept less assurance (such as 90%) of correctly estimating the population mean.

In general, the level of confidence is symbolized by $(1 - \alpha) \times 100\%$, where α is the proportion in the tails of the distribution which are outside of the confidence interval. Therefore to obtain the $(1 - \alpha) \times 100\%$ confidence interval estimate of the mean with σ_X known, we have

$$\overline{X} \pm Z \frac{\sigma_X}{\sqrt{n}}$$

or   **(10.1)**

$$\overline{X} - Z \frac{\sigma_X}{\sqrt{n}} \le \mu_X \le \overline{X} + Z \frac{\sigma_X}{\sqrt{n}}$$

where Z is the value corresponding to an area of $(1 - \alpha)/2$ from the center of a standardized normal distribution.

For example, $.025 \times 100 = 2.5\%$ of the values of the standard normal distribution are greater than 1.96, which is why 1.96 is used for constructing a $(1 - .05) \times 100 = 95\%$ confidence interval. The value of Z selected for constructing such a confidence interval is called the **critical value** from the distribution. There is a different critical value for each level of α.

A level of confidence of 95% led to a Z value of ± 1.96 (see Figure 10.2). If 99% confidence were desired, the area of .99 would be divided in half, leaving .495 between each limit and μ_X (see Figure 10.3). The Z value corresponding to an area of .495 from the center of the normal curve is approximately 2.58.

Now that we have presented various levels of confidence, one might wonder why we wouldn't want to make the confidence level as close to 100% as possible. But any increase in confidence is achieved only by simultaneously widening (and making less precise and less useful) the confidence interval obtained. Thus we would have more

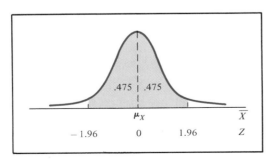

FIGURE 10.2
Normal curve for determining the Z value needed for 95% confidence.

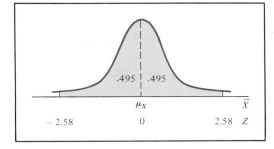

FIGURE 10.3
Normal curve for determining the Z value needed for 99% confidence.

confidence that the population mean is within a broader range of values. This tradeoff between the width of the confidence interval and the level of confidence will be discussed in greater depth when we investigate the determination of sample size (see Section 10.5).

We may illustrate the application of the confidence interval estimate by an example. A manufacturer of computer paper has a production process that operates continuously throughout an entire production shift. The paper is expected to have an average length of 11 inches and the standard deviation is known to be 0.02 inch. At periodic intervals, samples are selected to determine whether the average paper length is still equal to 11 inches or whether something has gone wrong in the production process to change the length of the paper produced. If indeed such a situation has occurred, corrective action must be contemplated. A random sample of 100 sheets has been selected and the average paper length is found to be 10.998 inches. If a 95% confidence interval estimate of the population average paper length were desired, using Equation (10.1), with $Z = 1.96$ for 95% confidence, we would have

$$10.998 \pm \frac{(1.96)(.02)}{\sqrt{100}}$$

$$10.998 \pm .00392$$

$$10.99408 \le \mu_X \le 11.00192$$

Thus we would estimate, with 95% confidence, that the population mean is between 10.99408 and 11.00192 inches. Since 11, the value that indicates the production process is working properly, is included within the interval, there is no reason to believe that anything is wrong with the production process. There is 95% confidence that the sample selected is one where the true population mean is included somewhere within the interval developed.

If 99% confidence were desired, then using Equation (10.1), with $Z = 2.58$, we would have

$$10.998 \pm \frac{(2.58)(.02)}{\sqrt{100}}$$

$$10.998 \pm .00516$$

$$10.99284 \le \mu_X \le 11.00316$$

Once again, since 11 is included within the interval, there is no reason to believe that anything is wrong with the production process.

Problems

10.1 A market researcher states that she has 95% confidence that the true average monthly sales of a product will be between $170,000 and $200,000. Explain the meaning of this statement.

10.2 Why can't the production manager in the example on page 310 have 100% confidence? Explain.

✗ **10.3** Is it true in the example on page 313 pertaining to the production of computer paper that 95% of the sample means will fall between 10.99408 and 11.00192 inches? Explain.

✗ **10.4** Is it true in the example on page 313 pertaining to the production of computer paper that we do not know for sure whether the true population mean is between 10.99408 and 11.00192 inches? Explain.

● **10.5** Suppose that a paint supply store wanted to estimate the correct amount of paint contained in one-gallon cans purchased from a nationally known manufacturer. It is known from the manufacturer's specifications that the standard deviation of the amount of paint is equal to .02 gallon. A random sample of 50 gallons is selected, and the average amount of paint per one-gallon can is 0.995 gallon.
  (a) Set up a 99% confidence interval estimate of the true population average amount of paint included in a one-gallon can.
  ✗**(b)** Based on your results, do you think that the store owner has a right to complain to the manufacturer? Why?
  (c) Does the population of amount of paint per can have to be normally distributed here? Explain.
  ✗**(d)** Tell why an observed value of .98 gallon for an individual can would not be unusual, even though it is outside the confidence interval you calculated.

10.6 The quality control manager at a light bulb factory needs to estimate the average life of a large shipment of light bulbs. The process standard deviation is known to be 100 hours. A random sample of 50 light bulbs indicated a sample average life of 350 hours.
  (a) Set up a 95% confidence interval estimate of the true average life of light bulbs in this shipment.
  (b) Does the population of light bulb life have to be normally distributed here? Explain.
  ✗**(c)** Tell why an observed value of 320 hours would not be unusual, even though it is outside the confidence interval you calculated.

10.7 The inspection division of the Lee County Weights and Measures Department is interested in estimating the actual amount of soft drink that is placed in 2-liter bottles at the local bottling plant of a large nationally known soft-drink company. The bottling plant has informed the inspection division that the standard deviation for 2-liter bottles is .05 liter. A random sample of 100 2-liter bottles obtained from this bottling plant indicated a sample average of 1.99 liters.
  (a) Set up a 95% confidence interval estimate of the true average amount of soft drink in each bottle.
  (b) Does the population of soft-drink fill have to be normally distributed here? Explain.
  ✗**(c)** Tell why an observed value of 2.02 liters would not be unusual, even though it is outside the confidence interval you calculated.

10.3 CONFIDENCE INTERVAL ESTIMATION OF THE MEAN (σ_X UNKNOWN)

As previously stated, just as the mean of the population μ_X is usually not known, the actual standard deviation of the population σ_X is also not likely to be known. Therefore, we need to obtain a confidence interval estimate of μ_X by using only the sample statistics of $\overline{X}$ and S. To achieve this we turn to the work of William S. Gosset.

10.3.1 Student's *t* Distribution

At the turn of this century a statistician named William S. Gosset, an employee of Guinness Breweries in Ireland (see Reference 3), was interested in making inferences about the mean when σ_X was unknown. Since Guinness employees were not permitted to publish research work under their own names, Gosset adopted the pseudonym "Student." The distribution that he developed has come to be known as **Student's *t* distribution.** If the random variable X is normally distributed, then the statistic

$$\frac{\overline{X} - \mu_X}{\dfrac{S}{\sqrt{n}}}$$

has a *t* distribution with $n - 1$ *degrees of freedom*. Notice that this expression has the same form as Equation (9.5) on page 293, except that S is used to estimate σ_X, which is presumed unknown in this case.

10.3.2 Properties of the *t* Distribution

In appearance the *t* distribution is very similar to the normal distribution. Both distributions are bell-shaped and symmetric. However the Student *t* distribution has more area in the tails and less in the center than does the normal distribution (see Figure 10.4). This is because σ_X is unknown, and we are using S to estimate it. Since we are uncertain of the value of σ_X, the values of *t* which we observe will be more variable than for Z. Therefore, we must go a larger number of standard deviations from 0 to include a certain percentage of values from the *t* distribution than is the case with the standard normal.

However, as the number of degrees of freedom increases, the *t* distribution gradually approaches the normal distribution until the two are virtually identical. This happens because as the sample size gets larger, S becomes a better estimate of σ_X. With a sample size of about 120 or more, S estimates σ_X precisely enough that there is little difference between the *t* and Z distributions. For this reason, most statisticians will use Z instead of *t* when the sample size is over 120.

In practice, as long as the sample size is not too small and the population is not very skewed, the *t* distribution can be used in estimating the population mean when σ_X is unknown. The critical values of *t* for the appropriate degrees of freedom can be obtained from the tables of the *t* distribution (see Table E.3). The top of each column of the *t* table indicates the area in the right tail of the *t* distribution (since positive

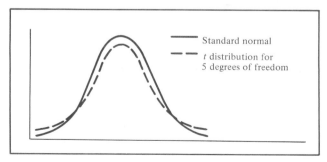

Standard normal
t distribution for 5 degrees of freedom

FIGURE 10.4
Standard normal distribution and *t* distribution for 5 degrees of freedom.

entries are supplied, the values are for the upper tail); each row represents the particular *t* value for each specific degree of freedom. For example, with 24 degrees of freedom, if 95% confidence were desired, the appropriate value of *t* would be found in the following manner (as shown in Table 10.1). The 95% confidence level indicates that there would be an area of .025 in each tail of the distribution. Looking in the column for an upper-tail area of .025 and in the row corresponding to 24 degrees of freedom results in a value of *t* of 2.0639, which for convenience is rounded to 2.064. Since *t* is a symmetrical distribution, if the upper tail value is +2.064, the value for the lower-tail area (lower .025) would be −2.064. A *t* value of 2.064 means that the probability that *t* would exceed +2.064 is .025 or 2.5% (see Figure 10.5).

TABLE 10.1 Determining the critical value from the *t* table for an area of .025 in each tail with 24 degrees of freedom

Degrees of Freedom	Upper-Tail Areas					
	.25	.10	.05	.025	.01	.005
1	1.0000	3.0777	6.3138	12.7062	31.8207	63.6574
2	0.8165	1.8856	2.9200	4.3027	6.9646	9.9248
3	0.7649	1.6377	2.3534	3.1824	4.5407	5.8409
4	0.7407	1.5332	2.1318	2.7764	3.7469	4.6041
5	0.7267	1.4759	2.0150	2.5706	3.3649	4.0322
.	.	.	.	.	.	.
.	.	.	.	.	.	.
21	0.6864	1.3232	1.7207	2.0796	2.5177	2.8314
22	0.6858	1.3212	1.7171	2.0739	2.5083	0.8188
23	0.6853	1.3195	1.7139	2.0687	2.4999	2.8073
24	0.6848	1.3178	1.7109	2.0639	2.4922	2.7969
25	0.6844	1.3163	1.7081	2.0595	2.4851	2.7874

SOURCE: Extracted from Table E.3.

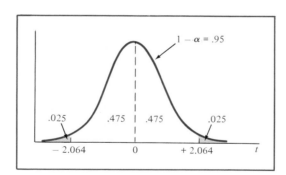

FIGURE 10.5
t distribution with 24 degrees of freedom.

10.3.2 The Concept of Degrees of Freedom

We may recall from Chapter 3 that the sample variance S^2 requires the computation of

$$\sum_{i=1}^{n} (X_i - \overline{X})^2$$

Thus, in order to compute S^2 we need to first know $\overline{X}$. Therefore we can say that only $n - 1$ of the sample values are "free" to vary. That is, there are $n - 1$ degrees of freedom.

We may illustrate this concept as follows: Suppose that we had a sample of five values which had a mean of 20. How many distinct values would we need to know before we could obtain the remainder? The fact that $n = 5$ and $\overline{X} = 20$ also tells us that $\sum_{i=1}^{n} X_i = 100$, since $\sum_{i=1}^{n} X_i/n = \overline{X}$. Thus, once we know four of the values, the fifth one will not be "free" to vary, since the sum must add to 100. For example, if four of the values are 18, 24, 19, and 16, the fifth value can only be 23, so that the sum equals 100.

10.3.4 The Confidence Interval Statement

The $(1 - \alpha) \times 100\%$ confidence interval estimate for the mean with σ_X unknown is expressed as follows:

$$\overline{X} \pm t_{n-1} \frac{S}{\sqrt{n}}$$

or **(10.2)**

$$\overline{X} - t_{n-1} \frac{S}{\sqrt{n}} \leq \mu_X \leq \overline{X} + t_{n-1} \frac{S}{\sqrt{n}}$$

where t_{n-1} is the critical value of the t distribution with $n - 1$ degrees of freedom for an area of $\alpha/2$ in the upper tail.

In order to see how confidence intervals for a mean can be constructed when the population standard deviation is unknown, let us turn to the following applications:

As a first example, suppose the marketing director for a large department store chain would like to take a sample of female credit card holders to obtain information concerning attitudinal and purchase behavior. Specifically, the marketing director would like to estimate the average amount that females in a particular community spend per month on personal clothing purchases. A random sample of 25 female credit card holders was selected and the respondents were asked to determine their clothing purchases in the previous month. The results indicated a sample average of $86.40 and a sample standard deviation of $37.50.

If the marketing director would like to have 95% confidence that the interval obtained includes the true population average amount spent on clothing, using $\overline{X} = \$86.40$, $S = \$37.50$, $n = 25$, and $t_{24} = 2.064$, we have

$$\overline{X} \pm t_{n-1} \frac{S}{\sqrt{n}} = 86.40 \pm 2.064 \frac{37.50}{\sqrt{25}}$$

$$= 86.40 \pm 15.48$$

$$\$70.92 \leq \mu_X \leq \$101.88$$

We would conclude with 95% confidence that the average amount spent per month on clothing by females is between $70.92 and $101.88. The 95% confidence interval states that we are 95% sure that the sample we have selected is one in which the true population mean is located within the interval. This 95% confidence actually means that if all possible samples of size 25 were selected (something that would never be done in practice), 95% of the intervals developed would include the true population mean *somewhere* within the interval.

As a second example, let us refer to our real estate survey. Suppose that the president would like to estimate the average appraised value (in thousands of dollars) for single-family houses in East Meadow. Using the responses to questions 1 and 9, which are contained in Figure 2.10, we can determine that from the sample of 74 houses in East Meadow, the average appraised value is 215.23 (thousands of dollars) and the standard deviation is 38.49 (thousands of dollars). If a 99% confidence interval were desired, the critical value from the t distribution (Table E.3) with $74 - 1 = 73$ degrees of freedom is 2.6449. Therefore, using Equation (10.2), we have

$$215.23 \pm (2.6449) \frac{38.49}{\sqrt{74}}$$

$$= 215.23 \pm 11.83$$

$$203.40 \le \mu_X \le 227.06$$

We would conclude with 99% confidence that the average appraised value of single-family houses in East Meadow is between 203.40 and 227.06 thousand dollars.

Problems

10.8   Determine the critical value of t in each of the following circumstances:
(a) $1 - \alpha = .95, n = 10$.
(b) $1 - \alpha = .99, n = 10$.
(c) $1 - \alpha = .95, n = 32$.
(d) $1 - \alpha = .95, n = 65$.
(e) $1 - \alpha = .90, n = 16$.

10.9   If σ_X was known and a sample size of 10 was selected, which distribution would be more appropriate, the normal or the t? Why?

• **10.10**   A new breakfast cereal is to be test-marketed for one month at stores of a large supermarket chain. The results for a sample of 16 stores indicated average sales of $1,200 with a sample standard deviation of $180. Set up a 99% confidence interval estimate of the true average sales of this new breakfast cereal.

10.11   The manager of a branch of a local savings bank wanted to estimate the average amount held in passbook savings accounts by depositors at the bank. A random sample of 30 depositors was selected and the results indicated a sample average of $4,750 and a sample standard deviation of $1,200.
(a) Set up a 95% confidence interval estimate of the population average amount held in passbook savings accounts.
(b) If an individual had $4,000 in a passbook savings account, would this be considered unusual? Explain your answer.

10.12   The personnel department of a large corporation would like to estimate the family dental expenses of its employees in order to determine the feasibility of providing a dental insurance plan. A random sample of 10 employees revealed the following family dental expenses in the previous year:

$$\$110, 362, 246, 85, 510, 208, 173, 425, 316, 179$$

(a) Set up a 90% confidence interval estimate of the average family dental expenses for all employees of this corporation.

(b) What assumption about the population distribution must be made in part (a)?

✗ (c) Give an example of a family dental expense that would be outside the confidence interval but would not be unusual for an individual family, and tell why this is not a contradiction.

➠(d) **ACTION** What should the personnel department tell the president of the corporation concerning family dental expenses?

10.13 Referring to the data of Problem 3.9 on page 43

(a) Set up a 95% confidence interval estimate of the average price of a single hotel room on a weekday in New York City.

➠(b) **ACTION** How would this information be of interest to a travel agent. A tourist? Discuss.

10.14 Referring to the data of Problem 3.7 on page 43, set up a 99% confidence interval estimate of the average amount in unpaid accounts.

10.15 Using the data on GNP projections (Problem 3.76 on page 78):

(a) Set up a 90% confidence interval estimate of the average projected change in GNP.

➠(b) **ACTION** Write a report to your economics professor discussing these results.

10.16 Referring to the data of Problem 3.68 on page 74, set up a 99% confidence interval estimate of the true population average price of sparkling spring and mineral water sold in New York City supermarkets.

● **10.17** The customer services department of a local gas utility would like to estimate the average length of time between the entry of the service request and the connection of service. A random sample of 15 houses was selected from the records available during the past year. The results in number of days were as follows:

$$114 \quad 78 \quad 96 \quad 137 \quad 78 \quad 103 \quad 117 \quad 126 \quad 86 \quad 99 \quad 114 \quad 72 \quad 104 \quad 73 \quad 86$$

(a) Set up a 95% confidence interval estimate of the population average waiting time in the past year.

(b) What assumption about the population distribution must be made in part (a) of this problem?

➠(c) **ACTION** Use the results in part (a) to provide information to your neighbor who is thinking about converting to gas heat.

✗ **10.18** Set up a 95% confidence interval estimate for each of the following batches of data:

$$\text{Batch 1: } 1, 1, 1, 1, 8, 8, 8, 8$$
$$\text{Batch 2: } 1, 2, 3, 4, 5, 6, 7, 8$$

Tell why they have different confidence intervals even though they have the same mean and range.

✗ **10.19** Compute a 95% confidence interval for the numbers 1, 2, 3, 4, 5, 6, 20. Change the number 20 to 7, and recalculate the confidence interval. Using these results, describe the effect of an outlier (or extreme value) on the confidence interval.

10.20 Referring to the data of Problem 3.73 on page 76,

(a) Set up a 95% confidence interval estimate of the population average cost per dose of pain relievers.

✗ (b) If an individual pain reliever had a cost of 7 cents per dose, would that be considered unusual? Explain.

➠(c) **ACTION** Incorporate the results in part (a) in the newspaper article you are writing dealing with consumer affairs.

10.21   Referring to the data of Problem 3.70 on page 75
  (a) Set up a 90% confidence interval estimate of the population average price of compact disk players.
  ➡**(b)** **ACTION**   How would the results of (a) help you if you were thinking of purchasing a compact disk player? Discuss.

10.22   Referring to the data of Problem 3.71 on page 75
  (a) Set up a 99% confidence interval estimate of the population average price of high fidelity video cassette recorders.
  ➡**(b)** **ACTION**   How would the results of (a) help you if you were thinking of purchasing a high fidelity video cassette recorder? Discuss.

10.23   Referring to the data of Problem 3.74 on page 77
  (a) Set up a 95% confidence interval estimate of the population average price of an IBM PC/XT compatible system.
  ✎**(b)** If an individual system had a price of $1,000, would that be considered unusual? What about a price of $500? Explain.
  ➡**(c)** **ACTION**   Use the results of part (a) as part of a report to be presented to the director of the computer center.

10.24   Referring to the data of Problem 3.75 on page 78
  (a) Set up a 90% confidence interval estimate of the population average price of the spreadsheet products.
  ✎**(b)** If an individual spreadsheet had a price of $400, would that be considered unusual? What about $1,000? Explain.
  ➡**(c)** **ACTION**   Use the results of part (a) as part of an article that you are writing for a computer magazine.

10.25   Referring to the data of Problem 3.72 on page 76
  (a) Set up a 99% confidence interval estimate of the population average price of compact microwave ovens.
  ➡**(b)** **ACTION**   Use the results of part (a) to provide information to your neighbor who is thinking about buying a compact microwave oven.

10.26   Referring to the data of Problem 3.67 on page 74
  (a) Set up a 95% confidence interval estimate of the population average selling price of auto alarm systems.
  ✎**(b)** The first 17 observations refer to professionally installed systems, while the last eight are do-it-yourself systems. Set up separate 95% confidence interval estimates for each type and comment on the difference in your results as compared to part (a).
  (c) Incorporate the results in part (a) in the newspaper article you are writing dealing with consumer affairs.

10.27   Referring to the data of Problem 3.77 on page 79
  (a) Set up a 99% confidence interval estimate of the population average cost per dose of laundry detergent.
  ➡**(b)** **ACTION**   How would the results in part (a) be useful to the manufacturer of a laundry detergent? To your family?

10.4 CONFIDENCE INTERVAL ESTIMATION FOR THE PROPORTION

In this section we extend the concept of the confidence interval to qualitative data to estimate the population proportion p from the sample proportion $p_S = X/n$. Recall from Chapters 8 and 9 that when both np and $n(1 - p)$ were at least 5, the binomial distribution could be approximated by the normal distribution. Hence, we could set up the following $(1 - \alpha) \times 100\%$ confidence interval estimate for the population proportion p:

$$p_S \pm Z \sqrt{\frac{p_S(1 - p_S)}{n}}$$

or $\qquad\qquad\qquad\qquad\qquad\qquad\qquad\qquad\qquad\qquad\qquad\qquad$ **(10.3)**

$$p_S - Z \sqrt{\frac{p_S(1 - p_S)}{n}} \leq p \leq p_S + Z \sqrt{\frac{p_S(1 - p_S)}{n}}$$

In order to see how this confidence interval estimate of the proportion can be utilized, we will examine two additional applications. First, returning to the earlier example concerning the shopping behavior of female credit card holders, suppose that the marketing director also wanted to determine the proportion of females who went shopping for clothing in the preceding week. In order to estimate this qualitative characteristic, a sample of 200 female credit card holders was selected. Of this sample of 200, 70 indicated that they had gone shopping for clothing in the preceding week. If the marketing director wanted to have 90% confidence in estimating the true population proportion, the confidence interval would be computed as follows:

$$p_S = 70/200 = .35, \text{ and with 90\% confidence } Z = 1.645$$

Using Equation (10.3), we have

$$
\begin{aligned}
p_S \pm Z \sqrt{\frac{p_S(1 - p_S)}{n}} &= .35 \pm (1.645) \sqrt{\frac{.35(.65)}{200}} \\
&= .35 \pm (1.645)(.0337) \\
&= .35 \pm .0554 \\
&\quad .2946 \leq p \leq .4054
\end{aligned}
$$

Therefore the marketing director would estimate with 90% confidence that between 29.46% and 40.54% of the female credit card holders went shopping for clothing in the preceding week.

In the second example, referring to our real estate survey, the president would like to estimate the proportion of houses that have a modern kitchen (question 19, code 1). From the sample of 233 houses selected (see Figure 2.10) it can be determined that 80 have a modern kitchen. A 95% confidence interval estimate of the true proportion of houses that have a modern kitchen can be developed as follows:

$$p_S = 80/233 = .343, \text{ and with 95\% confidence } Z = 1.96$$

Again from Equation (10.3)

$$
\begin{aligned}
p_S \pm Z \sqrt{\frac{p_S(1 - p_S)}{n}} &= .343 \pm (1.96) \sqrt{\frac{.343(.657)}{233}} \\
&= .343 \pm (1.96)(.0311) \\
&= .343 \pm .061 \\
&\quad .282 \leq p \leq .404
\end{aligned}
$$

Therefore it can be concluded with 95% confidence that between 28.2% and 40.4% of the houses have a modern kitchen.

We should note that in each of these examples the number of successes and failures was sufficiently large so that the normal distribution provides an excellent approximation for the binomial distribution. However, if the sample size is not large or the percentage of successes is either very low or very high, then the binomial distribution should be used rather than the normal distribution (References 1 and 5). The exact confidence intervals for various sample sizes and proportions of successes have been tabled by Fisher and Yates (Reference 2).

For a given sample size, confidence intervals for proportions often seem to be wider relative to those for continuous variables. With continuous variables, the measurement on each respondent contributes more information than for a dichotomous variable. In other words, a variable with only two possible values is a very crude measure compared with a continuous variable, so each subject contributes only a little information about the parameter we are estimating.

Problems

- **10.28** The manager of a bank in a small city would like to determine the proportion of its depositors who are paid on a weekly basis. A random sample of 100 depositors is selected and 30 state that they are paid weekly. Set up a 90% confidence interval estimate of the true proportion of the bank's depositors who are paid weekly.

  10.29 A suburban bus company is considering the institution of a commuter bus route from a particular suburb into the central business district of the city. A random sample of 50 commuters is selected, and 18 indicate that they would use this bus route.
  - **(a)** Set up a 95% confidence interval estimate of the true proportion of commuters who would utilize this new bus route.
  - ➠**(b)** **ACTION** How can the manager of the bus company use the results of part (a) in making a recommendation concerning the bus route?

  10.30 An auditor for the state insurance department would like to determine the proportion of claims that are paid by a health insurance company within two months of receipt of the claim. A random sample of 200 claims is selected, and it is determined that 80 were paid out within two months of the receipt of the claim.
  - **(a)** Set up a 99% confidence interval estimate of the true proportion of the claims paid within two months.
  - ➠**(b)** **ACTION** How can the results of part (a) be used in a report to the state insurance department?

- **10.31** An automobile dealer would like to estimate the proportion of customers who still own the same cars they purchased five years earlier. A random sample of 200 customers selected from the automobile dealer's records indicated that 82 still owned the cars that had been purchased five years earlier. Set up a 95% confidence interval estimate of the true proportion of all customers who still own the same cars five years after they were purchased.

  10.32 A stationery supply store receives a shipment of a certain brand of inexpensive ball point pens from the manufacturer. The owner of the store wishes to estimate the proportion of pens that are defective. A random sample of 300 pens is tested, and 30 are found to be defective.
  - **(a)** Set up a 90% confidence interval estimate of the proportion of defective pens in the shipment.

(b) The shipment can be returned if it is more than 5% defective; based on the sample results, can the owner return this shipment?

10.33 Referring to Problem 4.98 on page 129, set up a 95% confidence interval estimate of the true population proportion of persons who believe that police and fire protection is adequate in their neighborhood.

10.34 The advertising director for a fast-food chain would like to estimate the proportion of high-school students who are familiar with a particular commercial that has been broadcast on radio and television in the last month. A random sample of 400 high-school students indicated that 160 were familiar with the commercial. Set up a 95% confidence interval estimate of the true population proportion of high-school students who are familiar with the commercial.

10.5 SAMPLE SIZE DETERMINATION FOR THE MEAN

In each of our examples concerning confidence interval estimation, the sample size was arbitrarily determined without regard to the size of the confidence interval. In the business world the determination of the proper sample size is a complicated procedure which is subject to the constraints of budget, time, and ease of selection. For example, if the marketing director wished to estimate the average monthly amount spent on clothing by females, he would try to determine in advance how "good" an estimate would be required. This would mean that he would decide how much error he was willing to allow in estimating the population average monthly amount spent on clothing by females. Was accuracy required to be within $\pm \$1$, $\pm \$10$, $\pm \$20$, $\pm \$50$, etc? The marketing director would also determine in advance how sure (confident) he wanted to be of correctly estimating the true population parameter. In determining the sample size for estimating the mean, these requirements must be kept in mind along with information about the standard deviation.

To develop a formula for determining sample size recall Equation (9.5):

$$Z = \frac{\overline{X} - \mu_X}{\dfrac{\sigma_X}{\sqrt{n}}}$$

where Z is the value corresponding to an area of $(1 - \alpha)/2$ from the center of a standardized normal distribution. Multiplying both sides of Equation (9.5) by $\sigma_X/\sqrt{n}$ we have

$$Z \frac{\sigma_X}{\sqrt{n}} = \overline{X} - \mu_X$$

Thus, the value of Z will be positive or negative, depending on whether $\overline{X}$ is larger or smaller than μ_X. The difference between the sample mean $\overline{X}$ and the population mean μ_X is called the **sampling error.** The sampling error e can be defined as

$$e = \frac{Z\sigma_X}{\sqrt{n}} \qquad \text{(10.4a)}$$

Solving this equation for n, we have

$$n = \frac{Z^2 \sigma_X^2}{e^2}$$

(10.4b)

Therefore, to determine the sample size, three factors must be known:

1. The confidence level desired, which determines the value of Z, the critical value from the normal distribution.[2]
2. The sampling error permitted, e.
3. The standard deviation, σ_X.

In practice the determination of these three quantities may not be easy. How is one to know what level of confidence to use and what sampling error is desired? Typically these questions can be answered only by the individual who is familiar with the variables to be analyzed. Although 95% is the most common confidence level used (in which case $Z = 1.96$), if one desires greater confidence, 99% might be more appropriate, while if less confidence is deemed acceptable, then 90% (or even 80%) might be utilized.

For the sampling error, we should be thinking not of how much sampling error we would like to have (we really don't want any error) but of how much we can "live with" and still be able to provide adequate conclusions for the data. Even when the confidence level and the sampling error are specified, an estimate of the standard deviation must be available. Unfortunately, in very few cases is the population standard deviation σ_X known. In some instances the standard deviation can be estimated from past data. In other situations, one can develop an "educated guess" by taking into account the range and distribution of the variable. For example, if one assumes a normal distribution, the range is approximately equal to $6\sigma_X$ (that is, $\pm 3\sigma_X$ around the mean), so that σ_X can be estimated as range/6 for a normally distributed variable. If σ_X cannot be estimated in this manner, a **pilot study** can be conducted to estimate the standard deviation.

Returning to the earlier example, suppose that the marketing director would like to estimate the population mean to within $\pm\$10$ of the true value and desires to be 95% confident of correctly estimating the true mean. Based on studies taken in the last year, the marketing director feels that the standard deviation can be estimated as $40. With this information the sample size can be determined in the following manner for $e = \$10$, $\sigma_X = \$40$, and 95% confidence ($Z = 1.96$):

$$n = \frac{Z^2 \sigma_X^2}{e^2} = \frac{(1.96)^2(40)^2}{10^2}$$

$$= \frac{3.8416(1,600)}{100} = 61.47$$

---

[2] We use Z instead of t because (1) to determine the critical value of t we would need to know the sample size, which is what we don't know yet, and (2) for most studies the sample size needed will be large enough that the normal is a good approximation to the t distribution.

Therefore, $n = 62$.

We have chosen a sample of size 62 because the rule of thumb used in determining sample size is to always round up to the nearest integer value in order to slightly oversatisfy the criteria desired.

Therefore, if the marketing director utilized these criteria, a sample of 62 should have been taken—not a sample of 25. However, it should be noted that the standard deviation has been estimated at $40 based on previous surveys. If the actual sample standard deviation is very different from this value, the computed sampling error will be directly affected.

Problems

10.35 A survey is planned to determine the average annual family medical expenses of employees of a large company. The management of the company wishes to be 95% confident that the sample average is correct to within ±$50 of the true average family expenses. A pilot study indicates that the standard deviation can be estimated as $400. How large a sample size is necessary?

● **10.36** If the quality control manager in Problem 10.6 on page 314 wanted to estimate the average life to within ±20 hours with 95% confidence and also assumed that the process standard deviation remained at 100 hours, what sample size is needed?

10.37 If the supermarket chain in Problem 10.10 on page 318 wanted to estimate the population average amount of sales to within ±$100 with 99% confidence and the population standard deviation is assumed to be $200, what sample size is needed?

10.38 If the local gas utility in Problem 10.17 on page 319 wished to estimate the average waiting time in days to within ±5 days with 95% confidence and the population standard deviation is assumed to be 20 days, what sample size is needed?

● **10.39** A consumer group would like to estimate the average monthly electric bills for the month of July for one-family homes in a large city. Based upon studies conducted in other cities, the standard deviation is assumed to be $25. The group would like to estimate the average bill for July to within ±$5 of the true average with 99% confidence. What sample size is needed?

10.40 If the inspection division in Problem 10.7 on page 314 wanted to estimate the average amount of soft-drink fill to within ±.01 with 95% confidence and also assumed that the standard deviation remained at .05 liter, what sample size would be needed?

10.6 SAMPLE SIZE DETERMINATION FOR A PROPORTION

In Section 10.5 we discussed the determination of sample size needed for the estimation of a quantitative parameter (the mean). Now suppose that the marketing director wishes to determine the sample size necessary for estimating the true proportion of females who have gone shopping for clothing in the preceding week. The methods of sample size determination that are utilized in estimating a true proportion are similar to those employed in estimating a mean.

To develop a formula for determining sample size recall from Equation (9.8) that

$$Z \cong \frac{p_S - p}{\sqrt{\dfrac{p(1 - p)}{n}}}$$

where Z is the value corresponding to an area of $(1 - \alpha)/2$ from the center of a standardized normal distribution. Multiplying both sides of Equation (9.8) by $\sqrt{\dfrac{p(1 - p)}{n}}$ we have

$$Z\sqrt{\frac{p(1 - p)}{n}} = p_S - p$$

The sampling error is equal to $(p_S - p)$, the difference between the estimate from the sample p_S and the parameter to be estimated p. This sampling error can be defined as

$$e = Z\sqrt{\frac{p(1 - p)}{n}} \tag{10.5a}$$

Solving for n, we obtain

$$n = \frac{Z^2 p(1 - p)}{e^2} \tag{10.5b}$$

In determining the sample size for estimating a proportion, three unknowns must be defined:

1. The level of confidence desired.
2. The sampling error permitted, e.
3. The true proportion of success, p.

In practice the selection of these three quantities is often difficult. Once we determine the desired level of confidence, we will be able to obtain the appropriate Z value from the normal distribution. The sampling error e indicates the amount of error that we are willing to accept in estimating the population proportion. The third quantity—the true proportion of success, p—is actually the population parameter that we are trying to find! Thus, how can we state a value for the very thing that we are taking a sample in order to determine?

Here there are two alternatives. First, in many situations past information or relevant experience may be available that enables us to provide an "educated" estimate of p. Second, if past information or relevant experience is not available, we try to provide a value for p that would never *underestimate* the sample size needed. Referring to Equation (10.5b), we observe that the quantity $p(1 - p)$ appears in the numerator. Thus, we need to determine the value of p that will make $p(1 - p)$ as large as possible. It can be shown that when $p = .5$, then the product $p(1 - p)$ achieves its maximum result. Several values of p along with the accompanying products of $p(1 - p)$ are

$$p = .5, \quad p(1 - p) = .5(.5) \quad = .25$$
$$p = .4, \quad p(1 - p) = .4(.6) \quad = .24$$
$$p = .7, \quad p(1 - p) = .7(.3) \quad = .21$$
$$p = .1, \quad p(1 - p) = .1(.9) \quad = .09$$
$$p = .99, \quad p(1 - p) = .99(.01) = .0099$$

Therefore, when we have no prior knowledge or estimate of the true proportion p, we should use $p = .5$ as the most conservative way of determining the sample size. However, the use of $p = .5$ may result in an overestimate of the sample size. Since the actual sample proportion is utilized in the confidence interval, if it is very different from .5, the width of the confidence interval may be subtantially narrower than originally intended.

In our example, suppose that the marketing director wanted to have 90% confidence of estimating the proportion of shoppers to within $\pm .06$ of its true value. In addition, since this question has not been asked in previous surveys taken by the department store chain, no information is available from past data. Therefore p will be set equal to .5.

With these criteria in mind, the sample size needed can be determined in the following manner with 90% confidence ($Z = 1.645$), $e = .06$, $p = .5$, and

$$n = \frac{Z^2 p(1 - p)}{e^2} = \frac{(1.645)^2(.5)(.5)}{(.06)^2} = \frac{(2.7025)(.25)}{.0036} = 187.67$$

Thus, $n = 188$.

Therefore, in order to be 90% confident of estimating the proportion to within $\pm .06$ of its true value, a sample size of 188 would be needed.

Problems

10.41 A political pollster would like to estimate the proportion of voters who will vote for the Democratic candidate in a presidential campaign. The pollster would like 90% confidence that her prediction is correct to within $\pm .04$ of the true proportion. What sample size is needed?

● **10.42** A cable television company would like to estimate the proportion of its customers that would purchase a cable television program guide. The company would like to have 95% confidence that its estimate is correct to within $\pm .05$ of the true proportion. Past experience in other areas indicates that 30% of the customers will purchase the program guide. What sample size is needed?

● **10.43** A bank manager wants to be 90% confident of being correct to within $\pm .05$ of the true proportion of depositors who have both savings and checking accounts. What sample size is needed?

10.44 What sample size would be needed if the bus company in Problem 10.29 on page 322 wanted to conduct a survey in which they desired to be 95% confident of being correct to within $\pm .02$ of the true proportion of commuters who would utilize the bus service? Based upon past experience with other routes the true proportion is assumed to be approximately .40.

10.45 If the automobile dealer in Problem 10.31 on page 322 wanted to be 95% confident of being correct to within $\pm .025$ of the true proportion of customers who own their cars five years after purchasing them, what sample size would be needed? Based upon past experience we may assume that the true proportion is equal to .20.

10.7   ESTIMATION AND SAMPLE SIZE DETERMINATION FOR FINITE POPULATIONS

10.7.1   Estimating the Mean

In Section 9.4 we saw that when sampling without replacement from finite populations, the **finite population correction (fpc) factor** served to reduce the standard error by a factor equal to $\sqrt{(N - n)/(N - 1)}$. When estimating population parameters from such samples without replacement, the finite population correction factor should be used for developing confidence interval estimates.

Therefore, the $(1 - \alpha) \times 100\%$ confidence interval estimate for the mean would become

$$\overline{X} \pm t_{n-1} \frac{S}{\sqrt{n}} \sqrt{\frac{N - n}{N - 1}} \qquad \textbf{(10.6)}$$

In the marketing director's example, a sample of 25 female credit card holders was selected. Suppose that there was a population of 1,000 accounts. Using the finite population correction factor, we would have, with $\overline{X} = \$86.40$, $S = \$37.50$, $n = 25$, $N = 1,000$, and $t_{24} = 2.064$ (for 95% confidence):

$$\overline{X} \pm t_{n-1} \frac{S}{\sqrt{n}} \sqrt{\frac{N - n}{N - 1}} = 86.40 \pm 2.064 \frac{37.50}{\sqrt{25}} \sqrt{\frac{1,000 - 25}{1,000 - 1}}$$

$$= 86.40 \pm (15.48)(.988)$$
$$= 86.40 \pm (15.29)$$

$$\$71.11 \le \mu_X \le \$101.69$$

In this case, since the sample was a very small fraction of the population, the correction factor had little effect on the confidence interval estimate (as was computed in Section 10.3).

10.7.2   Estimating the Proportion

The $(1 - \alpha) \times 100\%$ confidence interval estimate of the proportion, when sampling without replacement, would be

$$p_S \pm Z \sqrt{\frac{p_S(1 - p_S)}{n}} \sqrt{\frac{N - n}{N - 1}} \qquad \textbf{(10.7)}$$

In the marketing director's study of the consumer behavior of females, a sample of 200 was selected from a population of 1,000 credit card holders. The 90% confidence interval estimate would be determined in the following manner when sampling without replacement. We have $p_S = 70/200 = .35$, $Z = 1.645$, $n = 200$, and $N = 1,000$. Thus

$$p_S \pm Z \sqrt{\frac{p_S(1 - p_S)}{n}} \sqrt{\frac{N - n}{N - 1}} = .35 \pm 1.645 \sqrt{\frac{35(.65)}{200}} \sqrt{\frac{1,000 - 200}{1,000 - 1}}$$

$$= .35 \pm (1.645)(.0337)\sqrt{(.801)}$$
$$= .35 \pm (.0554)(.895)$$
$$= .35 \pm .05$$

$$0.30 \leq p \leq .40$$

Here, since 20% of the population was to be sampled, the finite population correction factor had a moderate effect on the confidence interval estimate.

10.7.3 Determining the Sample Size

Just as the correction factor was used in developing confidence-interval estimates, it also should be used in determining sample size when sampling without replacement. For example, in estimating means the sampling error would be

$$e = Z \frac{\sigma_X}{\sqrt{n}} \sqrt{\frac{N - n}{N - 1}} \qquad (10.8)$$

while in estimating proportions the sampling error would be

$$e = Z \sqrt{\frac{p(1 - p)}{n}} \sqrt{\frac{N - n}{N - 1}} \qquad (10.9)$$

In determining the sample size in estimating the mean, we would have, from Equation (10.4b),

$$n_0 = \frac{Z^2 \sigma_X^2}{e^2}$$

where n_0 is the sample size without considering the finite population correction factor. Applying the correction factor to this results in

$$n = \frac{n_0 N}{n_0 + (N - 1)} \qquad (10.10)$$

In the marketing director's survey to estimate the monthly amount spent on clothing, the sample size needed in order to be 95% confident of being correct to within $\pm \$10$ (assuming a standard deviation of $40) was 62, since n_0 was computed as 61.47. Using the correction factor leads to the following:

$$n = \frac{(61.47)(1,000)}{61.47 + (1,000 - 1)} = 57.96$$

Thus $n = 58$.

Here the use of the correction factor made very little difference in the sample size selected. However, in general this may not be the case. For example, we may recall that in order to estimate the true proportion of females who went shopping for clothing in the preceding week, the marketing director needed a sample size of 188 (since n_0 was computed as 187.67). Using the correction factor leads to

$$n = \frac{n_0 N}{n_0 + (N - 1)} = \frac{187.67(1,000)}{187.67 + (1,000 - 1)} = 158.15$$

Thus $n = 159$.

Here, since almost 20% of the population was to be sampled, the finite population correction factor had a substantial effect on the sample size—reducing it from 188 to 159.

We may recall that in the real estate survey in Chapter 2 we stated that a sample of 233 houses had to be selected. This sample size is based on satisfying the requirements of those questions that are deemed the most important. In this study, the president of the real estate company and the statistician have determined that questions 1 and 19 are the most essential quantitative and qualitative questions, respectively.

Since the random variable "appraised value" is quantitative, in order to determine the sample size required we use Equations (10.4b) and (10.10). Three quantities are needed: the desired confidence level (Z), the sampling error (e), and the standard deviation (σ_X). After considerable thought and consultation, the statistician decided that he would like to have 95% confidence that the estimate of the average appraised value be correct to within ± 4.0 thousands of dollars of the true value. Based on surveys in similar geographical areas, the standard deviation of the appraised value is estimated as 31.5. With this information, the sample size can be determined in the following manner, with $e = 4.0$, $\sigma_X = 31.5$ (estimated), and 95% confidence ($Z = 1.96$):

$$n_0 = \frac{Z^2 \sigma_X^2}{e^2} = \frac{(1.96)^2 (31.5)^2}{(4.0)^2} = 238.24$$

Thus

$$n = \frac{n_0 N}{n_0 + (N - 1)} = \frac{238.24(9,660)}{238.24 + (9,660 - 1)} = 232.53$$

Therefore $n = 233$.

However, before deciding upon the sample size needed for the survey, we must evaluate the sample size required for the qualitative variable "does the house contain a modern kitchen?" This can be found by using Equations (10.5b) and (10.10) after determining three quantities—the confidence level desired (Z), the sampling error (e), and an estimate of the true proportion of houses that have a modern kitchen. Once again, as with the quantitative variable, considerable thought was given to determining the desired values. The statistician concluded that he would like 95% confidence that the estimate of the true proportion of houses with a modern kitchen (question 19, code 1) be correct to within $\pm .07$. Based on experience with similar geographical areas, the true proportion of houses in this category is assumed to be no more than .40. With this information, the sample size can be determined in the following manner with $e = .07$, $p = .40$, and 95% confidence ($Z = 1.96$):

$$n_0 = \frac{Z^2 p(1 - p)}{e^2} = \frac{(1.96)^2(.40)(.60)}{(.07)^2} = 188.16$$

Thus

$$n = \frac{n_0 N}{n_0 + (N - 1)} = \frac{188.16(9,660)}{188.16 + (9,660 - 1)} = 184.58$$

Therefore $n = 185$.

We have seen that a sample of 233 houses is needed to satisfy the requirements for the quantitative variable (appraised value) while a sample of 185 houses is required to satisfy the requirements for the qualitative variable (presence of a modern kitchen). However, since we must satisfy both requirements simultaneously with one sample, the larger sample size of 233 must be utilized for the real estate survey.

Problems

● **10.46** Refer to Problems 10.6 and 10.36 on pages 314 and 325. If the shipment contains a total of 2,000 light bulbs
(a) Set up a 95% confidence interval estimate of the true average life of light bulbs in this shipment.
(b) Determine the sample size needed to estimate the average life to within ± 20 hours with 95% confidence.

10.47 Refer to Problem 10.35 on page 325. What sample size is necessary if the company has 3,000 employees?

● **10.48** Refer to Problem 10.28 on page 322. If the bank has 1,000 depositors
(a) Set up a 90% confidence interval estimate of the true proportion of depositors who are paid weekly.
(b) Determine the sample size needed to estimate the true proportion to within $\pm .05$ with 90% confidence.

10.49 Refer to Problems 10.31 and 10.45 on pages 322 and 327. If the population consists of 4,000 owners
(a) Set up a 95% confidence interval estimate of the true proportion of customers who still own their cars five years after they purchased them.
(b) Determine what sample size is necessary to estimate the true proportion to within $\pm .025$ with 95% confidence.

10.50 Refer to Problems 10.7 and 10.40 on pages 314 and 325. If the population consists of 2,000 bottles
(a) Set up a 95% confidence interval estimate of the true population average of soft drink in each bottle.
(b) Determine the sample size that is necessary to estimate the true average amount to within $\pm .01$ liter with 95% confidence.

Supplementary Problems

10.51 Referring to Problem 10.6 (page 314), set up 99% and 90% confidence interval estimates of the true average life of light bulbs in the shipment. Compare and discuss the meaning of the three confidence interval estimates.

10.52 Referring to Problem 10.30 (page 322), set up 95% and 90% confidence interval estimates of the true proportion of claims paid within two months. Compare and discuss the meaning of the three confidence interval estimates.

● **10.53** A market researcher for a large consumer electronics company would like to study television viewing habits of residents of a particular small city. A random sample of 40 respondents was selected, and each respondent was instructed to keep a detailed record of all television viewing in a particular week. The results were as follows:

Amount of viewing per week: $\overline{X} = 15.3$ hours, $S = 3.8$ hours.
27 respondents watched the Evening News on at least three weeknights.

Set up 95% confidence interval estimates for each of the following:
   (a) The average amount of television watched per week in this city.
   (b) The proportion of respondents who watch the Evening News at least three nights per week.
➡**(c)** **ACTION**   How can the market researcher use the results of parts (a) and (b) to determine a plan for television advertising?
   If the market researcher wanted to take another survey in a different city
   (d) What sample size is required if he wishes to be 95% confident of being correct to within ±2 hours and assumes the population standard deviation is equal to 5 hours?
   (e) What sample size is needed if he wishes to be 95% confident of being within ±.035 of the true proportion who watch the Evening News on at least three weeknights if no previous estimate were available?

10.54 The real estate assessor for a county government wishes to study various characteristics concerning single-family houses in the county. A random sample of 70 houses revealed the following:

Heating area of the house: $\overline{X} = 1,759$ sq ft, $S = 380$ sq ft.
42 houses had central air conditioning.

   (a) Set up a 99% confidence interval estimate of the population average heating area of the house.
   (b) Set up a 95% confidence interval estimate of the population proportion of houses that have central air conditioning.

10.55 The personnel director of a large corporation wished to study absenteeism among clerical workers at the corporation's central office during last year. A random sample of 25 clerical workers revealed the following:

$\overline{X} = 9.7$ days, $S = 4.0$ days
12 employees were absent more than 10 days

Set up 95% confidence interval estimates of each of the following:
   (a) The average number of days absent for clerical workers last year.
   (b) The proportion of clerical workers absent more than 10 days last year.
➡**(c)** **ACTION**   How can the personnel director use the results of parts (a) and (b) to determine how absenteeism can be reduced in the coming year?
   If the personnel director also wishes to take a survey in a branch office
   (d) What sample size is needed if the director wishes to be 95% confident of being correct to ±1.5 days and the population standard deviation is assumed to be 4.5 days?

(e) What sample size is needed if the director wishes to be 90% confident of being correct to within $\pm .075$ of the true proportion of workers who are absent more than 10 days if no previous estimate were available?

10.56 The registrar's office of a local university wishes to estimate the number of credits taken by students during the past semester. A random sample of 50 students was selected with the following results:

$$\overline{X} = 14.2 \text{ credits}, \qquad S = 3.8 \text{ credits}$$
$$37 \text{ students were full-time students (taking 12 or more credits)}$$

(a) Set up a 99% confidence interval estimate of the population average number of credits taken by students at this university.
(b) Set up a 95% confidence interval estimate of the population proportion of students who are full-time students.
➡(c) **ACTION** How can the registrar use the results of parts (a) and (b) to plan for next semester's registration?

10.57 A representative for a large chain of hardware stores was interested in testing the product claims of a manufacturer of "ice melt" that reported to melt snow and ice at temperatures as low as 15 degrees Fahrenheit. A shipment of 400 five-pound bags was purchased by the chain for distribution. The representative wanted to know with 95% confidence, within $\pm .05$, what proportion of bags of ice melt would perform the job as claimed by the manufacturer.

(a) How many bags does the representative need to test? What assumption should be made concerning the true proportion in the population? (This is called *destructive testing*; that is, the product being tested is destroyed by the test and is then unavailable to be sold.)
(b) If the representative actually tested 50 bags, out of which 42 did the job as claimed, construct a 95% confidence interval estimate for the population proportion that will do the job as claimed.
➡(c) **ACTION** How can the representative use the results of part (b) to determine whether to sell the "ice melt" product?

10.58 Sixty accounting firms in a large city each hired individuals who had just received their bachelor's degree with a major in accounting. Suppose that, within a firm, everyone newly hired is paid the same amount.

(a) How many firms must be sampled to determine with 95% confidence the average starting salary per firm to within $\pm \$1,000$? (Assume a population standard deviation of $3,500.)
(b) How many firms must be sampled to determine within $\pm 4\%$, with 95% confidence, the percentage of firms that have hired at least five new accounting majors?
(c) Suppose that 18 firms are sampled and the average starting salary is $28,500 with a sample standard deviation of $3,750. Furthermore, suppose that seven of the firms have hired at least five new accountants. Compute 95% confidence interval estimates for the average starting salary and the proportion of firms hiring at least five new accountants.

10.59 Referring to the data of Problem 3.87 on page 87 that deal with the cost, the calories, and the amount of sodium in pancake mixes and pancake syrup

(a) Set up 95% confidence interval estimates of the cost, calories, and amount of sodium per pancake.
(b) Set up 95% confidence interval estimates of the cost, calories, and amount of sodium per serving of pancake syrup.
➡(c) **ACTION** Based on your results in parts (a) and (b), what conclusions can you draw in comparing the cost, calories, and sodium of pancakes with similar results for pancake syrup?

10.60 Referring to the data of Problem 3.82 on page 81

(a) Set up 90% confidence interval estimates of the population average cost per pound of frozen turkey and cost per pound of edible meat.

➠(b) **ACTION**   Use the results of part (a) as part of a newspaper article about the cost of frozen turkey.

10.61   Referring to the data of Problem 3.85 on page 84
   (a) Set up separate 95% confidence interval estimates of the population average cost, caffeine, and cocoa mass for dark chocolate bars and milk chocolate bars.
   ➠(b) **ACTION**   Based on the results in part (a), what conclusions can you draw in comparing the cost, caffeine, and cocoa mass of dark chocolate and milk chocolate? Write a newspaper article.

10.62   Referring to the data of Problem 3.83 on page 82
   (a) Set up 95% confidence interval estimates of the population average cost and average amount of sodium per serving of salted peanut butter.
   ➠(b) **ACTION**   Use the results of part (a) as part of a newspaper article about salted peanut butter.

10.63   Referring to the data of Problem 3.86 on page 85
   (a) Set up separate 90% confidence interval estimates of the population average cost per ounce, cost per pound of protein, calories per frank, and amount of sodium per frank for ''meat'' frankfurters and ''beef'' frankfurters.
   ➠(b) **ACTION**   Based on the results in part (a), what conclusions can you draw about the average cost per ounce, cost per pound of protein, calories per frank, and amount of sodium per frank of ''meat'' and ''beef'' frankfurters? Write a newspaper article.

10.64   Referring to the data of Problem 3.84 on page 83
   (a) Set up 95% confidence intervals estimates of the population average price, shelf area, cooking grid, and maximum heat output of gas barbecue grills.
   ➠(b) **ACTION**   Use the results of part (a) to provide information to your neighbor who is thinking about buying a gas barbecue grill.

Database Exercises

The following problems refer to the sample data obtained from the questionnaire of Figure 2.5 on page 15 and presented in Figure 2.10 on pages 24–29. They should be solved with the aid of an available computer package.

☐ **10.65**   Set up a 95% confidence interval estimate of the average appraised value (question 1).

☐ **10.66**   Set up a 99% confidence interval estimate of the average lot size (question 2).

☐ **10.67**   Set up a 90% confidence interval estimate of the average number of bedrooms (question 3).

☐ **10.68**   Set up a 95% confidence interval estimate of the average number of bathrooms (question 4).

☐ **10.69**   Set up a 99% confidence interval estimate of the average number of rooms (question 5).

☐ **10.70**   Set up a 90% confidence interval estimate of the average age of houses (question 6).

☐ **10.71**   Set up a 95% confidence interval estimate of the average annual taxes (question 7).

☐ **10.72**   Set up a 95% confidence interval estimate of the average appraised value (question 1) of houses in Levittown (question 9, code 3)

☐ **10.73**   Set up a 99% confidence interval estimate of the average annual taxes (question 7) of houses in East Meadow (question 9, code 1).

☐ **10.74**   Set up a 90% confidence interval estimate of the average number of rooms (question 5) in houses that are categorized as ''Cape'' (question 10, code 1).

☐ **10.75**   Set up a 95% confidence interval estimate of the average lot size (question 2) of houses that have an above-ground or in-ground swimming pool (question 13, codes 2 and 3).

☐ **10.76**   Set up a 95% confidence interval estimate of the population proportion of houses that have an eat-in kitchen (question 14, code 1).

□ **10.77**   Set up a 95% confidence interval estimate of the population proportion of houses that have central air conditioning (question 15, code 1).

□ **10.78**   Set up a 99% confidence interval estimate of the population proportion of houses that have a fireplace (question 16, code 1).

□ **10.79**   Set up a 90% confidence interval estimate of the population proportion of houses that do not have a connection to the local sewer system (question 17, code 0).

□ **10.80**   Set up a 95% confidence interval estimate of the population proportion of houses that have a basement (question 18, code 1).

□ **10.81**   Set up a 95% confidence interval estimate of the population proportion of houses that have modern bathrooms (question 20, code 1).

□ **10.82**   Set up a 99% confidence interval estimate of the population proportion of houses that have a one-car garage (question 8, code 1).

□ **10.83**   Set up a 90% confidence interval estimate of the population proportion of houses that are categorized as ''split level'' (question 10, code 5).

□ **10.84**   Set up a 95% confidence interval estimate of the population proportion of houses that have oil heat (question 11, code 2).

□ **10.85**   Set up a 95% confidence interval estimate of the population proportion of houses that have a hot water heating system (question 12, code 2).

□ **10.86**   Set up a 99% confidence interval estimate of the population proportion of houses that have an above-ground or in-ground swimming pool (question 13, codes 2 and 3).

References

1. COCHRAN, W. G., *Sampling Techniques*, 3d ed. (New York: Wiley, 1977).
2. FISHER, R. A., AND F. YATES, *Statistical Tables for Biological, Agricultural and Medical Research*, 5th ed. (Edinburgh: Oliver & Boyd, 1957).
3. KIRK, R. E., ed., *Statistical Issues: A Reader for the Behavioral Sciences* (Belmont, Calif.: Wadsworth, 1972).
4. LARSEN, R. L., AND M. L. MARX, *An Introduction to Mathematical Statistics and Its Applications*, 2d ed. (Englewood Cliffs, N.J.: Prentice-Hall, 1986).
5. SNEDECOR, G. W., AND W. G. COCHRAN, *Statistical Methods*, 7th ed. (Ames, Iowa: Iowa State University Press, 1980).

11

Hypothesis Testing I: Introduction and Concepts

11.1 INTRODUCTION

In Chapter 9 we began our study of statistical inference by developing the concept of a sampling distribution. In Chapter 10 we demonstrated how sample information can be used to estimate true population parameters. In this chapter we will begin to focus on another phase of statistical inference which is also based on sample information—hypothesis testing.

11.2 THE HYPOTHESIS TESTING PROCEDURE

In order to develop the hypothesis-testing procedure, we will focus on some examples based on the cereal box filling process discussed in Chapters 9 and 10. The production manager of the process had to deal with the following three issues:

1. Is the process working in a way that ensures that on average, the proper amount (i.e., 368 grams) is being filled in each box?
2. Since the filling process is subject to periodic inspection from representatives of the local Office of Consumer Affairs who are solely concerned about "shortweighting" of products, is there any evidence that the average amount of fill is below 368 grams?
3. Once the boxes are filled, each package is sealed so that it is air-tight. Based on past experience, it is known that .10 of the packages do not meet standards for sealing and must be "reworked" in order to pass inspection. A new packaging system has been developed. Is there any evidence that the proportion of defective packages has improved (i.e., the proportion has gotten lower)?

A sample of 25 boxes will be selected to answer the first two questions, and (because obtaining a proportion is a cruder and often cheaper process) a sample of 200 boxes will be used to answer the third question. Hence in order to answer each of these questions, a decision based upon sample information must be made. In the first example, one of the following two conclusions will be reached:

1. The average fill is 368 grams.
2. The average fill is not 368 grams; either it is less than 368 grams or it is more than 368 grams.

From the perspective of statistical hypothesis testing, these two conclusions would be represented as follows:

$$\text{(null hypothesis)} \qquad H_0: \quad \mu_X = 368$$

$$\text{(alternative hypothesis)} \quad H_1: \quad \mu_X \neq 368$$

In this example, the **null hypothesis H_0** represents the conclusion that would be drawn if the filling process was working properly (and μ_X was $= 368$ grams). The null hypothesis can also be viewed from the perspective of the American legal process, in which innocence is presumed until guilt is proven. Thus we assume that the average is ''not different'' unless evidence of ''guilt'' is found showing that the average has changed. The **alternative hypothesis, H_1,** which is usually the negation of the null hypothesis, represents the conclusion that would be drawn if evidence of ''guilt'' were found. In our example, ''guilt'' refers to the average amount of fill being different from 368 grams.

The null hypothesis is the hypothesis that is always tested. The alternative hypothesis represents the conclusion for which evidence is sought. In classical statistical inference

1. The null hypothesis always refers to a specified value of the population parameter (μ_X, σ_X, p), not a sample statistic ($\overline{X}$, S, p_S)
2. The statement of the null hypothesis always contains an equality (i.e., H_0: $\mu_X = 368$ grams).
3. The statement of the alternative hypothesis never contains an equality (i.e., H_1: $\mu_X \neq 368$ grams).

We may develop the logic underlying the hypothesis-testing procedure by contemplating how we can determine, based only on a sample, whether or not the population average is 368 grams. If our sample average is 367.6, for example, we will be inclined to conclude that the average has not changed ($\mu_X = 368$), since the sample mean is ''close to'' the hypothesized value of 368. Intuitively, we will be thinking that it is not unlikely that we could obtain a sample mean of 367.6 from a population whose mean was 368. On the other hand, if our sample average is 320, our instinct will be to conclude that the average is not 368 (that $\mu_X \neq 368$), since the sample mean is far away from the hypothesized value of 368. In this case we will be reasoning that it would be very unlikely that the sample mean of 320 could be obtained if the population mean was 368; therefore it is more reasonable to conclude that the population mean is not equal to 368.

Unfortunately, the decision-making process is not always so clear-cut. It would be arbitrary for us to determine what is ''close'' and what is ''far away'' from the population mean. For this reason statistical hypothesis testing is employed to quantify the decision-making process so that the probability of obtaining a given sample result can be found. This is achieved by first determining the sampling distribution that the sample statistic (i.e., the mean) follows and then computing the appropriate **test statistic.** This test statistic measures how close the sample value has come to the null hypothesis. The test statistic often follows a well-known statistical distribution (such as the normal, t, etc.).

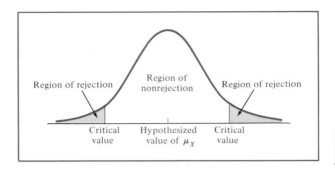

FIGURE 11.1
Regions of rejection and nonrejection in hypothesis testing.

The appropriate distribution of the test statistic is divided into two regions, a **region of rejection** (sometimes called the **critical region**) and a **region of nonrejection** (see Figure 11.1). If the test statistic falls into the region of nonrejection, the null hypothesis cannot be rejected, and the manager will conclude that the average amount filled has not changed. If the test statistic falls into the rejection region, the null hypothesis will be rejected and the manager will conclude that the population mean is not 368.

The region of rejection may be thought of as consisting of the values of the test statistic which are unlikely to occur if the null hypothesis is true. On the other hand, these values are not so unlikely to occur if the null hypothesis is false. Therefore, if we observe a value of the statistic which falls into the critical region, we reject the null hypothesis because the observation of that value would be unlikely to occur if the null hypothesis were true.

In order to make this decision concerning the null hypothesis, we must first determine the **critical value** for the statistical distribution of interest. The critical value divides the nonrejection region from the rejection region. However, the determination of this critical value depends on the size of the rejection region. As we will see in the next section, the size of the rejection region is directly related to the risks involved in using only sample evidence to make decisions about a population parameter.

11.3 TYPE I AND TYPE II ERRORS

In using a sample to draw conclusions about a population there is a risk that an incorrect conclusion will be reached. Indeed, two different errors can occur in applying the hypothesis-testing approach to decision making concerning population parameters.

The first error is called the **Type I error;** the probability of a Type I error is called **α.** (α is the lower-case Greek letter alpha.)

A **Type I error** occurs if the null hypothesis H_0 is rejected when in fact it is true.

In our cereal fill example, the Type I error would occur if we concluded (based on sample data) that the average population amount filled was *not* 368 when in fact it was 368.

The probability of a Type I error (α) is also called the **level of significance.** Traditionally, the statistician controls the Type I error rate by establishing the risk level he or she is willing to tolerate in terms of rejecting a true null hypothesis. The selection of a particular risk level α is, of course, dependent on the cost of making a Type I error. Once the value for α is specified, the size of the rejection region is known, since α is the probability of rejection under the null hypothesis. From this fact the critical value or values that divide the rejection and nonrejection regions can be determined.

The second error, called the **Type II error,** occurs with a probability called $\boldsymbol{\beta}$ (β is the lower-case Greek letter beta.)

> A **Type II error** occurs if the null hypothesis H_0 is not rejected when it is false and should be rejected.

In our cereal fill example, the Type II error would occur if we concluded (based on sample data) that the average population amount filled was 368 when in fact it was not 368. Unlike the Type I error rate α, which is preset at a specified value, the magnitude of the Type II error rate β is dependent on the actual population value of the mean. For example, if the true population average (which is unknown to us) were 320, there would be a small chance (β) of concluding that the average had not changed from 368. However, if the true population average were really 367, we would have a high probability of concluding that the population average amount filled had not changed from our stated 368 (and we would be making a Type II error).

The complement $(1 - \beta)$ of the probability of a Type II error is called the **power** of a statistical test.

> The **power** of a statistical test $(1 - \beta)$ is the probability of rejecting the null hypothesis when it is false (and should be rejected).

In our cereal fill example, the power of the test is the probability of concluding that the average amount of fill is not 368 when in fact it is actually not 368. A more detailed discussion of the power of a statistical test is presented in Section 11.11.

An easy way to remember which probability goes with which type of error is to note that α is the first letter of the Greek alphabet, and it is used to represent the probability of a Type I error. The letter β is the second letter of the Greek alphabet and is used to represent the probability of a Type II error. (If you have trouble remembering the Greek alphabet, note that the word ''alphabet'' tells you its first two letters.)

Table 11.1 illustrates the two types of errors, the probability of each, and the power of the test.

The usual procedure in research is to choose a level of α; this (along with sample size) will determine the level of β for a particular study design. Very often, α is chosen to be .05; sometimes it is .01; other values of α are less common. One way in which a researcher can control the probability of these errors is to increase the sample size. For a given level of α, increasing the sample size will decrease β and therefore increase the power to detect that H_0 is false.

TABLE 11.1   Hypothesis testing

Statistical Decision	Actual Situation	
	H_0 *True*	H_0 *False*
Do not reject H_0	$1 - \alpha$	Type II error (β)
Reject H_0	Type I error (α)	Power $= 1 - \beta$

For a given sample size the decision maker must balance the two types of errors. If α is to be decreased, then β will be increased. If β is to be decreased, then α will be increased. The values for α and β depend on the importance of each risk in a particular problem. The risk of a Type I error in the cereal filling process involves concluding that the average amount has changed when it has not changed. The risk of a Type II error involves concluding that the average amount has not changed when in truth it has changed.

The choice of reasonable levels of α and β depends on the costs inherent in each type of error. For example, if it were very costly to make changes from the status quo, then we would want to be very sure that a change would be beneficial, so the risk of a Type I error might be most important and α would be kept very low. On the other hand, if we wanted to be very certain of detecting changes from a hypothesized mean, the risk of a Type II error would be most important and we might choose a higher level of α. Of course, by increasing the sample size, we could control both α and β, but there is always a limit on our resources, so we still must consider the tradeoffs between making Type I and Type II errors.

Problems

11.1   Why is it possible for the null hypothesis to be rejected when in fact it is true?

11.2   For a given sample size, if the α risk is reduced from .05 to .01, what will happen to the β risk?

11.3   Why is it possible that the null hypothesis will not always be rejected when it is false?

11.4   What is the relationship of α to the Type I error?

11.5   What is the relationship of β to the Type II error?

11.6   For H_0: $\mu_X = 100$, H_1: $\mu_X \neq 100$, and for a sample of size n, β will be larger if the actual value of μ_X is 90 than if the actual value of μ_X is 75. Why?

11.7   In the American legal system, a defendant is presumed innocent until proven guilty. Consider then a null hypothesis H_0 that the defendant is innocent and an alternative hypothesis H_1 that the defendant is guilty. A jury has two possible decisions: convict the defendant (i.e., reject the null hypothesis) or do not convict the defendant (i.e., do not reject the null hypothesis). Explain the meaning of the α and β risks in this example.

11.8   Suppose the defendant in Problem 11.7 were presumed guilty until proven innocent. How would the null and alternative hypotheses differ from those in Problem 11.7? What would be the meaning of the α and β risks?

11.9   Explain what Type I and Type II errors are.

11.10   Explain in your own words what the terms *null hypothesis* and *alternative hypothesis* mean.

11.11   Which type of error (I or II) usually has its probability directly controlled by the choice of the person analyzing the data? What determines the probability of the other type of error?

11.12   How is power related to the probability of making a Type II error?

11.4   TEST OF HYPOTHESIS FOR THE MEAN (σ_X Known)

Now that we have defined the Type I and Type II errors, we may return to the first question of interest to the manager. For the cereal fill problem, the null and alternative hypothesis were

$$H_0: \quad \mu_X = 368$$

$$H_1: \quad \mu_X \neq 368$$

If we assume that the standard deviation σ_X is known, then based on the central limit theorem the sampling distribution of the mean would follow the normal distribution and the test statistic would be

$$Z = \frac{\overline{X} - \mu_X}{\dfrac{\sigma_X}{\sqrt{n}}} \qquad\qquad (11.1)$$

In this formula, the numerator measures how far (in an absolute sense) the observed mean $\overline{X}$ is from the hypothesized mean μ_X. The denominator is the standard error, so Z represents how many standard errors $\overline{X}$ is from μ_X. With σ_X known, Z has a standard normal distribution.

If the manager decided to choose a level of significance of .05, the size of the rejection region would be .05, and the critical values of the normal distribution could be determined. Since the rejection region is divided into the two tails of the distribution, the .05 is divided into two equal parts of .025 each.

Since we have a normal distribution, the critical values can be expressed in standard-deviation units. A rejection region of .025 in each tail of the normal distribution results in an area of .475 between the hypothesized mean and each critical value. Looking up this area in the normal distribution (Table E.2), we find that the critical values that divide the rejection and nonrejection regions are $+1.96$ and -1.96. Figure 11.2 illustrates this case; it shows that if the mean is actually 368, as H_0 claims, then the values of the test statistic Z will have a standard normal distribution centered at $\mu_X = 368$. Observed values of Z greater than 1.96 or less than -1.96 indicate that $\overline{X}$ is so far from 368 that it is unlikely that such a value would occur if H_0 were true.

Therefore the rejection rule would be

Reject H_0 if $Z > +1.96$

or if $Z < -1.96$;

otherwise do not reject H_0.

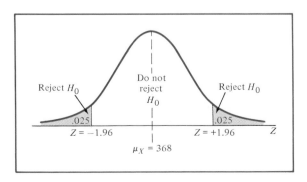

FIGURE 11.2
Testing a hypothesis about the mean (σ_X known) at the .05 level of significance.

Suppose that the sample of 25 cereal boxes indicated a sample mean of 364.1 grams and the population standard deviation was assumed to remain at 15 grams (see Section 9.2). Using Equation (11.1), we have

$$Z = \frac{\overline{X} - \mu_X}{\dfrac{\sigma_X}{\sqrt{n}}}$$

$$= \frac{364.1 - 368}{\dfrac{15}{\sqrt{25}}} = -1.30$$

Since $Z = -1.30$, we see that $-1.96 < -1.30 < +1.96$. Thus our decision is not to reject H_0. We would conclude that the average amount filled is 368 grams. Alternatively, to take into account the possibility of a Type II error, we may phrase the conclusion as ''there is no evidence that the average is different from 368 grams.''

Problems

- **11.13** Referring to Problem 10.6 on page 314, the production process is said to be ''in control'' (that is, working properly) when the population average life of the light bulbs is 375 hours.
  (a) State the null and alternative hypotheses.
  (b) Using the .05 level of significance, what should the quality control manager conclude about the process based on sample results?

11.14 Referring to Problem 10.5 on page 314, is there evidence that the average amount is different from 1.0 gallon? (Use the .05 level of significance.)

11.15 Referring to Problem 10.7 on page 314, is there evidence that the average amount in the bottles is not equal to 2.0 liters? (Use $\alpha = .05$.)

11.16 Referring to the example concerning the length of computer paper on page 313, is there evidence that the average length is different from 11 inches? (Use $\alpha = .05$.)

11.17 Suppose that scores on an aptitude test used for determining admission to graduate study in business are known to be normally distributed with a mean of 500 and a population standard deviation of 100. If a random sample of 12 applicants from Stephan College have a sample mean of 537, is there any evidence that their mean score is different from the mean expected of all applicants? (Use $\alpha = .01$.)

11.5 SUMMARIZING THE STEPS OF HYPOTHESIS TESTING

Now that we have used the hypothesis-testing procedure to draw a conclusion about the population mean, it will be useful to summarize the steps involved in the procedure.

1. State the null hypothesis, H_0.
2. State the alternative hypothesis, H_1.
3. Choose the level of significance, α.
4. Choose the sample size, n.
5. Determine the appropriate statistical technique and corresponding test statistic to use.
6. Set up the critical values that divide the rejection and nonrejection regions.
7. Collect the data and compute the sample value of the appropriate test statistic.
8. Determine whether the test statistic has fallen into the rejection or the nonrejection region.

9. Make the statistical decision.
10. Express the statistical decision in terms of the problem.

Steps 1 and 2. The null and alternative hypotheses must be stated in statistical terms. In testing whether the average amount filled was 368 grams, the null hypothesis was that μ_X equals 368, and the alternative hypothesis was that μ_X was not equal to 368 grams.

Step 3. The level of significance is specified according to the relative importance of Type I and Type II errors in the problem. We chose $\alpha = .05$; along with the sample size, this determines β.

Step 4. The sample size is determined after taking into account the desired α and β risks and considering budget constraints in carrying out the study. Here 25 cereal boxes were selected.

Step 5. The statistical technique that will be used to test the null hypothesis must be chosen. Since σ_X was known, a Z test was selected.

Step 6. Once the null and alternative hypotheses are specified and the level of significance and the sample size are determined, the critical values for the appropriate statistical distribution can be found so that the rejection and nonrejection regions can be indicated. Here the values 1.96 and -1.96 were used to define these regions.

Step 7. The data are collected and the value of the test statistic is computed. Here, $\overline{X} = 364.1$, so $Z = -1.30$.

Step 8. The value of the test statistic is compared with the critical values for the appropriate distribution to determine whether it falls into the rejection or nonrejection region. Here, $Z = -1.30$ is in the region of nonrejection, since $-1.96 < -1.30 < +1.96$.

Step 9. The hypothesis-testing decision is made. If the test statistic falls into the nonrejection region, the null hypothesis H_0 cannot be rejected. If the test statistic falls into the rejection region, the null hypothesis is rejected. Here, H_0 is not rejected.

Step 10. The consequences of the hypothesis-testing decision must be expressed in terms of the actual problem involved. Thus in our cereal fill problem we concluded that there was no evidence that the average amount of cereal fill was different from 368 grams.

11.6 TEST OF HYPOTHESIS FOR THE MEAN (σ_X UNKNOWN)

In most cases, however, the standard deviation σ_X of the population is unknown. The standard deviation is estimated by computing S, the standard deviation of the sample. If the population is assumed to be normal, the sampling distribution of the mean will follow a t distribution with $n - 1$ degrees of freedom. In practice it has been found that as long as the sample size is not very small and the population is not very skewed, the t distribution gives a good approximation to the sampling distribution of the mean.

The test statistic for determining the difference between the sample mean $\overline{X}$ and the population mean μ_X when the sample standard deviation S is used is given by

$$t_{n-1} = \frac{\overline{X} - \mu_X}{\dfrac{S}{\sqrt{n}}} \qquad (11.2)$$

Suppose that when the sample in Section 11.4 was selected the representative of the Office of Consumer Affairs was present and was unwilling to assume that the standard deviation was equal to the company's previously stated value of 15 grams. In such a case, we may use the sample standard deviation which was computed as 17.3 grams.

If a level of significance of .05 is selected, the critical values of the t distribution with $25 - 1 = 24$ degrees of freedom can be obtained from Table E.3, as illustrated in Table 11.2 and Figure 11.3. The rejection region of .05 is divided into two parts of .025 each. This is due to the fact that the alternative hypothesis is nondirectional, since it merely states that $\mu_X \neq 368$. Such a test is called a **two-tailed test.** Using the t table as given in Table E.3, the critical values are -2.0639 and $+2.0639$. The decision rule is

$$\text{Reject } H_0 \text{ if } t_{24} > +2.0639$$
$$\text{or if } t_{24} < -2.0639;$$
$$\text{otherwise do not reject } H_0.$$

Using Equation (11.2), we have

$$t_{24} = \frac{364.1 - 368}{\dfrac{17.3}{\sqrt{25}}} = -1.127$$

TABLE 11.2 Determining the critical value from the t table for an area of .025 in each tail with 24 degrees of freedom

Degrees of Freedom	Upper-Tail Areas					
	.25	.10	.05	.025	.01	.005
1	1.0000	3.0777	6.3138	12.7062	31.8207	63.6574
2	0.8165	1.8856	2.9200	4.3027	6.9646	9.9248
3	0.7649	1.6377	2.3534	3.1824	4.5407	5.8409
4	0.7407	1.5332	2.1318	2.7764	3.7469	4.6041
5	0.7267	1.4759	2.0150	2.5706	3.3649	4.0322
.	.	.	.	.	.	.
.	.	.	.	.	.	.
21	0.6864	1.3232	1.7207	2.0796	2.5177	2.8314
22	0.6858	1.3212	1.7171	2.0739	2.5083	2.8188
23	0.6853	1.3195	1.7139	2.0687	2.4999	2.8073
24	0.6848	1.3178	1.7109	2.0639	2.4922	2.7969
25	0.6844	1.3163	1.7081	2.0595	2.4851	2.7874

SOURCE: Extracted from Table E.3.

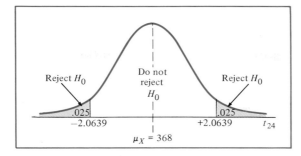

FIGURE 11.3
Testing a hypothesis about the mean (σ_x unknown) at the .05 level of significance with 24 degrees of freedom.

Since $t_{24} = -1.127$, we see that $-2.0639 < -1.127 < +2.0639$. Thus our decision is to not reject H_0. We would conclude that the average amount filled is 368 grams. Alternatively, to take into account the possibility of a Type II error, we may phrase the conclusion as "There is no evidence that the average is different from 368 grams."

Problems

11.18   Referring to Problem 10.11 on page 318, is there evidence that the average amount held in passbook savings accounts by depositors is different from $5,000? (Use the $\alpha = .05$ level of significance.)

● **11.19**   The manager of the credit department for an oil company would like to determine whether the average monthly balance of credit card holders is equal to $75. An auditor selects a random sample of 100 accounts and finds that the average owed is $83.40 with a sample standard deviation of $23.65. Using the .05 level of significance, should the auditor conclude that there is evidence that the average balance is different from $75?

11.20   Referring to Problem 10.12 on page 318, at the .10 level of significance is there evidence to enable the personnel manager to conclude that the average family dental expenses of all employees is different from $200?

11.21   Referring to Problem 3.73 on page 76, is there evidence that the average cost per dose of pain reliever is different from 6 cents? (Use the .01 level of significance.)

11.22   Referring to Problem 3.76 on page 78, is there any evidence that the average projected change in GNP is different from 2.0? (Use the .10 level of significance.)

11.23   Referring to Problem 3.70 on page 75, is there any evidence that the average price of compact disk players is different from $600? (Use the .05 level of significance.)

11.24   Referring to Problem 3.71 on page 75, is there any evidence that the average price of high fidelity video cassette recorders is different from $1,000? (Use the .01 level of significance.)

11.7 ONE-TAILED TESTS

In Section 11.4 we examined the question of whether the population average amount was 368 grams. The alternative hypothesis contained two possibilities: either the average could be less than 368 grams or the average could be more than 368 grams. For this reason the rejection region was divided into two tails of the distribution. In many instances, however, the alternative hypothesis focuses in a particular direction. For example, we mentioned in Section 11.2 that the representative of the Office of Consumer

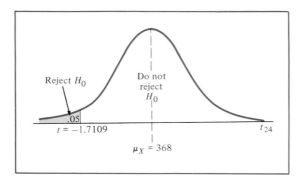

FIGURE 11.4
One-tailed test of hypothesis for a mean (σ_x unknown) at the .05 level of significance with 24 degrees of freedom.

Affairs would only be concerned with "shortweighting" and thus would only be interested in whether the average amount was *below* 368 grams. This would mean that unless the sample mean was "significantly" below 368 grams, the process would be considered to be working properly. The null and alternative hypotheses would be stated as follows:

$$H_0: \quad \mu_x \geq 368 \quad \text{(working properly)}$$

$$H_1: \quad \mu_x < 368 \quad \text{(not working properly)}$$

The rejection region would be entirely contained in the lower tail of the distribution since we want to reject H_0 only when the sample mean is significantly below 368 grams. If we again use an α level of .05, the critical value on the t distribution can be determined. Since the entire rejection region of .05 is in the lower tail of the distribution, the critical value (see Table E.3) will be -1.7109 (see Figure 11.4).

Thus the decision would be to reject the null hypothesis if the sample statistic is below -1.7109, otherwise do not reject the null hypothesis. For the data of Section 11.6, since $t_{24} = -1.127 > -1.7109$, our conclusion would be to not reject H_0 and state that there is no evidence that the average amount is below 368 grams.

Problems

● **11.25** Referring to Problem 10.7 on page 314, based on the sample data is there evidence that the true average amount of soft drink in the bottles is less than two liters? (Use the $\alpha = .01$ level of significance.)

11.26 The Glen Valley Steel Company manufactures steel bars. The production process turns out steel bars with an average length of at least 2.8 feet when the process is *working properly*. A sample of 25 bars is selected from the production line. The sample indicates an average length of 2.43 feet and a standard deviation of .20 foot. The company wishes to determine whether the production equipment needs any adjustment.
(a) State the null and alternative hypotheses.
(b) If the company wishes to test the hypothesis at the .05 level of significance, what decision would it make?

11.27 Referring to Problem 3.68 on page 74 and using the .05 level of significance:
(a) Is there evidence that the average price per 8 ounces of sparkling spring and mineral water is *greater than* 30 cents?
(b) What assumption is necessary to perform this test?

● **11.28**   Referring to Problem 10.17 on page 319 and using a level of significance of .01, is there evidence that the population mean waiting time in the past year is greater than 90 days?

11.29   A large nationwide chain of home improvement centers is having an end-of-season clearance of lawnmowers. The number of lawnmowers sold during this sale at a sample of 10 stores was as follows:

$$8 \quad 11 \quad 0 \quad 4 \quad 7 \quad 8 \quad 10 \quad 5 \quad 8 \quad 3$$

(a) At the .05 level of significance, is there evidence that an average of more than 5 lawnmowers per store have been sold during this sale?

(b) What assumption is necesssary to perform this test?

11.30   Referring to the data of Problem 3.74 on page 77, is there evidence that the average price of an IBM PC/XT compatible system is less than $1,000? (Use the .01 level of significance.)

11.31   Referring to the data of Problem 3.75 on page 78, is there evidence that the average price of spreadsheet products is below $400? (Use the .01 level of significance.)

11.32   Referring to the data of Problem 3.72 on page 76, is there evidence that the average price of compact microwave ovens is below $250? (Use the .05 level of significance.)

11.8 TEST OF HYPOTHESIS FOR A PROPORTION (ONE SAMPLE)

In the preceding sections we used hypothesis-testing procedures for quantitative data (means). The concept of hypothesis testing can also be used to test hypotheses about qualitative data. In our study, for example, the quality control manager wanted to determine whether there was evidence that (under the new system) the proportion of defective packages had been reduced below .10. In terms of proportions rather than percentages, the null and alternative hypotheses can be stated as follows:

$$H_0: \quad p \geq .10$$

$$H_1: \quad p < .10$$

We recall that although the *number of successes* follows a binomial distribution, if the sample size is large enough (both $np \geq 5$ and $n(1 - p) \geq 5$), the normal distribution provides a good approximation to the binomial distribution (see Section 8.4). Here our test statistic can be stated in two forms, in terms of either the *proportion* of successes [see Equation (11.3)] or the *number* of successes [see Equation (11.4)]:

$$Z \cong \frac{p_s - p}{\sqrt{\dfrac{p(1 - p)}{n}}} \tag{11.3}$$

where

$$p_s = \frac{X}{n} = \frac{\text{number of successes in sample}}{\text{sample size}} = \text{observed proportion of successes}$$

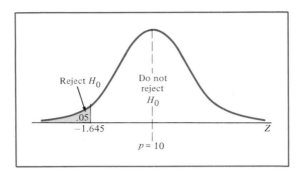

FIGURE 11.5
One-tailed test of hypothesis for a proportion at the .05 level of significance.

p = proportion of successes from the null hypothesis

or

$$Z \cong \frac{X - np}{\sqrt{np(1 - p)}} \qquad (11.4)$$

Aside from possible rounding errors, both formulas will provide the same solution for Z.

Suppose that the results of a sample of 200 packages indicate that 11 need rework. If a level of significance α of .05 is selected, the rejection and nonrejection regions would be set up as shown in Figure 11.5, and the decision rule would be

Reject H_0 if $Z < -1.645$; otherwise do not reject H_0.

From our data,

$$p_S = \frac{11}{200} = .055$$

Using Equation (11.3) we have

$$Z \cong \frac{p_S - p}{\sqrt{\dfrac{p(1 - p)}{n}}} = \frac{.055 - .10}{\sqrt{\dfrac{.10(.90)}{200}}} = \frac{-.045}{\sqrt{.00045}} = \frac{-.045}{.0212} = -2.12.$$

or using Equation (11.4), we have

$$Z = \frac{X - np}{\sqrt{np(1 - p)}} = \frac{11 - 200(.10)}{\sqrt{200(.10)(.90)}} = \frac{11 - 20}{\sqrt{18}} = \frac{-9}{4.243} = -2.12$$

Since $-2.12 < -1.645$, we reject H_0. Thus, the manager may conclude that there is evidence that the proportion of defectives with the new system is less than .10.

Problems

✗ **11.33**   Prove that the formula on the right-hand side of Equation (11.3) is equivalent to the formula on the right-hand side of Equation (11.4).

11.34   Referring to the data of Problem 10.34 on page 323, if the advertising director claims that at least 45% of all high-school students are familiar with the commercial, is this claim valid or is there evidence that the claim is not valid? (Use the .05 level of significance.)

11.35   A television manufacturer had claimed in its warranty that in the past only 10% of its television sets needed any repair during their first two years of operation. In order to test the validity of this claim a government testing agency selects a sample of 100 sets and finds that 14 sets required some repair within their first two years of operation. Using the .01 level of significance, is the manufacturer's claim valid or is there evidence that the claim is not valid?

11.36   Referring to Problem 10.30 on page 322, suppose that the health insurance company is expected to process half of all claims within two months of their receipt. Based upon the data of Problem 10.30, at the .05 level of significance is there evidence that the insurance company is not processing (within two months) the proportion of claims that is expected?

● **11.37**   Referring to Problem 10.31 on page 322, suppose that in the past, .35 of the customers of an automobile dealer owned the same cars that they purchased five years earlier. Based upon the data of Problem 10.31, is there evidence that the proportion has changed? (Use a level of significance of .10.)

11.38   Referring to Problem 4.102 on page 130, suppose that a random sample of 200 individuals, taken in 1988, indicates that 52 preferred Classic Coke to other soft drinks. At the .01 level of significance, is there evidence that the proportion has changed from the 1987 market share?

11.39   Referring to Problem 10.32 on page 322, is there evidence that the proportion of defective pens is greater than .05 (and that the shipment can be returned)? (Use the .10 level of significance.)

11.9   A CONNECTION BETWEEN CONFIDENCE INTERVALS AND HYPOTHESIS TESTING

In the last two chapters we have examined the two major areas of statistical inference: confidence intervals and hypothesis testing. They are based on the same set of concepts, but we have used them for different purposes. We used confidence intervals to estimate parameters, while we used hypothesis testing in making decisions about specified values of population parameters.

In many situations we can use confidence intervals to do a test of a null hypothesis. This can be illustrated for the test of a hypothesis for a mean. Referring back to the cereal filling process, we first attempted to determine whether the population average amount was different from 368 grams. We tested this in Section 11.6 using the formula

$$t_{n-1} = \frac{\overline{X} - \mu_X}{\dfrac{S}{\sqrt{n}}} \tag{11.2}$$

We could also solve the problem by obtaining a confidence-interval estimate of μ_X. If the hypothesized value of $\mu_X = 368$ fell into the interval, the null hypothesis would not be rejected. That is, the value 368 would not be considered unusual for the data observed. On the other hand, if it did not fall into the interval, the null hypothesis would be rejected, because 368 would then be an unusual value. Using Equation (10.2), the confidence-interval estimate could be set up from the following data:

$$n = 25, \quad S = 17.3, \quad \overline{X} = 364.1$$

For a confidence level of 95% (corresponding to a .05 level of significance—that is, $\alpha = .05$) we have

$$\overline{X} \pm t_{n-1} \frac{S}{\sqrt{n}}$$

$$364.1 \pm (2.0639) \frac{17.3}{\sqrt{25}} = 364.1 \pm 7.141$$

so that

$$356.959 \leq \mu_X \leq 371.241$$

Since the interval includes the hypothesized value of 368, we would not reject the null hypothesis. This, of course, was the same decision we reached by using the hypothesis-testing technique. However, we should realize that if a one-tailed test of hypothesis was utilized, we would not be able to directly compare it with the results of the confidence-interval estimate, which is based on an area on both sides of the sample statistic (i.e., the sample mean).

Problems

11.40 Compare the conclusions obtained from Problems 10.6 and 11.13 on pages 314 and 342. Are the conclusions the same? Why?

11.41 Compare the conclusions obtained from Problems 10.11 and 11.18 on pages 318 and 345. Are the conclusions the same? Why?

• **11.42** Referring to Problem 11.19 on page 345
(a) Set up a 95% confidence-interval estimate of the average monthly balance of credit-card holders.
(b) Is the value of $75 included within the confidence interval?
(c) Use the results of (b) to determine whether the average credit-card balance is equal to $75.

11.43 Compare the results obtained from Problems 10.17 and 11.28 on pages 319 and 347. Are the conclusions the same? Why?

11.44 Why shouldn't we compare the results obtained from the confidence interval in Problem 10.7 with the results of the test of hypothesis in Problem 11.25? (See pages 314 and 346.)

11.10 HYPOTHESIS TESTING AND THE REAL ESTATE SURVEY

Now that we have discussed the basic concepts of hypothesis testing by referring to the cereal filling process, we shall return to the real estate survey. Suppose that prior to the collection of the data, the president of the real estate company wanted answers to the following two questions:

1. Is the average appraised value in East Meadow equal to $200,000?
2. Do 30% of all the houses have a modern kitchen? (i.e., the same percentage as in other geographical areas in which the company is located)?

The results necessary to answer these questions are summarized in Table 11.3.

For the first question of interest to the president of the real estate company the null and alternative hypothesis would be

$$H_0: \quad \mu_X = 200$$

$$H_1: \quad \mu_X \neq 200$$

TABLE 11.3   Summary table from real estate survey

For East Meadow Residents

$\overline{X}$ = 215.23 thousands of dollars
S = 38.49 thousands of dollars
n = 74

For Three Geographic Locations

80 houses have a modern kitchen
n = 233 houses

Suppose it was desired to make this test at the .01 level of significance. Since there were 74 East Meadow residents in the sample, we would have $74 - 1 = 73$ degrees of freedom and, from Table E.3, the critical values at the .01 level of significance would be ± 2.6449 (since the rejection region is divided into the two tails of the distribution) as shown in Figure 11.6. The decision rule would be

$$\text{Reject } H_0 \text{ if } t_{73} > +2.6449$$
$$\text{or if } t_{73} < -2.6449;$$
$$\text{otherwise do not reject } H_0.$$

Since the sample results for East Meadow residents were $\overline{X} = 215.23$, $S = 38.49$, and $n = 74$, using Equation (11.2) we have

$$t = \frac{215.23 - 200}{\dfrac{38.49}{\sqrt{74}}} = \frac{15.23}{4.474} = +3.40$$

Since $t_{73} = 3.40 > 2.6449$, reject H_0.

Therefore we would conclude that the average appraised values of houses in East Meadow is different from \$200,000.

To evaluate the second question of interest to the president of the real estate

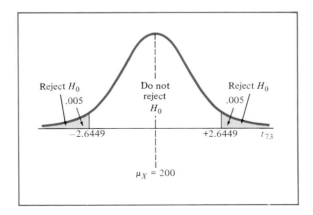

FIGURE 11.6
Testing a hypothesis about the mean (σ_X unknown) at the .01 level of significance with 73 degrees of freedom.

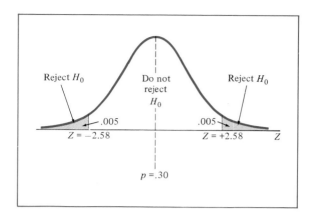

FIGURE 11.7
Two-tailed test of hypothesis for a proportion at the .01 level of significance.

company (regarding the proportion of houses that have a modern kitchen), the null and alternative hypotheses would be

$$H_0\!: p = .30$$

$$H_1\!: p \neq .30$$

Using Equation (11.4) for testing a hypothesis about a proportion and again selecting the .01 level of significance, we have the following decision rule (see Figure 11.7):

Reject H_0 if $Z > +2.58$
or if $Z < -2.58$;
otherwise do not reject H_0.

Out of a total of 233 houses in the overall sample, 80 had a modern kitchen. For these data, using Equation (11.4), we have

$$Z = \frac{X - np}{\sqrt{np(1-p)}} = \frac{80 - 233(.30)}{\sqrt{233(.30)(1-.30)}} = \frac{80 - 69.9}{\sqrt{48.93}} = \frac{10.1}{6.995} = +1.44$$

Since $-2.58 < Z = +1.44 < +2.58$, do not reject H_0.

The conclusion would be reached that there is no evidence that the proportion of houses with a modern kitchen is different from .30.

Problems

☐ **11.45** Referring to the first question of interest to the president of the real estate company (Is the average appraised value of houses in East Meadow equal to $200,000?)
(a) Explain the meaning of the Type I error in this situation.
(b) Explain the meaning of the Type II error in this situation.

☐ **11.46** Referring to the second question of interest to the president of the real estate company (Is the proportion of houses with a modern kitchen equal to .30?)
(a) Explain the meaning of the Type I error in this situation.
(b) Explain the meaning of the Type II error in this situation.

11.11 POWER OF A TEST

11.11.1 Development

In our initial discussions of statistical hypothesis testing we defined the two types of risks that are taken when decisions are made about population parameters based only upon sample evidence.

α represents the probability that the null hypothesis is rejected when in fact it is true and should not be rejected. β represents the probability that the null hypothesis is not rejected when in fact it is false and should be rejected. The power of the test (which is $1 - \beta$, the complement of β) indicates the sensitivity of the statistical procedure in detecting changes which have occurred by measuring the probability of rejecting the null hypothesis when it is false and should be rejected. The power of the statistical test depends upon how different the true mean really is from the value being hypothesized (under H_0). If there is a large difference between the true mean and the hypothesized mean, the power of the test will be much greater than if the difference between the population mean and the hypothesized mean is small.

In this section the concept of the power of a statistical test will be further developed from our cereal box filling example. In Section 11.7 we noted that the representative from the Office of Consumer Affairs was interested in determining whether there was evidence that the cereal boxes had an average amount that was less than 368 grams. The null and alternative hypotheses were set up as follows:

$$H_0: \quad \mu_X \geq 368 \text{ (process working properly)}$$
$$H_1: \quad \mu_X < 368 \text{ (process not working properly)}$$

Let us assume as in Section 11.4 that the true standard deviation σ_X is equal to 15 grams. If a level of significance (α risk) of .05 is selected and a random sample of 25 boxes is obtained, the value of $\overline{X}$ that will enable us to reject the null hypothesis can be found from Equation (9.6a) as follows:

$$\overline{X}_L = \mu_X - Z \frac{\sigma_X}{\sqrt{n}}$$

Since we have a one-tailed test with a level of significance of .05, the value of Z equal to 1.645 standard deviations *below* the hypothesized mean can be obtained from Table E.2 (see Figure 11.8). Therefore,

$$\overline{X}_L = 368 - (1.645) \frac{15}{\sqrt{25}} = 368 - 4.935 = 363.065$$

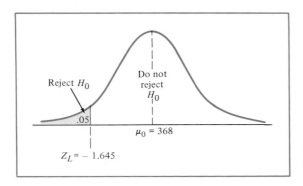

FIGURE 11.8
Determining the lower critical value for a one-tailed test for a population mean at the .05 level of significance.

The decision rule for this one-tailed test would be

$$\text{Reject } H_0 \text{ if } \overline{X} < 363.065; \text{ otherwise do not reject } H_0.$$

The decision rule states that if a random sample of 25 boxes reveals a sample mean of less than 363.065 grams, the null hypothesis will be rejected and the representative will conclude that the process is not working properly. If in fact this is the case, the power of the test measures the probability of concluding that the process is not working properly for differing values of the true population mean.

Suppose, for example, we would like to determine the chance of rejecting the null hypothesis when the true population mean is actually 360 grams. Based on our decision rule, we need to determine the probability or area under the normal curve below 363.065 grams. From the central limit theorem and the assumption of normality in the population, we may assume that the sampling distribution of the mean follows a normal distribution. Therefore the area under the normal curve below 363.065 grams can be expressed in standard deviation units, since we are finding the probability of rejecting the null hypothesis when the true mean has shifted to 360 grams (see Figure 11.9). Using Equation (11.1), we have

$$Z = \frac{\overline{X} - \mu_1}{\dfrac{\sigma_X}{\sqrt{n}}}$$

where μ_1 is the true population mean. Thus

$$Z = \frac{363.065 - 360}{\dfrac{15}{\sqrt{25}}} = +1.02$$

From Table E.2, there is a 34.61% chance of observing a Z value between the mean and $+1.02$ standard deviations. Since we wish to determine the area below 363.065, the area under the curve below the mean (50%) must be added to this value, and the power of the test is found to be 84.61%. β, the probability that the null hypothesis ($\mu_X = 368$) will not be rejected is $1 - .8461 = .1539$ (or 15.39%). This is the probability of committing a Type II error.

Now that we have determined the power of the test if the population mean were really equal to 360 we can also calculate the power for any other value that μ_X could attain. For example, what would be the power of the test if the population mean were

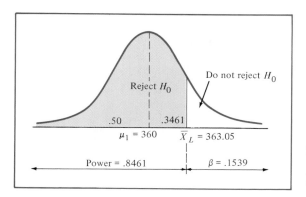

FIGURE 11.9
Determining the power of the test and the probability of a Type II error when $\mu_1 = 360$.

really equal to 352 grams? Assuming the same standard deviation, sample size, and level of significance, the decision rule would still be

$$\text{Reject } H_0 \text{ if } \overline{X} < 363.065; \text{ otherwise do not reject } H_0$$

Once again, since we are testing a hypothesis for a mean, from Equation (11.1) we have

$$Z = \frac{\overline{X} - \mu_1}{\dfrac{\sigma_X}{\sqrt{n}}}$$

If the population mean shifts down to 352 grams (see Figure 11.10), then

$$Z = \frac{363.065 - 352}{\dfrac{15}{\sqrt{25}}} = +3.69$$

From Table E.2, there is a 49.989% chance of observing a Z value between the mean and $+3.69$ standard deviations. Since we wish to determine the area below 363.065, the area under the curve below the mean (50%) must be added to this value, and the power of the test is found to be 99.989%. β, the probability that the null hypothesis ($\mu_X = 368$) will not be rejected is $1 - .99989 = .00011$ (or .011%). This is the probability of committing a Type II error.

In the preceding two cases we have found that the power of the test was quite high, while, conversely, the chance of committing a Type II error was quite low. In our next example we shall compute the power of the test if the population mean were really equal to 367 grams—a value which is very close to the hypothesized mean of 368 grams.

Once again, from Equation (11.1), since we are testing a hypothesis about a mean, we have

$$Z = \frac{\overline{X} - \mu_1}{\dfrac{\sigma_X}{\sqrt{n}}}$$

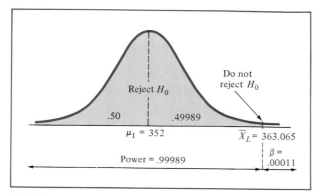

FIGURE 11.10
Determining the power of the test and the probability of a Type II error when $\mu_1 = 352$ grams.

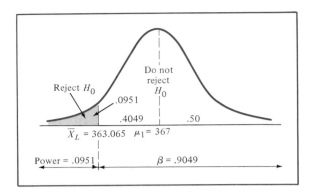

FIGURE 11.11
Determining the power of the test and the probability of a Type II error when $\mu_1 = 367$ grams.

If the population mean were really equal to 367 grams (see Figure 11.11), then

$$Z = \frac{363.065 - 367}{\dfrac{15}{\sqrt{25}}} = -1.31$$

so that

$$\begin{array}{r} .5000 \\ -.4049 \\ \hline .0951 \end{array} = \text{power} = 1 - \beta$$

From Table E.2, we can observe that the probability (area under the curve) between the mean and -1.31 standard deviation units is .4049 (40.49%).

Since, in this instance, the rejection region is in the lower tail of the distribution, the power of the test is 9.51%, while the chance of making a Type II error is 90.49%.

Figure 11.12 illustrates the power of the test for various possible values of μ_1 (including, of course, the three cases that we have examined). This is called a **power curve.** The computations for our three cases are summarized in Figure 11.13 on page 358.

From Figure 11.12 we observe that the power of this one-tailed test increases sharply (and approaches 100%) as the true population mean takes on values farther below the hypothesized 368 grams. Clearly, for this one-tailed test the smaller the true mean μ_1 is when compared to the hypothesized mean, the greater will be the power to detect this disparity.[1] On the other hand, for values of μ_1 close to 368 grams the power is rather small, since the test is unable to effectively detect small differences between the true population mean and the hypothesized value of 368 grams. If the population mean were actually 368 grams then the power of the test would be equal to α, the level of significance (which is .05 in this example), since the null hypothesis would actually be true.

The drastic changes in the power of the test for differing values of the true population means can be observed by reviewing the different panels of Figure 11.13.

---

[1] Of course, for situations involving one-tailed tests in which the actual mean μ_1 really exceeds the hypothesized mean, the converse would be true. The larger the actual mean μ_1 would be when compared with the hypothesized mean, the greater would be the power. On the other hand, for two-tailed tests, the greater the *distance* between the actual mean μ_1 and the hypothesized mean, the greater the power of the test.

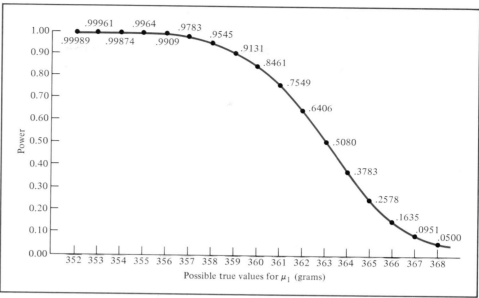

FIGURE 11.12
Power curve of the cereal fill process for an alternative hypothesis $\mu_x < 368$.

From panels A and B we can see that when the population mean does not greatly differ from 368 grams, the chance of rejecting the null hypothesis, based upon the decision rule involved, is not large. However, once the true population mean shifts substantially below the hypothesized 368 grams, the power of the test greatly increases, approaching its maximum value of 100%.

In our discussion of the power of a statistical test we have utilized a one-tailed test, a level of significance of .05, and a sample size of 25 boxes. With this in mind we can determine the effect on the power of the test by varying

1. The type of statistical test—one-tailed versus two-tailed.
2. The level of significance α.
3. The sample size n.

11.11.2 The Effects on Power of Changes in the Type of Statistical Test

In formulating the null hypothesis in Section 11.11.1, we noted that the representative desired to reject the null hypothesis only when the mean fill was significantly below 368 grams (one-tailed test). The question that we now wish to answer is: what would be the effect on the power of the test if the representative wanted to reject the null hypothesis when the mean fill was significantly *different* from 368 grams? In this case we would have a two-tailed test that would be set up as follows:

$$H_0: \quad \mu_X = 368 \text{ grams}$$
$$H_1: \quad \mu_X \neq 368 \text{ grams}$$

If we assume that the level of significance is still .05, the standard deviation is still 15 grams, and the sample size is still 25 boxes, then from Equations (9.6a) and

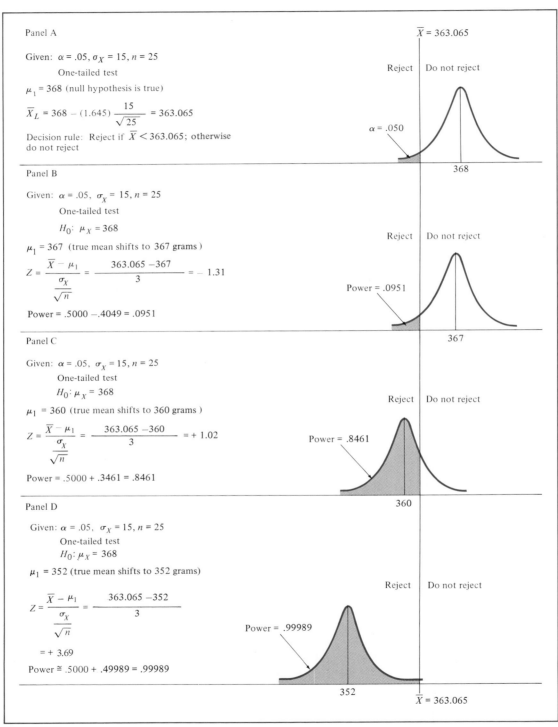

FIGURE 11.13
Determining statistical power for varying values of the true population mean.

(9.6b) we may determine the values of $\overline{X}_L$ and $\overline{X}_U$ which would cause us to reject the null hypothesis:

$$\overline{X}_L = \mu_X - Z\frac{\sigma_X}{\sqrt{n}}$$

and

$$\overline{X}_U = \mu_X + Z\frac{\sigma_X}{\sqrt{n}}$$

Here, however, the total level of significance of .05 is contained in both rejection regions, so that, from Table E.2, the appropriate Z value is 1.96 (see Figure 11.14). $\overline{X}_L$, the lower critical value of $\overline{X}$, would be obtained from

$$\overline{X}_L = 368 - (1.96)\frac{15}{\sqrt{25}} = 368 - 5.88 = 362.12$$

while $\overline{X}_U$, the upper critical value of $\overline{X}$, would be obtained from

$$\overline{X}_U = 368 + (1.96)\frac{15}{\sqrt{25}} = 368 + 5.88 = 373.88$$

Therefore, the decision rule for the two-tailed test would be

Reject H_0 if $\overline{X} > 373.88$
or if $\overline{X} < 362.12$;
otherwise do not reject H_0.

Now that the decision rule has been established, we can find the power of the test for the case in which the population mean is really 360 grams. We may recall from panel C of Figure 11.13 that for the particular one-tailed test the power was 84.61%. Using our decision rule for the two-tailed test, we now need to find the probability that a sample mean will fall below 362.12 grams or above 373.88 grams if the true mean is really 360 grams. Using Equation (11.1) for these data, we would have

$$Z_U = \frac{\overline{X}_U - \mu_1}{\dfrac{\sigma_X}{\sqrt{n}}} \quad \text{and} \quad Z_L = \frac{\overline{X}_L - \mu_1}{\dfrac{\sigma_X}{\sqrt{n}}}$$

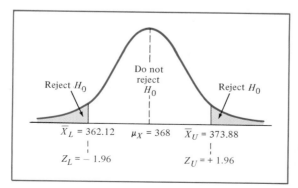

FIGURE 11.14
Determining the lower and upper critical values for a two-tailed test for a population mean at the .05 level of significance.

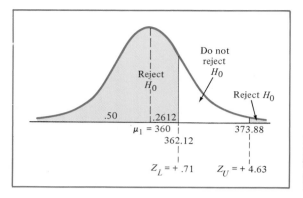

FIGURE 11.15
Determining the power of a two-tailed test and the probability of a Type II error when $\mu_1 = 360$ grams at the .05 level of significance.

Thus (see Figure 11.15)

$$Z_U = \frac{373.88 - 360}{\dfrac{15}{\sqrt{25}}} = +4.63$$

The area from the mean to Z_U is .5000. Moreover,

$$Z_L = \frac{362.12 - 360}{\dfrac{15}{\sqrt{25}}} = +0.71$$

The area from the mean to Z_L is .2612. The area between Z_L and $Z_U = .5000 - .2612 = .2388$. Hence,

$$\text{power} = 1 - .2388 = .7612$$

Since 373.88 grams is 4.63 standard deviation units above the population mean of 360, from Table E.2 we observe that the area under the normal curve between 373.88 and 360 grams is approximately .50. In a similar manner, the area between 362.12 and 360 grams is found to be .2612 (since 362.12 grams is .71 standard deviation unit above 360 grams). Therefore, the power of the test is equal to .7612 (or 76.12%) because the null hypothesis will be rejected if the sample mean is below 362.12 grams or above 373.88 grams. Comparing this result with the one obtained in panel C of Figure 11.13 illustrates that for given values of α, σ_X, and n, a one-tailed test is more powerful than a two-tailed test for a specified population mean. This result occurs because the one-tailed test places the rejection region entirely in one tail of the distribution. Thus the critical value of Z will be closer to zero than if a corresponding two-tailed test was performed, and rejection of the null hypothesis will be more likely.

Thus we may conclude that if we have prior information that leads us to test the null hypothesis against a specifically directed alternative, then a one-tailed test will provide a more powerful test than a two-tailed test. On the other hand, we should realize that if we are interested only in *differences* from the null hypothesis, not in the *direction* of the difference, the two-tailed test is the appropriate procedure to utilize.

11.11.3 Effects on Power of Changes in the Level of Significance

Now that we have examined the effect of a two-tailed test on the power of the test, we may also study the effect of the level of significance α on the power of the test. In Section 11.3 we mentioned that if α (the level of significance) is decreased, then, for a fixed sample size, the chance of a Type II error (β) will increase. Since β and power are complementary, if β were to increase, this would unfortunately result in a decrease in the power of the test. This effect can be observed by once again referring to panel C of Figure 11.13, where a one-tailed test was utilized with a sample size of 25 boxes. Now, however, let us select a level of significance of .01 rather than .05. Using Equation (9.6a), we have

$$\overline{X}_L = \mu_X - Z \frac{\sigma_X}{\sqrt{n}}$$

and, for these data (see Figure 11.16)

$$\overline{X}_L = 368 - (2.33) \frac{15}{\sqrt{25}} = 368 - 6.99 = 361.01$$

Therefore, the decision rule would be

Reject H_0 if $\overline{X} < 361.01$ grams;

otherwise do not reject H_0.

Now that the decision rule has been determined, the power of this one-tailed test can be found for the case in which the population mean is really 360 grams. Based on our decision rule, we would need to find the probability that the sample mean falls below 361.01 grams. Using Equation (11.1) with a population mean of 360 grams we have (see Figure 11.17 on page 362)

$$Z = \frac{361.01 - 360}{\frac{15}{\sqrt{25}}} = +0.34$$

so that

$$\text{power} = .50 + .1331 = .6331$$

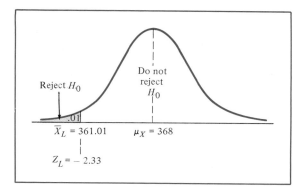

FIGURE 11.16
Determining the lower critical value for a one-tailed test for a population mean at the .01 level of significance.

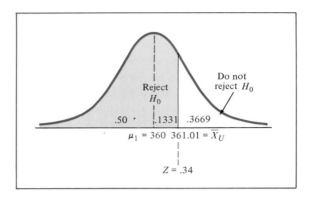

FIGURE 11.17
Determining the power of the test and the probability of a Type II error when $\mu_1 = 360$ grams at the .01 level of significance.

Since the critical value for 361.01 grams is .34 standard deviation unit above the population mean of 360 grams, from Table E.2 we may determine the probability to be .1331. Since the null hypothesis will be rejected when the sample mean is below 361.01 grams and since 50% of the values will be below the population mean of 360 grams, the power of the test will be 63.31%. Thus if we compare the resulting statistical power (63.31%) with the power of the test using a .05 level of significance (84.61%), we can see that the reduction in the level of significance from .05 to .01 produces a substantial reduction in the power of the test.

11.11.4 Effects on Power of Changes in Sample Size

Now that the effects on power of a two-tailed test and changes in the level of significance have each been studied using a fixed sample size, it becomes necessary to vary the sample size to determine its effect on statistical power. This effect can be seen by increasing the sample size from 25 to 100 boxes and determining the power of the one-tailed test at the .05 level of significance when the population mean is really 360 grams. Using Equation (9.6a), we have

$$\overline{X}_L = \mu_X - Z\frac{\sigma_X}{\sqrt{n}}$$

and thus, for a sample of 100 boxes (see Figure 11.18),

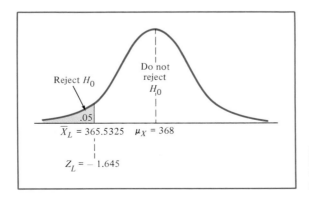

FIGURE 11.18
Determining the lower critical value for a one-tailed test for a population mean using a sample of size 100.

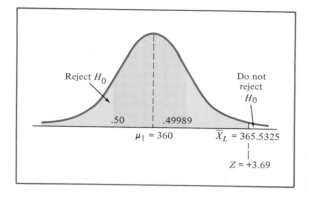

FIGURE 11.19
Determining the power of the test and the probability of a Type II error when $\mu_1 = 360$ grams with a sample of size 100.

$$\overline{X}_L = 368 - (1.645)\frac{15}{\sqrt{100}} = 368 - 2.4675 = 365.5325$$

Therefore, the decision rule for this problem containing a sample of 100 boxes would be

Reject H_0 if $\overline{X} < 365.5325$ grams; otherwise do not reject H_0.

The power of the test can be determined by finding the probability that the sample mean falls below 365.5325 grams when the population mean is actually 360 grams. Using Equation (11.1) for a true population mean of 360 grams, we have (see Figure 11.19)

$$Z = \frac{365.5325 - 360}{\dfrac{15}{\sqrt{100}}} = +3.69$$

Since 365.5325 is 3.69 standard deviation units above the population mean of 360 grams, from Table E.2 we may determine the probability of such an occurrence to be .49989. Since 50% of the mean values will be below 360 grams, the probability of obtaining a sample mean below 365.5325 miles will be .50000 + .49989 = .99989 (or 99.989%). Comparing this power with that which was obtained for a sample of 25 boxes (84.61%), as shown in Panel C of Figure 11.13, indicates that, other things remaining equal, an increase in sample size may sharply increase the power of the test.

11.11.5 Effects on Power: Summary of Findings

In examining the power of a statistical test we have observed that the type of test used (one-tailed versus two-tailed), the level of significance selected, and the sample size chosen each can seriously affect the results. A summary of our findings is presented in Figure 11.20 on page 364.

11.11.6 Determining Sample Size Based on α and β Risks

In planning a statistical study we have already seen in Section 10.5 that the desired sample size can be determined for a specified confidence level and sampling error. In a decision-making procedure such as hypothesis testing, however, assuming a one-

Conclusion 1—For a one-tailed test having a specified α, n, and σ_X, the greater the distance between
the actual mean μ_1 and the hypothesized mean, the
greater is the power of the test (provided the correct
direction of the alternative has been stated).
Note: For a two-tailed test having specified α, n, and
σ_X, the greater the distance between the actual mean
μ_1 and the hypothesized mean, the greater is the
power of the test.

Given: H_0: $\mu_X = 368$
$\alpha = .05$
$\sigma_X = 15$
$n = 25$
One-tailed test
If $\mu_1 = 360$, then power $= .8461$ (and $\beta = .1539$)
If $\mu_1 = 367$, then power $= .0951$ (and $\beta = .9049$)

Conclusion 2—For a specified α, n, σ_X, and actual
mean μ_1, a one-tailed test is more powerful than a
two-tailed test and, therefore, should be used whenever the researcher is able to specify the direction of
the alternative hypothesis.

Given: H_0: $\mu_X = 368$
$\alpha = .05$
$\sigma_X = 15$
$n = 25$
$\mu_1 = 360$
If a one-tailed test is used, then power $= .8461$ (and $\beta = .1539$)
If a two-tailed test is used, then power $= .7612$ (and $\beta = .2388$)

Conclusion 3—For a specified n, σ_X, type of test, and
actual mean μ_1, the larger the level of significance α
that is chosen, the smaller is the risk of Type II error
(β) and the greater is the power of the test.

Given: $\mu_X = 368$
$\sigma_X = 15$
$n = 25$
One-tailed test
$\mu_1 = 360$
If $\alpha = .05$, then power $= .8461$ (and $\beta = .1539$)
If $\alpha = .01$, then power $= .6331$ (and $\beta = .3669$)

Conclusion 4—For a specified α, σ_X, type of test, and
actual mean μ_1, the larger the sample size n that is
chosen, the greater is the power of the test.

Given: $\mu_X = 368$
$\sigma_X = 15$
$\alpha = .05$
One-tailed test
$\mu_1 = 360$
If $n = 25$, then power $= .8461$ (and $\beta = .1539$)
If $n = 100$, then power $= .99989$ (and $\beta = .00011$)

FIGURE 11.20
Studying the power of a test.

tailed test, we may determine the sample size needed for a desired level of significance α and the desired power of a test $(1 - \beta)$ as follows:

$$n = \frac{\sigma_X^2(Z_\alpha - Z_\beta)^2}{(\mu_0 - \mu_1)^2} \qquad (11.5)$$

where σ_X^2 = variance of the population
Z_α = Z value for a given α level of significance
Z_β = Z value for a given β risk of a Type II error
μ_0 = value of the population mean under the null hypothesis
μ_1 = value of the population mean under the alternative hypothesis

To demonstrate this sample-size determination procedure for a specified α and β risk, we may refer once again to our cereal filling process. If we assume that we wish to have an 80% chance (power) of rejecting the null hypothesis (of 368 grams) when the population mean is really equal to 360 grams and we are willing to accept

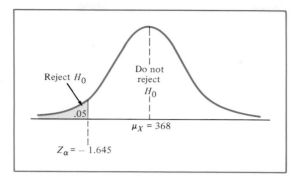

FIGURE 11.21
Determining the lower critical value in a one-tailed test for the population mean when the sample size is unknown.

an α risk of .05 (that is, 5%), what sample size is required? Using Equation (11.5), we have

$$ n = \frac{\sigma_X^2(Z_\alpha - Z_\beta)^2}{(\mu_0 - \mu_1)^2} $$

and, for the cereal filling process,

$$ \sigma_X = 15 \text{ grams} $$

$$ \mu_0 = 368 \text{ grams} $$

$$ \mu_1 = 360 \text{ grams} $$

Using a level of significance of $\alpha = .05$ for a one-tailed test, the rejection region can be established as follows (see Figure 11.21).

The Z_α value obtained from Table E.2 is equal to -1.645 because the rejection region contains .05 of the area under the normal curve (so that the area between the lower critical value and the null hypothesized mean of 368 grams is .45).

If a power of 80% is desired when the true population mean is 360 grams, the value of Z_β can also be obtained from Table E.2 (see Figure 11.22). Since we wish to have a power of 80% of rejecting a false null hypothesis (and hence a β risk of 20%), this results in an area of .30 between the true population mean of 360 grams and the critical value (which corresponds to .84 standard deviation unit above the true population mean).

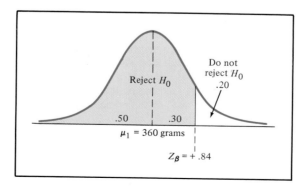

FIGURE 11.22
Determining the critical value for $\mu_1 = 360$ grams when the sample size is unknown.

Therefore, from Equation (11.5) the sample size would be found as follows:

$$n = \frac{(15)^2(-1.645 - .84)^2}{(368 - 360)^2}$$

$$n = \frac{(225)(-2.485)^2}{8^2} = 21.71$$

Hence $n = 22$.

A sample size of 22 boxes would be required if the manager were willing to have a .05 risk of making a Type I error and an 80% chance of rejecting the null hypothesis of 368 grams and detecting that the true population mean had actually shifted to 360 grams.

Problems

• **11.47** A coin-operated soft-drink machine was designed to discharge, when it is operating properly, at least 7 ounces of beverage per cup with a standard deviation of 0.2 ounce. If a random sample of 16 cupfuls is selected by a statistician for a consumer testing service, and the statistician is willing to have an α risk of .05, compute the power of the test and the probability of a Type II error (β) if the population average amount dispensed is
  (a) 6.9 ounces per cup
  (b) 6.8 ounces per cup
  (c) If the statistician wishes to have a power of 99% of detecting a shift in the population mean from 7.0 ounces to 6.9 ounces, what sample size must be selected?
  [*Note:* Assume the data are normally distributed.]

• **11.48** Refer to Problem 11.47. If the statistician wishes to have an α risk of .01, compute the power of the test and the probability of a Type II error (β) if the population average amount dispensed is
  (a) 6.9 ounces
  (b) 6.8 ounces
  (c) Compare the results in (a) and (b) of this problem and Problem 11.47.

• **11.49** Refer to Problem 11.47. If the statistician selected a random sample of 25 cupfuls, and used an α risk of .05, compute the power of the test and the probability of a Type II error (β) if the population average amount dispensed is
  (a) 6.9 ounces
  (b) 6.8 ounces
  (c) Compare the results in (a) and (b) of this problem and Problem 11.47.

11.50 A machine produces tires that last an average of at least 25,000 miles when it is working properly. Based upon past experience, the standard deviation of the tires is assumed to be 3,500 miles. The production manager will stop the production process if there is evidence that the average tire life is below 25,000 miles. If a random sample of 100 tires is selected (to be subjected to destructive testing), and the production manager is willing to have an α risk of .05, compute the power of the test and the probability of a Type II error (β) if the population average life is
  (a) 24,000 miles
  (b) 24,900 miles
  (c) If the production manager wishes to have 80% power of detecting a shift in the population mean from 25,000 miles to 24,000 miles, what sample size must be selected?
  [*Note:* Assume the data are normally distributed.]

11.51 Refer to Problem 11.50. If the production manager wishes to have an α risk of .01, compute the power of the test and the probability of a Type II error (β) if the population average life is
(a) 24,000 miles
(b) 24,900 miles
(c) Compare the results in (a) and (b) of this problem and (a) and (b) in Problem 11.50.

11.52 Refer to Problem 11.50. If the production manager selected a random sample of 25 tires and used an α risk of .05, compute the power of the test and the probability of a Type II error (β) if the population average life is
(a) 24,000 miles
(b) 24,900 miles
(c) Compare the results in (a) and (b) of this problem and (a) and (b) in Problem 11.50.

11.53 Refer to Problem 11.50. If the production manager will stop the process when there is evidence that the average life is different from 25,000 miles (either less than or greater than) and a random sample of 100 tires is selected with an α risk of .05, compute the power of the test and the probability of a Type II error (β) if the population average life is
(a) 24,000 miles
(b) 24,900 miles
(c) Compare the results in (a) and (b) of this problem and (a) and (b) in Problem 11.50.

11.54 A businessman was considering the establishment of a Sunday morning bagel delivery service in a local suburb. Based upon the cost of this service and the profits to be made, he has arrived at the following conclusion: If there is evidence that the average order will be more than 14 bagels per household in this suburban area, then the delivery service will be instituted. If no evidence can be demonstrated, the delivery service will not be instituted. Based on past experience with other suburbs, the standard deviation is estimated to be 3 bagels. A random sample of 36 households is to be surveyed. The businessman is willing to have a .01 risk that the service will be instituted when the average demand is at most 14 bagels per household.
(a) Compute the probability of instituting the bagel delivery service when the average demand is 15 bagels per household.
(b) Compute the probability of instituting the bagel delivery service when the average demand is 17 bagels per household.
(c) If the businessman wishes to have a 90% chance of instituting the bagel delivery service when the population average demand is 17 bagels, what sample size should be selected?
[*Note*: Assume the data are normally distributed.]

11.55 Refer to Problem 11.54. If the businessman is willing to have a .05 risk (rather than a .01 risk) that the service will be instituted when the average demand is at most 14 bagels per household, compute the probability of instituting the bagel delivery service when the average demand is
(a) 15 bagels per household
(b) 17 bagels per household
(c) Compare the results in (a) and (b) of this problem and Problem 11.54.

11.56 Refer to Problem 11.54. If the businessman selected a random sample of 64 households and is willing to have an α risk of .01, compute the probability of instituting the bagel delivery service when the average demand is
(a) 15 bagels per household
(b) 17 bagels per household
(c) Compare the results in (a) and (b) of this problem and Problem 11.54.

11.57 A large chain of discount toy stores would like to determine whether a certain toy should be sold. Based upon past experience with similar toys, the marketing director of the chain has decided that the toy will be marketed only if there is evidence that more than an average of 100 toys per month will be sold at each store. A random sample of 25 stores is selected for a test-marketing period of 1 month. Based on past experience, the standard deviation is estimated to be 10 toys. The marketing director is willing to have a .05 risk that the toy will be sold

when the average sale is no more than 100 toys per month. Compute the probability that the toy will be marketed when the population average number of toys sold is
(a) 105
(b) 108
(c) If the marketing director wishes to have a 98% chance of marketing the toy when the population average demand is 110 per month, how large a sample of stores must be selected?
[*Note*: Assume the data are normally distributed.]

11.58 Refer to Problem 11.57. If the marketing director is willing to have a .10 risk (rather than a .05 risk) of selling the toy when the average sale is no more than 100 toys per month, compute the probability that the toy will be marketed when the population average number of toys sold is
(a) 105
(b) 108
(c) Compare the results in (a) and (b) of this problem and Problem 11.57.

11.59 Refer to Problem 11.57. If the marketing director could only select a sample of 16 stores in which to test-market the toy, and is willing to have an α risk of .05, compute the probability of marketing that toy when the population average number of toys sold is
(a) 105
(b) 108
(c) Compare the results in (a) and (b) of this problem and Problem 11.57.

11.12 THE *p*-VALUE APPROACH TO HYPOTHESIS TESTING

In recent years an approach to hypothesis testing which has increasingly gained acceptance involves the concept of the ***p* value.**

The ***p* value** is the probability of obtaining a test statistic equal to or more extreme than the result observed, given H_0 is true.

The *p* value is often referred to as the *observed level of significance*, the smallest level at which H_0 can be rejected for a given set of data. If the *p* value is greater than or equal to α, the null hypothesis is not rejected; if the *p* value is smaller than α, the null hypothesis is rejected.

We may obtain a better understanding of the *p* value by referring to the examples studied in Sections 11.10 and 11.8.

In the real estate survey we tested whether or not the proportion of houses with a modern kitchen was equal to .30 (page 352). We obtained a Z value of +1.44 and did not reject the null hypothesis, since this was less than the upper critical value of +2.58. Using the *p* value approach, we could determine the probability of obtaining a Z value larger than +1.44. From Table E.2, this probability is .5000 − .4251 = .0749. Since we are performing a two-tailed test, we also need to find the probability of obtaining a value smaller than −1.44. Since the normal distribution is symmetric, this value is also .0749. Thus the *p* value for the two-tailed test is .1498 (see Figure 11.23). This result may be interpreted to mean that the probability of obtaining a more extreme result than the one observed is .1498. Since this is greater than α = .01, the null hypothesis is not rejected.

If a one-tailed test is under consideration, the *p* value represents the probability in only one tail of the distribution. In order to illustrate the computation of the *p* value for the one-tailed test, we may refer to the example concerning the proportion of defective packages (page 347). For this example, a Z value of −2.12 was obtained. Using the *p*-value approach, the probability of obtaining a Z value smaller than −2.12 is .5000 − .4830 = .0170 (see Figure 11.24). Since this is less than α = .05, the null hypothesis is rejected.

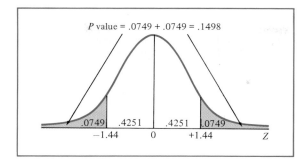

FIGURE 11.23
Determining the p value for a two-tailed test.

Unless we are dealing with the test statistic that follows the normal distribution, the computation of the exact p value is very difficult. Thus it is fortunate that statistical computer software such as SAS, SPSS^X, STATGRAPHICS, MYSTAT, and Minitab (see References 1–7) now present the p value as part of the output for many hypothesis-testing procedures. As an example, Figure 11.25 represents partial Minitab output for the average appraised value of East Meadow houses.

We may observe from Figure 11.25 that Minitab displays the null and alternative hypotheses and the level at which the test is significant (i.e., the p value). Here we observe that the p value is .0011. Since this is less than $\alpha = .01$, the null hypothesis may be rejected. If, on the other hand, the p value had exceeded .01, Minitab would have printed a message to inform the user of this lack of significance.

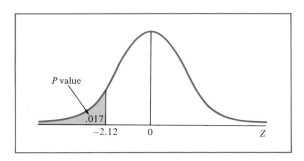

FIGURE 11.24
Determining the p value for a one-tailed test.

```
MTB > ttest of mu = 200 'value'

TEST OF MU = 200.00 VS MU N.E. 200.00
```

	N	MEAN	STDEV	SE MEAN	T	P VALUE
value	74	215.2	38.5	4.5	3.40	0.0011

FIGURE 11.25
Minitab output for a t test.

Problems

11.60   Why is it easier to compute the p value for a test statistic that follows the normal distribution than for one that follows the t distribution?

- **11.61** Compute the p value in Problem 11.13 on page 342 and interpret its meaning.
- **11.62** Compute the p value in Problem 11.25 on page 346 and interpret its meaning.
- **11.63** Compute the p value in Problem 11.36 on page 349 and interpret its meaning.
- **11.64** Compute the p value in Problem 11.34 on page 349 and interpret its meaning.
- **11.65** Compute the p value in Problem 11.35 on page 349 and interpret its meaning.
- **11.66** Using Table E.3, a t statistic of 2.25 with 25 degrees of freedom will have a p value that falls between .01 and .025 if the test is one tailed. Explain.
- **11.67** What will be the lower and upper limits of the p value for a t statistic of 1.0 with 35 degrees of freedom if the test is one-tailed?
- **11.68** In Problem 11.15 on page 342 find the p value and interpret its meaning.
- **11.69** In Problem 11.16 on page 342 find the p value and interpret its meaning.
- **11.70** In Problem 11.18 on page 345 find the lower and upper limits of the p value and interpret its meaning.
- **11.71** In Problem 11.24 on page 345 find the lower and upper limits of the p value and interpret its meaning.

Supplementary Problems

- **11.72** Distinguish between
  - **(a)** Null hypothesis and alternative hypothesis
  - **(b)** Type I error and Type II error
  - **(c)** One-tailed test and two-tailed test
  - **(d)** Region of nonrejection and region of rejection
- **11.73** The editor of a textbook publishing firm must decide whether to publish a textbook written by a particular professor. Based upon publication costs, the editor has arrived at the following conclusion. If there is evidence that more than 15% of the colleges in the country would consider adopting this textbook, then the textbook will be published. If no evidence can be demonstrated, the textbook will not be published. A random sample of 100 colleges will be selected.
  - **(a)** Explain the meaning of the Type I and Type II errors in this problem.
  - **(b)** Which error would be more important to the editor? Why?
  - **(c)** Which error would be more important to the professor? Why?
  - **(d)** Is this problem a one-tailed test or a two-tailed test? Explain.
  - **(e)** If the random sample of 100 colleges indicated that 25 would consider adopting this textbook, should the editor publish it? (Use a level of significance of .05.)
- **11.74** The personnel department of a large company would like to determine the amount of time it takes for employees to arrive at work. A random sample of 12 employees is selected and the time in minutes to arrive at work is recorded, with the following results:

  15   30   50   60   25   65   45   90   75   50   50   20

  - **(a)** At the .01 level of significance, is there evidence that the average travel time of employees is less than 60 minutes?
  - **(b)** What assumption is necessary to perform this test?
- **11.75** Referring to Problem 10.53 on page 332 and using a level of significance of .05, determine whether
  - **(a)** There is evidence that the average amount of viewing per week exceeds 12 hours.
  - **(b)** There is evidence that the proportion of respondents who watch the Evening News on at least three weeknights is different from .65.

11.76 Referring to Problem 10.55 on page 332 and using a level of significance of .01, determine whether
 (a) There is evidence that the population average number of days absent is greater than eight per year.
 (b) There is evidence that more than one-third of the clerical employees are absent more than 10 days.

11.77 Referring to Problem 10.56 on page 333 and using a level of significance of .10, determine whether
 (a) There is evidence that the average number of credits taken by students at the university is different from 16 per semester.
 (b) There is evidence that the proportion of full-time students is different from .80.

• **11.78** An auditor for the Department of Energy wishes to study the price of unleaded gasoline per gallon and the availability of diesel fuel in New York City. A random sample of 50 gas stations was selected, with the following results: $\bar{X} = \$1.20$; $S = \$.073$; 11 sold diesel fuel.
 (a) Is there evidence that the average price of unleaded gasoline is different from $1.30 per gallon? ($\alpha = .05$.)
 (b) Is there evidence that less than 25% of the gas stations sell diesel fuel? ($\alpha = .05$.)
 (c) If a similar study is to be planned for Westchester County and the auditor wishes to have 90% confidence of estimating the proportion of gas stations that sell diesel fuel to within $\pm .08$ of the true proportion, what sample size is needed?

11.79 Referring to Problem 3.87 on page 87 (pancake mixes and pancake syrup), at the .05 level of significance is there evidence
 (a) That the average cost per pancake is different from 10 cents?
 (b) That the average calories per pancake exceeds 70?
 (c) That the average amount of sodium is less than 250 mg?
 (d) That the average cost per serving of pancake syrup exceeds 30 cents?
 (e) That the average calories per serving of pancake syrup is less than 250 calories?
 (f) That the average amount of sodium per serving of pancake syrup is less than 120 mg?
 ➡**(g)** **ACTION** Do the results of parts (a)–(f) surprise you? Why? Discuss.

11.80 Referring to Problem 3.82 on page 81 (frozen turkey), at the .05 level of significance is there evidence
 (a) That the average cost per pound is different from $1.00?
 (b) That the average cost per pound of edible meat is different from $2.50?
 ➡**(c)** **ACTION** Incorporate the results in parts (a) and (b) in a newspaper article you are writing dealing with consumer affairs.

11.81 Referring to Problem 3.85 on page 84, at the .01 level of significance (for dark chocolate and milk chocolate separately) is there evidence
 (a) That the average cost per ounce is greater than 40 cents?
 (b) That the average amount of caffeine per ounce is different from 15 mg?
 (c) That the average percentage of cocoa mass is different from 15%?
 ➡**(d)** **ACTION** Based on the results of parts (a)–(c), what would you tell a meeting of Chocolate Lovers Anonymous concerning dark chocolate and milk chocolate?

11.82 Referring to Problem 3.83 on page 82, at the .01 level of significance is there evidence
 (a) That the average cost per ounce of salted peanut butter is greater than 15 cents?
 (b) That the average amount of sodium per ounce of salted peanut butter is greater than 200 mg?
 ➡**(c)** **ACTION** Use the results of parts (a) and (b) as part of a newspaper article about salted peanut butter.

11.83 Referring to Problem 3.86 on page 85, at the .10 level of significance (for beef, "meat," and poultry frankfurters separately) is there evidence
 (a) That the average cost per ounce is less than 15 cents?
 (b) That the average cost per pound of protein is greater than $15?

(c) That the average amount of calories per frank is less than 175?

(d) That the average amount of sodium per frank is greater than 450 mg?

➠**(e) ACTION**   Based on the results of parts (a)–(d), which type of frankfurter would you tell your neighbor to buy?

11.84   Referring to Problem 3.84 on page 83 (gas barbecue grills), at the .05 level of significance is there evidence

(a) That the average price exceeds $300?

(b) That the average shelf area is different from 500 square inches?

(c) That the average cooking grid area is less than 350 square inches?

(d) That the average maximum heat output is greater than 30 (in 000 BTU/hour)?

➠**(e) ACTION**   Use the results of parts (a)–(d) to provide information to your neighbor who is thinking of buying a gas barbecue grill.

Database Exercises

The following problems refer to the sample data obtained from the questionnaire of Figure 2.5 on page 15 and presented in Figure 2.10 on pages 24–29. They should be solved with the aid of an available computer package.

☐ **11.85**   At the .05 level of significance, is there evidence that the average appraised value (question 1) of houses in Levittown (question 9, code 3) is less than $175,000?

☐ **11.86**   At the .05 level of significance, is there evidence that the average number of bedrooms (question 3) is different from 3.5?

☐ **11.87**   At the .01 level of significance, is there evidence that the average number of rooms (question 5) in Levittown houses (question 9, code 3) is less than 7?

☐ **11.88**   At the .10 level of significance, is there evidence that the average age of houses (question 6) is less than 35 years?

☐ **11.89**   At the .05 level of significance, is there evidence that the average annual taxes (question 7) is different from $3,000?

☐ **11.90**   At the .05 level of significance, is there evidence that the average appraised value (question 1) of all houses is less than $200,000?

☐ **11.91**   At the .01 level of significance, is there evidence that the average lot size (question 2) in Levittown (question 9, code 3) exceeds 6,000 square feet?

☐ **11.92**   At the .10 level of significance, is there evidence that the average number of rooms (question 5) is different from 7.5?

☐ **11.93**   At the .05 level of significance

(a) Is there evidence that the proportion of houses in Levittown (question 9, code 3) with no indoor parking facility (question 8, code 1) is greater than .25?

(b) Determine the p value and interpret its meaning.

☐ **11.94**   At the .05 level of significance

(a) Is there evidence that the proportion of houses that are ''Capes'' (question 10, code 1) is different from .50?

(b) Determine the p value and interpret its meaning.

☐ **11.95**   At the .01 level of significance

(a) Is there evidence that more than 80% of the houses use oil heat (question 11, code 2)?

(b) Determine the p value and interpret its meaning.

☐ **11.96**   At the .10 level of significance

(a) Is there evidence that more than 80% of the houses have a hot water heating system (question 12, code 2)?

(b) Determine the p value and interpret its meaning.

☐ **11.97** At the .05 level of significance
(a) Is there evidence that the proportion of houses with either an in-ground or above-ground swimming pool (question 13, codes 2 and 3) is different from .20?
(ʋ) Determine the *p* value and interpret its meaning.

☐ **11.98** At the .01 level of significance
(a) Is there evidence that less than 10% of the houses have central air-conditioning (question 15, code 1)?
(b) Determine the *p* value and interpret its meaning.

☐ **11.99** At the .10 level of significance
(a) Is there evidence that the proportion of houses with a fireplace (question 16, code 1) is less than .50?
(b) Determine the *p* value and interpret its meaning.

☐ **11.100** At the .05 level of significance
(a) Is there evidence that the proportion of houses that are connected to a sewer system (question 17, code 1) is different from .90?
(b) Determine the *p* value and interpret its meaning.

☐ **11.101** At the .05 level of significance
(a) Is there evidence that the proportion of houses that have a basement (question 18, code 1) is greater than .50?
(b) Determine the *p* value and interpret its meaning.

☐ **11.102** At the .01 level of significance
(a) Is there evidence that the proportion of houses that have modern bathrooms (question 20, code 1) is greater than .25?
(b) Determine the *p* value and interpret its meaning.

References

1. LEVINE, D. M., M. L. BERENSON, AND D. F. STEPHAN, *Using Minitab with Basic Business Statistics*, 2d ed. (Englewod Cliffs, N.J.: Prentice-Hall, 1986).
2. LEVINE, D. M., M. L. BERENSON, AND D. F. STEPHAN, *Using SAS with Basic Business Statistics* (Englewood Cliffs, N.J.: Prentice-Hall, 1983).
3. *MYSTAT-A Personal Version of SYSTAT* (Evanston, IL: SYSTAT Inc., 1988).
4. RYAN, T. A., B. L. JOINER, AND B. F. RYAN, *Minitab Student Handbook*, 2d ed. (North Scituate, Mass.: Duxbury Press, 1985).
5. *SAS User's Guide*, 1982 ed. (Raleigh, N.C.: SAS Institute, 1982).
6. *SPSS^X User's Guide* (New York: McGraw-Hill, 1983).
7. *STATGRAPHICS User's Guide* (Rockville, Md.: STSC Inc., 1986).

12

Hypothesis Testing II: Differences between Quantitative Variables

12.1 INTRODUCTION

In the preceding chapter we examined hypothesis-testing procedures pertaining to whether a mean or a proportion was equal to some specified value. These usually are referred to as **one-sample tests,** since a single sample is selected from a population of interest and a computed statistic from the sample is compared with a hypothesized value. In this chapter we shall extend our discussion of hypothesis testing to consider additional procedures pertaining to quantitative data.

In Section 11.2 we considered various questions of interest to the production manager. In this chapter we consider other questions of concern. As examples, suppose that the manager and his supervisor also wanted to answer the following questions:

1. Is there evidence of a difference in the average amount of cereal filled per box in plant A as compared with plant B?
2. Since the manager wishes to minimize the amount of cereal spilled (and thereby wasted) during the filling process, is there evidence that the average amount spilled is less for a new type of machine than for the type currently being used?
3. Is there evidence that the variability of the amount being filled is higher for plant A than for plant B?

12.2 TESTING FOR THE DIFFERENCE BETWEEN THE MEANS OF TWO INDEPENDENT POPULATIONS HAVING EQUAL VARIANCES

Let us first extend the hypothesis-testing concepts developed in the previous chapter to situations in which we would like to determine whether there is any difference between the means of two independent populations. Suppose then that we consider two independent populations, each having a mean and standard deviation (symbolically represented as follows):

Population I	Population II
μ_1, σ_1	μ_2, σ_2

The test to be performed can be either two-tailed or one-tailed, depending on whether we are testing if the two population means are merely *different* or if one mean is *greater than* the other mean.[1]

Two-Tailed Test	One-Tailed Test	One-Tailed Test
$H_0: \mu_1 = \mu_2$ or $\mu_1 - \mu_2 = 0$	$H_0: \mu_1 \geq \mu_2$ or $\mu_1 - \mu_2 \geq 0$	$H_0: \mu_1 \leq \mu_2$ or $\mu_1 - \mu_2 \leq 0$
$H_1: \mu_1 \neq \mu_2$ or $\mu_1 - \mu_2 \neq 0$	$H_1: \mu_1 < \mu_2$ or $\mu_1 - \mu_2 < 0$	$H_1: \mu_1 > \mu_2$ or $\mu_1 - \mu_2 > 0$

where μ_1 = mean of population 1
μ_2 = mean of population 2

The statistic used to determine the difference between the population means is based upon the difference between the sample means $(\overline{X}_1 - \overline{X}_2)$. Because of the central limit theorem, the statistic will follow the normal distribution for large enough sample sizes. The test statistic is

$$Z = \frac{(\overline{X}_1 - \overline{X}_2) - (\mu_1 - \mu_2)}{\sqrt{\dfrac{\sigma_1^2}{n_1} + \dfrac{\sigma_2^2}{n_2}}} \qquad (12.1)$$

However, as we mentioned previously, in most cases we do not know the standard deviation of either of the two populations (σ_1, σ_2). The only information usually available is the sample means and sample standard deviations $(\overline{X}_1, \overline{X}_2; S_1, S_2)$. If the assumptions are made that each population is normally distributed and that the **population variances are equal** $(\sigma_1^2 = \sigma_2^2)$, a t test with $n_1 + n_2 - 2$ degrees of freedom can be used to determine whether there is any difference between the means of the two populations.

If a two-tailed test is to be used, the null and alternative hypotheses will be (see Figure 12.1 on page 376):

$$H_0: \quad \mu_1 = \mu_2 \text{ or } \mu_1 - \mu_2 = 0$$

$$H_1: \quad \mu_1 \neq \mu_2 \text{ or } \mu_1 - \mu_2 \neq 0$$

Since we have assumed equal variances in the two populations, the variances of the two samples (S_1^2, S_2^2) can be pooled together or combined to form one estimate (S_p^2) of the "common" population variance. The test statistic will be

---

[1] If the hypothesized difference is 0 (that is, $\mu_1 - \mu_2 = 0$ or $\mu_1 = \mu_2$), the numerator in Equations (12.1), (12.2), and (12.6) merely becomes $\overline{X}_1 - \overline{X}_2$.

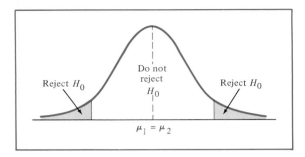

FIGURE 12.1
Rejection regions for the two-tailed test for the difference between two means.

$$t_{n_1 + n_2 - 2} = \frac{(\overline{X}_1 - \overline{X}_2) - (\mu_1 - \mu_2)}{\sqrt{S_p^2 \left(\frac{1}{n_1} + \frac{1}{n_2}\right)}}$$ (12.2)

where

$$S_p^2 = \frac{(n_1 - 1)S_1^2 + (n_2 - 1)S_2^2}{n_1 + n_2 - 2}$$

where S_p^2 = pooled variance of the two groups

$\overline{X}_1$ = sample mean in population 1

S_1^2 = sample variance in population 1

n_1 = sample size for population 1

$\overline{X}_2$ = sample mean in population 2

S_2^2 = sample variance in population 2

n_2 = sample size for population 2

In our study of the cereal-filling process, we may recall that we wanted to know whether there was any difference in the average amount filled per box between plants A and B. The results can be summarized as follows:

Plant A	Plant B
$\overline{X}_A = 366.35$	$\overline{X}_B = 369.74$
$S_A = 16.71$	$S_B = 14.20$
$n_A = 25$	$n_B = 20$

The null and alternative hypotheses for this example would be

$$H_0: \mu_A = \mu_B \text{ or } \mu_A - \mu_B = 0$$

$$H_1: \mu_A \neq \mu_B \text{ or } \mu_A - \mu_B \neq 0$$

If the test were conducted at the .01 level of significance, the t distribution with $25 + 20 - 2 = 43$ degrees of freedom would be utilized. Hence the critical values are $+2.6951$ and -2.6951 (see Figure 12.2), and the decision rule is

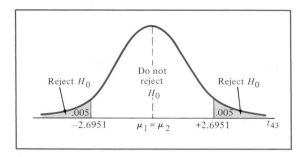

FIGURE 12.2
Two-tailed test of hypothesis for the difference between the means at the .01 level of significance.

Reject H_0 if $t_{43} > +2.6951$

or if $t_{43} < -2.6951$;

otherwise do not reject H_0.

For our data we have

$$t_{43} = \frac{\overline{X}_A - \overline{X}_B}{\sqrt{S_p^2 \left(\frac{1}{n_A} + \frac{1}{n_B}\right)}}$$

where[2]

$$S_p^2 = \frac{(n_A - 1)S_A^2 + (n_B - 1)S_B^2}{n_A + n_B - 2}$$

$$= \frac{24(16.71)^2 + 19(14.20)^2}{25 + 20 - 2}$$

$$= \frac{10{,}532.538}{43} = 244.943$$

$$t_{43} = \frac{366.35 - 369.74}{\sqrt{244.943 \left(\frac{1}{25} + \frac{1}{20}\right)}}$$

$$= \frac{-3.39}{\sqrt{22.045}} = \frac{-3.39}{4.695} = -0.72$$

Since we see that $-2.6951 < -0.72 < +2.6951$, we don't reject H_0.

The null hypothesis has not been rejected because the test statistic has not fallen into the rejection region. Therefore the manager and supervisor would conclude that there is no evidence of a difference in the average amount of fill per box between plant A and plant B.

In testing for the difference between the means, we have assumed normal distributions and equality of variances of the two populations. We must examine the

---

[2] In this example the two groups had unequal sample sizes. For the special case of equal sample sizes ($n_1 = n_2$), the formula for the pooled variance can be simplified. Thus if $n_1 = n_2$, then

$$S_p^2 = \frac{S_1^2 + S_2^2}{2}$$

consequences on the *t* test of departures from each of these assumptions. With respect to the assumption of normality, the *t* test is ''robust'' in that it is not sensitive to modest departures from normality. As long as the sample sizes are not extremely small, the assumption of normality can be violated without serious effect on the power of the test. The second assumption, equality of variances (see Section 12.4), creates what is called in statistics the **Behrens-Fisher problem** when it is violated. One widely used approach to this problem is presented in Section 12.5.

Problems

12.1 The quality control manager at a light bulb factory would like to determine if there is any difference in the average life of bulbs manufactured on two different types of machines. The process standard deviation for machine I is 110 hours and for machine II is 125 hours. A random sample of 25 light bulbs obtained from machine I indicated a sample mean of 375 hours, while a similar sample of 25 from machine II indicated a sample mean of 362 hours. Using the .05 level of significance, is there any evidence of a difference in the average life of bulbs produced by the two types of machines?

12.2 The purchasing director for an industrial parts factory is investigating the possibility of purchasing a new type of milling machine. She has determined that the new machine will be bought if there is evidence that the parts produced have a higher breaking strength than those from the old machine. The process standard deviation of the breaking strength for the old machine is 10 kilograms and for the new machine is 9 kilograms. A sample of 100 parts taken from the old machine indicated a sample mean of 65 kilograms, while a similar sample of 100 from the new machine indicated a sample mean of 72 kilograms. Using the .01 level of significance, is there evidence that the purchasing director should buy the new machine?

• **12.3** Management of the Sycamore Steel Co. wishes to determine if there is any difference in performance between the day shift of workers and the evening shift of workers. A sample of 100 day-shift workers reveals an average output of 74.3 parts per hour with a sample standard deviation of 16 parts per hour. A sample of 100 evening-shift workers reveals an average output of 69.7 parts per hour with a sample standard deviation of 18 parts per hour. At the .10 level of significance, is there evidence of a difference in output between the day shift and the evening shift?

12.4 An independent testing agency has been contracted to determine whether there is any difference in gasoline mileage output of two different gasolines on the same model automobile. Gasoline A was tested on 200 cars and produced a sample average of 18.5 miles per gallon with a sample standard deviation of 4.6 miles per gallon. Gasoline B was tested on a sample of 100 cars and produced a sample average of 19.34 miles per gallon with a sample standard deviation of 5.2 miles per gallon. At the .05 level of significance, is there evidence of a difference in performance of the two gasolines?

• **12.5** The advertising manager of a breakfast cereal company would like to determine whether a new package shape would improve sales of the product. In order to test the feasibility of the new package shape, a sample of 40 equivalent stores was selected and 20 were randomly assigned as the test market of the new package shape, while the other 20 were to continue receiving the old package shape. The weekly sales during the time period studied were as follows:

New	Old
$\bar{X}_1 = 130$ boxes	$\bar{X}_2 = 117$ boxes
$S_1 = 10$ boxes	$S_2 = 12$ boxes

Using the .05 level of significance, is there evidence that the new package shape resulted in increased sales?

12.6 Referring to Problem 3.79 on page 80

(a) Is there evidence that the average tuition is higher at private colleges in the Northeast than in the Midwest? (Use $\alpha = .01$.)

➡**(b) ACTION** What would you report to the guidance counselor at your local high school concerning tuition in these two regions?

12.7 Referring to Problem 3.80 on page 81

(a) Is there evidence of a difference in the average acceleration time between German and Japanese cars? (Use $\alpha = .05$.)

➡**(b) ACTION** What would you write concerning the results of part (a) in an article for an automotive magazine?

12.8 Referring to Problem 3.81 on page 81, is there evidence of a difference in the average age of automobile salespeople in the United States and Europe? (Use $\alpha = .10$.)

12.9 Referring to Problem 4.121 on page 142

(a) Is there evidence that average stock prices are higher on the New York Exchange than the American Exchange? (Use $\alpha = .05$.)

➡**(b) ACTION** Based on the results of part (a), what would you tell your stockbroker?

12.10 Referring to Problem 12.2, suppose the purchasing director decides to buy a new machine if there is evidence that the parts produced have a breaking strength more than two kilograms higher than those from the old machine. What decision should be made? (Use $\alpha = .01$.)

12.11 Referring to Problem 12.5, using the .05 level of significance, is there evidence that the new package shape increased sales by more than five boxes?

12.3 TESTING FOR THE DIFFERENCE BETWEEN THE MEANS FROM TWO RELATED POPULATIONS

12.3.1 Rationale

In Section 12.2 we discussed the test for the difference between the means of two independent populations. In this section we shall develop a procedure for analyzing the difference between the means of two groups when the sample data are obtained from populations that are **related**—that is, the results of the first group are not independent of the second group. This dependent characteristic of the two groups occurs either because the items or individuals are **paired** or **matched** according to some characteristic or because **repeated measurements** are obtained from the same set of items or individuals. In either case, the variable of interest becomes the *difference* between the values of the observations rather than the observations themselves.

The first approach to the related-samples problem involves matching of items or individuals according to some characteristic of interest. For example, if the manager wanted to study the effect of different filling machines on the amount of cereal that is spilled (and thereby wasted), a control for differences in the various types of cereals (which may themselves have different spillage patterns) should be established. In this situation two boxes of each cereal type can be tested, with one box assigned to the new machine and the other to the old machine.

The second approach to the related-samples problem involves taking repeated measurements on the same items or individuals. Under the theory that the same items or individuals will behave alike if treated alike, the objective of the analysis is to show that any differences between two measurements of the same items or individuals are due to different treatment conditions. For example, suppose that in the real estate survey, the statistician would like to validate the appraised value of the houses in order to assure himself that there is no real difference between the appraisers in evaluating the worth of real estate. Thus a sample of 12 houses will be selected for evaluation. It is beneficial to have each of the 12 houses evaluated by the same two appraisers rather than taking two different samples of houses, as discussed in Section 12.2. Such an approach serves to reduce the variability in the appraised value and enables us to focus on the differences between the two appraisers.

Regardless of whether matched (paired) samples or repeated measurements are utilized, the objective is to study the difference between two measurements by reducing the effect of the variability due to the items or individuals themselves.

12.3.2 Development

In order to determine whether any difference exists between two related groups, the individual values for each group must be obtained (as shown in Table 12.1).

From the central limit theorem, the average difference $\overline{D}$ follows a normal distribution when the population standard deviation of the difference σ_D is known and the sample size is large enough. Since only the sample standard deviation of the difference S_D is usually available, the test statistic[3] is

$$t_{n-1} = \frac{\overline{D} - \mu_D}{\dfrac{S_D}{\sqrt{n}}} \tag{12.3}$$

with $(n - 1)$ degrees of freedom, where

$$\overline{D} = \frac{\sum\limits_{i=1}^{n} D_i}{n}$$

$$S_D^2 = \frac{\sum\limits_{i=1}^{n} D_i^2 - \dfrac{\left(\sum\limits_{i=1}^{n} D_i\right)^2}{n}}{n - 1}$$

The three panels of Figure 12.3 indicate the null and alternative hypothesis and rejection regions for the possible one-tailed and two-tailed tests. If, as shown in panel A, the test of the hypothesis is two-tailed, the rejection region is split into the lower and upper tails of the t distribution. However, if the test is one-tailed, the rejection region is either in the upper tail (panel B of Figure 12.3) or in the lower tail (panel C of Figure 12.3) of the t distribution, depending on the direction of the alternative hypothesis.

---

[3] If the hypothesized difference is 0 (that is, $\mu_D = 0$), the numerator in Equation (12.3) merely becomes $\overline{D}$.

TABLE 12.1 Determining the difference between two related groups

Observation	Group 1	Group 2	Difference
1	X_{11}	X_{21}	$D_1 = X_{11} - X_{21}$
2	X_{12}	X_{22}	$D_2 = X_{12} - X_{22}$
$\vdots$	$\vdots$	$\vdots$	$\vdots$
i	X_{1i}	X_{2i}	$D_i = X_{1i} - X_{2i}$
$\vdots$	$\vdots$	$\vdots$	$\vdots$
n	X_{1n}	X_{2n}	$D_n = X_{1n} - X_{2n}$

where X_{1i} = ith value in group 1
$\quad\ X_{2i}$ = ith value in group 2
$\quad\ D_i = X_{1i} - X_{2i}$ = difference between the ith value in
$\qquad$ group 1 and the ith value in group 2

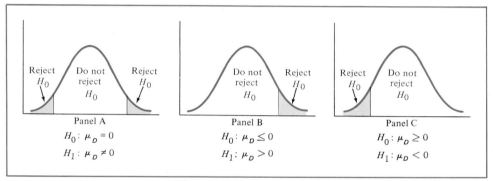

FIGURE 12.3
Testing for the difference between the means in related samples: Panel A, two-tailed test; Panel B, one-tailed test; Panel C, one-tailed test.

12.3.3 Applications

To apply the test for the difference between the means of two related groups, let us refer back to the first example mentioned in Section 12.3.1.

The manager wanted to determine whether there was evidence that the spillage was lower for the new machine than the old machine. In order to reduce the influence of the cereal type variability, a pair of boxes for each of ten cereal types was randomly selected. One box of each type was filled on the new machine and another box was filled on the old machine. The assignment of a member of each pair of boxes to a machine (new or old) was done randomly. The results are shown in Table 12.2 on page 382.

For these data,

$$\sum_{i=1}^{n} D_i = -15.60, \quad \sum_{i=1}^{n} D_i^2 = 38.1676, \quad n = 10$$

Thus

TABLE 12.2 Amount of cereal spilled (in grams) for a random sample of ten types of cereal filled on two machines

Cereal Type	Machine Type		Difference D_i $(X_{1i} - X_{2i})$
	New	Old	
1	12.73	13.89	-1.16
2	9.75	10.32	-0.57
3	13.78	17.01	-3.23
4	8.37	10.43	-2.06
5	11.71	11.39	$+0.32$
6	15.47	17.99	-2.52
7	14.56	16.02	-1.46
8	11.74	11.90	-0.16
9	9.76	13.11	-3.35
10	12.47	13.88	-1.41

$$\overline{D} = \frac{\sum_{i=1}^{n} D_i}{n} = \frac{-15.60}{10} = -1.56$$

and

$$S_D^2 = \frac{\sum_{i=1}^{n} D_i^2 - \frac{\left(\sum_{i=1}^{n} D_i\right)^2}{n}}{n-1} = \frac{38.1676 - \frac{(-15.6)^2}{10}}{9} = 1.537$$

so that

$$S_D = 1.24$$

Since the manager wishes to determine whether the average spillage will be less with the new machine than the old machine, we have a one-tailed test in which the null and alternative hypotheses can be stated as follows:

$$H_0: \quad \mu_D \geq 0 \ (\mu_{new} \geq \mu_{old} \text{ or } \mu_{new} - \mu_{old} \geq 0)$$
$$H_1: \quad \mu_D < 0 \ (\mu_{new} < \mu_{old} \text{ or } \mu_{new} - \mu_{old} < 0)$$

Since samples of ten cereal types have been taken, if a level of significance of .01 is selected, the decision rule can be stated as (see Figure 12.4):

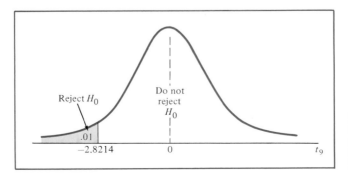

FIGURE 12.4
One-tailed test for the paired difference at the .01 level of significance with 9 degrees of freedom.

Reject H_0 if $t_9 < -2.8214$; otherwise do not reject H_0.

From Equation (12.3) we recall that the test statistic is

$$t_{n-1} = \frac{\overline{D}}{\dfrac{S_D}{\sqrt{n}}}$$

and thus for this example we have

$$t_9 = \frac{-1.56}{\dfrac{1.24}{\sqrt{10}}} = -3.978$$

Since $-3.978 < -2.8214$, we reject H_0.

Since the null hypothesis has been rejected, we would conclude that there is evidence that the average amount of cereal spillage is lower for the new machine than the old machine.

A second example of the paired difference t test can be illustrated by referring to the real estate survey. In Section 12.3.1 we may recall that the statistician was interested in determining whether there was any difference in the appraised value placed on houses by two different individuals. A sample of 12 houses was selected and each appraiser was assigned the task of placing an appraised value on the 12 houses. The results are summarized in Table 12.3.

TABLE 12.3 Appraised value (thousands of dollars) by two appraisers for a sample of 12 houses

House	Appraiser 1	Appraiser 2	Difference D_i $(X_{1i} - X_{2i})$
1	181.0	182.0	-1.0
2	179.9	180.0	-0.1
3	163.0	161.5	$+1.5$
4	218.0	215.0	$+3.0$
5	213.0	216.5	-3.5
6	175.0	175.0	0.0
7	217.9	219.5	-1.6
8	151.0	150.0	$+1.0$
9	164.9	165.5	-0.6
10	192.5	195.0	-2.5
11	225.0	222.7	$+2.3$
12	177.5	178.0	-0.5

For these data,

$$\sum_{i=1}^{n} D_i = -2.0, \quad \sum_{i=1}^{n} D_i^2 = 40.22, \quad n = 12$$

Thus

$$\overline{D} = \frac{\sum_{i=1}^{n} D_i}{n} = \frac{-2.0}{12} = -0.167$$

and

$$S_D^2 = \frac{\sum\limits_{i=1}^{n} D_i^2 - \dfrac{\left(\sum\limits_{i=1}^{n} D_i\right)^2}{n}}{n-1} = \frac{40.22 - \dfrac{(-2.0)^2}{12}}{11} = 3.626$$

so that

$$S_D = 1.904$$

Since we are interested in determining whether there is a difference between the two appraisers, we have a two-tailed test in which the null and alternative hypotheses can be stated as follows:

$$H_0: \quad \mu_D = 0 \text{ (that is, } \mu_1 = \mu_2 \text{ or } \mu_1 - \mu_2 = 0)$$

$$H_1: \quad \mu_D \neq 0 \text{ (that is, } \mu_1 \neq \mu_2 \text{ or } \mu_1 - \mu_2 \neq 0)$$

Since samples of 12 houses have been taken, if a level of significance of .05 is selected, the decision rule can be stated as (see Figure 12.5) follows:

$$\text{Reject } H_0 \text{ if } t_{11} > + 2.201$$

$$\text{or } t_{11} < - 2.201;$$

$$\text{otherwise do not reject } H_0.$$

From Equation (12.3) the test statistic is

$$t_{n-1} = \frac{\overline{D}}{\dfrac{S_D}{\sqrt{n}}}$$

Therefore, for the real estate survey example we have

$$t_{11} = \frac{-0.167}{\dfrac{1.904}{\sqrt{12}}} = -0.304$$

Since $-2.201 < -0.304 < +2.201$, we do not reject H_0.

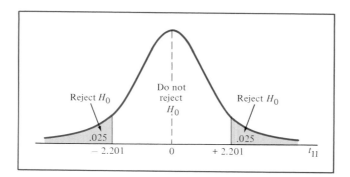

FIGURE 12.5
Two-tailed test for the paired difference at the .05 level of significance with 11 degrees of freedom.

Since the null hypothesis cannot be rejected, we would conclude that there is no evidence of a difference in the average appraised value given by the two appraisers.

Problems

12.12   A consumer reporting agency wished to determine whether an "unknown brand" calculator sells at a lower price than the "famous brand" calculator of the same type. A random sample of eight stores was selected, and the prices (at the stores) of each of the two calculators was recorded with the following results:

Store	Unknown Brand	Famous Brand
1	10	11
2	8	11
3	7	10
4	9	12
5	11	11
6	10	13
7	9	12
8	8	10

(a) At the .01 level of significance, is there evidence that the unknown brand sells for a lower price?

(b) What assumption is necessary to perform this test?

● **12.13**   A systems analyst is testing the feasibility of using a new computer system. The analyst will switch the processing to the new system only if there is evidence that the new system uses less processing time than the old system. In order to make a decision, a sample of seven jobs was selected and the processing time in seconds was recorded on the two systems with the following results:

Job	Old	New
1	8	6
2	4	3
3	10	7
4	9	8
5	8	5
6	7	8
7	12	9

(a) At the .01 level of significance, is there evidence that the old system uses more processing time?

(b) What assumption is necessary to perform this test?

12.14   Suppose that a shoe company wanted to test material for the soles of shoes. For each pair of shoes the new material was placed on one shoe and the old material was placed on the other shoe. After a given period of time a random sample of ten pairs of shoes was selected and the wear was measured on a ten-point scale with the following results (see top of page 386):

Material	Pair Number									
	I	*II*	*III*	*IV*	*V*	*VI*	*VII*	*VIII*	*IX*	*X*
New	2	4	5	7	7	5	9	8	8	7
Old	4	5	3	8	9	4	7	8	5	6
Differences	−2	−1	+2	−1	−2	+1	+2	0	+3	+1

At the .05 level of significance, is there evidence that the average wear is higher for the new material than the old material?

12.15 The project director for a large consumer products company was interested in studying the effect of a new product packaging design on sales of a laundry stain remover. The new package design was to be test-marketed over a period of a month in a sample of supermarkets in a particular city. A random sample of ten pairs of supermarkets were matched according to weekly sales volume and other demographic characteristics. One store of each pair (the experimental group) was to sell the laundry stain remover in its new package, while the other member of the pair (the control group) was to sell the laundry stain remover in its old package. The following data indicate the results over the test period of one month:

Pair	New Package	Old Package	Difference (D)
1	4.58	3.97	+0.61
2	5.19	4.88	+0.31
3	3.94	4.09	−0.15
4	6.32	5.87	+0.45
5	7.68	6.93	+0.75
6	3.48	4.00	−0.52
7	5.72	5.08	+0.64
8	7.04	6.95	+0.09
9	5.27	4.96	+0.31
10	5.84	5.13	+0.71

At the .05 level of significance, the project director would like to know whether there is evidence that average sales (in thousands of units sold) are higher for the new package design.

• **12.16** A group of engineering students decide to see whether cars which supposedly do not need high-octane gasoline get more miles per gallon using regular or high-octane gas. They test several cars, using both types of gas in each car at different times. The mileage in each condition for each car is:

Gas Type	Car									
	A	*B*	*C*	*D*	*E*	*F*	*G*	*H*	*I*	*J*
Regular	15	23	21	35	42	28	19	32	31	24
High-octane	18	21	25	34	47	30	19	27	34	20

Is there any evidence of a difference in the average gasoline mileage between regular and high-octane gas? (Use $\alpha = .05$.)

12.17 In order to measure the effect of a storewide sales campaign on nonsale items, the research director of a national supermarket chain took a random sample of 13 pairs of stores which were matched according to average weekly sales volume. One store of each pair (the experimental group) was exposed to the sales campaign, while the other member of the pair (the control group) was not. The following data indicate the results over a weekly period:

Store	Sales ($000) of Nonsale Items	
	With Sales Campaign	Without Sales Campaign
1	67.2	65.3
2	59.4	54.7
3	80.1	81.3
4	47.6	39.8
5	97.8	92.5
6	38.4	37.9
7	57.3	52.4
8	75.2	69.9
9	94.7	89.0
10	64.3	58.4
11	31.7	33.0
12	49.3	41.7
13	54.0	53.6

(a) At the .05 level of significance, can the research director conclude that there is evidence that the sales campaign has increased the sales of nonsale items?

(b) What assumption is necessary to perform this test?

12.18 Referring to Problem 12.13 on page 385, suppose the analyst will switch processing to the new system only if there is evidence that the old system uses in excess of two seconds more than the new system. What decision should be made?

12.4 TESTING FOR THE EQUALITY OF VARIANCES FROM TWO INDEPENDENT POPULATIONS

In many situations, we may also be interested in testing whether two populations have the same variability. Either we may be interested in testing the assumption of equal variances that we had made for the *t* test in Section 12.2 or we may be interested in studying the variances of two populations as an end in itself.

In order to examine the equality of the variances of two independent populations, a statistical procedure has been devised that is based upon the ratio of the two sample variances. If the data from each population are assumed to be normally distributed, then the ratio S_1^2/S_2^2 follows a distribution called the *F* distribution (see Table E.5), which was named after the famous statistician R. A. Fisher. From Table E.5, we can see that the critical values of the *F* distribution depend upon *two* sets of degrees of freedom—the degrees of freedom in the numerator and in the denominator. The test statistic for testing the equality between two variances would be

$$F_{(n_1-1),(n_2-1)} = \frac{S_1^2}{S_2^2} \qquad (12.4)$$

where n_1 = sample size in group 1

n_2 = sample size in group 2

$n_1 - 1$ = degrees of freedom in group 1

$n_2 - 1$ = degrees of freedom in group 2

$$S_1^2 = \text{sample variance in group 1}$$
$$S_2^2 = \text{sample variance in group 2}$$

In testing the equality of two variances, either one-tailed or two-tailed tests can be employed as indicated in Figure 12.6.

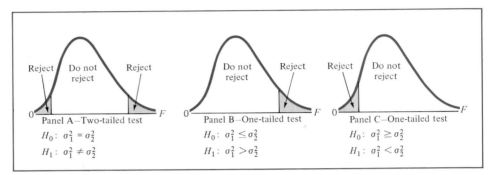

FIGURE 12.6
Testing a hypothesis about the equality of two population variances: one- and two-tailed tests: Panel A, two-tailed test; Panel B, one-tailed test; Panel C, one-tailed test.

In order to demonstrate how we may test for the equality of two variances, we can return to the cereal process study of Section 12.1. We recall that we wanted to determine whether the variability in the amount filled was higher in Plant A than in Plant B. Since the manager wishes to determine whether or not there is evidence of more variability in Plant A than in Plant B, a one-tailed test can be set up as follows:

$$H_0: \quad \sigma_A^2 \leq \sigma_B^2$$

$$H_1: \quad \sigma_A^2 > \sigma_B^2$$

For this example, since group 1 consists of cereal boxes filled at Plant A and group 2 consists of cereal boxes filled at Plant B, the rejection region is located in the upper tail of the distribution (see Figure 12.7 on page 389).

Using Equation (11.4),

$$F_{(n_1-1),(n_2-1)} = \frac{S_1^2}{S_2^2}$$

we have

$$F_{(25-1),(20-1)} = \frac{S_A^2}{S_B^2}$$

Since there are 24 degrees of freedom in the numerator and 19 degrees of freedom in the denominator, if a level of significance of .01 is selected, the critical value on the F distribution can be found from Table E.5 by looking in the column labeled "24" and the row labeled "19" and obtaining the value for the upper .01 of this F distribution, which is 2.92 (see Table 12.4). Therefore, the decision rule is as follows:

Reject H_0 if $F_{24,19} > 2.92$;

otherwise do not reject H_0.

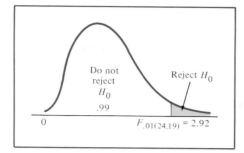

FIGURE 12.7
One-tailed test for the equality of two variances at the .01 level of significance with 24 and 19 degrees of freedom.

TABLE 12.4 Obtaining the critical value of F with 24 and 19 degrees of freedom at the .01 level of significance

Denominator df_2	Numerator df_1							
	1	*2*	*3*	. . .	*15*	*20*	*24*	*30*
1	4052	4999.5	5403	. . .	6157	6209	6235	6261
2	98.50	99.00	99.17	. . .	99.43	99.45	99.46	99.47
3	34.12	30.82	29.46	. . .	26.87	26.69	26.60	26.50
4	21.20	18.00	16.69	. . .	14.20	14.02	13.93	13.84
⋮	⋮	⋮	⋮	. . .	⋮	⋮	⋮	⋮
15	8.68	6.36	5.42	. . .	3.52	3.37	3.29	3.21
16	8.53	6.23	5.29	. . .	3.41	3.26	3.18	3.10
17	8.40	6.11	5.18	. . .	3.31	3.16	3.08	3.00
18	8.29	6.01	5.09	. . .	3.23	3.08	3.00	2.92
19	8.18	5.93	5.01	. . .	3.15	3.00	2.92	2.84
20	8.10	5.85	4.94	. . .	3.09	2.94	2.86	2.78
21	8.02	5.78	4.87	. . .	3.03	2.88	2.80	2.72
22	7.95	5.72	4.82	. . .	2.98	2.83	2.75	2.67

SOURCE: Extracted from Table E.5.

For our data, since $S_A = 16.71$ and $S_B = 14.20$

$$F_{24,19} = \frac{(16.71)^2}{(14.20)^2} = 1.385$$

Since $1.385 < 2.92$, do not reject H_0.

Since the null hypothesis cannot be rejected, the manager would conclude that there is no evidence that the variability in the amount of cereal filled is higher in Plant A than Plant B.

A second purpose for testing the differences between two variances arises from the assumption of equality of variances that is made in the t test for the difference between the means of two independent samples. Rather than just assuming equality of variances in two groups, it can be argued that the variances should be tested for equality prior to using the t test for the difference between the means.

This process may be illustrated with the following example. Suppose that a market researcher wanted to study the effect of product placement on the sales of disposable razor blades. In particular, she wanted to determine if there was any difference in sales depending on whether the razors were placed at the checkout counter or at the health and beauty section. A random sample of 13 equal-size stores within the supermarket chain was selected and the razors were placed at the checkout counter

TABLE 12.5 Weekly sales of disposable razors at checkout counters and health and beauty sections

Checkout Counter	Health and Beauty Section
107	90
153	83
82	86
158	94
141	89
87	93
119	

in seven stores and in the health and beauty section in six other stores. The results, in terms of number of packages of razors sold per week, are given in Table 12.5.

Using Equations (3.1) and (3.6) we may compute the sample mean and sample variance in each group. These results are summarized in Table 12.6.

TABLE 12.6 Sample means and variances of disposable razor sales

Checkout Counter	Health and Beauty Section
$\bar{X}_1 = 121.00$	$\bar{X}_1 = 89.17$
$S_1^2 = 945.00$	$S_2^2 = 17.37$
$n_1 = 7$	$n_2 = 6$

Since the market researcher wishes to determine whether there is a difference in the variability between the checkout counter and the health and beauty section, a two-tailed test can be set up as follows:

$$H_0: \quad \sigma_1^2 = \sigma_2^2$$

$$H_1: \quad \sigma_1^2 \neq \sigma_2^2$$

Because this is a two-tailed test, the rejection region is split into the lower and upper tails of the F distribution. If a level of significance of .05 were selected, each rejection region would contain .025 of the distribution (see Figure 12.8).

The upper critical value can be obtained directly from Table E.5, the tables of the F distribution. If we look up $7 - 1 = 6$ degrees of freedom in the numerator and $6 - 1 = 5$ degrees of freedom in the denominator, we observe an upper tail (.025) critical value of 6.98.

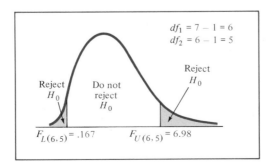

FIGURE 12.8
Two-tailed test for the equality of two variances at the .05 level of significance with 6 and 5 degrees of freedom.

Any lower-tail critical value on the F distribution can be obtained from

$$F_{L(a,b)} = \frac{1}{F_{U(b,a)}} \tag{12.5}$$

where F_L = lower critical value of F
$\quad F_U$ = upper critical value of F
$\quad a$ = number of degrees of freedom in group A
$\quad b$ = number of degrees of freedom in group B

Therefore, in this example we have

$$F_{L(6,5)} = \frac{1}{F_{U(5,6)}}$$

To compute our desired lower-tail critical value, we need to obtain the upper .025 value of F with 5 degrees of freedom in the numerator and 6 degrees of freedom in the denominator and take its reciprocal. From Table E.5 this upper-tail value is 5.99. Therefore from Equation (12.5)

$$F_{L(6,5)} = \frac{1}{F_{U(5,6)}} = \frac{1}{5.99} = .167$$

The decision rule for this example can then be stated as

Reject H_0 if $F_{6,5} > 6.98$

or if $F_{6,5} < .167$;

otherwise do not reject H_0.

For this example, $S_1^2 = 945$ and $S_2^2 = 17.37$. Using Equation (12.4), we have

$$F_{6,5} = \frac{945}{17.37} = 54.40$$

Therefore, since $F_{6,5} = 54.40 > 6.98$, we reject H_0.

The market researcher would reject the null hypothesis and conclude that there is a difference in the variability of the number of razors sold per week between placement at the checkout counter and the health and beauty section. Thus the t test of Section 12.2 would be inappropriate in this situation, since the population variances cannot be assumed to be equal. A test for difference in means that does not assume equality of variances in the populations will be the subject of discussion in Section 12.5.

In testing for the equality of two population variances, we should be aware that the test assumes that each of the two populations is normally distributed. Unfortunately, this test is not robust for departures from this assumption (Reference 1), particularly when the sample sizes in the two groups are not equal. Therefore if the populations are not at least approximately normally distributed, the accuracy of the procedure can be seriously affected (References 1–3 present other procedures for testing the equality of two variances).

Problems

- **12.19** Referring to Problem 12.5 on page 378, is there evidence that the variance is lower for the new package shape than the old package shape? (Use $\alpha = .05$.)

12.20 Referring to Problem 3.79 on page 80, is there evidence that the variance of tuition is higher at private colleges in the Northeast than in the Midwest? (Use $\alpha = .01$.)

12.21 Referring to Problem 3.80 on page 81, is there evidence of a difference in the variance of the acceleration time between German and Japanese cars? (Use $\alpha = .05$.)

12.22 Referring to Problem 3.81 on page 81, is there evidence of a difference in the variance of the age of automobile salespeople in the United States and Europe? (Use $\alpha = .10$.)

12.23 Referring to Problem 4.121 on page 142, is there evidence that the variance of stock prices are higher on the New York Exchange than the American Exchange? (Use $\alpha = .05$.)

12.5 TESTING FOR THE DIFFERENCE BETWEEN THE MEANS OF TWO INDEPENDENT POPULATIONS HAVING UNEQUAL VARIANCES

In our discussion of testing for the difference between the means of two independent populations in Section 12.2, we pooled the sample variances together into a common estimate because we assumed that the population variances were equal ($\sigma_1^2 = \sigma_2^2$). However, if we are either unwilling to assume equal population variances or we have evidence that the variances are not equal (as in Section 12.4), then we have what is referred to as the Behrens–Fisher problem. In such situations, the *pooled variances t test* [Equation (12.2)] is inappropriate.

In order to address this problem, we shall utilize an excellent approximation developed by Cochran (see Reference 8) in which separate variance estimates are included in the test statistic while the critical value of t is obtained by weighting the critical value of each sample by its variance of the mean (S^2/n).

The test statistic[4] is

$$t' = \frac{\overline{X}_1 - \overline{X}_2}{\sqrt{\dfrac{S_1^2}{n_1} + \dfrac{S_2^2}{n_2}}} \qquad (12.6)$$

and the decision rule (for a two-tailed test) is

$$\text{Reject } H_0 \text{ if } t' > \frac{+(t_1 W_1 + t_2 W_2)}{W_1 + W_2}$$

$$\text{or if } t' < \frac{-(t_1 W_1 + t_2 W_2)}{W_1 + W_2}; \qquad (12.7)$$

otherwise do not reject H_0

---
[4] See footnote 1 on page 375.

where t_1 = critical t value at the α level of significance with $(n_1 - 1)$ degrees of freedom

t_2 = critical t value at the α level of significance with $(n_2 - 1)$ degrees of freedom

$$W_1 = \frac{S_1^2}{n_1} \quad \text{and} \quad W_2 = \frac{S_2^2}{n_2}$$

This approximate t test may be demonstrated by referring to the problem of interest to the market researcher (see page 389). We recall from Section 12.4 that the market researcher wanted to determine whether there was any difference in the mean number of disposable razors sold per week in stores in which the product was placed at the checkout counter and stores in which the product was in the health and beauty section. That is,

$$H_0: \quad \mu_1 = \mu_2$$

$$H_1: \quad \mu_1 \neq \mu_2$$

Since there is evidence that the variability between these groups is different (see Section 12.4), the market researcher has decided to apply the *separate variances t test* [Equation (12.6)]. Thus, using the data of Table 12.6 on page 390, we have

$$t' = \frac{\bar{X}_1 - \bar{X}_2}{\sqrt{\dfrac{S_1^2}{n_1} + \dfrac{S_2^2}{n_2}}}$$

$$= \frac{121 - 89.17}{\sqrt{\dfrac{945}{7} + \dfrac{17.37}{6}}} = \frac{31.83}{11.743} = 2.71$$

If a level of significance of .05 is chosen, using Equation (12.7) we would have

$t_1 = 2.4469$, the critical value of t for a two-tailed test with $(7 - 1) = 6$ degrees of freedom

$t_2 = 2.5706$, the critical value of t for a two-tailed test with $(6 - 1) = 5$ degrees of freedom

$$W_1 = \frac{S_1^2}{n_1} = \frac{945}{7} = 135$$

$$W_2 = \frac{S_2^2}{n_2} = \frac{17.37}{6} = 2.895$$

Thus

$$\frac{t_1 W_1 + t_2 W_2}{W_1 + W_2} = \frac{(2.4469)(135) + (2.5706)(2.895)}{135 + 2.895} = 2.45$$

Therefore, the decision rule is as follows:

$$\text{Reject } H_0 \text{ if } t' > 2.45$$

$$\text{or if } t' < -2.45;$$

$$\text{otherwise do not reject } H_0.$$

Since we see that $t' = 2.71 > 2.45$, we reject H_0.

The market researcher can conclude that there is significant evidence of a difference in the mean sales of disposable razors depending on whether they are placed at the checkout counter or the health and beauty section.

Problems

- **12.24** Referring to Problem 12.5 on page 378 and assuming that the variances in the populations are not equal
  (a) Is there evidence that the average sales are higher for the new package shape? (Use $\alpha = .05$.)
  (b) Compare the results obtained in (a) with those of Problem 12.5. In light of the results of Problem 12.19, which result do you think is more valid, those of (a) or of Problem 12.5?

  12.25 Referring to Problem 3.79 on page 80 and assuming that the variances in the populations are not equal
  (a) Is there evidence that the average tuition is higher at private colleges in the Northeast than in the Midwest? (Use $\alpha = .01$.)
  (b) Compare the results obtained in (a) with those of Problem 12.6. In light of the results of Problem 12.20, which result do you think is more valid, those of (a) or of Problem 12.6?

  12.26 Referring to Problem 3.80 on page 81 and assuming that the variances in the populations are not equal
  (a) Is there evidence of a difference in the average acceleration time between German and Japanese cars? (Use $\alpha = .05$.)
  (b) Compare the results obtained in (a) with those of Problem 12.7. In light of the results of Problem 12.21, which result do you think is more valid, those of (a) or of Problem 12.7?

  12.27 Referring to Problem 3.81 on page 81 and assuming that the variances in the populations are not equal
  (a) Is there evidence of a difference in the average age of automobile salespeople in the United States and Europe? (Use $\alpha = .10$.)
  (b) Compare the results obtained in (a) with those of Problem 12.8. In light of the results of Problem 12.22, which result do you think is more valid, those of (a) or of Problem 12.8

  12.28 Referring to Problem 4.121 on page 142 and assuming that the variances in the populations are not equal
  (a) Is there evidence that average stock prices are higher on the New York Exchange than the American Exchange? (Use $\alpha = .05$.)
  (b) Compare the results obtained in (a) with those of Problem 12.9. In light of the results of Problem 12.23, which result do you think is more valid, those of (a) or of Problem 12.9?

12.6 HYPOTHESIS TESTING, COMPUTERS, AND THE REAL ESTATE SURVEY

12.6.1 Introduction

Having discussed methods for evaluating differences between two groups when examining a quantitative variable, we may return to the real estate survey. Suppose that the president and the statistician wanted to know whether the average age of houses without a modern kitchen was different from the average age of houses with a modern kitchen. Thus, if we refer to question 6 (age) in conjunction with question 19 (modern kitchen), we would have the following null and alternative hypotheses:

$$H_0: \quad \mu_1 = \mu_2$$

$$H_1: \quad \mu_1 \neq \mu_2$$

Certainly now that a multitude of statistical packages are readily available for either mainframes or microcomputers, we would want to access a particular package so that the computer can be used as a tool to assist in the analysis.

12.6.2 Presentation of SAS, Minitab, and STATGRAPHICS Output

Among the well-known and most widely available packages are SAS, Minitab, and STATGRAPHICS. For the data of interest to the president, Figure 12.9 represents partial SAS output, Figure 12.10 represents partial Minitab output, and Figure 12.11 represents partial STATGRAPHICS output. We may note that each output provides the mean, standard deviation, and sample size for each group. In addition, a t test is performed for the difference between means of the two groups (assuming either equal or unequal variances), an F test for the equality of variances is provided, and p values are indicated—for both the t tests and the F test.

```
TTEST PROCEDURE

VARIABLE: AGE              AGE IN YEARS

MODKIT        N             MEAN         STD DEV        STD ERROR

ABSENCE      80        34.36250000     7.46509812      0.83462334
PRESENCE    153        34.30065359     8.39414345      0.67862628

VARIANCES        T         DF     PROB > :T:

UNEQUAL       0.0575     177.6       0.9542
EQUAL         0.0554     231.0       0.9559

FOR HO: VARIANCES ARE EQUAL, F' =    1.26  WITH 152 AND 79 DF
                PROB > F' = 0.2472
```

FIGURE 12.9
SAS output for t test of differences in age based upon absence or presence of a modern kitchen.

```
TWOSAMPLE T FOR AGE
MODKIT      N        MEAN      STDEV    SE MEAN
0          80       34.36      7.47      0.83
1         153       34.30      8.39      0.68

95 PCT CI FOR MU 0 - MU 1: (-2.14, 2.26)
TTEST MU 0 = MU 1 (VS NE): T=0.06 P=0.96 DF=231.0
```

FIGURE 12.10
Minitab output for t test of differences in age based upon absence or presence of a modern kitchen.

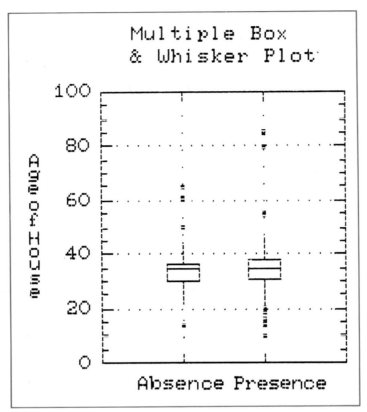

FIGURE 12.11
STATGRAPHICS output of data used in *t* test of differences in age based upon absence or presence of a modern kitchen.

Thus, for our data, we may first observe that the mean of the first group (those without a modern kitchen) is 34.36 years with a standard deviation of 7.47 years for a sample size of 80, while the mean of the second group (those with a modern kitchen) is 34.30 years with a standard deviation of 8.39 years for a sample size of 153.

12.6.3 Analysis and Interpretation

Before we may test for the difference between the means of two groups, it is appropriate that the assumption of equality of variances be evaluated using the *F* test. Our null and alternative hypothesis would be

$$H_0: \quad \sigma_1^2 = \sigma_2^2$$

$$H_1: \quad \sigma_1^2 \neq \sigma_2^2$$

From Figure 12.9 we may note that the *F* value is 1.26 and with 152 and 79 degrees of freedom the *p* value is given as .2472. If an α level of significance of .05 were selected, the null hypothesis would not be rejected, since .2472 > .05.[5] Thus we would conclude that there is no evidence of a difference between the variances in the two groups.

Now that the variances have been tested, we may obtain the t-test statistic from either Figure 12.9 or 12.10. Assuming equal variances,[6] we observe that the t statistic is equal to $+0.06$ and the corresponding two-tailed p value is .956. For a two-tailed test with $\alpha = .05$, since .956 > .05 (or since $+0.06 < +1.96$, the upper-tail critical value of t with 231 degrees of freedom), we are unable to reject the null hypothesis. We would conclude that there is no evidence that the average age of houses without a modern kitchen is different from the average age of houses with a modern kitchen.

Now that we have tested for the difference between the variances and also between the means of the two groups, we should evaluate the validity of the assumption of normality in each group. This can be done by obtaining a side-by-side box-and-whisker plot of the two groups from the STATGRAPHICS package (see Figure 12.11). We may observe from Figure 12.11 that aside from the few outliers, the box-and-whisker plots of each group do not appear to substantially differ from normality (see Section 3.11). Considering the large sample sizes, it is reasonable to conclude that there has not been any serious departure from the normality assumption and hence our preceding analysis can be considered appropriate.

Supplementary Problems

● **12.29** A product-testing organization was interested in studying Neveready and Pennysonic transistor radio batteries to determine the number of hours that the batteries lasted. Random samples of 25 Neveready batteries and 25 Pennysonic batteries indicated the following results:

Neveready	Pennysonic
$\overline{X}$ = 110.6 hours	$\overline{X}$ = 103.8 hours
S = 10 hours	S = 12 hours

Use hypothesis testing to draw conclusions about each of the following:
   (a) Is there evidence that Pennysonic batteries last, on average, more than 95 hours?
   (b) Is there evidence of a difference in the variances (in the number of hours the batteries last) between Neveready and Pennysonic batteries?
   (c) Is there evidence of a difference in the average number of hours between Neveready and Pennysonic batteries?
Note: Use a level of significance of .05 throughout the problem.
   ➠**(d)** **ACTION**   Based on the results of parts (a)–(c), what should the product-testing organization write about the two brands in its report?

---

[5] Since 152 and 79 degrees of freedom are not shown in Table E.5, rounding to the nearest tabular value of 120 and 60 degrees of freedom, the critical values are 1.58 and $1/1.53 = .65$. Since $.65 < 1.26 < 1.58$, the null hypothesis cannot be rejected.

[6] Had there been a difference between the variances, the t test of Section 12.5 would have been applied.

12.30 The R & M department store has two charge plans available for its credit account customers. The management of the store wishes to collect information about each plan and study the differences between the two plans. It is interested in the average monthly balance. A random sample of 25 accounts of plan A and 50 accounts of plan B was selected with the following results:

Plan A	Plan B
$n_A = 25$	$n_B = 50$
$\bar{X}_A = \$75$	$\bar{X}_B = \$110$
$S_A = \$15$	$S_B = \$14.14$

Use statistical inference (confidence intervals or tests of hypothesis) to draw conclusions about *each* of the following:

(a) Average monthly balance of plan B accounts.

(b) Is there evidence that the average monthly balance of plan A accounts is different from $105?

(c) Is there evidence of a difference in the variances (in the monthly balances) between plan A and plan B?

(d) Is there evidence of a difference in the average monthly balance between plan A and plan B?

Note: Use a level of significance of .01 (99% confidence) throughout the problem.

➡(e) **ACTION** Based on the results of parts (a)–(d), what would you tell the management about the two plans?

12.31 A large public utility wishes to compare the consumption of electricity during the summer season for single-family homes in three counties that it services. For each household, the monthly electric bill was recorded, with the following results:

County I	County II	County III
$n_1 = 25$	$n_2 = 21$	$n_3 = 16$
$\bar{X}_1 = \$85$	$\bar{X}_2 = \$68$	$\bar{X}_3 = \$91$
$S_1 = \$30$	$S_2 = \$18$	$S_3 = \$26$

Use hypothesis testing to draw conclusions about each of the following:

(a) Is there evidence that the average bill in County III is above $80?

(b) Is there evidence of a difference in the variances between bills in County I and County II?

(c) Is there evidence that the average monthly bill is higher in County I than County II?

Note: Use the .05 level of significance throughout the problem.

➡(d) **ACTION** Based on the results of parts (a)–(c), what would you tell the utility about the consumption of electricity in the three counties?

12.32 A statistician for a large automobile company would like to study the delivery time (in days) for custom-ordered subcompact, compact, and full-sized cars. A random sample of 16 subcompact cars, 25 compact cars, and 25 full-sized cars was selected. The results are summarized as follows:

Subcompact	Compact	Full-Sized
$\bar{X}_1 = 78$ days	$\bar{X}_2 = 64$ days	$\bar{X}_3 = 48$ days
$S_1 = 30$ days	$S_2 = 20$ days	$S_3 = 17$ days
$n_1 = 16$	$n_2 = 25$	$n_3 = 25$

Use hypothesis testing to draw conclusions about each of the following:
- **(a)** Is there evidence that the average delivery time for full-sized cars is different from 45 days?
- **(b)** Is there evidence of a difference in the variances between the subcompact and full-sized cars?
- **(c)** Is there evidence that the average delivery time for subcompact cars is greater than for full-sized cars?
- **(d)** Is there evidence of a difference between the variances between the compact and full-sized cars?
- **(e)** Is there evidence of a difference between compact and full-sized cars in the average delivery time?

Note: Use the level of significance of .10 throughout the problem.
- ➠**(f)** **ACTION** Based on the results of parts (a)–(e), what should the statistician report to the auto company concerning the delivery time of the three types of cars?

12.33 The manager of computer operations of a large company wishes to study computer usage of two departments within the company, the Accounting Department and the Research Department. A random sample of 5 jobs from the Accounting Department in the last month and 6 jobs from the Research Department in the last month were selected, and the processing time (in seconds) for each job was recorded with the following results:

Accounting	9	3	8	7	12	
Research	4	13	10	9	9	6

Use hypothesis testing to draw conclusions about each of the following:
- **(a)** Is there evidence that the average processing time in the Research Department is greater than 6 seconds?
- **(b)** Is there evidence of a difference in the variances between the two departments?
- **(c)** What assumption must be made in order to do (b)?
- **(d)** Is there evidence of a difference in the mean processing time between the Accounting Department and the Research Department?
- **(e)** What assumption(s) is (are) needed to do (d)?

Note: Use the .05 level of significance throughout the problem.
- ➠**(f)** **ACTION** Based on the results of parts (a)–(e), what should the manager write in his report to the Director of Information Systems concerning the two departments?

12.34 A consumer reporting agency wished to compare the price of a particular brand of a calculator in two different cities. A random sample of 6 stores in one city and 8 stores in a second city were selected with the following results:

City I	$10	12	9	14	12	10		
City II	$13	16	8	12	14	13	11	14

Use hypothesis testing to draw conclusions about each of the following:
- **(a)** Is there evidence of a difference in the variances between the two cities?
- **(b)** What assumption is necessary to do (a)?
- **(c)** Is there evidence of a difference in the mean price of the calculator in the two cities?
- **(d)** What assumptions(s) is (are) necessary to do (c)?

Note: Use a level of significance of .05 throughout this problem.
- ➠**(e)** **ACTION** Based on the results of parts (a)–(d), what should the consumer agency report concerning the price of this calculator in the two cities?

● **12.35** Referring to the monthly rental prices of unfurnished studio apartments in Manhattan and Brooklyn Heights (see Problem 3.64 on page 72), use hypothesis testing to draw conclusions about each of the following:

(a) Is there evidence of a difference in the variances in rental prices between apartments in Manhattan and Brooklyn Heights?

(b) What assumption is needed to do (a)?

(c) Is there evidence that the average rental price is higher in Manhattan than in Brooklyn Heights?

(d) What assumption(s) is (are) needed to do (c)?

Note: Use a level of significance of .01 throughout the problem.

➡(e) **ACTION**   Based on the results of parts (a)–(d), what would you tell a friend who is looking for an unfurnished studio apartment?

12.36   The director of marketing for a large banking services organization would like to estimate the number of credit cards held by two groups of banking customers: savings account holders and checking account holders. A random sample of 8 savings account holders and 8 checking account holders was selected with the following results:

Savings accounts	0	12	6	10	13	17	32	5
Checking accounts	4	9	40	20	1	27	38	9

Use hypothesis testing to draw conclusions about each of the following:

(a) Is there evidence of a difference in the variances between savings account holders and checking account holders?

(b) What assumption is needed to do (a)?

(c) Is there evidence that the number of credit cards held by savings account holders is less than that held by checking account holders?

(d) What assumption(s) is (are) necessary to do (c)?

Note: Use a .05 level of significance throughout the problem.

➡(e) **ACTION**   Based on the results of parts (a)–(d), what should the director of marketing report to the president of the organization about the two groups of account holders?

12.37   The following data represent the turning-circle capacity (in feet) of a sample of 10 compact cars and 10 medium-sized cars in 1987:

Compact	35	38	38	39	36	41	38	37	40	39
Medium	40	37	42	42	41	45	39	39	43	40

SOURCE: Copyright 1986 by Consumers Union of United States, Inc., Mount Vernon, NY 10453. Excerpted by permission from *Consumer Reports*, April, 1987, pp. 250–253

(a) Is there evidence of a difference in the variances of turning-circle capacity between compact and medium-size cars.

(b) What assumption is needed to do part (a)?

(c) Is there evidence that the average turning-circle capacity is lower for compact cars than for medium-size cars?

(d) What assumption(s) is (are) necessary to do (c)?

➡(e) **ACTION**   If you have a friend who is trying to decide whether to buy a compact or a medium-size car, what would you tell her concerning turning-circle capacity?

12.38   Crazy Dave, a nationally recognized baseball authority, would like to investigate the assertion that there was more offense in the 1987 season than during 1986. A random sample of 18 players who had at least 350 at bats in both the 1986 and 1987 seasons was selected and their batting average and number of home runs per 100 at bats was recorded for each season with the following results:

Player	Batting Average		Home Runs Per 100 At Bats	
	1987	1986	1987	1986
J. Franco	.319	.306	1.62	1.67
B. Jacoby	.300	.288	5.93	2.92
C. Lansford	.289	.284	3.43	3.21
L. Moseby	.282	.253	4.39	3.56
H. Reynolds	.275	.222	0.19	0.20
G. Gagne	.265	.250	2.29	2.54
J. Canseco	.257	.240	4.92	5.50
D. Schofield	.251	.249	1.88	2.84
F. White	.243	.272	3.02	3.75
S. Buechle	.237	.243	3.58	3.90
T. Raines	.330	.334	3.40	1.55
M. Wilson	.299	.289	2.34	2.36
M. Schmidt	.293	.290	6.70	6.70
T. Pendleton	.286	.239	2.06	0.17
M. Webster	.279	.290	2.55	1.39
V. Law	.272	.225	2.75	1.39
T. Herr	.263	.252	0.39	0.36
J. Davis	.248	.250	4.44	3.98

(a) At the .05 level of significance, is there evidence that the average batting average was higher in 1987 than in 1986?

(b) At the .05 level of significance, is there evidence that the average number of home runs per 100 at bats was higher in 1987 than in 1986?

➧(c) **ACTION** What conclusions should Crazy Dave broadcast in his nationally syndicated radio show based on these data?

✍(d) Why do you think that it was better to obtain repeated measurements from the same players for the 1987 and 1986 seasons than to take separate samples of players for each season?

12.39 Referring to Problem 3.67 on page 74

(a) Is there any evidence of a difference in the variances of the price of an alarm system between professionally installed and do-it-yourself systems?

(b) What assumption is needed to do part (a)?

(c) Is there evidence that the average price is higher for professionally installed systems than for do-it-yourself systems?

(d) What assumption(s) is (are) necessary to do (c)?

Note: Use the .01 level of significance throughout the problem.

➧(e) **ACTION** What would you tell your friend (who has just purchased a new car) about the auto alarm systems?

12.40 Referring to the data of Problem 3.85 (the chocolate bars) on page 84, for each of the three variables (cost, caffeine, and cocoa mass)

(a) Determine if there is a difference in the variances between dark chocolate and milk chocolate bars. (Use $\alpha = .05$.)

(b) Determine if there is a difference in the average between dark chocolate and milk chocolate bars. (Use $\alpha = .05$.)

➧(c) **ACTION** If you are making a presentation at your local chapter of Chocolate Lovers Anonymous, what would you say in your presentation?

12.41 Referring to the data of Problem 3.86 (frankfurters) on page 85, for each of the four variables (cost per ounce, cost per pound of protein, calories, and sodium)

(a) Is there evidence of a difference in the variances between beef and ''meat'' frankfurters? (Use $\alpha = .01$.)

(b) Is there evidence of a difference in the means between beef and ''meat'' frankfurters? (Use $\alpha = .01$.)

➡**(c)** **ACTION** If you were being interviewed by the health and science editor of your local television station concerning these two type of frankfurters, what statements would you make concerning their comparative characteristics?

12.42 Referring to the data of Problem 3.89 (football receptions) on page 89, for each of the five variables (number of receptions, yards, average yardage, number of touchdowns, and touchdown productivity)

(a) Is there evidence of a difference in the variances between the NFC and the AFC? (Use $\alpha = .05$.)

(b) Is there evidence of a difference in the means between the NFC and the AFC? (Use $\alpha = .05$.)

➡**(c)** **ACTION** If you were scheduled to present your results on Mad Mark's nationally telecast pregame show, what would you say?

12.43 Referring to the data of Problem 4.21 (life of light bulbs) on page 97,

(a) Is there evidence of a difference in the variances between Manufacturer A and B? (Use $\alpha = .10$.)

(b) Is there evidence of a difference in the average life between Manufacturer A and B? (Use $\alpha = .10$.)

➡**(c)** **ACTION** If you were scheduled to write an article for a consumer magazine comparing the two manufacturers, what conclusions would you draw?

✗ **12.44** A computer professor was interested in studying the amount of time it would take students enrolled in the Introduction to Computers course to write and run a program in PASCAL. The professor hires you to analyze the following results (in minutes) from a random sample of nine students:

10   13   9   15   12   13   11   13   12

(a) At the .05 level of significance, is there evidence that the population average amount is greater than 10 minutes? What would you tell the professor?

(b) Suppose that when checking her results, the computer professor realizes that the fourth student needed 51 minutes rather than the recorded 15 minutes to write and run the PASCAL program. At the .05 level of significance, reanalyze the revised data in (a). What would you tell the professor now?

(c) The professor is perplexed by these paradoxical results and requests an explanation from you regarding the justification for the difference in your findings in (a) and (b). Discuss.

(d) A few days later, the professor calls to tell you that the dilemma is completely resolved. The ''original'' number 15 (shown in part (a)) was correct, and therefore your findings in (a) are being used in the article she is writing for a computer magazine. Now she wants to hire you to compare the results from that group of Introduction to Computers students against those from a sample of 11 computer majors in order to determine whether there is evidence that computer majors can write a PASCAL program (on average) in less time than introductory students. The sample mean for the computer majors is 8.5 minutes and the sample standard deviation is 2.0 minutes. At the .05 level of significance, completely analyze these data. What would you tell the professor?

(e) A few days later the professor calls again to tell you that a reviewer of her article wants her to include the p value for the ''correct'' result in (a). In addition, the professor inquires about a ''Behrens-Fisher problem,'' which the reviewer wants her to discuss in her article. In your own words discuss the concept of p value and describe the Behrens-Fisher problem. Give the approximate p value in (a) and discuss whether or not the Behrens-Fisher problem had any meaning in the professor's study.

12.45   **(Class project)** Referring to the data of Problem 3.88 on page 88 (batting averages and home runs), have each student select a random sample of 10 players from the American League and 10 players from the National League. For each of the two variables (batting average and number of home runs)

    (a) Is there evidence of a difference between the variances in the American and National Leagues? (Use $\alpha = .05$.)

    (b) Is there evidence of a difference between the means in the American and National Leagues? (Use $\alpha = .05$.)

    (c) Compare the results obtained in (a) and (b) with the population results obtained in Problem 3.88. What explanation can you provide for the differences that may exist?

Database Exercises

The following problems refer to the sample data obtained from the questionnaire of Figure 2.5 on page 15 and presented in Figure 2.10 on pages 24–29. They should be solved with the aid of an available computer package.

□ **12.46**   Referring to the appraised value (question 1) and using a level of significance of .05

    (a) Determine whether there is a difference in the variances between houses located in Farmingdale and Levittown (question 9, codes 2 and 3).

    (b) Determine whether there is a difference in the means between houses located in Farmingdale and Levittown (question 9, codes 2 and 3).

    (c) Interpret the meaning of the p value in part (b).

□ **12.47**   Referring to the appraised value (question 1) and using a level of significance of .01

    (a) Determine whether there is a difference in the variances between colonial and split-level types of houses (question 10, codes 3 and 5).

    (b) Determine whether there is a difference in the means between colonial and split-level types of houses (question 10, codes 3 and 5).

    (c) Interpret the meaning of the p value in part (b).

□ **12.48**   Referring to the appraised value (question 1) and using a level of significance of .05

    (a) Determine whether there is a difference in the variances based on whether the house is connected to a local sewer system (question 17).

    (b) Determine whether there is evidence that the average appraised value is lower for houses that are not connected to a sewer system than for houses that are connected to a sewer system (question 17).

    (c) Interpret the meaning of the p value in part (b).

□ **12.49**   Referring to the appraised value (question 1) and using a level of significance of .10

    (a) Determine whether there is a difference in the variances based on whether the house has a modern kitchen (question 19).

    (b) Determine whether there is evidence that the average appraised value is higher for houses without a modern kitchen than for houses with a modern kitchen (question 19).

    (c) Interpret the meaning of the p value in part (b).

□ **12.50**   Referring to the lot size (question 2) and using a level of significance of .05

    (a) Determine whether there is a difference in the variances between houses without a garage and those with a two-car garage (question 8, codes 0 and 2).

    (b) Determine whether there is evidence that the average lot size is lower for houses without a garage than for houses with a two-car garage (question 8, codes 0 and 2).

    (c) Interpret the meaning of the p value in part (b).

□ **12.51**   Referring to the lot size (question 2) and using a level of significance of .01

    (a) Determine whether there is a difference in the variances between houses located in East Meadow and in Farmingdale (question 9, codes 1 and 2).

    (b) Determine whether there is a difference in the average lot size between houses located in East Meadow and in Farmingdale (question 9, codes 1 and 2).

    (c) Interpret the meaning of the p value in part (b).

☐ **12.52** Referring to the lot size (question 2) and using a level of significance of .10

    (a) Determine whether there is a difference in the variances between houses that are a colonial or split-level (question 10, codes 3 and 5) and houses that are Capes or ranches (question 10, codes 1 and 4).

    (b) Determine whether there is evidence that the average lot size is higher for houses that are colonial or split-level (question 10, codes 3 and 5) than for houses that are Capes or ranches (question 10, codes 1 and 4).

    (c) Interpret the meaning of the p value in part (b).

☐ **12.53** Referring to the lot size (question 2) and using a level of significance of .05

    (a) Determine whether there is a difference in the variances between houses without a swimming pool (question 13, code 1) and houses with a swimming pool (question 13, codes 2 and 3).

    (b) Determine whether there is evidence that the average lot size is lower for houses without a swimming pool (question 13, code 1) than for houses with a swimming pool (question 13, codes 2 and 3).

    (c) Interpret the meaning of the p value in part (b).

☐ **12.54** Referring to the number of bedrooms (question 3) and using a level of significance of .01

    (a) Determine whether there is a difference in the variances between houses in East Meadow (question 9, code 1) and houses in other communities (question 9, codes 2 and 3).

    (b) Determine whether there is evidence that the average number of bedrooms is lower in East Meadow (question 9, code 1) than in other communities (question 9, codes 2 and 3).

    (c) Interpret the meaning of the p value in part (b).

☐ **12.55** Referring to the number of bedrooms (question 3) and using a level of significance of .10

    (a) Determine whether there is a difference in the variances between colonials (question 10, code 3) and split-levels (question 10, code 5).

    (b) Determine whether there is a difference in the means between colonials (question 10, code 3) and split-levels (question 10, code 5).

    (c) Interpret the meaning of the p value in part (b).

☐ **12.56** Referring to the number of bedrooms (question 3) and using a level of significance of .05

    (a) Determine whether there is a difference in the variances based on whether the house has a fireplace (question 16).

    (b) Determine whether there is evidence of a difference in the average number of bedrooms based on whether the house has a fireplace (question 16).

    (c) Interpret the meaning of the p value in part (b).

☐ **12.57** Referring to the number of rooms (question 5) and using a level of significance of .01

    (a) Determine whether there is a difference in the variances between houses without a garage (question 8, code 0) and all other houses (question 8, codes 1–3).

    (b) Determine whether there is evidence that the average number of rooms is lower for houses without a garage (question 8, code 0) than for all other houses (question 8, codes 1–3).

    (c) Interpret the meaning of the p value in part (b).

☐ **12.58** Referring to the number of rooms (question 5) and using a level of significance of .10

    (a) Determine whether there is a difference in the variances between Capes (question 10, code 1) and all other types of houses (question 10, codes 2–5).

    (b) Determine whether there is a difference in the average number of rooms between Capes (question 10, code 1) and all other types of houses (question 10, codes 2–5).

    (c) Interpret the meaning of the p value in part (b).

□ **12.59**   Referring to the number of rooms (question 5) and using a level of significance of .05
    (a) Determine whether there is a difference in the variances based on whether the house has an eat-in kitchen (question 14).
    (b) Determine whether there is a difference in the average number of rooms based on whether the house has an eat-in kitchen (question 14).
    (c) Interpret the meaning of the p value in part (b).

□ **12.60**   Referring to the number of rooms (question 5) and using a level of significance of .01
    (a) Determine whether there is a difference in the variances based on whether the house has a modern kitchen (question 19).
    (b) Determine whether there is evidence that the average number of rooms is less for houses that do not have a modern kitchen than for houses that have a modern kitchen (question 19).
    (c) Interpret the meaning of the p value in part (b).

□ **12.61**   Referring to the age in years (question 6) and using a level of significance of .05
    (a) Determine whether there is a difference in the variances between houses without a garage (question 8, code 0) and houses with a garage (question 8, codes 1–3).
    (b) Determine whether there is evidence that the average age is higher for houses without a garage (question 8, code 0) than for houses with a garage (question 8, codes 1–3).
    (c) Interpret the meaning of the p value in part (b).

□ **12.62**   Referring to the age in years (question 6) and using a level of significance of .10
    (a) Determine whether there is a difference in the variances between Capes (question 10, code 1) and all other types of houses (question 10, codes 2–5).
    (b) Determine whether there is evidence that the average age of Capes (question 10, code 1) is greater than the average age of all other types of houses (question 10, codes 2–5).
    (c) Interpret the meaning of the p value in part (b).

□ **12.63**   Referring to the age in years (question 6) and using a level of significance of .05
    (a) Determine whether there is a difference in the variances based on whether the house has a fireplace (question 16).
    (b) Determine whether there is evidence of a difference in the average age based on whether the house has a fireplace (question 16).
    (c) Interpret the meaning of the p value in part (b).

□ **12.64**   Referring to the age in years (question 6) and using a level of significance of .01
    (a) Determine whether there is a difference in the variances based on whether the house has modern bathrooms (question 20).
    (b) Determine whether there is evidence that the average age of houses without modern bathrooms is greater than for houses that have modern bathrooms (question 20).
    (c) Interpret the meaning of the p value in part (b).

□ **12.65**   Referring to the annual taxes (question 7) and using a level of significance of .05
    (a) Determine whether there is a difference in the variances between East Meadow (question 9, code 1) and Farmingdale (question 9, code 2).
    (b) Determine whether there is evidence of a difference in the average annual taxes between East Meadow (question 9, code 1) and Farmingdale (question 9, code 2).
    (c) Interpret the meaning of the p value in part (b).

□ **12.66**   Referring to the annual taxes (question 7) and using a level of significance of .10
    (a) Determine whether there is a difference in the variances between houses that do not have a swimming pool (question 13, code 1) and houses that have a swimming pool (question 13, codes 2 and 3).
    (b) Determine whether there is evidence that the average annual taxes are lower for houses without a swimming pool (question 13, code 1) than for houses with a swimming pool (question 13, codes 2 and 3).
    (c) Interpret the meaning of the p value in part (b).

☐ **12.67** Referring to the annual taxes (question 7) and using a level of significance of .01
   (a) Determine whether there is a difference in the variances based on whether the house is connected to a local sewer system (question 17).
   (b) Determine whether there is evidence that the average annual taxes are lower for houses that are not connected to a local sewer system than for houses that are connected to a local sewer system (question 17).
   (c) Interpret the meaning of the *p* value in part (b).

Case Study D

As part of a work study project for the Office of Institutional Research at your college you have been assigned the task of analyzing faculty salary and administrative salary during the 1986–1987 academic year. Your task has two parts. First you are to compare the salary of administrators with various titles to determine whether differences exist between public and private institutions. Second you are to compare the salary of full professors from colleges in two states that include a wide variety of institutions of higher education—California and Massachusetts.

Table 12.7 provides data that indicates the median salary for a sample of administrative titles. Table 12.8 provides data that pertain to the average annual salary for full professors employed at colleges and universities offering baccalaureate degrees in the two aforementioned states.

The colleges have been divided into three categories.[7] Category I includes institutions that offer the doctorate degree. Category IIA includes institutions offering degrees above the bachelor's degree that have not been included in category I. Category IIB includes those institutions offering only the baccalaureate or equivalent degree.

Within each category you are to evaluate the differences in salary paid by colleges in the two states. You are to summarize your findings in a written report that includes a technical appendix for the statistical results obtained.

TABLE 12.7 Median salaries of administrators (thousands of dollars)

Title	Public	Private
Chief executive of a system	85.0	82.2
Executive vice-president	60.0	55.0
Chief academic officer	58.2	50.0
Chief public relations officer	38.8	31.0
Bursar	31.3	27.3
Registrar	37.5	28.1
Director, admissions	36.0	33.8
Director, computer center	44.2	34.8
Director, student financial aid	33.5	27.3
Dean, arts and sciences	57.7	57.0
Dean, engineering	68.9	68.0
Dean, business	55.7	55.8
Dean, law	86.6	90.0

SOURCE: Data are obtained from CUPA—The College and University Personnel Association—and reprinted with their permission. © 1987 by CUPA.

---

[7] Theological seminaries have been excluded from consideration, as have colleges reporting only combined average salary for clerical and lay faculty.

TABLE 12.8 Average salaries (excluding fringe benefits) of full professors in 1986–1987 in California and Massachusetts according to Institution Category (I, IIA , IIB)

California

Category I

65.8, 48.4, 46.9, 67.2, 68.9, 64.0, 56.9, 59.4, 62.3, 56.3, 60.4, 58.6, 55.7, 57.7

Category IIA

29.2, 35.3, 35.5, 48.8, 48.2, 48.5, 48.9, 49.0, 49.4, 49.2, 49.1, 48.5, 49.4, 48.9, 49.2, 49.5, 48.9, 49.0, 48.5, 49.4, 49.0, 49.0, 36.9, 30.0, 49.1, 44.5, 35.5, 26.6, 46.2, 42.0, 57.9, 34.3, 39.8, 40.5, 46.9, 58.0, 35.1

Category IIB

35.8, 48.8, 53.5, 32.5, 46.0, 44.6, 35.4, 52.4, 44.1, 33.7, 52.3, 33.7

Massachusetts

Category I

51.9, 52.4, 69.7, 62.4, 49.5, 51.2, 52.6

Category IIA

32.5, 39.0, 48.5, 48.6, 35.9, 46.7, 50.6, 42.0, 36.8, 48.4, 51.0, 45.9, 48.7

Category IIB

52.2, 38.0, 57.1, 33.6, 46.2, 34.5, 22.5, 38.5, 32.4, 40.5, 39.0, 45.9, 35.3, 35.8, 54.9, 44.4, 37.2, 52.2

SOURCE: Data extracted from "Economic Status of the Profession," *Academe* (Bulletin of the AAUP), Vol. 73, No. 2 (March–April 1987).

References

1. BRADLEY, J. V., *Distribution-Free Statistical Tests* (Englewood Cliffs, N.J.: Prentice-Hall, (1968).
2. CONOVER, W. J., *Practical Nonparametric Statistics*, 2d ed. (New York: Wiley, 1980).
3. DANIEL, W., *Applied Nonparametric Statistics* (Boston: Houghton Mifflin, 1978).
4. LEVINE, D. M., M. L. BERENSON, AND D. F. STEPHAN, *Using Minitab with Basic Business Statistics*, 2d ed. (Englewood Cliffs, N.J.: Prentice-Hall, 1986).
5. LEVINE, D. M., M. L. BERENSON, AND D. F. STEPHAN, *Using SAS with Basic Business Statistics* (Englewood Cliffs, N.J.: Prentice-Hall, 1983).
6. RYAN, T. A., B. L. JOINER, AND B. F. RYAN, *Minitab Student Handbook*, 2d ed. (North Scituate, Mass.: Duxbury Press, 1985).
7. *SAS User's Guide*, 1982 ed. (Cary, N.C.: SAS Institute, 1982).
8. SNEDECOR, G. W., AND W. G. COCHRAN, *Statistical Methods*, 7th ed. (Ames, Iowa: Iowa State University Press, 1980).
9. *STATGRAPHICS User's Guide* (Rockville, Md.: STSC, Inc., 1986).

13

Hypothesis Testing III: Differences between Proportions and Other Chi-Square Tests

13.1   INTRODUCTION

In the preceding chapter we examined hypothesis-testing procedures pertaining to the difference between two groups when dealing with a quantitative variable. In this chapter we shall extend our discussion of hypothesis testing to consider procedures that relate to differences between groups when dealing with a qualitative variable. We shall also introduce other hypothesis-testing techniques that involve test statistics based on the chi-square distribution.

Recall from Sections 11.2 and 12.1 that we considered various questions of interest to the production manager of a cereal filling process. Suppose that the manager and his supervisor also wanted to obtain answers to each of the following questions:

1. Is there evidence of a difference in the proportion of boxes that have to be "reworked" between Plant A and Plant B?
2. Is there evidence that the standard deviation of the amount of cereal filled in Plant A has increased from the previous value of 15 grams?

Statistical hypothesis-testing procedures for answering these questions will be described in Sections 13.2 and 13.8, respectively. For the moment, however, we may recall from Section 12.6 that we also applied hypothesis-testing procedures to answer questions of interest concerning the real estate survey. Suppose that the president and the statistician also wanted to obtain answers to each of the following:

1. Comparing houses that do not have a modern kitchen to those that do have a modern kitchen, is there a difference in the proportion of houses that have modern bathrooms?
2. Is there a difference in the proportion of houses that have a fireplace based on the geographic location of the house?
3. Is there a relationship between the style of house and the geographic location of the house?
4. Does the number of cars that can park in the indoor garage of the houses follow a Poisson distribution?
5. Does appraised value follow a normal distribution?

6. Is there evidence that the proportion of homeowners who stated that they intend to put their house up for sale in the next year differ from the actual proportion that placed their home up for sale during that year?

7. Is there evidence that the population standard deviation of the appraised value for houses without a connection to a local sewer system is different from the assumed population value of $39,000?

Statistical hypothesis-testing procedures for answering all these questions will be developed in the following sections.

13.2 TESTING FOR THE DIFFERENCE BETWEEN PROPORTIONS FROM TWO INDEPENDENT POPULATIONS USING THE NORMAL APPROXIMATION

A researcher is often concerned with the differences between two populations in terms of some qualitative characteristic. A test for the difference between two proportions based upon independent samples can be performed using two different methods. The results will be equivalent.

The first method of testing for the difference between two proportions involves the use of the normal distribution. This test is based on the difference between the two sample proportions, which may be approximated by a normal distribution for large sample sizes.

For the two populations involved, we are interested in either determining whether there is any *difference* in the proportion of successes in the two groups (two-tailed test) or whether one group had a *higher* proportion of successes than the other group (one-tailed test).[1]

Two-Tailed Test	One-Tailed Test	One-Tailed Test
H_0: $p_1 = p_2$ H_1: $p_1 \neq p_2$	H_0: $p_1 \geq p_2$ H_1: $p_1 < p_2$	H_0: $p_1 \leq p_2$ H_1: $p_1 > p_2$

where p_1 = proportion of successes in population 1
p_2 = proportion of successes in population 2

The test statistic would be

$$Z \cong \frac{(p_{S_1} - p_{S_2}) - (p_1 - p_2)}{\sqrt{\bar{p}(1 - \bar{p}) \left(\dfrac{1}{n_1} + \dfrac{1}{n_2} \right)}} \tag{13.1}$$

with

$$\bar{p} = \frac{X_1 + X_2}{n_1 + n_2}$$

---

[1] If the hypothesized difference is 0 (that is, $p_1 - p_2 = 0$ or $p_1 = p_2$), the numerator in Equation (13.1) merely becomes $p_{S_1} - p_{S_2}$.

$$p_{S_1} = \frac{X_1}{n_1}, \qquad p_{S_2} = \frac{X_2}{n_2}$$

where p_{S_1} = sample proportion obtained from population 1
  p_{S_2} = sample proportion obtained from population 2
  X_1 = number of successes in sample 1
  X_2 = number of successes in sample 2
  n_1 = size of sample taken from population 1
  n_2 = size of sample taken from population 2
  $\bar{p}$ = pooled estimate of the population proportion

Note that $\bar{p}$, the pooled estimate for the population proportion, is based on the null hypothesis. Under the null hypothesis it is assumed that the two population proportions are equal. Therefore we may obtain an overall estimate of the common population proportion by pooling together the two sample proportions. The estimate $\bar{p}$ is simply the number of successes in the two samples combined ($X_1 + X_2$) divided by the total sample size from the two groups ($n_1 + n_2$).

The test for the difference between two proportions can be applied in our cereal filling process to determine whether there is any difference between Plant A and Plant B in the proportion of boxes that need to be reworked. Samples of 200 boxes were selected from each of the two plants with the following results:

Plant A	Plant B
$n_A = 200$	$n_B = 200$
19 boxes need rework	21 boxes need rework

The null and alternative hypotheses are

$$H_0: \quad p_A = p_B$$

$$H_1: \quad p_A \neq p_B$$

If the test were to be carried out at the .10 level of significance, the critical values would be -1.645 and $+1.645$ (see Figure 13.1) and our decision rule would be

Reject H_0 if $Z > +1.645$

or if $Z < -1.645$;

otherwise do not reject H_0.

For our data,

$$p_{S_A} = \frac{X_A}{n_A} = \frac{19}{200} = .095 \qquad p_{S_B} = \frac{X_B}{n_B} = \frac{21}{200} = .105$$

and

$$\bar{p} = \frac{19 + 21}{200 + 200} = .10$$

and using Equation (13.1)

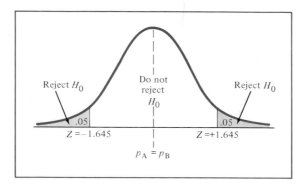

FIGURE 13.1
Testing a hypothesis about the difference between two proportions at the .10 level of significance.

$$Z \cong \frac{p_{S_1} - p_{S_2}}{\sqrt{\bar{p}(1 - \bar{p}) \left(\dfrac{1}{n_1} + \dfrac{1}{n_2} \right)}}$$

$$= \frac{.095 - .105}{\sqrt{(.1)(.9) \left(\dfrac{1}{200} + \dfrac{1}{200} \right)}}$$

$$= \frac{-.01}{\sqrt{(.09) \left(\dfrac{2}{200} \right)}} = \frac{-.01}{.03} = -.33$$

Since $Z = -.33$, we see that $-1.645 < -.33 < +1.645$, and the decision is not to reject H_0. There is no evidence of a difference in the proportion of boxes that need rework between Plant A and Plant B.

In this example the rejection region has been divided up into both tails of the distribution. Of course, if the alternative hypothesis had been a specific direction (such as $p_1 > p_2$), then the rejection region would be entirely contained in one tail of the normal distribution.

Problems

13.1   We wish to determine if there is any difference in the popularity of football between college-educated males and non-college-educated males. A sample of 100 college-educated males revealed 55 who considered themselves football fans. A sample of 200 non-college-educated males revealed 125 who considered themselves football fans. Is there any evidence of a difference in football popularity between college-educated and non-college-educated males at the .01 level of significance?

• **13.2**   A marketing study conducted in a large city showed that of 100 married women who worked full time, 43 ate dinner at a restaurant at least one night during a typical workweek, while a sample of 100 married women who did not work full time indicated that 27 ate dinner at a restaurant at least one night during the typical workweek. Using a .05 level of significance, is there evidence of a difference between the two groups of married women in the proportion that eat dinner in a restaurant at least once during the typical workweek?

● **13.3**   An accountant was studying the readability of the annual reports of two major companies. A random sample of 100 certified public accountants was selected. Fifty were randomly assigned to read the annual report of Company A, and the other 50 were to read the annual report of Company B. Based upon a standard measure of readability, 17 found Company A's annual report "understandable" and 23 found Company B's annual report "understandable." At the .10 level of significance, is there any evidence of a difference between the two companies in the proportion of CPAs who found the annual reports understandable?

13.4   Referring to Problem 6.64 on page 204, at the .05 level of significance, is there evidence of a difference between college graduates and non-college graduates in the proportion of applicants who have had their current job for at least five years?

13.5   Referring to Problem 6.7 on page 182, at the .01 level of significance, is there evidence of a difference between regular and nonregular customers in the proportion who pay cash?

13.6   A sample of 1,000 respondents were asked to compare two detergents, brand A and brand B. The respondents were asked to indicate their brand preference and whether the laundry temperature was high or low. Of 380 respondents who use a high temperature, 200 preferred brand A. Of 620 respondents who used a low temperature, 300 preferred brand A. At the .05 level of significance, is there evidence of a difference in brand preference based upon low and high laundry temperature?

13.3   TESTING FOR THE DIFFERENCE BETWEEN PROPORTIONS FROM TWO INDEPENDENT POPULATIONS USING THE CHI-SQUARE TEST

For the example of the preceding section, we may also view the data in terms of the frequency of rework from each of the two plants. A two-way table, called a **contingency table** (see Sections 4.11.1 and 6.3.2), can be developed to indicate the frequency of successes and failures for each group (Table 13.1).

The "cells" in the table indicate the frequency for each possible combination of outcomes (boxes to be reworked vs. boxes not to be reworked and Plant A vs. B). For example, the frequency of 19 indicates that 19 boxes sealed in Plant A need to be reworked, while 181 indicates that 181 boxes sealed in Plant A did not need to be reworked. The totals result from the sum of the values in the appropriate row or column of the table.

13.3.1   Test for the Difference Between Two Proportions

This contingency table is the basis for testing the difference between the two proportions using a second method of analysis, the **chi-square test.** The method begins from the null hypothesis that the proportion of successes is the same in the two populations ($p_1 = p_2$). If this null hypothesis were true, the frequencies that theoretically should be found in each cell could be computed. For example, under the null hypothesis we

TABLE 13.1   Contingency table for comparing the difference between Plant A and Plant B in the percentage of boxes needing rework

Result	Plant A	Plant B	Totals
Needed rework	19	21	40
Did not need rework	181	179	360
	200	200	400

can determine how many defectives (boxes needing rework) can theoretically be expected from boxes sealed in Plant A and Plant B. Immediately we note that a total of 40 out of 400 in the combined samples (10%) need to be reworked. If there was no difference between Plant A and Plant B, then theoretically 10% of each sample should require rework. This would mean a theoretical frequency of $.10 \times 200 = 20$ for Plant A and $.10 \times 200 = 20$ for Plant B. The number of boxes that theoretically should not need rework can be found by subtracting the theoretical number needing rework from the sample size in each plant. The actual observed frequencies and theoretical frequencies (circled numbers) are shown in Table 13.2.

TABLE 13.2   Observed and theoretical frequencies for cereal filling example

Result	Plant A	Plant B	Totals
Need rework	19 (20)	21 (20)	40
Do not need rework	181 (180) / 200	179 (180) / 200	360 / 400

The theoretical frequencies f_t for each cell can also be computed by using a simple formula:

$$f_t = \frac{n_R n_C}{n} \qquad (12.2)$$

where n_R = total number in row
n_C = total number in column
n = total sample size

Therefore, the theoretical frequency of 20 for the number that need rework in Plant A can be arrived at by taking the total number in the appropriate row (40), multiplying by the total number in the appropriate column (200), and dividing by the total sample size (400). The computation of the theoretical frequencies for each cell is illustrated below:

$$f_t = \frac{40(200)}{400} = 20.0 \qquad f_t = \frac{40(200)}{400} = 20.0$$

$$f_t = \frac{360(200)}{400} = 180.0 \qquad f_t = \frac{360(200)}{400} = 180.0$$

The chi-square method of analysis uses the squared difference between the observed frequency f_o and the theoretical frequency f_t in each cell. If there is no difference in the population proportions of success in the two groups, then the squared difference between the observed and theoretical frequencies should be small. If the proportions for the two groups are significantly different, then the squared difference between the observed and theoretical frequencies should be large. Of course, what is a "large" difference is relative; the same difference would mean more in a cell with only a few observations than in a cell where there are many observations. Therefore an adjustment is made for the size of the cell: The squared difference is divided by the expected frequency for the cell.

The test statistic is $(f_o - f_t)^2/f_t$ summed over all cells of the table. That is,

$$\chi^2_{(R-1)(C-1)} \cong \sum_{\substack{\text{all} \\ \text{cells}}} \frac{(f_o - f_t)^2}{f_t} \qquad \textbf{(13.3)}$$

where f_o = observed frequency in each cell
f_t = theoretical frequency in each cell
R = number of rows in the contingency table
C = number of columns in the contingency table

This statistic approximately follows a chi-square (χ^2) distribution, with the degrees of freedom equal to the number of rows in the contingency table minus 1 (that is, $R - 1$) times the number of columns in the contingency table minus 1 (that is, $C - 1$):

$$\text{degrees of freedom} = (R - 1)(C - 1)$$

The null hypothesis of equality between the two proportions ($p_1 = p_2$) will be rejected *only* when the computed value of the test statistic is greater than the critical value of the chi-square distribution with the appropriate number of degrees of freedom (see Figure 13.2).

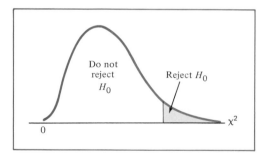

FIGURE 13.2
Testing a hypothesis for the difference between two proportions using the chi-square test.

The chi-square distribution is a skewed distribution whose shape depends solely on the number of degrees of freedom. As the number of degrees of freedom increases, the chi-square distribution becomes more symmetrical. Table E.4 contains various upper-tail areas of the chi-square distribution for different degrees of freedom. A portion of this table is displayed as Table 13.3.

The value at the top of each column indicates the area in the upper portion (or right side) of the chi-square distribution. For example, with 1 degree of freedom the value for an upper-tail area of .10 is 2.706 (see Figure 13.3). This means that for 1 degree of freedom the probability of exceeding a chi-square value of 2.706 is .10. Therefore, once we determine the level of significance and the degrees of freedom, the critical value of chi-square can be found.

Let us return to the computation of the chi-square value for the cereal filling example. There are two rows and two columns in Table 13.2. Therefore, there will be $(2 - 1) \times (2 - 1) = 1$ degree of freedom. The test statistic is

TABLE 13.3 Obtaining the critical value from the chi-square distribution for $\alpha = .10$ and 1 degree of freedom

Degrees of Freedom	Upper-Tail Area									
	.995	.99	.975	.95	.90	.75	.25	.10	.05	.025
1			0.001	0.004	0.016	0.102	1.323	2.706	3.841	5.024
2	0.010	0.020	0.051	0.103	0.211	0.575	2.773	4.605	5.991	7.378
3	0.072	0.115	0.216	0.352	0.584	1.213	4.108	6.251	7.815	9.348
4	0.207	0.297	0.484	0.711	1.064	1.923	5.385	7.779	9.488	11.143
5	0.412	0.554	0.831	1.145	1.610	2.675	6.626	9.236	11.071	12.833

SOURCE: Extracted from Table E.4.

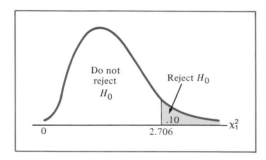

FIGURE 13.3
Finding the critical value of chi-square at the .10 level of significance with 1 degree of freedom.

$$\chi_1^2 \cong \sum_{\substack{\text{all} \\ \text{cells}}} \frac{(f_o - f_t)^2}{f_t}$$

The data are given in Table 13.4. χ_1^2 is computed to be .1111. If the test was being conducted at the .10 level, from Table 13.3 the critical value is 2.706 (see Figure 13.3). Therefore, since .1111 < 2.706, the null hypothesis would not be rejected. The conclusion would be reached that there is no evidence of a difference between Plant A and Plant B in the proportion of cereal boxes that need rework.

TABLE 13.4 Computation of the chi-square statistic for the cereal filling example

f_o	f_t	$(f_o - f_t)$	$(f_o - f_t)^2$	$(f_o - f_t)^2/f_t$
19	20	−1	1	.05000
181	180	+1	1	.00555
21	20	+1	1	.05000
179	180	−1	1	.00555
				.11110

The chi-square test assumes that there are at least five theoretical frequencies in each cell of the contingency table. This assumption is important particularly for the 2×2 contingency table which has only 1 degree of freedom. Other procedures, such as *Fisher's exact test* (References 1–3), can be utilized if this assumption is not met.

13.3.2 Test for Independence

The statement of no difference in the proportion needing rework between the two groups (Plant A and Plant B) also means that the two variables are independent (that is, there is no relationship between needing rework and the plant in which the box was filled). When the conclusions are stated in this manner, the chi-square test is called a **test of independence.** The null and alternative hypotheses would be

H_0: There is independence (no relationship) between needing rework and the plant in which the box is filled.

H_1: There is a relationship (dependence) between needing rework and the plant in which the box is filled.

If the null hypothesis cannot be rejected, the conclusion would be drawn that there is no evidence of a relationship between the two variables. If the null hypothesis is rejected, the conclusion would be drawn that there is evidence of a relationship between the two variables. Regardless of whether the chi-square test is considered a test for the difference between two proportions or a test of independence, the computations and results are exactly the same. Hence for our cereal filling example, we may conclude that there is no evidence of a relationship between needing rework and the plant in which the box was filled.

13.3.3 Testing for Equality of Proportions by Z and by χ^2: A Comparison of Results

The methods we have just developed can also be applied to the real estate survey. As a second example, we wish to determine if there is any difference between houses that do not have a modern kitchen and houses that have a modern kitchen with respect to the proportion that have modern bathrooms. The relevant information (obtained from Table 6.2 on page 181) is summarized below:

Houses That Do Not Have a Modern Kitchen	Houses That Have a Modern Kitchen
$n_N = 80$ 8 have modern bathrooms	$n_Y = 153$ 146 have modern bathrooms

The null and alternative hypotheses would be

$$H_0: \quad p_N = p_Y$$

$$H_1: \quad p_N \neq p_Y$$

If this test were to be performed using the normal distribution and a level of significance of .05 was selected, the critical values would be $+1.96$ and -1.96 (see Figure 13.4), and our decision rule would be

Reject H_0 if $Z > +1.96$

or if $Z < -1.96$;

otherwise do not reject H_0.

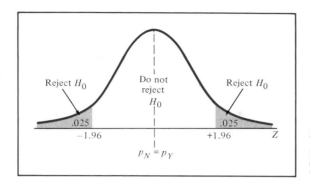

FIGURE 13.4
Testing for the difference between two proportions at the .05 level of signifi-cance using the normal approxima-tion.

Therefore, for our data we would have

$$p_{S_N} = \frac{X_N}{n_N} = \frac{8}{80} = .10 \qquad p_{S_Y} = \frac{X_Y}{n_Y} = \frac{146}{153} = .9542$$

Since we are testing for the difference between two proportions, from Equation (13.1) the test statistic would be

$$Z \cong \frac{p_{S_1} - p_{S_2}}{\sqrt{\bar{p}(1 - \bar{p}) \left(\frac{1}{n_1} + \frac{1}{n_2} \right)}}$$

where

$$\bar{p} = \frac{8 + 146}{80 + 153} = .661$$

so that

$$Z \cong \frac{.10 - .9542}{\sqrt{.661(.339) \left(\frac{1}{80} + \frac{1}{153} \right)}}$$

$$= \frac{-.8542}{\sqrt{.0042654}} = \frac{-.8542}{.06531} = -13.08$$

Since $Z = -13.08 < -1.96$, we reject H_0.

We conclude that there is evidence of a difference in the proportions.

This problem can also be examined (see Table 13.5) by using the chi-square test based on the contingency table previously developed as Table 6.2.

TABLE 13.5   Cross-classification of modern kitchen and modern bathrooms

Modern Kitchen	Modern Bathrooms		
	Absent	Present	Totals
Absent	72	8	80
Present	7	146	153
Totals	79	154	233

The theoretical frequencies can be obtained from Equation (13.2):

$$f_t = \frac{n_R n_C}{n}$$

so that

$$f_t = \frac{80(79)}{233} = 27.12 \qquad f_t = \frac{80(154)}{233} = 52.88$$

$$f_t = \frac{153(79)}{233} = 51.88 \qquad f_t = \frac{153(154)}{233} = 101.12$$

Since there are two rows and two columns in this table, there will be $(2 - 1)(2 - 1) = 1$ degree of freedom. From Table E.4, using a level of significance of .05 results in a critical value of 3.841 (see Figure 13.5).

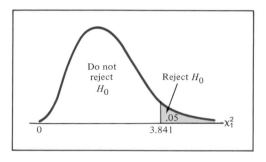

FIGURE 13.5
Testing for the difference between two proportions at the .05 level of significance using the chi-square test.

The chi-square test statistic, equal to

$$\sum_{\substack{\text{all} \\ \text{cells}}} \frac{(f_o - f_t)^2}{f_t}$$

would be computed as shown in Table 13.6. Since $\chi_1^2 = 171.1043 > 3.841$, we reject H_0.

Again the null hypothesis will be rejected and we would conclude that there is evidence of a difference in the proportions. Alternatively, we can conclude that there is evidence of a relationship between presence of a modern kitchen and presence of modern bathrooms.

We have seen in these examples that both the normal distribution and chi-square tests have led to the same conclusion. This can be explained by the interrelationship between the value for the normal distribution and that for the chi-square distribution with 1 degree of freedom. The chi-square statistic will always be the square of the

TABLE 13.6   Computation of the chi-square test statistic for data from Table 13.5

f_0	f_t	$(f_0 - f_t)$	$(f_0 - f_t)^2$	$(f_0 - f_t)^2/f_t$
72	27.12	+44.88	2014.2144	74.2704
7	51.88	−44.88	2014.2144	38.8245
8	52.88	−44.88	2014.2144	38.0903
146	101.12	+44.88	2014.2144	19.9191
				171.1043

test statistic based upon the normal distribution. For instance, our computed Z value was 13.08, while the chi-square value was $(13.08)^2 = 171.1043$. Also, if we compare the critical values of the two distributions, we can see that at the .05 level of significance the chi-square value of 3.841 is the square of the normal value of 1.96 (that is, $\chi_1^2 = Z^2$).

Therefore it is clear that in testing for the *difference* between two proportions, the normal distribution and the chi-square test provide equivalent methods. However, if we are interested specifically in determining a *directional difference*, such as $p_1 > p_2$, then the normal distribution test must be used with the entire rejection region located in one tail of the distribution.

In our examples to this point the chi-square test had 1 degree of freedom, since there were two rows and two columns in the contingency tables. We note that the 1 degree of freedom can be derived from the nature of the 2×2 contingency table. The theoretical frequencies are determined from the totals in the margins of the table. Once we have determined the theoretical frequency for one of the cells, the theoretical frequencies for the other three cells will be fixed. In the cereal-filling example, once the theoretical frequency of 20 for those needing rework in Plant A is found, we know that the theoretical number not needing rework in Plant A must be 180, since the total must add to 200. We also know that the theoretical number needing rework in Plant B must be 20, since the combined total needing rework must add to 40. Finally, for Plant B, if the theoretical number needing rework is 20, then the number not needing rework must be 180, since the total must add to 200. Therefore, since all other theoretical frequencies will be known once the theoretical frequency of one cell is known, the contingency table is said to have 1 degree of freedom.

Problems

13.7   Do Problem 13.1 on page 411 using the chi-square test.

● **13.8**   Do Problem 13.2 on page 411 using the chi-square test.

● **13.9**   Do problem 13.3 on page 412 using the chi-square test.

13.10   Do Problem 13.4 on page 412 using the chi-square test.

13.11   Do Problem 13.5 on page 412 using the chi-square test.

13.12   Do problem 13.6 on page 412 using the chi-square test.

13.4 TESTING FOR THE DIFFERENCE BETWEEN PROPORTIONS FROM C INDEPENDENT POPULATIONS

The chi-square method of testing for the difference between two proportions can be extended to the general case in which there are C independent populations to be compared. The null and alternative hypotheses would be

$$H_0: \quad p_1 = p_2 = p_3 = \cdots = p_C$$

$$H_1: \quad \text{At least one proportion is different from the others.}$$

The contingency table would have two rows and C columns, so that there would be $C - 1$ degrees of freedom in the chi-square test.

TABLE 13.7   Cross-classification of fireplace with geographical location

Fireplace	Geographical Location			
	East Meadow	Farmingdale	Levittown	Totals
Absent	61	45	48	154
Present	13	15	51	79
Totals	74	60	99	233

Referring to the real estate survey, one question that the president and the statistician wanted to study was whether there was a difference in the proportion of houses with a fireplace based upon geographical location. This information can be determined by cross-classifying presence of a fireplace (question 16) and the geographical location (question 9) as in Table 13.7.

The null and alternative hypotheses can be stated as follows:

$$H_0: \quad p_{EM} = p_F = p_L$$

$$H_1: \quad \text{At least one of the proportions differ}$$

where

$$p_{EM} = \text{proportion of houses in East Meadow that have a fireplace}$$

$$p_F = \text{proportion of houses in Farmingdale that have a fireplace}$$

$$p_L = \text{proportion of houses in Levittown that have a fireplace}$$

If the null hypothesis were to be tested at the .01 level of significance, the critical value (from Table E.4) would be 9.21 (since there would be $(2 - 1)(3 - 1) = 2$ degrees of freedom and the upper-tail area is .01). This is depicted in Figure 13.6.

Since the theoretical frequencies would be computed from Equation (13.2), $f_t = n_R n_C / n$, we would have for the six cells:

$$f_t = \frac{154(74)}{233} = 48.91 \qquad f_t = \frac{154(60)}{233} = 39.66 \qquad f_t = \frac{154(99)}{233} = 65.43$$

$$f_t = \frac{79(74)}{233} = 25.09 \qquad f_t = \frac{79(60)}{233} = 20.34 \qquad f_t = \frac{79(99)}{233} = 33.57$$

The chi-square test statistic is computed as in Table 13.8.

Since $\chi_2^2 = 24.6283 > 9.21$, the null hypothesis can be rejected, and we would conclude that there is evidence of a difference in the proportion of houses having a

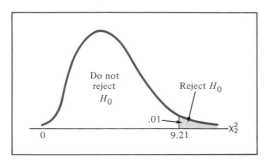

FIGURE 13.6
Testing for the equality of three proportions at the .01 level of significance with 2 degrees of freedom.

TABLE 13.8   Computation of the chi-square test statistic

f_0	f_t	$(f_0 - f_t)$	$(f_0 - f_t)^2$	$(f_0 - f_t)^2/f_t$
61	48.91	12.09	146.1681	2.9885
13	25.09	−12.09	146.1681	5.8258
45	39.66	5.34	28.5156	0.7190
15	20.34	−5.34	28.5156	1.4019
48	65.43	−17.43	303.8049	4.6432
51	33.57	17.43	303.8049	9.0499
				24.6283

fireplace based on geographical location. Alternatively, it can also be concluded that there is a relationship between presence of a fireplace and geographical location.

Problems

✗13.13   Why can't the normal approximation be used for determining differences in the proportion of successes in more than two groups?

13.14   Referring to Problem 6.65 on page 204, is there evidence of a difference in the proportion of foreign cars owned based upon area of residence? (Use $\alpha = .05$.)

13.15   An auditor would like to know if there is a difference in the proportion of improper travel expense vouchers in three different departments of a company. A random sample of 25 vouchers from department A, 25 vouchers from department B, and 50 vouchers from department C revealed the following information:

	Department		
Result	A	B	C
Improper vouchers	6	5	9
Proper vouchers	19	20	41

Is there any evidence of a difference in the proportion of improper vouchers between departments A, B, and C at the .05 level of significance?

● 13.16   The faculty council of a large university would like to determine the opinion of various groups toward a proposed trimester academic calendar. A random sample of 100 undergraduate students, 50 graduate students, and 50 faculty members is selected with the following results:

Opinion	Undergraduate	Graduate	Faculty
Favor trimester	63	27	30
Oppose trimester	37	23	20
Totals	100	50	50

(a)   At the .01 level of significance, is there evidence of a difference in attitude toward the trimester between the various groups?

➠(b)   ACTION   What should the faculty council report to the president of the university concerning the attitude toward the trimester academic calendar?

13.17   An agronomist is studying three different varieties of tomato to determine whether there is a difference in the proportion of seeds that germinate. Random samples of 100 seeds of each variety (beefsteak, plum, and cherry) are subjected to the same starting conditions with the following results:

| | Tomato Variety | | |
Number of Seeds	Beefsteak	Plum	Cherry
Germinated	82	70	58
Did not germinate	18	30	42
Totals	100	100	100

    (a) At the .10 level of significance, is there evidence of a difference between the varieties of tomatoes in the proportion of seeds that germinate?

➠**(b)** **ACTION**   If you have a relative who starts tomato plants from seeds, what would you tell her about the three varieties?

● **13.18**   The director of a large shopping center would like to know if there are differences in the proportion of women shoppers at various times during the week. Random samples of 300 weekday shoppers, 300 weeknight shoppers, and 400 weekend shoppers were selected with the following results:

Gender	Weekday	Weeknight	Weekend
Male	90	125	185
Female	210	175	215
Totals	300	300	400

At the .05 level of significance, is there evidence of a difference in the proportion of women shoppers at the various times of the week?

13.19   The Sudso Soap Company tested its new brand of detergent by having families try one box of the new brand and one box of the old brand and expressing a preference for one or the other. Families were classified by the softness of their water, resulting in the following table:

| | Preference | |
Water Softness	New	Old
Soft	19	29
Medium	23	47
Hard	24	43

    (a) Is there evidence that water softness is related to preference for the new detergent? (Use $\alpha = .01$.)

➠**(b)** **ACTION**   What would you report to the Director of Product Development concerning the new brand of detergent?

13.5   CHI-SQUARE TEST OF INDEPENDENCE IN THE $R \times C$ TABLE

We have just seen that the chi-square test can be used to determine differences between the proportion of successes in any number of populations. For a contingency table that

TABLE 13.9   Cross-classification of type of house and geographical location

| Style of House | Geographical Location | | | |
	East Meadow	Farmingdale	Levittown	Totals
Cape	31	14	52	97
Expanded ranch	2	1	12	15
Colonial	6	8	9	23
Ranch	16	20	24	60
Split level	19	17	2	38
Totals	74	60	99	233

has R rows and C columns, the chi-square test can be generalized as a test of independence. As an example from the real estate survey, the test of independence can be applied to determine whether there is a relationship between the style of house (question 10) and the geographical location of the house (question 9). The contingency table for these two categorical variables can be set up as shown in Table 13.9.
The null and alternative hypotheses for this table are:

H_0:   There is no relationship between style of house and geographic location.

H_1:   There is a relationship between style of house and geographic location.

If this null hypothesis were tested at the .01 level of significance, the critical value would be 20.09 since there are $(5 - 1)(3 - 1) = 8$ degrees of freedom. This is shown in Figure 13.7.
The theoretical frequencies for the 15 cells, computed from Equation (13.2) are

$$f_t = \frac{97(74)}{233} = 30.81 \qquad f_t = \frac{97(60)}{233} = 24.98 \qquad f_t = \frac{97(99)}{233} = 41.21$$

$$f_t = \frac{15(74)}{233} = 4.76 \qquad f_t = \frac{15(60)}{233} = 3.86 \qquad f_t = \frac{15(99)}{233} = 6.37$$

$$f_t = \frac{23(74)}{233} = 7.30 \qquad f_t = \frac{23(60)}{233} = 5.92 \qquad f_t = \frac{23(99)}{233} = 9.77$$

$$f_t = \frac{60(74)}{233} = 19.06 \qquad f_t = \frac{60(60)}{233} = 15.45 \qquad f_t = \frac{60(99)}{233} = 25.49$$

$$f_t = \frac{38(74)}{233} = 12.07 \qquad f_t = \frac{38(60)}{233} = 9.79 \qquad f_t = \frac{38(99)}{233} = 16.15$$

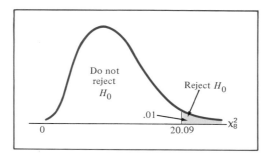

FIGURE 13.7
Testing for a relationship between style of house and geographic location at the .01 level of significance with 8 degrees of freedom.

TABLE 13.10 Computation of the chi-square test statistic for the style of house–geographical location contingency table

f_0	f_t	$(f_0 - f_t)$	$(f_0 - f_t)^2$	$(f_0 - f_t)^2/f_t$
31	30.81	0.19	.0361	.0012
2	4.76	−2.76	7.6176	1.6003
6	7.30	−1.30	1.6900	.2315
16	19.06	−3.06	9.3636	.4913
19	12.07	6.93	48.0249	3.9789
14	24.98	−10.98	120.5604	4.8263
1	3.86	−2.86	8.1796	2.1191
8	5.92	2.08	4.3264	.7308
20	15.45	4.55	20.7025	1.3400
17	9.79	7.21	51.9841	5.3099
52	41.21	10.79	116.4241	2.8251
12	6.37	5.63	31.6969	4.9760
9	9.77	−.77	.5929	.0607
24	25.49	−1.49	2.2201	.0871
2	16.15	−14.15	200.2225	12.3977
				40.9758

We may note that two cells (expanded ranch in East Meadow and expanded ranch in Farmingdale) have theoretical frequencies below 5 (4.76 and 3.86 respectively). However, in a large-sized contingency table (such as our 5 × 3 table), this will have little effect on the validity of the chi-square test and it would not be considered necessary to combine categories. As a general rule (see References 1–3), in a large contingency table, as long as no more than 20% of the cells have theoretical frequencies below 5 and as long as no cell has a theoretical frequency below 1, the validity of the chi-square test is not seriously affected.

The chi-square test statistic for these data would then be computed as indicated in Table 13.10. Since $\chi_8^2 = 40.9758 > 20.09$, the null hypothesis can be rejected. We would conclude that there is evidence of a relationship between style of house and geographic location.

Problems

13.20 If a contingency table had four rows and three columns, how many degrees of freedom would there be for the chi-square test?

13.21 Referring to Problem 6.11 on page 183, the statistics association at a large state university would like to determine whether there is a relationship between student interest in statistics and ability in mathematics. At the .05 level of significance, is there evidence of a relationship between interest in statistics and ability in mathematics?

13.22 A nationwide market research study was undertaken to determine the preferences of various age groups of males for different sports. A random sample of 1,000 men was selected, and each individual was asked to indicate his favorite sport. The results were as follows:

Age Group	Sport				
	Baseball	Football	Basketball	Hockey	Totals
Under 20	26	47	41	36	150
20–29	38	84	80	48	250
30–39	72	68	38	22	200
40–49	96	48	30	26	200
50 and over	134	44	18	4	200
Totals	366	291	207	136	1,000

At the .01 level of significance, is there evidence of a relationship between age of men and preference for sports?

13.23 Suppose that a survey has been undertaken to determine if there is a relationship between place of residence and automobile preference. A random sample of 200 car owners from large cities, 150 from suburbs, and 150 from rural areas were selected with the following results:

Residence	Automobile Preference					
	GM	Ford	Chrysler	European	Asian	Totals
Large city	64	40	26	8	62	200
Suburb	53	35	24	6	32	150
Rural	53	45	30	6	16	150
Totals	170	120	80	20	110	500

At the .05 level of significance, is there evidence of a relationship between place of residence and automobile preference?

• 13.24 The owner of a home-heating-oil delivery firm would like to investigate how fast bills are paid in three different suburban areas. Random samples of 100 accounts are selected in each area. The number of days between delivery of the oil and payment of the bill is recorded with the following results:

Days Before Payment	Area		
	I	II	III
1–15	34	42	40
16–30	48	50	46
More than 30	18	8	14
Totals	100	100	100

At the .10 level of significance, is there evidence of a difference between the three areas in how quickly the oil bills are paid?

13.25 During the Vietnam War a lottery system was instituted to choose males to be drafted into the military. Numbers representing days of the year were ''randomly'' selected; men born on days of the year with low numbers were drafted first, while those with high numbers were not drafted. The following shows how many low (1–122), medium (123–244), and high (245–366) numbers were drawn for birthdates in each quarter of the year (see page 426):

Number Set	Jan.–Mar.	Apr.–Jun.	Jul.–Sep.	Oct.–Dec.
Low	21	28	35	38
Medium	34	22	29	37
High	36	41	28	17

(a) Is there evidence that the numbers drawn were related to the time of year? (Use $\alpha = .05$.)

(b) Would you conclude that the lottery drawing appears to have been random?

13.6   THE CHI-SQUARE GOODNESS-OF-FIT TEST FOR PROBABILITY DISTRIBUTIONS

13.6.1   Introduction

In this section we shall examine still another important application of the chi-square test, that of testing the **goodness of fit** of a set of data to a specific probability distribution. In testing the goodness of fit of a set of data, we compare the actual frequencies in each category (or class interval) to the frequencies that theoretically would be expected to occur if the data followed the selected probability distribution.

To perform a chi-square goodness-of-fit test, several steps must be followed. First, we must hypothesize the probability distribution which is to be fitted to the data. Second, the values of each parameter of the selected probability distribution (such as the mean) must either be hypothesized or estimated from the actual data. Next, the selected probability distribution is used to determine the probability and then the theoretical frequency for each category or class interval. Finally, the chi-square test statistic [Equation (13.4) on page 428] can be employed to test whether the selected probability distribution is a ''good fit'' to the data.

13.6.2   The Chi-Square Goodness-of-Fit Test for a Poisson Distribution

The use of the chi-square goodness-of-fit test can be seen by referring to the real estate survey. We may recall from Section 13.1 that the president wanted to determine whether the size of the indoor garage of the houses followed a Poisson distribution. The information concerning ''type of indoor parking facility'' from the sample of 233 houses has been extracted from Figure 2.10 on pages 24–29 and presented in Table 13.11.

TABLE 13.11   Frequency distribution of "number of cars that can be parked in the indoor parking facility" for a random sample of 233 houses

Number of Cars	Frequency
0	61
1	151
2	$\underline{21}$
	233

SOURCE: Data are taken from Figure 2.10.

TABLE 13.12   Computation of the sample average number of parked cars from the frequency distribution

Number of Cars	Frequency f_j	$m_j f_j$
0	61	0
1	151	151
2	21	42
	$n = 233$	$\sum_{j=1}^{g} m_j f_j = 193$

In order to determine whether this variable follows a Poisson distribution, we may set up the following hypotheses:

H_0:   The number of parked cars follows a Poisson distribution.

H_1:   The number of parked cars does not follow a Poisson distribution.

Since the Poisson distribution has one parameter, its mean μ_X, we can either include a specified value for the mean as part of the null hypothesis or we can estimate the mean from the sample results. In our example, we will do the latter. We will hypothesize only that the data follow the Poisson distribution without specifying a population mean μ_X.

In order to obtain an estimate of the mean of the Poisson distribution we must refer back to Section 4.3, in which we computed the sample mean from a set of data grouped into a frequency distribution. In Table 13.11 each integer value may be considered the midpoint of a class. So, from Equation (4.1) we use $\overline{X} = \sum_{j=1}^{g} m_j f_j / n$, and we obtain the mean from Table 13.12. For this example

$$\overline{X} = \frac{\sum_{j=1}^{g} m_j f_j}{n} = \frac{193}{233} = 0.828$$

Therefore $\overline{X} \cong 0.80$.

This value of the sample mean would now be used as the estimate for μ_X for the purposes of finding probabilities from the table of the Poisson distribution (Table E.6). From Table E.6, for $\mu_X = \lambda = 0.8$, the probability of X successes ($X = 0, 1, 2, 3, \ldots, 6$) can be determined and the theoretical frequency for each is obtained by multiplying the appropriate probability by the sample size n. These results are summarized in Table 13.13.

TABLE 13.13   Actual and theoretical frequencies for "number of parked cars"

Number of Cars	Actual Frequency, f_o	Probability, $P(X)$, for Poisson with $\mu_X = 0.8$	Theoretical Frequency, $f_t = n \cdot P(X)$
0	61	.4493	104.687
1	151	.3595	87.764
2	21	.1438	33.505
3	0	.0383	8.924
4	0	.0077	1.794
5	0	.0012	.280
6	0	.0002	.047

We may observe from Table 13.13 that the theoretical frequency of having a parking facility that holds four or more cars is below five. However, we may recall that in our previous discussion of the chi-square test we assumed that each cell contained at least five theoretical frequencies. Thus we may combine all classes representing four or more cars with the class representing three cars in order to have all classes contain at least five theoretical frequencies.

The chi-square test for determining whether the data follow a specific probability distribution is computed from

$$\chi^2_{K-p-1} \cong \sum_K \frac{(f_o - f_t)^2}{f_t} \tag{13.4}$$

where f_o = observed frequency
f_t = theoretical frequency
K = number of categories or classes that remain after combining classes
p = number of parameters estimated from the data

In our example, after the combining of classes, four classes remain (0,1,2,3 or more). Since the mean of the Poisson distribution had been estimated from the actual data, the number of degrees of freedom would equal

$$K - p - 1 = 4 - 1 - 1 = 2 \text{ degrees of freedom}$$

On the other hand, it should be mentioned here that had a specific value of the mean been included as part of the null hypothesis, then the 1 degree of freedom p would not be lost and there would be $K - 1 = 3$ degrees of freedom for obtaining the critical value.

If a level of significance of .05 is selected, the critical value of chi-square with 2 degrees of freedom is 5.991 (from Table E.4). This is shown in Figure 13.8.

Therefore, the decision rule is

Reject H_0 if $\chi^2_2 > 5.991$; otherwise do not reject H_0.

The value of the chi-square statistic can be computed as shown in Table 13.14. Since $79.506 > 5.991$, we reject H_0. Thus we may conclude that the number of cars that can be parked at an indoor garage does not follow a Poisson distribution.

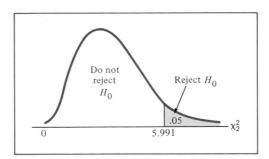

FIGURE 13.8
Testing the goodness of fit of the Poisson distribution at the .05 level of significance with 2 degrees of freedom.

TABLE 13.14 Computation of the chi-square test statistic for the number of parked cars problem

Number of Cars	f_o	f_t	$(f_o - f_t)$	$(f_o - f_t)^2$	$(f_o - f_t)^2/f_t$
0	61	104.687	−43.687	1908.5539	18.231
1	151	87.764	63.236	3998.7916	45.563
2	21	33.505	−12.505	156.3750	4.667
3 or more	0	11.045	−11.045	121.9920	11.045
					79.506

13.6.3 The Chi-Square Goodness-of-Fit Test for a Normal Distribution

In Chapters 10–12 we made the assumption of a normal distribution when developing confidence intervals and testing hypotheses about quantitative variables when σ_X is unknown. Suppose that in our real estate survey the statistician would like to determine whether the appraised value is normally distributed. Thus we have the following hypotheses:

H_0:   The appraised value follows a normal distribution.

H_1:   The appraised value does not follow a normal distribution.

In the case of the normal distribution, there are two parameters (the mean μ_X and the standard deviation σ_X) that can be estimated from the sample. If the raw data were available[2] as in the case of the real estate survey (see Figure 2.10), a statistical package such as SAS, SPSS^X, or Minitab could be used to compute the sample statistics. For these data, $\overline{X} = 190.85$ and $S = 34.54$ (in thousands of dollars).

The data are then tallied into a frequency distribution. For appraised value, our statistician has selected class interval widths of 20 (in thousands of dollars) with class boundaries beginning at 100. Since the normal distribution is continuous, we must determine the area in each class interval of the frequency distribution. In addition, since a normally distributed variable theoretically ranges from $-\infty$ to $+\infty$, we must also account for the area beyond the actual set of class intervals that have been established. For example, if we wish to find the area below 100, we merely subtract the area between 100 and the mean ($\overline{X} = 190.85$) from .5000 (which, of course, represents the area from $-\infty$ to the mean).

Thus for our data we have

$$Z = \frac{100 - 190.85}{34.54} = -2.63$$

and from Table E.2 we compute the area as $.5000 - .4957 = .0043$. Moreover, to compute the area in a particular class such as the interval between 100 but less than 120, we would compute the area between 120 and the mean and then subtract it from the area between 100 and the mean which we have previously obtained. Thus we have

---

[2] If only a frequency distribution were available, the grouped-data approximation formulas [Equations (4.1) and (4.3)] could be used.

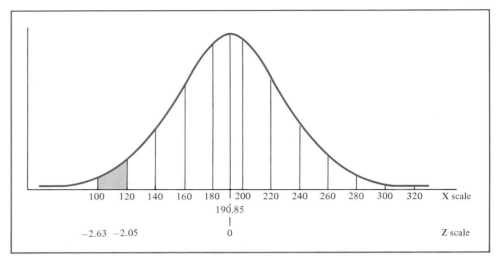

FIGURE 13.9
Finding the Z value for each class interval.

$$Z = \frac{120 - 190.85}{34.54} = -2.05$$

and from Table E.2 we can compute the area of interest as $.4957 - .4798 = .0159$ (as shown in Figure 13.9).

In a similar manner we may compute the area in each class interval—except for the class in which the mean is located. For this class we must add the area below the mean to the area above the mean. The complete set of computations needed to find the area and the theoretical frequency (the area or probability times the sample size) in each class are summarized in Table 13.15. From the table we may observe that for classes below the mean we have indicated the lower class boundary while for classes above the mean we have indicated the upper class boundary. By *subtracting* the area between the class boundary (X) and $\bar{X}$ for two *adjacent* classes, we have obtained the area in a *particular* class interval. On the other hand, for the class in which the mean is contained we must find two *separate* areas—the area from the lower boundary of this class to the mean and the area from the upper boundary of this class to the mean. These two portions are then *added together* to obtain the total area in this class interval (that is, between 180 and 200).

To perform the chi-square test we may recall that each cell or class should contain at least five theoretical frequencies. However, we can see from Table 13.15 that several classes have theoretical frequencies less than five. Since these classes are at the extreme lower and at the extreme upper portion of the distribution, they may be combined with respective adjacent categories for the purpose of performing the analysis.

The chi-square test for determining whether the data follow a specific probability distribution is computed from Equation (13.4). In our example, after the combining of the classes, eight classes remain. Since the true mean and standard deviation have been estimated from the sample data, the number of degrees of freedom would equal $K - p - 1 = 8 - 2 - 1 = 5$ degrees of freedom. If a level of significance of .05 is selected, the critical value of chi-square with 5 degrees of freedom is 11.071 (from Table E.4). This is shown in Figure 13.10.

TABLE 13.15   Computation of the area and theoretical frequencies in each class interval for the appraised value

Class Boundaries	X	$X - \bar{X}$	$Z = \dfrac{X - \bar{X}}{S}$	Area between X and $\bar{X}$	Area in Class	Theoretical Frequency $f_t = $ Area $\times n$	
Below 100	—	—	$-\infty$	.5000	.0043	1.0019 ⎫	
100 but < 120	100	−90.85	−2.63	.4957	.0159	3.7047 ⎬ combine	
120 but < 140	120	−70.85	−2.05	.4798	.0506	11.7898 ⎭	
140 but < 160	140	−50.85	−1.47	.4292	.1159	27.0047	
160 but < 180	160	−30.85	−0.89	.3133	.1916	44.6428	
180 but < 200	180	−10.85	−0.31	.1217 ⎫	.2243	52.2619	
	200	+9.15	+0.26	.1026 ⎭			
200 but < 220	220	+29.15	+0.84	.2995	.1969	45.8777	
220 but < 240	240	+49.15	+1.42	.4222	.1227	28.5891	
240 but < 260	260	+69.15	+2.00	.4772	.0550	12.8150	
260 but < 280	280	+89.15	+2.58	.4951	.0179	4.1707 ⎫	
280 but < 300	300	+109.15	+3.16	.49921	.00411	.95763 ⎬	
300 but < 320	320	+129.15	+3.74	.49991	.00070	.1631 ⎬ combine	
320 or above	—	—	$+\infty$	.5000	.00009	.02097 ⎭	

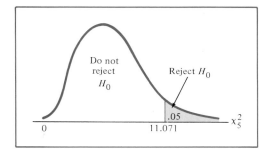

FIGURE 13.10
Testing the goodness of fit of the normal distribution at the .05 level of significance with 5 degrees of freedom.

After combining the classes in Table 13.15, the value of chi-square can be computed as shown in Table 13.16. Since $86.1195 > 11.071$, we reject H_0.

Since the null hypothesis has been rejected, the statistician can conclude that there is evidence that the appraised value follows other than a normal distribution.

In this section we have limited our discussion of the chi-square goodness-of-fit test to the Poisson and normal distributions. Other well-known probability distributions such as the uniform and binomial distributions can also be "fitted" to sets of data to

TABLE 13.16   Computation of the chi-square test statistic for appraised value example

Appraised Value	f_o	f_t	$f_o - f_t$	$(f_o - f_t)^2$	$(f_o - f_t)^2/f_t$
Under 140	2	16.4964	−14.4964	210.1456	12.7389
140 but < 160	23	27.0047	−4.0047	16.0376	.5939
160 but < 180	75	44.6428	30.3572	921.5596	20.6430
180 but < 200	73	52.2619	20.7381	430.0688	8.2291
200 but < 220	22	45.8777	−23.8777	570.1446	12.4275
220 but < 240	18	28.5891	−10.5891	112.1290	3.9221
240 but < 260	4	12.8150	−8.8150	77.7042	6.0635
260 or above	16	5.3124	10.6876	114.2248	21.5015
					86.1195

determine the goodness of fit. In each case the parameters of the distributions involved must be either hypothesized or estimated from the data so that the theoretical frequencies may be determined.

Problems

- **13.26** The manager of a computer facility has collected data on the number of times that service to users was interrupted (usually due to machine failure) in each day over the past 500 days.

Interruptions per Day	Number of Days
0	160
1	175
2	86
3	41
4	18
5	12
6	8
	500

Does the distribution of service interruptions come from a Poisson distribution at the .01 level of significance?

13.27 Referring to the data in Problem 13.26, at the .01 level of significance does the distribution of service interruptions follow a Poisson distribution with a population mean of 1.5 interruptions per day?

13.28 The manager of the commercial mortgage department of a large bank has collected data during the past two years concerning the number of commercial mortgages approved per week. The results from these two years (104 weeks) indicated the following:

Number of Commercial Mortgages Approved	Frequency
0	13
1	25
2	32
3	17
4	9
5	6
6	1
7	1
	104

Does the distribution of the number of commercial mortgages approved per week in the last two years follow a Poisson distribution at the .01 level of significance?

13.29 A random sample of 500 car batteries revealed the following distribution of battery life (in years):

Life (*in years*)	Frequency
0–under 1	12
1–under 2	94
2–under 3	170
3–under 4	188
4–under 5	28
5–under 6	8
	500

For these data $\bar{X} = 2.80$, $S = 0.97$.

Do these data fit a normal distribution at the .01 level of significance?

● **13.30** A random sample of 500 long-distance telephone calls revealed the following distribution of call length (in minutes):

Length (*in minutes*)	Frequency
0–under 5	48
5–under 10	84
10–under 15	164
15–under 20	126
20–under 25	50
25–under 30	28
	500

(a) Compute the mean and standard deviation of this frequency distribution.

(b) Do these data fit a normal distribution at the .01 level of significance?

13.31 To check the uniformity of the table of random numbers (Appendix E, Table E.1) make a tally of the 400 digits 0, 1, 2, . . . , 9 which appear in rows 1 through 10. Fit a uniform distribution to these data and, using a level of significance of .01, test for goodness of fit. *Hint*: The appropriate degrees of freedom for data fitted by a uniform distribution are the number of (remaining) groups or classes (after possible condensing) minus 1.

13.7 TESTING FOR THE DIFFERENCE BETWEEN PROPORTIONS FROM TWO RELATED POPULATIONS: THE MCNEMAR TEST

13.7.1 Rationale

In our discussion of the chi-square test in Sections 13.3–13.5, we have been concerned with situations in which the sample data were obtained from populations that were independent of each other. However, analogous to Section 12.3, it is often the case that we wish to compare the proportions from sample data taken from related populations. In our situation we might wish to determine whether there is a difference between two groups that have been matched according to some control characteristic. In a second circumstance we might wish to determine whether there has been a change in a particular group between one time period and another. For example, if we refer to the real estate survey, suppose that the president would like to know whether the proportion of homeowners who stated that they intend to put their house up for sale in the next year differs from the actual proportion that placed their home up for sale during that year. Since we would be evaluating the significance of the change, the chi-square test of Section 13.3 should not be used. In such situations, when two proportions (each with two categories) are involved, a test developed by McNemar may be employed.

13.7.2 Development

We may be interested in determining either whether there is a difference between the two proportions (two-tailed test) or whether one group has a higher proportion than the other group (one-tailed test).

Two-Tailed Test	One-Tailed Test	One-Tailed Test
$H_0: p_1 = p_2$ $H_1: p_1 \neq p_2$	$H_0: p_1 \geq p_2$ $H_1: p_1 < p_2$	$H_0: p_1 \leq p_2$ $H_1: p_1 > p_2$

where p_1 = proportion of successes in population 1
p_2 = proportion of successes in population 2

Thus we may set up a 2×2 contingency table as in Table 13.17. The sample proportions are

$$p_{S_1} = \frac{A + B}{n} = \text{the proportion of respondents in the sample who answer yes to condition 1}$$

$$p_{S_2} = \frac{A + C}{n} = \text{the proportion of respondents in the sample who answer yes to condition 2}$$

The test statistic for the McNemar test is

$$Z = \frac{B - C}{\sqrt{B + C}} \tag{13.5}$$

If homeowners were asked whether they intended to put their homes up for sale in the next year and each homeowner was contacted one year later to determine if the

TABLE 13.17 2×2 Contingency table for the McNemar test

		Condition (Group 2)		
		Yes	No	Total
Condition (Group 1)	Yes	A	B	A + B
	No	C	D	C + D
	Total	A + C	B + D	n

where A = number of respondents that answer yes to condition 1 and yes to condition 2
B = number of respondents that answer yes to condition 1 and no to condition 2
C = number of respondents that answer no to condition 1 and yes to condition 2
D = number of respondents that answer no to condition 1 and no to condition 2
n = the number of respondents in the sample (that is, the sample size)

house was actually put up for sale, we could form a contingency table (Table 13.18) to summarize the following results:

TABLE 13.18 Intended to put house up for sale and actually put house up for sale

Intended to Put House Up for Sale	Actually Put House Up for Sale		
	Yes	No	Total
Yes	23	3	26
No	11	196	207
Total	34	197	233

Since the president wanted to determine whether the proportion of houses that were intended to be put up for sale is different from the proportion that were actually put up for sale, the null and alternative hypotheses would be

$$H_0: \quad p_I = p_A$$

$$H_1: \quad p_I \neq p_A$$

If the test were carried out at the .05 level of significance, the critical values would be -1.96 and $+1.96$ (see Figure 13.11) and the decision rule would be

Reject H_0 if $Z < -1.96$ or if $Z > +1.96$;
otherwise do not reject H_0.

For our data A = 23, B = 3, C = 11, D = 196

$$p_{S_I} = \frac{23 + 3}{233} = .112 \quad p_{S_A} = \frac{23 + 11}{233} = .146$$

From Equation (13.5)

$$Z = \frac{3 - 11}{\sqrt{3 + 11}} = \frac{-8}{\sqrt{14}} = -2.138$$

Since $Z = -2.138 < -1.96$, the null hypothesis can be rejected.

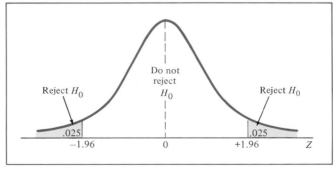

FIGURE 13.11
Two-tailed McNemar test at the .05 level of significance.

The president can conclude that there is evidence that the proportion of houses that are intended for sale is different from the proportion of houses that are actually put up for sale within one year.

Problems

- **13.32** Referring to Problem 6.8 on page 182, is there evidence of a difference in the proportion of individuals that planned to buy and actually purchased a new television? (Use $\alpha = .05$.)

13.33 A market researcher wanted to study the effect of an advertising campaign for Brand A cola to determine whether the proportion of cola drinkers that preferred Brand A would increase as a result of the campaign. A random sample of 200 cola drinkers were selected and they indicated their preference for either Brand A or Brand B prior to the beginning of the advertising campaign and at its completion. The results were as follows:

Preference Prior to Advertising Campaign	Preference after Completion of Advertising Campaign		Total
	Brand A	Brand B	
Brand A	101	9	110
Brand B	22	68	90
Total	123	77	200

At the .05 level of significance, is there evidence that the proportion of cola drinkers who prefer Brand A is higher at the end of the advertising campaign than at the beginning?

13.34 A political pollster wanted to evaluate the effect on voter preference of a televised debate between two candidates who were running for mayor of a city. A random sample of 500 registered voters was selected and each respondent was asked to indicate his or her preference prior to and after the debate. The results were as follows:

Preference Prior to Debate	Preference after Debate		Total
	Candidate A	Candidate B	
Candidate A	269	21	290
Candidate B	36	174	210
Total	305	195	500

At the .01 level of significance, is there evidence of a difference in the proportion of voters who favor Candidate A prior to and after the debate?

13.35 The coordinator of the Introduction to Computers course in a school of business would like to determine whether there is any difference in the proportion of students who intend to major in computers at the beginning of the course and after its completion. Each student enrolled in the course is asked to indicate on the first day of class and again after completion of the final exam whether he or she intends to major in computers. The results were as follows:

Computer Major Prior to Taking Computer Course	Computer Major after Completion of Computer Course		Total
	Yes	No	
Yes	52	32	84
No	13	230	243
Total	65	262	327

(a) At the .05 level of significance, is there evidence of a difference between the proportion of students who intend to major in computers prior to taking the computer course and after completion of the course?

✔(b) Tell why the following table gives less information than the table above, how it can be derived from the table above, and why the information in it is insufficient to test the hypothesis of interest:

Computer Major	Computer Major	
	Yes	No
Prior to course	84	243
After taking course	65	262

● **13.36** The personnel director of a large manufacturing company would like to reduce excessive absenteeism among assembly-line workers. She has decided to institute an experimental incentive plan that will provide financial rewards to employees who are absent less than 5 days in a given calendar year. A sample of 100 workers is selected at the end of the one-year trial period. For each of the two years, information is obtained for each employee selected that indicates whether the worker was absent less than 5 days in that year. The results were as follows:

Year 1	Year 2		Total
	<5 Days Absent	≥5 Days Absent	
<5 days absent	32	4	36
≥5 days absent	25	39	64
Total	57	43	100

(a) At the .01 level of significance, is there evidence that the proportion of employees absent less than 5 days is lower in year 1 than in year 2?

(b) What conclusion should the personnel director reach regarding the effect of the incentive plan?

✔(c) Tell why the following table on page 438 gives less information than the table above, how it can be derived from the table above, and why the information in it is insufficient to test the hypothesis of interest:

| | Days Absent | |
Year	<5	≥5
1	36	64
2	57	43

13.8 TESTING A HYPOTHESIS ABOUT A POPULATION VARIANCE (OR STANDARD DEVIATION)

In the preceding sections we have used the chi-square test to study equality of proportions, independence, and goodness of fit. In this section we demonstrate yet another application of this important distribution—the chi-square test for a population variance (or standard deviation).

When analyzing quantitative data, it is often important to draw conclusions about the variability as well as the average of a characteristic of interest. For example, in our cereal filling study the manager was interested in determining whether the standard deviation has increased above previously measured levels. Here, he would be interested in drawing conclusions about the population standard deviation.

In attempting to draw conclusions about the variability in the population, we first must determine what test statistic can be used to represent the distribution of the variability in the sample data. If the variable (amount of cereal filled) is assumed to be normally distributed, then the statistic $(n-1)S^2/\sigma_X^2$ will follow the chi-square (χ^2) distribution with $(n-1)$ degrees of freedom. Therefore, the test statistic for testing whether or not the population variance is equal to a specified value is

$$\chi^2_{n-1} = \frac{(n-1)S^2}{\sigma_X^2}$$

(13.6)

where n = sample size

S^2 = sample variance

σ_X^2 = hypothesized population variance

If, as shown in panel A of Figure 13.12, the test of hypothesis is two-tailed, the rejection region is split into both the lower and the upper tails of the chi-square distribution. However, if the test is one-tailed, the rejection region is either in the upper tail (panel B of Figure 13.12) or in the lower tail (panel C of Figure 13.12) of the chi-square distribution, depending on the direction of the alternative hypothesis.

To apply the test of hypothesis let us again refer back to the cereal filling study. We may recall from Section 9.2 that the population standard deviation was 15 grams. The manager is interested in determining whether the standard deviation has increased above 15 grams. Thus, we have a one-tailed test in which the null and alternative hypotheses can be stated as follows:

$$H_0: \sigma_X \leq 15 \text{ or } \sigma_X^2 \leq 225$$

$$H_1: \sigma_X > 15 \text{ or } \sigma_X^2 > 225$$

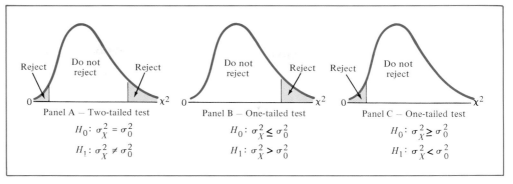

FIGURE 13.12
Testing a hypothesis about a population variance—one-tailed and two-tailed
tests: Panel A, two-tailed test; Panel B, one-tailed test; Panel C, one-tailed test.

Hence the null hypothesis would be rejected only if the test statistic were greater
than the critical value of the chi-square distribution.

Using Table E.4, since there are 24 degrees of freedom (25 − 1), if a level of
significance of .05 is selected, the following decision rule can be stated (see Figure
13.13):

Reject H_0 if $\chi^2_{24} > 36.415$; otherwise do not reject H_0.

For these data we have, from Equation (13.6),

$$\chi^2_{n-1} = \frac{(n-1)S^2}{\sigma^2_X} = \frac{(25-1)(17.3)^2}{(15)^2} = 31.92$$

Since $31.92 < 36.415$, we do not reject H_0. The manager would conclude that there
is no evidence that the standard deviation has increased above 15 grams.

As a second illustration of this test of hypothesis, let us refer to the real estate
survey. Here the president and the statistician would like to know whether the population
standard deviation of the appraised value of houses without a connection to a local
sewer system is different from $39,000, the value assumed when the sample size was
determined in Section 10.7. Using a computer package such as SAS, SPSS[x], or Minitab
enables us to determine that the sample standard deviation of the appraised value of
the 29 houses that are not connected to a local sewer system is $37,010.

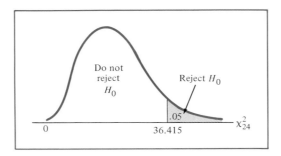

FIGURE 13.13
One-tailed test of hypothesis for a population variance at the .05 level of significance
with 24 degrees of freedom.

Since we wish to know whether the standard deviation differs from \$39,000, we have a two-tailed test and the null and alternative hypotheses can be stated as follows:

$$H_0: \sigma_X = 39 \text{ or } \sigma_X^2 = 1521$$

$$H_1: \sigma_X \neq 39 \text{ or } \sigma_X^2 \neq 1521$$

In this example the null hypothesis would be rejected if the test statistic fell into either the lower or upper tail of the chi-square distribution (Figure 13.14).

Since there are 28 degrees of freedom ($29 - 1 = 28$), if a level of significance of .05 was selected, the lower (χ_L^2) and upper (χ_U^2) critical values could be obtained from the table of the chi-square distribution (Table E.4). We may recall from Section 13.3 that the value at the top of the table of the chi-square distribution indicates the upper-tail area of the distribution. Therefore we can obtain the lower critical value χ_L^2 of 15.308 from Table E.4 by looking in the column labeled ''.975'' for 28 degrees of freedom. We can obtain the upper critical value χ_U^2 of 44.461 by looking in the column labeled ''.025'' for 28 degrees of freedom.

Therefore, the decision rule would be

$$\text{Reject } H_0 \text{ if } \chi_{28}^2 > 44.461$$

$$\text{or if } \chi_{28}^2 < 15.308;$$

$$\text{otherwise do not reject } H_0.$$

From Equation (13.6) we recall that the test statistic is

$$\chi_{n-1}^2 = \frac{(n-1)S^2}{\sigma_X^2}$$

and thus for this example we have

$$\chi_{28}^2 = \frac{(29-1)(37.01)^2}{(39)^2} = 25.22$$

Since $15.308 < 25.22 < 44.461$, we do not reject H_0.

Since the null hypothesis has not been rejected, the president and the statistician can conclude that there is no evidence that the population standard deviation of the

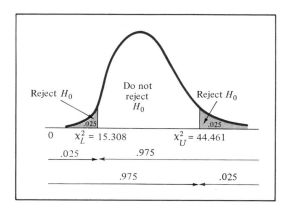

FIGURE 13.14
Two-tailed test of hypothesis about a population variance at the .05 level of significance with 28 degrees of freedom.

appraised value of houses that are not connected to a local sewer system is different from \$39,000.

In testing a hypothesis about a population variance, we should be aware that we have assumed that the data in the population are normally distributed. Unfortunately, this χ^2 test is sensitive to departures from this assumption, so that if the population is not normally distributed, particularly for small sample sizes, the accuracy of the test can be seriously affected (Reference 1).

Problems

13.37   In Problem 10.5 on page 314, we noted that the population standard deviation was expected to be equal to .02 gallon. If a random sample of 25 one-gallon cans of paint revealed a sample standard deviation of .025 gallon, at the .05 level of significance, is there evidence that the population standard deviation has changed?

• **13.38**   In Problem 10.6 on page 314, we noted that the process standard deviation of the life of electric light bulbs was known to be 314 hours. If a random sample of 20 light bulbs indicates a sample standard deviation of 110 hours, at the .05 level of significance, is there evidence that the process standard deviation has changed?

• **13.39**   In Problem 10.7 on page 314, we noted that the standard deviation for 2-liter soda bottles was .05 liter. As part of the quality control process, the bottling company wishes to know whether the standard deviation has increased above .05 liter. A random sample of ten 2-liter bottles indicated a sample standard deviation of .083 liter. At the .01 level of significance, is there evidence that the process standard deviation has increased?

13.40   Referring to Problem 10.12 on page 318, is there evidence that the population standard deviation of family dental expenses is above \$50? (Use $\alpha = .10$.)

13.41   In Problem 10.11 on page 318, is there evidence that the population standard deviation of the average amount held in passbook savings accounts is greater than \$1,000? (Use $\alpha = .05$.)

13.9   CHI-SQUARE TESTS, COMPUTERS, AND THE REAL ESTATE SURVEY

In this chapter various chi-square tests that involved cross-classifications of qualitative variables were applied to the real estate survey. As in the case of descriptive statistics (see Chapter 5) and t tests (see Section 12.6), one would certainly want to use available statistical software to assist in the analysis of data obtained from a survey.

We may illustrate such software by referring to the example of Section 13.3, in which we desired to study whether there was a relationship between presence of a modern kitchen and presence of modern bathrooms.

Figures 13.15, 13.16, and 13.17, respectively, represent partial SAS, MYSTAT, and Minitab output for this contingency table (see pages 442–443).

Figure 13.15 represents partial SAS output using PROC FREQ for these data. We may note that the FREQ procedure forms a contingency table and computes the chi-square test statistic (including the theoretical frequencies) as well as the p value. For these data the chi-square test statistic is 171.064 and the p value is .0000. Thus the probability of obtaining a value of chi-square greater than 171.064 is .0000. In

```
TABLE OF MODKIT BY MODBATH

MODKIT(MODERN KITCHEN)
          MODBATH(MODERN BATHROOMS)

FREQUENCY^
EXPECTED ^
DEVIATION^
 PERCENT ^
 ROW PCT ^
 COL PCT ^ABSENCE ^PRESENCE^    TOTAL
---------+--------+--------+
ABSENCE  ^    72 ^      8 ^      80
         ^  27.1 ^   52.9 ^
         ^  44.9 ^  -44.9 ^
         ^ 30.90 ^   3.43 ^   34.33
         ^ 90.00 ^  10.00 ^
         ^ 91.14 ^   5.19 ^
---------+--------+--------+
PRESENCE ^     7 ^    146 ^     153
         ^  51.9 ^  101.1 ^
         ^ -44.9 ^   44.9 ^
         ^  3.00 ^  62.66 ^   65.67
         ^  4.58 ^  95.42 ^
         ^  8.86 ^  94.81 ^
---------+--------+--------+
TOTAL         79      154      233
            33.91    66.09   100.00


STATISTICS FOR TABLE OF MODKIT BY MODBATH


STATISTIC                    DF    VALUE        PROB
---------------------------------------------------
CHI-SQUARE                    1   171.064      0.000
```

FIGURE 13.15
SAS output for chi-square test of independence for presence of a modern
kitchen and presence of modern bathrooms.

addition, a warning message will be printed whenever at least 5% of the cells have theoretical frequencies below 5.

Figure 13.16 represents partial MYSTAT output using TABULATE for these data. We may note that the TABULATE command forms a contingency table and computes the chi-square test statistic as well as the *p* value.

Figure 13.17 represents partial Minitab output using the TABLE command for these data. We may note that the TABLE command forms a contingency table and computes the chi-square test statistic (including the theoretical frequencies). However, category labels for each variable will not be printed; neither will the *p* value be displayed.

```
TABLE OF    MODKIT      (ROWS) BY   MODBATH      (COLUMNS)

FREQUENCIES

                0.000       1.000      TOTAL

    0.000         72           8         80

    1.000          7         146        153

  TOTAL           79         154        233


  TEST STATISTIC                      VALUE          DF          PROB
     PEARSON CHI-SQUARE              171.064          1          .000
```

FIGURE 13.16
MYSTAT output for chi-square test of independence for presence of a modern
kitchen and presence of modern bathrooms.

```
ROWS: modkit       COLUMNS: modbath

              0          1         ALL

    0         72          8          80
            27.12      52.88       80.00

    1          7        146         153
            51.88     101.12      153.00

   ALL        79        154         233
            79.00     154.00      233.00

   CHI-SQUARE =    171.064    WITH D.F. =    1

   CELL CONTENTS --
                        COUNT
                        EXP FREQ
```

FIGURE 13.17
Minitab output for chi-square test of independence for presence of a modern
kitchen and presence of modern bathrooms.

Supplementary Problems

13.42 (a) What is the difference between the McNemar test and the chi-square test for the difference between proportions?

(b) Under what circumstances should the McNemar test be used?

13.43 (a) Why shouldn't the chi-square test for independence be used when the theoretical frequencies in some of the cells are too small?

(b) What action can be taken in such circumstances to enable one to analyze that data from the contingency table?

13.44 A housing survey of single-family homes in two suburban New York City counties was conducted to determine the proportion of such homes that have gas heat. A sample of 300 single-family homes in County A indicated that 185 had gas heat, while a sample of 200 single-family homes in County B indicated that 75 had gas heat.

(a) Use *two* different statistical tests to determine whether there is evidence of a difference between the two counties in the proportion of single-family houses that have gas heat.

(b) Compare the results obtained by the two methods in (a). Are your conclusions the same?

(c) If you wanted to know whether there was evidence that County A had a higher proportion of single-family houses with gas heat, what method would you use to perform the statistical test?

Note: Use a level of significance of .01 throughout the problem.

• **13.45** Referring to Problem 6.9 on page 182, is there evidence of a difference in the proportion of males and females who enjoy shopping for clothing? (Use $\alpha = .05$.)

13.46 Referring to Problem 13.45, if you wanted to determine whether the proportion of females who enjoyed shopping for clothing was higher than the proportion of males, what method would you use and what would be your answer?

13.47 Referring to Problem 6.10 on page 183, is there evidence of a difference in the proportion of males and females who smoke cigarettes? (Use $\alpha = .10$.)

13.48 In 1954 a study was conducted on the efficacy of the Salk Polio vaccine on first, second, and third grade children (see J. Tanur, *Statistics: A Guide to the Unknown*, Oakland, CA: Holden-Day, 1972). Of 200,745 children who received the vaccine, 56 contracted polio. Of 201,229 who received a placebo (that is, a vaccine which, unknown to the participants in the study, contains no active ingredients), 142 contracted polio.

(a) At the .01 level of significance, is there evidence that the proportion contracting polio is lower for those children who received the vaccine than for those children who received the placebo?

(b) Compute the *p* value in part (a). Does this lead you to believe that the Salk vaccine was effective in reducing the incidence of polio? Explain.

(c) Why is it not appropriate to use the chi-square test of independence in part (a)?

13.49 A "physician's health study" of the effectiveness of aspirin in the reduction of heart attacks was begun in 1982 and completed in 1987 (see C. Hennekens, "The physician's health study," *New England Journal of Medicine*, January 28, 1988). Of 11,037 male medical doctors in the United States who took one 325 mg buffered aspirin tablet every other day, 104 suffered heart attacks during the five-year period of the study. Of 11,034 male medical doctors in the United States who took a placebo (that is, a pill which, unknown to the participants in the study, contains no active ingredients), 189 suffered heart attacks during the five-year period of the study.

(a) At the .01 level of significance, is there evidence that the proportion having heart attacks is lower for those male medical doctors in the United States who received the buffered aspirin every other day than for those who received the placebo?

(b) Compute the *p* value in part (a). Does this lead you to believe that taking one buffered

aspirin pill every other day was effective in reducing the incidence of heart attacks? Explain.
(c) Why is it not appropriate to use the chi-square test of independence in part (a)?

13.50 The quality control manager of an automobile parts factory would like to know if there is a difference in the proportion of defective parts produced on different days of the work week. Random samples of 100 parts produced on each day of the week were selected with the following results:

Result	Mon.	Tues.	Wed.	Thurs.	Fri.
Number of defective parts	12	7	7	10	14
Number of acceptable parts	88	93	93	90	86
Totals	100	100	100	100	100

At the .05 level of significance, is there evidence of a difference in the proportion of defective parts produced on the various days of the week?

13.51 A manufacturer of automobile batteries wishes to determine whether there are any differences in three different media (magazine, TV, radio) in terms of recall of an ad. The results of an advertising study were as follows:

	Media			
Recall Ability	Magazine	TV	Radio	Totals
Number of persons remembering ad	25	10	7	42
Number of persons not remembering ad	73	93	108	274
Totals	98	103	115	316

At the .10 level of significance, determine whether there is evidence of a relationship between media and ability to recall the ad.

• 13.52 The marketing director of a cable television company is interested in determining whether there is a difference in the proportion of households that adopt a cable television service based upon the type of residence (single-family dwelling, two- to four-family dwelling, and apartment house). A random sample of 400 households revealed the following:

	Type of Residence			
Adopt Cable TV?	Single-Family	Two- to Four-Family	Apartment House	Totals
Yes	94	39	77	210
No	56	36	98	190
Totals	150	75	175	400

At the .01 level of significance, is there evidence of a relationship between adopting the cable TV service and the type of residence?

13.53 A statistician wished to study the distribution of the three types of cars (subcompact, compact, and full size) in the four geographical regions of the United States (Northeast, South, Midwest, West). A random sample of 200 cars were selected with the following results:

Of 60 cars sold in the Northeast, 25 were subcompacts, 20 were compacts, and 15 were full size.

Of 40 cars sold in the South, 10 were subcompacts, 10 were compacts, and 20 were full size.

Of 50 cars sold in the Midwest, 15 were subcompacts, 15 were compacts, and 20 were full size.

Of 50 cars sold in the West, 20 were subcompacts, 15 were compacts, and 15 were full size.

At the .05 level of significance, is there evidence of a relationship between type of car and geographical region?

• **13.54** A large corporation was interested in determining whether an association exists between commuting time of their employees and the level of stress-related problems observed on the job. A study of 116 assembly-line workers revealed the following:

	Stress			
Commuting Time	High	Moderate	Low	Totals
Under 15 min.	9	5	18	32
15 min. to 45 min.	17	8	28	53
Over 45 min.	18	6	7	31
Totals	44	19	53	116

At the .01 level of significance, is there evidence of a relationship between commuting time and stress?

13.55 A statistician for a professional hockey team collected data on the number of goals scored per game by the team in an 80-game season. The results from last year indicated the following:

Number of Goals Scored	Frequency
0	5
1	10
2	15
3	18
4	14
5	11
6	3
7	2
8	0
9	1
10	1
	80

Does the distribution of number of goals scored follow a Poisson distribution at the .05 level of significance?

13.56 Referring to Problem 13.55, at the .05 level of significance does the distribution of goals scored follow a Poisson distribution with a population mean of 3 goals scored per game?

• **13.57** The number of customers waiting for service on the express checkout line of a large supermarket is examined at random on 50 occasions during a 12-hour period. The results are as follows:

3	5	1	4	0	6	4	3	4	2
0	4	8	3	5	5	6	5	7	4
4	2	6	9	3	4	1	2	3	3
4	3	3	5	1	3	4	5	2	5
7	1	4	2	12	2	7	4	6	3

Fit a Poisson distribution to the number of customers waiting for service per occasion and, using a level of significance of .01, test for goodness of fit.

13.58 The military historian Von Bortkewitsch (1898) obtained the following data on the number of deaths (per year per corps) in the Prussian cavalry due to being kicked in the head by a horse (Reference 2 of Chapter 7). Fit a Poisson distribution to these data and, using a level of significance of .05, test for goodness of fit.

Number of Deaths (per year per corps)	Frequency
0	109
1	65
2	22
3	3
4	1
	200

● **13.59** The scores of 500 students on the basic statistics final exam last term were recorded as follows:

Score	Frequency
40–under 50	36
50–under 60	60
60–under 70	118
70–under 80	170
80–under 90	76
90–under 100	40
	500

(a) Compute the mean and standard deviation of this frequency distribution.
(b) Do these data fit a normal distribution at the .05 level of significance?

13.60 An experimental psychologist wishes to determine whether the reaction time to a certain stimulus is normally distributed. A sample of 1,000 subjects revealed the following reaction-time distribution:

Reaction Time (msec)	Frequency
0–under 100	30
100–under 200	60
200–under 300	260
300–under 400	525
400–under 500	110
500–under 600	15
	1,000

For these data

$$\overline{X} = 317, \qquad S = 86$$

Does this distribution of reaction times fit a normal distribution at the .01 level of significance?

13.61 Roll a pair of dice 180 times and, for each roll, make a tally of the sum of the two numbers that appear. Fit a triangular distribution to these data (see Problem 7.6 on page 216) and, using a level of significance of .05, test for goodness of fit.

Hint: The appropriate degrees of freedom for data fitted by this triangular distribution are the number of (remaining) groups or classes (after possible condensing) minus 1.

13.62 The deluxe nut mixture produced by a food company is supposed to contain five types of nuts in a ratio of 5 peanuts to 3 cashews to 2 pecans to 1 almond to 1 walnut. Periodic checks of the composition of the mixture being processed are conducted. In a recent sample of 600 nuts, there were 282 peanuts, 138 cashews, 117 pecans, 32 almonds, and 31 walnuts. At the .05 level of significance, does the deluxe mixture contain the proper composition of the various nuts?

Hint: The appropriate degrees of freedom for data fitted by this distribution are the number of (remaining) groups or classes (after possible condensing) minus 1.

13.63 Referring to the example concerning the computer paper on page 313, if a random sample of 25 indicated a sample standard deviation of .031 inch, is there evidence that the population standard deviation is greater than .02 inch? (Use $\alpha = .05$.)

13.64 Referring to Problem 10.56 on page 333, is there evidence that the population standard deviation of the number of credits is different from 4? (Use $\alpha = .01$.)

13.65 Referring to Problem 3.68 on page 74, is there evidence that the population standard deviation of the price of sparkling and mineral water is different from 10 cents? (Use $\alpha = .05$.)

13.66 Referring to Problem 10.17 on page 319, is there evidence that the population standard deviation of the waiting time for gas installation is greater than 10 days? (Use $\alpha = .01$.)

13.67 Referring to Problem 10.55 on page 332, is there evidence that the population standard deviation is different from 5 days? (Use $\alpha = .10$.)

Database Exercises

The following problems refer to the sample data obtained from the questionnaire of Figure 2.5 on page 15 and presented in Figure 2.10 on pages 24–29. They should be solved with the aid of an available computer package.

☐ **13.68** Is there evidence of a relationship between whether the house has an eat-in kitchen (question 14) and whether it has a modern kitchen (question 19)? (Use $\alpha = .05$.)

☐ **13.69** Is there evidence of a relationship between whether the house has an eat-in kitchen (question 14) and whether it has a basement (question 18)? (Use $\alpha = .01$.)

☐ **13.70** Is there evidence of a relationship between whether the house has an eat-in kitchen (question 14) and whether it has a fireplace (question 16)? (Use $\alpha = .10$.)

☐ **13.71** Is there evidence of a relationship between whether the house has central air-conditioning (question 15) and whether it has a fireplace (question 16)? (Use $\alpha = .05$.)

☐ **13.72** Is there evidence of a relationship between whether the house has central air-conditioning (question 15) and whether it has a modern kitchen (question 19)? (Use $\alpha = .01$.)

☐ **13.73** Is there evidence of a relationship between whether the house has a fireplace (question 16) and whether it has a basement (question 18)? (Use $\alpha = .05$.)

☐ **13.74** Is there evidence of a relationship between whether the house has a basement (question 18) and whether it has modern bathrooms (question 20)? (Use $\alpha = .10$.)

☐ **13.75** Is there evidence of a relationship between the geographic location of the house[3] (question 9) and whether it has central air-conditioning (question 15)? (Use $\alpha = .05$.)

☐ **13.76** Is there evidence of a relationship between the geographic location of the house[3] (question 9) and whether the house has a connection to a local sewer system (question 17)? (Use $\alpha = .01$.)

---

[3] The categories of certain variables may have to be combined and recoded in order to meet the assumptions of the chi-square test (see Sections 13.3–13.5).

☐ **13.77** Is there evidence of a relationship between the geographic location of the house[3] (question 9) and whether the house has a modern kitchen (question 19)? (Use $\alpha = .05$.)

☐ **13.78** Is there evidence of a relationship between the style of house[3] (question 10) and whether the house has a fireplace (question 16)? (Use $\alpha = .10$.)

☐ **13.79** Is there evidence of a relationship between the style of house[3] (question 10) and whether the house has a modern kitchen (question 19)? (Use $\alpha = .05$.)

☐ **13.80** Is there evidence of a relationship between the type of heating fuel used (question 11) and whether the house has a basement (question 18)? (Use $\alpha = .01$.)

☐ **13.81** Is there evidence of a relationship between the type of swimming pool (question 13)[3] and whether the house has a fireplace (question 16)? (Use $\alpha = .05$.)

☐ **13.82** Is there evidence of a relationship between the type of indoor parking facility (question 8) and the geographic location of the house[3] (question 9)? (Use $\alpha = .10$.)

☐ **13.83** Is there evidence of a relationship between the geographic location of the house[3] (question 9) and type of heating fuel used (question 11)? (Use $\alpha = .05$.)

☐ **13.84** Is there evidence of a relationship between the geographic location (question 9) and the type of swimming pool (if any) present[3] (question 13)? (Use $\alpha = .01$.)

☐ **13.85** Is there evidence of a relationship between the style of house (question 10) and the type of swimming pool (if any) present[3] (question 13)? (Use $\alpha = .05$.)

☐ **13.86** Is there evidence of a relationship between the type of heating fuel used (question 11) and the type of heating system[3] (question 12)? (Use $\alpha = .05$.)

☐ **13.87** Fit a Poisson distribution to the data on the number of bedrooms (question 3) and test for goodness of fit. (Use $\alpha = .05$.)

☐ **13.88** Fit a Poisson distribution to the data on number of bathrooms (question 4) and test for goodness of fit. (Use $\alpha = .01$.) (*Note*: Be sure to round any fractional values up to the next highest integer, i.e., $1.5 = 2$, $2.5 = 3$.)

☐ **13.89** Fit a normal distribution to the data on the number of rooms (question 5) and test for goodness of fit. (Use $\alpha = .10$.)

☐ **13.90** Fit a normal distribution to the data on the age of houses (question 6) and test for goodness of fit. (Use $\alpha = .05$.)

☐ **13.91** Fit a normal distribution to the data on the annual taxes (question 7) and test for goodness of fit. (Use $\alpha = .05$.)

References

1. BRADLEY, J. V., *Distribution-Free Statistical Tests* (Englewood Cliffs, N.J.: Prentice-Hall, 1968).
2. CONOVER, W. J., *Practical Nonparametric Statistics*, 2d ed. (New York: Wiley, 1980).
3. DANIEL, W., *Applied Nonparametric Statistics* (Boston: Houghton Mifflin, 1978).
4. LEVINE, D. M., M. L. BERENSON, AND D. F. STEPHAN, *Using Minitab with Basic Business Statistics*, 2d ed. (Englewood Cliffs, N.J.: Prentice-Hall, 1986).
5. LEVINE, D. M., M. L. BERENSON, AND D. F. STEPHAN, *Using SAS with Basic Business Statistics* (Englewood Cliffs, N.J.: Prenctice-Hall, 1983).
6. MYSTAT: A Personal Version of SYSTAT (Evanston, IL.: 1988).
7. RYAN, T. A., B. L. JOINER, AND B. F. RYAN, *Minitab Student Handbook*, 2d ed. (North Scituate, Mass.: Duxbury Press, 1985).
8. *SAS User's Guide*, 1982 ed. (Cary, N.C.: SAS Institute, 1982).

---

[3] The categories of certain variables may have to be combined and recoded in order to meet the assumptions of the chi-square test (see Sections 13.3–13.5).

14

The Analysis of Variance

14.1 INTRODUCTION: WHAT'S AHEAD

In many fields of application we need to compare alternative methods, treatments, or materials, according to some predetermined criteria. A consumer organization, for example, may wish to determine which brand of tires lasts longer under highway conditions; an agricultural researcher would like to know which type of green beans provides the highest yield; a medical researcher would like to evaluate the effect of different brands of prescription medicine on the reduction of diastolic blood pressure.

In Chapter 12 we used statistical inference to draw conclusions about differences between the means of two groups. In this chapter we shall examine techniques that have been developed to test for differences in the means of several groups. This methodology is classified under the general title of **analysis of variance** or **ANOVA**. First, we shall consider a **completely randomized** or **one-way ANOVA** model having only one **factor** with several groups (such as type of tire, variety of green bean, or brand of drug). However, the analysis of variance can easily be extended to handle cases where more than one factor at a time is studied in one experiment. Some of these more sophisticated models will be discussed in the later sections of the chapter.

14.2 THE ONE-WAY ANALYSIS OF VARIANCE

14.2.1 Introduction

Suppose that the production manager at a plant in which cereal is being manufactured and packaged in 368-gram-sized boxes is considering the replacement of an old machine that directly affects output in the production process. Moreover, suppose that three competing suppliers have permitted the production manager to use their particular equipment on a trial basis and that the purchasing prices and servicing contracts for the three brands of machines are essentially the same. In order to make a purchasing decision, the production manager decides to conduct an experiment to determine whether there are any significant differences among the three brands of machines in the average time (in seconds) it takes factory workers using them to complete a production task. Fifteen factory workers of similar experience, ability, and age are randomly assigned to receive training on one of the three brands of machines in such a manner that there are five factory workers for each machine. After an appropriate amount of training and practice, the production manager measures the time (in seconds) it takes the factory workers to complete a task using their respective equipment. The results of this experiment are displayed in Table 14.1.

TABLE 14.1 Time (in seconds) to complete a task using three different machines

	Machine		
	I	*II*	*III*
	25.40	23.40	20.00
	26.31	21.80	22.20
	24.10	23.50	19.75
	23.74	22.75	20.60
	25.10	21.60	20.40
Mean	$\overline{X}_I = 24.93$	$\overline{X}_{II} = 22.61$	$\overline{X}_{III} = 20.59$

In general, to test whether several (that is, $c = 3$ or more) groups all have the same population average, the null and alternative hypotheses would be stated as follows:

$$H_0: \quad \mu_1 = \mu_2 = \mu_3 = \cdots = \mu_c$$

$$H_1: \quad \text{Not all the means are equal.}$$

For the above productivity study, since there are three machines, the null and alternative hypotheses would be

$$H_0: \quad \mu_I = \mu_{II} = \mu_{III}$$

$$H_1: \quad \text{Not all the machines have equal means.}$$

We see in Table 14.1 that there are differences in the *sample* means for the three machines. It takes, on average, 24.93 seconds to complete a task using machine I, 22.61 seconds using machine II, and 20.59 seconds using machine III. The question that must be answered is whether these sample results are sufficiently different for the production manager to decide that the *population* averages are not all equal.

14.2.2 Measures of Variation

Since under the null hypothesis the population means of the three groups are presumed equal, a measure of the **total variation** or sum of squares (SST) among all the workers can be obtained by summing up the squared differences between each observation (time) and an overall mean $\overline{\overline{X}}$ based upon all the observations. The total variation would be computed as

$$\text{total variation} = \text{total sum of squares (SST)} = \sum_{j=1}^{c} \sum_{i=1}^{n_j} (X_{ij} - \overline{\overline{X}})^2 \quad \textbf{(14.1)}$$

where $\overline{\overline{X}} = \dfrac{\sum\limits_{j=1}^{c} \sum\limits_{i=1}^{n_j} X_{ij}}{n}$ is called the **grand mean**

$X_{ij} = i$th observation in group j

n_j = number of observations in group j

n = total number of observations

c = number of groups

In the productivity study the total sum of squares (SST) would be computed as follows:

$$\overline{\overline{X}} = \frac{\sum\limits_{j=1}^{c} \sum\limits_{i=1}^{n_j} X_{ij}}{n} = \frac{25.40 + 26.31 + \cdots + 23.40 + \cdots + 20.40}{15}$$

$$= \frac{340.65}{15} = 22.71$$

$$\text{SST} = \sum_{j=1}^{c} \sum_{i=1}^{n_j} (X_{ij} - \overline{\overline{X}})^2$$

$$= \begin{pmatrix} (25.40 - 22.71)^2 \\ +(26.31 - 22.71)^2 \\ +(24.10 - 22.71)^2 \\ +(23.74 - 22.71)^2 \\ +(25.10 - 22.71)^2 \end{pmatrix} + \begin{pmatrix} (23.40 - 22.71)^2 \\ +(21.80 - 22.71)^2 \\ +(23.50 - 22.71)^2 \\ +(22.75 - 22.71)^2 \\ +(21.60 - 22.71)^2 \end{pmatrix} + \begin{pmatrix} (20.00 - 22.71)^2 \\ +(22.20 - 22.71)^2 \\ +(19.75 - 22.71)^2 \\ +(20.60 - 22.71)^2 \\ +(20.40 - 22.71)^2 \end{pmatrix}$$

$$= \begin{pmatrix} 7.2361 \\ +12.9600 \\ + 1.9321 \\ + 1.0609 \\ + 5.7121 \end{pmatrix} + \begin{pmatrix} .4761 \\ + .8281 \\ + .6241 \\ + .0016 \\ + 1.2321 \end{pmatrix} + \begin{pmatrix} 7.3441 \\ + .2601 \\ + 8.7616 \\ + 4.4521 \\ + 5.3361 \end{pmatrix}$$

$$= 58.2172$$

This total variation measures the sum of the squared differences between each value X_{ij} and the overall (grand) mean $\overline{\overline{X}}$.

Why is there variation among the values; that is, why are the observations not all the same? One reason is that by treating people differently (in this case, giving them different machines to use) we affect their productivity. This would explain part of the reason why the groups have different means: the bigger the effect of the treatment, the more variation in group means we will find. But there is another reason for variability in the results, which is that people are naturally variable whether we treat them alike or not. So even within a particular group, where everyone got the same treatment (i.e., machine) there is variability. Because it occurs within each group, it is called **within-group variation.**

The differences among the group means are called the **between-group variation.** Part of the between-group variation, as we noted above, is due to the effect of being in different groups. But even if there is no effect of being in different groups (that is, the null hypothesis is true), there will likely be differences among the group means. This is because variability among workers will make the sample means different just

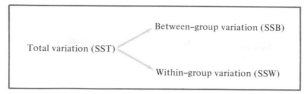

FIGURE 14.1
Partitioning the total variation.

because we have different samples. Therefore, if the null hypothesis is true, then the between-group variation will estimate the population variability just as well as the within-group variation. But if the null hypothesis is false, then the between-group variation will be larger. This fact forms the basis for the statistical test of group differences.

The total variation can therefore be subdivided (i.e., "analyzed") into two separate components (see Figure 14.1); one part consists of variation between the groups, and the other part consists of variation within the groups.

It is always true that

> total variation (SST) = between-group variation (SSB)
>
> + within-group variation (SSW)   **(14.2)**

The between-group variation is measured by the sum of the squared differences between the sample mean of each group $\overline{X}_j$ and the grand mean $\overline{\overline{X}}$, weighted by the sample size n_j in each group. The between-group variation, which is usually called the **sum of squares between** (or **SSB**), may be computed from

$$SSB = \sum_{j=1}^{c} n_j(\overline{X}_j - \overline{\overline{X}})^2 \qquad \textbf{(14.3)}$$

where n_j is the number of observations in group j

$\overline{X}_j$ is the sample mean of group j

$\overline{\overline{X}}$ is the grand mean

For our data the between-group variation would be computed as follows:

$$
\begin{aligned}
SSB &= 5(24.93 - 22.71)^2 + 5(22.61 - 22.71)^2 + 5(20.59 - 22.71)^2 \\
&= 5(2.22)^2 + 5(-.10)^2 + 5(-2.12)^2 \\
&= 24.642 + .05 + 22.472 \\
&= 47.164
\end{aligned}
$$

The within-group variation, usually called the **sum of squares within** (or **SSW**), measures the difference between each value and the mean of its own group and cumulates the squares of these differences over all groups. The within-group variation may be computed as

$$\text{SSW} = \sum_{j=1}^{c} \sum_{i=1}^{n_j} (X_{ij} - \overline{X}_j)^2 \qquad\qquad (14.4)$$

where $\overline{X}_j$ is the mean of group j

X_{ij} is the ith observation in group j

For the data of Table 14.1 the within-group variation would be computed as follows:

$$\text{SSW} = \begin{pmatrix} (25.40 - 24.93)^2 \\ +(26.31 - 24.93)^2 \\ +(24.10 - 24.93)^2 \\ +(23.74 - 24.93)^2 \\ +(25.10 - 24.93)^2 \end{pmatrix} + \begin{pmatrix} (23.40 - 22.61)^2 \\ +(21.80 - 22.61)^2 \\ +(23.50 - 22.61)^2 \\ +(22.75 - 22.61)^2 \\ +(21.60 - 22.61)^2 \end{pmatrix} + \begin{pmatrix} (20.00 - 20.59)^2 \\ +(22.20 - 20.59)^2 \\ +(19.75 - 20.59)^2 \\ +(20.60 - 20.59)^2 \\ +(20.40 - 20.59)^2 \end{pmatrix}$$

$$= \begin{pmatrix} .2209 \\ +1.9044 \\ +\ .6889 \\ +1.4161 \\ +\ .0289 \end{pmatrix} + \begin{pmatrix} .6241 \\ +\ .6561 \\ +\ .7921 \\ +\ .0196 \\ +1.0201 \end{pmatrix} + \begin{pmatrix} .3481 \\ +2.5921 \\ +\ .7056 \\ +\ .0001 \\ +\ .0361 \end{pmatrix}$$

$$= 11.0532$$

Referring back to the previous computations for the total variation and the between-group variation, we check to determine that

$$\text{SST} = \text{SSB} + \text{SSW}$$

$$58.2172 = 47.164 + 11.0532 = 58.2172$$

14.2.3 Computational Methods

So far in this chapter the formulas utilized in computing the between-group sum of squares, the within-group sum of squares, and the total sum of squares may be considered as conceptual (or definitional). Unfortunately, such formulas involve a large amount of tedious computations. However, as we saw in Section 3.5 when the variance was computed, a ''short-cut'' computational formula was derived from the definitional formula. There are similar computational formulas for the analysis of variance; they require the calculation of the following quantities:

1. $\sum_{j=1}^{c} \sum_{i=1}^{n_j} X_{ij}^2$, the sum of the squared values of each observation in the data

2. T_j, the total (or sum) of the values in group j

3. Grand total (GT) $= \sum_{j=1}^{c} \sum_{i=1}^{n_j} X_{ij}$, the sum of all values

4. $\sum_{j=1}^{c} T_j^2$, the sum of the squared totals of the values in each group

Using computational formulas, we can then compute the various sums of squares in the following way:

$$SSB = \sum_{j=1}^{c} \frac{T_j^2}{n_j} - \frac{(GT)^2}{n} \qquad (14.3a)$$

$$SSW = \sum_{j=1}^{c} \sum_{i=1}^{n_j} X_{ij}^2 - \sum_{j=1}^{c} \frac{T_j^2}{n_j} \qquad (14.4a)$$

$$SST = \sum_{j=1}^{c} \sum_{i=1}^{n_j} X_{ij}^2 - \frac{(GT)^2}{n} \qquad (14.1a)$$

Returning to the productivity study, the difference between the machines had been determined by using the definitional formulas. In order to use the simpler computational methods, the following four quantities must be computed:

$$\sum_{j=1}^{c} \sum_{i=1}^{n_j} X_{ij}^2 \qquad T_j \qquad \sum_{j=1}^{c} \frac{T_j^2}{n_j} \qquad \frac{(GT)^2}{n}$$

Referring back to Table 14.1 on page 451, there were three machines (I, II, and III). The results, giving the total and the mean for each, are summarized below:

	I	II	III
Sample size, n_j	$n_1 = 5$	$n_2 = 5$	$n_3 = 5$
Total, T_j	$T_1 = 124.65$	$T_2 = 113.05$	$T_3 = 102.95$
Sample mean, $\bar{X}_j$	$\bar{X}_1 = 24.93$	$\bar{X}_2 = 22.61$	$\bar{X}_3 = 20.59$

From this we compute

$$n = 5 + 5 + 5 = 15$$

$$GT = \sum_{j=1}^{c} \sum_{i=1}^{n_j} X_{ij} = 124.65 + 113.05 + 102.95 = 340.65$$

$$\frac{(GT)^2}{n} = \frac{(340.65)^2}{15} = 7{,}736.1615$$

$$\sum_{j=1}^{c} \sum_{i=1}^{n_j} X_{ij}^2 = 25.40^2 + 26.31^2 + \cdots + 23.40^2 + \cdots + 20.40^2$$
$$= 7{,}794.3787$$

$$\sum_{j=1}^{c} \frac{T_j^2}{n_j} = \frac{(124.65)^2 + (113.05)^2 + (102.95)^2}{5} = 7{,}783.3255$$

Using Equation (14.3a) we have

$$SSB = \sum_{j=1}^{c} \frac{T_j^2}{n_j} - \frac{(GT)^2}{n}$$
$$= 7{,}783.3255 - 7{,}736.1615$$
$$= 47.164$$

Using Equation (14.4a), we have

$$SSW = \sum_{j=1}^{c} \sum_{i=1}^{n_j} X_{ij}^2 - \sum_{j=1}^{c} \frac{T_j^2}{n_j}$$
$$= 7{,}794.3787 - 7{,}783.3255$$
$$= 11.0532$$

And, using Equation (14.1a), we have

$$SST = \sum_{j=1}^{c} \sum_{i=1}^{n_j} X_{ij}^2 - \frac{(GT)^2}{n}$$
$$= 7{,}794.3787 - 7{,}736.1615$$
$$= 58.2172$$

If we compare these calculations with those given on pages 452–454, we see, of course, that the two methods (definitional and computational) have produced exactly the same results. Therefore, it is recommended that the computational method be utilized for all calculations needed since these computations are less tedious and simpler to perform.

14.2.4 The *F* Distribution

In order to determine whether the means of the various groups are all equal, we can examine two different estimates of the population variance. One estimate is based on the sum of squares within groups (SSW); the other is based on the sums of squares between groups (SSB). If the null hypothesis is true, these estimates should be nearly the same; if it is false, the estimate based on the sum of squares between groups should be larger.

In Section 3.5.2 we said that a variance is estimated by dividing the sum of squared deviations by its appropriate degrees of freedom. In dividing by the degrees of freedom, we calculated the variance as a sort of average squared deviation. Since another word for "average" is "mean," we could call this the **mean squared deviation;** in statistics, this is shortened to the term **mean square.**

In the analysis of variance, the sum of squared deviations is represented by the component sums of squares we have computed. Within each group, the degrees of freedom are equal to the number of subjects in that group minus one. Since there are c groups, if we add the degrees of freedom within the groups together, we get $df_w = n - c$; this is the degrees of freedom for computing the variance estimate using the within sum of squares.[1] That is, the within-group mean square (also called the **mean square within,** or **MSW**), measures variability around the particular sample mean of each group. Since this variability is not affected by group differences, it can be considered a measure of the random variation of values within a group.

The between-group variance estimate (**mean square between** or **MSB**) is calculated by dividing the between-group sum of squares by the degrees of freedom between groups. The degrees of freedom is one less than the number of groups; i.e., $df_B = c - 1$. This is because SSB was calculated from the difference between the c

---

[1] Within each group there are $(n_j - 1)$ degrees of freedom. When these are summed over all c groups, there are $n - c$ degrees of freedom within groups:

$$(n_1 - 1) + (n_2 - 1) + \cdots + (n_c - 1) = (n_1 + n_2 + \cdots + n_c) + (-1 - 1 - \cdots - 1) = n - c$$

group means and the overall mean. Using the same logic as we did in calculating degrees of freedom for the variance in Chapter 3, we see that only $c - 1$ of the group means can vary; the last is determined because the overall mean is known.

The variance between groups, MSB, is estimated by

$$\text{MSB} = \frac{\substack{\text{sum of squares} \\ \text{between groups}}}{\substack{\text{degrees of freedom} \\ \text{between groups}}} = \frac{\text{SSB}}{df_B} = \frac{\sum\limits_{j=1}^{c} n_j(\bar{X}_j - \bar{\bar{X}})^2}{c - 1} = \frac{\sum\limits_{j=1}^{c} \dfrac{T_j^2}{n_j} - \dfrac{(GT)^2}{n}}{c - 1} \qquad \textbf{(14.5)}$$

The variance within groups, MSW, is estimated by

$$\text{MSW} = \frac{\substack{\text{sum of squares} \\ \text{within groups}}}{\substack{\text{degrees of freedom} \\ \text{within groups}}} = \frac{\text{SSW}}{df_W} = \frac{\sum\limits_{j=1}^{c} \sum\limits_{i=1}^{n_j} (X_{ij} - \bar{X}_j)^2}{n - c} = \frac{\sum\limits_{j=1}^{c} \sum\limits_{i=1}^{n_j} X_{ij}^2 - \sum\limits_{j=1}^{c} \dfrac{T_j^2}{n_j}}{n - c} \qquad \textbf{(14.6)}$$

The between-group variance estimate (MSB) not only takes into account random fluctuations from observation to observation, but also measures differences from one group to another. If there is no difference from group to group, any sample mean differences will be explainable by random variation, and the variance between groups, MSB, should be close to the variance within groups, MSW. If there is really a difference between the groups, however, the variance between groups, MSB, will be significantly *larger* than the variance within groups, MSW. The test statistic is based upon the ratio of the two variances, MSB/MSW. If the null hypothesis is true, this ratio should be near 1; if the null hypothesis is false, then the numerator should be bigger than the denominator, and the ratio should be bigger than 1. To know how big the ratio must be before we reject the null hypothesis, we need to know what the distribution of this statistic would be if the null hypothesis were true. As we may recall from Section 12.4, this distribution is called the ***F* distribution** (see Table E.5). That is,

$$F_{df_1, df_2} = \frac{\text{MSB}}{\text{MSW}} \qquad \textbf{(14.7)}$$

From Table E.5, we can see that the shape of the F distribution depends on two types of degrees of freedom: the degrees of freedom between the group means in the numerator (called df_1 in most tables of the F distribution) and the degrees of freedom within groups (df_2) in the denominator. Here, $df_1 = c - 1$ and $df_2 = n - c$.

The decision rule is to reject the null hypothesis of no difference between the groups if at the α level of significance

$$F_{(c-1),(n-c)} = \frac{\text{MSB}}{\text{MSW}} > F_{\alpha,(c-1),(n-c)}$$

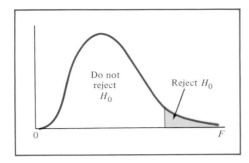

FIGURE 14.2
Regions of rejection and nonrejection in the analysis of variance.

where $F_{\alpha,(c-1),(n-c)}$ is the critical value of the F distribution with $c-1$ and $n-c$ degrees of freedom. This is depicted in Figure 14.2.

Returning to the productivity study, since SSB = 47.164, SSW = 11.0532, $n = 15$, and $c = 3$, we have

$$MSB = \frac{47.164}{3-1} = \frac{47.164}{2} = 23.582$$

$$MSW = \frac{11.0532}{15-3} = \frac{11.0532}{12} = .9211$$

Therefore, we have

$$F_{2,12} = \frac{MSB}{MSW} = \frac{23.582}{.9211} = 25.60$$

If a significance level of .01 was decided upon, the critical value of the F distribution could be determined from Table E.5. The values in the body of this table refer to selected *upper* percentage points of the F distribution. In this example, since there are 2 degrees of freedom in the numerator and 12 degrees of freedom in the denominator, the critical value of F at the .01 level of significance is 6.93 (see Table 14.2).

Thus the decision rule would be to reject the null hypothesis (H_0: $\mu_I = \mu_{II} = \mu_{III}$) if the calculated F equals or exceeds 6.93 (see Figure 14.3). In our example, since $F_{2,12} = 25.60 > 6.93$, the statistical decision is to reject the null hypothesis. The

TABLE 14.2 Obtaining the critical value of F with 2 and 12 degrees of freedom at the .01 level

Denominator, df_2	Numerator, df_1										
	1	2	3	4	5	6	7	8	9	10	12
6	13.75	10.92	9.78	9.15	8.75	8.47	8.26	8.10	7.98	7.87	7.72
7	12.25	9.55	8.45	7.85	7.46	7.19	6.99	6.84	6.72	6.62	6.47
8	11.26	8.65	7.59	7.01	6.63	6.37	6.18	6.03	5.91	5.81	5.67
9	10.56	8.02	6.99	6.42	6.06	5.80	5.61	5.47	5.35	5.26	5.11
10	10.04	7.56	6.55	5.99	5.64	5.39	5.20	5.06	4.94	4.85	4.71
11	9.65	7.21	6.22	5.67	5.32	5.07	4.89	4.74	4.63	4.54	4.40
12	9.33	6.93	5.95	5.41	5.06	4.82	4.64	4.50	4.39	4.30	4.16
13	9.07	6.70	5.74	5.21	4.86	4.62	4.44	4.30	4.19	4.10	3.96

SOURCE: Extracted from Table E.5.

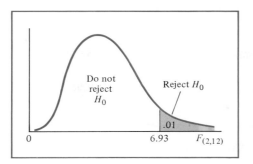

FIGURE 14.3
Regions of rejection and nonrejection for the analysis of variance at the .01 level of significance with 2 and 12 degrees of freedom.

production manager may conclude that there is a significant difference in the average time to complete a task on the three machines.

14.2.5 The Analysis-of-Variance Table

Since several steps are involved in the computation of both the between- and the within-group variances, the entire set of results may be organized into an *analysis-of-variance* (*ANOVA*) *table*. This table, which is presented as Table 14.3 using the definitional formulas and Table 14.4 using the computational formulas, includes the sources of variation, the sums of squares (i.e., variations), the degrees of freedom, the variances (i.e., mean squares), and the calculated *F* value.

TABLE 14.3 Analysis-of-variance table using definitional formulas

Source	*Sum of Squares*	*Degrees of Freedom*	*Mean Square (Variance)*	*F*
Between groups	$SSB = \sum_{j=1}^{c} n_j(\bar{X}_j - \bar{\bar{X}})^2$	$c - 1$	$MSB = \dfrac{SSB}{c-1}$	$F = \dfrac{MSB}{MSW}$
Within groups	$SSW = \sum_{j=1}^{c}\sum_{i=1}^{n_j}(X_{ij} - \bar{X}_j)^2$	$n - c$	$MSW = \dfrac{SSW}{n-c}$	
Total	$SST = \sum_{j=1}^{c}\sum_{i=1}^{n_j}(X_{ij} - \bar{\bar{X}})^2$	$n - 1$		

TABLE 14.4 Analysis-of-variance table using computational formulas

Source	*Sum of Squares*	*Degrees of Freedom*	*Mean Square (Variance)*	*F*
Between groups	$SSB = \sum_{j=1}^{c}\dfrac{T_j^2}{n_j} - \dfrac{(GT)^2}{n}$	$c - 1$	$MSB = \dfrac{SSB}{c-1}$	$F = \dfrac{MSB}{MSW}$
Within groups	$SSW = \sum_{j=1}^{c}\sum_{i=1}^{n_j}X_{ij}^2 - \sum_{j=1}^{c}\dfrac{T_j^2}{n_j}$	$n - c$	$MSW = \dfrac{SSW}{n-c}$	
Total	$SST = \sum_{j=1}^{c}\sum_{i=1}^{n_j}X_{ij}^2 - \dfrac{(GT)^2}{n}$	$n - 1$		

TABLE 14.5   Analysis-of-variance table for the productivity study

Source	Sum of Squares	Degrees of Freedom	Mean Square (Variance)	F
Between groups (machines)	47.164	$3 - 1 = 2$	23.582	25.60
Within groups (machines)	11.0532	$15 - 3 = 12$	.9211	
Total	58.2172	$15 - 1 = 14$		

In the productivity study the computations just completed can be summarized in the analysis-of-variance table shown as Table 14.5.

Problems

14.1   Explain the difference between the between-groups variance MSB and the within-groups variance MSW.

14.2   How does the one-way analysis of variance differ from the test for the differences between two variances of Section 12.4?

14.3   A consumer organization was interested in determining whether any difference existed in the average life of four different brands of transistor radio batteries. A random sample of four batteries of each brand was tested with the following results (in hours):

Brand 1	Brand 2	Brand 3	Brand 4
12	14	21	14
15	17	19	21
18	12	20	25
10	19	23	20

(a) At the .05 level of significance, is there evidence of a difference in the average life of these four brands of transistor radio batteries?

➡(b) **ACTION**   Write a memo to the Vice-President of Research at this organization explaining your findings.

14.4   A senior partner in a brokerage firm wishes to determine if there is really any difference between long-run performance of different categories of people hired as customers' representatives. The junior members of the firm are classified into four groups: professionals who have changed careers, recent business school graduates, former salesmen, and brokers hired from competing firms. A random sample of five individuals in each of these categories is selected and a "detailed performance score" is obtained.

Professionals	Business School Grads	Salesmen	Brokers
85	73	67	87
95	54	74	90
96	72	65	84
91	81	68	92
88	69	77	94

(a) Is there evidence of a difference in the average performance score for the various categories? (Use $\alpha = .05$.)

➡**(b) ACTION** Write a memo to the senior partner explaining your findings.

14.5 A consumer organization wanted to compare the price of a particular toy in three types of stores in a suburban county: discount toy stores, department stores, and variety stores. A random sample of 4 discount toy stores, 6 department stores, and 5 variety stores were selected. The results were as follows:

Discount Toy	Department	Variety
12	15	19
14	18	16
15	14	16
16	18	18
	18	15
	15	

(a) At the .05 level of significance, is there evidence of a difference in the average price between the types of stores?

➡**(b) ACTION** Write a memo to the Vice President of Research at this organization explaining your findings.

● 14.6 A professor of computer science wanted to conduct an experiment to investigate the relative efficiency of the three computer languages FORTRAN, COBOL, and PL/1 in solving a large-scale problem. A random sample of 15 computer science majors, equally proficient in all three languages, was selected. The 15 students were randomly assigned to a particular language and told to count the number of hours of work needed to solve the problem. The results were as follows:

FORTRAN	COBOL	PL/1
20	23	20
17	20	23
26	27	19
19	30	24
24	26	27

(a) At the .01 level of significance, is there any evidence of a difference in the average time in work-hours between the three computer languages?

➡**(b) ACTION** Write a memo to the professor explaining your findings.

14.7 A statistics professor wanted to study the difference in four different strategies of playing the game of Blackjack (Twenty-One). The four strategies were

1. Dealer's strategy
2. Five-count strategy
3. Basic ten-count strategy
4. Advanced ten-count strategy

A calculator that could play Blackjack was utilized and data from five sessions of each strategy were collected. The profits (or losses) from each session were as follows (top of page 462):

		Strategy	
Dealer's	Five Count	Basic Ten Count	Advanced Ten Count
−$56	−$26	+$16	+$60
−$78	−$12	+$20	+$40
−$20	+$18	−$14	−$16
−$46	−$8	+$6	+$12
−$60	−$16	−$25	+$4

(a) At the .01 level of significance, is there evidence of a difference in the average profitability for the four gambling strategies?

➡**(b)** **ACTION** Write a memo to the professor explaining your findings.

14.8 A metallurgist tested five different alloys for tensile strength. He tested several samples of each alloy; the tensile strength of each sample was

Alloy 1:	12.4, 19.8, 15.2, 14.8, 18.5
Alloy 2:	8.9, 11.6, 10.0, 10.3
Alloy 3:	10.5, 13.8, 12.1, 11.9, 12.6
Alloy 4:	12.8, 14.2, 15.9, 14.1
Alloy 5:	16.4, 15.9, 17.8, 20.3

(a) Construct an appropriate graph, plot, or chart of the data.

(b) Calculate the mean tensile strength for each group.

(c) Using your answers to (a) and (b), guess whether there is any difference among the groups.

➡**(d)** **ACTION** Do an analysis of variance of the data, and describe the results to the metallurgist in a memo. (Use $\alpha = .05$.)

14.9 In Problem 12.6 on page 379 you used a t test to compare the tuition at private colleges in the Northeast and Midwest. (The data are taken from Problem 3.79 on page 80.)

(a) Do an analysis of variance on this data set. (Use $\alpha = .01$.)

(b) Square the value of t you computed in Problem 12.6; notice that it is the same (except for rounding error) as the F value. Express in your own words the relationship between t and F.

14.10 In Problem 12.7 on page 379 you used a t test to compare the acceleration of German and Japanese cars. (The data are taken from Problem 3.80 on page 81.)

(a) Do an analysis of variance on this data set. (Use $\alpha = .05$.)

(b) Square the value of t you computed in Problem 12.7; notice that it is the same (except for rounding error) as the F value. Express in your own words the relationship between t and F.

14.3 ASSUMPTIONS OF THE ANALYSIS OF VARIANCE

In Chapters 12 and 13 we mentioned the assumptions made in applying each particular statistical procedure to a set of data and the consequences of departures from these assumptions. The analysis-of-variance technique also makes certain assumptions about the data being investigated. There are three major assumptions in the analysis of variance:

1. Normality
2. Homogeneity of variance
3. Independence of errors

The first assumption, normality, states that the values in each group are normally distributed. Just as in the case of the *t* test, the analysis-of-variance test is "robust" against departures from the normal distribution; that is, as long as the distributions are not extremely different from the normal distribution, the level of significance of the analysis-of-variance test is not greatly affected by lack of normality, particularly for large samples.

When only the normality assumption is seriously violated, alternatives to the analysis-of-variance *F* test are available (see Section 15.7).

The second assumption, homogeneity of variance, states that the variance within each population should be equal for all populations ($\sigma_1^2 = \sigma_2^2 = \cdots = \sigma_c^2$). This assumption is needed in order to combine or pool the variances within the groups into a single "within-group" source of variation SSW. If there are equal sample sizes in each group, inferences based upon the *F* distribution may not be seriously affected by unequal variances. If, however, there are unequal sample sizes in different groups, unequal variances from group to group can have serious effects on drawing inferences made from the analysis of variance. Thus, from the point of view of computational simplicity, robustness, and power, there should be equal sample sizes in all groups whenever possible.

When only the homogeneity-of-variance assumption is violated, procedures similar to those used in Section 12.5 are available (see Reference 1). However, if both the normality and homogeneity-of-variance assumptions have been violated, an appropriate "data transformation" may be used that will both normalize the data and reduce the differences in variances (see References 1 and 7).

The third assumption, independence of errors, refers not to mistakes, but to the difference of each value from its own group mean. The assumption is that these should be independent for each value. That is, the error for one observation should not be related to the error for any other observation. This assumption might be violated, for example, in the productivity study described in this chapter if one worker aided another in completing the task. The assumption would also be violated if two of the workers in one group were twins: their behavior would likely be more similar than would the behavior of any other two individuals in the study.

This assumption is often violated when data are collected over a period of time, because observations made at adjacent time points are often more alike than those made at very different times. Consider, for example, temperature recorded every day for a month. The temperature on a given day is likely to be near what it was the day before, but less likely to be close to the temperature several weeks later.

Departures from this assumption can seriously affect inferences from the analysis of variance. These problems are discussed more thoroughly in References 1 and 3.

Problems

✗ **14.11** Compare and contrast the assumptions of the analysis of variance and the assumptions of the *t* test for the difference between the means of two populations. Discuss fully.

✗ 14.12   Explain how the graphical methods of Chapters 3 and 4 might be used to evaluate the validity of the assumptions of the analysis of variance.

14.4 HARTLEY'S TEST FOR HOMOGENEITY OF VARIANCE

Although the one-way analysis of variance is relatively robust to the assumption of equal group variances, large departures from this assumption may seriously affect the α level and the power of the test. Therefore, various procedures have been developed to test the assumption of homogeneity of variance. Perhaps the simplest and best known is Hartley's F_{max} procedure (see Reference 1). To test

$$H_0: \quad \sigma_1^2 = \sigma_2^2 = \cdots = \sigma_c^2$$

against the alternative

$$H_1: \text{Not all } \sigma_j^2 \text{ are equal } (j = 1, 2, \ldots, c)$$

we obtain the test statistic

$$F_{max[c,(n-1)]} = \frac{S_{max}^2}{S_{min}^2} \tag{14.8}$$

where S_{max}^2 = largest sample variance
S_{min}^2 = smallest sample variance

$$\bar{n} = \frac{\sum_{j=1}^{c} n_j}{c} = \frac{n}{c} \quad \text{(only the integer portion of this value is utilized)}$$

The null hypothesis of the equality of group variances will be rejected only when the computed F_{max} equals or exceeds the upper-tail critical value of Hartley's F_{max} distribution based upon c and $(\bar{n} - 1)$ degrees of freedom (see Table E.8).

In order to illustrate Hartley's F_{max} procedure, let us return to the data for the productivity study, which is presented in Table 14.1 on page 451. Using Equation (3.6), we can compute the sample variances of the three groups as follows:

$$S_I^2 = 1.065, \quad S_{II}^2 = .778, \quad S_{III}^2 = .921$$

Since each group contains a sample of size 5, $\bar{n} = (5 + 5 + 5)/3 = 5$, and, testing the null hypothesis

$$H_0: \quad \sigma_I^2 = \sigma_{II}^2 = \sigma_{III}^2$$

against the alternative

$$H_1: \text{Not all } \sigma_j^2 \text{ are equal } (j = 1, 2, 3)$$

the F_{max} statistic is computed from Equation (14.8) as

$$F_{max[3,4]} = \frac{1.065}{.778} = 1.369$$

If the .05 level of significance is selected, the decision rule would be to reject H_0 if $F_{max[3,4]} \geq 15.5$ (see Table 14.6). In our example, since $F_{max[3,4]} = 1.369 <$

TABLE 14.6 Obtaining the critical value of F_{max} with 3 and 4 degrees of freedom at the .05 level of significance

Upper 5% points ($\alpha = .05$)

$\bar{n} - 1$ \ c	2	3	4	5	6	7	8	9
2	39.0	87.5	142	202	266	333	403	475
3	15.4	27.8	39.2	50.7	62.0	72.9	83.5	93.9
4	9.60	15.5	20.6	25.2	29.5	33.6	37.5	41.1
5	7.15	10.8	13.7	16.3	18.7	20.8	22.9	24.7
6	5.82	8.38	10.4	12.1	13.7	15.0	16.3	17.5
7	4.99	6.94	8.44	9.70	10.8	11.8	12.7	13.5
8	4.43	6.00	7.18	8.12	9.03	9.78	10.5	11.1
9	4.03	5.34	6.31	7.11	7.80	8.41	8.95	9.45
10	3.72	4.85	5.67	6.34	6.92	7.42	7.87	8.28
12	3.28	4.16	4.79	5.30	5.72	6.09	6.42	6.72
15	2.86	3.54	4.01	4.37	4.68	4.95	5.19	5.40
20	2.46	2.95	3.29	3.54	3.76	3.94	4.10	4.24
30	2.07	2.40	2.61	2.78	2.91	3.02	3.12	3.21
60	1.67	1.85	1.96	2.04	2.11	2.17	2.22	2.26
∞	1.00	1.00	1.00	1.00	1.00	1.00	1.00	1.00

SOURCE: Extracted from Table E.8.

15.5, we would not reject H_0 and we would conclude that there is no evidence of a difference in the variances of the three groups.

Although the F_{max} test is simple to utilize, unfortunately it is not robust. It is extremely sensitive to departures from normality in the data. Thus in situations where the researcher is unable to assume normality for each group, other alternative procedures should be applied (see Reference 1).

Problems

14.13 Referring to Problem 14.3 on page 460, at the .05 level of significance is there evidence of a difference in the variances of the life of the batteries?

• **14.14** Referring to Problem 14.4 on page 460, at the .05 level of significance is there evidence of a difference in the variances for the four categories?

14.15 Referring to Problem 14.5 on page 461, at the .05 level of significance is there evidence of a difference in the variances between the three types of stores?

• **14.16** Referring to Problem 14.6 on page 461, at the .01 level of significance is there evidence of a difference in the variances between the three computer languages?

14.17 Referring to Problem 14.7 on page 461, at the .01 level of significance is there evidence of a difference in the variances between the four gambling strategies?

14.18 Referring to Problem 14.8 on page 462, at the .05 level of significance is there evidence of a difference in the variances between the five alloys?

14.5 MULTIPLE COMPARISONS: THE TUKEY *T* METHOD

In the productivity study discussed thus far in this chapter, the analysis of variance was used to determine whether there was a difference in the average time to complete a task over several groups. Once differences in the means of the groups are found, it is important that we determine which particular groups are different.

Although many procedures are available (see References 1 and 3), we will focus on Tukey's T method in order to determine which of the c means are significantly different from each other. This method is an example of a *post hoc* (or *a posteriori*) comparison procedure, since the hypotheses of interest are formulated *after* the data have been inspected.

The Tukey T method enables us to simultaneously examine comparisons between all pairs of groups. The first step involved is to compute the differences $\bar{X}_j - \bar{X}_{j'}$ (where $j \neq j'$) among all $c(c-1)/2$ pairs of means. The critical range for the T method is then obtained from the quantity.[2]

$$\text{critical range} = Q_{\alpha, c, n-c} \sqrt{\frac{\text{MSW}}{n_j}} \qquad (14.9)$$

The final step is to compare each of the $c(c-1)/2$ pairs of means against the critical range. A specific pair would be declared significantly different if the absolute difference in the sample means $|\bar{X}_j - \bar{X}_{j'}|$ equals or exceeds the critical range.

To apply the T method, we return to the productivity study. Using the ANOVA procedure, we recall that we concluded that there was a difference in the average time to complete a task by using the three machines. Since there are three groups, there are $3(3-1)/2 = 3$ possible pairwise comparisons to be made. From Table 14.1, the absolute mean differences are

1. $|\bar{X}_{\text{I}} - \bar{X}_{\text{II}}| = |24.93 - 22.61| = 2.32$.
2. $|\bar{X}_{\text{I}} - \bar{X}_{\text{III}}| = |24.93 - 20.59| = 4.34$.
3. $|\bar{X}_{\text{II}} - \bar{X}_{\text{III}}| = |22.61 - 20.59| = 2.02$.

To determine the critical range, from Table 14.5 we have MSW = .9211 and $n_j = 5$. From Table E.12, for $\alpha = .05$, $c = 3$ and $n - c = 15 - 3 = 12$, the upper critical value of $Q_{.05, 3, 12}$ is 3.77 (see Table 14.7 on page 467). From Equation (14.9), we have

$$\text{critical range} = 3.77 \sqrt{\frac{.9211}{5}} = 1.618$$

Since $2.32 > 1.618$, $4.34 > 1.618$, and $2.02 > 1.618$, it would be concluded that there is a significant difference between each pair of means. Hence the production

---

[2] If there are unequal sample sizes in each group, n_j in Equation (14.9) is replaced by

$$\frac{c}{\sum_{j=1}^{c} \left(\frac{1}{n_j} \right)} = \frac{c}{\left(\frac{1}{n_1} \right) + \left(\frac{1}{n_2} \right) + \cdots + \left(\frac{1}{n_c} \right)}$$

Although the T method was originally devised for equal sample sizes, many statisticians have maintained that it is robust to moderate departures from the assumption of equal sample sizes.

TABLE 14.7 Obtaining the Studentized range Q statistic for $\alpha = .05$ with 3 and 12 degrees of freedom

Denominator Degrees of Freedom	Numerator Degrees of Freedom														
	2	3	4	5	6	7	8	9	10	11	12	13	14	15	16
1	18.0	27.0	32.8	37.1	40.4	43.1	45.4	47.4	49.1	50.6	52.0	53.2	54.3	55.4	56.3
2	6.09	8.3	9.8	10.9	11.7	12.4	13.0	13.5	14.0	14.4	14.7	15.1	15.4	15.7	15.9
3	4.50	5.91	6.82	7.50	8.04	8.48	8.85	9.18	9.46	9.72	9.95	10.15	10.35	10.52	10.69
4	3.93	5.04	5.76	6.29	6.71	7.05	7.35	7.60	7.83	8.03	8.21	8.37	8.52	8.66	8.79
5	3.64	4.60	5.22	5.67	6.03	6.33	6.58	6.80	6.99	7.17	7.32	7.47	7.60	7.72	7.83
6	3.46	4.34	4.90	5.31	5.63	5.89	6.12	6.32	6.49	6.65	6.79	6.92	7.03	7.14	7.24
7	3.34	4.16	4.68	5.06	5.36	5.61	5.82	6.00	6.16	6.30	6.43	6.55	6.66	6.76	6.85
8	3.26	4.04	4.53	4.89	5.17	5.40	5.60	5.77	5.92	6.05	6.18	6.29	6.39	6.48	6.57
9	3.20	3.95	4.42	4.76	5.02	5.24	5.43	5.60	5.74	5.87	5.98	6.09	6.19	6.28	6.36
10	3.15	3.88	4.33	4.65	4.91	5.12	5.30	5.46	5.60	5.72	5.83	5.93	6.03	6.11	6.20
11	3.11	3.82	4.26	4.57	4.82	5.03	5.20	5.35	5.49	5.61	5.71	5.81	5.90	5.99	6.06
12	3.08	3.77	4.20	4.51	4.75	4.95	5.12	5.27	5.40	5.51	5.62	5.71	5.80	5.88	5.95
13	3.06	3.73	4.15	4.45	4.69	4.88	5.05	5.19	5.32	5.43	5.53	5.63	5.71	5.79	5.86
14	3.03	3.70	4.11	4.41	4.64	4.83	4.99	5.13	5.25	5.36	4.46	5.55	5.64	5.72	5.79

SOURCE: Extracted from Table E.12.

manager would purchase machine III since the average time for completing a task on it is fastest.

Using the T method, we may also establish a set of simultaneous confidence-interval estimates for the true differences between each pair of means. This is achieved by adding and subtracting the critical range to the differences in each pair of sample means, so that

$$(\bar{X}_j - \bar{X}_{j'}) - Q_{\alpha,c,n-c}\sqrt{\frac{MSW}{n_j}} \le (\mu_j - \mu_{j'}) \le (\bar{X}_j - \bar{X}_{j'}) + Q_{\alpha,c,n-c}\sqrt{\frac{MSW}{n_j}} \quad (14.10)$$

Using Equation (14.10), we would obtain the following confidence-interval estimates:

1. $2.32 - 1.618 \le (\mu_I - \mu_{II}) \le 2.32 + 1.618$
   $.702 \le (\mu_I - \mu_{II}) \le 3.938$
2. $4.34 - 1.618 \le (\mu_I - \mu_{III}) \le 4.34 + 1.618$
   $2.722 \le (\mu_I - \mu_{III}) \le 5.958$
3. $2.02 - 1.618 \le (\mu_{II} - \mu_{III}) \le 2.02 + 1.618$
   $.402 \le (\mu_{II} - \mu_{III}) \le 3.638$

The set of confidence intervals provides us with the same conclusions that we obtained from the previously described set of tests. Since none of the intervals include 0, each paired comparison is deemed significantly different. Moreover, we should realize that we have 95% confidence that the entire set of confidence intervals is correct.

From these confidence intervals, the production manager can appreciate the gains in productivity from purchasing machine III. When compared to machine I, it is estimated that the task can be completed between 2.722 and 5.958 seconds faster on machine III; moreover, when compared with machine II, it is estimated that the task can be completed between .402 and 3.638 seconds faster on machine III. Since cost of purchase and service was similar, the production manager would select machine III.

Problems

14.19   Referring to Problem 14.3 on page 460, at the .05 level of significance, which brands are different?

● 14.20   Referring to Problem 14.4 on page 460, at the .05 level of significance, which categories differ in performance score?

14.21   Referring to Problem 14.5 on page 461, at the .05 level of significance, which types of stores differ in price?

● 14.22   Referring to Problem 14.6 on page 461, at the .01 level of significance, which languages differ in average work-hours?

14.23   Referring to Problem 14.7 on page 461, at the .01 level of significance, which gambling strategies differ in average profits?

14.24   Referring to Problem 14.8 on page 462, at the .05 level of significance, which alloys differ in average tensile strength?

14.6 THE RANDOMIZED BLOCK DESIGN

14.6.1 Introduction

In Sections 14.1–14.5 we have studied the one-way analysis-of-variance model to evaluate differences in the means of c groups. The one-way ANOVA model is also called a *completely randomized design*, since it includes experimental situations in which a set of n homogeneous individuals are randomly assigned to the c levels of a factor of interest (that is, the treatment groups).

We may recall from Section 12.3 that we used the paired t test for situations involving repeated measurements or matched samples in order to evaluate differences between two treatment conditions. Suppose, now, we wish to extend this to situations in which there are more than two treatment groups or conditions. In such cases the heterogeneous sets of individuals are called **blocks.** Information concerning the variable of interest may then be obtained for each treatment group. Thus, there would be two things to consider in developing the analysis-of-variance model: treatments and blocks. However, with respect to our tests of hypotheses, we focus on the differences between the treatments. As in the paired t test for two groups, the purpose for blocking is to remove from the model as much as possible of the variability that is due to the blocking variable so that we may focus on differences among the treatment conditions. Thus, when appropriate, the purpose of selecting a randomized block design instead of a completely randomized design is to provide a more efficient analysis by reducing the experimental error and thereby obtaining more precise results.

14.6.2 Development

To develop the ANOVA procedure for the randomized block model let us refer to the following example. Suppose that a fast-food chain having four branches in a particular geographical area would like to evaluate the service at these restaurants. The research director for the chain hires 24 investigators (raters) with varied experiences in food-service evaluations. After preliminary consultations, the 24 investigators are stratified into six blocks of four—based on food-service evaluation experience—so that the four most experienced investigators are placed in block 1, the next four most experienced investigators are placed in block 2, and so on. Within each of the six homogeneous blocks, the four raters are then randomly assigned to evaluate the service at a particular restaurant using a rating scale from 0 (low) to 100 (high). The results are summarized in Table 14.8.

TABLE 14.8 Restaurant ratings for four branches of a fast-food chain

Blocks of Raters	Restaurants				
	A	B	C	D	Totals
1	70	61	82	74	287
2	77	75	88	76	316
3	76	67	90	80	313
4	80	63	96	76	315
5	84	66	92	84	326
6	78	68	98	86	330
Totals	465	400	546	476	1887
Means	77.5	66.67	91	79.33	78.625

In order to extend our discussion of the analysis of variance to the randomized block model we need to define the following:

X_{ij} = the value in the ith block for the jth treatment

$X_{i.}$ = the summation of all the values in block i

$X_{.j}$ = the summation of all the values for treatment j

GT = the summation of the values over all blocks and all treatments— i.e., the grand total

r = the number of blocks

c = the number of treatments

We recall from Equation (14.2) that in the one-way analysis-of-variance model, the total sum of squares (SST) was subdivided into sum of squares between groups (SSB) and sum of squares within groups (SSW). For the randomized block model, we need to subdivide the total sum of squares (SST) into sum of squares due to treatments (SSTR), sum of squares due to blocks (SSBL), and sum of squares due to random error (SSE):

$$SST = SSTR + SSBL + SSE \qquad (14.11)$$

The total sum of squares (SST) measures the total variation among the observations. SST would be computed as

$$SST = \sum_{j=1}^{c} \sum_{i=1}^{r} (X_{ij} - \overline{\overline{X}})^2 = \sum_{j=1}^{c} \sum_{i=1}^{r} X_{ij}^2 - \frac{(GT)^2}{rc} \qquad (14.12)$$

where $\overline{\overline{X}} = \dfrac{\sum\limits_{j=1}^{c}\sum\limits_{i=1}^{r} X_{ij}}{rc}$ (i.e., the overall or grand mean)

The treatment sum of squares (SSTR) measures the differences between the various treatment groups. SSTR would be computed as

$$\text{SSTR} = \sum_{j=1}^{c}\sum_{i=1}^{r}(\overline{X}_{.j} - \overline{\overline{X}})^2 = \sum_{j=1}^{c}\frac{X_{.j}^2}{r} - \frac{(GT)^2}{rc} \qquad (14.13)$$

where $\overline{X}_{.j} = \dfrac{\sum\limits_{i=1}^{r} X_{ij}}{r}$ (i.e., the treatment means)

The sum of squares between blocks (SSBL) measures the differences between the various blocks. SSBL would be computed as

$$\text{SSBL} = \sum_{j=1}^{c}\sum_{i=1}^{r}(\overline{X}_{i.} - \overline{\overline{X}})^2 = \sum_{i=1}^{r}\frac{X_{i.}^2}{c} - \frac{(GT)^2}{rc} \qquad (14.14)$$

where $\overline{X}_{i.} = \dfrac{\sum\limits_{j=1}^{c} X_{ij}}{c}$ (i.e., the block means)

The error sum of squares (SSE) measures differences among all the observations after the effect of the particular treatments and blocks have been accounted for. SSE would be computed as

$$\text{SSE} = \sum_{j=1}^{c}\sum_{i=1}^{r}(X_{ij} - \overline{X}_{.j} - \overline{X}_{i.} + \overline{\overline{X}})^2 \qquad (14.15)$$

$$= \sum_{j=1}^{c}\sum_{i=1}^{r} X_{ij}^2 - \sum_{j=1}^{c}\frac{X_{.j}^2}{r} - \sum_{i=1}^{r}\frac{X_{i.}^2}{c} + \frac{(GT)^2}{rc}$$

If SSTR, SSBL, and SSE are divided by their respective number of degrees of freedom, we will obtain the variances or mean squares:

$$\text{MSTR} = \frac{\text{SSTR}}{c-1} \qquad (14.16)$$

$$\text{MSBL} = \frac{\text{SSBL}}{r - 1} \qquad (14.17)$$

$$\text{MSE} = \frac{\text{SSE}}{(r - 1)(c - 1)} \qquad (14.18)$$

Referring back to Table 14.8 on page 469 we have

$$r = 6, \quad c = 4, \quad X_{.1} = 465, \quad X_{.2} = 400, \quad X_{.3} = 546$$

$$X_{.4} = 476, \quad X_{1.} = 287, \quad X_{2.} = 316, \quad X_{3.} = 313$$

$$X_{4.} = 315, \quad X_{5.} = 326, \quad X_{6.} = 330, \quad GT = 1,887$$

$$\sum_{j=1}^{c} \sum_{i=1}^{r} X_{ij}^2 = 70^2 + 77^2 + \cdots + 86^2 = 150,661$$

$$\sum_{i=1}^{r} \frac{X_{i.}^2}{c} = \frac{287^2 + 316^2 + \cdots + 330^2}{4} = 148,648.75$$

$$\sum_{j=1}^{c} \frac{X_{.j}^2}{r} = \frac{465^2 + 400^2 + 546^2 + 476^2}{6} = 150,152.83$$

$$\frac{(GT)^2}{rc} = \frac{1,887^2}{6(4)} = 148,365.37$$

Using Equation (14.12),

$$\text{SST} = \sum_{j=1}^{c} \sum_{i=1}^{r} X_{ij}^2 - \frac{(GT)^2}{rc}$$

$$= 150,661 - 148,365.37 = 2,295.63$$

Using Equation (14.13),

$$\text{SSTR} = \sum_{j=1}^{c} \frac{X_{.j}^2}{r} - \frac{(GT)^2}{rc}$$

$$= 150,152.83 - 148,365.37 = 1,787.46$$

Using Equation (14.14),

$$\text{SSBL} = \sum_{i=1}^{r} \frac{X_{i.}^2}{c} - \frac{(GT)^2}{rc}$$

$$= 148,648.75 - 148,365.37 = 283.38$$

Using Equation (14.15),

$$\text{SSE} = \sum_{j=1}^{c} \sum_{i=1}^{r} X_{ij}^2 - \sum_{j=1}^{c} \frac{X_{.j}^2}{r} - \sum_{i=1}^{r} \frac{X_{i.}^2}{c} + \frac{(GT)^2}{rc}$$

$$= 150,661 - 150,152.83 - 148,648.75 + 148,365.37$$

$$= 224.79$$

Thus, using Equations (14.16), (14.17), and (14.18),

$$\text{MSTR} = \frac{\text{SSTR}}{c-1} = \frac{1{,}787.46}{3} = 595.820$$

$$\text{MSBL} = \frac{\text{SSBL}}{r-1} = \frac{283.38}{5} = 56.676$$

$$\text{MSE} = \frac{\text{SSE}}{(r-1)(c-1)} = \frac{224.79}{15} = 14.986$$

To test the null hypothesis of no treatment effects

$$H_0: \quad \mu_{.1} = \mu_{.2} = \cdots = \mu_{.c}$$

against the alternative

$$H_1: \quad \text{not all } \mu_{.j} \text{ are equal}$$

we form the F statistic

$$F_{c-1,(r-1)(c-1)} = \frac{\text{MSTR}}{\text{MSE}} \qquad\qquad \textbf{(14.19a)}$$

and the null hypothesis would be rejected at the α level of significance if

$$F_{c-1,(r-1)(c-1)} = \frac{\text{MSTR}}{\text{MSE}} > F_{\alpha,c-1,(r-1)(c-1)}$$

To examine whether it is advantageous to block, some researchers might want to test the null hypothesis of no block effects

$$H_0: \quad \mu_{1.} = \mu_{2.} = \cdots = \mu_{r.}$$

against the alternative

$$H_1: \quad \text{not all } \mu_{i.} \text{ are equal}$$

We form the F statistic

$$F_{r-1,(r-1)(c-1)} = \frac{\text{MSBL}}{\text{MSE}} \qquad\qquad \textbf{(14.19b)}$$

and the null hypothesis would be rejected at the α level of significance if

$$F_{r-1,(r-1)(c-1)} = \frac{\text{MSBL}}{\text{MSE}} > F_{\alpha,r-1,(r-1)(c-1)}$$

However, it may be argued that this is unnecessary, that the sole purpose of establishing the blocks was to provide a more efficient means of testing for treatment effects by reducing the experimental error.[3]

---

[3] In essence, in a randomized block design the blocks are not given the status of a factor. In Section 14.7 we shall see that when the blocks are considered important enough to be a second factor, the design is called a two-factor experiment, and tests for each factor effect would potentially be important.

TABLE 14.9 Analysis-of-variance table for the randomized block design

Source	Sum of Squares	Degrees of Freedom	Mean Square (Variance)	F
Among treatments	$SSTR = \sum_{j=1}^{c} \dfrac{X_{.j}^2}{r} - \dfrac{(GT)^2}{rc}$	$c - 1$	$MSTR = \dfrac{SSTR}{c-1}$	$F = \dfrac{MSTR}{MSE}$
Among blocks	$SSBL = \sum_{i=1}^{r} \dfrac{X_{i.}^2}{c} - \dfrac{(GT)^2}{rc}$	$r - 1$	$MSBL = \dfrac{SSBL}{r-1}$	$F = \dfrac{MSBL}{MSE}$
Error	$SSE = \sum_{j=1}^{c}\sum_{i=1}^{r} X_{ij}^2 - \sum_{j=1}^{c}\dfrac{X_{.j}^2}{r} - \sum_{i=1}^{r}\dfrac{X_{i.}^2}{c} + \dfrac{(GT)^2}{rc}$	$(r-1)(c-1)$	$MSE = \dfrac{SSE}{(r-1)(c-1)}$	
Total	$SST = \sum_{j=1}^{c}\sum_{i=1}^{r} X_{ij}^2 - \dfrac{(GT)^2}{rc}$	$rc - 1$		

As in Section 14.2.5, the entire set of steps for the randomized block design may be summarized in an analysis-of-variance table (Table 14.9).

In the fast-food-chain study the computations just completed can be summarized in the analysis-of-variance table shown in Table 14.10.

Testing for differences between the restaurants, using the .05 level of significance, the decision rule would be to reject the null hypothesis (H_0: $\mu_{.A} = \mu_{.B} = \mu_{.C} = \mu_{.D}$) if the calculated F value equals or exceeds 3.29 (see Figure 14.4 on page 474). Since $F_{3,15} = 39.758 > 3.29$, we may reject H_0 and conclude that there is evidence of a difference in the average rating between the different restaurants.

As a check on the effectiveness of blocking, we may test for the difference among the groups of raters. The decision rule, using the .05 level of significance, would be to reject the null hypothesis (H_0: $\mu_1. = \mu_2. = \cdots = \mu_6.$) if the calculated F value equals or exceeds 2.90 (see Figure 14.5 on page 474). Since $F_{5,15} = 3.782 > 2.90$, we may reject H_0 and conclude that there is evidence of a difference among the groups of raters. Thus we may conclude that the blocking has been advantageous in reducing the experimental error.

TABLE 14.10 Analysis-of-variance table for the fast-food chain study

Source	Sum of Squares	Degrees of Freedom	Mean Square (Variance)	F
Among treatments (branches)	$150,152.83 - 148,365.37 = 1,787.46$	$4 - 1 = 3$	$MSTR = \dfrac{1,787.46}{3} = 595.820$	$F = \dfrac{595.820}{14.986} = 39.758$
Among blocks (raters)	$148,648.75 - 148,365.37 = 283.38$	$6 - 1 = 5$	$MSBL = \dfrac{283.38}{5} = 56.676$	$F = \dfrac{56.676}{14.986} = 3.782$
Error	$150,661 - 150,152.83 - 148,648.75 + 148,365.37 = 224.79$	$(6-1)(4-1) = 15$	$MSE = \dfrac{224.79}{15} = 14.986$	
Total	$150,661 - 148,365.37 = 2,295.63$	$6(4) - 1 = 23$		

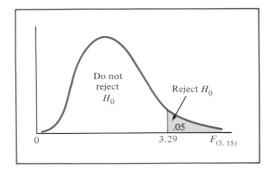

FIGURE 14.4
Regions of rejection and nonrejection for the fast-food-chain study at the .05 level of significance with 3 and 15 degrees of freedom.

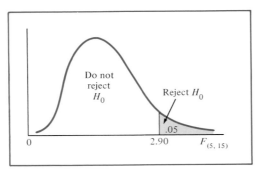

FIGURE 14.5
Regions of rejection and nonrejection for the fast-food-chain study at the .05 level of significance with 5 and 15 degrees of freedom.

In addition to the assumptions of the one-way analysis of variance previously mentioned in Section 14.3, we need to assume that there is no *interacting effect* between the treatments and the blocks. That is, we need to assume that any differences between the treatments (the restaurants) are consistent across the entire set of blocks (the groups of raters).[4]

14.6.3 Tukey's *T* Method for the Randomized Block Model

As in the case of the one-way ANOVA model, once the null hypothesis of no differences between the treatment groups has been rejected, we need to determine which of these treatment groups are significantly different from each other. For the randomized block model the critical range for the *T* method is given in Equation (14.20):

$$\text{critical range} = Q_{\alpha,c,(r-1)(c-1)}\sqrt{\frac{\text{MSE}}{r}} \qquad \text{(14.20)}$$

As in Section 14.5, each of the $c(c-1)/2$ pairs of means is compared against the critical range. A specific pair would be declared different if the absolute difference in the sample means $|\overline{X}_{.j} - \overline{X}_{.j'}|$ equals or exceeds this critical range.

To apply the *T* method, we return to our fast-food-chain study. Since there are

---

[4] This concept of interaction will be discussed further in Section 14.7 when two-factor models are considered.

four restaurants, there are $4(4 - 1)/2 = 6$ possible pairwise comparisons to be made. From Table 14.8 on page 469, the absolute mean differences are

1. $|\overline{X}_A - \overline{X}_B| = |77.5 - 66.67| = 10.83$.

2. $|\overline{X}_A - \overline{X}_C| = |77.5 - 91| = 13.5$.

3. $|\overline{X}_A - \overline{X}_D| = |77.5 - 79.33| = 1.83$.

4. $|\overline{X}_B - \overline{X}_C| = |66.67 - 91| = 24.33$.

5. $|\overline{X}_B - \overline{X}_D| = |66.67 - 79.33| = 12.66$.

6. $|\overline{X}_C - \overline{X}_D| = |91 - 79.33| = 11.67$.

To determine the critical range we use Table 14.10 to obtain MSE = 14.986 and $r = 6$. Moreover, from Table E.12 [for $\alpha = .05$, $c = 4$, and $(r - 1)(c - 1) = (6 - 1)(4 - 1) = 15$], the upper critical value of $Q_{.05,4,15}$ is 4.08. Therefore, using Equation (14.20) we have

$$\text{critical range} = 4.08 \sqrt{\frac{14.986}{6}} = 6.448$$

We note that all contrasts except $|\overline{X}_A - \overline{X}_D|$ are greater than the critical range. Therefore we may conclude that there is evidence of a significant difference in the average rating between all pairs of restaurant branches except for branches A and D. (Moreover, branch C has the highest ratings (i.e., is most preferred) while branch B has the lowest (i.e., is least preferred).

As in the case of the one-way ANOVA design, we may establish a set of simultaneous confidence intervals from Equation (14.21):

$$(\overline{X}_{.j} - \overline{X}_{.j'}) - Q_{\alpha,c,(r-1)(c-1)} \sqrt{\frac{\text{MSE}}{r}}$$

$$\le (\mu_{.j} - \mu_{.j'}) \le (\overline{X}_{.j} - \overline{X}_{.j'}) + Q_{\alpha,c,(r-1)(c-1)} \sqrt{\frac{\text{MSE}}{r}}$$

(14.21)

By using Equation (14.21) with a confidence level of 95%, we obtain the following set of confidence intervals:

1. $10.83 - 6.448 \le (\mu_A - \mu_B) \le 10.83 + 6.448$
   $ 4.382 \le (\mu_A - \mu_B) \le 17.278$
2. $-13.5 - 6.448 \le (\mu_A - \mu_C) \le -13.5 + 6.448$
   $ -19.948 \le (\mu_A - \mu_C) \le -7.052$
3. $-1.83 - 6.448 \le (\mu_A - \mu_D) \le -1.83 + 6.448$
   $ -8.278 \le (\mu_A - \mu_D) \le +4.618$
4. $-24.33 - 6.448 \le (\mu_B - \mu_C) \le -24.33 + 6.448$
   $ -30.778 \le (\mu_B - \mu_C) \le -17.882$

5. $-12.66 - 6.448 \leq (\mu_B - \mu_D) \leq -12.66 + 6.448$
$$-19.108 \leq (\mu_B - \mu_D) \leq -6.212$$
6. $11.67 - 6.448 \leq (\mu_C - \mu_D) \leq 11.67 + 6.448$
$$5.222 \leq (\mu_C - \mu_D) \leq 18.118$$

14.6.4 Comparing the Randomized Block Design to the One-Way (Completely Randomized) Design

Now that we have developed the randomized block model and have used it in the fast-food-chain study, the question arises as to what effect the blocking had on the analysis. That is, did the blocking result in an increase in precision in comparing the different treatment groups?

The estimated relative efficiency (*RE*) of the randomized block design as compared with the completely randomized design may be computed as in Equation (14.22):

$$RE = \frac{(r - 1)\,\text{MSBL} + r(c - 1)\,\text{MSE}}{(rc - 1)\,\text{MSE}} \tag{14.22}$$

Thus, from Table 14.10 on page 473 for the fast-food-chain study we have

$$RE = \frac{5(56.676) + 6(3)(14.986)}{23(14.986)} = 1.60$$

This means that 1.6 times as many observations in each treatment group would be needed in a one-way ANOVA design to obtain the same precision for comparison of treatment group means as would be needed for our randomized block design.

Problems

✗ **14.25** Explain the difference between the randomized block design and the completely randomized one-way ANOVA. Discuss fully.

● **14.26** A plant manager was interested in the effect of "time of day" on the productivity of workers in an automobile parts factory. A sample of five workers is randomly selected and the number of parts produced in a given hour is recorded with the following results:

| Worker | Time Periods | | | | |
	9–10 A.M.	11 A.M.–12 noon	2–3 P.M.	4–5 P.M.	Totals
A	42	36	54	27	159
B	40	43	51	35	169
C	38	32	47	30	147
D	28	25	35	20	108
E	36	30	43	22	131
Totals	184	166	230	134	714

(a) Using a level of significance of $\alpha = .05$, is there evidence of a difference in the output between the time periods?

(b) What assumptions must be made in part (a)? Comment on the appropriateness of these assumptions.

(c) Using the Tukey T method of multiple comparisons, set up interval estimates for all paired comparisons. $(1 - \alpha = .95)$. Which time periods are different?

(d) Determine the relative efficiency of the randomized block design as compared with the completely randomized design.

➠**(e)** **ACTION**   Draft a memo for the plant manager to the Vice-President of Production regarding your findings.

14.27   An agronomist wishes to study the yield (in pounds per plot) of four different strains of Gallipoli wheat. A field is divided into six blocks. Within each block the four strains are randomly assigned, one each, to four plots for planting. The results of the experiment are displayed below.

| | Gallipoli Wheat Strain | | | |
Blocks	A	B	C	D
I	30.4	28.8	33.0	31.8
II	33.9	25.5	32.7	33.5
III	32.7	27.3	34.5	34.5
IV	34.9	29.3	36.0	33.8
V	31.9	27.5	36.5	34.5
VI	35.4	28.3	34.2	36.0

(a) Using a level of significance of $\alpha = .05$, is there evidence of a difference in the yield of the four strains of Gallipoli wheat?

(b) Using the Tukey T method of multiple comparisons, set up interval estimates for all paired comparisons. $(1 - \alpha = .95)$. Which strains are different?

(c) Determine the relative efficiency of the randomized block design as compared with the one-way (completely randomized) design.

➠**(d)** **ACTION**   Draft a letter that the agronomist might send to the Department of Agriculture based on the findings of this experiment.

● **14.28**   Woody Woodward, a former professional baseball player, sought to determine the fastest approach for a base runner to reach second base. He devised an experiment in which the time trials of various Cincinnati Reds baseball players would be evaluated over three different methods of rounding first base: round out, narrow angle, and wide angle. Suppose, in an effort to replicate Woodward's experiment, the data below were obtained.

| | Methods | | |
Player	Round Out	Narrow Angle	Wide Angle
A	5.40	5.50	5.55
B	5.90	5.85	5.70
C	5.25	5.15	5.00
D	5.85	5.80	5.70
E	5.55	5.55	5.35
F	5.65	5.60	5.40

(a) Using a level of significance of $\alpha = .05$, is there evidence of a difference between the methods?

(b) What assumptions are necessary in part (a)?

(c) Using the Tukey T method of multiple comparisons, determine which methods are different. (Use $\alpha = .05$.)

(d) Determine the relative efficiency of the randomized block design as compared with the one-way (completely randomized) design.

➡️(e) **ACTION** Draft a letter to the sports editor of your local newspaper regarding these findings.

14.29 The following data represent the percentage change in real gross national product (GNP) on an annual rate forecast for the four quarters of 1988 by a sample of 12 econometric services:

Econometric Services	Quarter			
	I	*II*	*III*	*IV*
David A. Levine (Sanford C. Bernstein)	6.3	7.2	6.3	2.3
Charles B. Reeder (Charles Reeder Associates)	0.7	2.9	6.5	7.2
Robert J. Genetski (Harris Trust)	4.1	3.9	3.7	3.4
Rosalind Wells (J. C. Penney)	2.4	3.5	3.8	3.1
Gordon B. Pye (Irving Trust)	3.4	3.2	2.9	2.7
Jerry Jordan (First Interstate)	3.8	3.2	2.8	2.4
Joseph W. Duncan (Dun & Bradstreet)	1.9	2.3	3.5	3.0
David D. Hale (Kemper Financial)	2.0	3.5	3.5	3.0
M. Cathryn Eickhoff (Eickhoff Economics)	3.0	3.3	2.2	0.1
Peter L. Bernstein (Peter L. Bernstein)	3.2	3.9	1.2	0.2
Albert E. DePrince (Marine Midland)	2.9	3.3	3.1	2.1
Edward Yardeni (Prudential-Bache)	2.6	2.7	3.1	2.6

SOURCE: Extracted from *Business Week*, December 28, 1987, p. 111.

(a) Analyze the data ($\alpha = .05$) to determine if there are significant differences in the projections between the four quarters of 1988.

(b) Analyze the data ($\alpha = .05$) to determine if there are significant differences in the projections between the econometric services (i.e., the blocks).

(c) What assumptions must be made in order to perform the analyses of parts (a) and (b)?

➡️(d) **ACTION** Go to your library and find the true percentage changes for the four quarters of 1988. Which econometric services did best in the projections? Discuss fully in a letter to your economics professor.

14.30 In Problem 12.16 on page 386 you used a t test to compare average gasoline mileage between regular and high-octane gas.

(a) Do an analysis of variance on this data set. (Use $\alpha = .05$.)

(b) Square the value of t you computed in Problem 12.16; notice that it is the same (except for rounding error) as the F value. Express in your own words the relationship between t and F.

14.7 TWO-WAY ANALYSIS OF VARIANCE

14.7.1 Introduction

In Sections 14.1–14.5 we discussed the one-way analysis-of-variance model, while in Section 14.6 the randomized block model was introduced. In this section we shall extend our discussion to consider a model in which two factors are of interest. However, we shall be concerned only with situations in which there are equal sample sizes for each combination of the levels of factor A with those of factor B. (See References 1 and 10 for a discussion of ANOVA models with unequal sample sizes.)

14.7.2 Development

To develop the ANOVA procedure for the two-factor design with replication[5] let us refer to the following example. Suppose that the marketing research director for a supermarket chain was interested in studying the effect of shelf location on sales of a product. Four different shelf locations were to be studied: normal location (A), additional location in store (B), new location only and "shelf-talker" (C), and normal location and "ribboning" (D). Three different store sizes were to be considered: small, medium, and large. For each shelf location a random sample of two stores of each size was selected. The results in weekly sales are summarized in Table 14.11.

TABLE 14.11 Weekly sales by store size and shelf location

Store Size	Shelf Location				Totals	Means
	A	B	C	D		
Small	45	56	65	48		
	50	63	71	53	451	56.375
Medium	57	69	73	60		
	65	78	80	57	539	67.375
Large	70	75	82	71		
	78	82	89	75	622	77.750
Totals	365	423	460	364	1,612	
Means	60.83	70.50	76.67	60.67		67.167

In order to extend our discussion of the analysis of variance to the two-factor model with replication we need to define the following:

X_{ijk} = the value of the kth observation for level i of factor A and level j of factor B

$X_{ij.}$ = the sum of the values in cell ij (the observations at level i of factor A and level j of factor B)

$X_{i..}$ = the sum of the values for row i of factor A

$X_{.j.}$ = the sum of the values for column j of factor B

GT = the grand total of all values over all rows and columns

r = the number of levels of factor A

c = the number of levels of factor B

n = the number of values (replications) for each cell

We recall from Equation (14.2) that in the one-way ANOVA model, the total sum of squares (SST) was subdivided into sum of squares between groups (SSB) and sum of squares within groups (SSW), while in the randomized block model [see Equation (14.11)] the total sum of squares (SST) was subdivided into sum of squares between treatments (SSTR), sum of squares between blocks (SSBL), and error sum

---

[5] In this section we shall consider the general case in which there are n observations for each combination of factor A and factor B (i.e., each cell). If there is only one observation per cell, the notation of the randomized block design can be used with the blocks being considered a second factor of interest.

of squares (SSE). For the two-factor ANOVA model with replication ($n > 1$), we need to subdivide the total sum of squares (SST) into sum of squares due to factor A (SSFA), sum of squares due to factor B (SSFB), sum of squares due to the interacting effect of A and B (SSAB), and the sum of squares due to random error (SSE):

$$\text{SST} = \text{SSFA} + \text{SSFB} + \text{SSAB} + \text{SSE} \tag{14.23}$$

The total sum of squares (SST) measures the total variation among the observations. SST would be computed as

$$\text{SST} = \sum_{i=1}^{r} \sum_{j=1}^{c} \sum_{k=1}^{n} (X_{ijk} - \overline{\overline{X}})^2 = \sum_{i=1}^{r} \sum_{j=1}^{c} \sum_{k=1}^{n} X_{ijk}^2 - \frac{(GT)^2}{rcn} \tag{14.24}$$

where $\overline{\overline{X}} = \dfrac{\displaystyle\sum_{i=1}^{r} \sum_{j=1}^{c} \sum_{k=1}^{n} X_{ijk}}{rcn}$ (i.e., the overall or grand mean)

The sum of squares due to factor A represents differences among the various levels of factor A. SSFA would be computed as

$$\text{SSFA} = cn \sum_{i=1}^{r} (\overline{X}_{i..} - \overline{\overline{X}})^2 = \sum_{i=1}^{r} \frac{X_{i..}^2}{cn} - \frac{(GT)^2}{rcn} \tag{14.25}$$

where $\overline{X}_{i..} = \dfrac{\displaystyle\sum_{j=1}^{c} \sum_{k=1}^{n} X_{ijk}}{cn}$ (i.e., the mean of each level of factor A)

The sum of squares due to factor B represents differences among the various levels of factor B. SSFB would be computed as

$$\text{SSFB} = rn \sum_{j=1}^{c} (\overline{X}_{.j.} - \overline{\overline{X}})^2 = \sum_{j=1}^{c} \frac{X_{.j.}^2}{rn} - \frac{(GT)^2}{rcn} \tag{14.26}$$

where $\overline{X}_{.j.} = \dfrac{\displaystyle\sum_{i=1}^{r} \sum_{k=1}^{n} X_{ijk}}{rn}$ (i.e., the mean of each level of factor B)

The sum of squares due to interaction measures the effect of combinations of factor A and factor B. SSAB would be computed as

$$SSAB = n \sum_{i=1}^{r} \sum_{j=1}^{c} (\overline{X}_{ij.} - \overline{X}_{i..} - \overline{X}_{.j.} + \overline{\overline{X}})^2$$

$$= \sum_{i=1}^{r} \sum_{j=1}^{c} \frac{X_{ij.}^2}{n} - \sum_{i=1}^{r} \frac{X_{i..}^2}{cn} - \sum_{j=1}^{c} \frac{X_{.j.}^2}{rn} + \frac{(GT)^2}{rcn} \qquad (14.27)$$

where $\overline{X}_{ij.} = \sum_{k=1}^{n} \dfrac{X_{ijk}}{n}$ (i.e., the mean of each cell)

The error sum of squares measures differences within each cell. SSE would be computed as

$$SSE = \sum_{i=1}^{r} \sum_{j=1}^{c} \sum_{k=1}^{n} (X_{ijk} - \overline{X}_{ij.})^2 = \sum_{i=1}^{r} \sum_{j=1}^{c} \sum_{k=1}^{n} X_{ijk}^2 - \sum_{i=1}^{r} \sum_{j=1}^{c} \frac{X_{ij.}^2}{n} \qquad (14.28)$$

If SSFA, SSFB, SSAB, and SSE are divided by their respective degrees of freedom, we will obtain the variances or mean squares:

$$MSFA = \frac{SSFA}{r - 1} \qquad (14.29)$$

$$MSFB = \frac{SSFB}{c - 1} \qquad (14.30)$$

$$MSAB = \frac{SSAB}{(r - 1)(c - 1)} \qquad (14.31)$$

$$MSE = \frac{SSE}{rc(n - 1)} \qquad (14.32)$$

Referring back to Table 14.11 on page 479, we have

$r = 3, \quad c = 4, \quad n = 2, \quad X_{1..} = 451, \quad X_{2..} = 539, \quad X_{3..} = 622$

$X_{.1.} = 365, \quad X_{.2.} = 423, \quad X_{.3.} = 460, \quad X_{.4.} = 364, \quad GT = 1{,}612$

$X_{11.} = 95, \quad X_{12.} = 119, \quad X_{13.} = 136, \quad X_{14.} = 101, \quad X_{21.} = 122, \quad X_{22.} = 147$

$X_{23.} = 153, \quad X_{24.} = 117, \quad X_{31.} = 148, \quad X_{32.} = 157, \quad X_{33.} = 171, \quad X_{34.} = 146$

$$\sum_{i=1}^{r}\sum_{j=1}^{c}\sum_{k=1}^{n} X_{ijk}^2 = 45^2 + 50^2 + \cdots + 75^2 = 111{,}550$$

$$\sum_{i=1}^{r}\frac{X_{i..}^2}{cn} = \frac{451^2 + 539^2 + 622^2}{4(2)} = 110{,}100.75$$

$$\sum_{j=1}^{c}\frac{X_{.j.}^2}{rn} = \frac{365^2 + 423^2 + 460^2 + 364^2}{3(2)} = 109{,}375$$

$$\sum_{i=1}^{r}\sum_{j=1}^{c}\frac{X_{ij.}^2}{n} = \frac{95^2 + 119^2 + \cdots + 146^2}{2} = 111{,}292$$

$$\frac{(GT)^2}{rcn} = \frac{1{,}612^2}{3(4)(2)} = 108{,}272.66$$

Using Equation (14.24),

$$SST = \sum_{i=1}^{r}\sum_{j=1}^{c}\sum_{k=1}^{n} X_{ijk}^2 - \frac{(GT)^2}{rcn}$$
$$= 111{,}550 - 108{,}272.66 = 3{,}277.34$$

Using Equation (14.25),

$$SSFA = \sum_{i=1}^{r}\frac{X_{i..}^2}{cn} - \frac{(GT)^2}{rcn}$$
$$= 110{,}100.75 - 108{,}272.66 = 1{,}828.09$$

Using Equation (14.26),

$$SSFB = \sum_{j=1}^{c}\frac{X_{.j.}^2}{rn} - \frac{(GT)^2}{rcn}$$
$$= 109{,}375 - 108{,}272.66 = 1{,}102.34$$

Using Equation (14.27),

$$SSAB = \sum_{i=1}^{r}\sum_{j=1}^{c}\frac{X_{ij.}^2}{n} - \sum_{i=1}^{r}\frac{X_{i..}^2}{cn} - \sum_{j=1}^{c}\frac{X_{.j.}^2}{rn} + \frac{(GT)^2}{rcn}$$
$$= 111{,}292 - 110{,}100.75 - 109{,}375 + 108{,}272.66$$
$$= 88.91$$

Using Equation (14.28),

$$SSE = \sum_{i=1}^{r}\sum_{j=1}^{c}\sum_{k=1}^{n} X_{ijk}^2 - \sum_{i=1}^{r}\sum_{j=1}^{c}\frac{X_{ij.}^2}{n}$$
$$= 111{,}550 - 111{,}292 = 258$$

To compute the variances we use Equations (14.29) through (14.32). From Equation (14.29):

$$MSFA = \frac{SSFA}{r-1} = \frac{1{,}828.09}{3-1} = 914.045$$

From Equation (14.30):

$$\text{MSFB} = \frac{\text{SSFB}}{c - 1} = \frac{1{,}102.34}{4 - 1} = 367.447$$

From Equation (14.31):

$$\text{MSAB} = \frac{\text{SSAB}}{(r - 1)(c - 1)} = \frac{88.91}{(3 - 1)(4 - 1)} = 14.818$$

From Equation (14.32):

$$\text{MSE} = \frac{\text{SSE}}{rc(n - 1)} = \frac{258}{3(4)(2 - 1)} = 21.5$$

In the two-factor ANOVA model there are three distinct tests that may be performed. If we assume that the levels of factor A and factor B have been specifically selected for analysis (rather than being randomly selected from a population of possible levels), then we would have the following three tests of hypotheses:

To test the hypothesis of no difference due to factor A

$$H_0: \quad \mu_{1..} = \mu_{2..} = \cdots = \mu_{r..}$$

against the alternative

$$H_1: \quad \text{Not all } \mu_{i..} \text{ are equal}$$

we form the F statistic

$$F_{(r-1),rc(n-1)} = \frac{\text{MSFA}}{\text{MSE}} \tag{14.33}$$

and the null hypothesis would be rejected at the α level of significance if

$$F_{(r-1),rc(n-1)} = \frac{\text{MSFA}}{\text{MSE}} > F_{\alpha,(r-1),rc(n-1)}$$

To test the hypothesis of no difference due to factor B

$$H_0: \quad \mu_{.1.} = \mu_{.2.} = \cdots = \mu_{.c.}$$

against the alternative

$$H_1: \quad \text{Not all } \mu_{.j.} \text{ are equal.}$$

we form the F statistic

$$F_{(c-1),rc(n-1)} = \frac{\text{MSFB}}{\text{MSE}} \tag{14.34}$$

and the null hypothesis would be rejected at the α level of significance if

$$F_{(c-1),rc(n-1)} = \frac{\text{MSFB}}{\text{MSE}} > F_{\alpha,(c-1),rc(n-1)}$$

To test the hypothesis of no interaction of factors A and B

$$H_0: \quad AB_{ij} = 0 \qquad \text{(for all } i \text{ and } j\text{)}$$

against the alternative

$$H_1: \quad AB_{ij} \neq 0$$

we form the F statistic

$$F_{(r-1)(c-1),rc(n-1)} = \frac{\text{MSAB}}{\text{MSE}} \qquad\qquad (14.35)$$

and the null hypothesis would be rejected at the α level of significance if

$$F_{(r-1)(c-1),rc(n-1)} = \frac{\text{MSAB}}{\text{MSE}} > F_{\alpha,(r-1)(c-1),rc(n-1)}$$

As in Sections 14.2.5 and 14.6.2, the entire set of steps may be summarized in an analysis-of-variance (ANOVA) table such as Table 14.12.

In the supermarket study the computations just completed can be summarized in Table 14.13.

Using the .05 level of significance and testing for the difference between the store sizes, the decision rule would be to reject the null hypothesis ($H_0: \mu_{1..} = \mu_{2..} = \cdots = \mu_{r..}$) if the calculated F value equals or exceeds 3.89 (see Figure 14.6). Since $F_{2,12} = 42.51 > 3.89$, we may reject H_0 and conclude that there is evidence of a difference between the store sizes in terms of the average weekly sales.

Using the .05 level of significance and testing for the difference between the

TABLE 14.12 Analysis-of-variance table for the two-factor model with replication

Source	Sum of Squares	Degrees of Freedom	Mean Square (Variance)	F
A	$\displaystyle\sum_{i=1}^{r} \frac{X_{i..}^2}{cn} - \frac{(GT)^2}{rcn}$	$r-1$	$\text{MSFA} = \dfrac{\text{SSFA}}{r-1}$	$F = \dfrac{\text{MSFA}}{\text{MSE}}$
B	$\displaystyle\sum_{j=1}^{c} \frac{X_{.j.}^2}{rn} - \frac{(GT)^2}{rcn}$	$c-1$	$\text{MSFB} = \dfrac{\text{SSFB}}{c-1}$	$F = \dfrac{\text{MSFB}}{\text{MSE}}$
AB	$\displaystyle\sum_{i=1}^{r}\sum_{j=1}^{c} \frac{X_{ij.}^2}{n} - \sum_{i=1}^{r} \frac{X_{i..}^2}{cn} - \sum_{j=1}^{c} \frac{X_{.j.}^2}{rn} + \frac{(GT)^2}{rcn}$	$(r-1)(c-1)$	$\text{MSAB} = \dfrac{\text{SSAB}}{(r-1)(c-1)}$	$F = \dfrac{\text{MSAB}}{\text{MSE}}$
Error	$\displaystyle\sum_{i=1}^{r}\sum_{j=1}^{c}\sum_{k=1}^{n} X_{ijk}^2 - \sum_{i=1}^{r}\sum_{j=1}^{c} \frac{X_{ij.}^2}{n}$	$rc(n-1)$	$\text{MSE} = \dfrac{\text{SSE}}{rc(n-1)}$	
Total	$\displaystyle\sum_{i=1}^{r}\sum_{j=1}^{c}\sum_{k=1}^{n} X_{ijk}^2 - \frac{(GT)^2}{rcn}$	$rcn-1$		

TABLE 14.13 Analysis-of-variance table for the supermarket example

Source	Sum of Squares	Degrees of Freedom	Mean Square (Variance)	F
A (Store Size)	$110{,}100.75 - 108{,}272.66 = 1{,}828.09$	$3 - 1 = 2$	$\text{MSFA} = \dfrac{1{,}828.09}{2}$ $= 914.045$	$F = \dfrac{914.045}{21.5}$ $= 42.51$
B (Shelf Location)	$109{,}375 - 108{,}272.66 = 1{,}102.34$	$4 - 1 = 3$	$\text{MSFB} = \dfrac{1{,}102.34}{3}$ $= 367.447$	$F = \dfrac{367.447}{21.5}$ $= 17.09$
AB (Store Size × Shelf Location)	$111{,}292 - 110{,}100.75 - 109{,}375$ $+\ 108{,}272.66 = 88.91$	$(3-1)(4-1) = 6$	$\text{MSAB} = \dfrac{88.91}{6}$ $= 14.818$	$F = \dfrac{14.818}{21.5}$ $= .69$
Error	$111{,}550 - 111{,}292 = 258$	$(3)(4)(2-1) = 12$	$\text{MSE} = \dfrac{258}{12}$ $= 21.5$	
Total	$111{,}550 - 108{,}272.66 = 3{,}277.34$	$(3)(4)(2) - 1 = 23$		

shelf locations, the decision rule would be to reject the null hypothesis (H_0: $\mu_{.1.} = \mu_{.2.} = \cdots = \mu_{.c.}$) if the calculated F value equals or exceeds 3.49 (see Figure 14.7). Since $F_{3,12} = 17.09 > 3.49$, we may reject H_0 and conclude that there is evidence of a difference between the shelf locations in terms of the average weekly sales.

Finally, we can test whether there is an interacting effect between factor A (store size) and factor B (shelf location). Using the .05 level of significance, the decision

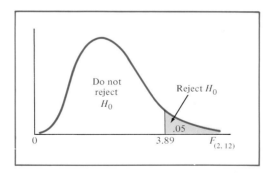

FIGURE 14.6
Regions of rejection and nonrejection at the .05 level of significance with 2 and 12 degrees of freedom.

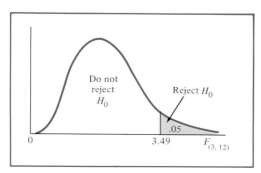

FIGURE 14.7
Regions of rejection and nonrejection at the .05 level of significance with 3 and 12 degrees of freedom.

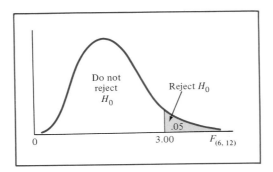

FIGURE 14.8
Regions of rejection and nonrejection at the .05 level of significance with 6 and 12 degrees of freedom.

rule would be to reject the null hypothesis [$AB_{ij} = 0$ (for all i and j)] if the calculated F value equals or exceeds 3.00 (see Figure 14.8). Since $F_{6,12} = .69 < 3.00$, we do not reject H_0 and we conclude that there is no evidence of an interacting effect between store size and shelf location.

14.7.3 Interpreting Interaction Effects

Now that the tests for the significance of factor A, factor B, and their interaction have been performed, we can get a better understanding of the interpretation of the concept of interaction by plotting the cell means as in Figure 14.9. Since $\overline{X}_{ij.} = X_{ij.}/n$, we have

$$\overline{X}_{11.} = \frac{95}{2} = 47.5, \quad \overline{X}_{12.} = \frac{119}{2} = 59.5, \quad \overline{X}_{13.} = \frac{136}{2} = 68.0, \quad \overline{X}_{14.} = \frac{101}{2} = 50.5$$

$$\overline{X}_{21.} = \frac{122}{2} = 61.0, \quad \overline{X}_{22.} = \frac{147}{2} = 73.5, \quad \overline{X}_{23.} = \frac{153}{2} = 76.5, \quad \overline{X}_{24.} = \frac{117}{2} = 58.5$$

$$\overline{X}_{31.} = \frac{148}{2} = 74.0, \quad \overline{X}_{32.} = \frac{157}{2} = 78.5, \quad \overline{X}_{33.} = \frac{171}{2} = 85.5, \quad \overline{X}_{34.} = \frac{146}{2} = 73.0$$

In Figure 14.9 we have plotted the average weekly sales for each level of store size and location. For our data the four lines (representing the four shelf locations) appear roughly parallel. This phenomenon can be interpreted to mean that the *difference* in weekly sales between the four shelf locations is virtually the same for the three store sizes. In other words, there is no interaction between these two factors—as was clearly substantiated from the F test on page 485.

What would be the interpretation if there were an interacting effect? In such a situation some levels of factor A would respond better with certain levels of factor B. For example, suppose that some shelf locations were better for large stores while other shelf locations were better for small stores. If this were true, the lines of Figure 14.9 would not be nearly as parallel and the interaction effect might be statistically significant. In such a situation, the differences between the various shelf locations would not be the same for all store sizes. Such an outcome would also serve to complicate the interpretation of the main effects, since differences in one factor (shelf locations) would not be consistent across the other factor (store sizes).

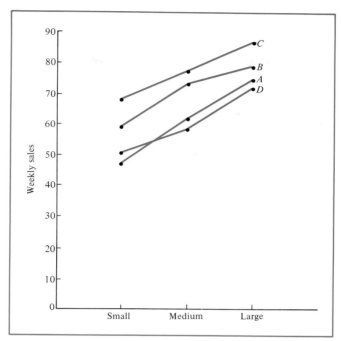

FIGURE 14.9
Average weekly sales based on store size for different shelf locations.

14.7.4 Tukey's *T* Method for the Two-Factor Model with Replication

As in the case of the one-way and randomized block models, once the null hypothesis of no differences in the levels of a factor has been rejected, we need to determine the particular groups or levels that are significantly different from each other. Tukey's *T* method may be used for factor A as well as for factor B.

For factor A we have

$$\text{critical range} = Q_{\alpha, r, rc(n-1)} \sqrt{\frac{\text{MSE}}{cn}} \qquad (14.36)$$

while for factor B we have

$$\text{critical range} = Q_{\alpha, c, rc(n-1)} \sqrt{\frac{\text{MSE}}{rn}} \qquad (14.37)$$

As in Section 14.5 and 14.6.3, each of the $c(c-1)/2$ or $r(r-1)/2$ pairs of means is compared against the appropriate critical range. A specific pair would be declared significantly different if the absolute difference in the sample means ($|\overline{X}_{i..} - \overline{X}_{i'..}|$ for factor A or $|\overline{X}_{.j.} - \overline{X}_{.j'.}|$ for factor B) equals or exceeds its respective critical range.

To apply the T method, we return to our supermarket example. With respect to factor A, since there are three groups, there are $3(3 - 1)/2 = 3$ possible paired comparisons to be made. From Table 14.11, on page 479, the absolute mean differences are

1. $|\overline{X}_{1..} - \overline{X}_{2..}| = |56.375 - 67.375| = 11.000$
2. $|\overline{X}_{1..} - \overline{X}_{3..}| = |56.375 - 77.750| = 21.375$
3. $|\overline{X}_{2..} - \overline{X}_{3..}| = |67.375 - 77.750| = 10.375$

To determine the critical range, from Table 14.13, we have MSE $= 21.5$, $r = 3$, and $c = 4$. From Table E.12, for $\alpha = .05$, $r = 3$, and $rc(n - 1) = (3)(4)(2 - 1) = 12$, the upper critical value of $Q_{3,12} = 3.77$. From Equation (14.36), we have

$$\text{critical range} = 3.77 \sqrt{\frac{21.5}{8}} = 6.18$$

We note that all the contrasts are greater than the critical range. Therefore we may conclude that small, medium, and large stores differ from each other in weekly sales.

With respect to factor B, since there are four groups, there are $4(4 - 1)/2 = 6$ possible pairwise comparisons to be made. From Table 14.11, on page 479, the absolute mean differences are

1. $|\overline{X}_{.1.} - \overline{X}_{.2.}| = |60.83 - 70.50| = 9.67$
2. $|\overline{X}_{.1.} - \overline{X}_{.3.}| = |60.83 - 76.67| = 15.84$
3. $|\overline{X}_{.1.} - \overline{X}_{.4.}| = |60.83 - 60.67| = .16$
4. $|\overline{X}_{.2.} - \overline{X}_{.3.}| = |70.50 - 76.67| = 6.17$
5. $|\overline{X}_{.2.} - \overline{X}_{.4.}| = |70.50 - 60.67| = 9.83$
6. $|\overline{X}_{.3.} - \overline{X}_{.4.}| = |76.67 - 60.67| = 16.00$

To determine the critical range, from Table 14.13 we have MSE $= 21.5$, $r = 3$, and $c = 4$. From Table E.12, for $\alpha = .05$, $c = 4$, and $rc(n - 1) = (3)(4)(2 - 1) = 12$, the upper critical value of $Q_{4,12} = 4.20$. From Equation (14.37), we have

$$\text{critical range} = 4.20 \sqrt{\frac{21.5}{6}} = 7.95$$

We note that $\overline{X}_{.1.}$ is different from $\overline{X}_{.2.}$ ($9.67 > 7.95$) and $\overline{X}_{.3.}$ ($15.84 > 7.95$) while $\overline{X}_{.4.}$ is different from $\overline{X}_{.2.}$ ($9.83 > 7.95$) and $\overline{X}_{.3.}$ ($16 > 7.95$). Thus we may conclude that shelf locations A (normal) and D (normal plus ''ribboning'') are each different from locations B (additional location in store) and C (new location only and ''shelf talker''). However, there is no evidence of a difference between locations A and D or between locations B and C.

As in the case of the one-way ANOVA and the randomized block design, we may establish a set of simultaneous confidence intervals.

For factor A we have

$$(\overline{X}_{i..} - \overline{X}_{i'..}) \pm Q_{\alpha,r,rc(n-1)} \sqrt{\frac{\text{MSE}}{cn}} \qquad (14.38)$$

By using Equation (14.38) with a confidence level of 95%, the following set of confidence intervals are obtained:

1. $-11.000 - 6.18 \le (\mu_{1..} - \mu_{2..}) \le -11.000 + 6.18$
   $-17.180 \le (\mu_{1..} - \mu_{2..}) \le -4.820$
2. $-21.375 - 6.18 \le (\mu_{1..} - \mu_{3..}) \le -21.375 + 6.18$
   $-27.555 \le (\mu_{1..} - \mu_{3..}) \le -15.195$
3. $-10.375 - 6.18 \le (\mu_{2..} - \mu_{3..}) \le -10.375 + 6.18$
   $-16.555 \le (\mu_{2..} - \mu_{3..}) \le -4.195$

For factor B we have

$$(\overline{X}_{.j.} - \overline{X}_{.j'.}) \pm Q_{\alpha,c,rc(n-1)} \sqrt{\frac{\text{MSE}}{rn}} \qquad (14.39)$$

By using Equation (14.39) with a confidence level of 95%, the following set of confidence intervals are obtained:

1. $-9.67 - 7.95 \le (\mu_{.1.} - \mu_{.2.}) \le -9.67 + 7.95$
   $-17.62 \le (\mu_{.1.} - \mu_{.2.}) \le -1.72$
2. $-15.84 - 7.95 \le (\mu_{.1.} - \mu_{.3.}) \le -15.84 + 7.95$
   $-23.79 \le (\mu_{.1.} - \mu_{.3.}) \le -7.89$
3. $.16 - 7.95 \le (\mu_{.1.} - \mu_{.4.}) \le .16 + 7.95$
   $-7.79 \le (\mu_{.1.} - \mu_{.4.}) \le +8.11$
4. $-6.17 - 7.95 \le (\mu_{.2.} - \mu_{.3.}) \le -6.17 + 7.95$
   $-14.12 \le (\mu_{.2.} - \mu_{.3.}) \le +1.78$
5. $9.83 - 7.95 \le (\mu_{.2.} - \mu_{.4.}) \le 9.83 + 7.95$
   $+1.88 \le (\mu_{.2.} - \mu_{.4.}) \le +17.78$
6. $16.00 - 7.95 \le (\mu_{.3.} - \mu_{.4.}) \le 16.00 + 7.95$
   $+8.05 \le (\mu_{.3.} - \mu_{.4.}) \le +23.95$

14.7.5 Fixed, Random, and Mixed Models

In our discussion of analysis-of-variance models we have not focused upon the manner in which the various levels of a factor have been selected. From this perspective, there are three alternative models:

1. Fixed-effects model (Model I)
2. Random-effects model (Model II)
3. Mixed-effects model (Model III)

The first model, the fixed-effects model (Model I), described thus far in this section, assumes that the levels of a factor have been *specifically* selected for analysis. This means that the levels of the factor have *not* been randomly selected from a population and that no inferences can be drawn about any other levels except the ones used in the study.

In contrast to the fixed-effects model, Model II, the random-effects model, contains factors in which the levels are *randomly selected* from a population. The objective for a random-effects model is not necessarily to examine differences among levels but, more important, to estimate the variability due to each factor (see Reference 2). For example, if we wished to study the effect on productivity of different workers and different machines, we might randomly select a sample of machines and assign a random sample of workers to each machine for a given number of days. Not only would we be able to measure whether workers and machines have significant effects on productivity, but we would also be able to estimate the variability due to different machines and the variability due to different workers.

The third model, the mixed-effects model (Model III), contains a mixture of fixed and random effects.

Although the random- and mixed-effect models can be discussed in much greater depth (see References 2 and 3), our focus involves the consequences of the various models on the F test. Since the components of the models differ in their assumptions, they also lead to different F tests in evaluating the significance of the main effects (factors A and B). Therefore, the appropriate F tests for each of the three models are summarized in Table 14.14.

TABLE 14.14 F tests for two-factor ANOVA models with replication

Null Hypothesis	Fixed Effects (A & B Fixed)	Random Effects (A & B Random)	Mixed Effects (A Fixed, B Random)	Mixed Effects (A Random, B Fixed)
$\mu_{i..} = 0$	$F = \dfrac{MSFA}{MSE}$	$F = \dfrac{MSFA}{MSAB}$	$F = \dfrac{MSFA}{MSAB}$	$F = \dfrac{MSFA}{MSE}$
$\mu_{.j.} = 0$	$F = \dfrac{MSFB}{MSE}$	$F = \dfrac{MSFB}{MSAB}$	$F = \dfrac{MSFB}{MSE}$	$F = \dfrac{MSFA}{MSAB}$
$AB_{ij} = 0$	$F = \dfrac{MSAB}{MSE}$	$F = \dfrac{MSAB}{MSE}$	$F = \dfrac{MSAB}{MSE}$	$F = \dfrac{MSAB}{MSE}$

As we observe in Table 14.14, the tests for the main effects differ depending on the type of model selected. For the fixed-effects model, the F tests involve the ratio of MSFA or MSFB to MSE. For the random-effects model, the F tests (for the main effects) involve the ratio of MSFA or MSFB to MSAB. For the mixed model with factor A fixed and factor B random, the F test for factor A involves the ratio of MSFA to MSAB, while the test for factor B involves the ratio of MSFB to MSE. For the mixed model with factor A random and factor B fixed, the F test for factor A involves the ratio of MSFA to MSE, while the test for factor B involves the ratio of MSFB to MSAB.

Problems

✗ **14.31** Explain the difference between the one-factor and two-factor ANOVA models.

✗ **14.32** Explain the difference between the randomized block model and the two-factor ANOVA model.

● **14.33** A videocassette recorder (VCR) repair service wished to study the effect of VCR brand and service center on the repair time measured in minutes. Three VCR brands (A, B, C) were specifically selected for analysis. Three service centers were also selected. Each service center was assigned to repair two VCRs of each brand. The results were as follows:

	VCR Brands		
Service Centers	A	B	C
1	52	48	59
	57	39	67
2	51	61	58
	43	52	64
3	37	44	65
	46	50	69

(a) At the .05 level of significance
  (1) Is there an effect due to service centers?
  (2) Is there an effect due to VCR brand?
  (3) Is there an interaction due to service center and VCR brand?

(b) Plot a graph of average service time for each service center for each VCR brand.

(c) If appropriate, use Tukey's T method to determine which service centers and which VCR brands differ in average service time. (Use $\alpha = .05$.)

(d) Based upon the results, what conclusions can you reach concerning average service time?

➠(e) **ACTION** Write a memo to the CEO of the repair service describing your findings.

(f) If the three service centers were *randomly* selected, how would your analysis in part (a) be affected?

14.34 An experiment was designed to study the effect of two factors on the amplification of a stereo recording. The factors were type of amplifier (four brands) and type of cartridge (two brands). For each combination of factor levels, three tests were performed in which decibel output was measured. A higher decibel output means a better result. The coded results were as follows:

	Amplifiers			
Cartridge	A	B	C	D
C_1	9	8	8	10
	4	11	7	15
	12	16	1	9
C_2	7	5	0	6
	1	9	1	7
	4	6	7	5

(a) At the .01 level of significance
  (1) Is there an effect due to cartridges?
  (2) Is there an effect due to amplifiers?
  (3) Is there an interaction between cartridges and amplifiers?
(b) Plot a graph of average decibel output for each cartridge for each amplifier.
(c) If appropriate, use Tukey's T method to determine which amplifiers differ in average decibel output. (Use $\alpha = .01$.)
➡(d) **ACTION** Based upon the results, what conclusions can you reach concerning average decibel output? Write a memo on this to your music professor.

● **14.35** An industrial psychologist would like to determine the effect of alcoholic consumption on the typing ability of a group of secretaries. Two factors are to be considered: the amount of consumption (0, 1, and 2 ounces) and the type of manuscript (technical, nontechnical). A group of 12 secretaries (of similar typing ability) were randomly assigned to an alcoholic consumption level and a manuscript type. Each secretary was instructed to type a standard page (either technical or nontechnical). The number of errors made by each secretary was recorded with the following results:

Alcoholic Consumption (ounces)	Type of Manuscript	
	Technical	Nontechnical
0	5	0
	3	2
1	12	3
	14	6
2	18	10
	21	7

(a) At the .01 level of significance
  (1) Is there an effect due to level of alcoholic consumption?
  (2) Is there an effect due to type of manuscript?
  (3) Is there an interaction between alcoholic consumption and manuscript type?
(b) Plot a graph of average errors for each level of alcoholic consumption for each type of manuscript.
(c) If appropriate, use Tukey's T method to determine which levels of alcoholic consumption differ in number of errors. (Use $\alpha = .01$.)
➡(d) **ACTION** Based on the results, what conclusions can you reach concerning the average number of errors? Draft a letter that the industrial psychologist might send to the ''daily living'' column of your local newspaper.

14.36 The Environmental Protection Agency of a large suburban county is studying coliform bacteria counts (in parts per thousand) at beaches within the county. Three types of beaches are to be considered—ocean, bay, and sound—in three geographic areas of the county—west, central, and east. Two beaches of each type are randomly selected in each region of the county. The coliform bacteria counts at each beach on a particular day were as follows (page 493):

Type of Beach	Geographical Area		
	West	Central	East
Ocean	25	9	3
	20	6	6
Bay	32	18	9
	39	24	13
Sound	27	16	5
	30	21	7

(a) At the .05 level of significance
  (1) Is there an effect due to type of beach?
  (2) Is there an effect due to geographical area?
  (3) Is there an interaction between type of beach and geographical area?
(b) Plot a graph of the average bacteria count for each type of beach in each geographical area.
(c) If appropriate, use Tukey's T method to determine which types of beaches and which geographical areas differ in average bacteria count. (Use $\alpha = .05$.)
(d) Based upon the results, what conclusions concerning average bacteria count can be reached?
➡(e) **ACTION** Draft a memo on these findings to the supervisor at the Environmental Protection Agency.

14.8 ANALYSIS OF VARIANCE, COMPUTERS, AND THE REAL ESTATE SURVEY

14.8.1 Introduction

Having discussed various analysis-of-variance models, we may return to the real estate survey. Suppose that the president of the realty company wanted to determine whether there is evidence of a difference in the number of rooms based on the geographic location of the house. Thus, if we refer to questions 5 and 9 from the questionnaire (Figure 2.5 on page 15), we may set up the following null and alternative hypotheses:

$$H_0: \quad \mu_{EM} = \mu_F = \mu_L$$

$$H_1: \quad \text{Not all the means are equal.}$$

Certainly, now that a multitude of statistical packages is readily available for either mainframe or microcomputers, we would want to access a selected package so that the computer can be used as a tool to assist in this analysis.

14.8.2 Presentation of SAS, MYSTAT, Minitab, and STATGRAPHICS Output

Among the most widely available packages are SAS, MYSTAT, Minitab, and STATGRAPHICS (see References 9, 6, 4 and 8, and 11, respectively). For the data of interest to the president of the realty company, Figure 14.10 represents partial SAS output, Figure 14.11 represents partial MYSTAT output, and Figure 14.12 represents

```
GENERAL LINEAR MODELS PROCEDURE

DEPENDENT VARIABLE: ROOMS          NUMBER OF ROOMS

SOURCE                    DF        SUM OF SQUARES        MEAN SQUARE

MODEL                      2          5.24047399          2.62023699

ERROR                    230        327.07712258          1.42207445

CORRECTED TOTAL          232        332.31759657


MODEL F =              1.84                          PR > F = 0.1607


R-SQUARE              C.V.              ROOT MSE          ROOMS MEAN

0.015769            16.7786           1.19250763          7.10729614


SOURCE                    DF            TYPE I SS   F VALUE    PR > F

LOCATE                     2          5.24047399     1.84      0.1607


SOURCE                    DF          TYPE III SS   F VALUE    PR > F

LOCATE                     2          5.24047399     1.84      0.1607


GENERAL LINEAR MODELS PROCEDURE

MEANS

      LOCATE          N          ROOMS

EAST MEADOW           74       7.12162162
FARMINGDALE           60       7.33333333
LEVITTOWN             99       6.95959596
```

FIGURE 14.10
Partial SAS output for the one-way ANOVA model of number of rooms based on geographic location of the house.

```
DEP VAR:   ROOMS      N:  233


                    ANALYSIS OF VARIANCE

    SOURCE    SUM-OF-SQUARES    DF    MEAN-SQUARE    F-RATIO        P

    LOCATE         5.240         2        2.620        1.843      0.161

    ERROR        327.077       230        1.422
```

FIGURE 14.11
Partial MYSTAT output for the one-way ANOVA model of number of rooms based on geographic location of the house.

```
ANALYSIS OF VARIANCE ON rooms
SOURCE      DF        SS        MS          F
locate       2      5.24      2.62       1.84
ERROR      230    327.08      1.42
TOTAL      232    332.32
                                    INDIVIDUAL 95 PCT CI'S FOR MEAN
                                    BASED ON POOLED STDEV
LEVEL        N      MEAN     STDEV  -----------------------------------
    1       74     7.122     1.292        (----------------------)
    2       60     7.333     1.258                 (-----------------------)
    3       99     6.960     1.068   (-------------------)
                                    -----------------------------------
POOLED STDEV =      1.193           6.75     7.00     7.25     7.50
```

FIGURE 14.12
Partial Minitab output for the one-way ANOVA model of number of rooms based
on geographic location of the house.

partial Minitab output. We may observe that SAS and Minitab provide the mean and
sample size for each group along with an accompanying ANOVA table. In SAS, the
between-groups source of variation is called MODEL and the within-groups is called
ERROR, while in MYSTAT and in Minitab the variable label (''locate'') for geographic
location of the house is substituted for between-groups and the within-groups is called
ERROR as is SAS. In addition, both SAS and MYSTAT provide the p value for the
F test.

14.8.3 Analysis and Interpretation

From Figures 14.10, 14.11, and 14.12 we observe that the F value for the one-way
ANOVA is 1.84 (with 2 and 230 degrees of freedom, respectively). In addition, we
may note from the output that the mean number of rooms for the three geographic
locations are 7.122 (for houses in East Meadow), 7.333 (for houses in Farmingdale),
and 6.960 (for houses in Levittown).

However, prior to interpreting these results we should evaluate the validity of the
assumptions of normality and homogeneity of variance by obtaining side-by-side box-
and-whisker plots of each group. This may be accomplished by using the STAT-
GRAPHICS package. Figure 14.13 on page 496 consists of side-by-side box-and-
whisker plots for the four groups of interest. From Figure 14.13 we may observe that
there do not appear to be any wide discrepancies in the variability of the three geographic
locations. In addition, none of the locations indicate a substantial departure from the
normality assumption. Since neither the assumption of normality nor the assumption
of homogeneity of variance appear to have been violated, we do not have to consider
appropriate data transformations (see Reference 1). More formally, however, using
Figure 14.12 we may compute the Hartley statistic for the equality of variances (which
assumes normality within the groups) as $(1.292^2)/(1.068^2) = 1.463$. Using Table E.8
(see Section 14.4), the critical value for the F_{max} statistic at the .05 level would be
approximately 1.85 (with 3 and $\frac{233}{3} - 1 = 76$ degrees of freedom).[6] Since 1.463 <

---

[6] This 1.85 value was found by selecting the printed tabular value for 60 degrees of freedom in the
denominator of the F_{max} statistic. This level of degrees of freedom is closest to the desired value of 76.

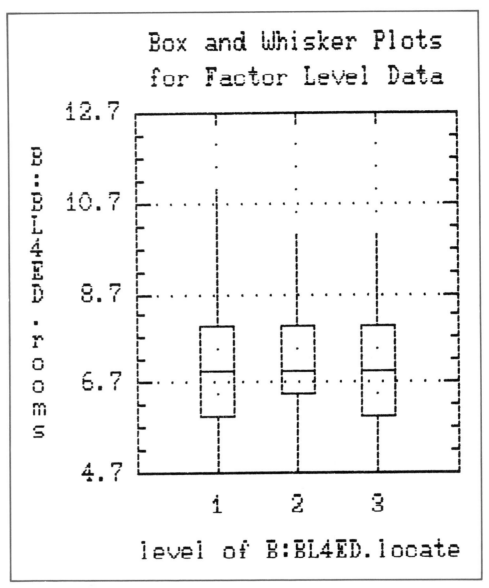

FIGURE 14.13
Box-and-whisker plots obtained from STATGRAPHICS for the one-way ANOVA
on number of rooms based on geographic location of the house.

1.85, we would not reject the null hypothesis of no difference in the variances of the
number of rooms per house over the three geographic locations—East Meadow, Farmingdale, and Levittown.

Now that we have evaluated the ANOVA assumptions, from Figures 14.10, 14.11,
and 14.12 we note that the F value for testing the difference between the means of the
three groups is 1.84. If a level of significance of $\alpha = .05$ were applied, the null

hypothesis of equal means[7] would not be rejected, since $1.84 < 3.07$. Thus we may conclude that there is no evidence of a difference in the mean number of rooms based on geographic location of the house.

Supplementary Problems

✗ **14.37** Explain the purpose of an analysis of variance.

✗ **14.38** Refer to Problem 14.5 on page 461. If the stores were not a sample but the only such stores in the county, would it make sense to do a statistical analysis? (You should be able to give arguments for and against the sensibility of doing an analysis). [*Hint*: Consider to what populations you might want to generalize and whether the sample could be considered a random sample for each possible population of interest.]

14.39 The retailing manager of a food chain wishes to determine whether product location has any effect on the sale of pet toys. Three different aisle locations are to be considered: front, middle, and rear. A random sample of 18 stores was selected with 6 stores randomly assigned to each aisle location. At the end of a one-week trial period, the sales of the product in each store were as follows:

Aisle Location		
Front	Middle	Rear
86	20	46
72	32	28
54	24	60
40	18	22
50	14	28
62	16	40

(a) At the .05 level of significance, is there evidence of a difference in the variances for the three aisle locations?

(b) At the .05 level of significance, is there evidence of a difference in average sales between the various aisle locations?

(c) If appropriate, use the Tukey T method to determine which aisle locations are different in average sales. (Use $\alpha = .05$.)

✗(d) What would the retailing manager conclude? Discuss fully the retailing manager's options with respect to aisle locations.

● **14.40** The owner of a home-heating-oil delivery company would like to investigate the speed with which bills are paid in three suburban areas. Random samples of five accounts are selected in each area, and the number of days between delivery and payment of the bill is recorded with the following results (top of page 498):

---

[7] Since 230 degrees of freedom are not shown in Table E.5, rounding to the nearest tabular value of 2 and 120 degrees of freedom leads to a critical value of 3.07.

	Area	
I	*II*	*III*
8	10	32
18	16	8
14	28	16
20	25	27
12	7	17

At the .01 level of significance

   (a) Is there evidence of a difference in the variances of the three suburban areas?

   (b) Is there any evidence of a difference in the average payment (as measured by days) between the three suburban areas?

   (c) If appropriate, use the Tukey T method to determine the areas that differ in average number of days between delivery and payment. (Use $\alpha = .01$.)

   ✓**(d)** What would the owner of the company conclude? Discuss some possible reasons for the results and some strategies that may be taken to counteract these results.

14.41 An agronomist wishes to study the yield (in pounds) of four different types of squash. A field was divided into 16 plots with 4 plots randomly assigned to each variety. The four varieties of squash were

   1. Butternut (winter) squash

   2. Acorn (winter) squash

   3. Zucchini (summer) squash

   4. Scallop (summer) squash

The results of the experiment (yield in pounds) were as follows:

1	*2*	*3*	*4*
86	40	30	48
74	48	36	54
88	54	42	42
76	46	34	56

   (a) At the .05 level of significance, is there evidence of a difference in the variances of the four types of squash?

   (b) At the .05 level of significance, is there evidence of a difference in the average yield between the four varieties of squash?

   (c) If appropriate, use the Tukey T method to determine the types of squash that differ in yield. (Use $\alpha = .05$.)

   ✓**(d)** What are the implications of the findings in this experiment? Discuss fully.

14.42 An auditor for the Internal Revenue Service would like to compare the efficiency of four regional tax processing centers. A random sample of five returns was selected at each center, and the number of days between receipt of the tax return and final processing was determined. The results (in days) were as follows (top of page 499):

Regional Center			
East	Midwest	South	West
49	47	39	52
54	56	55	42
40	40	48	57
60	51	43	46
43	55	50	50

(a) Is there evidence of a difference in the variances between the four regional centers? (Use $\alpha = .05$.)

(b) Is there evidence of a difference in the average processing time between the four regional centers? (Use $\alpha = .05$.)

(c) If appropriate, use the Tukey T method to determine the regional centers that differ in average processing time. (Use $\alpha = .05$.)

✔(d) What would the auditor conclude?

➠(e) ACTION What recommendations might the auditor give to the Internal Revenue Service based on these findings?

● 14.43 A new-car dealer would like to study the amount of money spent on optional equipment purchased for full-sized cars. A random sample of 20 purchases was selected. The respondents were divided into the following age classifications: 18–24, 25–29, 30–39, 40–59, 60 and over. The amount of optional equipment purchased (in hundreds of dollars) was organized by age groups as follows:

Age				
18–24	25–29	30–39	40–59	60 and Over
6.31	7.64	8.37	11.23	6.74
4.27	5.36	9.26	10.64	7.36
5.75	3.85	10.16	8.32	5.12
	6.24	6.48	9.00	
		7.86	7.53	

(a) At the .05 level of significance, is there evidence of a difference in the variances between the five age groups?

(b) At the .05 level of significance, is there evidence of a difference in the average amount of money spent on optional equipment purchased by the various age groups?

(c) If appropriate, use the Tukey T method to determine the age groups that differ in the average amount of money spent on optional equipment. (Use $\alpha = .05$.)

✔(d) What should the new car dealer conclude? How might these findings help in establishing sales promotion and inventory policies?

14.44 As a consulting industrial engineer you are hired to perform a "human factors experiment" at Burstiner & Lobel, a large law firm. A pool of 12 typists of similar ability and experience is selected to participate. The 12 subjects are randomly assigned to one of three groups of working conditions—very noisy atmosphere (90 Db constant), somewhat noisy atmosphere (65 Db constant), and pleasant atmosphere (40 Db constant). The subjects are then asked to type a technical manuscript. The data at the top of page 500 represent the number of mistakes on the manuscript made by the typists under the various working conditions.

Groups		
Very Noisy *(90 Db)*	*Somewhat Noisy* *(65 Db)*	*Pleasant* *(40 Db)*
14	2	2
12	5	6
13	8	6
13	5	2

(a) At the .01 level of significance, is there evidence of a difference in the variances of the number of errors between the three groups?

(b) At the .01 level of significance, is there evidence of a difference in the average number of errors between the three groups?

(c) If appropriate, use the Tukey T method to determine which groups differ in average number of errors. (Use $\alpha = .01$.)

➡(d) **ACTION**   Write a report for the CEO at Burstiner & Lobel explaining your findings and offering recommendations for productivity improvement.

14.45   As part of an evaluation of competitive utility packages for an important systems improvement, a director of MIS decided to survey other installations which already had each of the major alternative choices. After careful efforts to match up the respondents on all important characteristics, data were obtained concerning the number of minutes of run time for the key utility program with the following results:

"Utility Packages"			
Apple Cart	*Bomb-Shell*	*Orange Blossom*	*Data Fake*
9	5	12	11
12	9	14	13
10	8	7	10
11	6	11	14
14	6	14	15

(a) At the .05 level of significance
   (1) Is there evidence of a difference in the variances of the run time between the four utility packages?
   (2) Is there evidence of a difference in the average run time between the four utility packages?
   (3) If appropriate, use Tukey's T method to determine which utility packages differ in average run time. (Use $\alpha = .05$.)

✔(b) Based on the results, which utility package should the director of MIS choose? Why?

14.46   The following data represent the price per 8 ounces of sparkling spring and mineral water sold at a supermarket in New York City, classified by country of origin:

USA	France	Other
63	42	31
46	32	31
28	30	40
36	33	35
38	68	22
28		34
		38
		34
		34

(a) At the .05 level of significance, is there evidence of a difference in the variances of the price between the countries?

(b) At the .05 level of significance, is there evidence of a difference in the average price between the countries?

(c) If appropriate, use Tukey's T method to determine which countries differ in average price. (Use $\alpha = .05$.)

➠(d) **ACTION** Write an article for the food editor of your local newspaper based on your findings.

14.47 Suppose that the assistant superintendent for curriculum affairs wishes to evaluate three alternative sets of mathematics materials so that one set can be selected to be purchased by the entire school district. A third-grade teacher in the district has volunteered to make the comparison. The 24 students in her class are homogeneous with respect to their academic abilities. They are to be divided randomly into three groups, containing 7, 9, and 8 students, respectively. The first group is assigned to set I, the second to set II, and the third to set III.

At the end of the year all 24 students are given the same standardized mathematics test. The scores on a scale of 0–100 (low–high) are displayed below:

	Material Set	
I	*II*	*III*
87	58	81
80	63	62
74	64	70
82	75	64
74	70	70
81	73	72
97	80	92
	62	63
	71	

Based on these results, the assistant superintendent would like to know whether there is any difference among the sets in the scores achieved and, if so, which set(s) are superior to the others.

(a) Completely analyze the data. (Use $\alpha = .05$.)

➠(b) **ACTION** Draft a report that the third-grade teacher might send to the assistant superintendent.

14.48 A medical researcher decided to compare several over-the-counter sleep medications. People who had trouble sleeping came to the researcher's sleep laboratory and took either a placebo (a pill with no active ingredients), Nighty-night, Snooze-Away, or Mr. Sandman. The number of hours each one slept is given at the top of page 502:

Placebo:	2, 4, 3, 5, 2, 4, 3
Nighty-night:	3, 4, 5, 3, 5, 4, 6, 5
Snooze-Away:	6, 5, 7, 4, 8, 6
Mr. Sandman:	5, 4, 7, 5, 8, 6, 7

(a) Construct an appropriate graph, plot, or chart of the data.

(b) Calculate the mean time slept for each group.

(c) Using your answers to (a) and (b), guess whether there is any difference among the groups.

(d) Do an analysis of variance of the data, and describe the results. (Use $\alpha = .05$.)

(e) Does it appear that some drugs are more useful than others? (Use $\alpha = .05$.)

➡️(f) **ACTION** Write a draft of an article the medical researcher might send to the editor of the health column in your local newspaper.

14.49 Use the data from Problem 3.86 on page 85. Is there evidence of a difference in the mean amount of sodium among beef, "meat," and poultry frankfurters? (Use $\alpha = .05$.) Discuss.

14.50 An auditor for a supermarket chain wanted to study differences between stores within the chain in the prices of various products. Four stores were selected, one each from the "Inner City," "Outer City," "Nearby Suburb," and "Rural Suburb." The prices at these four stores for the seven products studied were as follows:

Product	Inner City	Outer City	Nearby Suburb	Rural Suburb
Corn flakes 12 oz.	1.25	1.19	1.19	1.09
Chunk light tuna 6.5 oz.	1.09	.99	1.09	.99
Butter 1 lb.	2.69	2.69	2.69	2.59
London broil 1 lb.	4.29	2.99	3.59	2.99
Mayonnaise 32 oz.	2.29	2.29	2.29	1.89
Large eggs—dozen	1.19	.89	.89	.89
Ice cream half gallon	3.49	2.89	3.09	2.99

(a) At the .05 level of significance, is there evidence of a difference in the average price between the store locations?

(b) What assumptions are necessary in part (a)?

(c) If appropriate, use the Tukey T method to determine the store locations that differ in average price. (Use $\alpha = .05$.)

(d) Determine the relative efficiency of the randomized block design as compared with the completely randomized design.

➡️(e) **ACTION** Draft a memo that the auditor might send the CEO based on these findings.

14.51 Suppose that a second supermarket chain was planning a similar study with a different set of products. Four stores of this chain were selected, one each from the "Inner City," "Outer City," "Nearby Suburb," and "Rural Suburb." The prices at these stores for the ten products studied were as follows:

Product	Inner City	Outer City	Nearby Suburb	Rural Suburb
Ground chuck 1 lb.	1.69	1.69	1.69	1.69
Bananas 1 lb.	.39	.39	.39	.39
Vegetable oil 24 oz.	1.69	1.69	1.69	1.69
Insect spray 11 oz.	2.39	2.39	2.39	2.39
Dish detergent 50 oz.	3.49	3.49	3.29	3.29
Six pack of beer 12 oz.	3.39	3.39	3.09	3.09
Tea 48 bags	1.69	1.69	1.59	1.59
Raisins 15 oz.	1.29	1.29	1.19	1.19
Vegetable soup 10.5 oz.	.37	.37	.35	.35
Pork chops 1 lb.	2.19	2.19	2.29	2.29

(a) At the .05 level of significance, is there evidence of a difference in the average price between the store locations?

(b) What assumptions are necessary in part (a)?

(c) If appropriate, use the Tukey T method to determine the store locations that differ in average price. (Use $\alpha = .05$.)

(d) Determine the relative efficiency of the randomized block design as compared with the completely randomized design.

✗(e) Can you directly compare the results obtained in parts (a)–(d) with those of Problem 14.50? Explain.

● 14.52 A recent wine tasting was held by the J. S. Wine Club in which eight wines were rated by twelve club members. Information concerning the country of origin and the price were not known to the club members until after the tasting took place. The wines rated (and the prices paid for them) were

1. French white $4.59
2. Italian white $2.50
3. Italian red $2.50
4. French burgundy (red) $4.69
5. French burgundy (red) $5.75
6. California Beaujolais (red) $4.50
7. French white $3.75
8. California white $7.59

The summated ratings over several characteristics for the twelve club members were as follows:

Respondent	Wine							
	1	2	3	4	5	6	7	8
A	10	17	15	9	12	6	15	9
B	9	14	11	5	16	2	15	7
C	10	18	10	5	18	5	10	10
D	9	11	13	10	17	11	14	9
E	10	16	12	8	18	8	10	10
F	6	16	3	8	4	2	2	5
G	9	12	14	9	9	6	6	5
H	7	12	11	8	15	9	12	8
I	10	18	12	12	16	10	10	16
J	16	9	10	13	18	11	15	14
K	14	16	13	12	15	15	17	11
L	15	17	10	13	15	16	16	13

(a) At the .01 level of significance, is there evidence of a difference in the average rating scores between the wines?

(b) What assumptions are necessary in order to do part (a) of this problem? Comment on the validity of these assumptions.

(c) If appropriate, use the Tukey T method to determine the wines that differ in average rating. (Use $\alpha = .01$)

✗(d) Based upon your results in part (c)
  (1) Do you think that country of origin has had an effect on the ratings?
  (2) Do you think that the type of wine (red versus white) has had an effect on the ratings?
  (3) Do you think that price has had an effect on the ratings?
  Discuss fully.

(e) Determine the relative efficiency of the randomized block design as compared with the completely randomized design.

14.53 A psychological experiment is designed to determine if there are any differences in recall ability due to different levels of exposure to an object. Three levels of exposure (in msec) are considered. Eight sets of triplets are chosen as subjects. In each of the eight sets of triplets, the members are randomly assigned to be examined under an exposure level.

| Set of Triplets | Exposure Level | | |
(Subjects)	Minimum	Moderate	High
I	55	68	67
II	78	83	84
III	34	53	54
IV	56	67	65
V	79	78	85
VI	20	29	30
VII	68	88	92
VIII	59	58	72

(a) At the .05 level of significance, is there evidence of a difference in the average recall ability between the exposure levels?

(b) What assumptions are necessary in order to do part (a) of this problem?

(c) If appropriate, use the Tukey T method to determine the exposure levels that differ in average recall ability. (Use $\alpha = .05$.)

(d) Determine the relative efficiency of the randomized block design as compared with the completely randomized design.

➡(e) **ACTION** Write a memo to your industrial psychology professor regarding the results and possible implications in advertising.

14.54 The retailing manager of a food chain wishes to determine whether product location will have any effect on the sale of pet toys. Two factors are to be studied: (1) height of shelf: top, middle, and bottom; and (2) location in aisle: front, middle, and rear. A random sample of 18 stores was selected, and 2 stores were randomly assigned to each combination of shelf height and aisle location. The size of the display area was constant for all 18 stores. At the end of a 1-week trial period, the sales of the product in each store were as follows:

Aisle Location	Height of Shelf		
	Top	Middle	Bottom
Front	86	62	50
	72	54	40
Middle	32	20	18
	24	14	16
Rear	60	40	28
	46	28	22

    (a) At the .05 level of significance
        (1) Is there an effect due to aisle location?
        (2) Is there an effect due to shelf height?
        (3) Is there an interaction between aisle location and shelf height?
    (b) Plot a graph of average sales for each aisle location for each shelf height.
    (c) If appropriate, use Tukey's T method to determine which aisle locations and which shelf heights differ in sales. (Use $\alpha = .05$.)
    (d) Based on the results, what conclusions can you reach concerning sales? Discuss.
    ✏(e) Compare and contrast your results here with those from the one-way experiment in Problem 14.39 on page 497.

● **14.55** An experiment was carried out to determine the effect of room size and wall color on the measured anxiety level of subjects. Two subjects were tested for each of three room sizes and three room colors. A large value means a high level of anxiety. The results were as follows:

Size	Room Color		
	Red	Yellow	Blue
Small	50	31	12
	65	26	16
Medium	63	48	26
	49	54	19
Large	68	63	20
	59	57	16

    (a) At the .01 level of significance
        (1) Is there an effect due to room size?
        (2) Is there an effect due to room color?
        (3) Is there an interaction due to room size and room color?
    (b) Plot the average anxiety for each room size for each room color.
    (c) If appropriate, use Tukey's T method to determine which room sizes and room colors differ in average anxiety levels. (Use $\alpha = .01$.)
    ➡**(d)** **ACTION** Write a memo to your industrial psychology professor regarding these findings and their implications on office design in large firms.

14.56 The board of education of a large state wishes to study differences in class size between elementary, intermediate, and high schools in various cities. A random sample of three cities within the state was selected. Two schools at each level were chosen within each city, and the average class size for the school was recorded with the following results (page 506):

	City		
Educational Level	*A*	*B*	*C*
Elementary	32	26	20
	34	30	23
Intermediate	35	33	24
	39	30	27
High School	43	37	31
	38	34	28

(a) At the .05 level of significance
    (1) Is there an effect due to educational level?
    (2) Is there an effect due to cities?
    (3) Is there an interaction due to educational level and city?
(b) Plot the average class size for each educational level for each city.
(c) If appropriate, use Tukey's T method to determine which educational levels differ in class size. (Use $\alpha = .05$.)
➡**(d)** **ACTION** What should the board conclude? Discuss.
✎**(e)** If the three cities had been specifically (not randomly) selected, how would your analysis in part (a) be affected?

14.57 A hospital administrator wished to examine postsurgical hospitalization periods following knee surgery. A random sample of 30 patients was selected, five for each combination of age group and type of surgery. The results, in number of postsurgical hospitalization days, were as follows:

	Age Group		
Type of Knee Surgery	*Under 30*	*30 to 50*	*Over 50*
Arthroscopy	1	4	3
	3	3	5
	2	2	2
	6	3	3
	2	2	3
Arthrotomy	3	4	4
	10	5	8
	6	11	12
	7	5	10
	8	6	3

(a) At the .05 level of significance
    (1) Is there a difference between the types of surgery?
    (2) Is there a difference between the age groups?
    (3) Is there an interaction between type of knee surgery and age group?
(b) Plot a graph of the average number of days of postsurgical hospitalization for each type of surgery for each age group.
(c) If appropriate, use the Tukey T method to determine the age groups that differ in average number of postsurgical hospitalization days. (Use $\alpha = .05$.)

➠**(d)** **ACTION** Based on the results, what conclusions can the hospital administrator draw? Discuss.

Database Exercises

The following problems refer to the sample data obtained from the questionnaire of Figure 2.5 on page 15 and presented in Figure 2.10 on pages 24–29. They should be solved with the aid of an available computer package.

Suppose you are hired as a research assistant to the president of the realty company. For Problems 14.58–14.74 which follow

(a) Completely analyze the data at the .05 level.

➠**(b)** **ACTION** Write a memo to the president of the realty company discussing your findings and their implications.

☐ **14.58** Is there evidence of a difference in appraised value based on type of indoor parking facility (questions 1 and 8)?

☐ **14.59** Is there evidence of a difference in appraised value based on geographic location (questions 1 and 9)?

☐ **14.60** Is there evidence of a difference in appraised value based on architectural style of house (questions 1 and 10)?

☐ **14.61** Is there evidence of a difference in appraised value based on type of heating system used (questions 1 and 12)?

☐ **14.62** Is there evidence of a difference in lot size based on geographic location (questions 2 and 9)?

☐ **14.63** Is there evidence of a difference in number of bedrooms based on geographic location (questions 3 and 9)?

☐ **14.64** Is there evidence of a difference in number of bedrooms based on architectural style of house (questions 3 and 10)?

☐ **14.65** Is there evidence of a difference in number of rooms based on architectural style of house (questions 5 and 10)?

☐ **14.66** Is there evidence of a difference in the age of the house based on geographic location (questions 6 and 9)?

☐ **14.67** Is there evidence of a difference in the age of the house based on architectural style (questions 6 and 10)?

☐ **14.68** Is there evidence of a difference in annual taxes based on type of indoor parking facility (questions 7 and 8)?

☐ **14.69** Is there evidence of a difference in annual taxes based on geographic location (questions 7 and 9)?

☐ **14.70** Is there evidence of a difference in annual taxes based on architectural style of house (questions 7 and 10)?

☐ **14.71** Is there evidence of a difference in annual taxes based on type of heating system used (questions 7 and 12)?

☐ **14.72** Is there evidence of a difference in appraised value based on architectural style in East Meadow (questions 1, 10, and 9)?

☐ **14.73** Is there evidence of a difference in appraised value based on architectural style in Farmingdale (questions 1, 10, and 9)?

☐ **14.74** Is there evidence of a difference in appraised value based on architectural style in Levittown (questions 1, 10, and 9)?

Case Study E

As research director of a large advertising agency you have decided to initiate a study of the effect of advertising on product perception. Five different advertisements were to be compared in the marketing of a ball-point pen. Advertisement A tended to greatly undersell the pen's characteristics. Advertisement B tended to slightly undersell the pen's characteristics. Advertisement C tended to slightly oversell the pen's characteristics. Advertisement D tended to greatly oversell the pen's characteristics. Advertisement E attempted to correctly state the pen's characteristics. A sample of 30 *adult* respondents were randomly assigned to the five advertisements (so that there were six respondents to each). After reading the advertisement and developing a sense of "product expectation," all respondents unknowingly received the same pen to evaluate. The respondents were permitted to test their pen and the plausibility of the advertising copy. The respondents were then asked to rate the pen from 1 to 7 on three product characteristic scales as shown below:

	Extremely Poor $\longrightarrow$ *Neutral* $\longrightarrow$					*Extremely Good*
Appearance	1	2	3	4	5	6	7
Durability	1	2	3	4	5	6	7
Writing performance	1	2	3	4	5	6	7

The *combined scores* of three ratings (appearance, durability, and writing performance) are given in Table 14.15.

TABLE 14.15 Product ratings for five advertisements

A	B	C	D	E
15	16	8	5	12
18	17	7	6	19
17	21	10	13	18
19	16	15	11	12
19	19	14	9	17
20	17	14	10	14

A detailed report that summarizes your findings based upon this study is to be prepared. Included as an appendix is a discussion of the statistical analysis utilized.

References

1. BERENSON, M. L., D. M. LEVINE, AND M. GOLDSTEIN, *Intermediate Statistical Methods and Applications: A Computer Package Approach* (Englewood Cliffs, N.J.: Prentice-Hall, 1983).
2. HICKS, C. R., *Fundamental Concepts in the Design of Experiments*, 3d ed. (New York: Holt, Rinehart and Winston, 1982).
3. KIRK, R. E., *Experimental Design*, 2d ed. (Belmont, Cal.: Brooks-Cole, 1982).

4. LEVINE, D. M., M. L. BERENSON, AND D. F. STEPHAN, *Using Minitab with Basic Business Statistics*, 2d ed. (Englewood Cliffs, N.J.: Prentice-Hall, 1986).

5. LEVINE, D. M., M. L. BERENSON, AND D. F. STEPHAN, *Using SAS with Basic Business Statistics* (Englewood Cliffs, N.J.: Prentice-Hall, 1983).

6. *MYSTAT*: *A Personal Version of SYSTAT*, (Evanston, Ill.: 1988).

7. NETER, J., W. WASSERMAN, AND M. H. KUTNER, *Applied Linear Statistical Models*, 2d ed. (Homewood, Ill.: Richard D. Irwin, 1985).

8. RYAN, T. A., B. L. JOINER, AND B. F. RYAN, *Minitab Student Handbook*, 2d ed. (North Scituate, Mass.: Duxbury Press, 1985).

9. *SAS User's Guide*: *Statistics*, 1982 ed. (Cary, N.C.: SAS Institute, 1982).

10. SNEDECOR, G. W., AND W. G. COCHRAN, *Statistical Methods*, 7th ed. (Ames, Iowa: Iowa State University Press, 1980).

11. *STATGRAPHICS User's Guide* (Rockville, Md.: STSC, 1986).

15

Nonparametric Methods

15.1 INTRODUCTION

In the preceding four chapters a variety of hypothesis-testing situations were described. In most of these situations the so-called "classical" or **parametric methods** of hypothesis testing were employed. Nevertheless, often the researcher in the social sciences or in business must decide what kinds of testing procedures to choose if

1. The measurements attained on the data are only qualitative (i.e., *nominally* scaled) or in ranks (i.e., *ordinally* scaled).
2. The assumptions underlying the use of the classical methods cannot be met.
3. The situation requires a study of such features as *randomness*, *trend*, *independence*, *symmetry*, or *goodness-of-fit* rather than the testing of hypotheses about particular population parameters.

For such circumstances as these, **nonparametric methods** of hypothesis testing have been devised. In fact, three such methods have already been discussed—the McNemar test for changes in proportions (see Section 13.7) and the chi-square tests for independence (see Section 13.5) and for goodness of fit (see Section 13.6).[1] This chapter will focus on the development and use of seven additional nonparametric methods:

1. The Wald-Wolfowitz one-sample runs test for randomness
2. The Wilcoxon one-sample signed-ranks test
3. The Wilcoxon paired-sample signed-ranks test
4. The Wilcoxon rank-sum test for two independent samples
5. The Kruskal-Wallis test for c independent samples
6. The Friedman rank test for c related samples
7. The Spearman rank-correlation procedure

---

[1] The first two methods deal with qualitative data and are not (necessarily) concerned with parameters. The McNemar procedure may be viewed as a test for symmetry, while the chi-square technique seeks to determine whether or not a relationship between two qualitative variables is present. The third technique is concerned with how well a set of data fit a hypothesized probability distribution.

The goals of this chapter are

1. To show the need for nonparametric methods.
2. To demonstrate the usefulness of nonparametric methods by comparing a selected set against their classical counterparts.

15.2 CLASSICAL VERSUS NONPARAMETRIC PROCEDURES

15.2.1 Classical Procedures

Classical or **parametric procedures** have three distinguishing characteristics. First, they require that the level of measurement attained on the collected data be in the form of an *interval* scale or *ratio* scale (as described in Chapter 2). Second, they involve hypothesis testing of specified parameters (such as $\mu_X = 30$ or $\beta_1 = 0$ or $\rho = 0$). Third, classical procedures require very stringent assumptions and are valid only if these assumptions hold. Among these assumptions are

1. That the sample data be randomly drawn from a population which is normally distributed.
2. That the observations be independent of each other.
3. For situations concerning central tendency for which two or more samples have been drawn, that they be drawn from normal populations having equal variances (so that any differences between the populations will be in central tendency).[2]

The sensitivity of classical procedures to violations in the assumptions has been considered in the statistical literature (References 1 and 2). Some test procedures are said to be ''robust'' because they are relatively insensitive to slight violations in the assumptions. However, with gross violations in the assumptions both the true level of significance and the power of a test may differ sharply from what otherwise would be expected.

15.2.2 Nonparametric Procedures

When classical methods of hypothesis testing are not applicable, an appropriate **nonparametric procedure** (References 2 and 3) can be selected.

> **Nonparametric test procedures** may be broadly defined as either (1) those whose test statistic does not depend upon the form of the underlying population distribution from which the sample data were drawn, (2) those which are not concerned with the parameters of a population, or (3) those for which the data are of ''insufficient strength'' to warrant meaningful arithmetic operations.

The one-, two-, and c-sample tests for proportions as well as the chi-square tests for independence and for goodness of fit and the McNemar test for changes (all of which were discussed in Chapters 11 and 13) fit such a broad definition. Indeed, when testing a hypothesis about a proportion, we have previously employed what is called

---

[2] One exception to this is presented in Section 12.5 and an approximate solution is described therein. Recall that the Behrens–Fisher problem is said to exist whenever the researcher desires to test for differences in the means when the samples are drawn from normal populations but the equality of variances cannot be assumed.

(in the nonparametric literature) the **binomial test.** For example, the responses to question 7 from the real estate survey indicate annual tax payments. Suppose, however, that instead of evaluating the quantitative responses to this random variable, the president of the realty company merely classifies the results as high or low annual tax payments, depending on whether the actual amount exceeds $3,000. For such data, a binomial test could be broadly categorized as nonparametric for two reasons. First, each observation would be ''grossly measured'' (that is, categorized as above $3,000 or at most $3,000). Second, the test statistic would not depend upon the underlying population from which the sample data would be drawn. For example, regardless of whether the variable ''annual tax payments''actually follows a normal (or any other shaped) distribution, the variable ''tax payment grouping'' (high or low) would be derived from an arbitrarily selected classification point of $3,000. The binomial test statistic then would be independent of the form of the particular underlying distribution for the quantitative random variable of interest, ''annual tax payments.''

On the other hand, aside from the fact that the data gathered are qualitative (nominally scaled), the chi-square test for independence may be broadly classified as nonparametric for a different reason—it is not concerned with parameters.[3] In Section 13.5 the president of the realty company sought to ascertain whether or not the architectural style of the house (question 10) was independent of its geographic location (question 9). Other kinds of nonparametric procedures that are in this category are tests for randomness (see Section 15.4), tests for trend (see Reference 4), tests for symmetry (see Section 13.7), and tests for goodness of fit (see Section 13.6).

15.3 ADVANTAGES AND DISADVANTAGES OF USING NONPARAMETRIC METHODS

The use of nonparametric methods offers numerous advantages. Six are summarized below.

1. Nonparametric methods may be used on all types of data—qualitative data (nominal scaling), data in rank form (ordinal scaling), as well as data that have been measured more precisely (interval or ratio scaling).
2. Nonparametric methods are generally easy to apply and quick to compute when the sample sizes are small. Sometimes they are as simple as just counting how often some feature appears in the data. Thus they are often used for pilot or preliminary studies and/or in situations in which quick answers are desired.
3. Nonparametric methods make fewer, less stringent assumptions (which are more easily met) than do the classical procedures. Hence they enjoy wider applicability and yield a more general, broad-based set of conclusions.
4. Nonparametric methods permit the solution of problems that do not involve the testing of population parameters.
5. Nonparametric methods may be more economical than classical procedures, since the researcher may increase power and yet save money, time, and labor by collecting larger samples of data which are more grossly measured (that is, qualitative data or data in rank form), thereby solving the problem more quickly.
6. Depending on the particular procedure selected, nonparametric methods may be equally

---

[3] That is, traditionally this test has not been considered as parametric. The development of new techniques for analyzing qualitative data—specifically log-linear models—have changed that situation.

(or almost) as powerful as the classical procedure when the assumptions of the latter are met, and when they are not met may be quite a bit more powerful.

It should now be apparent that nonparametric methods may be advantageously employed in a variety of situations. On the other hand, nonparametric procedures have some shortcomings.

1. It is disadvantageous to use nonparametric methods when all the assumptions of the classical procedures can be met and the data are measured on either an interval or ratio scale. Unless classical procedures are employed in these instances, the researcher is not taking full advantage of the data. Information is lost when we convert such collected data (from an interval or ratio scale) to either ranks (ordinal scale) or categories (nominal scale). In particular, in such circumstances, some very quick and simple nonparametric tests have much less power than the classical procedures and should usually be avoided.
2. As the sample size gets larger, data manipulations required for nonparametric procedures are sometimes laborious unless appropriate computer software is available.
3. Often special tables of critical values are needed, and these are not as readily available as are the tables of the normal, t, χ^2, and F critical values.

Now that we have discussed some of the advantages and disadvantages of nonparametric methods, it is apparent that such procedures do not provide a panacea for all problems of statistical data analysis. Nevertheless, they comprise an important and useful body of statistical techniques. In the sections that follow we will consider the development of simple but important nonparametric techniques that may prove highly useful under differing circumstances.

15.4 WALD-WOLFOWITZ ONE-SAMPLE RUNS TEST FOR RANDOMNESS

In statistical inference it is usually assumed that the collected data constitute a random sample. Such an assumption, however, may be tested by the employment of a nonparametric procedure called the **Wald-Wolfowitz one-sample runs test for randomness.**

The null hypothesis of randomness may be tested by observing the *order* or *sequence* in which the items are obtained. If each item is assigned one of two symbols, such as S and F (for success and failure), depending either on whether the item possesses a particular property or on the amount or magnitude in which the property is possessed, the randomness of the sequence may be investigated. If the sequence is randomly generated, the items will be independent and identically distributed. This means that the value of an item will be independent both of its position in the sequence and of the values of the items which precede it and follow it. On the other hand, if an item in the sequence is affected by the items which precede it or succeed it so that the probability of its occurrence varies from one position to another, the process is not considered random. In such cases either similar items would tend to cluster together (such as when a trend in the data is present) or the similar items would alternatingly mix so that some systematic periodic effect would exist.

To study whether or not an observed sequence is random, we will consider as the test statistic the **number of runs** present in the data.

A **run** is defined as a consecutive series of similar items which are bounded by items of a different type (or by the beginning or ending of the sequence).

For instance, suppose that the following is the observed occurrence of an experiment of flipping a coin 20 times:

HHHHHHHHHHHTTTTTTTTTT

In this sequence there are two runs—a run of 10 heads followed by a run of 10 tails. With similar items tending to cluster, such a sequence would not be considered random even though, as would theoretically be expected, 10 of the 20 outcomes are heads, and 10 are tails.

At the other extreme, suppose that the following sequence is obtained when flipping a coin 20 times:

HTHTHTHTHTHTHTHTHTHT

In this sequence there are 20 runs—10 runs of one head each and 10 runs of one tail each. With such an alternating pattern, this sequence could not be considered random because there are too many runs.

On the other hand, if, as shown below, the sequence of responses to the 20 coin tosses is thoroughly mixed, the number of runs will neither be too few nor too many, and the process may then be considered random:

HHTTHHHHTTTTTHTHTTHH

Therefore, in testing for randomness, what is essential is the ordering or positioning of the items in the sequence, not the frequency of items of each type.

15.4.1   Procedure

To perform the test of the null hypothesis of randomness, let the total sample size n be decomposed into two parts, n_1 successes and n_2 failures. The test statistic U, the total number of runs, is then obtained by counting. For a two-tailed test, if U is either too large or too small, we may reject the null hypothesis of randomness in favor of the alternative that the sequence is not random. If both n_1 and n_2 are less than or equal to 20, Table E.9, Parts 1 and 2, presents the critical values for the test statistic U at the .05 level of significance (two-tailed). If, for a given combination of n_1 and n_2, U is either greater than or equal to the upper critical value or less than or equal to the lower critical value, the null hypothesis of randomness may be rejected at the .05 level. However, if U lies between these limits, the null hypothesis of randomness cannot be rejected.

On the other hand, tests for randomness are not always two-tailed. If we are interested in testing for randomness against the specific alternative of a **trend effect**—that there is a tendency for like items to cluster together—a one-tailed test is needed. Here we reject the null hypothesis only if too few runs occur—if the observed value of U is less than or equal to the critical value presented in Table E.9, Part 1, at the .025 level of significance. At the other extreme, if we are interested in testing for randomness against a **systematic** or **periodic effect,** we use a one-tailed test that rejects only if too many runs occur—if the observed value of U is greater than or equal to the critical value given in Table E.9, Part 2, at the .025 level of significance.

Regardless of whether the test is one-tailed or two-tailed, however, for a sample size n greater than 40 (or when either n_1 or n_2 exceeds 20) the test statistic U is approximately normally distributed. Therefore, the following large-sample approximation formula may be used to test the hypothesis of randomness.

$$Z = \frac{U - \mu_U}{\sigma_U} \tag{15.1}$$

where U = total number of runs

μ_U = mean value of U; $\mu_U = \dfrac{2n_1n_2}{n} + 1$

σ_U = standard deviation of U; $\sigma_U = \sqrt{\dfrac{2n_1n_2(2n_1n_2 - n)}{n^2(n - 1)}}$

n_1 = number of successes in sample

n_2 = number of failures in sample

n = sample size; $n = n_1 + n_2$

That is,

$$Z = \frac{U - \left(\dfrac{2n_1n_2}{n} + 1\right)}{\sqrt{\dfrac{2n_1n_2(2n_1n_2 - n)}{n^2(n - 1)}}} \tag{15.2}$$

and, based on the level of significance selected, the null hypothesis may be rejected if the computed Z value falls in the appropriate region of rejection, depending on whether a two-tailed test or a one-tailed test is used (see Figure 15.1).

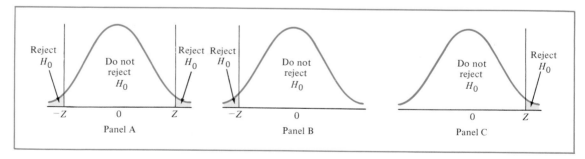

FIGURE 15.1
Determining the rejection region; Panel A, two-tailed test; Panel B, one-tailed test, trend effect; Panel C, one-tailed test, periodic effect.

15.4.2 Applications

To illustrate the use of the Wald–Wolfowitz one-sample runs test suppose that a quality control engineer was observing the production process of a new brand of tires at a manufacturing plant. To check whether the process was in control, she examined a sample of 50 consecutive tires emerging from the production line and classified each as defective or nondefective. The resulting sequence follows:

Sequence NNNNNNDNNN NNNNNDNNNDN NNNNNNNNNN NNNDDNNNNN NNNNNNNNNDN

Runs 1 2 3 4 5 6 7 8 9 10 11

The null and alternative hypotheses are

H_0: The process generates defective and nondefective tires randomly.

H_1: The process does not generate defective and nondefective tires randomly but in clusters (one tailed).

If the null hypothesis is not rejected, the production process is said to be in control. If the null hypothesis is rejected, the process is said to be generating defective items in clusters.

From the sequence above it is observed that 6 of the 50 tires (12%) in the sample are defective and that the data contain a total of 11 runs; that is, $n = 50$, $n_1 = 6$, $n_2 = 44$, and $U = 11$.

Since the sample size exceeds 40, the large-sample approximation formula [Equation (15.2)] is used to test the null hypothesis. If the level of significance is selected as .05, the null hypothesis of randomness would be rejected if $Z < -1.645$, since the test is one-tailed. For our data,

$$Z = \frac{U - \left(\dfrac{2n_1 n_2}{n} + 1\right)}{\sqrt{\dfrac{2n_1 n_2(2n_1 n_2 - n)}{n^2(n-1)}}} = \frac{11 - \left(\dfrac{(2)(6)(44)}{50} + 1\right)}{\sqrt{\dfrac{[(2)(6)(44)][(2)(6)(44) - 50]}{(50)^2(49)}}}$$

$$= \frac{-.56}{\sqrt{2.0602}}$$

$$= -.39$$

Since $Z = -.39$ exceeds the critical Z value of -1.645, the null hypothesis of randomness cannot be rejected, and the process is said to be in control in terms of the ways in which the defective items emerge mixed in the sequence. On the other hand, if it is company policy that no more than 8% of the tires being produced can be defective, Equation (11.3) or (11.4) would now be used to test whether the process is in control in terms of the proportion of defective items in the sample (see Section 11.8).

In the example above, the data were measured on the strength of a nominal scale. Each tire was merely classified as defective or nondefective. As a second application of the runs test of randomness, Table 15.1 presents the unemployment rates (per thousand) of clerical workers in the United States from 1960 through 1987.

A distinguishing feature of the Wald–Wolfowitz one-sample runs test for randomness is that it may be used not only on data which constitute a nominal scale—where each of the items is classified as success or failure—but also on data measured in the strength of an interval or ratio scale—where each of the items is classified according to its position with respect to the median of the sequence. For example, from Table 15.1 we may wish to test the null hypothesis that the unemployment rates

TABLE 15.1 U.S. clerical workers' unemployment rates*
(1960–1987)

Year	Unemployment Rates (per thousand)	Relationship to Median Rate of 4.6†
1960	3.8	B
1961	4.6	A
1962	4.0	B
1963	4.0	B
1964	3.7	B
1965	3.3	B
1966	2.9	B
1967	3.1	B
1968	3.0	B
1969	3.0	B
1970	4.0	B
1971	4.8	A
1972	4.7	A
1973	4.2	B
1974	4.6	A
1975	6.6	A
1976	6.4	A
1977	5.9	A
1978	4.9	A
1979	4.6	A
1980	5.3	A
1981	5.7	A
1982	7.0	A
1983	6.4	A
1984	5.1	A
1985	4.9	A
1986	4.7	A
1987	4.2	B

* In 1983 the occupational classifications were changed. From that year to the present, clerical workers comprise the major component of administrative support services.

† A, equal or above; B, below.

SOURCES: Data are extracted from Table 28, *Handbook of Labor Statistics Bulletin* 2175, U.S. Department of Labor, Bureau of Labor Statistics, December 1984, and from Table 10, *Employment & Earnings*, U.S. Department of Labor, Bureau of Labor Statistics, January 1985, 1986, 1988.

of clerical workers are randomly distributed with respect to the median over time against the alternative that these rates are not randomly distributed with respect to the median over time—that is,

H_0: Unemployment rates of clerical workers are random over time.

H_1: Unemployment rates of clerical workers are not random over time (two-tailed).

To perform the runs test we assign the symbol A to each rate that equals or exceeds the median rate and the symbol B to each rate that is below the median rate. From Table 15.1 the median rate is 4.6. Thus for the 28 rates, 16 are equal to or above the median rate, while 12 are below it.

Parts 1 and 2 of Table E.9 present the critical values of the runs test at the .05 level of significance. As demonstrated in Table 15.2 (which is a replica of Table E.9), since $n_1 = 16$ and $n_2 = 12$ we would reject the null hypothesis at the .05 level if $U \geq 21$ or if $U \leq 9$ for this two-tailed test. Since the observed number of runs is 7,

TABLE 15.2   Obtaining the lower and upper tail critical values U for the runs test where $n_1 = 16$, $n_2 = 12$, and $\alpha = .05$

Part 1. Lower Tail
($\alpha = .025$)

n_1 \ n_2	2	3	4	5	6	7	8	9	10	11	12	13	14	15	16	17	18	19	20
2											2	2	2	2	2	2	2	2	2
3					2	2	2	2	2	2	2	2	2	3	3	3	3	3	3
4				2	2	2	3	3	3	3	3	3	3	3	4	4	4	4	4
5			2	2	3	3	3	3	3	4	4	4	4	4	4	4	5	5	5
6		2	2	3	3	3	3	4	4	4	5	5	5	5	5	6	6	6	6
7		2	2	3	3	3	4	5	5	5	5	6	6	6	6	6	7	7	7
8		2	3	3	3	4	4	5	5	5	6	6	6	6	7	7	7	7	7
9		2	3	3	4	4	5	5	5	6	6	7	7	7	7	8	8	8	8
10		2	3	3	4	5	5	5	6	6	7	7	7	8	8	8	8	8	9
11		2	3	4	4	5	5	6	6	7	7	8	8	8	9	9	9	9	9
12	2	2	3	4	4	5	6	6	7	7	7	8	8	9	9	9	9	10	10
13	2	2	3	4	5	5	6	6	7	7	8	8	9	9	9	10	10	10	10
14	2	2	3	4	5	5	6	7	7	8	8	9	9	9	10	10	10	11	11
15	2	3	3	4	5	6	6	7	7	8	8	9	9	10	10	11	11	11	12
16	2	3	4	4	5	6	6	7	8	8	9	9	10	10	11	11	11	12	12
17	2	3	4	4	5	6	7	7	8	9	9	10	10	11	11	11	12	12	13
18	2	3	4	5	5	6	7	8	8	9	9	10	10	11	11	12	12	13	13
19	2	3	4	5	6	6	7	8	8	9	10	10	11	11	12	12	13	13	13
20	2	3	4	5	6	6	7	8	9	9	10	10	11	12	12	13	13	13	14

Part 2. Upper Tail
($\alpha = .025$)

n_1 \ n_2	2	3	4	5	6	7	8	9	10	11	12	13	14	15	16	17	18	19	20
2																			
3																			
4				9	9														
5			9	10	10	11	11												
6			9	10	11	12	12	13	13	13	13								
7					11	12	13	13	14	14	14	14	15	15	15				
8					11	12	13	14	14	15	15	16	16	16	16	17	17	17	17
9						13	14	14	15	16	16	16	17	17	18	18	18	18	18
10						13	14	15	16	16	17	17	18	18	18	19	19	19	20
11						13	14	15	16	17	17	18	19	19	19	20	20	20	21
12						13	14	16	16	17	18	19	19	20	20	21	21	21	22
13							15	16	17	18	19	19	20	20	21	21	22	22	23
14							15	16	17	18	19	20	20	21	22	22	23	23	24
15							15	16	18	18	19	20	21	22	22	23	23	24	25
16							17	18	19	20	21	21	22	23	23	24	25	25	25
17							17	18	19	20	21	22	22	23	23	24	25	25	26
18							17	18	19	20	21	22	23	23	24	25	25	26	27
19							17	18	20	21	22	23	23	24	25	26	26	27	27
20							17	18	20	21	22	23	24	25	25	26	27	27	28

SOURCE: Extracted from Table E.9, Parts 1 and 2.

we may reject the null hypothesis of randomness in favor of the alternative. There is apparently a cyclical pattern over time to the rates of unemployment for clerical workers. If the null hypothesis were true, the *p*-value or probability of obtaining such a result as this or one even more extreme would be less than .05.

Problems

15.1   Flip a coin 50 times recording the sequence of heads (H) and tails (T). Can the resulting sequence be considered random? (Use $\alpha = .05$.)

15.2   Roll a die 30 times recording the sequence of odd faces (1, 3, 5) and even faces (2, 4, 6). Can the resulting sequence be considered random? (Use $\alpha = .05$.)

15.3   Starting at the beginning of the table of random numbers (Table E.1), record the sequence of high digits (5, 6, 7, 8, 9) and low digits (0, 1, 2, 3, 4) for the first 100 digits observed. Can this resulting sequence of high and low digits be considered random? (Use $\alpha = .05$).

15.4   Select a page from your local telephone directory and, examining only the last digit of each telephone number, record the sequence of high (5, 6, 7, 8, 9) and low (0, 1, 2, 3, 4) digits. Can the resulting sequence be considered random? (Use $\alpha = .05$.)

15.5   During the period from 1960 to 1987 there was an increase in the federal budget outlays for veterans' benefits and services. During this period, however, total federal outlays for all functions also increased. The data in the accompanying table present the percentage of total federal outlays for veterans' benefits and services during the 28-year period from 1960 to 1987. With respect to fluctuations above and below the median, is there any evidence of trend over the 28-year period? (Use $\alpha = .025$.)

Percentage of total federal outlays to veterans' benefits and services

Year	Percentage
1960	5.9
1961	5.8
1962	5.3
1963	5.0
1964	4.8
1965	4.8
1966	4.4
1967	4.4
1968	3.9
1969	4.1
1970	4.4
1971	4.6
1972	4.6
1973	4.9
1974	5.0
1975	5.1
1976	5.0
1977	4.5
1978	4.2
1979	4.0
1980	3.6
1981	3.4
1982	3.2
1983	3.1
1984	3.0
1985	2.8
1986	2.7
1987	2.6

SOURCE: Data are extracted from Table 476, *Statistical Abstract of the United States*, U.S. Department of Commerce, 1988.

15.6 In Figure 3.7 on page 54, 24 companies comprising the natural resource industrial grouping are listed alphabetically along with their PE ratios. A digidot plot for these data is displayed in Figure 4.17 on page 124. With respect to the fluctuations above and below the median PE ratio of 16.0, can the resulting sequence be considered random? (Use $\alpha = .05$.)

15.7 Use the data in Problem 4.96 on page 125. Is there evidence from the resulting sequence of 30 consecutive pairs of manufactured jeans that the manufacturing process is out-of-control? (Use $\alpha = .05$.)

15.8 Use the data in Problem 4.97 on page 125. With respect to fluctuations above and below the median, is there evidence of a trend in Victor Sternberg's time trials over the 27-day period? (Use $\alpha = .025$.)

15.5 WILCOXON SIGNED-RANKS TEST

In the preceding section the nonparametric procedure was not concerned with the testing of any particular parameters and as such has no classical counterpart. However, the procedure presented in this section may be used when we want to test a hypothesis regarding a parameter reflecting central tendency. This procedure, known as the **Wilcoxon signed-ranks test,** may be chosen over its respective classical counterpart—the one-sample t test (Section 11.5) or the paired-difference t test (Section 12.3)—when the researcher is able to obtain data measured at a higher level than an ordinal scale but does not believe that the assumptions of the classical procedure are sufficiently met. When the assumptions of the t test are violated, the Wilcoxon procedure (which makes fewer and less stringent assumptions than does the t test) is likely to be more powerful in detecting the existence of significant differences than its corresponding classical counterpart. Moreover, even under conditions appropriate to the classical t test, the Wilcoxon signed-ranks test has proven to be almost as powerful.

15.5.1 Procedure

To perform the Wilcoxon signed-ranks test the following six-step procedure may be used:

1. For each item in a sample of n' items we obtain a **difference score** D_i (to be described in Sections 15.5.3 and 15.5.5 for the one-sample and paired-sample tests, respectively).
2. We then neglect the $+$ and $-$ signs and obtain a set of n' absolute differences $|D_i|$.
3. We omit from further analysis any absolute difference score of zero, thereby yielding a set of n nonzero absolute difference scores where $n \le n'$.
4. We then assign ranks R_i from 1 to n to each of the $|D_i|$ such that the smallest absolute difference score gets rank 1 and the largest gets rank n. Owing to a lack of precision in the measuring process, if two or more $|D_i|$ are equal, they are each assigned the "average rank" of the ranks they otherwise would have individually been assigned had ties in the data not occurred.
5. We now reassign the symbol $+$ or $-$ to each of the n ranks R_i, depending on whether D_i was originally positive or negative.
6. The Wilcoxon test statistic W is obtained as the sum of the $+$ ranks.

$$W = \sum_{i=1}^{n} R_i^{(+)} \qquad (15.3)$$

Since the sum of the first n integers $(1, 2, \ldots, n)$ is given by $n(n + 1)/2$, the Wilcoxon test statistic W may range from a minimum of 0 (where all the observed difference scores are negative) to a maximum of $n(n + 1)/2$ (where all the observed difference scores are positive). If the null hypothesis were true, we would expect the test statistic W to take on a value close to its mean, $\mu_W = n(n + 1)/4$, while if the null hypothesis were false, we would expect the observed value of the test statistic to be close to one of the extremes.

For samples of $n \leq 20$, Table E.10 may be used for obtaining the critical values of the test statistic W for both one- and two-tailed tests at various levels of significance. For a two-tailed test and for a particular level of significance, if the observed value of W equals or exceeds the upper critical value or is equal to or less than the lower critical value, the null hypothesis may be rejected. For a one-tailed test in the positive direction the decision rule is to reject the null hypothesis if the observed value of W equals or exceeds the upper critical value, while for a one-tailed test in the negative direction the decision rule is to reject the null hypothesis if the observed value of W is less than or equal to the lower critical value.

For samples of $n > 20$, the test statistic W is approximately normally distributed, and the following large-sample approximation formula may be used for testing the null hypothesis:

$$Z = \frac{W - \mu_W}{\sigma_W} \qquad \textbf{(15.4)}$$

where W is the sum of positive ranks; $\quad W = \sum_{i=1}^{n} R_i^{(+)}$

μ_W is the mean value of W; $\quad \mu_W = \dfrac{n(n + 1)}{4}$

σ_W is the standard deviation of W; $\quad \sigma_W = \sqrt{\dfrac{n(n + 1)(2n + 1)}{24}}$

n is the number of nonzero absolute difference scores in the sample

That is,

$$Z = \frac{W - \left(\dfrac{n(n + 1)}{4}\right)}{\sqrt{\dfrac{n(n + 1)(2n + 1)}{24}}} \qquad \textbf{(15.5)}$$

and, based on the level of significance selected, the null hypothesis may be rejected if the computed Z value falls in the appropriate region of rejection, depending on whether a two-tailed test or a one-tailed test is used (see Figure 15.2 on page 522).

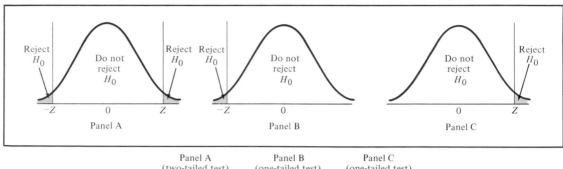

	Panel A (two-tailed test)	Panel B (one-tailed test)	Panel C (one-tailed test)
One-sample procedure:	Median $\neq M_0$	Median $< M_0$	Median $> M_0$
Paired-difference procedure:	$M_D \neq 0$	$M_D < 0$	$M_D > 0$

FIGURE 15.2
Determining the rejection region using the Wilcoxon signed-ranks test.

The *only* difference between the one-sample and the paired-sample tests is in how the ranks are computed. After that step is done, the computational procedures are identical.

15.5.2 One-Sample Test

If the researcher is interested in testing a hypothesis regarding a specified population median M_0 based on data from a single sample, the Wilcoxon (one-sample) signed-ranks test may be used. The test of the null hypothesis may be one-tailed or two-tailed:

Two-Tailed Test	One-Tailed Test	One-Tailed Test
H_0: Median $= M_0$	H_0: Median $\geq M_0$	H_0: Median $\leq M_0$
H_1: Median $\neq M_0$	H_1: Median $< M_0$	H_1: Median $> M_0$

The assumptions necessary for performing the one-sample test are

1. That the observed data $(X_1, X_2, \ldots, X_{n'})$ constitute a random sample of n' independent values from a population with the unknown median.
2. That the underlying random phenomenon of interest be continuous.
3. That the observed data be measured at a higher level than the ordinal scale.
4. That the underlying population be (approximately) symmetrical.[4]

15.5.3 Application

To demonstrate the use of the Wilcoxon (one-sample) signed-ranks test suppose that a manufacturer of batteries claims that the median capacity of a certain type of battery the company produces is at least 140 ampere-hours. An independent consumer protection agency wishes to test the credibility of the manufacturer's claim and measures

---

[4] Such an assumption as symmetry, however, is not as stringent as an assumption of normality. Recall that not all symmetrical distributions are normal, although all normal distributions are symmetrical.

the capacity of a random sample of $n' = 20$ batteries from a recently produced batch. The results are as follows:

137.0   140.0   138.3   139.0   144.3   139.1   141.7   137.3   133.5   138.2

141.1   139.2   136.5   136.5   135.6   138.0   140.9   140.6   136.3   134.1

Since the consumer protection agency is interested in whether or not the manufacturer's claim is being overstated, the test is one-tailed and the following null and alternative hypotheses are established:

$$H_0: \quad \text{Median} \geq 140.0 \text{ ampere-hours}$$

$$H_1: \quad \text{Median} < 140.0 \text{ ampere-hours}$$

To perform the one-sample test the first step is to obtain a set of difference scores D_i between each of the observed values X_i and the hypothesized median M_0—that is,

$$D_i = X_i - M_0$$

where $i = 1, 2, \ldots, n'$.

The remaining steps of the six-step procedure are developed in Table 15.3.

The test statistic W is obtained as the sum of the positive ranks.

$$W = \sum_{i=1}^{n=19} R_i^{(+)} = 16 + 7.5 + 6 + 3.5 + 1 = 34$$

From Table 15.3 we note that only 5 of the 19 nonzero absolute-difference scores exceed the claimed median of at least 140 ampere-hours. Thus to test for significance we compare the observed value of the test statistic, $W = 34$, to the lower-tail critical value presented in Table E.10 for $n = 19$ and for an α level selected at .05. As shown in Table 15.4 (which is a replica of Table E.10), this critical value is 53. Since $W < 53$, the null hypothesis may be rejected at the .05 level of significance. There is

TABLE 15.3   Setting up the Wilcoxon (one-sample) signed-ranks test

Capacity X_i	$D_i = X_i - 140.0$	$\lvert D_i \rvert$	R_i	Sign of D_i
137.0	−3.0	3.0	12.0	−
140.0	.0	.0	. . .	Discard
138.3	−1.7	1.7	7.5	−
139.0	−1.0	1.0	5.0	−
144.3	+4.3	4.3	16.0	+
139.1	−.9	.9	3.5	−
141.7	+1.7	1.7	7.5	+
137.3	−2.7	2.7	11.0	−
133.5	−6.5	6.5	19.0	−
138.2	−1.8	1.8	9.0	−
141.1	+1.1	1.1	6.0	+
139.2	−.8	.8	2.0	−
136.5	−3.5	3.5	13.5	−
136.5	−3.5	3.5	13.5	−
135.6	−4.4	4.4	17.0	−
138.0	−2.0	2.0	10.0	−
140.9	+.9	.9	3.5	+
140.6	+.6	.6	1.0	+
136.3	−3.7	3.7	15.0	−
134.1	−5.9	5.9	18.0	−

TABLE 15.4 Obtaining lower-tail critical value W for Wilcoxon one-sample signed-ranks test where $n = 19$ and $\alpha = .05$

	One-Tailed:	$\alpha = .05$	$\alpha = .025$	$\alpha = .01$	$\alpha = .005$
	Two-Tailed:	$\alpha = .10$	$\alpha = .05$	$\alpha = .02$	$\alpha = .01$
n			(Lower, Upper)		
5		0,15	—,—		
6		2,19	0,21	—,—	—,—
7		3,25	2,26	0,28	—,—
.		.	.	.	.
.		.	.	.	.
.		.	.	.	.
17		41,112	34,119	27,126	23,130
18		47,124	40,131	32,139	27,144
19		53,137	46,144	37,153	32,158
20		60,150	52,158	43,167	37,173

SOURCE: Extracted from Table E.10.

evidence to believe that the manufacturing claim is overstated, and the protection agency should initiate some corrective measure against the manufacturer.

It is interesting to note that the large-sample approximation formula [Equation (15.5)] for the test statistic W yields excellent results for samples as small as 8. With the data above, for a sample of $n = 19$ (nonzero differences),

$$Z = \frac{W - \dfrac{n(n+1)}{4}}{\sqrt{\dfrac{n(n+1)(2n+1)}{24}}} = \frac{34 - 95}{\sqrt{617.5}} = \frac{-61}{24.89} = -2.45$$

Since $Z = 2.45$ is less than the critical Z value of -1.645, the null hypothesis would also be rejected. However, since Table E.10 is available for $n \leq 20$, it is both simpler and more accurate to merely look up the critical value in the table and avoid these computations when possible.

15.5.4 Paired-Sample Test

In the social sciences and in marketing research it is frequently of interest to examine differences between two *related* groups. We discussed this situation in Section 12.3. For example, in test-marketing a product under two different advertising conditions, a sample of test markets can be *matched (paired)* based on the test-market population size and/or other socioeconomic and demographic variables. Moreover, when performing a taste-testing experiment, each subject in the sample could be used as his or her own control so that *repeated measurements* on the same individual are obtained. For such situations, involving either matched (paired) items or repeated measurements of the same item, the Wilcoxon (paired-sample) signed-ranks test may be used when the t test is not appropriate. The test of the null hypothesis that the population median difference M_D is zero may be one-tailed or two-tailed:

	Two-Tailed Test	One-Tailed Test	One-Tailed Test
	H_0: $M_D = 0$ H_1: $M_D \neq 0$	H_0: $M_D \geq 0$ H_1: $M_D < 0$	H_0: $M_D \leq 0$ H_1: $M_D > 0$

The assumptions necessary for performing the paired-sample test are that

1. The observed data constitute a random sample of n' independent items or individuals, each with two measurements (X_{11}, X_{21}), (X_{12}, X_{22}), . . . , $(X_{1n'}, X_{2n'})$, or the observed data constitute a random sample of n' independent pairs of items or individuals so that (X_{1i}, X_{2i}) represents the observed values for each member of the matched pair ($i = 1, 2,$ . . . , n').
2. The underlying variable of interest be continuous.
3. The observed data be measured at a higher level than the ordinal scale—i.e., at the interval or ratio level.
4. The distribution of the population of difference scores between repeated measurements or between matched (paired) items or individuals be (approximately) symmetric.[5]

15.5.5 Application

Influenza and its effects are considered dangerous for adults over 60, and many doctors recommend that their patients in this age group be inoculated with an anti-influenza vaccine each fall. To demonstrate the use of the Wilcoxon (paired-sample) signed-ranks test, suppose that a pharmaceutical manufacturer is producing a new vaccine for a particular strain of influenza. In testing the effects of this vaccine it is desired to study the change in body temperature taken immediately before and one hour after the inoculation. If the vaccine is effective, symptoms of a mild case of influenza—a slightly stuffy nose, sore throat, chills, and a rise in bodily temperature—are noted within one hour after the vaccine is administered.

The results which follow are for a sample of $n' = 10$ male patients (aged 60 and over) who volunteered for the experiment.

	Volunteer									
	a	b	c	d	e	f	g	h	i	j
Temperature before (°F)	98.8	98.6	97.5	98.0	98.7	98.4	98.7	98.6	98.3	98.6
Temperature after (°F)	99.8	98.8	98.4	99.9	99.4	98.4	98.6	101.2	99.0	99.1

The question that must be answered is whether or not this new vaccine is effective. That is, for males aged 60 and over, is there any evidence of a significant increase in the body temperature one hour after the vaccination?

---

[5] See footnote 4 on page 522.

The following null and alternative hypotheses are established:

$$H_0: \quad M_D \leq 0$$
$$H_1: \quad M_D > 0$$

and the test is one-tailed.

To perform the paired-sample test, the first step of the six-step procedure is to obtain a set of difference scores D_i between each of the n' paired observations:

$$D_i = X_{1i} - X_{2i}$$

where $i = 1, 2, \ldots, n'$.

In our example, we obtain a set of n' difference scores from

$$D_i = X_{\text{after}_i} - X_{\text{before}_i}$$

If the vaccine is effective, bodily temperature is expected to rise, so that the difference scores will tend to be *positive* values (and H_0 will be rejected). On the other hand, if the vaccine is not effective, we can expect some D_i values to be positive, others to be negative, and some to show no change (that is, $D_i = 0$). If this is the case, the difference scores will average near zero (that is, $\overline{D} \cong 0$) and H_0 will not be rejected.

The remaining steps of the six-step procedure are developed in Table 15.5. Notice that these are exactly the same steps as for the one-sample test. From this table we note that volunteer f is discarded from the study (because his difference score is zero) and that eight of the remaining $n = 9$ difference scores have a positive sign. The test statistic W is obtained as the sum of the positive ranks:

$$W = \sum_{i=1}^{n} R_i^{(+)} = 7 + 2 + 6 + 8 + 4.5 + 9 + 4.5 + 3 = 44$$

Since $n = 9$, we use Table E.10 to determine the upper tail critical value for this one-tailed test for an α level selected at .05. The upper tail critical value is 37. Since $W > 37$, the null hypothesis may be rejected at the .05 level of significance. There is evidence to support the contention that bodily temperature significantly increases among males over 60 years of age within one hour of the vaccination.

TABLE 15.5   Setting up the Wilcoxon (paired-sample) signed-ranks test

Volunteer	Temperature (°F) After, X_{1i}	Before, X_{2i}	$D_i = X_{1i} - X_{2i}$	$\lvert D_i \rvert$	R_i	Sign of D_i
a	99.8	98.8	+1.0	1.0	7.0	+
b	98.8	98.6	+0.2	0.2	2.0	+
c	98.4	97.5	+0.9	0.9	6.0	+
d	99.9	98.0	+1.9	1.9	8.0	+
e	99.4	98.7	+0.7	0.7	4.5	+
f	98.4	98.4	0.0	0.0	. . .	Discard
g	98.6	98.7	−0.1	0.1	1.0	−
h	101.2	98.6	+2.6	2.6	9.0	+
i	99.0	98.3	+0.7	0.7	4.5	+
j	99.1	98.6	+0.5	0.5	3.0	+

Problems

- **15.9**   A cigarette manufacturer claims that the tar content of a new brand of cigarettes is 17 milligrams. A random sample of 24 cigarettes is selected and the tar content measured. The results are shown below in milligrams:

  | 16.9 | 16.6 | 17.3 | 17.5 | 17.0 | 17.2 | 16.1 | 16.4 | 17.3 | 15.9 | 17.7 | 18.3 |
  | 15.6 | 16.8 | 17.1 | 17.2 | 16.4 | 18.1 | 17.4 | 16.7 | 16.9 | 16.0 | 16.5 | 17.8 |

  Is there evidence that the median tar content of this new brand is different from 17 milligrams? (Use $\alpha = .01$.)

- **15.10**   An actuary of a particular insurance company wants to examine the records of larceny claims filed by persons insured under a household goods policy. In the past the median claim was for $85. A random sample of 18 claims is taken and the results are as follows:

  | $140 | $92 | $35 | $202 | $80 | $87 | $80 | $100 | $47 |
  | $25 | $160 | $68 | $50 | $65 | $310 | $90 | $75 | $120 |

  Is there evidence that the median claim significantly increased? (Use $\alpha = .05$).

- **15.11**   Using the data from Problem 3.7 on page 43, is there evidence that the median amount owed to the company by individuals purchasing books by mail is different from $20? (Use $\alpha = .05$.)

- **15.12**   Using the data from Problem 11.74 on page 370, determine whether there is evidence that the median travel time of employees is less than 60 minutes. (Use $\alpha = .01$.) Are there any differences between your present results and those obtained using the t test? Discuss.

- **15.13**   Use the data from Problem 3.87 on page 87. Is there evidence that the median calories per pancake exceeds 70? (Use $\alpha = .05$.) Are there any differences between your present results and those obtained using the t test in part (a) of Problem 11.79 on page 371? Discuss.

- **15.14**   Use the data from Problem 3.82 on page 81. Is there evidence that the median cost per pound of edible meat is different from $2.50? (Use $\alpha = .05$.) Are there any differences between your present results and those obtained using the t test in part (b) of Problem 11.80 on page 371? Discuss.

- **15.15**   Use the data from Problem 3.83 on page 82. Is there evidence that the median cost per ounce of salted peanut butter is greater than 15 cents? (Use $\alpha = .01$.) Are there any differences between your present results and those obtained using the t test in part (a) of Problem 11.82 on page 371? Discuss.

- **15.16**   Use the data from Problem 3.86 on page 85. Is there evidence that the median amount of sodium per beef frank is greater than 450 mg? (Use $\alpha = .10$.) Are there any differences between your present results and those obtained using the t test in part (a) of Problem 11.83 on page 371? Discuss.

- **15.17**   Use the data from Problem 3.84 on page 83. Is there evidence that the median price of gas barbecue grills exceeds $300? (Use $\alpha = .05$.) Are there any differences between your present results and those obtained using the t test in part (a) of Problem 11.84 on page 372? Discuss.

- **15.18**   The T & A Blech Tax Preparation Company Inc. claimed that taxpayers would save money by having their firm prepare the individual's tax return. A consumer agency had people who had already prepared their return go to Blech's offices to get their taxes done by Blech's preparers. The taxes each person would pay if they paid what they calculated and if they paid what Blech calculated are presented at the top of page 528:

	Tax-Return Preparer	
Taxpayer	Blech	Self
Jose	1,459	1,910
Marcia	3,250	2,900
Alexis	1,190	1,200
Harry	8,100	7,650
Jean	13,200	15,390
Marc	9,120	9,100
JR	255,970	33,120
Billy	210	140
Richard	1,290	1,320
Ted	130	0
Bruce	5,190	6,123

Is there evidence that the claim is not valid? (Use $\alpha = .05$.)

15.19 The ratings of the television shows of two networks are shown below; the ratings are for shows which compete in the same time slots:

Time slot:	1	2	3	4	5	6	7	8	9
Network A:	14.5	21.4	9.9	12.8	19.2	28.1	14.2	23.6	13.2
Network B:	12.3	21.9	8.8	11.1	18.1	26.4	11.0	20.1	11.5

(The ratings are the percentages of homes with a television which are watching the show.) Decide whether there is evidence of a difference between the networks in these time slots. (Use $\alpha = .05$.)

15.20 Refer to Problem 12.12 on page 385.
   (a) Use the Wilcoxon signed-ranks test to determine (at the .01 level of significance) whether there is evidence that the unknown brand sells for a lower price.
   (b) Are there any differences in your present results from those obtained using the t test? Discuss.

15.21 Refer to Problem 12.13 on page 385.
   (a) Use the Wilcoxon signed-ranks test to determine (at the .01 level of significance) whether there is evidence that the old system uses more processing time.
   (b) Are there any differences in your present results from those obtained using the t test? Discuss.

15.22 Refer to Problem 12.15 on page 386.
   (a) Use the Wilcoxon signed-ranks test to determine (at the .05 level of significance) whether there is evidence that sales are higher for the new package design.
   (b) Are there any differences in your present results from those obtained using the t test? Discuss.

15.23 Refer to Problem 12.16 on page 386.
   (a) At the .05 level of significance, is there evidence of a difference in the median gasoline mileage?
   (b) Are there any differences in your present results from those obtained using the t test? Discuss.

15.24 Refer to Problem 12.17 on page 386.
   (a) At the .05 level of significance, can the research director conclude that there is evidence that the sales campaign has increased the sales of nonsale items?

(b) Are there any differences in your present results from those obtained using the *t* test? Discuss.

15.6 WILCOXON RANK-SUM TEST

In Section 12.2, when the researcher was interested in testing for differences in the means of two independent groups of data, the two-sample *t* test [Equation (12.2)] was selected. To use the two-sample *t* test, however, it is necessary to make a set of stringent assumptions. In particular, it is necessary that the two independent samples be randomly drawn from normal populations having equal variances and that the data be measured on at least an interval scale. However, it is frequently the case in studies of consumer behavior, marketing research, and experimental psychology that only ordinal type data can be obtained. Since the classical two-sample *t* test could not be used in such situations, an appropriate nonparametric technique is needed. On the other hand, even if data possessing the properties of an interval or ratio scale are obtained, the researcher may feel that the assumptions of the *t* test are unrealistic for the set of data. In such a circumstance a very simple but powerful nonparametric procedure known as the **Wilcoxon rank-sum test** may be used. Like the Wilcoxon signed-ranks test of the previous section, the Wilcoxon rank-sum test has proven to be almost as powerful as its classical counterpart under conditions appropriate to the latter and is likely to be more powerful when the assumptions of the *t* test are not met.

15.6.1 Procedure

To perform the Wilcoxon rank-sum test we must replace the observations in the two samples of size n_1 and n_2 with their combined ranks (unless, of course, the obtained data contained the ranks initially). The ranks are assigned in such manner that rank 1 is given to the smallest of the $n = n_1 + n_2$ combined observations, rank 2 is given to the second smallest, and so on until rank n is given to the largest. If several values are tied, we assign each the average of the ranks that would otherwise have been assigned.

For convenience we must establish that whenever the two sample sizes are unequal, we will let n_1 represent the *smaller*-sized sample and n_2 the *larger*-sized sample. The Wilcoxon rank-sum test statistic T_1 is merely the sum of the ranks assigned to the n_1 observations in the smaller sample. (For equal-sized samples, either group may be selected for determining T_1.)

For any integer value n, the sum of the first n consecutive integers may easily be calculated as $n(n + 1)/2$. The test statistic T_1 plus the sum of the ranks assigned to the n_2 items in the second sample, T_2, must therefore be equal to this value; that is,

$$T_1 + T_2 = \frac{n(n + 1)}{2} \qquad (15.6)$$

so that Equation (15.6) can serve as a check on the ranking procedure.

The test of the null hypothesis may be one-tailed or two-tailed:

Two-Tailed Test	One-Tailed Test	One-Tailed Test
H_0: $M_1 = M_2$	H_0: $M_1 \geq M_2$	H_0: $M_1 \leq M_2$
H_1: $M_1 \neq M_2$	H_1: $M_1 < M_2$	H_1: $M_1 > M_2$

where M_1 = population median for the first group, having n_1 sample observations
M_2 = population median for the second group, having n_2 sample observations

When both samples n_1 and n_2 are ≤ 10, Table E.11 may be used to obtain the critical values of the test statistic T_1 for both one- and two-tailed tests at various levels of significance. For a two-tailed test and for a particular level of significance, if the computed value of T_1 equals or exceeds the upper critical value or is less than or equal to the lower critical value, the null hypothesis may be rejected. For one-tailed tests having the alternative H_1: $M_1 > M_2$, the decision rule is to reject the null hypothesis if the observed value of T_1 equals or exceeds the upper critical value, while for one-tailed tests having the alternative H_1: $M_1 < M_2$ the decision rule is to reject the null hypothesis if the observed value of T_1 is less than or equal to the lower critical value.

For large sample sizes the test statistic T_1 is approximately normally distributed. The following large-sample approximation formula may be used for testing the null hypothesis when sample sizes are outside the range of Table E.11.

$$Z = \frac{T_1 - \mu_{T_1}}{\sigma_{T_1}} \tag{15.7}$$

where T_1 is the sum of the ranks assigned to the n_1 observations in the first sample
  μ_{T_1} is the mean value of T_1; $\mu_{T_1} = n_1(n + 1)/2$
  σ_{T_1} is the standard deviation of T_1; $\sigma_{T_1} = \sqrt{n_1 n_2(n + 1)/12}$
 and $n_1 \leq n_2$

That is,

$$Z = \frac{T_1 - \dfrac{n_1(n + 1)}{2}}{\sqrt{\dfrac{n_1 n_2(n + 1)}{12}}} \tag{15.8}$$

Based on the level of significance selected, the null hypothesis may be rejected if the computed Z value falls in the appropriate region of rejection depending on whether a two-tailed or a one-tailed test is used (see Figure 15.3)

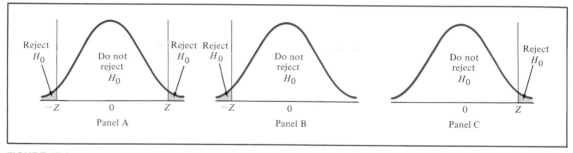

FIGURE 15.3
Determining the rejection region: Panel A, two-tailed test, $M_1 \neq M_2$; Panel B, one-tailed test, $M_1 < M_2$; Panel C, one-tailed test, $M_1 > M_2$.

15.6.2 Application

As an example using the Wilcoxon rank-sum test, suppose that a security analyst wishes to compare the dividend yields of stocks traded on the American Stock Exchange with those traded on the New York Stock Exchange. Random samples of 8 issues from the American Stock Exchange and 10 issues from the New York Stock Exchange are selected; the results are presented in Table 15.6.

If the security analyst is specifically concerned with comparing the median dividend yields rather than just any differences whatsoever in the dividend yields, it must be assumed that the distributions of dividend yields in both populations from which the random samples were drawn are identical, except possibly for differences in location (the medians).

Since the security analyst is not specifying which of the two groups is likely to possess a greater median dividend yield, the test is two-tailed, and the following null and alternative hypotheses are established:

$$H_0: \quad M_1 = M_2 \text{ (the median dividend yields are equal)}$$
$$H_1: \quad M_1 \neq M_2 \text{ (the median dividend yields are different)}$$

TABLE 15.6   Computing dividend yields of selected issues from the American and New York Stock Exchanges

American Stock Exchange ($n_1 = 8$)			New York Stock Exchange ($n_2 = 10$)		
(1) Dividends per Share	*(2)* Price per Share	Dividend Yield (%) *(1) ÷ (2)*	*(1)* Dividends per Share	*(2)* Price per Share	Dividend Yield (%) *(1) ÷ (2)*
$ .60	$11.88	5.1	$ .22	$ 8.00	2.8
.12	8.75	1.4	.60	8.25	7.3
.24	14.75	1.6	2.00	20.38	9.8
.20	3.50	5.7	1.08	15.50	7.0
.80	8.25	9.7	1.59	16.75	9.5
1.30	14.25	9.1	1.00	18.25	5.5
.35	3.12	11.2	.80	14.25	5.6
.32	3.88	8.2	3.60	33.25	10.8
			.80	17.12	4.7
			.50	7.75	6.5

TABLE 15.7 Forming the combined ranks

American Stock Exchange Dividend Yield Rankings ($n_1 = 8$)	New York Stock Exchange Dividend Yield Rankings ($n_2 = 10$)
5	3
1	11
2	16
8	10
15	14
13	6
18	7
12	17
	4
	9

SOURCE: Data are extracted from Table 15.6.

To perform the Wilcoxon rank-sum test we form the combined ranking of the $n_1 = 8$ dividend yields from the issues on the American Stock Exchange with the $n_2 = 10$ dividend yields from the issues on the New York Stock Exchange as in Table 15.7.

We then obtain the test statistic T_1, the sum of the ranks assigned to the smaller sample:

$$T_1 = 5 + 1 + 2 + 8 + 15 + 13 + 18 + 12 = 74$$

As a check on the ranking procedure we also obtain T_2 and use Equation (15.6) to show that the sum of the first $n = 18$ integers in the combined ranking is equal to $T_1 + T_2$:

$$T_1 + T_2 = \frac{n(n + 1)}{2}$$

$$74 + 97 = \frac{18(19)}{2} = 171$$

Had one or both of the samples been greater than 10, the large-sample approximation formula [Equation (15.8)] would have been used for testing. Here, since both n_1 and $n_2 \leq 10$, Table E.11 is employed to obtain the critical values for the T_1 statistic. With $n_1 = 8$ and $n_2 = 10$, it is observed (see Table 15.8, which is a replica of Table E.11)

TABLE 15.8 Obtaining the lower- and upper-tail critical values T_1 for the Wilcoxon rank-sum test where $n_1 = 8$, $n_2 = 10$, and $\alpha = .05$

	α					n_1			
			4	5	6	7	8	9	10
n_2	One-Tailed	Two-Tailed				(Lower, Upper)			
9	.025	.05	14,42	22.53	31,65	40,79	51,93	62,109	
	.01	.02	13,43	20,55	28,68	37,82	47,97	59,112	
	.005	.01	11,45	18,57	26,70	35,84	45,99	56,115	
	.05	.10	17,43	26,54	35,67	45,81	56,96	69,111	82,128
10	.025	.05	15,45	23,57	32,70	42,84	53,99	65,115	78,132
	.01	.02	13,47	21,59	29,73	39,87	49,103	61,119	74,136
	.005	.01	12,48	19,61	27,75	37,89	47,105	58,122	71,139

SOURCE: Extracted from Table E.11.

that at the .05 level of significance the lower and upper critical values for the two-tailed test are, respectively, 53 and 99. Since the observed value of the test statistic $T_1 = 74$ falls between these critical values, the null hypothesis cannot be rejected. It may therefore be said that there is no evidence of any differences between the median dividend yield of stocks traded on the American Stock Exchange and that of stocks traded on the New York Stock Exchange.

Problems

● 15.25 A statistics professor taught two special sections of a basic course in which the 10 students in each section were considered outstanding. She used a "traditional" method of instruction (T) in one section and an "experimental" method (E) in the other. At the end of the semester she ranked the students based on their performance from 1 (worst) to 20 (best).

T	1	2	3	5	9	10	12	13	14	15
E	4	6	7	8	11	16	17	18	19	20

For this instructor was there any evidence of a difference in performance based on the two methods? (Use $\alpha = .05$.)

15.26 A consumer protection agency wishes to perform a "life test" to investigate the differences in the median time to failure of electronic calculators supplied with AAA alkaline batteries operated under normal-temperature versus high-temperature conditions. A total of 16 electronic calculators of the same type are randomly assigned to the two groups so that 8 are examined under normal temperature and 8 are examined under high temperature. All the calculators are started simultaneously, and the following data are the times to failure (in hours):

Normal temperature	9.3	12.7	12.9	14.9	16.1	16.3	17.9	23.1
High temperature	6.0	8.2	8.8	11.9	12.3	14.7	14.8	15.6

Is there evidence that calculators operating under high temperature have a significantly shorter life than those operating under normal temperature? (Use $\alpha = .05$.)

15.27 A New York television station decided to do a story comparing two commuter railroads in the area—the Long Island Rail Road (LIRR) and New Jersey Transit (NJT). The researchers at the station sampled the performance of several scheduled train runs of each railroad. The data on how many minutes early (negative numbers) or late (positive numbers) each train was are presented below:

> LIRR: 5 −1 39 9 12 21 15 52 18 23
> NJT: 8 4 10 4 12 5 4 9 15 33 14 7

(a) Is there evidence that the railroads differ in their median tendencies to be late? (Use $\alpha = .01$.)

✓(b) What conclusions about the lateness of the two railroads can be made?

✗ **15.28** For the data on television show ratings in Problem 15.19 on page 528, pretend that there was no pairing, and analyze the data using the methods of this section. Discuss any differences in the outcomes of the two analyses. (Use $\alpha = .05$.)

15.29 Using the data from Problem 3.64 on page 72, test whether there is evidence that the median rent paid for unfurnished studio apartments in Manhattan is significantly higher than in Brooklyn Heights. (Use $\alpha = .05$.)

15.30 Using the data from Problem 3.81 on page 81, test whether there is evidence of a difference in the median ages of United States versus Western European automobile salespersons. (Use $\alpha = .01$.)

15.31 Using the data from Problem 4.121 on page 142, test whether there is evidence of a difference in the median closing prices of stocks traded on the New York Stock Exchange versus the American Stock Exchange. (Use $\alpha = .01$).

15.32 Using the data from Problem 12.33 on page 399, determine whether there is evidence of a difference in the median processing time between the Accounting Department and the Research Department. (Use $\alpha = .05$.) Are there any differences in your present results from those obtained using the *t* test? Discuss.

15.33 Using the data from Problem 3.85 on page 84, test whether there is evidence of a difference in the median price between dark chocolate and milk chocolate bars. (Use $\alpha = .05$.) Are there any differences in your present results from those using the *t* test (see Problem 12.40, page 401)? Discuss.

15.7 KRUSKAL-WALLIS TEST FOR *c* INDEPENDENT SAMPLES

The **Kruskal-Wallis test for *c* independent samples** (where $c > 2$) may be considered an extension of the Wilcoxon rank-sum test for two independent samples discussed in Section 15.6. Thus the Kruskal-Wallis test enjoys the same power properties relative to the analysis-of-variance *F* test (Chapter 14) as does the Wilcoxon rank-sum test relative to the *t* test for two independent samples (Section 12.2). That is, the Kruskal-Wallis procedure has proven to be almost as powerful as the *F* test under conditions appropriate to the latter and even more powerful than the classical procedure when its assumptions (see Section 14.3) are violated.

15.7.1 Procedure

The Kruskal-Wallis procedure is most often used to test whether *c* independent sample groups have been drawn from populations possessing equal medians. That is,

$$H_0: \quad M_1 = M_2 = M_3 = \ldots = M_c$$

$$H_1: \quad \text{Not all } M_j\text{'s are equal (where } j = 1, 2, \ldots, c).$$

For such situations, it is necessary to assume that

1. The *c* samples are randomly and independently drawn from their respective populations.
2. The underlying random phenomenon of interest is continuous (to avoid ties).
3. The observed data constitute at least an ordinal scale of measurement, both within and between the *c* samples.
4. The *c* populations have the same *spread*.
5. The *c* populations have the same *shape*.

Interestingly, the Kruskal-Wallis procedure still makes less stringent assumptions than does the *F* test. To employ the Kruskal-Wallis procedure the measurements need only be ordinal over all sample groups, and the common population distributions need only be continuous—their common shapes are irrelevant. On the other hand, to utilize the classical *F* test the level of measurement must be more sophisticated, and we must assume that the c samples are coming from underlying normal populations having equal variances.

The Kruskal-Wallis test is very simple to use. To perform the test we must first (if necessary) replace the observations in the c samples with their combined ranks such that rank 1 is given to the smallest of the combined observations and rank n to the largest of the combined observations (where $n = n_1 + n_2 + \cdots + n_c$). If any values are tied, they are assigned the average of the ranks they would otherwise have been assigned if ties had not been present in the data.

The Kruskal-Wallis test statistic H may be computed from

$$H = \left[\frac{12}{n(n + 1)} \sum_{j=1}^{c} \frac{T_j^2}{n_j} \right] - 3(n + 1) \qquad (15.9)$$

where n is the total number of observations over the combined samples, i.e.,
$n = n_1 + n_2 + \cdots + n_c$
n_j is the number of observations in the jth sample; $j = 1, 2, \ldots, c$
T_j^2 is the square of the sum of the ranks assigned to the jth sample

Part of this formula may look familiar: (T_j^2/n_j) is very much like part of the formula for computing the between-groups sum of squares in the analysis of variance. In fact, if we were to compute the between sum of squares using the ranks instead of the raw data, and then multiply by the constant $12/\{n(n + 1)\}$, we would get H. H is, therefore, a measure of discrepancy among the mean ranks of the groups, rather than a measure of discrepancy among the mean scores of the groups as in ANOVA.

As the sample sizes in each group get large (greater than 5), the test statistic H may be approximated by the χ^2 distribution with $c - 1$ degrees of freedom. Thus for any selected level of significance α, the decision rule would be to reject the null hypothesis if the computed value of H exceeds the critical χ^2 value and not to reject the null hypothesis if H is less than or equal to the critical χ^2 value (see Figure 15.4). The critical χ^2 values are given in Table E.4.

15.7.2 Application

Let us look at an application of the Kruskal-Wallis procedure. Suppose the personnel manager of a large insurance company wished to evaluate the effectiveness of four different sales-training programs designed for new employees. Thirty recently hired

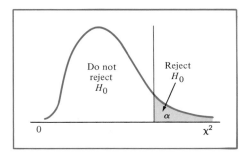

FIGURE 15.4
Determining the rejection region.

TABLE 15.9 Examination results of subjects assigned to four programs

A	B	C	D
66	72	61	63
74	51	60	61
82	59	57	76
75	62	60	84
73	74	81	58
97	64	55	65
87	78	70	69
		71	80

college graduates were randomly assigned to the four programs so that there were seven subjects each in programs A and B and eight subjects each in programs C and D. At the end of the month-long training period a standard exam was administered to the 30 subjects; the scores are given in Table 15.9.

The null hypothesis to be tested is that the median scores for the four groups are equal; the alternative is that at least two of the groups possess median scores which differ. Thus, substituting 1, 2, 3, 4 for A, B, C, D we have

$$H_0: \quad M_1 = M_2 = M_3 = M_4$$

$$H_1: \quad \text{Not all } M_j\text{'s are equal (where } j = 1, 2, 3, 4).$$

Converting the 30 test scores to ranks, we obtain Table 15.10.

We note that in the combined ranking, the second subject in program B had the lowest score, 51, and received a rank of 1; the sixth subject in program C had the second lowest score, 55, and received the rank of 2; and so on. We also note, for example, that in program C the second and fourth subjects both had scores of 60 and received a rank of 6.5, since they were tied for the sixth and seventh lowest scores.

After all the ranks are assigned, we then obtain the sum of the ranks for each group:

Rank sums: $\quad T_1 = 161.5, \quad T_2 = 90.5, \quad T_3 = 85.5, \quad T_4 = 127.5$

As a check on the rankings we have

$$T_1 + T_2 + T_3 + T_4 = \frac{n(n + 1)}{2}$$

TABLE 15.10 Converting data to ranks

A	B	C	D
14.0	18.0	8.5	11.0
20.5	1.0	6.5	8.5
27.0	5.0	3.0	23.0
22.0	10.0	6.5	28.0
19.0	20.5	26.0	4.0
30.0	12.0	2.0	13.0
29.0	24.0	16.0	15.0
		17.0	25.0

SOURCE: Data are taken from Table 15.9.

$$161.5 + 90.5 + 85.5 + 127.5 = \frac{(30)(31)}{2}$$

$$465 = 465$$

Now Equation (15.9) is employed to test the null hypothesis:

$$H = \left[\frac{12}{n(n+1)}\sum_{j=1}^{c}\frac{T_j^2}{n_j}\right] - 3(n+1)$$

$$= \left\{\frac{12}{(30)(31)}\left[\frac{(161.5)^2}{7} + \frac{(90.5)^2}{7} + \frac{(85.5)^2}{8} + \frac{(127.5)^2}{8}\right]\right\} - 3(31)$$

$$= \left(\frac{12}{930}\right)[7,841.89] - 93$$

$$= 101.19 - 93 = 8.19$$

Using Table E.4, the critical χ^2 value having $c - 1 = 3$ degrees of freedom and corresponding to a .05 level of significance is 7.815 (see Table 15.11, which is a replica of Table E.4). Since the computed value of the test statistic H exceeds this critical value, we may reject the null hypothesis and conclude that not all the training programs were the same with respect to median test performance.[6] (That is, if the null hypothesis were really true, the probability of obtaining such a result or one even more extreme is less than .05.)

TABLE 15.11 Obtaining the approximate χ^2 critical value for the Kruskal-Wallis test at the .05 level of significance with 3 degrees of freedom

Degrees of Freedom	Upper-Tail Area									
	.995	.99	.975	.95	.90	.75	.25	.10	.05	.025
1	—	—	0.001	0.004	0.016	0.102	1.323	2.706	3.841	5.024
2	0.010	0.020	0.051	0.103	0.211	0.575	2.773	4.605	5.991	7.378
3	0.072	0.115	0.216	0.352	0.584	1.213	4.100	6.251	7.815	9.348
4	0.207	0.297	0.484	0.711	1.064	1.923	5.385	7.779	9.488	11.143
5	0.412	0.554	0.831	1.145	1.610	2.675	6.626	9.236	11.071	12.833
6	0.676	0.872	1.237	1.635	2.204	3.455	7.841	10.645	12.592	14.449
7	0.989	1.239	1.690	2.167	2.833	4.255	9.037	12.017	14.067	16.013
8	1.344	1.646	2.180	2.733	3.490	5.071	10.219	13.362	15.507	17.535
9	1.735	2.088	2.700	3.325	4.168	5.899	11.389	14.684	16.919	19.023
10	2.156	2.558	3.247	3.940	4.865	6.737	12.549	15.987	18.307	20.483
11	2.603	3.053	3.816	4.575	5.578	7.584	13.701	17.275	19.675	21.920
12	3.074	3.571	4.404	5.226	6.304	8.438	14.845	18.549	21.026	23.337
13	3.565	4.107	5.009	5.892	7.042	9.299	15.984	19.812	22.362	24.736

SOURCE: Extracted from Table E.4.

---

[6] Once the null hypothesis is rejected, nonparametric a posteriori multiple-comparison procedures analogous to the Tukey T method presented in Section 14.5 are available for determining which group or groups differ from which others. These procedures, however, are beyond the scope of this text. (See Reference 4.)

Problems

- **15.34** An industrial psychologist desires to test whether the reaction times of assembly-line workers are equivalent under three different learning methods. From a group of 25 new employees, nine are randomly assigned to method A, eight to method B, and eight to method C. The data below present the rankings from 1 (fastest) to 25 (slowest) of the reaction times to complete a task given by the industrial psychologist after the learning period.

	Method	
A	B	C
2	1	5
3	6	7
4	8	11
9	15	12
10	16	13
14	17	18
19	21	24
20	22	25
23		

Is there evidence of a difference in the reaction times for these learning methods? (Use $\alpha = .01$.)

15.35 The percentage increase in the price of stocks of companies in four different industry groups over a ten-year period were

Industry	Percentage Increase in Stock Prices						
A	213	1040	321	112	421		
B	155	240	121	290	174	226	
C	490	381	402	648			
D	280	178	310	249	281	353	399

Is there evidence that the prices of stocks in the industries have increased at different rates? (Use $\alpha = .05$.)

15.36 Use the Kruskal-Wallis test to solve Problem 14.4 (performance scores) on page 460. (Use $\alpha = .01$) Are there any differences in your present results from those of the analysis-of-variance *F* test? Discuss.

15.37 Use the Kruskal-Wallis test to solve Problem 14.5 (toy prices) on page 461. (Use $\alpha = .01$) Are there any differences in your present results from those of the analysis-of-variance *F* test? Discuss.

15.38 Use the Kruskal-Wallis test to solve Problem 14.6 (time) on page 461. (Use $\alpha = .05$) What differences are there in the assumptions for your selected nonparametric test and those for the analysis-of-variance *F* test? Discuss.

15.39 Use the Kruskal-Wallis test to solve Problem 14.7 (profitability) on page 461. (Use $\alpha = .01$) What differences are there in the assumptions for your selected nonparametric test and those for the analysis-of-variance *F* test? Discuss.

15.8 FRIEDMAN RANK TEST FOR c RELATED SAMPLES

It often happens that, although the randomized complete block design (see Section 14.6) is deemed appropriate for a particular experiment, the researcher may prefer some nonparametric alternative to the classical two-way F test for analyzing the data. If the data collected are only in rank form within each block or if normality cannot be assumed, a simple but fairly powerful nonparametric approach called the **Friedman test** can be utilized. The Friedman test is essentially a two-way analysis of variance (ANOVA) on ranked data.

15.8.1 Procedure

The Friedman rank test is primarily used to test whether c sample groups have been drawn from populations having equal medians. To develop the test we first replace the data by their ranks on a block-to-block basis. That is, in each of the n independent blocks we replace the c observations by their corresponding ranks such that the rank 1 is given to the smallest observation in the block and the rank c to the largest. If any values in a block are tied, they are assigned the average of the ranks that they would otherwise have been given. Thus, R_{ij} is the rank (from 1 to c) associated with the jth group (where $j = 1, 2, \ldots, c$) in the ith block (where $i = 1, 2, \ldots, n$).

Under the null hypothesis of no differences in the c groups, each ranking within a block is equally likely. Thus there are $c!$ possible ways of ranking within a particular block and $(c!)^n$ possible arrangements of ranks over all n independent blocks. Moreover, if the null hypothesis is true, there would be no real differences among the average ranks for each group (taken over all n blocks).

From the above the following test statistic F_R may be derived:

$$F_R = \frac{12}{nc(c+1)} \sum_{j=1}^{c} R_j^2 - 3n(c+1) \qquad \text{(15.10)}$$

where R_j^2 is the square of the rank total for group j; $(j = 1, 2, \ldots, c)$
n is the number of independent blocks
c is the number of groups

As the number of blocks in the experiment gets large (greater than 5), the test statistic F_R may be approximated by the χ^2 distribution with $c - 1$ degrees of freedom. Thus for any selected level of significance α, the decision rule would be to reject the null hypothesis if the computed value of F_R exceeds the upper-tail critical value for the χ^2 distribution having $c - 1$ degrees of freedom as shown in Figure 15.5 on page 540. The critical χ^2 values are presented in Table E.4.

15.8.2 Application

As an application of the Friedman rank test, suppose that a taste-testing experiment has been designed so that four brands of Colombian coffee are to be rated by nine experts. To avoid any *carryover* effects, the tasting sequence for the four brews is

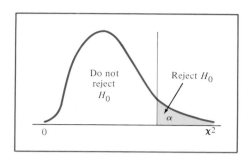

FIGURE 15.5
Determining the rejection region.

randomly determined for each of the nine expert tasters until a rating on a 7-point scale (1 = extremely unpleasing, 7 = extremely pleasing) is given for each of the following four characteristics: taste, aroma, richness, and acidity.

Table 15.12 displays the *summated* ratings—accumulated over all four characteristics. The data in each block (that is, for each expert) are converted to ranks, as shown in Table 15.13.

The null hypothesis to be tested is that the median summated rating scores for the four brands are equal; the alternative is that at least two of the brands have median summated rating scores which differ. Thus

TABLE 15.12 Summated ratings of four brands of Colombian coffee

	Brand			
Expert	A	B	C	D
1	24	26	25	22
2	27	27	26	24
3	19	22	20	16
4	24	27	25	23
5	22	25	22	21
6	26	27	24	24
7	27	26	22	23
8	25	27	24	21
9	22	23	20	19

TABLE 15.13 Converting the data to ranks

	Brand			
Expert	A	B	C	D
1	2.0	4.0	3.0	1.0
2	3.5	3.5	2.0	1.0
3	2.0	4.0	3.0	1.0
4	2.0	4.0	3.0	1.0
5	2.5	4.0	2.5	1.0
6	3.0	4.0	1.5	1.5
7	4.0	3.0	1.0	2.0
8	3.0	4.0	2.0	1.0
9	3.0	4.0	2.0	1.0
Rank totals:	25.0	34.5	20.0	10.5

SOURCE: Table 15.12.

$$H_0: \quad M_1 = M_2 = M_3 = M_4$$

H_1: Not all M_j's are equal (where $j = 1, 2, 3, 4$).

As shown in Table 15.13, the sum of the ranks for each group are obtained

Rank sums: $\quad R_{.1} = 25.0 \quad R_{.2} = 34.5 \quad R_{.3} = 20.0 \quad R_{.4} = 10.5$

As a check on the rankings we have

$$R_{.1} + R_{.2} + R_{.3} + R_{.4} = \frac{nc(c + 1)}{2} \qquad \textbf{(15.11)}$$

For our data,

$$25.0 + 34.5 + 20.0 + 10.5 = \frac{9(4)(5)}{2}$$

$$90 = 90$$

Using Equation (15.10), we obtain

$$
\begin{aligned}
F_R &= \frac{12}{nc(c + 1)} \sum_{j=1}^{c} R_{.j}^2 - 3n(c + 1) \\
&= \left\{ \frac{12}{9(4)(5)} [25.0^2 + 34.5^2 + 20.0^2 + 10.5^2] \right\} - 3(9)(5) \\
&= \left(\frac{12}{180} \right)(2{,}325.5) - 135 \\
&= 155.03 - 135 = 20.03
\end{aligned}
$$

Since the computed F_R statistic exceeds 7.815, upper-tail critical value under the χ^2 distribution having $c - 1 = 3$ degrees of freedom (see Table E.4), the null hypothesis may be rejected at the $\alpha = .05$ level. We may conclude that there are significant differences (perceived by the experts) with respect to the quality of the four brands of coffee.[7]

Problems

● **15.40** The President's Council on Physical Fitness and Sports asked a panel of medical experts to rank five diverse forms of exercise with respect to their special contributions to physical fitness and overall well-being. The rankings (1 = least beneficial, 5 = most beneficial) are displayed at the top of page 542 for each of nine equally important characteristics of fitness and well-being. Is there evidence of a difference in the "perceived benefit" ratings of the five forms of exercise? (Use $\alpha = .05$.)
[*Hint*: Treat the nine characteristics as blocks.]

---

[7] Once the null hypothesis is rejected, a posteriori multiple-comparison techniques may be used to determine which group or groups differ significantly from which others. (See Reference 4.)

	Exercise				
Characteristic	*Bicycling*	*Calisthenics*	*Jogging*	*Swimming*	*Tennis*
Balance	5.0	2.0	4.0	1.0	3.0
Digestion	2.5	1.0	4.5	4.5	2.5
Flexibility	1.5	5.0	1.5	4.0	3.0
Muscular definition	4.0	5.0	2.5	2.5	1.0
Muscular endurance	3.0	1.0	4.5	4.5	2.0
Muscular strength	3.5	3.5	5.0	1.5	1.5
Sleep	3.0	2.0	4.5	4.5	1.0
Stamina	3.0	1.0	4.5	4.5	2.0
Weight control	4.0	1.0	5.0	2.0	3.0

15.41 Use an appropriate nonparametric technique to solve Problem 14.27 (wheat yield) on page 477. (Use $\alpha = .05$.) Are there any differences in your present results from those of the analysis-of-variance F test? Discuss.

15.42 Use an appropriate nonparametric technique to solve Problem 14.28 (base running methods) on page 477. (Use $\alpha = .05$.) Are there any differences in your present results from those of the analysis-of-variance F test? Discuss.

15.43 Use an appropriate nonparametric technique to solve part (a) of Problem 14.53 (recall ability) on page 504. (Use $\alpha = .05$.) Are there any differences in your present results from those of the analysis-of-variance F test? Discuss.

15.9 SPEARMAN'S RANK-CORRELATION PROCEDURE

Among the various statistical methods based on ranks, the **Spearman rank-correlation** procedure was the earliest to be developed. For more than three-quarters of a century this procedure has continued to be widely used for studying the association between two variables—primarily because of its simplicity and its power. That is, we shall observe that the Spearman rank-correlation procedure is simple to use and easy to apply. Moreover, it has proven to be almost as powerful as its classical counterpart—the **Pearson (product-moment) correlation** method (described in Chapter 16)—under conditions favorable to the latter and even more powerful than the parametric method when its assumptions are violated.

15.9.1 Procedure

Let us suppose that we obtain a sample of n subjects, each measured on two variables, X and Y. To investigate the degree of possible association between X and Y we must focus on how the values of X ''relate'' to the values of Y. A *direct* or *positive association* is said to exist if subjects possessing high values of X also possess high values of Y while subjects having low values of X also contain low values of Y. At the other extreme, an *indirect* or *negative association* is said to exist if subjects possessing high values of X also contain low values of Y, and vice versa.

To study the amount or degree of association between the two variables X and Y, we may compute r_S, the **Spearman coefficient of rank correlation,** provided that in our data we have attained at least an ordinal level of measurement for each variable.

The Spearman coefficient of rank correlation may be obtained using the following five steps:

1. Replace the n values of X by their ranks R_x by giving the rank of 1 to the smallest X and the rank of n to the largest. If two or more X values are tied, they are each assigned

the average rank of the rank positions they otherwise would have been assigned individually had ties not occurred.

2. Replace the n values of Y by their ranks R_Y as in step 1.

3. For each of the n subjects, obtain a set of **rank difference scores**

$$d_{R_i} = R_{X_i} - R_{Y_i}$$

where $i = 1, 2, \ldots, n$.

4. Obtain $\sum_{i=1}^{n} d_{R_i}^2$, the sum of each of the squared rank difference scores.

5. The Spearman coefficient of rank correlation, r_S, is given by the following formula:

$$r_s = 1 - \frac{6 \sum_{i=1}^{n} d_{R_i}^2}{n(n^2 - 1)} \tag{15.12}$$

The rank correlation coefficient is a relative measure which varies from -1 (a perfect negative relationship between X and Y) to $+1$ (a perfect positive relationship between X and Y). The closer r_S is to these extremes, the *stronger* is the relationship between X and Y. The closer r_S is to 0, the *weaker* is the relationship between X and Y. If X and Y are independent of each other, there is no relationship and thus the coefficient of rank correlation is 0.

From Equation (15.12) a perfect positive association between X and Y would be observed in our sample if the ranks assigned to the X values were to "completely match" the ranks assigned to the Y values. In such a case each $d_{R_i} = R_{X_i} - R_{Y_i}$ would be 0, so that $\sum_{i=1}^{n} d_{R_i}^2$ would also be 0 and r_s would be equal $+1$. At the other extreme, a perfect negative association would be observed in our sample if the ranks assigned to the X values were in "complete disagreement" with those assigned to the Y values. That is, if R_X is 1, then R_Y is n; if R_X is 2, then R_Y is $n - 1$; if R_X is 3, then R_Y is $n - 2$; and so on. In such a case, where the R_X and R_Y ranks for each subject were the reverse of each other, $\sum_{i=1}^{n} d_{R_i}^2$ would achieve its maximum possible value, $n(n^2 - 1)/3$. Using Equation (15.12), r_s would equal -1. These results are noted below:

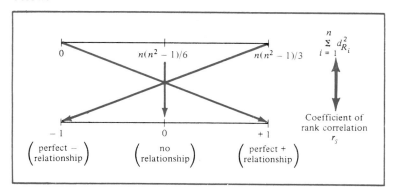

To evaluate whether or not a significant relationship between X and Y exists, we may test the null hypothesis of *independence* against the alternative that there is a *relationship*. The test may either be one-tailed or two-tailed. For a two-tailed test, the null and alternative hypotheses are

H_0:   The two variables X and Y are independent ($\rho_S = 0$).

H_1:   There is either a positive or negative association between X and Y ($\rho_S \neq 0$).

On the other hand, if the researcher is specifically interested in a particular type of relationship, a one-tailed test would be needed. For a test of positive correlation between X and Y the hypotheses are

H_0:   There is no positive association between X and Y ($\rho_S \leq 0$).

H_1:   There is a positive association between X and Y ($\rho_S > 0$).

while for a test of negative correlation between X and Y the hypotheses are

H_0:   There is no negative association between X and Y ($\rho_S \geq 0$).

H_1:   There is a negative association between X and Y ($\rho_S < 0$).

To test the null hypothesis the following large-sample approximation formula may be used (provided that the sample size n is not very small):

$$Z = r_s \sqrt{n-1} \qquad\qquad \textbf{(15.13)}$$

and, based on the level of significance selected, the null hypothesis may be rejected if the computed Z value falls in the appropriate region of rejection, depending on whether a two-tailed or one-tailed test is employed (see Figure 15.6).

15.9.2 Application

As one application of the Spearman rank-correlation procedure, let us suppose that a financial analyst was interested in determining whether or not there is evidence of a significant positive association between sales revenues (in millions of dollars) and the number of employees (in thousands of workers) for companies in the aerospace industry.

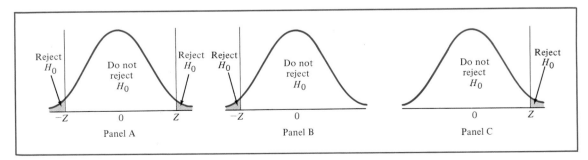

FIGURE 15.6
Determining the rejection region: Panel A, two-tailed test; Panel B, one-tailed test, negative association; Panel C, one-tailed test, positive association.

TABLE 15.14   Determining Spearman's coefficient of rank correlation

Company	Sales, X (in millions)	Rank, R_x	Employees, Y (in thousands)	Rank, R_y	d_R	d_R^2
Allied Signal	11,597	5	115,300	4	1	1
Boeing	15,355	2	136,100	2	0	0
Colt Industries	1,642	13	16,600	13	0	0
Fairchild Industries	897	15	4,877	17	−2	4
General Dynamics	9,344	7	105,300	6	1	1
Grumman	3,325	11	33,700	11	0	0
Kaman	707	16	6,473	16	0	0
Lockheed	11,370	6	99,300	7	−1	1
Martin Marietta	5,165	10	70,000	8	2	4
McDonnell Douglas	13,146	3	112,400	5	−2	4
Northrop	6,053	8	48,200	10	−2	4
Parker Hannifin	1,877	12	27,608	12	0	0
Rockwell International	12,123	4	116,148	3	1	1
Rohr Industries	663	17	10,300	15	2	4
Sundstrand	1,365	14	14,200	14	0	0
Textron	5,661	9	61,000	9	0	0
United Technologies	17,170	1	190,000	1	0	0
						24

SOURCE: "The Fortune Directory of the 500 Largest U.S. Industrial Corporations," *Fortune Magazine*, vol. 113 (April 5, 1988), p. D37.

Using the directory compiled by *Fortune* (based on sales revenues), the analyst takes a random sample of 17 companies from the aerospace industry, with the results recorded in Table 15.14. Since the direction of the alternative has been specified (that is, the analyst is interested in determining whether there is evidence of a significant positive association), the test is one-tailed. If the analyst does not wish to make the more rigorous assumptions of the classical correlation procedure (to be described in Chapter 16), the following null and alternative hypotheses may be stated:

H_0:   There is no positive association.

H_1:   There is a positive association (one-tailed).

The five-step procedure to obtain the Spearman coefficient of rank correlation r_s is developed in Table 15.14. From this we observe that $\sum_{i=1}^{n=17} d_{R_i}^2 = 24$ and, using Equation (15.12),

$$
\begin{aligned}
r_s &= 1 - \frac{6 \sum_{i=1}^{n} d_{R_i}^2}{n(n^2 - 1)} \\
&= 1 - \frac{6(24)}{17(288)} \\
&= 1 - .029 \\
&= .971
\end{aligned}
$$

To test the null hypothesis we have

$$
\begin{aligned}
Z &= r_s \sqrt{n - 1} \\
&= (.971)\sqrt{16} \\
&= 3.88
\end{aligned}
$$

Using a level of significance of .05, the one-tailed test has a critical Z value of $+1.645$. Since $Z = 3.88$ exceeds this critical value of $+1.645$, the null hypothesis may be rejected, and the financial analyst may conclude that there is evidence of a positive correlation between sales revenues and number of employees per firm in the aerospace industry.

Problems

✗ **15.44** A chemical reaction is timed at several different temperatures; the results are

Temperature (°F)	100	150	200	250	300	350
Time needed (seconds)	843	211	164	69	22	17

Without doing any calculations, tell what the Spearman correlation is between the variables.

● **15.45** The director of personnel of a large company would like to determine whether two personnel interviewers have been evaluating job applicants in a similar manner. It is important for the company to have consistency (high correlation) between its interviewers, so that job placement is independent of the interviewer. Two interviewers were asked to rank a set of 14 applicants in order of preference, with rank 1 given to the most preferred applicant and rank 14 to the least preferred applicant. The results were as follows:

	Interviewer	
Applicant	X	Y
Al	3	2
Ben	5	4
Clare	1	3
Dave	2	1
Ethel	7	5
Fred	4	7
Gil	6	8
Harry	8	6
Ilana	11	11
Judy	12	12
Ken	10	9
Lou	9	10
Milt	13	13
Nat	14	14

Measure the rank correlation between the two interviewers. Is there evidence of a significantly *positive* relationship? (Use $\alpha = .05$.)

15.46 Given the following set of "social status striving scores" (X) and "conformity ratings" (Y) for a sample of $n = 12$ male college seniors majoring in business at a large university (see top of page 547):

Student	1	2	3	4	5	6	7	8	9	10	11	12
Social status (*X*)	49	65	38	50	72	83	79	95	71	66	68	62
Conformity (*Y*)	13	16	15	21	22	25	24	23	19	18	20	17

Using $\alpha = .05$, is there evidence of a significance *positive* association between social status striving and conformity among male business majors?

15.47 A market researcher would like to determine the factors that are most important in predicting whether an individual will purchase a subcompact car. Seven factors are to be ranked: luxuriousness, reliability, ease of parking, ease of driving, purchase price, economy of maintenance, and gas mileage. The following composite ranking (with rank 1 given to the most important factor) is obtained from a group of domestic subcompact owners and from a group of foreign subcompact owners:

Factor	Domestic	Foreign
Luxuriousness	7	7
Reliability	6	3
Ease of parking	5	5
Ease of driving	4	4
Purchase price	3	6
Economy of maintenance	1	1
Gas mileage	2	2

Measure the rank correlation between domestic and foreign car owners. Is there evidence of a significant relationship? (Use $\alpha = .05$).

15.48 The Quantitative Methods Society of a business school wanted to study the preferences of statistics majors and computer majors for different academic subjects. A composite ranking for each of the two majors is presented below (rank 1 = most preferred).

Subject	Statistics Majors	Computer Majors
Accounting	6	8
Mathematics	2	5
Statistics	1	3
Computers	3	1
Psychology	8	6
Finance	5	7
Marketing	9	10
Management	10	4
Law	11	11
English	13	12
Political science	12	13
History	14	14
Biology	7	9
Economics	4	2

Measure the correlation in the preferences of statistics and computer majors. Is there evidence of a significantly *positive* relationship? (Use $\alpha = .05$.)

15.49 In a study of attitudes toward travel, the managers of two branches of a travel agency (one located in New York, one in Los Angeles) were asked to rank 10 countries according to their "desirability" for vacation travel (rank 1 = most desirable). The results are displayed at the top of page 548.

Country	New York	Los Angeles
Australia	10	2
USSR	9	4
China	6	1
France	3	6
West Germany	4	7
England	2	5
Japan	7	3
Denmark	1	9
Israel	5	8
India	8	10

Measure the correlation in ''desirability'' between the managers of the two branches. Is there evidence of a significant relationship? (Use $\alpha = .05$.)

15.50   An educational psychologist wishes to study whether or not a significant positive relationship exists between verbal facility (as measured by the Peabody test) and geometrical intuition (as measured by the Raven test). A sample of 15 ten-year-old girls yields the following results:

Subject	Verbal, X	Geometrical, Y
Alice	67	24
Clare	84	37
Dora	77	21
Ethel	85	38
Kathy	89	40
Kiki	72	32
Laurie	93	36
Lila	65	26
Lola	78	25
Lori	88	39
Merri	80	31
Nina	79	27
Patsy	75	29
Sandi	81	22
Terri	82	30

At the .05 level of significance, is there evidence that a positive relationship between the two variables exists?

15.10 NONPARAMETRIC PROCEDURES, COMPUTERS, AND THE REAL ESTATE SURVEY

We may recall from Section 15.3 that in using nonparametric procedures the numerical manipulations sometimes become laborious as the sample sizes get larger. Fortunately, various packaged computer programs can be utilized to ease the computational complexity. If the SPSS[X] package (see References 6 and 11) were being accessed, the NPAR TESTS and NONPAR CORR commands could be utilized for a variety of nonparametric procedures including all those discussed in this chapter. Moreover, if the SAS package (see References 7 and 9) were being accessed, the NPAR1WAY procedure could be utilized for the Wilcoxon rank-sum test and the Kruskal-Wallis test, while the CORR procedure could be utilized to compute Spearman's rank-cor-

```
Mann-Whitney Confidence Interval and Test

 nobasemt   N = 106    MEDIAN =       37.000
 basement   N = 127    MEDIAN =       32.000
 POINT ESTIMATE FOR ETA1-ETA2 IS       3.9998
 95.0  PCT C.I. FOR ETA1-ETA2 IS (     3.00,      5.00)
 W =   16010.0
 TEST OF ETA1 = ETA2  VS.  ETA1 N.E. ETA2 IS SIGNIFICANT AT   0.0000
```

FIGURE 15.7
Partial output obtained from Minitab MANN-WHITNEY-WILCOXON command to
perform Wilcoxon rank-sum test.

relation coefficient. Furthermore, if the Minitab package (see References 5 and 8) were being accessed, the RUNS, WTEST, MANN-WHITNEY-WILCOXON, KRUSKAL-WALLIS, TWOWAYAOV (on the ranks), and CORR (on the ranks) commands could be used for the respective nonparametric procedures addressed in Sections 15.4 through 15.9 of this chapter. To demonstrate how various computer packages may be utilized for analyses involving nonparametric methods, we return to our real estate survey. Some applications are presented in Figures 15.7 through 15.9.

Figure 15.7 represents partial Minitab output obtained from a comparison of ages of houses with and without basements. We note that the Wilcoxon rank-sum test statistic is 16,010.0 with a p value of .0000. Since .0000 < .05, there is evidence of

```
ANALYSIS FOR VARIABLE LOTSIZE CLASSIFIED BY VARIABLE  LOCATE
AVERAGE SCORES WERE USED FOR TIES


ANALYSIS OF VARIANCE

LEVEL               N       MEAN           AMONG MS   WITHIN MS
                                           29.1697    8.08799
EAST MEADOW         74      7.24
FARMINGDALE         60      8.32           F VALUE    PROB>F
LEVITTOWN           99      7.13             3.61     0.0287


WILCOXON SCORES (RANK SUMS)

                            SUM OF    EXPECTED    STD DEV      MEAN
LEVEL               N       SCORES    UNDER HO    UNDER HO    SCORE

EAST MEADOW         74     8674.00    8658.00     462.79     117.22
FARMINGDALE         60     8778.50    7020.00     434.68     146.31
LEVITTOWN           99     9808.50   11583.00     491.40      99.08


KRUSKAL-WALLIS TEST (CHI-SQUARE APPROXIMATION)
CHISQ=   19.65     DF=  2     PROB > CHISQ=0.0001
```

FIGURE 15.8
Partial output obtained from SAS PROC NPAR1WAY to perform Kruskal-Wallis
test.

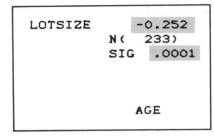

FIGURE 15.9
Partial output obtained from SPSS^X NONPAR CORR command to obtain Spearman's rank-correlation statistics.

a difference in the medians. Houses in those communities without basements are significantly older than houses with basements.

Figure 15.8 presents partial SAS output comparing lot size based on geographic location. We note that the Kruskal-Wallis statistic is 19.65 with 2 degrees of freedom and has a *p* value of .0001. Since *p* < .05, there is evidence of a difference in the median lot size based on geographic location. Median lot size in Levittown appears to be smaller than in the other communities.

Figure 15.9 represents partial SPSS^X output obtained from using the NONPAR CORR command to investigate whether or not a relationship exists between the lot size and the age of the houses. We note that the Spearman rank-correlation coefficient is −0.252 and the *p* value is .0001. Since .0001 < .05, we may conclude that the correlation is significant and there is evidence of a negative relationship between lot size and age.

15.11 SUMMARY

In this chapter we have provided but a brief introduction to the very broad subject of nonparametric methods of hypothesis testing. The need for such methods arose for the following three reasons:

1. The measurements attained on behavioral science data were often only qualitative (nominal scale) or in ranks (ordinal scale), and procedures were required to make appropriate tests.
2. The researcher often had no knowledge of the form of the population from which the sample data were drawn and believed that the assumptions for the classical procedure were unrealistic for a given endeavor.
3. The researcher was not always interested in testing hypotheses about particular population parameters and required methods for treating problems regarding randomness, trend, symmetry, and goodness of fit.

For these reasons a set of nonparametric procedures was devised. Six such nonparametric methods were presented here. Such methods may be broadly described as those which make fewer and less stringent assumptions than do their parametric counterparts, are generally easier to apply and quicker to compute than their classical counterparts, and yield a more general set of conclusions than do their parametric counterparts. In addition, nonparametric methods are applicable to very small sample sizes (from which exact probabilities may be computed) and also lend themselves readily to preliminary or pilot studies from which more detailed and sophisticated analyses can later be undertaken. Finally, for those situations in which the researcher has a choice, it has been found that some of the nonparametric techniques are either as powerful or almost as powerful in their ability to detect statistically significant differences (when they do exist) as their classical counterparts under conditions appropriate to the latter, and they may actually be much more powerful than the classical procedures when their assumptions do not hold.

On the other hand, especially with larger sample sizes, when the conditions of the classical methods are met it would be considered wasteful of information to merely convert sophisticated levels of measurement into ranks (ordinal scale) or into categorized groupings (nominal scale) just so that a nonparametric procedure could be employed. Thus, in such circumstances as these, the classical procedures should be utilized.

For a more detailed study of nonparametric methods and their applications, the reader may wish to consult References 1 through 4 and 10.

Supplementary Problems

15.51   What three general conditions define nonparametric tests?

15.52   What are the advantages and disadvantages of nonparametric tests?

15.53   Give an example of a sequence of results from tossing a coin which (a) has a clear pattern (and is therefore unlikely to be random) *but* (b) is not detected by the Wald-Wolfowitz test as being nonrandom. This demonstrates that the Wald-Wolfowitz test is sensitive to certain departures from randomness but not to others.

15.54   Suppose we walk down a street on a Sunday and notice which stores are open (Y) and which are not (N). The results are

YYYNNYNNNYNNYYYYYNYNYYY

Is there evidence that the tendency of stores to be open or closed is not random? (Use $\alpha = .05$.)

15.55   Sampling with replacement from a deck of cards, record the sequence of red (r = diamonds or hearts) and black (b = clubs or spades) cards for a sample of 20 selections. Be sure to shuffle the deck thoroughly before each selection is made. Can the resulting sequence be considered random? (Use $\alpha = .05$.)

15.56   A psychologist wishes to construct a true-false examination containing 30 questions. She desires the sequence of correct responses to be random so that nobody taking the examination can merely guess at the answers by following a particular pattern. The following sequence is obtained:

FTTTFTFFFTTFTFFFTTTTFFTTTFFTFF

Can this sequence be considered random? (Use $\alpha = .05$.)

15.57   Use the data from Problem 4.138 on page 150. With respect to fluctuations above and below the median, is there evidence of some pattern in the gross sales receipts for Ethel's over the 29-day period? (Use $\alpha = .05$.)

15.58   Use the data from the **Student Project** in Problem 4.139 on page 150.

(a) Is there evidence of a trend in the closing prices of the stock over the 20 days? (Use $\alpha = .025$.)

(b) Is there evidence of some pattern in the changes in closing prices of the stock over the 20 days? (Use $\alpha = .05$.)

15.59   A machine being used for packaging seedless golden raisins has been set so that on the average

15 ounces of raisins will be packaged per box. The quality control engineer wishes to test the machine setting and selects a sample of 30 consecutive raisin packages filled during the production process. Their weights are recorded below in row sequence (from left to right):

15.2	15.3	15.1	15.7	15.3	15.0	15.1	14.3	14.6	14.5
15.0	15.2	15.4	15.6	15.7	15.4	15.3	14.9	14.8	14.6
14.3	14.4	15.5	15.4	15.2	15.5	15.6	15.1	15.3	15.1

Do these data indicate a lack of randomness in the sequence of underfills and overfills, or can the production process be considered as "in control"? (Use $\alpha = .05$.)

15.60 In Problem 15.59 a machine used for packaging seedless golden raisins has been set so that on the average 15 ounces of raisins will be packaged per box. Using the data of Problem 15.59, the weights from a sample of 30 raisin packages are obtained. Is there evidence that the (median) weight per box is different from 15 ounces? (Use $\alpha = .05$.)

[*Note*: To test this claim we must assume that the observed sequence is random. Therefore, let us assume that the data were collected in column sequence (from top to bottom) rather than in row sequence (from left to right).]

● **15.61** A task on an assembly line has, in the past, required 30 seconds to complete. An industrial engineer has developed a new method for performing the task which she believes will speed up the process. A random sample of 15 trials is obtained for a worker trained under the new method as shown below:

27.2	31.1	29.0	26.7	28.1	27.3	29.6	30.5
30.0	30.2	25.9	31.3	28.8	27.4	27.0	

Is there evidence to suggest that the median time under the new method is significantly less than 30 seconds? What would you recommend to the management? (Use $\alpha = .05$.)

● **15.62** A federal agency tested the relative effectiveness of two brands of disinfectants designed for use in hospitals to prevent infections. Nine hospitals used the two disinfectants; each used one disinfectant in one ward, the other in another (similar) ward. The percentage of patients getting an infection during the six-month test period was as follows:

	Hospital								
Disinfectant	1	2	3	4	5	6	7	8	9
Brand X	12	5	3	9	14	4	2	5	6
Brand Y	10	6	6	10	14	5	8	4	9

Is there any evidence of a difference between brand X and brand Y in the median percentage of patients getting an infection? (Use $\alpha = .10$.)

● **15.63** A women's organization wishes to know whether starting salaries of men and women entering business differ. A random sample of 10 male seniors with B+ grade-point indexes and a random sample of 9 female seniors with B+ grade-point indexes are selected, and each person is permitted a total of three interviews with companies in marketing, public relations, or advertising. The following data are the reported "best offers" made to the individuals:

Male		Female	
$21,000	$22,200	$21,200	$17,000
$18,800	$21,500	$17,250	$19,750
$24,000	$17,500	$20,100	$18,250
$20,000	$19,500	$16,000	$19,000
$21,000	$22,000	$18,500	

Is there any evidence that women are not as well paid as men when their qualifications are similar? (Use $\alpha = .05$.)

15.64 An industrial psychologist wishes to study the effects of motivation on sales in a particular firm. Of 24 new sales persons being trained, 12 are to be paid at an hourly rate and 12 on a commission basis. The 24 persons were randomly assigned to the two groups. The following data represent the sales volume achieved during the first month on the job.

Hourly Rate		Commission	
256	212	224	261
239	216	254	228
222	236	273	234
207	219	285	225
228	225	237	232
241	230	277	245

Is there any evidence that wage incentives (through commission) yield significantly greater sales volume? (Use $\alpha = .01$.)

15.65 To examine the effects of the work environment on attitude toward work, an industrial psychologist randomly assigned a group of 18 recently hired sales trainees to three "home rooms"—six trainees per room. Each room was identical except for wall color. One was light green, another was light blue, and the third was deep red.

During the week-long training program, the trainees stayed mainly in their respective home rooms. At the end of the program, an attitude scale was used to measure each trainee's attitude toward work. The following data were obtained:

Room Color		
Light Green	Light Blue	Deep Red
46	59	34
51	54	29
48	47	43
42	55	40
58	49	45
50	44	34

A low score indicates a poor attitude, a high score a good attitude. Using a level of significance of .05, is there evidence that work environment has an effect on attitude toward work?

● **15.66** A batch of 20 AAA carbon-zinc batteries are randomly assigned to four groups (so that there are five batteries per group.) Each group of batteries is then subjected to a particular temperature level—low, normal, high, and very high. The batteries are simultaneously tested under these temperatures, and the times to failure (in hours) are recorded below:

Low	Normal	High	Very High
8.0	7.6	6.0	5.1
8.1	8.2	6.3	5.6
9.2	9.8	7.1	5.9
9.4	10.9	7.7	6.7
11.7	12.3	8.9	7.8

Do the four temperature levels yield the same median battery lives? (Use $\alpha = .05$.)

15.67 The following data represent the percentage of fat content for samples of eight 1-pound packages of pork sausages for each of five brands tested by a consumer's interest group:

		Brand of Pork Sausages		
A	B	C	D	E
26	25	31	33	21
19	23	20	36	29
31	28	25	30	20
28	18	31	35	30
22	27	23	32	28
20	26	30	39	26
27	20	22	34	25
24	24	29	37	23

Using a level of significance of .05, is there evidence of a difference in the percentage of fat content for these five brands?

15.68 Use the data from Problem 3.86 on page 85. Is there evidence of a difference in the median amount of sodium among beef, "meat," and poultry frankfurters? (Use $\alpha = .05$.) Compare your present results to those obtained from the ANOVA F test in Problem 14.49 on page 502. Discuss.

• **15.69** In November 1983 the American Telephone & Telegraph Company released its report on the divestiture planned for January 1, 1984. The data below represent the 1983 earnings-per-share estimates made in November 1983 by three brokerage firms for the regional telephone companies and for the remainder of AT&T. Was there evidence of a difference among the three brokerage firms with respect to median earnings-per-share estimates? (Use $\alpha = .05$.)

	1983 Earnings-Per-Share Estimates		
Company	Bernstein & Co.	Solomon Bros.	Sutro & Co.
Ameritech	9.82	8.76	9.70
Bell Atlantic	10.85	9.12	9.50
Bell South	16.02	12.17	12.95
Nynex	9.77	8.54	10.00
Pacific Telesis	10.00	6.43	6.50
Southwestern Bell	10.74	8.15	8.50
US West	10.48	8.12	8.70
Remaining AT&T	1.49	1.32	1.06

15.70 The following data at the top of page 555 represent the overall length and luggage capacity for a random sample of 10 types of small cars.

Car	Length (in.)	Capacity (cu. ft.)
Acura Integra	171	14
Chevrolet Spectrum	160	11
Ford Escort	167	16
Honda Civic	163	12
Hyundai Excel	168	13
Mazda 323	170	15
Nissan Sentra	169	12
Subaru Justy	139	9
Toyota Tercel	157	10
Volkswagen Jetta	172	17

SOURCE: Copyright © by Consumers Union of United States, Inc., Mount Vernon, NY 10553. Excerpted by permission from *Consumer Reports*, April 1987, p. 255.

Measure the rank correlation between overall length and luggage capacity for these 10 small cars. Is there evidence of a significant relationship? (Use $\alpha = .05$.)

15.71   The following data represent the leverage and the return on equity for 12 bank holding companies in a recent year:

Leverage	Return on Equity
32.2	−16.3
21.2	16.3
22.4	13.2
21.9	14.2
25.8	13.8
20.4	13.3
19.3	13.0
16.1	19.0
25.3	12.1
19.7	9.9
22.4	15.5
21.6	14.8

Measure the rank correlation between the leverage and the return on equity for these 12 bank holding companies. Is there evidence of a significant relationship? (Use $\alpha = .05$.)

15.72   You are having cocktails with a client. Someone has suggested to her that nonparametric techniques might be helpful for her current project. As her statistical confidant, she asks you: "What are nonparametric techniques and when or why may they be helpful?" You sip your drink and you reply. . . .

Database Exercises

The following problems refer to the sample data obtained from the questionnaire of Figure 2.5 on page 15 and presented in Figure 2.10 on pages 24–29. They should be solved with the aid of an available computer package.

15.73   At the .01 level of significance, is there evidence that the median appraised value (question 1) exceeds $200,000?

☐ **15.74** At the .05 level of significance, is there evidence that the median age (question 6) is different from 40 years?

☐ **15.75** At the .10 level of significance, is there evidence that the median annual taxes paid (question 7) is under $3,000?

☐ **15.76** At the .05 level of significance, is there evidence that the median appraised value (question 1) is higher in houses with a fireplace (question 16) than in those without it?

☐ **15.77** At the .05 level of significance, is there evidence that the median appraised value (question 1) is higher in houses with a basement (question 18) than in those without it?

☐ **15.78** At the .05 level of significance, is there evidence that the median appraised value (question 1) is higher in houses with a modern kitchen (question 19) than in those without it?

☐ **15.79** At the .05 level of significance, is there evidence that the median appraised value (question 1) is higher in houses with modern bathrooms (question 20) than in those without them?

☐ **15.80** At the .05 level of significance, is there evidence that the median annual taxes paid (question 7) is higher in houses with a fireplace (question 18) than in those without it?

☐ **15.81** At the .05 level of significance, is there evidence that the median annual taxes paid (question 7) is higher in houses with a basement (question 18) than in those without it?

☐ **15.82** At the .05 level of significance, is there evidence that the median annual taxes paid (question 7) is higher in houses with a modern kitchen (question 19) than in those without it?

☐ **15.83** At the .05 level of significance, is there evidence that the median annual taxes paid (question 7) is higher in houses with modern bathrooms (question 20) than in those without them?

☐ **15.84** At the .05 level of significance, is there evidence of a difference between the median appraised values (question 1) based on geographic location (question 9)?

☐ **15.85** At the .05 level of significance, is there evidence of a difference between the median appraised values (question 1) based on architectural style (question 10)?

☐ **15.86** At the .05 level of significance, is there evidence of a difference between the median number of rooms in the house (question 5) based on geographic location (question 9)?

☐ **15.87** At the .05 level of significance, is there evidence of a difference between the median number of rooms in the house (question 5) based on architectural style (question 10)?

☐ **15.88** At the .05 level of significance, is there evidence of a difference between the median age of houses (question 6) based on geographic location (question 9)?

☐ **15.89** At the .05 level of significance, is there evidence of a difference between the median age of houses (question 6) based on architectural style (question 10)?

☐ **15.90** At the .05 level of significance, is there evidence of a correlation between appraised value (question 1) and lot size (question 2)?

☐ **15.91** At the .05 level of significance, is there evidence of a correlation between appraised value (question 1) and number of rooms (question 5)?

☐ **15.92** At the .05 level of significance, is there evidence of a correlation between appraised value (question 1) and age (question 6)?

☐ **15.93** At the .05 level of significance, is there evidence of a correlation between appraised value (question 1) and annual taxes paid (question 7)?

☐ **15.94** At the .05 level of significance, is there evidence of a correlation between lot size (question 2) and number of rooms (question 5)?

☐ **15.95** At the .05 level of significance, is there evidence of a correlation between lot size (question 2) and annual taxes paid (question 7)?

☐ **15.96** At the .05 level of significance, is there evidence of a correlation between number of rooms (question 5) and age (question 6)?

☐ **15.97** At the .05 level of significance, is there evidence of a correlation between number of rooms (question 5) and annual taxes paid (question 7)?

□ **15.98**   At the .05 level of significance, is there evidence of a correlation between age (question 6) and annual taxes paid (question 7)?

□ **15.99**   At the .01 level of significance, is there evidence that the median appraised value (question 1) exceeds $200,000 in East Meadow (question 9, code 1)?

□ **15.100**   At the .05 level of significance, is there evidence that the median age (question 6) is different from 40 years in Farmingdale (question 9, code 2)?

□ **15.101**   At the .10 level of significance, is there evidence that the median annual taxes paid (question 7) is under $3,000 in Levittown (question 9, code 3)?

□ **15.102**   At the .05 level of significance, is there evidence that in East Meadow (question 9, code 1) the median appraised value (question 1) is higher in houses with a modern kitchen (question 19) than in those without it?

□ **15.103**   At the .05 level of significance, is there evidence that in Farmingdale (question 9, code 2) the median age (question 6) is greater in houses with a fireplace (question 16) than in those without it?

□ **15.104**   At the .05 level of significance, is there evidence that in Levittown (question 9, code 3) the median annual taxes paid (question 7) is higher in houses with a basement (question 18) than in those without it?

Case Study F

In Case Study E (see page 508) the research director of a large advertising agency conducted a study of the effect of advertising on product perception. Five different types of advertising copy were evaluated in the marketing of a ball-point pen. A detailed report was to be prepared. Included as an appendix was to be a discussion of the statistical analysis used.

At a meeting with the agency's consulting statistician it was suggested that an appropriate nonparametric method be considered for analyzing the data displayed in Table 14.15. Many researchers would argue, the statistician observed, that the "product characteristic scales" used do not truly satisfy the criteria of *interval* or *ratio* scaling and, therefore, that nonparametric methods are more appropriate. Since the classical analysis has already been completed, you decide to perform a nonparametric analysis of the data to see whether or not there are any differences in the conclusions. You also decide to extend your research effort to include the following (using nonparametric methods):

1. A determination of whether there is evidence of a difference in the combined ratings of *adult* versus *high-school student* respondents subjected to advertisement E (which attempted to correctly state the pen's characteristics).

2. A determination of whether there is evidence that the median combined ratings for the *high-school student* respondents subjected to advertisement E exceeds 11.

The aforementioned combined ratings data for a sample of 8 *high-school student* respondents are:

14   13   15   9   11   13   12   16

References

1. BRADLEY, J. V., *Distribution-Free Statistical Tests* (Englewood Cliffs, N.J.: Prentice-Hall, 1968).
2. CONOVER, W. J., *Practical Nonparametric Statistics*, 2d ed. (New York: Wiley, 1980).
3. DANIEL, W. W., *Applied Nonparametric Statistics* (Boston: Houghton Mifflin, 1978).
4. HOLLANDER, M., AND D. A. WOLFE, *Nonparametric Statistical Methods* (New York: Wiley, 1973).
5. LEVINE, D. M., M. L. BERENSON, AND D. F. STEPHAN, *Using Minitab with Basic Business Statistics*, 2d ed. (Englewood Cliffs, N.J.: Prentice-Hall, 1986).
6. LEVINE, D. M., M. L. BERENSON, AND D. F. STEPHAN, *Using the SPSS Batch System with Basic Business Statistics* (Englewood Clifs, N.J.: Prentice-Hall, 1983).
7. LEVINE, D. M., M. L. BERENSON, AND D. F. STEPHAN, *Using SAS with Basic Business Statistics* (Englewood Cliffs, N.J.: Prentice-Hall, 1983).
8. RYAN, T. A., B. L. JOINER, AND B. F. RYAN, *Minitab Student Handbook*, 2d ed. (North Scituate, Mass.: Duxbury Press, 1985).
9. *SAS User's Guide: Statistics*, 1982 ed. (Cary, N.C.: SAS Institute, 1982).
10. SIEGEL, S., *Nonparametric Statistics for the Behavioral Sciences* (New York: McGraw-Hill, 1956).
11. *SPSS^X User's Guide* (New York: McGraw-Hill, 1983).

16

The Simple Linear Regression Model and Correlation

16.1 INTRODUCTION

In previous chapters we have focused primarily upon a single quantitative response variable such as the age of a house. We examined various measures of statistical description (see Chapter 3) and applied different techniques of statistical inference to make estimates and draw conclusions about our quantitative response variable (see Chapters 10 to 15). In this and the following chapter we will concern ourselves with problems involving two or more quantitative variables as a means of viewing the relationships that exist between them. Two techniques will be discussed: regression and correlation.

Regression analysis is used for the purpose of prediction. Our goal in regression analysis is the development of a statistical model that can be used to predict the values of a dependent or response variable based upon the values of at least one explanatory or independent variable. In this chapter we shall focus on a "simple" regression model—one which would utilize a single quantitative independent variable X to predict the quantitative dependent variable Y—while in Chapter 17 we shall develop a multiple regression model—one which could utilize several explanatory variables ($X_1, X_2, \ldots, X_p$) to predict a quantitative dependent variable Y.[1]

Referring to our real estate survey, for example, the president and the statistician would like to develop a statistical model that can assist in predicting the appraised value of houses in a particular community. Although in practice several variables would actually be considered, it would seem that the number of rooms might be a useful predictor of appraised value. For this model, the dependent or response variable Y (the one to be predicted) would be appraised value and the variable X used to obtain the prediction (the explanatory or independent variable) is the number of rooms.

Correlation analysis, in contrast to regression, *is used to measure the strength*

---

[1] In Section 17.12 we shall investigate multiple regression problems in which at least one of the independent variables is *qualitative* (see dummy variable models).

of the association between quantitative variables. For example, in the real estate survey we could determine the correlation between the lot size and taxes paid on those houses that have an in-ground swimming pool. In this instance, the objective is not to use one variable to predict another, but rather to measure the strength of the association or "covariation" that exists between two quantitative variables.

16.2 THE SCATTER DIAGRAM

Methods of regression and correlation analysis will be applied to two problems in this chapter. In the first, suppose that the dean of a college of business would like to predict the performance of students (as measured by their graduate grade point index) in a Masters of Business Administration (MBA) program. A random sample of 20 students who have taken at least 30 credits in the program was selected in order to develop a statistical model to predict their grade point index. In developing such a model, many explanatory variables could be considered. These include such quantitative variables as score on the Graduate Management Aptitude Test (GMAT) and undergraduate grade point index, as well as such qualitative variables as graduate major and whether or not the individual is enrolled as a full-time graduate student.

TABLE 16.1 GMAT score and grade point index for a random sample of 20 graduate students

Student	GMAT Score	GPI	Student	GMAT Score	GPI
Todd K.	688	3.72	Kim B.	567	3.07
Tamara K.	647	3.44	Jason L.	542	2.86
Jessica G.	652	3.21	Matthew B.	551	2.91
Seth K.	608	3.29	Walter M.	573	2.79
Lauren E.	680	3.91	Timothy D.	536	3.00
Ryan R.	617	3.28	Douglas L.	639	3.55
Charles Y.	557	3.02	Shelby K.	619	3.47
Jason S.	599	3.13	Neil G.	694	3.60
Michael W.	616	3.45	Jordana E.	718	3.88
Brooke G.	594	3.33	Sharyn L.	759	3.76

For pedagogical purposes, we shall begin our discussion with a simple regression model in which only one quantitative explanatory variable is used to predict the values of a dependent variable. Thus we will develop a model to predict grade point index (the dependent variable Y) based upon the GMAT score (the explanatory or independent variable X). The results for a sample of 20 students are summarized in Table 16.1. Such data, however, can be presented in a form that is more visually interpretable.

In Chapter 4, when information concerning the PE ratios of companies in the natural resources industry was studied, various graphs (such as histograms, polygons, and ogives) were developed for data presentation. In a regression analysis involving one independent and one dependent variable the individual values are plotted on a two-dimensional graph called a **scatter diagram.** Each value is plotted at its particular X and Y coordinates. The scatter diagram for the data in Table 16.1 is shown in Figure 16.1.

A brief examination of Figure 16.1 indicates a clearly increasing relationship between GMAT score (X) and grade point index (Y). As GMAT score increases, grade point index also increases. The exact mathematical form of the model expressing the

dependent

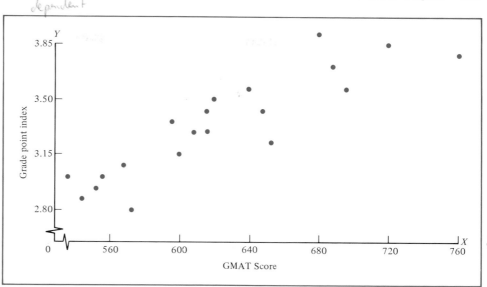

independent

FIGURE 16.1
Scatter diagram of grade point index versus GMAT score.

Source: Data are taken from Table 16.1.

relationship as well as methods for estimating the grade point index for a given GMAT score will be examined in subsequent sections of this chapter.

Problems

● **16.1** The marketing manager of a large supermarket chain would like to determine the effect of shelf space on the sales of pet food. A random sample of 12 equal-sized stores was selected and the results are presented below:

Pet food sales problem

Store	Shelf Space, X (feet)	Weekly Sales, Y (hundreds of dollars)
1	5	1.6
2	5	2.2
3	5	1.4
4	10	1.9
5	10	2.4
6	10	2.6
7	15	2.3
8	15	2.7
9	15	2.8
10	20	2.6
11	20	2.9
12	20	3.1

Set up a scatter diagram.

16.2 A personnel manager for a large corporation feels that there may be a relationship between absenteeism and age and would like to use the age of a worker to develop a model to predict the number of days absent during a calendar year. A random sample of 10 workers was selected with the results presented below:

Absenteeism problem

Worker	Age, X (in years)	Days Absent, Y
1	27	15
2	61	6
3	37	10
4	23	18
5	46	9
6	58	7
7	29	14
8	36	11
9	64	5
10	40	8

Set up a scatter diagram

● 16.3 A company manufacturing parts would like to develop a model to estimate the number of worker-hours required for production runs of varying lot size. A random sample of 14 production runs (2 each for lot size 20, 30, 40, 50, 60, 70, and 80) was selected with the results shown below:

Production worker-hours problem

Lot Size	Worker-Hours
20	50
20	55
30	73
30	67
40	87
40	95
50	108
50	112
60	128
60	135
70	148
70	160
80	170
80	162

Set up a scatter diagram.

16.4 An agronomist would like to determine the effect of a natural organic fertilizer on the yield of tomatoes. Five differing amounts of fertilizer are to be used on 10 equivalent plots of land: 0, 10, 20, 30, and 40 pounds per 100 square feet. The levels of fertilizer are randomly assigned to the plots of land with the results given at the top of page 563:

Tomato yield problem

Plot	Amount of Fertilizer, X (in pounds per 100 square feet)	Yield, Y (in pounds)
1	0	6
2	0	8
3	10	11
4	10	14
5	20	18
6	20	23
7	30	25
8	30	28
9	40	30
10	40	34

Set up a scatter diagram.

16.5 The manager of an educational computer facility would like to develop a model to predict the number of service calls per annum for interactive terminals based upon the age of the terminal. A sample of 10 terminals was selected. The data follows:

Terminal maintenance problem

Terminal	Number of Service Calls	Age (years)
1	3	1
2	4	1
3	3	2
4	5	2
5	5	3
6	7	3
7	8	4
8	10	4
9	10	5
10	12	5

Set up a scatter diagram.

16.3 TYPES OF REGRESSION MODELS

In the scatter diagram plotted in Figure 16.1 a rough idea of the type of relationship that exists between the variables can be observed. The nature of the relationship can take many forms, ranging from simple mathematical functions to extremely complicated ones. The simplest relationship consists of a straight-line or **linear** relationship. An example of this relationship is shown in Figure 16.2 on page 564.

The straight-line (linear) model can be represented as

$$Y_i = \beta_0 + \beta_1 X_i + \epsilon_i \tag{16.1}$$

where β_0 = true Y intercept for the population
β_1 = true slope for the population
ϵ_i = random error in Y for observation i

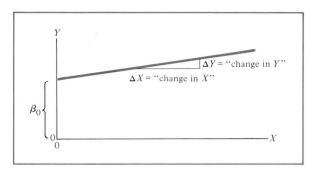

FIGURE 16.2
A positive straight-line relationship.

In this model, the slope of the line β_1 represents the unit change in Y per unit change in X; that is, it represents the amount that Y changes (either positively or negatively) for a particular unit change in X. On the other hand, the Y intercept β_0 represents a constant factor that is included in the equation. It represents the value of Y when X equals zero. Moreover, the last component of the model, ϵ_i, represents the random error in Y for each observation i that occurs. This term is included because the statistical model is only an approximation of the exact relationship between the two variables.

The proper mathematical model to be selected is influenced by the distribution of the X and Y values on the scatter diagram. This can be seen readily from an examination of panels A through F in Figure 16.3. Clearly, from panel A in Figure 16.3 it can be seen that the values of Y are generally increasing linearly as X increases. This panel is similar to Figure 16.1, which illustrates the relationship between GMAT score and GPI. Panel B is an example of a negative linear relationship. As X increases, we note that the values of Y are decreasing. An example of this type of relationship might be the price of a particular product and the amount of sales. Panel C shows a set of data in which there is very little or no relationship between X and Y. High and low values of Y appear at each value of X. The data in panel D show a positive curvilinear relationship between X and Y. The values of Y are increasing as X increases, but this increase tapers off beyond certain values of X. An example of this positive curvilinear relationship might be the age and maintenance cost of a machine. As a machine gets older, the maintenance cost may rise rapidly at first, but then level off beyond a certain number of years. Panel E shows a parabolic or U-shaped relationship between X and Y. As X increases, at first Y decreases; but as X continues to increase, Y not only stops decreasing but actually increases above its minimum value. An example of this type of relationship could be the number of errors per hour at a task and the number of hours worked. The number of errors per hour would decrease as the individual becomes more proficient at the task, but then would increase beyond a certain point due to factors such as fatigue and boredom. Finally, panel F indicates an exponential or negative curvilinear relationship between X and Y. In this case Y decreases very rapidly as X first increases, but then decreases much less rapidly as X increases further. An example of this exponential relationship could be the resale value of a particular type of automobile and its age. In the first year the resale value drops drastically from its original price; however, the resale value then decreases much less rapidly in subsequent years.

In this section we have briefly examined a variety of different models that could be used to represent the relationship between two variables. Although scatter diagrams can be extremely helpful in determining the mathematical form of the relationship, more sophisticated statistical procedures are available to determine the most appropriate

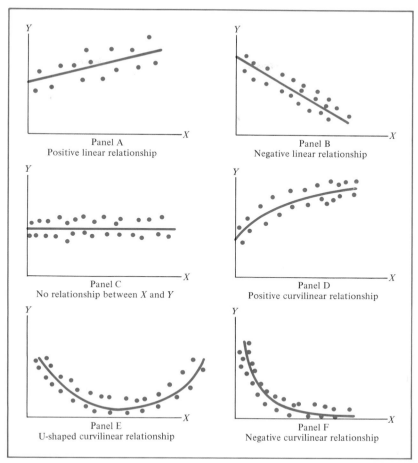

FIGURE 16.3
Examples of types of relationships found in scatter diagrams.

model for a set of variables. In subsequent sections of this chapter we shall primarily focus on building statistical models for fitting *linear* relationships between variables.

16.4 DETERMINING THE SIMPLE LINEAR REGRESSION EQUATION

If we refer to the scatter diagram in Figure 16.1, we notice that grade point index appears to increase linearly as a function of GMAT score. The question that must be addressed in regression analysis involves the determination of the particular straight-line model that is the best fit to these data.

16.4.1 The Least-Squares Method

In the preceding section we hypothesized a statistical model to represent the relationship between two variables in a population. However, as noted in Table 16.1, we have obtained data from only a random sample of the population. If certain assumptions are valid (see Section 16.11), the sample Y intercept (b_0) and the sample slope (b_1) can be used as estimates of the respective population parameters (β_0 and β_1). Thus the sample regression equation representing the straight-line regression model would be

$$\hat{Y}_i = b_0 + b_1 X_i \qquad (16.1a)$$

where $\hat{Y}_i$ is the predicted value of Y for observation i and X_i is the value of X for observation i.

This equation requires the determination of two coefficients—b_0 (the Y intercept) and b_1 (the slope) in order to predict values of Y. Once b_0 and b_1 are obtained, the straight line is known and can be plotted on the scatter diagram. We could then make a visual comparison of how well our particular statistical model (a straight line) fits the original data. That is, we can see whether the original data lie close to the fitted line or deviate greatly from the fitted line.

Simple linear regression analysis is concerned with finding the straight line that ''fits'' the data best. The best fit means that we wish to find the straight line for which the differences between the actual values (Y_i) and the values that would be predicted from the fitted line of regression ($\hat{Y}_i$) are as small as possible. Because these differences will be both positive and negative for different observations, mathematically we minimize

$$\sum_{i=1}^{n} (Y_i - \hat{Y}_i)^2$$

where Y_i = actual value of Y for observation i
$\hat{Y}_i$ = predicted value of Y for observation i

Since $\hat{Y}_i = b_0 + b_1 X_i$, we are minimizing

$$\sum_{i=1}^{n} [Y_i - (b_0 + b_1 X_i)]^2$$

which has two unknowns, b_0 and b_1. A mathematical technique which determines the values of b_0 and b_1 that best fit the observed data is known as the **least-squares method.** Any values for b_0 and b_1 other than those determined by the least-squares method would result in a greater sum of squared differences between the actual value of Y and the predicted value of Y.

In using the least-squares method, we obtain the following two equations, called the normal equations:

$$\text{I.} \qquad \sum_{i=1}^{n} Y_i = nb_0 + b_1 \sum_{i=1}^{n} X_i \qquad (16.2a)$$

$$\text{II.} \qquad \sum_{i=1}^{n} X_i Y_i = b_0 \sum_{i=1}^{n} X_i + b_1 \sum_{i=1}^{n} X_i^2 \qquad (16.2b)$$

Since there are two equations with two unknowns, we can solve these equations simultaneously for b_1 and b_0 as follows:

$$b_1 = \frac{n \sum_{i=1}^{n} X_i Y_i - \left(\sum_{i=1}^{n} X_i \right) \left(\sum_{i=1}^{n} Y_i \right)}{n \sum_{i=1}^{n} X_i^2 - \left(\sum_{i=1}^{n} X_i \right)^2} \qquad \text{(16.3)}$$

$$b_0 = \bar{Y} - b_1 \bar{X} \qquad \text{(16.4)}$$

where

$$\bar{Y} = \frac{\sum_{i=1}^{n} Y_i}{n} \quad \text{and} \quad \bar{X} = \frac{\sum_{i=1}^{n} X_i}{n}$$

or, alternatively,

$$b_1 = \frac{\sum_{i=1}^{n} X_i Y_i - \dfrac{\left(\sum_{i=1}^{n} X_i \right) \left(\sum_{i=1}^{n} Y_i \right)}{n}}{\sum_{i=1}^{n} X_i^2 - \dfrac{\left(\sum_{i=1}^{n} X_i \right)^2}{n}} \qquad \text{(16.3a)}$$

and

$$b_0 = \frac{\sum_{i=1}^{n} Y_i}{n} - b_1 \frac{\sum_{i=1}^{n} X_i}{n} \qquad \text{(16.4a)}$$

Examining Equations (16.3) and (16.4), we see that there are five quantities that must be calculated in order to determine b_0 and b_1. These are n, the sample size; $\sum_{i=1}^{n} X_i$, the sum of the X values; $\sum_{i=1}^{n} Y_i$, the sum of the Y values; $\sum_{i=1}^{n} X_i^2$, the sum of the squared X values, and $\sum_{i=1}^{n} X_i Y_i$, the sum of the cross product of X and Y. For our data in Table 16.1 the GMAT score was used to predict the grade point index in the MBA program. The computation of the various sums needed (including $\sum_{i=1}^{n} Y_i^2$, the sum of the squared Y values which will be used in Section 16.5) are presented in Table 16.2.

Using Equations (16.3) and (16.4), we can compute the values of b_0 and b_1:

$$b_1 = \frac{n \sum_{i=1}^{n} X_i Y_i - \left(\sum_{i=1}^{n} X_i \right) \left(\sum_{i=1}^{n} Y_i \right)}{n \sum_{i=1}^{n} X_i^2 - \left(\sum_{i=1}^{n} X_i \right)^2}$$

$$= \frac{20(41,876.42) - (12,456)(66.67)}{20(7,830,354) - (12,456)^2}$$

$$= \frac{7,086.88}{1,455,144} = +.00487$$

$$b_0 = \overline{Y} - b_1 \overline{X}$$

$$\overline{Y} = \frac{\sum_{i=1}^{n} Y_i}{n} = \frac{66.67}{20} = 3.3335$$

$$\overline{X} = \frac{\sum_{i=1}^{n} X_i}{n} = \frac{12,456}{20} = 622.8$$

$$b_0 = 3.3335 - (.00487)(622.8) = +0.30$$

Thus the equation for the "best" straight line for these data is

$$\hat{Y}_i = 0.30 + .00487 \, X_i$$

The slope b_1 was computed as $+.00487$. This means that for each increase of one unit in X, the value of Y increases by .00487 units. That is, for each increase of one point in GMAT score, the fitted model predicts that the grade point index will increase by .00487 points (or we can say that for each 100-point increase in GMAT score, grade point index will increase by .487 points). Hence the slope can be viewed as representing the portion of the grade point index that varies according to GMAT score.

The Y intercept b_0 was computed to be $+.30$. The Y intercept represents the value of Y when X equals zero. Since the GMAT score can never be zero, this Y intercept can be viewed as expressing the portion of the grade point index that varies with factors other than GMAT score.

The regression model that has been fit to the data can now be used to predict the grade point index. For example, let us say that we would like to use the fitted model to predict the average grade point index for students with a GMAT score of

TABLE 16.2   Computations for the student performance problem

Student	GMAT Score X	GPI Y	X^2	Y^2	XY
Todd K.	688	3.72	473,344	13.8384	2,559.36
Tamara K.	647	3.44	418,609	11.8336	2,225.68
Jessica G.	652	3.21	425,104	10.3041	2,092.92
Seth K.	608	3.29	369,664	10.8241	2,000.32
Lauren E.	680	3.91	462,400	15.2881	2,658.80
Ryan R.	617	3.28	380,689	10.7584	2,023.76
Charles Y.	557	3.02	310,249	9.1204	1,682.14
Jason S.	599	3.13	358,801	9.7969	1,874.87
Michael W.	616	3.45	379,456	11.9025	2,125.20
Brooke G.	594	3.33	352,836	11.0889	1,978.02
Kim B.	567	3.07	321,489	9.4249	1,740.69
Jason L.	542	2.86	293,764	8.1796	1,550.12
Matthew B.	551	2.91	303,601	8.4681	1,603.41
Walter M.	573	2.79	328,329	7.7841	1,598.67
Timothy D.	536	3.00	287,296	9.0000	1,608.00
Douglas L.	639	3.55	408,321	12.6025	2,268.45
Shelby K.	619	3.47	383,161	12.0409	2,147.93
Neil G.	694	3.60	481,636	12.9600	2,498.40
Jordana E.	718	3.88	515,524	15.0544	2,785.84
Sharyn L.	759	3.76	576,081	14.1776	2,853.84
Totals	12,456	66.67	7,830,354	224.4075	41,876.42

600. We can determine the predicted value by substituting $X = 600$ into our regression equation,

$$\hat{Y}_i = .30 + .00487(600) = 3.222$$

Thus the predicted grade point index for students with a GMAT score of 600 is 3.222.

16.4.2 Predictions in Regression Analysis: Interpolation versus Extrapolation

When using a regression model for prediction purposes, it is important that we consider only the relevant range of the independent variable in making our predictions. This relevant range encompasses all values from the smallest to the largest X used in developing the regression model. Hence, when predicting Y for a given value of X, we may *interpolate* within this relevant range of the X values, but we may not *extrapolate* beyond the range of X values. For example, when we use the GMAT score to predict grade point index, we note from Table 16.2 that the GMAT score varies from 536 to 759. Therefore, predictions of grade point index should be made only for students who have achieved a GMAT score between 536 and 759. Any prediction of grade point index outside this range of GMAT scores presumes that the fitted relationship holds outside the 536 to 759 range.

Problems

● **16.6**   Referring to Problem 16.1, the pet food sales problem, on page 561,
(a) Assuming a linear relationship, use the least-squares method to compute the regression coefficients b_0 and b_1.

(b) Interpret the meaning of the slope b_1 in this problem.

(c) Predict the average weekly sales (in hundreds of dollars) of pet food for stores with 8 feet of shelf space for pet food.

16.7   Referring to Problem 16.2, the absenteeism problem, on page 562,

(a) Assuming a linear relationship, use the least-squares method to find the regression coefficients b_0 and b_1.

(b) Interpret the meaning of the slope b_1 in this problem.

(c) How many days (on the average) would you predict that a 40-year-old worker would be absent?

● **16.8**   Referring to Problem 16.3, the production worker-hours problem, on page 562,

(a) Assuming a linear relationship, use the least-squares method to find the regression coefficients b_0 and b_1.

(b) Interpret the meaning of the Y intercept b_0 and the slope b_1 in this problem.

(c) Predict the average number of worker-hours required for a production run with a lot size of 45.

(d) Why would it not be appropriate to predict the average number of worker-hours required for a production run with lot size of 100? Explain.

16.9   Referring to Problem 16.4, the tomato yield problem, on page 562,

(a) Assuming a linear relationship, use the least-squares method to find the regression coefficients b_0 and b_1.

(b) Interpret the meaning of the Y intercept b_0 and the slope b_1 in this problem.

(c) Predict the average yield of tomatoes for a plot that has been given 15 pounds per 100 square feet of natural organic fertilizer.

(d) Why would it not be appropriate to predict the average yield for a plot that has been fertilized with 100 pounds per 100 square feet? Explain.

16.10   Referring to Problem 16.5, the terminal maintenance problem, on page 563,

(a) Assuming a linear relationship, use the least-squares method to find the regression coefficients b_0 and b_1.

(b) Interpret the meaning of the Y intercept b_0 and the slope b_1 in this problem.

(c) Use the regression model developed in (a) to predict the average number of service calls for a terminal that is four years old.

16.5   STANDARD ERROR OF THE ESTIMATE

In the preceding section we used the least-squares method to develop an equation to predict the grade point index based on the GMAT score. Although the least-squares method results in the line that fits the data with the minimum amount of variation, the regression equation is not a perfect predictor, unless all the observed data points fall on the predicted regression line. Just as we cannot expect all data values to be located exactly at their arithmetic mean, in the same way we cannot expect all data points to fall exactly on the regression line. The regression line serves only as an approximate predictor of a Y value for a given value of X. Therefore, we need to develop a statistic that measures the variability of the actual Y values, from the predicted Y values, in the same way that we developed (see Chapter 3) a measure of the variability of each observation around its mean. The measure of variability around the line of regression is called the **standard error of the estimate.**

The variability around the line of regression is illustrated in Figure 16.4 for the student performance problem. We can see from Figure 16.4 that, although the predicted

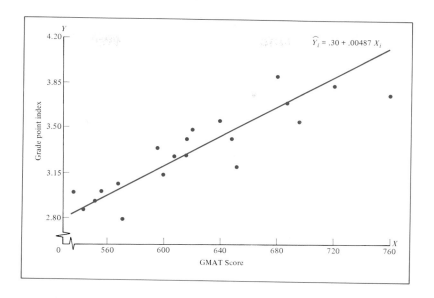

FIGURE 16.4
Scatter diagram and line of regression for the student performance problem.

line of regression falls near many of the actual values of Y, there are several values above the line of regression as well as below the line of regression, so that

$$\sum_{i=1}^{n} (Y_i - \hat{Y}_i) = 0$$

The standard error of the estimate, given by the symbol S_{YX}, is defined as

$$S_{YX} = \sqrt{\frac{\sum_{i=1}^{n} (Y_i - \hat{Y}_i)^2}{n - 2}} \qquad (16.5)$$

where Y_i = actual value of Y for a given X_i
  $\hat{Y}_i$ = predicted value of Y for a given X_i

The computation of the standard error of the estimate using Equation (16.5) would first require the determination of the predicted value of Y for each X value in the sample. The computation can be simplified, however, because of the following identity:

$$\sum_{i=1}^{n} (Y_i - \hat{Y}_i)^2 = \sum_{i=1}^{n} Y_i^2 - b_0 \sum_{i=1}^{n} Y_i - b_1 \sum_{i=1}^{n} X_i Y_i$$

The standard error of the estimate S_{YX} can thus be obtained using the following computational formula:

$$S_{YX} = \sqrt{\frac{\sum_{i=1}^{n} Y_i^2 - b_0 \sum_{i=1}^{n} Y_i - b_1 \sum_{i=1}^{n} X_i Y_i}{n - 2}} \qquad (16.6)$$

For the student performance problem, from Table 16.2 on page 569 we have determined that

$$\sum_{i=1}^{n} Y_i^2 = 224.4075 \qquad \sum_{i=1}^{n} Y_i = 66.67 \qquad \sum_{i=1}^{n} X_i Y_i = 41,876.42$$

$$b_0 = .30 \quad b_1 = + .00487$$

Therefore, using Equation (16.6), the standard error of the estimate S_{YX} can be computed as

$$
\begin{aligned}
S_{YX} &= \sqrt{\frac{\sum_{i=1}^{n} Y_i^2 - b_0 \sum_{i=1}^{n} Y_i - b_1 \sum_{i=1}^{n} X_i Y_i}{n - 2}} \\
&= \sqrt{\frac{224.4075 - (.30)(66.67) - (.00487)(41,876.42)}{20 - 2}} \\
&= \sqrt{\frac{.4483}{18}} = \sqrt{.0249} \\
&= .158
\end{aligned}
$$

This standard error of the estimate, equal to .158, represents a measure of the variation around the fitted line of regression. It is measured in units of the dependent variable Y. The interpretation of the standard error of the estimate, then, is analogous to that of the standard deviation. Just as the standard deviation measured variability around the arithmetic mean, the standard error of the estimate measures variability around the fitted line of regression. Moreover, as we shall see in Sections 16.8–16.10, the standard error of the estimate can be used in making inferences about a predicted value of Y and in determining whether a statistically significant relationship exists between the two variables.

Problems

- **16.11**　Referring to the pet food sales problem (pages 561 and 569), compute the standard error of the estimate.

  16.12　Referring to the absenteeism problem (pages 562 and 570), compute the standard error of the estimate.

- **16.13**　Referring to the production worker-hours problem (pages 562 and 570), compute the standard error of the estimate.

  16.14　Referring to the tomato yield problem (pages 562 and 570), compute the standard error of the estimate.

16.15   Referring to the terminal maintenance problem (pages 563 and 570), compute the standard error of the estimate.

16.6   MEASURES OF VARIATION IN REGRESSION AND CORRELATION

In order to examine how well the independent variable predicts the dependent variable in our statistical model, we need to develop several measures of variation. The first measure, the **total sum of squares** (SST), is a measure of variation of the Y_i values around their mean, $\overline{Y}$. As we have seen previously in Section 14.2, the total sum of squares can be subdivided into two components. In a regression analysis the total sum of squares can be subdivided into **explained variation** or **sum of squares due to regression** (SSR), that which is attributable to the relationship between X and Y, and **unexplained variation** or **error sum of squares** (SSE), that which is attributable to factors other than the relationship between X and Y. These different measures of variation can be seen in Figure 16.5.

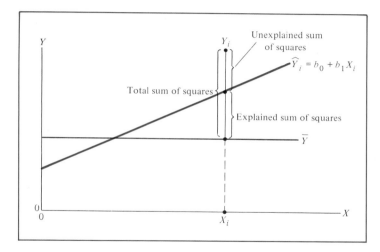

FIGURE 16.5
Measures of variation in regression.

The regression sum of squares (SSR) represents the difference between $\overline{Y}$ (the average value of Y) and $\hat{Y}_i$ (the value of Y that would be predicted from the regression relationship). The error sum of squares (SSE) represents that part of the variation in Y that is not explained by the regression. It is based upon the difference between Y_i and $\hat{Y}_i$.

These measures of variation can be represented as follows:

$$
\begin{aligned}
\text{total sum of squares} &= \text{explained sum of squares} \\
&\quad + \text{unexplained sum of squares} \qquad \textbf{(16.7)} \\
\text{SST} &= \text{SSR} + \text{SSE}
\end{aligned}
$$

where

$$\text{SST} = \text{total sum of squares} = \sum_{i=1}^{n} (Y_i - \bar{Y})^2 = \sum_{i=1}^{n} Y_i^2 - \frac{\left(\sum_{i=1}^{n} Y_i\right)^2}{n} \qquad \textbf{(16.8)}$$

$$\text{SSE} = \text{unexplained or error sum of squares}$$
$$= \sum_{i=1}^{n} (Y_i - \hat{Y}_i)^2 \qquad \textbf{(16.9)}$$
$$= \sum_{i=1}^{n} Y_i^2 - b_0 \sum_{i=1}^{n} Y_i - b_1 \sum_{i=1}^{n} X_i Y_i$$

$$\text{SSR} = \text{explained or regression sum of squares}$$
$$= \sum_{i=1}^{n} (\hat{Y}_i - \bar{Y})^2$$
$$= \text{SST} - \text{SSE} \qquad \textbf{(16.10)}$$
$$= b_0 \sum_{i=1}^{n} Y_i + b_1 \sum_{i=1}^{n} X_i Y_i - \frac{\left(\sum_{i=1}^{n} Y_i\right)^2}{n}$$

Examining the unexplained or error sum of squares [Equation (16.9)], we may recall that $\sum_{i=1}^{n} (Y_i - \hat{Y}_i)^2$ was the numerator under the square root in the computation of the standard error of the estimate [see Equation (16.5)]. Therefore, in the process of computing the standard error of the estimate, we have already computed the following unexplained sum of squares:

$$\text{SSE} = \text{unexplained or error sum of squares}$$
$$= \sum_{i=1}^{n} Y_i^2 - b_0 \sum_{i=1}^{n} Y_i - b_1 \sum_{i=1}^{n} X_i Y_i$$
$$= 224.4075 - (.30)(66.67) - (.00487)(41,876.42)$$
$$= .4483$$

Moreover,

$$\text{SST} = \text{total sum of squares}$$
$$= \sum_{i=1}^{n} Y_i^2 - \frac{\left(\sum_{i=1}^{n} Y_i\right)^2}{n}$$
$$= 224.4075 - \frac{(66.67)^2}{20}$$
$$= 224.4075 - 222.2444$$
$$= 2.1631$$

so that

$$SSR = \text{explained or regression sum of squares}$$
$$= SST - SSE$$
$$= 2.1631 - .4483 = 1.7148$$

Now the **coefficient of determination** r^2 can be defined as

$$r^2 = \frac{\text{regression sum of squares}}{\text{total sum of squares}} = \frac{SSR}{SST} \qquad \textbf{(16.11a)}$$

That is, the coefficient of determination measures the proportion of variation that is explained by the independent variable in the regression model. For the student performance problem,

$$r^2 = \frac{1.7148}{2.1631} = .793$$

Therefore, 79.3% of the variation in grade point index can be explained by the variability in GMAT score from student to student. This is an example where there is a strong linear relationship between two variables, since the use of a regression model has reduced the variability in predicting grade point index by 79.3%. Only 20.7% of the variability in grade point index can be explained by factors other than what is accounted for by the linear regression model.

To interpret the coefficient of determination—particularly when dealing with multiple regression models—some researchers suggest that an "adjusted" r^2 be computed to reflect both the number of predictor or explanatory variables in the model and the sample size. In simple linear regression, however, we may denote such an adjusted r^2 as

$$r^2_{adj} = 1 - \left[(1 - r^2) \frac{n - 1}{n - 2} \right] \qquad \textbf{(16.11b)}$$

Thus for our student performance data, since $r^2 = .793$ and $n = 20$,

$$r^2_{adj} = 1 - \left[(1 - r^2) \frac{20 - 1}{20 - 2} \right]$$
$$= 1 - \left[(1 - .793) \frac{19}{18} \right]$$
$$= 1 - .219$$
$$= .781$$

This result is similar to the one obtained without adjustment for degrees of freedom.

Problems

- **16.16**   Referring to Problem 16.11 (pet food sales) on page 572
  (a) Compute the coefficient of determination r^2 and interpret its meaning.
  (b) Compute the adjusted r^2.

  16.17   Referring to Problem 16.12 (absenteeism) on page 572
  (a) Compute the coefficient of determination r^2 and interpret its meaning.
  (b) Compute the adjusted r^2.

- **16.18**   Referring to Problem 16.13 (production worker-hours) on page 572
  (a) Compute the coefficient of determination r^2 and interpret its meaning.
  (b) Compute the adjusted r^2.

  16.19   Referring to Problem 16.14 (tomato yield) on page 572
  (a) Compute the coefficient of determination r^2 and interpret its meaning.
  (b) Compute the adjusted r^2.

  16.20   Referring to Problem 16.15 (terminal maintenance) on page 573
  (a) Compute the coefficient of determination r^2 and interpret its meaning.
  (b) Compute the adjusted r^2.

  16.21   When will the unexplained or error sum of squares be equal to 0?

  16.22   When will the explained or regression sum of squares be equal to 0?

16.7 CORRELATION—MEASURING THE STRENGTH OF THE ASSOCIATION

In our discussion of the relationship between two variables thus far in this chapter we have been concerned with the prediction of the dependent variable Y based upon the independent variable X. On the other hand, as we have previously mentioned, correlation measures the degree of association between two variables. Figure 16.6 illustrates three different types of association between variables: perfect negative correlation, no correlation, and perfect positive correlation.

The strength of a relationship between two variables in a population is usually measured by the coefficient of correlation ρ, whose values range from -1 for perfect negative correlation up to $+1$ for perfect positive correlation. Panel A of Figure 16.6

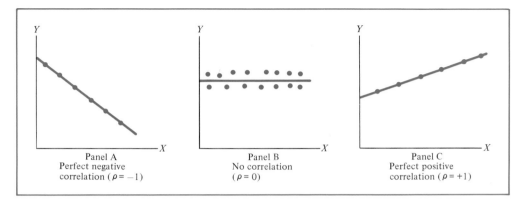

FIGURE 16.6
Types of association between variables.

illustrates a perfect negative linear relationship between X and Y. Thus there is a perfect one-to-one relationship between X and Y so that Y will decrease in a perfectly predictable manner as X increases. Panel B of Figure 16.6 illustrates an example in which there is no relationship between X and Y. As X increases, there is no change in Y, so that there is no association between the values of X and the values of Y. On the other hand, panel C of Figure 16.6 depicts a perfect positive correlation between X and Y. In this case Y increases in a perfectly predictable manner as X increases.

For regression-oriented problems, the sample coefficient of correlation (r) may easily be obtained from Equation (16.11a) as follows:

$$r^2 = \frac{\text{regression sum of squares}}{\text{total sum of squares}} = \frac{\text{SSR}}{\text{SST}}$$

so that

$$r = \sqrt{r^2} \tag{16.12}$$

In simple linear regression r takes the sign of b_1. If b_1 is positive, r is positive. If b_1 is negative, r is negative. If b_1 is zero, r is zero.

In the student performance problem, since $r^2 = .793$ and the slope b_1 is positive, the coefficient of correlation is computed as $+.891$. The closeness of the correlation coefficient to $+1.0$ implies a strong association between GMAT score and grade point index.

We have now computed and interpreted the correlation coefficient in terms of its regression viewpoint. As we mentioned at the beginning of this chapter, however, regression and correlation are two separate techniques, with regression being concerned with prediction and correlation with association. In many applications, particularly in the social sciences, the researcher is concerned only with measuring association between variables, not with using one variable to predict another. This can be illustrated by reference to the real estate survey. If, for example, the president and the statistician were interested in studying the association between lot size (question 2) and taxes (question 7) for houses that have an in-ground swimming pool, the problem would be one of correlation, not regression. The objective of the correlation analysis would be to measure the strength of the association between the two variables—not to use one variable to predict values of the other.

If only correlation analysis is being performed on a set of data, the sample correlation coefficient r can be computed directly using the following formula:

$$r = \frac{\sum_{i=1}^{n} (X_i - \bar{X})(Y_i - \bar{Y})}{\sqrt{\sum_{i=1}^{n} (X_i - \bar{X})^2} \sqrt{\sum_{i=1}^{n} (Y_i - \bar{Y})^2}} \tag{16.13a}$$

or, alternatively,

$$r = \cfrac{\sum_{i=1}^{n} X_i Y_i - \cfrac{\left(\sum_{i=1}^{n} X_i\right)\left(\sum_{i=1}^{n} Y_i\right)}{n}}{\sqrt{\sum_{i=1}^{n} X_i^2 - \cfrac{\left(\sum_{i=1}^{n} X_i\right)^2}{n}} \; \sqrt{\sum_{i=1}^{n} Y_i^2 - \cfrac{\left(\sum_{i=1}^{n} Y_i\right)^2}{n}}} \qquad (16.13b)$$

Thus for our real estate survey, the lot size (in thousands of square feet) and the taxes paid for the sample of nine houses with an in-ground swimming pool are shown in Table 16.3.

TABLE 16.3 Lot size and taxes for houses which have an in-ground swimming pool

House	Lot Size	Taxes
1	7.20	2,860
2	6.00	3,460
3	6.00	3,200
4	6.00	3,250
5	12.24	4,400
6	8.00	2,900
7	7.00	4,163
8	6.00	4,000
9	8.30	3,440

For the data of Table 16.3 we can compute the following values:

$$\sum_{i=1}^{n} X_i = 66.74 \qquad \sum_{i=1}^{n} X_i^2 = 527.5476 \qquad \sum_{i=1}^{n} Y_i = 31,673$$

$$n = 9 \qquad \sum_{i=1}^{n} Y_i^2 = 113,887,869 \qquad \sum_{i=1}^{n} X_i Y_i = 238,801$$

Using Equation (16.13b), we obtain

$$r = \cfrac{\sum_{i=1}^{n} X_i Y_i - \cfrac{\left(\sum_{i=1}^{n} X_i\right)\left(\sum_{i=1}^{n} Y_i\right)}{n}}{\sqrt{\sum_{i=1}^{n} X_i^2 - \cfrac{\left(\sum_{i=1}^{n} X_i\right)^2}{n}} \; \sqrt{\sum_{i=1}^{n} Y_i^2 - \cfrac{\left(\sum_{i=1}^{n} Y_i\right)^2}{n}}}$$

$$= \frac{238,801 - \frac{(66.74)(31,673)}{9}}{\sqrt{527.5476 - \frac{(66.74)^2}{9}} \sqrt{113,887,869 - \frac{(31,673)^2}{9}}}$$

$$= \frac{3,928.12}{\sqrt{32.6334} \sqrt{2,423,543.6}}$$

$$= +.442$$

The coefficient of correlation between lot size and taxes paid for houses with an in-ground swimming pool indicates at best a moderate association—that is, an increased lot size might be somewhat associated with increased taxes. In Section 16.10 we shall use these sample results to determine whether there is any evidence of significant association between these variables in the population.

Problems

16.23 Under what circumstances will the coefficient of correlation be negative?

● **16.24** Referring to Problem 16.16 (pet food sales) on page 576, compute the coefficient of correlation.

16.25 Referring to Problem 16.17 (absenteeism) on page 576, compute the coefficient of correlation.

● **16.26** Referring to Problem 16.18 (production worker-hours) on page 576, compute the coefficient of correlation.

16.27 Referring to Problem 16.19 (tomato yield) on page 576, compute the coefficient of correlation.

16.28 Referring to Problem 16.20 (terminal maintenance) on page 576, compute the coefficient of correlation.

● **16.29** Referring to the data of Problem 15.50 on page 548
   (a) Compute the coefficient of correlation r between verbal facility and geometrical intuition.
   (b) Compare this result to the value of Spearman's rho obtained in Problem 15.50.

16.30 The following table presents data obtained from a sample of 10 of the 100 largest commercial banking companies in 1986:

Company	Deposits (billions of $)	Loans (billions of $)
First Interstate Bancorp	39.46	33.99
Marine Midland	17.42	18.42
Texas Commerce Bancshares	14.14	12.70
First City Bancorp (Texas)	11.05	9.58
Harris Bancorp	7.60	5.70
Northern Trust	6.21	3.92
State Street Boston Corp.	5.27	2.13
First American Corp.	4.68	3.50
Continental Bancorp.	4.51	3.54
South Carolina National Corp.	3.33	3.08

SOURCE: *Fortune*, Vol. 115, No. 12, June 8, 1987, pp. 200–203. © Time Inc., 1987. All rights reserved.

Compute the coefficient of correlation r between amount of deposits and amount of loans at commercial banks.

16.31 The following data represent the percentage of flights of United States airlines that arrived within 15 minutes of scheduled arrival time during December 1987 and January 1988.

Airline	January 1988	December 1987
Southwest	85.0	74.2
America West	83.9	76.4
Pacific Southwest	81.6	57.6
Alaska	76.4	59.2
American	75.7	73.1
US Air	73.2	71.7
Pan Am	72.6	77.3
United	69.8	62.6
Delta	65.6	61.8
T.W.A.	65.5	63.5
Continental	64.8	60.5
Piedmont	62.4	67.2
Northwest	61.6	63.3
Eastern	61.5	69.5

SOURCE: U.S. Department of Transportation.

(a) Compute the coefficient of correlation of on-time performance for January 1988 and December 1987 of United States airlines.

(b) What factors might explain the difference in performance between December and January?

➠**(c)** **ACTION** If you were to present a memo to the Secretary of Transportation concerning this matter what would you conclude?

16.8 CONFIDENCE-INTERVAL ESTIMATE FOR PREDICTING μ_{YX}

In our discussion of regression and correlation analysis in the preceding sections of this chapter we have been concerned with the use of these methods solely for the purpose of description. The least-squares method has been utilized to determine the regression coefficients and to predict the value of Y from a given value of X. In addition, the standard error of the estimate has been discussed along with the coefficients of correlation and determination. Nevertheless, since we are usually sampling from large populations, we are often concerned with making inferences about the relationship between the variables in the entire population based upon our sample results. In this section, then, we will discuss methods of making predictive inferences about the mean of Y, while in the following section we will predict an individual response value $\hat{Y}_I$.

We may recall that in Section 16.4 the fitted regression equation was used to make predictions about the value of Y for a given X. In the student performance problem, for example, we predicted that the average grade point index of students with a GMAT score of 600 would be 3.222. This estimate, however, is merely a point estimate of the true average value. In Chapter 10 we developed the concept of the confidence interval as an estimate of the true population value. In a similar fashion, a confidence-interval estimate can now be developed to make inferences about the predicted value of Y.

$$\hat{Y}_i \pm t_{n-2}S_{YX} \sqrt{h_i} \qquad (16.14)$$

where[2]

$$h_i = \frac{1}{n} + \frac{(X_i - \overline{X})^2}{\displaystyle\sum_{i=1}^{n} X_i^2 - \frac{\left(\displaystyle\sum_{i=1}^{n} X_i\right)^2}{n}}$$

$\hat{Y}_i$ = predicted value of Y;　$\hat{Y}_i = b_0 + b_1X_i$

S_{YX} = standard error of the estimate

n = sample size

X_i = given value of X

An examination of Equation (16.14) indicates that the width of the confidence interval is dependent on several factors. For a given level of confidence, increased variation around the line of regression, as measured by the standard error of the estimate, results in a wider interval. However, as would be expected, increased sample size reduces the width of the interval. Moreover, the width of the interval also varies at different values of X. When predicting Y for values of X close to $\overline{X}$, the interval is much narrower than for predictions for X values more distant from the mean. This effect can be seen from the square-root portion of Equation (16.14) and from Figure 16.7.

As indicated in Figure 16.7, the interval estimate of the true mean of Y varies *hyperbolically* as a function of the closeness of the given X to $\overline{X}$. When predictions are to be made for X values which are distant from the average value of X, the much

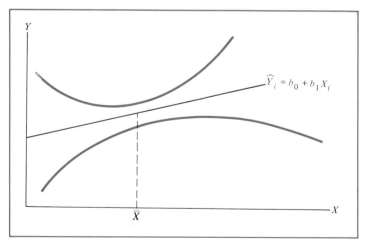

FIGURE 16.7
Interval estimates of μ_{YX} for different values of X.

---

[2] h_i are the "hat matrix diagonal elements" which reflect the influence (see Section 16.13) of each X_i in the simple linear regression model.

wider interval is the tradeoff for predicting at such values of X. Thus, as depicted in Figure 16.7, we observe a *confidence-band effect* for the predictions.

Let us now use Equation (16.14) for our student performance problem. Suppose that we desire a 95% confidence interval estimate of the true average grade point index for all students with a GMAT score of 600. We compute the following:

$$\hat{Y}_i = .30 + .00487 X_i$$

and for $X_i = 600$ we obtain $\hat{Y}_i = 3.222$.

Also,

$$\bar{X} = 622.8 \qquad S_{YX} = .158$$

$$\sum_{i=1}^{n} X_i = 12,456 \qquad \sum_{i=1}^{n} X_i^2 = 7,830,354$$

From Table E.3, $t_{18} = 2.1009$. Thus

$$\hat{Y}_i \pm t_{n-2} S_{YX} \sqrt{h_i}$$

where

$$h_i = \frac{1}{n} + \frac{(X_i - \bar{X})^2}{\sum_{i=1}^{n} X_i^2 - \frac{\left(\sum_{i=1}^{n} X_i\right)^2}{n}}$$

so that we have

$$\hat{Y}_i \pm t_{n-2} S_{YX} \sqrt{\frac{1}{n} + \frac{(X_i - \bar{X})^2}{\sum_{i=1}^{n} X_i^2 - \frac{\left(\sum_{i=1}^{n} X_i\right)^2}{n}}}$$

and

$$3.222 \pm (2.1009)(.158) \sqrt{\frac{1}{20} + \frac{(600 - 622.8)^2}{7,830,354 - \frac{(12,456)^2}{20}}}$$

$$= 3.222 \pm (.3319) \sqrt{\frac{1}{20} + \frac{(-22.8)^2}{7,830,354 - 7,757,596.8}}$$

$$= 3.222 \pm (.3319)\sqrt{.0571}$$

$$= 3.222 \pm .079$$

so

$$3.143 \le \mu_{YX} \le 3.301$$

Therefore, our estimate is that the true average grade point index is between 3.143 and 3.301 for all students with GMAT scores of 600.

Problems

- 16.32   Referring to the pet food sales problem (pages 561, 569, and 572), set up a 90% confidence interval estimate of the average weekly sales for all stores that have 8 feet of shelf space for pet food.
- 16.33   Referring to the absenteeism problem (pages 562, 570, and 572), set up a 99% confidence interval estimate of the average number of days absent for all 40-year-old workers.
- 16.34   Referring to the production worker-hours problem (pages 562, 570, and 572), set up a 90% confidence interval estimate of the average worker hours for all production runs with a lot size of 45.
- 16.35   Referring to the tomato yield problem (pages 562, 570, and 572), set up a 90% confidence interval estimate of the average yield for all tomatoes that have been fertilized with 15 pounds per 100 square feet of natural organic fertilizer.
- 16.36   Referring to the terminal maintenance problem (pages 563, 570, and 573), set up a 95% confidence interval estimate of the average number of service calls for all terminals that are four years old.

16.9   PREDICTION INTERVAL FOR AN INDIVIDUAL RESPONSE $\hat{Y}_i$

In addition to the need to obtain a confidence-interval estimate for the average value, it is often important to be able to predict the response that would be obtained for a particular value. Although the form of the prediction interval is similar to the confidence-interval estimate of Equation (16.14), the prediction interval is merely estimating an individual value, not a parameter. Thus the prediction interval for an individual response $\hat{Y}_i$ at a particular value X_i is provided in Equation (16.15).

$$\hat{Y}_i \pm t_{n-2} S_{YX} \sqrt{1 + h_i} \qquad \qquad \textbf{(16.15)}$$

where h_i, $\hat{Y}_i$, S_{YX}, n, and X_i are defined as in Equation (16.14).

Suppose we desire a 95% prediction interval estimate of the grade point index for an individual student with a GMAT score of 600. We compute the following:

$$\hat{Y}_i = .30 + .00487 X_i$$

and for $X_i = 600$, $\hat{Y}_i = 3.222$.
Also

$$\overline{X} = 622.8 \qquad S_{YX} = .158$$

$$\sum_{i=1}^{n} X_i = 12,456 \qquad \sum_{i=1}^{n} X_i^2 = 7,830,354$$

From Table E.3, $t_{18} = 2.1009$. Thus

$$\hat{Y}_i \pm t_{n-2} S_{YX} \sqrt{1 + h_i}$$

so that

$$\hat{Y}_i \pm t_{n-2} S_{YX} \sqrt{1 + \frac{1}{n} + \frac{(X_i - \overline{X})^2}{\displaystyle\sum_{i=1}^{n} X_i^2 - \frac{\left(\displaystyle\sum_{i=1}^{n} X_i\right)^2}{n}}}$$

and

$$= 3.222 \pm (2.1009)(.158) \sqrt{1 + \frac{1}{20} + \frac{(600 - 622.8)^2}{7{,}830{,}354 - \dfrac{(12{,}456)^2}{20}}}$$

$$= 3.222 \pm (.3319) \sqrt{1 + \frac{1}{20} + \frac{(-22.8)^2}{7{,}830{,}354 - 7{,}757{,}596.8}}$$

$$= 3.222 \pm (.3319)\sqrt{1.0571}$$

$$= 3.222 \pm .341$$

so

$$2.881 \leq \hat{Y}_I \leq 3.563$$

Therefore with 95% confidence, our estimate is that the grade point index for an individual student with a GMAT score of 600 is between 2.881 and 3.563. We note that this prediction interval is much wider than the confidence interval estimate obtained in Section 16.8 for the average value.

Problems

16.37 Explain the difference between the confidence interval for an average value and the prediction interval for an individual value.

16.38 Referring to Problem 16.32 on page 583 (the pet food sales problem)
   (a) Set up a 90% prediction interval of the weekly sales of an individual store that has 8 feet of shelf space for pet food.
   (b) Explain the difference in the results obtained in part (a) and those obtained in Problem 16.32.

16.39 Referring to Problem 16.33 on page 583 (the absenteeism problem)
   (a) Set up a 99% prediction interval of the number of days absent of an individual 40-year-old worker.
   (b) Explain the difference in the results obtained in part (a) and those obtained in Problem 16.33.

• **16.40** Referring to Problem 16.34 on page 583 (the production worker-hours problem), set up a 90% prediction interval of the number of worker-hours for a single lot size of 45.

16.41 Referring to Problem 16.35 on page 583 (the tomato yield problem), set up a 90% prediction interval of the yield of tomatoes for an individual plot that has been fertilized with 25 pounds per 100 square feet of natural organic fertilizer.

16.42 Referring to Problem 16.36 on page 583 (the terminal maintenance problem), set up a 95% prediction interval of the number of service calls for a particular terminal that is two years old.

16.10 INFERENCES ABOUT THE POPULATION PARAMETERS IN REGRESSION AND CORRELATION

In the preceding two sections we used statistical inference to develop a confidence interval estimate for μ_{YX}, the true mean value of Y, and a prediction interval for $\hat{Y}_I$ an individual observation. In this section, statistical inference will be used to draw conclusions about the population slope β_1 and the population correlation coefficient ρ.

We can determine whether a significant relationship between the variables X and Y exists by testing whether β_1 (the true slope) is equal to zero. If this hypothesis is rejected, one could conclude that there is evidence of a linear relationship. The null and alternative hypotheses could be stated as follows:

$$H_0: \quad \beta_1 = 0 \quad \text{(There is no relationship)}$$
$$H_1: \quad \beta_1 \neq 0 \quad \text{(There is a relationship)}$$

and the test statistic for this is given by

$$t_{n-2} = \frac{b_1 - \beta_1}{S_{b_1}} \tag{16.16}$$

where

$$S_{b_1} = \frac{S_{YX}}{\sqrt{\sum_{i=1}^{n} X_i^2 - \dfrac{\left(\sum_{i=1}^{n} X_i\right)^2}{n}}}$$

Turning to our student performance problem, let us now test whether the sample results enable us to conclude that a significant relationship between the GMAT score and the grade point index exists at the .05 level of significance. The results from Sections 16.4 and 16.5 gave the following information:

$$b_1 = +.00487 \quad n = 20 \quad S_{YX} = .158$$

$$\sum_{i=1}^{n} X_i = 12{,}456 \quad \sum_{i=1}^{n} X_i^2 = 7{,}830{,}354$$

Therefore, to test the existence of a relationship at the .05 level of significance we have (see Figure 16.8 on page 586)

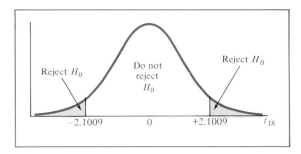

FIGURE 16.8
Testing a hypothesis about the population slope at the .05 level of significance with 18 degrees of freedom.

$$S_{b_1} = \frac{S_{YX}}{\sqrt{\sum\limits_{i=1}^{n} X_i^2 - \dfrac{\left(\sum\limits_{i=1}^{n} X_i\right)^2}{n}}}$$

$$= \frac{.158}{\sqrt{7,830,354 - \dfrac{(12,456)^2}{20}}} = \frac{.158}{\sqrt{72,757.2}} = .00058576$$

and, under the null hypothesis, $\beta_1 = 0$ so that

$$t_{n-2} = \frac{b_1}{S_{b_1}}$$

$$t_{18} = \frac{.00487}{.00058576} = 8.31$$

Since $8.31 > 2.1009$, we reject H_0. Hence, we can conclude that there is a significant linear relationship between grade point index and GMAT score.

A second, equivalent method for testing the existence of a linear relationship between the variables is to set up a confidence-interval estimate of β_1 and to determine whether the hypothesized value ($\beta_1 = 0$) is included in the interval. The confidence-interval estimate of β_1 would be obtained by using the following formula:

$$b_1 \pm t_{n-2}S_{b_1} \qquad\qquad (16.17)$$

If a 95% confidence interval estimate was desired, we would have $b_1 = .00487$, $t_{18} = 2.1009$ and $S_{b_1} = .00058576$. Thus

$$b_1 \pm t_{n-2}S_{b_1} = .00487 \pm (2.1009)(.00058576)$$
$$= .00487 \pm .00123$$
$$+ .00364 \le \beta_1 \le + .00610$$

From Equation (16.17) the true slope is estimated with 95% confidence to be between $+.00364$ and $+.00610$. Since these values are above zero, we can conclude that there is a significant linear relationship between grade point index and GMAT score. On the other hand, had the interval included zero, no relationship would have been determined.

A third method for examining the existence of a linear relationship between two variables involves the sample correlation coefficient r. The existence of a relationship between X and Y, which was tested using Equation (16.16), could be tested in terms of the correlation coefficient with equivalent results. Testing for the existence of a linear relationship between two variables is the same as determining whether there is any significant correlation between them. The population correlation coefficient ρ is hypothesized as equal to zero. Thus the null and alternative hypotheses would be

$$H_0: \quad \rho = 0 \qquad \text{(There is no correlation.)}$$
$$H_1: \quad \rho \neq 0 \qquad \text{(There is correlation.)}$$

The test statistic for determining the existence of correlation is given by

$$t_{n-2} = \frac{r}{\sqrt{\dfrac{1 - r^2}{n - 2}}} \tag{16.18}$$

In order to demonstrate that this statistic produces the same result, except for rounding errors, as the test for the existence of a slope [Equation (16.16)], we will use the student performance data. For these data $r = +.891$, $r^2 = .793$, and $n = 20$ so we have

$$t_{n-2} = \frac{r}{\sqrt{\dfrac{1 - r^2}{n - 2}}}$$

$$t_{18} = \frac{.891}{\sqrt{\dfrac{1 - .793}{20 - 2}}} = 8.31$$

We may note that this t value is, except for possible rounding error, the same as that obtained by using Equation (16.16). Therefore, in a linear regression analysis Equations (16.16) and (16.18) give equivalent alternative ways of determining the existence of a relationship between two variables. However, if the sole purpose of a particular study is to determine the existence of correlation, then Equation (16.18) is more appropriate. For instance, in Section 16.7 we studied the association of lot size and taxes paid for houses that have an in-ground swimming pool. Had we wanted to determine the significance of the correlation between these two variables, we could have used Equation (16.18) as follows:

$$H_0: \quad \rho = 0 \qquad \text{(There is no correlation.)}$$
$$H_1: \quad \rho \neq 0 \qquad \text{(There is correlation.)}$$

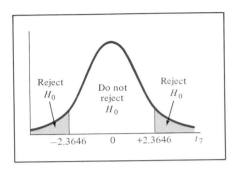

FIGURE 16.9
Testing for the existence of correlation at the .05 level of significance with 7 degrees of freedom.

If a level of significance of .05 was selected, we would have (see Figure 16.9)

$$t_{n-2} = \frac{r}{\sqrt{\dfrac{1 - r^2}{n - 2}}}$$

$$t_7 = \frac{.442}{\sqrt{\dfrac{1 - (.442)^2}{9 - 2}}} = \frac{.442}{.3391} = 1.303$$

Since $1.303 < 2.3646$, we do not reject H_0.

Since the null hypothesis has not been rejected, the statistician would inform the president that there is no evidence of any real association between the lot size and taxes paid for houses that have an in-ground swimming pool.

When inferences concerning the population slope were discussed, confidence intervals and tests of hypothesis were used interchangeably. However, when examining the correlation coefficient, the development of a confidence interval becomes more complicated because the shape of the sampling distribution of the statistic r varies for different values of the true correlation coefficient. Methods for developing a confidence interval estimate for the correlation coefficient are presented in Reference 4.

Problems

• **16.43** Referring to the pet food sales problem (pages 569, 572, and 576), at the .10 level of significance, is there evidence of a linear relationship between shelf space and sales?

16.44 Referring to the absenteeism problem (pages 570, 572, and 576), at the .01 level of significance, is there evidence of a linear relationship between age and absenteeism?

• **16.45** Referring to the production worker-hours problem (pages 570, 572, and 576), at the .10 level of significance, is there evidence of a linear relationship between lot size and worker-hours?

16.46 Referring to the tomato yield problem (pages 570, 572, and 576), at the .10 level of significance, is there evidence of a linear relationship between the amount of fertilizer used and the yield of tomatoes?

16.47 Referring to the terminal maintenance problem (pages 570, 573, and 576), at the .05 level of significance, is there evidence of a linear relationship between age and number of service calls?

• **16.48** Referring to Problem 16.29 on page 579, at the .05 level of significance, is there evidence of a positive linear relationship between verbal facility and geometrical intuition?

16.49 Referring to Problem 16.30 on page 579, at the .01 level of significance, is there evidence of a linear relationship between deposits and loans?

16.50 Referring to Problem 16.31 on page 580, at the .10 level of significance, is there evidence of a linear relationship between the percentage of on-time arrivals in the two months?

16.11 ASSUMPTIONS OF REGRESSION AND CORRELATION

In our investigations into hypothesis testing and the analysis of variance we have noted that the appropriate application of a particular statistical procedure is dependent on how well a set of assumptions for that procedure are met. The assumptions necessary for regression and correlation analysis are analogous to those of the analysis of variance, since they fall under the general heading of "linear models" (References 4 and 12). Although there are some differences in the assumptions made by the regression model and by correlation (see References 4 and 12), this topic is beyond the scope of this text and we will consider only the former.

The three major assumptions of regression are

1. Normality
2. Homoscedasticity
3. Independence of error

The first assumption, **normality,** requires that the values of Y be normally distributed at each value of X (see Figure 16.10). Like the t test and analysis-of-variance F test, regression analysis is "robust" against departures from the normality assumption; that is, as long as the distribution of Y_i values around each level of X is not extremely different from a normal distribution, inferences about the line of regression and the regression coefficients will not be seriously affected.

The second assumption, **homoscedasticity,** requires that the variation around the line of regression be constant for all values of X. This means that Y varies the same amount when X is a low value as when X is a high value (see Figure 16.10). The homoscedasticity assumption is important for using the least-squares method of determining the regression coefficients. If there are serious departures from this assumption, either data transformations or weighted least-squares methods (References 4 and 12) can be applied.

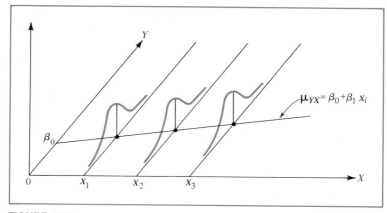

FIGURE 16.10
Assumptions of regression.

The third assumption, **independence of error,** requires that the error (''residual'' difference between an observed and predicted value of Y) should be independent for each value of X. This assumption often refers to data that are collected over a period of time. For example, in economic data the values for a particular time period are often correlated with the values of the previous time period. (See Reference 4.) These types of models fall under the general heading of time series and will be considered in Chapter 18.

16.12 REGRESSION DIAGNOSTICS: RESIDUAL ANALYSIS

16.12.1 Introduction

In our discussion of our student performance data throughout this chapter we have relied upon a simple regression model in which the dependent variable was predicted based upon a straight-line relationship with a single independent variable. In this section we shall use a graphical approach called **residual analysis** to evaluate the appropriateness of the regression model that has been fitted to the data. In addition, this approach will also allow us to study potential violations in the assumptions of our regression model (see Section 16.11).

16.12.2 Evaluating the Aptness of the Fitted Model

The residual or error values (ϵ_i) may be defined as the difference between the observed (Y_i) and predicted ($\hat{Y}_i$) values of the dependent variable for given values X_i. Thus

$$\epsilon_i = Y_i - \hat{Y}_i \qquad (16.19)$$

We may evaluate the aptness of the fitted regression model by plotting the residuals on the vertical axis against the corresponding X_i values of the independent variable on the horizontal axis. If the fitted model is appropriate for the data, there will be no apparent pattern in this plot of the residuals versus X_i. However, if the fitted model is not appropriate, there will be a relationship between the X_i values and the residuals ϵ_i. Such a pattern can be observed in Figure 16.11. Figure 16.11(a) depicts a situation in which there is a significant simple linear relationship between X and Y. However, it would seem possible that a curvilinear model between the two variables might be more appropriate. This effect appears to be highlighted in Figure 16.11(b), the residual plot of ϵ_i versus X_i. In (b) there is an obvious curvilinear effect between X and ϵ. By plotting the residuals we have essentially ''filtered out'' or removed the *linear* trend of X with Y, thereby exposing the ''lack of fit'' in the simple linear model. Thus from (a) and (b) we may conclude that the curvilinear model may be a better fit and should be evaluated in place of the simple linear model (see Section 17.10 for further discussion of fitting curvilinear models).

Now that we have considered Figure 16.11, we may return to the evaluation of the student performance data. Table 16.4 represents the observed, predicted, and residual values of the response variable (grade point index) in the simple linear model we have fitted. Note that we have also computed the ''standardized residuals.'' These

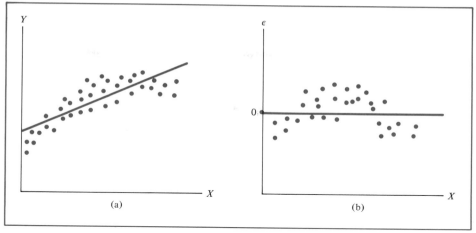

FIGURE 16.11
Studying the appropriateness of the simple linear regression model.

represent each residual divided by its standard error. The standardized residual is expressed as Equation (16.20):

$$Standardized\ Residual$$

$$SR_i = \frac{\epsilon_i}{S_{YX}\sqrt{1 - h_i}} \qquad (16.20)$$

TABLE 16.4 Observed, predicted, and residual values for the student performance data

Observation	GMAT Score X_i	Grade Point Index			Standardized Residual, SR_i
		Observed	Predicted	Residual	
1	688	3.7200	3.6510	0.0690	0.47
2	647	3.4400	3.4514	−0.0114	−0.08
3	652	3.2100	3.4757	−0.2657	−1.76
4	608	3.2900	3.2614	0.0286	0.19
5	680	3.9100	3.6121	0.2979	2.01
6	617	3.2800	3.3053	−0.0253	−0.17
7	557	3.0200	3.0130	0.0070	0.05
8	599	3.1300	3.2176	−0.0876	−0.58
9	616	3.4500	3.3004	0.1496	0.99
10	594	3.3300	3.1932	0.1368	0.91
11	567	3.0700	3.0617	0.0083	0.06
12	542	2.8600	2.9400	−0.0800	−0.55
13	551	2.9100	2.9838	−0.0738	−0.51
14	573	2.7900	3.0910	−0.3010	−2.02
15	536	3.0000	2.9108	0.0892	0.62
16	639	3.5500	3.4124	0.1376	0.91
17	619	3.4700	3.3150	0.1550	1.02
18	694	3.6000	3.6803	−0.0803	−0.55
19	718	3.8800	3.7971	0.0829	0.59
20	759	3.7600	3.9968	−0.2368	−1.82

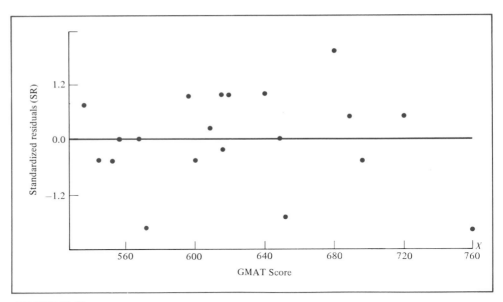

FIGURE 16.12
Plotting the standardized residuals versus GMAT score.

where

$$h_i = \frac{1}{n} + \frac{(X_i - \overline{X})^2}{\displaystyle\sum_{i=1}^{n} X_i^2 - \frac{\left(\displaystyle\sum_{i=1}^{n} X_i\right)^2}{n}}$$

These standardized values allow us to consider the magnitude of the residuals in units that reflect the standardized variation around the line of regression. The standardized residuals have been plotted against the independent variable (GMAT scores) in Figure 16.12. From this we may observe that although there is widespread scatter in the residual plot, there is no apparent pattern or relationship between the standardized residuals and X_i. The residuals appear to be evenly spread above and below 0 for differing values of X. Thus we may conclude that the fitted model appears to be appropriate.

16.12.3   Evaulating the Assumptions

Homoscedasticity

The assumption of homoscedasticity (see Section 16.11) can also be evaluated from a plot of SR_i with X_i. For the student performance data, there do not appear to be major differences in the variability of SR_i for different X_i values (see Figure 16.12). Thus we may conclude that for our fitted model there is no apparent violation in the assumption of equal variance at each level of X.

Nevertheless, if we observe the *hypothetical* plot of SR_i with X_i in Figure 16.13, there is an obvious violation of the homogeneity-of-variance assumption. In this hypothetical plot there appears to be a "fanning effect" in which the variability of the

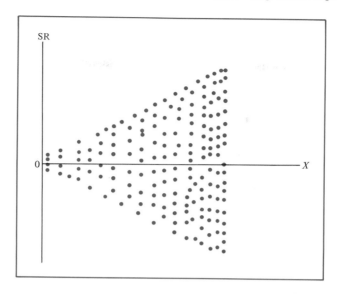

FIGURE 16.13
Violations in homoscedasticity.

residuals increases as X increases, thereby demonstrating the lack of homogeneity in the variances of Y_i at each level of X.

Normality

The normality assumption of regression (see Section 16.11) can also be evaluated from a residual analysis by tallying the standardized residuals into a frequency distribution and displaying the results in a histogram (see Chapter 4). In addition, if the sample size is large enough, the normality assumption can be tested by using a chi-square goodness-of-fit test as shown in Section 13.6.

For the student performance data, the standardized residuals have been tallied into a frequency distribution as indicated in Table 16.5 with the results displayed in Figure 16.14 on page 594. We must realize that it is difficult to evaluate the normality assumption for a sample of only 20 observations and available test procedures are beyond the scope of this text. (See Reference 6.) From Figure 16.14 we may note that the data do not appear to be exactly "bell shaped." However, in view of the small sample size and the fact that most of the residuals are located near the center of the distribution, it seems reasonable to conclude that there is no overwhelming evidence of a violation of the normality assumption.

TABLE 16.5 Frequency distribution of 20 standardized residual values for the student performance data

Standardized Residuals	No.
-2.8 but less than -2.0	1
-2.0 but less than -1.2	2
-1.2 but less than -0.4	4
-0.4 but less than $+0.4$	5
$+0.4$ but less than $+1.2$	7
$+1.2$ but less than $+2.0$	0
$+2.0$ but less than $+2.8$	1
Totals	20

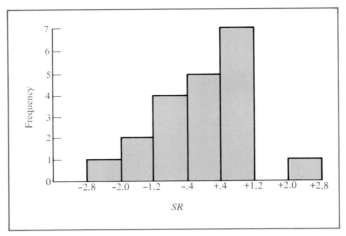

FIGURE 16.14
Plotting the standardized residuals for the student performance data.

SOURCE: Data taken from Table 16.5.

Independence

The independence assumption discussed in Section 16.11 can be evaluated by plotting the residuals in the order or sequence in which the observed data were obtained. Although it was not the case for the model considered in this chapter, data collected over periods of time (see Chapter 18) often exhibit an "autocorrelation" effect among successive observations. That is, there exists a correlation between a particular observation and those values that precede and succeed it. Such patterns, which violate the assumption of independence, are readily apparent in the plot of the residuals versus the time in which they were collected.

Problems

16.51 What is the difference between the residuals and the standardized residuals?

16.52 What is the purpose of residual analysis?

● **16.53** Referring to the pet food sales problem (pages 569, 572, and 576), perform a residual analysis on your results and determine the adequacy of the fit of the model.

16.54 Referring to the absenteeism problem (pages 570, 572, and 576), perform a residual analysis on your results and determine the adequacy of the fit of the model.

● **16.55** Referring to the production worker-hours problem (pages 570, 572, and 576), perform a residual analysis on your results and determine the adequacy of the fit of the model.

16.56 Referring to the tomato yield problem (pages 570, 572, and 576), perform a residual analysis on your results and determine the adequacy of the fit of the model.

16.57 Referring to the terminal maintenance problem (pages 570, 573, and 576), perform a residual analysis on your results and determine the adequacy of the fit of the model.

16.13 REGRESSION DIAGNOSTICS: INFLUENCE ANALYSIS

16.13.1 Introduction

Regression diagnostics deals with both the evaluation of the aptness of a particular model and the potential effect or "influence" of each particular point on that fitted model. In Section 16.12 we have utilized methods of residual analysis to study the aptness of our fitted model. In this section we will consider several methods that measure the influence of particular data points. Among a variety of recently developed criteria (see References 1–3, 5, 9, 19) we shall consider the following:

1. The hat matrix elements, h_i
2. The Studentized deleted residuals, t_i^*
3. Cook's distance statistic, D_i

Table 16.6 represents the values of these statistics for the student performance data of Table 16.1, which have been obtained from the Minitab computer package. We note from Table 16.6 that certain data points have been highlighted for further analysis.

TABLE 16.6 Influence statistics for the student performance data

Observation	GMAT Score X_i	Grade Point Index Y_i	Residual	h_i	Studentized Deleted Residual, t_i^*	Cook's D_i
1	688	3.72	0.46856	0.108428	0.45816	0.013350
2	647	3.44	−0.07509	0.058049	−0.07299	0.000174
3	652	3.21	−1.75986	0.061719	−1.87961	0.101862
4	608	3.29	0.18841	0.053011	0.18329	0.000994
5	680	3.91	2.00914	0.094969	2.21686	0.211791
6	617	3.28	−0.16626	0.050462	−0.16170	0.000735
7	557	3.02	0.04732	0.109508	0.04599	0.000138
8	599	3.13	−0.57891	0.057785	−0.56791	0.010277
9	616	3.45	0.98515	0.050636	0.98430	0.025882
10	594	3.33	0.90566	0.061400	0.90090	0.026828
11	567	3.07	0.05563	0.092795	0.05406	0.000158
12	542	2.86	−0.55326	0.139732	−0.54231	0.024860
13	551	2.91	−0.50509	0.120855	−0.49437	0.017535
14	573	2.79	−2.01754	0.084087	−2.22884	0.186847
15	536	3.00	0.62226	0.153553	0.61134	0.035122
16	639	3.55	0.90746	0.053607	0.90278	0.023322
17	619	3.47	1.02040	0.050198	1.02164	0.027515
18	694	3.60	−0.54880	0.119676	−0.53786	0.020472
19	718	3.88	0.58508	0.174566	0.57408	0.036197
20	759	3.76	−1.82247	0.304964	−1.96129	0.728670

16.13.2 The Hat Matrix Elements, h_i

We may recall from Section 16.8 that when we developed a confidence-interval estimate μ_{YX} we defined the "hat matrix diagonal elements," h_i, as

$$h_i = \frac{1}{n} + \frac{(X_i - \bar{X})^2}{\sum_{i=1}^{n} X_i^2 - \dfrac{\left(\sum_{i=1}^{n} X_i\right)^2}{n}}$$

(16.21)

Each h_i reflects the "influence" of each X_i on the fitted regression model. If such influential points are present, we may need to reevaluate the necessity for keeping them in the model. In simple linear regression[3] Hoaglin and Welsch (see Reference 9) suggest the following decision rule:

If $h_i > 4/n$, then X_i is an influential point and may be considered a candidate for removal from the model.

For our student performance data, since $n = 20$, our criteria would be to "flag" any h_i value greater than $4/20 = .200$. Referring to Table 16.6, we note that the value (X_{20}) is .305. This twentieth X observation then is a potential candidate for removal from our student performance model. However, other criteria for measuring influence must be considered prior to making such a decision.

16.13.3 The Studentized Deleted Residuals, t_i^*

In our discussion of residual analysis in Section 16.12, we defined the standardized residuals in Equation (16.20) as

$$SR_i = \frac{\epsilon_i}{S_{YX} \sqrt{1 - h_i}}$$

In an effort to better measure the adverse impact of each individual case on the model, Hoaglin and Welsch (see Reference 9) also developed the Studentized deleted residual t_i^* given in Equation (16.22):

$$t_i^* = \frac{\epsilon_i}{S_{(i)} \sqrt{1 - h_i}}$$

(16.22)

where $S_{(i)} =$ the standard error of the estimate for a model that includes all observations except observation i.

Thus this Studentized deleted residual measures the difference of each observation Y_i from that predicted by a model that includes all other observations. For example, t_1^* represents a measure of the difference between the actual grade point index for the first student ($Y_1 = 3.72$) and the grade point index that would be predicted for this student based on a model that included only the second through the twentieth students. In simple linear regression, Hoaglin and Welsch suggest that if

$$|t_i^*| > t_{.10, n-3}$$

---

[3] The more general criteria for multiple regression will be discussed in Section 17.16.

then this would mean that the observed and predicted Y values are so different that X_i is an influential point that adversely affects the model and may be considered a candidate for removal.

For our student performance data, since $n = 20$, our criteria would be to "flag" any t_i^* value greater than 1.7396 (see Table E.3). Referring to Table 16.6, we note that $t_3^* = -1.879$, $t_5^* = +2.216$, $t_{14}^* = -2.228$, and $t_{20}^* = -1.961$. Thus, the third, fifth, fourteenth, and twentieth students may each have an adverse effect on the model. The twentieth observation was also "flagged" according to the h_i criterion but the third, fifth, and fourteenth students were not. Hence, with this lack of consistency we should consider another criterion, Cook's D_i, which is based on both the h_i and the standardized residual statistics.

16.13.4 Cook's Distance Statistic, D_i

The use of h_i and t_i^* in the search for potential troublesome data points is complementary. Neither criterion is sufficient by itself. When h_i is small, t_i^* may be large (see observations 3, 5, and 14). On the other hand, when h_i is large, t_i^* may be moderate or small because the observed Y_i is consistent with the model and the rest of the data. To decide whether a point which has been flagged by either the h_i or t_i^* criterion is unduly affecting the model, Cook and Weisberg (see Reference 5) suggest the use of the D_i statistic. In the simple linear regression model[4] D_i is shown in Equation (16.23):

$$D_i = \frac{SR_i^2 h_i}{2(1 - h_i)} \tag{16.23}$$

where SR_i is the standardized residual of Equation (16.20).

In simple linear regression, Cook and Weisberg suggest that if

$$D_i > F_{.50,2,n-2}$$

this would mean that the observation may have an impact on the results of fitting the linear regression model.

For our student performance data, since $n = 20$, our criterion would be to "flag" any $D_i > F_{.50,2,18} = .720$. (See Table E.5a.) Referring to Table 16.6, we note that $D_{20} = .729 > .720$. The next largest D_i value, for observation 5 ($D_5 = .21$) is much smaller than .720. Thus it would appear that an alternative model should be explored in which observation 20 is deleted. Figure 16.15 on page 598 represents partial Minitab output for the new model. Here, we note that $r^2 = .819$ and the fitted model can be expressed as

$$\hat{Y}_i = -.0799 + .0055081\, X_i$$

From this we may conclude that for each increase of one point in GMAT score, the fitted model predicts that the grade point index will increase by .005508 points

---

[4] See footnote 3 on page 596.

```
The regression equation is
gpi = - 0.080 + 0.00551 gmat

Predictor          Coef          Stdev        t-ratio
Constant         -0.0799        0.3879         -0.21
gmat            0.0055081      0.0006278        8.77

s = 0.1448        R-sq = 81.9%      R-sq(adj) = 80.8%

Analysis of Variance

SOURCE           DF           SS            MS
Regression        1         1.6150        1.6150
Error            17         0.3566        0.0210
Total            18         1.9716
```

FIGURE 16.15

Minitab REGRESS output with observation 20 deleted from the data of Table 16.1.

(or we can say that for each 100-point increase in GMAT score, the grade point index will increase by .551 points). This slope can be viewed as representing the portion of the grade point index that varies according to GMAT score. The Y intercept b_0 was computed to be $-.08$. The Y intercept represents the value of Y when X equals zero (in this problem $-.08$). Since the GMAT score can never be zero, this Y intercept can be viewed as expressing the portion of the grade point index that varies with factors other than GMAT score. The removal of the twentieth observation has changed the regression coefficients somewhat and has produced a slightly better fitting model. However, the range for which predictions of GPI can be made has been narrowed from GMAT scores of 536 to 759 to GMAT scores of 536 to 718.

16.13.5 Summary

In this section we have discussed several criteria for evaluating the influence of each observation on the regression model. As we have noted, the various statistics often do not yield consistent results. Under such circumstances, most statisticians would conclude that there is insufficient evidence for the removal of such observations from the model.

In addition to the three criteria presented here, numerous other measures of influence have recently been developed (see References 1 and 8). While different researchers seem to prefer particular measures, currently there is no consensus as to the "best" measures. Hence, only when there is consistency in a selected set of measures is it appropriate to consider the removal of particular observations.

In conclusion, we should also realize that because of the computations involved in both residual analysis and influence analysis, diagnostic evaluation is not practical without the aid of a computer package. However, as Tukey (see Reference 17) has noted, the actual decision concerning the deletion of any observation is best left in the hands of the researcher rather than delegating such a decision to the computer package itself.

Problems

16.58   What is the difference between residual analysis and influence analysis?

16.59   Explain the difference between the h_i measure and the Studentized deleted residual.

● **16.60**   Referring to the pet food sales problem (pages 569, 572, and 576), perform an influence analysis and determine whether any observations may be deleted from the model. If necessary, reanalyze the regression model after deleting these observations and compare your results with the original model.

16.61   Referring to the absenteeism problem (pages 570, 572, and 576), perform an influence analysis and determine whether any observations may be deleted from the model. If necessary, reanalyze the regression model after deleting these observations and compare your results with the original model.

● **16.62**   Referring to the production worker-hours problem (pages 570, 572, and 576), perform an influence analysis and determine whether any observations may be deleted from the model. If necessary, reanalyze the regression model after deleting these observations and compare your results with the original model.

16.63   Referring to the tomato yield problem (pages 570, 572, and 576), perform an influence analysis and determine whether any observations may be deleted from the model. If necessary, reanalyze the regression model after deleting these observations and compare your results with the original model.

16.64   Referring to the terminal maintenance problem (pages 570, 573, and 576), perform an influence analysis and determine whether any observations may be deleted from the model. If necessary, reanalyze the regression model after deleting these observations and compare your results with the original model.

16.14   REGRESSION, COMPUTERS, AND THE REAL ESTATE SURVEY

16.14.1   Introduction

When we discussed descriptive statistics and hypothesis testing, we used the real estate survey to illustrate the role of the computer as an aid in data analysis. The role of computer software becomes even more important when applied to regression and correlation analysis and, in particular, to problems in multiple regression that will be discussed in Chapter 17. It is reasonable to state that with the development of residual analysis and influence analysis techniques, the role of the computer has become crucial even when only a simple linear regression model is being considered.

16.14.2   Using SAS, STATGRAPHICS, and Minitab for Regression Analysis

We may illustrate the role of the computer in regression and correlation analysis by referring to the complete data set of Table 16.1 on page 560. If the SAS package was being accessed (see References 10 and 15), procedures such as GLM, PLOT, and REG could be utilized. Figure 16.16 represents partial output from PROC REG for the student performance data. We may note that in addition to the various regression

```
DEP VARIABLE: GPI        GRADUATE GRADE POINT INDEX
ANALYSIS OF VARIANCE

                    SUM OF          MEAN
SOURCE      DF      SQUARES         SQUARE        F VALUE      PROB>F

MODEL       1       1.72573533      1.72573533    71.031       0.0001
ERROR       18      0.43731967      0.02429554
C TOTAL     19      2.16305500

        ROOT MSE       0.1558703     R-SQUARE      0.7978
        DEP MEAN       3.3335        ADJ R-SQ      0.7866
        C.V.           4.675874

PARAMETER ESTIMATES

                    PARAMETER            STANDARD           T FOR HO:
VARIABLE    DF      ESTIMATE             ERROR              PARAMETER=0

INTERCEP    1     $b_0$  0.30032331      0.36157714  $S_{b_0}$      0.831
GMAT        1     $b_1$  0.004870226     0.000577864 $S_{b_1}$      8.428


VARIABLE    DF      PROB > |T|     TYPE I SS        TYPE II SS

INTERCEP    1       0.4171         222.24444        0.01676111
GMAT        1       0.0001         1.72573533       1.72573533

                    VARIABLE
VARIABLE    DF      LABEL

INTERCEP    1       INTERCEPT
GMAT        1       SCORE ON GMAT EXAM




                    PREDICT      STD ERR                 STD ERR
OBS         ACTUAL  VALUE        PREDICT     RESIDUAL    RESIDUAL

    1       3.7200  3.6510       0.0513      0.0690      0.1472
    2       3.4400  3.4514       0.0376      -0.0114     0.1513
    3       3.2100  3.4757       0.0387      -0.2657     0.1510
    4       3.2900  3.2614       0.0359      0.0286      0.1517
    5       3.9100  3.6121       0.0480      0.2979      0.1483
    6       3.2800  3.3053       0.0350      -0.0253     0.1519
    7       3.0200  3.0130       0.0516      .0069609    0.1471
    8       3.1300  3.2176       0.0375      -0.0876     0.1513
    9       3.4500  3.3004       0.0351      0.1496      0.1519
   10       3.3300  3.1932       0.0386      0.1368      0.1510
   11       3.0700  3.0617       0.0475      .0082586    0.1485
   12       2.8600  2.9400       0.0583      -0.0800     0.1446
   13       2.9100  2.9838       0.0542      -0.0738     0.1461
   14       2.7900  3.0910       0.0452      -0.3010     0.1492
   15       3.0000  2.9108       0.0611      0.0892      0.1434
   16       3.5500  3.4124       0.0361      0.1376      0.1516
   17       3.4700  3.3150       0.0349      0.1550      0.1519
   18       3.6000  3.6803       0.0539      -0.0803     0.1462
   19       3.8800  3.7971       0.0651      0.0829      0.1416
   20       3.7600  3.9968       0.0861      -0.2368     0.1299
```

FIGURE 16.16
SAS output for the student performance data.

OBS	STUDENT RESIDUAL	-2-1-0 1 2	COOK'S D
1	0.4686	^ ^ ^	0.013
2	-0.0751	^ ^ ^	0.000
3	-1.7599	^ ***^ ^	0.102
4	0.1884	^ ^ ^	0.001
5	2.0091	^ ^**** ^	0.212
6	-0.1663	^ ^ ^	0.001
7	0.0473	^ ^ ^	0.000
8	-0.5789	^ *^ ^	0.010
9	0.9852	^ ^* ^	0.026
10	0.9057	^ ^* ^	0.027
11	0.0556	^ ^ ^	0.000
12	-0.5533	^ *^ ^	0.025
13	-0.5051	^ , *^ ^	0.018
14	-2.0175	^ ****^ ^	0.187
15	0.6223	^ ^* ^	0.035
16	0.9075	^ ^* ^	0.023
17	1.0204	^ ^** ^	0.028
18	-0.5488	^ *^ ^	0.020
19	0.5851	^ ^* ^	0.036
20	-1.8225	^ ***^ ^	0.729

OBS	RESIDUAL	RSTUDENT	HAT DIAG H
1	0.0690	0.4582	0.1084
2	-0.0114	-0.0730	0.0580
3	-0.2657	-1.8796	0.0617
4	0.0286	0.1833	0.0530
5	0.2979	2.2169	0.0950
6	-0.0253	-0.1617	0.0505
7	.0069609	0.0460	0.1095
8	-0.0876	-0.5679	0.0578
9	0.1496	0.9843	0.0506
10	0.1368	0.9009	0.0614
11	.0082586	0.0541	0.0928
12	-0.0800	-0.5423	0.1397
13	-0.0738	-0.4944	0.1209
14	-0.3010	-2.2288	0.0841
15	0.0892	0.6113	0.1536
16	0.1376	0.9028	0.0536
17	0.1550	1.0216	0.0502
18	-0.0803	-0.5379	0.1197
19	0.0829	0.5741	0.1746
20	-0.2368	-1.9613	0.3050

FIGURE 16.16 (Continued)

```
Regression Analysis - Linear model: Y = a+bX

Dependent variable: B:TABLE161.GPI        Independent variable: B:TABLE161.GMAT

                         Standard          T              Prob.
Parameter     Estimate    Error          Value            Level

Intercept  b₀  0.300323    0.361577 Sb₀   0.830593        0.417085
Slope      b₁ 4.87023E-3  5.77864E-4 Sb₁  8.42799         1.15758E-7


                    Analysis of Variance

Source          Sum of Squares   Df   Mean Square   F-Ratio    Prob. Level
Model               1.725735      1    1.725735    71.030959      .00000
Error                .437320     18     .024296

Total (Corr.)       2.163055     19

Correlation Coefficient = 0.893209        R-squared =  79.78 percent
Stnd. Error of Est. = 0.15587
```

FIGURE 16.17
STATGRAPHICS output for the student performance data.

statistics such as the regression coefficients, standard errors, and r^2, we may obtain several statistics that relate to residual analysis and influence analysis.

In a similar manner, the STATGRAPHICS package (see Reference 16) may also be accessed for regression and correlation analysis. Figure 16.17 represents partial output obtained from the multiple regression choice on the REGRESS menu. We may note that in addition to the regression coefficients, standard errors, and r^2 that are

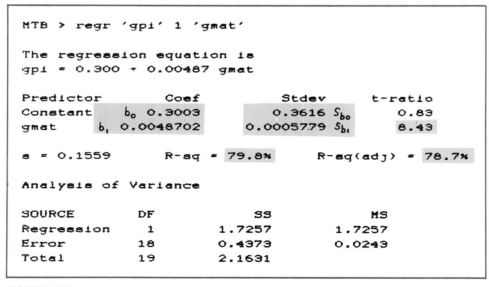

```
MTB > regr 'gpi' 1 'gmat'

The regression equation is
gpi = 0.300 + 0.00487 gmat

Predictor       Coef           Stdev         t-ratio
Constant   b₀  0.3003         0.3616 Sb₀      0.83
gmat       b₁  0.0048702      0.0005779 Sb₁   8.43

s = 0.1559      R-sq = 79.8%      R-sq(adj) = 78.7%

Analysis of Variance

SOURCE        DF          SS            MS
Regression     1        1.7257        1.7257
Error         18        0.4373        0.0243
Total         19        2.1631
```

FIGURE 16.18
Minitab output for the student performance data.

displayed, we could also obtain the standardized residuals and the DFFITS statistic (see Reference 3) which is an alternative to Cook's D_i statistic.

If the Minitab package was being accessed (see References 11 and 14), the REGRESS command could be used for a regression analysis. Figure 16.18 represents partial output from this command for the student performance data. We may observe that the regression coefficients, standard errors, and r^2 are provided here. The various statistics related to residual analysis and influence analysis were already displayed in Table 16.6 on page 595. We note from the highlighted regression statistics displayed in Figures 16.16–16.18 some discrepancies with the results presented earlier in the chapter. These differences are due to rounding errors. The results from the computer packages are more precise.

16.14.3   Computers and the Real Estate Survey

Now that we have illustrated how packages such as SAS, STATGRAPHICS, and Minitab can be used in regression analysis, we may return to the real estate survey. Suppose that the president would like to develop a statistical model to predict the appraised value of houses in East Meadow. Although realistically one may need to include several explanatory variables in an analysis, the statistician has decided to begin by initially using only a single independent variable for prediction—the number of rooms in the house. The data for these variables is illustrated in Table 16.7 on page 604.

We may begin our analysis by examining Figure 16.19 on page 605, a scatter diagram of these two variables provided by the Minitab package. We may observe that there appears to be a moderately increasing relationship between rooms and appraised value. Although there is some variability in the plotted data, it seems reasonable to begin by assuming a linear relationship between the two variables. Using the Minitab package, we obtain the output presented in Figure 16.20 on page 605.

We first note that the regression equation is

$$\hat{Y}_i = 74.80 + 19.718\, X_i$$

We may interpret the slope 19.718 to mean that for each additional one room in the house, the predicted appraised value increases by 19.718 thousand dollars. We note that since X varies from 5 to 11, the model may be used to predict appraised value for houses in East Meadow that have between five and eleven rooms. The Y intercept 74.80 represents the predicted appraised value for a house that has zero rooms. Since such a house is certainly not feasible, we can also view the intercept as the portion of the appraised value that does not vary with the number of rooms.

Now that the regression coefficients have been interpreted, we need to evaluate whether there is a significant linear relationship between these two variables. From Figure 16.20 we observe that r^2 is .438 or 43.8%. Thus 43.8% of the variation in appraised value can be explained by variation in the number of rooms. We note that the t statistic for the significance of the slope is 7.49, which, with $74 - 2 = 72$ degrees of freedom, is clearly significant even at the .01 level ($7.49 > 2.6459$). Thus there is reason to believe that there is evidence of a linear relationship between the two variables.

Although the relationship was significant, since r^2 was only of moderate value, more than half of the variation is explained by other factors. This might lead one to consider using additional explanatory variables in the model or curvilinear regression

TABLE 16.7 Appraised value and number of rooms for houses in East Meadow

Observation	Y_i (Appraised Value)	X_i (Rooms)	Observation	Y_i (Appraised Value)	X_i (Rooms)
1	215.0	7	38	297.5	9
2	195.0	8	39	229.0	7
3	160.0	7	40	215.0	7
4	189.0	6	41	190.0	6
5	249.0	8	42	290.0	9
6	267.0	9	43	310.0	11
7	199.9	6	44	206.0	7
8	169.0	6	45	224.5	7
9	179.0	6	46	220.0	7
10	218.0	7	47	270.0	7
11	247.0	8	48	205.0	8
12	218.0	7	49	240.0	8
13	299.9	8	50	210.0	7
14	172.0	6	51	215.0	7
15	230.0	7	52	210.0	8
16	235.0	7	53	229.0	6
17	190.0	8	54	280.0	8
18	180.0	5	55	280.0	7
19	213.0	8	56	174.5	6
20	175.0	6	57	185.0	6
21	170.0	6	58	180.0	7
22	215.0	7	59	205.0	7
23	229.5	7	60	190.0	7
24	180.0	6	61	195.0	7
25	225.0	6	62	260.0	10
26	155.0	5	63	168.0	5
27	179.0	6	64	180.0	6
28	195.0	7	65	185.0	7
29	179.9	6	66	286.5	11
30	225.0	7	67	165.9	6
31	197.5	8	68	265.0	6
32	195.0	8	69	230.0	6
33	190.0	7	70	194.0	6
34	245.0	7	71	295.0	8
35	206.7	10	72	169.5	6
36	199.0	6	73	275.0	9
37	190.0	6	74	225.0	10

(see Chapter 17). We also note that the standard error of the estimate (denoted as S by Minitab) equals 29.05.

Now that a preliminary regression analysis has been completed, we turn to the use of regression diagnostics (residual analysis and influence analysis) to determine the aptness of the model and the influence of individual observations on the model. First we may examine several plots of the standardized residuals (see Section 16.12). Figure 16.21 on page 606 represents a Minitab plot of the standardized residuals versus the independent variable, number of rooms. We observe from Figure 16.21 that there appears to be little or no pattern in this plot; there are both high and low standardized residuals at many different levels of X. In addition, we observe little evidence of heterogeneity of variance at different levels of X.

We may also evaluate the normality assumption by plotting the standardized residuals as in Figure 16.22 on page 606. From Figure 16.22 we note very little

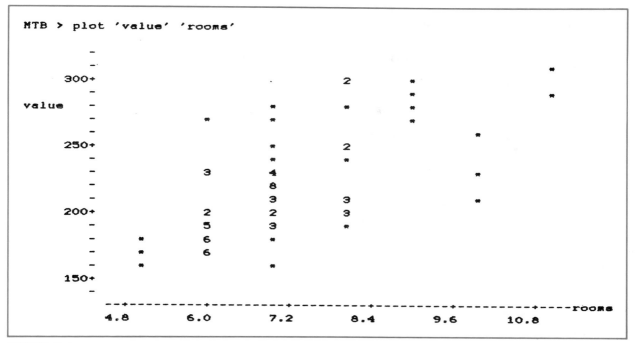

FIGURE 16.19
Minitab PLOT output for the data of Table 16.7.

departure from normality. Thus we may conclude from the perspective of residual analysis that the linear model appears to be an appropriate fit to the data.

Although the residual analysis has shown little departure from either linearity or the set of regression assumptions, it is important that we continue with our diagnostic

```
The regression equation is
value = 74.8 + 19.7 rooms

Predictor      Coef        Stdev      t-ratio
Constant      74.80        19.04        3.93
rooms         19.718        2.631       7.49

s = 29.05        R-sq = 43.8%     R-sq(adj) = 43.0%

Analysis of Variance

SOURCE        DF          SS             MS
Regression     1        47398          47398
Error         72        60775            844
Total         73       108173
```

FIGURE 16.20
Minitab REGRESS output for the data of Table 16.7.

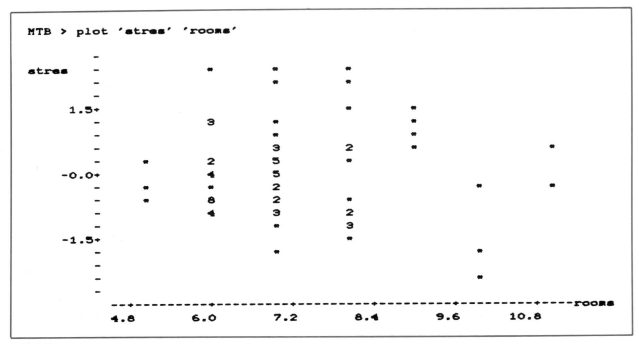

FIGURE 16.21
Minitab PLOT of standardized residuals versus number of rooms.

analysis through the use of influence measures. This approach will enable us to determine whether any observations are unduly affecting the model. Figure 16.23 represents additional Minitab output obtained for our model. Included are the residual, standardized residual, h_i value, Studentized deleted residual, and Cook's D_i statistic

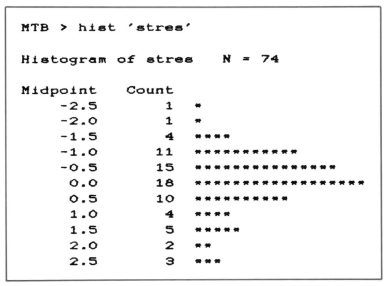

FIGURE 16.22
Minitab HISTOGRAM output of standardized residuals.

ROW	value	rooms	stres	hi	tresids	cookd
1	215.0	7	0.07524	0.013635	0.07472	0.000039
2	195.0	8	-1.30537	0.019843	-1.31189	0.017248
3	160.0	7	-1.83087	0.013635	-1.86197	0.023168
4	189.0	6	-0.14320	0.023833	-0.14223	0.000250
5	249.0	8	0.57200	0.019843	0.56931	0.003312
6	267.0	9	0.51828	0.042456	0.51563	0.005955
7	199.9	6	0.23652	0.023833	0.23496	0.000683
8	169.0	6	-0.83995	0.023833	-0.83821	0.008613
9	179.0	6	-0.49157	0.023833	-0.48897	0.002950
10	218.0	7	0.17921	0.013635	0.17800	0.000222
11	247.0	8	0.50247	0.019843	0.49985	0.002556
12	218.0	7	0.17921	0.013635	0.17800	0.000222
13	299.9	8	2.34160	0.019843	2.41922	0.055501
14	172.0	6	-0.73543	0.023833	-0.73307	0.006603
15	230.0	7	0.59509	0.013635	0.59240	0.002448
16	235.0	7	0.76837	0.013635	0.76617	0.004081
17	190.0	8	-1.47920	0.019843	-1.49173	0.022147
18	180.0	5	0.23339	0.050438	0.23185	0.001447
19	213.0	8	-0.67958	0.019843	-0.67701	0.004675
20	175.0	6	-0.63092	0.023833	-0.62827	0.004859
21	170.0	6	-0.80511	0.023833	-0.80312	0.007913
22	215.0	7	0.07524	0.013635	0.07472	0.000039
23	229.5	7	0.57776	0.013635	0.57507	0.002307
24	180.0	6	-0.45674	0.023833	-0.45421	0.002547
25	225.0	6	1.11093	0.023833	1.11277	0.015066
26	155.0	5	-0.64965	0.050438	-0.64703	0.011209
27	179.0	6	-0.49157	0.023833	-0.48897	0.002950
28	195.0	7	-0.61789	0.013635	-0.61521	0.002639
29	179.9	6	-0.46022	0.023833	-0.45769	0.002586
30	225.0	7	0.42181	0.013635	0.41939	0.001230
31	197.5	8	-1.21845	0.019843	-1.22263	0.015028
32	195.0	8	-1.30537	0.019843	-1.31189	0.017248
33	190.0	7	-0.79117	0.013635	-0.78909	0.004326
34	245.0	7	1.11494	0.013635	1.11685	0.008592
35	206.7	10	-2.34457	0.081477	-2.42254	0.243802
36	199.0	6	0.20517	0.023833	0.20380	0.000514
37	190.0	6	-0.10837	0.023833	-0.10762	0.000143
38	297.5	9	1.59110	0.042456	1.60854	0.056124
39	229.0	7	0.56044	0.013635	0.55775	0.002171
40	215.0	7	0.07524	0.013635	0.07472	0.000039
41	190.0	6	-0.10837	0.023833	-0.10762	0.000143
42	290.0	9	1.32729	0.042456	1.33447	0.039056
43	310.0	11	0.67793	0.136903	0.67536	0.036450
44	206.0	7	-0.23667	0.013635	-0.23511	0.000387

FIGURE 16.23
Minitab output for influence analysis for the data of Table 16.7.

45	224.5	7	0.40448	0.013635	0.40212	0.001131
46	220.0	7	0.24853	0.013635	0.24690	0.000427
47	270.0	7	1.98135	0.013635	2.02348	0.027134
48	205.0	8	-0.95770	0.019843	-0.95715	0.009284
49	240.0	8	0.25911	0.019843	0.25742	0.000680
50	210.0	7	-0.09804	0.013635	-0.09736	0.000066
51	215.0	7	0.07524	0.013635	0.07472	0.000039
52	210.0	8	-0.78387	0.019843	-0.78175	0.006220
53	229.0	6	1.25028	0.023833	1.25527	0.019083
54	280.0	8	1.64975	0.019843	1.67013	0.027549
55	280.0	7	2.32792	0.013635	2.40393	0.037456
56	174.5	6	-0.64834	0.023833	-0.64571	0.005131
57	185.0	6	-0.28255	0.023833	-0.28074	0.000975
58	180.0	7	-1.13774	0.013635	-1.14010	0.008947
59	205.0	7	-0.27132	0.013635	-0.26957	0.000509
60	190.0	7	-0.79117	0.013635	-0.78909	0.004326
61	195.0	7	-0.61789	0.013635	-0.61521	0.002639
62	260.0	10	-0.43037	0.081477	-0.42792	0.008215
63	168.0	5	-0.19047	0.050438	-0.18919	0.000964
64	180.0	6	-0.45674	0.023833	-0.45421	0.002547
65	185.0	7	-0.96445	0.013635	-0.96398	0.006429
66	286.5	11	-0.19272	0.136903	-0.19142	0.002946
67	165.9	6	-0.94794	0.023833	-0.94726	0.010970
68	265.0	6	2.50442	0.023833	2.60292	0.076567
69	230.0	6	1.28512	0.023833	1.29106	0.020161
70	194.0	6	0.03098	0.023833	0.03077	0.000012
71	295.0	8	2.17125	0.019843	2.23037	0.047719
72	169.5	6	-0.82253	0.023833	-0.82066	0.008259
73	275.0	9	0.79968	0.042456	0.79765	0.014177
74	225.0	10	-1.68735	0.081477	-1.70973	0.126276

FIGURE 16.23 (Continued)

for each observation. We may note that any standardized residual in excess of 2.0 (or below −2.0) is denoted with an *R* by Minitab. In addition, any observation whose h_i is >6/n in simple linear regression will be denoted with an *X* by Minitab.

We may begin our influence analysis by first examining the h_i statistic. Using the Hoaglin-Welsch criterion ($h_i > 4/n$), with $n = 74$, we would consider an observation influential if $h_i > 4/74 = .054$. From Figure 16.23 we observe that observations 43 and 66 (whose $h_i = .137$) and observations 35, 62, and 74 (whose $h_i = .081$) exceed this criterion. Thus, based on the h_i criterion, observations 35, 43, 62, 66 and 74 are candidates for removal from the model. However, other criteria for measuring influence must be considered prior to making such a decision.

The second criterion for measuring influence is the t_i^* statistic that involves the Studentized deleted residuals. Using the Hoaglin-Welsch criterion, ($|t_i^*| > t_{.10,n-3}$), for $n = 74$ we would consider an observation influential if $|t_i^*| > 1.6666$. From Figure 16.23 we observe that t_i^* equals −1.86 for observation 3, 2.42 for observation 13,

−2.42 for observation 35, 2.02 for observation 47, 2.40 for observation 55, 2.60 for observation 68, 2.23 for observation 71, and −1.71 for observation 74. We also observe that t_i^* for observation 43 is .68 while for observation 66 t_i^* is −.19. Thus observations 43 and 66, which had high h_i values, did not adversely affect the model.

In order to complete our influence analysis we need to look at Cook's D_i statistic, which measures the combined effect of h_i and SR_i. Using Cook and Weisberg's criterion for linear regression ($D_i > F_{.50,2,n-2}$), for $n = 74$ we should consider an observation influential if $D_i > .700$. Referring to Figure 16.23, we note that there are no D_i values that meet this criterion. However, the largest values are for observations 35 (.244) and 74 (.126). These results are not consistent with those obtained from the h_i and t_i^* criteria. Hence the researcher would have no clear basis for removing any of the observations from the fitted regression model. Regardless of whether any observations are to be deleted from this model, it is clear that, at best, this model is only a moderately useful predictor of appraised value and that other independent variables and/or a curvilinear relationship should be investigated for possible inclusion in a model. This subject will be the topic of our next chapter.

16.15 REGRESSION AND CORRELATION—SOME CAVEATS

Regression and correlation analysis are perhaps the most widely used, and unfortunately, the most widely abused, statistical techniques that are applied in business and economics. The difficulties that often accompany regression and correlation analysis may arise from several sources. One common difficulty in regression analysis is the lack of awareness on the part of the user of the assumptions of least-squares regression, how they can be evaluated, and what can be done if they are seriously violated (see Sections 16.11–16.13). This phenomenon unfortunately has been compounded by the easy access to statistical software.

A second difficulty is the mistaken belief that correlation implies causation. In many instances the co-variation between the variables is "spurious" in that the relationship is caused by a third factor that has not been or cannot be measured.

A third difficulty involves the fact that a good-fitting model does not necessarily mean that the model can truly be used for prediction. The researcher with knowledge of the subject matter would have to be convinced that the process that produced the data will remain stable in the future in order to use the model for predictive purposes.

Supplementary Problems

16.65 Referring to Problems 16.1 and 16.6 (pages 561 and 569), what assumptions about the relationship between shelf space and profits do we need to make in order to use this regression model for predictive purposes?

16.66 Referring to Problems 16.4 and 16.9 (pages 562 and 570), what assumptions about the relationship between amount of fertilizer and yield do we need to make in order to use this regression model for predictive purposes?

16.67   Referring to Problems 16.5 and 16.10 (pages 563 and 570), what assumptions about the relationship between age and the number of service calls do we need to make in order to use this regression model for predictive purposes?

• **16.68**   A statistician for a large American automobile manufacturer would like to develop a statistical model for predicting delivery time (the days between the ordering of the car and the actual delivery of the car) of custom-ordered new automobiles. The statistician believes that there is a *linear* relationship between the number of options ordered on the car and delivery time. A random sample of 16 cars is selected with the results given below.

Relating delivery time with options ordered (Problem 16.68)

Car	Number of Options, Ordered, X	Delivery Time, Y (in days)
1	3	25
2	4	32
3	4	26
4	7	38
5	7	34
6	8	41
7	9	39
8	11	46
9	12	44
10	12	51
11	14	53
12	16	58
13	17	61
14	20	64
15	23	66
16	25	70

(a) Set up a scatter diagram.

(b) Use the least-squares method to find the regression coefficients b_0 and b_1.

(c) Interpret the meaning of the Y intercept b_0 and the slope b_1 in this problem.

(d) If a car was ordered that had 16 options, how many days would you predict it would take to be delivered?

(e) Compute the standard error of the estimate.

(f) Compute the coefficient of determination r^2 and interpret its meaning in this problem.

(g) Compute the coefficient of correlation r.

(h) Compute the adjusted r^2 and compare it to the coefficient of determination r^2.

(i) Set up a 95% confidence interval estimate of the average delivery time for all cars ordered with 16 options.

(j) Set up a 95% prediction interval estimate of the delivery time for an individual car that was ordered with 16 options.

(k) At the .05 level of significance, is there evidence of a linear relationship between number of options and delivery time?

(l) Set up a 95% confidence-interval estimate of the true slope.

(m) Perform a residual analysis on your results and determine the adequacy of the fit of the model.

(n) Perform an influence analysis and determine whether any observations should be deleted from the model. If necessary, reanalyze the regression model after deleting these observations and compare your results to the original model.

(o) What assumptions about the relationship between the number of options and delivery time would the statistician need to make in order to use this regression model for predictive purposes in the future?

16.69 An official of a local racetrack would like to develop a model to forecast the amount of money bet (in millions of dollars) based on attendance. A random sample of 10 days is selected with the results given in the table below.

Relating betting with attendance (Problem 16.69)

Day	Attendance (thousands)	Amount Bet (millions of dollars)
1	14.5	.70
2	21.2	.83
3	11.6	.62
4	31.7	1.10
5	46.8	1.27
6	31.4	1.02
7	40.0	1.15
8	21.0	.80
9	16.3	.71
10	32.1	1.04

Hint: Determine which are the independent and dependent variables.
(a) Set up a scatter diagram.
(b) Assuming a linear relationship, use the least-squares method to find the regression coefficients b_0 and b_1.
(c) Interpret the meaning of the slope b_1 in this problem.
(d) Predict the amount bet for a day on which attendance is 20,000.
(e) Compute the standard error of the estimate.
(f) Compute the coefficient of determination r^2 and interpret its meaning in this problem.
(g) Compute the coefficient of correlation r.
(h) Set up a 99% confidence-interval estimate of the average amount of money bet when attendance is 20,000.
(i) Set up a 99% prediction interval for the amount of money bet on a day in which attendance is 20,000.
(j) At the .01 level of significance, is there evidence of a linear relationship between the amount of money bet and attendance?
(k) Set up a 99% confidence-interval estimate of the true slope.
(l) Discuss why you should not predict the amount bet on a day on which the attendance exceeded 46,800 or was below 11,600.
(m) Perform a residual analysis on your results and determine the adequacy of the fit of the model.
(n) Perform an influence analysis and determine whether any observations should be deleted from the model. If necessary, reanalyze the regression model after deleting these observations and compare your results with the original model.

16.70 The controller's office of a state government would like to be able to estimate the amount turned over to the state government as profit once a proposed lottery has been operating for at least one year. The following information (on page 612) is available for the latest year from 23 states.

Relating profit to sales (Problem 16.70)

State	Sales ($ millions)	Profit ($ millions)
Arizona	142.3	51.6
California	1,400.0	504.0
Colorado	113.3	35.7
Connecticut	489.0	214.0
Delaware	45.9	17.1
District of Columbia	118.0	40.0
Illinois	1,330.0	553.0
Iowa	94.5	26.9
Maine	58.0	18.2
Maryland	760.5	332.2
Massachusetts	1,270.0	410.0
Michigan	1,005.0	410.0
Missouri	177.0	80.0
New Hampshire	58.7	20.7
New Jersey	1,100.0	472.2
New York	1,460.0	666.8
Ohio	1,070.0	376.0
Oregon	100.4	33.2
Pennsylvania	1,338.0	570.0
Rhode Island	57.9	21.5
Vermont	25.3	8.0
Washington	194.0	78.0
West Virginia	66.0	28.0

Hint: Determine which are the independent and dependent variables.
(a) Set up a scatter diagram.
(b) Assuming a linear relationship, use the least-squares method to find the regression co-efficients b_0 and b_1.
(c) Interpret the meaning of the slope b_1 in this problem.
(d) Predict the profit for a state that has a sales of lottery tickets of $700 million.
(e) Compute the standard error of the estimate.
(f) Compute the coefficient of determination r^2 and interpret its meaning in this problem.
(g) Compute the coefficient of correlation r.
(h) Compute the adjusted r^2 and compare it with the coefficient of determination r^2.
(i) Set up a 95% confidence interval estimate of the average profit for all states which have sales of $700 million.
(j) Set up a 95% prediction interval of the profit for an individual state which has sales of $700 million.
(k) At the .05 level of significance, is there evidence of a linear relationship between sales and profits?
(l) Set up a 95% confidence interval estimate of the true population slope.
(m) Perform a residual analysis on your results and determine the adequacy of the fit of the model.
(n) Perform an influence analysis and determine whether any observations should be deleted from the model. If necessary, reanalyze the regression model after deleting these observations and compare your results with the original model.
(o) What assumptions about the relationship between sales and profits do we need to make in order to use this regression model for predictive purposes?

16.71 The owner of a large chain of ice-cream stores would like to study the effect of atmospheric temperature on sales during the summer season. A random sample of 14 days is selected with the results given at the top of page 613.

Relating sales to temperature (Problem 16.71)

Day	Temperature (°F)	Sales per Store (in $ 000)
1	63	1.52
2	70	1.68
3	73	1.80
4	75	2.05
5	80	2.36
6	82	2.25
7	85	2.68
8	88	2.90
9	90	3.14
10	91	3.06
11	92	3.24
12	75	1.92
13	98	3.40
14	100	3.28

(a) Set up a scatter diagram.

(b) Assuming a linear relationship, use the least-squares method to compute the regression coefficients b_0 and b_1.

(c) Interpret the meaning of the slope b_1 in this problem.

(d) Predict the sales per store for a day in which the temperature is 83°F.

(e) Compute the standard error of the estimate.

(f) Compute the coefficient of determination r^2 and interpret its meaning in this problem.

(g) Compute the coefficient of correlation r.

(h) Compute the adjusted r^2 and compare it with the coefficient of determination r^2.

(i) Set up a 95% confidence-interval estimate of the average sales per store for all days in which the temperature is 83°F.

(j) Set up a 95% prediction interval for the sales per store on a day in which the temperature is 80°F.

(k) At the .05 level of significance, is there evidence of a linear relationship between temperature and sales?

(l) Set up a 95% confidence-interval estimate of the true slope.

(m) Discuss how different your results might be if the model had been based upon temperature measured according to the Celsius (°C) scale.

(n) Perform a residual analysis on your results and determine the adequacy of the fit of the model.

(o) Perform an influence analysis and determine whether any observations should be deleted from the model. If necessary, reanalyze the regression model after deleting these observations and compare your results with the original model.

16.72 A member of the controller's office in a state government would like to develop a model to estimate the amount of highway users' tax that will be collected based upon the number of trucks registered. Data available from 49 states and the District of Columbia are summarized on page 614.

(a) Assuming a linear relationship, use the least-squares method to compute the regression coefficients b_0 and b_1.

(b) Interpret the meaning of the Y intercept b_0 and the slope b_1 in this problem.

(c) Use the regression model developed in (a) to predict the highway users' tax collected for a state that has 300,000 registered trucks.

(d) Compute the standard error of the estimate.

(e) Compute the coefficient of determination r^2 and interpret its meaning in this problem.

(f) Compute the coefficient of correlation r.

Highway tax data by state (Problem 16.72)

State	Trucks Registered (in thousands)	Highway Taxes (in $ millions))
Alabama	596.0	170.0
Arkansas	86.8	24.7
Arizona	390.4	124.2
California	2,690.5	909.1
Colorado	491.6	107.0
Connecticut	142.5	50.6
Delaware	60.1	24.1
District of Columbia	12.9	7.8
Florida	922.3	263.3
Georgia	700.2	165.3
Hawaii	66.6	15.6
Idaho	240.2	60.2
Illinois	1,094.5	372.1
Indiana	764.0	255.7
Iowa	560.5	155.9
Kansas	568.2	120.6
Kentucky	596.8	180.4
Louisiana	620.7	148.7
Maine	132.2	40.9
Maryland	342.2	125.3
Massachusetts	299.9	90.6
Michigan	921.9	307.3
Minnesota	659.1	172.8
Mississippi	387.6	105.6
Missouri	684.6	179.5
Montana	237.7	56.6
Nebraska	369.4	90.8
Nevada	123.7	38.4
New Hampshire	75.2	24.0
New Jersey	354.1	163.1
New Mexico	275.7	72.5
New York	824.2	269.3
North Carolina	812.7	245.3
North Dakota	219.6	39.1
Ohio	907.2	339.1
Oklahoma	683.2	148.8
Oregon	332.4	107.2
Pennsylvania	1,114.5	376.7
Rhode Island	68.4	19.3
South Carolina	342.8	93.3
South Dakota	187.1	41.3
Tennessee	617.3	178.1
Texas	2,248.7	653.0
Utah	262.1	55.5
Vermont	56.4	22.5
Virginia	506.3	207.5
Washington	668.0	186.4
West Virginia	224.6	83.9
Wisconsin	412.5	130.8
Wyoming	138.9	47.1

(g) Compute the adjusted r^2 and compare it to the coefficient of determination r^2.

(h) At the .05 level of significance, is there evidence of a linear relationship between registered trucks and highway users' tax collected?

(i) Perform a residual analysis on your results and determine the adequacy of the fit of the model.

(j) Perform an influence analysis and determine whether any observations may be deleted from the model. If necessary, reanalyze the regression model after deleting these observations and compare your results with the original model.

● **16.73** Suppose that a researcher for the Environmental Protection Agency would like to develop a model to predict gasoline mileage as measured by miles per gallon (MPG) based upon the horsepower of the car's engine. A sample of 50 recent car models was selected and the results are shown below.

Relating MPG to horsepower (Problem 16.73)

Model	MPG	Horsepower	Model	MPG	Horsepower
1	43.1	48	26	23.9	90
2	19.9	110	27	29.9	65
3	19.2	105	28	30.4	67
4	17.7	165	29	36.0	74
5	18.1	139	30	22.6	110
6	20.3	103	31	36.4	67
7	21.5	115	32	27.5	95
8	16.9	155	33	33.7	75
9	15.5	142	34	44.6	67
10	18.5	150	35	32.9	100
11	27.2	71	36	38.0	67
12	41.5	76	37	24.2	120
13	46.6	65	38	38.1	60
14	23.7	100	39	39.4	70
15	27.2	84	40	25.4	116
16	39.1	58	41	31.3	75
17	28.0	88	42	34.1	68
18	24.0	92	43	34.0	88
19	20.2	139	44	31.0	82
20	20.5	95	45	27.4	80
21	28.0	90	46	22.3	88
22	34.7	63	47	28.0	79
23	36.1	66	48	17.6	85
24	35.7	80	49	34.4	65
25	20.2	85	50	20.6	105

Hint: First determine which is the independent variable and which is the dependent variable.

(a) Plot a scatter diagram and, assuming a linear relationship, use the least-squares method to find the regression coefficients b_0 and b_1.

(b) Interpret the meaning of the Y intercept b_0 and the slope b_1 in this problem.

(c) Use the regression model developed in (a) to predict the miles per gallon for a car with 100 horsepower.

(d) Compute the standard error of the estimate.

(e) Compute the coefficient of determination r^2 and interpret its meaning in this problem.

(f) Compute the coefficient of correlation r.

(g) Compute the adjusted r^2 and compare it with the coefficient of determination r^2.

(h) At the .10 level of significance, is there evidence of a linear relationship between miles per gallon and horsepower?

(i) Set up a 90% confidence-interval estimate for the average miles per gallon for cars that have 100 horsepower.

(j) Set up a 90% prediction-interval estimate of the miles per gallon for an individual car that has 100 horsepower.

(k) Perform a residual analysis on your results and determine the adequacy of the fit of the model.

(l) Perform an influence analysis and determine whether any observations may be deleted from the model. If necessary, reanalyze the regression model after deleting these observations and compare your results with the original model.

16.74   A sample of 30 recently sold single-family houses in a small western city was selected. The selling price and the assessed value (the houses in the city had been reassessed at full value one year prior to the study) was recorded with the following results:

Relating selling price to assessed value (Problem 16.74)

Observation	Assessed Value ($000)	Selling Price ($000)
1	78.17	94.10
2	80.24	101.90
3	74.03	88.65
4	86.31	115.50
5	75.22	97.50
6	65.54	72.00
7	72.43	91.50
8	85.61	113.90
9	60.80	69.34
10	81.88	96.90
11	79.11	96.00
12	59.93	61.90
13	75.27	83.00
14	85.88	109.50
15	76.64	93.75
16	84.36	106.70
17	72.94	81.50
18	86.50	94.50
19	66.28	69.00
20	79.74	96.90
21	72.78	86.50
22	77.90	97.90
23	74.31	83.00
24	79.85	87.30
25	84.78	100.80
26	81.61	97.90
27	74.92	90.50
28	79.98	97.00
29	77.96	92.00
30	79.07	95.90

Suppose that we wanted to develop a model to predict selling price based on assessed value.

Hint: First determine which is the independent variable and which is the dependent variable.

(a) Plot a scatter diagram and, assuming a linear relationship, use the least-squares method to find the regression coefficients b_0 and b_1.

(b) Interpret the meaning of the Y intercept b_0 and the slope b_1 in this problem.

(c) Use the regression model developed in (a) to predict the selling price for a house whose assessed value is $70,000.

(d) Compute the standard error of the estimate.

(e) Compute the coefficient of determination r^2 and interpret its meaning in this problem.

(f) Compute the coefficient of correlation r.

(g) Compute the adjusted r^2 and compare it with the coefficient of determination r^2.

(h) At the .10 level of significance, is there evidence of a linear relationship between selling price and assessed value?

(i) Set up a 90% confidence-interval estimate for the average selling price for houses that have an assessed value of $70,000.

(j) Set up a 90% prediction-interval estimate of the selling price of an individual house which has an assessed value of $70,000.

(k) Set up a 90% confidence-interval estimate of the population slope.

(l) Perform a residual analysis on your results and determine the adequacy of the fit of the model.

(m) Perform an influence analysis and determine whether any observations may be deleted from the model. If necessary, reanalyze the regression model after deleting these observations and compare your results with the original model.

16.75 Suppose that a sample of 15 single-family houses was selected in a different city. The assessed value (in thousands of dollars) and the heating area of the houses (in thousands of square feet) was recorded with the following results:

Relating assessed value to heating area (Problem 16.75)

House Number	Assessed Value ($ 000)	Heating Area of Dwelling (thousands of square feet)
1	84.4	2.00
2	77.4	1.71
3	75.7	1.45
4	85.9	1.76
5	79.1	1.93
6	70.4	1.20
7	75.8	1.55
8	85.9	1.93
9	78.5	1.59
10	79.2	1.50
11	86.7	1.90
12	79.3	1.39
13	74.5	1.54
14	83.8	1.89
15	76.8	1.59

Suppose we wanted to develop a model to predict assessed value based on heating area.

Hint: First determine which is the independent variable and which is the dependent variable.

(a) Plot a scatter diagram and, assuming a linear relationship, use the least-squares method to find the regression coefficients b_0 and b_1.

(b) Interpret the meaning of the Y intercept b_0 and the slope b_1 in this problem.

(c) Use the regression model developed in (a) to predict the assessed value for a house whose heating area is 1,750 square feet.

(d) Compute the standard error of the estimate.

(e) Compute the coefficient of determination r^2 and interpret its meaning in this problem.

(f) Compute the coefficient of correlation r.

(g) Compute the adjusted r^2 and compare it with the coefficient of determination r^2

(h) At the .10 level of significance, is there evidence of a linear relationship between assessed value and heating area?

(i) Set up a 90% confidence-interval estimate for the average assessed value for houses with a heating area of 1,750 square feet.

(j) Set up a 90% prediction-interval estimate of the assessed value of an individual house which has a heating area of 1,750 square feet.

(k) Set up a 90% confidence-interval estimate of the population slope.

(l) Perform a residual analysis on your results and determine the adequacy of the fit of the model.

(m) Perform an influence analysis and determine whether any observations may be deleted from the model. If necessary, reanalyze the regression model after deleting these observations and compare your results with the original model.

16.76 The production manager of a factory would like to develop a model to predict performance time for a manual assembly task based upon the amount of time spent in training. A sample of 18 recent employees was selected; the training time in hours and the performance time in minutes are presented below.

Relating performance time to training (Problem 16.76)

Observation	Training Time (hours)	Performance Time (minutes)
1	27	19
2	24	16
3	12	12
4	22	17
5	13	10
6	29	19
7	14	15
8	20	14
9	16	15
10	21	21
11	22	14
12	25	22
13	23	22
14	18	15
15	20	14
16	15	15
17	13	16
18	20	15

Hint: First determine which is the independent variable and which is the dependent variable.
   (a) Plot a scatter diagram and, assuming a linear relationship, use the least-squares method to find the regression coefficients b_0 and b_1.
   (b) Interpret the meaning of the Y intercept b_0 and the slope b_1 in this problem.
   (c) Use the regression model developed in (a) to predict the performance time for a worker who has had a training time of 15 hours.
   (d) Compute the standard error of the estimate.
   (e) Compute the coefficient of determination r^2 and interpret its meaning in this problem.
   (f) Compute the coefficient of correlation r.
   (g) Compute the adjusted r^2 and compare it with the coefficient of determination r^2.
   (h) At the .05 level of significance, is there evidence of a linear relationship between training time and performance time?
   (i) Set up a 95% confidence-interval estimate for the average performance time for workers who have had a training time of 15 hours.
   (j) Set up a 95% prediction-interval estimate of the performance time for a worker who has had a training time of 15 hours.
   (k) Set up a 95% confidence-interval estimate of the population slope.
   (l) Perform a residual analysis on your results and determine the adequacy of the fit of the model.
   (m) Perform an influence analysis and determine whether any observations may be deleted from the model. If necessary, reanalyze the regression model after deleting these observations and compare your results with the original model.

16.77 The following data at the top of page 619 represent the weight (in pounds) and the fuel capacity (in gallons) of a sample of fourteen 1987 compact cars:

Relating weight and fuel capacity (Problem 16.77)

Model	Weight (lbs.)	Fuel Capacity (gallons)
Audi 4000S	2,360	15.8
BMW325	2,550	14.5
Buick Skyhawk	2,500	13.6
Chevrolet Cavalier	2,485	13.6
Dodge Shadow	2,670	14.0
Honda Accord	2,590	15.9
Mercedes-Benz 190E	2,780	14.5
Nissan Stanza	2,905	16.1
Oldsmobile Firenza	2,535	13.6
Plymouth Reliant	2,620	14.0
Pontiac Sunbird	2,435	13.6
Saab 900	2,775	16.6
Toyota Camry	2,925	15.9
Volvo DL/GL	2,985	15.8

SOURCE: Copyright 1987 by Consumers Union of United States, Inc., Mount Vernon, NY 10553. Excerpted by permission from *Consumer Reports*, April, 1987, pp. 250–252.

(a) Compute the coefficient of correlation r between weight and fuel capacity.

(b) At the .05 level of significance is there evidence of a significant correlation between weight and fuel capacity?

16.78 The following data represent the number of beds and the number of employees of the largest 25 hospitals in New York City in 1987 (ranked by number of beds):

Relating hospital beds and employees (Problem 16.78)

Hospital	Number of Beds	Number of Employees
New York	1,418	6,373
St. Luke's–Roosevelt	1,315	7,220
Columbia–Presbyterian	1,291	6,246
King's County	1,269	5,500
Bellevue	1,197	5,000
Montefiore	1,176	8,000
Catholic Medical Center	1,145	5,300
Mount Sinai	1,112	5,334
Coler Memorial	1,045	1,825
Beth Israel	916	4,332
Goldwater	912	1,400
St. Vincent's	817	3,707
Elmhurst City	780	3,252
New York University	726	8,000
Harlem	725	4,375
Maimonides	700	3,500
Lenox Hill	690	3,064
Metropolitan	631	2,895
Interfaith	620	2,660
Bronx-Lebanon	614	2,741
Long Island College	567	2,570
Memorial Sloan-Kettering	565	3,083
Lincoln	557	2,500
Lutheran	532	2,188
Queens	527	3,235

SOURCE: *Crain's New York Business*, 1988 Edition, p. 53.

(a) Compute the coefficient of correlation r between the number of beds and the number of employees.

(b) At the .05 level of significance, is there evidence of a significant correlation between number of beds and number of employees?

16.79 The following data represent the number of partners and the number of associates at the 25 largest law firms in New York City in 1987 (ranked by total number of lawyers):

Relating partners and associates (Problem 16.79)

Firm	Partners	Associates
Skadden, Arps, Slate, Meagher, and Flom	99	365
Sherman and Sterling	99	313
Simpson, Thacher, and Bartlett	85	288
Weil, Gotshal, and Manges	72	263
Sullivan and Cromwell	92	225
Davis, Polk, and Wardwell	76	233
Paul, Weiss, Rifkind, Wharton, and Garrison	77	225
Cravath, Swaine, and Moore	63	231
Kaye, Scholer, Fierman, Hays, and Handler	73	211
Cahill, Gordon, and Reindel	63	202
Milbank, Tweed, Hadley, and McCloy	82	195
Shea and Gould	84	183
Proskauer, Rose, Goetz, and Mendelsohn	88	162
White and Case	68	183
Stroock and Stroock and Lavan	70	165
Fried, Frank, Harris, Silver, and Jacobson	67	169
Cadwalader, Wickersham, and Taft	62	158
Mudge, Rose, Guthrie, Alexander, and Ferdon	67	156
Wilkie, Farr, and Gallagher	67	156
LeBoeuf, Lamb, Leiby, and MacRae	62	151
Rosenman and Colin	68	128
Brown and Wood	60	146
Cleary, Gottlieb, Steen, and Hamilton	52	149
Finley, Kumble, Wagner, Underberg, Manley, Meyerson, and Casey	63	131
Rogers and Wells	65	115

SOURCE: *Crain's New York Business*, 1988 Edition, p. 54.

(a) Compute the coefficient of correlation r between the number of partners and the number of associates.

(b) At the .05 level of significance, is there evidence of a significant correlation between number of partners and number of associates?

● **16.80** The following data represent the price per pound and number of grams of protein per 100 grams of different types of meat sold at a local supermarket:

Relating price and protein (Problem 16.80)

Meat	Price per Pound ($)	Protein (grams)	Meat	Price per Pound ($)	Protein (grams)
Beef chuck (lean and fat)	1.82	24.9	Beef rib (lean only)	7.89	25.3
Beef chuck (lean only)	1.89	30.7	Beef roast (lean and fat)	2.36	26.2
Beef bottom (lean and fat)	4.06	29.5	Beef roast (lean only)	2.79	28.3
Beef bottom (lean only)	4.49	31.8	Sirloin steak (lean and fat)	3.76	26.8
Beef rib (lean and fat)	5.55	20.9	Sirloin steak (lean only)	4.12	30.1

(a) Compute the coefficient of correlation r between price and amount of protein.

(b) At the .10 level of significance, is there evidence of a significant correlation between price and amount of protein?

16.81 The following data represent the graduation rate and amount spent per pupil in 1986 for each of the 50 states and the District of Columbia:

Relating graduation rate and expenditures (Problem 16.81)

State	Graduation Rate (%)	Amount Spent per Pupil ($)
Alabama	67.3	2,565
Alaska	68.3	8,253
Arizona	63.0	3,093
Arkansas	78.0	2,658
California	66.7	3,543
Colorado	73.1	3,975
Connecticut	89.8	4,743
Delaware	70.7	4,610
Dist. of Columbia	56.8	5,337
Florida	62.0	3,529
Georgia	62.7	2,966
Hawaii	70.8	3,807
Idaho	79.0	2,484
Illinois	75.8	3,781
Indiana	71.7	3,275
Iowa	87.5	3,619
Kansas	81.5	3,829
Kentucky	68.6	2,486
Louisiana	62.7	3,187
Maine	76.5	3,472
Maryland	76.6	4,450
Massachusetts	76.7	4,562
Michigan	67.8	4,176
Minnesota	91.4	3,941
Mississippi	63.3	2,362
Missouri	75.6	3,189
Montana	87.2	4,091
Nebraska	88.1	3,634
Nevada	65.2	3,440
New Hampshire	73.3	3,542
New Jersey	77.6	5,395
New Mexico	72.3	3,195
New York	64.2	6,011
North Carolina	70.0	2,982
North Dakota	89.7	3,481
Ohio	80.4	3,527
Oklahoma	71.6	3,146
Oregon	74.1	4,141
Pennsylvania	78.5	4,416
Rhode Island	67.3	4,667
South Carolina	64.5	3,058
South Dakota	81.5	3,051
Tennessee	67.4	2,612
Texas	64.3	3,298
Utah	80.3	2,390
Vermont	77.6	4,031
Virginia	73.9	3,520
Washington	75.2	3,881
West Virginia	75.2	3,528
Wisconsin	86.3	4,168
Wyoming	81.2	5,114

    (a) Compute the coefficient of correlation r between graduation rate and the amount spent per pupil.

    (b) At the .05 level of significance, is there evidence of a significant correlation between graduation rate and the amount spent per pupil?

    ✗**(c)** Indicate what other factors might be present that would make you believe that any correlation between these two variables is merely spurious correlation.

16.82 Referring to Problem 3.82 on page 81
    (a) Compute the coefficient of correlation r between the cost per pound as purchased and the cost per pound of edible meat for the 19 brands of whole frozen turkey.

    (b) At the .01 level of significance, is there evidence of a significant positive correlation between the cost per pound as purchased and the cost per pound of edible meat?

    (c) Are these results about what you would have expected prior to analyzing the data? Explain.

16.83 Referring to Problem 3.84 (gas barbecue grills) on page 83
    (a) Compute the coefficient of correlation r between shelf area and cooking grid.

    (b) At the .05 level of significance, is there evidence of a positive correlation between shelf area and cooking grid?

    (c) Are these results about what you would have expected prior to analyzing the data? Explain.

Database Exercises

The following problems refer to the sample data obtained from the questionnaire of Figure 2.5 on page 15 and presented in Figure 2.10 on pages 24–29. They should be solved with the aid of an available computer package.

☐ **16.84** For houses located in Farmingdale (question 9, code 2), develop a model to predict appraised value (question 1) based upon the number of rooms (question 5).

    (a) Plot a scatter diagram and, assuming a linear relationship, use the least-squares method to find the regression coefficients b_0 and b_1.

    (b) Interpret the meaning of the Y intercept b_0 and the slope b_1 in this problem.

    (c) Use the regression model developed in (a) to predict the appraised value for a house which has 8 rooms.

    (d) Compute the standard error of the estimate.

    (e) Compute the coefficient of determination r^2 and interpret its meaning in this problem.

    (f) Compute the coefficient of correlation r.

    (g) Compute the adjusted r^2 and compare it with the coefficient of determination r^2.

    (h) At the .05 level of significance, is there evidence of a linear relationship between appraised value and number of rooms?

    (i) Set up a 95% confidence interval estimate for the average appraised value for houses which have 8 rooms.

    (j) Set up a 95% prediction interval estimate for the appraised value of an individual house that has 8 rooms.

    (k) Set up a 95% confidence interval estimate of the population slope.

    (l) Perform a residual analysis on your results and determine the adequacy of the fit of the model.

    (m) Perform an influence analysis and determine whether any observations may be deleted from the model. If necessary, reanalyze the regression model after deleting these observations and compare your results with the original model.

    (n) Compare the results obtained in parts (a)–(m) with those obtained for houses in East Meadow (see Section 16.14) and houses in Levittown (see Problem 16.85). What conclusions can you draw?

☐ **16.85** Perform a similar analysis for houses located in Levittown (question 9, code 3) as was done for houses in Farmingdale in Problem 16.84. Compare the results obtained with those obtained for houses in East Meadow (see Section 16.14) and houses in Farmingdale (see Problem 16.84). What conclusions can you draw?

☐ **16.86** For houses located in East Meadow (question 9, code 1), develop a model to predict annual taxes (question 7) based on appraised value (question 1).
  - **(a)** Plot a scatter diagram and, assuming a linear relationship, use the least-squares method to find the regression coefficients b_0 and b_1.
  - **(b)** Interpret the meaning of the Y intercept b_0 and the slope b_1 in this problem.
  - **(c)** Use the regression model developed in (a) to predict the annual taxes for a house which has an appraised value of $200,000.
  - **(d)** Compute the standard error of the estimate.
  - **(e)** Compute the coefficient of determination r^2 and interpret its meaning in this problem.
  - **(f)** Compute the coefficient of correlation r.
  - **(g)** Compute the adjusted r^2 and compare it with the coefficient of determination r^2.
  - **(h)** At the .05 level of significance, is there evidence of a linear relationship between annual taxes and appraised value?
  - **(i)** Set up a 95% confidence interval estimate for the average annual taxes for houses which have an appraised value of $200,000.
  - **(j)** Set up a 95% prediction interval estimate for the annual taxes paid in an individual house that has an appraised value of $200,000.
  - **(k)** Set up a 95% confidence interval estimate of the population slope.
  - **(l)** Perform a residual analysis on your results and determine the adequacy of the fit of the model.
  - **(m)** Perform an influence analysis and determine whether any observations may be deleted from the model. If necessary, reanalyze the regression model after deleting these observations and compare your results with the original model.
  - **(n)** Compare the results obtained in parts (a)–(m) with those obtained for houses in Farmingdale (see Problem 16.87) and houses in Levittown (see Problem 16.88). What conclusions can you draw?

☐ **16.87** Perform a similar analysis for houses located in Farmingdale (question 9, code 2) as was done for houses in East Meadow in Problem 16.86. Compare the results obtained with those obtained for houses in East Meadow (see Problem 16.86) and houses in Levittown (see Problem 16.88). What conclusions can you draw?

☐ **16.88** Perform a similar analysis for houses located in Levittown (question 9, code 3) as was done for houses in East Meadow in Problem 16.86. Compare the results obtained with those obtained for houses in East Meadow (see Problem 16.86) and houses in Farmingdale (see Problem 16.87). What conclusions can you draw?

Case Study G

You are employed in the marketing department of a large nationwide newspaper chain. The parent company is interested in investigating the feasibility of beginning a Sunday edition for some of its newspapers. However, before proceeding with a final decision, it needs to estimate the amount of Sunday circulation that would be expected. In particular, it wishes to predict the Sunday circulation that would be obtained by newspapers (in three different cities) that have a daily circulation of 200,000, 400,000, and 600,000, respectively.

Toward this end, data (summarized in Table 16.8 on page 624) have been collected from a sample of 20 newspapers.

TABLE 16.8   U.S. newspapers—daily versus Sunday

Newspaper	Sunday (thousands)	Daily (thousands)
Des Moines Register	364.73	221.87
Philadelphia Inquirer	989.25	494.84
Tampa Tribune	298.78	218.95
New York Times	1,645.06	1,056.92
New York News	1,631.69	1,278.12
Long Island Newsday	680.62	624.29
Sacramento Bee	289.08	245.38
Los Angeles Times	1,397.19	1,117.95
Boston Globe	798.12	500.11
Cincinnati Enquirer	323.39	191.65
Orange Co. Register	300.56	307.78
Miami Herald	546.98	437.23
Chicago Tribune	1,126.29	758.46
Detroit News	839.32	678.40
Houston Chronicle	531.53	406.08
Kansas City Star	433.48	223.13
Omaha World Herald	290.20	120.06
Denver Post	425.45	227.11
St. Louis Post-Dispatch	548.96	357.31
Portland Oregonian	404.19	321.68

SOURCE: From *Gale Directory of Publications*: *1988*, 120th edition. Edited by Kay Gill and Donald P. Boyden. Gale Research, 1988. Copyright © 1988 by Gale Research, Inc. Reprinted by permission of the publisher.

You have been asked to develop a model that would enable you to make a prediction of the expected Sunday circulation, and to write a report that presents your results and summarizes your findings.

References

1. ANDREWS, D. F., AND D. PREGIBON, "Finding the Outliers that Matter," *Journal of the Royal Statistical Society.* Ser. B., 1978, Vol. 40, pp. 85–93.
2. ATKINSON, A. C., "Robust and Diagnostic Regression Analysis," *Communications in Statistics*, 1982, Vol. 11, pp. 2559–2572.
3. BELSLEY, D. A., E. KUH, AND R. WELSCH, *Regression Diagnostics*: *Identifying Influential Data and Sources of Collinearity* (New York: John Wiley, 1980).
4. BERENSON, M. L., D. M. LEVINE, AND M. GOLDSTEIN, *Intermediate Statistical Methods and Applications*: *A Computer Package Approach* (Englewood Cliffs, N.J.: Prentice-Hall, 1983).
5. COOK, R. D., AND S. WEISBERG, *Residuals and Influence in Regression* (New York: Chapman and Hall, 1982).
6. CONOVER, W. J., *Practical Nonparametric Statistics*, 2d ed. (New York: John Wiley, 1980).
7. DRAPER, N. R., AND H. SMITH, *Applied Regression Analysis*, 2d ed. (New York: John Wiley, 1981).
8. HOCKING, R. R., "Developments in Linear Regression Methodology: 1959–1982," *Technometrics*, 1983, Vol. 25, pp. 219–250.
9. HOAGLIN, D. C. AND R. WELSCH, "The Hat Matrix in Regression and ANOVA," *The American Statistician*, 1978, Vol. 32, pp. 17–22.

10. LEVINE, D. M., M. L. BERENSON, AND D. STEPHAN, *Using SAS with Basic Business Statistics* (Englewood Cliffs, N.J.: Prentice-Hall, 1983).

11. LEVINE, D. M., M. L. BERENSON, AND D. STEPHAN, *Using Minitab with Basic Business Statistics*, 2d ed. (Englewood Cliffs, N.J.: Prentice-Hall, 1986).

12. NETER, J. W. WASSERMAN, AND M. H. KUTNER, *Applied Linear Statistical Models*, 2d ed. (Homewood, Ill.: Richard D. Irwin, 1985).

13. PREGIBON, D. "Logistic Regression Diagnostics," *Annals of Statistics*, 1981, Vol. 9, pp. 705–724.

14. RYAN, T. A., B. L. JOINER, AND B. F. RYAN, *Minitab Student Handbook*, 2d ed. (North Scituate, Mass.: Duxbury Press, 1985).

15. *SAS User's Guide*, 1982 ed. (Cary, N.C.: SAS Institute, 1982).

16. *STATGRAPHICS User's Guide* (Rockville, Md.: STSC, Inc., 1986).

17. TUKEY, J. W. "Data Analysis, Computation and Mathematics," *Quarterly Journal of Applied Mathematics*, 1972, Vol. 30, pp. 51–65.

18. VELLEMAN, P. F., AND R. WELSCH, "Efficient Computing of Regression Diagnostics," *The American Statistician*, 1981, Vol. 35, pp. 234–242.

19. WEISBERG, S., *Applied Linear Regression* (New York: John Wiley, 1980).

17

Multiple Regression Models

17.1 INTRODUCTION

In our discussion of the simple regression model in the preceding chapter, we focused upon a model in which one independent or explanatory variable X was used to predict the value of a dependent or response variable Y. That is, we may recall that a simple regression model was developed in order to predict the grade point index based upon GMAT score. In this chapter we shall extend our discussion to consider multiple regression models in which several explanatory variables can be used to predict the value of a dependent variable.

Suppose, for example, that we now wish to develop a regression model in order

TABLE 17.1 Consumption of heating oil, atmospheric temperature, and amount of attic insulation for a random sample of 15 single-family homes

Observation	Monthly Consumption of Heating Oil, (Gallons)	Average Daily Atmospheric Temperature, (°F)	Amount of Attic Insulation, (Inches)
1	275.3	40	3
2	363.8	27	3
3	164.3	40	10
4	40.8	73	6
5	94.3	64	6
6	230.9	34	6
7	366.7	9	6
8	300.6	8	10
9	237.8	23	10
10	121.4	63	3
11	31.4	65	10
12	203.5	41	6
13	441.1	21	3
14	323.0	38	3
15	52.5	58	10

to predict the consumption of home heating oil during the month of January. A sample of 15 similar homes built by a particular housing developer throughout the country was selected for analysis. Although many variables could be considered, for simplicity only two explanatory variables are to be evaluated here—the average daily atmospheric temperature, as measured in Fahrenheit degrees, outside the house during that month (X_1) and the amount of insulation, as measured in inches, in the attic of the house (X_2). The results are presented in Table 17.1 on page 626.

With two explanatory variables in the multiple regression model, a scatter diagram of the points can be plotted on a three-dimensional graph as shown in Figure 17.1.

For a particular investigation, when there are several explanatory variables present, the simple linear regression model of the preceding chapter [Equation (16.1)] can merely be extended by assuming a linear relationship between each explanatory variable

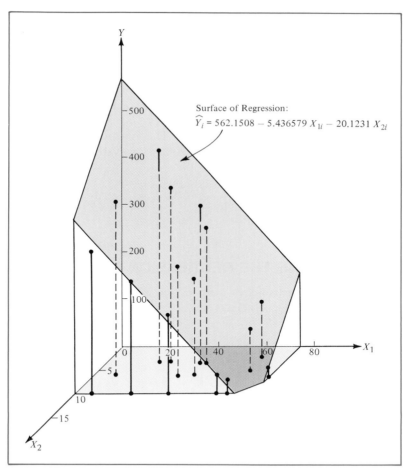

Surface of Regression:
$$\widehat{Y}_i = 562.1508 - 5.436579\,X_{1i} - 20.1231\,X_{2i}$$

FIGURE 17.1
Scatter diagram of average daily atmospheric temperature X_1, amount of attic insulation X_2, and monthly consumption of heating oil Y with indicated regression plane fitted by least-squares method.

and the dependent variable. For example, as in our current problem with two explanatory variables, the multiple linear regression model is expressed as

$$Y_i = \beta_0 + \beta_1 X_{1i} + \beta_2 X_{2i} + \epsilon_i \qquad \text{(17.1)}$$

where $\beta_0 = Y$ intercept

$\qquad \beta_1 =$ slope of Y with variable X_1 holding variable X_2 constant

$\qquad \beta_2 =$ slope of Y with variable X_2 holding variable X_1 constant

$\qquad \epsilon_i =$ random error in Y for observation i

This multiple linear regression model can be compared to the simple linear regression model [Equation (16.1)] expressed as

$$Y_i = \beta_0 + \beta_1 X_i + \epsilon_i$$

In the case of the simple linear regression model we should note that the slope β_1 represents the unit change in Y per unit change in X and does not take into account any other variables besides the single independent variable that is included in the model. On the other hand, in the multiple linear regression model [Equation (17.1)], the slope β_1 represents the unit change in Y per unit change in X_1, taking into account the effect of X_2. It is referred to as a **net regression coefficient.**

As in the case of simple linear regression, when sample data are analyzed, the sample regression coefficients (b_0, b_1, and b_2) are used as estimates of the true parameters (β_0, β_1, and β_2). Thus the regression equation for the multiple linear regression model with two explanatory variables would be

$$\hat{Y}_i = b_0 + b_1 X_{1i} + b_2 X_{2i} \qquad \text{(17.1a)}$$

17.2 FINDING THE REGRESSION COEFFICIENTS

If the least-squares method (see Section 16.4.1) is utilized to compute the sample regression coefficients (b_0, b_1, and b_2), we will have the following three normal equations:

$$\text{I.} \quad \sum_{i=1}^{n} Y_i = nb_0 + b_1 \sum_{i=1}^{n} X_{1i} + b_2 \sum_{i=1}^{n} X_{2i} \qquad \text{(17.2a)}$$

$$\text{II.} \quad \sum_{i=1}^{n} X_{1i} Y_i = b_0 \sum_{i=1}^{n} X_{1i} + b_1 \sum_{i=1}^{n} X_{1i}^2 + b_2 \sum_{i=1}^{n} X_{1i} X_{2i} \qquad \text{(17.2b)}$$

$$\text{III.} \quad \sum_{i=1}^{n} X_{2i} Y_i = b_0 \sum_{i=1}^{n} X_{2i} + b_1 \sum_{i=1}^{n} X_{1i} X_{2i} + b_2 \sum_{i=1}^{n} X_{2i}^2 \qquad \text{(17.2c)}$$

For the data of Table 17.1, the values of the various sums needed to solve Equations (17.2a), (17.2b), and (17.2c) are given below:

$$\sum_{i=1}^{n} Y_i = 3{,}247.4 \qquad \sum_{i=1}^{n} X_{1i}Y_i = 98{,}060.1 \qquad \sum_{i=1}^{n} X_{1i} = 604$$

$$\sum_{i=1}^{n} X_{2i} = 95 \qquad \sum_{i=1}^{n} X_{2i}Y_i = 18{,}057.0 \qquad \sum_{i=1}^{n} X_{1i}^2 = 30{,}308$$

$$\sum_{i=1}^{n} X_{2i}^2 = 725 \qquad \sum_{i=1}^{n} X_{1i}X_{2i} = 3{,}833 \qquad n = 15$$

$$\sum_{i=1}^{n} Y_i^2 = 939{,}175.68$$

Therefore, for these data the three normal equations are

I. $3{,}247.4 = 15b_0 + 604b_1 + 95b_2$

II. $98{,}060.1 = 604b_0 + 30{,}308b_1 + 3{,}833b_2$

III. $18{,}057.0 = 95b_0 + 3{,}833b_1 + 725b_2$

The values of the three sample regression coefficients may be obtained by solving this set of simultaneous equations or by using an appropriate computer package (see References 10–12, 15, 17, 18, 20, 21). Figure 17.2 (see pages 630–631) presents partial output from the SAS REG and GLM procedures for the data of Table 17.1. Figure 17.22 (see page 680) presents output from MYSTAT, Figure 17.23 (see page 681) presents output from the REGRESSION command in SPSS[X], and Figure 17.24 (see page 682) presents output from the REGRESS command in Minitab.

From Figure 17.2, we observe that the computed values of the regression coefficients in this problem are

$$b_0 = 562.151, \qquad b_1 = -5.43658, \qquad b_2 = -20.0123$$

Therefore, the multiple regression equation can be expressed as

$$\hat{Y}_i = 562.151 - 5.43658X_{1i} - 20.0123X_{2i}$$

where $\hat{Y}_i$ = predicted amount of home heating oil consumed (gallons) during January for observation i

X_{1i} = average daily atmospheric temperature (°F) during January for observation i

X_{2i} = amount of attic insulation (inches) for observation i

The interpretation of the regression coefficients is analogous to that of the simple linear regression model. The Y intercept b_0, computed as 562.151, represents the number of gallons of home heating oil that would be consumed in January when the average daily atmospheric temperature was 0°F for a home that was not insulated (that is, a house with 0 inches of attic insulation). The slope of average daily atmospheric temperature with consumption of heating oil (b_1, computed as −5.43658) can be interpreted to mean that for a home with a *given* number of inches of attic insulation,

Panel (a)

```
DEP VARIABLE: OIL            (VARIANCE)
                     SUM OF      MEAN
SOURCE      DF      SQUARES     SQUARE      F VALUE     PROB>F
MODEL        2       228015     114007      168.471     0.0001
ERROR       12     8120.603     676.717
C TOTAL     14       236135
     ROOT MSE      26.013783   R-SQUARE          0.9656
     DEP MEAN      216.493     ADJ R-SQ          0.9599
     C.V.          12.01597


                     PARAMETER    STANDARD    T FOR HO:
VARIABLE    DF       ESTIMATE      ERROR      PARAMETER=0   PROB > !T!

INTERCEP    1  b₀     562.151     21.093104 s_{b₀}   26.651     0.0001
TEMPF       1  b₁    -5.436581     0.336216 s_{b₁}  -16.170     0.0001
INSU        1  b₂   -20.012321     2.342505 s_{b₂}   -8.543     0.0001


VARIABLE    DF     TYPE I SS    TYPE II SS

INTERCEP    1        703040       480653
TEMPF       1        178624       176938
INSU        1     49390.202    49390.202


                 PREDICT    STD ERR  LOWER95%  UPPER95%
OBS    ACTUAL    VALUE      PREDICT    MEAN      MEAN   RESIDUAL

 1     275.300   284.651     10.300   262.210   307.092   -9.351
 2     363.800   355.326     11.196   330.932   379.721    8.474
 3     164.300   144.565     10.905   120.805   168.324   19.735
 4      40.800    45.207     12.923    17.050    73.363   -4.407
 5      94.300    94.136     10.465    71.335   116.936  0.164072
 6     230.900   257.233      7.081   241.806   272.661  -26.333
 7     366.700   393.148     12.493   365.927   420.369  -26.448
 8     300.600   318.535     15.435   284.905   352.165  -17.935
 9     237.800   236.986     12.389   209.994   263.979  0.813551
10     121.400   159.609     12.867   131.574   187.645  -38.209
11      31.400     8.650     13.666   -21.126    38.426   22.750
12     203.500   219.177      6.767   204.434   233.921  -15.677
13     441.100   387.946     12.130   361.516   414.375   53.154
14     323.000   295.524     10.323   273.033   318.015   27.476
15      52.500    46.706     12.390    19.710    73.703    5.794
```

FIGURE 17.2
Partial output for the data of Table 17.1 obtained from SAS:
Panel (a) PROC REG; Panel (b) PROC GLM.

the consumption of heating oil will *decrease* by 5.43658 gallons per month for each 1°F increase in average daily atmospheric temperature. Furthermore, the slope of amount of attic insulation with consumption of heating oil (b_2, computed as -20.0123) can be interpreted to mean that for a month with a *given* average daily atmospheric temperature, the consumption of heating oil will *decrease* by 20.0123 gallons for each additional inch of attic insulation.

Problems

17.1   Explain the difference in the interpretation of the regression coefficients in simple linear regression and multiple linear regression.

Panel (b)

```
GENERAL LINEAR MODELS PROCEDURE

DEPENDENT VARIABLE: OIL
```

SOURCE	DF	SUM OF SQUARES	MEAN SQUARE
MODEL	2	228014.62631736	114007.31315868
ERROR	12	8120.60301597	676.71691800
CORRECTED TOTAL	14	236135.22933333	

MODEL F =	168.47		PR > F = 0.0001

R-SQUARE	C.V.	ROOT MSE	OIL MEAN
0.965610	12.0160	26.01378323	216.49333333

SOURCE	DF	TYPE I SS	F VALUE	PR > F
TEMPF	1	178624.42421986	263.96	0.0001
INSU	1	49390.20209750	72.99	0.0001

SOURCE	DF	TYPE III SS	F VALUE	PR > F
TEMPF	1	176938.16130835	261.47	0.0001
INSU	1	49390.20209750	72.99	0.0001

PARAMETER	ESTIMATE	T FOR H0: PARAMETER=0	PR > :T:	STD ERROR OF ESTIMATE
INTERCEPT	$562.15100923\,b_0$	26.65	0.0001	$21.09310433\,S_{b_0}$
TEMPF	$-5.43658059\,b_1$	-16.17	0.0001	$0.33621617\,S_{b_1}$
INSU	$-20.01232067\,b_2$	-8.54	0.0001	$2.34250523\,S_{b_2}$

FIGURE 17.2
(Continued)

● **17.2** A marketing analyst for a major shoe manufacturer is considering the development of a new brand of running shoes. In particular, the marketing analyst wishes to determine the variables that can be used in predicting durability (or the effect of long-term impact). The following two independent variables are to be considered:

X_1 (FOREIMP), a measurement of the forefoot shock-absorbing capability

X_2 (MIDSOLE), a measurement of the change in impact properties over time

along with the dependent variable Y (LTIMP) which is a measure of the long-term ability to absorb shock after a repeated impact test. A random sample of 15 types of currently manufactured running shoes was selected for testing. Using SAS, the following (partial) output is provided at the top of page 632:

Shoe durability problem

STATISTICAL ANALYSIS SYSTEM
GENERAL LINEAR MODELS PROCEDURE
DEPENDENT VARIABLE: LTIMP LONG-TERM IMPACT

SOURCE	DF	SS	MS	F	P VALUE
MODEL	2	12.61020	6.30510	97.69	0.0001
ERROR	12	0.77453	0.06454		
CORRECTED TOTAL	14	13.38473	STD DEV = 0.25406		

SOURCE	DF	TYPE I SS	F	DF	TYPE III SS	F
FOREIMP	1	8.02166	124.28	1	10.19682	157.98
MIDSOLE	1	4.58854	71.09	1	4.58854	71.09

PARAMETER	ESTIMATE	T FOR HO PARAMETER = 0	STD ERROR OF ESTIMATE (S_{b_i})
INTERCEPT	−0.02686	−0.39	.06905
FOREIMP	0.79116	12.57	.06295
MIDSOLE	0.60484	8.43	.07174

(a) Assuming that each independent variable is linearly related to long-term impact, state the multiple regression equation.

(b) Interpret the meaning of the slopes in this problem.

17.3 Referring to Problem 16.2 on page 562, the absenteeism problem, the personnel manager feels that there may be a relationship between a second independent variable, salary, and absenteeism. The annual salary (in thousands of dollars) of the workers in the sample was

Worker	Annual Salary (Thousands of Dollars)
1	18.5
2	26.4
3	24.3
4	18.0
5	24.7
6	24.0
7	21.2
8	25.3
9	26.9
10	27.2

Access a computer package and perform a multiple linear regression analysis. Based on the results obtained

(a) State the multiple regression equation.

(b) Interpret the meaning of the slopes in this problem.

● 17.4 Suppose that a large consumer products company wanted to measure the effectiveness of different types of advertising media in the promotion of its products. Specifically, two types of advertising media were to be considered: radio and television advertising and newspaper advertising (including the cost of discount coupons). A sample of 22 cities with approximately equal populations was selected for study during a test period of one month. Each city was allocated a specific expenditure level for both radio and television advertising as well as newspaper advertising. The sales of the product (in thousands of dollars) during the test month was recorded along with the levels of media expenditure with the following results (see top of page 633):

Advertising media problem

City	Sales ($000)	Radio and Television Advertising ($000)	Newspaper Advertising ($000)
1	973	0	40
2	1,119	0	40
3	875	25	25
4	625	25	25
5	910	30	30
6	971	30	30
7	931	35	35
8	1,177	35	35
9	882	40	25
10	982	40	25
11	1,628	45	45
12	1,577	45	45
13	1,044	50	0
14	914	50	0
15	1,329	55	25
16	1,330	55	25
17	1,405	60	30
18	1,436	60	30
19	1,521	65	35
20	1,741	65	35
21	1,866	70	40
22	1,717	70	40

Access a computer package and perform a multiple linear regression analysis. Based on the results obtained

(a) State the multiple regression equation.

(b) Interpret the meaning of the slopes in this problem.

17.5　The personnel department of a large industrial corporation would like to develop a model to predict the weekly salary based upon the length of employment and age of its managerial employees. A random sample of 16 managerial employees is selected with the results displayed below.

Employee salary problem

Employee	Weekly Salary	Length of Employment (Months)	Age (Years)
1	$639	330	46
2	746	569	65
3	670	375	57
4	518	113	47
5	602	215	41
6	612	343	59
7	548	252	45
8	591	348	57
9	552	352	55
10	529	256	61
11	456	87	28
12	674	337	51
13	406	42	28
14	529	129	37
15	528	216	46
16	592	327	56

Access a computer package and perform a multiple linear regression analysis. Based on the results obtained

(a) State the multiple regression equation.

(b) Interpret the meaning of the slopes in this problem.

17.6 A financial analyst would like to develop a regression model to predict the current selling price of stocks in the publishing industry based upon the book value of the company (in dollars per share) and the return on common equity. A sample of 19 companies was selected with the following results:

Stock price problem

Company	Current Selling Price	Book Value (in $ per share)	Return on Common Equity (%)
Dun and Bradstreet	52	10.81	23.6
Gannett	39	9.61	19.8
Time	93	22.04	19.3
Times Mirror	39	11.30	18.5
Dow Jones	35	8.84	24.0
Tribune	41	14.75	12.9
Washington Post	224	42.67	34.1
McGraw-Hill	59	17.88	20.0
New York Times	32	10.16	19.5
Knight-Ridder	44	15.83	17.2
Affiliated Publications	64	10.44	39.7
Macmillan	62	13.60	20.2
Commerce Clearing House	64	10.56	28.1
Lee Enterprises	27	6.12	23.3
Media General	47	24.10	12.7
Meredith	29	18.71	13.3
A. H. Belo	26	5.03	9.9
Houghton Mifflin	35	12.54	13.3
Grolier	25	6.96	11.9

SOURCE: "Business Week Top 1000," *Business Week*, April 15, 1988, pp. 276, 280. Reprinted by special permission. © 1988 by McGraw-Hill, Inc.

Access a computer package and perform a multiple linear regression analysis. Based on the results obtained

(a) State the multiple regression equation.

(b) Interpret the meaning of the slopes in this problem.

17.3 PREDICTION OF THE DEPENDENT VARIABLE Y FOR GIVEN VALUES OF THE EXPLANATORY VARIABLES

Now that the multiple regression model has been fitted to these data, various procedures, analogous to those discussed for simple linear regression, could be developed. In this section we shall use the multiple regression model to predict the monthly consumption of heating oil.

Suppose that we wanted to predict the number of gallons of heating oil consumed in a house that had 6 inches of attic insulation during a month in which the average daily atmospheric temperature was 30°F. Using our multiple regression equation

$$\hat{Y}_i = 562.151 - 5.43658X_{1i} - 20.0123X_{2i}$$

with $X_{1i} = 30$ and $X_{2i} = 6$, we have

$$\hat{Y}_i = 562.151 - 5.43658(30) - 20.0123(6)$$

and thus

$$\hat{Y}_i = 278.9798$$

Therefore, we would predict that approximately 278.98 gallons of heating oil would be used by that particular house.

Problems

17.7   Referring to Problem 17.3 (the absenteeism problem) on page 632, predict the number of days absent for a 40-year old worker who earns $23,000 per year.

● **17.8**   Referring to Problem 17.4 (the advertising media problem) on page 632, predict the sales for a city in which radio and television advertising is $20,000 and newspaper advertising is $20,000.

17.9   Referring to Problem 17.5 (the employee salary problem) on page 633, predict the weekly salary for a managerial employee who has been employed for 15 years and is 47 years old.

17.10   Referring to Problem 17.6 (the stock price problem) on page 634, predict the current selling price for a company with a book value of $20 per share and a return on equity of 15%.

17.4   TESTING FOR THE SIGNIFICANCE OF THE RELATIONSHIP BETWEEN THE DEPENDENT VARIABLE AND THE EXPLANATORY VARIABLES

Once a regression model has been fitted to a set of data, we can determine whether there is a significant relationship between the dependent variable and the set of explanatory variables. Since there is more than one explanatory variable, the null and alternative hypotheses can be set up as follows:

H_0: $\beta_1 = \beta_2 = 0$ (There is no linear relationship between the dependent variable and the explanatory variables)

H_1: $\beta_1 \neq \beta_2 \neq 0$ (At least one regression coefficient is not equal to zero)

This null hypothesis may be tested by utilizing an F test, as indicated in Table 17.2 on page 636.

We may recall from Sections 12.4 and 14.2 that the F test is used when testing the ratio of two variances. When testing for the significance of the regression coefficients, the measure of random error is called the **error variance,** so that the F test is the ratio of the variance due to the regression divided by the error variance as shown in Equation (17.3)

$$F_{p,n-p-1} = \frac{\text{MSR}}{\text{MSE}} \tag{17.3}$$

where p is the number of explanatory variables in the regression model.

TABLE 17.2 Analysis-of-variance table for testing the significance of a set of regression coefficients in a multiple regression model containing p explanatory variables

Source	df	Sums of Squares	Mean Square (Variance)	F
Regression	p	$SSR = b_0 \sum_{i=1}^{n} Y_i + b_1 \sum_{i=1}^{n} X_{1i}Y_i + b_2 \sum_{i=1}^{n} X_{2i}Y_i - \dfrac{\left(\sum_{i=1}^{n} Y_i\right)^2}{n}$	$MSR = \dfrac{SSR}{p}$	$F = \dfrac{MSR}{MSE}$
Error	$n - p - 1$	$SSE = \sum_{i=1}^{n} Y_i^2 - b_0 \sum_{i=1}^{n} Y_i - b_1 \sum_{i=1}^{n} X_{1i}Y_i - b_2 \sum_{i=1}^{n} X_{2i}Y_i$	$MSE = \dfrac{SSE}{n - p - 1}$	
Total	$n - 1$	$SST = \sum_{i=1}^{n} Y_i^2 - \dfrac{\left(\sum_{i=1}^{n} Y_i\right)^2}{n}$		

Interestingly, the error variance (MSE) is also the square of the standard error of the estimate (S_{YX}), which was described in Section 16.5.

For the data of the heating oil consumption problem, the ANOVA table (also displayed as part of Figure 17.2) is presented in Table 17.3.

If a level of significance of .05 is chosen, from Table E.5 we determine that the critical value on the F distribution (with 2 and 12 degrees of freedom) is 3.89, as depicted in Figure 17.3. From Equation (17.3), since $F_{2,12} = MSR/MSE = 168.47 > 3.89$, we can reject H_0 and conclude that *at least* one of the explanatory variables (temperature and/or insulation) is related to heating oil consumption.

TABLE 17.3 Analysis-of-variance table for testing the significance of a set of regression coefficients for the heating oil consumption problem

Source	df	Sums of Squares	Mean Square (Variance)	F
Regression	2	$(562.151)(3,247.4) + (-5.43658)(98,060.1)$ $+ (-20.0123)(18,057) - \dfrac{(3,247.4)^2}{15}$ $= 228,014.6263$	$\dfrac{228,014.6263}{2}$ $= 114,007.31315$	$\dfrac{114,007.31315}{676.71692}$ $= 168.47$
Error	$15 - 2 - 1 = 12$	$939,175.68 - (562.151)(3,247.4)$ $- (-5.43658)(98,060.1) - (-20.0123)(18,057)$ $= 8,120.6030$	$\dfrac{8,120.6030}{12}$ $= 676.71692$	
Total	$15 - 1 = 14$	$939,175.68 - \dfrac{(3,247.4)^2}{15} = 236,135.2293$		

SOURCE: Format of Table 17.2.

Problems

- **17.11** Referring to Problem 17.2 (the shoe durability problem) on page 631, determine whether there is a significant relationship between long-term impact and the two explanatory variables at the .05 level of significance.

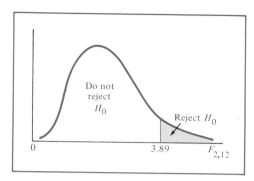

FIGURE 17.3
Testing for the significance of a set of regression coefficients at the .05 level of significance with 2 and 12 degrees of freedom.

17.12 Referring to Problem 17.3 (the absenteeism problem) on page 632, determine whether there is a significant relationship between absenteeism and the two explanatory variables (age and salary) at the .05 level of significance.

● **17.13** Referring to Problem 17.4 (the advertising media problem) on page 632, determine whether there is a significant relationship between sales and the two explanatory variables (radio and television advertising and newspaper advertising) at the .05 level of significance.

17.14 Referring to Problem 17.5 (the employee salary problem) on page 633, determine whether there is a significant relationship between weekly salary and the two explanatory variables (length of employment and age) at the .05 level of significance.

17.15 Referring to Problem 17.6 (the stock price problem) on page 634, determine whether there is a significant relationship between current stock price and the two explanatory variables (book value and return on common equity) at the .05 level of significance.

17.5 MEASURING ASSOCIATION IN THE MULTIPLE REGRESSION MODEL

We may recall from Section 16.6 that once a regression model has been developed, the coefficient of determination r^2 could be computed. In multiple regression, since there are at least two explanatory variables, the coefficient of multiple determination represents the proportion of the variation in Y that is explained by the set of explanatory variables selected. In our example, containing two explanatory variables, the coefficient of multiple determination ($r_{Y.12}^2$) is given by

$$r_{Y.12}^2 = \frac{\text{SSR}}{\text{SST}} \qquad (17.4)$$

where

$$\text{SSR} = b_0 \sum_{i=1}^{n} Y_i + b_1 \sum_{i=1}^{n} X_{1i} Y_i + b_2 \sum_{i=1}^{n} X_{2i} Y_i - \frac{\left(\sum_{i=1}^{n} Y_i \right)^2}{n}$$

$$\text{SST} = \sum_{i=1}^{n} Y_i^2 - \frac{\left(\sum_{i=1}^{n} Y_i \right)^2}{n}$$

In the home-heating-oil consumption problem we have already computed SSR = 228,014.6263 and SST = 236,135.2293. Thus, as is displayed in the SAS output of Figure 17.2 on pages 630–631,

$$r^2_{Y.12} = \frac{SSR}{SST} = \frac{228,014.6263}{236,135.2293} = .96561$$

This coefficient of multiple determination, computed as .96561, can be interpreted to mean that 96.561% of the variation in the consumption of home heating oil can be explained by the variation in the average daily atmospheric temperature and the variation in the amount of attic insulation.

Nevertheless, we may recall from Section 16.6 that when dealing with multiple regression models some researchers suggest that an "adjusted" r^2 be computed to reflect both the number of explanatory variables in the model and the sample size. This is especially necessary when we are comparing two or more regression models that predict the same dependent variable but have different numbers of explanatory or predictor variables. Thus, in multiple regression, we may denote an adjusted r^2 as

$$r^2_{adj} = 1 - \left[(1 - r^2_{Y.12\ldots p})\frac{n-1}{n-p-1}\right] \qquad (17.5)$$

where p is the number of explanatory variables in the regression equation.

Thus, for our heating oil data, since $r^2_{Y.12} = .96561$, $n = 15$, and $p = 2$,

$$r^2_{adj} = 1 - \left[(1 - r^2_{Y.12})\frac{15-1}{15-2-1}\right]$$

$$= 1 - \left[(1 - .96561)\frac{14}{12}\right]$$

$$= 1 - .04$$

$$= .96$$

Hence 96% of the variation in home heating oil usage can be explained by our multiple regression model—adjusted for number of predictors and sample size.

In order to further study the relationship among the variables, it is often useful to examine the correlation between each pair of variables included in the model. Such a correlation "matrix" that indicates the coefficient of correlation between each pair of variables is displayed in Table 17.4.

TABLE 17.4   Correlation matrix for the heating oil consumption problem

	Y (Heating Oil)	X_1 (Temperature)	X_2 (Attic Insulation)
Y (Heating Oil)	$r_{YY} = 1.0$	$r_{Y1} = -.86974$	$r_{Y2} = -.46508$
X_1 (Temperature)	$r_{Y1} = -.86974$	$r_{11} = 1.0$	$r_{12} = .00892$
X_2 (Attic Insulation)	$r_{Y2} = -.46508$	$r_{12} = .00892$	$r_{22} = 1.0$

From Table 17.4, we observe that the correlation between the amount of heating oil consumed and temperature is $-.86974$, indicating a strong negative association between the variables. We may also observe that the correlation between the amount of heating oil consumed and attic insulation is $-.46508$, indicating a moderate negative correlation between these variables. Furthermore, we also note that there is virtually no correlation ($.00892$) between the two explanatory variables, temperature and attic insulation. Finally, we may note that the correlation coefficients along the main diagonal of the matrix (r_{YY}, r_{11}, r_{22}) are each 1.0, since there will be perfect correlation between a variable and itself.

Problems

- **17.16** Referring to Problem 17.2 (the shoe durability problem) on page 631
  - **(a)** Compute the coefficient of multiple determination $r^2_{Y.12}$ and interpret its meaning.
  - **(b)** Compute the adjusted r^2.
- **17.17** Referring to Problem 17.3 (the absenteeism problem) on page 632
  - **(a)** Interpret the meaning of the coefficient of multiple determination $r^2_{Y.12}$.
  - **(b)** Compute the adjusted r^2.
- **17.18** Referring to Problem 17.4 (the advertising media problem) on page 632
  - **(a)** Interpret the meaning of the coefficient of multiple determination $r^2_{Y.12}$.
  - **(b)** Compute the adjusted r^2.
- **17.19** Referring to Problem 17.5 (the employee salary problem) on page 633
  - **(a)** Interpret the meaning of the coefficient of multiple determination $r^2_{Y.12}$.
  - **(b)** Compute the adjusted r^2.
- **17.20** Referring to Problem 17.6 (the stock price problem) on page 634
  - **(a)** Interpret the meaning of the coefficient of multiple determination $r^2_{Y.12}$.
  - **(b)** Compute the adjusted r^2.

17.6 TESTING PORTIONS OF A MULTIPLE REGRESSION MODEL

In developing a multiple regression model, the objective is to utilize only those explanatory variables that are useful in predicting the value of a dependent variable. If an explanatory variable is not helpful in making this prediction, then it could be deleted from the multiple regression model and a model with fewer explanatory variables could be utilized in its place.

One method for determining the contribution of an explanatory variable is called **the partial F test criterion** (see Reference 4). It involves determining the contribution to the regression sum of squares made by each explanatory variable after all the other explanatory variables have been included in a model. The new explanatory variable would only be included if it significantly improved the model. To apply the partial F test criterion in our heating oil consumption problem containing two explanatory variables, we need to evaluate the contribution of the variable attic insulation (X_2) once average daily atmospheric temperature (X_1) has been included in the model and, conversely, we also must evaluate the contribution of the variable average daily atmospheric temperature (X_1) once attic insulation (X_2) has been included in the model.

17.6.1 Determining the Contribution of an Explanatory Variable by Comparing Different Regression Models

The contribution of each explanatory variable to be included in the model can be determined in two ways, depending upon the information provided by the particular computer package utilized. In this section we shall evaluate the contribution of each explanatory variable by taking into account the regression sum of squares of a model that includes all explanatory variables except the one of interest, SSR (*all variables except k*). Thus, in general, to determine the contribution of variable k given that all other variables are already included, we would have

$$
\begin{aligned}
\text{SSR}(X_k|\text{\textit{all variables except k}}) \\
= \text{SSR}(\textit{all variables including } k) \\
- \text{SSR}(\textit{all variables except } k)
\end{aligned}
\tag{17.6a}
$$

If, as in the heating oil consumption problem, there are two explanatory variables, the contribution of each can be determined from Equations (17.6b) and (17.6c).

Contribution of Variable X_1 Given X_2 Has Been Included

$$
\text{SSR}(X_1|X_2) = \text{SSR}(X_1 \text{ and } X_2) - \text{SSR}(X_2)
\tag{17.6b}
$$

Contribution of Variable X_2 Given X_1 Has Been Included

$$
\text{SSR}(X_2|X_1) = \text{SSR}(X_1 \text{ and } X_2) - \text{SSR}(X_1)
\tag{17.6c}
$$

The term $\text{SSR}(X_2)$ represents the regression sum of squares for a model that includes only the explanatory variable X_2 (amount of attic insulation); the term $\text{SSR}(X_1)$ represents the regression sum of squares for a model that includes only the explanatory variable X_1 (average daily atmospheric temperature). Computer output obtained from the SAS REG procedure for these two models is presented in Figures 17.4 and 17.5. We can observe from Figure 17.4 that

$$
\text{SSR}(X_2) = 51{,}076.4650
$$

and, therefore, from Equation (17.6b),

$$
\text{SSR}(X_1|X_2) = \text{SSR}(X_1 \text{ and } X_2) - \text{SSR}(X_2)
$$

we have

$$
\text{SSR}(X_1|X_2) = 228{,}014.6263 - 51{,}076.4650 = 176{,}938.1613
$$

We should note that this value, except for rounding, is also shown as the *Type II Sum of Squares* (*SS*) obtained from the SAS REG procedure or the *Type III Sum*

```
DEP VARIABLE: OIL                 (VARIANCE)
                        SUM OF       MEAN
    SOURCE     DF       SQUARES     SQUARE     F VALUE      PROB>F
    MODEL       1        51076       51076       3.59        .0807
    ERROR      13     185058.76      14235
    C TOTAL    14       236135
         ROOT MSE    119.31051     R-SQUARE     0.2163
         DEP MEAN     216.493      ADJ R-SQ     0.1560


                        PARAMETER    STANDARD    T FOR HO:
    VARIABLE   DF       ESTIMATE      ERROR     PARAMETER=0    PROB > :T:

    INTERCEP    1        345.378    74.690659      4.62        0.0005
    INSU        1      -  20.351    10.743429     -1.89        0.0807


    VARIABLE   DF     TYPE I SS    TYPE II SS

    INSU        1     51076.465    51076.465
```

FIGURE 17.4
Partial output of simple linear regression model of amount of heating oil consumed and amount of attic insulation (obtained from SAS PROC REG).

```
DEP VARIABLE: OIL                 (VARIANCE)
                        SUM OF       MEAN
    SOURCE     DF       SQUARES     SQUARE     F VALUE      PROB>F
    MODEL       1       178624      178624      40.38        0.0001
    ERROR      13     57510.805      4424
    C TOTAL    14       236135
         ROOT MSE     66.513       R-SQUARE     0.7565
         DEP MEAN    216.493       ADJ R-SQ     0.7378


                        PARAMETER    STANDARD    T FOR HO:
    VARIABLE   DF       ESTIMATE      ERROR     PARAMETER=0    PROB > :T:

    INTERCEP    1        436.438    38.639709     11.30        0.0001
    TEMPF       1      -5.462208     0.859609     - 6.35       0.0001


    VARIABLE   DF     TYPE I SS    TYPE II SS

    TEMPF       1       178624       178624
```

FIGURE 17.5
Partial output of simple linear regression model of amount of heating oil consumed and average daily atmospheric temperature (obtained from SAS PROC REG).

of Squares from the SAS GLM procedure for the regression model with two explanatory variables (see Figure 17.2 on pages 630–631).

In order to determine whether X_1 significantly improves the model after X_2 has been included, we can now subdivide the regression sum of squares into two component parts as shown in Table 17.5 on page 642.

The null and alternative hypotheses to test for the contribution of X_1 to the model would be:

TABLE 17.5 Analysis-of-variance table dividing the regression sum of squares into components to determine the contribution of variable X_1

Source	df	Sums of Squares	Mean Square (Variance)	F
Regression	2	228,014.6263	114,007.31315	
$\left\{\begin{array}{c} X_2 \\ X_1\|X_2 \end{array}\right\}$	$\left\{\begin{array}{c} 1 \\ 1 \end{array}\right\}$	$\left\{\begin{array}{c} 51,076.4650 \\ 176,938.1613 \end{array}\right\}$	$\begin{array}{c} 51,076.4650 \\ 176,938.1613 \end{array}$	261.47
Error	12	8,120.6030	MSE = 676.71692	
Total	14	236,135.2293		

H_0: Variable X_1 does not significantly improve the model once variable X_2 has been included.

H_1: Variable X_1 significantly improves the model once variable X_2 has been included.

The partial F-test criterion is expressed by

$$F_{1, n-p-1} = \frac{\text{SSR}(X_k | \text{all variables except } k)}{\text{MSE}} \tag{17.7}$$

where p = number of explanatory variables in the regression model.

Thus, from Table 17.5 we have

$$F_{1,12} = \frac{176,938.1613}{676.71692} = 261.47$$

If a level of significance of .05 is selected, from Table E.5 we can observe that the critical value is 4.75 (see Figure 17.6). Since the computed F value exceeds this critical F value ($261.47 > 4.75$), our decision would be to reject H_0 and conclude that the addition of variable X_1 (average daily atmospheric temperature) significantly improves a multiple regression model that already contains variable X_2 (attic insulation).

In order to evaluate the contribution of variable X_2 (attic insulation) to a model in which variable X_1 has been included, we need to compute

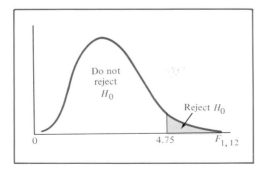

FIGURE 17.6
Testing for the contribution of a regression coefficient to a multiple regression model at the .05 level of significance with 1 and 12 degrees of freedom.

$$\text{SSR}(X_2|X_1) = \text{SSR}(X_1 \text{ and } X_2) - \text{SSR}(X_1) \tag{17.6c}$$

From Figures 17.2 and 17.5 we determine that

$$\text{SSR}(X_1) = 178{,}624.4242$$

Therefore,

$$\text{SSR}(X_2|X_1) = 228{,}014.6263 - 178{,}624.4242 = 49{,}390.2021$$

Thus, in order to determine whether X_2 significantly improves a model after X_1 has been included, the regression sum of squares can be subdivided into two component parts as shown in Table 17.6.

TABLE 17.6 Analysis-of-variance table subdividing the regression sum of squares into components to determine the contribution of variable X_2

Source	df	Sums of Squares	Mean Square (Variance)	F
Regression	2	228,014.6263	114,007.31315	
$\begin{cases} X_1 \\ X_2\|X_1 \end{cases}$	$\begin{cases} 1 \\ 1 \end{cases}$	$\begin{cases} 178{,}624.4242 \\ 49{,}390.2021 \end{cases}$	178,624.4242 49,390.2021	72.99
Error	12	8,120.6030	MSE = 676.71692	
Total	14	236,135.2293		

The null and alternative hypotheses to test for the contribution of X_2 to the model would be:

H_0: Variable X_2 does not significantly improve the model once variable X_1 has been included.

H_1: Variable X_2 significantly improves the model once variable X_1 has been included.

Using Equation (17.7), we obtain

$$F_{1,12} = \frac{49{,}390.2021}{676.71692} = 72.99$$

as indicated in Table 17.6. Since there are 1 and 12 degrees of freedom, respectively, if a .05 level of significance is selected, we again observe from Figure 17.6 that the critical value of F is 4.75. Since the computed F value exceeds this critical value (72.99 > 4.75), our decision is to reject H_0 and conclude that the addition of variable X_2 (attic insulation) significantly improves the multiple regression model already containing X_1 (average daily atmospheric temperature).

Thus, by testing for the contribution of each explanatory variable after the other had been included in the model, we determined that each of the two explanatory variables contributed by significantly improving the model. Therefore, our multiple regression model should include both average daily atmospheric temperature X_1 and the amount of attic insulation X_2 in predicting the consumption of home heating oil.

17.6.2 Determining the Contribution of an Explanatory Variable Based on the Standard Error of Its Regression Coefficient

A second approach to evaluating the contribution made by an explanatory variable is based upon the standard error of its regression coefficient. Since the standard errors of the regression coefficients S_{b_k} (see Sections 16.10 and 17.7) are available from the output of a computer package (see Figures 17.2, 17.22, 17.23, and 17.24), the contribution of a particular variable to the regression sum of squares can be determined in the following manner:

$$\text{SSR}(X_k | \textit{all variables except } k) = \frac{b_k^2 \text{MSE}}{S_{b_k}^2} \qquad (17.8)$$

We can observe from Figure 17.2 that the standard errors of the regression coefficients for each explanatory variable (S_{b_1} and S_{b_2}) are available as part of the SAS output. Thus if we wish to determine the contribution of variable X_2 after X_1 has been included, from Equation (17.8) we have

$$\text{SSR}(X_2 | X_1) = \frac{b_2^2 \text{MSE}}{S_{b_2}^2} = \frac{(-20.0123)^2(676.71692)}{(2.3425)^2} = 49{,}390.2021$$

However, as indicated in Table 17.6, we can observe that this result is the same as that obtained by using Equation (17.6c) on page 640.

Problems

- **17.21** Referring to Problem 17.2 (the shoe durability problem) on page 631, at the .05 level of significance, determine whether each explanatory variable makes a significant contribution to the regression model. Based upon these results, indicate the regression model that should be utilized in this problem.

  17.22 Referring to Problem 17.3 (the absenteeism problem) on page 632, at the .05 level of significance, determine whether each explanatory variable makes a significant contribution to the regression model. Based upon these results, indicate the regression model that should be used in this problem.

- **17.23** Referring to Problem 17.4 (the advertising media problem) on page 632, at the .05 level of significance, determine whether each explanatory variable makes a significant contribution to the regression model. Based upon these results, indicate the regression model that should be utilized in this problem.

  17.24 Referring to Problem 17.5 (the employee salary problem) on page 633, at the .05 level of significance, determine whether each explanatory variable makes a significant contribution to the regression model. Based upon these results, indicate the regression model that should be utilized in this problem.

  17.25 Referring to Problem 17.6 (the stock price problem) on page 634, at the .05 level of significance, determine whether each explanatory variable makes a significant contribution to the regression model. Based upon these results, indicate the regression model that should be utilized in this problem.

17.7 INFERENCES CONCERNING THE POPULATION REGRESSION COEFFICIENTS

In Section 16.10 we may recall that tests of hypotheses were performed on the regression coefficients in a simple linear regression model in order to determine the significance of the relationship between X and Y. In addition, confidence intervals were used to estimate the population values of these regression coefficients. In this section, these procedures will be ε ended to situations involving multiple regression.

17.7.1 Tests of Hypothesis

To test a hypothesis regarding a regression coefficient, we used Equation (16.16):

$$t_{n-2} = \frac{b_1}{S_{b_1}}$$

However, this equation can be generalized for multiple regression as follows:

$$t_{n-p-1} = \frac{b_k}{S_{b_k}} \tag{17.9}$$

where p = number of explanatory variables in the regression equation
S_{b_k} = standard error of the regression coefficient b_k

Since the formulas for the standard errors of the regression coefficients are unwieldy with a large number of variables, it is fortunate that the results are provided as part of the output obtained from a computer package (see Figures 17.2, 17.22, 17.23, and 17.24).

Thus, if we wish to determine whether variable X_2 (amount of attic insulation) has a significant effect on the consumption of home heating oil, taking into account the average daily atmospheric temperature, the null and alternative hypotheses would be

$$H_0: \quad \beta_2 = 0$$
$$H_1: \quad \beta_2 \neq 0$$

From Equation (17.9) we have

$$t_{n-p-1} = \frac{b_2}{S_{b_2}}$$

and from the data of this problem,

$$b_2 = -20.0123 \quad \text{and} \quad S_{b_2} = 2.3425$$

so that

$$t_{12} = \frac{-20.0123}{2.3425} = -8.5431$$

If a level of significance of .05 is selected, from Table E.3 we can observe that for 12 degrees of freedom the critical values of t are -2.1788 and $+2.1788$ (see Figure 17.7 on page 646).

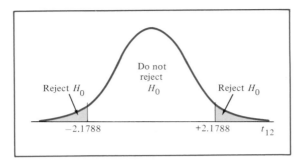

FIGURE 17.7
Testing for the significance of a regression coefficient at the .05 level of significance with 12 degrees of freedom.

Since we have $t_{12} = -8.5431 < -2.1788$, we reject H_0 and conclude that there is a significant relationship between variable X_2 (amount of attic insulation) and the consumption of heating oil, taking into account the average daily atmospheric temperature X_1.

In order to focus upon the interpretation of this conclusion, we should note that there is a relationship between the value of the t-test statistic obtained from Equation (17.9) and the partial F-test statistic [Equation (17.7)] used to determine the contribution of X_2 to the multiple regression model. While the t value was computed to be -8.5431, the corresponding computed value of F was 72.99—which happens to be the square of -8.5431. This points up the following relationship between t and F:[1]

$$t_a^2 = F_{1,a} \qquad \textbf{(17.10)}$$

where a is the number of degrees of freedom.

Thus the test of significance for a particular regression coefficient (in this case b_2) is actually a test for the significance of adding a particular variable into a regression model given that the other variables have been included. Therefore, we see that the t test for the regression coefficient is equivalent to testing for the contribution of each explanatory variable as discussed in Section 17.6.

17.7.2 Confidence-Interval Estimation

Rather than attempting to determine the significance of a regression coefficient, we may be more concerned with estimating the true population value of a regression coefficient. In multiple regression analysis a confidence-interval estimate can be obtained from

$$b_k \pm t_{n-p-1} S_{b_k} \qquad \textbf{(17.11)}$$

For example, if we wish to obtain a 95% confidence-interval estimate of the true slope β_1 (that is, the effect of average daily temperature X_1 on consumption of heating

---

[1] The relationship between t and F indicated in Equation (17.10) holds when t is a two-tailed test.

oil Y, holding constant the effect of attic insulation X_2), we would have, from Equation (17.11) and Figure 17.2,

$$b_1 \pm t_{12}S_{b_1}$$

Since the critical value of t at the 95% confidence level with 12 degrees of freedom is 2.1788 (see Table E.3), we have

$$-5.43658 \pm (2.1788)(.33622)$$

$$-5.43658 \pm .732556$$

$$-6.169136 \leq \beta_1 \leq -4.704024$$

Thus, taking into account the effect of attic insulation, we estimate that the true effect of average daily atmospheric temperature is to reduce consumption of heating oil by between approximately 4.7 and 6.17 gallons for each 1°F increase in temperature. Furthermore, we have 95% confidence that this interval correctly estimates the true relationship between these variables. Of course, from a hypothesis-testing viewpoint, since this confidence interval does not include zero, the regression coefficient β_1 would be considered to have a significant effect.

Problems

- **17.26** Referring to Problem 17.2 (the shoe durability problem) on page 631, set up a 95% confidence-interval estimate of the true population slope between long-term impact and forefoot impact.

  17.27 Referring to Problem 17.3 (the absenteeism problem) on page 632, set up a 95% confidence-interval estimate of the true population slope between absenteeism and age.

- **17.28** Referring to Problem 17.4 (the advertising media problem) on page 632, set up a 95% confidence-interval estimate of the true population slope between sales and radio and television advertising.

  17.29 Referring to Problem 17.5 (the employee salary problem) on page 633, set up a 95% confidence-interval estimate of the true population slope between weekly salary and length of employment.

  17.30 Referring to Problem 17.6 (the stock price problem) on page 634, set up a 95% confidence-interval estimate of the true population slope between stock price and book value.

17.8 CONFIDENCE-INTERVAL ESTIMATES FOR PREDICTING μ_{YX} and $\hat{Y}_I$

In Section 17.3, we used the multiple regression equation to obtain a prediction of the consumption of heating oil for a house that has 6 inches of attic insulation in a month in which the average daily temperature was 30°F. A confidence-interval estimate of μ_{YX}, the true mean value of Y, and a prediction-interval estimate of an individual value $\hat{Y}_I$ can be obtained by extending the procedures discussed in Sections 16.8 and 16.9 to the multiple regression model. However, as indicated in the previous section in our discussion of the standard error of the regression coefficients, the formulas used for predicting μ_{YX} and $\hat{Y}_I$ also become unwieldy when there are several explanatory variables included in a multiple regression model and therefore they usually are expressed in terms of matrix notation (see Reference 4). Nevertheless, as displayed in Figure 17.8 on page 648, these interval estimates are obtained for each observation in the sample by using the SAS REG or GLM procedure.

OBS	ACTUAL	PREDICT VALUE	STD ERR PREDICT	LOWER95% MEAN	UPPER95% MEAN	RESIDUAL
1	275.300	284.651	10.300	262.210	307.092	-9.351
2	363.800	355.326	11.196	330.932	379.721	8.474
3	164.300	144.565	10.905	120.805	168.324	19.735
4	40.800	45.207	12.923	17.050	73.363	-4.407
5	94.300	94.136	10.465	71.335	116.936	0.164072
6	230.900	257.233	7.081	241.806	272.661	-26.333
7	366.700	393.148	12.493	365.927	420.369	-26.448
8	300.600	318.535	15.435	284.905	352.165	-17.935
9	237.800	236.986	12.389	209.994	263.979	0.813551
10	121.400	159.609	12.867	131.574	187.645	-38.209
11	31.400	8.650	13.666	-21.126	38.426	22.750
12	203.500	219.177	6.767	204.434	233.921	-15.677
13	441.100	387.946	12.130	361.516	414.375	53.154
14	323.000	295.524	10.323	273.033	318.015	27.476
15	52.500	46.706	12.390	19.710	73.703	5.794

OBSERVATION	OBSERVED	PREDICTED RESIDUAL	LOWER 95% CLI UPPER 95% CLI
1	275.30000000	284.65082371	223.69081563
		-9.35082371	345.61083179
2	363.80000000	355.32637135	293.62026727
		8.47362865	417.03247544
3	164.30000000	144.56457905	83.10703569
		19.73542095	206.02212241
4	40.80000000	45.20670231	-18.08084005
		-4.40670231	108.49424466
5	94.30000000	94.13592760	33.04259214
		0.16407240	155.22926307
6	230.90000000	257.23334524	198.49211244
		-26.33334524	315.97457804
7	366.70000000	393.14785994	330.27085527
		-26.44785994	456.02486461
8	300.60000000	318.53515786	252.62970178
		-17.93515786	384.44061395
9	237.80000000	236.98644904	174.20794227
		0.81355096	299.76495582
10	121.40000000	159.60947019	96.37550756
		-38.20947019	222.84343281
11	31.40000000	8.65006435	-55.37457834
		22.74993565	72.67470704
12	203.50000000	219.17728112	160.61191173
		-15.67728112	277.74265052
13	441.10000000	387.94585488	325.40738800
		53.15414512	450.48432177
14	323.00000000	295.52398489	234.54532672
		27.47601511	356.50264305
15	52.50000000	46.70612846	-16.07399549
		5.79387154	109.48625242

FIGURE 17.8
Confidence and prediction intervals obtained from SAS PROC REG and PROC GLM for the heating oil usage model.

17.9 COEFFICIENT OF PARTIAL DETERMINATION

In Section 17.5 we discussed the coefficient of multiple determination ($r_{Y.12}^2$) which measured the proportion of the variation in Y that was explained by variation in the two explanatory variables. Now that we have examined ways in which the contribution of each explanatory variable to the multiple regression model can be evaluated, we can also compute the coefficients of partial determination ($r^2_{Y1.2}$ and $r^2_{Y2.1}$). The coefficients measure the proportion of the variation in the dependent variable that is explained by each explanatory variable while controlling for, or holding constant, the other explanatory variable(s). Thus in a multiple regression model with two explanatory variables we have

$$r^2_{Y1.2} = \frac{SSR(X_1|X_2)}{SST - SSR(X_1 \text{ and } X_2) + SSR(X_1|X_2)} \qquad \textbf{(17.12a)}$$

and also

$$r^2_{Y2.1} = \frac{SSR(X_2|X_1)}{SST - SSR(X_1 \text{ and } X_2) + SSR(X_2|X_1)} \qquad \textbf{(17.12b)}$$

where $SSR(X_1|X_2)$ = sum of squares of the contribution of variable X_1 to the regression model given that variable X_2 has been included in the model

SST = total sum of squares for Y

$SSR(X_1 \text{ and } X_2)$ = regression sum of squares when variables X_1 and X_2 are both included in the multiple-regression model

$SSR(X_2|X_1)$ = sum of squares of the contribution of variable X_2 to the regression model given that variable X_1 has been included in the model

while in a multiple regression model containing several (p) explanatory variables, we have

$$r^2_{Yk.(\text{all variables except } k)} = \frac{SSR(X_k|\text{all variables except } k)}{SST - SSR(\text{all variables including } k) + SSR(X_k|\text{all variables except } k)} \qquad \textbf{(17.13)}$$

For our heating oil consumption problem we can compute

$$r^2_{Y1.2} = \frac{176{,}938.1613}{236{,}135.2293 - 228{,}014.6263 + 176{,}938.1613}$$
$$= 0.9561$$

and

$$r^2_{Y2.1} = \frac{49{,}390.2021}{236{,}135.2293 - 228{,}014.6263 + 49{,}390.2021}$$
$$= 0.8588$$

The coefficient of partial determination of variable Y with X_1 while holding X_2 constant ($r^2_{Y1.2}$) can be interpreted to mean that for a fixed (constant) amount of attic insulation,

95.61% of the variation in the consumption of heating oil in January can be explained by the variation in the average daily atmospheric temperature in that month. Moreover, the coefficient of partial determination of variable Y with X_2 while holding X_1 constant ($r_{Y2.1}^2$) can be interpreted to mean that for a given (constant) average daily atmospheric temperature, 85.88% of the variation in the consumption of heating oil in January can be explained by variation in the amount of attic insulation.

Problems

17.31   Explain the difference between the coefficient of multiple determination $r_{Y.12}^2$ and the coefficient of partial determination $r_{Y.12}^2$.

● **17.32**   Referring to Problem 17.2 (the shoe durability problem) on page 631, compute the coefficients of partial determination $r_{Y1.2}^2$ and $r_{Y2.1}^2$ and interpret their meaning.

17.33   Referring to Problem 17.3 (the absenteeism problem) on page 632, compute the coefficients of partial determination $r_{Y1.2}^2$ and $r_{Y2.1}^2$ and interpret their meaning.

● **17.34**   Referring to Problem 17.4 (the advertising media problem) on page 632, compute the coefficients of partial determination $r_{Y1.2}^2$ and $r_{Y2.1}^2$ and interpret their meaning.

17.35   Referring to Problem 17.5 (the employee salary problem) on page 633, compute the coefficients of partial determination $r_{Y1.2}^2$ and $r_{Y2.1}^2$ and interpret their meaning.

17.36   Referring to Problem 17.6 (the stock price problem) on page 634, compute the coefficients of partial determination $r_{Y1.2}^2$ and $r_{Y2.1}^2$ and interpret their meaning.

17.10   THE CURVILINEAR REGRESSION MODEL

In our discussion of simple regression in Chapter 16 and multiple regression in this chapter, we have thus far assumed that the relationship between Y and each explanatory variable is linear. However, we may recall that several different types of relationships between variables were introduced in Section 16.3. One of the more common nonlinear relationships that was illustrated was a curvilinear polynomial relationship between two variables (see Figure 16.3 on page 565, panels D to F) in which Y increases (or decreases) at a *changing rate* for various values of X. This model of a polynomial relationship between X and Y can be expressed as

$$Y_i = \beta_0 + \beta_1 X_{1i} + \beta_{11} X_{1i}^2 + \epsilon_i \qquad (17.14)$$

where $\beta_0 = Y$ intercept
$\quad \beta_1 = $ *linear* effect on Y
$\quad \beta_{11} = $ *curvilinear* effect on Y
$\quad \epsilon_i = $ random error in Y for observation i

This regression model is similar to the multiple regression model with two explanatory variables [see Equation (17.1) on page 628] except that the second ''explanatory'' variable in this instance is merely the square of the first explanatory variable.

As in the case of multiple linear regression, when sample data are analyzed the sample regression coefficients (b_0, b_1, and b_{11}) are used as estimates of the true parameters (β_0, β_1, and β_{11}). Thus the regression equation for the curvilinear polynomial model having one explanatory variable (X_1) and a dependent variable (Y) is

$$\hat{Y}_i = b_0 + b_1 X_{1i} + b_{11} X_{1i}^2 \qquad \textbf{(17.14a)}$$

An alternative approach to the curvilinear regression model expressed in Equation (17.14a) is to center the data by subtracting the mean of the explanatory variable from each value in the model. This centered regression model is expressed as Equation (17.15).

$$\hat{Y}_i = b_0' + b_1'(X_{1i} - \overline{X}_1) + b_{11}(X_{1i} - \overline{X}_1)^2 \qquad \textbf{(17.15)}$$

Centering such a model may be done both for numerical and statistical reasons. First, from a computational perspective, more accuracy may be achieved if the mean is subtracted from each value before a regression equation is solved numerically. Second, and perhaps more important, the variance of the explanatory variable may be greatly inflated because X_1 and X_1^2 are positively correlated. Since X_1 and X_1^2 carry essentially the same information, it is sometimes difficult to determine whether the X_1 term is truly statistically significant. Moreover, it is also possible that the slope of the X_1 term will have a sign opposite of the trend indicated by a scatter diagram. To avoid such problems, some researchers (see Reference 19) recommend centering the X_1 variable in a curvilinear regression model.

Mathematically, Equation (17.14a) and Equation (17.15) are equivalent. They give the same values for $\hat{Y}_i$ and b_{11} and they explain the same amount of the total variation. The difference between the two models occurs in the *intercept* (b_0 versus b_0') and *linear effect* (b_1 versus b_1') terms.

17.10.1 Finding the Regression Coefficients and Predicting Y

In order to illustrate the curvilinear regression model, let us suppose that the marketing department of a large supermarket chain wanted to study the price elasticity of packages of disposable razors. A sample of 15 stores with equal store traffic and product placement (i.e., at the checkout counter) was selected. Five stores were randomly assigned to each of three price levels (79 cents, 99 cents, and $1.19) for the package of razors. The number of packages sold and the price at each store are presented in Table 17.7 on page 652.

In order to investigate the selection of the proper model expressing the relationship between price and sales, a scatter diagram is plotted as in Figure 17.9 on page 652. An examination of Figure 17.9 indicates that the decrease in sales levels off for an increasing price. Therefore, it appears that it may be more appropriate to use a curvilinear model to estimate sales based upon price than a linear model.

As in the case of multiple regression, the values of the three sample regression coefficients (b_0', b_1', and b_{11}) can be obtained most easily by accessing a computer package (see References 10–12, 15, 17, 18, 20, 21).

TABLE 17.7   Sales and price of packages of disposable razors for a sample of 15 stores

Sales	Price (*cents*)
142	79
151	79
163	79
168	79
176	79
91	99
100	99
107	99
115	99
126	99
77	119
86	119
95	119
100	119
106	119

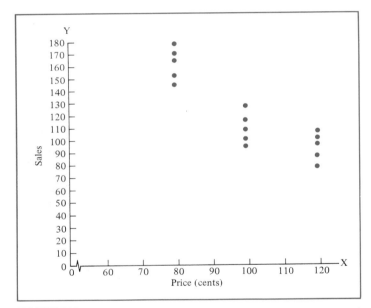

FIGURE 17.9
Scatter diagram of price (*X*) and sales (*Y*).

Figure 17.10 presents partial output from the Minitab REGRESS command for the data of Table 17.7 using the centered model (Equation 17.15). From Figure 17.10 we observe that

$$b_0' = 107.8, \; b_1' = -1.68, \; b_{11} = .0465$$

Therefore the centered curvilinear model can be expressed as

$$\hat{Y}_i = 107.8 - 1.68(X_{1i} - \overline{X}_1) + .0465 \, (X_{1i} - \overline{X}_1)^2$$

```
The regression equation is
sales = 108 - 1.68 pricecen + 0.0465 prcensq

Predictor          Coef           Stdev         t-ratio
Constant         107.800          5.756          18.73
pricecen          -1.6800         0.2035         -8.26
prcensq            0.04650        0.01762          2.64

s = 12.87          R-sq = 86.2%          R-sq(adj) = 83.9%

Analysis of Variance

SOURCE          DF           SS             MS
Regression       2        12442.8         6221.4
Error           12         1987.6          165.6
Total           14        14430.4

SOURCE          DF          SEQ SS
pricecen         1         11289.6
prcensq          1          1153.2
```

FIGURE 17.10
Partial output for the data of Table 17.7 using Minitab.

where $\hat{Y}_i$ = predicted sales for store i
X_{1i} = price of disposable razors in store i

As depicted in Figure 17.11, this curvilinear regression equation is plotted on the scatter diagram to indicate how well the selected regression model fits the original data. Moreover, Figure 17.11 helps us to interpret the meaning of our computed regression coefficients. From our curvilinear regression equation and Figure 17.11, the Y intercept (b_0', computed as 107.80) can be interpreted to mean that the predicted sales for $X_{1i} = \overline{X}_1 = 99$ is 107.8 packages. To interpret the coefficients b_1' and b_{11}, we see from Figure 17.11 that the sales decrease with increasing price; nevertheless, we also observe that these decreases in sales level off or become reduced with increasing price. This can be seen by predicting average sales for packages priced at 79 cents, 99 cents, and 119 cents ($1.19). Using our curvilinear regression equation

$$\hat{Y}_i = 107.8 - 1.68(X_{1i} - \overline{X}_1) + .0465(X_{1i} - \overline{X}_1)^2$$

with $\overline{X}_1 = 99$,

for $X_{1i} = 79$ we have:

$$\hat{Y}_i = 107.8 - 1.68(79 - 99) + .0465(79 - 99)^2 = 160$$

for $X_{1i} = 99$ we have:

$$\hat{Y}_i = 107.8 - 1.68(99 - 99) + .0465(99 - 99)^2 = 107.8$$

for $X_{1i} = 119$ we have:

$$\hat{Y}_i = 107.8 - 1.68(119 - 99) + .0465(119 - 99)^2 = 92.8$$

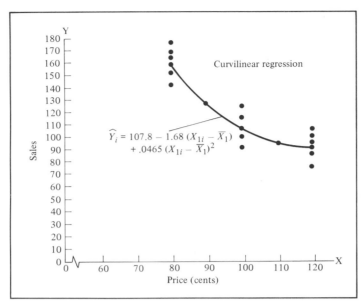

FIGURE 17.11
Scatter diagram expressing the curvilinear relationship between price *X* and sales *Y*.

Thus we observe that a store selling the razors for 79 cents is expected to sell 52.2 more packages than a store selling them for 99 cents, but a store selling them for 99 cents is expected to sell only 15 more packages than a store selling them for $1.19.

17.10.2 Testing for the Significance of the Curvilinear Model

Now that the curvilinear model has been fitted to the data, we can determine whether there is a significant curvilinear relationship between sales *Y* and price *X*. In a manner similar to multiple regression (see Section 17.4), the null and alternative hypotheses can be set up as follows:

H_0: $\beta_1 = \beta_{11} = 0$ (There is no relationship between X_1 and *Y*.)

H_1: $\beta_1 \neq \beta_{11} \neq 0$ (At least one regression coefficient is not equal to zero.)

The null hypothesis can be tested by utilizing an *F* test [Equation (17.3)] as indicated in Table 17.8.

For the data of Table 17.7 the ANOVA table is displayed as part of the computer output in Figure 17.10 on page 653.

If a level of significance of .05 is chosen, from Table E.5 we find that for 2 and 12 degrees of freedom the critical value on the *F* distribution is 3.89 (see Figure 17.12). Utilizing Equation (17.3), since

$$F_{2,12} = \frac{\text{MSR}}{\text{MSE}} = \frac{6,221.4}{165.6} = 37.57 > 3.89,$$

we can reject the null hypothesis (H_0) and conclude that there is a significant curvilinear relationship between sales and price of razors.

TABLE 17.8 Analysis-of-variance table testing the significance of a curvilinear polynomial relationship

Source	df	Sums of Squares	Mean Square (Variance)	F
Regression	2	$SSR = b_0' \sum_{i=1}^{n} Y_i + b_1' \sum_{i=1}^{n} (X_{1i} - \overline{X}_1)Y_i + b_{11}' \sum_{i=1}^{n} (X_{1i} - \overline{X}_1)^2 Y_i - \dfrac{\left(\sum_{i=1}^{n} Y_i\right)^2}{n}$	$MSR = \dfrac{SSR}{2}$	$\dfrac{MSR}{MSE}$
Error	$n - 3$	$SSE = \sum_{i=1}^{n} Y_i^2 - b_0' \sum_{i=1}^{n} Y_i - b_1' \sum_{i=1}^{n} (X_{1i} - \overline{X}_1)Y_i - b_{11}' \sum_{i=1}^{n} (X_{1i} - \overline{X}_1)^2 Y_i$	$MSE = \dfrac{SSE}{n - 3}$	
Total	$n - 1$	$SST = \sum_{i=1}^{n} Y_i^2 - \dfrac{\left(\sum_{i=1}^{n} Y_i\right)^2}{n}$		

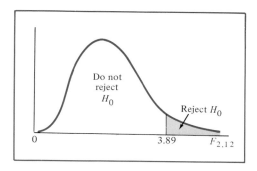

FIGURE 17.12
Testing for the existence of a curvilinear relationship at the .05 level of significance with 2 and 12 degrees of freedom.

In the multiple regression model we computed the coefficient of multiple determination $r_{Y.12}^2$ (see Section 17.5) to represent the proportion of variation in Y that is explained by variation in the explanatory variables. In curvilinear regression analysis, this coefficient can be computed from Equation (17.4):

$$r_{Y.12}^2 = \frac{SSR}{SST}$$

From Figure 17.10,

$$SSR = 12{,}442.8 \qquad SST = 14{,}430.4$$

Thus, as displayed in Figure 17.10,

$$r_{Y.12}^2 = \frac{SSR}{SST} = \frac{12{,}442.8}{14{,}430.4} = .862$$

This coefficient of multiple determination, computed as .862, can be interpreted to mean that 86.2% of the variation in sales can be explained by the curvilinear relationship between sales Y and price X. We may also recall from Section 17.4 that we computed an "adjusted" $r_{Y.12}^2$ to take into account the number of explanatory variables and the number of degrees of freedom. In our curvilinear regression problem $p = 2$, since we have two explanatory variables, X_1 and its square (X_1^2). Thus, using Equation (17.5) for the razor sales data, we have

$$r^2_{adj} = 1 - \left[(1 - r^2_{Y.12}) \frac{(15 - 1)}{(15 - 2 - 1)} \right]$$

$$= 1 - \left[(1 - .862) \frac{(14)}{12} \right]$$

$$= 1 - .161$$

$$= .839$$

Problems

17.37 Explain the difference between the curvilinear polynomial regression model and the multiple linear regression model with two explanatory variables.

• **17.38** A researcher for a major oil company wished to develop a model to predict miles per gallon based upon highway speed. An experiment was designed in which a test car was driven during two trial periods at a particular speed which ranged from 10 miles per hour to 75 miles per hour. The results are summarized below.

Observation	Miles per Gallon	Speed (Miles per Hour)
1	4.8	10
2	5.7	10
3	8.6	15
4	7.3	15
5	9.8	20
6	11.2	20
7	13.7	25
8	12.4	25
9	18.2	30
10	16.8	30
11	19.9	35
12	19.0	35
13	22.4	40
14	23.5	40
15	21.3	45
16	22.0	45
17	20.5	50
18	19.7	50
19	18.6	55
20	19.3	55
21	14.4	60
22	13.7	60
23	12.1	65
24	13.0	65
25	10.1	70
26	9.4	70
27	8.4	75
28	7.6	75

Assuming a curvilinear polynomial relationship between speed and mileage, access a computer package to perform a regression analysis. Based on the results obtained

(a) Set up a scatter diagram between speed and miles per gallon.
(b) State the equation for the curvilinear model.
(c) Predict the mileage obtained when the car is driven at 55 miles per hour.
(d) Determine whether there is a significant curvilinear relationship between mileage and speed at the .05 level of significance.
(e) Interpret the meaning of the coefficient of multiple determination $r_{Y.12}^2$.
(f) Compute the adjusted r^2.

17.39 An industrial psychologist would like to develop a model to predict the number of typing errors based upon the amount of alcoholic consumption. A random sample of 15 typists was selected with the following results:

Typist	X Alcoholic Consumption (Ounces)	Y Number of Errors
1	0	2
2	0	6
3	0	3
4	1	7
5	1	5
6	1	9
7	2	12
8	2	7
9	2	9
10	3	13
11	3	18
12	3	16
13	4	24
14	4	30
15	4	22

Assuming a curvilinear relationship between alcoholic consumption and the number of errors, access a computer package to perform the regression analysis. Based on the results obtained
(a) Set up a scatter diagram between alcoholic consumption X and the number of errors Y.
(b) State the equation for the curvilinear model.
(c) Predict the number of errors made by a typist who has consumed 2.5 ounces of alcohol.
(d) Determine whether there is a significant curvilinear relationship between alcoholic consumption and the number of errors made at the .05 level of significance.
(e) Interpret the meaning of the coefficient of multiple determination $r_{Y.12}^2$.
(f) Compute the adjusted r^2.

17.11 TESTING PORTIONS OF THE CURVILINEAR MODEL

17.11.1 Testing the Curvilinear Effect

In using a regression model to examine a relationship between two variables, we would like to fit not only the most accurate model but also the simplest model expressing that relationship. Therefore, it becomes important to examine whether there is a significant difference between the curvilinear model

$$Y_i = \beta_0' + \beta_1'(X_{1i} - \overline{X}_1) + \beta_{11}(X_{1i} - \overline{X}_1)^2 + \epsilon_i$$

and the linear model

$$Y_i = \beta_0 + \beta_1 X_i + \epsilon_i$$

These two models may be compared by determining the regression effect of adding the curvilinear term, given that the linear term has already been included, $SSR(b_{11}|b_1)$.

We may recall that in Section 17.7.1 we used the *t* test for the regression coefficient to determine whether each particular variable made a significant contribution to the regression model. From Figure 17.10 on page 653, we observe that the standard error of each regression coefficient and its corresponding *t* statistic is available as part of the Minitab output.

Thus we may test the significance of the contribution of the curvilinear effect with the following null and alternative hypotheses:

H_0: Including the curvilinear effect does not significantly improve the model ($\beta_{11} = 0$).

H_1: Including the curvilinear effect significantly improves the model ($\beta_{11} \neq 0$).

For our data

$$t_{n-3} = \frac{b_{11}}{S_{b_{11}}}$$

$$t_{12} = \frac{.0465}{.01762} = 2.64$$

If a level of significance of .05 is selected, from Table E.3, we find with 12 degrees of freedom that the critical values are -2.1788 and $+2.1788$ (see Figure 17.13). Since $t_{12} = 2.64 > 2.1788$, our decision would be to reject H_0 and conclude that the curvilinear model is significantly better than the linear model in representing the relationship between sales and price.

17.11.2 Testing the Linear Effect

Now that we have tested for the curvilinear effect, we should also determine whether there is a significant difference between the curvilinear model

$$Y_i = \beta_0' + \beta_1'(X_{1i} - \overline{X}_1) + \beta_{11}(X_{1i} - \overline{X}_1)^2 + \epsilon_i$$

and the model that includes *only* the curvilinear effect,

$$Y_i = \beta_0' + \beta_{11}(X_{1i} - \overline{X}_1)^2 + \epsilon_i$$

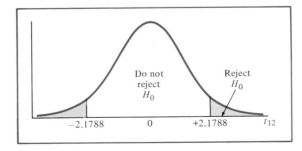

FIGURE 17.13
Testing for the contribution of the curvilinear effect to a regression model at the .05 level of significance with 12 degrees of freedom.

As in the case of the curvilinear effect, we may use the t test to determine the contribution of the linear effect given that the curvilinear effect is already in the model. For our data,

$$t_{n-3} = \frac{b_1'}{S_{b_1'}}$$

$$t_{12} = \frac{-1.68}{.2035} = -8.26$$

The null and alternative hypotheses to test for the contribution of the linear effect to the regression model are

H_0: $\beta_1' = 0$ (Including the linear effect does not improve the curvilinear effect model.)

H_1: $\beta_1' \neq 0$ (Including the linear effect does improve the curvilinear effect model.)

If a level of significance of .05 is selected, from Table E.3, we find with 12 degrees of freedom that the critical values are -2.1788 and $+2.1788$ (see Figure 17.13). Since $t_{12} = -8.26 < -2.1788$, our decision would be to reject H_0 and conclude that the curvilinear model that includes the linear effect is significantly better than the model that includes only the curvilinear effect.

Problems

- **17.40**   Referring to Problem 17.38 on page 656, at the .05 level of significance, determine whether the curvilinear model is a better fit than the linear regression model.
- **17.41**   Referring to Problem 17.39 on page 657, at the .05 level of significance, determine whether the curvilinear model is a better fit than the linear regression model.

17.12 DUMMY-VARIABLE MODELS

In our discussion of multiple regression models we have thus far assumed that each explanatory (or independent) variable was *quantitative*. However, there are many occasions in which categorical variables need to be considered as part of the model development process. For example, if we refer to the real estate survey, we recall that in Section 16.14 we used the number of rooms to develop a model to predict the appraised value of houses in East Meadow. In addition, we may also wish to include the effect of the presence or absence of such amenities as central air conditioning, a fireplace, a basement, or a modern kitchen.

The use of **dummy variables** is the vehicle that permits the researcher to consider qualitative explanatory variables as part of the regression model. If a given qualitative explanatory variable has two categories, then only one dummy variable will be needed to represent the two categories. The particular dummy variable (X_d) would be defined as

$$X_d = \begin{cases} 0 & \text{if the observation was in category 1} \\ 1 & \text{if the observation was in category 2} \end{cases}$$

In order to illustrate the application of dummy variables in regression, let us examine a model for predicting the appraised value of houses in East Meadow based upon the number of rooms and whether or not the house has central air conditioning. Thus a dummy variable for central air conditioning (X_2) could be defined as

$$X_2 = \begin{cases} 0 & \text{if the house does not have central air conditioning} \\ 1 & \text{if the house has central air conditioning} \end{cases}$$

Assuming that the slope between appraised value and number of rooms is the same for both groups,[2] the regression model could be stated as

$$Y_i = \beta_0 + \beta_1 X_{1i} + \beta_2 X_{2i} + \epsilon_i \qquad \text{(17.16)}$$

where Y_i = appraised value for house i

β_0 = Y intercept

β_1 = slope of appraised value with number of rooms holding central air-conditioning constant

β_2 = incremental effect of the presence of central air conditioning holding number of rooms constant

ϵ_i = random error in Y for house i

Using the sample of 74 houses, the model stated in Equation (17.16) was fitted. The resulting sample regression coefficients (b_0, b_1, and b_2), standard errors, and t values are summarized in Table 17.9.

TABLE 17.9   Summary of results for dummy variable model

Variable Name	Regression Coefficient	Standard Error	t
Constant	78.910	18.730	4.21
No. of Rooms	18.757	2.616	7.17
Central Air Cond.	20.251	9.820	2.06

Note the following:

1. Holding constant the effect of central air conditioning, each additional room is estimated to be worth $18,757 toward the appraised value of a house.
2. b_2 measures the effect on appraised value of having central air conditioning ($X_2 = 1$) as compared with not having central air conditioning ($X_2 = 0$). Thus we estimate that, holding the number of rooms constant, a house with central air conditioning will have an appraised value $20,251 above that of a corresponding house without central air conditioning.

---

[2] If the two groups have different slopes, an *interaction* term needs to be included in the model (see Section 17.13 and Reference 4).

Using the results of Table 17.9, the model for these data may be stated as

$$\hat{Y}_i = 78.91 + 18.757X_{1i} + 20.251X_{2i}$$

so that for houses without central air conditioning, since $X_2 = 0$

$$\hat{Y}_i = 78.91 + 18.757X_{1i}$$

while for houses with central air conditioning, since $X_2 = 1$

$$\hat{Y}_i = 78.91 + 18.757X_{1i} + 20.251(1)$$

$$\hat{Y}_i = 99.161 + 18.757X_{1i}$$

The fitted models for the two types of houses are displayed in Figure 17.14.

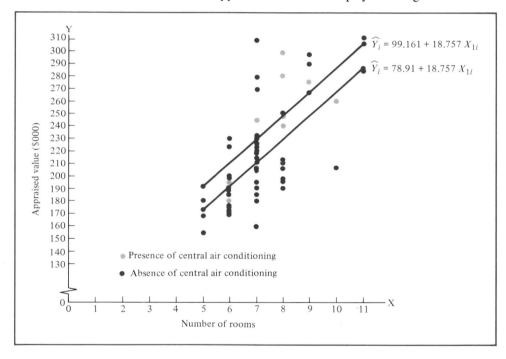

FIGURE 17.14
Regression models for houses with and without central air conditioning.

Problems

17.42 Under what circumstances would we want to include a "dummy variable" in a regression model?

17.43 What assumption concerning the slope between the response variable Y and the explanatory variable X must be made when a dummy variable is included in a regression model?

• **17.44** Referring to Problem 16.1 on page 561, suppose that in addition to studying the effect of shelf space on the sales of pet food, the marketing manager also wanted to study the effect of product placement on sales. Suppose that in stores 2, 6, 9, and 12 the pet food was placed at the front of the aisle while in the other stores it was placed at the back of the aisle. Access an available computer package to perform a multiple linear regression analysis. Based on the results obtained

(a) State the multiple regression equation.

(b) Interpret the meaning of the slopes in this problem.

(c) Predict the weekly sales of pet food for a store with 8 square feet of shelf space that is situated at the back of the aisle.

(d) Determine whether there is a significant relationship between sales and the two explanatory variables (shelf space and the dummy variable aisle position) at the .05 level of significance.

(e) Interpret the meaning of the coefficient of multiple determination $r^2_{Y.12}$.

(f) Compute the adjusted r^2.

(g) Compare $r^2_{Y.12}$ with the value computed in Problem 16.16(a) on page 576 and the adjusted r^2 of part (f) with the adjusted r^2 computed in Problem 16.16(b). Explain the results.

(h) At the .05 level of significance, determine whether each explanatory variable makes a contribution to the regression model. Based upon these results, indicate the regression model that should be used in this problem.

(i) Set up 95% confidence-interval estimates of the true population slope for the relationship between sales and shelf space and between sales and aisle location.

(j) Compare the slope obtained in part (b) with the slope for the simple linear regression model of Problem 16.6 on page 569. Explain the difference in the results.

(k) Compute the coefficients of partial determination and interpret their meaning.

(l) What assumption about the slope of shelf space with sales must be made in this problem?

17.45 Referring to Problem 16.2 on page 562, suppose that the personnel manager also wanted to study whether there was a difference between males and females in absenteeism. Suppose that workers 3, 6, 7, and 10 are females and workers 1, 2, 4, 5, 8, and 9 are male. Access an available computer package to perform a multiple linear regression analysis. Based on the results obtained

(a) State the multiple regression equation.

(b) Interpret the meaning of the slopes in this problem.

(c) Predict the number of days absent for a 40-year old male worker.

(d) Determine whether there is a significant relationship between days absent and the two explanatory variables (age and the dummy variable gender) at the .05 level of significance.

(e) Interpret the meaning of the coefficient of multiple determination $r^2_{Y.12}$.

(f) Compute the adjusted r^2.

(g) Compare $r^2_{Y.12}$ with the value computed in Problem 16.17(a) on page 576 and the adjusted r^2 of part (f) with the adjusted r^2 computed in Problem 16.17(b). Explain the results.

(h) At the .05 level of significance, determine whether each explanatory variable makes a contribution to the regression model. Based upon these results, indicate the regression model that should be used in this problem.

(i) Set up 95% confidence-interval estimates of the true population slope for the relationship between absenteeism and age and between absenteeism and gender.

(j) Compare the slope obtained in part (b) with the slope for the simple linear regression model of Problem 16.7 on page 570. Explain the difference in the results.

(k) Compute the coefficients of partial determination and interpret their meaning.

(l) What assumption about the slope of absenteeism with age must be made in this problem?

17.46 Referring to Problem 16.5 on page 563, suppose that the manager of the educational computing facility wishes to study the effect of brand on the number of service calls. Suppose that terminals 1, 3, 5, 7, and 9 were manufactured by Company A and terminals 2, 4, 6, 8, and 10 were manufactured by Company B. Access an available computer package to perform a multiple linear regression analysis. Based on the results obtained

(a) State the multiple regression equation.

(b) Interpret the meaning of the slopes in this problem.

(c) Predict the number of service calls for a terminal that is four years old and was manufactured by Company A.

(d) Determine whether there is a significant relationship between service calls and the two explanatory variables (age and the dummy-variable company) at the .05 level of significance.

(e) Interpret the meaning of the coefficient of multiple determination $r^2_{Y.12}$.

(f) Compute the adjusted r^2.

(g) Compare $r^2_{Y.12}$ with the value computed in Problem 16.20(a) on page 576 and the adjusted r^2 of part (f) with the adjusted r^2 computed in Problem 16.20(b). Explain the results.

(h) At the .05 level of significance, determine whether each explanatory variable makes a contribution to the regression model. Based upon the these results, indicate the regression model that should be used in this problem.

(i) Set up 95% confidence-interval estimates of the true population slope for the relationship between service calls and age and between service calls and company.

(j) Compare the slope obtained in part (b) with the slope for the simple linear regression model of Problem 16.10 on page 570. Explain the difference in the results.

(k) Compute the coefficients of partial determination and interpret their meaning.

(l) What assumption about the slope of service calls with age must be made in this problem?

17.13 OTHER TYPES OF REGRESSION MODELS

In our discussion of multiple regression models we have thus far examined the multiple linear model [Equation (17.1)], the curvilinear polynomial model [Equations (17.14) and (17.15)], and the dummy variable model [Equation (17.16)]. See pages 628, 651, and 660.

17.13.1 Interaction Terms in Regression Models

In the multiple linear regression model [Equation (17.1)] we have included only terms that express a relationship between the explanatory variables and a dependent variable Y. However, in some situations the relationship between X_1 and Y changes for differing values of X_2. In such a case, an *interaction* term involving the product of explanatory variables may be included. With two explanatory variables, such an interaction model may be stated as

$$Y_i = \beta_0 + \beta_1 X_{1i} + \beta_2 X_{2i} + \beta_3 X_{1i} X_{2i} + \epsilon_i \qquad \textbf{(17.17)}$$

As an example of an interaction model we may refer back to the dummy-variable model discussed in Section 17.12. We may recall that Equation (17.16) postulated a dummy-variable model in which the slope of X_1 was constant for each category of the dummy variable (X_2).

If in fact the slope of appraised value with number of rooms was different for houses with and without central air conditioning, an interaction term consisting of the product of the two explanatory variables should be included. For that example the model would be stated as

$$Y_i = \beta_0 + \beta_1 X_{1i} + \beta_2 X_{2i} + \beta_3 X_{1i} X_{2i} + \epsilon_i$$

where Y_i = appraised value for house i

β_0 = Y intercept

β_1 = slope of appraised value with number of rooms holding central air conditioning constant

β_2 = incremental effect of the presence of central air conditioning holding number of rooms constant

β_3 = slope representing interaction effect of number of rooms and presence of central air conditioning

ϵ_1 = random error in Y for house i

17.13.2 Regression Models Using Transformations

In Section 16.11 we discussed the assumptions of normality, homoscedasticity, and independence of error that are involved in the regression model. In many circumstances the effect of violations of these assumptions can be overcome by transforming the dependent variable, the explanatory variables, or both.

By using the transformed variables we are often able to obtain a simpler model than had we maintained the original variables. By reexpressing X and/or Y we may simplify the relationship to one that is linear in its transformation. Unfortunately, the choice of an appropriate transformation is often not an easy one to make. Among the transformations along a "ladder of powers" discussed by Tukey (see Reference 23) are the square-root transformation, the logarithmic transformation, and the reciprocal transformation. If a square-root transformation were applied to the values of each of two explanatory variables, the multiple regression model would be

$$Y_i = \beta_0 + \beta_1 \sqrt{X_{1i}} + \beta_2 \sqrt{X_{2i}} + \epsilon_i \qquad (17.18)$$

Moreover, if a logarithmic transformation had been applied, the model would be

$$Y_i = \beta_0 + \beta_1 \ln X_{1i} + \beta_2 \ln X_{2i} + \epsilon_i \qquad (17.19)$$

Furthermore, if a reciprocal transformation were applied, the model would be

$$Y_i = \beta_0 + \beta_1 \frac{1}{X_{1i}} + \beta_2 \frac{1}{X_{2i}} + \epsilon_i \qquad (17.20)$$

Interestingly, in some situations the use of a transformation can change what appears to be a nonlinear model into a linear model. For example, the multiplicative model

$$Y_i = \beta_0 X_{1i}^{\beta_1} X_{2i}^{\beta_2} \epsilon_i \qquad (17.21)$$

can be transformed (by taking natural logarithms of both the dependent and explanatory variables) to the model

$$\ln Y_i = \ln \beta_0 + \beta_1 \ln X_{1i} + \beta_2 \ln X_{2i} + \ln \epsilon_i \qquad \textbf{(17.22)}$$

Hence Equation (17.22) is linear in the natural logarithms. In a similar fashion the exponential model

$$Y_i = e^{\beta_0 + \beta_1 X_{1i} + \beta_2 X_{2i}} \epsilon_i \qquad \textbf{(17.23)}$$

can also be transformed to linear form (by taking natural logarithms of both the dependent and explanatory variables). The resulting model is

$$\ln Y_i = \beta_0 + \beta_1 X_{1i} + \beta_2 X_{2i} + \ln \epsilon_i \qquad \textbf{(17.24)}$$

Problems

- **17.47** Referring to Problem 17.44 on page 661, suppose that we wish to include a term in the multiple regression model that represents the interaction of shelf space and aisle location. Reanalyze the data by accessing a computer package for this model. Based on the results obtained
  - **(a)** State the multiple regression equation.
  - **(b)** At the .05 level of significance, determine whether the inclusion of the interaction term made a significant contribution to the model that already included shelf space and aisle location. Based on these results indicate the regression model that should be used in this problem.

- **17.48** Referring to Problem 17.45 on page 662, suppose that we wish to include a term in the multiple regression model that represents the interaction of age and gender. Reanalyze the data by accessing a computer package for this model. Based on the results obtained
  - **(a)** State the multiple regression equation.
  - **(b)** At the .05 level of significance, determine whether the inclusion of an interaction term made a significant contribution to the model that already included age and gender. Based on these results indicate the regression model that should be used in this problem.

- **17.49** Referring to Problem 17.46 on page 662, suppose that we wish to include a term in the multiple regression model that represents the interaction of age and company. Reanalyze the data by accessing a computer package for this model. Based on the results obtained
  - **(a)** State the multiple regression equation.
  - **(b)** At the .05 level of significance, determine whether the inclusion of the interaction term made a significant contribution to the model that already included age and company. Based on these results indicate the regression model that should be used in this problem.

- **17.50** Referring to the data of Problem 17.38 on page 656, use a square-root transformation of the explanatory variable (speed) as in Equation (17.18) and access a computer package to reanalyze the data using this model. Based on your results
  - **(a)** State the regression equation.
  - **(b)** Predict the mileage obtained when the car is driven at 55 miles per hour.
  - **(c)** At the .05 level of significance, is there a significant relationship between mileage and the square root of speed?

(d) Interpret the meaning of the coefficient of determination r^2 in this problem.

(e) Compute the adjusted r^2.

(f) Compare your results with those obtained in Problem 17.38. Which model would you choose? Why?

17.51 Referring to the data of Problem 17.38 on page 656, use a logarithmic transformation of the explanatory variable (speed) as in Equation (17.19) and access a computer package to reanalyze the data using this model. Based on your results

(a) State the regression equation.

(b) Predict the mileage obtained when the car is driven at 55 miles per hour.

(c) At the .05 level of significance, is there a significant relationship between mileage and the natural logarithm of speed?

(d) Interpret the meaning of the coefficient of determination r^2 in this problem.

(e) Compute the adjusted r^2.

(f) Compare your results with those obtained in Problems 17.38 and 17.50. Which model would you choose? Why?

17.14 MULTICOLLINEARITY

One important problem in the application of multiple regression analysis involves the possible multicollinearity of the explanatory variables. This condition refers to situations in which some of the explanatory variables are highly correlated with each other. In such situations collinear variables do not provide new information, and it becomes difficult to separate the effect of such variables on the dependent or response variable. In such cases, the values of the regression coefficients for the correlated variables may fluctuate drastically, depending on which variables are included in the model.

One method of measuring collinearity uses the variance inflationary factor (VIF) for each explanatory variable. This VIF is defined as in Equation (17.25):

$$\text{VIF}_j = \frac{1}{1 - R_j^2} \qquad (17.25)$$

where R_j^2 represents the coefficient of multiple determination of explanatory variable X_j with all other X variables.

If there are only two explanatory variables, R_j^2 is merely the coefficient of determination between X_1 and X_2. If, for example, there were three explanatory variables, then R_1^2 would be the coefficient of multiple determination of X_1 with X_2 and X_3.

If a set of explanatory variables are uncorrelated, then VIF_j will be equal to 1. If the set were highly intercorrelated, then VIF_j might even exceed 10. Marquandt (see Reference 13) suggests that if VIF_j is greater than 10, there is too much correlation between variable X_j and the other explanatory variables. However, other researchers (see Reference 19) suggest a more conservative criterion that would employ alternatives to least-squares regression if the maximum VIF_j were to exceed 5.

If we examine our heating oil data, we note from Table 17.4 on page 638 that the correlation between the two explanatory variables, temperature and attic insulation, is only .00892. Therefore since there are only two explanatory variables in the model, we may compute the VIF_j from Equation (17.25):

$$\text{VIF}_1 = \text{VIF}_2 = \frac{1}{1 - (.00892)^2}$$

$$\text{VIF}_1 = \text{VIF}_2 \cong 1.00$$

Thus we may conclude that there is no reason to suspect any multicollinearity for the heating oil data.

We shall return to this subject of multicollinearity in Section 17.17 when we discuss model building.

Problems

17.52 Explain the difference between the variance inflationary factor and the coefficient of partial determination.

17.53 Referring to Problem 17.3 on page 632, the absenteeism problem, determine the VIF for each explanatory variable in the model. Is there reason to suspect the existence of multicollinearity?

• **17.54** Referring to Problem 17.4 on page 632, the advertising media problem, determine the VIF for each explanatory variable in the model. Is there reason to suspect the existence of multicollinearity?

17.55 Referring to Problem 17.5 on page 633, the employee salary problem, determine the VIF for each explanatory variable in the model. Is there reason to suspect the existence of multicollinearity?

17.56 Referring to Problem 17.6 on page 634, the stock price problem, determine the VIF for each explanatory variable in the model. Is there reason to suspect the existence of multicollinearity?

17.15 RESIDUAL ANALYSIS IN MULTIPLE REGRESSION

In Section 16.12 we utilized residual analysis to evaluate whether the simple linear regression model was appropriate for the set of data being studied. When examining a multiple linear regression model with two explanatory variables, the following residual plots are of particular interest:

1. Standardized residuals versus $\hat{Y}_i$
2. Standardized residuals versus X_{1i}
3. Standardized residuals versus X_{2i}
4. Standardized residuals versus X_{1i} for different levels of X_2

The first residual plot examines the pattern of residuals for the predicted values of Y. If the standardized residuals appear to vary for different levels of the predicted Y value, it provides evidence of a possible curvilinear effect in at least one explanatory variable and/or the need to transform the dependent variable. The second and third residual plots involve the explanatory variables. Patterns in the plot of the standardized residuals versus an explanatory variable may indicate the existence of a curvilinear effect and, therefore, lead to the possible transformation of that explanatory variable. The fourth type of plot is used to investigate the possible interaction of the two explanatory variables. Separate residual plots can be obtained for variable X_1 at low values of X_2 and high values of X_2. If the pattern of standardized residuals were different between the two plots, it would lead to the possible inclusion of an interaction term (such as $X_1 X_2$) in the regression model.

The residual plots are available as part of the output obtained from the SAS REG procedure (see References 11 and 18), the REGRESSION command in SPSS^X (see

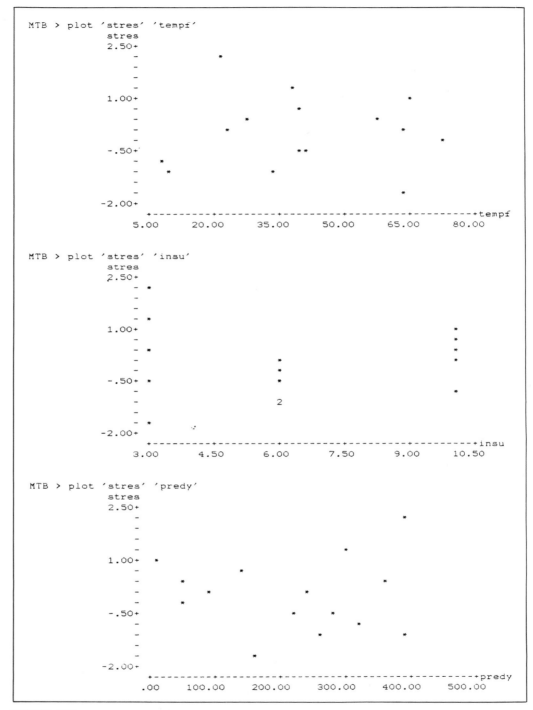

FIGURE 17.15
Residual plots for the heating oil usage model obtained from the Minitab
REGRESS and PLOT commands.

Reference 20), or the REGRESS and PLOT commands (see References 12 and 17) in Minitab. Figure 17.15 consists of the residual plots obtained from the Minitab REGRESS and PLOT commands for the heating oil problem. We can observe from Figure 17.15 that there appears to be very little or no pattern in the relationship between the standardized residuals and either the predicted value of Y, the value of X_1 (temperature), or the value of X_2 (attic insulation). Thus we may conclude that the multiple linear regression model is appropriate for predicting heating oil usage.

Problems

17.57 Referring to the absenteeism problem (pages 632, 635, and 637), perform a residual analysis on your results and determine the adequacy of the fit of the model.

● **17.58** Referring to the advertising media problem (pages 632, 635, and 637), perform a residual analysis on your results and determine the adequacy of the fit of the model.

17.59 Referring to the employee salary problem (pages 633, 635, and 637), perform a residual analysis on your results and determine the adequacy of the fit of the model.

17.60 Referring to the stock prices problem (pages 634, 635, and 637), perform a residual analysis on your results and determine the adequacy of the fit of the model.

● **17.61** Referring to Problem 17.38 on page 656, perform a residual analysis on your results and determine the adequacy of the fit of the model.

17.62 Referring to Problem 17.39 on page 657, perform a residual analysis on your results and determine the adequacy of the fit of the model.

17.63 Referring to Problem 17.44 on page 661
  (a) Perform a residual analysis on your results and determine the adequacy of the fit of the model.
  (b) Compare the results of part (a) with those obtained in Problem 16.1 on page 561.

17.64 Referring to Problem 17.45 on page 662, perform a residual analysis on your results and determine the adequacy of the fit of the model.

17.65 Referring to Problem 17.46 on page 662, perform a residual analysis on your results and determine the adequacy of the fit of the model.

17.66 Referring to Problem 17.50 on page 665
  (a) Perform a residual analysis on your results and determine the adequacy of the fit of the model.
  (b) Compare the results of part (a) with those of Problem 17.61.

17.67 Referring to Problem 17.51 on page 666
  (a) Perform a residual analysis on your results and determine the adequacy of the fit of the model.
  (b) Compare the results of part (a) with those of Problem 17.61 and 17.66.

17.16 INFLUENCE ANALYSIS IN MULTIPLE REGRESSION

17.16.1 Introduction

Now that we have considered the issue of whether multicollinearity exists between the explanatory variables and we have evaluated the aptness of the fitted model through the use of residual analysis, we are ready to utilize the influence-analysis techniques

ROW	htngoil	predy	stres	hi	stdelres	cookd
1	275.3	284.651	-0.39144	0.156757	-0.37720	0.009495
2	363.8	355.326	0.36087	0.185246	0.34740	0.009870
3	164.3	144.565	0.83561	0.175717	0.82438	0.049616
4	40.8	45.207	-0.19519	0.246777	-0.18717	0.004161
5	94.3	94.136	0.00689	0.161823	0.00660	0.000003
6	230.9	257.233	-1.05200	0.074084	-1.05714	0.029517
7	366.7	393.148	-1.15911	0.230654	-1.17765	0.134267
8	300.6	318.535	-0.85651	0.352057	-0.84632	0.132868
9	237.8	236.986	0.03557	0.226801	0.03405	0.000124
10	121.4	159.609	-1.69004	0.244667	-1.85367	0.308398
11	31.4	8.650	1.02779	0.275988	1.03043	0.134224
12	203.5	219.177	-0.62414	0.067663	-0.60751	0.009424
13	441.1	387.946	2.30980	0.217438	2.96740	0.494131
14	323.0	295.524	1.15068	0.157465	1.16802	0.082488
15	52.5	46.706	0.25330	0.226864	0.24317	0.006276

FIGURE 17.16
Influence statistics obtained from Minitab for the heating oil data.

discussed in Section 16.13 to determine whether any individual observations have undue influence on the fitted model.

We may recall that in Section 16.13 we considered three measures:

1. The hat matrix elements h_i
2. The Studentized deleted residuals t_i^*
3. Cook's distance statistic D_i

Figure 17.16 represents the values of these statistics for the heating oil data of Table 17.1, which have been obtained from the Minitab computer package. We note from Figure 17.16 that certain data points have been highlighted for further analysis.

17.16.2 Using the Hat Matrix Elements h_i

We may recall from Section 16.13 that each h_i reflects the influence of each X_i value on the fitted regression model. In a multiple regression model containing p explanatory variables, Hoaglin and Welsch (see Reference 9) suggest the following decision rule:

$$\text{If } h_i > 2(p + 1)/n$$

then X_i is an influential point and may be considered a candidate for removal from the model.

For our heating oil data, since $n = 15$ and $p = 2$, our criterion would be to "flag" any h_i value greater than .40. Referring to Figure 17.16, we observe that none of the h_i values exceed .35; therefore, based upon this criterion, there do not appear to be any observations that can be considered for removal from the model.

17.16.3 Using the Studentized Deleted Residuals t_i^*

We may recall from Section 16.13 that the Studentized deleted residual measures the difference between each observed value Y_i and predicted value $\hat{Y}_i$ obtained from a model that includes all observations other than i. In the multiple regression model, Hoaglin and Welsch suggested that

$$\text{if } |t_i^*| > t_{.10, n-p-2}$$

then the observed and predicted values are so different that observation i is an influential point that adversely affects the model and may be considered a candidate for removal.

For our heating oil data, since $n = 15$ and $p = 2$, our criterion would be to "flag" any t_i^* value greater than $|1.7959|$ (see Table E.3). Referring to Figure 17.16, we note that $t_{10}^* = -1.854$ and $t_{13}^* = 2.967$. Thus the tenth and thirteenth observations may each have an adverse effect on the model. We should note that these points were not previously "flagged" according to the h_i criterion. Hence, we shall consider Cook's D_i statistic that is based on both h_i and the standardized residual.

17.16.4 Using Cook's Distance Statistic D_i

Now that the h_i and t_i^* statistics have been considered, we turn to the D_i statistic that was discussed in Section 16.13.4. In the multiple regression model, Cook and Weisberg (see Reference 5) suggest that

$$\text{if } D_i > F_{.50, p+1, n-p-1}$$

then the observation may have an impact on the results of fitting a multiple regression model.

For our heating oil data, since $n = 15$ and $p = 2$, our criterion would be to flag any $D_i > F_{.50, 3, 12} = .835$. Referring to Figure 17.16, we note that none of the D_i values exceed .494, so that according to this criterion there are no values that may be deleted (although we should note that the largest D_i values are for observations 13 and 10, respectively). Hence, the researcher would have no clear basis for removing any of the observations from the multiple regression model.

17.16.5 Summary

In this section we have discussed several criteria for evaluating the influence of each observation on the multiple regression model. The various statistics did not lead to a consistent set of conclusions. According to both the h_i and D_i criteria, none of the observations are candidates for removal from the model. However, according to the t_i^* criterion, observations 13 and 10 may be adversely affecting the fit of the model. Although some statisticians might argue for their removal, it seems reasonable to keep them in the model both because of the inconsistency of the influence statistics and because the model fits extremely well ($r_{Y.12}^2 = .96$) regardless of whether or not these observations are included.

The use of regression diagnostics (such as residual analysis and influence analysis) has provided us with the opportunity to closely evaluate each point in the data. Perhaps we might be able to explain the large residuals in observations 13 and 10 as being due to other factors beside the atmospheric temperature and amount of attic insulation. For example, it is quite possible that the large positive residual for observation 13 might be explained by the fact that the thermostatic control was turned to an especially high level in a month in which the average monthly temperature was only 21 degrees Fahrenheit. On the other hand, the large negative residual of observation 10 might be explained by the fact that in a month in which the average atmospheric temperature was 63 degrees Fahrenheit, the thermostat was turned on less than what would have been expected for such situations.

Problems

17.68   Referring to the absenteeism problem (see pages 632, 635, and 637), perform an influence analysis and determine whether any observations should be deleted from the model. If necessary, reanalyze the regression model after deleting these observations and compare your results to the original model.

● **17.69**   Referring to the advertising media problem (see pages 632, 635, and 637), perform an influence analysis and determine whether any observations should be deleted from the model. If necessary, reanalyze the regression model after deleting these observations and compare your results with the original model.

17.70   Referring to the employee salary problem (see pages 633, 635, and 637), perform an influence analysis and determine whether any observations should be deleted from the model. If necessary, reanalyze the regression model after deleting these observations and compare your results with the original model.

17.71   Referring to the stock price problem (see pages 634, 635, and 637), perform an influence analysis and determine whether any observations should be deleted from the model. If necessary, reanalyze the regression model after deleting these observations and compare your results with the original model.

● **17.72**   Referring to Problem 17.38 on page 656, perform an influence analysis and determine whether any observations should be deleted from the model. If necessary, reanalyze the regression model after deleting these observations and compare your results with the original model.

17.73   Referring to Problem 17.39 on page 657, perform an influence analysis and determine whether any observations should be deleted from the model. If necessary, reanalyze the regression model after deleting these observations and compare your results with the original model.

● **17.74**   Referring to Problem 17.44 on page 661
   (a) Perform an influence analysis and determine whether any observations should be deleted from the model. If necessary, reanalyze the regression model after deleting these observations and compare your results with the original model.
   (b) Compare the results in (a) with those obtained in Problem 16.60 on page 599.

17.75   Referring to Problem 17.45 on page 662
   (a) Perform an influence analysis and determine whether any observations should be deleted from the model. If necessary, reanalyze the regression model after deleting these observations and compare your results with the original model.
   (b) Compare the results in (a) with those obtained in Problems 16.61 (on page 599) and 17.68.

17.76   Referring to Problem 17.46 on page 662
   (a) Perform an influence analysis and determine whether any observations should be deleted from the model. If necessary, reanalyze the regression model after deleting these observations and compare your results with the original model.
   (b) Compare the results in (a) with those obtained in Problem 16.64 on page 599.

17.77   Referring to Problem 17.50 on page 665
   (a) Perform an influence analysis and determine whether any observations should be deleted from the model. If necessary, reanalyze the regression model after deleting these observations and compare your results with the original model.
   (b) Compare the results in (a) with those obtained in Problem 17.72.

17.78   Referring to Problem 17.51 on page 666
   (a) Perform an influence analysis and determine whether any observations should be deleted from the model. If necessary, reanalyze the regression model after deleting these observations and compare your results with the original model.
   (b) Compare the results in (a) with those obtained in Problems 17.72 and 17.77.

17.17   AN EXAMPLE OF MODEL BUILDING

In the last two chapters we have investigated several different types of regression models. In Chapter 16 we focused primarily on the simple linear regression model, while in this chapter we have developed the multiple linear regression model and subsequently discussed the curvilinear polynomial model, models involving dummy variables, and models involving transformations of variables. In this section we shall conclude our discussion of regression by developing a model that includes a set of several qualitative and quantitative explanatory variables.

We may recall that in Chapter 16, only one quantitative variable (number of rooms) was used in the development of a regression model for predicting appraised value. Let us now reevaluate this regression model by also considering such other quantitative explanatory variables as lot size, the number of bedrooms, the number of bathrooms, and the age of the house. In addition, let us also consider such qualitative explanatory variables as the presence of an eat-in kitchen, central air conditioning, a fireplace, a connection to a local sewer system, a basement, a modern kitchen, and modern bathrooms.

Before we begin to develop a model to predict assessed value, we should keep in mind that a widely used criterion of model building is "parsimony." This means that we wish to develop a regression model that includes the *least number* of explanatory variables that permits an adequate interpretation of the dependent variable of interest. Regression models with fewer explanatory variables are inherently easier to interpret, particularly since they are less likely to be affected by the problem of multicollinearity (see Section 17.14).

Nevertheless, we should realize that the selection of an appropriate model when 12 explanatory variables are to be considered involves complexities that are not present for a model that contains only two explanatory variables. First, the evaluation of all possible regression models (see Reference 4) becomes more computationally complex and costly. Second, although competing models can be quantitatively evaluated, there may not exist a uniquely "best" model but rather several equally appropriate models.

We shall begin our analysis of the real estate data by first measuring the amount of collinearity that exists between the explanatory variables through the use of the variance inflationary factor [see Equation (17.25)]. Figure 17.17 on page 674 represents partial Minitab output for a multiple linear regression model in which appraised value is predicted from the 12 explanatory variables. We may observe that most of the VIF values are relatively small, ranging from a high of 7.1 for the presence of modern bathrooms to a low of 1.2 for the presence of an eat-in-kitchen. Thus, based on the criteria developed by Marquardt (see References 13 and 14), there is little evidence of multicollinearity among the set of explanatory variables. We also note that the coefficient of multiple determination is .695 and the adjusted r^2 is .635.

We may now continue our analysis of these data by attempting to determine the explanatory variables that might be deleted from the complete model. We shall apply a widely used "search" procedure called **stepwise regression** that attempts to find the "best" regression model without examining all possible regressions. Once a "best" model has been found, residual analysis is utilized to evaluate the aptness of the model and influence measures are computed to determine whether any observations may be deleted.

We may recall that in Section 17.6 the partial *F*-test criterion was used to evaluate portions of a multiple regression model. Stepwise regression extends this partial

```
The regression equation is
value = 95.6 + 1.07 lotsize + 1.41 bed + 25.1 bath + 10.7 rooms - 0.717 age
      + 0.5 eik + 13.0 cac + 12.2 firepl - 0.7 sewer + 3.00 base
      + 47.1 modkit - 46.7 modbath

Predictor        Coef         Stdev      t-ratio        VIF
Constant        95.56        34.63         2.76
lotsize          1.066        1.787        0.60          1.6
bed              1.405        4.291        0.33          1.4
bath            25.149        6.857        3.67          2.4
rooms           10.737        2.866        3.75          1.9
age             -0.7169       0.5969      -1.20          1.8
eik              0.55        18.49         0.03          1.2
cac             12.960        9.348        1.39          1.4
firepl          12.237        8.629        1.42          1.5
sewer           -0.731        9.997       -0.07          1.3
base             2.999        9.048        0.33          1.3
modkit          47.07        14.59         3.23          7.0
modbath        -46.73        14.52        -3.22          7.1

s = 23.26       R-sq = 69.5%        R-sq(adj) = 63.5%
```

FIGURE 17.17
Minitab output for the full regression model with 12 explanatory variables.

F-test criterion to a model with any number of explanatory variables. An important feature of this stepwise process is that an explanatory variable which has entered into the model at an early stage may subsequently be removed once other explanatory variables are considered. That is, in stepwise regression, variables are either "added to" or "deleted from" the regression model at each step of the model-building process. The stepwise procedure terminates with the selection of a "best fitting" model when no variables can be added to or deleted from the last model fitted.

We may now observe this stepwise process for our data. Figure 17.18 represents a partial output obtained from the SAS STEPWISE procedure. For this example a significance level of .05 was utilized to either enter a variable into the model or delete a variable from the model. The first variable entered into the model is BATH (number of bathrooms). Since the F value of 68.90 is greater than the critical value for $\alpha = .05$ (that is $F_{.05,1,72} = 3.99$), BATH is included in the regression model.

The next step involves the evaluation of the second variable to be included in this model. The variable to be chosen is that which will make the largest contribution to the model, given that the first explanatory variable has already been selected. For this model the second variable is ROOMS (number of rooms). Note that the contribution of each variable, given that the other variables are already included, is provided by the Type II Sum of Squares in the STEPWISE procedure. Since the F value of 18.13 for SSR(ROOMS|BATH) is greater than the critical value for $\alpha = .05$ (that is $F_{.05,1,71} = 3.99$), ROOMS is included in the regression model.

Now that ROOMS has been entered into the model, we may determine whether BATH is still an important contributing variable or whether it may be eliminated from the model. Since the F value of 26.99 for SSR(BATH|ROOMS) is also greater than the critical value for F at $\alpha = .05$ (that is, $F_{.05,1,71} = 3.99$), BATH should remain in the regression model.

The next step involves the determination of whether any of the remaining variables should be added to the model. From Figure 17.18, since none of the other variables meet the $\alpha = .05$ criterion for entry into the model, the stepwise procedure terminates with a model that includes the number of bathrooms and the number of rooms.

Before we use residual analysis to test the aptness of this model, it would be

```
STEPWISE REGRESSION PROCEDURE FOR DEPENDENT VARIABLE VALUE

STEP 1      VARIABLE BATH ENTERED           R SQUARE = 0.48900350
                                            C(P) =    32.19682006

                DF    SUM OF SQUARES    MEAN SQUARE       F     PROB>F

REGRESSION       1     52896.8120423    52896.81204    68.90    0.0001
ERROR           72     55275.8539036      767.72019
TOTAL           73    108172.6659459

                B VALUE    STD ERROR    TYPE II SS        F     PROB>F

INTERCEPT    135.973351
BATH          43.930876   5.29244800   52896.81204     68.90    0.0001

BOUNDS ON CONDITION NUMBER:                     1,             1
-------------------------------------------------------------------

STEP 2      VARIABLE ROOMS ENTERED          R SQUARE = 0.59292374
                                            C(P) =    13.41327582

                DF    SUM OF SQUARES    MEAN SQUARE       F     PROB>F

REGRESSION       2     64138.1418069    32069.07090    51.71    0.0001
ERROR           71     44034.5241390      620.20457
TOTAL           73    108172.6659459

                B VALUE    STD ERROR    TYPE II SS        F     PROB>F

INTERCEPT     78.1000944
BATH          29.9977339   5.77395785   16740.35394    26.99    0.0001
ROOMS         11.6559688   2.73783336   11241.32976    18.13    0.0001

BOUNDS ON CONDITION NUMBER:       1.473337,      5.893347
-------------------------------------------------------------------

NO OTHER VARIABLES MET THE 0.0500 SIGNIFICANCE LEVEL FOR ENTRY
```

FIGURE 17.18
Partial output for the real estate model obtained from SAS STEPWISE.

appropriate to determine whether or not a model containing an interaction term between BATH and ROOMS is justified (see Section 17.13). Figure 17.19 presents partial output from the Minitab REGRESS procedure for a model that includes the interaction between the number of bathrooms and the number of rooms. From this model we observe that the t value for the contribution of BATH*ROOMS|BATH, ROOMS is 1.85. Since 1.85 < 1.9944 (that is, when $\alpha = .05$, $t_{.05,70} = 1.9944$), we may conclude that the interaction term should not be included as part of the model. Thus, the model selected to predict appraised value includes only the number of bathrooms and the number of rooms.

Now that the explanatory variables to be included in the model have been selected, a residual analysis may be undertaken to evaluate the aptness of the fitted model. Figure 17.20 presents partial output obtained from Minitab for these purposes. We may observe from Figure 17.20 that the plots of the standardized residuals versus the number of bathrooms and the number of rooms reveal no apparent pattern. In addition, a histogram of the standardized residuals indicate only moderate departure from normality. (See pages 677–678.)

Since the residual analysis appeared to confirm the aptness of the fitted model,

```
The regression equation is
value = 187 - 24.1 bath - 4.44 rooms + 7.80 bth*rms

Predictor         Coef         Stdev      t-ratio
Constant        186.52        60.78         3.07
bath            -24.07        29.78        -0.81
rooms            -4.436        9.107       -0.49
bth*rms           7.803        4.219        1.85

s = 24.49        R-sq = 61.2%      R-sq(adj) = 59.5%

Analysis of Variance

SOURCE          DF            SS            MS
Regression       3          66190         22063
Error           70          41983           600
Total           73         108173
```

FIGURE 17.19
Partial output for the interaction model obtained from Minitab.

we may now utilize various influence measures to determine whether any of the observations have unduly influenced the fitted model. Figure 17.21 represents the values of the h_i, t_i^*, and Cook's D_i statistics for our fitted model. We note from Figure 17.21 that certain data points have been highlighted for further analysis. (See pages 679–680.)

For our fitted model, since $n = 74$ and $p = 3$, using the decision rule suggested by Hoaglin and Welsch (see Section 17.16.2), our criterion would be to "flag" any h_i value greater than $2(2 + 1)/74 = .081$. Referring to Figure 17.21, we observe that observations 13 ($h_i = .134405$), 35 ($h_i = .099413$), 43 ($h_i = .143353$), 62 ($h_i = .081801$), 66 ($h_i = .143353$), and 74 ($h_i = .081801$), have h_i values that exceed .081 and therefore are considered to be possible candidates for deletion from the model.

Now that the h_i criterion has been considered, we turn to the Studentized deleted residual measure t_i^*. For our model, since $p = 2$ and $n = 74$, using the decision rule suggested by Hoaglin and Welsch (see Section 17.16.3), our criterion would be to "flag" any $|t_i^*|$ value greater than 1.6669 (see Table E.3). Referring to Figure 17.21, we note that $t_{32}^* = -2.14715$, $t_{35}^* = -2.07586$, $t_{53}^* = 2.13771$, $t_{55}^* = 1.89268$, $t_{68}^* = 3.89907$, and $t_{74}^* = -1.90558$. Thus these observations may have an adverse effect on the model. We note that observations 35 and 74 were also "flagged" according to the h_i criteria, but observations 32, 53, 55, and 68 were not.

Thus, because of the lack of consistency between h_i and t_i^*, we should consider a third criterion, Cook's D_i statistic, which is based on both h_i and the standardized residual.

For our model, in which $p = 2$ and $n = 74$, using the decision rule suggested by Cook and Weisberg (see Section 17.16.4), our criterion would be to "flag" any $D_i > F_{.50,3,71} = .797$. Referring to Figure 17.21, we note that none of the D_i values exceed .164, so that according to this criterion there are no values that may be deleted. Hence, we would have no clear basis for removing any observations from the multiple regression model.

```
The regression equation is
value = 78.1 + 30.0 bath + 11.7 rooms

Predictor        Coef         Stdev      t-ratio         VIF
Constant        78.10         16.33        4.78
bath            29.998        5.774        5.20          1.5
rooms           11.656        2.738        4.26          1.5

s = 24.90         R-sq = 59.3%        R-sq(adj) = 58.1%

Analysis of Variance

SOURCE           DF            SS           MS
Regression        2          64138        32069
Error            71          44035          620
Total            73         108173

SOURCE           DF          SEQ SS
bath              1          52897
rooms             1          11241

MTB > hist 'stres'

Histogram of stres     N = 74

Midpoint       Count
    -2.0           3    ***
    -1.5           3    ***
    -1.0           7    *******
    -0.5          15    ***************
     0.0          23    ***********************
     0.5           8    ********
     1.0           6    ******
     1.5           6    ******
     2.0           2    **
     2.5           0
     3.0           0
     3.5           1    *
```

FIGURE 17.20
Minitab output for a model that includes number of bathrooms and number of rooms. (continued on page 678)

From Figure 17.20 we note that the VIF values are 1.5, so that there appears to be very little multicollinearity between the two explanatory variables. The r^2 coefficient of multiple determination is .593 and the adjusted r^2 is .581. This compares favorably with the adjusted r^2 of .635 for the 12 explanatory variable model. The fitted model can be expressed as

$$\hat{Y}_i = 78.1 + 29.998 \text{ BATH} + 11.656 \text{ ROOMS}$$

where BATH = number of bathrooms
      ROOMS = number of rooms

From this model we may conclude that for each additional bathroom, appraised value increases by \$29,998, holding constant the effect of number of rooms. For each

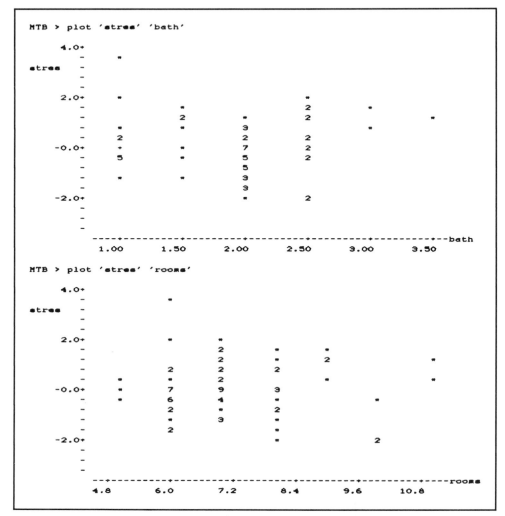

FIGURE 17.20
(Continued)

additional room, we may conclude that appraised value increases by \$11,656, holding constant the effect of number of bathrooms.

17.18 COMPUTER PACKAGES AND MULTIPLE REGRESSION

17.18.1 Overview

Throughout this chapter we have emphasized how to interpret the results that may be obtained from computer packages. Indeed, it is this widespread availability of various computer packages that has led to a great expansion in the application of regression models in business and economics. Among the packages that are commonly accessed when developing regression models for business applications are the Statistical Analysis

```
MTB > print 'value' 'stres' 'yhat' 'hi' 'stdelres' 'cookd'
ROW   value      stres        yhat          hi     stdelres      cookd

  1   215.0   -0.18978      219.687    0.016445    -0.18849    0.000201
  2   195.0   -1.47410      231.343    0.019929    -1.48661    0.014729
  3   160.0   -1.22033      189.690    0.045619    -1.22461    0.023728
  4   189.0   -0.16389      193.033    0.023834    -0.16276    0.000219
  5   249.0    0.10843      246.342    0.031211     0.10767    0.000126
  6   267.0    0.36977      257.998    0.044420     0.36751    0.002119
  7   199.9   -0.33275      208.031    0.037132    -0.33065    0.001423
  8   169.0   -0.36972      178.034    0.037412    -0.36746    0.001771
  9   179.0    0.03955      178.034    0.037412     0.03927    0.000020
 10   218.0   -0.06832      219.687    0.016445    -0.06784    0.000026
 11   247.0    0.63504      231.343    0.019929     0.63235    0.002733
 12   218.0   -0.06832      219.687    0.016445    -0.06784    0.000026
 13   299.9    1.01684      276.340    0.134405     1.01709    0.053516
 14   172.0   -0.24694      178.034    0.037412    -0.24530    0.000790
 15   230.0   -0.19227      234.686    0.042173    -0.19096    0.000543
 16   235.0    1.22799      204.688    0.017593     1.23247    0.009002
 17   190.0   -1.07715      216.344    0.035525    -1.07838    0.014245
 18   180.0    0.56221      166.378    0.053377     0.55948    0.005941
 19   213.0   -0.74401      231.343    0.019929    -0.74165    0.003752
 20   175.0   -0.12416      178.034    0.037412    -0.12329    0.000200
 21   170.0   -1.55629      208.031    0.037132    -1.57235    0.031135
 22   215.0   -0.18978      219.687    0.016445    -0.18849    0.000201
 23   229.5    1.00517      204.688    0.017593     1.00525    0.006031
 24   180.0   -1.14708      208.031    0.037132    -1.14968    0.016914
 25   225.0    0.69438      208.031    0.037132     0.69182    0.006198
 26   155.0   -0.46957      166.378    0.053377    -0.46697    0.004144
 27   179.0    0.03955      178.034    0.037412     0.03927    0.000020
 28   195.0   -0.39250      204.688    0.017593    -0.39015    0.000920
 29   179.9    0.07638      178.034    0.037412     0.07585    0.000076
 30   225.0    0.21510      219.687    0.016445     0.21365    0.000258
 31   197.5   -0.16082      201.346    0.077997    -0.15971    0.000729
 32   195.0   -2.09456      246.342    0.031211    -2.14715    0.047112
 33   190.0   -1.20200      219.687    0.016445    -1.20584    0.008052
 34   245.0    1.63311      204.688    0.017593     1.65291    0.015921
 35   206.7   -2.02911      254.655    0.099413    -2.07586    0.151499
 36   199.0   -0.36958      208.031    0.037132    -0.36732    0.001756
 37   190.0   -0.73787      208.031    0.037132    -0.73548    0.006999
 38   297.5    1.62262      257.998    0.044420     1.64188    0.040796
 39   229.0    0.37706      219.687    0.016445     0.37477    0.000792
 40   215.0   -0.18978      219.687    0.016445    -0.18849    0.000201
 41   190.0   -0.73787      208.031    0.037132    -0.73548    0.006999
 42   290.0    1.31454      257.998    0.044420     1.32143    0.026775
 43   310.0    1.24469      281.310    0.143353     1.24960    0.086419
 44   206.0    0.67040      189.690    0.045619     0.66778    0.007161
 45   224.5    0.19486      219.687    0.016445     0.19353    0.000212
 46   220.0    0.62031      204.688    0.017593     0.61760    0.002297
 47   270.0    1.44888      234.686    0.042173     1.46040    0.030810
 48   205.0    0.15282      201.346    0.077997     0.15177    0.000659
 49   240.0   -0.25874      246.342    0.031211    -0.25703    0.000719
 50   210.0   -0.39223      219.687    0.016445    -0.38988    0.000857
 51   215.0   -0.18978      219.687    0.016445    -0.18849    0.000201
 52   210.0   -0.86570      231.343    0.019929    -0.86415    0.005080
 53   229.0    2.08591      178.034    0.037412     2.13771    0.056369
 54   280.0    0.77666      261.341    0.069369     0.77447    0.014988
 55   280.0    1.85917      234.686    0.042173     1.89268    0.050730
 56   174.5   -0.14462      178.034    0.037412    -0.14362    0.000271
 57   185.0    0.28511      178.034    0.037412     0.28326    0.001053
 58   180.0   -0.39827      189.690    0.045619    -0.39590    0.002527
```

FIGURE 17.21
Influence statistics obtained from Minitab for the real estate model of Figure 17.20.

```
MTB > print 'value' 'stres' 'yhat' 'hi' 'stdelres' 'cookd'
ROW    value     stres       yhat         hi    stdelres     cookd

 59    205.0    -0.59467    219.687    0.016445   -0.59194    0.001971
 60    190.0    -1.20200    219.687    0.016445   -1.20584    0.006052
 61    195.0    -0.99956    219.687    0.016445   -0.99955    0.005568
 62    260.0    -0.40455    269.654    0.081801   -0.40216    0.004860
 63    168.0     0.06696    166.378    0.053377    0.06648    0.000084
 64    180.0     0.08048    178.034    0.037412    0.07991    0.000084
 65    185.0    -0.19276    189.690    0.045619   -0.19144    0.000592
 66    286.5     0.22516    281.310    0.143353    0.22365    0.002828
 67    165.9    -0.49660    178.034    0.037412   -0.49395    0.003195
 68    265.0     3.55929    178.034    0.037412    3.89907    0.164127
 69    230.0     0.89898    208.031    0.037132    0.89776    0.010389
 70    194.0    -0.57418    208.031    0.037132   -0.57145    0.004238
 71    295.0     1.40102    261.341    0.069369    1.41076    0.048770
 72    169.5    -1.57675    208.031    0.037132   -1.59376    0.031959
 73    275.0     1.31668    242.999    0.047585    1.32363    0.028872
 74    225.0    -1.87122    269.654    0.081801   -1.90558    0.103980
```

FIGURE 17.21
(Continued)

System (SAS) (References 11 and 18), MYSTAT (Reference 15), the Statistical Package for the Social Sciences (SPSS[X]) (Reference 20), and Minitab (References 12 and 17). In order to observe some of the similarities and differences between these packages, the data for the heating oil usage model (Table 17.1) that had been analyzed by using the SAS REG and GLM procedures (see Figure 17.2) are also analyzed using the MYSTAT ESTIMATE command, the SPSS[X] REGRESSION command and the Minitab REGRESS command. Figure 17.22 illustrates partial MYSTAT output, Figure 17.23 illustrates partial SPSS[X] output, and Figure 17.24 illustrates partial Minitab output.

17.18.2 A Comparison of Packages

Although the basic elements of regression may be obtained from each computer package, there are differences among the packages in the range of options that are available.

```
DEP VAR: HTNGOIL      N:   15    MULTIPLE R:  .983    SQUARED MULTIPLE R:  .966
ADJUSTED SQUARED MULTIPLE R:  .960     STANDARD ERROR OF ESTIMATE:      26.014

    VARIABLE    COEFFICIENT    STD ERROR    STD COEF TOLERANCE    T     P(2 TAIL)

    CONSTANT      562.151        21.093       0.000    .          26.651   0.000
       TEMPF       -5.437         0.336      -0.866  0.9999204   -16.170   0.000
        INSU      -20.012         2.343      -0.457  0.9999204    -8.543   0.000


                        ANALYSIS OF VARIANCE

    SOURCE      SUM-OF-SQUARES    DF    MEAN-SQUARE     F-RATIO      P

    REGRESSION     228014.626      2    114007.313     168.471    0.000
      RESIDUAL       8120.603     12       676.717
```

FIGURE 17.22
Partial MYSTAT output for heating oil data.

```
EQUATION NUMBER 1 DEPENDENT VARIABLE HTNGOIL HEATING OIL

BEGINNING BLOCK NUMBER 1. METHOD:    ENTER

VARIABLE(S) ENTERED ON STEP NUMBER 1.  HTNGOIL HEATING OIL

MULTIPLE R            .98265
R SQUARE              .96561
ADJUSTED R SQUARE     .95988


ANALYSIS OF VARIANCE
                   DF        SUM OF SQUARES      MEAN SQUARE
REGRESSION          2           228014.45924    114007.22962
RESIDUAL           12             8120.59574       676.71631

F = 168.47123           SIGNIF F =    .0000


----------------VARIABLES IN THE EQUATION -----------------

VARIABLE            B          SE B    95% CONFDENCE INTRVL B          T

TEMPF      b₁ -5.43658      0.33622    - 6.16914   - 4.70402    -16.170
INSU       b₂-20.01231      2.34250    -25.11615  -14.90847    - 8.543
(CONSTANT) b₀562.15082     21.09309    516.19320   608.10844     26.651


----- IN  -------

VARIABLE   SIG T

TEMPF      .0000
INSU       .0000
(CONSTANT) .0000
```

FIGURE 17.23
Partial SPSSˣ output for heating oil data.

Table 17.10 contains a comparison of SPSS^X, SAS, Minitab, STATGRAPHICS, and MYSTAT in terms of the current availability of five features: stepwise regression, all possible regressions, residual plots, influence measures, and confidence intervals for the mean response μ_{YX}. Several different programs within each package are listed.

We may observe from Table 17.10 that residual plots and influence measures are available from each package and stepwise regression procedures are available for each package except MYSTAT. However, the output for all possible regressions is currently available only from SAS PROC RSQUARE, and confidence interval estimates for μ_{YX} are currently available only from SAS PROC REG and GLM and Minitab's RE-GRESSION command. Nevertheless, the choice of a package is often dependent upon (1) the microcomputer a user has available, (2) the type of mainframe or minicomputer to which one has access, and (3) the packages that are available at such a computer facility.

Interested readers are referred to References 4, 10–12, 15, 17, 18, 20, and 21 for further information.

```
THE REGRESSION EQUATION IS
htngoil = 562 - 5.44 tempf - 20.0 insu

                                     ST. DEV.     T-RATIO =
   COLUMN        COEFFICIENT         OF COEF.     COEF/S.D.       V.I.F.
                 b₀  562.15            21.09         26.65
   tempf         b₁  -5.4366            0.3362       -16.17         1.0
   insu          b₂  -20.012            2.343         -8.54         1.0

   S = 26.01

   R-SQUARED =  96.6 PERCENT
   R-SQUARED = 96.0 PERCENT, ADJUSTED FOR D.F.

   ANALYSIS OF VARIANCE

   DUE TO        DF          SS        MS=SS/DF
   REGRESSION     2        228015        114007
   RESIDUAL      12          8121           677
   TOTAL         14        236135

   FURTHER ANALYSIS OF VARIANCE
   SS EXPLAINED BY EACH VARIABLE WHEN ENTERED IN THE ORDER GIVEN
   DUE TO        DF          SS
   REGRESSION     2        228015
   tempf          1        178624
   insu           1         49390

                      Y       PRED. Y      ST.DEV.
   ROW    tempf    htngoil     VALUE      PRED. Y    RESIDUAL     ST.RES.
    1     40.0     275.30      284.65      10.30       -9.35       -0.39
    2     27.0     363.80      355.33      11.20        8.47        0.36
    3     40.0     164.30      144.56      10.90       19.74        0.84
    4     73.0      40.80       45.21      12.92       -4.41       -0.20
    5     64.0      94.30       94.14      10.46        0.16        0.01
    6     34.0     230.90      257.23       7.08      -26.33       -1.05
    7      9.0     366.70      393.15      12.49      -26.45       -1.16
    8      8.0     300.60      318.54      15.44      -17.94       -0.86
    9     23.0     237.80      236.99      12.39        0.81        0.04
   10     63.0     121.40      159.61      12.87      -38.21       -1.69
   11     65.0      31.40        8.65      13.67       22.75        1.03
   12     41.0     203.50      219.18       6.77      -15.68       -0.62
   13     21.0     441.10      387.95      12.13       53.15        2.31R
   14     38.0     323.00      295.52      10.32       27.48        1.15
   15     58.0      52.50       46.71      12.39        5.79        0.25

   R DENOTES AN OBS. WITH A LARGE ST. RES.
```

FIGURE 17.24
Partial Minitab output for heating oil data.

TABLE 17.10   Comparison of regression features of SPSS^X, SAS, Minitab, STATGRAPHICS, and MYSTAT

Name of Package	Stepwise Regression	All Possible Regressions	Residual Plots	Influence Measures	Confidence Intervals for μ_{YX}
SPSS^X					
REGRESSION	Yes	No	Yes	Yes	No
SAS					
PROC GLM	No	No	Yes	No	Yes
PROC STEPWISE	Yes	No	No	No	No
PROC RSQUARE	No	Yes	No	No	No
PROC REG	No	No	Yes	Yes	Yes
Minitab					
REGRESS	No	No	Yes	Yes	Yes
STEPWISE	Yes	No	No	No	No
STATGRAPHICS	Yes	No	Yes	Yes	No
MYSTAT	No	No	Yes	Yes	No

• **17.79** Referring to Problem 16.68 on page 610, the statistician for the automobile manufacturer believes that a second explanatory variable, shipping mileage, may be related to delivery time. The shipping mileage (in hundreds of miles) for the 16 cars in the sample was

Car	Shipping Mileage (Hundreds of Miles)
1	7.5
2	13.3
3	4.7
4	14.6
5	8.4
6	12.6
7	6.2
8	16.4
9	9.7
10	17.2
11	10.6
12	11.3
13	9.0
14	12.3
15	8.2
16	11.5

Access a computer package and perform a multiple linear regression analysis. Based on the results obtained

(a) State the multiple regression equation.

(b) Interpret the meaning of the slopes in this problem.

(c) If a car was ordered with 10 options and had to be shipped 800 miles, what would you predict the delivery time to be?

(d) Determine whether there is a significant relationship between delivery time and the two explanatory variables (number of options and shipping mileage) at the .05 level of significance.

(e) Interpret the meaning of the coefficient of multiple determination $r^2_{Y.12}$ in this problem.

(f) Compute the adjusted r^2.

(g) At the .05 level of significance, determine whether each explanatory variable makes a significant contribution to the regression model. Based upon these results, indicate the regression model that should be utilized in this problem.

(h) Set up a 95% confidence-interval estimate of the true population slope between delivery time and shipping mileage.

(i) Compute the coefficients of partial determination $r^2_{Y1.2}$ and $r^2_{Y2.1}$ and interpret their meaning.

(j) Determine the VIF for each explanatory variable in the model. Is there reason to suspect the existence of multicollinearity?

(k) Perform a residual analysis on your results and determine the adequacy of the fit of the model.

(l) Perform an influence analysis and determine whether any observations should be deleted from the model. If necessary, reanalyze the regression model after deleting these observations and compare your results with the original model.

17.80 The *Fortune* 500 consists of the 500 largest industrial corporations ranked by sales. We would like to be able to predict the net income of a corporation based upon sales and assets. A random sample of 25 corporations was selected from the *Fortune* 500 for the year 1987 with the results shown in the table below:

Access a computer package and perform a multiple regression analysis. Based on the results obtained

(a) State the multiple regression equation.
(b) Interpret the meaning of the slopes in this problem.
(c) Predict the net income for a corporation that has sales of $2 billion and assets of $2 billion.
(d) Determine whether there is a significant linear relationship between net income and the two explanatory variables (sales and assets) at the .05 level of significance.
(e) Compute the coefficient of multiple determination $r^2_{Y.12}$ and interpret its meaning in this problem.
(f) Compute the adjusted r^2.
(g) At the .05 level of significance, determine whether each explanatory variable makes a significant contribution to the regression model. Based upon these results, indicate the regression model that should be utilized in this problem.
(h) Compute the standard error of the estimate.
(i) Set up a 95% confidence-interval estimate of the true population slope between sales and net income.
(j) Compute the coefficients of partial determination $r^2_{Y1.2}$ and $r^2_{Y2.1}$ and interpret their meaning.
(k) Determine the VIF for each explanatory variable in the model. Is there reason to suspect the existence of multicollinearity?
(l) Perform a residual analysis on your results and determine the adequacy of the fit of the model.
(m) Perform an influence analysis and determine whether any observations should be deleted

Predicting net income for the *Fortune* 500

Company	Net Income ($ Millions)	Sales ($ Millions)	Assets ($ Millions)
Stanley Works	86.6	1,763.1	1,387.5
Computervision	19.5	564.0	466.8
Xidex	−44.5	572.8	675.7
Procter and Gamble	327.0	17,000.0	13,715.0
Amer. Maize-Products	12.7	506.8	401.7
General Mills	222.0	5,208.3	2,280.4
Rohm and Haas	195.5	2,203.0	1,954.0
M/A Com.	−35.4	542.9	581.7
Ford Motor	4,625.2	71,643.4	44,955.7
Wilson Foods	5.6	1,347.6	203.4
Telex	77.2	821.9	618.2
Morton Thiokol	138.0	1,987.3	1,666.0
Amerada Hess	229.9	4,784.6	5,304.8
EG and G	55.5	1,235.9	515.5
Magnetek	4.9	608.9	483.5
North Amer. Phillips	−18.1	4,846.9	3,102.3
Eaton	201.2	4,053.5	3,026.2
GAF	237.6	836.9	1,297.8
Envirodyne Ind.	38.7	475.7	425.4
Sherwin Wiilliams	96.6	2,094.8	1,140.0
Danaher	19.0	802.7	655.3
Holly Farms	71.7	1,406.6	685.4
Nat. Starch and Chem.	92.2	1,207.9	940.5
Cyprus Minerals	26.2	795.3	1,147.6
Foster Wheeler	3.0	1,219.1	1,079.7

SOURCE: *Fortune Magazine*, Vol. 117, No. 9, April 25, 1988, pp. D11–D30..

from the model. If necessary, reanalyze the regression model after deleting these observations and compare your results with the original model.

17.81 The *Fortune* Retailing Service 50 consists of the retailing service corporations that are ranked first to fiftieth in sales. As in Problem 17.80 for the *Fortune* 500, we would like to predict the net income of a corporation based on sales and assets. The table below represents a sample of 15 companies selected from the Retailing Service 50. Perform the same kind of analysis for the *Fortune* Retailing Service 50 as you did for the *Fortune* 500 in Problem 17.80 and compare the results.

Predicting net income for the Retailing Service 50

Company	Net Income ($ Millions)	Sales ($ Millions)	Assets ($ Millions)
Tandy	197.7	3,036.0	2,078.1
Price	58.9	2,590.3	492.9
Payless Cashways	42.4	1,525.6	709.4
Service Merchandise	− 46.9	2,740.8	1,525.1
K Mart	582.0	24,246.0	10,578.0
Ames Dept. Stores	27.1	1,888.5	745.4
Carter Hawley Hale	4.2	4,089.8	2,161.9
Walgreen	103.1	3,660.6	1,197.1
Circle K	39.8	2,111.3	852.8
Sears Roebuck	1,351.3	44,281.5	65,994.6
The Limited	227.8	3,142.7	1,377.1
Rapid American	− 20.5	1,893.5	1,654.2
Great Atl. and Pac.	88.3	6,615.4	1,663.8
Mercantile Stores	111.1	2,028.2	1,262.4
Albertson's	100.2	5,379.6	1,264.7

SOURCE: *Fortune Magazine*, Vol. 115, No. 12, June 8, 1987, p. 210.

17.82 Referring to Problem 16.73 on page 615, suppose that the researcher also would like to include the weight of the automobile in the regression model. The table at the top of page 686 represents the weight in pounds for each of the sample of 50 automobiles.

Access a computer package and perform a multiple regression analysis. Based on the results obtained

(a) State the multiple regression equation.

(b) Interpret the meaning of the slopes in this problem.

(c) If a car weighs 2,000 pounds and has 60 horsepower, what would you predict the miles per gallon to be?

(d) Determine whether there is a significant relationship between miles per gallon and the two explanatory variables (horsepower and weight) at the .05 level of significance.

(e) Interpret the meaning of the coefficient of multiple determination $r^2_{Y.12}$ in this problem.

(f) Compute the adjusted r^2.

(g) At the .05 level of significance, determine whether each explanatory variable makes a significant contribution to the regression model. Based on these results, indicate the regression model that should be used in this problem.

(h) Set up a 95% confidence-interval estimate of the true population slope between miles per gallon and horsepower.

(i) Compute the coefficients of partial determination $r^2_{Y1.2}$ and $r^2_{Y2.1}$ and interpret their meaning.

(j) Determine the VIF for each explanatory variable in the model. Is there reason to suspect the existence of multicollinearity?

(k) Perform a residual analysis on your results and determine the adequacy of the fit of the model.

(l) Perform an influence analysis and determine whether any observations should be deleted

Weight of 50 automobiles

Automobile	Weight	Automobile	Weight
1	1,985	26	3,420
2	3,365	27	2,380
3	3,535	28	3,250
4	3,445	29	1,980
5	3,205	30	2,800
6	2,830	31	2,950
7	3,245	32	2,560
8	4,360	33	2,210
9	4,054	34	1,850
10	3,940	35	2,615
11	3,190	36	1,965
12	2,144	37	2,930
13	2,110	38	1,968
14	2,420	39	2,070
15	2,490	40	2,900
16	1,755	41	2,542
17	2,605	42	1,985
18	2,865	43	2,395
19	3,570	44	2,720
20	3,155	45	2,670
21	2,678	46	2,890
22	2,215	47	2,625
23	1,800	48	3,465
24	1,915	49	2,045
25	2,965	50	3,380

from the model. If necessary, reanalyze the regression model after deleting these observations and compare your results with the original model.

17.83 Referring to Problem 16.74 on page 616, suppose that we also wish to include the time period in which the house was sold in the model. The table below represents the time period (in months) in which each of the 30 houses was sold.

Access a computer package and perform a multiple regression analysis. Based on the results obtained

Time period for the sample of 30 houses

House	Time Period (Months)	House	Time Period (Months)
1	10	16	12
2	10	17	5
3	11	18	14
4	2	19	1
5	5	20	3
6	4	21	14
7	17	22	12
8	13	23	11
9	6	24	12
10	5	25	2
11	7	26	6
12	4	27	12
13	11	28	4
14	10	29	9
15	17	30	12

(a) State the multiple regression equation.

(b) Interpret the meaning of the slopes in this equation.

(c) Predict the selling price for a house that has an assessed value of $70,000 and was sold in time period 12.

(d) Determine whether there is a significant relationship between selling price and the two explanatory variables (assessed value and time period) at the .05 level of significance.

(e) Interpret the meaning of the coefficient of multiple determination $r^2_{Y.12}$ in this problem.

(f) Compute the adjusted r^2.

(g) At the .05 level of significance, determine whether each explanatory variable makes a significant contribution to the regression model. Based on these results, indicate the regression model that should be used in this problem.

(h) Set up a 95% confidence-interval estimate of the true population slope between selling price and assessed value. How does the interpretation of the slope here differ from Problem 16.74(k)?

(i) Compute the coefficients of partial determination $r^2_{Y1.2}$ and $r^2_{Y2.1}$ and interpret their meaning.

(j) Determine the VIF for each explanatory variable in the model. Is there reason to suspect the existence of multicollinearity?

(k) Perform a residual analysis on your results and determine the adequacy of the fit of the model.

(l) Perform an influence analysis and determine whether any observations should be deleted from the model. If necessary, reanalyze the regression model after deleting these observations and compare your results with the original model.

17.84 Suppose that the agronomist in Problem 16.4 on page 562 wanted to design a study in which a wider range of fertilizer levels (pounds per hundred square feet) were to be used in order to determine whether the relationship between yield and amount of fertilier would be fit by a curvilinear model. Six fertilizer levels were to be utilized: 0, 20, 40, 60, 80, and 100 pounds per hundred square feet. These six levels were randomly assigned to plots of land with the following results:

Plot	Amount of Fertilizer (Pounds Per 100 Square Feet)	Yield (Pounds)
1	0	6
2	0	9
3	20	19
4	20	24
5	40	32
6	40	38
7	60	46
8	60	50
9	80	48
10	80	54
11	100	52
12	100	58

Assuming a curvilinear relationship between the amount of fertilizer used and tomato yield, access a computer package to perform the regression analysis.

(a) Set up a scatter diagram between amount of fertilizer and yield.

(b) State the regression equation for the curvilinear model.

(c) Predict the yield of tomatoes (in pounds) for a plot that has been fertilized with 70 pounds per hundred square feet of natural organic fertilizer.

(d) Determine whether there is a significant relationship between the amount of fertilizer used and tomato yield at the .05 level of significance.

(e) Compute the coefficient of multiple determination $r^2_{Y.12}$ and interpret its meaning.

(f) Compute the adjusted r^2.

(g) At the .05 level of significance, determine whether the curvilinear model is superior to the linear regression model.

(h) Perform a residual analysis on your results and determine the adequacy of the fit of the model.

(i) Perform an influence analysis and determine whether any observations should be deleted from the model. If necessary, reanalyze the regression model after deleting these observations and compare your results with the original model.

17.85 Referring to the data of Problem 16.69 on page 611, suppose that we wish to fit a curvilinear model to predict the amount bet based upon attendance. Access a computer package to perform the regression analysis.

(a) State the regression equation.

(b) Predict the amount bet for a day in which attendance is 30,000.

(c) Determine whether there is a significant relationship between attendance and amount bet at the .05 level of significance.

(d) Compute the coefficient of multiple determination $r^2_{Y.12}$ and interpret its meaning.

(e) Compute the adjusted r^2.

(f) At the .05 level of significance, determine whether the curvilinear model is superior to the linear regression model.

(g) Perform a residual analysis on your results and determine the adequacy of the fit of the model.

(h) Perform an influence analysis and determine whether any observations should be deleted from the model. If necessary, reanalyze the regression model after deleting these observations and compare your results with the original model.

● **17.86** Referring to Problem 16.73 on page 615, suppose that in addition to studying the effect of horsepower on miles per gallon, we wanted to study the effect of whether the car was manufactured in the United States or in a foreign country. Automobiles 2, 3, 4, 7–10, 15, 17–27, and 43–50 were manufactured in the United States and the other cars were manufactured in a foreign country. Access a computer package and perform a multiple regression analysis. Based on the results obtained

(a) State the multiple regression equation.

(b) Interpret the meaning of the slopes in this problem.

(c) Predict the miles per gallon for a car that has 60 horsepower and was manufactured in the United States.

(d) Determine whether there is a significant relationship between miles per gallon and the two explanatory variables (horsepower and country of origin) at the .05 level of significance.

(e) Interpret the meaning of the coefficient of multiple determination $r^2_{Y.12}$.

(f) Compute the adjusted r^2.

(g) At the .05 level of significance, determine whether each explanatory variable makes a significant contribution to the regression model. Based upon these results, indicate the regression model that should be used in this problem.

(h) Set up a 95% confidence-interval estimate of the true population slope between miles per gallon and horsepower.

(i) Compute the coefficients of partial determination $r^2_{Y1.2}$ and $r^2_{Y2.1}$ and interpret their meaning.

(j) Determine the VIF for each explanatory variable in the model. Is there reason to suspect the existence of multicollinearity?

(k) What assumption about the slope of miles per gallon and horsepower must be made in this problem?

(l) At the .05 level of significance, determine whether the inclusion of an interaction term makes a significant contribution to the model that already contains horsepower and country of origin. Based upon these results, indicate the regression model that should be used in this problem.

(m) Perform a residual analysis on your results and determine the adequacy of the fit of the model.

(n) Perform an influence analysis and determine whether any observations should be deleted from the model. If necessary, reanalyze the regression model after deleting these observations and compare your results with the original model.

17.87 Referring to Problem 16.74 on page 616, suppose that in addition to using assessed value to predict sales price, we also wanted to use information concerning whether the house was brand new. Houses 1, 2, 10, 14, 18, 20, 22, 24, 25, 26, 28, and 30 are brand new. Access a computer package and perform a multiple regression analysis. Based on the results obtained

(a) State the multiple regression equation.

(b) Interpret the meaning of the slopes in this problem.

(c) Predict the selling price for a brand new house with an assessed value of $75,000.

(d) Determine whether there is a significant relationship between selling price and the two explanatory variables (assessed value and whether the house is brand new) at the .05 level of significance.

(e) Interpret the meaning of the coefficient of multiple determination $r^2_{Y.12}$.

(f) Compute the adjusted r^2.

(g) At the .05 level of significance, determine whether each explanatory variable makes a significant contribution to the regression model. Based upon these results, indicate the regression model that should be used in this problem.

(h) Set up a 95% confidence-interval estimate of the true population slope between selling price and assessed value.

(i) Compute the coefficients of partial determination $r^2_{Y1.2}$ and $r^2_{Y2.1}$ and interpret their meaning.

(j) Determine the VIF for each explanatory variable in the model. Is there reason to suspect the existence of multicollinearity?

(k) What assumption about the slope of selling price and assessed value must be made in this problem?

(l) At the .05 level of significance, determine whether the inclusion of an interaction term makes a significant contribution to the model that already contains assessed value and whether the house is brand new. Based upon these results, indicate the regression model that should be used in this problem.

(m) Perform a residual analysis on your results and determine the adequacy of the fit of the model.

(n) Perform an influence analysis and determine whether any observations should be deleted from the model. If necessary, reanalyze the regression model after deleting these observations and compare your results with the original model.

17.88 A cost analyst for a large university would like to develop a regression model to predict library expenditures for materials and salaries (in thousands of dollars). Three explanatory variables are available for consideration:

X_1, volumes in the library (in thousands)

X_2, volumes to be added in a given year (in thousands)

X_3, current serials (in thousands)

A sample of 21 large research libraries was selected, and the results are presented in the table at the top of page 690.

With the assistance of a computer package, develop a regression model to predict the cost of materials and salaries. Be sure to perform a thorough residual analysis and evaluate the various measures of influence. In addition, provide a detailed explanation of your results.

• **17.89** In Problem 16.73 on page 615, we used horsepower to develop a regression model to predict gasoline mileage; in Problem 17.82 on page 685, we also considered vehicle weight and in Problem 17.86 we considered the country of origin. Suppose that in addition to these three

Expenditures for research libraries

University Library	X_1	X_2	X_3	Y
Yale	8,236.7	174.7	57.4	19.850.4
Columbia	5,551.7	121.7	63.4	18,031.2
Minnesota	4,286.4	116.5	44.6	14,956.7
Indiana	3,787.0	118.3	32.6	11.906.5
U. of Pennsylvania	3,376.9	106.2	30.5	12,468.6
New York Univ.	2,932.1	74.7	29.8	12,801.8
Duke Univ.	3,510.6	92.1	35.7	11,074.0
U. of Florida	2,539.4	78.9	29.5	9,875.5
Louisiana State U.	2,210.8	65.3	22.8	8,008.8
Mass. Inst. of Tech	2,029.5	81.9	21.1	8,719.2
U. of West. Ont.	1,868.9	62.0	19.0	7,130.9
Washington U. (Mo)	2,069.7	43.3	16.5	8,103.6
Emory	1,951.1	66.9	18.0	8,340.1
U. of S. Carolina	2,175.8	65.9	18.9	5,788.8
U of Cal. at Irvine	1,239.1	61.0	15.9	9,089.0
U of Nebraska	1,833.6	62.8	23.8	5,941.3
Geo. Inst. of Tech.	1,468.6	49.9	28.6	4,308.4
McMaster University	1,218.1	47.5	18.2	6,069.8
U. of Cal. at Riverside	1,250.4	47.2	13.7	6,303.2
U. of Saskatchewan	1,254.0	47.9	10.1	5,241.2
Oklahoma State Univ.	1,420.6	30.3	10.4	4,699.8

SOURCE: Association of Research Libraries, 1987.

explanatory variables, we also would like to consider three other explanatory variables—the number of cylinders, the displacement, and the acceleration. The table below provides information pertaining to these variables for the sample of 50 automobiles.

Number of cylinders, displacement, and acceleration for 50 automobiles

Automobile	Cylinders	Displacement	Acceleration	Automobile	Cylinders	Displacement	Acceleration
1	4	90	21.5	26	8	260	22.2
2	8	260	15.5	27	4	98	20.7
3	6	231	19.2	28	4	146	21.8
4	6	231	13.4	29	4	105	15.3
5	8	302	11.2	30	4	121	15.4
6	5	131	15.9	31	5	121	19.9
7	6	231	15.4	32	4	134	14.2
8	8	350	14.9	33	4	107	14.4
9	8	351	14.3	34	4	91	13.8
10	8	360	13.0	35	4	119	14.8
11	4	141	24.8	36	4	91	15.0
12	4	98	14.7	37	6	146	13.8
13	4	86	17.9	38	4	89	18.8
14	3	70	12.5	39	4	85	18.6
15	4	135	15.7	40	6	168	12.6
16	4	79	16.9	41	4	120	17.5
17	4	112	19.6	42	4	91	16.0
18	4	140	16.4	43	4	112	18.0
19	8	302	12.8	44	4	119	19.4
20	6	200	18.2	45	4	121	15.0
21	4	151	16.5	46	4	140	17.3
22	4	105	14.9	47	4	120	18.6
23	4	98	14.4	48	6	225	16.6
24	4	98	14.4	49	4	98	16.2
25	6	200	15.8	50	6	231	15.8

With the assistance of a computer package, develop a regression model to predict the miles per gallon. Be sure to perform a thorough residual analysis and evaluate the various measures of influence. In addition, provide a detailed explanation of your results.

17.90 In Problem 16.74 on page 616 we used assessed value to predict the selling price of houses; in Problem 17.83 on page 686 we also considered the time period in which the house was purchased, and in Problem 17.87 we considered whether or not the house was brand new. Suppose that we wanted to consider all three of these explanatory variables—assessed value, time period, and whether or not the house was brand new. With the assistance of a computer package, develop a regression model to predict the selling price of houses. Be sure to perform a thorough residual analysis and evaluate the various measures of influence. In addition, provide a detailed explanation of your results.

17.91 The *Fortune* Banking 100 consists of the 100 largest commercial banks (ranked by assets). Suppose that we would like to predict net income in 1986 based upon assets, deposits, loans, and number of employees. The table below represents the results of a random sample of 20 banks selected from the *Fortune* Banking 100.

With the assistance of a computer package, develop a regression model to predict the net income. Be sure to perform a thorough residual analysis and evaluate the various measures of influence. In addition, provide a detailed explanation of your results.

Predicting net income of banks

Bank	Assets ($ Bill.)	Deposits ($ Bill.)	Loans ($ Bill.)	Employees (000)	Net Income ($ Mill.)
Mellon Bank	34.50	21.65	23.03	19.8	276.2
Cit. and S. Geo.	18.76	14.03	11.57	13.3	155.8
Fidelcor	11.39	9.03	6.44	8.7	104.8
Shawmut Corp.	10.70	7.75	6.76	6.7	78.6
SunTrust Banks	26.17	21.28	16.64	19.7	245.1
U. S. Bancorp.	9.49	5.76	5.47	5.5	77.2
Signet Banking	9.47	6.66	5.89	6.1	86.3
First Amer. Ban.	7.21	5.92	4.31	4.4	41.1
Florida National	6.88	5.82	4.39	4.7	34.4
Mercantile Ban.	6.59	5.06	4.36	4.6	55.3
AmSouth Bancorp	5.94	4.45	3.82	4.3	61.0
SouthTrust Corp.	5.10	3.97	2.98	3.7	53.7
Harris Bancorp.	10.28	7.60	5.70	4.9	68.2
First Florida	4.85	4.04	2.79	3.5	47.2
Huntington Ban.	7.72	5.95	4.80	4.9	64.7
United Virginia	9.41	6.90	6.42	6.3	81.9
First Bank Sys.	28.01	16.26	14.64	10.0	202.9
United Jersey	8.02	6.67	4.99	5.3	71.5
Allied Bancshares	9.86	8.10	6.23	3.4	−17.6
Union Bancorp.	9.90	7.74	6.92	4.5	48.3

SOURCE: *Fortune Magazine*, Vol. 115, No. 12, June 8, 1987, pp. 202–203.

Database Exercises

The following problems refer to the sample data obtained from the questionnaire in Figure 2.5 on page 15 and presented in Figure 2.10 on pages 24–29. They should be solved with the aid of an available computer package.

☐ **17.92**   For houses in Farmingdale (question 9, code 2), we would like to develop a regression model to predict appraised value (question 1) based upon lot size (question 2), the number of bedrooms (question 3), the number of bathrooms (question 4), the number of rooms (question 5), the age of the house (question 6), the presence of an eat-in kitchen (question 14), central air conditioning (question 15), a fireplace (question 16), a connection to a local sewer system (question 17), a basement (question 18), a modern kitchen (question 19), and modern bathrooms (question 20). Be sure to perform a thorough residual analysis and to consider the various influence measures in your analysis. Provide a detailed explanation of your results including a comparison with the results obtained for East Meadow in Section 17.17.

☐ **17.93**   Perform a similar analysis for houses in Levittown (question 9, code 3) as was done for houses in Farmingdale in Problem 17.92.

☐ **17.94**   For houses in East Meadow (question 9, code 1), we would like to develop a regression model to predict annual taxes (question 7) based upon lot size (question 2), the number of bedrooms (question 3), the number of bathrooms (question 4), the number of rooms (question 5), the age of the house (question 6), the presence of an eat-in kitchen (question 14), central air conditioning (question 15), a fireplace (question 16), a connection to a local sewer system (question 17), a basement (question 18), a modern kitchen (question 19), and modern bathrooms (question 20). Be sure to perform a thorough residual analysis and to consider the various influence measures in your analysis. Provide a detailed explanation of your results.

☐ **17.95**   Perform a similar analysis for houses in Farmingdale (question 9, code 2) as was done for houses in East Meadow in Problem 17.94.

☐ **17.96**   Perform a similar analysis for houses in Levittown (question 9, code 3) as was done for houses in East Meadow in Problem 17.94.

Case Study H

Suppose that, as part of your job as personnel manager for a company that produces an industrial product, you have been assigned the task of analyzing the salaries of workers involved in the production process. To accomplish this, you have decided to develop a multiple regression model to predict their weekly salaries. The following information (explanatory variables) is available from the personnel files of each worker in the company:

X_1 = length of employment in months

X_2 = age in years

$$X_3 = \begin{cases} 0 & \text{for female employees} \\ 1 & \text{for male employees} \end{cases}$$

$$X_4 = \begin{cases} 0 & \text{for employees with technical jobs} \\ 1 & \text{for employees with clerical jobs} \end{cases}$$

Using the personnel files, you have selected a random sample of 49 workers involved in the production process. The data corresponding to their current weekly salaries, lengths of employment, ages, gender, and job classifications are summarized in Table 17.11.

With the assistance of a computer package, you plan to use the stepwise regression procedure to develop the "best"-fitting multiple regression model. Moreover, you plan to perform a thorough residual analysis and influence analysis on the model selected to ensure its appropriateness.

TABLE 17.11 Company employee data

Employee	Y	X_1	X_2	X_3	X_4	Employee	Y	X_1	X_2	X_3	X_4
1	395	69	47	1	0						
2	306	46	40	0	0	26	378	19	24	1	0
3	467	125	39	1	0	27	545	229	58	1	0
4	423	20	45	1	0	28	477	276	58	0	0
5	475	173	56	1	0	29	454	330	52	1	0
6	337	37	25	0	0	30	554	331	60	1	0
7	564	237	48	1	0	31	466	72	41	1	0
8	391	52	28	1	0	32	333	85	27	0	0
9	372	67	46	0	0	33	366	84	47	1	0
10	307	124	30	1	0	34	265	25	21	0	1
11	278	12	20	1	0	35	577	220	39	0	1
12	625	313	46	1	0	36	373	31	25	1	1
13	500	291	47	0	0	37	544	300	55	1	1
14	340	34	23	0	0	38	585	311	50	1	1
15	562	275	48	1	0	39	256	6	32	0	1
16	423	111	56	1	0	40	344	18	44	1	1
17	328	14	27	1	0	41	378	89	46	0	1
18	435	89	29	1	0	42	308	76	40	0	1
19	433	188	58	0	0	43	356	53	47	0	1
20	428	44	34	1	0	44	309	17	53	0	1
21	346	21	24	0	0	45	591	354	58	0	1
22	428	35	26	1	0	46	363	64	42	0	1
23	398	46	21	1	0	47	336	88	34	0	1
24	378	43	25	1	0	48	313	11	21	1	1
25	407	27	22	0	0	49	634	407	53	0	1

A detailed report that includes an explanation of your results as well as a summary of your findings is to be submitted to the company president next week.

References

1. ANDREWS, D. F., AND D. PREGIBON, "Finding the Outliers That Matter," *Journal of the Royal Statistical Society*, Ser. B., 1978, Vol. 40, pp. 85–93.
2. ATKINSON, A. C., "Robust and Diagnostic Regression Analysis," *Communications in Statistics*, 1982, Vol. 11, pp. 2559–2572.
3. BELSLEY, D. A., E. KUH, AND R. WELSCH, *Regression Diagnostics: Identifying Influential Data and Sources of Collinearity* (New York: John Wiley, 1980).
4. BERENSON, M. L., D. M. LEVINE, AND M. GOLDSTEIN, *Intermediate Statistical Methods and Applications: A Computer Package Approach* (Englewood Cliffs, N.J.: Prentice-Hall, 1983).
5. COOK, R. D., AND S. WEISBERG, *Residuals and Influence in Regression* (New York: Chapman and Hall, 1982).
6. DILLON, W. R., AND M. GOLDSTEIN, *Multivariate Analysis: Methods and Applications* (New York: John Wiley, 1984).
7. DRAPER, N. R., AND H. SMITH, *Applied Regression Analysis*, 2d ed. (New York: John Wiley, 1981).
8. HOCKING, R. R., "Developments in Linear Regression Methodology: 1959–1982," *Technometrics*, 1983, Vol. 25, 219–250.

9. HOAGLIN, D. C. AND R. WELSCH, "The Hat Matrix in Regression and ANOVA," *The American Statistician*, 1978, Vol. 32, pp. 17–22.

10. LEVINE, D. M., M. L. BERENSON, AND D. STEPHAN, *Using the SPSS Batch System with Basic Business Statistics* (Englewood Cliffs, N.J.: Prentice-Hall, 1983).

11. LEVINE, D. M., M. L. BERENSON, AND D. STEPHAN, *Using SAS with Basic Business Statistics* (Englewood Cliffs, N.J.: Prentice-Hall, 1983).

12. LEVINE, D. M., M. L. BERENSON, AND D. STEPHAN, *Using Minitab with Basic Business Statistics*, 2d ed. (Englewood Cliffs, N.J.: Prentice-Hall, 1986).

13. MARQUANDT, D. W., "You Should Standardize the Predictor Variables in Your Regression Models," discussion of "A Critique of Some Ridge Regression Methods," by G. Smith and F. Campbell, *Journal of the American Statistical Association*, 1980, Vol. 75, pp. 87–91.

14. MARQUANDT, D. W., AND R. D. SNEE, "Ridge Regression in Practice," *The American Statistician*, 1975, Vol. 29, pp. 3–19.

15. *MYSTAT—A Personal Version of SYSTAT* (Evanston, Ill.: SYSTAT Inc., 1988).

16. PREGIBON, D., "Logistic Regression Diagnostics," *Annals of Statistics*, 1981, Vol. 9, pp. 705–724.

17. RYAN, T. A., B. L. JOINER, AND B. F. RYAN, *Minitab Student Handbook*, 2d ed. (North Scituate, Mass.: Duxbury Press, 1985).

18. *SAS User's Guide*, 1982 ed. (Cary, N.C.: SAS Institute, 1982).

19. SNEE, R. D., "Some Aspects of Nonorthogonal Data Analysis, Part I. Developing Prediction Equations," *Journal of Quality Technology*, 1973, Vol. 5, pp. 67–79.

20. *SPSS^X User's Guide* (New York: McGraw-Hill, 1983).

21. *STATGRAPHICS User's Guide* (Rockville, Md.: STSC, Inc., 1986).

22. TUKEY, J. W., "Data Analysis, Computation and Mathematics," *Quarterly Journal of Applied Mathematics*, 1972, Vol. 30, pp. 51–65.

23. TUKEY, J. W., *Exploratory Data Analysis* (Reading, Mass.: Addison-Wesley, 1977).

24. VELLEMAN, P. F., AND R. WELSCH, "Efficient Computing of Regression Diagnostics," *The American Statistician*, 1981, Vol. 35, pp. 234–242.

25. WEISBERG, S., *Applied Linear Regression* (New York: John Wiley, 1980).

Index Numbers, Time Series, and Business Forecasting

18.1 INTRODUCTION

In the preceding two chapters we discussed the topic of regression analysis as a tool for model building and prediction. In these respects, regression analysis provides a useful guide to managerial decision making. In this chapter we shall develop an understanding of the concepts behind index numbers construction and time-series analysis as well as consider other business forecasting methods so that more timely and pertinent information will be available for managerial decision-making purposes.

18.2 INDEX NUMBERS

Over the years, **index numbers** have become increasingly important to management as indicators of changing economic or business activity. In fact, the use of index numbers has become the most widely accepted procedure for measuring changes in business conditions.

> **Index numbers** measure the size or magnitude of some object at a particular point in time as a percentage of some base or reference object in the past.

Many kinds of index numbers can be constructed. As examples, numerous price indexes, quantity indexes, value indexes, quality indexes, and sociological indexes (Reference 1) have been devised. For business forecasting purposes, however, we shall consider the construction of price indexes in this chapter.

18.3 THE PRICE INDEX

Price indexes reflect the percentage change in the price of some commodity (or group of commodities) in a given period of time over the price paid for that commodity (or group of commodities) at a particular point of time in the past. Price indexes are computed over numerous consecutive time periods in order to indicate changing economic or business activity.

18.3.1   Selecting the Base Period for a Price Index

2 rules :
1. normal economic period.
2. as recent as poss.

The base period or reference point is the year or time period in the past against which all these comparisons are made. In selecting the base period for a particular index, two rules should be observed. First, the period selected should, as much as possible, be one of economic normalcy or stability rather than one at or near the *peak* of an expanding economy or the *trough* of a recession or declining economy. Second, the base period should be recent, so that comparisons will not be unduly affected by changing technology, changing product quality, and/or changing consumer attitudes, interests, tastes, and habits.

18.3.2   Forming a Price Index for a Particular Commodity

As an example of a price index for a particular commodity, Table 18.1 depicts the average annual prices received by fishermen and vessel owners (in cents per pound) for flounder caught between the years of 1960 and 1984. Using 1960 as the base period or reference point, we may construct a price index for flounder by simply forming the ratio of the price paid for flounder in any given year to the price paid in the base year, and then multiply the result by 100 to express the index as a percentage. Thus if we let the symbol $I_i^{(t)}$ represent the price index for the *i*th commodity in time period (year) *t*, we have

$$I_i^{(t)} = \frac{P_i^{(t)}}{P_i^{(0)}} \times 100 \qquad\qquad \text{(18.1)}$$

where $P_i^{(t)}$ = price paid for the *i*th commodity in time period *t*
$P_i^{(0)}$ = price paid for the *i*th commodity in time period 0—the base period

From Table 18.1 and using Equation (18.1), the price index for the year 1961 is

$$I^{(1)} = \frac{P^{(1)}}{P^{(0)}} \times 100 = \frac{10.6}{12.2} \times 100 = 86.9$$

where the base year is selected as 1960. Obviously, from Equation (18.1) the price index for the base period must be 100.0.

18.3.3   Shifting the Base of a Price Index

In studying index numbers the decision maker is interested in comparing the current value of the index to some base period or reference point. Nevertheless, it becomes difficult to relate to price comparisons with reference points too far in the distant past. Under such circumstances, shifting the base period is desirable. Furthermore, a decision maker is frequently involved in comparing two series of index numbers—each with

TABLE 18.1 Prices paid to fishermen and vessel owners for flounder (1960 = 100.0) (annual average price in cents per pound)

Year	Price	Price Index	Year	Price	Price Index
1960	12.2	100.0	1973	23.7	194.3
1961	10.6	86.9	1974	26.5	217.2
1962	9.7	79.5	1975	34.9	286.1
1963	8.4	68.9	1976	39.9	327.0
1964	8.0	65.6	1977	41.7	341.8
1965	9.5	77.9	1978	50.5	413.9
1966	12.7	104.1	1979	47.2	386.9
1967	11.5	94.3	1980	42.4	347.5
1968	11.4	93.4	1981	57.9	474.6
1969	13.7	112.3	1982	56.7	464.8
1970	15.3	125.4	1983	54.0	442.6
1971	16.7	136.9	1984	96.5	791.0
1972	21.4	175.4			

SOURCES: Data are taken from *Statistical Abstract of the United States*, U.S. Department of Commerce, 1980, 1976, 1973; B. Wattenberg, ed., *Statistical History of the United States: From Colonial Times to the Present* (New York: Basic Books, 1976); and U.S. National Oceanic and Atmospheric Administration, *Prices Received by Fishermen*, H.S. No. 12 (C.F.S. No. 4657 Revised); *Fishery Statistics of the United States*, annual; and *Fisheries of the United States*, annual.

differing reference points. In these cases, too, it is feasible to shift the base period of one of the index-number series so that it matches that of the other series.

To shift the base we merely divide each index number in the series by the value of the index number in the newly desired base period. Each result is then multiplied by 100 to yield the new set of index numbers with the shifted base. Hence, symbolically, we have

$$I_{\text{new}}^{(t)} = \frac{I_{\text{old}}^{(t)}}{I_{\text{desired base}}^{(0)}} \times 100 \qquad (18.2)$$

where $I_{\text{new}}^{(t)}$ = index number in time period t under the shifted base

$I_{\text{old}}^{(t)}$ = index number in time period t under the old base

$I_{\text{desired base}}^{(0)}$ = value of the index number under the old base which is to be established as the new base

In other words, we create a series of *new* index numbers relative to the *old* value of the desired (shifted) base period. Hence this new point of reference must have a value of 100.0.

To demonstrate the shifting of the base, suppose we return to the simple price index we had constructed in Table 18.1. This price index represented the annual average prices paid to fishermen and vessel owners for flounder caught from 1960 through 1984. The base period that had been selected was 1960. If we now desire to shift the base to the year 1967 so that the results are more comparable to some of the more well-known government price indexes, Equation (18.2) may be used as indicated in Table 18.2 on page 698.

TABLE 18.2 Shifting the base of a price index: prices paid to fishermen and vessel owners for flounder

Year	Price index with 1960 Base	Price Index with 1967 Base
1960	100.0	$(100.0/94.3) \times 100.0 = 106.0$
1961	86.9	$(86.9/94.3) \times 100.0 = 92.1$
1962	79.5	$(79.5/94.3) \times 100.0 = 84.3$
1963	68.9	$(68.9/94.3) \times 100.0 = 73.1$
1964	65.6	$(65.6/94.3) \times 100.0 = 69.6$
1965	77.9	$(77.9/94.3) \times 100.0 = 82.6$
1966	104.1	$(104.1/94.3) \times 100.0 = 110.4$
1967	94.3	$(94.3/94.3) \times 100.0 = 100.0$
1968	93.4	$(93.4/94.3) \times 100.0 = 99.0$
1969	112.3	$(112.3/94.3) \times 100.0 = 119.1$
1970	125.4	$(125.4/94.3) \times 100.0 = 133.0$
1971	136.9	$(136.9/94.3) \times 100.0 = 145.2$
1972	175.4	$(175.4/94.3) \times 100.0 = 186.0$
1973	194.3	$(194.3/94.3) \times 100.0 = 206.0$
1974	217.2	$(217.2/94.3) \times 100.0 = 230.3$
1975	286.1	$(286.1/94.3) \times 100.0 = 303.4$
1976	327.0	$(327.0/94.3) \times 100.0 = 346.8$
1977	341.8	$(341.8/94.3) \times 100.0 = 362.5$
1978	413.9	$(413.9/94.3) \times 100.0 = 438.9$
1979	386.9	$(386.9/94.3) \times 100.0 = 410.3$
1980	347.5	$(347.5/94.3) \times 100.0 = 368.5$
1981	474.6	$(474.6/94.3) \times 100.0 = 503.3$
1982	464.8	$(464.8/94.3) \times 100.0 = 492.9$
1983	442.6	$(442.6/94.3) \times 100.0 = 469.4$
1984	791.0	$(791.0/94.3) \times 100.0 = 838.8$

SOURCE: Data are taken from Table 18.1.

Thus, for example, from Table 18.2 the computation of the price index for the year 1983 using the shifted (1967) base period is

$$I_{\text{new}}^{(1983)} = \frac{I_{\text{old}}^{(1983)}}{I_{\text{desired base}}^{(1967)}} \times 100$$

$$= \frac{442.6}{94.3} \times 100 = 469.4$$

The results indicate that prices paid to fishermen and vessel owners for flounder more than quadrupled (in terms of 1983 dollars) from 1967 to 1983. Interestingly, the prices paid in 1984 almost doubled that which was paid in 1983.

18.3.4 Forming a Price Index for a Group of Commodities

While a price index for any individual commodity [as described by Equation (18.1)] may be of interest, it is not usually considered important for most decision-making purposes. What is important is an index constituting a group of commodities—taken together—which may affect the quality of life enjoyed by a large number of consumers.

TABLE 18.3 Prices paid to fishermen and vessel owners for selected types of fish

Fish	Quantities* and Prices†	Year						
		1960	1965	1970	1975	1980	1982	1984
Cod	Q	40	36	53	56	118	104	97
	P	6.5	8.0	11.2	24.2	27.3	36.2	37.9
Flounder	Q	127	180	169	162	217	228	220
	P	12.2	9.5	15.3	34.9	42.4	56.7	96.5
Haddock	Q	119	134	27	16	55	45	26
	P	7.9	8.9	22.7	32.8	38.7	49.5	71.5
Ocean perch	Q	141	84	55	32	24	19	12
	P	4.0	4.1	4.9	10.3	23.0	27.4	28.8
Tuna	Q	298	319	393	393	399	261	212
	P	15.7	15.7	26.2	33.3	80.1	69.1	62.3

* Q, quantity caught in millions of pounds.

† P, price received in cents per pound.

SOURCE: *Statistical Abstract of the United States*, U.S. Department of Commerce, 1980, 1984, 1987 (extracted from data provided by the U.S. National Oceanic and Atmospheric Administration.)

Basically, two such types of price indexes concerning a group of commodities may be considered: simple aggregate price indexes and weighted aggregate price indexes.[1]

Simple Aggregate Price Index

When developing a price index for a group of commodities, the easiest index to construct is the simple aggregate price index given by

$$I_{SA}^{(t)} = \frac{\sum_{i=1}^{n} P_i^{(t)}}{\sum_{i=1}^{n} P_i^{(0)}} \times 100 \qquad (18.3)$$

where the superscript (t) in the symbol $I_{SA}^{(t)}$ represents the value of the simple aggregate index in time period t, and

$$\sum_{i=1}^{n} P_i^{(t)} = \text{sum of the prices paid for each of the } n \text{ commodities in time period } t$$

$$\sum_{i=1}^{n} P_i^{(0)} = \text{sum of the prices paid for the same commodities in time period 0—the base period}$$

As an example, Table 18.3 depicts the average prices received by fishermen and vessel owners from processors for various quantities of selected types of fish caught during selected periods from 1960 to 1984. Using 1960 as the base period, the simple aggregate price index is obtained as shown in Table 18.4 on page 700.

---

[1] In this context a ''simple'' index is one which is unweighted or equally weighted.

TABLE 18.4 Constructing a simple aggregate price index (1960 = 100.0)

Fish	Year						
	1960 $P_i^{(0)}$	1965 $P_i^{(1)}$	1970 $P_i^{(2)}$	1975 $P_i^{(3)}$	1980 $P_i^{(4)}$	1982 $P_i^{(5)}$	1984 $P_i^{(6)}$
Cod	6.5	8.0	11.2	24.2	27.3	36.2	37.9
Flounder	12.2	9.5	15.3	34.9	42.4	56.7	96.5
Haddock	7.9	8.9	22.7	32.8	38.7	49.5	71.5
Ocean perch	4.0	4.1	4.9	10.3	23.0	27.4	28.8
Tuna	15.7	15.7	26.2	33.3	80.1	69.1	62.3
Totals	46.3	46.2	80.3	135.5	211.5	238.9	297.0
Index	$\dfrac{46.3}{46.3} \times 100$	$\dfrac{46.2}{46.3} \times 100$	$\dfrac{80.3}{46.3} \times 100$	$\dfrac{135.5}{46.3} \times 100$	$\dfrac{211.5}{46.3} \times 100$	$\dfrac{238.9}{46.3} \times 100$	$\dfrac{297.0}{46.3} \times 100$
	$I_{SA}^{(0)} = 100.0$	$I_{SA}^{(1)} = 99.8$	$I_{SA}^{(2)} = 173.4$	$I_{SA}^{(3)} = 292.7$	$I_{SA}^{(4)} = 456.8$	$I_{SA}^{(5)} = 516.0$	$I_{SA}^{(6)} = 641.5$

SOURCE: Data are taken from Table 18.3.

An aggregate price index represents the changes in prices, over time, for an entire group of commodities. Such an index, while easy to compute, possesses two distinct shortcomings. First, the index considers each commodity in the group as equally important and thereby permits the most expensive commodities per unit to be overly influential. Second, any change in the unit of measurement of any commodity (for example, tuna could be priced in cents per kilogram while the other fish continue to be priced per pound) alters the value of the index.[2]

Weighted Aggregate Price Index

To overcome these difficulties we may use the weighted aggregate price index as defined by

$$I_{WA}^{(t)} = \frac{\sum\limits_{i=1}^{n} P_i^{(t)} W_i}{\sum\limits_{i=1}^{n} P_i^{(0)} W_i} \times 100 \qquad (18.4)$$

where W_i represents the "weight of importance" attached to the ith commodity ($i = 1, 2, \ldots, n$) in the group.

Now how should these weights of importance be determined? Subjectively, as discussed in Chapters 6 and 7, each individual or decision maker could assign his or her own set of weights to each commodity and obtain a personal, subjective price index. Clearly, if the weights assigned to each commodity are the same (that is, $W_i = 1/n$ for all $i = 1, 2, \ldots, n$), then the weighted aggregate price index would be identical to the simple aggregate price index ($I_{WA}^{(t)} = I_{SA}^{(t)}$). More objectively, the

---

[2] This latter drawback is overcome by constructing a simple arithmetic mean of price relatives for the group of commodities considered (see Reference 12).

importance of the individual commodities comprising the aggregate index may be accounted for by choosing as weights the *quantities* or amounts of each commodity that are produced, used, or consumed.

When constructing the price index over time it seems reasonable to hold the weights constant so that changes attributable to price movements may be isolated. Obviously, if both prices and quantities are varying, it would not be possible to isolate the fluctuations in price. But for which periods of time should these weights be chosen? Different approaches to this problem were taken by such researchers as Laspeyres, Paasche, and I. Fisher (see Reference 12). Each of these approaches has certain advantages and disadvantages with respect to cost, labor, and applicability.

The "Fixed"-Weight Indexes

Thus a "compromise" approach which has become widely accepted in practice is one based on a "fixed" set of weights—established at a particular point in time or developed as an average over several periods of time. Using the fixed quantity weights $W_i = Q_i^{(f)}$ we obtain the fixed-weight aggregate price index as

$$I_{FWA}^{(t)} = \frac{\sum_{i=1}^{n} P_i^{(t)} Q_i^{(f)}}{\sum_{i=1}^{n} P_i^{(0)} Q_i^{(f)}} \times 100 \tag{18.5}$$

The construction of the index is demonstrated in Table 18.5. The fixed quantity weights used are the quantities of the selected types of fish caught, in millions of pounds, in the year 1970.

The major advantages of this more general fixed weight index are that it avoids the price biases inherent in the aforementioned Laspeyres and Paasche indexes, and it

TABLE 18.5 Constructing a fixed-weight aggregate price index (1960 = 100.0)

Fish	1970 Fixed weight, $Q_i^{(2)}$	1960		1970		1984	
		$P_i^{(0)}$	$P_i^{(0)}Q_i^{(2)}$	$P_i^{(2)}$	$P_i^{(2)}Q_i^{(2)}$	$P_i^{(6)}$	$P_i^{(6)}Q_i^{(2)}$
Cod	53	6.5	344.5	11.2	593.6	37.9	2,008.7
Flounder	169	12.2	2,061.8	15.3	2,585.7	96.5	16,308.5
Haddock	27	7.9	213.3	22.7	612.9	71.5	1,930.5
Ocean perch	55	4.0	220.0	4.9	269.5	28.8	1,584.0
Tuna	393	15.7	6,170.1	26.2	10,296.6	62.3	24,483.9
Totals			9.009.7		14,358.3		46,315.6
Index		$\dfrac{9,009.7}{9,009.7} \times 100$		$\dfrac{14,358.3}{9,009.7} \times 100$		$\dfrac{46,315.6}{9,009.7} \times 100$	
		$I_{FWA}^{(0)} = 100.0$		$I_{FWA}^{(2)} = 159.4$		$I_{FWA}^{(6)} = 514.1$	

SOURCE: Data are taken from Table 18.3.

permits a direct period-to-period comparison of price movements in addition to comparisons from each period to the base.

Problems

18.1 Using the resources of your college library (see, for example, Reference 1 or Reference 12 or other texts), describe the Laspeyres price index.

18.2 Using the resources of your college library (see, for example, Reference 1 or Reference 12 or other texts), describe the Paasche price index.

18.3 Using the resources of your college library (see, for example, Reference 1 or Reference 12 or other texts), describe the "ideal" price index of Irving Fisher.

18.4 The Connie and Clare Cat Center is a retail outlet for feline pet supplies in a large northeastern city. Its net revenues (in $000) over the past decade are as follows:

Year	1979	1980	1981	1982	1983	1984	1985	1986	1987	1988
Net Revenues ($000)	40.1	41.3	44.8	52.5	41.6	43.2	50.7	59.3	61.8	67.1

(a) Form the price index for the net revenues over the ten years using 1979 as the base-year period.

(b) Shift the base-year period to 1983 and reformulate the price index for the net revenues over the ten years.

18.5 Monsieur Toulouse is another retail outlet for feline pet supplies. It began its operations in 1983 as a competitor of the Connie and Clare Cat Center (Problem 18.4). Its net revenues (in $000) over the six-year period, 1983 to 1988 are as follows:

Year	1983	1984	1985	1986	1987	1988
Net Revenues ($000)	23.1	25.4	33.3	30.4	31.6	34.5

(a) Form the price index for the net revenues over the six years using 1983 as the base-year period.

(b) Compare the price indexes for Monsieur Toulouse with those obtained for the Connie and Clare Cat Center in part (b) of Problem 18.4:

1. Which company has experienced the higher rate of growth in net revenues since 1983?

2. What is the annual growth rate in net revenues for each company since 1983?

Hint:

annual growth rate $(\%) =$

$$\left[\left(\frac{\text{latest value} - \text{earliest value}}{\text{earliest value}} \right) \div \left(\text{no. years since earliest value} \right) \right] \times 100\%$$

● **18.6**   The table below presents the wages paid to full-time civilian employees having certain types of federal government positions.

Paid civilian employment in full-time positions in federal government

Pay System	Number* and Pay†	1960	1965	1970	1975	1980	1985
General schedule	Q	973	1,112	1,287	1,349	1,402	1,450
	P	5,705	7,707	11,065	14,483	17,299	26,186
Wage system	Q	667	621	674	528	456	418
	P	4,935	5,887	6,976	11,197	17,644	23,288
Postal pay system	Q	483	534	673	566	528	528•
	P	4,854	6,219	8,120	13,329	17,799	17,799•
Other‡	Q	114	131	172	139	113	136
	P	5,344	7,032	8,741	13,951	20,344	34,413

* Q, number of employees in thousands.

† P, average pay per annum in dollars.

‡ Excludes Congress and Federal Court employees and Department of Commerce maritime seamen.

• 1985 data not available; 1980 figures used.

SOURCE: Data are taken from *Statistical Abstract of the United States*, Table 411, 1976, and Table 474, 1980 and Table 511, 1987.

(a) Using 1960 as the wage pay base year, construct the following indexes of wages paid to full-time civilian federal government employees:

   1. simple aggregate index.

   2. fixed-weight aggregate index (using 1970 as the weight period)

(b) Shift the wage pay base year from 1960 to 1970 for both indexes.

18.7   The table on page 704 depicts the prices paid for selected timber from 1969 through 1984.

(a) Using 1969 as the price base year, develop the following indexes of prices paid for selected timber species:

   1. simple aggregate price index.

   2. fixed-weight aggregate index (using 1972 as the weight period)

(b) Shift the wage pay base year from 1969 to 1972 for both indexes.

(c) The following table depicts the Producer Price Index for lumber and wood products from 1969 through 1984.

Producer price index for lumber and wood products (1967 = 100.0)

	1969	1970	1971	1972	1973	1974	1975	1976	1977	1978	1979	1980	1981	1982	1983	1984
Index (1967 = 100.0)	125.3	113.6	127.0	144.3	177.2	183.6	176.9	205.6	236.3	276.0	300.4	288.9	292.8	284.7	307.1	307.4

SOURCE: Data are taken from U.S. Department of Commerce, Bureau of Economic Analysis. *Business Statistics*: 1986, Washington, DC: USGPO, 1987.

   1. Shift the base of this index to 1972.

   2. Compare this index with your results from (b). Discuss.

Selected timber species (Problem 18.7)

Timber	Quantities* and Prices†	Year							
		1969	1970	1971	1972	1973	1974	1975	1976
Soft woods									
Douglas fir	Q	8,059	7,727	8,211	8,459	8,686	7,901	7,329	8,207
	P	82,200	41,900	49,100	71,700	138,100	202,400	169,500	176,200
Southern pine	Q	7,181	7,063	7,736	7,884	7,895	6,921	6,967	7,598
	P	51,700	44,100	52,200	65,600	93,400	76,200	57,000	87,000
Ponderosa pine	Q	3,684	3,429	3,780	4,001	4,030	3,580	3,544	4,032
	P	71,000	32,100	37,600	65,800	92,300	100,600	71,200	103,200
Hemlock	Q	1,902	1,980	2,367	2,692	2,711	2,105	2,020	2,454
	P	45,100	20,500	20,600	49,000	99,200	110,800	68,800	79,700
Hard woods									
Oak	Q	3,410	3,250	3,177	3,121	3,227	3,160	2,724	2,996
	P	28,200	26,600	21,200	26,600	43,600	54,700	29,700	43,400
Maple	Q	745	742	735	624	623	574	531	569
	P	41,100	34,400	37,800	59,400	71,400	79,500	39,600	36,600

Selected timber species (Problem 18.7 continued)

Timber	Quantities* and Prices†	Year							
		1977	1978	1979	1980	1981	1982	1983	1984
Soft woods									
Douglas fir	Q	8,543	8,601	8,425	6,853	5,868	4,842	6,434	7,740
	P	225,900	250,300	394,400	432,200	350,200	118,200	161,200	132,900
Southern pine	Q	8,239	8,267	9,283	8,217	8,415	8,754	10,181	10,674
	P	100,300	134,500	155,200	155,400	172,000	127,200	140,600	139,400
Ponderosa pine	Q	4,167	4,175	3,966	3,269	2,894	2,350	2,869	3,627
	P	131,400	164,700	239,000	206,100	195,200	66,900	104,000	122,700
Hemlock	Q	2,439	2,728	2,505	1,855	1,501	1,284	1,316	1,870
	P	89,300	113,600	200,800	212,700	163,400	44,500	62,200	61,800
Hard woods									
Oak	Q	3,103	3,220	3,461	3,356	1,922	1,855	2,163	2,488
	P	60,000	59,200	68,800	65,600	63,200	70,800	87,900	145,000
Maple	Q	563	561	217	225	426	367	524	526
	P	42,100	57,400	33,900	37,400	41,500	34,300	25,000	48,600

* *Q*, quantities in millions of board feet.
† *P*, prices in dollars per million board feet.
SOURCE: Data are taken from *Statistical Abstract of the United States*, Tables 1157 and 1160, 1976; Tables 1296 and 1298, 1980; and Tables 1179 and 1180, 1987.
Data compiled by U.S. Forest Service and Mackay-Shields Economics, Inc.

18.4 THE CONSUMER PRICE INDEX

18.4.1 The Consumer Price Index: A Historical Perspective

Perhaps the most important and certainly the most familiar of the price indexes developed by the federal government is the Consumer Price Index. Essentially, this index measures average changes in prices of a fixed ''market basket'' of goods and services usually bought by urban wage earners and clerical workers from one period of time to another. Since 1940 the index has been computed and published *monthly* by the Bureau of Labor Statistics. Although the fixed "market basket" consisted of some 400 goods and services, it was widely believed in recent years that the Consumer Price Index needed to be updated in order to better reflect changes in urban consumer purchasing habits. Thus in 1978 the Bureau of Labor Statistics introduced two versions of the index—a *new* **Consumer Price Index for All Urban Consumers** as well as an updated, *revised* **Consumer Price Index for All Urban Wage Earners and Clerical Workers.** The *new* Consumer Price Index for All Urban Consumers includes, in addition to wage earners and clerical workers, groups that historically had been excluded from coverage— professional, managerial, and technical workers; the self-employed; short-term workers; the unemployed; retirees; and others not in the labor force. Thus, this *new*, broad index covers approximately 80% of the total civilian noninstitutional population, roughly twice the size of the population covered by the *revised* Consumer Price Index for Urban Wage Earners and Clerical Workers.[3] Nevertheless, the *revised* index was still needed because organized labor believed that it better reflected the purchasing habits of the blue-collar family than did the new index, and hence many union contracts are tied to it.

18.4.2 The Consumer Price Index: How It Is Constructed

The Consumer Price Index is, in its most basic form, essentially a fixed-weight aggregate price index as shown in Equation (18.5). The price base for the items was established in one period of time while the value weights were obtained from a survey on consumer expenditures in another period of time. This massive undertaking involved both a probability sample and a judgment sample (as discussed in Chapter 2). Complete details as to the history, development, and construction of this index are given in Reference 6, while information pertaining to the revision is presented in References 7 and 9.

18.4.3 The Consumer Price Index: How It Is Used

Almost all Americans are affected in some manner by the Consumer Price Index— because of the many ways that it is used. In fact it is rather startling to note that a 1% change in the index may trigger up to a $3 billion change in extra federal spending (that is, income payments to workers, social security beneficiaries, retired military and federal civil service employees and survivors, as well as to food stamp recipients). Hence the accuracy and timeliness of the index are of major concern for both government and industrial decision making. Basically, the index has three major uses:

1. As an escalator
2. An an economic indicator
3. As a price deflator

---

[3] Neither index, however, includes persons in the military services or in institutions, or persons living outside urban areas such as farm families.

TABLE 18.6 Cost-of-living adjustment at the International Harvester Co. for a three-year period (October 1976 through September 1979)

Consumer Price Index (three-month average) (1967 = 100)	Hourly Cost-of-Living Allowance (in cents)
168.7 or less	None
168.8–169.0	1
169.1–169.3	2
169.4–169.6	3
169.7–169.9	4
170.0–170.2	5
170.3–170.5	6
170.6–170.8	7
170.9–171.1	8
171.2–171.4	9
171.5–171.7	10
171.8–172.0	11
172.1–172.3	12
172.4–172.6	13
172.7–172.9	14
173.0–173.2	15
173.3–173.5	16
173.6–173.8	17
173.9–174.1	18
174.2–174.4	19
174.5–174.7	20

and so forth with 1-cent adjustment for each .3-point change in the average index for the appropriate three months (rounded to the nearest .1).

SOURCE: Data are taken from B.L.S. Bulletin No. 1887, *Supplement to Wage Chronology-International Harvester and the Auto Workers, 1976–1979*, U.S. Department of Labor, June 1979.

The CPI as an Escalator

The Consumer Price Index was originally devised by the Bureau of Labor Statistics in 1919 so that the effects of inflationary tendencies resulting from World War I could be accounted for in wage negotiations in various industries. Subsequently, the index has been tied into numerous pension plans and escalator clauses in union contracts which affect the lives of millions of workers in the United States today. Hence the index has gained acceptance by the public as a measure of the "cost of living."[4] As an example, Table 18.6 presents the cost-of-living adjustment negotiated by the International Harvester Co. and the International Union, United Automobile, Aerospace and Agricultural Implement Workers of America (UAW) for the contractural period, October 1976 through September 1979. The agreement provided for cost-of-living adjustments each December, March, June, and September based on three-month averages of the respective published Consumer Price Indexes for the months ending October, January, April, and July.

[4] Although the Consumer Price Index is often thought of as a cost-of-living index it is, in fact, a price index. It denotes changes in prices for a fixed group of goods and services but does not reflect changes in purchasing patterns resulting from the changes in prices. Moreover, a complete cost-of-living index would also take into account income and social security taxes, which (unlike sales taxes) are excluded from the Consumer Price Index because they do not directly relate to prices of specific goods and services.

The CPI as an Economic Indicator

Aside from its ties to collective bargaining contracts and pensions as well as other income payments to individual Americans, the Consumer Price Index is widely used as an economic indicator. It is watched closely as a measure of success or failure of government economic policy and, in this sense, is utilized by both business and union leaders as well as by individuals as a guide to making economic decisions. Although the Bureau of Labor Statistics is quick to point out that it is a price index rather than a true cost-of-living index (see footnote 4), nevertheless, the public has ''adopted' the Consumer Price Index as the best available indicator of changes in monthly living costs.

The CPI as a Price Deflator

Another important use of the Consumer Price Index is as a price deflator. This results from the fact that economists, forecasters, and business decision makers are concerned with economic models which are representative of the complex workings of our economy. Since such models, when used for predictive purposes, deal with *real* wages, the Consumer Price Index is often used to adjust *nominal* wages (in current dollars) to *real* wages (in constant base-year dollars) by adjusting for changes in the cost of living. Using the Consumer Price Index as a ''deflator,'' we have

$$\text{real wages (in constant dollars)} = \frac{\text{nominal wages (in current dollars)}}{\text{Consumer Price Index (current)}} \times 100 \qquad (18.6)$$

This computation transforms current price levels into constant price levels which are more comparable to those of a prior period. To illustrate this, suppose, for example, your uncle's 1987 salary had been \$36,500 while his 1967 salary was \$10,000. Now it may be noted that while his *nominal* income would have increased by 265.0% $\left[\text{that is, } \left(\dfrac{\$36{,}500 - \$10{,}000}{\$10{,}000}\right) \times 100\right]$ over the 20-year period, the purchasing power of his *real* income certainly would not have. Using the Consumer Price Index as a deflator of *nominal* income [Equation (18.6)] we compute

$$\text{real wages (constant 1987 dollars)} = \frac{\$36{,}500}{340.4} \times 100 = \$10{,}722.68$$

and

$$\text{real wages (constant 1967 dollars)} = \frac{\$10{,}000}{100.0} \times 100 = \$10{,}000.00$$

Your uncle's *real* income would have increased not by 265.0% but only by approximately 7.2% $\left[\text{that is, } \left(\dfrac{\$10{,}722.68 - \$10{,}000}{\$10{,}000}\right) \times 100\right]$ since consumer prices increased (from 100.0 to 340.4 as measured by the Consumer Price Index) by 240.4% in the same period of time. On an annual basis, this corresponds to a real growth rate of only one-third of a percent. Essentially, this indicates that your uncle's income has just about kept pace with inflation.

18.4.4   The Consumer Price Index: Problems and Future Directions

Figure 18.1 shows percentage pie diagrams depicting the relative importance of the major categories comprising both versions (that is, *new* and *revised*) of the Consumer Price Index. The relative importance factors were developed by the Bureau of Labor Statistics from information collected in its 1982–84 Consumer Expenditure Survey—updated to December 1986 by price changes. These relative importance factors are adjusted each December to reflect annual price changes occurring in the major components in both versions of the index.

In recent years, as interest rates soared, many economists argued that the Consumer Price Index (in both its *new* and *revised* forms) had overstated inflation and that this had triggered billions of dollars in federal spending in excess of what was actually warranted—adding further upward pressure on the rate of inflation. This complaint was due primarily to exaggeration in the computation of housing costs, which represents by far the largest component of the index (see Figure 18.1). In recognition of this problem, the government conducted many studies. Based on their findings, in 1983 the Bureau of Labor Statistics altered the housing component of the

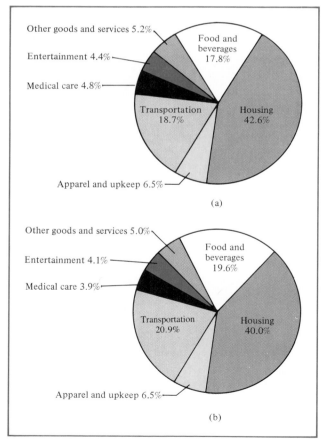

FIGURE 18.1
Relative importance of major components of the Consumer Price Index for All Urban Consumers (a) and the Revised Consumer Price Index for Urban Wage Earners and Clerical Workers (b)—January 1987.

SOURCE: U.S. Bureau of Labor Statistics

new Consumer Price Index for All Urban Consumers so as to include more data on rentals in lieu of data on purchases and mortgages. It was felt by government economists that such changes in the housing component would better approximate true shelter costs and hence yield a more viable index. Nevertheless, a similar alteration in the housing component of the *revised* Consumer Price Index for Urban Wage Earners and Clerical Workers was not effectuated until 1985 so as to permit the numerous existing union contracts which were tied to it to expire.

It is important to note that since 1985 the Consumer Price Index has had an even greater impact on the American economy through the process of **indexation of taxes.** That is, in 1981 legislation was passed which tied the index to the income tax rate tables so that purely inflationary increases in salary would not push the taxpayer into a higher tax bracket.

Problems

● **18.8**   The table below depicts the Consumer Price Index for selected periods from 1960 through 1985.

Consumer Price Index (1967 = 100.0)*

	Year																		
	1960	1965	1970	1971	1972	1973	1974	1975	1976	1977	1978	1979	1980	1981	1982	1983	1984	1985
Index (1967)	88.7	94.5	116.3	121.3	125.3	133.1	147.7	161.2	170.5	181.5	195.4	217.4	246.8	272.4	289.1	298.4	311.1	322.2

* CPI for all urban consumers since 1978.

SOURCE: Data are taken from Table 806. *Statistical Abstract of the United States*, 1980, and from Table 30, U.S. Bureau of Labor Statistics, *Monthly Labor Review*, February, 1988.

Using the data from Problem 18.6 on page 703
- **(a)** Determine the percentage growth rate in *nominal* wages paid in the postal pay system over the 20-year period 1960 to 1980.
- **(b)** Deflate the 1960 and 1980 figures by the Consumer Price Index for those years.
- **(c)** Determine the percentage growth rate in *real* wages paid in the postal pay system over the 20-year period 1960 to 1980.
- ➠**(d)** **ACTION**   Discuss how purchasing power for employees under the postal pay system had changed from 1960 to 1980.

18.9   Using the data from Problem 18.6 on page 703 and the Consumer Price Index from Problem 18.8
- **(a)** Determine the percentage growth rate in *nominal* wages paid in the general schedule pay system over the 25-year period 1960 to 1985.
- **(b)** Deflate the 1960 and 1985 figures by the Consumer Price Index for those years.
- **(c)** Determine the percentage in *real* wages paid in the general schedule pay system over the 25-year period 1960 to 1985.
- ➠**(d)** **ACTION**   Discuss how purchasing power for employees under the general schedule pay system had changed from 1960 to 1985.

18.10   Using the data from Problem 18.6 on page 703 and the Consumer Price Index from Problem 18.8
- **(a)** Determine the percentage growth rate in *nominal* wages paid in the wage system over the 25-year period 1960 to 1985.

(b) Deflate the 1960 and 1985 figures by the Consumer Price Index for those years.

(c) Determine the percentage growth rate in *real* wages paid in the wage system over the 25-year period 1960 to 1985.

➡(d) **ACTION** Discuss how purchasing power for employees under the wage system had changed from 1960 to 1985.

18.5 INDEX NUMBERS: AN OVERVIEW

We have noted that index numbers are useful to economists, forecasters, and business decision makers who study the magnitude and direction of price movements in our economy. Index numbers then are barometers of business change. Index numbers are also important in forecasting future economic activity. They are often used in **time-series analysis**—*the historical study of long-term trends, seasonal variations, and business cycle developments*—so that business leaders may keep pace with changing economic and business conditions and have better information available for decision-making purposes. Time-series analysis and business forecasting methods comprise the remaining sections of this chapter.

18.6 THE IMPORTANCE OF BUSINESS FORECASTING

18.6.1 Introduction to Forecasting

Since economic and business conditions vary over time, business leaders must find ways to keep abreast of the effects that such changes will have on their particular operations. One technique which business leaders may use as an aid in controlling present operations and in planning for future needs is **forecasting**. Although numerous forecasting methods have been devised, they all have one common goal—to make predictions of future events so that these projections can then be incorporated into the decision-making process. As examples, the government must be able to forecast such things as unemployment, inflation, industrial production, and expected revenues from personal and corporate income taxes in order to formulate its policies, while the marketing department of a large retailing corporation must be able to forecast product demand, sales revenues, consumer preferences, inventory, etc., in order to make timely decisions regarding its advertising strategies.

18.6.2 Types of Forecasting Methods

There are basically two approaches to forecasting: *qualitative* and *quantitative*. Qualitative forecasting methods are especially important when historical data are unavailable, as would be the case, for example, if the marketing department wanted to predict the sales of a new product. Qualitative forecasting methods are considered to be highly subjective and judgmental. These include the factor listing method, expert opinion, and the Delphi technique (see Reference 11). On the other hand, quantitative forecasting methods make use of historical data. The goal is to study past happenings in order to better understand the underlying structure of the data and thereby provide the means necessary for predicting future occurrences.

Quantitative forecasting methods can be subdivided into two types: *time-series* and *causal*. Causal forecasting methods involve the determination of factors which relate to the variable to be predicted. These include multiple regression analysis with lagged variables, econometric modeling, leading indicator analysis, and diffusion indexes and other economic barometers (see References 11 and 16). On the other hand, time-series forecasting methods involve the projection of future values of a variable based entirely on the past and present observations of that variable. It is these methods that we shall be concerned with here.

18.6.3 Introduction to Time-Series Analysis

A **time series** is a set of quantitative data that are obtained at regular periods over time. For example, the *daily* closing prices of a particular stock on the New York Stock Exchange constitutes a time series. Other examples of economic or business time series are the *weekly* percentage changes in department store sales; the *monthly* publication of the Consumer Price Index; the *quarterly* statements of gross national product (GNP); as well as the *annually* recorded total sales revenues of a particular firm. Time series, however, are not restricted to economic or business data (see Reference 22). As an example, the Dean of Students at your college may wish to investigate whether there is an indication of persistent ''grade inflation'' during the past decade. To accomplish this, on an annual basis either the percentage of freshmen and sophomore students on the Dean's List may be examined or the percentage of seniors graduating with honors may be studied.

18.6.4 Objectives of Time-Series Analysis

The basic assumption underlying time-series analysis is that those factors which have influenced patterns of economic activity in the past and present will continue to do so in more or less the same manner in the future. Thus the major goals of time-series analysis are to identify and isolate these influencing factors for predictive (forecasting) purposes as well as for managerial planning and control.

18.7 COMPONENT FACTORS OF THE CLASSICAL MULTIPLICATIVE TIME-SERIES MODEL

To achieve these goals, many mathematical models have been devised for exploring the fluctuations among the component factors of a time series. Perhaps the most fundamental is the **classical multiplicative model** for data recorded annually, quarterly, or monthly. It is this model that will be considered in this text.

To demonstrate the classical multiplicative time-series model, Figure 18.2 presents the annual retail sales (in millions of dollars) for a well-known department store chain from 1963 through 1987. If we may characterize these time-series data, it is clear that retail sales revenues have shown a tendency to increase (in a curvilinear manner as indicated in Figure 18.4 on page 713) over this 25-year period. This overall long-term tendency or impression (of upward or downward movements) is known as **trend.**

However, trend is not the only component factor influencing either these particular data or other annual time series. Two other factors—the **cyclical** component and the **irregular** component—are also present in the data. While these two factors will be more easily observed when we ''decompose'' the classical multiplicative time-series model in Section 18.8.6, it suffices here for us to get some general impression of what

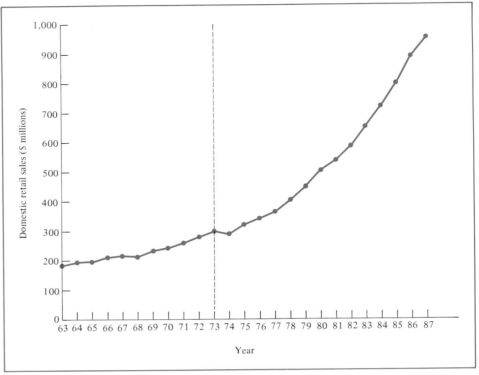

FIGURE 18.2
Annual retail sales (in millions of dollars) from 1963–1987.

these component factors are from the data at hand. As presented in Figure 18.3, the **cyclical** component depicts the up and down swings or movements through the series. Cyclical movements vary in length—usually lasting from 2 to 10 years—and also differ in intensity or amplitude. If we visualize a smooth curve representing trend[5] which passes through the time series (see Figure 18.4), several data points are found to dip far below the trend curve and others are found to be protruding above it. As examples, from Figure 18.4 the observed values for the years 1968, 1974, 1977, and 1982 are dipping below the trend curve and are representing the "bottoming out" or "trough" of their respective cycles.[6] At the other extreme, the observed data for the years 1966, 1973, 1975, and 1980 are protruding above the smoothly fitted trend curve. Therefore they are representing the peaks of their respective business cycles. Any observed data which do not follow the smoothly fitted trend curve modified by the aforementioned cyclical movements are indicative of the irregular or random factors of influence. These random fluctuations will be more easily observed in Figure 18.5. (See pages 714 and 715).

---

[5] The nonlinear trend curve was obtained by a 7-year moving average. The method of moving averages will be discussed in Section 18.10.1.
[6] Although the data here reflect the sales performance of one company, the time series for total annual domestic retail sales is considered by economists as one which generally "coincides" with the cyclical movements of the overall economy. Thus forecasters have referred to the overall series of retail sales as a "coinciding indicator" of economic conditions (Reference 10).

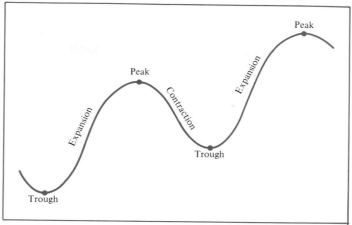

FIGURE 18.3
The four phases of the business cycle.

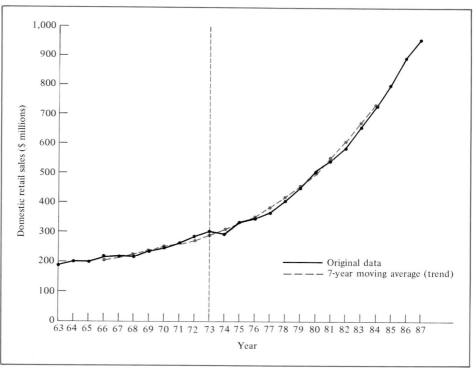

FIGURE 18.4
Seven-year moving average fitted to retail sales (1963–1987).
SOURCE: Data are taken from Figure 18.2.

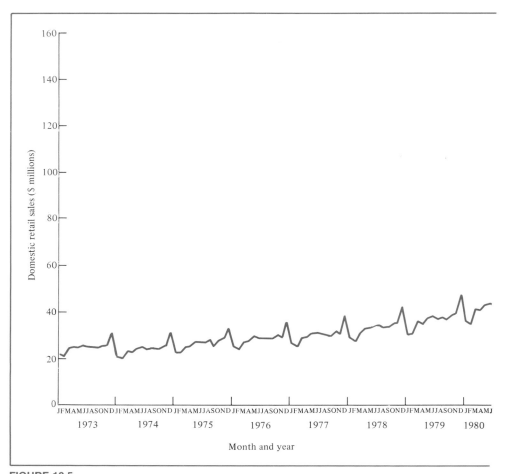

FIGURE 18.5
Domestic retail sales (in millions of dollars) for all stores in the department store
chain (January 1973 to December 1987).

When data are recorded monthly rather than annually, an additional component factor has an effect on the time series. This fourth factor is called the **seasonal** component. To demonstrate the seasonal effects on a time series, Figure 18.5 presents the monthly domestic retail sales (in millions of dollars) for all retail outlets in this department store chain from January 1973 through December 1987. (The annual results for this 15-year period can be observed to the right of the vertical dashed line in Figures 18.2 and 18.4.) In each of the 15 years the seasonal influences on retail sales revenues are clearly indicated. The peak retail sales volume in each year is seen to occur in December (as the nation prepares for the holiday season) while lulls in sales volume are observed in every January and February.

On the other hand, the irregular or random fluctuations influencing the time series may be observed more or less by comparing the recorded sales revenues for the months of June and August. It is seen from Figure 18.5 that August retail sales revenues exceeded June retail sales revenues in 8 of the 15 years. However, if we were also to compare June and August sales revenues for the years 1963 through 1972, we would

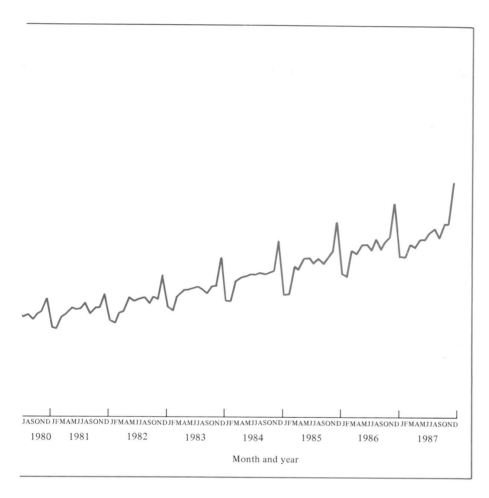

JASOND JFMAMJJASOND JFMAMJJASOND JFMAMJJASOND JFMAMJJASOND JFMAMJJASOND JFMAMJJASOND JFMAMJJASOND JFMAMJJASOND

1980   1981   1982   1983   1984   1985   1986   1987

Month and year

observe that over the 10-year period June revenues were higher on seven occasions and August revenues were higher on three occasions. In total, then, over the 25 years there is no systematic or observable pattern to the changes in the retail sales revenues for the months of June and August. Thus the obtained results are influenced by irregular or random factors.

In addition, from the monthly time-series data of Figure 18.5, the overall tendency (the curvilinearly increasing trend) is again readily observed. Unfortunately, for this particular set of data we are not able to visualize the cyclical factors which are influencing the time series. However, cyclical effects on monthly time series will be discussed and computed in Section 18.13.5.

From the annual data in Figure 18.2 and from the monthly data in Figure 18.5 we have thus far determined that there are three or four component factors, respectively, which influence an economic or business time series. These are summarized in Table 18.7 on page 716. Hence the classical multiplicative time-series model states that any observed value in a time series is the *product* of these influencing factors; that is, when

TABLE 18.7   Factors influencing time-series data

Component	Classification of Component	Definition	Reason for Influence	Duration
Trend	Systematic	Overall or persistent, long-term upward or downward pattern of movements	Due to changes in technology, population, wealth, values	Several years
Seasonal	Systematic	Fairly regular periodic fluctuations which occur within each 12-month period year after year	Due to weather conditions, social customs, religious customs	Within 12 months (or monthly or quarterly data)
Cyclical	Systematic	Repeating up-and-down swings or movements through four phases: from peak (prosperity) to contraction (recession) to trough (depression) to expansion (recovery or growth)	Due to interactions of numerous combinations of factors influencing the economy	Usually 2–10 years with differing intensity for a complete cycle
Irregular	Unsystematic	The erratic or "residual" fluctuations in a time series which exist after taking into account the systematic effects—trend, seasonal, and cyclical	Due to random variations in data or due to unforeseen events such as strikes, hurricanes, floods, political assassinations, etc.	Short duration and nonrepeating

the data are obtained annually, an observation Y_i recorded in the year i may be expressed as

$$Y_i = T_i \cdot C_i \cdot I_i \qquad (18.7)$$

where in the year i,

T_i = value of the trend component
C_i = value of the cyclical component
I_i = value of the irregular component

On the other hand, when the data are obtained either quarterly or monthly, an observation Y_i recorded in time period i may be given as

$$Y_i = T_i \cdot S_i \cdot C_i \cdot I_i \qquad (18.8)$$

where, in the time period i, T_i, C_i, and I_i are the values of the trend, cyclical, and irregular components, respectively, and S_i is the value of the seasonal component.

18.8   TIME-SERIES ANALYSIS OF ANNUAL DATA: FITTING TRENDS AND ISOLATING COMPONENTS

The component factor of a time series most often studied is trend. Primarily, we study trend for predictive purposes; that is, we either may wish to study trend directly as an aid in making intermediate and long-range forecasting projections, or we may wish to merely isolate and then eliminate its influencing effects on the time-series model as a guide to short-run (1 year or less) forecasting of general business cycle conditions.[7] As depicted in Figures 18.2 and 18.5, to obtain some visual impression or feeling of the overall long-term movements in a time series we construct a chart in which the observed data (dependent variable) are plotted on the vertical axis and the time periods (independent variable) are plotted on the horizontal axis. If it appears that a straight-line trend could be adequately fitted to the data, the two most widely used methods of trend fitting are the method of least squares (see Section 16.4) and the method of "double" exponential smoothing (References 2, 3, and 5). However, if the time-series data indicate some long-run downward or upward (see Figure 18.2) curvilinear movement, the two most widely used trend-fitting methods are the method of least squares (see Section 17.10) and the method of "triple" exponential smoothing (References 2, 3, and 5). In this section we shall focus on least-squares methods for fitting linear and curvilinear trends as guides to forecasting. In Sections 18.11 and 18.12 other, more elaborate, forecasting approaches will be described.

18.8.1 Fitting and Forecasting Linear Trends

We recall from Section 16.4 that the least-squares method permits us to fit a straight line of the form

$$\hat{Y}_i = b_0 + b_1 X_i \tag{18.9}$$

such that the values we calculate for the two coefficients—the intercept b_0 and the slope b_1—result in the sum of squared differences between each observed value Y_i in the data and each predicted value $\hat{Y}_i$ along the trend line being minimized; that is

$$\sum_{i=1}^{n} (Y_i - \hat{Y}_i)^2 = \text{Minimum} \tag{18.10}$$

To obtain such a line, we recall that in linear regression analysis we compute the slope from

$$b_1 = \frac{\displaystyle\sum_{i=1}^{n} X_i Y_i - \frac{\left(\sum_{i=1}^{n} X_i\right)\left(\sum_{i=1}^{n} Y_i\right)}{n}}{\displaystyle\sum_{i=1}^{n} X_i^2 - \frac{\left(\sum_{i=1}^{n} X_i\right)^2}{n}} \tag{18.11}$$

---

[7] Before we do this, however, it would not be at all unreasonable if we tested the time-series data for the existence of a statistically significant trend effect. One such procedure which could be used for this purpose is the Wald-Wolfowitz one-sample-runs test, which was discussed in Section 15.4. In this chapter, however, we will be examining the time-series components for descriptive rather than inferential purposes.

and the intercept from

$$b_0 = \bar{Y} - b_1\bar{X} \qquad (18.12)$$

Once this is accomplished and the line $\hat{Y}_i = b_0 + b_1X_i$ is obtained, we may substitute values for X into Equation (18.9) to predict various values for Y. We may note, however, that when using the method of least squares for fitting linear trends in time series, the observed values of the series (Y values) are usually recorded annually over several consecutive years (X values). Therefore, when dealing with annual time-series data, our computational efforts can be simplified if we properly "code" the X values. However, the coding scheme that we choose depends on whether our time-series data have been obtained over an odd number of years or an even number of years.

18.8.2 Fitting a Least-Squares Linear Trend for an Odd Number of Years

For time-series data observed over an odd number of years, the most efficient coding scheme to facilitate our computations is the selection of the middle year in the sequence as the designated origin, having a code $X = 0$. All successive years are then assigned consecutively increasing integer codes while all preceding years are assigned consecutively decreasing integer codes. Thus, for example, if a time series has $n = 7$ years of data, the middle (fourth) year would be given a code of $X = 0$, and the coded sequence from the first year to the last would be

$$-3 \quad -2 \quad -1 \quad 0 \quad 1 \quad 2 \quad 3$$

Interestingly, by coding the middle year in the series as $X = 0$ it will always happen that $\sum_{i=1}^{n} X_i = 0$, and, therefore, the formulas for the slope and intercept [Equations (18.11) and (18.12)] will be altered as follows:

$$b_1 = \frac{\sum_{i=1}^{n} X_iY_i}{\sum_{i=1}^{n} X_i^2} \qquad (18.11a)$$

$$b_0 = \bar{Y} = \frac{\sum_{i=1}^{n} Y_i}{n} \qquad (18.12a)$$

and the computational effort is reduced.

To fit a least-squares trend line to annual data having an odd number of years the time series presented in Table 18.8 and plotted in Figure 18.6 represents the annual

TABLE 18.8 Annual income taxes paid to federal government (1973–1987)

Year	Taxes (millions of dollars)
1973	55.4
1974	61.5
1975	68.7
1976	87.2
1977	90.4
1978	86.2
1979	94.7
1980	103.2
1981	119.0
1982	122.4
1983	131.6
1984	157.6
1985	181.0
1986	217.8
1987	244.1

income taxes paid to the federal government for the 15-year period 1973 through 1987 by residents of a midwestern city.

The computations needed for fitting a linear trend to this 15-year series by the method of least squares are shown in Table 18.9 on page 720.

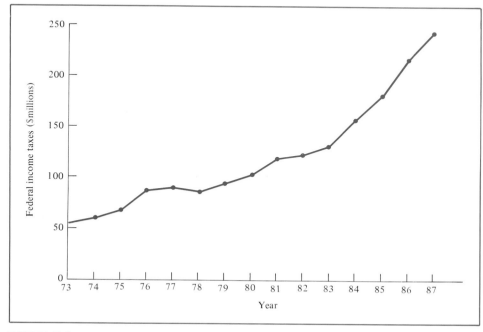

FIGURE 18.6
Annual income taxes paid to federal government (1973–1987).
SOURCE: Data are taken from Table 18.8.

TABLE 18.9   Computation of least-squares trend for 15 years of data

Year	X_i	Y_i ($ millions)	$X_i Y_i$	X_i^2
1973	-7	55.4	-387.8	49
1974	-6	61.5	-369.0	36
1975	-5	68.7	-343.5	25
1976	-4	87.2	-348.8	16
1977	-3	90.4	-271.2	9
1978	-2	86.2	-172.4	4
1979	-1	94.7	-94.7	1
1980	0	103.2	0	0
1981	1	119.0	119.0	1
1982	2	122.4	244.8	4
1983	3	131.6	394.8	9
1984	4	157.6	630.4	16
1985	5	181.0	905.0	25
1986	6	217.8	1,306.8	36
1987	7	244.1	1,708.7	49
$n = 15$	0	1,820.8	3,322.1	280

SOURCE: Data are taken from Table 18.8.

Using the adjusted formulas for slope and intercept [Equations (18.11a) and (18.12a)], we compute

$$b_1 = \frac{\sum_{i=1}^{n} X_i Y_i}{\sum_{i=1}^{n} X_i^2} = \frac{3,322.1}{280} \cong 11.9$$

and

$$b_0 = \overline{Y} = \frac{\sum_{i=1}^{n} Y_i}{n} = \frac{1,820.8}{15} \cong 121.4$$

Since the designated origin was the middle year (1980) of the series, we have

$$\hat{Y}_i = 121.4 + 11.9 X_i$$

where the origin is 1980 and X units = 1 year.

This equation may be interpreted as follows: For the designated origin year, 1980, the fitted trend line indicates that 121.4 millions of dollars of income taxes was expected to have been paid to the federal government by residents of this city. Moreover, the slope $b_1 = 11.9$ indicates that such payments of individual income taxes to the federal government were increasing there at the rate of 11.9 millions of dollars per year.

To fit the trend line to the observed years of the series we merely substitute the appropriate coded values of X into the equation. As an example, for the year 1982, where $X = 2$, the predicted (fitted) trend value is given by

$$\hat{Y}_{10} = 121.4 + (11.9)(2) = 145.2 \text{ millions of dollars}$$

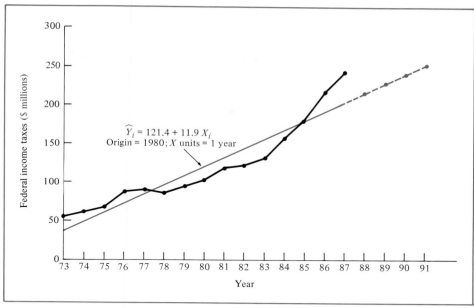

FIGURE 18.7
Fitting the least-squares trend line.
SOURCE: Data are taken from Tables 18.8 and 18.9.

To use the trend line for forecasting purposes, we may project the fitted line into the future by mathematical extrapolation.[8] For example, to predict the trend in payments for the year 1988, we substitute $X = 8$, the code for the year 1988, into the equation, and we forecast the trend to be

$$1988 \qquad \hat{Y}_{16} = 121.4 + (11.9)(8) = 216.6 \text{ millions of dollars}$$

Moreover, for the years 1989 through 1991 we forecast the trend in payments to be

$$1989 \qquad \hat{Y}_{17} = 121.4 + (11.9)(9) = 228.5 \text{ millions of dollars}$$

$$1990 \qquad \hat{Y}_{18} = 121.4 + (11.9)(10) = 240.4 \text{ millions of dollars}$$

$$1991 \qquad \hat{Y}_{19} = 121.4 + (11.9)(11) = 252.3 \text{ millions of dollars}$$

The fitted trend line projected to 1991 is plotted in Figure 18.7 along with the original time series. While the trend demonstrates the overall long-term movement of the series, we note that there are large discrepancies between the actual data and the fitted linear model. Thus a curvilinear model would likely be more indicative of the historical patterns in the data and perhaps provide better projections of future trend movements (see Sections 18.8.4 and 18.8.5).

---

[8] The method of least squares is an objective mathematical technique for fitting a trend line or curve. Of course, the obtained trend equation may mechanically be projected into the future for predictive purposes. However, we may recall from Section 16.4.2 in our discussion of interpolation versus extrapolation that any such extrapolation beyond the range of the observed data makes assumptions about the continuity of the process that cannot be verified in a probabilistic sense.

18.8.3 Fitting a Least-Squares Linear Trend for an Even Number of Years

For time-series data observed over an even number of years we choose the first year in our series as the origin and assign that year a code $X = 0$. All successive years are then assigned consecutively increasing integer codes: 1, 2, 3, 4 , . . . , so that the last year in the series, the *n*th year, has code $n - 1$. Thus, for example, if a time series has $n = 6$ years of data, the codes would be 0, 1, 2, 3, 4, 5.

To fit a least-squares trend line to annual data having an even number of years, the time series presented in Table 18.10 and plotted in Figure 18.8 represents the annual payments (in millions of dollars) to a life-insurance company both for interest on policy loans and for premium notes over the 14-year period of 1974 through 1987. The necessary computations are given in Table 18.11.

Using Equations (18.11) and (18.12), we determine that

$$b_1 = \frac{\sum_{i=1}^{n} X_i Y_i - \dfrac{\left(\sum_{i=1}^{n} X_i\right)\left(\sum_{i=1}^{n} Y_i\right)}{n}}{\sum_{i=1}^{n} X_i^2 - \dfrac{\left(\sum_{i=1}^{n} X_i\right)^2}{n}} = \frac{2{,}520.4 - \dfrac{(91)(313.9)}{14}}{819 - \dfrac{(91)^2}{14}} \cong 2.1$$

and since

$$\overline{Y} = \frac{\sum_{i=1}^{n} Y_i}{n} = \frac{313.9}{14} = 22.42 \quad \text{and} \quad \overline{X} = \frac{\sum_{i=1}^{n} X_i}{n} = \frac{91}{14} = 6.5$$

then

$$b_0 = \overline{Y} - b_1\overline{X} = 22.42 - (2.1)(6.5) \cong 8.8$$

TABLE 18.10 Annual payments on policy loans and premium notes to a life-insurance company (1974–1987)

Year	Payments (millions of dollars)
1974	10.1
1975	11.3
1976	13.8
1977	16.1
1978	17.1
1979	18.0
1980	20.2
1981	22.9
1982	24.5
1983	25.9
1984	27.6
1985	30.1
1986	34.8
1987	41.5

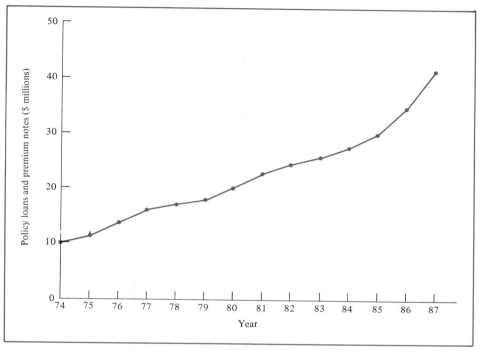

FIGURE 18.8
Annual payments on policy loans and premium notes to a life-insurance
company (1974–1987).
SOURCE: Data are taken from Table 18.10.

TABLE 18.11   Computation of least-squares trend line for
14 years of data

Year	X_i	Y_i (millions of dollars)	X_iY_i	X_i^2
1974	0	10.1	0	0
1975	1	11.3	11.3	1
1976	2	13.8	27.6	4
1977	3	16.1	48.3	9
1978	4	17.1	68.4	16
1979	5	18.0	90.0	25
1980	6	20.2	121.2	36
1981	7	22.9	160.3	49
1982	8	24.5	196.0	64
1983	9	25.9	233.1	81
1984	10	27.6	276.0	100
1985	11	30.1	331.1	121
1986	12	34.8	417.6	144
1987	13	41.5	539.5	169
$n = 14$	91	313.9	2,520.4	819

SOURCE: Data are taken from Table 18.10.

Since our first observed value in the time series was obtained for the year 1974, our origin is referenced in the middle of that year. Thus we have

$$\hat{Y}_i = 8.8 + 2.1X_i$$

where the origin is 1974 and X units $= 1$ year.

The intercept $b_0 = 8.8$ is the fitted trend value reflecting the amount of money (in millions of dollars) paid to the life-insurance company for interest on loans and for premium notes during the origin or base year, 1974. The slope $b_1 = 2.1$ indicates that such payments are increasing at a rate of 2.1 millions of dollars per year.

To project the trend in payments to the life-insurance company for interest on loans and for premium notes to the year 1991, we substitute $X = 17$, the code for the year 1991, into the equation and our forecast is

$$1991 \qquad \hat{Y}_{18} = 8.8 + (2.1)(17) = 44.5 \text{ millions of dollars}$$

The fitted trend line projected to 1991 is plotted in Figure 18.9 along with the original time series. A careful examination of Figure 18.9 reveals that a marked increase has occurred in the more recent years of the series. Perhaps, then, a curvilinear trend model would better fit the series? Two such models—a *quadratic* trend model and an *exponential* trend model—are presented in Sections 18.8.4 and 18.8.5, respectively.

18.8.4 Fitting a Quadratic Trend by the Method of Least Squares

A quadratic model or "second-degree polynomial" is the simplest of the curvilinear models. Using the least-squares method of Section 17.10, we may fit a quadratic trend equation of the form

$$\hat{Y}_i = b_0 + b_1X_i + b_{11}X_i^2 \tag{18.13}$$

where $b_0 =$ estimated Y intercept
$b_1 =$ estimated *linear* effect on Y
$b_{11} =$ estimated *curvilinear* effect on Y

The sample coefficients b_0, b_1, and b_{11} would have the following three normal equations:

$$\text{I.} \qquad \sum_{i=1}^{n} Y_i = nb_0 + b_1 \sum_{i=1}^{n} X_i + b_{11} \sum_{i=1}^{n} X_i^2 \tag{18.14a}$$

$$\text{II.} \qquad \sum_{i=1}^{n} X_iY_i = b_0 \sum_{i=1}^{n} X_i + b_1 \sum_{i=1}^{n} X_i^2 + b_{11} \sum_{i=1}^{n} X_i^3 \tag{18.14b}$$

$$\text{III.} \qquad \sum_{i=1}^{n} X_i^2Y_i = b_0 \sum_{i=1}^{n} X_i^2 + b_1 \sum_{i=1}^{n} X_i^3 + b_{11} \sum_{i=1}^{n} X_i^4 \tag{18.14c}$$

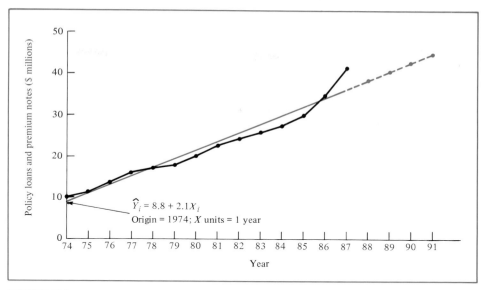

FIGURE 18.9
Fitting the least-squares trend line.
SOURCE: Data are taken from Tables 18.10 and 18.11.

The necessary computations for the data on payments to the life-insurance company for interest on loans and for premium notes are:

$$\sum_{i=1}^{n} X_i = 91, \quad \sum_{i=1}^{n} Y_i = 313.9, \quad \sum_{i=1}^{n} X_i Y_i = 2{,}520.4, \quad\quad n = 14$$

$$\sum_{i=1}^{n} X_i^2 = 819, \quad \sum_{i=1}^{n} X_i^3 = 8{,}281, \quad \sum_{i=1}^{n} X_i^4 = 89{,}271, \quad \sum_{i=1}^{n} X_i^2 Y_i = 24{,}877.0$$

The three normal equations would be

$$\text{I.} \quad\quad 313.9 = 14b_0 + 91b_1 + 819b_{11}$$

$$\text{II.} \quad\quad 2{,}520.4 = 91b_0 + 819b_1 + 8{,}281b_{11}$$

$$\text{III.} \quad 24{,}877.0 = 819b_0 + 8{,}281b_1 + 89{,}271b_{11}$$

The values of the coefficients b_0, b_1, and b_{11} can be obtained either by solving simultaneous equations or by using an available computer package (see Sections 17.10 and 17.18). The computed values for these data are

$$b_0 \cong 11.1, \quad\quad b_1 \cong .89, \quad\quad b_{11} \cong .094$$

Since our first observed value in the time series was obtained for the year 1974, the fitted quadratic trend equation can be expressed as

$$\hat{Y}_i = 11.1 + .89X_i + .094X_i^2$$

where the origin is 1974 and X units $= 1$ year.

To use the quadratic trend equation for forecasting purposes we substitute the

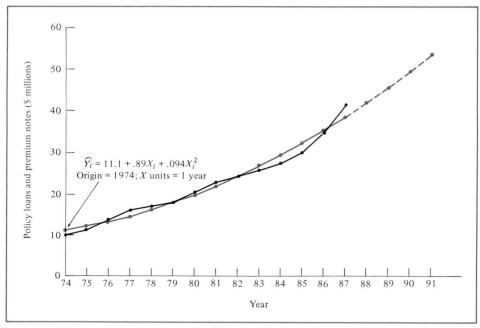

FIGURE 18.10
Fitting the quadratic trend equation.
SOURCE: Data are taken from Table 18.10.

appropriate coded values of X into the equation. For example, to predict the trend in payments for the year 1991, we have

$$1991 \qquad \hat{Y}_{18} = 11.1 + (.89)(17) + (.094)(17^2) = 53.4 \text{ millions of dollars}$$

The fitted quadratic trend equation projected to 1991 is plotted in Figure 18.10 together with the original time series.

18.8.5. Fitting an Exponential Trend by the Method of Least Squares

When a series appears to be increasing at an increasing rate such that the percent difference from observation to observation is constant, we may fit an exponential trend equation of the form

$$\hat{Y}_i = b_0 b_1^{X_i} \qquad\qquad (18.15)$$

where $b_0 =$ estimated Y intercept

$(b_1 - 1) \times 100\% =$ estimated annual *compound growth rate* (in percent)

If we take the logarithm (base 10) of both sides of Equation (18.15), we have

$$\log \hat{Y}_i = \log b_0 + X_i \log b_1 \qquad \text{(18.16)}$$

Since Equation (18.16) is *linear* in form, we may use the method of least squares to obtain the slope of this line ($\log b_1$) and its intercept ($\log b_0$).[9] Thus

$$\log b_1 = \frac{\sum\limits_{i=1}^{n} (X_i \log Y_i) - \dfrac{\left(\sum\limits_{i=1}^{n} X_i\right)\left(\sum\limits_{i=1}^{n} \log Y_i\right)}{n}}{\sum\limits_{i=1}^{n} X_i^2 - \dfrac{\left(\sum\limits_{i=1}^{n} X_i\right)^2}{n}} \qquad \text{(18.17)}$$

and

$$\log b_0 = \frac{\sum\limits_{i=1}^{n} \log Y_i}{n} - \bar{X} \log b_1 \qquad \text{(18.18)}$$

The necessary computations are displayed in Table 18.12 on page 728 for the data on payments to the life-insurance company for interest on loans and for premium notes.
Using Equations (18.17) and (18.18), we determine that

$$\log b_1 = \frac{\sum\limits_{i=1}^{n} (X_i \log Y_i) - \dfrac{\left(\sum\limits_{i=1}^{n} X_i\right)\left(\sum\limits_{i=1}^{n} \log Y_i\right)}{n}}{\sum\limits_{i=1}^{n} X_i^2 - \dfrac{\left(\sum\limits_{i=1}^{n} X_i\right)^2}{n}} = \frac{129.55270 - \dfrac{(91)(18.43915)}{14}}{819 - \dfrac{(91)^2}{14}}$$

$$\cong .0426296$$

---

[9] Note that Equations (18.17) and (18.18) are similar in form to Equations (18.11) and (18.12), respectively. When fitting a *linear* trend [Equation (18.9)] we plot Y_i versus X_i and compute b_1 and b_0; when fitting an *exponential* trend [Equation (18.16)] we plot $\log Y_i$ versus X_i and compute $\log b_1$ and $\log b_0$.

TABLE 18.12   Computations for exponential trend model

Year	X_i	Y_i ($ millions)	log Y_i	X_i log Y_i	X_i^2
1974	0	10.1	1.00432	0	0
1975	1	11.3	1.05308	1.05308	1
1976	2	13.8	1.13988	2.27976	4
1977	3	16.1	1.20683	3.62049	9
1978	4	17.1	1.23300	4.93200	16
1979	5	18.0	1.25527	6.27635	25
1980	6	20.2	1.30535	7.83210	36
1981	7	22.9	1.35984	9.51888	49
1982	8	24.5	1.38917	11.11336	64
1983	9	25.9	1.41330	12.71970	81
1984	10	27.6	1.44091	14.40910	100
1985	11	30.1	1.47857	16.26427	121
1986	12	34.8	1.54158	18.49896	144
1987	13	41.5	1.61805	21.03465	169
$n = 14$	91	313.9	18.43915	129.55270	819

SOURCE: Data are taken from Table 18.10.

and since

$$\overline{X} = \frac{\sum\limits_{i=1}^{n} X_i}{n} = \frac{91}{14} = 6.5$$

then

$$\log b_0 = \frac{\sum\limits_{i=1}^{n} \log Y_i}{n} - \overline{X} \log b_1 = \frac{18.43915}{14} - (6.5)(.0426296) \cong 1.03999$$

Since our first observed value in the time series was obtained for the year 1974, the fitted "trend line" can be expressed as

$$\log \hat{Y}_i = 1.03999 + .0426296X_i$$

where the origin is 1974 and X units $= 1$ year. However, the values for b_0 and b_1 may readily be obtained by taking the antilogs of the coefficients in this equation:

$$b_0 = \text{antilog } 1.03999 \cong 11.0$$

$$b_1 = \text{antilog } .0426296 \cong 1.1031$$

Thus the fitted exponential trend equation can be expressed as

$$\hat{Y}_i = 11.0(1.1031)^{X_i}$$

where the origin is 1974 and X units $= 1$ year.

The intercept $b_0 = 11.0$ is the fitted trend value representing payments (in millions of dollars) during the base year 1974. The value $(b_1 - 1) \times 100\% = 10.31\%$ is the annual compound growth rate in payments to the life-insurance company for interest on loans and for premium notes.

For forecasting purposes we may substitute the appropriate coded values of X into either of the two equations—depending on the type of calculator we have available. For example, to predict the trend in payments for the year 1991, we have

$$1991 \qquad \log \hat{Y}_{18} = 1.03999 + .0426296(17) = 1.7646932$$

$$\hat{Y}_{18} = \text{antilog } 1.7646932 = 58.2 \text{ millions of dollars}$$

or

$$1991 \qquad \hat{Y}_{18} = 11.0(1.1031)^{17} = 58.3 \text{ millions of dollars}$$

The differences in the forecasts are due to rounding.

The fitted exponential trend equation projected to 1991 is plotted in Figure 18.11 together with the original time series.

We have now seen the time-series data on payments to the life-insurance company for interest on loans and for premium notes fitted by three different models: linear, quadratic, and exponential. In Section 18.9 we will compare the results of these and other forecasting models to determine, *a posteriori*, the best fit. In Problems 18.51 and 18.52 on pages 775 and 776 the student will have the opportunity to use *a priori* methods to determine the appropriate model for a given series of data.

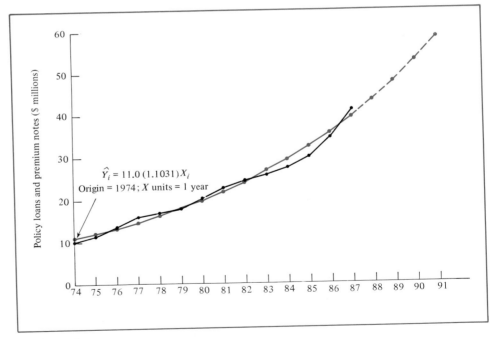

FIGURE 18.11
Fitting the exponential trend equation.
SOURCE: Data are taken from Table 18.12.

18.8.6 Isolating and Removing Trend from Annual Data: The Cyclical-Irregular Relatives

In the previous sections we studied trend as an aid to intermediate and long-term forecasting. However, as we have already noted, economists and/or business forecasters may also wish to study trend so that its influencing effects may be removed from the classical multiplicative time-series model and thereby provide the framework for short-run forecasting of general business activity. The procedure of isolating and eliminating a component factor from the data is called **decomposing the time series.** Since the method of least squares provides us with "fitted" trend values $\hat{Y}_i$ for each year in the series, we can easily remove the trend component T_i from our classical multiplicative time-series model (because in any given year the trend component T_i is estimated by $\hat{Y}_i$). Thus from Equation (18.7) the trend component may be removed through division as follows:

$$Y_i = T_i \cdot C_i \cdot I_i$$

so that

$$\frac{Y_i}{\hat{Y}_i} = \frac{T_i \cdot C_i \cdot I_i}{\hat{Y}_i}$$

but since $\hat{Y}_i = T_i$ we have

$$\frac{Y_i}{\hat{Y}_i} = \frac{T_i \cdot C_i \cdot I_i}{T_i} = C_i \cdot I_i$$

The ratios of the observed values to fitted trend values, $Y_i/\hat{Y}_i$, which are computed each year in the series, are called the **cyclical–irregular relatives.** These values, which fluctuate around a base of 1.0, depict both cyclical and irregular activity in the series.

TABLE 18.13   Obtaining the cyclical-irregular relatives

(1) Year	*(2)* X_i	*(3)* Y_i *($ millions)*	*(4)* *Fitted Trend,* $\hat{Y}_i = 8.8 + 2.1X_i$	*(5)* $Y_i/\hat{Y}_i$
1974	0	10.1	8.8	1.148
1975	1	11.3	10.9	1.037
1976	2	13.8	13.0	1.062
1977	3	16.1	15.1	1.066
1978	4	17.1	17.2	.994
1979	5	18.0	19.3	.933
1980	6	20.2	21.4	.944
1981	7	22.9	23.5	.974
1982	8	24.5	25.6	.957
1983	9	25.9	27.7	.935
1984	10	27.6	29.8	.926
1985	11	30.1	31.9	.944
1986	12	34.8	34.0	1.024
1987	13	41.5	36.1	1.150

SOURCE: Data are taken from Table 18.10.

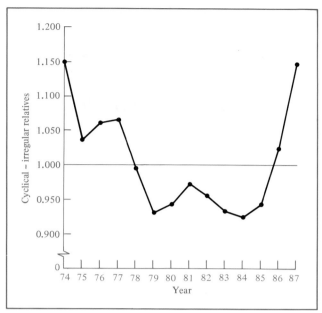

FIGURE 18.12
Plotting the cyclical–irregular relatives.
SOURCE: Data are taken from Table 18.13.

Returning to the previous example, the cyclical-irregular relatives are displayed in Table 18.13 for the 14-year time-series data reflecting annual payments to the life-insurance company both for interest on policy loans and for premium notes. To demonstrate the computations of these cyclical–irregular relatives the linear trend equation obtained in Section 18.8.3 by the method of least squares is utilized. In Table 18.13 the fitted trend values [column (4)] are determined by merely substituting the appropriately coded X values [column (2)] into the linear trend model. For each year in the series we see that the observed value [column (3)] is then divided by the fitted trend value [column (4)] to yield the cyclical–irregular relative [column (5)]. This series of cyclical–irregular relatives is plotted in Figure 18.12. With annual data, no further "decomposition" of the time series is undertaken.

Problems

18.11 Refer to the data from Problem 18.4 on page 702 on net revenues.
  (a) Plot the data on a chart.
  (b) Fit a least-squares linear trend line to the data and plot the line on your chart.
  (c) What are your trend forecasts for the years 1989, 1990, and 1991?

● **18.12** The data given in the table at the top of page 732 represent the annual net sales (in billions of dollars) obtained by General Motors Corporation from 1967 through 1986.

Annual net sales: General Motors Corporation

Year	1967	1968	1969	1970	1971	1972	1973	1974	1975	1976
Net sales	20.0	22.8	24.3	18.8	28.3	30.4	35.8	31.6	35.7	47.2

Year	1977	1978	1979	1980	1981	1982	1983	1984	1985	1986
Net sales	55.0	63.2	66.3	57.7	62.8	60.8	74.6	83.9	96.4	102.8

SOURCE: Data are taken from "Standard N.Y.S.E. Stock Reports," Vol. 48,
Standard & Poor's Corp., July 1981, and "Moody's Handbook of Common Stocks,"
Fall 1987 Edition.

(a) Plot the data on a chart.
(b) Fit a least-squares linear trend line to the data and plot the line on your chart.
(c) What was the annual growth in net sales over the 20 years?
(d) Determine the cyclical–irregular relatives for the data and plot your results on a separate chart.
(e) Before the data became available, what trend forecasts could you have made for the years 1987 through 1989?

18.13 The data given in the accompanying table represent the annual amount of corporate income taxes paid (in millions of dollars) to the federal government from 1974 through 1988 by a large construction company.

Corporate income taxes paid

Year	1974	1975	1976	1977	1978	1979	1980	1981	1982	1983	1984	1985	1986	1987	1988
Taxes paid	30.1	34.0	28.7	36.7	32.8	26.8	32.2	36.2	38.6	42.6	55.7	54.9	60.0	65.7	64.6

(a) Plot the data on a chart.
(b) Fit a least-squares linear trend line to the data and plot the line on your chart.
(c) What was the annual growth in corporate income tax payments over the 15 years?
(d) Determine the cyclical–irregular relatives for the data and plot your results on a separate chart.
(e) What are your trend forecasts for the years 1989, 1990, and 1991?

18.14 The data given in the accompanying table represent the annual gross passenger revenues (in billions of dollars) obtained by Pan American World Airways, Inc., over the 18-year period 1969 through 1986.

Annual passenger revenues: Pan American World Airways, Inc.

Year	1969	1970	1971	1972	1973	1974	1975	1976	1977	1978	1979	1980	1981	1982	1983	1984	1985	1986
Passenger revenues	1.05	1.13	1.18	1.31	1.43	1.53	1.61	1.66	1.91	2.20	2.48	4.02	3.80	3.72	3.79	3.68	3.48	3.04

SOURCE: Data are taken from "Moody's Handbook of Common Stocks," Summer,
1979 Edition and Fall, 1987 Edition.

(a) Plot the data on a chart.
(b) Fit a quadratic trend equation to the data and plot the curve on your chart.

(c) Fit an exponential trend equation to the data and plot the curve on your chart.

(d) For the exponential trend model, what has been the annual growth in passenger revenues over the 18 years.

(e) Before the data became available, what trend forecasts could you have made for the years 1987 through 1989

  (1) Using the quadratic trend model?

  (2) Using the exponential trend model?

18.15 The data given in the table below represent the amount of consumer (short-term and intermediate-term) installment credit (in millions of dollars) held annually by a large commercial bank from 1974 through 1988.

Consumer installment credit (Problem 18.15)

Year	1974	1975	1976	1977	1978	1979	1980	1981	1982	1983	1984	1985	1986	1987	1988
Credit held	31.3	33.2	37.9	42.4	45.4	51.2	59.8	69.5	72.5	78.7	85.4	112.4	136.2	154.2	145.8

(a) Plot the data on a chart.

(b) Fit a quadratic trend equation to the data and plot the curve on your chart.

(c) Fit an exponential trend equation to the data and plot the curve on your chart.

(d) For the exponential trend model, what has been the annual growth in the amount of consumer installment credit held by this commercial bank over the 15 years?

(e) For each of the models, what are the trend forecasts for the years 1989, 1990, and 1991?

18.9 CHOOSING THE APPROPRIATE FORECASTING MODEL

In Section 18.8 three commonly used time-series forecasting models were described: the linear-trend model, the quadratic trend model, and the exponential trend model. In Section 18.10 we shall examine two other widely used time-series forecasting models, one based on *moving averages* and the other based on *exponential smoothing*. Among such models as these (and others), which one should the researcher select for forecasting purposes? Three approaches are offered as guidelines for model selection:

1. Perform a residual analysis.
2. Measure the magnitude of the forecasting error.
3. Use the principal of parsimony.

The most widely used methods of determining the adequacy of a particular forecasting model are based on a judgment of how well it has fit a given set of time-series data. These methods, of course, assume that future movements in the series can be projected by a study of past behavior patterns. One such method is to perform a residual analysis; a second method is to measure the magnitude of the forecasting error.

The *forecast error* (e_t) in time period t may be defined as the difference between the actual value of the series (Y_t) and the predicted value of the series ($\hat{Y}_t$). That is,

$$\text{forecast error in time period } t = e_t = Y_t - \hat{Y}_t \qquad (18.20)$$

734 Chapter 18/Index Numbers, Time Series, and Business Forecasting

We may recall from our study of regression analysis in Sections 16.12 and 17.15 that such differences between the observed (Y_i) and fitted ($\hat{Y}_i$) data are known as *residuals*.

18.9.1 Residual Analysis

Once a particular model has been fitted to a given time series we may plot the residuals over the n time periods. As depicted in Figure 18.13(a), if the particular model fits adequately, the residuals represent the irregular component of the time series and, therefore, they should be randomly distributed throughout the series. On the other hand, as illustrated in the three remaining panels of Figure 18.13, if the particular model does not fit adequately, the residuals may demonstrate some systematic pattern such as a failure to account for trend (b), a failure to account for cyclical variation (c), or, with monthly data, a failure to account for seasonal variation (d).

18.9.2 Measuring the Forecast Error

If, after performing a residual analysis, the researcher still believes that two or more models appear to fit the data adequately, then a second method used for model selection is based on some measure of the magnitude of the forecast error. Numerous measures have been proposed (see References 2, 3, and 16) and, unfortunately, there is no consensus among researchers as to which particular measure is best for determining the most appropriate forecasting model.

Based on the principle of least squares, one measure which we have already used in regression analysis (see Sections 16.5 and 16.6) is the *unexplained variation*:

$$\text{unexplained variation} = \sum_{i=1}^{n} (Y_i - \hat{Y}_i)^2 \qquad \textbf{(18.20)}$$

For a particular model, this measure is based on the sum of squared differences between the actual and fitted values in a given time series. If a model were to fit the past time-series data *perfectly*, then unexplained variation would be zero. On the other hand, if a model were to fit the past time-series data *poorly*, the unexplained variation would be large. Thus when comparing the adequacy of two or more forecasting models, the one with the *minimum* unexplained variation can be selected as most appropriate based on past fits of the given time series.

Nevertheless, a major drawback to using the unexplained variation measure when comparing forecasting models is that it penalizes a model too much for large forecasting errors. That is, whenever there is a large discrepancy between Y_i and $\hat{Y}_i$ the computation for unexplained variation becomes magnified through the squaring process. For this reason, a measure that most researchers seem to prefer for assessing the appropriateness of various forecasting models is the **mean absolute deviation (MAD):**

$$\text{MAD} = \frac{\sum_{i=1}^{n} |Y_i - \hat{Y}_i|}{n} \qquad \textbf{(18.21)}$$

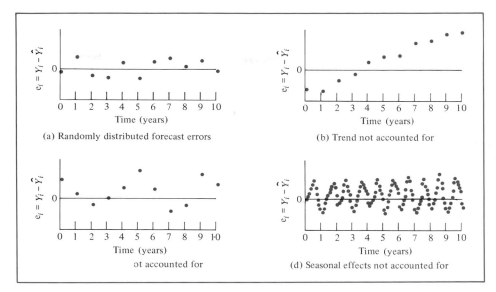

FIGURE 18.13
A residual analysis to study error patterns.

For a particular model, the MAD is a measure of the average of the absolute discrepancies between the actual and fitted values in a given time series. If a model were to fit the past time-series data *perfectly*, the MAD would be zero; if a model were to fit the past time-series data *poorly*, the MAD would be large. Hence when comparing the merits of two or more forecasting models, the one with the *minimum* MAD can be selected as most appropriate based on past fits of the given time series.

18.9.3 Principle of Parsimony

If, after performing a residual analysis and comparing the obtained MAD measures, the researcher still believes that two or more models appear to adequately fit the data, then a third method for model selection is based on the **principle of parsimony.** That is, the researcher should select the *simplest* model that gets the job done adequately.

18.9.4 A Comparison of Five Forecasting Methods

To illustrate the model selection process we again consider the time-series data on payments to the life-insurance company for interest on loans and for premium notes. Five forecasting methods are to be compared: two very simple methods and the three increasingly sophisticated trend models (linear, quadratic, and exponential) developed in Sections 18.8.3 through 18.8.5. The actual values (Y_i), the fitted values ($\hat{Y}_i$), and the residuals (e_i) for each of the five forecasting methods are displayed in Table 18.14 on page 736. At this time the reader is asked to perform a residual analysis for each of the forecasting methods in order to better understand the ensuing discussion (see Problem 18.22 on page 739).

TABLE 18.14   Comparison of five forecasting methods using the mean absolute deviation (MAD)

| | | Policy Loans and Premium Notes (millions of dollars) | Forecasting Method | | | | | | | | | |
| | | | Mean, $\hat{Y}_i = \overline{Y} = 22.4$ | | Naïve, $\hat{Y}_i = Y_{i-1}$ | | Linear, $\hat{Y}_i = 8.8 + 2.1X_i$ | | Quadratic, $\hat{Y}_i = 11.1 + 0.89X_i + 0.094X_i^2$ | | Exponential, $\hat{Y}_i = 11.0 \times (1.1031^{X_i})$ | |
Year	X_i	Y_i	$\hat{Y}_i$	e_i	$\hat{Y}_i$	e_i	$\hat{Y}_i$	e_i	$\hat{Y}_i$	e_i	$\hat{Y}_i$	e_i
1974	0	10.1	22.4	−12.3	****	****	8.8	1.3	11.1	−1.0	11.0	−.9
1975	1	11.3	22.4	−11.1	10.1	1.2	10.9	.4	12.1	−.8	12.1	−.8
1976	2	13.8	22.4	−8.6	11.3	2.5	13.0	.8	13.3	.5	13.4	.4
1977	3	16.1	22.4	−6.3	13.8	2.3	15.1	1.0	14.6	1.5	14.8	1.3
1978	4	17.1	22.4	−5.3	16.1	1.0	17.2	−.1	16.2	.9	16.3	.8
1979	5	18.0	22.4	−4.4	17.1	.9	19.3	−1.3	17.9	.1	18.0	.0
1980	6	20.2	22.4	−2.2	18.0	2.2	21.4	−1.2	19.8	.4	19.8	.4
1981	7	22.9	22.4	.5	20.2	2.7	23.5	−.6	21.9	1.0	21.9	1.0
1982	8	24.5	22.4	2.1	22.9	1.6	25.6	−1.1	24.2	.3	24.1	.4
1983	9	25.9	22.4	3.5	24.5	1.4	27.7	−1.8	26.7	−.8	26.6	−.7
1984	10	27.6	22.4	5.2	25.9	1.7	29.8	−2.2	29.4	−1.8	29.3	−1.7
1985	11	30.1	22.4	7.7	27.6	2.5	31.9	−1.8	32.3	−2.2	32.4	−2.3
1986	12	34.8	22.4	12.4	30.1	4.7	34.0	.8	35.3	−.5	35.7	−.9
1987	13	41.5	22.4	19.1	34.8	6.7	36.1	5.4	38.6	2.9	39.4	2.1
Absolute sum				100.7		31.4		19.8		14.7		13.7
MAD			$\dfrac{100.7}{14} = 7.193$		$\dfrac{31.4}{13} = 2.415$		$\dfrac{19.8}{14} = 1.414$		$\dfrac{14.7}{14} = 1.050$		$\dfrac{13.7}{14} = .979$	

The simplest forecasting method is the **mean forecast.** That is, in time period t we forecast the value of the series to be equal to the mean of the series:

$$\hat{Y}_t = \overline{Y} \qquad (18.22)$$

An analysis of the residuals listed in Table 18.14 indicates that this forecasting method is not adequate for these data. The trend effects and the cyclical effects in the series have been missed completely.

Another simple forecasting method is the **naïve autoregressive** (or **random walk) forecast.** That is, by taking advantage of the fact that there may be a high correlation between successive pairs of values in a time series, we may forecast the value in the series at time period t to be equal to the actual value observed in the previous period (that is, time period $t - 1$):

$$\hat{Y}_t = Y_{t-1} \qquad (18.23)$$

Here, too, an analysis of the residuals listed in Table 18.14 indicates that this forecasting method is inappropriate. The overall level of the time series has been entirely missed (all the e_i values are positive), as have the cyclical effects.[10]

Aside from the fact that the cyclical effects were unaccounted for in each case, a residual analysis for the three more sophisticated time-series models (linear, quadratic, and exponential) presented in Table 18.14 do not appear to exhibit any other systematic patterns. Since only 14 data points are observed, however, caution must be used when drawing such conclusions—particularly for the linear model, wherein the last residual (5.4) is so much larger than any of the others that it may very well be signaling a missed exponential type of trend effect.

To aid further in the selection process, the computations of the mean absolute deviation (MAD) for the five forecasting methods are also presented in Table 18.14. Interestingly, a comparison of the various MAD results for these data indicate that the more sophisticated the model, the better the fit. Therefore, based on these findings the exponential model may be selected for forecasting purposes with this time series. Nevertheless, it is to be noted that since the MAD values are fairly similar, many researchers might use the principle of parsimony and choose the quadratic model instead.

18.9.5 Model Selection: A Warning

Once a particular forecasting model is selected, it becomes imperative that the researcher appropriately monitor the chosen model. After all, the objective in selecting the model is to be able to project or forecast future movements in a set of time-series data. Unfortunately, such forecasting models are generally poor at detecting changes in the underlying structure of the time series. It is important then that such projections be examined together with those obtained through other types of forecasting methods such as the use of leading indicators. As soon as a *new* data value (Y_t) is observed in time period t it must be compared to its projection ($\hat{Y}_t$). If the difference is too large, the forecasting model should be revised. Such *adaptive-control procedures* are described in Reference 3.

Problems

18.16 Refer to Problem 18.11—net revenues—on page 731.
   (a) Perform a residual analysis.
   (b) Compute the MAD for your fitted model.
   (c) Does the linear trend model appear to give a good fit to these data?

● **18.17** Refer to Problem 18.12—annual net sales for General Motors Corporation—on page 731.
   (a) Perform a residual analysis.
   (b) Compute the MAD for your fitted model.

---

[10] Although such simple forecasting methods as the mean forecast and the naïve autoregressive forecast were inadequate for the particular time series studied here, it should be noted that if a given time series does not possess an overall upward or downward movement (that is, no long-term trend effect), such models may be useful. In these situations the two simple methods could be compared to models based on *moving averages* and *exponential smoothing* (to be described in Section 18.10) when attempting to make an appropriate selection for purposes of forecasting.

(c) Does the linear trend model appear to give a good fit to these data?
(d) Go to your library and, using appropriate sources, record the actual annual net sales for the years 1987 to the present.
  (1) Compare the actual net sales (Y_i) with the predicted net sales ($\hat{Y}_i$) from part (e) of Problem 18.12. Compute the MAD for the years 1987 to the present.
  (2) Compare the MAD for the fitted model in part (b) with the MAD for the predicted values in part (d)(1). Discuss.

18.18 Refer to Problem 18.13—corporate income tax payments—on page 732.
(a) Perform a residual analysis.
(b) Compute the MAD for your fitted model.
(c) Does the linear trend model appear to give a good fit to these data?

18.19 Refer to Problem 18.14—annual passenger revenues for Pan American World Airways—on page 732.
(a) Perform a residual analysis for each of your fitted models.
(b) Compute the MAD for each of your fitted models.
(c) Based on parts (a) and (b), which of the two models would you say is more appropriate?
(d) Go to your library and, using appropriate sources, record the actual annual passenger revenues for the years 1987 to the present.
  (1) Compare the actual passenger revenues (Y_i) with the predicted passenger revenues ($\hat{Y}_i$) from part (e) of Problem 18.14. Compute the MAD for the years 1987 to the present.
  (2) Compare the MAD for the fitted model in part (b) with the corresponding MAD based on the predicted values in part (d)(1). Do your conclusions in part (c) still hold? Discuss.

18.20 Refer to Problem 18.15—consumer installment credit—on page 733.
(a) Perform a residual analysis for each of your fitted models.
(b) Compute the MAD for each of your fitted models.
(c) Based on parts (a) and (b), which of the two models would you say is more appropriate?

18.21 The data given in the accompanying table represent the earnings per share of common stock (in dollars) held for the Minnesota Mining and Manufacturing Company over the 20-year period of 1967 through 1986.

Earnings per share

Year	1967	1968	1969	1970	1971	1972	1973	1974	1975	1976
Earnings per share	1.38	1.50	1.61	1.68	1.87	2.17	2.62	2.66	2.29	2.94

Year	1977	1978	1979	1980	1981	1982	1983	1984	1985	1986
Earnings per share	3.57	4.83	5.59	5.69	5.74	5.40	2.83	3.13	2.88	3.40

SOURCE: Data are taken from "Standard N.Y.S.E. Stock Reports," Standard & Poor's Corp., July 1981, April 1984, September 1987.

(a) Using the method of least squares, fit
  (1) the linear trend equation
  (2) the quadratic trend equation
  (3) the exponential trend equation
(b) Determine the most appropriate model through residual analysis. Discuss.
(c) Determine the most appropriate model by comparing the MADs. Do your results here concur with your findings in (b)? Discuss.

(d) Using your selected model, what trend forecasts for the years 1987 through 1989 could you have made?

(e) Go to your library and, using the most recent issue of "Standard N.Y.S.E. Reports," record the actual annual earnings per share for the years 1987 to the present.

    (1) Compare the actual earnings per share (Y_i) with the predicted earnings per share ($\hat{Y}_i$) from part (d). Compute the MAD for the years 1987 to the present.

    (2) Compare the MAD for the selected model in part (c) with the MAD for the predicted values in part (e)(1). Discuss.

18.22 Using the data displayed in Table 18.14 on page 736, perform a residual analysis for each of the five forcasting methods in order to assist in the process of model selection for forecasting purposes. Discuss your findings.

18.10 OTHER METHODS OF ANNUAL TIME-SERIES ANALYSIS: MOVING AVERAGES AND EXPONENTIAL SMOOTHING

Figure 18.14 depicts the number of passenger cars sold annually from automobile plants in the United States over the 27-year period of 1960 through 1986. When examining annual data such as these, our visual impression of the overall long-term tendencies or movements in the series is obscured by wide fluctuations in the cyclical and irregular components. It is then difficult to judge whether a linear or curvilinear trend will better fit a particular set of data, or, as in Figure 18.14, whether there is really any long-term downward or upward trend effect present in the data at all.

Under such conditions as these, the **method of moving averages** or the **method of exponential smoothing** may be utilized to "smooth" a series and thereby provide us with an impression as to the overall long-term pattern of movement in the data—free from unwanted cyclical or irregular disturbances.

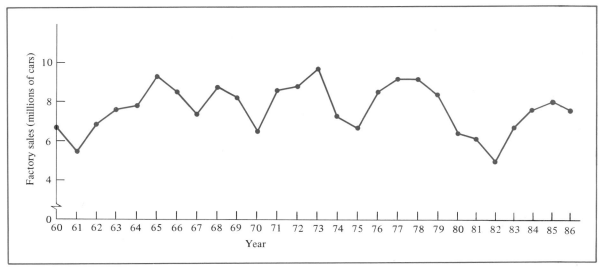

FIGURE 18.14
Factory sales of passenger cars from U.S. plants (1960–1986).
SOURCE: Data are taken from Series S-32, *Survey of Current Business* and *Business Statistics Supplement*, U.S. Department of Commerce.

18.10.1 Moving Averages

Unlike the method of least squares, the moving-averages method of studying trend is highly subjective and dependent upon the length of the period selected for constructing the averages. To eliminate the cylical fluctuations, the period chosen should be an integer value which corresponds to (or is a multiple of) the estimated average length of a cycle in the series. Thus for the retail sales data (Figure 18.2) it was subjectively estimated that the average cyclical length—measured from peak to peak or from trough to trough—was 3.5 years; therefore, since 7 is a multiple of 3.5, 7-year moving averages were fitted to the data in order to indicate the overall trend (Figure 18.4 on page 713).

But what are moving averages and how are they computed?

Moving averages for a chosen period of length L consist of a series of arithmetic means computed over time such that each mean is calculated for a sequence of observed values having that particular length L.

For example, 5-year moving averages consist of a series of means obtained over time by averaging out consecutive sequences containing five observed values. In general, for any series composed of n years, a moving average of length L (given by the symbol $\overline{Y}_i^L$) can be computed at year i as follows:

$$\overline{Y}_i^L = \frac{1}{L} \sum_{t=(1-L)/2}^{(L-1)/2} Y_{i+t} \tag{18.24}$$

where L = an *odd* number of years

$$i = \left(\frac{L-1}{2}\right) + 1, \left(\frac{L-1}{2}\right) + 2, \ldots, n - \left(\frac{L-1}{2}\right)$$

To illustrate the use of Equation (18.24), suppose we desire to compute 5-year moving averages from a series containing $n = 11$ years. Since $L = 5$, then $i = 3$, 4, 5, . . . , 9. Therefore we have

$$\overline{Y}_3^5 = 1/5(Y_1 + Y_2 + Y_3 + Y_4 + Y_5)$$

$$\overline{Y}_4^5 = 1/5(Y_2 + Y_3 + Y_4 + Y_5 + Y_6)$$

$$\overline{Y}_5^5 = 1/5(Y_3 + Y_4 + Y_5 + Y_6 + Y_7)$$

$$\overline{Y}_6^5 = 1/5(Y_4 + Y_5 + Y_6 + Y_7 + Y_8)$$

$$\overline{Y}_7^5 = 1/5(Y_5 + Y_6 + Y_7 + Y_8 + Y_9)$$

$$\overline{Y}_8^5 = 1/5(Y_6 + Y_7 + Y_8 + Y_9 + Y_{10})$$

$$\overline{Y}_9^5 = 1/5(Y_7 + Y_8 + Y_9 + Y_{10} + Y_{11})$$

We note that when the chosen period of length L is an odd number,[11] the moving average $\overline{Y}_i^L$ at year i is "centered" on i, the middle year in the consecutive sequence

---

[11] As we shall see in Section 18.13.2, moving averages with an even number of terms are more cumbersome to construct than those with an odd number of terms.

of L yearly values used to compute it. Moreover, we note that no moving averages can be obtained for the first $(L - 1)/2$ years or the last $(L - 1)/2$ years in the series.

Let us now take another look at the car sales series displayed in Figure 18.14. Table 18.15 presents the annual data on passenger car sales along with the computations for 3-year moving averages and 7-year moving averages. Both of these constructed series are plotted in Figure 18.15 with the original data (see page 742).

In practice, to compute 3-year moving averages, we first obtain a series of 3-year moving totals as indicated in column (3) of Table 18.15 and then divide each of these totals by 3. The results are given in column (4). For example, since our observed time series was first recorded in 1960, the first 3-year moving total consists of the sum of the first three annually recorded values—6.7, 5.5, and 6.9. This moving total, 19.1, is then "centered" so that the recording is made against the year 1961. To obtain the moving total for the year 1962—which consists of the observed annual sales data for the years 1961, 1962, and 1963—we merely add the next observed value in the time series (year 1963) to the previous moving total and then subtract the first (oldest) value in the series. This process continues so that the 3-year moving total for any particular year i in the series represents the sum of the observed value for year i along with the observed values for the year preceding it and the year following it. On the other hand, with 7-year moving totals, the result computed and recorded for the year i consists of the observed value in the time series for year i plus the three observed

TABLE 18.15   Three-year and seven-year moving averages of factory sales of passenger cars from U.S. plants (1960–1986)

(1) Year	(2) Millions of Cars Sold	(3) 3-Year Moving Total	(4) 3-Year Moving Average	(5) 7-Year Moving Total	(6) 7-Year Moving Average
1960	6.7	—	—	—	—
1961	5.5	19.1	6.4	—	—
1962	6.9	20.0	6.7	—	—
1963	7.6	22.3	7.4	52.4	7.5
1964	7.8	24.7	8.2	53.1	7.6
1965	9.3	25.7	8.6	56.4	8.1
1966	8.6	25.3	8.4	57.7	8.2
1967	7.4	24.8	8.3	56.6	8.1
1968	8.8	24.4	8.1	57.4	8.2
1969	8.2	23.5	7.8	56.9	8.1
1970	6.5	23.3	7.8	58.0	8.3
1971	8.6	23.9	8.0	57.9	8.3
1972	8.8	27.1	9.0	55.8	8.0
1973	9.7	25.8	8.6	56.1	8.0
1974	7.3	23.7	7.9	58.8	8.4
1975	6.7	22.5	7.5	59.4	8.5
1976	8.5	24.4	8.1	59.0	8.4
1977	9.2	26.9	9.0	55.7	8.0
1978	9.2	26.8	8.9	54.6	7.8
1979	8.4	24.0	8.0	52.9	7.6
1980	6.4	21.0	7.0	51.1	7.3
1981	6.2	17.6	5.9	49.5	7.1
1982	5.0	17.9	6.0	48.3	6.9
1983	6.7	19.3	6.4	47.4	6.8
1984	7.6	22.3	7.4	—	—
1985	8.0	23.1	7.7	—	—
1986	7.5	—	—	—	—

SOURCE: Data are taken from Series S-32, *Survey of Current Business* and *Business Statistics Supplement*, U.S. Department of Commerce.

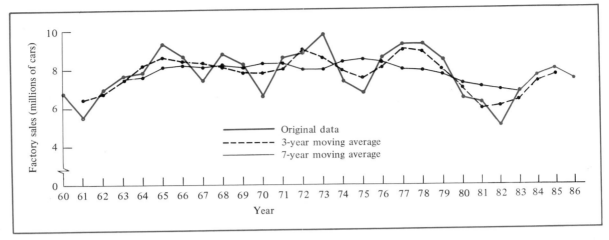

FIGURE 18.15
Plotting the 3-year and 7-year moving averages.
SOURCE: Data are taken from Table 18.15.

values which precede it and the three observed values which follow it. To "move the 7-year total" from one year to the next, we merely add on to the previous total the next observed value in the time series and remove the oldest value that had appeared in the previous total. This process continues through the series. The 7-year moving averages are then obtained by dividing the series of moving totals by 7.

We note from columns (3) and (4) of Table 18.15 that, in obtaining the 3-year moving averages, no result can be computed for the first or last observed value in the time series. Moreover, as seen in columns (5) and (6), when computing 7-year moving averages there are no results for the first three observed values or the last three values. This, of course, occurs because the first 7-year moving total for the data at hand consists of the number of passenger cars sold during the years 1960 through 1966, which is centered at 1963, while the last moving total consists of the number of car sales recorded in 1980 through 1986, which is centered at 1983.

From Figure 18.15 we can clearly see that the 7-year moving averages smooth the series a great deal more than do the 3-year moving averages, since the period is of longer duration. Unfortunately, however, as we previously had noted, the longer the period, the fewer the number of moving average values that can be computed and plotted. Therefore, selecting moving averages with periods of length greater than 7 years is usually undesirable since too many computed data points would be missing at the beginning and end of the series, making it more difficult to obtain an overall impression of the trend through the entire series.

18.10.2 Exponential Smoothing

Exponential smoothing is another technique that may be used to smooth a time series and thereby provide us with an impression as to the overall long-term movements in the data. In addition, the method of exponential smoothing can be utilized for obtaining short-term (one period into the future) forecasts for such time series as depicted in Figure 18.14 for which it is questionable as to what type of long-term trend effect, if any, is present in the data. In this respect, the technique possesses a distinct advantage over the method of moving averages. Essentially, the method of exponential smoothing derives its name because it provides us with an *exponentially weighted* moving average through the time series; that is, throughout the series each smoothing calculation or forecast is dependent upon all previously observed values. This is another advantage over the method of moving averages, which does not take into account all the observed values in this manner. With exponential smoothing, the weights assigned to the observed values decrease over time so that when a calculation is made, the most recently observed value receives the highest weight, the previously observed value receives the second highest weight, and so on, with the initially observed value receiving the lowest weight.

While the magnitude of work involved from this description may seem formidable, the calculations are really quite simple. If we may focus on the smoothing aspects of the technique (rather than the forecasting aspects), the formulas developed for exponentially smoothing a series in any time period i are based only on three terms—the presently observed value in the time series Y_i, the previously computed exponentially smoothed value ϵ_{i-1}, and some subjectively assigned weight or smoothing coefficient W. Thus to smooth a series at any time period i we have the following expression:[12]

$$\epsilon_i = WY_i + (1 - W)\epsilon_{i-1} \qquad (18.25)$$

where ϵ_i = value of the exponentially smoothed series being computed in time period i

ϵ_{i-1} = value of the exponentially smoothed series already computed in time period $i - 1$

Y_i = observed value of the times series in period i

W = subjectively assigned weight or smoothing coefficient (where $0 < W < 1$)

The choice of a smoothing coefficient or weight which we should assign to our time series is quite important since it will affect our results. Unfortunately, this selection

---

[12] That all i observed values in the time series are included in the computation of the exponentially smoothed value in time period i can be seen by noting that the present smoothed value is calculated using the smoothed value of the previous period, and that value, in turn, was calculated using the smoothed value from its previous period, and so on. Algebraically, this can be stated as follows:

In time period 1,

$$\epsilon_1 = Y_1$$

In time period 2,

$$\epsilon_2 = WY_2 + (1 - W)\epsilon_1 = WY_2 + (1 - W)Y_1$$

In time period 3,

$$\epsilon_3 = WY_3 + (1 - W)\epsilon_2 = WY_3 + (1 - W)[WY_2 + (1 - W)Y_1]$$
$$= WY_3 + W(1 - W)Y_2 + (1 - W)^2 Y_1$$

In general, in time period i,

$$\epsilon_i = WY_i + (1 - W)\epsilon_{i-1} = WY_i + W(1 - W)Y_{i-1} + W(1 - W)^2 Y_{i-2} + \cdots + (1 - W)^{(i-1)}Y_1$$

Thus we see that over time, as the integer value i gets large, the weights assigned to the earlier (older) values in the time series may become negligible.

is rather subjective. However, in regard to smoothing ability, we may observe from Figures 18.15 and 18.16 that a series of L term moving averages is related to an exponentially smoothed series having weight W as follows:

$$W = \frac{2}{L + 1} \qquad \text{(18.26)}$$

or

$$L = \frac{2}{W} - 1 \qquad \text{(18.27)}$$

From Equations (18.26) and (18.27) we note that with respect to smoothing ability, similarities are found between the 3-year series of moving averages (Figure 18.15) and the exponentially smoothed series having weight $W = .50$ (see Figure 18.16). In addition, we see that the series of 7-year moving averages (Figure 18.15) corresponds to the exponentially smoothed series having weight $W = .25$ (see Figure 18.16). By examining how our two smoothing series (one with $W = .25$ and the other with $W = .50$) fit the observed data in Figure 18.16, we may realize that the choice of a particular smoothing coefficient W is dependent upon the purpose of the user. If we desire only to smooth a series by eliminating unwanted cyclical and irregular variations, we should select a small value for W (closer to zero). On the other hand, if our goal is forecasting, we should choose a larger value for W (closer to 1). In the former case, the overall long-term tendencies of the series will be apparent; in the latter case, future short-term directions may be more adequately predicted.

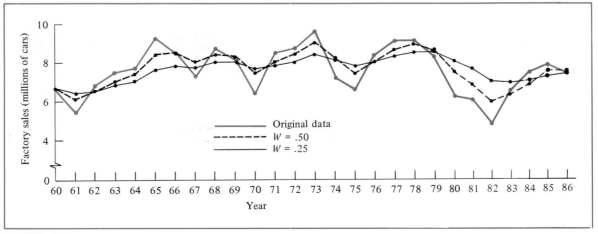

FIGURE 18.16
Plotting the exponentially smoothed series ($W = .50$ and $W = .25$).
SOURCE: Data are taken from Table 18.16.

TABLE 18.16   Exponentially smoothed series of factory sales of passenger cars from U.S. plants (1960–1986)

Year	Millions of Cars Sold	W = .50	W = .25
1960	6.7	6.7	6.7
1961	5.5	6.1	6.4
1962	6.9	6.5	6.5
1963	7.6	7.0	6.8
1964	7.8	7.4	7.0
1965	9.3	8.4	7.6
1966	8.6	8.5	7.8
1967	7.4	8.0	7.7
1968	8.8	8.4	8.0
1969	8.2	8.3	8.0
1970	6.5	7.4	7.6
1971	8.6	8.0	7.8
1972	8.8	8.4	8.0
1973	9.7	9.0	8.4
1974	7.3	8.2	8.1
1975	6.7	7.4	7.8
1976	8.5	8.0	8.0
1977	9.2	8.6	8.3
1978	9.2	8.9	8.5
1979	8.4	8.6	8.5
1980	6.4	7.5	8.0
1981	6.2	6.8	7.6
1982	5.0	5.9	7.0
1983	6.7	6.3	6.9
1984	7.6	7.0	7.1
1985	8.0	7.5	7.3
1986	7.5	7.5	7.4

SOURCE: Data are taken from Table 18.15

To use the exponentially weighted moving average for purposes of forecasting rather than for smoothing, we merely take the smoothed value in our current period of time (say time period i) as our projected estimate of the observed value of the time series in the following time period, $i + 1$—that is,

$$\hat{Y}_{i+1} = \epsilon_i \tag{18.28}$$

Thus, for example, to forecast the number of passenger cars to be sold from automobile plants in the United States during the year 1987, we would use the smoothed value for the year 1986 as its estimate. From Table 18.16, for a smoothing coefficient of $W = .50$, that projection is 7.5 million cars. Once the observed data for the year 1987 become available, we can use Equation (18.25) to make a forecast for the year 1988 (by obtaining the smoothed value for 1987) as follows:

$$\epsilon_{1987} = WY_{1987} + (1 - W)\epsilon_{1986}$$

current smoothed value = (W) (current observed value)
$+ (1 - W)$ (previous smoothed value)

or, in terms of forecasting,

$$\hat{Y}_{1988} = WY_{1987} + (1 - W)\hat{Y}_{1987}$$

$$\text{new forecast} = (W)(\text{current observed value})$$
$$+ (1 - W)(\text{current forecast})$$

The computations for the two smoothed series (using respective weights of $W = .25$ and $W = .50$) are listed in Table 18.16 and, as previously indicated, are plotted in Figure 18.16 along with the original time series. To demonstrate the computations, let us consider for a moment the exponentially smoothed series having weight $W = .25$. For example, as a starting point we merely use the initial observed value $Y_{1960} = 6.7$ as our first smoothed value ($\epsilon_{1960} = 6.7$) and as our first forecast value ($\hat{Y}_{1961} = 6.7$). Now using the observed value of the time series for the year 1961 ($Y_{1961} = 5.5$) we may smooth the series for the year 1961 by computing

$$\epsilon_{1961} = WY_{1961} + (1 - W)\epsilon_{1960}$$
$$= (.25)(5.5) + (.75)(6.7) = 6.4 \text{ million}$$

Of course, this smoothed value also serves as the forecast value for the following year ($\hat{Y}_{1962} = 6.4$). The process continues in the same manner until all the values in the series have been smoothed and the results plotted in Figure 18.16 on page 744.

The exponentially weighted moving-average methods for smoothing and forecasting have gained wide recognition over the past two decades as guides to managerial planning and control. Available computer packages are invaluable for handling the laborious calculations (References 13, 14, 19, and 20) inherent in these methods.

Problems

● **18.23** The data given in the accompanying table represent the annual number of employees (in thousands) in an oil supply company for the years 1969 through 1988.

Number of employees

Year	Number	Year	Number	Year	Number
1969	1.45	1977	2.06	1985	1.88
1970	1.55	1978	1.80	1986	2.00
1971	1.61	1979	1.73	1987	2.08
1972	1.60	1980	1.77	1988	1.88
1973	1.74	1981	1.90		
1974	1.92	1982	1.82		
1975	1.95	1983	1.65		
1976	2.04	1984	1.73		

(a) Plot the data on a chart.
(b) Fit a 3-year moving average to the data and plot the results on your chart.
(c) Using a smoothing coefficient of .50, exponentially smooth the series and plot the results on your chart.
(d) What is your exponentially smoothed forecast for the trend in 1989?
(e) Compute the MAD for each fitted model. Compare the results.

18.24 The data given in the accompanying table on page 747 represent the annual sales dollars (in millions) for a food-processing company for the years 1963 through 1988.

Annual sales dollars (millions)

Year	Sales Dollars	Year	Sales Dollars	Year	Sales Dollars
1963	41.6	1972	53.2	1981	36.4
1964	48.0	1973	53.3	1982	38.4
1965	51.7	1974	51.6	1983	42.6
1966	55.9	1975	49.0	1984	34.8
1967	51.8	1976	38.6	1985	28.4
1968	57.0	1977	37.3	1986	23.9
1969	64.4	1978	43.8	1987	27.8
1970	60.8	1979	41.7	1988	42.1
1971	56.3	1980	38.3		

(a) Plot the data on a chart.

(b) Fit a 7-year moving average to the data and plot the results on your chart.

(c) Using a smoothing coefficient of .25, exponentially smooth the series and plot the results on your chart.

(d) What is your exponentially smoothed forecast for the trend in 1989?

(e) Compute the MAD for each fitted model. Compare the results.

18.25 Refer to the data in Problem 18.13—corporate income tax payments—on page 732.

(a) Fit a 3-year moving average to the data.

(b) Using a smoothing coefficient of .50, exponentially smooth the series.

(c) What is your exponentially smoothed forecast for the trend in 1989?

(d) Compute the MAD for each fitted model. Compare the results with those from Problem 18.18 [part (b)] on page 738. Discuss.

18.11 THE HOLT-WINTERS FORECASTING METHOD

The **Holt-Winters forecasting method** (Reference 17) is a sophisticated extension of the exponential smoothing approach described in the previous section. Whereas the exponential smoothing procedure provides an impression of the overall, long-term movements in the data and permits short-term forecasting, the more elaborate Holt-Winters technique also allows for the study of trend through intermediate and/or long-term forecasting into the future. The differences between the two procedures are highlighted in Figure 18.17.

From panel (a) we observe that exponential smoothing can be used most effectively

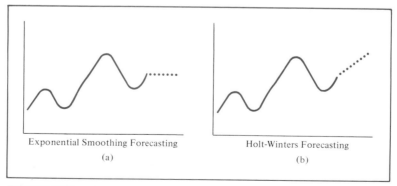

FIGURE 18.17
Exponential smoothing and the Holt-Winters method.

for short-term forecasting (one period into the future). We can, of course, extend this forecast numerous time periods into the future. This would be meaningful if there were no overall upward or downward trend in the series. However, if any upward or downward movement does exist, such a horizontal projection, like that of the mean forecast method of Section 18.9.4, will entirely miss it. On the other hand, the Holt-Winters forecasting method of panel (b) is designed to detect such phenomena. Hence, the Holt-Winters technique concurrently provides for study of overall movement level and future trend in a series.

To use the Holt-Winters forecasting method at any time period i we must continuously estimate the level of the series (that is, the smoothed value ϵ_i) and the value of trend (T_i). This is achieved through the solution to the following equations:

Level	$\epsilon_i = U(\epsilon_{i-1} + T_{i-1}) + (1 - U)Y_i$	(18.29a)
Trend	$T_i = VT_{i-1} + (1 - V)(\epsilon_i - \epsilon_{i-1})$	(18.29b)

where ϵ_i = level of the smoothed series being computed in time period i

ϵ_{i-1} = level of the smoothed series already computed in time period $i - 1$

T_i = value of the trend component being computed in time period i

T_{i-1} = value of the trend component already computed in time period $i - 1$

Y_i = observed value of the time series in period i

U = subjectively assigned smoothing constant (where $0 < U < 1$)

V = subjectively assigned smoothing constant (where $0 < V < 1$)

To begin computations, we set $\epsilon_2 = Y_2$ and $T_2 = Y_2 - Y_1$ and choose smoothing constants for U and V. We then compute ϵ_i and T_i for all i years, $i = 3, 4, \ldots, n$.

To illustrate the Holt-Winters forecasting method, let us return to the time series presented in Table 18.8 (on page 719) and plotted in Figure 18.6 (on page 719), which represents the annual income taxes paid to the federal government for the 15-year period 1973 through 1987 by residents of a midwestern city. The computations are shown in Table 18.17 with selected constants $U = .3$ and $V = .3$.

To begin, we set

$$\epsilon_2 = Y_2 = 61.5$$

and

$$T_2 = Y_2 - Y_1 = 61.5 - 55.4 = 6.1$$

Choosing smoothing constants $U = .3$ and $V = .3$, Equations (18.29a) and (18.29b) become

$$\epsilon_i = .3\,(\epsilon_{i-1} + T_{i-1}) + .7(Y_i)$$

and

$$T_i = .3\,(T_{i-1}) + .7\,(\epsilon_i - \epsilon_{i-1})$$

As an example, for 1975, the third year, $i = 3$ and we have

$$\epsilon_3 = .3\,(61.5 + 6.1) + .7\,(68.7) = 68.4$$

TABLE 18.17 Using the Holt-Winters method on annual income taxes paid to the federal government (1973–1987)

Year	i	Y_i Taxes (millions of dollars)	$U(\epsilon_{i-1} + T_{i-1}) + (1 - U)Y_i = \epsilon_i$	$VT_{i-1} + (1 - V)(\epsilon_i - \epsilon_{i-1}) = T_i$
1973	1	55.4		
1974	2	61.5	$\cdots$ 61.5	$\cdots$ 6.1
1975	3	68.7	.3 (61.5 + 6.1) + .7 (68.7) = 68.4	.3 (6.1) + .7 (68.4 − 61.5) = 6.7
1976	4	87.2	.3 (68.4 + 6.7) + .7 (87.2) = 83.6	.3 (6.7) + .7 (83.6 − 68.4) = 12.7
1977	5	90.4	.3 (83.6 + 12.7) + .7 (90.4) = 92.2	.3 (12.7) + .7 (92.2 − 83.6) = 9.8
1978	6	86.2	.3 (92.2 + 9.8) + .7 (86.2) = 90.9	.3 (9.8) + .7 (90.9 − 92.2) = 2.0
1979	7	94.7	.3 (90.9 + 2.0) + .7 (94.7) = 94.2	.3 (2.0) + .7 (94.2 − 90.9) = 2.9
1980	8	103.2	.3 (94.2 + 2.9) + .7 (103.2) = 101.4	.3 (2.9) + .7 (101.4 − 94.2) = 5.9
1981	9	119.0	.3 (101.4 + 5.9) + .7 (119.0) = 115.5	.3 (5.9) + .7 (115.5 − 101.4) = 11.6
1982	10	122.4	.3 (115.5 + 11.6) + .7 (122.4) = 123.8	.3 (11.6) + .7 (123.8 − 115.5) = 9.3
1983	11	131.6	.3 (123.8 + 9.3) + .7 (131.6) = 132.0	.3 (9.3) + .7 (132.0 − 123.8) = 8.5
1984	12	157.6	.3 (132.0 + 8.5) + .7 (157.6) = 152.5	.3 (8.5) + .7 (152.5 − 132.0) = 16.9
1985	13	181.0	.3 (152.5 + 16.9) + .7 (181.0) = 177.5	.3 (16.9) + .7 (177.5 − 152.5) = 22.6
1986	14	217.8	.3 (177.5 + 22.6) + .7 (217.8) = 212.5	.3 (22.6) + .7 (212.5 − 177.5) = 31.3
1987	15	244.1	.3 (212.5 + 31.3) + .7 (244.1) = 244.0	.3 (31.3) + .7 (244.0 − 212.5) = 31.4

SOURCE: Data are taken from Table 18.8.

and

$$T_3 = .3 \,(6.1) + .7 \,(68.4 - 61.5) = 6.7$$

Continuing, these values would then be used in Equations (18.29a) and (18.29b) to obtain ϵ_4 and T_4, and so on, yielding the results shown in Table 18.17.

To use the Holt-Winters method for forecasting we assume that all future trend movements will continue from the most recent smoothed level ϵ_n. Hence, to forecast j years into the future we have

$$\hat{Y}_{n+j} = \epsilon_n + j(T_n) \qquad (18.30)$$

where $\hat{Y}_{n+j}$ = forecasted value j years into the future

ϵ_n = level of the smoothed series computed in the most recent time period n

T_n = value of the trend component computed in the most recent time period n

j = number of years into the future

Using ϵ_{15} and T_{15}, the latest estimates of current level and trend, respectively, our forecasts of federal income tax payments for the years 1988 through 1991 are obtained from Equation (18.30) as follows:

$$\hat{Y}_{n+j} = \epsilon_n + j(T_n)$$

1988:   1 year ahead $\hat{Y}_{16} = \epsilon_{15} + 1(T_{15}) = 244.0 + 31.4$
  = 275.4 millions of dollars

1989:   2 years ahead $\hat{Y}_{17} = \epsilon_{15} + 2(T_{15}) = 244.0 + 2(31.4)$
  = 306.8 millions of dollars

1990:   3 years ahead $\hat{Y}_{18} = \epsilon_{15} + 3(T_{15}) = 244.0 + 3(31.4)$
                                               $= 338.2$ millions of dollars

1991:   4 years ahead $\hat{Y}_{19} = \epsilon_{15} + 4(T_{15}) = 244.0 + 4(31.4)$
                                               $= 369.6$ millions of dollars

The data and the forecasts are plotted in Figure 18.18.

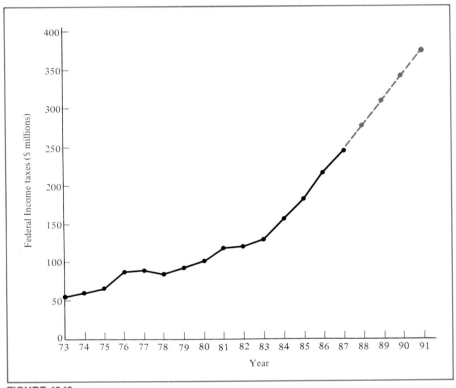

FIGURE 18.18
Using the Holt-Winters method on annual income taxes paid to the federal government.

Problems

✗ **18.26**   Refer to Figure 18.17 on page 747. Describe why the Holt-Winters forecasting method is superior to the exponential smoothing approach when dealing with such a time series.

● **18.27**   Given an annual time series with 20 consecutive observations, if the smoothed level for the most recent value is 34.2 and the corresponding trend level is computed to be 5.6,
(a) What is your forecast for the coming year?
(b) What is your forecast five years from now?

18.28   Given the following series from $n = 15$ consecutive time periods:

3   5   6   8   10   10   12   15   16   13   16   17   22   19   24

use the Holt-Winters method (with $U = .30$ and $V = .30$) to forecast the series for the sixteenth through twentieth periods.

18.29 Given the following series from $n = 10$ consecutive time periods:

$$137 \quad 125 \quad 116 \quad 110 \quad 103 \quad 96 \quad 86 \quad 79 \quad 72 \quad 66$$

use the Holt-Winters method (with $U = .20$ and $V = .20$) to forecast the series for the eleventh through fourteenth periods.

18.30 Refer to Problem 18.12—annual net sales for General Motors Corporation—on page 731.
 (a) Use the Holt-Winters method (with $U = .20$ and $V = .20$) to forecast annual net sales from 1987 through 1989.
 (b) Compare your results with the forecasts based on the linear trend model.
  (1) Compute the MAD for these Holt-Winters forecasts. Compare this MAD with that obtained from the linear trend model in part (d)(1) of Problem 18.17 on page 737.
  (2) Which of the two forecasting models would you say is more appropriate? Discuss.

18.12 AUTOREGRESSIVE MODELING FOR ANNUAL TIME-SERIES FORECASTING

Another useful approach to forecasting with annual time-series data is based on **autoregressive modeling.**[13] Frequently, we find that the values of a series of financial data at particular points in time are highly correlated with the values which precede and succeed them. A first-order autocorrelation refers to the magnitude of the association between consecutive values in a time series. A second-order autocorrelation refers to the magnitude of the relationship between values two periods apart. Moreover, a pth-order autocorrelation refers to the size of the correlation between values in a time series that are p periods apart. To obtain a better historical fit of our data and, at the same time, be able to make useful forecasts of their future behavior, we may take advantage of the potential autocorrelation features inherent in such data by considering autoregressive modeling methods.

A set of autoregressive models are expressed by Equations (18.31), (18.32), and (18.33).

First-Order Autoregressive Model
$$Y_i = \omega + \psi_1 Y_{i-1} + \delta_i \qquad \text{(18.31)}$$

Second-Order Autoregressive Model
$$Y_i = \omega + \psi_1 Y_{i-1} + \psi_2 Y_{i-2} + \delta_i \qquad \text{(18.32)}$$

p^{TH}-Order Autoregressive Model
$$Y_i = \omega + \psi_1 Y_{i-1} + \psi_2 Y_{i-2} + \cdots + \psi_p Y_{i-p} + \delta_i \qquad \text{(18.33)}$$

where Y_i = the observed value of the series at time i
Y_{i-1} = the observed value of the series at time $i - 1$

---

[13] It should be noted that the exponential smoothing model of Section 18.10, the Holt-Winters model of Section 18.11, and the autoregressive models described herein are all special cases of **autoregressive integrated moving average (ARIMA)** models developed by Box and Jenkins (Reference 4). The Box-Jenkins approach, however, is beyond the scope of this text.

$$Y_{i-2} = \text{the observed value of the series at time } i - 2$$
$$Y_{i-p} = \text{the observed value of the series at time } i - p$$
$$\omega = \text{fixed parameter to be estimated from least-squares regression analysis}$$
$$\psi_1, \psi_2, \ldots, \psi_p = \text{autoregression parameters to be estimated from least-squares regression analysis}$$
$$\delta_i = \text{a nonautocorrelated random (error) component (with 0 mean and constant variance)}$$

A first-order autoregressive model [Equation (18.31)] is concerned with only the correlation between consecutive values in a series. A second-order autoregressive model [Equation (18.32)] considers the effects of the relationship between consecutive values in a series as well as the correlation between values two periods apart. A pth-order autoregressive model [Equation (18.33)] deals with the effects of relationships between consecutive values, values two periods apart, and so on—up to values p periods apart. The selection of an appropriate autoregression model, then, is no easy task. We must weigh the advantages due to parsimony with the concern of failing to take into account important autocorrelation behavior inherent in the data. On the other hand, we must be equally concerned with selecting a high-order model requiring the estimation of numerous, unnecessary parameters—especially if n, the number of observations in the series, is not too large. The reason for this is that p out of n data values will be lost in obtaining an estimate of ψ_p when comparing each data value Y_i with its "fairly near neighbor" Y_{i-p} which is p periods apart (that is, the comparisons are Y_{1+p} versus Y_1, Y_{2+p} versus Y_2, $\ldots$, and Y_n versus Y_{n-p}). To illustrate this, suppose we have the following series of $n = 7$ consecutive values:

$$31 \quad 34 \quad 37 \quad 35 \quad 36 \quad 43 \quad 40$$

Comparison schema for autoregressive models of order one and order two are established in the accompanying table:

i	First-Order Autoregressive Model (Y_i versus Y_{i-1})	Second-Order Autoregressive Model (Y_i versus Y_{i-1} and Y_i versus Y_{i-2})
1	31 ↔ ⋯	31 ↔ ⋯ and 31 ↔ ⋯
2	34 ↔ 31	34 ↔ 31 and 34 ↔ ⋯
3	37 ↔ 34	37 ↔ 34 and 37 ↔ 31
4	35 ↔ 37	35 ↔ 37 and 35 ↔ 34
5	36 ↔ 35	36 ↔ 35 and 36 ↔ 37
6	43 ↔ 36	43 ↔ 36 and 43 ↔ 35
7	40 ↔ 43	40 ↔ 43 and 40 ↔ 36
	(1 comparison is lost for regression analysis)	(2 comparisons are lost for regression analysis)

Once a model is selected and least-squares regression methods are used to obtain estimates of the parameters, the next step would be to determine the appropriateness of this model. Either the researcher has selected a given pth-order autoregressive model based on previous experiences with similar data, or else he would select, as a starting point, a model with several parameters and then eliminate those which do not contribute significantly. In this latter approach, Newbold (Reference 17) suggests the following test for the significance of the highest-order autoregressive parameter in the fitted model:

$$H_0: \quad \psi_p = 0 \qquad \text{(The highest-order parameter is 0)}$$

against the two-sided alternative

$$H_1: \quad \psi_p \neq 0 \qquad \text{(The parameter } \psi_p \text{ is significantly meaningful)}$$

The test statistic, readily obtainable from the output of various multiple regression programs (which provide estimates of regression coefficients and standard errors), is approximated by

$$Z \cong \frac{\hat{\psi}_p}{S_{\hat{\psi}_p}} \tag{18.34}$$

where $\hat{\psi}_p$ = the estimate of the highest-order parameter ψ_p in the autoregressive model
$S_{\hat{\psi}_p}$ = the standard deviation of $\hat{\psi}_p$

Using an α level of significance, the decision rule is to reject H_0 if $Z > Z_{\alpha/2}$ (the upper-tail critical value from a standardized normal distribution) or if $Z < -Z_{\alpha/2}$ (the lower-tail critical value from a standardized normal distribution), and not to reject H_0 if $-Z_{\alpha/2} \leq Z \leq Z_{\alpha/2}$.

If the null hypothesis that $\psi_p = 0$ is not rejected, we may conclude that the selected model contains too many estimated parameters. The highest-order term would then be discarded and an autoregressive model of order $p - 1$ would be obtained through least-squares regression. A test of the hypothesis that the "new" highest-order term is 0 would then be repeated.

This testing and modeling procedure continues until we reject H_0. When this occurs, we know that our highest-order parameter is significant and we are ready to use the particular model for forecasting purposes.

The fitted pth-order autoregressive model has the following form:

$$\hat{Y}_i = \hat{\omega} + \hat{\psi}_1 Y_{i-1} + \hat{\psi}_2 Y_{i-2} + \cdots + \hat{\psi}_p Y_{i-p} \tag{18.35}$$

where $\hat{Y}_i$ = the fitted value of the series at time i
Y_{i-1} = the observed value of the series at time $i - 1$
Y_{i-2} = the observed value of the series at time $i - 2$
Y_{i-p} = the observed value of the series at time $i - p$
$\hat{\omega}, \hat{\psi}_1, \hat{\psi}_2, \ldots, \hat{\psi}_p$ = regression estimates of the parameters $\omega, \psi_1, \psi_2, \ldots, \psi_p$

To forecast j years into the future from the current nth time period we have

$$\hat{Y}_{n+j} = \hat{\omega} + \hat{\psi}_1 \hat{Y}_{n+j-1} + \hat{\psi}_2 \hat{Y}_{n+j-2} + \cdots + \hat{\psi}_p \hat{Y}_{n+j-p} \tag{18.36}$$

where $\hat{\omega}$, $\hat{\psi}_1$, $\hat{\psi}_2$, . . . , $\hat{\psi}_p$ are the regression estimates of the parameters ω, ψ_1, ψ_2, . . . , ψ_p; where j is the number of years into the future; and where, for $k > 0$, $\hat{Y}_{n+k}$ is the forecast of Y_{n+k} from the current time period, while for $k \leq 0$, $\hat{Y}_{n+k}$ is the observed value Y_{n+k}.

Thus, to make forecasts j years into the future from, say, a $p = $ 3rd-order autoregressive model, we need only the most recent $p = 3$ observed data values Y_n, Y_{n-1}, and Y_{n-2} and the estimates of the parameters ω, ψ_1, ψ_2, and ψ_3 from a multiple regression program. To forecast one year ahead, Equation (18.36) becomes

$$\hat{Y}_{n+1} = \hat{\omega} + \hat{\psi}_1 Y_n + \hat{\psi}_2 Y_{n-1} + \hat{\psi}_3 Y_{n-2}$$

To forecast two years ahead, Equation (18.36) becomes

$$\hat{Y}_{n+2} = \hat{\omega} + \hat{\psi}_1 \hat{Y}_{n+1} + \hat{\psi}_2 Y_n + \hat{\psi}_3 Y_{n-1}$$

To forecast three years ahead, Equation (18.36) becomes

$$\hat{Y}_{n+3} = \hat{\omega} + \hat{\psi}_1 \hat{Y}_{n+2} + \hat{\psi}_2 \hat{Y}_{n+1} + \hat{\psi}_3 Y_n$$

To forecast four years ahead, Equation (18.36) becomes

$$\hat{Y}_{n+4} = \hat{\omega} + \hat{\psi}_1 \hat{Y}_{n+3} + \hat{\psi}_2 \hat{Y}_{n+2} + \hat{\psi}_3 \hat{Y}_{n+1}$$

and so on.

To demonstrate the autoregressive modeling technique let us return once more to the time series presented in Table 18.8 (on page 719) and plotted in Figure 18.6 (on page 719) which represents the annual income tax payments to the federal government for the 15-year period 1973 through 1987 by residents of a midwestern city. Table 18.18 displays the set-up for a third-order autoregressive model. Note that $p = 3$ observations out of $n = 15$ are lost in the comparisons needed for developing the (multiple regression) autoregressive model.

TABLE 18.18   Developing the third-order autoregressive model on annual income taxes paid to the federal government (1973–1987)

Year	i	"Dependent" Variable Y_i	Predictor Variables		
			Y_{i-1}	Y_{i-2}	Y_{i-3}
1973	1	55.4	*	*	*
1974	2	61.5	55.4	*	*
1975	3	68.7	61.5	55.4	*
1976	4	87.2	68.7	61.5	55.4
1977	5	90.4	87.2	68.7	61.5
1978	6	86.2	90.4	87.2	68.7
1979	7	94.7	86.2	90.4	87.2
1980	8	103.2	94.7	86.2	90.4
1981	9	119.0	103.2	94.7	86.2
1982	10	122.4	119.0	103.2	94.7
1983	11	131.6	122.4	119.0	103.2
1984	12	157.6	131.6	122.4	119.0
1985	13	181.0	157.6	131.6	122.4
1986	14	217.8	181.0	157.6	131.6
1987	15	244.1	217.8	181.0	157.6

Using the LAG and REGRESS commands in Minitab (Reference 15), the following third-order autoregressive model is fitted to the income tax data:

$$\hat{Y}_i = -11.04 + 1.154 Y_{i-1} - .199 Y_{i-2} + .290 Y_{i-3}$$

Next, one might test for the significance of the highest-order parameter. On the other hand, if a researcher's experiences with similar data permit him to hypothesize that a third-order autoregressive model is appropriate for this time series, our fitted model can be used directly for forecasting purposes without the need for testing for parameter significance. Therefore, to demonstrate the forecasting procedure for our third-order autoregressive model, we use the estimates

$$\hat{\omega} = -11.04, \quad \hat{\psi}_1 = 1.154, \quad \hat{\psi}_2 = -.199, \quad \hat{\psi}_3 = .290$$

as well as the three most current data values

$$Y_{13} = 181.0, \quad Y_{14} = 217.8, \quad Y_{15} = 244.1$$

Our forecasts of federal income tax payments for the years 1988 to 1991 in this midwestern city are obtained from Equation (18.36) as follows:

$$\hat{Y}_{n+j} = -11.04 + 1.154 \hat{Y}_{n+j-1} - .199 \hat{Y}_{n+j-2} + .290 \hat{Y}_{n+j-3}$$

1988: 1 year ahead
$$\hat{Y}_{16} = -11.04 + 1.154 (244.1) - .199 (217.8) + .290 (181.0)$$
$$= 279.8 \text{ millions of dollars}$$

1989: 2 years ahead
$$\hat{Y}_{17} = -11.04 + 1.154 (279.8) - .199 (244.1) + .290 (217.8)$$
$$= 326.4 \text{ millions of dollars}$$

1990: 3 years ahead
$$\hat{Y}_{18} = -11.04 + 1.154 (326.4) - .199 (279.8) + .290 (244.1)$$
$$= 380.7 \text{ millions of dollars}$$

1991: 4 years ahead
$$\hat{Y}_{19} = -11.04 + 1.154 (380.7) - .199 (326.4) + .290 (279.8)$$
$$= 444.5 \text{ millions of dollars}$$

Prior to forecasting, however, most researchers would have preferred to test for the significance of the parameters of a fitted model. Using the output from the REGRESS command in Minitab, the highest-order parameter estimate $\hat{\psi}_3$ for the fitted third-order autoregressive model is .290 with a standard deviation $S_{\hat{\psi}_3}$ of .449.

To test

$$H_0: \quad \psi_3 = 0$$

against

$$H_1: \quad \psi_3 \neq 0$$

we have, from Equation (18.34),

$$Z \cong \frac{\hat{\psi}_3}{S_{\hat{\psi}_3}} = \frac{.290}{.499} = .65$$

Using a .05 level of significance, the two-tailed test has critical Z values of ± 1.96. Since $Z = +.65 < +1.96$, the upper-tail critical value under the standardized normal distribution (Table E.2), we may not reject H_0, and we would conclude that the third-order parameter of the autoregressive model is not significantly important and it can be deleted.

Using the REGRESS command once again, a second-order autoregressive model is run. From the Minitab output the highest-order parameter estimate $\hat{\psi}_2$ is .022 with a standard deviation $S_{\hat{\psi}_2} = .400$.

To test

$$H_0: \quad \psi_2 = 0$$

against

$$H_1: \quad \psi_2 \neq 0$$

we have, from Equation (18.34),

$$Z \cong \frac{\hat{\psi}_2}{S_{\hat{\psi}_2}} = \frac{.022}{.400} = .06$$

Testing again at the .05 level of significance, since $Z = +.06 < +1.96$, we may not reject H_0, and we would conclude that the second-order parameter of the autoregressive model is not significantly important and it can be eliminated.

Using the REGRESS command once more, a first-order autoregressive model is obtained. From the Minitab output we now write the fitted model as

$$\hat{Y}_i = -5.992 + 1.173 Y_{i-1}$$

Moreover, $S_{\hat{\psi}_1}$, the standard deviation of the estimated first-order autoregressive parameter, is .0494. To test

$$H_0: \quad \psi_1 = 0$$

against

$$H_1: \quad \psi_1 \neq 0$$

we have, from Equation (18.34),

$$Z \cong \frac{\hat{\psi}_1}{S_{\hat{\psi}_1}} = \frac{1.173}{.0494} = 23.74$$

Testing again at the $\alpha = .05$ level of significance, since $Z = +23.74 > +1.96$, we this time reject H_0, and we would conclude that the first-order parameter of the autoregressvie model is significantly important.

Our "model-building" approach has led to the selection of the parsimonious first-order autoregressive model as the most appropriate for the given data. Using the estimates $\hat{\omega} = -5.992$ and $\hat{\psi}_1 = 1.173$ as well as the most recent data value $Y_{15} = 244.1$, our forecasts of federal income tax payments for the years 1988 to 1991 are obtained from Equation (18.36) as follows:

$$\hat{Y}_{n+j} = -5.992 + 1.173 \hat{Y}_{n+j-1}$$

1988: 1 year ahead $\quad \hat{Y}_{16} = -5.992 + 1.173\,(244.1)$
$\qquad\qquad\qquad\qquad\qquad = 280.3$ millions of dollars

1989: 2 years ahead $\quad \hat{Y}_{17} = -5.922 + 1.173\,(280.3)$
$\qquad\qquad\qquad\qquad\qquad = 322.8$ millions of dollars

1990: 3 years ahead $\quad \hat{Y}_{18} = -5.992 + 1.173\,(322.8)$
$\qquad\qquad\qquad\qquad\qquad = 372.7$ millions of dollars

$$1991: \quad 4 \text{ years ahead} \quad \hat{Y}_{19} = -5.992 + 1.173\,(372.7)$$
$$= 431.2 \text{ millions of dollars}$$

The data and the forecasts are plotted in Figure 18.19.

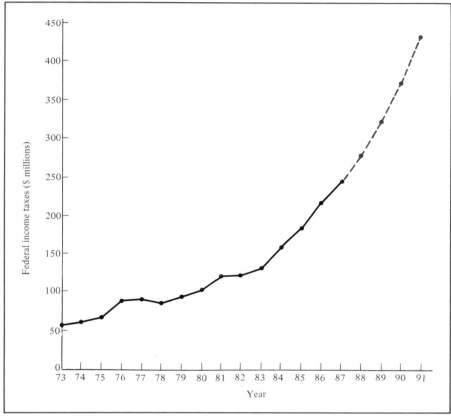

FIGURE 18.19
Using a first-order autoregressive model on annual income taxes paid to the
federal government.

Problems

● **18.31** Given an annual time series with 40 consecutive observations. If you were to fit a fifth-order autoregression model,
  (a) How many comparisons would be lost in the development of the autoregressive model?
  (b) How many parameters would you need to estimate?
  (c) Which of the original 40 values would you need for forecasting?
  (d) Express the model.
  (e) Write a general equation to indicate how you would forecast j years into the future.

  18.32 The following second-order autoregressive model at the top of page 758 would be fitted to the federal income tax data in Table 18.18 on page 754:

$$\hat{Y}_i = -7.155 + 1.162Y_{i-1} + .022Y_{i-2}$$

(a) Write a general expression to be used for forecasting over the next j years.

(b) Obtain your forecasts from 1988 through 1991.

(c) Discuss the similarities/differences between these results and those obtained from the first-order autoregressive model on page 756 and from the third-order model on page 755.

18.33 An annual time series with 17 consecutive values is obtained. A third-order autoregressive model is fitted to the data and has the following estimated parameters and standard deviations:

$$\hat{\omega} = 4.50, \quad \hat{\psi}_1 = 1.80, \quad \hat{\psi}_2 = .70, \quad \hat{\psi}_3 = .20$$
$$S_{\hat{\psi}_1} = .50, \quad S_{\hat{\psi}_2} = .30, \quad S_{\hat{\psi}_3} = .10$$

At the .05 level of significance, test the appropriateness of the fitted model.

18.34 Refer to Problem 18.33. The three most recent observations are

$$Y_{15} = 23, \quad Y_{16} = 28, \quad Y_{17} = 34$$

(a) Forecast the series for the next year and the following year.

(b) Suppose, when testing for the appropriateness of the fitted model in Problem 18.33, the standard deviations were

$$S_{\hat{\psi}_1} = .45, \quad S_{\hat{\psi}_2} = .35, \quad S_{\hat{\psi}_3} = .15$$

(1) What would you conclude?

(2) Discuss how you would proceed if forecasting were still your main objective.

18.35 Refer to Problem 18.12—annual net sales for General Motors Corporation—on page 731.

(a) Fit a first-order autoregressive model.

(b) Test for the significance of the first-order autoregressive parameter.

(c) If appropriate, forecast annual net sales from 1987 through 1989.

(1) Compare your results with the forecasts based on the linear trend model and the Holt-Winters method (Problems 18.17 on page 737 and 18.30 on page 751) by computing the MAD for the first-order autoregressive model.

(2) What model would you say did the best forecasting of this series since 1986? Discuss.

18.13 TIME-SERIES ANALYSIS OF MONTHLY DATA

Figure 18.20 depicts the monetary value (in millions of dollars) of residential construction contracts issued on a monthly basis from January 1982 through December 1987 for a well-known construction company. For such monthly time series as these the classical multiplicative time-series model includes the **seasonal** component in addition to the trend, cyclical, and irregular components. The model is expressed by Equation (18.8) on page 716 as

$$Y_i = T_i \cdot S_i \cdot C_i \cdot I_i$$

Basically, there are two major goals of time-series analysis with monthly data. Either we are interested in *forecasting* some future monthly movements, or we are interested in *decomposing* the time series by isolating and removing the trend, seasonal, and irregular components so that we can concentrate on how a particular series correlates with overall business activity; that is, we may determine whether a particular series can be considered as a *leading*, *coinciding*, or *lagging* indicator of overall economic activity based upon whether the cyclical component of the series exhibits tendencies to precede, match, or follow, respectively, the cyclical behavior of the overall economy.

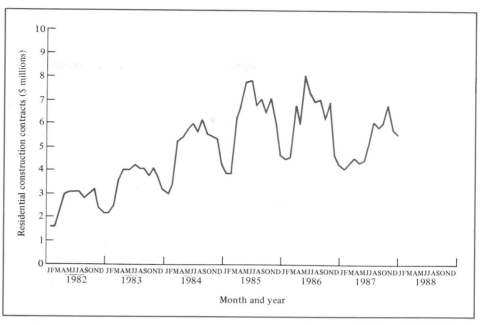

FIGURE 18.20
Value of monthly residential construction contracts issued (in millions of dollars, January 1982 to December 1987), for a well-known construction company.

18.13.1 Fitting and Forecasting Linear Trends: Converting Annual Series to Monthly Series

When dealing with monthly time series which can be fitted with a linear trend, much labor can be saved without too much loss in accuracy if we form the *annual aggregates* from our monthly totals and fit a least-squares trend line to the annual data. The resulting expression, in annual terms, can easily be converted to monthly terms by dividing the intercept by 12 and the slope by 144 and then "shifting the series." To demonstrate this, Table 18.19 presents the calculations necessary for fitting a least-squares trend line to the annual value of residential construction contracts issued over the 6-year period of 1982 through 1987.

TABLE 18.19 Computation of least-squares trend line for 6 years of data

Year	X_i	Y_i (millions of dollars)	$X_i Y_i$	X_i^2
1982	0	31.3	0	0
1983	1	43.7	43.7	1
1984	2	62.0	124.0	4
1985	3	74.9	224.7	9
1986	4	74.7	298.8	16
1987	5	63.2	316.0	25
$n = 6$	15	349.8	1,007.2	55

SOURCE: Data are taken from construction company annual reports.

Since this series contains an even number of years, the appropriate coding scheme given in Section 18.8.3 is employed, and, using Equations (18.11) and (18.12), we have

$$b_1 = \frac{\sum_{i=1}^{n} X_i Y_i - \frac{\left(\sum_{i=1}^{n} X_i\right)\left(\sum_{i=1}^{n} Y_i\right)}{n}}{\sum_{i=1}^{n} X_i^2 - \frac{\left(\sum_{i=1}^{n} X_i\right)^2}{n}} = \frac{132.7}{17.5} = 7.5829$$

and since

$$\overline{Y} = \frac{\sum_{i=1}^{n} Y_i}{n} = \frac{349.8}{6} = 58.3 \quad \text{and} \quad \overline{X} = \frac{\sum_{i=1}^{n} X_i}{n} = \frac{15}{6} = 2.5$$

then

$$b_0 = \overline{Y} - b_1\overline{X} = 58.3 - (7.5829)(2.5) = 39.34$$

Thus the annually fitted trend line is given by

$$\hat{Y}_i = 39.34 + 7.5829X_i$$

where origin = 1982 and X units = 1 year.

To convert this annual trend model to a monthly basis we first divide the intercept by 12 and the slope by 144. This gives us

$$\hat{Y}_i = \frac{39.34}{12} + \frac{7.5829}{144}X_i = 3.2786 + .05266X_i$$

where origin = June 30–July 1, 1982 and X units = 1 month.

We may recall that when dealing with data on an annual basis, the data representing the entire year are recorded in the middle of the year. Hence when converting from an annual trend equation to a monthly trend equation, our resulting origin also falls in the middle of the year—between June 30 and July 1. Rather than stating that the monthly trend equation has an origin between the two months June and July, we merely shift the origin of the series to the middle of July by adding in one half the value of the slope. That is, to shift to July 15, 1982, we have

$$\hat{Y}_i = 3.2786 + .05266(X_i + .5)$$
$$= 3.2786 + .05266X_i + .02633$$

so that

$$\hat{Y}_i = 3.3049 + .05266X_i$$

where origin = July 15, 1982, and X units = 1 month.

For this series the new slope indicates that (on a monthly basis) the monetary values of residential construction contracts issued for this company have been increasing at a rate of 0.05266 millions of dollars (that is, 52.66 thousands of dollars) per month.

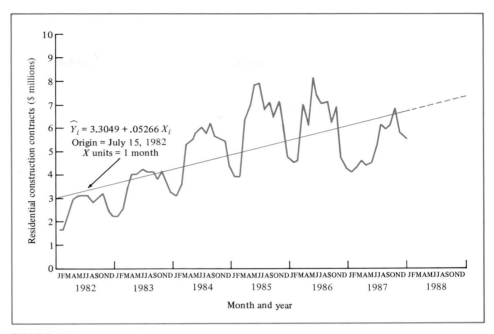

FIGURE 18.21
Fitting the least-squares trend line.
SOURCE: Data are taken from Tables 18.19 and 18.20.

This is depicted in Figure 18.21, where the slope of the fitted monthly trend line exhibits a slight tendency to increase over time. Of course, this equation may be used to project future monthly trend values in residential construction contracts. However, since such monthly time series are influenced by seasonal factors, we shall not make any future forecasts until we have developed a **seasonal index** which accounts for the month-to-month fluctuations. This will be accomplished in the following section.

18.13.2 Computing the Seasonal Index

It is important to isolate and study the seasonal movements in a monthly time series for two reasons. First, by knowing the value of the seasonal component for any particular month, the economist can easily adjust and improve upon trend projections for forecasting purposes. Second, by knowing the value of the seasonal component the economist can decompose the time series by eliminating its influences—along with those pertaining to trend and irregular fluctuations—and thereby concentrate on the cyclical movements of the series. If, as often it is assumed, the seasonal movements are fairly constant over time, the construction of a seasonal index may be illustrated from Tables 18.20 and 18.21 on pages 762–763.

To start, a series of 12-month moving totals is obtained. However, as depicted in column (3) of Table 18.20, when recording these moving totals the results are centered between the two middle months comprising each respective moving total. For example, the first moving total, which consists of the months of January 1982 through December 1982, is recorded between June and July 1982; the second moving total, which consists of the months of February 1982 through January 1983, is recorded

TABLE 18.20 Developing the seasonal index

(1) Year and Month		(2) Residential Construction Contracts ($ millions)	(3) 12-Month Moving Totals	(4) 2-Month Moving Totals of 12-Month Moving Totals	(5) Centered 12-Month Moving Averages	(6) Ratios to Moving Average	(7) Seasonal Index	(8) Deseasonalized Data
1982	Jan	1.6	—	—	—	—	.698	2.3
	Feb	1.6		—	—	—	.765	2.1
	Mar	2.3	—	—	—	—	1.080	2.1
	Apr	3.0	—	—	—	—	1.114	2.7
	May	3.1	—	—	—	—	1.158	2.7
	Jun	3.1		—	—	—	1.172	2.6
	Jul	3.1	31.4	63.4	2.64	1.174	1.116	2.8
	Aug	2.8	32.0	64.9	2.70	1.037	1.121	2.5
	Sep	3.0	32.9	67.1	2.80	1.071	1.033	2.9
	Oct	3.2	34.2	69.4	2.89	1.107	1.103	2.9
	Nov	2.4	35.2	71.3	2.97	.808	.895	2.7
	Dec	2.2	36.1	73.3	3.05	.721	.746	2.9
1983	Jan	2.2	37.2	75.4	3.14	.701	.698	3.2
	Feb	2.5	38.2	77.7	3.24	.772	.765	3.3
	Mar	3.6	39.5	79.8	3.32	1.084	1.080	3.3
	Apr	4.0	40.3	81.5	3.40	1.176	1.114	3.6
	May	4.0	41.2	83.7	3.49	1.146	1.158	3.5
	Jun	4.2	42.5	86.0	3.58	1.173	1.172	3.6
	Jul	4.1	43.5	87.8	3.66	1.120	1.116	3.7
	Aug	4.1	44.3	89.6	3.73	1.099	1.121	3.7
	Sep	3.8	45.3	92.3	3.85	.987	1.033	3.7
	Oct	4.1	47.0	95.5	3.98	1.030	1.103	3.7
	Nov	3.7	48.5	98.8	4.12	.898	.895	4.1
	Dec	3.2	50.3	102.4	4.27	.749	.746	4.3
1984	Jan	3.0	52.1	105.8	4.41	.680	.698	4.3
	Feb	3.5	53.7	109.5	4.56	.768	.765	4.6
	Mar	5.3	55.8	113.4	4.72	1.123	1.080	4.9
	Apr	5.5	57.6	116.6	4.86	1.132	1.114	4.9
	May	5.8	59.0	119.7	4.99	1.162	1.158	5.0
	Jun	6.0	60.7	122.5	5.10	1.176	1.172	5.1
	Jul	5.7	61.8	124.5	5.19	1.098	1.116	5.1
	Aug	6.2	62.7	125.8	5.24	1.183	1.121	5.5
	Sep	5.6	63.1	127.2	5.30	1.057	1.033	5.4
	Oct	5.5	64.1	129.5	5.40	1.019	1.103	5.0
	Nov	5.4	65.4	132.8	5.53	.976	.895	6.0
	Dec	4.3	67.4	136.7	5.70	.754	.746	5.8
1985	Jan	3.9	69.3	139.7	5.82	.670	.698	5.6
	Feb	3.9	70.4	141.7	5.90	.661	.765	5.1
	Mar	6.3	71.3	143.5	5.98	1.054	1.080	5.8
	Apr	6.8	72.2	146.0	6.08	1.118	1.114	6.1
	May	7.8	73.8	148.2	6.18	1.262	1.158	6.7
	Jun	7.9	74.4	149.2	6.22	1.270	1.172	6.7
	Jul	6.8	74.8	150.2	6.26	1.086	1.116	6.1
	Aug	7.1	75.4	151.5	6.31	1.125	1.121	6.3
	Sep	6.5	76.1	152.8	6.37	1.020	1.033	6.3
	Oct	7.1	76.7	152.6	6.36	1.116	1.103	6.4
	Nov	6.0	75.9	152.1	6.34	.946	.895	6.7
	Dec	4.7	76.2	151.8	6.32	.744	.746	6.3
1986	Jan	4.5	75.6	151.4	6.31	.713	.698	6.4
	Feb	4.6	75.8	151.6	6.32	.728	.765	6.0
	Mar	6.9	75.8	151.3	6.30	1.095	1.080	6.4
			75.5					

(continued on next page)

TABLE 18.20   (Continued)

(1) Year and Month		(2) Residential Construction Contracts ($ millions)	(3) 12-Month Moving Totals	(4) 2-Month Moving Totals of 12-Month Moving Totals	(5) Centered 12-Month Moving Averages	(6) Ratios to Moving Average	(7) Seasonal Index	(8) Deseasonalized Data
	Apr	6.0	75.3	150.8	6.28	.955	1.114	5.4
	May	8.1	74.0	149.3	6.22	1.302	1.158	7.0
	Jun	7.3	73.6	147.6	6.15	1.187	1.172	6.2
	Jul	7.0	73.2	146.8	6.12	1.144	1.116	6.3
	Aug	7.1	72.9	146.1	6.09	1.166	1.121	6.3
	Sep	6.2	70.6	143.5	5.98	1.037	1.033	6.0
	Oct	6.9	69.0	139.6	5.82	1.186	1.103	6.3
	Nov	4.7	65.4	134.4	5.60	.839	.895	5.3
	Dec	4.3	63.2	128.6	5.36	.802	.746	5.8
1987	Jan	4.1	62.3	125.5	5.23	.784	.698	5.9
	Feb	4.3	61.1	123.4	5.14	.837	.765	5.6
	Mar	4.6	61.0	122.1	5.09	.904	1.080	4.3
	Apr	4.4	60.9	121.9	5.08	.866	1.114	3.9
	May	4.5	62.0	122.9	5.12	.879	1.158	3.9
	Jun	5.1	63.3	125.3	5.22	.977	1.172	4.4
	Jul	6.1	—	—	—	—	1.116	5.5
	Aug	5.9	—	—	—	—	1.121	5.3
	Sep	6.1	—	—	—	—	1.033	5.9
	Oct	6.8	—	—	—	—	1.103	6.2
	Nov	5.8	—	—	—	—	.895	6.5
	Dec	5.6	—	—	—	—	.746	7.5

SOURCE: Data are taken from construction company annual reports.

TABLE 18.21   Computing the seasonal index from the median of monthly ratios to moving averages

Month	Year 1982	1983	1984	1985	1986	1987	Median	Seasonal Index
January	—	{ .701}	.680	.670	.713	.784	.701	.698
February	—	.772	{ .768}	.661	.728	.837	.768	.765
March	—	{1.084}	1.123	1.054	1.095	.904	1.084	1.080
April	—	1.176	1.132	{1.118}	.955	.866	1.118	1.114
May	—	1.146	{1.162}	1.262	1.302	.879	1.162	1.158
June	—	1.173	{1.176}	1.270	1.187	.977	1.176	1.172
July	1.174	{1.120}	1.098	1.086	1.144	—	1.120	1.116
August	1.037	1.099	1.183	{1.125}	1.166	—	1.125	1.121
September	1.071	.987	1.057	1.020	{1.037}	—	1.037	1.033
October	{1.107}	1.030	1.019	1.116	1.186	—	1.107	1.103
November	.808	{.898}	.976	.946	.839	—	.898	.895
December	.721	{.749}	.754	.744	.802	—	.749	.746
Totals							12.045	12.001 ↓ 12.000

$$\text{seasonal index} = \frac{(12.000)(\text{median})}{12.045}$$

SOURCE: Data are taken from Table 18.20.

between July and August 1982; and so on. To center these results within a particular month, "2-month moving totals of the 12-month moving totals" are obtained as indicated in column (4) of Table 18.20. The first result, which consists of the total indicated between June and July plus that between July and August, is centered in July 1982.[14] By dividing these totals in column (4) by 24, the **centered moving averages** are obtained as shown in column (5). *These centered moving averages are said to consist of the trend and cyclical components of the series.* The original data [column (2)] are then divided by the respective centered moving averages [column (5)] yielding the **ratio to moving averages** depicted in column (6). *Essentially, these ratios to moving averages represent the seasonal and irregular fluctuations in the series,* since the division of the observed data [column (2)] by the centered moving averages [column (5)] effectively eliminates trend and cyclical influences as demonstrated in Equation (18.37):

$$\frac{Y_i}{\text{centered moving average}_i} = \frac{T_i \cdot S_i \cdot C_i \cdot I_i}{T_i \cdot C_i} = S_i \cdot I_i \qquad \textbf{(18.37)}$$

To form the seasonal index, the ratios to moving averages data from Table 18.20 are rearranged according to monthly values as depicted in Table 18.21.

From Table 18.21 it is seen that for each month the irregular variations can be eliminated if the median of the various obtained ratios to moving averages is used as an indicator of seasonal activity over time. As shown in Table 18.21, these median values are then adjusted so that the total value of the seasonal indexes over the year is 12.0 and the average value of each (monthly) seasonal index is 1.0. Thus we note that a seasonal index of .698 for the month of January indicates that the value of residential construction contracts issued in January is only 69.8% of the monthly average, while a seasonal index is 1.172 for the month of June indicates that the value of contracts issued in June is 17.2% better than average.

18.13.3   Graphing the Seasonal Index: The Seasonal Subseries Plot

A modern graphical device for studying the seasonal indexes and their component ratios to moving averages is the **seasonal subseries plot** (Reference 18).

Figure 18.22 depicts the seasonal subseries plot for our data on residential construction contracts. It is developed from the data contained in Table 18.21. To obtain such a graph, we first plot the twelve monthly seasonal indexes with a series of equally spaced horizontal lines. For each month, we then plot the consecutive sequence of annual ratios to moving averages and connect these points to their seasonal index line with a series of vertical lines.[15]

---

[14] If we reflect on this computation, we will realize that these centered values presented in column (4) really represent a 13-month weighted moving total where the results are centered in the middle of the series (the seventh month). Moreover, the centered month receives a weight of 2, the 5 months preceding it receive a weight of 2, the 5 months following it receive a weight of 2, while the extremes—the first and last months in the moving total—receive a weight of 1.

[15] A seasonal subseries plot can be obtained by using the Exec*U*Stat package (Reference 14).

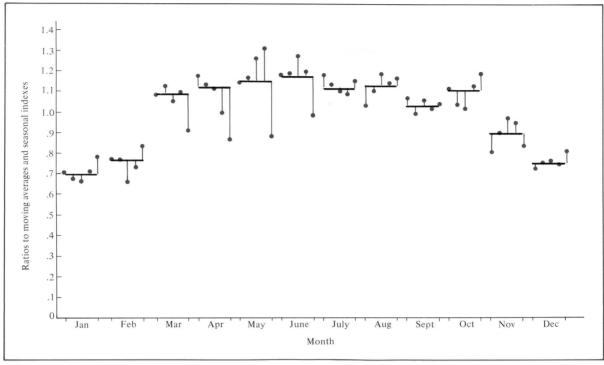

FIGURE 18.22
Seasonal subseries plot of value of residential construction contracts issued.

The vertical distances between the ratios to moving averages and their corresponding seasonal indexes indicate

1. The magnitude of the fluctuations within a particular month
2. Potential trends within a month over time
3. Possible patterns of change (which may obviate the value of the indexes)

From Figure 18.22, the most striking visual impression is the large negative discrepancies between the March through June seasonal indexes and the corresponding 1987 ratios to moving averages. Since these values were the last four recorded, it may be indicative of a change in seasonal patterns and require a recomputation of a new index as the next twelve months of data become available.

18.13.4 Using the Seasonal Index in Forecasting

To use the seasonal index to adjust a trend projection for forecasting purposes, we merely multiply the projected trend value for a particular month by the corresponding seasonal index for that month. For example, using our model, the projected monthly trend values in residential construction contracts to be issued for this company over the year 1990 are listed in column (1) of Table 18.22 on page 766. The respective monthly seasonal indexes are displayed in column (2). Adjusting for seasonal fluctuations, the product of the various projected monthly trend values with their respective seasonal indexes yields the set of monthly forecasts shown in column (3).

TABLE 18.22 Adjusting least-squares trend projections by seasonal indexes for forecasting purposes

Month	(1) Monthly Trend Projection for Year 1990	(2) Seasonal Index	(3) Forecast
January	7.7283	.698	5.3944
February	7.7810	.765	5.9525
March	7.8337	1.080	8.4604
April	7.8863	1.114	8.7853
May	7.9390	1.158	9.1934
June	7.9916	1.172	9.3662
July	8.0443	1.116	8.9774
August	8.0970	1.121	9.0767
September	8.1496	1.033	8.4185
October	8.2023	1.103	9.0471
November	8.2549	.895	7.3881
December	8.3076	.746	6.1975

SOURCE: Data are taken from Table 18.21 and the annual trend model.

18.13.5 Deseasonalizing the Data

The seasonal index may also be used for isolating and removing the effects of seasonal influences on the data. When this is achieved in conjunction with the elimination of trend and irregular effects, the cyclical component may be examined. Hence from

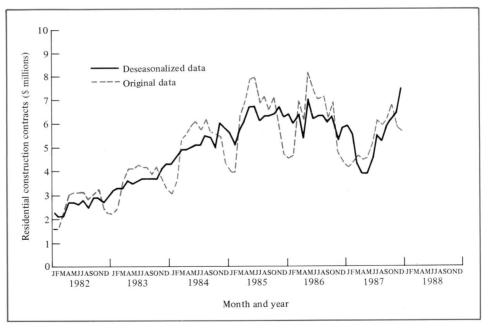

FIGURE 18.23
Value of residential construction contracts issued—original data and deseasonalized data.
SOURCE: Data are taken from table 18.20.

Table 18.20, to ''deseasonalize'' the data and thereby eliminate the seasonal effects, we merely divide each observed value in the monthly time series [column (2)] by the seasonal index for that month [column (7)]. The results are shown in column (8), and the deseasonalized series is plotted in Figure 18.23 along with the original series on page 766.

In terms of our classical multiplicative time-series model,

$$Y_i = T_i \cdot S_i \cdot C_i \cdot I_i$$

the deseasonalized series[16] is given by

$$\frac{Y_i}{S_i} = \frac{T_i \cdot S_i \cdot C_i \cdot I_i}{S_i} = T_i \cdot C_i \cdot I_i \qquad (18.38)$$

Therefore if the trend component were also removed, we would be left with a series of **cyclical–irregular relatives**—$C_i \cdot I_i$. Hence from Table 18.23 the fitted trend values [column (3)], which were obtained from the linear trend model, are divided into the deseasonalized series [column (2)] yielding the cyclical–irregular relatives in column (4)—that is,

$$\frac{T_i \cdot C_i \cdot I_i}{\hat{Y}_i} = \frac{T_i \cdot C_i \cdot I_i}{T_i} = C_i \cdot I_i \qquad (18.39)$$

18.13.6 Studying the Cyclical Component

Unlike annual data, the irregular fluctuations of a monthly time series are often removed by using 3-month weighted moving averages in which the middle value receives a weight of 2 while the two end values each receive a weight of 1. Thus from Table 18.23, for the series of cyclical–irregular relatives [column (4)], the set of 3-month weighted moving totals [column (5)] is obtained. These weighted moving totals are then divided by 4 to yield a series of isolated **cyclical relatives** [column (6)], and the time-series decomposition is completed; that is,

$$\frac{C_i \cdot I_i}{I_i} = C_i \qquad (18.40)$$

These cyclical relatives are plotted in Figure 18.24. Business forecasters have considered the series concerning monetary value of residential construction contracts in the entire construction industry to be a leading indicator of overall economic activity. Nevertheless, our construction company may or may not be typical of the industry.

---

[16] Many researchers refer to a *deseasonalized series* as a *seasonally adjusted series*.

TABLE 18.23   Isolating the cyclical component by time-series decomposition

(1) Year and Month		(2) Deseasonalized Data	(3) Trend $\hat{Y}_i$	(4) Cyclical-Irregular Relatives	(5) 3-Month Weighted Moving Totals	(6) Cyclical Relatives
1982	Jan	2.3	2.9889	.770	—	—
	Feb	2.1	3.0416	.690	2.829	.707
	Mar	2.1	3.0943	.679	2.906	.726
	Apr	2.7	3.1469	.858	3.239	.810
	May	2.7	3.1996	.844	3.345	.836
	Jun	2.6	3.2522	.799	3.289	.822
	Jul	2.8	3.3049	.847	3.238	.810
	Aug	2.5	3.3576	.745	3.187	.797
	Sep	2.9	3.4102	.850	3.282	.820
	Oct	2.9	3.4629	.837	3.292	.823
	Nov	2.7	3.5155	.768	3.186	.796
	Dec	2.9	3.5682	.813	3.278	.820
1983	Jan	3.2	3.6209	.884	3.479	.870
	Feb	3.3	3.6735	.898	3.566	.892
	Mar	3.3	3.7262	.886	3.623	.906
	Apr	3.6	3.7788	.953	3.705	.926
	May	3.5	3.8315	.913	3.706	.926
	Jun	3.6	3.8842	.927	3.707	.927
	Jul	3.7	3.9368	.940	3.734	.934
	Aug	3.7	3.9895	.927	3.709	.927
	Sep	3.7	4.0421	.915	3.661	.915
	Oct	3.7	4.0948	.904	3.712	.928
	Nov	4.1	4.1475	.989	3.906	.976
	Dec	4.3	4.2001	1.024	4.048	1.012
1984	Jan	4.3	4.2528	1.011	4.114	1.028
	Feb	4.6	4.3054	1.068	4.271	1.068
	Mar	4.9	4.3581	1.124	4.427	1.107
	Apr	4.9	4.4108	1.111	4.466	1.116
	May	5.0	4.4634	1.120	4.480	1.120
	Jun	5.1	4.5161	1.129	4.494	1.124
	Jul	5.1	4.5687	1.116	4.551	1.138
	Aug	5.5	4.6214	1.190	4.651	1.163
	Sep	5.4	4.6741	1.155	4.558	1.140
	Oct	5.0	4.7267	1.058	4.526	1.132
	Nov	6.0	4.7794	1.255	4.768	1.192
	Dec	5.8	4.8320	1.200	4.801	1.200
1985	Jan	5.6	4.8847	1.146	4.525	1.131
	Feb	5.1	4.9374	1.033	4.374	1.094
	Mar	5.8	4.9900	1.162	4.567	1.142
	Apr	6.1	5.0427	1.210	4.897	1.224
	May	6.7	5.0953	1.315	5.141	1.285
	Jun	6.7	5.1480	1.301	5.090	1.272
	Jul	6.1	5.2007	1.173	4.846	1.212
	Aug	6.3	5.2533	1.199	4.758	1.190
	Sep	6.3	5.3060	1.187	4.767	1.192
	Oct	6.4	5.3586	1.194	4.813	1.203
	Nov	6.7	5.4113	1.238	4.823	1.206
	Dec	6.3	5.4640	1.153	4.704	1.176
1986	Jan	6.4	5.5166	1.160	4.550	1.138
	Feb	6.0	5.5693	1.077	4.452	1.113
	Mar	6.4	5.6219	1.138	4.305	1.076
	Apr	5.4	5.6746	.952	4.264	1.066
	May	7.0	5.7273	1.222	4.469	1.117
	Jun	6.2	5.7799	1.073	4.448	1.112
	Jul	6.3	5.8326	1.080	4.303	1.076
	Aug	6.3	5.8852	1.070	4.230	1.058
	Sep	6.0	5.9379	1.010	4.142	1.036

TABLE 18.23   (Continued)

(1) Year and Month		(2) Deseasonalized Data	(3) Trend $\hat{Y}_i$	(4) Cyclical- Irregular Relatives	(5) 3-Month Weighted Moving Totals	(6) Cyclical Relatives
	Oct	6.3	5.9906	1.052	3.991	.998
	Nov	5.3	6.0432	.877	3.757	.939
	Dec	5.8	6.0959	.951	3.739	.935
1987	Jan	5.9	6.1485	.960	3.774	.944
	Feb	5.6	6.2012	.903	3.454	.864
	Mar	4.3	6.2539	.688	2.897	.724
	Apr	3.9	6.3065	.618	2.537	.634
	May	3.9	6.3592	.613	2.530	.632
	Jun	4.4	6.4118	.686	2.836	.709
	Jul	5.5	6.4645	.851	3.201	.800
	Aug	5.3	6.5172	.813	3.375	.844
	Sep	5.9	6.5698	.898	3.545	.886
	Oct	6.2	6.6225	.936	3.744	.936
	Nov	6.5	6.6751	.974	3.999	1.000
	Dec	7.5	6.7278	1.115	—	—

SOURCE: Data are taken from Table 18.20.

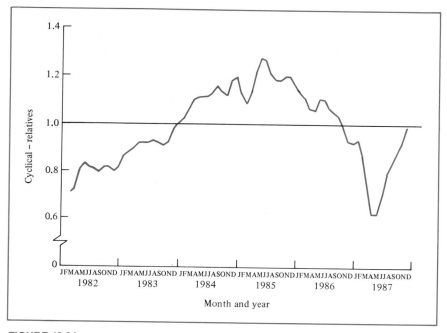

FIGURE 18.24
Plotting the cyclical relatives.
SOURCE: Data are taken from Table 18.23.

Problems

18.36 The data given in the accompanying table represent the number of persons employed on a monthly basis from January 1979 through December 1988 by a food-processing distributor.

Monthly employment

Month	Year									
	1979	1980	1981	1982	1983	1984	1985	1986	1987	1988
January	2,877	2,869	2,955	3,197	2,888	2,853	2,672	2,868	2,762	2,782
February	2,846	2,909	2,956	3,283	2,890	2,802	2,709	2,771	2,796	2,836
March	3,042	3,094	3,131	3,334	2,988	2,897	2,804	2,913	2,925	2,962
April	3,505	3,287	3,295	3,437	3,171	3,273	3,140	3,151	3,074	3,081
May	3,598	3,531	3,467	3,604	3,622	3,415	3,478	3,369	3,309	3,436
June	3,920	3,976	4,053	3,895	3,869	3,780	3,820	3,983	3,785	3,737
July	3,971	4,061	4,165	4,024	4,090	3,931	3,790	3,997	3,857	3,853
August	3,764	4,031	3,826	3,851	3,886	3,842	3,682	3,856	3,795	3,636
September	3,444	3,658	3,436	3,563	3,626	3,396	3,326	3,549	3,545	3,635
October	3,470	3,721	3,525	3,536	3,524	3,447	3,408	3,553	3,467	3,501
November	3,262	3,363	3,419	3,224	3,156	3,081	3,181	3,100	3,257	3,214
December	2,948	3,163	3,202	2,959	2,856	2,850	2,914	2,990	2,995	3,057

(a) Plot the data on a chart.

(b) Compute the seasonal index and construct a seasonal subseries plot.

(c) Fit a least-squares linear-trend line to the *average* annual employment.

(d) Convert the *annual* least-squares trend equation to a *monthly* trend equation. *Hint:* To convert an annual trend equation which is based on monthly averages to a monthly trend equation, keep the same intercept but divide the slope by 12. Adjust the results so as to center the origin within a particular month.

(e) Use the monthly trend equation and seasonal index to forecast the number of persons employed by this distributor for all twelve months of 1989 and 1990.

(f) Isolate and plot (on a separate chart) the cyclical relatives by detrending, deseasonalizing and smoothing the irregular component with a three-term weighted moving average.

● **18.37** The data given in the table at the top of page 771 represent the monthly outlays (in thousands of dollars) by a municipality to its sanitation department from January 1979 through December 1988.

(a) Plot the data on a chart.

(b) Compute the seasonal index and construct a seasonal subseries plot.

(c) Fit a least-squares linear-trend line to the *aggregate* annual outlays.

(d) Use the monthly trend equation and seasonal index to forecast the monthly outlays for all twelve months of 1989 and 1990.

(e) Isolate and plot (on a separate chart) the cyclical relatives by detrending, deseasonalizing, and smoothing the irregular component with a three-term weighted moving average.

Monthly outlays (Problem 18.37)

Month	Year									
	1979	1980	1981	1982	1983	1984	1985	1986	1987	1988
January	262	259	271	251	298	260	275	315	354	417
February	295	276	241	231	283	291	321	342	365	408
March	333	310	301	252	315	307	352	370	389	416
April	252	238	265	293	287	293	322	316	198	398
May	274	270	255	278	301	279	309	361	366	397
June	245	292	301	447	185	287	314	320	389	452
July	377	289	278	216	368	344	299	324	341	423
August	291	289	262	247	310	359	355	320	413	456
September	273	273	246	267	313	250	324	344	387	356
October	266	271	249	281	312	368	310	300	384	479
November	286	272	246	297	325	359	339	350	415	425
December	285	284	221	288	326	345	320	333	328	499

18.38 The data given in the accompanying table represent the number of cans (in millions) shipped by a soft-drink distributor from January 1980 through December 1988.

Monthly number of cans

Month	Year								
	1980	1981	1982	1983	1984	1985	1986	1987	1988
January	1.51	1.22	1.57	2.80	3.12	2.63	2.60	2.23	2.23
February	1.50	1.21	1.57	3.02	2.90	2.63	2.61	2.30	2.48
March	1.52	1.21	1.56	2.95	2.88	2.70	2.50	2.44	2.46
April	1.48	1.23	1.65	2.64	2.95	2.66	2.39	2.80	2.58
May	1.54	1.23	2.02	2.61	2.90	2.80	2.42	2.62	2.74
June	1.52	1.20	2.30	2.80	2.86	2.87	2.26	2.52	2.72
July	1.43	1.22	2.33	3.27	2.93	2.94	2.04	2.47	2.90
August	1.29	1.21	2.70	3.53	3.15	2.79	1.86	2.31	2.69
September	1.13	1.28	2.40	3.46	2.95	2.71	1.80	2.24	2.33
October	1.11	1.28	2.35	3.69	2.73	3.46	1.86	2.27	2.90
November	1.09	1.30	2.39	3.46	2.58	2.40	2.08	2.15	2.88
December	1.20	1.54	2.58	3.42	2.57	2.48	2.23	2.34	2.60

(a) Plot the data on a chart.

(b) Compute the seasonal index and construct a seasonal subseries plot.

(c) Fit a least-squares linear-trend line to the *mean* annual number of cans shipped.

(d) Convert the *annual* least-squares trend equation to a *monthly* trend equation. *Hint:* To convert an annual trend equation which is based on monthly averages to a monthly trend equation, keep the same intercept but divide the slope by 12. Adjust the results so as to center the origin within a particular month.

(e) Use the monthly trend equation and seasonal index to forecast the number of cans shipped for all 12 months of 1989 and 1990.

(f) Isolate and plot (on a separate chart) the cyclical relatives by detrending, deseasonalizing and smoothing the irregular component with a three-term weighted moving average.

18.39 The data given in the table at the top of page 772 represent the closing quarterly stock market averages based on 30 industrial stocks for the 72 quarters ended March 31, 1970, through December 31, 1987.

Quarterly closing stock market averages

Quarterly Ending	Year								
	1970	1971	1972	1973	1974	1975	1976	1977	1978
March	785.57	904.37	940.70	951.01	846.68	768.15	999.45	919.13	757.36
June	683.53	891.14	929.03	891.71	802.41	878.99	1002.78	916.30	818.95
September	760.68	887.19	953.27	947.10	607.87	793.88	990.19	847.11	865.82
December	838.92	890.20	1020.02	850.86	616.24	852.41	1004.65	831.17	805.01

Quarterly Ending	Year								
	1979	1980	1981	1982	1983	1984	1985	1986	1987
March	862.18	785.75	1003.87	822.77	1130.03	1164.89	1266.78	1818.61	2304.69
June	841.98	867.92	976.88	811.93	1221.96	1132.40	1335.46	1892.72	2418.53
September	878.67	932.42	849.98	896.25	1233.13	1206.71	1328.63	1767.58	2596.28
December	838.74	963.99	875.00	1046.54	1258.64	1211.51	1546.67	1895.95	1938.83

(a) Plot the data on a chart.

(b) Compute the seasonal index and construct a seasonal subseries plot.

(c) Fit a least-squares linear-trend line to these closing quarterly industrial stock market averages.

(d) Use the quarterly trend equation and seasonal index to forecast the closing industrial stock market averages for all four quarters of 1988, 1989, 1990, and 1991.

18.14 TIME-SERIES ANALYSIS: AN OVERVIEW

The value of such forecasting methodology as time-series analysis, which utilizes past and present information as a guide to the future, was recognized and most eloquently expressed more than two centuries ago by the American statesman Patrick Henry, who said:

> I have but one lamp by which my feet are guided, and that is the lamp of experience. I know no way of judging the future but by the past. [*Speech at Virginia Convention (Richmond) March 23, 1775*]

If it were true (as time-series analysis assumes) that those factors which have affected particular patterns of economic activity in the past and present will continue to do so in a similar manner in the future, time-series analysis, by itself, would certainly be a most appropriate and effective forecasting tool as well as an aid in the managerial control of present activities.

On the other hand, critics of classical time-series methods have argued that these techniques are overly "naïve" and "mechanical"; that is, a mathematical model based on the past should not be utilized for mechanically extrapolating trends into the future without consideration as to personal judgments, business experiences, or changing technologies, habits, and needs. (See Problem 18.49.) Thus in recent years, econometricians have been concerned with including such factors in developing highly sophisticated computerized models of economic activity for forecasting purposes. Such forecasting methods, however, are beyond the scope of this text (References 2, 3, 11, 13, and 19).

Nevertheless, as we have seen from the previous sections of this chapter, time-series methods provide useful guides to business leaders as to projecting future trends (on a long-term and short-term basis) or as to measuring overall cyclical activity. If used properly—in conjunction with other forecasting methods as well as business judgment and experience—time-series methods will continue to be an excellent managerial tool for decision making.

Supplementary Problems

18.40 Go to your college library and, using *The Statistical History of the United States from Colonial Times to the Present*, write a report that briefly describes the composition, characteristics, and uses of the Indexes of Prices Received and Paid by Farmers and the Parity Ratio.

18.41 Go to your college library and use appropriate resources to write a brief report that describes the composition, characteristics, and uses of the Producer Price Index.

18.42 Go to your college library and use appropriate resources to write a brief report that describes the composition, characteristics, and uses of the Sotheby Art Index.

18.43 Go to your college library and use appropriate resources to write a brief report that describes the composition, characteristics, and uses of the Dow Jones Industrial Averages.

18.44 Go to your college library and use appropriate resources to write a brief report that describes the composition, characteristics, and uses of the Standard & Poor's Stock Price Index.

18.45 Go to your college library and use appropriate resources to write a brief report that describes the composition, characteristics, and uses of the Federal Reserve Board's Index of Industrial Production.

18.46 The minimum wage rates in the United States over ten-year periods from 1938 through 1968 are presented in the accompanying table:

Minimum wage rates (1938–1968)

	Year			
	1938	*1948*	*1958*	*1968*
Minimum wage rate (per hour)	$.25	$.40	$1.00	$1.60

Moreover, the following table displays the minimum wage rates in the United States approved by Congress in 1977 under the Fair Labor Standards Act for the years 1978 through 1981.

Minimum wage rates (1978–1981)

	Year			
	1978	*1979*	*1980*	*1981*
Minimum wage rate (per hour)	$2.65	$2.90	$3.10	$3.35

Since 1977 there has been no further legislation on this matter. At the present time, $3.35 remains the minimum wage rate. Nevertheless, the table below depicts the Consumer Price Indexes for these time periods.

Consumer Price Index (1967 = 100.0)*

	Year													
	1938	1948	1958	1968	1978	1979	1980	1981	1982	1983	1984	1985	1986	1987
Index	42.2	72.1	86.6	104.2	195.4	217.4	246.8	272.4	289.1	298.4	311.1	322.2	328.4	340.4

* CPI for all urban consumers since 1978.
SOURCE: Data are taken from *Statistical Abstract of the United States*,
Table 806, 1980, and Table 774, 1987 and U.S. Bureau of Labor Statistics,
Montly Labor Review, February 1988, p. 104.

In recent years many Americans have voiced complaints that their wages have not kept pace with the cost of living. In particular, many feel that those hardest hit by this problem are the lowest-paid workers.

(a) Examine the nominal and real growth rates over the decade from 1968 to 1978 to determine how the purchasing power of persons paid at the minimum wage rate had changed during that period of time.

(b) Study the nominal and real growth rates on an annual basis from 1978 through 1981 to determine how the purchasing power of persons paid at the minimum wage rate had changed in these more recent time periods.

➡(c) **ACTION**   Based on your findings write an appropriate letter to your Congressional Representative

(1) regarding the equitability of the 1977 bill.

(2) recommending an appropriate minimum wage rate structure for the years 1988, 1989, and 1990.

18.47 Using the data in the various tables presented in Problem 18.46, determine the year in which those American workers paid at the minimum wage rate had their highest purchasing power. Discuss.

18.48 What are the advantages and disadvantages of time-series analysis as a forecasting tool?

18.49 The data given below represent the annual incidence rates (per 100,000 persons) of reported acute poliomyelitis recorded over 5-year periods from 1915–1955.

Incidence rates of reported acute poliomyelitis

Year	1915	1920	1925	1930	1935	1940	1945	1950	1955
Rate	3.1	2.2	5.3	7.5	8.5	7.4	10.3	22.1	17.6

SOURCE: Data are taken from B. Wattenberg, ed., *The Statistical History of the United States: From Colonial Times to the Present* (Series B303), (New York: Basic Books, 1976).

(a) Plot the data on a chart.

(b) Fit a least-squares linear trend line to the data and plot the line on your chart.

(c) What are your trend forecasts for the years 1960, 1965, and 1970?

(d) Go to your library and, using the above reference, look up the actually reported incidence rates of acute poliomyelitis for the years 1960, 1965, and 1970. Record your results.

(e) Why are the mechanical trend extrapolations from your least-squares model not useful? Discuss.

18.50 Refer to the data on percentage of total federal outlays for veterans' benefits and services displayed in the table accompanying Problem 15.5 on page 519.

(a) Plot the data on a chart.

(b) Fit a least-squares trend line and plot the line on your chart.

(c) What is your least-squares trend forecast for the year 1988?

(d) Using a smoothing coefficient of .20, exponentially smooth the series and plot the results on your chart.

(e) What is your exponentially smoothed trend forecast for the year 1988?

(f) Compute the MAD for each fitted model. Compare the results.

(g) Go to your library and compare your forecasts [parts (c) and (e)] against the actual 1988 value presented in the *Statistical Abstract of the United States*. Discuss.

18.51 If a linear trend model were to *perfectly fit* a time series, then the "first differences" would be constant. That is, the differences between consecutive observations in the series would be the same throughout:

$$Y_2 - Y_1 = Y_3 - Y_2 = \cdots = Y_{i+1} - Y_i = \cdots = Y_n - Y_{n-1}$$

Moreover, if a quadratic trend model were to *perfectly fit* a time series, then the "second differences" would be constant. That is,

$$[(Y_3 - Y_2) - (Y_2 - Y_1)] = [(Y_4 - Y_3) - (Y_3 - Y_2)]$$
$$= \cdots = [(Y_{i+2} - Y_{i+1}) - (Y_{i+1} - Y_i)]$$
$$= \cdots = [(Y_n - Y_{n-1}) - (Y_{n-1} - Y_{n-2})]$$

Furthermore, if an exponential trend model were to *perfectly fit* a time series, then the percentage differences between consecutive observations would be constant. That is,

$$\left(\frac{Y_2 - Y_1}{Y_1}\right) \times 100\% = \left(\frac{Y_3 - Y_2}{Y_2}\right) \times 100\%$$
$$= \cdots$$
$$= \left(\frac{Y_{i+1} - Y_i}{Y_i}\right) \times 100\%$$
$$= \cdots$$
$$= \left(\frac{Y_n - Y_{n-1}}{Y_{n-1}}\right) \times 100\%$$

Although we should not expect a perfectly fitting model for any particular set of time-series data, we nevertheless can evaluate the first differences, second differences, and percentage differences for a given series as a guide for determining an appropriate model to choose.

For each of the time-series data sets presented below:

(a) Determine the most appropriate model to fit.

(b) Develop this trend equation.

(c) Forecast the trend value for the year 1992.

	Year									
	1979	*1980*	*1981*	*1982*	*1983*	*1984*	*1985*	*1986*	*1987*	*1988*
Time series I	10.0	15.1	24.0	36.7	53.8	74.8	100.0	129.2	162.4	199.0
Time series II	30.0	33.1	36.4	39.9	43.9	48.2	53.2	58.2	64.5	70.7
Time series III	60.0	67.9	76.1	84.0	92.2	100.0	108.0	115.8	124.1	132.0

18.52 A time-series plot often aids the forecaster in determining an appropriate model to use. For each of the time-series data sets presented below:

(a) Plot the observed data (Y) over time (X) and plot the logarithm of the observed data (log Y) over time (X) to determine whether a linear trend model or an exponential trend model is more appropriate. *Hint*: Recall from Section 18.8.5 that if the plot of log Y versus X appears to be linear, an exponential trend model provides an appropriate fit.

(b) Develop this trend equation.

(c) Forecast the trend value for the year 1992.

					Year					
	1979	1980	1981	1982	1983	1984	1985	1986	1987	1988
Time series I	100.0	115.2	130.1	144.9	160.0	175.0	189.8	204.9	219.8	235.0
Time series II	100.0	115.2	131.7	150.8	174.1	200.0	230.8	266.1	305.5	351.8

18.53 The data given in the accompanying table represent the annual gross revenues (in millions of dollars) obtained by a utility company for the years 1975 through 1988.

Annual gross revenues

Year	1975	1976	1977	1978	1979	1980	1981	1982	1983	1984	1985	1986	1987	1988
Gross revenues	13.0	14.1	15.7	17.0	18.4	20.9	23.5	26.2	29.0	32.8	36.5	41.0	45.4	50.8

(a) Compare the first differences, second differences, and percent differences (see Problem 18.51) to determine the most appropriate model to fit.

(b) Develop this trend equation.

(c) What has been the annual growth in gross revenues over the 14 years?

(d) Forecast the trend value for the year 1990.

18.54 The data given in the accompanying table represent the annual revenues (in millions of dollars) of a well-known advertising agency for the years 1969 through 1988.

Annual revenues (millions of dollars)

Year	Revenues	Year	Revenues	Year	Revenues
1969	51.0	1977	102.8	1985	133.3
1970	54.1	1978	98.0	1986	192.8
1971	56.4	1979	83.6	1987	234.0
1972	58.1	1980	81.0	1988	238.9
1973	69.5	1981	87.0		
1974	79.2	1982	102.9		
1975	89.2	1983	100.9		
1976	93.0	1984	110.9		

(a) Plot the data over time and plot the logarithm of the data over time to determine whether a linear trend model or an exponential trend model is more appropriate (see Problem 18.52).

(b) Develop this trend equation.

(c) What has been the annual growth in advertising revenues over the 20 years?

(d) Forecast the trend value for the year 1992.

18.55 The data given in the table on page 777 represent the average weekly gross hours per production worker for a well-known clothing manufacturer from 1969 through 1988.

Average weekly gross hours

Year	Hours	Year	Hours	Year	Hours
1969	37.4	1977	37.2	1985	36.9
1970	37.6	1978	37.2	1986	37.1
1971	37.5	1979	37.7	1987	36.5
1972	37.9	1980	38.3	1988	36.7
1973	38.2	1981	37.9		
1974	38.6	1982	37.2		
1975	38.1	1983	37.4		
1976	38.3	1984	37.3		

(a) Plot the data on a chart.

(b) Using a smoothing coefficient of .10, exponentially smooth the series and plot the results on your chart.

(c) Using a smoothing coefficient of .30, exponentially smooth the series and plot the results on your chart.

(d) Using a smoothing coefficient of .50, exponentially smooth the series and plot the results on your chart.

(e) Fit a least-squares linear trend line to the data and plot the line on your chart.

(f) Obtain a forecast for the trend in 1989 using the three exponential smoothing models in (b), (c), and (d) as well as the linear trend model in (e).

(g) Obtain a forecast for the trend in 1989 using the mean forecasting method.

(h) Obtain a forecast for the trend in 1989 using the naïve autoregression forecasting method.

(i) Obtain a forecast for the trend in 1989 using the Holt-Winters method (with $U = .30$ and $V = .30$).

(j) Obtain a forecast for the trend in 1989 using a first-order autoregressive model.

(k) Perform a residual analysis for each of the eight forecasting methods.

(l) Compute the MAD for each of the eight fitted models.

(m) Based on your results in (k) and (l), which of your forecasts do you believe is most reliable? Discuss fully.

Case Study I

Suppose that in June 1988 you are hired as a Research Economist for an affiliate of the United Garment Workers of America. The union leadership has asked you to examine the monthly hourly wage structure at a particular apparel company in order to ascertain whether the wages have kept pace with monthly movements in the Consumer Price Index. Contractual negotiations will be commencing in the next few months, and the union leadership wants to ensure an equitable contract for its membership at this company. Previous contracts have contained escalator clauses tying wage increments to movements in the index.

At the present time, you are specifically asked to accomplish the following:

1. Determine if there is a significant *positive correlation* between *annual* average hourly gross earnings at this company and the Consumer Price Index for the 10-year period from 1978–1987.

2. Determine if there is a significant *positive correlation* between the 12 *monthly* seasonal indexes of average hourly gross earnings at this company and the *monthly* Consumer Price Index for the year 1987.

3. Develop a *monthly* (simple) linear regression model based on the past five years so that average hourly gross earnings (Y) at this company in a particular month can be predicted from a knowledge of the (lagged) Consumer Price Index (X) from the previous month (that is, $\hat{Y}_i = b_0 + b_1 X_{i-1}$).

4. Comment on the company's ten-year payment records versus the minimum wage structure.

Using the *Survey of Current Business* as well as *Business Statistics Supplement* from your library, you obtain the needed data for the Consumer Price Index. The monthly average hourly gross earnings per production worker in this company from January 1978 through December 1987 are obtained from company records and are presented below. Also shown is the minimum wage rate structure in effect throughout the United States during this time period.

Monthly average hourly gross earnings

Month	Year									
	1978	1979	1980	1981	1982	1983	1984	1985	1986	1987
January	2.45	2.55	2.73	2.85	3.14	3.33	3.57	3.85	4.17	4.44
February	2.47	2.58	2.72	2.86	3.13	3.33	3.53	3.85	4.17	4.45
March	2.47	2.57	2.74	2.87	3.16	3.37	3.57	3.89	4.17	4.49
April	2.46	2.58	2.75	2.89	3.16	3.37	3.56	3.91	4.19	4.46
May	2.46	2.57	2.74	2.96	3.15	3.38	3.56	3.89	4.20	4.45
June	2.47	2.60	2.76	2.98	3.16	3.40	3.62	3.91	4.21	4.51
July	2.47	2.58	2.75	3.01	3.16	3.39	3.59	3.91	4.23	4.50
August	2.49	2.62	2.79	3.05	3.16	3.42	3.61	3.93	4.21	4.60
September	2.52	2.65	2.84	3.09	3.22	3.49	3.68	3.99	4.28	4.70
October	2.51	2.67	2.85	3.10	3.24	3.49	3.69	4.01	4.32	4.73
November	2.51	2.69	2.86	3.10	3.25	3.50	3.71	4.03	4.32	4.74
December	2.54	2.70	2.84	3.11	3.27	3.52	3.76	4.09	4.39	4.81
Minimum Wage (1977 Fair Labor Standards Act)	2.65	2.90	3.10	3.35	3.35	3.35	3.35	3.35	3.35	3.35

References

1. ARKIN, H., AND R. COLTON, *Statistical Methods*, 5th ed. (New York: Barnes & Noble College Outline Series, 1970).
2. BAILS, D. G., AND L. C. PEPPERS, *Business Fluctuations: Forecasting Techniques and Applications* (Englewood Cliffs, N.J.: Prentice-Hall, 1982).
3. BOWERMAN, B. L., AND R. T. O'CONNELL, *Forecasting and Times-Series*, 2d ed. (North Scituate, Mass.: Duxbury Press, 1986).
4. BOX, G. E. P., AND G. M. JENKINS, *Time Series Analysis: Forecasting and Control*, 2d ed. (San Francisco: Holden-Day, 1977).
5. BROWN, R. G., *Smoothing, Forecasting, and Prediction* (Englewood Cliffs, N.J.: Prentice-Hall, 1963).
6. Bureau of Labor Statistics Bulletin No. 1517, *The Consumer Price Index: History and Techniques*, U.S. Department of Labor, 1966.

7. Bureau of Labor Statistics Report No. 517, *The Consumer Price Index: Concepts and Content over the Years*, U.S. Department of Labor, 1977.
8. Bureau of Labor Statistics Bulletin No. 1887, *Supplement to Wage Chronology—International Harvester and the Auto Workers, 1976–1979*, U.S. Department of Labor, June 1979.
9. Bureau of Labor Statistics Report No. 736, *The Consumer Price Index: 1987 Revision*, U.S. Department of Labor, January 1987.
10. *Business Conditions Digest*, U.S. Department of Commerce, 1981.
11. CHAMBERS, J. C., S. K. MULLICK, AND D. D. SMITH, "How to Choose the Right Forecasting Technique," *Harvard Business Review*, Vol. 49, No. 4, July–August 1971, pp. 45–74.
12. CROXTON, F., D. COWDEN, AND S. KLEIN, *Applied General Statistics*, 3d ed. (Englewood Cliffs, N.J.: Prentice-Hall, 1967).
13. CURTIS, G. A., *ESP: Economic Software Package* (Chicago: Graduate School of Business, University of Chicago, January 1976).
14. EDMONSTON, B., *Exec *U* Stat User's Manual* (Princeton, N.J.: Exec *U* Stat, Inc., 1985).
15. LEVINE, D. M., M. L. BERENSON, AND D. F. STEPHAN, *Using Minitab With Basic Business Statistics*, 2d ed. (Englewod Cliffs, N.J.: Prentice-Hall, 1986).
16. MAHMOUD, E., "Accuracy in Forecasting: A Survey," *Journal of Forecasting*, Vol. 3, 1984, pp. 139–159.
17. NEWBOLD, P., *Statistics for Business and Economics*, 2d ed. (Englewood Cliffs, N.J.: Prentice-Hall, 1988).
18. POLHEMUS, N., "Quantitative Graphics on Microcomputers: Problems and Prospects," invited presentation at the 1985 Annual Meeting of the *Northeast American Institute for Decision Sciences*, New York City, March 29, 1985.
19. RADUCHEL, W. J., "*RAPFE*: The Regression Analysis Program for Economists Reference Guide,' Tech. Paper 10, Harvard Institute of Economic Research, Harvard University, Cambridge, Mass., April 1973.
20. *SAS-ETS User's Guide* (Cary, N.C.: SAS Institute, 1980).
21. *Statistical Abstract of the United States*, U.S. Department of Commerce, 1980, 1985, 1987.
22. WATTENBERG, B. J., ed., *The Statistical History of the United States from Colonial Times to the Present* (New York: Basic Books, 1976).

19

Statistical Applications in Quality and Productivity Management

19.1 INTRODUCTION

In this chapter we culminate our discussion of statistical concepts and methods with a focus on statistical applications in quality and productivity management. The pioneer of this methodology, W. A. Shewhart, said a half century ago (see Reference 17) that

> The long range contribution of statistics depends not so much upon getting a lot of highly trained statisticians into industry as it does in creating a statistically minded generation of physicists, chemists, engineers and others who will in any way have a hand in developing and directing the production processes of tomorrow.

Although we will be using concepts and methods learned in other chapters, including descriptive measures, probability distributions, and time series, this chapter differs from the preceding ones in that we will be focusing on applications from both a managerial and statistical perspective and providing detailed coverage of a managerial approach developed by W. Edwards Deming (see References 2, 12, 14, and 21).

19.2 QUALITY AND PRODUCTIVITY: A HISTORICAL PERSPECTIVE

By the mid-1980s it had become clear that among the nations of the industrialized world, the system of commerce had become global in nature so that each country must deal with competition from all parts of the world. Such a global economy had developed because of many factors, including the rapid expansion in worldwide communications and the exponential increase in the availability and power of computer systems. In such an environment, it is of vital importance for their survival that business organizations be prepared to face the challenges presented with the most effective managerial approaches available.

Perhaps the fundamental issues can be better understood by briefly examining the historical development of management in four phases (see Reference 10). We may think of first-generation management as *"Management by Doing,"* in which each individual produced something for himself or his family unit whenever the product was required. Beginning in the Middle Ages, the rise of craft guilds in Europe led to the second generation of management, *"Management by Directing,"* in which craft guilds protected and fostered the interest of the craftsmen by training apprentices in the best possible manner for learning a craft.

The development of Watt's steam engine, Whitney's system of interchangeable parts, along with many other inventions led to the Industrial Revolution of the nineteenth century (see Reference 4). The creation of the factory environment brought a third generation of management, *"Management by Control,"* in which workers were divided into those who actually did the work and those who planned and supervised the work (i.e., the managers). This sharp division was emphasized in the work of American engineer Frederick W. Taylor (see Reference 4) and this managerial style contains a hierarchical structure that emphasizes individual accountability to a set of predetermined goals. This third generation of management has been commonly practiced in the United States since the early part of the twentieth century.

In recent years, however, the United States has seen the competitive advantage it enjoyed in the post-World War II period gradually eliminated because of several factors. First, the United States emerged from World War II with its industrial base intact, unlike most European countries and Japan. Thus, the United States was in a monopolistic position in which the rest of the world eagerly waited for whatever consumer products it was able to produce. With ever-expanding markets, both labor and management had little incentive to critically examine the ways in which they were operating with the goal of making production more efficient.

Second, the redevelopment of Japanese industry, beginning in 1950, was based on a managerial style that took advantage of the only real resource available in Japan, its labor force (since that country is devoid of abundant natural resources). With the assistance of individuals such as W. Edwards Deming, Joseph Juran, A. V. Feigenbaum, Kaoru Ishikawa, and others, a different managerial style was developed that emphasized the continuous improvement of the quality of a product. This fourth generation of management called *"Management by Process,"* views management as a process (see Figure 19.1 on page 782) in which the goal is to (1) work on the methods for constantly improving a product or service and (2) develop new technology. This managerial style is characterized by interdependency of functional areas, a focus on the customer, and a fast reaction to changes and improvements. Management by process has a strong statistical foundation, based on a deep knowledge of variability, a systems perspective, and belief in continuous improvement. Control charts are one tool that make the variability of the system apparent. Thus, they are a good place to start to explore these ideas. They will be the focus of our next section.

19.3 THE THEORY OF CONTROL CHARTS

If we are examining data over a period of time or in sequential order, it is imperative that a graph of the variable of interest be plotted at successive time periods or intervals. One such graph, originally developed by Shewhart (see References 15, 16, and 17) is the control chart.

The **control chart** is a means of studying variation in a product or service by focusing on (1) the time dimension in which the system (which may be changing)

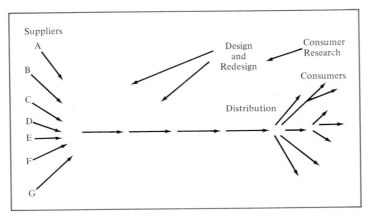

FIGURE 19.1
Management by process.

SOURCE: Reprinted from *Out of the Crisis* by W. Edwards Deming by permission of MIT and W. Edwards Deming. Published by MIT, Center for Advanced Engineering Study, Cambridge, MA 02139. Copyright 1986 by W. Edwards Deming.

produces products or services, and (2) capturing the natural variability in the system. The primary purpose of control charts is to monitor a process, whereas other methods such as design of experiments (see Chapter 14) catalyze improvements. Control charts enable the user to study the behavior of the variation that exists in any phenomenon, be it the amount filled in successive sets of one liter bottles of juice or the proportion of late arrivals of an airplane flight. The control chart can be used to study past performance, as an ongoing operation to evaluate present conditions, and as the basis for taking corrective action.

In addition to providing a visual display of data representing a process, the principal focus of the control chart is the attempt to separate "special or assignable causes" of variation from "common causes" of variation.

> **Special** or **assignable causes** of variation are signaled by individual fluctuations or patterns in the data. These fluctuations are caused by a change in the system which are either problems to be fixed or opportunities to exploit.
>
> **Common causes** of variation represent variation due to the inherent variability in the particular system of operation.

The distinction between the two causes of variation is crucial because special causes of variation are considered to be outside the system and are often correctable or exploitable without modifying the system, whereas common causes of variation can be reduced only by changing a system. Such changes in a system are the reponsibility of management.

There are two types of errors that control charts help prevent. The first type of error involves the belief that a mistake is due to a special cause when it is caused by the system. This is the error that occurs when a system that is in control is overadjusted or "tampered" with, resulting in excess variation in the process. The second type of error involves treating special cause variation as if it is common cause variation and

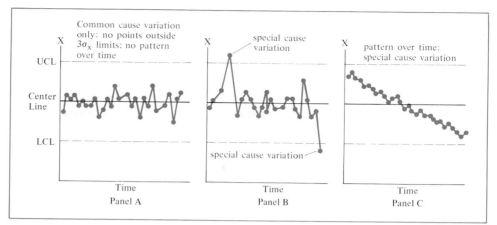

FIGURE 19.2
Three control chart patterns.

thus not taking immediate corrective action when it is necessary. Although these errors can still occur when a control chart is used, they are far less likely.

The most typical form of control chart will set "control limits" that are within ±3 standard deviations[1] of the statistical measure of interest (be it the average, the proportion, the range, etc.). The 3 standard deviation limits also serve to reduce the likelihood of "tampering" with the process. Once these control limits are set, the control chart would be evaluated from the perspective of (1) discerning any pattern that might exist in the values over time and (2) determining whether any points fall outside the control limits. Figure 19.2 illustrates three different situations.

In Panel A of Figure 19.2, we observe a process that is "stable," one in which there does not appear to be any pattern in the ordering of values over time, and one in which there are no points that fall outside the 3 standard deviation limits of variability. Panel B, on the contrary, contains several points that fall outside the 3 standard deviation control limits. Each of these points would have to be further investigated to determine any special situations that could have caused the result. Although Panel C does not have any points that are beyond the control limits, it has a series of consecutive points that are above the expected (or average) value as well as a series of consecutive points that are below the expected (or average) value. In addition, a long-term overall downward trend in the value of the variable is clearly visible. Such a situation would call for corrective action to determine what might account for this pattern prior to initiating any changes in the system.

Once all special causes of variation have been explained and eliminated, the process involved can be examined on a continuing basis until there are no patterns over time or points outside the three standard deviation limits. When the process contains only common cause variation, its performance is predictable (at least in the near future). In order to reduce common cause variation, it is necessary to alter the system that is producing the product or service. Such actions are the *responsibility of*

---

[1] We recall from Section 8.2 that in the normal distribution $\mu_X \pm 3\sigma_X$ includes almost all (99.73%) of the observations in the population. Although the calculations used in control charts are based on the normal distribution, we should stress that in *analytical* studies the concept of population has no applicability. The subject of interest is a *process*, not a population from which a sample is taken of what has been produced.

management. In our next section, we will discuss how such system changes might be accomplished by applying the fourteen points of Deming's management theory.

19.4   DEMING'S FOURTEEN POINTS: A THEORY OF MANAGEMENT BY PROCESS

The high quality of Japanese products along with the economic "miracle" of Japanese development after World War II are commonly known facts. What is not as readily known, particularly by young people today, is the fact that, prior to the 1950s, Japan had acquired the unenviable reputation of producing shoddy consumer products of poor quality. Thus, the question must surely be asked, what happened to change this reputation? Part of the answer lies in the fact that by 1950, top management of Japanese companies, in alliance with the Union of Japanese Science and Engineering (JUSE), realized that quality was a vital factor for the exporting of consumer products. Some Japanese engineers had been exposed to the contribution that the Shewhart control charts had made toward the American war effort during World War II (see References 8 and 20). Thus, several American experts, including W. Edwards Deming, were invited to Japan during the early 1950s. The rigorous application of a total quality approach including tools such as control charts led to improved productivity in Japanese industry as variation was reduced. Over a period of time, the continued focus on this total quality approach led Deming to develop his theory of *management by process* based on the following fourteen points:

1. Create constancy of purpose for improvement of product and service.
2. Adopt the new philosophy.
3. Cease dependence on inspection to achieve quality.
4. End the practice of awarding business on the basis of price tag alone. Instead, minimize total cost by working with a single supplier.
5. Improve constantly and forever every process for planning, production, and service.
6. Institute training on the job.
7. Adopt and institute leadership.
8. Drive out fear.
9. Break down barriers between staff areas.
10. Eliminate slogans, exhortations, and targets for the work force.
11. Eliminate numerical quotas for the work force and numerical goals for management.
12. Remove barriers that rob people of pride of workmanship. Eliminate the annual rating or merit system.
13. Institute a vigorous program of education and self-improvement for everyone.
14. Put everyone in the company to work to accomplish the transformation.

Point 1, regarding constancy of purpose, refers to how an organization deals with problems that arise both at present and in the future. The focus is on the constant improvement of a product or service. This improvement process is illustrated by the Shewhart[2] cycle of Figure 19.3. Unlike the traditional manufacturing approach of "design it, make it, try to sell it," the Shewhart cycle represents a continuous cycle of "plan, do, check, and act." The first step, **planning,** represents the initial design phase for planning a change in a manufacturing or service process. The second step,

---

[2] In Japan the Shewhart cycle is known as the Deming cycle. This cycle is an application of the scientific method.

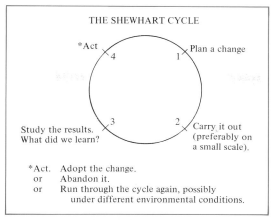

THE SHEWHART CYCLE

*Act   Plan a change

    4   1

    3   2

Study the results.   Carry it out
What did we learn?   (preferably on
                      a small scale).

*Act.   Adopt the change.
or   Abandon it.
or   Run through the cycle again, possibly
             under different environmental conditions.

FIGURE 19.3
The Shewhart cycle.

SOURCE: Reprinted from *Out of the Crisis* by W. Edwards Deming by permission of MIT and W. Edwards Deming. Published by MIT, Center for Advanced Engineering Study, Cambridge, MA 02139. Copyright 1986 by W. Edwards Deming. Adapted from Figure 5, p. 88.

doing, involves carrying out the change, preferably on a small scale. In doing this, planned experiments (see Chapter 14) can be a particularly valuable approach. The third step, **checking,** involves a study of the results using statistical tools to determine what was learned. The fourth step, **acting,** involves the acceptance of the change, its abandonment, or further study of the change under different conditions. With this approach, the business process starts with the customer as the most important part of the production line or service rendered.

The key aspect of this approach is the dominance of the concern for future problems. Improvement of processes must go hand in hand with innovation and the development of new products. The importance of innovation can be illustrated by an analogy to the "Fosbury Flop" technique[3] of high jumping. Prior to the development of this technique of high jumping, the accepted approach was to use a technique called the "Western Roll." If someone had just worked at improving his ability using the Western Roll, he still would not have been able to compete with others who had adopted what was at that time the newer and better Fosbury Flop technique. Thus, innovation must go hand in hand with process improvement.

Point 2, regarding the adoption of the new philosophy, refers to the urgency with which American companies need to realize that we are in a new economic age that differs drastically from the post-World War II period of American dominance (see Reference 8). It is a commonly accepted fact that, as "part of human nature," people will not act until a crisis is at hand, since they prefer to continue doing things in ways that they believe have produced successful results in the past. However, in this new economic age, American management is often afflicted with what Deming calls a set of "deadly diseases"—including lack of constancy of purpose, emphasis on short-term profits, fear of unfriendly takeover, evaluation of performance and merit rating systems, and excessive mobility of management. Finally, management philosophy needs to accept the notion that higher quality costs less *not* more. However, it does require

---

[3] This example was related to the authors by Brian Joiner of Joiner Associates who credits it to Ed Pindy of Philadelphia Electric Company.

an upfront investment to get quality. This investment pays off with tremendous dividends.

Point 3, regarding ceasing dependence on mass inspection, implies that any inspection whose purpose is to improve quality is too late since the quality is already built into the product. Among the difficulties involved in mass inspection (besides high costs) are the failure of inspectors to agree on nonconforming items and the problem of separating good and bad items. Such difficulties can be illustrated from an example taken from Scherkenbach (see Reference 14) and depicted in Figure 19.4. Suppose that your job here is to read the sentence displayed in Figure 19.4. The process involves proofreading the sentence with the objective of counting the number of occurrences of the letter *"f."* Read the sentence and note the number of occurrences of the letter *f* that you discover.

```
FINISHED FILES ARE THE RESULT
OF YEARS OF SCIENTIFIC STUDY
COMBINED WITH THE
EXPERIENCE
OF MANY YEARS
```

FIGURE 19.4
An example of the Proofreading Process.

SOURCE: W. W. Scherkenbach, *The Deming Route to Quality and Productivity: Road Maps and Roadblocks* (Washington: D.C.: CEEPress, 1987).

People see either three *f*s or six *f*s. The correct number is six *f*s. The number seen is dependent on the method used in reading the paragraph. One is likely to find three *f*s if the paragraph is read phonetically and six *f*s if one forces onself to carefully count the number of *f*s. The point of the exercise is to show that, if we have such a simple process as counting *f*s leading to inconsistency of "inspector's" results, what will happen when a process fails to contain a clear operational definition of "nonconforming"? Certainly, in such situations much more variability from inspector to inspector will occur. However, it may be a mistake to remove inspection completely before control of the process has been established.

Point 4, regarding ending the practice of awarding business on the basis of price tag alone, represents the antithesis of lowest bidder awards. It focuses on the fact that there can be no real long-term meaning to price without a knowledge of the quality of the product. A lowest-bidder approach ignores the advantages in reduced variation of a single supplier and fails to consider the advantages of the development of a long-term relationship between purchaser and supplier. Such a relationship would allow the supplier to be innovative and would tend to make the supplier and purchaser partners in achieving success.

Point 5, regarding improving constantly and forever the system of production and services, reinforces the importance of the continuous focus of the Shewhart cycle and the belief that quality needs to be built in at the design stage.[4] Attaining quality is viewed as a never-ending process in which smaller variation translates into a reduction in the economic losses that occur in the production of a product whose characteristics are variable. Such an approach stands in contrast to one whose only concern *is in*

---

[4] Design of experiments is a statistical tool that is particularly useful at the design stage.

meeting specifications. This latter ''all or none'' approach does not associate any economic loss with products whose characteristics are within specification limits.

Point 6, regarding instituting training, reflects needs for all employees including production workers, engineers, and managers. It is critically important for management to understand the differences between special causes and common causes of variation, so that proper action can be taken in each circumstance. In particular, training needs to focus on developing standards for acceptable work that do not change on a daily basis. Also, management needs to realize that people learn in different ways; some learn better with written instructions, some learn better with verbal instructions. In addition, management must decide who should be trained in what. Often corporate training in statistics is wasted because of (1) limited screening of who gets trained, (2) little planning on how to sequence awareness versus how to use review courses, (3) no emphasis on how to manage the use of statistical tools, and (4) little insistence on their use.

Point 7, regarding adopting and instituting leadership, relates to the distinction between leadership and supervision. The aim of leadership should be to improve the system and achieve greater consistency of performance.

Points 8 through 12 [regarding driving out fear (this may be the most important point), breaking down barriers between staff areas, eliminating slogans, etc., eliminating numerical quotas for the workforce and numerical goals for management, and removing barriers to pride of workmanship including the annual rating and merit system (this may be the most controversial point)] are all related to how the performance of an employee is to be evaluated.

The quota system for the production worker is viewed as detrimental for several reasons. First, it has a negative effect on the quality of the product since supervisors are more inclined to pass inferior products through the system when they need to meet work quotas. Such flexible standards of work reduce the pride of workmanship of the individual and perpetuate a system in which peer pressure holds the upper half of the workers to no more than the quota rate. Second, the annual performance rating system can rob the manager of his or her pride of workmanship because this system of evaluation more often than not fails to provide a meaningful measure of performance. For many managers, the only ''customer'' is his or her supervisor. In too many cases (see Reference 18), efforts are focused on either distoring figures or distorting the system to produce the desired set of results, rather than on efforts to improve the system. Such an approach stifles teamwork, since there is often reduced tangible reward for working together across functional areas. Finally, it rewards people who work successfully within the system, rather than people who work to improve the system.

Point 13, regarding encouraging education and self-improvement for everyone, reflects the notion that the most important resource of any organization is its people. Efforts that improve the knowledge of people in the organization also serve to increase the assets of the organization.

Point 14, regarding taking action to accomplish the transformation, again reflects the approach of management as a process in which one continuously strives toward improvement in a never-ending cycle.

Now that we have provided a brief introduction to the Deming philosophy and linked *management by process* to fundamental control chart ideas, in the following sections we shall develop several control charts that are used in industry.

19.5   THE RUN CHART: A CONTROL CHART FOR A SEQUENCE OF INDIVIDUAL *X* VALUES

19.5.1   The Importance of the Time Order Plot

In our discussion of graphical methods for presenting quantitative variables in Chapter 4, we took into account the order in which the data had been collected when we discussed the digidot plot in Section 4.7. Unfortunately, there are many situations in which the failure to consider the order or sequence leads to improper conclusions concerning a process that is being studied.

To illustrate such a situation, suppose that we are studying the filling operation in a plant in which one-liter bottles of apple juice are being manufactured. Table 19.1 represents the amount of apple juice contained in a subgroup of 50 consecutive one-liter bottles selected from the bottling process.

The data presented in Table 19.1 can be tabulated into the frequency distribution presented in Table 19.2 and depicted in the histogram of Figure 19.5.

TABLE 19.1   Amount of apple juice filled in a subgroup of 50 one-liter bottles (listed horizontally from left to right in order of being filled)

1.109	1.086	1.066	1.075	1.065	1.057	1.052	1.044	1.036	1.038
1.031	1.029	1.025	1.029	1.023	1.020	1.015	1.014	1.013	1.014
1.012	1.012	1.012	1.010	1.005	1.003	0.999	0.996	0.997	0.992
0.994	0.986	0.984	0.981	0.973	0.975	0.971	0.969	0.966	0.967
0.963	0.957	0.951	0.951	0.947	0.941	0.941	0.938	0.908	0.894

TABLE 19.2   Frequency distribution of the amount of fill for a subgroup of 50 one-liter bottles

Amount of Fill (in liters)	Number of Bottles
0.85 but under 0.90	1
0.90 but under 0.95	5
0.95 but under 1.00	18
1.00 but under 1.05	19
1.05 but under 1.10	6
1.10 but under 1.15	1
Totals	50

An examination of Figure 19.5 indicates that the distribution of the amount of fill appears to be approximately bell-shaped and symmetric around a central value of about 1.0 liter, precisely the value that we would expect to obtain for one-liter bottles. Unfortunately, if the analysis merely concluded after examining this frequency distribution and histogram, the most important information concerning the bottling process would not be obtained. This fact can be readily seen from the run chart (a control chart for a series of individual *X* values).

19.5.2   The Run Chart when the Process Average and Process Standard Deviation Are Known

As mentioned in Section 19.3, the most common form of control chart will set ''control limits'' that are within ± 3 standard deviations of the statistical measure of interest.

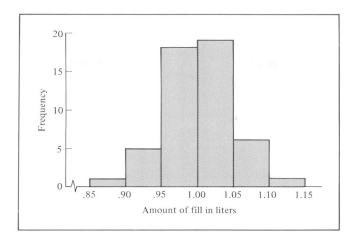

FIGURE 19.5
Frequency histogram of the amount of fill of 50 apple juice bottles.

For the case of a sequence of individual *X* values that have a process average and process standard deviation, the center line would be located at this long term process average, the upper control limit (*UCL*) would be the process average + 3 standard deviations, and the lower control limit (*LCL*) would be the process average − 3 standard deviations. This is expressed as Equation (19.1).

$$\text{process average} \pm 3 \text{ standard deviations} \qquad (19.1)$$

We can now refer back to the data of Table 19.2 to determine whether any pattern exists in the bottling of the apple juice. If we assume that the data have been recorded consecutively in row sequence (from left to right in each row), and we assume that the process average is 1.0 liter and the process standard deviation is 0.05 liter, a control chart can be set up as depicted in Figure 19.6 on page 790.

We can observe from Figure 19.6 that although none of the 50 points fall outside the control limits, there is a clear discernible downward pattern in the amount of fill in the bottles. Thus, any conclusions about the stability of the process would be inappropriate. It would appear in this case that corrective action should be taken to determine the special cause of this problem.

19.5.3   The Run Chart when the Process Average and Process Standard Deviation Are Unknown

When the process average is unknown, the subgroup mean $\overline{X}$ is used instead. When the process standard deviation is unknown, there are several methods for estimating it from the individual observations. It is usually preferable (see Reference 19) to estimate the standard deviation by using the *moving range*.

The **moving range** is defined as the difference between the largest and smallest observations in a subset of *n* observations.

Since it is most common to use subsets of $n = 2$ observations, the *i*th moving range (MR_i) can be defined as in Equation (19.2)

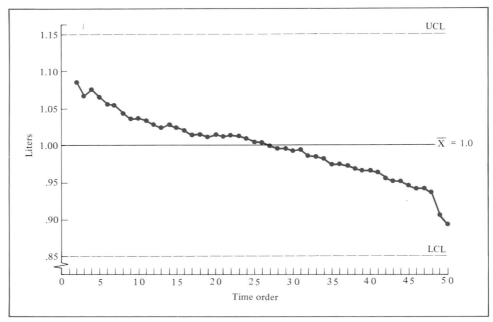

FIGURE 19.6
Run chart for amount of fill with process average 1.0 and process standard
deviation 0.05.

$$MR_i = |X_{i+1} - X_i| \text{ for } i = 1, \ldots, k - 1 \qquad (19.2)$$

This produces $(k - 1)$ moving ranges from which the average moving range $(\overline{MR})$ is
computed in Equation (19.3)

$$\overline{MR} = \frac{\sum_{i=1}^{k-1} MR_i}{k - 1} \qquad (19.3)$$

Since the relationship of the range to the standard deviation varies with sample
size, when this moving range is used as an estimate of the process standard deviation,
a constant factor called d_2 that reflects this relationship is used to develop the control
limits.[5] The d_2 factor is obtained from Table E.13 on page 864. The control limits are

$$\overline{X} \pm \frac{3 \, \overline{MR}}{d_2} \qquad (19.4)$$

---

[5] In industry the E_2 factor (see Reference 19), equal to $3/d_2$ is used to simplify the computations.

From Table E.13, for subgroups of size $n = 2$, the d_2 factor is 1.128.

If we return to our apple juice filling example, and assume that both the process mean and standard deviation are unknown, the moving range can be computed as summarized in Table 19.3.

TABLE 19.3 Computation of the moving range

Observation	Sample	High	Low	Moving Range
1.109	1	1.109	1.086	0.023
1.086	2	1.086	1.066	0.020
1.066	3	1.075	1.066	0.009
1.075	4	1.075	1.065	0.010
1.065	5	1.065	1.057	0.008
1.057	6	1.057	1.052	0.005
1.052	7	1.052	1.044	0.008
1.044	8	1.044	1.036	0.008
1.036	9	1.038	1.036	0.002
1.038	10	1.038	1.031	0.007
1.031	11	1.031	1.029	0.002
1.029	12	1.029	1.025	0.004
1.025	13	1.029	1.025	0.004
1.029	14	1.029	1.023	0.006
1.023	15	1.023	1.020	0.003
1.020	16	1.020	1.015	0.005
1.015	17	1.015	1.014	0.001
1.014	18	1.014	1.013	0.001
1.013	19	1.014	1.013	0.001
1.014	20	1.014	1.012	0.002
1.012	21	1.012	1.012	0.000
1.012	22	1.012	1.012	0.000
1.012	23	1.012	1.010	0.002
1.010	24	1.010	1.005	0.005
1.005	25	1.005	1.003	0.002
1.003	26	1.003	0.999	0.004
0.999	27	0.999	0.996	0.003
0.996	28	0.997	0.996	0.001
0.997	29	0.997	0.992	0.005
0.992	30	0.994	0.992	0.002
0.994	31	0.994	0.986	0.008
0.986	32	0.986	0.984	0.002
0.984	33	0.984	0.981	0.003
0.981	34	0.981	0.973	0.008
0.973	35	0.975	0.973	0.002
0.975	36	0.975	0.971	0.004
0.971	37	0.971	0.969	0.002
0.969	38	0.969	0.966	0.003
0.966	39	0.967	0.966	0.001
0.967	40	0.967	0.963	0.004
0.963	41	0.963	0.957	0.006
0.957	42	0.957	0.951	0.006
0.951	43	0.951	0.951	0.000
0.951	44	0.951	0.947	0.004
0.947	45	0.947	0.941	0.006
0.941	46	0.941	0.941	0.000
0.941	47	0.941	0.938	0.003
0.938	48	0.938	0.908	0.030
0.908	49	0.908	0.894	0.014
0.894				

$$\sum_{i=1}^{k} X_i = 50.036 \qquad\qquad \sum_{i=1}^{k-1} MR_i = 0.259$$

SOURCE: Table 19.1.

Thus,

$$\overline{X} = \frac{50.036}{50} = 1.00072$$

and

$$\overline{MR} = \frac{0.259}{49} = .0053$$

Using Equation (19.4), we may set up control limits as

$$1.00072 \pm \frac{3(.0053)}{1.128} = 1.00072 \pm .014$$

Thus the *LCL* = 0.98672 and *UCL* = 1.01472.

Figure 19.7 represents the revised control chart based on these new control limits and center line. We may observe that the moving range (and consequently the revised control limits) differ drastically from the corresponding values in Figure 19.6. This is due to the fact that the moving range is emphasizing variation between consecutive values. When there is a trend in the data, as in Figure 19.7, it is preferable to use control limits based on the moving range rather than the sample standard deviation *S*, so that the out-of-control condition (the trend in this case) can be highlighted.

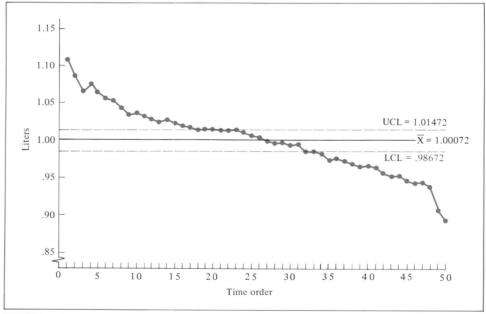

FIGURE 19.7
Run chart for the amount of fill using the moving range.

Problems

- **19.1**   A machine produces ''softballs'' that historically have a circumference that averages 12 inches with a standard deviation of 0.04 inches. A subgroup of 25 consecutive balls manufactured during the production process is selected. The circumferences are recorded below in row sequence (from left to right).

11.965	11.983	12.058	12.080	12.080
11.985	11.981	11.927	11.969	12.017
11.955	12.012	12.019	12.035	11.983
11.956	12.031	11.969	11.998	11.996
12.008	11.975	11.972	11.989	12.052

(a) Set up a control chart for these data using 3 standard deviation limits.
(b) Suppose that you do not wish to assume that the process average and process standard deviation have remained at their historical values. Set up a control chart for this situation.
(c) Compare the control charts obtained in parts (a) and (b). What conclusions can you reach?

19.2   Referring to the data on the length of jeans in Problem 4.96 on page 125
(a) Assume that from past experience a stable system of common causes results in data with an estimated standard deviation of 0.07 inches. Set up a control chart for these data using 3 standard deviation limits.
(b) What conclusions can you reach about whether the process is in control?
(c) Suppose that you do not wish to assume that the process average and process standard deviation have remained at their historical values. Set up a control chart for this situation.
(d) Compare the control charts obtained in parts (a) and (c). What conclusions can you reach?
(e) Compare the control charts obtained in parts (a) and (c) with the digidot plot obtained in Problem 4.96. What conclusions can you reach?

19.3   A machine being used for packaging table salt historically has a process average of 737 grams (26 ounces) of salt per box and a process standard deviation of 5 grams. A subgroup of 50 consecutive table salt packages is selected. The weights of these packages are recorded below in row sequence (from left to right).

739	745	741	749	746	754	748	745	746	740
738	735	733	734	729	725	726	721	726	732
734	733	736	740	742	741	745	748	749	751
750	748	745	746	741	740	739	737	736	732
729	730	725	720	730	732	735	738	740	744

(a) Set up a control chart for these data using 3 standard deviation limits.
(b) What conclusions can you reach about whether the process is in control?
(c) Suppose that you do not wish to assume that the process average and process standard deviation have remained at their historical values. Set up a control chart for this situation.
(d) Compare the control charts obtained in parts (a) and (c). What conclusions can you reach?

19.4   Referring to the data of Problem 4.97 on page 126
(a) Set up a control chart for Victor Sternberg's time trials.
(b) Do you think his time trials are ''in control''?
(c) Compare the control chart obtained in part (a) with the digidot plot of Problem 4.97.

19.5   Referring to the data of Problem 4.138 on page 150
(a) Set up a control chart of gross daily sales receipts.
(b) What patterns, if any, can you observe from the control chart?

19.6   CONTROL CHARTS FOR THE MEAN ($\overline{X}$)

19.6.1   Introduction

The most commonly used control chart is the control chart for the average. Because measurements are obtained from homogenous subgroups, the attained results are more sensitive to detecting special cause variation than the charts developed from the individual values. The $\overline{X}$ chart of this section is almost always used in conjunction with the R chart of Section 19.7 to detect out-of-control conditions in either the central tendency or the dispersion of a process.

19.6.2   Development

The control chart for $\overline{X}$ uses subgroups of size n that are obtained over k consecutive sequences or periods of time. If the process mean and standard deviation are known, we may use Equation (9.5) to develop control limits for the mean.

$$\text{average} \pm \frac{3 \text{ standard deviations}}{\sqrt{n}} \tag{19.5}$$

so that

$$LCL = \text{average} - \frac{3 \text{ standard deviations}}{\sqrt{n}}$$

and

$$UCL = \text{average} + \frac{3 \text{ standard deviations}}{\sqrt{n}}$$

However, we often wish to develop control limits without reference to any historical values. In such circumstances, as in the case of the control chart for the individual X values, the range and the d_2 factor can be used to estimate the standard deviation.[6] Thus, we may set up the following control limits:

$$\overline{\overline{X}} \pm \frac{3\overline{R}}{d_2\sqrt{n}} \tag{19.6}$$

where

$$\overline{\overline{X}} = \frac{\sum_{i=1}^{k} \overline{X}_i}{k} \quad \text{and} \quad \overline{R} = \frac{\sum_{i=1}^{k} R_i}{k}$$

where $\overline{X}_i$ = the sample mean of n observations at time i
R_i = the range of n observations at time i
and k = number of subgroups

so that

$$LCL = \overline{\overline{X}} - \frac{3\overline{R}}{d_2\sqrt{n}} \quad \text{and} \quad UCL = \overline{\overline{X}} + \frac{3\overline{R}}{d_2\sqrt{n}}$$

---

[6] In industry, the A_2 factor (see Reference 19), equal to $3/d_2\sqrt{n}$, is used to simplify the computations.

As an application of the $\overline{X}$ chart let us refer to the following example. Suppose that the management of a large hotel chain wanted to analyze the check-in process at a certain hotel located in a large northeastern city. In particular, it wanted to study the amount of time it took for the delivery of luggage (as measured from the time the guest completed check-in procedures to the time the luggage arrived in the guest's room). Data were recorded over a four-week (Sunday–Saturday) period and subgroups of 5 deliveries were selected (on a certain shift) on each day for analysis. The summary results (in minutes) are recorded in Table 19.4.

TABLE 19.4   Subgroup average and range for luggage delivery times over a four-week period

Day	Subgroup Average $\overline{X}_i$ (in minutes)	Subgroup Range R_i (in minutes)
1	5.32	3.85
2	6.59	4.27
3	4.88	3.28
4	5.70	2.99
5	4.07	3.61
6	7.34	5.04
7	6.79	4.22
8	4.93	3.69
9	5.01	3.33
10	3.92	2.96
11	5.66	3.77
12	4.98	3.09
13	6.83	5.21
14	5.27	3.84
15	5.21	3.26
16	4.68	2.92
17	5.32	3.37
18	4.90	3.55
19	4.44	3.73
20	5.80	3.86
21	5.61	3.65
22	4.77	3.38
23	4.37	3.02
24	4.79	3.80
25	5.03	4.11
26	5.11	3.75
27	6.94	4.57
28	5.71	4.29

For these data

$$k = 28 \qquad \sum_{i=1}^{k} \overline{X}_i = 149.97 \qquad \sum_{i=1}^{k} R_i = 104.41.$$

Thus,

$$\overline{\overline{X}} = \frac{149.97}{28} = 5.356 \quad \text{and} \quad \overline{R} = \frac{104.41}{28} = 3.729$$

Using Equation (19.6)

$$\overline{\overline{X}} \pm \frac{3\overline{R}}{d_2\sqrt{n}}$$

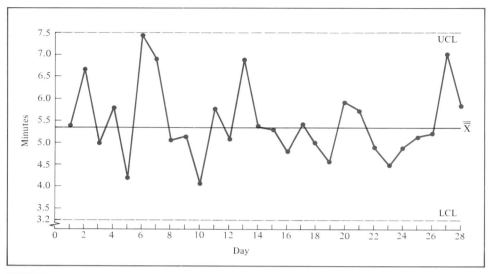

FIGURE 19.8
$\bar{X}$ chart for average luggage delivery time.
SOURCE: Table 19.4.

so that, using Table E.13, for $d_2 = 2.326$

$$5.356 \pm \frac{3\,(3.729)}{2.326\,(\sqrt{5})}$$

$$5.356 \pm 2.151$$

Thus $LCL = 3.205$ and $UCL = 7.507$.

The control chart for the data of Table 19.4 is displayed in Figure 19.8. An examination of Figure 19.8 does not reveal any points outside the control limits, although there is a large amount of variability among the 28 subgroup means. However, a closer evaluation does seem to indicate a series of six consecutive points and a series of five consecutive points that are below the overall average. Since these occurred on days 14–19 and 22–26, which correspond to Saturday–Thursday and Sunday–Thursday, it would seem that further study might be necessary to determine whether a different system of delivery exists during the midweek and weekend periods. For example, the proportion of filled rooms may vary or the number of available workers may vary during these times. After conclusion of such a study, any further improvements in the delivery times would have to be brought about by changes in the management of the delivery service.

Problems

19.6   Explain the difference between the control chart for an individual value and the control chart for the average.

19.7 Explain the differences in the development of the control chart for the average when historical values for the process average and standard deviation are available as compared with when there is no historical data.

• **19.8** Referring to the data of Problem 19.1 (softball production) on page 793, consider each row as a subgroup of size 5.
 (a) Assuming that the process average and standard deviation have not changed from the values given in Problem 19.1(a), set up a control chart for the average.
 (b) Suppose that you do not wish to assume that the process average and standard deviation have remained at their historical values. Set up a control chart for the average.
 (c) Compare the results of parts (a) and (b) of this problem. What differences in the results, if any, do you observe?
 (d) Compare the results of part (a) with those of part (a) of Problem 19.1 and the results of part (b) with those of part (b) of Problem 19.1. What differences in the control charts for the individual X values and for the average can you observe?

19.9 Referring to the data of Problem 19.2 (jeans production) on page 793, consider each consecutive set of three to represent a separate subgroup of size 3.
 (a) Suppose that you do not wish to assume that the process average and standard deviation have remained at their historical values. Set up a control chart for the average.
 (b) Compare the results of part (a) with those of part (c) of Problem 19.2. What differences can you observe?

19.10 Referring to the data of Problem 19.3 (table salt packaging) on page 793, consider each consecutive set of five to represent a separate subgroup of size 5.
 (a) Suppose that you do not wish to assume that the process average and standard deviation have remained at their historical values. Set up a control chart for the average.
 (b) Compare the results of part (a) with those of part (c) of Problem 19.3. What differences can you observe?

19.11 The manager of a private swimming pool facility monitors the pH (alkalinity–acidity) level of the swimming pool by taking hourly readings from 8 A.M. to 6 P.M. daily. The results for a three-week period summarized on a daily basis are presented below:

Day	Average ($\bar{X}_i$)	Range (R_i)
1	7.34	0.16
2	7.41	0.12
3	7.30	0.11
4	7.28	0.19
5	7.23	0.17
6	7.30	0.20
7	7.35	0.15
8	7.38	0.19
9	7.32	0.14
10	7.38	0.19
11	7.43	0.23
12	7.39	0.16
13	7.40	0.18
14	7.35	0.17
15	7.39	0.22
16	7.42	0.20
17	7.40	0.18
18	7.37	0.18
19	7.41	0.22
20	7.36	0.15
21	7.40	0.12

Set up a control chart for the average daily pH level.

19.12 The following data pertaining to incandescent light bulbs represents the average life and range for 30 subgroups of 5 light bulbs each. The results were as follows:

Subgroup Number	Subgroup Mean $\overline{X}_i$	Subgroup Range R_i
1	790	52
2	845	56
3	857	116
4	846	89
5	843	65
6	877	73
7	861	38
8	891	84
9	866	76
10	816	72
11	806	61
12	835	55
13	797	59
14	803	47
15	818	69
16	845	42
17	891	38
18	859	65
19	826	70
20	828	37
21	854	52
22	847	49
23	868	40
24	851	43
25	870	64
26	857	53
27	851	59
28	834	68
29	842	57
30	825	74

Set up a control chart for the average light bulb life.

19.7 THE R CHART: A CONTROL CHART FOR DISPERSION

In addition to evaluating whether an individual X value or the process average is in control, we usually wish to determine whether the variability in a process is also in control or whether shifts are occurring over time. One common control chart for dispersion is the R chart, a control chart for the range. The control limits for the range are a function not only of the d_2 factor, which represents the relationship between the standard deviation and the range for varying sample sizes, but also the d_3 factor, which represents the relationship between the standard deviation and the standard deviation of the range for varying sample sizes.[7] Values for the d_3 factor are also presented in Table E.13. Thus, we may set up the following control limits for the range over k consecutive sequences or periods of time.

---

[7] In industry the D_3 factor equal to $1 - 3d_3/d_2$, and the D_4 factor equal to $1 + 3\,d_3/d_2$ (see Reference 19), are used to simplify the computations.

$$\overline{R} \pm \frac{3\, d_3\, \overline{R}}{d_2} \qquad\qquad (19.7)$$

$$\text{where } \overline{R} = \frac{\sum\limits_{i=1}^{k} R_i}{k}$$

so that

$$LCL = \overline{R} - \frac{3\, d_3\, \overline{R}}{d_2} \quad \text{and} \quad UCL = \overline{R} + \frac{3\, d_3\, \overline{R}}{d_2}$$

We may observe the application of the R chart by returning to the luggage delivery data of Table 19.4 on page 795. Since $\overline{R} = 3.729$, and from Table E.13 we obtain $d_3 = .864$, using Equation 19.7, we have

$$3.729 \pm \frac{3\,(.864)\,(3.729)}{2.326}$$

$$3.729 \pm 4.155$$

so that

$$UCL = 7.884$$

We note that the lower control limit for R does not exist since a negative range is impossible to attain. The R control chart is displayed in Figure 19.9. An examination of Figure 19.9 does not indicate any individual ranges outside the control limits. However, there does seem to be some pattern in the ranges with higher values on Fridays and Saturdays (points 6, 7, 13, 20, 21). Thus, as with the $\overline{X}$ chart, a different system of delivery may be operating on the weekends as compared with the weekdays.

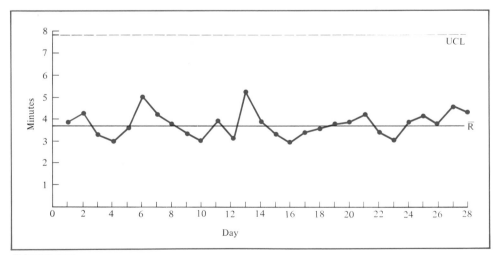

FIGURE 19.9
The R chart for luggage delivery times.
SOURCE: Table 19.4.

> ### *Problems*

- **19.13**   Referring to Problem 19.8 (softball production) on page 797.
     (a) Set up an *R* chart and determine whether the range chart gives an out of control signal.
     (b) How might you use the conclusions of part (a) in conjunction with those of Problem 19.8(b) to evaluate the process involved?

  19.14   Referring to Problem 19.9 (jeans production) on page 797, set up an *R* chart and determine whether the range chart gives an out of control signal.

  19.15   Referring to Problem 19.10 (table salt packaging) on page 797, set up an *R* chart and determine whether the range chart gives an out of control signal.

  19.16   Referring to Problem 19.11 (swimming pool pH level) on page 797, set up an *R* chart and determine whether the range chart gives an out of control signal.

  19.17   Referring to Problem 19.12 (light bulb life) on page 798, set up an *R* chart and determine whether the range chart gives an out of control signal.

19.8   THE *p*-CHART: A CONTROL CHART FOR THE FRACTION OF NONCONFORMING ITEMS (THE PROPORTION OF "SUCCESSES")

Now that we have studied control charts for an individual value, for the sample mean, and for the sample range, we may turn our attention to a different type of control chart—one that is used for a qualitative variable possessing an attribute that can be classified as conforming or nonconforming (i.e., "success" or "failure").

We may recall that we studied proportions in Chapters 6–9. We defined the proportion in Equation (6.1) as X/n; we then discussed the binomial distribution in Section 7.6 and the normal approximation to the binomial distribution in Section 8.4.2; moreover, in Section 9.3, we defined the standard error of the proportion as

$$\sigma_{p_S} = \sqrt{\frac{p(1 - p)}{n}}$$

Thus, using the normal approximation to the binomial distribution, we may set up control limits for the proportion of "successes"[8] given that a historical value for the proportion is provided:

$$p \pm 3 \sqrt{\frac{p(1 - p)}{n}} \tag{19.8}$$

However, in many instances, either there is no historical estimate of the proportion of nonconforming items (i.e., "successes") or one does not wish to assume that a specified value for *p* has remained constant. In such situations, we need to estimate the proportion from the subgroup data. Thus, we would have

---

[8] As in the case of our discussion of proportions in Section 7.6, we may define a "success" as a defective or nonconforming item.

$$\bar{p} \pm 3 \sqrt{\frac{\bar{p}(1 - \bar{p})}{n}} \tag{19.9}$$

where

X_i = number of "successes" in subgroup i

n_i = subgroup size for subgroup i

$p_{S_i} = X_i/n_i$

k = number of subgroups taken

$\bar{n}$ = average subgroup size

For equal n_i,

$$\bar{n} = n_i \qquad \text{and} \qquad \bar{p} = \frac{\sum_{i=1}^{k} p_{S_i}}{k}$$

or, in general,

$$\bar{n} = \frac{\sum_{i=1}^{k} n_i}{k} \qquad \text{and} \qquad \bar{p} = \frac{\sum_{i=1}^{k} X_i}{\sum_{i=1}^{n} n_i}$$

and

$$LCL = \bar{p} - 3 \sqrt{\frac{\bar{p}(1 - \bar{p})}{n}} \qquad \text{and} \qquad UCL = \bar{p} + 3 \sqrt{\frac{\bar{p}(1 - \bar{p})}{n}}$$

Any negative value for the lower control limit will mean that the lower control limit does not exist.

We may observe an application of the p chart by referring back to the hotel chain previously studied in Sections 19.6 and 19.7. Suppose that in addition to studying luggage delivery times, the hotel chain also wanted to study the proportion of guest rooms that were not ready at the time the individual guest checked in. A subgroup of 100 guest rooms were selected each day. Table 19.5 on page 802 represents the proportion of rooms that were not ready at check-in time for each day in the four-week period.

For these data, $k = 28$, $\sum_{i=1}^{k} p_{S_i} = 1.16$ and $n_i = 100$

Thus,

$$\bar{p} = \frac{1.16}{28} = .0414$$

so that we have

$$.0414 \pm 3 \sqrt{\frac{.0414 (.9586)}{100}}$$

$$= .0414 \pm .0598$$

TABLE 19.5 Proportion of rooms not ready for a four-week period

Day	Proportion	Day	Proportion
1	0.04	15	0.05
2	0.02	16	0.03
3	0.05	17	0.04
4	0.04	18	0.03
5	0.06	19	0.04
6	0.05	20	0.06
7	0.04	21	0.05
8	0.04	22	0.03
9	0.03	23	0.02
10	0.03	24	0.03
11	0.05	25	0.04
12	0.05	26	0.04
13	0.04	27	0.05
14	0.06	28	0.05

Thus, $UCL = .1012$, and the LCL does not exist..

The control chart for the data of Table 19.5 is displayed in Figure 19.10. An examination of Figure 19.10 seems to indicate a process in a state of statistical control, with the individual points distributed around p without any pattern. However, the points appear to be tightly distributed around the control limits. Thus, any improvement in this system of making rooms ready for guests must come from the reduction of common cause variation. As we have stated previously, such system alterations are the responsibility of management.

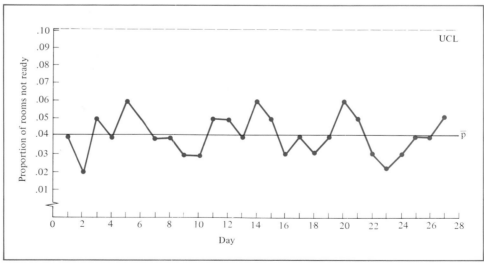

FIGURE 19.10
p chart for the proportion of rooms not ready.
SOURCE: Figure 19.5.

Problems

● **19.18**   The Commuters Watchdog Council of a railroad that serves a large metropolitan area wishes to monitor the on-time performance of the railroad during the morning rush hour. Suppose that a train is defined as being late if it arrives more than five minutes after the scheduled arrival time. A total of 235 trains are scheduled during the rush hour each morning. The results for a four-week period (based on a five-day work week) were as follows:

Day	Proportion of Late Arrivals	Day	Proportion of Late Arrivals
1	0.073	11	0.089
2	0.108	12	0.097
3	0.095	13	0.287
4	0.116	14	0.103
5	0.137	15	0.147
6	0.096	16	0.076
7	0.069	17	0.098
8	0.102	18	0.103
9	0.086	19	0.111
10	0.154	20	0.151

(a) Set up a p chart for the proportion of late arrivals and indicate whether the arrival process is in statistical control during this period.

(b) What effect would it have on your conclusions if you knew that there had been a four-inch snowstorm on the morning of day 13?

19.19   A professional basketball player has embarked on a program to study his ability to successfully shoot ''foul shots.'' On each day in which a game is not scheduled, he intends to shoot 100 foul shots. He maintains records over a period of 40 days of practice, with the following results:

Day	Proportion of Foul Shots Made	Day	Proportion of Foul Shots Made
1	0.73	21	0.64
2	0.75	22	0.67
3	0.69	23	0.72
4	0.72	24	0.70
5	0.77	25	0.74
6	0.71	26	0.76
7	0.68	27	0.75
8	0.70	28	0.78
9	0.67	29	0.76
10	0.74	30	0.80
11	0.75	31	0.78
12	0.72	32	0.83
13	0.70	33	0.84
14	0.74	34	0.81
15	0.73	35	0.86
16	0.76	36	0.85
17	0.69	37	0.86
18	0.68	38	0.87
19	0.72	39	0.85
20	0.70	40	0.85

(a) Set up a *p* chart for the percentage of successful foul shots. Do you think that the player's foul-shooting process is in statistical control? If not, why not?

(b) What if you were told that after the first 20 days, the player changed his method of shooting foul shots? How might this information change the conclusions you drew in part (a)?

(c) If you knew this information prior to doing part (a), how might you have done the *p* chart differently?

19.20 A private mail delivery service has a policy of guaranteeing delivery by 10:30 A.M. of the morning after a package is picked up. Suppose that management of the service wishes to study delivery performance in a particular geographic area over a four-week time period based on a five-day work week. The total number of packages delivered daily and the number of packages that were not delivered by 10:30 A.M. were recorded with the following results:

Day	Number of Packages Delivered	Number of Packages Not Arriving before 10:30 A.M.
1	136	4
2	153	6
3	127	2
4	157	7
5	144	5
6	122	5
7	154	6
8	132	3
9	160	8
10	142	7
11	157	6
12	150	9
13	142	8
14	137	10
15	147	8
16	132	7
17	136	6
18	137	7
19	153	11
20	141	7

(a) Set up a *p* chart for the proportion of packages that are not delivered before 10:30 A.M. Does the process give an out of control signal?

(b) Suppose that, based on past experience, a system of common causes results in 5% of the packages for this geographical area not arriving by 10:30 A.M. In light of this past experience, revise the center line and the control limits that you developed in part (a). What conclusions about the process are you able to draw now?

19.21 The superintendent of a school district was interested in studying student absenteeism at a particular elementary school during December and January. The school had 537 students registered during this time period. The results were recorded as shown at the top of page 805:

Day	Proportion of Students Absent	Day	Proportion of Students Absent
1	0.073	19	0.101
2	0.085	20	0.097
3	0.071	21	0.086
4	0.086	22	0.084
5	0.098	23	0.079
6	0.097	24	0.082
7	0.104	25	0.091
8	0.113	26	0.073
9	0.095	27	0.135
10	0.102	28	0.102
11	0.096	29	0.093
12	0.091	30	0.078
13	0.082	31	0.089
14	0.073	32	0.085
15	0.099	33	0.084
16	0.127	34	0.091
17	0.188	35	0.076
18	0.130	36	0.087

NOTE: The first seventeen days were from December and the last nineteen days were from January.

(a) Set up a *p* chart for the proportion of students who were absent during December and January. Does the process give an out of control signal?

(b) If the superintendent wants to develop a process to reduce absenteeism, how should she proceed?

19.22 A bottling company of Sweet Suzy's Sugarless Cola maintains daily records of the occurrences of unacceptable cans flowing from the filling and sealing machine. Nonconformities such as improper filling amount, dented cans, and cans that are improperly sealed are noted. Data for one month's production (based on a five-day work week) were as follows:

Day	Number of Cans Filled	Number of Unacceptable Cans
1	5,043	47
2	4,852	51
3	4,908	43
4	4,756	37
5	4,901	78
6	4,892	66
7	5,354	51
8	5,321	66
9	5,045	61
10	5,113	72
11	5,247	63
12	5,314	70
13	5,097	64
14	4,932	59
15	5,023	75
16	5,117	71
17	5,099	68
18	5,345	78
19	5,456	88
20	5,554	83
21	5,421	82
22	5,555	87

(a) Set up a *p* chart for the proportion of unacceptable cans for the month. Does the process give an out of control signal?

(b) If management wants to develop a process for reducing the proportion of unacceptable cans, how should it proceed?

19.9 THE c CHART: A CONTROL CHART FOR THE NUMBER OF OCCURRENCES PER UNIT

In Section 19.8 we considered the *p* chart, a control chart for the proportion of nonconforming items. In other instances we may be interested in determining the number of nonconformities (or "occurrences") in a unit, where the subgroup size per unit is very large and the probability of a nonconformity occurring in any part of the unit is very small. We may recall from Section 7.8 that such a situation fits the assumptions of a Poisson distribution. Among the phenomena that could be described by this process would be the number of flaws in a square foot of material, the number of typographical errors on a printed page, the number of breakdowns per day in an academic computer center, and the number of "turnovers" per game by a college basketball team.

In Section 7.8, we defined the standard deviation of the number of occurrences as being equal to the square root of the average number of occurrences. Thus, if the average number of occurrences is called λ,

$$\sigma_c = \sqrt{\lambda} \qquad\qquad \textbf{(19.10)}$$

Assuming that the size of each subgroup unit remains constant,[9] we may set up control limits for the number of occurrences using the normal approximation to the Poisson distribution. If an estimate is available from a stable system for the average number of occurrences per unit ($\bar{c}_0$) the control limits would be

$$\bar{c}_0 \pm 3\sqrt{\bar{c}_0} \qquad\qquad \textbf{(19.11)}$$

If no prior estimate is given, the average number of occurrences ($\bar{c}$) would be estimated from the data as

$$\bar{c} = \frac{\sum_{i=1}^{k} c_i}{k}$$

where $k =$ the number of units sampled
$c_i =$ the number of occurrences in unit i

---

[9] If the size of the sample unit varies appreciably, the *u* chart may be used instead of the *c* chart (see References 5, 7, 19).

Thus, for the situation where no prior estimate was available, the control limits for the average number of occurrences would be obtained from

$$\bar{c} \pm 3 \sqrt{\bar{c}} \qquad\qquad \textbf{(19.12)}$$

so that

$$LCL = \bar{c} - 3 \sqrt{\bar{c}} \quad \text{and} \quad UCL = \bar{c} + 3 \sqrt{\bar{c}}$$

Once again, we understand that any negative value for the lower control limit will mean that the lower control limit does not exist.

As an application of the *c* chart, suppose that the production manager of a large baking factory that makes Marilyn's pumpkin chocolate chip cupcakes for the Halloween holiday season needed to study the baking process to determine the number of chocolate chips that were contained in the cupcakes being baked. A subgroup of 50 cupcakes was selected from the production line. The results, listed in the order of selection, are summarized in Table 19.6.

For these data, $k = 50$ and $\sum_{i=1}^{k} c_i = 316$

Thus,

$$\bar{c} = \frac{316}{50} = 6.32$$

TABLE 19.6 Number of chocolate chips in a subgroup of 50 cupcakes

Cupcake	Number of Chocolate Chips	Cupcake	Number of Chocolate Chips
1	8	26	7
2	10	27	5
3	6	28	8
4	7	29	6
5	5	30	7
6	7	31	5
7	9	32	5
8	8	33	4
9	7	34	4
10	9	35	3
11	10	36	5
12	7	37	2
13	8	38	4
14	11	39	3
15	10	40	3
16	9	41	4
17	8	42	2
18	7	43	4
19	10	44	5
20	11	45	5
21	8	46	3
22	7	47	2
23	8	48	5
24	6	49	4
25	7	50	4

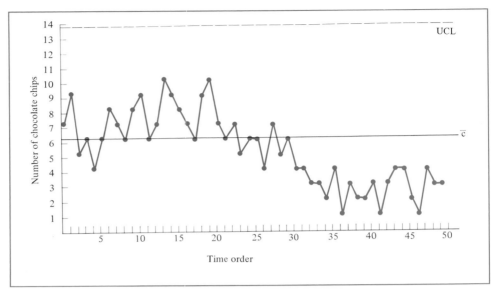

FIGURE 19.11
c chart for number of chocolate chips.

so that we have

$$6.32 \pm 3 \sqrt{6.32}$$

$$= 6.32 \pm 7.542$$

Thus, *UCL* = 13.862 and the *LCL* does not exist.

The control chart for the data of Table 19.6 is displayed in Figure 19.11. An examination of Figure 19.11 does not indicate any points outside the control limits. However, there is a clear pattern to the number of chocolate chips per cupcake over time, with cupcakes baked in the first half of the sequence almost always having more than the average number of chocolate chips and cupcakes in the latter half of the sequence having fewer than the average number of chocolate chips. Thus, the production manager should immediately investigate the process to determine the special causes that have produced this pattern of variation. The best place to start would be to ask the workers on the production line.

Problems

19.23   Explain the difference between the *p* chart and the *c* chart and indicate the circumstances in which each would be the most appropriate chart for a particular variable.

19.24   The owner of a dry cleaning business, in an effort to measure the quality of the services provided, would like to study the number of dry cleaned items that are returned for rework per day. Records were kept for a four-week period (the store is open Monday–Saturday) with the results indicated at the top of page 809:

Day	Items Returned for Rework	Day	Items Returned for Rework
1	4	13	5
2	6	14	8
3	3	15	3
4	7	16	4
5	6	17	10
6	8	18	9
7	6	19	6
8	4	20	5
9	8	21	8
10	6	22	6
11	5	23	7
12	12	24	9

(a) Set up a *c* chart for the number of items per day that are returned for rework. Do you think that the process is in a state of statistical control?

(b) Should the owner of the dry cleaning store take action to investigate why 12 items were returned for rework on day 12? Explain. Would your answer be the same if 20 items were returned for rework on day 12?

➠(c) **ACTION**   Based on the results in part (a), how should the owner of the dry cleaning store proceed in setting up a process to reduce the number of items per day that are returned for rework?

(d) Suppose that the previous long run average for number of items returned was 5 per day. Set up a *c* chart based on this number and evaluate the results in light of this.

19.25   The branch manager of a savings bank has recorded the number of errors of a particular type that each of 12 tellers has made during the past year. The results were as follows:

Teller	Number of Errors
Alice	4
Carl	7
Gina	12
Jane	6
Linda	2
Marla	5
Mitchell	6
Nora	3
Paul	5
Susan	4
Thomas	7
Vera	5

(a) Do you think the bank manager will single out Gina for any disciplinary action regarding her performance in the last year?

(b) Set up a *c* chart for the number of errors committed by the 12 tellers. Is the number of errors in a state of statistical control?

(c) Based on the *c* chart developed in part (b), do you now think that Gina should be singled out for disciplinary action regarding her performance? Does your conclusion now agree with what you expected the manager to do?

➠(d) **ACTION**   Based on the results in part (b), how should the branch manager go about setting up a program to reduce this particular type of error?

19.26 Referring to the data of Problem 19.20 on page 804
  (a) Set up a c chart for the number of packages per day that do not arrive before 10:30 A.M. Is the process in a state of statistical control?
  ✔(b) Compare the results of part (a) with the p chart developed in part (a) of Problem 19.20. Comment on the similarities and differences in the results obtained. Which chart do you think is more appropriate for these data? Why?
  ✔(c) What pitfalls might be involved in using the c chart for these data?

19.27 Referring to the data of Problem 19.22 on page 805
  (a) Set up a c chart for the number of unacceptable cans per day. Is the process in a state of statistical control?
  ✔(b) Compare the results of part (a) with the p chart developed in part (a) of Problem 19.22. Comment on the similarities and differences in the results obtained. Which chart do you think is more appropriate for these data? Why?
  ✔(c) What pitfalls might be involved in using the c chart for these data?

19.28 The University of Southwest North Carolina has recently completed its basketball season. Its basketball coach, the legendary Raving Rick Rawng, has maintained records of the number of turnovers (times the ball was lost without taking a shot) per game. The results were as follows:

Game	Number of Turnovers	Game	Number of Turnovers
1	16	14	18
2	12	15	26
3	25	16	14
4	17	17	12
5	11	18	16
6	19	19	29
7	17	20	11
8	23	21	7
9	12	22	15
10	9	23	12
11	13	24	17
12	16	25	22
13	21	26	14

  (a) Set up a c chart for the number of turnovers per game. Is the process in a state of statistical control?
  ➠(b) **ACTION** Based on the results of part (a), how should the coach proceed in setting up a process to reduce the number of turnovers in the future?

19.10 INSPECTION OF INCOMING MATERIAL AND FINAL PRODUCT

Although suppliers and industrial customers may work together to reduce the proportion of nonconforming items, it is necessary that there be decision criteria for use in evaluating incoming or outgoing items. In this section, we will briefly discuss three approaches for dealing with the issue of inspection of finished products: **mass inspection, acceptance sampling,** and **all-or-none** inspection.

19.10.1 Mass Inspection

Perhaps the first approach to controlling quality was one in which all finished products were subjected to inspection by a single inspector or by multiple inspectors. Such an approach contains several drawbacks. First, the cost of such massive inspection may likely be prohibitive, or at least much more in some circumstances than the total cost of no inspection. Second, as pointed out by Dodge (see Reference 3) and by Deming (see Reference 2), mass inspection will not improve the actual quality of an item, since the item already produced either has or does not have a given level of quality. Finally, for some products, (matches, for example) inspection is destructive. In such situations, sampling must be employed if there is to be any product left to sell after the inspection phase!

19.10.2 Acceptance Sampling

Acceptance sampling may be defined as sampling procedures in which a decision is made to accept an entire lot of a product or service based only on a sampling of the lot.

A rejected lot is returned to the supplier for rework or total inspection. We may recall from our discussion of hypothesis testing in Chapters 11–13 that there are two types of errors associated with making decisions based on sample information. From an acceptance sampling viewpoint, the Type I error represents the rejection of a lot that should have been accepted. This is referred to as the **producer's risk,** since the producer is incurring the risk that an acceptable lot will be returned. The Type II error represents the acceptance of a lot that should have been rejected. This is referred to as the **consumer's risk,** since the consumer is incurring the risk of accepting a lot that should have been rejected.

The producer's risk is usually stated in terms of a probability (α) that a lot will be rejected even though it is at or exceeds a certain **acceptable quality level** (called AQL). The consumer's risk is usually stated in terms of the probability (β) that a lot whose quality is below a certain level [called the **lot tolerance percent defective** (LTPD)] is accepted.

A wide variety of sampling plans have been developed (see References 5, 7, and 19) in acceptance sampling. One set of plans, referred to as **Military Standard 105D,** develops sampling plans for varying lot sizes and sample sizes indexed by the acceptable quality level (AQL). However, as Deming (see Reference 2) has noted, these plans do not take into account the total cost of inspection. Even more important is the fact that they do not take into account the ''invisible costs'' of lost customers. In addition, such plans specify that the producer is willing to send out products that have a defective rate at the AQL.

A second set of plans, called the **Dodge-Romig** plans, are based on the **Average Outgoing Quality Limit** (AOQL), which takes into account lots that have been screened after inspection. The tables of the Dodge-Romig plan are based either on AOQL or on LTPD (lot tolerance percent defective). The advantage of the Dodge-Romig plans as compared with Military Standard 105D is that at least these plans minimize the cost of inspection for a given quality level.

19.10.3 All-or-None Inspection

A third approach, suggested by Deming (see Reference 2), for most products attempts to minimize the average total cost of inspection along with the cost to repair and retest a product that failed downstream in the production process. This approach involves all-or-none rules that attempt to minimize the average total cost. These rules depend on the average fraction of nonconforming incoming parts, the cost of inspection, the cost to dismantle, repair, reassemble, and test an assembly that failed because of a nonconforming part, and the importance of the product's function to the customer. Some products, such as cardiac pacemakers, are so important to the customer that 100% testing is needed.

19.11 SUMMARY AND OVERVIEW

In this chapter we have introduced the topic of quality and productivity by discussing the Deming approach to management, by developing several different types of control charts, and by briefly discussing alternative approaches to the inspection of finished products. Those readers interested in the Deming approach are encouraged to examine References 2, 12, 14, and 21. Readers interested in additional control chart procedures should access References 1, 5, 7, and 19. Moreover, those interested in acceptance sampling methods (including their pitfalls) should examine References 2, 3, 5, 6, 7, and 19.

Supplementary Problems

19.29 On each morning for a period of four weeks, record your pulse rate (in beats per minute) just after you get out of bed. Set up a control chart for the pulse rate and determine whether it is in a state of statistical control. Explain.

19.30 On each day for a period of four weeks, record the time (in minutes) that it takes you to get from where you reside to your first class. Set up a control chart for this commuting time. Do you think that your commuting time is "stable" or it is out of statistical control? Explain.

19.31 In Problem 3.88 on page 88, although the batting averages are listed in order from highest to lowest, the listing of the number of home runs is based on the ordering of the batting averages of the players. For each league, set up a control chart of the number of home runs in the order listed. Would you say that there is a pattern in the number of home runs based on batting average?

19.32 In Problem 3.89 on page 89, although the number of receptions are listed in order from highest to lowest, the ordering of the average yardage per reception and the number of touchdowns is based on the ordering of the number of receptions of the players. For each conference, set up control charts of the average yardage per reception and the number of touchdowns in the order listed. Would you say that there is a pattern in the average yardage per reception and/or the number of touchdowns based on number of receptions?

● **19.33** The service manager of a large automobile dealership wanted to study the length of time required for a particular type of repair in his shop. A subgroup of 10 cars needing this repair was selected on each day for a period of four weeks. The results (service time in hours) were recorded in the table at the top of page 813:

Day	Subgroup Mean $\bar{X}_i$	Subgroup Range R_i
1	3.73	5.23
2	3.16	4.82
3	3.56	4.98
4	3.01	4.28
5	3.87	5.74
6	3.90	5.42
7	3.54	4.08
8	3.32	4.55
9	3.29	4.48
10	3.83	5.09
11	3.64	5.37
12	3.27	4.42
13	3.16	4.85
14	3.39	4.44
15	3.85	5.06
16	3.90	4.99
17	3.72	4.67
18	3.51	4.37
19	3.34	4.53
20	3.99	5.28

(a) Set up all appropriate control charts and determine whether the service time process is in a state of statistical control.

➡(b) **ACTION** If the service manager wanted to develop a process to reduce service time, how should he proceed?

19.34 A paper-cutting machine is operating in a process that is producing paper of a standard length (in this case, 11.5 inches). As the paper is being cut by the machine, periodically subgroups of five pieces are selected. The results for a set of 20 consecutive subgroups were as follows:

Subgroup Number	Subgroup Mean $\bar{X}_i$ (in inches)	Subgroup Range R_i (in inches)
1	11.523	0.043
2	11.507	0.049
3	11.502	0.037
4	11.498	0.048
5	11.507	0.052
6	11.501	0.046
7	11.492	0.049
8	11.504	0.053
9	11.500	0.047
10	11.489	0.037
11	11.494	0.061
12	11.506	0.054
13	11.498	0.051
14	11.503	0.046
15	11.505	0.040
16	11.494	0.053
17	11.487	0.038
18	11.507	0.046
19	11.493	0.064
20	11.483	0.061

(a) Set up all appropriate control charts and determine whether the paper length is in a state of statistical control.

(b) Assuming that the process standard deviation has remained at its historical value of .01, set up a control chart for the mean and determine whether the process is in a state of statistical control.

(c) Compare the results of parts (a) and (b) of this problem. What differences in the results, if any, do you observe?

19.35 The director of operations for an airline was interested in studying the number of pieces of baggage that are lost (temporarily or permanently) at a large airport. Records indicating the number of lost baggage claims filed per day over a one-month period were as follows:

Day	Number of Claims	Day	Number of Claims
1	14	16	28
2	23	17	20
3	17	18	13
4	25	19	26
5	27	20	42
6	42	21	38
7	35	22	23
8	29	23	28
9	30	24	19
10	23	25	26
11	15	26	14
12	27	27	30
13	41	28	37
14	50	29	17
15	23	30	24

(a) Set up a control chart for the number of claims per day. Is the process of number of claims in a state of statistical control? Explain.

✔(b) Suppose that the total number of pieces of baggage per day was available for the 30-day period. Explain how you might proceed with a different control chart than the one you used in part (a). Indicate what the advantages could be of using this alternative control chart as compared with the control chart that was used in part (a).

19.36 **(CLASS PROJECT)** The table of random numbers (Table E.1) can be used to simulate the operation of an urn of different colored balls as follows:

1. Start in the row corresponding to the day of the month you were born plus the year in which you were born. For example, if you were born on Oct. 15, 1969, you would start in row 15 + 69 = 84.
2. Two-digit random numbers are to be selected.
3. If the random number between 00 and 94 is selected, consider the ball to be white; if the random number is 95–99, consider the ball to be red.

Each student is to select 100 such two-digit random numbers and report the number of "red balls" in the sample. A control chart is to be set up of the number of (or the proportion of) red balls. What conclusions can you draw about the system of selecting red balls? Are all the students "part of the system"? Is anyone "outside the system"? If so, what explanation can you give for someone who has too many red balls? If a bonus was paid to the top 10% of the students (those 10% with the fewest red balls), what effect would that have on the rest of the students? Discuss.

Case Study J

As Chief Operating Officer of a local community hospital, you have just returned from a three-day seminar on quality and productivity. It is your intention to implement many of the ideas that you learned at the seminar in your own hospital. You have decided to maintain control charts for the upcoming month for the following variables: number of daily admissions, proportion of rework in the laboratory (based on 1000 daily samples), and time (in hours) between receipt of a specimen at the laboratory and completion of the work (based on a subgroup of 10 specimens per day). The data collected are summarized in Table 19.7.

TABLE 19.7   Hospital summary data

Day	Number of Admissions	Processing Time $\overline{X}_i$	Processing Time R_i	Proportion of Rework in Laboratory
1	27	1.72	3.57	0.048
2	36	2.03	3.98	0.052
3	23	2.18	3.54	0.047
4	28	1.90	3.49	0.046
5	19	2.53	3.99	0.039
6	22	2.26	3.34	0.086
7	18	2.11	3.36	0.051
8	30	2.35	3.52	0.043
9	33	2.06	3.39	0.046
10	35	2.01	3.24	0.040
11	29	2.13	3.62	0.045
12	28	2.18	3.37	0.036
13	22	2.31	3.97	0.048
14	26	2.37	4.06	0.057
15	32	2.78	4.27	0.052
16	30	2.12	3.21	0.046
17	28	2.27	3.48	0.041
18	27	2.49	3.62	0.032
19	27	2.32	3.19	0.042
20	18	2.43	3.67	0.053
21	19	2.25	3.10	0.041
22	25	2.31	3.58	0.037
23	23	2.07	3.26	0.039
24	28	2.33	3.40	0.050
25	34	2.36	3.52	0.048
26	25	2.47	3.82	0.054
27	21	2.28	3.97	0.046
28	20	2.17	3.60	0.035
29	40	2.54	3.92	0.075
30	31	2.63	3.86	0.046

You are to make a presentation to the Chief Executive Officer of the hospital and the Board of Directors. You need to prepare a report that summarizes the conclusions obtained from analyzing control charts for these variables. In addition, it is expected that you will recommend additional variables for which control charts are to be maintained. Finally, it is your intention to explain how the Deming philosophy of management by process can be implemented in the context of your hospital's environment.

References

1. ALWAN, L. C., AND H. V. ROBERTS, "Time series modeling for statistical process control." *Journal of Business and Economic Statistics*, 1988, Vol. 6, pp. 87–96.
2. DEMING, W. E., *Out of the Crisis* (Cambridge, Mass.: MIT Center for Advanced Engineering Study, 1986).
3. DODGE, H. F., "Administration of a sampling inspection plan," *Industrial Quality Control*, 1948, Vol. 5, pp. 12–19.
4. DOBSON, J. M., *A History of American Enterprise* (Englewood Cliffs, N.J.: Prentice-Hall, 1988).
5. DUNCAN, A. J., *Quality Control and Industrial Statistics*, 5th ed. (Homewood, Ill.: Richard D. Irwin, 1986).
6. FEIGENBAUM, A. V., *Total Quality Control* (New York: McGraw-Hill, 1983).
7. GRANT, E. L., AND R. S. LEAVENWORTH, *Statistical Quality Control*, 6th ed. (New York: McGraw-Hill, 1988).
8. HALBERSTAM, D., *The Reckoning* (New York: William Morrow and Company, 1986).
9. JOINER, B. J., "Lurking variables," *American Statistician*, 1981, Vol. 35, pp. 227–233.
10. JOINER, B. J., "The key role of statisticians in the transformation of North American industry," *American Statistician*, 1985, Vol. 39, pp. 224–234.
11. MAIN, J., "The curmudgeon who talks tough on quality," *Fortune*, June 25, 1984, pp. 118–122.
12. MANN, N. R., *The Keys to Excellence: The Story of the Deming Philosophy* (Los Angeles: Prestwick Books, 1987).
13. PORT, O., "The push for quality," *Business Week*, June 8, 1987, pp. 130–135.
14. SCHERKENBACH, W. W., *The Deming Route to Quality and Productivity: Road Maps and Roadblocks* (Washington, D.C.: CEEP Press, 1986).
15. SHEWHART, W. A., "The applications of statistics as an aid in maintaining quality of manufactured products," *Journal of the American Statistical Association*, 1925, Vol. 20, pp. 546–548.
16. SHEWHART, W. A., *Economic Control of Quality of Manufactured Products* (New York: Van Nostrand-Reinhard, 1931, reprinted by the American Society for Quality Control, Milwaukee, 1980).
17. SHEWHART, W. A., AND W. E. DEMING, *Statistical Methods from the Viewpoint of Quality Control* (Washington, D.C.: Graduate School, Dept. of Agriculture, 1939, Dover Press, 1986).
18. SHOLTES, P. R., *An Elaboration on Deming's Teaching on Performance Appraisal* (Madison, Wisc.: Joiner Associates, 1987).
19. WADSWORTH, H. M., K. S. STEPHENS, AND A. B. GODFREY, *Modern Methods for Quality Control and Improvement* (New York: John Wiley and Sons, 1986).
20. WALLIS, W. A., "The statistical research group 1942–1945," *Journal of the American Statistical Association*, 1980, Vol. 75, pp. 320–335.
21. WALTON, M., *The Deming Management Method* (New York: Perigee Books, Putnam Publishing Group, 1986).

Appendix A: Review of Arithmetic and Algebra

A.1 RULES FOR ARITHMETIC OPERATIONS

The following is a summary of various rules for arithmetic operations with each rule illustrated by a numerical example:

Rule	*Example*
1. $a + b = c$ and $b + a = c$	$2 + 1 = 3$ and $1 + 2 = 3$
2. $a + (b + c) = (a + b) + c$	$5 + (7 + 4) = (5 + 7) + 4 = 16$
3. $a - b = c$ but $b - a \neq c$	$9 - 7 = 2$ but $7 - 9 = -2$
4. $a \times b = b \times a$	$7 \times 6 = 6 \times 7 = 42$
5. $a \times (b + c) = (a \times b) + (a \times c)$	$2 \times (3 + 5) = (2 \times 3) + (2 \times 5) = 16$
6. $a \div b \neq b \div a$	$12 \div 3 \neq 3 \div 12$
7. $\dfrac{a + b}{c} = \dfrac{a}{c} + \dfrac{b}{c}$	$\dfrac{7 + 3}{2} = \dfrac{7}{2} + \dfrac{3}{2} = 5$
8. $\dfrac{a}{b + c} \neq \dfrac{a}{b} + \dfrac{a}{c}$	$\dfrac{3}{4 + 5} \neq \dfrac{3}{4} + \dfrac{3}{5}$
9. $\dfrac{1}{a} + \dfrac{1}{b} = \dfrac{b + a}{ab}$	$\dfrac{1}{3} + \dfrac{1}{5} = \dfrac{5 + 3}{(3)(5)} = \dfrac{8}{15}$
10. $\dfrac{a}{b} \times \dfrac{c}{d} = \dfrac{a \times c}{b \times d}$	$\dfrac{2}{3} \times \dfrac{6}{7} = \dfrac{2 \times 6}{3 \times 7} = \dfrac{12}{21}$
11. $\dfrac{a}{b} \div \dfrac{c}{d} = \dfrac{a \times d}{b \times c}$	$\dfrac{5}{8} \div \dfrac{3}{7} = \dfrac{5 \times 7}{8 \times 3} = \dfrac{35}{24}$

A.2 RULES FOR ALGEBRA: EXPONENTS AND SQUARE ROOTS

The following is a summary of various rules for algebraic operations with each rule illustrated by a numerical example:

Rule	*Example*
1. $X^a \cdot X^b = X^{a+b}$	$4^2 \cdot 4^3 = 4^5$
2. $(X^a)^b = X^{ab}$	$(2^2)^3 = 2^6$
3. $(X^a/X^b) = X^{a-b}$	$\dfrac{3^5}{3^3} = 3^2$
4. $\dfrac{X^a}{X^a} = X^0 = 1$	$\dfrac{3^4}{3^4} = 3^0 = 1$
5. $\sqrt{XY} = \sqrt{X}\sqrt{Y}$	$\sqrt{(25)(4)} = \sqrt{25}\sqrt{4} = 10$
6. $\sqrt{\dfrac{X}{Y}} = \dfrac{\sqrt{X}}{\sqrt{Y}}$	$\sqrt{\dfrac{16}{100}} = \dfrac{\sqrt{16}}{\sqrt{100}} = .40$

Appendix B:
Summation Notation

Since the operation of addition occurs so frequently in statistics, the special symbol $\sum$ (sigma) is used to denote "taking the sum of." Suppose, for example, that we have a set of n values for some variable X. The expression $\sum_{i=1}^{n} X_i$ means that these n values are to be added together. Thus

$$\sum_{i=1}^{n} X_i = X_1 + X_2 + X_3 + \cdots + X_n$$

The use of the summation notation can be illustrated in the following problem. Suppose that we have five observations of a variable X: $X_1 = 2$, $X_2 = 0$, $X_3 = -1$, $X_4 = 5$, and $X_5 = 7$. Thus

$$\begin{aligned} \sum_{i=1}^{5} X_i &= X_1 + X_2 + X_3 + X_4 + X_5 \\ &= 2 + 0 + (-1) + 5 + 7 = 13 \end{aligned}$$

In statistics we are also frequently involved with summing the squared values of a variable. Thus

$$\sum_{i=1}^{n} X_i^2 = X_1^2 + X_2^2 + X_3^2 + \cdots + X_n^2$$

and, in our example, we have

$$\begin{aligned} \sum_{i=1}^{5} X_i^2 &= X_1^2 + X_2^2 + X_3^2 + X_4^2 + X_5^2 \\ &= 2^2 + 0^2 + (-1)^2 + 5^2 + 7^2 \\ &= 4 + 0 + 1 + 25 + 49 \\ &= 79 \end{aligned}$$

We should realize here that $\sum_{i=1}^{n} X_i^2$, the summation of the squares, is not the same as $\left(\sum_{i=1}^{n} X_i\right)^2$, the square of the sum, that is,

$$\sum_{i=1}^{n} X_i^2 \neq \left(\sum_{i=1}^{n} X_i\right)^2$$

In our example the summation of squares is equal to 79. This is not equal to the square of the sum, which is $13^2 = 169$.

Another frequently used operation involves the summation of the product. That is, suppose that we have two variables, X and Y, each having n observations. Then,

$$\sum_{i=1}^{n} X_i Y_i = X_1 Y_1 + X_2 Y_2 + X_3 Y_3 + \cdots + X_n Y_n$$

Continuing with our previous example, suppose that there is also a second variable Y whose five values are $Y_1 = 1$, $Y_2 = 3$, $Y_3 = -2$, $Y_4 = 4$, and $Y_5 = 3$. Then,

$$\begin{aligned}
\sum_{i=1}^{5} X_i Y_i &= X_1 Y_1 + X_2 Y_2 + X_3 Y_3 + X_4 Y_4 + X_5 Y_5 \\
&= 2(1) + 0(3) + (-1)(-2) + 5(4) + 7(3) \\
&= 2 + 0 + 2 + 20 + 21 \\
&= 45
\end{aligned}$$

In computing $\sum_{i=1}^{n} X_i Y_i$ we must realize that the first value of X is multiplied by the first value of Y, the second value of X is multiplied by the second value of Y, etc. These cross products are then summed in order to obtain the desired result. However, we should note here that the summation of cross products is not equal to the product of the individual sums, that is,

$$\sum_{i=1}^{n} X_i Y_i \neq \left(\sum_{i=1}^{n} X_i\right)\left(\sum_{i=1}^{n} Y_i\right)$$

In our example, $\sum_{i=1}^{5} X_i = 13$ and $\sum_{i=1}^{5} Y_i = 1 + 3 + (-2) + 4 + 3 = 9$, so that $\left(\sum_{i=1}^{5} X_i\right)\left(\sum_{i=1}^{5} Y_i\right) = 13(9) = 117$. This is not the same as $\sum_{i=1}^{5} X_i Y_i$, which equals 45.

Before studying the four basic rules of performing operations with summation notation, it would be helpful to present the values for each of the five observations of X and Y in a tabular format.

Observation	X_i	Y_i
1	2	1
2	0	3
3	−1	−2
4	5	4
5	7	3
	$\sum_{i=1}^{5} X_i = 13$	$\sum_{i=1}^{5} Y_i = 9$

Rule 1: The summation of the values of two variables is equal to the sum of the values of each summed variable.

$$\sum_{i=1}^{n} (X_i + Y_i) = \sum_{i=1}^{n} X_i + \sum_{i=1}^{n} Y_i$$

Thus, in our example,

$$\sum_{i=1}^{5} (X_i + Y_i) = (2 + 1) + (0 + 3) + (-1 + (-2)) + (5 + 4) + (7 + 3)$$

$$= 3 + 3 + (-3) + 9 + 10$$

$$= 22 = \sum_{i=1}^{5} X_i + \sum_{i=1}^{5} Y_i = 13 + 9 = 22$$

Rule 2: The summation of a difference between the values of two variables is equal to the difference between the summed values of the variables.

$$\sum_{i=1}^{n} (X_i - Y_i) = \sum_{i=1}^{n} X_i - \sum_{i=1}^{n} Y_i$$

Thus, in our example,

$$\sum_{i=1}^{5} (X_i - Y_i) = (2 - 1) + (0 - 3) + (-1 - (-2)) + (5 - 4) + (7 - 3)$$

$$= 1 + (-3) + 1 + 1 + 4$$

$$= 4 = \sum_{i=1}^{5} X_i - \sum_{i=1}^{5} Y_i = 13 - 9 = 4$$

Rule 3: The summation of a constant times a variable is equal to that constant times the summation of the values of the variable.

$$\sum_{i=1}^{n} cX_i = c \sum_{i=1}^{n} X_i$$

where c is a constant.

Thus, in our example, if $c = 2$,

$$\sum_{i=1}^{5} cX_i = \sum_{i=1}^{5} 2X_i = 2(2) + 2(0) + 2(-1) + 2(5) + 2(7)$$

$$= 4 + 0 + (-2) + 10 + 14$$

$$= 26 = 2 \sum_{i=1}^{5} X_i = 2(13) = 26$$

Rule 4: A constant summed n times will be equal to n times the value of the constant.

$$\sum_{i=1}^{n} c = nc$$

where c is a constant.

Thus, if the constant $c = 2$ is summed five times, we would have

$$\sum_{i=1}^{5} c = 2 + 2 + 2 + 2 + 2$$

$$= 10 = 5(2) = 10$$

To illustrate how these summation rules are used, we may demonstrate one of the mathematical properties pertaining to the average or arithmetic mean (see Section 3.5.2), that is,

$$\sum_{i=1}^{n} (X_i - \bar{X}) = 0$$

This property states that the summation of the differences between each observation and the arithmetic mean is zero. This can be proven mathematically in the following manner.

1. From Equation (3.1),

$$\bar{X} = \frac{\sum_{i=1}^{n} X_i}{n}$$

Thus, using summation rule 2, we have

$$\sum_{i=1}^{n} (X_i - \bar{X}) = \sum_{i=1}^{n} X_i - \sum_{i=1}^{n} \bar{X}$$

2. Since, for any fixed set of data, $\bar{X}$ can be considered a constant, from summation rule 4 we have

$$\sum_{i=1}^{n} \bar{X} = n\bar{X}$$

Therefore,

$$\sum_{i=1}^{n} (X_i - \overline{X}) = \sum_{i=1}^{n} X_i - n\overline{X}$$

3. However, from Equation (3.1), since

$$\overline{X} = \frac{\sum_{i=1}^{n} X_i}{n} \quad \text{then} \quad n\overline{X} = \sum_{i=1}^{n} X_i$$

Therefore,

$$\sum_{i=1}^{n} (X_i - \overline{X}) = \sum_{i=1}^{n} X_i - \sum_{i=1}^{n} X_i$$

Thus we have shown that

$$\sum_{i=1}^{n} (X_i - \overline{X}) = 0$$

Problem

Suppose that there are six observations for the variables X and Y such that $X_1 = 2$, $X_2 = 1$, $X_3 = 5$, $X_4 = -3$, $X_5 = 1$, $X_6 = -2$, and $Y_1 = 4$, $Y_2 = 0$, $Y_3 = -1$, $Y_4 = 2$, $Y_5 = 7$, and $Y_6 = -3$. Compute each of the following.

(a) $\displaystyle\sum_{i=1}^{6} X_i$ **(b)** $\displaystyle\sum_{i=1}^{6} Y_i$

(c) $\displaystyle\sum_{i=1}^{6} X_i^2$ **(d)** $\displaystyle\sum_{i=1}^{6} Y_i^2$

(e) $\displaystyle\sum_{i=1}^{6} X_i Y_i$ **(f)** $\displaystyle\sum_{i=1}^{6} (X_i + Y_i)$

(g) $\displaystyle\sum_{i=1}^{6} (X_i - Y_i)$ **(h)** $\displaystyle\sum_{i=1}^{6} (X_i - 3Y_i + 2X_i^2)$

(i) $\displaystyle\sum_{i=1}^{6} (cX_i)$, where $c = -1$ **(j)** $\displaystyle\sum_{i=1}^{6} (X_i - 3Y_i + c)$, where $c = +3$

Reference

BASHAW, W. L., *Mathematics for Statistics* (New York: Wiley, 1969).

Appendix C:
Statistical Symbols
and Greek Alphabet

C.1 STATISTICAL SYMBOLS

$+$	add	$\times$	multiply
$-$	subtract	$\div$	divide
$=$	equals	$\neq$	not equal
$\cong$	approximately equal to		
$>$	greater than	$<$	less than
$\geq$ or $\geqslant$	greater than or equal to	$\leq$ or $\leqslant$	less than or equal to

C.2 GREEK ALPHABET

Greek Letter	Greek Name	English Equivalent	Greek Letter	Greek Name	English Equivalent
A α	Alpha	a	N ν	Nu	n
B β	Beta	b	Ξ ξ	Xi	x
Γ γ	Gamma	g	O o	Omicron	ŏ
Δ δ	Delta	d	Π π	Pi	p
E ϵ	Epsilon	ĕ	P ρ	Rho	r
Z ζ	Zeta	z	Σ σ ς	Sigma	s
H η	Eta	ē	T τ	Tau	t
Θ θ ϑ	Theta	th	Υ υ	Upsilon	u
I ι	Iota	i	Φ ϕ φ	Phi	ph
K κ	Kappa	k	X χ	Chi	ch
Λ λ	Lambda	l	Ψ ψ	Psi	ps
M μ	Mu	m	Ω ω	Omega	ō

Appendix D:
The Metric System

The current system of measurement used in the United States is called the English system. In this appendix we will discuss the much more widely used metric system of measurement.

There are several reasons for adopting the metric system of measurement. One major advantage of converting to the metric system is found in the area of international trade and commerce. The manufacturing process will become much more efficient if, in the production of goods for export, different machinery and/or different production setups were not needed. A second advantage to the metric system is found in the area of travel and communications. Whether for reasons of business or pleasure, as more and more Americans spend time traveling abroad, and, at the same time, we accept visitors from other countries to our shores, this ''exchange process'' would greatly be facilitated if we used the same system of measurement as is used throughout most of the world. A third major advantage to using the metric system is its simplicity. The metric system of measurement is a decimal system, and, therefore, is much simpler to use and work with than our current English system.

Metric conversions

Type of Measurement	From Metric to Metric	From English to Metric	From Metric to English
Length (linear measurement)	1 micrometer $= \dfrac{1}{1,000,000}$ meter 1 millimeter $= \dfrac{1}{1,000}$ meter 1 centimeter $= \dfrac{1}{100}$ meter 1 hectometer $=$ 100 meters 1 kilometer $=$ 1,000 meters 1 megameter $=$ 1,000,000 meters	1 inch $=$ 25.4 millimeters 1 inch $=$ 2.54 centimeters 1 foot $=$ 0.3 meter 1 yard $=$ 0.9 meter 1 mile $=$ 1.6 kilometers	1 millimeter $=$ 0.04 inch 1 centimeter $=$ 0.4 inch 1 meter $=$ 3.3 feet 1 meter $=$ 1.1 yards 1 kilometer $=$ 0.621 mile
Area (square measure)		1 square inch $=$ 6.5 square centimeters 1 square foot $=$ 0.09 square meter 1 square yard $=$ 0.8 square meter 1 acre $=$ 0.4 square hectometer	1 square centimeter $=$ 0.16 square inch 1 square meter $=$ 11 square feet 1 square meter $=$ 1.2 square yards 1 square hectometer $=$ 2.5 acres
Weight (mass)	1 microgram $= \dfrac{1}{1,000,000}$ gram 1 milligram $= \dfrac{1}{1,000}$ gram 1 centigram $= \dfrac{1}{100}$ gram 1 hectogram $=$ 100 grams 1 kilogram $=$ 1,000 grams 1 megagram $=$ 1,000,000 grams	1 ounce $=$ 28.3 grams 1 pound $=$ 0.45 kilogram	1 gram $=$ 0.035 ounce 1 kilogram $=$ 2.2 pounds
Volume (capacity)	1 microliter $= \dfrac{1}{1,000,000}$ liter 1 milliliter $= \dfrac{1}{1,000}$ liter 1 centiliter $= \dfrac{1}{100}$ liter 1 hectoliter $=$ 100 liters 1 kiloliter $=$ 1,000 liters 1 megaliter $=$ 1,000,000 liters	1 quart $=$ 0.9463 liter 1 gallon $=$ 3.7853 liters	1 liter $=$ 1.06 quarts 1 liter $=$ 0.26 gallon

E

Appendix E: Tables

TABLE E.1   Table of random numbers

Row	00000 12345	00001 67890	11111 12345	11112 67890	22222 12345	22223 67890	33333 12345	33334 67890
				Column				
01	49280	88924	35779	00283	81163	07275	89863	02348
02	61870	41657	07468	08612	98083	97349	20775	45091
03	43898	65923	25078	86129	78496	97653	91550	08078
04	62993	93912	30454	84598	56095	20664	12872	64647
05	33850	58555	51438	85507	71865	79488	76783	31708
06	97340	03364	88472	04334	63919	36394	11095	92470
07	70543	29776	10087	10072	55980	64688	68239	20461
08	89382	93809	00796	95945	34101	81277	66090	88872
09	37818	72142	67140	50785	22380	16703	53362	44940
10	60430	22834	14130	96593	23298	56203	92671	15925
11	82975	66158	84731	19436	55790	69229	28661	13675
12	39087	71938	40355	54324	08401	26299	49420	59208
13	55700	24586	93247	32596	11865	63397	44251	43189
14	14756	23997	78643	75912	83832	32768	18928	57070
15	32166	53251	70654	92827	63491	04233	33825	69662
16	23236	73751	31888	81718	06546	83246	47651	04877
17	45794	26926	15130	82455	78305	55058	52551	47182
18	09893	20505	14225	68514	46427	56788	96297	78822
19	54382	74598	91499	14523	68479	27686	46162	83554
20	94750	89923	37089	20048	80336	94598	26940	36858
21	70297	34135	53140	33340	42050	82341	44104	82949
22	85157	47954	32979	26575	57600	40881	12250	73742
23	11100	02340	12860	74697	96644	89439	28707	25815
24	36871	50775	30592	57143	17381	68856	25853	35041
25	23913	48357	63308	16090	51690	54607	72407	55538
26	79348	36085	27973	65157	07456	22255	25626	57054
27	92074	54641	53673	54421	18130	60103	69593	49464
28	06873	21440	75593	41373	49502	17972	82578	16364
29	12478	37622	99659	31065	83613	69889	58869	29571
30	57175	55564	65411	42547	70457	03426	72937	83792
31	91616	11075	80103	07831	59309	13276	26710	73000
32	78025	73539	14621	39044	47450	03197	12787	47709
33	27587	67228	80145	10175	12822	86687	65530	49325
34	16690	20427	04251	64477	73709	73945	92396	68263
35	70183	58065	65489	31833	82093	16747	10386	59293
36	90730	35385	15679	99742	50866	78028	75573	67257
37	10934	93242	13431	24590	02770	48582	00906	58595
38	82462	30166	79613	47416	13389	80268	05085	96666
39	27463	10433	07606	16285	93699	60912	94532	95632
40	02979	52997	09079	92709	90110	47506	53693	49892
41	46888	69929	75233	52507	32097	37594	10067	67327
42	53638	83161	08289	12639	08141	12640	28437	09268
43	82433	61427	17239	89160	19666	08814	37841	12847
44	35766	31672	50082	22795	66948	65581	84393	15890
45	10853	42581	08792	13257	61973	24450	52351	16602
46	20341	27398	72906	63955	17276	10646	74692	48438
47	54458	90542	77563	51839	52901	53355	83281	19177
48	26337	66530	16687	35179	46560	00123	44546	79896
49	34314	23729	85264	05575	96855	23820	11091	79821
50	28603	10708	68933	34189	92166	15181	66628	58599

TABLE E.1   *(Continued)*

Row	Column							
	00000 *12345*	*00001* *67890*	*11111* *12345*	*11112* *67890*	*22222* *12345*	*22223* *67890*	*33333* *12345*	*33334* *67890*
51	66194	28926	99547	16625	45515	67953	12108	57846
52	78240	43195	24837	32511	70880	22070	52622	61881
53	00833	88000	67299	68215	11274	55624	32991	17436
54	12111	86683	61270	58036	64192	90611	15145	01748
55	47189	99951	05755	03834	43782	90599	40282	51417
56	76396	72486	62423	27618	84184	78922	73561	52818
57	46409	17469	32483	09083	76175	19985	26309	91536
58	74626	22111	87286	46772	42243	68046	44250	42439
59	34450	81974	93723	49023	58432	67083	36876	93391
60	36327	72135	33005	28701	34710	49359	50693	89311
61	74185	77536	84825	09934	99103	09325	67389	45869
62	12296	41623	62873	37943	25584	09609	63360	47270
63	90822	60280	88925	99610	42772	60561	76873	04117
64	72121	79152	96591	90305	10189	79778	68016	13747
65	95268	41377	25684	08151	61816	58555	54305	86189
66	92603	09091	75884	93424	72586	88903	30061	14457
67	18813	90291	05275	01223	79607	95426	34900	09778
68	38840	26903	28624	67157	51986	42865	14508	49315
69	05959	33836	53758	16562	41081	38012	41230	20528
70	85141	21155	99212	32685	51403	31926	69813	58781
71	75047	59643	31074	38172	03718	32119	69506	67143
72	30752	95260	68032	62871	58781	34143	68790	69766
73	22986	82575	42187	62295	84295	30634	66562	31442
74	99439	86692	90348	66036	48399	73451	26698	39437
75	20389	93029	11881	71685	65452	89047	63669	02656
76	39249	05173	68256	36359	20250	68686	05947	09335
77	96777	33605	29481	20063	09398	01843	35139	61344
78	04860	32918	10798	50492	52655	33359	94713	28393
79	41613	42375	00403	03656	77580	87772	86877	57085
80	17930	00794	53836	53692	67135	98102	61912	11246
81	24649	31845	25736	75231	83808	98917	93829	99430
82	79899	34061	54308	59358	56462	58166	97302	86828
83	76801	49594	81002	30397	52728	15101	72070	33706
84	36239	63636	38140	65731	39788	06872	38971	53363
85	07392	64449	17886	63632	53995	17574	22247	62607
86	67133	04181	33874	98835	67453	59734	76381	63455
87	77759	31504	32832	70861	15152	29733	75371	39174
88	85992	72268	42920	20810	29361	51423	90306	73574
89	79553	75952	54116	65553	47139	60579	09165	85490
90	41101	17336	48951	53674	17880	45260	08575	49321
91	36191	17095	32123	91576	84221	78902	82010	30847
92	62329	63898	23268	74283	26091	68409	69704	82267
93	14751	13151	93115	01437	56945	89661	67680	79790
94	48462	59278	44185	29616	76537	19589	83139	28454
95	29435	88105	59651	44391	74588	55114	80834	85686
96	28340	29285	12965	14821	80425	16602	44653	70467
97	02167	58940	27149	80242	10587	79786	34959	75339
98	17864	00991	39557	54981	23588	81914	37609	13128
99	79675	80605	60059	35862	00254	36546	21545	78179
00	72335	82037	92003	34100	29879	46613	89720	13274

SOURCE: Partially extracted from The Rand Corporation, *A Million Random Digits with 100,000 Normal Deviates* (Glencoe, Ill.: The Free Press, 1955).

TABLE E.2   The standardized normal distribution

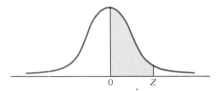

Entry represents area under the standardized normal distribution from the mean to *Z*

Z	.00	.01	.02	.03	.04	.05	.06	.07	.08	.09
0.0	.0000	.0040	.0080	.0120	.0160	.0199	.0239	.0279	.0319	.0359
0.1	.0398	.0438	.0478	.0517	.0557	.0596	.0636	.0675	.0714	.0753
0.2	.0793	.0832	.0871	.0910	.0948	.0987	.1026	.1064	.1103	.1141
0.3	.1179	.1217	.1255	.1293	.1331	.1368	.1406	.1443	.1480	.1517
0.4	.1554	.1591	.1628	.1664	.1700	.1736	.1772	.1808	.1844	.1879
0.5	.1915	.1950	.1985	.2019	.2054	.2088	.2123	.2157	.2190	.2224
0.6	.2257	.2291	.2324	.2357	.2389	.2422	.2454	.2486	.2518	.2549
0.7	.2580	.2612	.2642	.2673	.2704	.2734	.2764	.2794	.2823	.2852
0.8	.2881	.2910	.2939	.2967	.2995	.3023	.3051	.3078	.3106	.3133
0.9	.3159	.3186	.3212	.3238	.3264	.3289	.3315	.3340	.3365	.3389
1.0	.3413	.3438	.3461	.3485	.3508	.3531	.3554	.3577	.3599	.3621
1.1	.3643	.3665	.3686	.3708	.3729	.3749	.3770	.3790	.3810	.3830
1.2	.3849	.3869	.3888	.3907	.3925	.3944	.3962	.3980	.3997	.4015
1.3	.4032	.4049	.4066	.4082	.4099	.4115	.4131	.4147	.4162	.4177
1.4	.4192	.4207	.4222	.4236	.4251	.4265	.4279	.4292	.4306	.4319
1.5	.4332	.4345	.4357	.4370	.4382	.4394	.4406	.4418	.4429	.4441
1.6	.4452	.4463	.4474	.4484	.4495	.4505	.4515	.4525	.4535	.4545
1.7	.4554	.4564	.4573	.4582	.4591	.4599	.4608	.4616	.4625	.4633
1.8	.4641	.4649	.4656	.4664	.4671	.4678	.4686	.4693	.4699	.4706
1.9	.4713	.4719	.4726	.4732	.4738	.4744	.4750	.4756	.4761	.4767
2.0	.4772	.4778	.4783	.4788	.4793	.4798	.4803	.4808	.4812	.4817
2.1	.4821	.4826	.4830	.4834	.4838	.4842	.4846	.4850	.4854	.4857
2.2	.4861	.4864	.4868	.4871	.4875	.4878	.4881	.4884	.4887	.4890
2.3	.4893	.4896	.4898	.4901	.4904	.4906	.4909	.4911	.4913	.4916
2.4	.4918	.4920	.4922	.4925	.4927	.4929	.4931	.4932	.4934	.4936
2.5	.4938	.4940	.4941	.4943	.4945	.4946	.4948	.4949	.4951	.4952
2.6	.4953	.4955	.4956	.4957	.4959	.4960	.4961	.4962	.4963	.4964
2.7	.4965	.4966	.4967	.4968	.4969	.4970	.4971	.4972	.4973	.4974
2.8	.4974	.4975	.4976	.4977	.4977	.4978	.4979	.4979	.4980	.4981
2.9	.4981	.4982	.4982	.4983	.4984	.4984	.4985	.4985	.4986	.4986
3.0	.49865	.49869	.49874	.49878	.49882	.49886	.49889	.49893	.49897	.49900
3.1	.49903	.49906	.49910	.49913	.49916	.49918	.49921	.49924	.49926	.49929
3.2	.49931	.49934	.49936	.49938	.49940	.49942	.49944	.49946	.49948	.49950
3.3	.49952	.49953	.49955	.49957	.49958	.49960	.49961	.49962	.49964	.49965
3.4	.49966	.49968	.49969	.49970	.49971	.49972	.49973	.49974	.49975	.49976
3.5	.49977	.49978	.49978	.49979	.49980	.49981	.49981	.49982	.49983	.49983
3.6	.49984	.49985	.49985	.49986	.49986	.49987	.49987	.49988	.49988	.49989
3.7	.49989	.49990	.49990	.49990	.49991	.49991	.49992	.49992	.49992	.49992
3.8	.49993	.49993	.49993	.49994	.49994	.49994	.49994	.49995	.49995	.49995
3.9	.49995	.49995	.49996	.49996	.49996	.49996	.49996	.49996	.49997	.49997

TABLE E.3   Critical values of *t*

For a particular number of degrees of freedom,
entry represents the critical value of *t*
corresponding to a specified upper tail area α

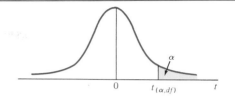

Degrees of Freedom	Upper Tail Areas					
	.25	.10	.05	.025	.01	.005
1	1.0000	3.0777	6.3138	12.7062	31.8207	63.6574
2	0.8165	1.8856	2.9200	4.3027	6.9646	9.9248
3	0.7649	1.6377	2.3534	3.1824	4.5407	5.8409
4	0.7407	1.5332	2.1318	2.7764	3.7469	4.6041
5	0.7267	1.4759	2.0150	2.5706	3.3649	4.0322
6	0.7176	1.4398	1.9432	2.4469	3.1427	3.7074
7	0.7111	1.4149	1.8946	2.3646	2.9980	3.4995
8	0.7064	1.3968	1.8595	2.3060	2.8965	3.3554
9	0.7027	1.3830	1.8331	2.2622	2.8214	3.2498
10	0.6998	1.3722	1.8125	2.2281	2.7638	3.1693
11	0.6974	1.3634	1.7959	2.2010	2.7181	3.1058
12	0.6955	1.3562	1.7823	2.1788	2.6810	3.0545
13	0.6938	1.3502	1.7709	2.1604	2.6503	3.0123
14	0.6924	1.3450	1.7613	2.1448	2.6245	2.9768
15	0.6912	1.3406	1.7531	2.1315	2.6025	2.9467
16	0.6901	1.3368	1.7459	2.1199	2.5835	2.9208
17	0.6892	1.3334	1.7396	2.1098	2.5669	2.8982
18	0.6884	1.3304	1.7341	2.1009	2.5524	2.8784
19	0.6876	1.3277	1.7291	2.0930	2.5395	2.8609
20	0.6870	1.3253	1.7247	2.0860	2.5280	2.8453
21	0.6864	1.3232	1.7207	2.0796	2.5177	2.8314
22	0.6858	1.3212	1.7171	2.0739	2.5083	2.8188
23	0.6853	1.3195	1.7139	2.0687	2.4999	2.8073
24	0.6848	1.3178	1.7109	2.0639	2.4922	2.7969
25	0.6844	1.3163	1.7081	2.0595	2.4851	2.7874
26	0.6840	1.3150	1.7056	2.0555	2.4786	2.7787
27	0.6837	1.3137	1.7033	2.0518	2.4727	2.7707
28	0.6834	1.3125	1.7011	2.0484	2.4671	2.7633
29	0.6830	1.3114	1.6991	2.0452	2.4620	2.7564
30	0.6828	1.3104	1.6973	2.0423	2.4573	2.7500
31	0.6825	1.3095	1.6955	2.0395	2.4528	2.7440
32	0.6822	1.3086	1.6939	2.0369	2.4487	2.7385
33	0.6820	1.3077	1.6924	2.0345	2.4448	2.7333
34	0.6818	1.3070	1.6909	2.0322	2.4411	2.7284
35	0.6816	1.3062	1.6896	2.0301	2.4377	2.7238
36	0.6814	1.3055	1.6883	2.0281	2.4345	2.7195
37	0.6812	1.3049	1.6871	2.0262	2.4314	2.7154
38	0.6810	1.3042	1.6860	2.0244	2.4286	2.7116
39	0.6808	1.3036	1.6849	2.0227	2.4258	2.7079
40	0.6807	1.3031	1.6839	2.0211	2.4233	2.7045
41	0.6805	1.3025	1.6829	2.0195	2.4208	2.7012
42	0.6804	1.3020	1.6820	2.0181	2.4185	2.6981
43	0.6802	1.3016	1.6811	2.0167	2.4163	2.6951
44	0.6801	1.3011	1.6802	2.0154	2.4141	2.6923
45	0.6800	1.3006	1.6794	2.0141	2.4121	2.6896

TABLE E.3 *(Continued)*

Degrees of Freedom	Upper Tail Areas					
	.25	.10	.05	.025	.01	.005
46	0.6799	1.3002	1.6787	2.0129	2.4102	2.6870
47	0.6797	1.2998	1.6779	2.0117	2.4083	2.6846
48	0.6796	1.2994	1.6772	2.0106	2.4066	2.6822
49	0.6795	1.2991	1.6766	2.0096	2.4049	2.6800
50	0.6794	1.2987	1.6759	2.0086	2.4033	2.6778
51	0.6793	1.2984	1.6753	2.0076	2.4017	2.6757
52	0.6792	1.2980	1.6747	2.0066	2.4002	2.6737
53	0.6791	1.2977	1.6741	2.0057	2.3988	2.6718
54	0.6791	1.2974	1.6736	2.0049	2.3974	2.6700
55	0.6790	1.2971	1.6730	2.0040	2.3961	2.6682
56	0.6789	1.2969	1.6725	2.0032	2.3948	2.6665
57	0.6788	1.2966	1.6720	2.0025	2.3936	2.6649
58	0.6787	1.2963	1.6716	2.0017	2.3924	2.6633
59	0.6787	1.2961	1.6711	2.0010	2.3912	2.6618
60	0.6786	1.2958	1.6706	2.0003	2.3901	2.6603
61	0.6785	1.2956	1.6702	1.9996	2.3890	2.6589
62	0.6785	1.2954	1.6698	1.9990	2.3880	2.6575
63	0.6784	1.2951	1.6694	1.9983	2.3870	2.6561
64	0.6783	1.2949	1.6690	1.9977	2.3860	2.6549
65	0.6783	1.2947	1.6686	1.9971	2.3851	2.6536
66	0.6782	1.2945	1.6683	1.9966	2.3842	2.6524
67	0.6782	1.2943	1.6679	1.9960	2.3833	2.6512
68	0.6781	1.2941	1.6676	1.9955	2.3824	2.6501
69	0.6781	1.2939	1.6672	1.9949	2.3816	2.6490
70	0.6780	1.2938	1.6669	1.9944	2.3808	2.6479
71	0.6780	1.2936	1.6666	1.9939	2.3800	2.6469
72	0.6779	1.2934	1.6663	1.9935	2.3793	2.6459
73	0.6779	1.2933	1.6660	1.9930	2.3785	2.6449
74	0.6778	1.4931	1.6657	1.9925	2.3778	2.6439
75	0.6778	1.2929	1.6654	1.9921	2.3771	2.6430
76	0.6777	1.2928	1.6652	1.9917	2.3764	2.6421
77	0.6777	1.2926	1.6649	1.9913	2.3758	2.6412
78	0.6776	1.2925	1.6646	1.9908	2.3751	2.6403
79	0.6776	1.2924	1.6644	1.9905	2.3745	2.6395
80	0.6776	1.2922	1.6641	1.9901	2.3739	2.6387
81	0.6775	1.2921	1.6639	1.9897	2.3733	2.6379
82	0.6775	1.2920	1.6636	1.9893	2.3727	2.6371
83	0.6775	1.2918	1.6634	1.9890	2.3721	2.6364
84	0.6774	1.2917	1.6632	1.9886	2.3716	2.6356
85	0.6774	1.2916	1.6630	1.9883	2.3710	2.6349
86	0.6774	1.2915	1.6628	1.9879	2.3705	2.6342
87	0.6773	1.2914	1.6626	1.9876	2.3700	2.6335
88	0.6773	1.2912	1.6624	1.9873	2.3695	2.6329
89	0.6773	1.2911	1.6622	1.9870	2.3690	2.6322
90	0.6772	1.2910	1.6620	1.9867	2.3685	2.6316
91	0.6772	1.2909	1.6618	1.9864	2.3680	2.6309
92	0.6772	1.2908	1.6616	1.9861	2.3676	2.6303
93	0.6771	1.2907	1.6614	1.9858	2.3671	2.6297
94	0.6771	1.2906	1.6612	1.9855	2.3667	2.6291
95	0.6771	1.2905	1.6611	1.9853	2.3662	2.6286

TABLE E.3   *(Continued)*

Degrees of Freedom	Upper Tail Areas					
	.25	.10	.05	.025	.01	.005
96	0.6771	1.2904	1.6609	1.9850	2.3658	2.6280
97	0.6770	1.2903	1.6607	1.9847	2.3654	2.6275
98	0.6770	1.2902	1.6606	1.9845	2.3650	2.6269
99	0.6770	1.2902	1.6604	1.9842	2.3646	2.6264
100	0.6770	1.2901	1.6602	1.9840	2.3642	2.6259
110	0.6767	1.2893	1.6588	1.9818	2.3607	2.6213
120	0.6765	1.2886	1.6577	1.9799	2.3578	2.6174
130	0.6764	1.2881	1.6567	1.9784	2.3554	2.6142
140	0.6762	1.2876	1.6558	1.9771	2.3533	2.6114
150	0.6761	1.2872	1.6551	1.9759	2.3515	2.6090
∞	0.6745	1.2816	1.6449	1.9600	2.3263	2.5758

TABLE E.4 Critical values of χ^2

For a particular number of degrees of freedom, entry represents the critical value of χ^2 corresponding to a specified upper tail area (α)

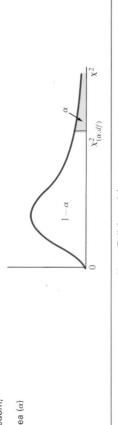

Degrees of Freedom	Upper Tail Areas (α)													
---	.995	.99	.975	.95	.90	.75	.25	.10	.05	.025	.01	.005
1			0.001	0.004	0.016	0.102	1.323	2.706	3.841	5.024	6.635	7.879
2	0.010	0.020	0.051	0.103	0.211	0.575	2.773	4.605	5.991	7.378	9.210	10.597
3	0.072	0.115	0.216	0.352	0.584	1.213	4.108	6.251	7.815	9.348	11.345	12.838
4	0.207	0.297	0.484	0.711	1.064	1.923	5.385	7.779	9.488	11.143	13.277	14.860
5	0.412	0.554	0.831	1.145	1.610	2.675	6.626	9.236	11.071	12.833	15.086	16.750
6	0.676	0.872	1.237	1.635	2.204	3.455	7.841	10.645	12.592	14.449	16.812	18.548
7	0.989	1.239	1.690	2.167	2.833	4.255	9.037	12.017	14.067	16.013	18.475	20.278
8	1.344	1.646	2.180	2.733	3.490	5.071	10.219	13.362	15.507	17.535	20.090	21.955
9	1.735	2.088	2.700	3.325	4.168	5.899	11.389	14.684	16.919	19.023	21.666	23.589
10	2.156	2.558	3.247	3.940	4.865	6.737	12.549	15.987	18.307	20.483	23.209	25.188
11	2.603	3.053	3.816	4.575	5.578	7.584	13.701	17.275	19.675	21.920	24.725	26.757
12	3.074	3.571	4.404	5.226	6.304	8.438	14.845	18.549	21.026	23.337	26.217	28.299
13	3.565	4.107	5.009	5.892	7.042	9.299	15.984	19.812	22.362	24.736	27.688	29.819
14	4.075	4.660	5.629	6.571	7.790	10.165	17.117	21.064	23.685	26.119	29.141	31.319
15	4.601	5.229	6.262	7.261	8.547	11.037	18.245	22.307	24.996	27.488	30.578	32.801
16	5.142	5.812	6.908	7.962	9.312	11.912	19.369	23.542	26.296	28.845	32.000	34.267
17	5.697	6.408	7.564	8.672	10.085	12.792	20.489	24.769	27.587	30.191	33.409	35.718
18	6.265	7.015	8.231	9.390	10.865	13.675	21.605	25.989	28.869	31.526	34.805	37.156
19	6.844	7.633	8.907	10.117	11.651	14.562	22.718	27.204	30.144	32.852	36.191	38.582
20	7.434	8.260	9.591	10.851	12.443	15.452	23.828	28.412	31.410	34.170	37.566	39.997
21	8.034	8.897	10.283	11.591	13.240	16.344	24.935	29.615	32.671	35.479	38.932	41.401
22	8.643	9.542	10.982	12.338	14.042	17.240	26.039	30.813	33.924	36.781	40.289	42.796
23	9.260	10.196	11.689	13.091	14.848	18.137	27.141	32.007	35.172	38.076	41.638	44.181
24	9.886	10.856	12.401	13.848	15.659	19.037	28.241	33.196	36.415	39.364	42.980	45.559
25	10.520	11.524	13.120	14.611	16.473	19.939	29.339	34.382	37.652	40.646	44.314	46.928
26	11.160	12.198	13.844	15.379	17.292	20.843	30.435	35.563	38.885	41.923	45.642	48.290
27	11.808	12.879	14.573	16.151	18.114	21.749	31.528	36.741	40.113	43.194	46.963	49.645
28	12.461	13.565	15.308	16.928	18.939	22.657	32.620	37.916	41.337	44.461	48.278	50.993
29	13.121	14.257	16.047	17.708	19.768	23.567	33.711	39.087	42.557	45.722	49.588	52.336
30	13.787	14.954	16.791	18.493	20.599	24.478	34.800	40.256	43.773	46.979	50.892	53.672

TABLE E.4 (Continued)

Degrees of Freedom	Upper Tail Areas (α)											
	.995	.99	.975	.95	.90	.75	.25	.10	.05	.025	.01	.005
31	14.458	15.655	17.539	19.281	21.434	25.390	35.887	41.422	44.985	48.232	52.191	55.003
32	15.134	16.362	18.291	20.072	22.271	26.304	36.973	42.585	46.194	49.480	53.486	56.328
33	15.815	17.074	19.047	20.867	23.110	27.219	38.058	43.745	47.400	50.725	54.776	57.648
34	16.501	17.789	19.806	21.664	23.952	28.136	39.141	44.903	48.602	51.966	56.061	58.964
35	17.192	18.509	20.569	22.465	24.797	29.054	40.223	46.059	49.802	53.203	57.342	60.275
36	17.887	19.233	21.336	23.269	25.643	29.973	41.304	47.212	50.998	54.437	58.619	61.581
37	18.586	19.960	22.106	24.075	26.492	30.893	42.383	48.363	52.192	55.668	59.892	62.883
38	19.289	20.691	22.878	24.884	27.343	31.815	43.462	49.513	53.384	56.896	61.162	64.181
39	19.996	21.426	23.654	25.695	28.196	32.737	44.539	50.660	54.572	58.120	62.428	65.476
40	20.707	22.164	24.433	26.509	29.051	33.660	45.616	51.805	55.758	59.342	63.691	66.766
41	21.421	22.906	25.215	27.326	29.907	34.585	46.692	52.949	56.942	60.561	64.950	68.053
42	22.138	23.650	25.999	28.144	30.765	35.510	47.766	54.090	58.124	61.777	66.206	69.336
43	22.859	24.398	26.785	28.965	31.625	36.436	48.840	55.230	59.304	62.990	67.459	70.616
44	23.584	25.148	27.575	29.787	32.487	37.363	49.913	56.369	60.481	64.201	68.710	71.893
45	24.311	25.901	28.366	30.612	33.350	38.291	50.985	57.505	61.656	65.410	69.957	73.166
46	25.041	26.657	29.160	31.439	34.215	39.220	52.056	58.641	62.830	66.617	71.201	74.437
47	25.775	27.416	29.956	32.268	35.081	40.149	53.127	59.774	64.001	67.821	72.443	75.704
48	26.511	28.177	30.755	33.098	35.949	41.079	54.196	60.907	65.171	69.023	73.683	76.969
49	27.249	28.941	31.555	33.930	36.818	42.010	55.265	62.038	66.339	70.222	74.919	78.231
50	27.991	29.707	32.357	34.764	37.689	42.942	56.334	63.167	67.505	71.420	76.154	79.490
51	28.735	30.475	33.162	35.600	38.560	43.874	57.401	64.295	68.669	72.616	77.386	80.747
52	29.481	31.246	33.968	36.437	39.433	44.808	58.468	65.422	69.832	73.810	78.616	82.001
53	30.230	32.018	34.776	37.276	40.308	45.741	59.534	66.548	70.993	75.002	79.843	83.253
54	30.981	32.793	35.586	38.116	41.183	46.676	60.600	67.673	72.153	76.192	81.069	84.502
55	31.735	33.570	36.398	38.958	42.060	47.610	61.665	68.796	73.311	77.380	82.292	85.749
56	32.490	34.350	37.212	39.801	42.937	48.546	62.729	69.919	74.468	78.567	83.513	86.994
57	33.248	35.131	38.027	40.646	43.816	49.482	63.793	71.040	75.624	79.752	84.733	88.236
58	34.008	35.913	38.844	41.492	44.696	50.419	64.857	72.160	76.778	80.936	85.950	89.477
59	34.770	36.698	39.662	42.339	45.577	51.356	65.919	73.279	77.931	82.117	87.166	90.715
60	35.534	37.485	40.482	43.188	46.459	52.294	66.981	74.397	79.082	83.298	88.379	91.952

For larger values of degrees of freedom (DF) the expression $z = \sqrt{2\chi^2} - \sqrt{2(DF) - 1}$ may be used and the resulting upper tail area can be obtained from the table of the standardized normal distribution (Table E.2).

835

TABLE E.5 Critical values of F

For a particular combination of numerator and denominator degrees of freedom, entry represents the critical values of F corresponding to a specified upper tail area (α).

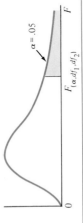

$F_{(\alpha, df_1, df_2)}$

$\alpha = .05$

F

Denominator df_2	\multicolumn{19}{c}{Numerator df_1}
	1	2	3	4	5	6	7	8	9	10	12	15	20	24	30	40	60	120	∞
1	161.4	199.5	215.7	224.6	230.2	234.0	236.8	238.9	240.5	241.9	243.9	245.9	248.0	249.1	250.1	251.1	252.2	253.3	254.3
2	18.51	19.00	19.16	19.25	19.30	19.33	19.35	19.37	19.38	19.40	19.41	19.43	19.45	19.45	19.46	19.47	19.48	19.49	19.50
3	10.13	9.55	9.28	9.12	9.01	8.94	8.89	8.85	8.81	8.79	8.74	8.70	8.66	8.64	8.62	8.59	8.57	8.55	8.53
4	7.71	6.94	6.59	6.39	6.26	6.16	6.09	6.04	6.00	5.96	5.91	5.86	5.80	5.77	5.75	5.72	5.69	5.66	5.63
5	6.61	5.79	5.41	5.19	5.05	4.95	4.88	4.82	4.77	4.74	4.68	4.62	4.56	4.53	4.50	4.46	4.43	4.40	4.36
6	5.99	5.14	4.76	4.53	4.39	4.28	4.21	4.15	4.10	4.06	4.00	3.94	3.87	3.84	3.81	3.77	3.74	3.70	3.67
7	5.59	4.74	4.35	4.12	3.97	3.87	3.79	3.73	3.68	3.64	3.57	3.51	3.44	3.41	3.38	3.34	3.30	3.27	3.23
8	5.32	4.46	4.07	3.84	3.69	3.58	3.50	3.44	3.39	3.35	3.28	3.22	3.15	3.12	3.08	3.04	3.01	2.97	2.93
9	5.12	4.26	3.86	3.63	3.48	3.37	3.29	3.23	3.18	3.14	3.07	3.01	2.94	2.90	2.86	2.83	2.79	2.75	2.71
10	4.96	4.10	3.71	3.48	3.33	3.22	3.14	3.07	3.02	2.98	2.91	2.85	2.77	2.74	2.70	2.66	2.62	2.58	2.54
11	4.84	3.98	3.59	3.36	3.20	3.09	3.01	2.95	2.90	2.85	2.79	2.72	2.65	2.61	2.57	2.53	2.49	2.45	2.40
12	4.75	3.89	3.49	3.26	3.11	3.00	2.91	2.85	2.80	2.75	2.69	2.62	2.54	2.51	2.47	2.43	2.38	2.34	2.30
13	4.67	3.81	3.41	3.18	3.03	2.92	2.83	2.77	2.71	2.67	2.60	2.53	2.46	2.42	2.38	2.34	2.30	2.25	2.21
14	4.60	3.74	3.34	3.11	2.96	2.85	2.76	2.70	2.65	2.60	2.53	2.46	2.39	2.35	2.31	2.27	2.22	2.18	2.13
15	4.54	3.68	3.29	3.06	2.90	2.79	2.71	2.64	2.59	2.54	2.48	2.40	2.33	2.29	2.25	2.20	2.16	2.11	2.07
16	4.49	3.63	3.24	3.01	2.85	2.74	2.66	2.59	2.54	2.49	2.42	2.35	2.28	2.24	2.19	2.15	2.11	2.06	2.01
17	4.45	3.59	3.20	2.96	2.81	2.70	2.61	2.55	2.49	2.45	2.38	2.31	2.23	2.19	2.15	2.10	2.06	2.01	1.96
18	4.41	3.55	3.16	2.93	2.77	2.66	2.58	2.51	2.46	2.41	2.34	2.27	2.19	2.15	2.11	2.06	2.02	1.97	1.92
19	4.38	3.52	3.13	2.90	2.74	2.63	2.54	2.48	2.42	2.38	2.31	2.23	2.16	2.11	2.07	2.03	1.98	1.93	1.88
20	4.35	3.49	3.10	2.87	2.71	2.60	2.51	2.45	2.39	2.35	2.28	2.20	2.12	2.08	2.04	1.99	1.95	1.90	1.84
21	4.32	3.47	3.07	2.84	2.68	2.57	2.49	2.42	2.37	2.32	2.25	2.18	2.10	2.05	2.01	1.96	1.92	1.87	1.81
22	4.30	3.44	3.05	2.82	2.66	2.55	2.46	2.40	2.34	2.30	2.23	2.15	2.07	2.03	1.98	1.94	1.89	1.84	1.78
23	4.28	3.42	3.03	2.80	2.64	2.53	2.44	2.37	2.32	2.27	2.20	2.13	2.05	2.01	1.96	1.91	1.86	1.81	1.76
24	4.26	3.40	3.01	2.78	2.62	2.51	2.42	2.36	2.30	2.25	2.18	2.11	2.03	1.98	1.94	1.89	1.84	1.79	1.73
25	4.24	3.39	2.99	2.76	2.60	2.49	2.40	2.34	2.28	2.24	2.16	2.09	2.01	1.96	1.92	1.87	1.82	1.77	1.71
26	4.23	3.37	2.98	2.74	2.59	2.47	2.39	2.32	2.27	2.22	2.15	2.07	1.99	1.95	1.90	1.85	1.80	1.75	1.69
27	4.21	3.35	2.96	2.73	2.57	2.46	2.37	2.31	2.25	2.20	2.13	2.06	1.97	1.93	1.88	1.84	1.79	1.73	1.67
28	4.20	3.34	2.95	2.71	2.56	2.45	2.36	2.29	2.24	2.19	2.12	2.04	1.96	1.91	1.87	1.82	1.77	1.71	1.65
29	4.18	3.33	2.93	2.70	2.55	2.43	2.35	2.28	2.22	2.18	2.10	2.03	1.94	1.90	1.85	1.81	1.75	1.70	1.64
30	4.17	3.32	2.92	2.69	2.53	2.42	2.33	2.27	2.21	2.16	2.09	2.01	1.93	1.89	1.84	1.79	1.74	1.68	1.62
40	4.08	3.23	2.84	2.61	2.45	2.34	2.25	2.18	2.12	2.08	2.00	1.92	1.84	1.79	1.74	1.69	1.64	1.58	1.51
60	4.00	3.15	2.76	2.53	2.37	2.25	2.17	2.10	2.04	1.99	1.92	1.84	1.75	1.70	1.65	1.59	1.53	1.47	1.39
120	3.92	3.07	2.68	2.45	2.29	2.17	2.09	2.02	1.96	1.91	1.83	1.75	1.66	1.61	1.55	1.50	1.43	1.35	1.25
∞	3.84	3.00	2.60	2.37	2.21	2.10	2.01	1.94	1.88	1.83	1.75	1.67	1.57	1.52	1.46	1.39	1.32	1.22	1.00

TABLE E.5 (Continued)

$F_{(\alpha, df_1, df_2)}$, $\alpha = .025$

Denominator df_2	Numerator df_1																		
	1	2	3	4	5	6	7	8	9	10	12	15	20	24	30	40	60	120	∞
1	647.8	799.5	864.2	899.6	921.8	937.1	948.2	956.7	963.3	968.6	976.7	984.9	993.1	997.2	1001	1006	1010	1014	1018
2	38.51	39.00	39.17	39.25	39.30	39.33	39.36	39.37	39.39	39.40	39.41	39.43	39.45	39.46	39.46	39.47	39.48	39.49	39.50
3	17.44	16.04	15.44	15.10	14.88	14.73	14.62	14.54	14.47	14.42	14.34	14.25	14.17	14.12	14.08	14.04	13.99	13.95	13.90
4	12.22	10.65	9.98	9.60	9.36	9.20	9.07	8.98	8.90	8.84	8.75	8.66	8.56	8.51	8.46	8.41	8.36	8.31	8.26
5	10.01	8.43	7.76	7.39	7.15	6.98	6.85	6.76	6.68	6.62	6.52	6.43	6.33	6.28	6.23	6.18	6.12	6.07	6.02
6	8.81	7.26	6.60	6.23	5.99	5.82	5.70	5.60	5.52	5.46	5.37	5.27	5.17	5.12	5.07	5.01	4.96	4.90	4.85
7	8.07	6.54	5.89	5.52	5.29	5.12	4.99	4.90	4.82	4.76	4.67	4.57	4.47	4.42	4.36	4.31	4.25	4.20	4.14
8	7.57	6.06	5.42	5.05	4.82	4.65	4.53	4.43	4.36	4.30	4.20	4.10	4.00	3.95	3.89	3.84	3.78	3.73	3.67
9	7.21	5.71	5.08	4.72	4.48	4.32	4.20	4.10	4.03	3.96	3.87	3.77	3.67	3.61	3.56	3.51	3.45	3.39	3.33
10	6.94	5.46	4.83	4.47	4.24	4.07	3.95	3.85	3.78	3.72	3.62	3.52	3.42	3.37	3.31	3.26	3.20	3.14	3.08
11	6.72	5.26	4.63	4.28	4.04	3.88	3.76	3.66	3.59	3.53	3.43	3.33	3.23	3.17	3.12	3.06	3.00	2.94	2.88
12	6.55	5.10	4.47	4.12	3.89	3.73	3.61	3.51	3.44	3.37	3.28	3.18	3.07	3.02	2.96	2.91	2.85	2.79	2.72
13	6.41	4.97	4.35	4.00	3.77	3.60	3.48	3.39	3.31	3.25	3.15	3.05	2.95	2.89	2.84	2.78	2.72	2.66	2.60
14	6.30	4.86	4.24	3.89	3.66	3.50	3.38	3.29	3.21	3.15	3.05	2.95	2.84	2.79	2.73	2.67	2.61	2.55	2.49
15	6.20	4.77	4.15	3.80	3.58	3.41	3.29	3.20	3.12	3.06	2.96	2.86	2.76	2.70	2.64	2.59	2.52	2.46	2.40
16	6.12	4.69	4.08	3.73	3.50	3.34	3.22	3.12	3.05	2.99	2.89	2.79	2.68	2.63	2.57	2.51	2.45	2.38	2.32
17	6.04	4.62	4.01	3.66	3.44	3.28	3.16	3.06	2.98	2.92	2.82	2.72	2.62	2.56	2.50	2.44	2.38	2.32	2.25
18	5.98	4.56	3.95	3.61	3.38	3.22	3.10	3.01	2.93	2.87	2.77	2.67	2.56	2.50	2.44	2.38	2.32	2.26	2.19
19	5.92	4.51	3.90	3.56	3.33	3.17	3.05	2.96	2.88	2.82	2.72	2.62	2.51	2.45	2.39	2.33	2.27	2.20	2.13
20	5.87	4.46	3.86	3.51	3.29	3.13	3.01	2.91	2.84	2.77	2.68	2.57	2.46	2.41	2.35	2.29	2.22	2.16	2.09
21	5.83	4.42	3.82	3.48	3.25	3.09	2.97	2.87	2.80	2.73	2.64	2.53	2.42	2.37	2.31	2.25	2.18	2.11	2.04
22	5.79	4.38	3.78	3.44	3.22	3.05	2.93	2.84	2.76	2.70	2.60	2.50	2.39	2.33	2.27	2.21	2.14	2.08	2.00
23	5.75	4.35	3.75	3.41	3.18	3.02	2.90	2.81	2.73	2.67	2.57	2.47	2.36	2.30	2.24	2.18	2.11	2.04	1.97
24	5.72	4.32	3.72	3.38	3.15	2.99	2.87	2.78	2.70	2.64	2.54	2.44	2.33	2.27	2.21	2.15	2.08	2.01	1.94
25	5.69	4.29	3.69	3.35	3.13	2.97	2.85	2.75	2.68	2.61	2.51	2.41	2.30	2.24	2.18	2.12	2.05	1.98	1.91
26	5.66	4.27	3.67	3.33	3.10	2.94	2.82	2.73	2.65	2.59	2.49	2.39	2.28	2.22	2.16	2.09	2.03	1.95	1.88
27	5.63	4.24	3.65	3.31	3.08	2.92	2.80	2.71	2.63	2.57	2.47	2.36	2.25	2.19	2.13	2.07	2.00	1.93	1.85
28	5.61	4.22	3.63	3.29	3.06	2.90	2.78	2.69	2.61	2.55	2.45	2.34	2.23	2.17	2.11	2.05	1.98	1.91	1.83
29	5.59	4.20	3.61	3.27	3.04	2.88	2.76	2.67	2.59	2.53	2.43	2.32	2.21	2.15	2.09	2.03	1.96	1.89	1.81
30	5.57	4.18	3.59	3.25	3.03	2.87	2.75	2.65	2.57	2.51	2.41	2.31	2.20	2.14	2.07	2.01	1.94	1.87	1.79
40	5.42	4.05	3.46	3.13	2.90	2.74	2.62	2.53	2.45	2.39	2.29	2.18	2.07	2.01	1.94	1.88	1.80	1.72	1.64
60	5.29	3.93	3.34	3.01	2.79	2.63	2.51	2.41	2.33	2.27	2.17	2.06	1.94	1.88	1.82	1.74	1.67	1.58	1.48
120	5.15	3.80	3.23	2.89	2.67	2.52	2.39	2.30	2.22	2.16	2.05	1.94	1.82	1.76	1.69	1.61	1.53	1.43	1.31
∞	5.02	3.69	3.12	2.79	2.57	2.41	2.29	2.19	2.11	2.05	1.94	1.83	1.71	1.64	1.57	1.48	1.39	1.27	1.00

TABLE E.5 (Continued)

$\alpha = .01$

$F_{(\alpha, df_1, df_2)}$

Numerator df_1

Denominator df_2	1	2	3	4	5	6	7	8	9	10	12	15	20	24	30	40	60	120	∞
1	4052	4999.5	5403	5625	5764	5859	5928	5982	6022	6056	6106	6157	6209	6235	6261	6287	6313	6339	6366
2	98.50	99.00	99.17	99.25	99.30	99.33	99.36	99.37	99.39	99.40	99.42	99.43	99.45	99.46	99.47	99.47	99.48	99.49	99.50
3	34.12	30.82	29.46	28.71	28.24	27.91	27.67	27.49	27.35	27.23	27.05	26.87	26.69	26.60	26.50	26.41	26.32	26.22	26.13
4	21.20	18.00	16.69	15.98	15.52	15.21	14.98	14.80	14.66	14.55	14.37	14.20	14.02	13.93	13.84	13.75	13.65	13.56	13.46
5	16.26	13.27	12.06	11.39	10.97	10.67	10.46	10.29	10.16	10.05	9.89	9.72	9.55	9.47	9.38	9.29	9.20	9.11	9.02
6	13.75	10.92	9.78	9.15	8.75	8.47	8.26	8.10	7.98	7.87	7.72	7.56	7.40	7.31	7.23	7.14	7.06	6.97	6.88
7	12.25	9.55	8.45	7.85	7.46	7.19	6.99	6.84	6.72	6.62	6.47	6.31	6.16	6.07	5.99	5.91	5.82	5.74	5.65
8	11.26	8.65	7.59	7.01	6.63	6.37	6.18	6.03	5.91	5.81	5.67	5.52	5.36	5.28	5.20	5.12	5.03	4.95	4.86
9	10.56	8.02	6.99	6.42	6.06	5.80	5.61	5.47	5.35	5.26	5.11	4.96	4.81	4.73	4.65	4.57	4.48	4.40	4.31
10	10.04	7.56	6.55	5.99	5.64	5.39	5.20	5.06	4.94	4.85	4.71	4.56	4.41	4.33	4.25	4.17	4.08	4.00	3.91
11	9.65	7.21	6.22	5.67	5.32	5.07	4.89	4.74	4.63	4.54	4.40	4.25	4.10	4.02	3.94	3.86	3.78	3.69	3.60
12	9.33	6.93	5.95	5.41	5.06	4.82	4.64	4.50	4.39	4.30	4.16	4.01	3.86	3.78	3.70	3.62	3.54	3.45	3.36
13	9.07	6.70	5.74	5.21	4.86	4.62	4.44	4.30	4.19	4.10	3.96	3.82	3.66	3.59	3.51	3.43	3.34	3.25	3.17
14	8.86	6.51	5.56	5.04	4.69	4.46	4.28	4.14	4.03	3.94	3.80	3.66	3.51	3.43	3.35	3.27	3.18	3.09	3.00
15	8.68	6.36	5.42	4.89	4.56	4.32	4.14	4.00	3.89	3.80	3.67	3.52	3.37	3.29	3.21	3.13	3.05	2.96	2.87
16	8.53	6.23	5.29	4.77	4.44	4.20	4.03	3.89	3.78	3.69	3.55	3.41	3.26	3.18	3.10	3.02	2.93	2.84	2.75
17	8.40	6.11	5.18	4.67	4.34	4.10	3.93	3.79	3.68	3.59	3.46	3.31	3.16	3.08	3.00	2.92	2.83	2.75	2.65
18	8.29	6.01	5.09	4.58	4.25	4.01	3.84	3.71	3.60	3.51	3.37	3.23	3.08	3.00	2.92	2.84	2.75	2.66	2.57
19	8.18	5.93	5.01	4.50	4.17	3.94	3.77	3.63	3.52	3.43	3.30	3.15	3.00	2.92	2.84	2.76	2.67	2.58	2.49
20	8.10	5.85	4.94	4.43	4.10	3.87	3.70	3.56	3.46	3.37	3.23	3.09	2.94	2.86	2.78	2.69	2.61	2.52	2.42
21	8.02	5.78	4.87	4.37	4.04	3.81	3.64	3.51	3.40	3.31	3.17	3.03	2.88	2.80	2.72	2.64	2.55	2.46	2.36
22	7.95	5.72	4.82	4.31	3.99	3.76	3.59	3.45	3.35	3.26	3.12	2.98	2.83	2.75	2.67	2.58	2.50	2.40	2.31
23	7.88	5.66	4.76	4.26	3.94	3.71	3.54	3.41	3.30	3.21	3.07	2.93	2.78	2.70	2.62	2.54	2.45	2.35	2.26
24	7.82	5.61	4.72	4.22	3.90	3.67	3.50	3.36	3.26	3.17	3.03	2.89	2.74	2.66	2.58	2.49	2.40	2.31	2.21
25	7.77	5.57	4.68	4.18	3.85	3.63	3.46	3.32	3.22	3.13	2.99	2.85	2.70	2.62	2.54	2.45	2.36	2.27	2.17
26	7.72	5.53	4.64	4.14	3.82	3.59	3.42	3.29	3.18	3.09	2.96	2.81	2.66	2.58	2.50	2.42	2.33	2.23	2.13
27	7.68	5.49	4.60	4.11	3.78	3.56	3.39	3.26	3.15	3.06	2.93	2.78	2.63	2.55	2.47	2.38	2.29	2.20	2.10
28	7.64	5.45	4.57	4.07	3.75	3.53	3.36	3.23	3.12	3.03	2.90	2.75	2.60	2.52	2.44	2.35	2.26	2.17	2.06
29	7.60	5.42	4.54	4.04	3.73	3.50	3.33	3.20	3.09	3.00	2.87	2.73	2.57	2.49	2.41	2.33	2.23	2.14	2.03
30	7.56	5.39	4.51	4.02	3.70	3.47	3.30	3.17	3.07	2.98	2.84	2.70	2.55	2.47	2.39	2.30	2.21	2.11	2.01
40	7.31	5.18	4.31	3.83	3.51	3.29	3.12	2.99	2.89	2.80	2.66	2.52	2.37	2.29	2.20	2.11	2.02	1.92	1.80
60	7.08	4.98	4.13	3.65	3.34	3.12	2.95	2.82	2.72	2.63	2.50	2.35	2.20	2.12	2.03	1.94	1.84	1.73	1.60
120	6.85	4.79	3.95	3.48	3.17	2.96	2.79	2.66	2.56	2.47	2.34	2.19	2.03	1.95	1.86	1.76	1.66	1.53	1.38
∞	6.63	4.61	3.78	3.32	3.02	2.80	2.64	2.51	2.41	2.32	2.18	2.04	1.88	1.79	1.70	1.59	1.47	1.32	1.00

TABLE E.5 *(Continued)*

$\alpha = .005$

$F_{(\alpha, df_1, df_2)}$

Denominator df_2	\ Numerator df_1																		
	1	2	3	4	5	6	7	8	9	10	12	15	20	24	30	40	60	120	∞
1	16211	20000	21615	22500	23056	23437	23715	23925	24091	24224	24426	24630	24836	24940	25044	25148	25253	25359	25465
2	198.5	199.0	199.2	199.2	199.3	199.3	199.4	199.4	199.4	199.4	199.4	199.4	199.4	199.5	199.5	199.5	199.5	199.5	199.5
3	55.55	49.80	47.47	46.19	45.39	44.84	44.43	44.13	43.88	43.69	43.39	43.08	42.78	42.62	42.47	42.31	42.15	41.99	41.83
4	31.33	26.28	24.26	23.15	22.46	21.97	21.62	21.35	21.14	20.97	20.70	20.44	20.17	20.03	19.89	19.75	19.61	19.47	19.32
5	22.78	18.31	16.53	15.56	14.94	14.51	14.20	13.96	13.77	13.62	13.38	13.15	12.90	12.78	12.66	12.53	12.40	12.27	12.14
6	18.63	14.54	12.92	12.03	11.46	11.07	10.79	10.57	10.39	10.25	10.03	9.81	9.59	9.47	9.36	9.24	9.12	9.00	8.88
7	16.24	12.40	10.88	10.05	9.52	9.16	8.89	8.68	8.51	8.38	8.18	7.97	7.75	7.65	7.53	7.42	7.31	7.19	7.08
8	14.69	11.04	9.60	8.81	8.30	7.95	7.69	7.50	7.34	7.21	7.01	6.81	6.61	6.50	6.40	6.29	6.18	6.06	5.95
9	13.61	10.11	8.72	7.96	7.47	7.13	6.88	6.69	6.54	6.42	6.23	6.03	5.83	5.73	5.62	5.52	5.41	5.30	5.19
10	12.83	9.43	8.08	7.34	6.87	6.54	6.30	6.12	5.97	5.85	5.66	5.47	5.27	5.17	5.07	4.97	4.86	4.75	4.64
11	12.23	8.91	7.60	6.88	6.42	6.10	5.86	5.68	5.54	5.42	5.24	5.05	4.86	4.76	4.65	4.55	4.44	4.34	4.23
12	11.75	8.51	7.23	6.52	6.07	5.76	5.52	5.35	5.20	5.09	4.91	4.72	4.53	4.43	4.33	4.23	4.12	4.01	3.90
13	11.37	8.19	6.93	6.23	5.79	5.48	5.25	5.08	4.94	4.82	4.64	4.46	4.27	4.17	4.07	3.97	3.87	3.76	3.65
14	11.06	7.92	6.68	6.00	5.56	5.26	5.03	4.86	4.72	4.60	4.43	4.25	4.06	3.96	3.86	3.76	3.66	3.55	3.44
15	10.80	7.70	6.48	5.80	5.37	5.07	4.85	4.67	4.54	4.42	4.25	4.07	3.88	3.79	3.69	3.58	3.48	3.37	3.26
16	10.58	7.51	6.30	5.64	5.21	4.91	4.69	4.52	4.38	4.27	4.10	3.92	3.73	3.64	3.54	3.44	3.33	3.22	3.11
17	10.38	7.35	6.16	5.50	5.07	4.78	4.56	4.39	4.25	4.14	3.97	3.79	3.61	3.51	3.41	3.31	3.21	3.10	2.98
18	10.22	7.21	6.03	5.37	4.96	4.66	4.44	4.28	4.14	4.03	3.86	3.68	3.50	3.40	3.30	3.20	3.10	2.99	2.87
19	10.07	7.09	5.92	5.27	4.85	4.56	4.34	4.18	4.04	3.93	3.76	3.59	3.40	3.31	3.21	3.11	3.00	2.89	2.78
20	9.94	6.99	5.82	5.17	4.76	4.47	4.26	4.09	3.96	3.85	3.68	3.50	3.32	3.22	3.12	3.02	2.92	2.81	2.69
21	9.83	6.89	5.73	5.09	4.68	4.39	4.18	4.01	3.88	3.77	3.60	3.43	3.24	3.15	3.05	2.95	2.84	2.73	2.61
22	9.73	6.81	5.65	5.02	4.61	4.32	4.11	3.94	3.81	3.70	3.54	3.36	3.18	3.08	2.98	2.88	2.77	2.66	2.55
23	9.63	6.73	5.58	4.95	4.54	4.26	4.05	3.88	3.75	3.64	3.47	3.30	3.12	3.02	2.92	2.82	2.71	2.60	2.48
24	9.55	6.66	5.52	4.89	4.49	4.20	3.99	3.83	3.69	3.59	3.42	3.25	3.06	2.97	2.87	2.77	2.66	2.55	2.43
25	9.48	6.60	5.46	4.84	4.43	4.15	3.94	3.78	3.64	3.54	3.37	3.20	3.01	2.92	2.82	2.72	2.61	2.50	2.38
26	9.41	6.54	5.41	4.79	4.38	4.10	3.89	3.73	3.60	3.49	3.33	3.15	2.97	2.87	2.77	2.67	2.56	2.45	2.33
27	9.34	6.49	5.36	4.74	4.34	4.06	3.85	3.69	3.56	3.45	3.28	3.11	2.93	2.83	2.73	2.63	2.52	2.41	2.29
28	9.28	6.44	5.32	4.70	4.30	4.02	3.81	3.65	3.52	3.41	3.25	3.07	2.89	2.79	2.69	2.59	2.48	2.37	2.25
29	9.23	6.40	5.28	4.66	4.26	3.98	3.77	3.61	3.48	3.38	3.21	3.04	2.86	2.76	2.66	2.56	2.45	2.33	2.21
30	9.18	6.35	5.24	4.62	4.23	3.95	3.74	3.58	3.45	3.34	3.18	3.01	2.82	2.73	2.63	2.52	2.42	2.30	2.18
40	8.83	6.07	4.98	4.37	3.99	3.71	3.51	3.35	3.22	3.12	2.95	2.78	2.60	2.50	2.40	2.30	2.18	2.06	1.93
60	8.49	5.79	4.73	4.14	3.76	3.49	3.29	3.13	3.01	2.90	2.74	2.57	2.39	2.29	2.19	2.08	1.96	1.83	1.69
120	8.18	5.54	4.50	3.92	3.55	3.28	3.09	2.93	2.81	2.71	2.54	2.37	2.19	2.09	1.98	1.87	1.75	1.61	1.43
∞	7.88	5.30	4.28	3.72	3.35	3.09	2.90	2.74	2.62	2.52	2.36	2.19	2.00	1.90	1.79	1.67	1.53	1.36	1.00

SOURCE: Reprinted from E. S. Pearson and H. O. Hartley, eds., *Biometrika Tables for Statisticians*, 3rd ed., 1966, by permission of the *Biometrika* Trustees.

TABLE E.5a Selected critical values of F for Cook's D_i statistic

Denominator df $= n - p - 1$	$\alpha = .50$											
	Numerator df $= p + 1$											
	2	3	4	5	6	7	8	9	10	12	15	20
10	.743	.845	.899	.932	.954	.971	.983	.992	1.00	1.01	1.02	1.03
11	.739	.840	.893	.926	.948	.964	.977	.986	.994	1.01	1.02	1.03
12	.735	.835	.888	.921	.943	.959	.972	.981	.989	1.00	1.01	1.02
15	.726	.826	.878	.911	.933	.949	.960	.970	.977	.989	1.00	1.01
20	.718	.816	.868	.900	.922	.938	.950	.959	.966	.977	.989	1.00
24	.714	.812	.863	.895	.917	.932	.944	.953	.961	.972	.983	.994
30	.709	.807	.858	.890	.912	.927	.939	.948	.955	.966	.978	.989
40	.705	.802	.854	.885	.907	.922	.934	.943	.950	.961	.972	.983
60	.701	.798	.849	.880	.901	.917	.928	.937	.945	.956	.967	.978
120	.697	.793	.844	.875	.896	.912	.923	.932	.939	.950	.961	.972
∞	.693	.789	.839	.870	.891	.907	.918	.927	.934	.945	.956	.967

TABLE E.6   Table of Poisson probabilities

For a given value of λ, entry indicates the probability of obtaining a specified value of X

X	0.1	0.2	0.3	0.4	0.5	0.6	0.7	0.8	0.9	1.0
0	.9048	.8187	.7408	.6703	.6065	.5488	.4966	.4493	.4066	.3679
1	.0905	.1637	.2222	.2681	.3033	.3293	.3476	.3595	.3659	.3679
2	.0045	.0164	.0333	.0536	.0758	.0988	.1217	.1438	.1647	.1839
3	.0002	.0011	.0033	.0072	.0126	.0198	.0284	.0383	.0494	.0613
4	.0000	.0001	.0003	.0007	.0016	.0030	.0050	.0077	.0111	.0153
5	.0000	.0000	.0000	.0001	.0002	.0004	.0007	.0012	.0020	.0031
6	.0000	.0000	.0000	.0000	.0000	.0000	.0001	.0002	.0003	.0005
7	.0000	.0000	.0000	.0000	.0000	.0000	.0000	.0000	.0000	.0001

X	1.1	1.2	1.3	1.4	1.5	1.6	1.7	1.8	1.9	2.0
0	.3329	.3012	.2725	.2466	.2231	.2019	.1827	.1653	.1496	.1353
1	.3662	.3614	.3543	.3452	.3347	.3230	.3106	.2975	.2842	.2707
2	.2014	.2169	.2303	.2417	.2510	.2584	.2640	.2678	.2700	.2707
3	.0738	.0867	.0998	.1128	.1255	.1378	.1496	.1607	.1710	.1804
4	.0203	.0260	.0324	.0395	.0471	.0551	.0636	.0723	0812	.0902
5	.0045	.0062	.0084	.0111	.0141	.0176	.0216	.0260	.0309	.0361
6	.0008	.0012	.0018	.0026	.0035	.0047	.0061	.0078	.0098	.0120
7	.0001	.0002	.0003	.0005	.0008	.0011	.0015	.0020	.0027	.0034
8	.0000	.0000	.0001	.0001	.0001	.0002	.0003	.0005	.0006	.0009
9	.0000	.0000	.0000	.0000	.0000	.0000	.0001	.0001	.0001	.0002

X	2.1	2.2	2.3	2.4	2.5	2.6	2.7	2.8	2.9	3.0
0	.1225	.1108	.1003	.0907	.0821	.0743	.0672	.0608	.0550	.0498
1	.2572	.2438	.2306	.2177	.2052	.1931	.1815	.1703	.1596	.1494
2	.2700	.2681	.2652	.2613	.2565	.2510	.2450	.2384	.2314	.2240
3	.1890	.1966	.2033	.2090	.2138	.2176	.2205	.2225	.2237	.2240
4	.0992	.1082	.1169	.1254	.1336	.1414	.1488	.1557	.1622	.1680
5	.0417	.0476	.0538	.0602	.0668	.0735	.0804	.0872	.0940	.1008
6	.0146	.0174	.0206	.0241	.0278	.0319	.0362	.0407	.0455	.0504
7	.0044	.0055	.0068	.0083	.0099	.0118	.0139	.0163	.0188	.0216
8	.0011	.0015	.0019	.0025	.0031	.0038	.0047	.0057	.0068	.0081
9	.0003	.0004	.0005	.0007	.0009	.0011	.0014	.0018	.0022	.0027
10	.0001	.0001	.0001	.0002	.0002	.0003	.0004	.0005	.0006	.0008
11	.0000	.0000	.0000	.0000	.0000	.0001	.0001	.0001	.0002	.0002
12	.0000	.0000	.0000	.0000	.0000	.0000	.0000	.0000	.0000	.0001

X	3.1	3.2	3.3	3.4	3.5	3.6	3.7	3.8	3.9	4.0
0	.0450	.0408	.0369	.0334	.0302	.0273	.0247	.0224	.0202	.0183
1	.1397	.1304	.1217	.1135	.1057	.0984	.0915	.0850	.0789	.0733
2	.2165	.2087	.2008	.1929	.1850	.1771	.1692	.1615	.1539	.1465
3	.2237	.2226	.2209	.2186	.2158	.2125	.2087	.2046	.2001	.1954
4	.1734	.1781	.1823	.1858	.1888	.1912	.1931	.1944	.1951	.1954
5	.1075	.1140	.1203	.1264	.1322	.1377	.1429	.1477	.1522	.1563
6	.0555	.0608	.0662	.0716	.0771	.0826	.0881	.0936	.0989	.1042
7	.0246	.0278	.0312	.0348	.0385	.0425	.0466	.0508	.0551	.0595
8	.0095	.0111	.0129	.0148	.0169	.0191	.0215	.0241	.0269	.0298
9.	.0033	.0040	.0047	.0056	.0066	.0076	.0089	.0102	.0116	.0132

TABLE E.6   *(Continued)*

X	3.1	3.2	3.3	3.4	3.5	λ 3.6	3.7	3.8	3.9	4.0
10	.0010	.0013	.0016	.0019	.0023	.0028	.0033	.0039	.0045	.0053
11	.0003	.0004	.0005	.0006	.0007	.0009	.0011	.0013	.0016	.0019
12	.0001	.0001	.0001	.0002	.0002	.0003	.0003	.0004	.0005	.0006
13	.0000	.0000	.0000	.0000	.0001	.0001	.0001	.0001	.0002	.0002
14	.0000	.0000	.0000	.0000	.0000	.0000	.0000	.0000	.0000	.0001

X	4.1	4.2	4.3	4.4	4.5	λ 4.6	4.7	4.8	4.9	5.0
0	.0166	.0150	.0136	.0123	.0111	.0101	.0091	.0082	.0074	.0067
1	.0679	.0630	.0583	.0540	.0500	.0462	.0427	.0395	.0365	.0337
2	.1393	.1323	.1254	.1188	.1125	.1063	.1005	.0948	.0894	.0842
3	.1904	.1852	.1798	.1743	.1687	.1631	.1574	.1517	.1460	.1404
4	.1951	.1944	.1933	.1917	.1898	.1875	.1849	.1820	.1789	.1755
5	.1600	.1633	.1662	.1687	.1708	.1725	.1738	.1747	.1753	.1755
6	.1093	.1143	.1191	.1237	.1281	.1323	.1362	.1398	.1432	.1462
7	.0640	.0686	.0732	.0778	.0824	.0869	.0914	.0959	.1002	.1044
8	.0328	.0360	.0393	.0428	.0463	.0500	.0537	.0575	.0614	.0653
9	.0150	.0168	.0188	.0209	.0232	.0255	.0280	.0307	.0334	.0363
10	.0061	.0071	.0081	.0092	.0104	.0118	.0132	.0147	.0164	.0181
11	.0023	.0027	.0032	.0037	.0043	.0049	.0056	.0064	.0073	.0082
12	.0008	.0009	.0011	.0014	.0016	.0019	.0022	.0026	.0030	.0034
13	.0002	.0003	.0004	.0005	.0006	.0007	.0008	.0009	.0011	.0013
14	.0001	.0001	.0001	.0001	.0002	.0002	.0003	.0003	.0004	.0005
15	.0000	.0000	.0000	.0000	.0001	.0001	.0001	.0001	.0001	.0002

X	5.1	5.2	5.3	5.4	5.5	λ 5.6	5.7	5.8	5.9	6.0
0	.0061	.0055	.0050	.0045	.0041	.0037	.0033	.0030	.0027	.0025
1	.0311	.0287	.0265	.0244	.0225	.0207	.0191	.0176	.0162	.0149
2	.0793	.0746	.0701	.0659	.0618	.0580	.0544	.0509	.0477	.0446
3	.1348	.1293	.1239	.1185	.1133	.1082	.1033	.0985	.0938	.0892
4	.1719	.1681	.1641	.1600	.1558	.1515	.1472	.1428	.1383	.1339
5	.1753	.1748	.1740	.1728	.1714	.1697	.1678	.1656	.1632	.1606
6	.1490	.1515	.1537	.1555	.1571	.1584	.1594	.1601	.1605	.1606
7	.1086	.1125	.1163	.1200	.1234	.1267	.1298	.1326	.1353	.1377
8	.0692	.0731	.0771	.0810	.0849	.0887	.0925	.0962	.0998	.1033
9	.0392	.0423	.0454	.0486	.0519	.0552	.0586	.0620	.0654	.0688
10	.0200	.0220	.0241	.0262	.0285	.0309	.0334	.0359	.0386	.0413
11	.0093	.0104	.0116	.0129	.0143	.0157	.0173	.0190	.0207	.0225
12	.0039	.0045	.0051	.0058	.0065	.0073	.0082	.0092	.0102	.0113
13	.0015	.0018	.0021	.0024	.0028	.0032	.0036	.0041	.0046	.0052
14	.0006	.0007	.0008	.0009	.0011	.0013	.0015	.0017	.0019	.0022
15	.0002	.0002	.0003	.0003	.0004	.0005	.0006	.0007	.0008	.0009
16	.0001	.0001	.0001	.0001	.0001	.0002	.0002	.0002	.0003	.0003
17	.0000	.0000	.0000	.0000	.0000	.0000	.0001	.0001	.0001	.0001

X	6.1	6.2	6.3	6.4	6.5	λ 6.6	6.7	6.8	6.9	7.0
0	.0022	.0020	.0018	.0017	.0015	.0014	.0012	.0011	.0010	.0009
1	.0137	.0126	.0116	.0106	.0098	.0090	.0082	.0076	.0070	.0064
2	.0417	.0390	.0364	.0340	.0318	.0296	.0276	.0258	.0240	.0223
3	.0848	.0806	.0765	.0726	.0688	.0652	.0617	.0584	.0552	.0521
4	.1294	.1249	.1205	.1162	.1118	.1076	.1034	.0992	.0952	.0912

TABLE E.6 *(Continued)*

X	6.1	6.2	6.3	6.4	6.5	6.6	6.7	6.8	6.9	7.0
5	.1579	.1549	.1519	.1487	.1454	.1420	.1385	.1349	.1314	.1277
6	.1605	.1601	.1595	.1586	.1575	.1562	.1546	.1529	.1511	.1490
7	.1399	.1418	.1435	.1450	.1462	.1472	.1480	.1486	.1489	.1490
8	.1066	.1099	.1130	.1160	.1188	.1215	.1240	.1263	.1284	.1304
9	.0723	.0757	.0791	.0825	.0858	.0891	.0923	.0954	.0985	.1014
10	.0441	.0469	.0498	.0528	.0558	.0588	.0618	.0649	.0679	.0710
11	.0245	.0265	.0285	.0307	.0330	.0353	.0377	.0401	.0426	.0452
12	.0124	.0137	.0150	.0164	.0179	.0194	.0210	.0227	.0245	.0264
13	.0058	.0065	.0073	.0081	.0089	.0098	.0108	.0119	.0130	.0142
14	.0025	.0029	.0033	.0037	.0041	.0046	.0052	.0058	.0064	.0071
15	.0010	.0012	.0014	.0016	.0018	.0020	.0023	.0026	.0029	.0033
16	.0004	.0005	.0005	.0006	.0007	.0008	.0010	.0011	.0013	.0014
17	.0001	.0002	.0002	.0002	.0003	.0003	.0004	.0004	.0005	.0006
18	.0000	.0001	.0001	.0001	.0001	.0001	.0001	.0002	.0002	.0002
19	.0000	.0000	.0000	.0000	.0000	.0000	.0000	.0001	.0001	.0001

X	7.1	7.2	7.3	7.4	7.5	7.6	7.7	7.8	7.9	8.0
0	.0008	.0007	.0007	.0006	.0006	.0005	.0005	.0004	.0004	.0003
1	.0059	.0054	.0049	.0045	.0041	.0038	.0035	.0032	.0029	.0027
2	.0208	.0194	.0180	.0167	.0156	.0145	.0134	.0125	.0116	.0107
3	.0492	.0464	.0438	.0413	.0389	.0366	.0345	.0324	.0305	.0286
4	.0874	.0836	.0799	.0764	.0729	.0696	.0663	.0632	.0602	.0573
5	.1241	.1204	.1167	.1130	.1094	.1057	.1021	.0986	.0951	.0916
6	.1468	.1445	.1420	.1394	.1367	.1339	.1311	.1282	.1252	.1221
7	.1489	.1486	.1481	.1474	.1465	.1454	.1442	.1428	.1413	.1396
8	.1321	.1337	.1351	.1363	.1373	.1382	.1388	.1392	.1395	.1396
9	.1042	.1070	.1096	.1121	.1144	.1167	.1187	.1207	.1224	.1241
10	.0740	.0770	.0800	.0829	.0858	.0887	.0914	.0941	.0967	.0993
11	.0478	.0504	.0531	.0558	.0585	.0613	.0640	.0667	.0695	.0722
12	.0283	.0303	.0323	.0344	.0366	.0388	.0411	.0434	.0457	.0481
13	.0154	.0168	.0181	.0196	.0211	.0227	.0243	.0260	.0278	.0296
14	.0078	.0086	.0095	.0104	.0113	.0123	.0134	.0145	.0157	.0169
15	.0037	.0041	.0046	.0051	.0057	.0062	.0069	.0075	.0083	.0090
16	.0016	.0019	.0021	.0024	.0026	.0030	.0033	.0037	.0041	.0045
17	.0007	.0008	.0009	.0010	.0012	.0013	.0015	.0017	.0019	.0021
18	.0003	.0003	.0004	.0004	.0005	.0006	.0006	.0007	.0008	.0009
19	.0001	.0001	.0001	.0002	.0002	.0002	.0003	.0003	.0003	.0004
20	.0000	.0000	.0001	.0001	.0001	.0001	.0001	.0001	.0001	.0002
21	.0000	.0000	.0000	.0000	.0000	.0000	.0000	.0000	.0001	.0001

X	8.1	8.2	8.3	8.4	8.5	8.6	8.7	8.8	8.9	9.0
0	.0003	.0003	.0002	.0002	.0002	.0002	.0002	.0002	.0001	.0001
1	.0025	.0023	.0021	.0019	.0017	.0016	.0014	.0013	.0012	.0011
2	.0100	.0092	.0086	.0079	.0074	.0068	.0063	.0058	.0054	.0050
3	.0269	.0252	.0237	.0222	.0208	.0195	.0183	.0171	.0160	.0150
4	.0544	.0517	.0491	.0466	.0443	.0420	.0398	.0377	.0357	.0337
5	.0882	.0849	.0816	.0784	.0752	.0722	.0692	.0663	.0635	.0607
6	.1191	.1160	.1128	.1097	.1066	.1034	.1003	.0972	.0941	.0911
7	.1378	.1358	.1338	.1317	.1294	.1271	.1247	.1222	.1197	.1171
8	.1395	.1392	.1388	.1382	.1375	.1366	.1356	.1344	.1332	.1318
9	.1256	.1269	.1280	.1290	.1299	.1306	.1311	.1315	.1317	.1318

TABLE E.6 *(Continued)*

					λ					
X	8.1	8.2	8.3	8.4	8.5	8.6	8.7	8.8	8.9	9.0
10	.1017	.1040	.1063	.1084	.1104	.1123	.1140	.1157	.1172	.1186
11	.0749	.0776	.0802	.0828	.0853	.0878	.0902	.0925	.0948	.0970
12	.0505	.0530	.0555	.0579	.0604	.0629	.0654	.0679	.0703	.0728
13	.0315	.0334	.0354	.0374	.0395	.0416	.0438	.0459	.0481	.0504
14	.0182	.0196	.0210	.0225	.0240	.0256	.0272	.0289	.0306	.0324
15	.0098	.0107	.0116	.0126	.0136	.0147	.0158	.0169	.0182	.0194
16	.0050	.0055	.0060	.0066	.0072	.0079	.0086	.0093	.0101	.0109
17	.0024	.0026	.0029	.0033	.0036	.0040	.0044	.0048	.0053	.0058
18	.0011	.0012	.0014	.0015	.0017	.0019	.0021	.0024	.0026	.0029
19	.0005	.0005	.0006	.0007	.0008	.0009	.0010	.0011	.0012	.0014
20	.0002	.0002	.0002	.0003	.0003	.0004	.0004	.0005	.0005	.0006
21	.0001	.0001	.0001	.0001	.0001	.0002	.0002	.0002	.0002	.0003
22	.0000	.0000	.0000	.0000	.0001	.0001	.0001	.0001	.0001	.0001

					λ					
X	9.1	9.2	9.3	9.4	9.5	9.6	9.7	9.8	9.9	10
0	.0001	.0001	.0001	.0001	.0001	.0001	.0001	.0001	.0001	.0000
1	.0010	.0009	.0009	.0008	.0007	.0007	.0006	.0005	.0005	.0005
2	.0046	.0043	.0040	.0037	.0034	.0031	.0029	.0027	.0025	.0023
3	.0140	.0131	.0123	.0115	.0107	.0100	.0093	.0087	.0081	.0076
4	.0319	.0302	.0285	.0269	.0254	.0240	.0226	.0213	.0201	.0189
5	.0581	.0555	.0530	.0506	.0483	.0460	.0439	.0418	.0398	.0378
6	.0881	.0851	.0822	.0793	.0764	.0736	.0709	.0682	.0656	.0631
7	.1145	.1118	.1091	.1064	.1037	.1010	.0982	.0955	.0928	.0901
8	.1302	.1286	.1269	.1251	.1232	.1212	.1191	.1170	.1148	.1126
9	.1317	.1315	.1311	.1306	.1300	.1293	.1284	.1274	.1263	.1251
10	.1198	.1210	.1219	.1228	.1235	.1241	.1245	.1249	.1250	.1251
11	.0991	.1012	.1031	.1049	.1067	.1083	.1098	.1112	.1125	.1137
12	.0752	.0776	.0799	.0822	.0844	.0866	.0888	.0908	.0928	.0948
13	.0526	.0549	.0572	.0594	.0617	.0640	.0662	.0685	.0707	.0729
14	.0342	.0361	.0380	.0399	.0419	.0439	.0459	.0479	.0500	.0521
15	.0208	.0221	.0235	.0250	.0265	.0281	.0297	.0313	.0330	.0347
16	.0118	.0127	.0137	.0147	.0157	.0168	.0180	.0192	.0204	.0217
17	.0063	.0069	.0075	.0081	.0088	.0095	.0103	.0111	.0119	.0128
18	.0032	.0035	.0039	.0042	.0046	.0051	.0055	.0060	.0065	.0071
19	.0015	.0017	.0019	.0021	.0023	.0026	.0028	.0031	.0034	.0037
20	.0007	.0008	.0009	.0010	.0011	.0012	.0014	.0015	.0017	.0019
21	.0003	.0003	.0004	.0004	.0005	.0006	.0006	.0007	.0008	.0009
22	.0001	.0001	.0002	.0002	.0002	.0002	.0003	.0003	.0004	.0004
23	.0000	.0001	.0001	.0001	.0001	.0001	.0001	.0001	.0002	.0002
24	.0000	.0000	.0000	.0000	.0000	.0000	.0000	.0001	.0001	.0001

					λ					
X	11	12	13	14	15	16	17	18	19	20
0	.0000	.0000	.0000	.0000	.0000	.0000	.0000	.0000	.0000	.0000
1	.0002	.0001	.0000	.0000	.0000	.0000	.0000	.0000	.0000	.0000
2	.0010	.0004	.0002	.0001	.0000	.0000	.0000	.0000	.0000	.0000
3	.0037	.0018	.0008	.0004	.0002	.0001	.0000	.0000	.0000	.0000
4	.0102	.0053	.0027	.0013	.0006	.0003	.0001	.0001	.0000	.0000
5	.0224	.0127	.0070	.0037	.0019	.0010	.0005	.0002	.0001	.0001
6	.0411	.0255	.0152	.0087	.0048	.0026	.0014	.0007	.0004	.0002
7	.0646	.0437	.0281	.0174	.0104	.0060	.0034	.0018	.0010	.0005
8	.0888	.0655	.0457	.0304	.0194	.0120	.0072	.0042	.0024	.0013
9	.1085	.0874	.0661	.0473	.0324	.0213	.0135	.0083	.0050	.0029

TABLE E.6 *(Continued)*

X	11	12	13	14	15	λ 16	17	18	19	20
10	.1194	.1048	.0859	.0663	.0486	.0341	.0230	.0150	.0095	.0058
11	.1194	.1144	.1015	.0844	.0663	.0496	.0355	.0245	.0164	.0106
12	.1094	.1144	.1099	.0984	.0829	.0661	.0504	.0368	.0259	.0176
13	.0926	.1056	.1099	.1060	.0956	.0814	.0658	.0509	.0378	.0271
14	.0728	.0905	.1021	.1060	.1024	.0930	.0800	.0655	.0514	.0387
15	.0534	.0724	.0885	.0989	.1024	.0992	.0906	.0786	.0650	.0516
16	.0367	.0543	.0719	.0866	.0960	.0992	.0963	.0884	.0772	.0646
17	.0237	.0383	.0550	.0713	.0847	.0934	.0963	.0936	.0863	.0760
18	.0145	.0256	.0397	.0554	.0706	.0830	.0909	.0936	.0911	.0844
19	.0084	.0161	.0272	.0409	.0557	.0699	.0814	.0887	.0911	.0888
20	.0046	.0097	.0177	.0286	.0418	.0559	.0692	.0798	.0866	.0888
21	.0024	.0055	.0109	.0191	.0299	.0426	.0560	.0684	.0783	.0846
22	.0012	.0030	.0065	.0121	.0204	.0310	.0433	.0560	.0676	.0769
23	.0006	.0016	.0037	.0074	.0133	.0216	.0320	.0438	.0559	.0669
24	.0003	.0008	.0020	.0043	.0083	.0144	.0226	.0328	.0442	.0557
25	.0001	.0004	.0010	.0024	.0050	.0092	.0154	.0237	.0336	.0446
26	.0000	.0002	.0005	.0013	.0029	.0057	.0101	.0164	.0246	.0343
27	.0000	.0001	.0002	.0007	.0016	.0034	.0063	.0109	.0173	.0254
28	.0000	.0000	.0001	.0003	.0009	.0019	.0038	.0070	.0117	.0181
29	.0000	.0000	.0001	.0002	.0004	.0011	.0023	.0044	.0077	.0125
30	.0000	.0000	.0000	.0001	.0002	.0006	.0013	.0026	.0049	.0083
31	.0000	.0000	.0000	.0000	.0001	.0003	.0007	.0015	.0030	.0054
32	.0000	.0000	.0000	.0000	.0001	.0001	.0004	.0009	.0018	.0034
33	.0000	.0000	.0000	.0000	.0000	.0001	.0002	.0005	.0010	.0020
34	.0000	.0000	.0000	.0000	.0000	.0000	.0001	.0002	.0006	.0012
35	.0000	.0000	.0000	.0000	.0000	.0000	.0000	.0001	.0003	.0007
36	.0000	.0000	.0000	.0000	.0000	.0000	.0000	.0001	.0002	.0004
37	.0000	.0000	.0000	.0000	.0000	.0000	.0000	.0000	.0001	.0002
38	.0000	.0000	.0000	.0000	.0000	.0000	.0000	.0000	.0000	.0001
39	.0000	.0000	.0000	.0000	.0000	.0000	.0000	.0000	.0000	.0001

SOURCE: Extracted from William H. Beyer, ed., *CRC Basic Statistical Tables* (Cleveland, Ohio: The Chemical Rubber Co., 1971). Reprinted with permission. © The Chemical Rubber Co., CRC Press, Inc.

TABLE E.7 Table of binomial probabilities

For a given combination of n and p, entry indicates the probability of obtaining a specified value of X. To locate entry: **when $p \le .50$,** read p across the top heading and both n and X down the left margin; **when $p \ge .50$,** read p across the bottom heading and both n and X up the right margin

n	X	0.01	0.02	0.03	0.04	0.05	0.06	0.07	0.08	0.09	0.10	0.11	0.12	0.13	0.14	0.15	0.16	0.17	0.18	X	n
2	0	0.9801	0.9604	0.9409	0.9216	0.9025	0.8836	0.8649	0.8464	0.8281	0.8100	0.7921	0.7744	0.7569	0.7396	0.7225	0.7056	0.6889	0.6724	2	2
	1	0.0198	0.0392	0.0582	0.0768	0.0950	0.1128	0.1302	0.1472	0.1638	0.1800	0.1958	0.2112	0.2262	0.2408	0.2550	0.2688	0.2822	0.2952	1	
	2	0.0001	0.0004	0.0009	0.0016	0.0025	0.0036	0.0049	0.0064	0.0081	0.0100	0.0121	0.0144	0.0169	0.0196	0.0225	0.0256	0.0289	0.0324	0	
3	0	0.9703	0.9412	0.9127	0.8847	0.8574	0.8306	0.8044	0.7787	0.7536	0.7290	0.7050	0.6815	0.6585	0.6361	0.6141	0.5927	0.5718	0.5514	3	3
	1	0.0294	0.0576	0.0847	0.1106	0.1354	0.1590	0.1816	0.2031	0.2236	0.2430	0.2614	0.2788	0.2952	0.3106	0.3251	0.3387	0.3513	0.3631	2	
	2	0.0003	0.0012	0.0026	0.0046	0.0071	0.0102	0.0137	0.0177	0.0221	0.0270	0.0323	0.0380	0.0441	0.0506	0.0574	0.0645	0.0720	0.0797	1	
	3	0.0000	0.0000	0.0000	0.0001	0.0001	0.0002	0.0003	0.0005	0.0007	0.0010	0.0013	0.0017	0.0022	0.0027	0.0034	0.0041	0.0049	0.0058	0	
4	0	0.9606	0.9224	0.8853	0.8493	0.8145	0.7807	0.7481	0.7164	0.6857	0.6561	0.6274	0.5997	0.5729	0.5470	0.5220	0.4979	0.4746	0.4521	4	4
	1	0.0388	0.0753	0.1095	0.1416	0.1715	0.1993	0.2252	0.2492	0.2713	0.2916	0.3102	0.3271	0.3424	0.3562	0.3685	0.3793	0.3888	0.3970	3	
	2	0.0006	0.0023	0.0051	0.0088	0.0135	0.0191	0.0254	0.0325	0.0402	0.0486	0.0575	0.0669	0.0767	0.0870	0.0975	0.1084	0.1195	0.1307	2	
	3	0.0000	0.0000	0.0001	0.0002	0.0005	0.0008	0.0013	0.0019	0.0027	0.0036	0.0047	0.0061	0.0076	0.0094	0.0115	0.0138	0.0163	0.0191	1	
	4	0.0000	—	0.0000	0.0000	0.0000	0.0000	0.0000	0.0000	0.0001	0.0001	0.0001	0.0002	0.0003	0.0004	0.0005	0.0007	0.0008	0.0010	0	
5	0	0.9510	0.9039	0.8587	0.8154	0.7738	0.7339	0.6957	0.6591	0.6240	0.5905	0.5584	0.5277	0.4984	0.4704	0.4437	0.4182	0.3939	0.3707	5	5
	1	0.0480	0.0922	0.1328	0.1699	0.2036	0.2342	0.2618	0.2866	0.3086	0.3280	0.3451	0.3598	0.3724	0.3829	0.3915	0.3983	0.4034	0.4069	4	
	2	0.0010	0.0038	0.0082	0.0142	0.0214	0.0299	0.0394	0.0498	0.0610	0.0729	0.0853	0.0981	0.1113	0.1247	0.1382	0.1517	0.1652	0.1786	3	
	3	0.0000	0.0001	0.0003	0.0006	0.0011	0.0019	0.0030	0.0043	0.0060	0.0081	0.0105	0.0134	0.0166	0.0203	0.0244	0.0289	0.0338	0.0392	2	
	4	—	0.0000	0.0000	0.0000	0.0000	0.0001	0.0001	0.0002	0.0003	0.0004	0.0007	0.0009	0.0012	0.0017	0.0022	0.0028	0.0035	0.0043	1	
	5	—	0.0000	0.0000	—	0.0000	0.0000	0.0000	0.0000	0.0000	0.0000	0.0000	0.0000	0.0000	0.0001	0.0001	0.0001	0.0001	0.0002	0	
6	0	0.9415	0.8858	0.8330	0.7828	0.7351	0.6899	0.6470	0.6064	0.5679	0.5314	0.4970	0.4644	0.4336	0.4046	0.3771	0.3513	0.3269	0.3040	6	6
	1	0.0571	0.1085	0.1546	0.1957	0.2321	0.2642	0.2922	0.3164	0.3370	0.3543	0.3685	0.3800	0.3888	0.3952	0.3993	0.4015	0.4018	0.4004	5	
	2	0.0014	0.0055	0.0120	0.0204	0.0305	0.0422	0.0550	0.0688	0.0833	0.0984	0.1139	0.1295	0.1452	0.1608	0.1762	0.1912	0.2057	0.2197	4	
	3	0.0000	0.0002	0.0005	0.0011	0.0021	0.0036	0.0055	0.0080	0.0110	0.0146	0.0188	0.0236	0.0289	0.0349	0.0415	0.0486	0.0562	0.0643	3	
	4	—	0.0000	0.0000	0.0000	0.0001	0.0002	0.0003	0.0005	0.0008	0.0012	0.0017	0.0024	0.0032	0.0043	0.0055	0.0069	0.0086	0.0106	2	
	5	—	—	0.0000	0.0000	0.0000	0.0000	0.0000	0.0000	0.0000	0.0001	0.0001	0.0001	0.0002	0.0003	0.0004	0.0005	0.0007	0.0009	1	
	6	—	—	—	0.0000	0.0000	0.0000	0.0000	0.0000	0.0000	0.0000	0.0000	0.0000	0.0000	0.0000	0.0000	0.0000	0.0000	0.0000	0	

P

Binomial probabilities — P

x	0.82	0.83	0.84	0.85	0.86	0.87	0.88	0.89	0.90	0.91	0.92	0.93	0.94	0.95	0.96	0.97	0.98	0.99	X	n
7	0.2493	0.2714	0.2951	0.3206	0.3479	0.3773	0.4087	0.4423	0.4783	0.5168	0.5578	0.6017	0.6485	0.6983	0.7514	0.8080	0.8681	0.9321	0	7
6	0.3830	0.3891	0.3935	0.3960	0.3965	0.3946	0.3901	0.3827	0.3720	0.3578	0.3396	0.3170	0.2897	0.2573	0.2192	0.1749	0.1240	0.0659	1	
5	0.2523	0.2391	0.2248	0.2097	0.1936	0.1769	0.1596	0.1419	0.1240	0.1061	0.0886	0.0716	0.0555	0.0406	0.0274	0.0162	0.0076	0.0020	2	
4	0.0923	0.0816	0.0714	0.0617	0.0525	0.0441	0.0363	0.0292	0.0230	0.0175	0.0128	0.0090	0.0059	0.0036	0.0019	0.0008	0.0003	0.0000	3	
3	0.0203	0.0167	0.0136	0.0109	0.0086	0.0066	0.0049	0.0036	0.0026	0.0017	0.0011	0.0007	0.0004	0.0002	0.0001	0.0000	0.0000	—	4	
2	0.0027	0.0021	0.0016	0.0012	0.0008	0.0006	0.0004	0.0003	0.0002	0.0001	0.0001	0.0000	0.0000	0.0000	0.0000	—	—	—	5	
1	0.0002	0.0001	0.0001	0.0001	0.0000	0.0000	0.0000	0.0000	0.0000	0.0000	0.0000	—	—	—	—	—	—	—	6	
0	0.0000	0.0000	0.0000	0.0000	0.0000	0.0000	0.0000	0.0000	0.0000	—	—	—	—	—	—	—	—	—	7	

x	0.82	0.83	0.84	0.85	0.86	0.87	0.88	0.89	0.90	0.91	0.92	0.93	0.94	0.95	0.96	0.97	0.98	0.99	X	n
8	0.2044	0.2252	0.2479	0.2725	0.2992	0.3282	0.3596	0.3937	0.4305	0.4703	0.5132	0.5596	0.6096	0.6634	0.7214	0.7837	0.8508	0.9227	0	8
7	0.3590	0.3691	0.3777	0.3847	0.3897	0.3923	0.3923	0.3892	0.3826	0.3721	0.3570	0.3370	0.3113	0.2793	0.2405	0.1939	0.1389	0.0746	1	
6	0.2758	0.2646	0.2518	0.2376	0.2220	0.2052	0.1872	0.1684	0.1488	0.1288	0.1087	0.0888	0.0695	0.0515	0.0351	0.0210	0.0099	0.0026	2	
5	0.1211	0.1084	0.0959	0.0839	0.0723	0.0613	0.0511	0.0416	0.0331	0.0255	0.0189	0.0134	0.0089	0.0054	0.0029	0.0013	0.0004	0.0001	3	
4	0.0332	0.0277	0.0228	0.0185	0.0147	0.0115	0.0087	0.0064	0.0046	0.0031	0.0021	0.0013	0.0007	0.0004	0.0002	0.0001	0.0000	0.0000	4	
3	0.0058	0.0045	0.0035	0.0026	0.0019	0.0014	0.0009	0.0006	0.0004	0.0002	0.0001	0.0001	0.0000	0.0000	0.0000	0.0000	—	—	5	
2	0.0006	0.0005	0.0003	0.0002	0.0002	0.0001	0.0001	0.0000	0.0000	0.0000	0.0000	0.0000	—	—	—	—	—	—	6	
1	0.0000	0.0000	0.0000	0.0000	0.0000	0.0000	0.0000	—	—	—	—	—	—	—	—	—	—	—	7	
0	0.0000	0.0000	0.0000	—	—	—	—	—	—	—	—	—	—	—	—	—	—	—	8	

x	0.82	0.83	0.84	0.85	0.86	0.87	0.88	0.89	0.90	0.91	0.92	0.93	0.94	0.95	0.96	0.97	0.98	0.99	X	n
9	0.1676	0.1869	0.2082	0.2316	0.2573	0.2855	0.3165	0.3504	0.3874	0.4279	0.4722	0.5204	0.5730	0.6302	0.6925	0.7602	0.8337	0.9135	0	9
8	0.3312	0.3446	0.3569	0.3679	0.3770	0.3840	0.3884	0.3897	0.3874	0.3809	0.3695	0.3525	0.3292	0.2985	0.2597	0.2116	0.1531	0.0830	1	
7	0.2908	0.2823	0.2720	0.2597	0.2455	0.2295	0.2119	0.1927	0.1722	0.1507	0.1285	0.1061	0.0840	0.0629	0.0433	0.0262	0.0125	0.0034	2	
6	0.1489	0.1349	0.1209	0.1069	0.0933	0.0800	0.0674	0.0556	0.0446	0.0348	0.0261	0.0186	0.0125	0.0077	0.0042	0.0019	0.0006	0.0001	3	
5	0.0490	0.0415	0.0345	0.0283	0.0228	0.0179	0.0138	0.0103	0.0074	0.0052	0.0034	0.0021	0.0012	0.0006	0.0003	0.0001	0.0000	0.0000	4	
4	0.0108	0.0085	0.0066	0.0050	0.0037	0.0027	0.0019	0.0013	0.0008	0.0005	0.0003	0.0002	0.0001	0.0000	0.0000	0.0000	0.0000	0.0000	5	
3	0.0016	0.0012	0.0008	0.0006	0.0004	0.0003	0.0002	0.0001	0.0001	0.0001	0.0000	0.0000	0.0000	0.0000	0.0000	0.0000	—	—	6	
2	0.0001	0.0001	0.0001	0.0000	0.0000	0.0000	0.0000	0.0000	0.0000	0.0000	0.0000	0.0000	—	—	—	—	—	—	7	
1	0.0000	0.0000	0.0000	0.0000	0.0000	0.0000	0.0000	0.0000	0.0000	—	—	—	—	—	—	—	—	—	8	
0	0.0000	0.0000	0.0000	—	—	—	—	—	—	—	—	—	—	—	—	—	—	—	9	

x	0.82	0.83	0.84	0.85	0.86	0.87	0.88	0.89	0.90	0.91	0.92	0.93	0.94	0.95	0.96	0.97	0.98	0.99	X	n
10	0.1374	0.1552	0.1749	0.1969	0.2213	0.2484	0.2785	0.3118	0.3487	0.3894	0.4344	0.4840	0.5386	0.5987	0.6648	0.7374	0.8171	0.9044	0	10
9	0.3017	0.3178	0.3331	0.3474	0.3603	0.3712	0.3798	0.3854	0.3874	0.3851	0.3777	0.3643	0.3438	0.3151	0.2770	0.2281	0.1667	0.0914	1	
8	0.2980	0.2929	0.2856	0.2759	0.2639	0.2496	0.2330	0.2143	0.1937	0.1714	0.1478	0.1234	0.0988	0.0746	0.0519	0.0317	0.0153	0.0042	2	
7	0.1745	0.1600	0.1450	0.1298	0.1146	0.0995	0.0847	0.0706	0.0574	0.0452	0.0343	0.0248	0.0168	0.0105	0.0058	0.0026	0.0008	0.0001	3	
6	0.0670	0.0573	0.0483	0.0401	0.0326	0.0260	0.0202	0.0153	0.0112	0.0078	0.0052	0.0033	0.0019	0.0010	0.0004	0.0001	0.0000	0.0000	4	
5	0.0177	0.0141	0.0111	0.0085	0.0064	0.0047	0.0033	0.0023	0.0015	0.0009	0.0005	0.0003	0.0001	0.0001	0.0000	0.0000	0.0000	0.0000	5	
4	0.0032	0.0024	0.0018	0.0012	0.0009	0.0006	0.0004	0.0002	0.0001	0.0001	0.0001	0.0000	0.0000	0.0000	0.0000	0.0000	0.0000	—	6	
3	0.0004	0.0003	0.0002	0.0001	0.0001	0.0000	0.0000	0.0000	0.0000	0.0000	0.0000	0.0000	0.0000	0.0000	—	—	—	—	7	
2	0.0000	0.0000	0.0000	0.0000	0.0000	0.0000	0.0000	0.0000	0.0000	0.0000	0.0000	—	—	—	—	—	—	—	8	
1	0.0000	0.0000	0.0000	0.0000	0.0000	0.0000	0.0000	0.0000	—	—	—	—	—	—	—	—	—	—	9	
0	0.0000	0.0000	0.0000	—	—	—	—	—	—	—	—	—	—	—	—	—	—	—	10	

| n X | 0.99 | 0.98 | 0.97 | 0.96 | 0.95 | 0.94 | 0.93 | 0.92 | 0.91 | 0.90 | 0.89 | 0.88 | 0.87 | 0.86 | 0.85 | 0.84 | 0.83 | 0.82 |

P

TABLE E.7 (Continued)

n	X	0.01	0.02	0.03	0.04	0.05	0.06	0.07	0.08	0.09	0.10	0.11	0.12	0.13	0.14	0.15	0.16	0.17	0.18	X	n
12	0	0.8864	0.7847	0.6938	0.6127	0.5404	0.4759	0.4186	0.3677	0.3225	0.2824	0.2470	0.2157	0.1880	0.1637	0.1422	0.1234	0.1069	0.0924	12	
	1	0.1074	0.1922	0.2575	0.3064	0.3413	0.3645	0.3781	0.3837	0.3827	0.3766	0.3663	0.3529	0.3372	0.3197	0.3012	0.2821	0.2627	0.2434	11	
	2	0.0060	0.0216	0.0438	0.0702	0.0988	0.1280	0.1565	0.1835	0.2082	0.2301	0.2490	0.2647	0.2771	0.2863	0.2924	0.2955	0.2960	0.2939	10	
	3	0.0002	0.0015	0.0045	0.0098	0.0173	0.0272	0.0393	0.0532	0.0686	0.0852	0.1026	0.1203	0.1380	0.1553	0.1720	0.1876	0.2021	0.2151	9	
	4	0.0000	0.0001	0.0003	0.0009	0.0021	0.0039	0.0067	0.0104	0.0153	0.0213	0.0285	0.0369	0.0464	0.0569	0.0683	0.0804	0.0931	0.1062	8	
	5	—	0.0000	0.0000	0.0001	0.0002	0.0004	0.0008	0.0014	0.0024	0.0038	0.0056	0.0081	0.0111	0.0148	0.0193	0.0245	0.0305	0.0373	7	
	6	—	—	—	0.0000	0.0000	0.0000	0.0001	0.0001	0.0003	0.0005	0.0008	0.0013	0.0019	0.0028	0.0040	0.0054	0.0073	0.0096	6	
	7	—	—	—	—	—	—	0.0000	0.0000	0.0000	0.0000	0.0001	0.0001	0.0002	0.0004	0.0006	0.0009	0.0013	0.0018	5	
	8	—	—	—	—	—	—	—	—	—	—	0.0000	0.0000	0.0000	0.0000	0.0001	0.0001	0.0002	0.0002	4	
	9	—	—	—	—	—	—	—	—	—	—	0.0000	0.0000	0.0000	0.0000	0.0000	0.0000	0.0000	0.0000	3	
	10	—	—	—	—	—	—	—	—	—	—	—	—	—	—	—	—	—	—	2	
	11	—	—	—	—	—	—	—	—	—	—	—	—	—	—	—	—	—	—	1	
	12	—	—	—	—	—	—	—	—	—	—	—	—	—	—	—	—	—	—	0	12
15	0	0.8601	0.7386	0.6333	0.5421	0.4633	0.3953	0.3367	0.2863	0.2430	0.2059	0.1741	0.1470	0.1238	0.1041	0.0874	0.0731	0.0611	0.0510	15	
	1	0.1303	0.2261	0.2938	0.3388	0.3658	0.3785	0.3801	0.3734	0.3605	0.3432	0.3228	0.3006	0.2775	0.2542	0.2312	0.2090	0.1878	0.1678	14	
	2	0.0092	0.0323	0.0636	0.0988	0.1348	0.1691	0.2003	0.2273	0.2496	0.2669	0.2793	0.2870	0.2903	0.2897	0.2856	0.2787	0.2692	0.2578	13	
	3	0.0004	0.0029	0.0085	0.0178	0.0307	0.0468	0.0653	0.0857	0.1070	0.1285	0.1496	0.1696	0.1880	0.2044	0.2184	0.2300	0.2389	0.2452	12	
	4	0.0000	0.0002	0.0008	0.0022	0.0049	0.0090	0.0148	0.0223	0.0317	0.0428	0.0555	0.0694	0.0843	0.0998	0.1156	0.1314	0.1468	0.1615	11	
	5	—	0.0000	0.0001	0.0002	0.0006	0.0013	0.0024	0.0043	0.0069	0.0105	0.0151	0.0208	0.0277	0.0357	0.0449	0.0551	0.0662	0.0780	10	
	6	—	—	0.0000	0.0000	0.0000	0.0001	0.0003	0.0006	0.0011	0.0019	0.0031	0.0047	0.0069	0.0097	0.0132	0.0175	0.0226	0.0285	9	
	7	—	—	—	—	—	0.0000	0.0000	0.0001	0.0001	0.0003	0.0005	0.0008	0.0013	0.0020	0.0030	0.0043	0.0059	0.0081	8	
	8	—	—	—	—	—	—	—	0.0000	0.0000	0.0000	0.0001	0.0001	0.0002	0.0003	0.0005	0.0008	0.0012	0.0018	7	
	9	—	—	—	—	—	—	—	—	—	—	0.0000	0.0000	0.0000	0.0000	0.0001	0.0001	0.0002	0.0003	6	
	10	—	—	—	—	—	—	—	—	—	—	—	—	—	—	0.0000	0.0000	0.0000	0.0000	5	
	11	—	—	—	—	—	—	—	—	—	—	—	—	—	—	—	—	—	—	4	
	12	—	—	—	—	—	—	—	—	—	—	—	—	—	—	—	—	—	—	3	
	13	—	—	—	—	—	—	—	—	—	—	—	—	—	—	—	—	—	—	2	
	14	—	—	—	—	—	—	—	—	—	—	—	—	—	—	—	—	—	—	1	
	15	—	—	—	—	—	—	—	—	—	—	—	—	—	—	—	—	—	—	0	15

n	X	0.99	0.98	0.97	0.96	0.95	0.94	0.93	0.92	0.91	0.90	0.89	0.88	0.87	0.86	0.85	0.84	0.83	0.82	X	n
20	0	0.8179	0.6676	0.5438	0.4420	0.3585	0.2901	0.2342	0.1887	0.1516	0.1216	0.0972	0.0776	0.0617	0.0490	0.0388	0.0306	0.0241	0.0189	20	20
	1	0.1652	0.2725	0.3364	0.3683	0.3774	0.3703	0.3526	0.3282	0.3000	0.2702	0.2403	0.2115	0.1844	0.1595	0.1368	0.1165	0.0986	0.0829	19	
	2	0.0159	0.0528	0.0988	0.1458	0.1887	0.2246	0.2521	0.2711	0.2818	0.2852	0.2822	0.2740	0.2618	0.2466	0.2293	0.2109	0.1919	0.1730	18	
	3	0.0010	0.0065	0.0183	0.0364	0.0596	0.0860	0.1139	0.1414	0.1672	0.1901	0.2093	0.2242	0.2347	0.2409	0.2428	0.2410	0.2358	0.2278	17	
	4	0.0000	0.0006	0.0024	0.0065	0.0133	0.0233	0.0364	0.0523	0.0703	0.0898	0.1099	0.1299	0.1491	0.1666	0.1821	0.1951	0.2053	0.2125	16	
	5	—	0.0000	0.0002	0.0009	0.0022	0.0048	0.0088	0.0145	0.0222	0.0319	0.0435	0.0567	0.0713	0.0868	0.1028	0.1189	0.1345	0.1493	15	
	6	—	—	0.0000	0.0001	0.0003	0.0008	0.0017	0.0032	0.0055	0.0089	0.0134	0.0193	0.0266	0.0353	0.0454	0.0566	0.0689	0.0819	14	
	7	—	—	—	0.0000	0.0000	0.0001	0.0002	0.0005	0.0011	0.0020	0.0033	0.0053	0.0080	0.0115	0.0160	0.0216	0.0282	0.0360	13	
	8	—	—	—	—	0.0000	0.0000	0.0000	0.0001	0.0002	0.0004	0.0007	0.0012	0.0019	0.0030	0.0046	0.0067	0.0094	0.0128	12	
	9	—	—	—	—	—	—	—	0.0000	0.0000	0.0001	0.0001	0.0002	0.0004	0.0007	0.0011	0.0017	0.0026	0.0038	11	
	10	—	—	—	—	—	—	—	—	0.0000	0.0000	0.0000	0.0000	0.0001	0.0001	0.0002	0.0004	0.0006	0.0009	10	
	11	—	—	—	—	—	—	—	—	—	—	—	—	0.0000	0.0000	0.0000	0.0001	0.0001	0.0002	9	
	12	—	—	—	—	—	—	—	—	—	—	—	—	—	—	—	0.0000	0.0000	0.0000	8	
	13	—	—	—	—	—	—	—	—	—	—	—	—	—	—	—	—	—	—	7	
	14	—	—	—	—	—	—	—	—	—	—	—	—	—	—	—	—	—	—	6	
	15	—	—	—	—	—	—	—	—	—	—	—	—	—	—	—	—	—	—	5	
	16	—	—	—	—	—	—	—	—	—	—	—	—	—	—	—	—	—	—	4	
	17	—	—	—	—	—	—	—	—	—	—	—	—	—	—	—	—	—	—	3	
	18	—	—	—	—	—	—	—	—	—	—	—	—	—	—	—	—	—	—	2	
	19	—	—	—	—	—	—	—	—	—	—	—	—	—	—	—	—	—	—	1	
	20	—	—	—	—	—	—	—	—	—	—	—	—	—	—	—	—	—	—	0	20
n	X	0.99	0.98	0.97	0.96	0.95	0.94	0.93	0.92	0.91	0.90	0.89	0.88	0.87	0.86	0.85	0.84	0.83	0.82	X	n

P

TABLE E.7 (Continued)

n	X								P												X	n
		0.19	0.20	0.21	0.22	0.23	0.24	0.25	0.26	0.27	0.28	0.29	0.30	0.31	0.32	0.33	0.34	0.35	0.36		
2	0	0.6561	0.6400	0.6241	0.6084	0.5929	0.5776	0.5625	0.5476	0.5329	0.5184	0.5041	0.4900	0.4761	0.4624	0.4489	0.4356	0.4225	0.4096	2	
	1	0.3078	0.3200	0.3318	0.3432	0.3542	0.3648	0.3750	0.3848	0.3942	0.4032	0.4118	0.4200	0.4278	0.4352	0.4422	0.4488	0.4550	0.4608	1	
	2	0.0361	0.0400	0.0441	0.0484	0.0529	0.0576	0.0625	0.0676	0.0729	0.0784	0.0841	0.0900	0.0961	0.1024	0.1089	0.1156	0.1225	0.1296	0	2
3	0	0.5314	0.5120	0.4930	0.4746	0.4565	0.4390	0.4219	0.4052	0.3890	0.3732	0.3579	0.3430	0.3285	0.3144	0.3008	0.2875	0.2746	0.2621	3	
	1	0.3740	0.3840	0.3932	0.4015	0.4091	0.4159	0.4219	0.4271	0.4316	0.4355	0.4386	0.4410	0.4428	0.4439	0.4444	0.4443	0.4436	0.4424	2	
	2	0.0877	0.0960	0.1045	0.1133	0.1222	0.1313	0.1406	0.1501	0.1597	0.1693	0.1791	0.1890	0.1989	0.2089	0.2189	0.2289	0.2389	0.2488	1	
	3	0.0069	0.0080	0.0093	0.0106	0.0122	0.0138	0.0156	0.0176	0.0197	0.0220	0.0244	0.0270	0.0298	0.0328	0.0359	0.0393	0.0429	0.0467	0	3
4	0	0.4305	0.4096	0.3895	0.3702	0.3515	0.3336	0.3164	0.2999	0.2840	0.2687	0.2541	0.2401	0.2267	0.2138	0.2015	0.1897	0.1785	0.1678	4	
	1	0.4039	0.4096	0.4142	0.4176	0.4200	0.4214	0.4219	0.4214	0.4201	0.4180	0.4152	0.4116	0.4074	0.4025	0.3970	0.3910	0.3845	0.3775	3	
	2	0.1421	0.1536	0.1651	0.1767	0.1882	0.1996	0.2109	0.2221	0.2331	0.2439	0.2544	0.2646	0.2745	0.2841	0.2933	0.3021	0.3105	0.3185	2	
	3	0.0222	0.0256	0.0293	0.0332	0.0375	0.0420	0.0469	0.0520	0.0575	0.0632	0.0693	0.0756	0.0822	0.0891	0.0963	0.1038	0.1115	0.1194	1	
	4	0.0013	0.0016	0.0019	0.0023	0.0028	0.0033	0.0039	0.0046	0.0053	0.0061	0.0071	0.0081	0.0092	0.0105	0.0119	0.0134	0.0150	0.0168	0	4
5	0	0.3487	0.3277	0.3077	0.2887	0.2707	0.2536	0.2373	0.2219	0.2073	0.1935	0.1804	0.1681	0.1564	0.1454	0.1350	0.1252	0.1160	0.1074	5	
	1	0.4089	0.4096	0.4090	0.4072	0.4043	0.4003	0.3955	0.3898	0.3834	0.3762	0.3685	0.3601	0.3513	0.3421	0.3325	0.3226	0.3124	0.3020	4	
	2	0.1919	0.2048	0.2174	0.2297	0.2415	0.2529	0.2637	0.2739	0.2836	0.2926	0.3010	0.3087	0.3157	0.3220	0.3275	0.3323	0.3364	0.3397	3	
	3	0.0450	0.0512	0.0578	0.0648	0.0721	0.0798	0.0879	0.0962	0.1049	0.1138	0.1229	0.1323	0.1418	0.1515	0.1613	0.1712	0.1811	0.1911	2	
	4	0.0053	0.0064	0.0077	0.0091	0.0108	0.0126	0.0146	0.0169	0.0194	0.0221	0.0251	0.0283	0.0319	0.0357	0.0397	0.0441	0.0488	0.0537	1	
	5	0.0002	0.0003	0.0004	0.0005	0.0006	0.0008	0.0010	0.0012	0.0014	0.0017	0.0021	0.0024	0.0029	0.0034	0.0039	0.0045	0.0053	0.0060	0	5
6	0	0.2824	0.2621	0.2431	0.2252	0.2084	0.1927	0.1780	0.1642	0.1513	0.1393	0.1281	0.1176	0.1079	0.0989	0.0905	0.0827	0.0754	0.0687	6	
	1	0.3975	0.3932	0.3877	0.3811	0.3735	0.3651	0.3560	0.3462	0.3358	0.3251	0.3139	0.3025	0.2909	0.2792	0.2673	0.2555	0.2437	0.2319	5	
	2	0.2331	0.2458	0.2577	0.2687	0.2789	0.2882	0.2966	0.3041	0.3105	0.3160	0.3206	0.3241	0.3267	0.3284	0.3292	0.3290	0.3280	0.3261	4	
	3	0.0729	0.0819	0.0913	0.1011	0.1111	0.1214	0.1318	0.1424	0.1531	0.1639	0.1746	0.1852	0.1957	0.2061	0.2162	0.2260	0.2355	0.2446	3	
	4	0.0128	0.0154	0.0182	0.0214	0.0249	0.0287	0.0330	0.0375	0.0425	0.0478	0.0535	0.0595	0.0660	0.0727	0.0799	0.0873	0.0951	0.1032	2	
	5	0.0012	0.0015	0.0019	0.0024	0.0030	0.0036	0.0044	0.0053	0.0063	0.0074	0.0087	0.0102	0.0119	0.0137	0.0157	0.0180	0.0205	0.0232	1	
	6	0.0000	0.0001	0.0001	0.0001	0.0001	0.0002	0.0002	0.0003	0.0004	0.0005	0.0006	0.0007	0.0009	0.0011	0.0013	0.0015	0.0018	0.0022	0	6

Binomial probability table (continued). Column headers are values of p; row labels are X (left-side, ascending) and X (right-side, descending) for each value of n.

$n = 7$

X	0.64	0.65	0.66	0.67	0.68	0.69	0.70	0.71	0.72	0.73	0.74	0.75	0.76	0.77	0.78	0.79	0.80	0.81	X
0	0.0440	0.0490	0.0546	0.0606	0.0672	0.0745	0.0824	0.0910	0.1003	0.1105	0.1215	0.1335	0.1465	0.1605	0.1757	0.1920	0.2097	0.2288	7
1	0.1732	0.1848	0.1967	0.2090	0.2215	0.2342	0.2471	0.2600	0.2731	0.2860	0.2989	0.3115	0.3237	0.3356	0.3468	0.3573	0.3670	0.3756	6
2	0.2922	0.2985	0.3040	0.3088	0.3127	0.3156	0.3177	0.3186	0.3186	0.3174	0.3150	0.3115	0.3067	0.3007	0.2935	0.2850	0.2753	0.2643	5
3	0.2740	0.2679	0.2610	0.2535	0.2452	0.2363	0.2269	0.2169	0.2065	0.1956	0.1845	0.1730	0.1614	0.1497	0.1379	0.1263	0.1147	0.1033	4
4	0.1541	0.1442	0.1345	0.1248	0.1154	0.1062	0.0972	0.0886	0.0803	0.0724	0.0648	0.0577	0.0510	0.0447	0.0389	0.0336	0.0287	0.0242	3
5	0.0520	0.0466	0.0416	0.0369	0.0326	0.0286	0.0250	0.0217	0.0187	0.0161	0.0137	0.0115	0.0097	0.0080	0.0066	0.0054	0.0043	0.0034	2
6	0.0098	0.0084	0.0071	0.0061	0.0051	0.0043	0.0036	0.0030	0.0024	0.0020	0.0016	0.0013	0.0010	0.0008	0.0006	0.0005	0.0004	0.0003	1
7	0.0008	0.0006	0.0005	0.0004	0.0003	0.0003	0.0002	0.0002	0.0001	0.0001	0.0001	0.0000	0.0000	0.0000	0.0000	0.0000	0.0000	0.0000	0

$n = 8$

X	0.64	0.65	0.66	0.67	0.68	0.69	0.70	0.71	0.72	0.73	0.74	0.75	0.76	0.77	0.78	0.79	0.80	0.81	X
0	0.0281	0.0319	0.0360	0.0406	0.0457	0.0514	0.0576	0.0646	0.0722	0.0806	0.0899	0.1001	0.1113	0.1236	0.1370	0.1517	0.1678	0.1853	8
1	0.1267	0.1373	0.1484	0.1600	0.1721	0.1847	0.1977	0.2110	0.2247	0.2386	0.2527	0.2670	0.2812	0.2953	0.3092	0.3226	0.3355	0.3477	7
2	0.2494	0.2587	0.2675	0.2758	0.2835	0.2904	0.2965	0.3017	0.3058	0.3089	0.3108	0.3115	0.3108	0.3087	0.3052	0.3002	0.2936	0.2855	6
3	0.2805	0.2786	0.2756	0.2717	0.2668	0.2609	0.2541	0.2464	0.2379	0.2285	0.2184	0.2076	0.1963	0.1844	0.1722	0.1596	0.1468	0.1339	5
4	0.1973	0.1875	0.1775	0.1673	0.1569	0.1465	0.1361	0.1258	0.1156	0.1056	0.0959	0.0865	0.0775	0.0689	0.0607	0.0530	0.0459	0.0393	4
5	0.0888	0.0808	0.0732	0.0659	0.0591	0.0527	0.0467	0.0411	0.0360	0.0313	0.0270	0.0231	0.0196	0.0165	0.0137	0.0113	0.0092	0.0074	3
6	0.0250	0.0217	0.0188	0.0162	0.0139	0.0118	0.0100	0.0084	0.0070	0.0058	0.0047	0.0038	0.0031	0.0025	0.0019	0.0015	0.0011	0.0009	2
7	0.0040	0.0033	0.0028	0.0023	0.0019	0.0015	0.0012	0.0010	0.0008	0.0006	0.0005	0.0004	0.0003	0.0002	0.0002	0.0001	0.0001	0.0001	1
8	0.0003	0.0002	0.0002	0.0001	0.0001	0.0001	0.0001	0.0001	0.0000	0.0000	0.0000	0.0000	0.0000	0.0000	0.0000	0.0000	0.0000	0.0000	0

$n = 9$

X	0.64	0.65	0.66	0.67	0.68	0.69	0.70	0.71	0.72	0.73	0.74	0.75	0.76	0.77	0.78	0.79	0.80	0.81	X
0	0.0180	0.0207	0.0238	0.0272	0.0311	0.0355	0.0404	0.0458	0.0520	0.0589	0.0665	0.0751	0.0846	0.0952	0.1069	0.1199	0.1342	0.1501	9
1	0.0912	0.1004	0.1102	0.1206	0.1317	0.1433	0.1556	0.1685	0.1820	0.1960	0.2104	0.2253	0.2404	0.2558	0.2713	0.2867	0.3020	0.3169	8
2	0.2052	0.2162	0.2270	0.2376	0.2478	0.2576	0.2668	0.2754	0.2831	0.2899	0.2957	0.3003	0.3037	0.3056	0.3061	0.3049	0.3020	0.2973	7
3	0.2693	0.2716	0.2729	0.2731	0.2721	0.2701	0.2668	0.2624	0.2569	0.2502	0.2424	0.2336	0.2238	0.2130	0.2014	0.1891	0.1762	0.1627	6
4	0.2272	0.2194	0.2109	0.2017	0.1921	0.1820	0.1715	0.1608	0.1499	0.1388	0.1278	0.1168	0.1060	0.0954	0.0852	0.0754	0.0661	0.0573	5
5	0.1278	0.1181	0.1086	0.0994	0.0904	0.0818	0.0735	0.0657	0.0583	0.0513	0.0449	0.0389	0.0335	0.0285	0.0240	0.0200	0.0165	0.0134	4
6	0.0479	0.0424	0.0373	0.0326	0.0284	0.0245	0.0210	0.0179	0.0151	0.0127	0.0105	0.0087	0.0070	0.0057	0.0045	0.0036	0.0028	0.0021	3
7	0.0116	0.0098	0.0082	0.0069	0.0057	0.0047	0.0039	0.0031	0.0025	0.0020	0.0016	0.0012	0.0010	0.0007	0.0005	0.0004	0.0003	0.0002	2
8	0.0016	0.0013	0.0011	0.0008	0.0007	0.0005	0.0004	0.0003	0.0002	0.0002	0.0001	0.0001	0.0001	0.0001	0.0000	0.0000	0.0000	0.0000	1
9	0.0001	0.0001	0.0001	0.0001	0.0000	0.0000	0.0000	0.0000	0.0000	0.0000	0.0000	0.0000	0.0000	0.0000	—	—	—	—	0

$n = 10$

X	0.64	0.65	0.66	0.67	0.68	0.69	0.70	0.71	0.72	0.73	0.74	0.75	0.76	0.77	0.78	0.79	0.80	0.81	X
0	0.0115	0.0135	0.0157	0.0182	0.0211	0.0245	0.0282	0.0326	0.0374	0.0430	0.0492	0.0563	0.0643	0.0733	0.0834	0.0947	0.1074	0.1216	10
1	0.0649	0.0725	0.0808	0.0898	0.0995	0.1099	0.1211	0.1330	0.1456	0.1590	0.1730	0.1877	0.2030	0.2188	0.2351	0.2517	0.2684	0.2852	9
2	0.1642	0.1757	0.1873	0.1990	0.2107	0.2222	0.2335	0.2444	0.2548	0.2646	0.2735	0.2816	0.2885	0.2942	0.2984	0.3011	0.3020	0.3010	8
3	0.2462	0.2522	0.2573	0.2614	0.2644	0.2662	0.2668	0.2662	0.2642	0.2609	0.2563	0.2503	0.2429	0.2343	0.2244	0.2134	0.2013	0.1883	7
4	0.2424	0.2377	0.2320	0.2253	0.2177	0.2093	0.2001	0.1903	0.1798	0.1689	0.1576	0.1460	0.1343	0.1225	0.1108	0.0993	0.0881	0.0773	6
5	0.1636	0.1536	0.1434	0.1332	0.1229	0.1128	0.1029	0.0933	0.0839	0.0750	0.0664	0.0584	0.0509	0.0439	0.0375	0.0317	0.0264	0.0218	5
6	0.0767	0.0689	0.0616	0.0547	0.0482	0.0422	0.0368	0.0317	0.0272	0.0231	0.0195	0.0162	0.0134	0.0109	0.0088	0.0070	0.0055	0.0043	4
7	0.0247	0.0212	0.0181	0.0154	0.0130	0.0108	0.0090	0.0074	0.0060	0.0049	0.0039	0.0031	0.0024	0.0019	0.0014	0.0011	0.0008	0.0006	3
8	0.0052	0.0043	0.0035	0.0028	0.0023	0.0018	0.0014	0.0011	0.0009	0.0007	0.0005	0.0004	0.0003	0.0002	0.0002	0.0001	0.0001	0.0001	2
9	0.0006	0.0005	0.0004	0.0003	0.0002	0.0002	0.0001	0.0001	0.0001	0.0001	0.0001	0.0000	0.0000	0.0000	0.0000	0.0000	0.0000	0.0000	1
10	0.0000	0.0000	0.0000	0.0000	0.0000	0.0000	0.0000	0.0000	0.0000	0.0000	—	—	—	—	—	—	—	—	0

p

TABLE E.7 (Continued)

n	X	0.19	0.20	0.21	0.22	0.23	0.24	0.25	0.26	0.27	0.28	0.29	0.30	0.31	0.32	0.33	0.34	0.35	0.36	X	n
12	0	0.0798	0.0687	0.0591	0.0507	0.0434	0.0371	0.0317	0.0270	0.0229	0.0194	0.0164	0.0138	0.0116	0.0098	0.0082	0.0068	0.0057	0.0047	12	
	1	0.2245	0.2062	0.1885	0.1717	0.1557	0.1407	0.1267	0.1137	0.1016	0.0906	0.0804	0.0712	0.0628	0.0552	0.0484	0.0422	0.0368	0.0319	11	
	2	0.2897	0.2835	0.2756	0.2663	0.2558	0.2444	0.2323	0.2197	0.2068	0.1937	0.1807	0.1678	0.1552	0.1429	0.1310	0.1197	0.1088	0.0986	10	
	3	0.2265	0.2362	0.2442	0.2503	0.2547	0.2573	0.2581	0.2573	0.2549	0.2511	0.2460	0.2397	0.2324	0.2241	0.2151	0.2055	0.1954	0.1849	9	
	4	0.1195	0.1329	0.1460	0.1589	0.1712	0.1828	0.1936	0.2034	0.2122	0.2197	0.2261	0.2311	0.2349	0.2373	0.2384	0.2382	0.2367	0.2340	8	
	5	0.0449	0.0532	0.0621	0.0717	0.0818	0.0924	0.1032	0.1143	0.1255	0.1367	0.1477	0.1585	0.1688	0.1787	0.1879	0.1963	0.2039	0.2106	7	
	6	0.0123	0.0155	0.0193	0.0236	0.0285	0.0340	0.0401	0.0469	0.0542	0.0620	0.0704	0.0792	0.0885	0.0981	0.1079	0.1180	0.1281	0.1382	6	
	7	0.0025	0.0033	0.0044	0.0057	0.0073	0.0092	0.0115	0.0141	0.0172	0.0207	0.0246	0.0291	0.0341	0.0396	0.0456	0.0521	0.0591	0.0666	5	
	8	0.0004	0.0005	0.0007	0.0010	0.0014	0.0018	0.0024	0.0031	0.0040	0.0050	0.0063	0.0078	0.0096	0.0116	0.0140	0.0168	0.0199	0.0234	4	
	9	0.0000	0.0001	0.0001	0.0001	0.0002	0.0003	0.0004	0.0005	0.0007	0.0009	0.0011	0.0015	0.0019	0.0024	0.0031	0.0038	0.0048	0.0059	3	
	10	0.0000	0.0000	0.0000	0.0000	0.0000	0.0000	0.0000	0.0001	0.0001	0.0001	0.0001	0.0002	0.0003	0.0003	0.0005	0.0006	0.0008	0.0010	2	
	11	—	0.0000	0.0000	0.0000	0.0000	0.0000	0.0000	0.0000	0.0000	0.0000	0.0000	0.0000	0.0000	0.0000	0.0000	0.0001	0.0001	0.0001	1	
	12	—	—	—	—	—	—	—	0.0000	0.0000	0.0000	0.0000	0.0000	0.0000	0.0000	0.0000	0.0000	0.0000	0.0000	0	12
15	0	0.0424	0.0352	0.0291	0.0241	0.0198	0.0163	0.0134	0.0109	0.0089	0.0072	0.0059	0.0047	0.0038	0.0031	0.0025	0.0020	0.0016	0.0012	15	
	1	0.1492	0.1319	0.1162	0.1018	0.0889	0.0772	0.0668	0.0576	0.0494	0.0423	0.0360	0.0305	0.0258	0.0217	0.0182	0.0152	0.0126	0.0104	14	
	2	0.2449	0.2309	0.2162	0.2010	0.1858	0.1707	0.1559	0.1416	0.1280	0.1150	0.1029	0.0916	0.0811	0.0715	0.0627	0.0547	0.0476	0.0411	13	
	3	0.2489	0.2501	0.2490	0.2457	0.2405	0.2336	0.2252	0.2156	0.2051	0.1939	0.1821	0.1700	0.1579	0.1457	0.1338	0.1222	0.1110	0.1002	12	
	4	0.1752	0.1876	0.1986	0.2079	0.2155	0.2213	0.2252	0.2273	0.2276	0.2262	0.2231	0.2186	0.2128	0.2057	0.1977	0.1888	0.1792	0.1692	11	
	5	0.0904	0.1032	0.1161	0.1290	0.1416	0.1537	0.1651	0.1757	0.1852	0.1935	0.2005	0.2061	0.2103	0.2130	0.2142	0.2140	0.2123	0.2093	10	
	6	0.0353	0.0430	0.0514	0.0606	0.0705	0.0809	0.0917	0.1029	0.1142	0.1254	0.1365	0.1472	0.1575	0.1671	0.1759	0.1837	0.1906	0.1963	9	
	7	0.0107	0.0138	0.0176	0.0220	0.0271	0.0329	0.0393	0.0465	0.0543	0.0627	0.0717	0.0811	0.0910	0.1011	0.1114	0.1217	0.1319	0.1419	8	
	8	0.0025	0.0035	0.0047	0.0062	0.0081	0.0104	0.0131	0.0163	0.0201	0.0244	0.0293	0.0348	0.0409	0.0476	0.0549	0.0627	0.0710	0.0798	7	
	9	0.0005	0.0007	0.0010	0.0014	0.0019	0.0025	0.0034	0.0045	0.0058	0.0074	0.0093	0.0116	0.0143	0.0174	0.0210	0.0251	0.0298	0.0349	6	
	10	0.0001	0.0001	0.0002	0.0002	0.0003	0.0005	0.0007	0.0009	0.0013	0.0017	0.0023	0.0030	0.0038	0.0049	0.0062	0.0078	0.0096	0.0118	5	
	11	0.0000	0.0000	0.0000	0.0000	0.0000	0.0001	0.0001	0.0002	0.0002	0.0003	0.0004	0.0006	0.0008	0.0011	0.0014	0.0018	0.0024	0.0030	4	
	12	—	0.0000	0.0000	0.0000	0.0000	0.0000	0.0000	0.0000	0.0000	0.0000	0.0001	0.0001	0.0001	0.0002	0.0002	0.0003	0.0004	0.0006	3	
	13	—	—	—	—	—	—	0.0000	0.0000	0.0000	0.0000	0.0000	0.0000	0.0000	0.0000	0.0000	0.0000	0.0001	0.0001	2	
	14	—	—	—	—	—	—	—	—	—	—	0.0000	0.0000	0.0000	0.0000	0.0000	0.0000	0.0000	0.0000	1	
	15	—	—	—	—	—	—	—	—	—	—	—	—	—	—	—	—	—	—	0	15

n = 20

X	0.81	0.80	0.79	0.78	0.77	0.76	0.75	0.74	0.73	0.72	0.71	0.70	0.69	0.68	0.67	0.66	0.65	0.64	X
0	0.0148	0.0115	0.0090	0.0069	0.0054	0.0041	0.0032	0.0024	0.0018	0.0014	0.0011	0.0008	0.0006	0.0004	0.0003	0.0002	0.0002	0.0001	20
1	0.0693	0.0576	0.0477	0.0392	0.0321	0.0261	0.0211	0.0170	0.0137	0.0109	0.0087	0.0068	0.0054	0.0042	0.0033	0.0025	0.0020	0.0015	19
2	0.1545	0.1369	0.1204	0.1050	0.0910	0.0783	0.0669	0.0569	0.0480	0.0403	0.0336	0.0278	0.0229	0.0188	0.0153	0.0124	0.0100	0.0080	18
3	0.2175	0.2054	0.1920	0.1777	0.1631	0.1484	0.1339	0.1199	0.1065	0.0940	0.0823	0.0716	0.0619	0.0531	0.0453	0.0383	0.0323	0.0270	17
4	0.2168	0.2182	0.2169	0.2131	0.2070	0.1991	0.1897	0.1790	0.1675	0.1553	0.1429	0.1304	0.1181	0.1062	0.0947	0.0839	0.0738	0.0645	16
5	0.1627	0.1746	0.1845	0.1923	0.1979	0.2012	0.2023	0.2013	0.1982	0.1933	0.1868	0.1789	0.1698	0.1599	0.1493	0.1384	0.1272	0.1161	15
6	0.0954	0.1091	0.1226	0.1356	0.1478	0.1589	0.1686	0.1768	0.1833	0.1879	0.1907	0.1916	0.1907	0.1881	0.1839	0.1782	0.1712	0.1632	14
7	0.0448	0.0545	0.0652	0.0765	0.0883	0.1003	0.1124	0.1242	0.1356	0.1462	0.1558	0.1643	0.1714	0.1770	0.1811	0.1836	0.1844	0.1836	13
8	0.0171	0.0222	0.0282	0.0351	0.0429	0.0515	0.0609	0.0709	0.0815	0.0924	0.1034	0.1144	0.1251	0.1354	0.1450	0.1537	0.1614	0.1678	12
9	0.0053	0.0074	0.0100	0.0132	0.0171	0.0217	0.0271	0.0332	0.0402	0.0479	0.0563	0.0654	0.0750	0.0849	0.0952	0.1056	0.1158	0.1259	11
10	0.0014	0.0020	0.0029	0.0041	0.0056	0.0075	0.0099	0.0128	0.0163	0.0205	0.0253	0.0308	0.0370	0.0440	0.0516	0.0598	0.0686	0.0779	10
11	0.0003	0.0005	0.0007	0.0010	0.0015	0.0022	0.0030	0.0041	0.0055	0.0072	0.0094	0.0120	0.0151	0.0188	0.0231	0.0280	0.0336	0.0398	9
12	0.0001	0.0001	0.0001	0.0002	0.0003	0.0005	0.0008	0.0011	0.0015	0.0021	0.0029	0.0039	0.0051	0.0066	0.0085	0.0108	0.0136	0.0168	8
13	0.0000	0.0000	0.0000	0.0000	0.0001	0.0001	0.0002	0.0002	0.0003	0.0005	0.0007	0.0010	0.0014	0.0019	0.0026	0.0034	0.0045	0.0058	7
14	—	—	—	—	0.0000	0.0000	0.0000	0.0000	0.0001	0.0001	0.0001	0.0002	0.0003	0.0005	0.0006	0.0009	0.0012	0.0016	6
15	—	—	—	—	—	—	—	—	0.0000	0.0000	0.0000	0.0000	0.0001	0.0001	0.0001	0.0002	0.0003	0.0004	5
16	—	—	—	—	—	—	—	—	—	—	—	—	0.0000	0.0000	0.0000	0.0000	0.0000	0.0001	4
17	—	—	—	—	—	—	—	—	—	—	—	—	—	—	—	—	—	0.0000	3
18	—	—	—	—	—	—	—	—	—	—	—	—	—	—	—	—	—	—	2
19	—	—	—	—	—	—	—	—	—	—	—	—	—	—	—	—	—	—	1
20	—	—	—	—	—	—	—	—	—	—	—	—	—	—	—	—	—	—	0
X	0.81	0.80	0.79	0.78	0.77	0.76	0.75	0.74	0.73	0.72	0.71	0.70	0.69	0.68	0.67	0.66	0.65	0.64	X

P

n = 20

TABLE E.7 (Continued)

n	X	0.37	0.38	0.39	0.40	0.41	0.42	0.43	0.44	0.45	0.46	0.47	0.48	0.49	0.50	X	n
2	0	0.3969	0.3844	0.3721	0.3600	0.3481	0.3364	0.3249	0.3136	0.3025	0.2916	0.2809	0.2704	0.2601	0.2500	2	
	1	0.4662	0.4712	0.4758	0.4800	0.4838	0.4872	0.4902	0.4928	0.4950	0.4968	0.4982	0.4992	0.4998	0.5000	1	
	2	0.1369	0.1444	0.1521	0.1600	0.1681	0.1764	0.1849	0.1936	0.2025	0.2116	0.2209	0.2304	0.2401	0.2500	0	2
3	0	0.2500	0.2383	0.2270	0.2160	0.2054	0.1951	0.1852	0.1756	0.1664	0.1575	0.1489	0.1406	0.1327	0.1250	3	
	1	0.4406	0.4382	0.4354	0.4320	0.4282	0.4239	0.4191	0.4140	0.4084	0.4024	0.3961	0.3894	0.3823	0.3750	2	
	2	0.2587	0.2686	0.2783	0.2880	0.2975	0.3069	0.3162	0.3252	0.3341	0.3428	0.3512	0.3594	0.3674	0.3750	1	
	3	0.0507	0.0549	0.0593	0.0640	0.0689	0.0741	0.0795	0.0852	0.0911	0.0973	0.1038	0.1106	0.1176	0.1250	0	3
4	0	0.1575	0.1478	0.1385	0.1296	0.1212	0.1132	0.1056	0.0983	0.0915	0.0850	0.0789	0.0731	0.0677	0.0625	4	
	1	0.3701	0.3623	0.3541	0.3456	0.3368	0.3278	0.3185	0.3091	0.2995	0.2897	0.2799	0.2700	0.2600	0.2500	3	
	2	0.3260	0.3330	0.3396	0.3456	0.3511	0.3560	0.3604	0.3643	0.3675	0.3702	0.3723	0.3738	0.3747	0.3750	2	
	3	0.1276	0.1361	0.1447	0.1536	0.1627	0.1719	0.1813	0.1908	0.2005	0.2102	0.2201	0.2300	0.2400	0.2500	1	
	4	0.0187	0.0209	0.0231	0.0256	0.0283	0.0311	0.0342	0.0375	0.0410	0.0448	0.0488	0.0531	0.0576	0.0625	0	4
5	0	0.0992	0.0916	0.0845	0.0778	0.0715	0.0656	0.0602	0.0551	0.0503	0.0459	0.0418	0.0380	0.0345	0.0312	5	
	1	0.2914	0.2808	0.2700	0.2592	0.2484	0.2376	0.2270	0.2164	0.2059	0.1956	0.1854	0.1755	0.1657	0.1562	4	
	2	0.3423	0.3441	0.3452	0.3456	0.3452	0.3442	0.3424	0.3400	0.3369	0.3332	0.3289	0.3240	0.3185	0.3125	3	
	3	0.2010	0.2109	0.2207	0.2304	0.2399	0.2492	0.2583	0.2671	0.2757	0.2838	0.2916	0.2990	0.3060	0.3125	2	
	4	0.0590	0.0646	0.0706	0.0768	0.0834	0.0902	0.0974	0.1049	0.1128	0.1209	0.1293	0.1380	0.1470	0.1562	1	
	5	0.0069	0.0079	0.0090	0.0102	0.0116	0.0131	0.0147	0.0165	0.0185	0.0206	0.0229	0.0255	0.0282	0.0312	0	5
6	0	0.0625	0.0568	0.0515	0.0467	0.0422	0.0381	0.0343	0.0308	0.0277	0.0248	0.0222	0.0198	0.0176	0.0156	6	
	1	0.2203	0.2089	0.1976	0.1866	0.1759	0.1654	0.1552	0.1454	0.1359	0.1267	0.1179	0.1095	0.1014	0.0937	5	
	2	0.3235	0.3201	0.3159	0.3110	0.3055	0.2994	0.2928	0.2856	0.2780	0.2699	0.2615	0.2527	0.2436	0.2344	4	
	3	0.2533	0.2616	0.2693	0.2765	0.2831	0.2891	0.2945	0.2992	0.3032	0.3065	0.3091	0.3110	0.3121	0.3125	3	
	4	0.1116	0.1202	0.1291	0.1382	0.1475	0.1570	0.1666	0.1763	0.1861	0.1958	0.2056	0.2153	0.2249	0.2344	2	
	5	0.0262	0.0295	0.0330	0.0369	0.0410	0.0455	0.0503	0.0554	0.0609	0.0667	0.0729	0.0795	0.0864	0.0937	1	
	6	0.0026	0.0030	0.0035	0.0041	0.0048	0.0055	0.0063	0.0073	0.0083	0.0095	0.0108	0.0122	0.0138	0.0156	0	6

n	X	0.50	0.51	0.52	0.53	0.54	0.55	0.56	0.57	0.58	0.59	0.60	0.61	0.62	0.63
7	7	0.0078	0.0090	0.0103	0.0117	0.0134	0.0152	0.0173	0.0195	0.0221	0.0249	0.0280	0.0314	0.0352	0.0394
	6	0.0547	0.0604	0.0664	0.0729	0.0798	0.0872	0.0950	0.1032	0.1119	0.1211	0.1306	0.1407	0.1511	0.1619
	5	0.1641	0.1740	0.1840	0.1940	0.2040	0.2140	0.2239	0.2336	0.2431	0.2524	0.2613	0.2698	0.2778	0.2853
	4	0.2734	0.2786	0.2830	0.2867	0.2897	0.2918	0.2932	0.2937	0.2934	0.2923	0.2903	0.2875	0.2838	0.2793
	3	0.2734	0.2676	0.2612	0.2543	0.2468	0.2388	0.2304	0.2216	0.2125	0.2031	0.1935	0.1838	0.1739	0.1640
	2	0.1641	0.1543	0.1447	0.1353	0.1261	0.1172	0.1086	0.1003	0.0923	0.0847	0.0774	0.0705	0.0640	0.0578
	1	0.0547	0.0494	0.0445	0.0400	0.0358	0.0320	0.0284	0.0252	0.0223	0.0196	0.0172	0.0150	0.0131	0.0113
	0	0.0078	0.0068	0.0059	0.0051	0.0044	0.0037	0.0032	0.0027	0.0023	0.0019	0.0016	0.0014	0.0011	0.0009
8	8	0.0039	0.0046	0.0053	0.0062	0.0072	0.0084	0.0097	0.0111	0.0128	0.0147	0.0168	0.0192	0.0218	0.0248
	7	0.0312	0.0352	0.0395	0.0442	0.0493	0.0548	0.0608	0.0672	0.0742	0.0816	0.0896	0.0981	0.1071	0.1166
	6	0.1094	0.1183	0.1275	0.1371	0.1469	0.1569	0.1672	0.1776	0.1880	0.1985	0.2090	0.2194	0.2297	0.2397
	5	0.2187	0.2273	0.2355	0.2431	0.2503	0.2568	0.2627	0.2679	0.2723	0.2759	0.2787	0.2806	0.2815	0.2815
	4	0.2734	0.2730	0.2717	0.2695	0.2665	0.2627	0.2580	0.2526	0.2465	0.2397	0.2322	0.2242	0.2157	0.2067
	3	0.2187	0.2098	0.2006	0.1912	0.1816	0.1719	0.1622	0.1525	0.1428	0.1332	0.1239	0.1147	0.1058	0.0971
	2	0.1094	0.1008	0.0926	0.0848	0.0774	0.0703	0.0637	0.0575	0.0517	0.0463	0.0413	0.0367	0.0324	0.0285
	1	0.0312	0.0277	0.0244	0.0215	0.0188	0.0164	0.0143	0.0124	0.0107	0.0092	0.0079	0.0067	0.0057	0.0048
	0	0.0039	0.0033	0.0028	0.0024	0.0020	0.0017	0.0014	0.0012	0.0010	0.0008	0.0007	0.0005	0.0004	0.0004
9	9	0.0020	0.0023	0.0028	0.0033	0.0039	0.0046	0.0054	0.0064	0.0074	0.0087	0.0101	0.0117	0.0135	0.0156
	8	0.0176	0.0202	0.0231	0.0263	0.0299	0.0339	0.0383	0.0431	0.0484	0.0542	0.0605	0.0673	0.0747	0.0826
	7	0.0703	0.0776	0.0853	0.0934	0.1020	0.1110	0.1204	0.1301	0.1402	0.1506	0.1612	0.1721	0.1831	0.1941
	6	0.1641	0.1739	0.1837	0.1933	0.2027	0.2119	0.2207	0.2291	0.2369	0.2442	0.2508	0.2567	0.2618	0.2660
	5	0.2461	0.2506	0.2543	0.2571	0.2590	0.2600	0.2601	0.2592	0.2573	0.2545	0.2508	0.2462	0.2407	0.2344
	4	0.2461	0.2408	0.2347	0.2280	0.2207	0.2128	0.2044	0.1955	0.1863	0.1769	0.1672	0.1574	0.1475	0.1376
	3	0.1641	0.1542	0.1445	0.1348	0.1253	0.1160	0.1070	0.0983	0.0900	0.0819	0.0743	0.0671	0.0603	0.0539
	2	0.0703	0.0635	0.0571	0.0512	0.0458	0.0407	0.0360	0.0318	0.0279	0.0244	0.0212	0.0184	0.0158	0.0136
	1	0.0176	0.0153	0.0132	0.0114	0.0097	0.0083	0.0071	0.0060	0.0051	0.0042	0.0035	0.0029	0.0024	0.0020
	0	0.0020	0.0016	0.0014	0.0011	0.0009	0.0008	0.0006	0.0005	0.0004	0.0003	0.0003	0.0002	0.0002	0.0001
10	10	0.0010	0.0012	0.0014	0.0017	0.0021	0.0025	0.0030	0.0036	0.0043	0.0051	0.0060	0.0071	0.0084	0.0098
	9	0.0098	0.0114	0.0133	0.0155	0.0180	0.0207	0.0238	0.0273	0.0312	0.0355	0.0403	0.0456	0.0514	0.0578
	8	0.0439	0.0494	0.0554	0.0619	0.0688	0.0763	0.0843	0.0927	0.1017	0.1111	0.1209	0.1312	0.1419	0.1529
	7	0.1172	0.1267	0.1364	0.1464	0.1564	0.1665	0.1765	0.1865	0.1963	0.2058	0.2150	0.2237	0.2319	0.2394
	6	0.2051	0.2130	0.2204	0.2271	0.2331	0.2384	0.2427	0.2462	0.2488	0.2503	0.2508	0.2503	0.2487	0.2461
	5	0.2461	0.2456	0.2441	0.2417	0.2383	0.2340	0.2289	0.2229	0.2162	0.2087	0.2007	0.1920	0.1829	0.1734
	4	0.2051	0.1966	0.1878	0.1786	0.1692	0.1596	0.1499	0.1401	0.1304	0.1209	0.1115	0.1023	0.0934	0.0849
	3	0.1172	0.1080	0.0991	0.0905	0.0824	0.0746	0.0673	0.0604	0.0540	0.0480	0.0425	0.0374	0.0327	0.0285
	2	0.0439	0.0389	0.0343	0.0301	0.0263	0.0229	0.0198	0.0171	0.0147	0.0125	0.0106	0.0090	0.0075	0.0063
	1	0.0098	0.0083	0.0070	0.0059	0.0050	0.0042	0.0035	0.0029	0.0024	0.0019	0.0016	0.0013	0.0010	0.0008
	0	0.0010	0.0008	0.0006	0.0005	0.0004	0.0003	0.0003	0.0002	0.0002	0.0001	0.0001	0.0001	0.0001	0.0000

P

| n | X |

TABLE E.7 (Continued)

n	X	0.37	0.38	0.39	0.40	0.41	0.42	0.43	0.44	0.45	0.46	0.47	0.48	0.49	0.50	X	n
12	0	0.0039	0.0032	0.0027	0.0022	0.0018	0.0014	0.0012	0.0010	0.0008	0.0006	0.0005	0.0004	0.0003	0.0002	12	
	1	0.0276	0.0237	0.0204	0.0174	0.0148	0.0126	0.0106	0.0090	0.0075	0.0063	0.0052	0.0043	0.0036	0.0029	11	
	2	0.0890	0.0800	0.0716	0.0639	0.0567	0.0502	0.0442	0.0388	0.0339	0.0294	0.0255	0.0220	0.0189	0.0161	10	
	3	0.1742	0.1634	0.1526	0.1419	0.1314	0.1211	0.1111	0.1015	0.0923	0.0836	0.0754	0.0676	0.0604	0.0537	9	
	4	0.2302	0.2254	0.2195	0.2128	0.2054	0.1973	0.1886	0.1794	0.1700	0.1602	0.1504	0.1405	0.1306	0.1208	8	
	5	0.2163	0.2210	0.2246	0.2270	0.2284	0.2285	0.2276	0.2256	0.2225	0.2184	0.2134	0.2075	0.2008	0.1934	7	
	6	0.1482	0.1580	0.1675	0.1766	0.1851	0.1931	0.2003	0.2068	0.2124	0.2171	0.2208	0.2234	0.2250	0.2256	6	
	7	0.0746	0.0830	0.0918	0.1009	0.1103	0.1198	0.1295	0.1393	0.1489	0.1585	0.1678	0.1768	0.1853	0.1934	5	
	8	0.0274	0.0318	0.0367	0.0420	0.0479	0.0542	0.0611	0.0684	0.0762	0.0844	0.0930	0.1020	0.1113	0.1208	4	
	9	0.0071	0.0087	0.0104	0.0125	0.0148	0.0175	0.0205	0.0239	0.0277	0.0319	0.0367	0.0418	0.0475	0.0537	3	
	10	0.0013	0.0016	0.0020	0.0025	0.0031	0.0038	0.0046	0.0056	0.0068	0.0082	0.0098	0.0116	0.0137	0.0161	2	
	11	0.0001	0.0002	0.0002	0.0003	0.0004	0.0005	0.0006	0.0008	0.0010	0.0013	0.0016	0.0019	0.0024	0.0029	1	
	12	0.0000	0.0000	0.0000	0.0000	0.0000	0.0000	0.0000	0.0001	0.0001	0.0001	0.0001	0.0001	0.0002	0.0002	0	12
15	0	0.0010	0.0008	0.0006	0.0005	0.0004	0.0003	0.0002	0.0002	0.0001	0.0001	0.0001	0.0001	0.0000	0.0000	15	
	1	0.0086	0.0071	0.0058	0.0047	0.0038	0.0031	0.0025	0.0020	0.0016	0.0012	0.0010	0.0008	0.0006	0.0005	14	
	2	0.0354	0.0303	0.0259	0.0219	0.0185	0.0156	0.0130	0.0108	0.0090	0.0074	0.0060	0.0049	0.0040	0.0032	13	
	3	0.0901	0.0805	0.0716	0.0634	0.0558	0.0489	0.0426	0.0369	0.0318	0.0272	0.0232	0.0197	0.0166	0.0139	12	
	4	0.1587	0.1481	0.1374	0.1268	0.1163	0.1061	0.0963	0.0869	0.0780	0.0696	0.0617	0.0545	0.0478	0.0417	11	
	5	0.2051	0.1997	0.1933	0.1859	0.1778	0.1691	0.1598	0.1502	0.1404	0.1304	0.1204	0.1106	0.1010	0.0916	10	
	6	0.2008	0.2040	0.2059	0.2066	0.2060	0.2041	0.2010	0.1967	0.1914	0.1851	0.1780	0.1702	0.1617	0.1527	9	
	7	0.1516	0.1608	0.1693	0.1771	0.1840	0.1900	0.1949	0.1987	0.2013	0.2028	0.2030	0.2020	0.1997	0.1964	8	
	8	0.0890	0.0985	0.1082	0.1181	0.1279	0.1376	0.1470	0.1561	0.1647	0.1727	0.1800	0.1864	0.1919	0.1964	7	
	9	0.0407	0.0470	0.0538	0.0612	0.0691	0.0775	0.0863	0.0954	0.1048	0.1144	0.1241	0.1338	0.1434	0.1527	6	
	10	0.0143	0.0173	0.0206	0.0245	0.0288	0.0337	0.0390	0.0450	0.0515	0.0585	0.0661	0.0741	0.0827	0.0916	5	
	11	0.0038	0.0048	0.0060	0.0074	0.0091	0.0111	0.0134	0.0161	0.0191	0.0226	0.0266	0.0311	0.0361	0.0417	4	
	12	0.0007	0.0010	0.0013	0.0016	0.0021	0.0027	0.0034	0.0042	0.0052	0.0064	0.0079	0.0096	0.0116	0.0139	3	
	13	0.0001	0.0001	0.0002	0.0003	0.0003	0.0004	0.0006	0.0008	0.0010	0.0013	0.0016	0.0020	0.0026	0.0032	2	
	14	0.0000	0.0000	0.0000	0.0000	0.0000	0.0000	0.0001	0.0001	0.0001	0.0002	0.0002	0.0003	0.0004	0.0005	1	
	15	—	0.0000	0.0000	0.0000	—	—	0.0000	0.0000	0.0000	0.0000	0.0000	0.0000	0.0000	0.0000	0	15

n = 20

n	X	0.50	0.51	0.52	0.53	0.54	0.55	0.56	0.57	0.58	0.59	0.60	0.61	0.62	0.63	X	n
20	0	—	—	—	0.0000	0.0000	0.0000	0.0000	0.0000	0.0000	0.0000	0.0000	0.0001	0.0001	0.0001	20	20
	1	0.0000	0.0000	0.0000	0.0001	0.0001	0.0001	0.0001	0.0002	0.0003	0.0004	0.0005	0.0007	0.0009	0.0011	19	
	2	0.0002	0.0002	0.0003	0.0005	0.0006	0.0008	0.0011	0.0014	0.0018	0.0024	0.0031	0.0040	0.0050	0.0064	18	
	3	0.0011	0.0014	0.0019	0.0024	0.0031	0.0040	0.0051	0.0064	0.0080	0.0100	0.0123	0.0152	0.0185	0.0224	17	
	4	0.0046	0.0059	0.0074	0.0092	0.0113	0.0139	0.0170	0.0206	0.0247	0.0295	0.0350	0.0412	0.0482	0.0559	16	
	5	0.0148	0.0180	0.0217	0.0260	0.0309	0.0365	0.0427	0.0496	0.0573	0.0656	0.0746	0.0843	0.0945	0.1051	15	
	6	0.0370	0.0432	0.0501	0.0577	0.0658	0.0746	0.0839	0.0936	0.1037	0.1140	0.1244	0.1347	0.1447	0.1543	14	
	7	0.0739	0.0830	0.0925	0.1023	0.1122	0.1221	0.1318	0.1413	0.1502	0.1585	0.1659	0.1722	0.1774	0.1812	13	
	8	0.1201	0.1296	0.1388	0.1474	0.1553	0.1623	0.1683	0.1732	0.1768	0.1790	0.1797	0.1790	0.1767	0.1730	12	
	9	0.1602	0.1661	0.1708	0.1742	0.1763	0.1771	0.1763	0.1742	0.1707	0.1658	0.1597	0.1526	0.1444	0.1354	11	
	10	0.1762	0.1755	0.1734	0.1700	0.1652	0.1593	0.1524	0.1446	0.1359	0.1268	0.1171	0.1073	0.0974	0.0875	10	
	11	0.1602	0.1533	0.1455	0.1370	0.1280	0.1185	0.1089	0.0991	0.0895	0.0801	0.0710	0.0624	0.0542	0.0467	9	
	12	0.1201	0.1105	0.1007	0.0911	0.0818	0.0727	0.0642	0.0561	0.0486	0.0417	0.0355	0.0299	0.0249	0.0206	8	
	13	0.0739	0.0653	0.0572	0.0497	0.0429	0.0366	0.0310	0.0260	0.0217	0.0178	0.0146	0.0118	0.0094	0.0074	7	
	14	0.0370	0.0314	0.0264	0.0221	0.0183	0.0150	0.0122	0.0098	0.0078	0.0062	0.0049	0.0038	0.0029	0.0022	6	
	15	0.0148	0.0121	0.0098	0.0078	0.0062	0.0049	0.0038	0.0030	0.0023	0.0017	0.0013	0.0010	0.0007	0.0005	5	
	16	0.0046	0.0036	0.0028	0.0022	0.0017	0.0013	0.0009	0.0007	0.0005	0.0004	0.0003	0.0002	0.0001	0.0001	4	
	17	0.0011	0.0008	0.0006	0.0005	0.0003	0.0002	0.0002	0.0001	0.0001	0.0001	0.0000	0.0000	0.0000	0.0000	3	
	18	0.0002	0.0001	0.0001	0.0001	0.0000	0.0000	0.0000	0.0000	0.0000	0.0000	—	—	—	—	2	
	19	0.0000	0.0000	0.0000	0.0000	—	—	—	—	—	—	—	—	—	—	1	
	20	—	—	—	—	—	—	—	—	—	—	—	—	—	—	0	20
n	X	0.50	0.51	0.52	0.53	0.54	0.55	0.56	0.57	0.58	0.59	0.60	0.61	0.62	0.63	X	n

P

TABLE E.8 Critical values of Hartley's F_{max} Test $(F_{max} = \dfrac{s^2_{largest}}{s^2_{smallest}} \sim F_{max_{1-\alpha(c,v)}})$

Upper 5% points ($\alpha = .05$)

c / v	2	3	4	5	6	7	8	9	10	11	12
2	39.0	87.5	142	202	266	333	403	475	550	626	704
3	15.4	27.8	39.2	50.7	62.0	72.9	83.5	93.9	104	114	124
4	9.60	15.5	20.6	25.2	29.5	33.6	37.5	41.1	44.6	48.0	51.4
5	7.15	10.8	13.7	16.3	18.7	20.8	22.9	24.7	26.5	28.2	29.9
6	5.82	8.38	10.4	12.1	13.7	15.0	16.3	17.5	18.6	19.7	20.7
7	4.99	6.94	8.44	9.70	10.8	11.8	12.7	13.5	14.3	15.1	15.8
8	4.43	6.00	7.18	8.12	9.03	9.78	10.5	11.1	11.7	12.2	12.7
9	4.03	5.34	6.31	7.11	7.80	8.41	8.95	9.45	9.91	10.3	10.7
10	3.72	4.85	5.67	6.34	6.92	7.42	7.87	8.28	8.66	9.01	9.34
12	3.28	4.16	4.79	5.30	5.72	6.09	6.42	6.72	7.00	7.25	7.48
15	2.86	3.54	4.01	4.37	4.68	4.95	5.19	5.40	5.59	5.77	5.93
20	2.46	2.95	3.29	3.54	3.76	3.94	4.10	4.24	4.37	4.49	4.59
30	2.07	2.40	2.61	2.78	2.91	3.02	3.12	3.21	3.29	3.36	3.39
60	1.67	1.85	1.96	2.04	2.11	2.17	2.22	2.26	2.30	2.33	2.36
∞	1.00	1.00	1.00	1.00	1.00	1.00	1.00	1.00	1.00	1.00	1.00

Upper 1% points ($\alpha = .01$)

c / v	2	3	4	5	6	7	8	9	10	11	12
2	199	448	729	1036	1362	1705	2063	2432	2813	3204	3605
3	47.5	85	120	151	184	21(6)	24(9)	28(1)	31(0)	33(7)	36(1)
4	23.2	37	49	59	69	79	89	97	106	113	120
5	14.9	22	28	33	38	42	46	50	54	57	60
6	11.1	15.5	19.1	22	25	27	30	32	34	36	37
7	8.89	12.1	14.5	16.5	18.4	20	22	23	24	26	27
8	7.50	9.9	11.7	13.2	14.5	15.8	16.9	17.9	18.9	19.8	21
9	6.54	8.5	9.9	11.1	12.1	13.1	13.9	14.7	15.3	16.0	16.6
10	5.85	7.4	8.6	9.6	10.4	11.1	11.8	12.4	12.9	13.4	13.9
12	4.91	6.1	6.9	7.6	8.2	8.7	9.1	9.5	9.9	10.2	10.6
15	4.07	4.9	5.5	6.0	6.4	6.7	7.1	7.3	7.5	7.8	8.0
20	3.32	3.8	4.3	4.6	4.9	5.1	5.3	5.5	5.6	5.8	5.9
30	2.63	3.0	3.3	3.4	3.6	3.7	3.8	3.9	4.0	4.1	4.2
60	1.96	2.2	2.3	2.4	2.4	2.5	2.5	2.6	2.6	2.7	2.7
∞	1.00	1.0	1.0	1.0	1.0	1.0	1.0	1.0	1.0	1.0	1.0

$s^2_{largest}$ is the largest and $s^2_{smallest}$ the smallest in a set of c independent mean squares, each based on v degrees of freedom.

TABLE E.9 Lower and upper critical values U for the runs test for randomness

Part 1. Lower Tail
$(\alpha = .025)$

$n_1 \backslash n_2$	2	3	4	5	6	7	8	9	10	11	12	13	14	15	16	17	18	19	20
2															2	2	2	2	2
3					2	2	2	2	2	2	2	2	2	3	3	3	3	3	3
4			2	2	2	2	3	3	3	3	3	3	3	3	4	4	4	4	4
5		2	2	3	3	3	3	3	3	4	4	4	4	4	4	5	5	5	5
6		2	2	3	3	3	3	4	4	4	5	5	5	5	5	5	6	6	6
7		2	3	3	3	3	4	4	5	5	5	5	6	6	6	6	6	6	6
8		2	3	3	3	4	4	5	5	5	6	6	6	6	6	7	7	7	7
9		2	3	3	4	4	5	5	5	6	6	6	7	7	7	7	8	8	8
10		2	3	3	4	5	5	5	6	6	7	7	7	7	8	8	8	8	9
11		2	3	4	4	5	5	6	6	7	7	7	8	8	8	9	9	9	10
12	2	2	3	4	4	5	6	6	7	7	7	8	8	9	9	9	10	10	10
13	2	2	3	4	5	5	6	6	7	7	8	8	9	9	9	10	10	11	11
14	2	2	3	4	5	5	6	7	7	8	8	9	9	9	10	10	11	11	12
15	2	3	3	4	5	6	6	7	7	8	8	9	9	10	10	11	11	12	12
16	2	3	4	4	5	6	6	7	8	8	9	9	10	10	11	11	11	12	12
17	2	3	4	4	5	6	7	7	8	8	9	9	10	10	11	11	12	12	13
18	2	3	4	5	5	6	7	8	8	9	9	10	10	11	11	12	12	13	13
19	2	3	4	5	6	6	7	8	8	9	10	10	11	11	12	12	13	13	13
20	2	3	4	5	6	6	7	8	9	9	10	10	11	12	12	13	13	13	14

Part 2. Upper Tail
$(\alpha = .025)$

$n_1 \backslash n_2$	2	3	4	5	6	7	8	9	10	11	12	13	14	15	16	17	18	19	20
2																			
3																			
4				9	9														
5			9	10	10	11	11												
6			9	10	11	12	12	13	13	13	13								
7				11	12	13	13	14	14	14	14	15	15	15					
8				11	12	13	14	14	15	15	16	16	16	16	17	17	17	17	
9					13	14	14	15	16	16	16	17	17	18	18	18	18		
10					13	14	15	16	16	17	17	18	18	18	19	19	20	20	
11					13	14	15	16	17	17	18	19	19	19	20	20	21	21	
12					13	14	16	16	17	18	19	19	20	20	21	21	21	22	
13						15	16	17	18	19	19	20	20	21	22	22	23	23	
14						15	16	17	18	19	20	20	21	22	22	23	23	24	
15						15	16	18	18	19	20	21	22	22	23	23	24	25	
16							17	18	19	20	21	21	22	23	23	24	25	25	
17							17	18	19	20	21	22	23	23	24	25	25	26	
18							17	18	20	21	22	23	23	24	25	25	26	26	
19							17	18	20	21	22	23	24	25	25	26	26	27	
20							17	18	20	21	22	23	24	25	26	27	27	28	

SOURCE: Adapted from F. S. Swed and C. Eisenhart, *Ann. Math. Statist.*, vol. 14, 1943, pp. 83–86.

TABLE E.10   Lower and upper critical values *W* of Wilcoxon signed-ranks test

n	One Tailed: $\alpha = .05$ Two-Tailed: $\alpha = .10$	$\alpha = .025$ $\alpha = .05$	$\alpha = .01$ $\alpha = .02$	$\alpha = .005$ $\alpha = .01$
	(Lower, Upper)			
5	0,15	—,—	—,—	—,—
6	2,19	0,21	—,—	—,—
7	3,25	2,26	0,28	—,—
8	5,31	3,33	1,35	0,36
9	8,37	5,40	3,42	1,44
10	10,45	8,47	5,50	3,52
11	13,53	10,56	7,59	5,61
12	17,61	13,65	10,68	7,71
13	21,70	17,74	12,79	10,81
14	25,80	21,84	16,89	13,92
15	30,90	25,95	19,101	16,104
16	35,101	29,107	23,113	19,117
17	41,112	34,119	27,126	23,130
18	47,124	40,131	32,139	27,144
19	53,137	46,144	37,153	32,158
20	60,150	52,158	43,167	37,173

SOURCE: Adapted from Table 2 of F. Wilcoxon and R. A. Wilcox, *Some Rapid Approximate Statistical Procedures* (Pearl River, N.Y.: Lederle Laboratories, 1964), with permission of the American Cyanamid Company.

TABLE E.11 Lower and upper critical values T_{n_1} of Wilcoxon rank sum test

n_2	α One-Tailed	Two-Tailed	4	5	6	7	8	9	10
4	.05	.10	11,25						
	.025	.05	10,26						
	.01	.02	—,—						
	.005	.01	—,—						
5	.05	.10	12,28	19,36					
	.025	.05	11,29	17,38					
	.01	.02	10,30	16,39					
	.005	.01	—,—	15,40					
6	.05	.10	13,31	20,40	28,50				
	.025	.05	12,32	18,42	26,52				
	.01	.02	11,33	17,43	24,54				
	.005	.01	10,34	16,44	23,55				
7	.05	.10	14,34	21,44	29,55	39,66			
	.025	.05	13,35	20,45	27,57	36,69			
	.01	.02	11,37	18,47	25,59	34,71			
	.005	.01	10,38	16,49	24,60	32,73			
8	.05	.10	15,37	23,47	31,59	41,71	51,85		
	.025	.05	14,38	21,49	29,61	38,74	49,87		
	.01	.02	12,40	19,51	27,63	35,77	45,91		
	.005	.01	11,41	17,53	25,65	34,78	43,93		
9	.05	.10	16,40	24,51	33,63	43,76	54,90	66,105	
	.025	.05	14,42	22,53	31,65	40,79	51,93	62,109	
	.01	.02	13,43	20,55	28,68	37,82	47,97	59,112	
	.005	.01	11,45	18,57	26,70	35,84	45,99	56,115	
10	.05	.10	17,43	26,54	35,67	45,81	56,96	69,111	82,128
	.025	.05	15,45	23,57	32,70	42,84	53,99	65,115	78,132
	.01	.02	13,47	21,59	29,73	39,87	49,103	61,119	74,136
	.005	.01	12,48	19,61	27,75	37,89	47,105	58,122	71,139

SOURCE: Adapted from Table 1 of F. Wilcoxon and R. A. Wilcox, *Some Rapid Approximate Statistical Procedures* (Pearl River, N.Y., Lederle Laboratories, 1964), with permission of the American Cyanamid Company.

TABLE E.12 Critical values[a] of the Studentized range Q

Upper 5% points ($\alpha = .05$)

v \ η	2	3	4	5	6	7	8	9	10	11	12	13	14	15	16	17	18	19	20
1	18.0	27.0	32.8	37.1	40.4	43.1	45.4	47.4	49.1	50.6	52.0	53.2	54.3	55.4	56.3	57.2	58.0	58.8	59.6
2	6.09	8.3	9.8	10.9	11.7	12.4	13.0	13.5	14.0	14.4	14.7	15.1	15.4	15.7	15.9	16.1	16.4	16.6	16.8
3	4.50	5.91	6.82	7.50	8.04	8.48	8.85	9.18	9.46	9.72	9.95	10.15	10.35	10.52	10.69	10.84	10.98	11.11	11.24
4	3.93	5.04	5.76	6.29	6.71	7.05	7.35	7.60	7.83	8.03	8.21	8.37	8.52	8.66	8.79	8.91	9.03	9.13	9.23
5	3.64	4.60	5.22	5.67	6.03	6.33	6.58	6.80	6.99	7.17	7.32	7.47	7.60	7.72	7.83	7.93	8.03	8.12	8.21
6	3.46	4.34	4.90	5.31	5.63	5.89	6.12	6.32	6.49	6.65	6.79	6.92	7.03	7.14	7.24	7.34	7.43	7.51	7.59
7	3.34	4.16	4.68	5.06	5.36	5.61	5.82	6.00	6.16	6.30	6.43	6.55	6.66	6.76	6.85	6.94	7.02	7.09	7.17
8	3.26	4.04	4.53	4.89	5.17	5.40	5.60	5.77	5.92	6.05	6.18	6.29	6.39	6.48	6.57	6.65	6.73	6.80	6.87
9	3.20	3.95	4.42	4.76	5.02	5.24	5.43	5.60	5.74	5.87	5.98	6.09	6.19	6.28	6.36	6.44	6.51	6.58	6.64
10	3.15	3.88	4.33	4.65	4.91	5.12	5.30	5.46	5.60	5.72	5.83	5.93	6.03	6.11	6.20	6.27	6.34	6.40	6.47
11	3.11	3.82	4.26	4.57	4.82	5.03	5.20	5.35	5.49	5.61	5.71	5.81	5.90	5.99	6.06	6.14	6.20	6.26	6.33
12	3.08	3.77	4.20	4.51	4.75	4.95	5.12	5.27	5.40	5.51	5.62	5.71	5.80	5.88	5.95	6.03	6.09	6.15	6.21
13	3.06	3.73	4.15	4.45	4.69	4.88	5.05	5.19	5.32	5.43	5.53	5.63	5.71	5.79	5.86	5.93	6.00	6.05	6.11
14	3.03	3.70	4.11	4.41	4.64	4.83	4.99	5.13	5.25	5.36	5.46	5.55	5.64	5.72	5.79	5.85	5.92	5.97	6.03
15	3.01	3.67	4.08	4.37	4.60	4.78	4.94	5.08	5.20	5.31	5.40	5.49	5.58	5.65	5.72	5.79	5.85	5.90	5.96
16	3.00	3.65	4.05	4.33	4.56	4.74	4.90	5.03	5.15	5.26	5.35	5.44	5.52	5.59	5.66	5.72	5.79	5.84	5.90
17	2.98	3.63	4.02	4.30	4.52	4.71	4.86	4.99	5.11	5.21	5.31	5.39	5.47	5.55	5.61	5.68	5.74	5.79	5.84
18	2.97	3.61	4.00	4.28	4.49	4.67	4.82	4.96	5.07	5.17	5.27	5.35	5.43	5.50	5.57	5.63	5.69	5.74	5.79
19	2.96	3.59	3.98	4.25	4.47	4.65	4.79	4.92	5.04	5.14	5.23	5.32	5.39	5.46	5.53	5.59	5.65	5.70	5.75
20	2.95	3.58	3.96	4.23	4.45	4.62	4.77	4.90	5.01	5.11	5.20	5.28	5.36	5.43	5.49	5.55	5.61	5.66	5.71
24	2.92	3.53	3.90	4.17	4.37	4.54	4.68	4.81	4.92	5.01	5.10	5.18	5.25	5.32	5.38	5.44	5.50	5.54	5.59
30	2.89	3.49	3.84	4.10	4.30	4.46	4.60	4.72	4.83	4.92	5.00	5.08	5.15	5.21	5.27	5.33	5.38	5.43	5.48
40	2.86	3.44	3.79	4.04	4.23	4.39	4.52	4.63	4.74	4.82	4.91	4.98	5.05	5.11	5.16	5.22	5.27	5.31	5.36
60	2.83	3.40	3.74	3.98	4.16	4.31	4.44	4.55	4.65	4.73	4.81	4.88	4.94	5.00	5.06	5.11	5.16	5.20	5.24
120	2.80	3.36	3.69	3.92	4.10	4.24	4.36	4.48	4.56	4.64	4.72	4.78	4.84	4.90	4.95	5.00	5.05	5.09	5.13
∞	2.77	3.31	3.63	3.86	4.03	4.17	4.29	4.39	4.47	4.55	4.62	4.68	4.74	4.80	4.85	4.89	4.93	4.97	5.01

TABLE E.12 (Continued)

Upper 1% points ($\alpha = .01$)

v \ η	2	3	4	5	6	7	8	9	10	11	12	13	14	15	16	17	18	19	20
1	90.0	135	164	186	202	216	227	237	246	253	260	266	272	277	282	286	290	294	298
2	14.0	19.0	22.3	24.7	26.6	28.2	29.5	30.7	31.7	32.6	33.4	34.1	34.8	35.4	36.0	36.5	37.0	37.5	37.9
3	8.26	10.6	12.2	13.3	14.2	15.0	15.6	16.2	16.7	17.1	17.5	17.9	18.2	18.5	18.8	19.1	19.3	19.5	19.8
4	6.51	8.12	9.17	9.96	10.6	11.1	11.5	11.9	12.3	12.6	12.8	13.1	13.3	13.5	13.7	13.9	14.1	14.2	14.4
5	5.70	6.97	7.80	8.42	8.91	9.32	9.67	9.97	10.24	10.48	10.70	10.89	11.08	11.24	11.40	11.55	11.68	11.81	11.93
6	5.24	6.33	7.03	7.56	7.97	8.32	8.61	8.87	9.10	9.30	9.49	9.65	9.81	9.95	10.08	10.21	10.32	10.43	10.54
7	4.95	5.92	6.54	7.01	7.37	7.68	7.94	8.17	8.37	8.55	8.71	8.86	9.00	9.12	9.24	9.35	9.46	9.55	9.65
8	4.74	5.63	6.20	6.63	6.96	7.24	7.47	7.68	7.87	8.03	8.18	8.31	8.44	8.55	8.66	8.76	8.85	8.94	9.03
9	4.60	5.43	5.96	6.35	6.66	6.91	7.13	7.32	7.49	7.65	7.78	7.91	8.03	8.13	8.23	8.32	8.41	8.49	8.57
10	4.48	5.27	5.77	6.14	6.43	6.67	6.87	7.05	7.21	7.36	7.48	7.60	7.71	7.81	7.91	7.99	8.07	8.15	8.22
11	4.39	5.14	5.62	5.97	6.25	6.48	6.67	6.84	6.99	7.13	7.25	7.36	7.46	7.56	7.65	7.73	7.81	7.88	7.95
12	4.32	5.04	5.50	5.84	6.10	6.32	6.51	6.67	6.81	6.94	7.06	7.17	7.26	7.36	7.44	7.52	7.59	7.66	7.73
13	4.26	4.96	5.40	5.73	5.98	6.19	6.37	6.53	6.67	6.79	6.90	7.01	7.10	7.19	7.27	7.34	7.42	7.48	7.55
14	4.21	4.89	5.32	5.63	5.88	6.08	6.26	6.41	6.54	6.66	6.77	6.87	6.96	7.05	7.12	7.20	7.27	7.33	7.39
15	4.17	4.83	5.25	5.56	5.80	5.99	6.16	6.31	6.44	6.55	6.66	6.76	6.84	6.93	7.00	7.07	7.14	7.20	7.26
16	4.13	4.78	5.19	5.49	5.72	5.92	6.08	6.22	6.35	6.46	6.56	6.66	6.74	6.82	6.90	6.97	7.03	7.09	7.15
17	4.10	4.74	5.14	5.43	5.66	5.85	6.01	6.15	6.27	6.38	6.48	6.57	6.66	6.73	6.80	6.87	6.94	7.00	7.05
18	4.07	4.70	5.09	5.38	5.60	5.79	5.94	6.08	6.20	6.31	6.41	6.50	6.58	6.65	6.72	6.79	6.85	6.91	6.96
19	4.05	4.67	5.05	5.33	5.55	5.73	5.89	6.02	6.14	6.25	6.34	6.43	6.51	6.58	6.65	6.72	6.78	6.84	6.89
20	4.02	4.64	5.02	5.29	5.51	5.69	5.84	5.97	6.09	6.19	6.29	6.37	6.45	6.52	6.59	6.65	6.71	6.76	6.82
24	3.96	4.54	4.91	5.17	5.37	5.54	5.69	5.81	5.92	6.02	6.11	6.19	6.26	6.33	6.39	6.45	6.51	6.56	6.61
30	3.89	4.45	4.80	5.05	5.24	5.40	5.54	5.65	5.76	5.85	5.93	6.01	6.08	6.14	6.20	6.26	6.31	6.36	6.41
40	3.82	4.37	4.70	4.93	5.11	5.27	5.39	5.50	5.60	5.69	5.77	5.84	5.90	5.96	6.02	6.07	6.12	6.17	6.21
60	3.76	4.28	4.60	4.82	4.99	5.13	5.25	5.36	5.45	5.53	5.60	5.67	5.73	5.79	5.84	5.89	5.93	5.98	6.02
120	3.70	4.20	4.50	4.71	4.87	5.01	5.12	5.21	5.30	5.38	5.44	5.51	5.56	5.61	5.66	5.71	5.75	5.79	5.83
∞	3.64	4.12	4.40	4.60	4.76	4.88	4.99	5.08	5.16	5.23	5.29	5.35	5.40	5.45	5.49	5.54	5.57	5.61	5.65

^{a}Range/$S_Y \sim Q_{1-\alpha;\,\eta,\,v}$. η is the size of the sample from which the range is obtained, and v is the number of degrees of freedom of S_Y.

SOURCE: Reprinted from E. S. Pearson and H. O. Hartley, eds., Table 29 of *Biometrika Tables for Statisticians, Vol. 1*, 3rd ed., 1966, by permission of the *Biometrika* Trustees, London.

TABLE E.13   Control Chart Factors

Number of Observations in Sample	d_2	d_3
2	1.128	0.853
3	1.693	0.888
4	2.059	0.880
5	2.326	0.864
6	2.534	0.848
7	2.704	0.833
8	2.847	0.820
9	2.970	0.808
10	3.078	0.797
11	3.137	0.787
12	3.258	0.778
13	3.336	0.770
14	3.407	0.762
15	3.472	0.755
16	3.532	0.749
17	3.588	0.743
18	3.640	0.738
19	3.689	0.733
20	3.735	0.729
21	3.778	0.724
22	3.819	0.720
23	3.858	0.716
24	3.895	0.712
25	3.931	0.709

SOURCE: Reprinted from ASTM-STP 15D by kind permission of the American Society for Testing and Materials.

Answers to Selected Problems (·)

CHAPTER 2

2.31 **(a)** Quantitative (continuous)*; **(b)** Quantitative (discrete); **(c)** Qualitative; **(d)** Quantitative (continuous); **(e)** Qualitative; **(f)** Quantitative (discrete); **(g)** Qualitative.

2.32 **(1)** Qualitative—nominal scale.
(2) Qualitative—nominal scale.
(3) Quantitative (continuous)—ratio scale.†
(4) Quantitative (continuous)—ratio scale.*
(5) Qualitative—nominal scale.
(6) Qualitative—nominal scale.
(7) Quantitative (discrete)
(8) Quantitative (discrete)
(9) Quantitative (continuous)—ratio scale.*
(10) Quantitative (continuous)—ratio scale.*
(11) Qualitative—nominal scale.
(12) Quantitative (discrete)
(13) Quantitative (continuous)—ratio scale.*
(14) Quantitative (continuous)—ratio scale.
(15) Qualitative—nominal scale.
(16) Quantitative (continuous)—ratio scale.*

2.35 12 47 83 76 22 65 93 10 61 36 89 58 86 92 71

2.43 Line 1—columns 19–20 indicate that the home contains 99 rooms.
Line 1—column 48 has a 2 for absence or presence of a connection to a local sewer system.
Line 2—column 36 has a 4 for type of heating fuel used.
Line 3—column 32 has a 4 for geographical location.
Line 4—columns 15–17 indicate that there are no bathrooms in the home.
Line 5—column 42 has a 2 for absence or presence of an eat-in kitchen.

---

* Some researchers consider money as a discrete quantitative variable because it can be ''counted.''
† Age is measured on a ratio scale although calendar time is measured on an interval scale.

CHAPTER 3

3.2 **(a)**

	Mean	Median	Mode	Midrange
Batch 1:	4.0	3.0	2.0	6.0
Batch 2:	14.0	13.0	12.0	16.0

(b), (c) Every value in Batch 2 is 10 units higher than in Batch 1; thus, each measure of central tendency is 10 units greater in Batch 2 than in Batch 1.

3.14 **(a)**

	Range	Variance	Standard Deviation	Coeff. of Variation
Batch 1:	8.0	8.33	2.89	72.2%
Batch 2:	8.0	8.33	2.89	20.6%

(b) The batches differ only with respect to relative dispersion.

3.23 **(a)** and **(b)** For each batch the data are positive or right-skewed since $\overline{X}$ > median.

3.30 **(a)** Revised stem-and-leaf display: **(b)** Ordered array:

9	147
10	02238
11	135566777
12	223489
13	02

$n = 25$

91	102	115	117	124
94	103	115	117	128
97	108	116	122	129
100	111	116	122	130
102	113	117	123	132

(c) The stem-and-leaf display provides more information. It shows how the data are distributed (central tendency, dispersion, shape).

3.36 $Q_1 = 102.5$ and $Q_3 = 122.5$.

3.42 Midhinge $= 112.5$ and Interquartile range $= 20.0$.

3.48 **(a)** Five-number summary:
$X_{\text{smallest}} = 91$ $Q_1 = 102.5$ Median $= 116$ $Q_3 = 122.5$ $X_{\text{largest}} = 132$
(b) Box-and-whisker plot:

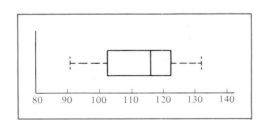

The data are approximately symmetric in shape.

3.54 **(a)** $\mu_X = 6.0$ Median $= 6.5$ Mode $= 8.0$ Midrange $= 6.0$ Midhinge $= 5.5$
(b) Range $= 10.0$ Interquartile range $= 5.0$ $\sigma_X^2 = 9.40$ $\sigma_X = 3.07$ $CV_{\text{pop}} = 51.1\%$
(c) Data are approximately symmetrical.

3.65 **(a)**   **(1)** $\overline{X} = 5.29$.   **(6)** Range $= 14.20$.
              (2) Median $= 4.10$.   **(7)** Interquartile range $= 6.30$.
              (3) Mode $=$ none.   **(8)** $S^2 = 16.0355$.
              (4) Midrange $= 7.70$.   **(9)** $S = 4.00$.
              (5) Midhinge $= 5.05$.   **(10)** CV $= 75.7\%$.

(b) Stem-and-leaf display:

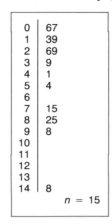

```
 0 | 67
 1 | 39
 2 | 69
 3 | 9
 4 | 1
 5 | 4
 6 |
 7 | 15
 8 | 25
 9 | 8
10 |
11 |
12 |
13 |
14 | 8
        n = 15
```

Box-and-whisker plot:

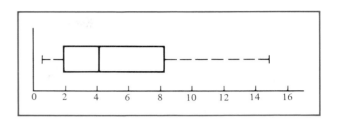

(c) Five-number summary:
$X_{\text{smallest}} = 0.6$ $Q_1 = 1.9$ Median $= 4.1$ $Q_3 = 8.2$ $X_{\text{largest}} = 14.8$.

(d) Data are positive or right-skewed since $\overline{X} >$ Median.

3.69 **(a)** **(1)** $\overline{X} = 9.8$. **(6)** Range $= 19.0$.
   (2) Median $= 9.0$. **(7)** Interquartile range $= 4.0$.
   (3) Mode $= 8.0$. **(8)** $S^2 = (3.7)^2$.
   (4) Midrange $= 13.5$. **(9)** $S = 3.7$.
   (5) Midhinge $= 9.0$. **(10)** CV $= 37.8\%$.

(b) Stem-and-leaf display:

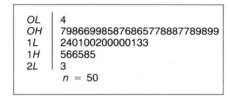

```
OL | 4
OH | 798669985876865778887789899
1L | 240100200000133
1H | 566585
2L | 3
        n = 50
```

Box-and-whisker plot:

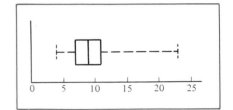

(c) Five-number summary:
$X_{\text{smallest}} = 4$ $Q_1 = 7$ Median $= 9$ $Q_3 = 11$ $X_{\text{largest}} = 23$.

(d) Data are positive or right-skewed since $\overline{X} >$ Median.

(e) 2.4 to 17.2.

(f) 96.0%.

CHAPTER 4

4.2 **(a)** $15,000 but less than $20,000, $20,000 but less than $25,000, and so on.
(b) $5,000.
(c) $17,500 $22,500 $27,500 $32,500 $37,500 $42,500 $47,500 $52,500 $57,500 $62,500.

4.4   **(a)** Revised stem-and-leaf display:

8	2
9	056
10	289
11	1469
12	3789
13	00579
14	1347899
15	013478
16	35678
17	1258
18	357
19	17
20	26
21	3
	$n = 50$

5 Classes

Utility Charges	Frequency
$70 < $100	4
$100 < $130	11
$130 < $160	18
$160 < $190	12
$190 < $220	5
Total	50

6 Classes

Utility Charges	Frequency
$75 < $100	4
$100 < $125	8
$125 < $150	15
$150 < $175	13
$175 < $200	7
$200 < $225	3
Total	50

7 Classes

Utility Charges	Frequency
$75 < $95	2
$95 < $115	7
$115 < $135	8
$135 < $155	14
$155 < $175	9
$175 < $195	6
$195 < $215	4
Total	50

(b)

Utility Charges	No. of Apartments
$80 but less than $100	4
$100 but less than $120	7
$120 but less than $140	9
$140 but less than $160	13
$160 but less than $180	9
$180 but less than $200	5
$200 but less than $220	3
Total	50

4.23   **(a)**   **(1)** $\bar{X} \cong \$147.20$.
             (2) Mode $\cong \$150.00$.
             (3) Midrange $\cong \$150.00$.
             (4) Range $\cong \$140.00$.
             (5) $S \cong \$32.33$.
             (6) CV $\cong 22.0\%$.
       (b) $82.54 to $211.86.
       (c) 96.0%.

4.41

Utility Charges	% of Apartments
$80 but less than $100	8.0
$100 but less than $120	14.0
$120 but less than $140	18.0
$140 but less than $160	26.0
$160 but less than $180	18.0
$180 but less than $200	10.0
$200 but less than $220	6.0
Total	100.0

4.59   **(a)** Percentage histogram:

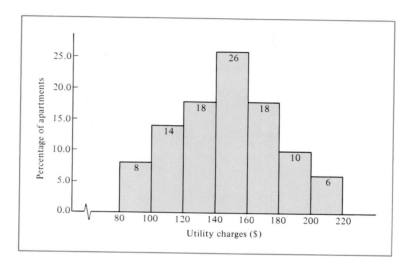

(b) Percentage polygon:

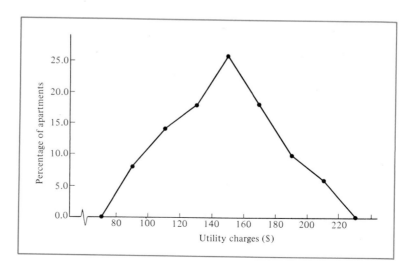

4.77   (a) and (b) Cumulative frequency and percentage distributions:

Utility Charges	Number < Value	Percentage < Value
$ 80	0	0.0
100	4	8.0
120	11	22.0
140	20	40.0
160	33	66.0
180	42	84.0
200	47	94.0
220	50	100.0

(c) Ogive:

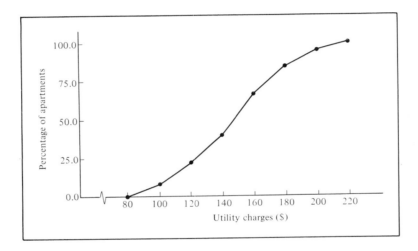

(d)   **(1)** Median $\cong$ $148.00.
　　(2) $Q_1 \cong$ $123.00 and $Q_3 \cong$ $173.00.
　　(3) Midhinge $\cong$ $148.00.
　　(4) Interquartile range $\cong$ $50.00.
(e) Data are approximately symmetrical.

4.98

Response	No.	%
Yes	293	69.93
No	80	19.09
Do not know or refused to answer	46	10.98
	419	100.00

(a) (1) Bar chart: **(2)** Pie chart:

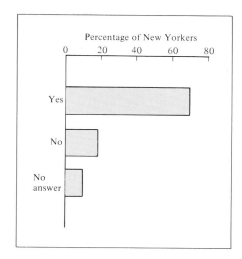

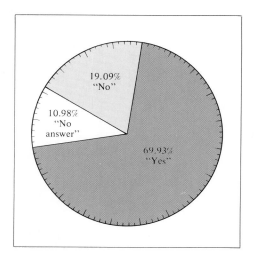

(3) Dot chart:

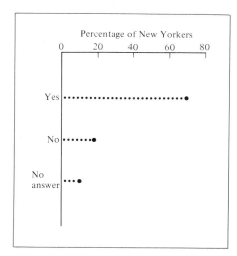

4.110 **(a)**

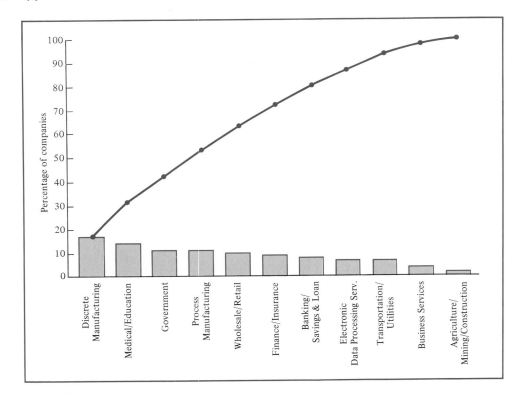

(b) Companies involved in discrete manufacturing and in medicine/education express the greatest interest in purchasing main frame computers; companies involved in business services and in agriculture/mining/construction have the least interest in such computers.

(c) It must be assumed that the industrial groupings are roughly of the same size.

4.121 **(a)** Frequency and percentage distribution of closing prices of issues traded on the American and New York Stock Exchanges.

Closing Prices	American Exchange		New York Exchange	
	Frequency	Percentage	Frequency	Percentage
$ 0 and under 10	16	64.0	13	26.0
10 and under 20	6	24.0	8	16.0
20 and under 30	1	4.0	15	30.0
30 and under 40	1	4.0	7	14.0
40 and under 50	1	4.0	2	4.0
50 and under 60	—	—	3	6.0
60 and under 70	—	—	1	2.0
70 and under 80	—	—	0	0.0
80 and under 90	—	—	1	2.0
Totals	25	100.0	50	100.0

(b) Frequency histograms:

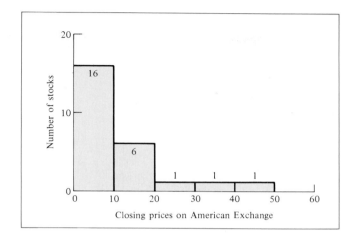

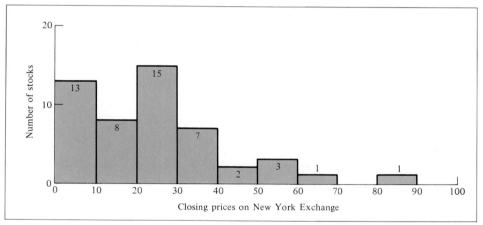

(c) Percentage polygons:

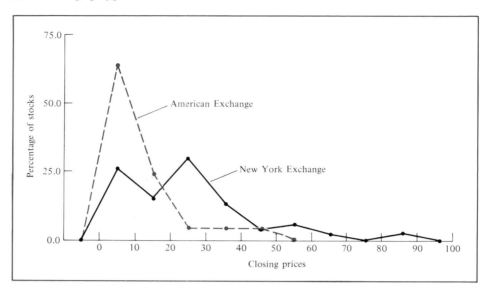

(d) Cumulative percentage distribution of closing prices of issues traded on the American and New York Stock Exchanges:

Closing prices	American Exchange < Value	New York Exchange < Value
$ 0	0.0	0.0
10	64.0	26.0
20	88.0	42.0
30	92.0	72.0
40	96.0	86.0
50	100.0	90.0
60	100.0	96.0
70	100.0	98.0
80	100.0	98.0
90	100.0	100.0

(e) Ogives:

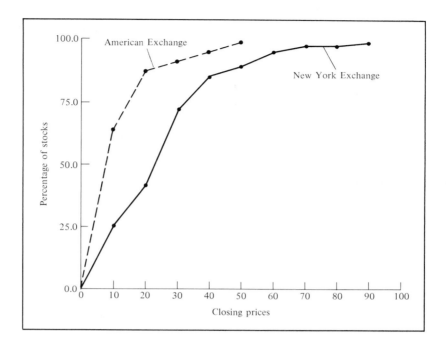

(f) The closing prices of issues on the New York Exchange are much higher than those on the American Exchange.

4.122

			American Exchange	New York Exchange
(a)	**(1)**	$\overline{X}$	$11.00	$24.20
	(2)	Median	$ 7.81	$22.67
	(3)	Mode	$ 5.00	$25.00
	(4)	Midrange	$25.00	$45.00
	(5)	Midhinge	$ 9.25	$20.88
	(6)	Range	$50.00	$90.00
	(7)	Interquartile range	$10.67	$22.52
	(8)	S^2	$(\$10.41)^2$	$(\$17.71)^2$
	(9)	S	$10.41	$17.71
	(10)	CV	94.6%	73.2%

(b) The summary measures, approximated from the distributions and ogives, indicate that closing prices of issues on the New York Exchange are much higher than those on the American Exchange. Nevertheless, as evidenced by CV, there is perhaps even a greater relative variability with respect to the American Exchange issues.

4.138   **(a)** Digidot plot

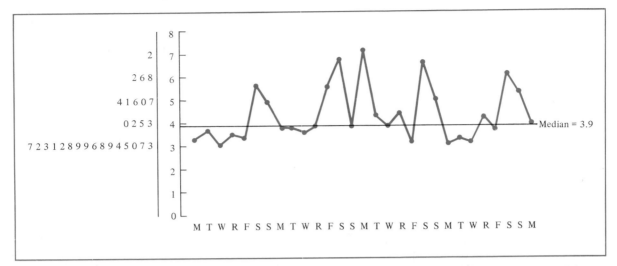

Saturday sales were highest. Sunday sales were good except for the holiday on February 14. Holiday sales were high on Friday, February 12, and on Monday, February 15.

(b) There does not appear to be any pattern in gross sales receipts over time.

CHAPTER 6

6.7   **(a)** Paying on credit;   **(b)** A regular customer and paying cash;   **(c)** Credit payment;   **(d)** It satisfies two criteria: being a regular customer and making a cash payment.

6.9   **(a)**

Enjoy Shopping	Male	Female	Total
Yes	136	224	360
No	104	36	140
Total	240	260	500

(b) Enjoying shopping for clothing.
(c) A male who enjoys shopping for clothing.
(d) Not enjoying shopping for clothing.

6.12   **(a)** 120/200;   **(b)** 110/200;   **(c)** 90/200;   **(d)** 80/200.

6.14   **(a)** 240/500;   **(b)** 360/500;   **(c)** 260/500;   **(d)** 140/500.

6.17   **(a)** 70/200;   **(b)** 40/200;   **(c)** 50/200.

6.19   **(a)** 224/500;   **(b)** 104/500;   **(c)** 136/500.

6.25   **(a)** 160/200;   **(b)** 150/200;   **(c)** 1.0.

6.27   **(a)** 396/500;   **(b)** 276/500;   **(c)** 1.0.

6.30   **(a)** 70/120;   **(b)** 50/90;   **(c)** 50/90 $\neq$ 120/200: not statistically independent.

6.32   **(a)** 36/260;   **(b)** 136/360;   **(c)** 36/260 $\neq$ 140/500: not statistically independent.

6.35   (120/200)(110/200) $\neq$ 70/200: not statistically independent.

6.37   (360/500)(240/500) $\neq$ 136/500: not statistically independent.

6.46   **(a)** 2/3;   **(b)** .36.

6.48   **(a)** $P(S_1|F) = .2157$ $P(S_2|F) = .3050$ $P(S_3|F) = .3486$ $P(S_4|F) = .1307$.
(b) $P(F) = .4590$.

6.50   **(a)** 27,000;   **(b)** .000037.

6.52   240.

6.56   5,040.

6.58   1,320.

6.60   35.

6.64   **(a)** **(1)** 80/200;   **(2)** 55/200;   **(3)** 125/200;   **(b)** 55/80;   **(c)** (25/200) ≠ (70/200)(80/200): not statistically independent.

CHAPTER 7

7.1

	Distribution A	Distribution B
(a)	$\mu_X = 1.00$	$\mu_X = 3.00$
(b)	$\sigma_X = 1.22$	$\sigma_X = 1.22$
(c)	Right-skewed	Left-skewed

7.6   **(a)** $\mu_X = 7.0$;   **(b)** $\sigma_X = 2.42$;
(c) Let V represent the results of one field bet:

V	$P(V)$
$\$-1$	20/36
$+1$	14/36
$+2$	2/26
	1

(d) $\mu_V = -.056$;   **(e)** Player loses 5.6 cents per bet;   **(f)** House wins 5.6 cents per bet.

7.10

	Actions		
Demand	500	1000	2000
500	+250	−125	−875
1000	+250	+500	−250
2000	+250	+500	+1000

$E(500) = \$250$. $E(1000) = \$375$. $E(2000) = \$125$. The fishing company should purchase 1000 pounds of clams.

7.12 E(Soda) $= \$49$. E(Ice Cream) $= \$56$. The vendor should sell ice cream.

7.24   **(a)** .1488;   **(b)** .8131;   **(c)** Histogram shows distribution is right-skewed.

7.28   **(a)** **(1)** .4691;   **(2)** .5854;   **(b)** Probability of audit increases.

7.35   **(a)** .2851;   **(b)** .1606;   **(c)** .7149;   **(d)** .2945.

7.43   **(a)** E(Service) $= \$1100$. Therefore the gardening service should be instituted.

(b) $P\left(p = .01 \;\middle|\; \begin{matrix} n = 20 \\ X = 3 \end{matrix}\right) = .0025$

$P\left(p = .05 \;\middle|\; \begin{matrix} n = 20 \\ X = 3 \end{matrix}\right) = .3361$

$P\left(p = .10 \;\middle|\; \begin{matrix} n = 20 \\ X = 3 \end{matrix}\right) = .3661$

$P\left(p = .25 \;\middle|\; \begin{matrix} n = 20 \\ X = 3 \end{matrix}\right) = .1646$

(c) E(Service) $= \$6,635.20$. The gardening service should be instituted.

7.48 (a) (1) .6496; (2) .1503; (3) .1493
    (c) 7 items is the expected number Donna will get right. She should get that number right on .2668 of the occasions she takes such 10-item exams.
    (d) σ_X = 1.45 items. $\mu_X \pm 2\sigma_X$ ranges from 4.1 to 9.9 items. The probability of getting between 5 and 9 items right is .9244. The Bienayme-Chebyshev rule says the result must be at least .7500.

7.53 (a) (1) .8171; (2) .1667; (3) .0162.
    (b) P(none will malfunction) $\cong$ .8187; P(one will malfunction) $\cong$ .1637; P(at least two will malfunction) $\cong$ .0176.
    (c) (1) .3679; (2) .3679; (3) .2642.

CHAPTER 8

8.2 (a) .0901; (b) .8790; (c) .3790; (d) .1210; (e) .7889; (f) .1875.

8.7 (a) (1) .7605; (2) .6599; (3) .1814; (b) 6.31 minutes (using Z = 1.645).

8.14 (a)

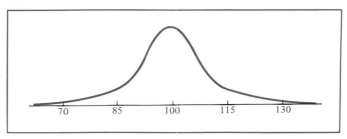

    (b) (1) .5000; (2) .8413; (3) .0228; (4) .00135
    (c) (1) .6826; (2) .9544.

8.17 Answers to (a) are obtained from Table E.7:
    (a) (1) .1208; (2) .9269; (3) .1937; (4) .0729; (5) .8063; (6) .7332.

    Answers to (b) are obtained from Table E.2:
    (b) (1) .1173; (2) .9251; (3) .1922; (4) .0749; (5) .8078; (6) .7329.

8.22 (a) (1) .0821; (2) .5438.
    (b) (1) .1587; (2) .6826.

8.30 (a) 6.68%; (b) .8664; (c) 133.6; (d) 6.622%; (e) 146.8 seconds; (f) .5556.

8.31 (a) (1) .5324; (2) .9961; (b) (1) .2388; (2) .99889.

8.34 (a) .3758; (b) .0043.

8.35 .0287.

8.37 (a) .9999+; (b) .9750; (c) .4522.

CHAPTER 9

9.6 (a) .1915; (b) .0254; (c) (1) $\mu_{\bar{X}}$ = 5, $\sigma_{\bar{X}}$ = .25; (2) normal; (3) .4772; (4) .00013. (5) Since samples of size 16 are being taken, rather than individual values, more values lie closer to the mean and fewer values lie farther away from the mean. (d) They are equally likely to occur (probability = .3085) since as n increases, more sample means will be closer to the population mean.

9.8 (a) .8413; (b) 3.204 minutes.

(c) That the population is symmetrically distributed such that the central limit theorem will hold for samples of $n = 16$.

(d) (1) 3.152; (2) We assume that the central limit theorem holds for samples of $n = 64$.

(e) An individual time below 2.0 is most likely to occur (probability $= .003$) since it is 2.75 standard deviation units below the population mean of 3.1.

9.10 (a) .2486; (b) .0918; (c) .1293 and .2514.

9.15 (1) $\mu_{\bar{X}} = 5$, $\sigma_{\bar{X}} = .24$; (2) normal; (3) .4812; (4) .00009.

9.20 6.726.

CHAPTER 10

10.5 (a) $[.9877 \le \mu_X \le 1.0023]$. (b) Since the confidence interval includes the specified amount of 1.0 gallon, the store owner has no reason to believe that the weight is below 1.0 gallon. (c) Since σ_X is known and $n = 50$, from the central limit theorem we may assume that $\bar{X}$ is approximately normally distributed.

10.10 $[\$1,067.40 \le \mu_X \le \$1,332.60]$.

10.17 (a) $[87.769 \le \mu_X \le 109.963]$; (b) That the length of time is normally distributed.

10.28 $[.2246 \le p \le .3754]$.

10.31 $[.342 \le p \le .478]$.

10.36 $n = 96$.

10.39 $n = 167$.

10.42 $n = 323$.

10.43 $n = 271$.

10.46 (a) $[322.62 \le \mu_X \le 377.38]$; (b) $n = 92$.

10.48 (a) $[.2284 \le p \le .3716]$; (b) $n = 214$.

10.53 (a) $[14.085 \le \mu_X \le 16.515]$.

(b) $[.601 \le p \le .749]$.

(d) $n = 24$.

(e) $n = 784$.

CHAPTER 11

11.13 (a) H_0: $\mu_X = 375$; H_1: $\mu_X \ne 375$.

(b) $Z = -1.768 > -1.96$. Don't reject H_0. There is no evidence that the mean is different from 375 hours.

11.19 $t_{99} = 3.552 > +1.9842$. Reject H_0. The average balance is different from $75.

11.25 $Z = -2.0 > -2.33$. Don't reject H_0. There is no evidence that the population average amount is less than 2 liters.

11.28 $t_{14} = 1.714 < 2.6245$. Don't reject H_0. There is no evidence that the average waiting time is greater than 90 days.

11.37 $Z = 1.779 > 1.645$. Reject H_0. There is evidence that the proportion has changed.

11.42 (a) $[\$78.71 \le \mu_X \le \$88.09]$.

(b) No.

(c) Since $75 is not included in the interval, the null hypothesis is rejected.

11.47 (a) Power $= .6387$; $\beta = .3613$.

(b) Power $= .9908$; $\beta = .0092$.

(c) $n = 64$.

11.48 (a) Power = .3707; β = .6293.
(b) Power = .9525; β = .0475.
(c) The decrease in α has caused an increase in β and a reduction in power.

11.49 (a) Power = .8037; β = .1963.
(b) Power = .9996; β = .0004.
(c) The increase in sample size has increased the power.

11.61 $P[Z < -1.77 \text{ or } Z > +1.77] = .0768$.
There is a 7.68% chance (under H_0) of obtaining a Z value $> |1.77|$.

11.73 (a) $H_0: p \le .15$ (Don't publish), $H_1: p > .15$ (Publish).

$$\text{Type I error } (\alpha) = P \text{ (Publish when } p \le .15)$$
$$\text{Type II error } (\beta) = P \text{ (Don't publish when } p > .15)$$

(b) Type I since the editor does not want to publish a book that will not sell enough copies.
(c) Type II since the professor wants to make sure the book is published if there is sufficient demand.
(d) A one-tailed test since we will publish only when there is evidence that $p > .15$.
(e) $Z = 2.801 > +1.645$. Reject H_0. There is evidence to indicate the editor should publish the book.

11.78 (a) $t_{49} = -9.686 < -2.0096$. Reject H_0. There is evidence that the average price of unleaded gas is different from \$1.30/gallon.
(b) $Z = -.49 > -1.645$. Don't reject H_0. There is no evidence that less than 25% of the gas stations sell diesel fuel.
(c) $n = 106$.

CHAPTER 12

12.3 $t_{198} = 1.91 > 1.645$. Reject H_0. There is evidence of a difference between shifts.

12.5 $t_{38} = 3.72 > 1.686$. Reject H_0. There is evidence that the new package shape resulted in increased sales.

12.13 (a) $t_6 = 3.03 < 3.1427$. Don't reject H_0. There is no evidence that the old system uses more processing time.
(b) That the difference in processing time is normally distributed.

12.16 $t_9 = -0.46 > -2.2622$. Don't reject H_0. There is no evidence of a difference in the average gasoline mileage between regular and high-octane gas.

12.19 $F_{19,19} = .694 > .46$ or $F_{19,19} = 1.44 < 2.18$. Don't reject H_0. No evidence that the variance is lower for the new package shape than for the old package shape.

12.24 (a) $t' = 3.722 > 1.7291$. Reject H_0. There is evidence that the new package shape resulted in increased sales.
(b) It seems reasonable to assume that the variances are equal. The results of Problems 12.5 and 12.24(a) are very similar.

12.29 (a) $t_{24} = 3.667 > 1.7109$. Reject H_0. There is evidence that Pennysonic batteries last more than 95 hours.
(b) $.441 < F_{24,24} = 1.44 < 2.27$. Don't reject H_0. No evidence of a difference in the variances between the two groups.
(c) $t_{48} = 2.18 > 2.0106$. Reject H_0. There is evidence of a difference in the average number of hours between Neveready and Pennysonic batteries.

12.35 (a) $.153 < F_{9,9} = 2.383 < 6.54$. Don't reject H_0. There is no evidence of a difference between Manhattan and Brooklyn Heights in the variance of the rental prices.
(b) The rental prices are normally distributed in each region.
(c) $t_{18} = 8.363 > 2.5524$. Reject H_0. There is evidence that the average rental price is higher in Manhattan than in Brooklyn Heights.

(d) That the variance in rental price is the same in the two regions and the rental price in each region is normally distributed.

CHAPTER 13

13.2 $Z = 2.372 > 1.96$. Reject H_0. There is evidence of a difference in the proportion of women in the two groups who eat dinner in a restaurant during the work week.

13.3 $Z = -1.225 > -1.645$. Don't reject H_0. No evidence of a difference in readability between the two reports.

13.8 $\chi_1^2 = 5.627 > 3.841$ (see Problem 13.2 for conclusions).

13.9 $\chi_1^2 = 1.50 < 2.706$ (see Problem 13.3 for conclusions).

13.16 $\chi_2^2 = 1.125 < 9.21$. Don't reject H_0. There is no evidence of a difference in attitude toward the trimester between the various groups.

13.18 $\chi_2^2 = 19.358 > 5.991$. Reject H_0. There is a difference in the proportion of woman shoppers at the various times of the week.

13.24 $\chi_4^2 = 5.0382 < 7.779$. Don't reject H_0. There is no evidence of a relationship between area and days between payment.

13.26 $\chi_4^2 = 54.1039 > 13.277$. Reject H_0. The distribution of service interruptions/day does not follow a Poisson distribution.

13.30 (a) $\overline{X} = 13.8$, $S = 6.41$.
(b) $\chi_4^2 = 21.933 > 13.277$. Reject H_0. The distribution of the length of long-distance telephone calls does not follow the normal distribution.

13.32 $Z = 4.082 > 1.96$. Reject H_0. There is evidence of a difference in the proportion of individuals that planned to buy and actually purchased a new television.

13.36 (a) $Z = -3.90 < -2.33$. Reject H_0. There is evidence that the proportion is lower in year 1.
(b) The incentive plan significantly reduced absenteeism.
(c) This table does *not* contain repeated information from the individual workers. The cells of this table represent the respective row and column totals of the original table.

13.38 $\chi_{19}^2 = 22.99 < 32.852$. Don't reject H_0. There is no evidence that the standard deviation has changed from 100 hours.

13.39 $\chi_9^2 = 24.8004 > 21.666$. Reject H_0. There is evidence that the process standard deviation has increased.

13.45 $\chi_1^2 = 53.826 > 3.841$. Reject H_0. There is evidence of a difference in the proportion of males and females who enjoy shopping for clothing.

13.52 $\chi_2^2 = 11.308 > 9.21$. Reject H_0. There is evidence of a relationship between adopting cable TV service and type of residence.

13.54 $\chi_4^2 = 9.83 < 13.277$. Don't reject H_0. No evidence of a relationship between commuting time and stress.

13.57 $\overline{X} = 3.98$. $\chi_5^2 = 1.2489 < 15.086$. Don't reject H_0. There is no evidence that the number of customers waiting for service follows other than a Poisson distribution.

13.59 (a) $\overline{X} = 71.2$ $S = 13.02$.
(b) $\chi_4^2 = 23.689 > 9.488$. Reject H_0. There is evidence that the distribution of final exam scores does not follow the normal distribution.

CHAPTER 14

14.4 $F_{3,16} = 16.98 > 3.24$. Reject H_0. There is evidence of a difference in the average performance for the various categories.

14.6 $F_{2,12} = 1.597 < 6.93$. Do not reject H_0. There is no evidence of a difference in the average time spent using the three computer languages.

14.14 $F_{max4,4} = 6.184 < 20.6$. Do not reject H_0. There is no evidence of a difference in the variances.

14.16 $F_{max3,4} = 1.424 < 37.0$. Do not reject H_0. There is no evidence of a difference in the variances.

14.20 Critical range $= 11.48$. Professionals and brokers each differ significantly from business school graduates and salesmen.

14.22 Since H_0 was not rejected, there is no evidence of any differences in the three computer languages with respect to average amount of time spent (in working hours).

14.26 (a) $F_{3,12} = 44.19 > 3.49$. Reject H_0. There is evidence of a difference in the output over the various time periods.
   (c) Critical range $= 5.064$;

9–10 versus 11–12:	$-1.464 \le (\mu_1 - \mu_2) \le 8.664$	(not significant)
9–10 versus 2–3:	$-14.264 \le (\mu_1 - \mu_3) \le -4.136$	(significant)
9–10 versus 4–5:	$4.936 \le (\mu_1 - \mu_4) \le 15.064$	(significant)
11–12 versus 2–3:	$-17.864 \le (\mu_2 - \mu_3) \le -7.736$	(significant)
11–12 versus 4–5:	$1.336 \le (\mu_2 - \mu_4) \le 11.464$	(significant)
2–3 versus 4–5:	$14.136 \le (\mu_3 - \mu_4) \le 24.264$	(significant)

   (d) RE $= 4.98$.

14.28 (a) $F_{2,10} = 6.37 > 4.10$. Reject H_0. There is evidence of a difference between the base-running methods.
   (c) Critical range $= 0.124$. The wide angle method is significantly better than either of the others.
   (d) RE $= 9.63$.

14.33 (a) (1) $F_{2,9} = 0.51 < 4.26$; not significant.
      (2) $F_{2,9} = 17.58 > 4.26$. Reject H_0. There is evidence of a brand effect.
      (3) $F_{4,9} = 3.36 < 3.63$; not significant.
   (c) Critical range $= 8.364$; Brand C requires a significantly greater amount of time for repair than either of the others.

14.35 (a) (1) $F_{2,6} = 40.79 > 10.92$. Reject H_0. There is evidence of an effect due to level of alcoholic consumption.
      (2) $F_{1,6} = 51.92 > 13.75$. Reject H_0. There is evidence of an effect due to type of manuscript.
      (3) $F_{2,6} = 5.15 < 10.92$; not significant.
   (c) Critical range $= 5.71$. Significantly fewer errors were made by secretaries who had not consumed alcohol than by secretaries who had consumed either one or two ounces of alcohol.

14.40 (a) $F_{max3,4} = 3.969 < 37.0$. Do not reject H_0. There is no evidence of a difference in the variances.
   (b) $F_{2,12} = 0.597 < 6.93$. Do not reject H_0. There is no evidence of a difference in time until payment between the three suburban areas.

14.43 (a) $F_{max5,3} = 2.272 < 50.7$. Do not reject H_0. There is no evidence of a difference in the variances.
   (b) $F_{4,15} = 6.15 > 3.06$. Reject H_0. There is evidence of a difference in the average amount of money spent on optional equipment between these age groups.
   (c) Critical range $= 3.171$; buyers in the 40–59 age group spend significantly more on average for optional equipment than do buyers in either the 18–24 age group or the 25–29 age group.

14.52 (a) $F_{7,77} = 7.69 > 2.90$ (interpolation). Reject H_0. There is evidence of a difference in rating scores between the wines.

(c) Critical range $= 4.31$; Wine #2 and Wine #5 each had significantly higher ratings than either Wine #4, Wine #6, or Wine #8.

(e) RE $= 1.56$.

14.55 (a) (1) $F_{2,9} = 8.04 > 8.02$. Reject H_0. There is evidence of an effect due to room size.
  (2) $F_{2,9} = 69.48 > 8.02$. Reject H_0. There is evidence of an effect due to room color.
  (3) $F_{4,9} = 3.84 < 6.42$; not significant.
(c) Room Size: Critical range $= 13.63$. There was a significantly higher level of anxiety in large rooms than in small rooms. Room Color: Critical range $= 13.63$. There was a significantly lower level of anxiety in blue rooms than in either red rooms or yellow rooms.

CHAPTER 15

15.9 $n = 23$; $W = 126.5$; $Z = -0.35$. Don't reject H_0, since $-2.58 < -0.35 < +2.58$; there is no evidence that M differs from 17.

15.18 $n = 11$; $W = 36$; $W_L = 13$. Don't reject H_0 since $W > 13$; there is no evidence that taxpayers would save money using the services of Blech.

15.25 Don't reject H_0 since $78 < T_1 = 84 < 132$. There is no evidence of a difference.

15.34 $H = 0.635 < \chi^2 = 9.210$. Don't reject H_0. There is no evidence of a difference.

15.40 $F_R = 8.244 < \chi^2 = 9.488$. Don't reject H_0. There is no evidence of a difference.

15.45 $r_s = +0.934$; $Z = 3.37 > 1.645$. Reject H_0. There is evidence of a significant positive correlation.

15.56 $10 < U = 15 < 22$. Do not reject H_0. There is no evidence that the sequence is not random.

15.61 $W = 16 < 25$. Reject H_0. There is evidence that $M < 30$.

15.62 $5 < W = 7.5 < 31$. Don't reject H_0. There is no evidence of a difference.

15.63 $T_1 = 62 < 69$. Reject H_0. There is evidence that $M_W < M_M$.

15.66 $H = 11.914 > \chi^2 = 7.815$. Reject H_0. There is evidence of a difference in median battery lives.

15.69 $F_R = 12.250 > \chi^2 = 5.991$. Reject H_0. There is evidence of a difference in the median earnings-per-share estimates given by the three brokerage firms.

CHAPTER 16

16.6 (a) $b_0 = 1.45$; $b_1 = .074$.
(b) For each increase of 1 foot of shelfspace, sales will increase by $7.40 per week.
(c) $\hat{Y}_i = 2.042$ or $204.20.

16.8 (a) $b_0 = 12.6786$; $b_1 = 1.9607$.
(b) The Y intercept b_0 (equal to 12.6786) represents the portion of the worker hours that is not affected by variation in lot size. The slope b_1 (equal to 1.96) means that for each increase in lot size of one unit, worker hours are predicted to increase by 1.96.
(c) $\hat{Y}_i = 100.91$.
(d) Lot size varied from 20 to 80, so that predicting for a lot size of 100 would be extrapolating beyond the range of the X variable.

16.11 $S_{YX} = 0.308$.

16.13 $S_{YX} = 4.71$.

16.16 (a) $r^2 = .684$; 68.4% of the variation in sales can be explained by variation in shelf space.
(b) $r^2_{adj} = .652$.

16.18 (a) $r^2 = .9878$. 98.78% of the variation in worker hours can be explained by variation in lot size.
(b) $r^2_{adj} = .987$.

16.24 $r = +.827$.

16.26 $r = +.9939$.

16.29 (a) $r = +.676$.
(b) $r_S = +.696$, so the Pearson correlation is similar here.

16.32 $[1.835 \leq \mu_{YX} \leq 2.249]$.

16.34 $[98.597 \leq \mu_{YX} \leq 103.223]$.

16.38 (a) $[1.547 \leq \hat{Y}_I \leq 2.637]$.
(b) This is an estimate for an individual response rather than an average predicted value.

16.40 (a) $[92.20 \leq \hat{Y}_I \leq 109.62]$.
(b) This is an estimate for an individual response rather than an average predicted value.

16.43 $t_{10} = 4.653 > 1.8125$. Reject H_0. There is evidence of a linear relationship.

16.45 $t_{12} = 31.15 > 1.7823$. Reject H_0. There is evidence of a significant relationship between lot size and worker hours.

16.48 $t_{13} = 3.31 > 2.1664$. Reject H_0. There is evidence of a linear relationship.

16.53 Based on a residual analysis the model appears to be adequate.

16.55 Based on a residual analysis the model appears to be adequate.

16.60 Max $h_i = .2333 < .3333$; max $|t_i^*| = 1.49 < 1.8331$; max $D_i = .369 < .743$. Thus there is no evidence that any observations should be removed from the model.

16.62 Max $h_i = .232 < .286$; observations 12 and 14 have large Studentized deleted residuals ($|t_i^*| = 2.967$ and $|t_i^*| = 2.057 > 1.7823$); Cook's D_i for these observations are .445 and .504 $< .735$. However, these are the largest D_i values. Thus, one might wish to consider these observations as being influential and delete them from the model; however, the model is an extremely good-fitting one with or without them.

16.68 (b) $b_0 = 21.9256$; $b_1 = +2.0687$.
(c) If the cars have no options, delivery time averages approximately 22 days; for each option ordered delivery time increases by 2.0687 days.
(d) 55.0248 days.
(e) $S_{YX} = 3.0448$.
(f) $r^2 = .9575$; 95.75% of the variation in delivery time can be explained by variation in the number of options ordered.
(g) $r = +.9785$.
(h) $r^2_{adj} = .955$.
(i) $[53.1115 \leq \mu_{YX} \leq 56.9381]$.
(j) $[48.22 \leq \hat{Y}_I \leq 61.83]$.
(k) $t_{14} = 17.769 > 2.1448$. Reject H_0. There is evidence of a linear relationship.
(l) $[+1.8187 \leq \beta_1 \leq +2.3187]$.
(m) Based on a residual analysis the model appears to be adequate.
(n) h_i for observation 16 $= .3096 > .25$. Therefore this observation is an influential point. However, $|t_i^*|$ for observation 16 $= 1.50 < 1.76$, so that this observation does not adversely affect the model. The largest $|t_i^*| = 1.57 < 1.76$. The largest Cook's D_i is for observation 16 $= .465 < .73$. Thus, we may conclude that there is insufficient reason to delete this observation from the model.

16.73 $Y =$ miles per gallon; $X =$ horsepower.
(a) $b_0 = 50.005$; $b_1 = -.2363$.
(b) The slope b_1 means that for each increase of 1 horsepower, it is predicted that miles per gallon will decrease by .2363 mile. The Y intercept, equal to 50.005, is the portion of the miles per gallon that is not affected by horsepower.

(c) $\hat{Y}_i = 26.375$ miles per gallon.
(d) $S_{YX} = 5.081$.
(e) $r^2 = .621$; 62.1% of the variation in miles per gallon can be explained by variation in horsepower.
(f) $r = -.788$.
(g) $r^2_{adj} = .613$.
(h) $t_{48} = -8.87 < -1.6772$. Reject H_0. There is evidence of a significant linear relationship between miles per gallon and horsepower.
(i) $[25.097 \le \mu_{YX} \le 27.653]$.
(j) $[17.758 \le \hat{Y}_I \le 34.992]$.
(k) Based upon a residual analysis the model appears adequate.
(l) Observations 4 ($h_i = .171$), 5 ($h_i = .083$), and 8 ($h_i = .133$) each are $> .08$. However, none of these observations has significantly affected the fit of the model. The $|t_i^*|$ values for observations 12, 13, 25, 34, and 48 (equal to 1.93, 2.53, 1.99, 2.17, and 2.59 respectively) are > 1.6779. However, the largest Cook's D_i value of .215 (for observation 4) is substantially less than the critical value of .703. Thus, owing to the inconsistency of the influence measures, there is insufficient reason to delete any observations from the model.

16.80 **(a)** $r = -.292$.
(b) $t_8 = -.864 > -1.8595$. Do not reject H_0. There is no evidence of a linear relationship between price per pound and proteins per gram.

CHAPTER 17

17.2 **(a)** $\hat{Y}_i = -.02686 + .79116 X_{1_i} + .60484 X_{2_i}$.
(b) For a given midsole impact, each increase of one unit in forefoot impact absorbing capability results in an increase in the long term ability to absorb shock by .79116 units. For a given forefoot impact absorbing capability, each increase in one unit in midsole impact results in an increase in the long term ability to absorb shock by .60484 units.

17.4 **(a)** $\hat{Y}_i = 156.4 + 13.081 X_{1_i} + 16.795 X_{2_i}$ where X_1 = radio and television advertising in thousands of dollars and X_2 = newspaper advertising in thousands of dollars.
(b) Holding the amount of newspaper advertising constant, for each increase of $1,000 in radio and television advertising, sales are predicted to increase by $13,081. Holding the amount of radio and television advertising constant, for each increase of $1,000 in newspaper advertising, sales are predicted to increase by $16,795.

17.8 $\hat{Y}_i = \$753,920$.

17.11 $F_{2,12} = 97.69 > 3.89$. Reject H_0. At least one of the independent variables is related to the dependent variable Y.

17.13 $F_{2,19} = 40.16 > 3.52$. Reject H_0. There is a significant relationship between sales and radio and television advertising and newspaper advertising.

17.16 **(a)** $r^2_{Y.12} = .9421$; 94.21% of the variation in the long-term ability to absorb shock can be explained by variation in forefoot impact-absorbing capability and variation in midsole impact.
(b) $r^2_{adj} = .9263$.

17.18 **(a)** $r^2_{Y.12} = .809$; 80.9% of the variation in sales can be explained by variation in radio and television advertising and in newspaper advertising.
(b) $r^2_{adj} = .789$.

17.21 $F_{1,12} = 157.98 > 4.75$ and $F_{1,12} = 71.09 > 4.75$ or $t_{12} = 12.57 > 2.1788$ and $t_{12} = 8.43 > 2.1788$; each independent variable makes a significant contribution in the presence of the other variable, and both variables should be included in the model.

17.23 $t_{19} = 7.43 > 2.093$ and $t_{19} = 5.67 > 2.093$. Each explanatory variable makes a significant contribution and should be included in the model.

17.26 $[.654 \leq \beta_1 \leq .928]$.

17.28 $[9.399 \leq \beta_1 \leq 16.763]$.

17.32 $r^2_{Y1.2} = .9294$; holding the effect of midsole impact constant, 92.94% of the variation in the long-term ability to absorb shock can be explained by variation in forefoot impact-absorbing capability. $r^2_{Y2.1} = .8556$; holding the effect of forefoot impact-absorbing capability constant, 85.56% of the variation in the long-term ability to absorb shock can be explained by variation in midsole impact.

17.34 $r^2_{Y1.2} = .7172$. For a given amount of newspaper advertising, 71.72% of the variation in sales can be explained by variation in radio and television advertising. $r^2_{Y2.1} = .5686$. For a given amount of radio and television advertising, 56.86% of the variation in sales can be explained by variation in newspaper advertising.

17.38 (a) $\hat{Y}_i = 20.2983 + .03908(X_i - \overline{X}) - .0145(X_i - \overline{X})^2$.

(c) $\hat{Y}_i = 18.52$.

(d) $F_{2,25} = 141.46 > 3.39$. Reject H_0. There is evidence of a curvilinear relationship between speed and miles per gallon.

(e) $r^2_{Y.12} = .9188$; 91.88% of the variation in miles per gallon can be explained by the curvilinear relationship with speed.

(f) $r^2_{adj} = .912$.

17.40 $t_{25} = 2.51 > 2.0595$ and $t_{25} = -16.63 < -2.0595$. Both the linear and curvilinear effects make significant contributions to the model and should be included in the model.

17.44 (a) $\hat{Y}_i = 1.30 + .074X_{1i} + .45X_{2i}$, where $X_1 =$ shelf space, $X_2 = 0$ for back of aisle and 1 for front of aisle.

(b) Holding constant the effect of aisle location, for each additional foot of shelf space predicted sales increase by .074 hundreds of dollars ($7.40). For a given amount of shelf space, a front-of-aisle location increases sales by .45 hundreds of dollars ($45).

(c) $\hat{Y}_i = 1.892$ or $189.20.

(d) $F_{2,9} = 28.562 > 4.26$. Reject H_0. There is evidence of a relationship between sales and the two independent variables.

(e) $r^2_{Y.12} = .864$; 86.4% of the variation in sales can be explained by variation in shelf space and variation in aisle location.

(f) $r^2_{adj} = .834$.

(g) $r^2_{Y.12} = .864$ while $r^2 = .684$; $r^2_{adj} = .834$ as compared to .652. The inclusion of the aisle-location variable has resulted in an increase in the r^2.

(h) $t_9 = 6.72 > 2.2622$ and $t_9 = 3.45 > 2.2622$. Therefore each explanatory variable makes a significant contribution and should be included in the model.

(i) $[.049 \leq \beta_1 \leq .099]$.
$[.155 \leq \beta_2 \leq .745]$.

(j) The slope $b_1 = .074$ is unchanged in this case because shelf space and aisle location are not correlated.

(k) $r^2_{Y1.2} = .834$. Holding constant the effect of aisle location, 83.4% of the variation in sales can be explained by variation in shelf space; $r^2_{Y2.1} = .569$; for a given amount of shelf space 56.9% of the variation in sales can be explained by variation in aisle location.

(l) That the slope of shelf space and sales is the same regardless of whether the aisle location is front or back.

17.47 (a) $\hat{Y}_i = 1.20 + .082X_{1i} + .75 X_{2i} - .024X_{1i}X_{2i}$, where $X_1 =$ shelf space, $X_2 = 0$ for back of aisle and 1 for front of aisle.

(b) $t_8 = -1.03 > -2.306$. Do not reject H_0. No evidence that the interaction term makes a contribution to the model. Therefore we should use the $\hat{Y}_i = b_0 + b_1X_{1i} + b_2X_{2i}$ model.

17.54 $VIF_1 = 1.0$. $VIF_2 = 1.0$. There is no reason to suspect the existence of multicollinearity.

17.58 There appears to be a curvilinear relationship in the plot of the residuals against both radio and television advertising and against newspaper advertising. Thus, curvilinear terms for each of these explanatory variables should be considered for inclusion in the model.

17.61 A residual analysis indicates both positive and negative values for low and high values of X, but only positive residuals for intermediate values of X. This would suggest the possibility of a logarithmic transformation of the Y variable.

17.69 Observations 1, 2, 13, 14 are influential (h_1 and h_2 = .2924, and h_{13} and h_{14} = .3564 > .2727). Observations 2, 4, 7, and 13 had an effect on the model (t_2^* = 2.44, t_4^* = 1.98, t_7^* = 1.87, and t_{13}^* = 1.96 > $|1.7341|$. The largest values for Cook's D_i are .652 for observation 2 and .619 for observation 13, which was less than .82. However, since these values were substantially above the D_i values for the other observations and were also found to have had an effect on the model and to be influential, a model was studied with observations 2 and 13 deleted. In this model, r^2 was .88, while b_0 = -24.7, b_1 = 14.932, and b_2 = 19.107.

17.72 None of the observations exceeds h_i = .214. However, observation 14 has $|t_i^*|$ = 2.30 > 1.7081. Since the largest Cook's D_i is for observation 27 (D_{27} = .238) and the second largest is for observation 14 (D_{14} = .131), each < .81, there is insufficient evidence that any observations should be removed from the model.

17.74 **(a)** Max h_i = .40 < .50; max $|t_i^*|$ = 2.16 > 1.8331; max D_i = .28 < .845. Observation 5, which has $|t_5^*|$ = 2.16, has D_5 = .183. Thus there is insufficient evidence that this observation should be deleted from the model.

 (b) The model in Problem 16.60 did not have any observations to be deleted; it did not have any significant $|t_i^*|$ observations.

17.79 **(a)** $\hat{Y}_i$ = 16.19567 + 2.03779 X_{1i} + 0.56262 X_{2i}.

 (b) For a given shipping mileage, each additional option ordered increases delivery time by 2.03779 days. For a given number of options, each 100-mile increase in shipping mileage increases delivery time by 0.56262 days.

 (c) 41.07 days.

 (d) $F_{2,13}$ = 270.58 > 3.81, so we may reject H_0. There is a significant relationship between delivery time and number of options ordered and shipping mileage.

 (e) $r_{Y.12}^2$ = .9765; 97.65% of the variation in delivery time can be explained by variation in the number of options ordered and the shipping mileage.

 (f) r_{adj}^2 = .973.

 (g) $F_{1,13}$ = 509.16 > 4.67 and $F_{1,13}$ = 10.53 > 4.67. Each independent variable makes a significant contribution and should be included in the model.

 (h) $\{.18794 \le \beta_2 \le .93730\}$.

 (i) $r_{Y1.2}^2$ = .9751. For a given shipping mileage, 97.51% of the variation in delivery time can be explained by variation in the number of options.

 $r_{Y2.1}^2$ = .4474. For a given number of options, 44.74% of the variation in delivery time can be explained by variation in shipping mileage.

 (j) VIF_1 = 1.0. VIF_2 = 1.0. There is no reason to suspect the existence of multicollinearity.

 (k) Based on a residual analysis the model appears adequate.

 (l) Max h_i = .333 < .375; no reason to indicate influential observations. $|t_i^*|$ for observations 13 (2.91) and 16 (2.07) are each > 1.7709. D_{13} = .253 and D_{16} = .511 < .826, so that there appears to be insufficient evidence to delete any observations. However, since these D_i values are far in excess of all others, the counterargument can be made that they should be deleted from the analysis.

17.86 **(a)** $\hat{Y}_i$ = 50.208 $-$ .21184X_{1i} $-$ 4.487X_{2i}, where X_1 = horsepower and X_2 = 0 if the car was manufactured in a foreign country and X_2 = 1 if the car was manufactured in the United States.

 (b) For a given country of manufacture, each increase of 1 horsepower reduces the predicted gas mileage by .21184 gallons. Holding constant the horsepower, a car manufactured in the United States has a predicted 4.487 miles per gallon less than that of a car manufactured in a foreign country.

 (c) $\hat{Y}_i$ = 33.01 miles per gallon.

(d) $F_{2,47} = 52.58 > 3.20$. Reject H_0. There is evidence of a relationship between miles per gallon and horsepower and/or country of origin.

(e) $r_{Y.12}^2 = .691$; 69.1% of the variation in miles per gallon can be explained by variation in horsepower and variation in country of origin.

(f) $r_{adj}^2 = .678$.

(g) $t_{47} = -8.33 < -2.0117$ and $t_{47} = -3.26 < -2.0117$. Each independent variable makes a significant contribution and should be included in the model.

(h) $[-.26304 \le \beta_1 \le -.16064]$.

(i) $r_{Y1.2}^2 = .596$. For a given country of origin, 59.6% of the variation in miles per gallon can be explained by variation in horsepower. $r_{Y2.1}^2 = .184$. For a given amount of horsepower, 18.4% of the variation in miles per gallon can be explained by variation in country of origin.

(j) $VIF_1 = 1.1$; $VIF_2 = 1.1$. There is no reason to suspect the existence of multicollinearity.

(k) It is assumed that the slope of miles per gallon with horsepower is the same regardless of country of origin.

(l) $t_{46} = 2.31 > 2.0139$. Reject H_0. There is evidence that the interaction of horsepower and country of origin improves the model. Therefore the regression model becomes $\hat{Y}_i = 56.384 - .28696X_{1i} - 14.804X_{2i} + .1173X_{1i}X_{2i}$.

(m) Based on a residual analysis the fit of the model appears adequate.

(n) Observations 4 ($h_4 = .247$), 5 ($h_5 = .313$), 8 ($h_8 = .189$), and 37 ($h_{37} = .163$) appear to be influential ($h_i > .16$). However, none of these observations has adversely affected the model ($|t_i^*| < 1.6787$). Observations 11 ($|t_{11}^*| = 2.117$), 13 ($|t_{13}^*| = 2.15$), 24 ($|t_{24}^*| = 1.826$), and 48 ($|t_{48}^*| = 2.306$) are > 1.6787. Since the largest $D_i = .093 < .85$, there is insufficient evidence to delete any observations from the model.

17.89 The model that is evaluated includes the six explanatory variables plus the interaction of variables X_1 (horsepower) and X_2 (country of origin). A preliminary analysis of the full model indicates a high level of multicollinearity present ($VIF = 10.1, 16.1, 12.2, 11.6, 28.9, 3.3$, and 24.8). Using the stepwise approach with forward selection leads to the investigation of a model that includes horsepower (X_1), country of origin (X_2), weight in hundreds of pounds (X_3), acceleration in seconds from 0 to 60 miles per hour (X_6), and the interaction of X_1 and X_2. Further analysis indicated that variable X_6 could be deleted from the model ($t_{44} = 0.50$). Thus the fitted model was:

$$\hat{Y}_i = 67.796 - .18146X_{1i} - 17.28X_{2i} - .8218X_{3i} + .16939X_{1i}X_{2i}$$

The model for foreign manufactured cars ($X_2 = 0$) is:

$$\hat{Y}_i = 67.796 - .18146X_{1i} - .8218X_{3i}$$

while for cars manufactured in the United States the model is:

$$\hat{Y}_i = 50.516 - .01207X_{1i} - .8218X_{3i}$$

For this model $VIF_1 = 4.0$, $VIF_2 = 13.8$, $VIF_3 = 3.0$, VIF_4 (for X_1X_2) $= 19.3$. Since we can expect multicollinearity between X_2 (the dummy variable) and X_1X_2, there is insufficient reason to suspect multicollinearity in the other explanatory variables. Based on a residual analysis, involving the plot of the standardized residuals versus each explanatory variable, the model appears adequate.

Observations 4 ($h_4 = .347$), 5 ($h_5 = .313$), 8 ($h_8 = .203$), and 28 ($h_{28} = .217$) appear to be influential ($h_i > .20$). However, none of these observations has adversely affected the model ($|t_i^*| < 1.6794$). Observations 6 ($|t_6^*| = 1.844$), 13 ($|t_{13}^*| = 2.732$) and 14 ($|t_{14}^*| = 2.028$)

are > 1.6794. Since the largest $D_i = .099 < .884$, there is insufficient evidence to delete any observations from the model.

CHAPTER 18

18.6 **(a)**

Year		I_{SA}	I_{FWA}
1960	(Base)	100.0	100.0
1965		128.8	129.8
1970		167.5	174.4
1975		254.2	252.8
1980		350.7	334.1
1985		488.0	453.0

(b)

Year		I_{SA}	I_{FWA}
1960		59.7	57.3
1965		76.9	74.4
1970	(Base)	100.0	100.0
1975		151.8	145.0
1980		209.4	191.6
1985		291.3	259.7

18.8 **(a)** 266.7% over 20 years or 13.3% per annum.
(b) 1960: $5,472.38; 1980: $7,211.91.
(c) 31.8% over 20 years or 1.6% per annum.
(d) Purchasing power has remained just about the same over the 20-year period.

18.12 **(b)** $\hat{Y}_i = 11.56 + 4.14 X_i$, where origin $= 1967$ and X units $= 1$ year.
(c) Annual nominal growth rate: 4.14 billions of dollars per year.

(d)

X_i	Y_i	$\hat{Y}_i$	$Y_i/\hat{Y}_i$
0.0	20.0	11.5629	1.72968
1.0	22.8	15.7057	1.45170
2.0	24.3	19.8486	1.22427
3.0	18.8	23.9914	0.78361
4.0	28.3	28.1343	1.00589
5.0	30.4	32.2771	0.94184
6.0	35.8	36.4200	0.98298
7.0	31.6	40.5629	0.77904
8.0	35.7	44.7057	0.79856
9.0	47.2	48.8486	0.96625
10.0	55.0	52.9914	1.03790
11.0	63.2	57.1343	1.10617
12.0	66.3	61.2771	1.08197
13.0	57.7	65.4200	0.88199
14.0	62.8	69.5629	0.90278
15.0	60.8	73.7057	0.82490
16.0	74.6	77.8486	0.95827
17.0	83.9	81.9914	1.02328
18.0	96.4	86.1343	1.11918
19.0	102.8	90.2771	1.13872

(e) 1987: 94.42.
     1988: 98.56.
     1989: 102.71.

18.17 **(b)** 5.79.
  (c) A linear trend model appears to give a good fit to the data but a curvilinear model might fit the data better.

18.23 **(b) and (c)**

Pd.	Year	Y_i	3-Year Moving Total	3-Year Moving Avg.	$(W = .50)$ ϵ_i
1	1969	1.45	**	**	1.45
2	1970	1.55	4.61	1.54	1.50
3	1971	1.61	4.76	1.59	1.55
4	1972	1.60	4.95	1.65	1.58
5	1973	1.74	5.26	1.75	1.66
6	1974	1.92	5.61	1.87	1.79
7	1975	1.95	5.91	1.97	1.87
8	1976	2.04	6.05	2.02	1.95
9	1977	2.06	5.90	1.97	2.01
10	1978	1.80	5.59	1.86	1.90
11	1979	1.73	5.30	1.77	1.82
12	1980	1.77	5.40	1.80	1.79
13	1981	1.90	5.49	1.83	1.85
14	1982	1.82	5.37	1.79	1.83
15	1983	1.65	5.20	1.73	1.74
16	1984	1.73	5.26	1.75	1.74
17	1985	1.88	5.61	1.87	1.81
18	1986	2.00	5.96	1.99	1.90
19	1987	2.08	5.96	1.99	1.99
20	1988	1.88	**	**	1.94

  (d) $\hat{Y}_{1989} = \epsilon_{1988} = 1.94$.
  (e) $MAD_{MA} = 0.0411$; $MAD_{ES} = 0.0657$.

18.27 **(a)** 39.8.
  (b) 62.2.

18.31 **(a)** 5.
  (b) 6.
  (c) The most recent five observed values—Y_{36}, Y_{37}, Y_{38}, Y_{39}, and Y_{40}.
  (d) $\hat{Y}_i = \hat{\omega} + \hat{\psi}_1 Y_{i-1} + \hat{\psi}_2 Y_{i-2} + \cdots + \hat{\psi}_5 Y_{i-5}$.
  (e) $\hat{Y}_{n+j} = \hat{\omega} + \hat{\psi}_1 \hat{Y}_{n+j-1} + \hat{\psi}_2 \hat{Y}_{n+j-2} + \cdots + \hat{\psi}_5 \hat{Y}_{n+j-5}$.

18.37 **(c)** $\hat{Y}_i = 244.909 + 1.192 X_i$, where origin $=$ Jan. 15, 1979, and X units $= 1$ month.

(d)

Year	Month	S_i	$\hat{Y}_i$	Forecast
1989	Jan.	0.941	387.97	364.884
	Feb.	0.985	389.16	383.165
	Mar.	1.072	390.35	418.389
	Apr.	0.964	391.54	377.389
	May	0.964	392.73	378.620
	Jun.	1.045	393.93	411.640
	Jul.	1.033	395.12	407.969
	Aug.	1.027	396.31	407.136
	Sep.	0.985	397.50	391.649
	Oct.	0.964	398.70	384.482
	Nov.	1.024	399.89	409.323
	Dec.	0.997	401.08	399.923
1990	Jan.	0.941	402.27	378.339
	Feb.	0.985	403.46	397.250
	Mar.	1.072	404.66	433.722
	Apr.	0.964	405.85	391.177
	May	0.964	407.04	392.412
	Jun.	1.045	408.23	426.589
	Jul.	1.033	409.42	422.740
	Aug.	1.027	410.62	421.832
	Sep.	0.985	411.81	405.744
	Oct.	0.964	413.00	398.278
	Nov.	1.024	414.19	423.967
	Dec.	0.997	415.39	414.187

(e) Obtaining the cyclical relatives (C_i) for 1987 and 1988.

Year	Month	Y_i	S_i	$T_iC_iI_i$	$\hat{Y}_i$	C_iI_i	Weighted Moving Total	C_i
1987	Jan.	354.00	0.941	376.39	359.35	1.047	4.055	1.014
	Feb.	365.00	0.985	370.71	360.55	1.028	4.107	1.027
	Mar.	389.00	1.072	362.93	361.74	1.003	3.601	0.900
	Apr.	198.00	0.964	205.43	362.93	0.566	3.178	0.794
	May	366.00	0.964	379.64	364.12	1.043	3.670	0.918
	Jun.	389.00	1.045	372.26	365.32	1.019	3.982	0.995
	Jul.	341.00	1.033	330.26	366.51	0.901	3.915	0.979
	Aug.	413.00	1.027	402.02	367.70	1.093	4.153	1.038
	Sep.	387.00	0.985	392.78	368.89	1.065	4.299	1.075
	Oct.	384.00	0.964	398.19	370.08	1.076	4.309	1.077
	Nov.	415.00	1.024	405.43	371.28	1.092	4.143	1.036
	Dec.	328.00	0.997	328.95	372.47	0.883	4.045	1.011
1988	Jan.	417.00	0.941	443.38	373.66	1.187	4.362	1.090
	Feb.	408.00	0.985	414.38	374.85	1.105	4.430	1.107
	Mar.	416.00	1.072	388.12	376.04	1.032	4.264	1.066
	Apr.	398.00	0.964	412.93	377.24	1.095	4.310	1.077
	May	397.00	0.964	411.80	378.43	1.088	4.410	1.103
	Jun.	452.00	1.045	432.55	379.62	1.139	4.443	1.111
	Jul.	423.00	1.033	409.68	380.81	1.076	4.453	1.113
	Aug.	456.00	1.027	443.88	382.01	1.162	4.343	1.086
	Sep.	356.00	0.985	361.32	383.20	0.943	4.340	1.085
	Oct.	479.00	0.964	496.71	384.39	1.292	4.604	1.151
	Nov.	425.00	1.024	415.20	385.58	1.077	4.740	1.185
	Dec.	499.00	0.997	500.44	386.77	1.294	**	**

CHAPTER 19

19.1

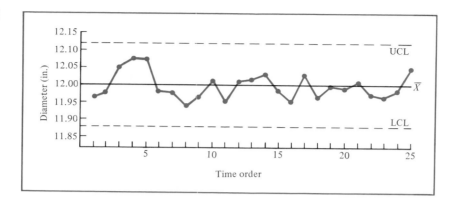

(a) $LCL = 11.88$; $UCL = 12.12$.
(b) $\overline{X} = 11.9998$; $\overline{MR} = .03648$; $LCL = 11.903$; $UCL = 12.097$.
(c) The results are similar because the subgroup estimates are similar to the historical values.

19.8 **(a)** The sample means are 12.0332, 11.9758, 12.0008, 11.99, and 11.9992. $LCL = 11.9463$ and $UCL = 12.0537$. The process appears to be in control since there are no points outside the lower and upper control limits and there is no pattern in the results over time.
(b) $\overline{\overline{X}} = 11.9998$; $\overline{R} = .088$; $LCL = 11.949$; $UCL = 12.0506$. The process appears to be in control since there are no points outside the lower and upper control limits and there is no pattern in the results over time.
(c) The results are similar because the subgroup estimates are similar to the historical values.

19.13 **(a)** The sample ranges are .115, .090, .080, .075, and .080. $\overline{R} = .088$; $UCL = .182$. The process appears to be in control since there are no points outside the upper control limit and there is no pattern in the results over time.
(b) The $\overline{X}$ and R charts can be used together to determine whether either the central tendency or the dispersion of the process are out of control.

19.18 **(a)** $p = .1149$; $LCL = .0525$; $UCL = .1773$. The proportion of late arrivals on day 13 is substantially out of control. Possible special causes of this value should be investigated. In addition, the next four highest points all occur on Friday.
(b) The snowstorm would explain why the proportion of late arrivals was so high on day 13.

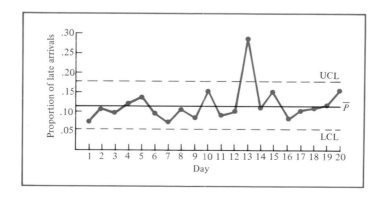

19.24

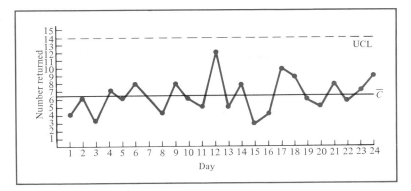

(a) $\bar{c} = 6.458$; $UCL = 14.082$. The process appears to be in control since there are no points outside the upper control limit and there is no pattern in the results over time.

(b) The value of 12 is within the control limits, so that it should be identified as a source of common cause variation. Thus, no action should be taken concerning this value. If the value was 20 instead of 12, $\bar{c}$ would be 6.792 and UCL would be 13.794. In this situation, a value of 20 would be substantially above the UCL, and action should be taken to explain this special cause of variation.

(c) Since the process is in control, it is up to management to reduce the common cause variation by application of the 14 points of the Deming theory of management by process.

(d) $UCL = 11.708$. In this case the value of 12 is outside the control limit and should be investigated as a source of special cause variation.

19.33

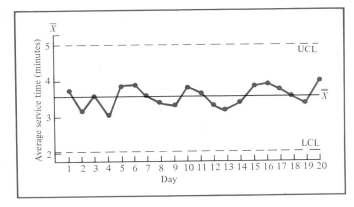

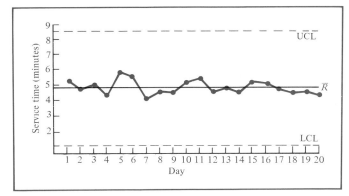

(a) For $\bar{X}$, $\bar{\bar{X}} = 3.549$, $LCL = 2.06$, and $UCL = 5.038$. For R, $\bar{R} = 4.8325$, $LCL = 1.0786$, $UCL = 8.5864$. The process appears to be in control since there are no points outside the lower and upper control limits and there is no pattern in the results over time.

(b) Since the process is in control, it is up to management to reduce the common cause variation by application of the 14 points of the Deming theory of management by process.

Index